# HISTORICAL DICTIONARY OF THE INDOCHINA WAR (1945–1954)

# HISTORICAL DICTIONARY OF THE INDOCHINA WAR (1945–1954)

## An International and Interdisciplinary Approach

Christopher E. Goscha

University of Hawai'i Press
Honolulu

Published in North America by
University of Hawai'i Press
2840 Kolowalu Street
Honolulu, Hawai'i 96822
www.uhpress.hawaii.edu

First published in Europe by
NIAS Press
Nordic Institute of Asian Studies
Leifsgade 33
2300 Copenhagen S, Denmark


Paperback edition 2015
Printed in the United States of America

20 19 18 17 16 15 6 5 4 3 2 1

**Library of Congress Cataloging-in-Publication Data**

Goscha, Christopher E.
Historical dictionary of the Indochina War (1945-1954) : an international and interdisciplinary approach / Christopher E. Goscha.
p. cm.
Includes bibliographical references and index.
ISBN 978-0-8248-3604-7 (hardcover : alk. paper)
1. Indochinese War, 1946-1954--Dictionaries. I. Title.
DS553.1.G67 2011
959.704'103--dc22
2011003823

ISBN 978-0-8248-5646-5 (pbk. : alk. paper)

Cover image: War memorial at Dien Bien Phu, 2004 (Associated Press).
Reproduced with permission.

# *Contents*

Acknowledgements vii

A Brief Chronology of the Indochina War (1945–1954) ix

Maps xx

The Indochina War: A Pictorial Essay xxvii

Introduction 1

Historical Dictionary of the Indochina War 21

Selected Bibliography 505

Name Index 537

Place Index 554

Events Index 555

General Index 557

# *Maps and Figures*

## Maps

1: Indochina peninsula xx
2: Ethnic populations xxi
3: French Indochina, 1862–1936 xxii
4: Indochina partition, 1945 xxiii
5: Territorial control, 1950–54 xxiv
6: Indochina regrouping zones after Geneva, 1954 xxv
7: South East Asia Treaty Organization, 1954 xxvi

## Figures

1: Battle of Hanoi, January 1947 xxvii
2: Militarizing childhood xxviii
3: Tomb of French soldier, Tonkin 1952 xxviii
4: Women praying for their men at war, Tonkin 1952 xxix
5: Wiring war, Southern Vietnam xxx
6: Viet Minh prisoners of war working for French Union xxxi
7: Troops of the Associated State of Vietnam xxxii
8: French return of female prisoners, August 1954 xxxiii
9: Refugees of war, Nam Dinh 1954 xxxiii
10: Freed French prisoner of war xxxiv
11: John Foster Dulles, SEATO meeting 1954 xxxv
12: Touching his father's name at the war memorial at Dien Bien Phu, 2004 xxxv

# Acknowledgements

It is my pleasure here to acknowledge the help and work of scores of friends and colleagues across the world, without whom this dictionary would never have seen the light of day. I have been extremely fortunate to be able to work with a team of French, Vietnamese, and Canadian research assistants, all of whom helped me track down vital yet often difficult to find information. In France, I'm thinking of Marjolaine Bouté, Antoine Boué, and Mathieu Lehunsec. I owe a particular debt to Nguyen Quoc Thanh and Elise Virely, who have helped me locate a wide variety of information in Vietnamese and French over the years. Since my arrival in Canada in 2005, I have been able to work with a dynamic group of young scholars, including Frédéric Renaud, Simon Abdela, Jean-Marc Ryan, Karine Laplante, Jade Canape, Guillaume Marceau, Phi Van Nguyen, Bui Thanh Ha, and Genviève Anaïs-Proulx. A special thanks goes to Simon Abdela and Guillaume Marceau whose help was vital to bringing this dictionary to fruition.

A number of archivists of the Indochina War have provided me with invaluable information and advice. In France, I owe a large debt to General André Bach, former head of the *Service historique de la Défense*, who first urged me to undertake this project. I also benefited from the friendly support of Colonels Gilbert Bodinier and Frédéric Guélton, who administered the historical section there and who allowed me to draw upon the rich sources of the military archives. In Aix-en-Provence, Lucette Vachier, former archivist in charge of the colonial holdings there on Indochina, provided me with precious advice for where to 'dig'. A special thanks to Paul and Marie-Catherine Villatoux, who work at the Air Force archives in Vincennes and who provided me with rich documentation, excellent counsel, and helped me to avoid many egregious errors.

On that note, I also owe a great deal to colleagues working on the Indochina War or aspects of it. They provided expert critiques, invaluable sources, and also helped me avoid embarrassing errors. In France, I'm thinking of Maurice Vaïsse, Pierre Grosser, Pierre Journoud, Pierre Brocheux, Claire Tran Thi Lien, Laurent Césari, Isabelle Tracol, Philippe Papin, François Guillemot, Christophe Dutrône, Etienne Lebaube, Jean-Marc Lepage, Nasir Carime Abdoul, Vatthana Pholsena, Gilles de Gantès, and Philippe Devillers. Hugues Tertrais kindly allowed me to use maps from his wonderful historical atlas of the Indochina War.[1]

In Vietnam, my thanks to Phan Huy Le, Cao Minh Chong, Andrew Hardy, Olivier Tessier, Philippe Lefailler, Phan Trac Canh, the late Dang Phong, Do Kien, Ton Nu Quynh Tran, Le Van Nam, Dinh Xuan Lam, Nguyen Vu Tung, the late Luu Doan Huynh, Nguyen Hong Thach, Truong Hong Truong, and Luu Van Loi.

In Europe and North America, I am grateful to the late Judy Stowe who read the first draft of the dictionary before passing away and who encouraged me to carry on despite the red she had wreaked upon my work. I'm also grateful to Oscar Salemink and Jean Michaud for their help on ethnic minorities. Susan Bayly was an inspiration when it came to working on French and Vietnamese intellectuals of all political

1. Hugues Tertrais, *Atlas des guerres d'Indochine, 1940–1990: De l'Indochine française à l'ouverture internationale* (Paris: Autrement, 2004).

stripes. In the United States, my sincere thanks go to a range of friends and scholars, including Edward Miller, Charles Keith, Shawn McHale, Julie Pham, Larry Berman, Christina Firpo, Chen Jian, Keith Taylor, Mark Lawrence, Edwin Moïse, Jay Veith, Fredrik Logevall, Penny Edwards, Qiang Zhai, Lorraine Patterson, Hannah Phan, Tuong Vu, and Ronald Spector. I owe a special debt to Peter Zinoman and Nguyen Cam Nguyet, who came to my rescue at a time when I was seriously thinking of throwing in the towel. Nguyen Cam Nguyet and Phi Van Nguyen also kindly helped me provide the correct diacritics for the Vietnamese names.

In the course of researching and writing this dictionary, I have also had the pleasure of getting to know and then working with two of the unsung specialists of the Vietnam War and walking encyclopedias, Merle Pribbenow and James Nach. In Canada, Eric Jennings, Lorenz Luthi, and Kathyrn Edwards provided excellent suggestions. In Australia, David Marr graciously shared information and his renowned expertise on the Indochina War. Grant Evans and Martin Rathie provided help on Laos.

Thanks to Gerald Jackson, my editor at the Nordic Institute of Asian Studies, for believing in this project and for helping me to bring it to fruition here. Stein Tønnesson, Edwin Moïse, and Laurent Césari deserve special mention for carefully going through the dictionary and providing invaluable comments, suggestions, and improvements. Stein Tønnesson read every single entry, perhaps even every single sentence of this dictionary, an extraordinary (and no doubt painful) feat for which I am deeply grateful. In the final stages, Jonathan Price provided expert copy-editing. And without the support of my wife and scholar, Agathe Larcher, I would have long ago abandoned the mad idea of writing a dictionary.

I take full responsibility for all errors, inaccuracies, and shortcomings in this dictionary and its entries.

Christopher E. Goscha
Université du Québec à Montréal (UQAM)
Montreal, Canada

# A Brief Chronology of the Indochina War (1945–1954)

## 1945

| | |
|---|---|
| February 8 | Creation of the French Interministerial Committee for Indochina (Cominindo). |
| March 9 | Japanese *coup d'état* ending French colonial rule in Indochina. |
| March 11 | The emperor of Annam, Bao Dai, backed by the Japanese, denounces the French protectorate and proclaims Vietnam's independence. |
| March 13 | Cambodia's King Norodom Sihanouk declares Cambodia's independence. |
| April 17 | Installation of the Tran Trong Kim government at the head of the state of Vietnam, with nominal national authority over the colonial territories of Cochinchina, Annam, and Tonkin. |
| May 8 | Germany surrenders. |
| July 17 | The Allied leaders in Potsdam divide Indochina at the 16th parallel, with the China Theatre in charge of the north and the British South East Asia Command the south. |
| August 6 | The Americans drop atomic bomb on Hiroshima. |
| August 9 | The Americans drop atomic bomb on Nagasaki. |
| August 14 | Japan surrenders. |
| August 15 | Charles de Gaulle names Admiral Georges Thierry d'Argenlieu as high commissioner of France in Indochina. |
| August 16–19 | The Viet Minh call for insurrection and take Hanoi on August 19th. |
| August 18–28 | Viet Minh power seizure in the country's main provinces. |
| August 22 | Jean Sainteny arrives in Hanoi on the same plane as Archimedes Patti. |
| August 27–28 | Emergence of the Vietnamese Provisional Government in Hanoi. |
| August 28 | British General Douglas Gracey named commander of Allied forces south of the 16th parallel, including French forces. |
| August 30 | Official abdication of Bao Dai in Hue before a delegate from the new government in Hanoi. The ex-emperor agrees to become supreme advisor to the Provisional government. |

| | |
|---|---|
| September 2 | At Ba Dinh square in Hanoi, proclamation confirming Vietnam's independence by Ho Chi Minh; birth of the Democratic Republic of Vietnam (DRV). |
| September 9 | In conformity with the Potsdam agreements and the issuance of Order No. 1 by Harry Truman, Chinese troops enter northern Indochina to disarm the Japanese and maintain order. |
| September 13 | Entry of British troops in southern Indochina to disarm the Japanese. |
| September 17–24 | Organizing of the "gold week" to help fill the DRV's empty coffers. |
| September 23 | French launch *coup de force* in Saigon, with British green light, driving the DRV out of the city before going on to retake major roads, bridges, and provincial capitals in Vietnam below the 16th parallel. The Indochina War begins in the south, while the DRV remains in power in Hanoi thanks to Chinese decision not to overthrow the government or allow a rapid French return. |
| September 24–25 | Hérault massacre in Saigon. |
| October 3 | Arrival of the first contingents of the Expeditionary Corps to southern Vietnam. |
| October 5 | Arrival of General Leclerc at Tan Son Nhut airbase. |
| October 10 | Inter-allied conference in Singapore (Mountbatten, Leclerc and Gracey). |
| October 15 | Leclerc orders the arrest of Cambodian leader Son Ngoc Thanh. |
| October 23 | First accord between the Viet Minh and the non-communist opposition parties in northern Vietnam: the Vietnam Nationalist Party (VNQDD) and the Dong Minh Hoi (DMH). |
| October 31 | Admiral Thierry d'Argenlieu arrives in Saigon. |
| November 4 | Prince Phetsarath of Laos, leader of a pro-independence government, deposes King Sīsāvangvong. |
| November 9–13 | Exchange of letters between Cambodia's King Norodom Sihanouk and the French high commissioner. |
| November 10–11 | Self-dissolution of the Indochinese Communist Party. |
| December 10 | Franco-Chinese monetary negotiations open in Hanoi following the withdrawal of 500-piastre bills. |
| December 22 | Second accord between Viet Minh and opposition parties. |
| December 25 | Revaluation of the *piastre* to 17 francs. |

## 1946

| | |
|---|---|
| January 6 | First DRV elections boycotted by nationalist opposition (DMH – VNQDD). |
| January 7 | Franco-Cambodian *modus vivendi* according Cambodia autonomy within the French Union. |

| | |
|---|---|
| January 20: | Charles de Gaulle resigns as leader of the French provisional government. |
| January 26 | General Alessandri's troops, who had taken refuge in China in March 1945, enter Tonkin and occupy the Lao Kay region. |
| January 31 | Issuing of "Ho Chi Minh bills" in the South. |
| February 25–26 | Vote in the French National Assembly on the French Union. |
| February 28 | Franco-Chinese accord in Chongqing. |
| March 2 | First session of the Democratic Republic of Vietnam's National Assembly: Ho Chi Minh is elected president and is in charge of establishing a government. |
| March 6 | Signing of Franco-Vietnamese accords of 6 March by Ho Chi Minh, Vu Hong Khanh and Jean Sainteny which stipulates: (1) Recognition by France of the DRV as a "free state" within the French Union; (2) Organization of a referendum on the reunion of the 3 *ky* (Tonkin, Annam, and Cochinchina); (3) Entry of French troops into Hanoi and establishment of combined Franco-Vietnamese garrisons in northern centers for a limited time-period. |
| March 18 | Arrival of General Leclerc's troops in Hanoi. First meeting between Leclerc and Ho Chi Minh. French war prisoners of Hanoi Citadel (held there since 9 March 1945) are rearmed and form *3e bataillon de marche (9e R.I.C., 19e R.I.C. and 5e R.E.I.).* |
| March 21 | Reoccupation of Thakhek by French forces. |
| March 24–25 | Meeting in Ha Long Bay between Ho Chi Minh and High Commissioner Admiral Georges Thierry d'Argenlieu. |
| April 17 | French reoccupation of Poulo Condor prison. |
| April 17–May 11 | First Dalat Conference (between France and the DRV). |
| April 19 | Creation in Paris of the French Union. |
| April 25 | French enter Vientiane. Exile of Lao Issara leaders to Thailand. |
| April 30 | Repatriation of Japanese troops from Cochinchina begins. |
| May 31 | Ho Chi Minh and a DRV delegation leave for France to continue negotiations there. |
| June 1 | Proclamation of the Provisional Government of the Republic of Cochinchina. General Leclerc recalled to France, and replaced by General Valluy. |
| June 10 | Withdrawal of Chinese troops begins. |
| June 13 | Ho Chi Minh arrives in France. |
| June 26 | Chinese troops headquarters leaves Hanoi. |
| July 2 | Ho Chi Minh is officially received in France by Georges Bidault, French prime minister. |
| July 6–August 1 | Fontainebleau conference. Pham Van Dong deplores the creation of the Provisional Government of the Republic of Cochinchina and accuses France of violating the 6 March Accords. |

| | |
|---|---|
| July 8 | Chinese troops withdraw from Langson. |
| July 22 | Creation of the Vietnamese Socialist Party. |
| August 1–15 | Second Dalat Conference organized by Thierry d'Argenlieu with representatives of all of Indochina except the DRV. |
| August 1 | The Vietnamese delegation suspends negotiations at Fontainebleau after learning of the Second Dalat Conference. |
| August 3 | Bac Ninh incident: DRV attack on a French convoy. |
| August 27 | Franco-Laotian *modus vivendi*" according Laos autonomy within the French Union. |
| September 1 | Elections in Cambodia: Democratic Party obtains 50 of 55 seats in parliament. |
| September 16 | *Modus vivendi* signed between Ho Chi Minh and Marius Moutet. |
| October 13 | Adoption by referendum of the French Fourth Republic's constitution. |
| October 18 | Thierry d'Argenlieu–Ho Chi Minh meeting. |
| October 28 | Ho Chi Minh returns to Hanoi by boat |
| October 31 | Provisional cease-fire implemented in Cochinchina and South Annam. |
| November 10 | Dr. Nguyen Van Thinh commits suicide |
| November 17 | Treaty of Washington by which Thailand returns territories taken in Cambodia and Laos from France in 1941. |
| November 20–21 | Clash leading to full French occupation of Langson. |
| November 20–23 | Clash leading to bombing and full French occupation of Haiphong. |
| December 6 | Le Van Hoach replaces the deceased Nguyen Van Thinh as head of the Provisional Government of the Republic of Cochinchina. |
| December 12 | Socialist (SFIO) Léon Blum is elected by the French National Assembly to form a new government. |
| December 18 | The last provisional French government formed by Blum comes into being before the entry into force of the new constitution |
| December 19–20 | Outbreak of war in Hanoi and other Vietnamese cities above the $16^{th}$ parallel, leading to full-scale Indochina War. |

## 1947

| | |
|---|---|
| January 14 | Admiral Thierry d'Argenlieu proposes restoration of ex-emperor Bao Dai. |
| January 16 | Vincent Auriol elected first president of the Fourth Republic. |
| February 17 | End of battle of Hanoi; withdrawal of last DRV forces. |

| | |
|---|---|
| April–May | Rallying of the Hoa Hao south-based sect to the French after the assassination of their religious leader Huynh Phu So by the Viet Minh. |
| March 5 | Émile Bollaert is named high commissioner in Indochina, replacing Georges Thierry d'Argenlieu. |
| March 12 | Truman doctrine is announced. |
| March 15–22 | Non-communist nationalists give their support to Bao Dai in China. |
| May 12 | Failed Ho Chi Minh–Paul Mus meeting |
| May 19 | 300 French intellectuals sign a petition in favor of negotiations with Ho Chi Minh government |
| May 20 | Ho Chi Minh and Hoang Minh Giam reject cease-fire conditions proposed by France. |
| June 27 | Signing in Washington of the Franco-Thai conciliation commission report. |
| July 5 | Bao Dai declares from exile in Hong Kong that he would not refuse a role in ending the war. |
| September 10 | In a speech at Hadong, Emile Bollaert, French high commissioner, offers an Indochina Charter but rules out concessions to the DRV. |
| September 18 | Message from Bao Dai to the Vietnamese people: the ex-emperor agrees to make contact with the French to obtain Vietnam's total independence. |
| October 1: | General Nguyen Van Xuan, supported by socialists and radicals, is elected president of the Cochinchina government, now renamed the "provisional government of South Vietnam". |
| October 5 | Creation of *Kominform.* |
| October 7 | Launching of Operation "Lea" aiming to capture the DRV leadership and sever the government's trading routes to China |
| December 6 | Bollaert–Bao Dai talks in Ha Long Bay lead to signing of provisional protocol promising recognition of Vietnam's unity and independence. |

## 1948

| | |
|---|---|
| January 27 | Military convention between Cao Dai and Hoa Hao to coordinate their military actions against Viet Minh in their respective zones in southern Vietnam. |
| March 8 | Letters exchanged between French President Vincent Auriol and Bao Dai. |
| March 26 | Bao Dai proclaims the creation of a central Vietnamese provisional government. |

| | |
|---|---|
| May 20 | Nguyen Van Xuan forms the first provisional government of a unified Vietnam under French auspices. |
| June 5 | Halong Bay accords signed. |
| June 18 | Bilateral Franco-American accords on the introduction of the Marshall plan – Indochina is among the French Union territories benefiting from it. |
| October 20 | Léon Pignon becomes high commissioner. |
| November 2 | Truman re-elected President. |
| During 1948 | Creation of the Tai Federation and of Muong and Nung autonomous territories near the Chinese border. |

## 1949

| | |
|---|---|
| January 3 | Dean Acheson becomes Secretary of State. |
| January 22 | Chinese Liberation Army takes Beijing |
| March 8 | Signing of the Elysée accords between Bao Dai and Vincent Auriol stipulating "unity and independence" of the Associated State of Vietnam. |
| April 24 | Chinese Liberation Army captures Nanjing. |
| April 28 | Bao Dai leaves Nice for Vietnam aboard the French presidential plane. Franco-Lao accord signed opening the way to the creation of an Associated State |
| May–June | General Revers's mission to Indochina. |
| June 3 | French National Assembly casts its first vote to approve the attachment of Cochinchina to Vietnam. |
| June 13 | Return of Bao Dai to Saigon. |
| June 14 | Creation of the Associated State of Vietnam led by Bao Dai. |
| June 30 | Bao Dai constitutes his government in Dalat. |
| June | Revers report submitted |
| July 19 | Franco-Lao treaty signed in Paris: creation of the Associated State of Laos within the French Union. |
| August 29 | The "Generals affair" begins. |
| September 19 | Dissolution of the Cambodian National Assembly |
| September | French troops occupy the independent Catholics areas of Bui Chu and Phat Diem |
| October 1 | Mao Zedong proclaims the creation of the People's Republic of China in Beijing. |
| October 24 | The Lao Issara government in Bangkok pronounces its own dissolution. |
| November 8 | Treaty signed in Paris making Cambodia an Associated State within the French Union. |

## 1950

| | |
|---|---|
| January 5 | Bao Dai charges Nguyen Phan Long with the formation of a new Vietnamese government. |
| January 6 | The United Kingdom recognizes the People's Republic of China. |
| January 17 | Paris: debates over the "Generals' affair" and investigation launched. |
| January 18 | People's Republic of China recognizes the Democratic Republic of Vietnam. |
| January 30 | The USSR recognizes the DRV. |
| January 29 | French National Assembly ratifies the Elysée treaty establishing autonomy for Laos, Cambodia, and Vietnam within the French Union. |
| February 7 | Britain and the US recognize the Associated State of Vietnam. |
| February 12 | Vatican recognizes the Associated States of Indochina. |
| February 19 | Violent student demonstrations in Saigon. |
| March 16 | Three ships of the US 7th fleet arrive in Saigon port. |
| May 1 | US President Harry Truman approves a 10-million-dollar military aid package for Indochina. |
| June 11–18 | Arrival in Saigon of US arms and supplies |
| June 25 | Outbreak of the Korean War. |
| June 29 | Pau Conference |
| July 15 | Arrival in Saigon of US military information mission led by US State Department officer John Melby and Major General B. Erskine. |
| August 3 | Arrival in Saigon of the first members of the US Military Assistance Advisor Group (MAAG). |
| October 3–8 | French retreat from the Route Coloniale 4 near Chinese border |
| October 18 | French evacuation of Langson |
| October 19 | Pierre Mendès France expresses for the first time his opposition to the Indochina War. |
| October 25 | Chinese military intervention in the Korean conflict. |
| November 1–3 | French evacuation of Lao Kay and Lai Chau. |
| November 27 | End of Pau conference. |
| December 6 | General de Lattre de Tassigny is named supreme commander and high commissioner for Indochina. |
| December 23 | Representatives of France, the US, Cambodia, Laos, and Vietnam sign a Mutual Defense Accord for Indochina. |

## 1951

| | |
|---|---|
| January 12–20 | Battle of Vinh Yen, a defeat for the DRV. |
| January 29–30 | French Premier Pleven and General Allard, chief of staff of the Expeditionary Corps, travel to Washington to sollicit more US support. |
| February | Creation of the Lao Dong Party, or Vietnamese Workers' Party, to replace the Indochinese Communist Party |
| March 23–May 29 | Battles of Mao Khe and Dong Trieu. DRV fails to take the Red River Delta |
| May 28–June 4 | Battle of the Day River. |
| June 15 | Bao Dai signs the draft into law |
| July 19 | The sentencing of Henri Martin, a French naval officer favorable to the Vietnamese resistance, launches a campaign of Leftist protests and demonstrations/ |
| July 11 | General de Lattre issues his "call to Vietnamese youth". |
| September 1 | Signing of the ANZUS Treaty (Australia, New Zealand, United States) |
| September 8 | Signing in San Francisco of Peace Treaty with Japan. |
| September 10 | General de Lattre starts a visit to the US. |
| October 2–6 | Battle of Nghia Lo, a DRV victory. |
| November 14 | General de Lattre launches an attack against the Viet Minh in the town of Hoa Binh on the Black River. |

## 1952

| | |
|---|---|
| January 11 | General de Lattre dies, replaced by General Raoul Salan. |
| February 22–24 | French evacuation of Hoa Binh. |
| June 3 | In Cambodia, King Sihanouk assumes command of the government. |
| September 12 | Soviet veto French demand for the membership of Bao Dai's Vietnam in the UN. |
| December 1–2 | Battle of Na San. Defeat for the DRV. |
| December 17 | The NATO council declares that "the campaign in Indochina led by French Union forces deserves support without compromise". |

## 1953

| | |
|---|---|
| Most of 1953 | Cambodian King Sihanouk launches his "royal crusade for independence". |
| January 14 | Sihanouk dissolves Cambodia's National Assembly and assumes presidency of the government with Penn Nouth as vice president. |
| March 5 | Death of Stalin in Moscow. |
| March 25 | Auriol – Sihanouk talks. |
| April 12 | DRV forces invade Laos. |
| April 13–15 | Sam Neua is evacuated. |
| May 11 | Devaluation of the piastre. |
| May 22 | General Henri Navarre named new French commander in Indochina |
| June 15 | Rupture between France and Cambodia. Sihanouk leaves Phnom Penh for Thailand and then settles in Battambang. |
| End of June | Creation of the *Groupement de commandos mixtes aéroportés*. |
| July 3 | The French government announces its intention to give total independence to the Associated States. |
| July 25 | For the first time, General Navarre considers an airborne operation at Dien Bien Phu. He believes the location will serve to block the enemy's access to Laos. |
| July 27 | Signing of armistice ending hostilities in Korea. |
| September 7 | Franco-Cambodian convention reached on military transfers. |
| September 9 | The United States donates an additional 385 million dollars to help France finance the war in Indochina. |
| October 17 | Franco-Cambodian military accord: all territorial command is transferred to the Royal Army, but leaving to the Expeditionary Corps operational freedom on the Mekong's left bank. |
| October 22 | Franco-Lao treaty of friendship giving complete independence to Laos. |
| October 30 | Nixon's visit to Indochina. |
| November 9 | France accords Cambodia full independence. |
| November 14 | Navarre decides to take a stand at Dien Bien Phu. |
| November 20 | Landing of French paratroopers at Dien Bien Phu. |
| November 29 | In an interview with the Swedish newspaper *Expressen*, Ho Chi Minh declares himself ready to negotiate with France. |
| December 8 | Colonel de Castries takes command of the entrenched Dien Bien Phu camp. |
| December 19 | Promulgation of a law on land reform in DRV. |
| December 21–29 | DRV invades Laos for a second time. |

## 1954

January 20 — Beginning of French Operation *Atlante* in south central Vietnam.

January 25–February 18 — Berlin Conference fails to agree on Korea but its final communiqué announces that another conference, in Geneva, will address Asian topics, mainly Indochina.

March 13 — Beginning of the battle of Dien Bien Phu.

March 15 — Viet Minh neutralizes Dien Bien Phu air strip.

March 23 — U.S. Secretary of State John Foster Dulles's declaration on Indochina.

March 24–26 — General Ely's visit to Washington. Technical preparation for Operation Vulture

April 2 — Eisenhower refuses to endorse Operation Vulture.

April 26 — Beginning of the Geneva conference.

April 28 — Franco-Vietnamese declaration on Associated State of Vietnam's independence.

April 29 — U.S. President Eisenhower's declaration on Indochina.

May 7 — French camp at Dien Bien Phu capitulates at 17H30.

May 7–9 — Letters exchanged between President Eisenhower and French President Coty. Negotiations on Indochina begin at Geneva

May 25 — In Geneva, Pham Van Dong hints at possibility of accepting preliminary partition of Vietnam.

June 16 — Bao Dai appoints Ngo Dinh Diem as prime minister.

June 18 — Pierre Mendès France resumes talks at the Geneva conference on Indochina. He gives one month to all parties to find a solution or else he will resign.

June 23 — Mendès France and Zhou Enlai meet in Bern.

June 25 — Ngo Dinh Diem arrives in Saigon to form a new government.

July 3–5 — Liuzhou talks between Zhou Enlai and Ho Chi Minh.

July 6 — Diem forms his government.

July 10 — Mendès France and Molotov meet in Geneva.

July 20 — Accord to end hostilities in Cambodia and Laos.

July 21 — Signing at Geneva of the armistices ending the Indochina War.

August 1 — Cease-fire in central Vietnam.

August 6 — Cease-fire in Laos.

August 7 — Cease-fire in Cambodia.

August 10 — Arrival in Hanoi of the International Control and Supervision Commission.

August — Exodus of Vietnamese Catholics from north to south, while DRV cadres and troops leave the south for the north.

| | |
|---|---|
| September 8 | Signing of the Manila pact, creation of SEATO. |
| October 9 | Hanoi evacuated by French forces. |
| October 10 | Viet Minh forces enter Hanoi. |
| November 1 | Beginning of the Algerian War. |
| December 30 | Signature in Paris of the accords and conventions between Cambodia, Laos, Vietnam, and France. The states are now monetarily independent and may receive direct American aid starting 1 January 1955. |
| December 31 | Declaration from the U.S. State Department on direct assistance to Vietnam, Cambodia, and Laos. |

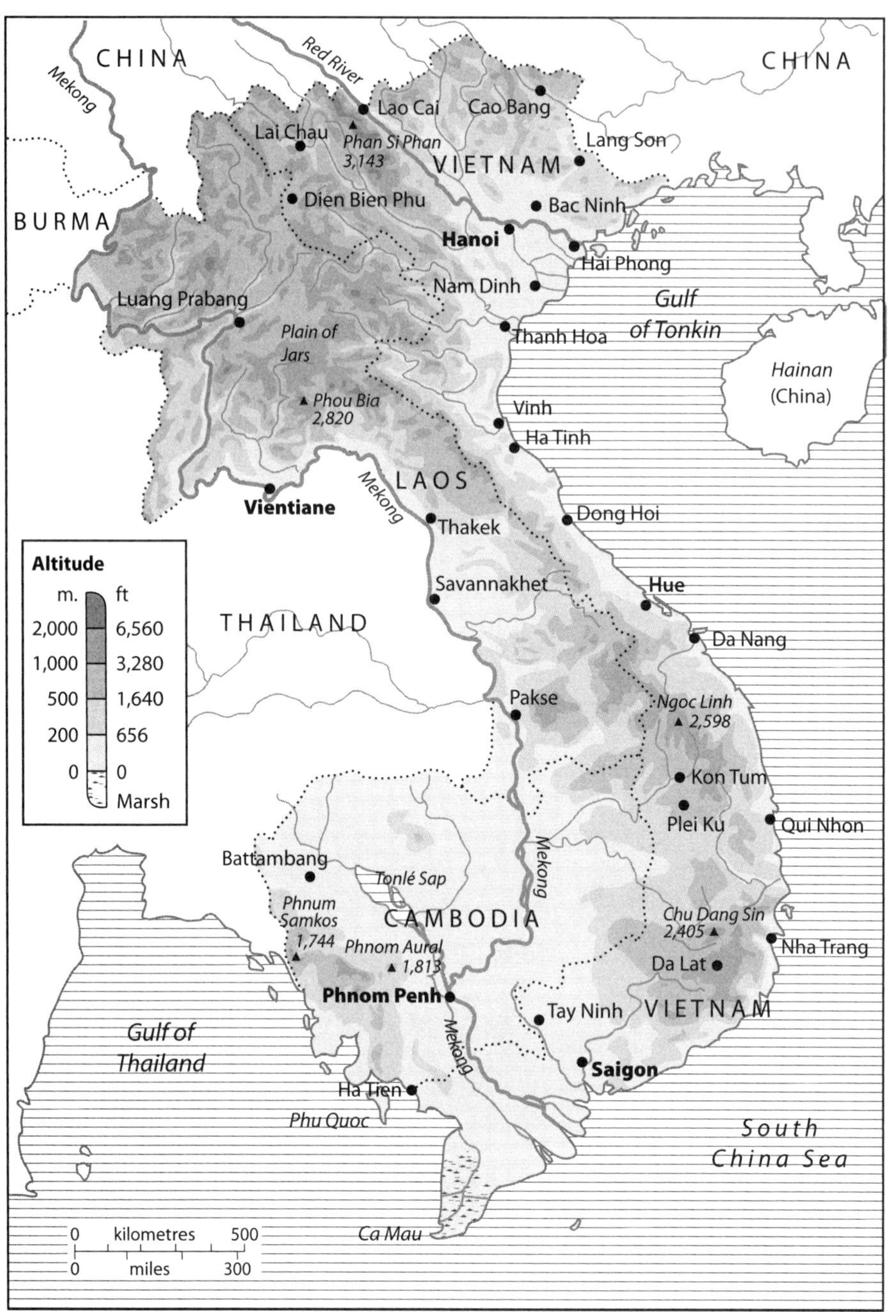


**Map 1**: Indochina peninsula. Adapted with permission from a map in Hugues Tertrais, *Atlas des guerres d'Indochine, 1940–1990: De l'Indochine française à l'ouverture internationale* (Paris: Autrement, 2004), p. 6.

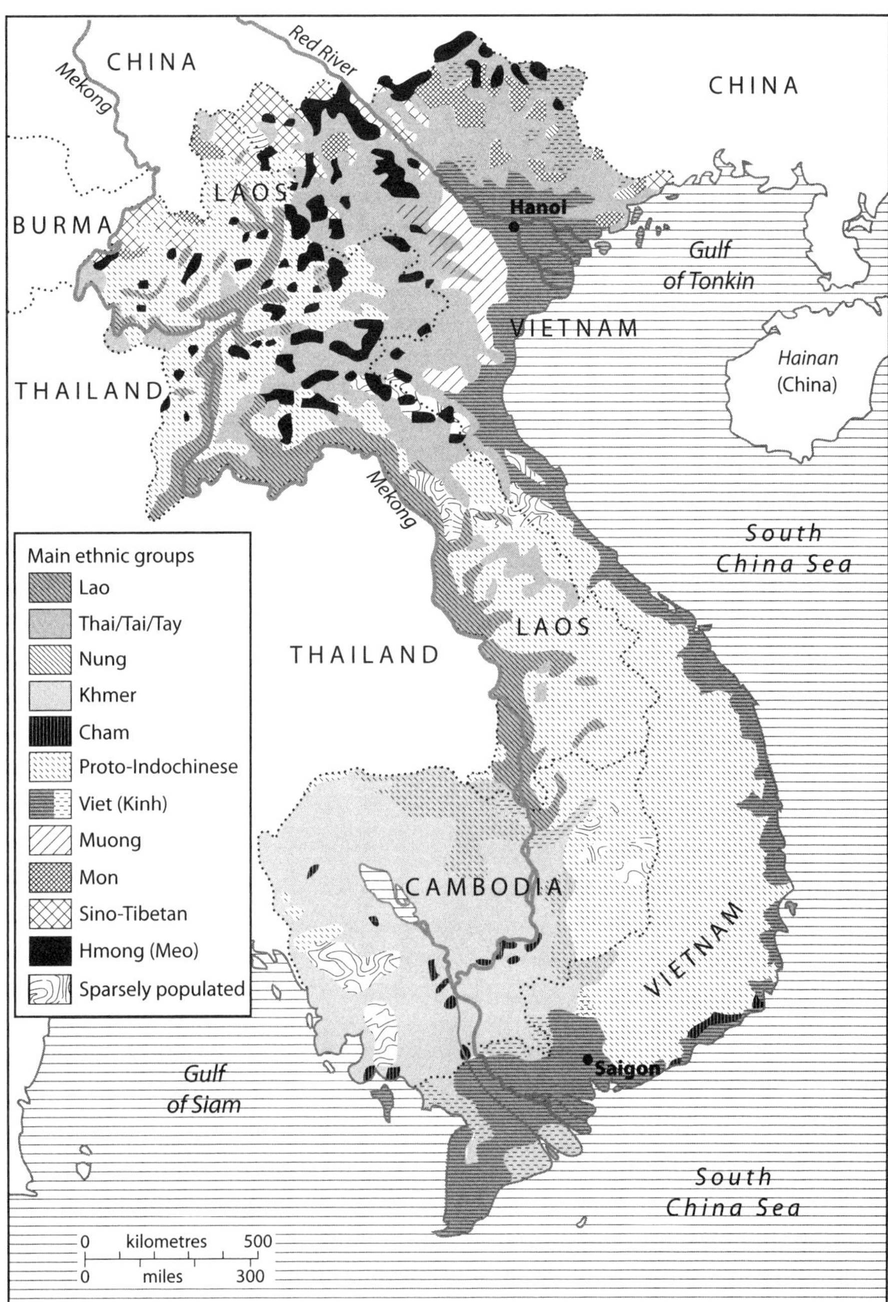


**Map 2**: Ethnic Populations. Adapted with permission from a map in Hugues Tertrais, *Atlas des guerres d'Indochine, 1940–1990: De l'Indochine française à l'ouverture internationale* (Paris: Autrement, 2004), p. 7.

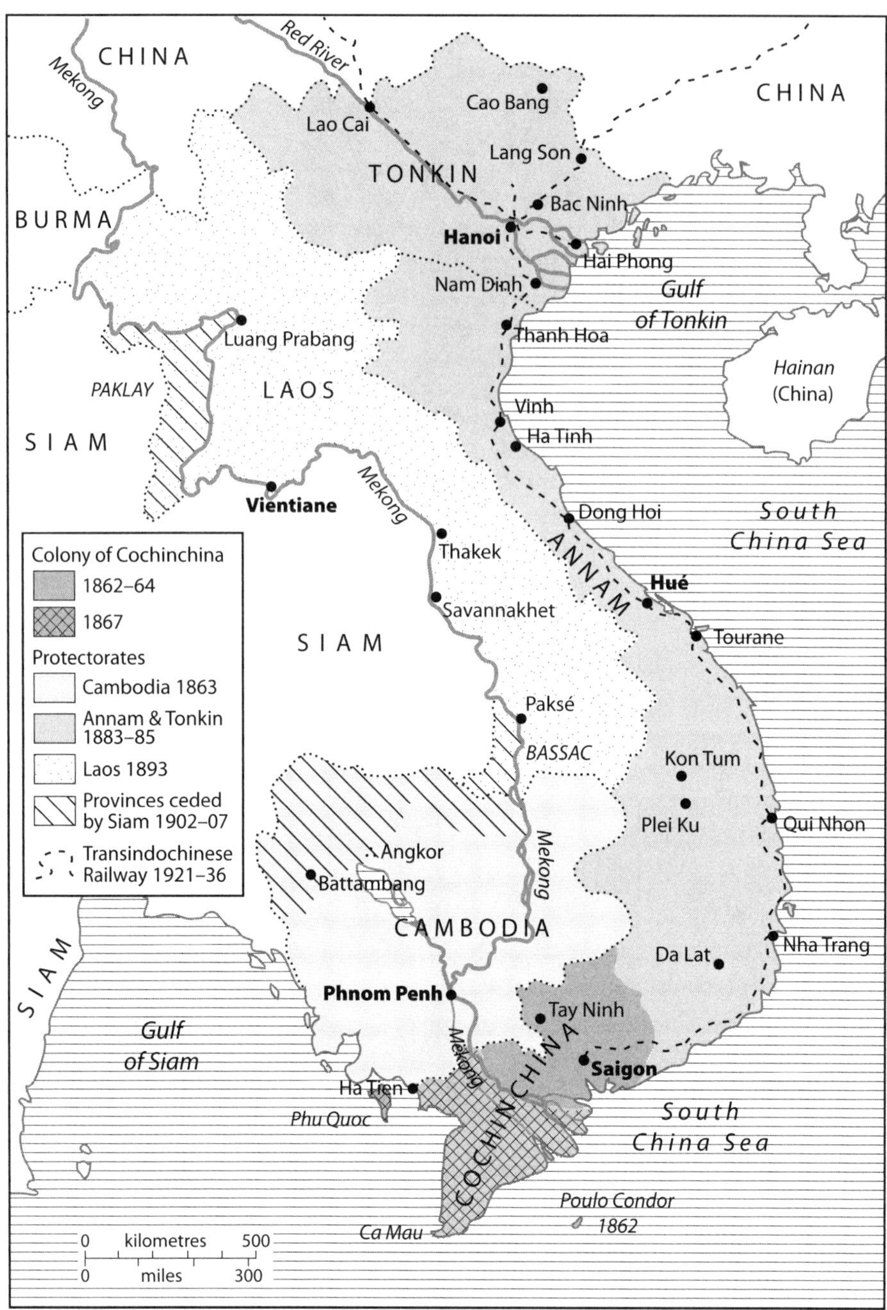


**Map 3**: French Indochina, 1862–1936. Adapted with permission from a map in Hugues Tertrais, *Atlas des guerres d'Indochine, 1940–1990: De l'Indochine française à l'ouverture internationale* (Paris: Autrement, 2004), p. 11.

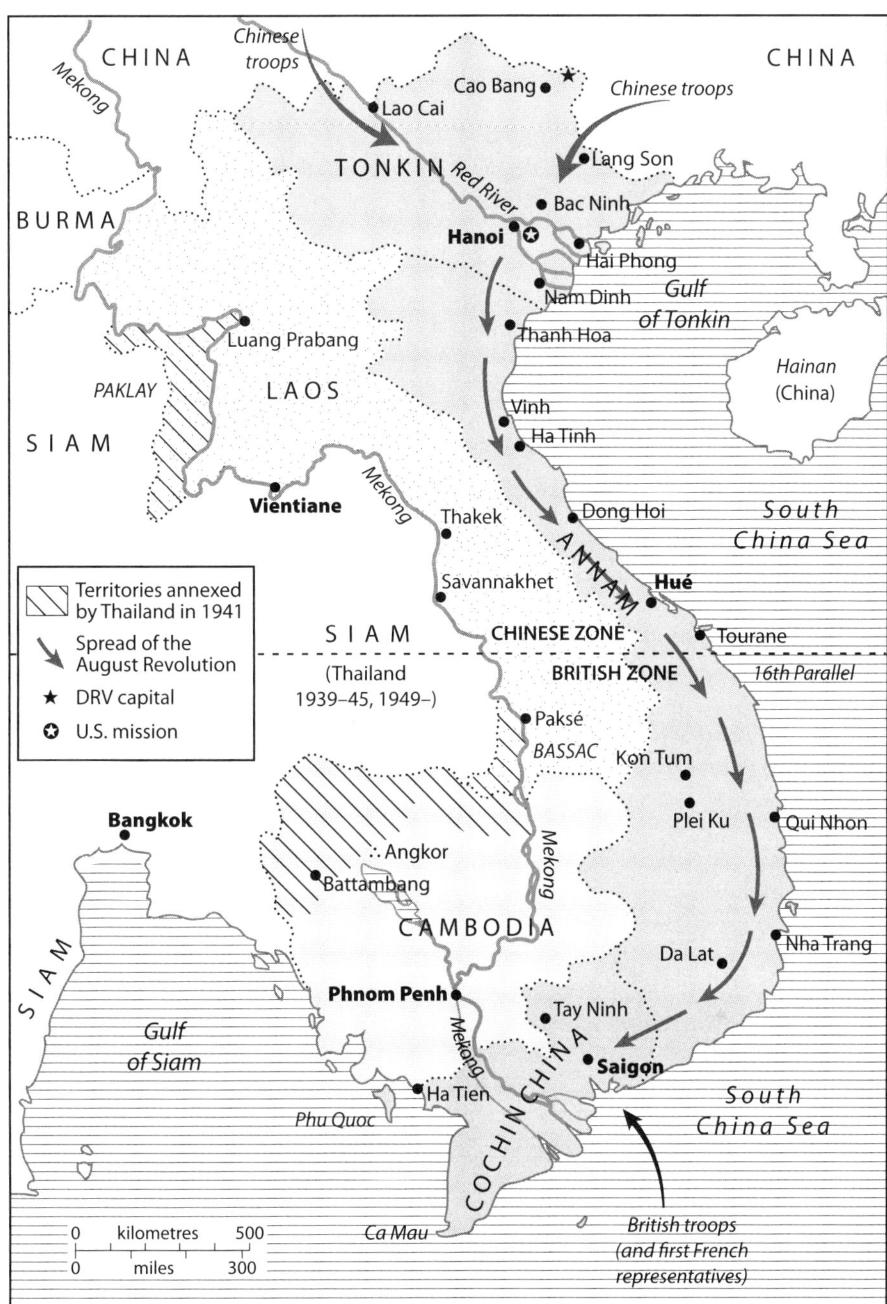


**Map 4**: Indochina partition, 1945. Adapted with permission from a map in Hugues Tertrais, *Atlas des guerres d'Indochine, 1940–1990: De l'Indochine française à l'ouverture internationale* (Paris: Autrement, 2004), p. 17.

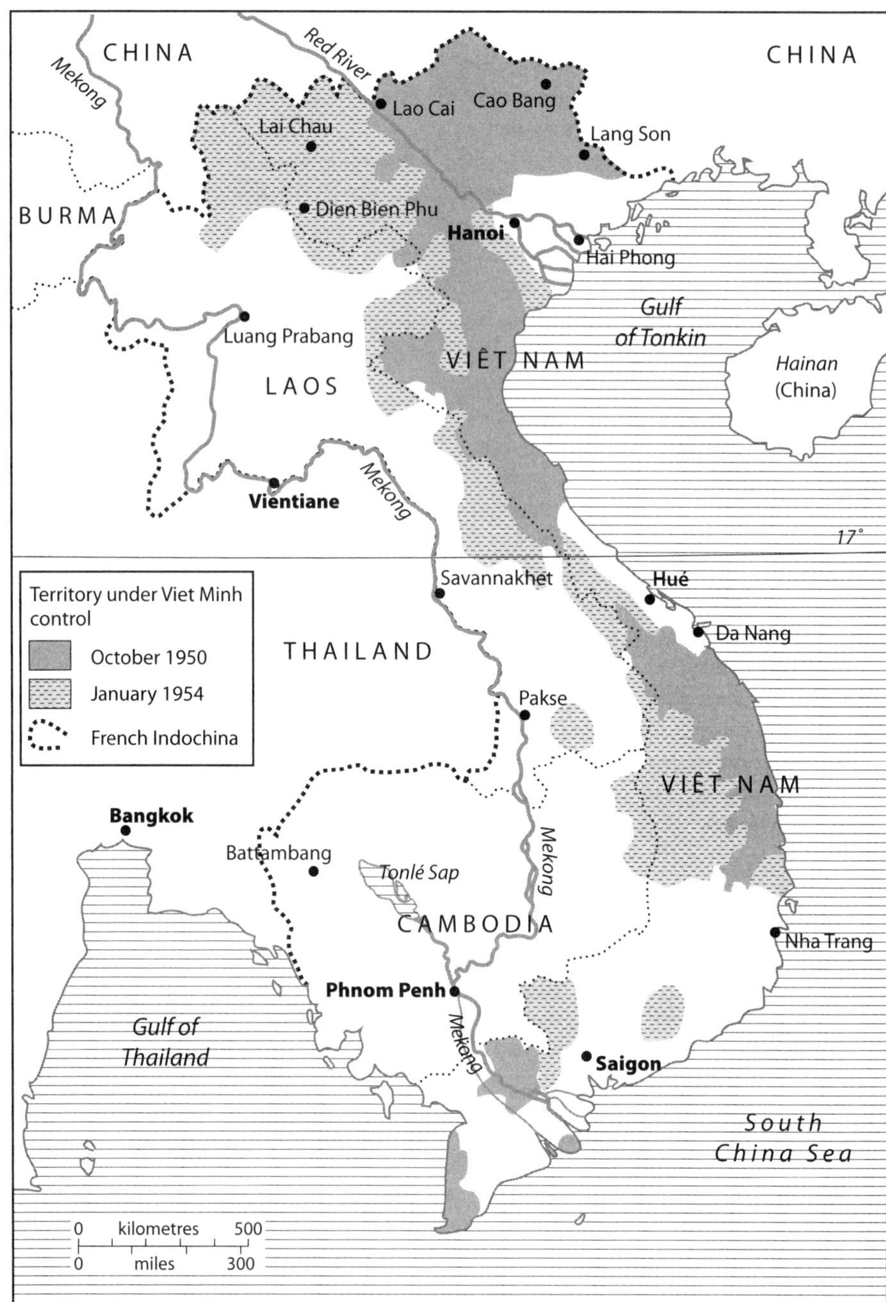


**Map 5**: Territorial control, 1950–54. Adapted with permission from a map in Hugues Tertrais, *Atlas des guerres d'Indochine, 1940–1990: De l'Indochine française à l'ouverture internationale* (Paris: Autrement, 2004), p. 26.

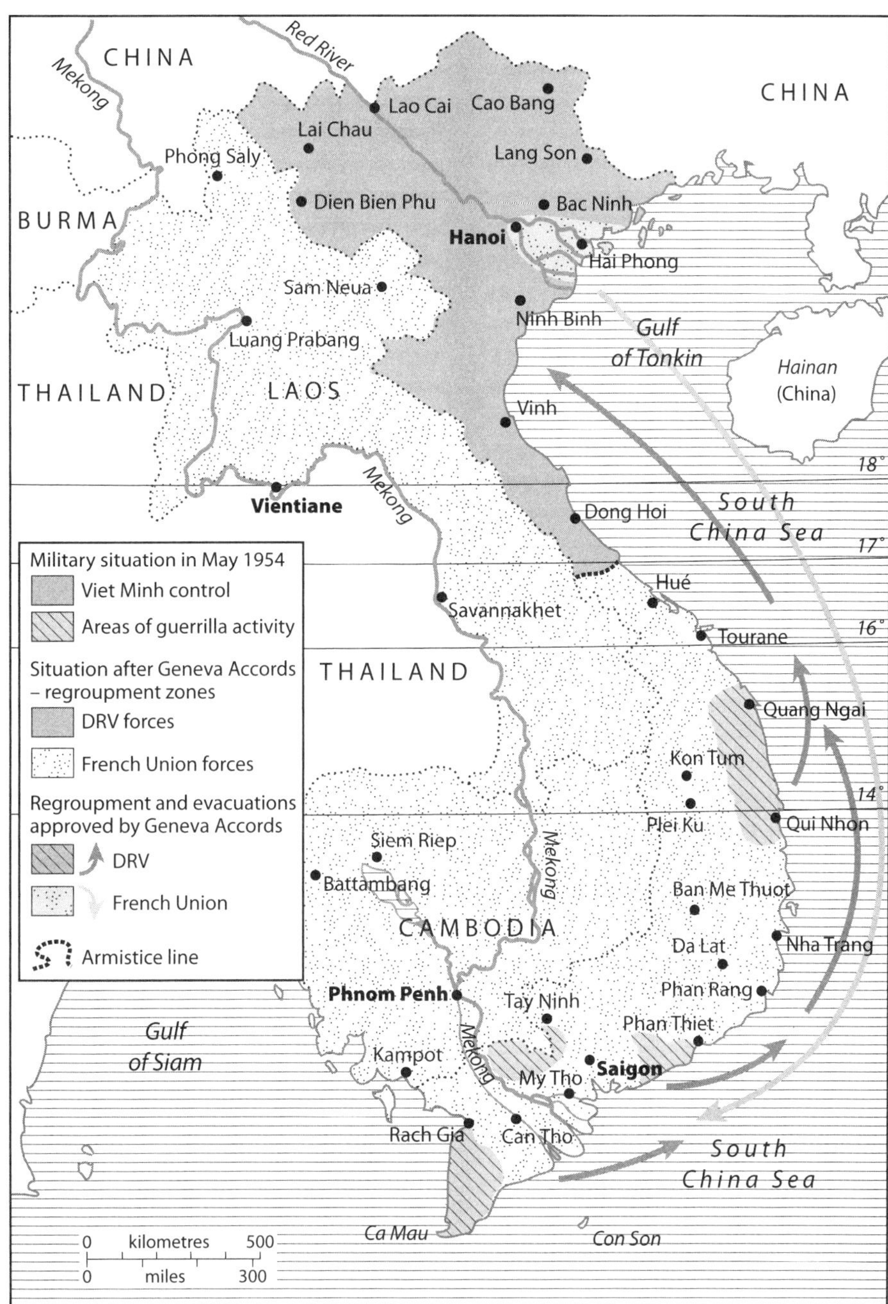


**Map 6**: Indochina regrouping zones after Geneva, 1954. Adapted with permission from a map in Hugues Tertrais, *Atlas des guerres d'Indochine, 1940–1990: De l'Indochine française à l'ouverture internationale* (Paris: Autrement, 2004), pp. 30–31.

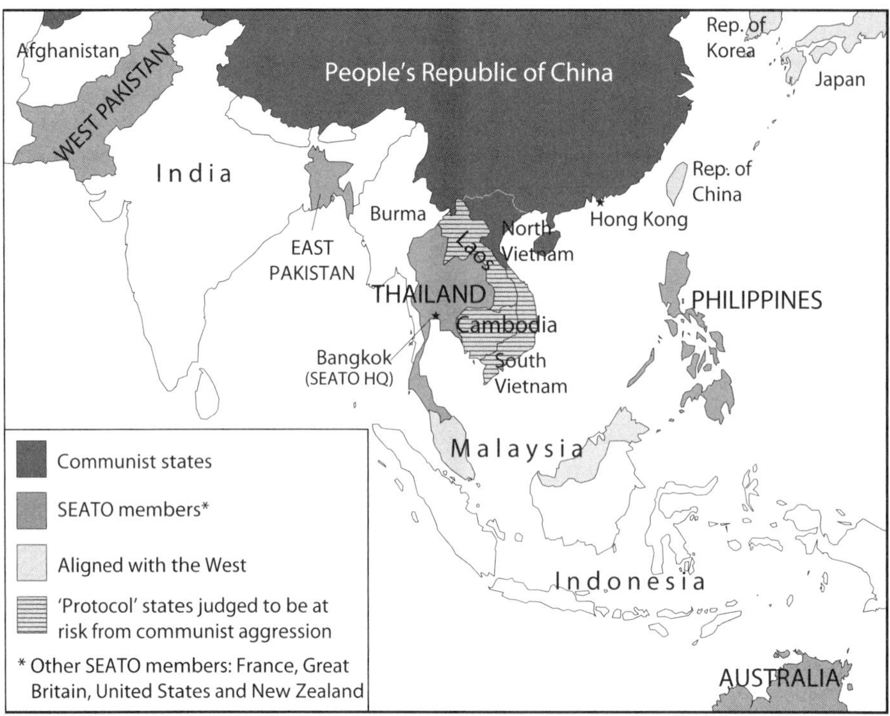


**Map 7**: South East Asia Treaty Organization, 1954. Adapted with permission from a map in Hugues Tertrais, *Atlas des guerres d'Indochine, 1940–1990: De l'Indochine française à l'ouverture internationale* (Paris: Autrement, 2004), p. 31. Further details courtesy Robert Cribb, from his *Digital Atlas of Indonesian History* (Copenhagen: NIAS Press, 2010).

# *The Indochina War: A Pictorial Essay*

**Figure 1**: Battle of Hanoi, January 1947 (Associated Press). Reproduced with permission.

**Figure 2** (left): Militarizing childhood (Getty Images). Reproduced with permission.

**Figure 3** (below): Tomb of French soldier, Tonkin 1952 (Magnum). Reproduced with permission.

**Figure 4**: Women praying for their men at war, Tonkin 1952 (Magnum). Reproduced with permission.

**Figure 5**: Wiring war, Southern Vietnam (Associated Press). Reproduced with permission.

**Figure 6**: Viet Minh prisoners of war working for French Union (Getty Images). Reproduced with permission.

**Figure 7**: Troops of the Associated State of Vietnam (Getty Images). Reproduced with permission.

**Figure 8**: French return of female prisoners, August 1954 (Associated Press). Reproduced with permission.

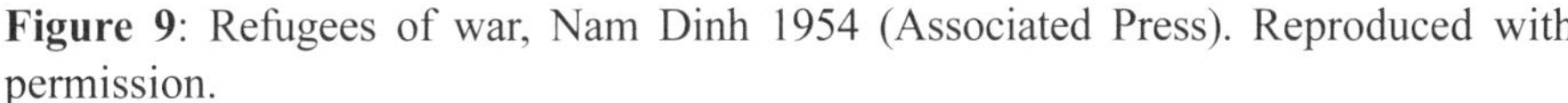

**Figure 9**: Refugees of war, Nam Dinh 1954 (Associated Press). Reproduced with permission.

**Figure 10**: Freed French prisoner of war (Getty Images). Reproduced with permission.

**Figure 11**: John Foster Dulles (left), SEATO meeting 1954 (Getty Images). Reproduced with permission.

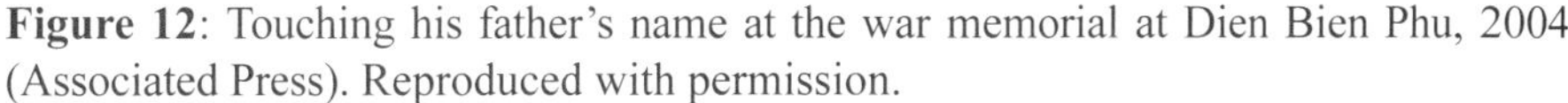

**Figure 12**: Touching his father's name at the war memorial at Dien Bien Phu, 2004 (Associated Press). Reproduced with permission.

# *Introduction*

## Why a Dictionary of the Indochina War?

Upon finishing the work at hand, I should have never revisited British comedian Rowan Atkinson's take on those poor souls who write dictionaries. But I simply could not resist. In the side-splitting episode, *Ink and Incapability,* our intrepid butler to Crown Prince George, Edmund Blackadder, engages Dr. Samuel Johnson himself in a sly tryst to learn more of the latter's newly completed dictionary. It is, Johnson declares, "the very cornerstone of English scholarship", containing every single word of the English language. Visibly unimpressed, Blackadder proposes one of his "most enthusiastic contrafribularities". "Damn!" Johnson responds, bewildered, "What is that?" He has just learned that he has failed to include an important regional term in his masterpiece. And that's not all. Unbeknownst to our renowned lexicographer, Blackadder has written a novel (*not* a dictionary, mind) and simply cannot contain his contempt for Johnson's lexicographical claim to fame. Blackadder suggests to his dimwitted boss that Johnson's dictionary really was much ado about nothing. In an unforgettable line, he scoffed it off as the "the most pointless book since *How To Learn French* was translated into French".

Ouch! I laughed of course. Who couldn't? But it hurt nonetheless. And now some 1,600 entries and six years of my life later, I'm going to have to defend "the" dictionary or at least "my" dictionary against Blackadder's charge of pointlessness. While I would never dream of speaking for Dr. Samuel Johnson, I will rebut Blackadder with a number of arguments to justify the production of this dictionary of the Indochina War.

*Motivations and Methods*

Six goals have guided me in the selection and crafting of this dictionary's entries. The first was a common one: to fill in a gap. When an intellectual field comes of age and produces a sufficiently important amount of "knowledge", it is useful to take stock, order, and synthesize that information in the form of a dictionary, both as a work of synthesis and as a reference tool. The state of the field on the Indochina War now justifies such an exercise and no English-language historical dictionary of the Indochina War exists. Given the importance of this conflict in Vietnamese, Lao, Cambodian, French, colonial, Asian, war, and international history studies, I felt that such a dictionary could be a useful resource for professionals, scholars, students, and general readers.

My second goal in writing this reference work was to use the dictionary as a way of liberating the study of the Indochina War from its nationalist and ideological straitjackets. French scholarship remains remarkably *franco-français* in its approach to this war, despite the crucial role played by others in it from the outset.[1] Vietnamese communist

1. A prolific writer on the French side of the war is Alain Ruscio. This French author specifically refers to the war as a "French" one. Alain Ruscio, *La guerre française d'Indochine* (Paris: Editions Complexes, 1992). Ten years later, in his massive bibliography of the war, Ruscio kept "French" but put it in quotes. Alain Ruscio, *La Guerre « Française » d'Indochine (1945–1954). Les Sources de la Connaissance : Bibliographie, Filmographie, Documents Divers* (Paris: Les Indes Savantes, 2002). Ruscio's bibliography focuses mainly on the French side of the war. A complete bibliography of the Vietnamese sides of the war remains to be done.

historiography reproduces this nationalist spin from the other side by focusing uniquely on the Democratic Republic of Vietnam's (DRV) "ineluctable victory" (*nhat dinh thang loi*).[2] This is not to say that the main actors in this decade-long war were not French and DRV Vietnamese; they most certainly were, as the majority of entries in this dictionary attest. However, what is striking about the Indochina War, especially as a new generation of postcolonial, transnational, and international work emerges, is the degree to which it touched upon, implicated, and connected with the region and the world from start to finish. Readers of this dictionary will thus find entries for a wide variety of non-French and non-Vietnamese actors, including the Japanese, British, Chinese, and their roles in the early stages of the war. This dictionary also contains information on the internationalization of the war, symbolized best by the involvement of the People's Republic of China and the United States in the Cold War endgame for Vietnam. A number of entries take up the connections between the Indochina War on the one hand and the European Defense Community, the North Atlantic Treaty Organization, (West) German rearmament, and the Korean War on the other. Transnational linkages cut in other ways, too. Take for example the role of a large number of Japanese, German, Soviet, Greek, and Austrian crossovers working in the DRV armed forces or the Foreign Legion, or colonial troops fighting for the French in what was in the end a very multi-national French Union army.[3] Almost 70% of the French Union troops fighting those of the DRV during the battle of Dien Bien Phu were not "metropolitan" French. They were African, North African, Foreign Legion (mainly European) and above all Vietnamese soldiers. Instructions may have been given in French, but a cacophony of languages echoed across battlefields during the entire conflagration. A handful of entries even explore such topics as the Chinese, Indian, and Vietnamese diasporas linking Indochina to the rest of Asia and beyond in a time of violent decolonization. In short, one cannot grasp the full significance of this conflict without situating it in its wider, global, transnational context, which Franco- and Vietnamo-centric approaches consistently miss. As the entry for the Algerian War suggests, the Vietnamese communist victory over the French at Dien Bien Phu in May 1954 not only inspired national liberation movements across the "South", but it also influenced the ways by which Western powers, their intelligence services, and armies understood decolonization – and sometimes did not.

My third goal in writing this dictionary was to adopt an interdisciplinary approach to the war, something that is also missing in the existing historiography. The Indochina conflict exercised profound effects upon local societies, economies, cultures, state-making (and -collapsing), art, and memory. The intertwining of colonial, civil, and Cold wars in the Indochina conflict only reinforced this. This is not to say that battles, weapons, soldiers, and officers are not important. Nor do I neglect diplomacy, diplomats, and their negotiations and accords. These things are all extremely important and occupy a large number of entries in this dictionary. However, a satisfactory dictionary of the Indochina War must now consider how violence impacted upon society, culture, gender, the economy, state-building, and the realm of ideas. This is particularly true for wars of decolonization or national liberation. Not only did national and colonial powers go to war to determine the nature of the state; they were simultaneously building their own states and underlying ideologies and discourses of legitimization in the midst of that violent confrontation. As instructions issued by the

---

2. DRV Vietnamese largely refer to the war as the "first resistance war against the French colonialists" (*cuoc khang chien chong thuc dan Phap*), followed by the "American imperialists", and the "Chinese expansionists". While things are now changing as a new generation of Vietnamese historians slowly makes its way on to the academic scene, Vietnamese communist historiography is most interested in the Vietnamese side, its side, the winning side.

3. Veterans of the French Union army and the Indochina War, Christophe Soglo and Saye Zerbo, later became presidents of Dahomey and Upper Volta, respectively.

Indochinese Communist Party on 23 November 1945 put it, the Vietnamese war of national liberation was one of "resistance and state-building" (*vua khang chien vua kien quoc*). "Those two tasks", the document added, "are inextricably linked together". Vietnamese communists even spoke of "comprehensive" or "total" war (*toan dien*), referring to the full-scale mobilization of all aspects of society, culture, economy, and politics. Similar things can be said for the non-communist Associated States of Vietnam, Laos, and Cambodia. Readers will thus find information on wartime state-building by the French and the Vietnamese, communists and non-communists, and their competing attempts to control and mobilize populations, build bureaucracies, and develop ideologies to legitimate and guide them along their ways. This dictionary also provides numerous entries on less studied socio-cultural and economic aspects of the war, such as currencies, finances, intellectuals, ideas, women, children, cities, ethnic minorities, *métis*, massacres, cinema, and novels. Even memory, grief, and cemeteries must find their place here. Lest we forget, for thousands of parents, wives, husbands, and children, the war did not end when the guns fell silent. These people carried the scars of war with them to their graves. While some might object to this wider approach, I hope nevertheless that this dual track – global and interdisciplinary – will be of some use to the reader and perhaps provide a new way of looking at the conflict, even if it means doing so through the lenses of a dictionary.

Fourth, while this dictionary is focused on the period of the war itself, 1945–1954, I have consciously tried to provide relevant biographical and thematic information on the pre-1945 period and, where relevant, I have tried to point out what a certain actor or theme became after the Indochina War ended in 1954, but only in so far as this throws light on the importance of the Indochina story at hand.[4] Such a choice has admittedly increased the size of many entries; but I feel that this has also improved the overall quality of the entries and usefulness of the dictionary. For example, the so-called Bao Dai Solution as it became known in the late 1940s, cannot be fully grasped without tracing its origins from the immediate post-World War I period, when colonial Republican thinkers such as Albert Sarraut created what was for all intents and purposes the first experiment. In the early 1930s (1930–1935), during the Vichy period (1940–1944), and again in the late 1940s, the French attempted to mobilize the Vietnamese monarch and his symbolic power to legitimate colonial rule in Vietnamese eyes and thwart communist and nationalist attempts to end that same foreign presence. Similarly, fuller biographical information on colonial administrators during the interwar period throws new light on the relationships among those who stayed on or returned during the Indochina War, such as Jean Cousseau, Léon Pignon, Albert Torel, and many others. Many of these names will be unfamiliar to non-French and younger Vietnamese and French readers; however, it is hard to underestimate their importance during the conflict. Similar things could be said for many military officers whose Indochinese experiences reached back to the colonial period and both World Wars.

Fifth, this dictionary attempts to include as many of the different actors of the Indochina War as possible, regardless of their ethnicity, political and religious beliefs, or alliances. I have tried to avoid two problems here. As noted earlier, French and Vietnamese dictionaries and historians are remarkably nationalist in their approach to the war. And when they say "Indochina", both tend to forget that colonial Indochina at the time also included the Lao, Cambodians, and minority peoples, many of whom were deeply affected by the violent Franco-Vietnamese showdown. A dictionary

4. Demarcating clear lines between the Indochina War and World War II on the one hand and between the Indochina conflict and the Vietnam War on the other turned out to be surprisingly difficult. For many French officers, as the entries in this volume show, the Indochina War flowed out of the World War II and into the Algerian one, whereas for just as many Vietnamese the Indochina conflict melded into the American War in Vietnam.

claiming an "Indochinese" tack thus must do more than simply pay lip service to these non-French and non-Vietnamese groups. Second, because the winners tend to write their history (*duoc lam vua thua lam giac* in Vietnamese[5]), the losers often vanish from the picture. Few would dispute this common assertion. However, a dictionary of the Indochina conflict must restore the vanquished to our purview. As recent scholarship on local strategies of accommodation with the Germans and Japanese during World War II shows, it is no longer permissible to write off groups working with the Axis powers as simple "collaborators", "lackeys", or "puppets".[6] Nor can one cast the Associated States of Indochina or their avatars as simple Franco-American "inventions" or "pawns" devoid of all agency and legitimacy.[7] Moreover, the Indochina War was not just a conflict opposing the French against the Democratic Republic of Vietnam. It was also a civil war, one that mutually opposed the Vietnamese in particular. Readers will thus find entries for a wide variety of non-communist Vietnamese, Lao, and Cambodian politicians, parties, and governments, all of which were a part of the making of postcolonial Indochina. This, too, has admittedly increased the length of this book; but I feel that it has also improved the quality and may make it more useful to a wider range of readers. In every case, I have tried to provide accurate information and non-polemical analysis where necessary. In short, there was more to "Vietnam" than the "Viet Minh", the state driving it, or the communist party behind it.[8]

Lastly, I should note here that I am not the only one to attempt a dictionary of

5. "Win and you are king; lose and you become a pirate".

6. See among others: Istvan Deak, Jan T. Gross, and Tony Judt (eds.). *The Politics of Retribution in Europe* (Princeton: Princeton University Press, 2000); Timothy Brook, *Collaboration: Japanese Agents and Local Elites in Wartime China* (Cambridge: Harvard University Press, 2005); Mark Mazower, *Hitler's Empire: How the Nazis Ruled Europe,* (London: Penguin, 2009); Simon Kitson and Hanna Diamond, eds., *Vichy, Resistance, Liberation: New Perspectives on Wartime France,* (London: Berg Publishers, 2005); Simon Kitson, *The Hunt for Nazi Spies: Fighting Espionage in Vichy France* (Chicago: The University of Chicago Press, 2007); Julian Jackson, *France: The Dark Years* (New York: Oxford University Press, 2003); and Michael Kim, 'Regards sur la collaboration coréenne', *Vingtième Siècle,* no. 94 (April–June 2007), pp. 35–44.

7. Frances Fitzgerald's Pulitzer prize-winning *Fire in the Lake* (1972) is largely premised on the illegitimacy of the Associated State of Vietnam and its postcolonial successor, the Republic of Vietnam led by Ngo Dinh Diem, whereas she champions Ho Chi Minh's Democratic Republic of Vietnam as the legitimate Vietnam, the receptacle of the historical "mandate of heaven". For a more nuanced, even handed approach to the Republic of Vietnam, allowing for Vietnamese agency and non-communist legitimacy, see: Philip E. Catton, *Diem's Final Failure: Prelude to America's War in Vietnam* (Lawrence: University of Kansas Press, 2003). On non-communist nationalism during the Indochina War, see François Guillemot's landmark study, *Dai Viêt, indépendance et révolution au Viêt-Nam. L'échec de la troisième voie (1938–1955),* (Paris: Les Indes Savantes, 2011). There exists no sustained, analytical account of the birth, evolution, and disappearance of the Associated State of Vietnam or its Cambodian and Lao counterparts.

8. I have done my best to factor in non-communist Vietnamese, Lao and Cambodians, despite serious difficulties encountered in obtaining reliable information. While I was able to locate biographical information on many Associated State personages, I have largely failed to obtain information allowing me to pen entries on cemeteries, memorials, children, women, history, intellectuals, and other vital socio-cultural matters for the Associated States of Vietnam, Laos, Cambodia and ethnic minority groups. To at least some extent this reflects the research agendas of scholarship over the last fifty years. I have every intention of updating these matters in a revised edition of this dictionary as more information becomes available and scholarship shifts in new directions. There are signs that this is occurring.

Indochina or the war of 1945–1954.[9] Recently, French historian Michel Bodin and the late and eminent Jacques Dalloz published French-language dictionaries of the Indochina War (1945–1954).[10] Bodin focuses mainly on the French military aspects of the war whereas Dalloz is interested in French politics and intellectuals. While I have benefited immensely from both books in the making of mine and recommend them to readers, they are hindered by the fact that their dictionaries reflect their respective specializations and failure to conceive of the war in wider international and interdisciplinary terms. Bodin and Dalloz are focused mainly on the French side and military and political issues.[11] One looks in vain for pertinent information on the Vietnamese, Lao, and Cambodian actors as well as social, cultural, gender, and economic matters. Moving along the lines described above, the dictionary I propose here seeks to provide a fuller, deeper, and more connected account of the war than is currently available. While I have done my utmost to be fair, dispassionate, and objective in researching and writing each of the following entries, this dictionary as a whole and many of its entries in particular are designed to move us in new directions in our understanding of the Indochina War. After all, as Diderot and Voltaire demonstrated in the eighteenth century, dictionaries are not simple *contrafribularities*. They can also provide an original way of looking at and engaging a subject intellectually. This is probably the main reason explaining my mad decision to undertake this project in the first place.[12]

*Sources*

As noted at the outset, the literature on the Indochina War has developed greatly since Philippe Devillers and Paul Mus first published their classic studies in 1952.[13] In addition to the work of these pioneers, I have relied heavily on the studies of scores of scholars from across the world now working on the Indochina War, including Vietnamese ones. To try to name some here and not others would be unfair and incomplete. The reader can find their main works cited in the bibliography. For a number of important entries, I have mentioned a certain author's contribution or interpretation of a person, event, or idea. My idea is to alert the reader to an important historiographical

---

9. For the Vietnam War, there are several dictionaries currently available. Of particular importance is Edwin E. Moïse's *Historical Dictionary of the Vietnam War* (Lanham: Scarecrow Press, 2001).

10. Jacques Dalloz, *Dictionnaire de la Guerre d'Indochine*, 1945–1954 (Paris: Armand Colin, 2006) (preface written by Bernard Droz) and Michel Bodin, *Dictionnaire de la Guerre d'Indochine, 1945–1954* (Paris: Economica, 2004). Another French historian, Hugues Tertrais, has provided us with an excellent atlas of the wars for Indochina. Hugues Tertrais, *Atlas des guerres d'Indochine, 1940–1990: De l'Indochine française à l'ouverture internationale* (Paris: Autrement, 2004). Leading French historians have recently produced beautifully crafted thematic dictionaries of "colonial France". Jean-Pierre Rioux (editor), *Dictionnaire de la France coloniale* (Paris: Flammarion, 2007) and the late Claude Liauzu (editor), *Dictionnaire de la colonisation française* (Paris: Larousse, 2007).

11. Michel Bodin is also involved in Indochinese memory making in France. See: http://www.souvenirfrancais-issy.com/article-15858099-6.html.

12. On madness and the crafting of dictionaries, see in particular: Simon Winchester, *The Professor and the Madman: A Tale of Murder, Insanity, and the Making of the Oxford English Dictionary* (Harper Perennial, 2005).

13. Philippe Devillers, *Histoire du Vietnam de 1940 à 1952* (Paris: Le Seuil, 1952) and Paul Mus, *Viêt-Nam : Sociologie d'une guerre* (Paris: Editions du Seuil, 1952). For mainly French publications and films on the Indochina War, see: Alain Ruscio, et. al., *La Guerre « Française » d'Indochine (1945–1954). Les Sources de la Connaissance: Bibliographie, Filmographie, Documents Divers* (Paris: Les Indes Savantes, 2002). See also Edwin Moïse's excellent *Bibliography of the Vietnam War* at http://www.clemson.edu/caah/history/facultypages/EdMoise/bibliography.html.

point, which remains a subject of debate (see, for example, the entries for 19 December 1946 or the Accords of 6 March 1946).

I have also relied on a wide variety of primary sources. I will forever be grateful to the staffs at the *Centre des Archives d'Outre-mer* (CAOM) in Aix-en-Provence and the *Service historique de la Défense* (SHD) in Vincennes for granting me special permission to consult and to use the personnel records (*les états des services*) for a large number of French military officers and colonial administrators, not to mention the biographical holdings on the Indochina War held in the *Service de documentation* at the SHD in the Château de Vincennes. A special thanks to Mme Lucette Vachier at the CAOM and Colonel Frédéric Guélton, General André Bach, and Madame Bernard (chi Son) at the SHD. Without their help and the access all of them provided, this dictionary would have been much poorer. I was also fortunate to discover in various French archives detailed biographies created and updated by various intelligence and security services during the war. While I always did my best to verify and discard questionable information and interpretations, the *Sûreté fédérale*'s biographies of Indochinese political personalities were a gold mine of information, often based on birth certificates, personnel records, and a variety of official internal documentation of their career tracks. The recent opening of the service files of the Office of Strategic Services in the National Archives and Records Administration (NARA) in the United States allowed me to fill in missing pieces concerning Americans involved in Vietnamese history at its most important historical juncture in 1945 and 1946. Access to recently declassified Department of State "airgrams" also provided me with some extraordinary biographical information on non-communist Vietnamese figures. I also benefited from access to the Georges Boudarel archives and papers now held at the *Institut d'Asie orientale* held in the *Ecole normale supérieure* in Lyon, France. The same is true for the remarkable collection of biographical cards kept by the American journalist Ellen Hammer during her coverage of the Indochina war, a copy of which is now held in the Cornell University library. My thanks to Prof. David Marr, who kindly made available his biographical database of Vietnamese historical figures. Lastly, I gleaned invaluable details from a mass of Vietnamese language memoirs, dictionaries, journals, and historical studies of the war, all of which have been pouring off the presses inside and outside Vietnam since the late 1980s (see the bibliography).

It would be absurd and pretentious to think that this dictionary is perfect. It is not. I can only hope that the reader will be so kind as to send me any suggestions, corrections, or other *contrafribularities* to goscha.christopher@uqam.ca. I have included an index at the end of the dictionary to assist the reader in locating people, places, things, and themes related to the Indochina War.

### *Naming and Periodizing the War*

A dictionary such as this must name the war and delineate the period it seeks to treat. On the first matter, there is still no unanimous agreement as to what exactly we should call this conflict. There may never be. Authors writing in French, Vietnamese, and English refer to it variously as the French Indochina War, the First Indochina War, the First Vietnam War, the First War of National Resistance, the Anti-French War, the Franco-Vietnamese War, the Franco-Vietminh War, and even the Vietnamese Civil War. The need to decide upon an acceptable formula for this dictionary is nevertheless obligatory. For several reasons, I have chosen to refer to this conflict as the "First Indochina War". I could have used the "French Indochina War", as Alain Ruscio does, but I feel that it is important to go beyond the French-centered, nationalist approach this term implies. For similar reasons, I have also avoided using the terms "Anti-French War" or the "Franco-Vietnamese War". The "First Vietnam War" could work, but the problem is that it is too narrow and is too easily confused with "the" Vietnam War involving the Americans later on. Moreover, the term "Vietnam" or

"Vietnamese" implicitly rules out others involved in the war, especially the Lao and the Cambodians. It also tends to equate "the" Vietnamese with those running the DRV, when in fact other Vietnamese states and nationalists came to life to compete with it and its leaders during the conflict.

Use of the wider term, "Indochina War", thus allows us to avoid these pitfalls. "Indochina" is a geopolitical term that came to refer to the colonial state created by the French by the late nineteenth century.[14] It included Tonkin, Annam, Cochinchina, Laos, and Cambodia, all of which became parts of an Indochinese Union created in 1887. It is useful to maintain this colonial framework since the war was at the outset a battle over the reality of French Indochina – and not just Vietnam. General Charles de Gaulle's reformist-minded colonial project for Indochina was based on the creation of a pentagonal Indochinese Federation, including Tonkin, Annam and Cochinchina (collectively, Vietnam to nationalists), as well as Laos and Cambodia. If the French conceded by 1947 that this pentagonal federal structure was not going to fly in the face of competing nationalisms and moved towards creating three Associated States along national lines from 1948, they nonetheless continued to situate and associate those states within an Indochinese context as the *Etats associés d'Indochine*. Monetary and commercial accords linked the three states in a quadripartite relationship with the French more or less until the end of the war. Even the French Ministry in charge of relations with these associated states was for all intents and purposes an Indochinese one until the eve of the Geneva Accords (1954).

Significantly, Vietnamese communists also operated in Indochinese terms. The creation of the Khmer Issarak and Pathet Lao "resistance governments" in 1949–1950 represented communist efforts to create their own associated states of an Indochinese kind to counter those being crafted by the French. And like the French, communist Vietnamese also had to give up on the idea of creating their own federation in 1950 in the light of Lao and Cambodian nationalist aspirations of a non-Indochinese kind. However, it is not at all clear that Vietnamese communists ever abandoned their internationalist communist vision of themselves at the head of an Indochinese revolution. Lastly, the use of the term "Indochina" is warranted by the fact that from 1950 military operations extended beyond Vietnam as Chinese aid allowed the DRV's army to take the battle to the French across the "Indochinese battlefield", as Vo Nguyen Giap put it in 1950.[15]

As for the periodization of the war, I have chosen the rather classic dates, starting with the Japanese capitulation on 15 August 1945 and ending with the signing of the Geneva Accords on 21 July 1954. These dates are admittedly arbitrary. I could have conceivably started with the Franco-Thai conflict of 1940–41 and Thai premier's Phibun Songkram's attempts to incorporate western parts of French colonial Indochina into "Thailand". Similarly, I could have easily extended the end of the dictionary to say 1956, closing with the final French military withdrawal from Indochina or the failure to hold elections to unify Vietnam according to the Geneva agreements. I was not opposed to either idea (indeed, I was favorably inclined to both), but in the end I thought it best to limit the period under study. All it takes is expanding the time frame by one year on either side of the conflagration to increase almost exponentially the number of entries one would have to include in order to do justice to the wider

14. Daniel Hémery, 'Inconstante Indochine … L'invention et les dérives d'une catégorie géographique', *Revue française d'histoire d'outre-mer* (1er semestre 2000), pp. 137–158 and Christopher Goscha, *Vietnam or Indochina? Contesting Concepts of Space in Vietnamese Nationalism* (Copenhagen: Nordic Institute of Asian Studies), 1995, part I.

15. Goscha, *Vietnam or Indochina?*, parts I and II, and Christopher Goscha, 'The Revolutionary Laos of the Democratic Republic of Vietnam: The Making of a Transnational Pathet Lao Solution', in Christopher Goscha and Karine Laplante, eds., *The Failure of Peace in Indochina* (Paris: Les Indes Savantes, 2010), pp. 61–84.

purview proposed in this dictionary. In short, one has to start and stop somewhere. I decided to begin in August 1945 and to end in July 1954.

## The Indochina War: A Connected History

The Indochina War was not one conflagration, but several. It was a colonial and civil conflict, a hotspot in the Cold War, as well as a social, cultural, intellectual, ideological, and economic battle for many. The conflict not only divided the French and the Vietnamese, but it also affected the Lao, Cambodians, and ethnic minorities and involved the Chinese, British, Soviets, Thais, Indians, and Americans. The Indochina War was all of this and more.

At the outset, it was above all a clash between opposing French and Vietnamese nationalist projects over who would control the Indochinese space left blank after the Japanese brought down the colonial house in Indochina in March 1945 and were then defeated themselves a few months later. Would Indochina remain a part of the French "imperial nation-state" which Charles de Gaulle counted on rebuilding or would it be decolonized into one or more modern nation-states under the leadership of Ho Chi Minh and his Lao and Cambodian partners?[16] Or perhaps something in between, defined along the lines of the British Commonwealth?

Both of these men's projects had crystallized during World War II, a global conflict that had unleashed momentous change. On the one hand, the French empire had been crucial to the national survival of Charles de Gaulle's resistance government contesting the reality of Vichy's France.[17] For de Gaulle, Algeria was French and so was Indochina. In 1943, following the Allied liberation of North Africa, de Gaulle established the *Comité français de la libération nationale* (CFLN) in Algiers. Less than a year later, thanks to the Allies and his remarkably multi-ethnic imperial army, de Gaulle returned from exile to lead a newly liberated France.[18] And for de Gaulle and many other French nationalists of all political stripes, the restoration of France's national and international identity would turn on the liberation, maintenance, and recovery of all of the empire, including the missing Indochinese piece. In Brazzaville in early 1944 and again in the declaration on Indochina in late March 1945, Free French colonial officials such as Henri Laurentie and Léon Pignon hammered out a package of seemingly liberal colonial reforms designed to provide increased autonomy to restless colonies in order to counter the growing tide of colonial nationalism generated by the rapid French defeat in 1940, by global war, and by the intrusion of international actors, not least of all the United States (in both North Africa and Indochina).[19] The term "French Union" replaced the suddenly outdated word "Empire", while Indochina would serve as the litmus test for a new federal conception of colonial renewal. However, decolonization, even cast within the framework of a commonwealth such as that proposed eventually by the British, was unimaginable in the official French mind of 1945, tantamount to another national humiliation, a debacle

16. On the notion of the imperial nation-state, see: Frederick Cooper, *Colonialism in Question* (Berkeley: University of California Press, 2005, pp. 153–203) and Gary Wilder, *The French Imperial Nation-State: Négritude and Colonial Humanism between the Two World Wars* (Chicago: The University of Chicago Press, 2005). Stein Tønnesson also underscores the emergence of two opposing national projects in his *Vietnam 1946: How the War Began* (Berkeley: University of California Press, 2009).

17. Martin Thomas, *The French Empire at War, 1940–1945,* (Manchester: Manchester University Press, 2007).

18. Indeed, the Free French Army was largely a colonial, not an ethnic French one. As was the British army that landed in southern Indochina in September 1945 to accept the Japanese surrender and maintain order.

19. Martin Shipway, *The Road to War: France and Vietnam, 1944–1947,* (Oxford: Berghahn Books, 1996).

on the scale of June 1940.[20] In September 1945, de Gaulle chose an Admiral, Georges Thierry d'Argenlieu, to serve as his new High Commissioner for Indochina. The latter's orders were to retake and to re-establish French sovereignty over all of Indochina in the form of an eventual Indochinese Federation.[21]

Like de Gaulle, Ho Chi Minh had also created a nationalist front during World War II.[22] It was located just outside Japanese-controlled Indochina and was designed to prepare for the recovery of Vietnamese national sovereignty once the Allies had defeated the Japanese in Asia. In 1941, in Pac Bo, a collection of caves located along the Sino-Vietnamese border, Ho Chi Minh presided over the formation of the *Viet Minh Doc Lap Dong Minh* or the Vietnamese Independence League (or, for short, Viet Minh). Led by the Indochinese Communist Party, this broad-based nationalist front was designed to attract support from all segments of Vietnamese society in favor of national independence. On 19 August 1945, a few days after the Japanese capitulation to the Allies, but before the Gaullists could land their troops, the communist-led Viet Minh rode a famine-driven wave of popular discontent to power in Hanoi and then throughout the rest of the country in the following weeks.[23] On 2 September 1945, the charismatic Ho Chi Minh electrified thousands of listeners in Hanoi when he declared the reality of the Democratic Republic of Vietnam (DRV). When Ho Chi Minh, "he who enlightens" as he now styled himself, stepped up to the microphone and asked his "compatriots" if they could hear him clearly, the crowd roared back "yes" (*co*!). Communist though he most certainly was, Ho Chi Minh was also a nationalist, now moving to personify Vietnamese nationalist aspirations as the father of the nation.[24] In this sense, two new states and two new nationalist leaders had emerged from World War II, one French, the other Vietnamese, both charismatic and each of whom held opposing yet deeply nationalist conceptions about the future of Indochina. This was a potentially very explosive mix.

International players also profoundly influenced the nature of the Indochina War from beginning to end. This was particularly true because of the globalizing effects of World War II and the Cold War. Consider the first case for a moment. Not only had Nazi Germany incorporated France into its European Empire, as Mark Mazower has demonstrated, but the Japanese also incorporated Western empires in Southeast Asia into their own imperial order. This meant that Vichy's subordination to the Axis gave rise to an "empire within an empire" in Indochina. It lasted until the Japanese finally

---

20. Stanley Hoffmann, 'Le trauma de 1940', in Jean-Pierre Azéma and François Bédarida, eds., *La France des années noires, 1. De la défaite à Vichy* (Paris: Editions du Seuil, 2000), p. 152. On Indochina, decolonization and the French colonial mind, see the essay signed by none other than Paul Mus, head of the Colonial Academy between 1946 and 1950. Paul Mus, *Le destin de l'Union française, de l'Indochine à l'Afrique* (Paris: Editions du Seuil, 1954) and David Chandler and Christopher Goscha (eds.), *L'espace d'un regard: Paul Mus* (Paris: Les Indes Savantes, 2006).

21. Frédéric Turpin, *De Gaulle, les gaullistes et l'Indochine (1940–1956)* (Paris: Les Indes Savantes, 2005). Admiral Thierry d'Argenlieu landed at Bayeux with de Gaulle on 14 June 1944.

22. It should be recalled that, whatever their limitations, nationalist minded governments emerged in Vietnam under Tran Trong Kim and Emperor Bao Dai, in Cambodia under Son Ngoc Thanh and King Norodom Sihanouk, and in Laos under Prince Phetxarāt and King Sīsāvangvong.

23. David Marr, *Vietnam 1945: The Quest for Power* (Berkeley: University of California Press, 1995) and Stein Tønnesson, *The Vietnamese Revolution of 1945: Roosevelt, Ho Chi Minh and de Gaulle in a World at War* (London: Sage Publications, 1991).

24. On this process, see: Pierre Brocheux, *Ho Chi Minh: du révolutionnaire à l'icône* (Paris: Payot, 2003) and Daniel Hémery, 'Ho Chi Minh: Vie singulière et nationalisation des esprits', in Christopher E. Goscha and Benoît de Tréglodé, eds., *The Birth of a Party-State: Vietnam since 1945* (Paris: Les Indes Savantes, 2004), pp. 135–148.

brought down the French in March 1945 and the Allies put an end to the Empire of Japan a few months later. This, in turn, gave rise to an important conjuncture in Southeast Asia, whereby the combination of the Japanese overthrow of European colonial states and the Allied defeat of the Japanese empire set decolonization into motion as nationalists such as Ho Chi Minh and Sukarno declared the independence of their respective countries. Of course, there was nothing inevitable about this as newly liberated French and Dutch nationalists moved to rebuild their colonial empires in Indochina and Indonesia. However, the emergence of Vietnamese and Indonesian nationalists determined to keep their newly formed nation-states alive against this "second colonial conquest" ensured that violence would come early to Southeast Asia.

International actors were deeply involved in France's attempt to hold on to Indochina as the Pacific War came to a close. Having been knocked out of World War II at the start, de Gaulle's France was not privy to many major global decisions taken by the British, Americans, Soviets, and the Chinese as the war ended. On several occasions, in fact, the American President Franklin Roosevelt spoke of taking Indochina away from the French altogether and putting it under an international trusteeship. Nor was de Gaulle consulted about the Allied decision taken at Potsdam in July 1945 allowing the British to occupy and accept the Japanese surrender in Indochina below the sixteenth parallel while the Republic of China would do the same above that line. Indeed, World War II and the rise of the Americans in the Pacific during the war strengthened Republican China's international stature to the detriment of the French. The Potsdam decision allowing the Chinese to occupy northern Indochina reflected this geopolitical reality, something that would have been simply unthinkable a few years earlier.[25] Thus, even before the Japanese had capitulated in mid August 1945, the French had to take into account the wartime internationalization of colonial matters. Neither French Indochina (Vietnam) nor North Africa (Algeria) for that matter could be considered as simple *chasses gardées coloniales*.

The internationally imposed division of Indochina at the sixteenth parallel remains the best example of how global events impinged on colonial and national ones, essential to understanding the complex events of 1945–47 in Indochina. For one, Chinese officers blocked the French return to northern Indochina until the Franco-Chinese accord of 28 February 1946 allowed the French to begin replacing Chinese troops north of the sixteenth parallel. In exchange, however, the French had to give up many of their colonial privileges in China and accord special ones to the overseas Chinese living in Indochina. The British, worried by the preservation of their own Asian empire, allowed local French forces to execute a *coup de force* in Saigon on 23 September 1945, pushing the DRV's southern forces into the countryside as the arriving Expeditionary Corps under General Philippe Leclerc began taking control of the major cities, routes, and bridges in southern Indochina from early October. British and Indian forces were involved in this fighting while Japanese troops now under British command took some of the heaviest casualties fighting the Viet Minh. The idea that the French marched in and restored order alone in the south is inaccurate. British, Indian, and Japanese troops helped them fight the Viet Minh.[26]

Indeed, Vietnamese nationalists resisted, with Nguyen Binh taking charge of southern forces from late 1945. The thirty-year war for Vietnam thus began in the south in September 1945 and would end there in April 1975. North of the 16$^{th}$ parallel, however, the presence of the Chinese occupation forces continued to protect the

25. Initially, given that the Potsdam meeting occurred before the Japanese capitulation, the British and Chinese received authorization to conduct military operations in these two areas. Upon the Japanese defeat, Harry Truman issued Order no. 1 putting the Chinese and British in charge of accepting the Japanese surrender in their respective operational zones.

26. Peter Dunn, who can hardly be accused of being hostile to the French, demonstrates this in his *The First Vietnam War*, (London: C. Hurst & Company, 1985).

DRV against immediate French attack or a *coup d'état*, thereby allowing the fledgling nation-state to survive and to strengthen itself for over a year.[27] As onerous as Chinese nationalist occupation was for the Vietnamese economy and society, local Chinese Republican troops – not Chinese communists ones – first helped the new Vietnamese nation-state get off the ground. For both the French and the Viet Minh, foreign forces were vital to their abilities to hang on in Indochina in the early months of the war.[28]

While full-scale war was still not inevitable in early 1946, the French determination to apply the federal project at the expense of Vietnamese independence aspirations set the two states on a dangerous collision course. We now know, thanks to Stein Tønnesson, that even the signing of the famous 6 March Accords in 1946 recognizing the DRV as a "free state" (*État libre*) within the Indochinese Federation and the French Union was due less to a liberal moment in the French colonial mind than to the intense pressure Chinese commanders applied to local French negotiators to sign a preliminary agreement with the Vietnamese before General Leclerc could disembark his troops in Haiphong.[29] Local Chinese leaders had no intention of getting drawn into a chaotic Franco-Vietnamese war, as had happened to the British a few months earlier in the south.

By signing the 6 March Accords, both the French and the Vietnamese sides nonetheless gained precious time for strengthening their respective forces as the Chinese began to withdraw their troops. The March accords also offered a chance for peace, for a negotiated, peaceful decolonization of Vietnam. Ho Chi Minh clearly understood this and hoped to seize the moment to avoid letting war engulf all of Indochina. The key dividing issue was the unification of Cochinchina/Nam Bo with the rest of the DRV situated above the sixteenth parallel. French negotiators considered the DRV to be one "free state" (*État libre*) among three – perhaps four – other "free states" that would constitute, together, the pentagonal Indochinese Federation. Vietnam would have no more legal right to absorb the French colony of Cochinchina than the Kingdom of Laos in this federal framework. In colonial eyes, the DRV (Vietnam), Cochinchina, Laos, and Cambodia made up or could make up the *Fédération indochinoise*, in its turn a part of the French Union.[30] For French nationalists determined to restore their colonial rule after WWII, there was nothing inevitable about decolonization.

Many Vietnamese nationalists emerging from the same war saw the tide of history flowing countercurrent. A real problem turned upon the French colonial division of "Vietnam" into three parts, considered by the majority of Vietnamese (though not all) to constitute an historical aberration. There were not three ethnically Vietnamese regional territories or *pays* or *ky*, but there was one unitary Vietnamese nation-state run by the DRV from its national capital now located in Hanoi and with deep roots

27. See Lin Hua, *Chiang Kai-Shek, De Gaulle contre Hô Chi Minh: Viêt-Nam, 1945–1946* (Paris: L'Harmattan, 1994).

28. Defeated Japanese troops fought on both sides of the colonial line. On the one hand, they helped the French reconquer southern Vietnam in late 1945. On the other hand, hundreds crossed over to the DRV and fought against that very colonial reconquest. See my 'Alliés tardifs : Le rôle technico-militaire joué par les déserteurs japonais dans les rangs du Viet Minh (1945–1950)', *Guerres mondiales et conflits contemporains,* nos. 202–203, (April-September 2001), pp. 81–109.

29. Stein Tønnesson, 'La paix imposée par la Chine: l'accord franco-vietnamien du 6 mars 1946', *Cahiers de l'Institut d'histoire du temps présent* (1996), pp. 35–56 and Tønnesson, *Vietnam 1946,* pp. 39–64.

30. As long as the March accords were valid, the French apparently accepted to put the question of "Tonkin" and "Annam" on hold as separate ethnic Viet states. In other words, the DRV "free state" embodied Tonkin and upper Annam (that part located north of the 16th parallel). It remained unclear whether "Annam" below the 16th parallel would eventually be reunified with DRV northern Annam or given a new status.

located in the pre-colonial past. In national eyes, Cochinchina or rather "Nam Bo" was an integral part of Vietnam and that Vietnam was in 1945–1946 the nation-state of the Democratic Republic of Vietnam. Except for the short-lived Tran Trong Kim government of mid 1945, non-communist Vietnamese nationalists never proposed an alternative, unitary one before 1947.[31] While Ho Chi Minh sought to avoid war, he could only compromise on this issue so far without discrediting himself and his cause. Anticommunist and anti-French nationalist parties within the coalition government, like the Vietnamese National Party (VNQDD) and the Greater Vietnam parties (Dai Viet), were highly critical of negotiations with the French in late 1945 and early 1946. They too believed in an independent and unified Vietnam, without the French. Indeed, Ho gambled dangerously when he agreed in the March Accords to place the DRV into the Indochinese Federation as a "free state" (minus Cochinchina), counting on the French promise to hold a referendum on the unification of Cochinchina with the rest of "Vietnam" (the DRV above the sixteenth parallel). Ho bet that this would allow him to realize the unity of Vietnam as a "free state" via peaceful means, even if it meant putting on hold for a few years complete national independence or *doc lap,* a word which the French had refused to pronounce in signing the March accords (and Ho Chi Minh agreed knowing perfectly well that "independence" was legally incompatible with federalism).

Ho lost his gamble when follow-up conferences designed to take up the unresolved issues of the 6 March accords failed, first in Dalat and then most importantly in France, at Fontainebleau, in mid 1946. In an ominous sign, on 1 June 1946, as Ho Chi Minh left to negotiate Vietnam's future with the French government, the High Commissioner for Indochina, Georges Thierry d'Argenlieu, announced the existence of the "free state" of Cochinchina as the cornerstone of the emerging Indochinese Federation of which the DRV (minus Cochinchina) was still technically a part, along with Laos and Cambodia. The failure of the French and the Vietnamese to find a peaceful solution at Fontainebleau on the status of Cochinchina allowed hardliners on both sides of the divide to take matters into their hands along national and colonial lines, making a compromise solution increasingly difficult to achieve. In a desperate move, Ho Chi Minh pleaded with Marius Moutet, socialist minister of overseas France, to sign a *modus vivendi* in September 1946 prescribing among other things a cease-fire in the south. While Moutet agreed, the lack of political will in France, exacerbated by ever-changing governments in Paris, allowed local authorities in Indochina led by Thierry d'Argenlieu to apply de Gaulle's instructions to the letter, rolling back the DRV's national sovereignty in favor of that of the colonial Federation. Such brinkmanship led to serious clashes in Lang Son and especially in Haiphong in November 1946, before the Vietnamese, their backs up against the wall, lashed out in Hanoi on the evening of 19 December 1946. Long spoiling for a fight, local French authorities were ready to reply with force. And they did in a two-month, bloody street battle for Hanoi that left the northern capital largely deserted until 1948.[32] In short, full-scale war had now broken out in all of Indochina and would rage for almost ten more years across Vietnam, Laos, and Cambodia, sowing death, destruction, and sorrow in its path before an international conference in Geneva put a temporary end to the fighting in mid 1954.

Wars of decolonization almost always spawn civil violence, if not revolution at some level, as different groups vie for control over the postcolonial state and its ideological soul. The Indochinese War was no exception. The civil war was most prominent in eastern Indochina, where communism had divided Vietnamese national-

31. To my knowledge, we have no cool-headed study of "Cochinchinese separatism", neither its historical roots nor its interface with French policies.

32. William Turley, 'Urbanization in War : Hanoi, 1946–1973', *Pacific Affairs,* vol. 48, no. 3 (Autumn 1975), pp. 370–397.

ists since the 1920s.[33] The roots of this conflict reached back to the revolts led by the VNQDD and the Indochinese Communist Party (ICP) in central and upper Vietnam in the early 1930s. Crushed by the French, nationalists from both groups took refuge mainly in southern China and northeast Thailand. There, sometimes violent ideological breaks occurred between leaders of both sides, divided as to the type of political regime, economic model, and social program that should be instituted in Vietnam upon its future liberation from French colonialism. Vietnamese communism and anti-communism emerged in this wider historical context and conjuncture. Mirroring the violent break between Chinese communists and nationalists in 1927, the VNQDD and the ICP entered into something of a low-intensity, microcosmic civil war in southern Chinese cities in Yunnan and Guangxi provinces, each allied with its respective Chinese ideological and military partners.

Similar "micro" breaks among Vietnamese nationalist elites occurred behind the bars of the colonial prison on Poulo Condor island, when nationalists and communists suddenly found themselves arguing, even rumbling, over the future of Vietnam. After intense debate and no doubt some serious soul-searching, Tran Huy Lieu crossed over to the communist side in this prison reflection of Vietnamese politics.[34] Many did not, however; and this became a source of verbal and physical violence. As the future communist chief of the security services for southern Vietnam recalled a nationalist taunting him in Poulo Condor: "Communists are our enemy no. 1; imperialists are the enemy no. 2".[35] The matter was put on hold until the Japanese brought down French Indochina in March 1945. Then, the question as to who would rule the new nation-state following the Japanese defeat became very real. The low-scale political violence confined to Poulo Condor cells and southern Chinese backstreets rapidly transformed into a civil war when communists and nationalists exited colonial cell blocks or returned to Vietnam from Yunnan and Guangxi in mid 1945, armed, and determined to impose their vision of the national future, even it meant using force against fellow Vietnamese. The colonial war breaking out between the French and the DRV in 1945–1946 was thus doubled by a civil conflict with roots in the interwar period and transnational linkages running from Poulo Condor to Kunming via the Vietnamese diaspora. In mid 1946, with the Chinese out of the way and Ho Chi Minh in Paris, Vo Nguyen Giap successfully attacked non-communist nationalist parties hostile to the communists, pushing most of them back into southern China and, this time, into DRV jails, from which many never returned.

Although the French army had initially supported Vo Nguyen Giap's destruction of the nationalist forces (who had been much more hostile to the French than the communists in 1945–1946),[36] French political leaders, above all Léon Pignon, now regretted that the French found themselves face-to-face with the DRV, increasingly dominated by communists. With the Indochinese Federation already in trouble by late 1946, Pignon understood that the French would have to work with non-communist Vietnamese nationalists to hold on colonially. As early as January 1947, he had secretly advised his superiors that the French war with the DRV had to "be transposed"

33. François Guillemot, 'La tentation "fasciste" des luttes anticoloniales Dai Viet: Nationalisme et anticommunisme dans le Viêt-Nam des années 1932–1945', *Vingtième siècle,* no. 104, vol. 4 (2009), pp. 45–66.

34. Peter Zinoman, *The Colonial Bastille: A History of Imprisonment in Vietnam, 1862–1940* (Berkeley: University of California Press, 2001).

35. Cited in *Pham Hung Tieu Su* (Hanoi: Nha Xuat Ban Chinh Tri Quoc Gia, 2007), pp. 58–64. For a particularly vivid example of the mobilization of civil violence in the colonial prison (cell block rumbles), see *Ibid.,* pp. 59–60.

36. Jean Crépin, *Souvenirs d'Indochine,* box T443, Service historique de la défense. See also: Guillemot, *Dai Viêt, indépendance et révolution au Viêt-Nam.*

to a Vietnamese playing field, using the Viet Minh's adversaries to do the fighting.[37] The French turned to the former Emperor Bao Dai, now living in exile in China and apparently unhappy with the DRV, in order to build a counter-revolutionary state, around which non-communist nationalists would rally. This was the third (not the first) time that French strategists had turned to Bao Dai to find a solution to their political problems in Indochina.[38] Vietnamese non-communists hoped that their anticommunism, nationalist credentials, and the Cold War would force Paris to accord them the independence the French had denied to the DRV and to them in 1945–1946.

They would be profoundly disappointed. Although the French persuaded Bao Dai to return eventually to Vietnam and albeit that an Associated State of Vietnam (ASV) emerged in 1949 under limited American pressure, the French only slowly granted non-communist nationalists full sovereignty. And yet this did not prevent the French from pushing the ASV to increase the number of Vietnamese fighting against the DRV.[39] From 1950, as the Cold War bore down upon Indochina, tens of thousands of Vietnamese began fighting in the French Union forces against the Vietnamese forces of the DRV. Military service became mandatory in the DRV in late 1949 and in the ASV in 1951. By "Vietnamizing" the war (what the French called *jaunissement,* or "yellowing"), the French exacerbated an already intense civil war among the Vietnamese. Indeed, more Vietnamese from the ASV than French nationals ended up dying in the Indochina War. In short, colonialism, communism, nationalism, and anticommunism made for a deadly combination in Indochina from the mid 1940s.

On top of this, the Indochina War was also one of the hottest and deadliest battlegrounds of the Cold War and this well into the 1980s. While the onset of the Cold War in Europe may have made itself felt in Indochina shortly after World War II, it was the Chinese communist victory of October 1949 in Asia and the outbreak of the Korean War in June 1950 that firmly shifted the Cold War along that Eurasian axis into East Asia, creating a communist bloc stretching from the Elbe to the Sino-Vietnamese border of Southeast Asia, as Truong Chinh himself approvingly put it. While Stalin handed over the Asian side of the world revolution to Mao Zedong,[40] who supported his longtime communist allies in Korea and Vietnam, the Americans were determined to hold the line in Indochina against the further spread of Eurasian communism into the region, even if it meant prolonging the French colonial presence in Indochina to the national detriment of the Associated States of Vietnam, Laos, and Cambodia. By its end, the Americans were financing almost 80% of the cost of the Indochina War while the Chinese communists were heavily backing the DRV. Unprecedented Sino-

37. Léon Pignon wrote on 4 January 1947, as war raged in Hanoi: "Notre objectif est clairement déterminé: transporter sur le plan intérieur annamite la querelle que nous avons avec le parti Viet Minh et nous engager nous-mêmes le moins possible dans des campagnes et des représailles qui doivent être le fait des adversaires autochtones de ce parti [...]". Cited by Philippe Devillers, *Paris, Saigon, Hanoi: Les archives de la guerre, 1944–1947* (Paris: Gallimard, 1988), p. 334.

38. See my 'Un « *cul de plomb* » et un « *fou génial* »: La mobilisation corporelle des rois coloniaux Bao Dai et Sihanouk en Indochine (1919–1945)', forthcoming in Agathe Larcher-Goscha and François Guillemot (éds.), *Le Corps au Vietnam* (Lyon: Editions de l'Ecole normale supérieure).

39. The hypocrisy of the French position was clearly lost on General Jean de Lattre de Tassigny when he exhorted young Vietnamese men in 1951 to sign up to fight with the French on national grounds: 'Soyez des hommes, c'est-à-dire, si vous êtes communistes, rejoignez le Viet Minh, il y a là des individus qui se battent bien pour une cause mauvaise. Mais, si vous êtes des patriotes, combattez pour votre patrie, car cette guerre est la vôtre ... Cette guerre, que vous l'ayez voulue ou non est la guerre du Vietnam pour le Vietnam. Et la France ne la fera pour vous que si vous la faites avec elle"'.

40. Chen Jian, *Mao's China and the Cold War* (Chapel Hill: University of North Carolina Press, 2001).

American intervention in Indochina began in 1950 (paralleling the Korean conflict to the northeast) and put its stamp on the nature of the war well into the 1960s. As the negotiations entered their decisive stage at Geneva in early July 1954, Zhou Enlai put it nicely when he emphasized to Ho Chi Minh in a crucial meeting in the southern Chinese city of Liuzhou that "in terms of scope and degree of internationalization, the Indochina issue even surpasses the Korean one", before adding: "the war in Indochina not only has involved the three (Indochina) countries, but has also influenced all of Southeast Asia, and has influenced Europe and the whole world as well".[41]

Like World War II, the coming of the Cold War to Indochina offered both opportunities as well as dangers. For one, the Cold War allowed the French to prolong their colonial foothold in Indochina by recasting their neo-colonial war and the Bao Dai solution as an integral part of the global fight against communist expansion.[42] Unlike the Dutch in Indonesia, fighting an anticommunist nationalist movement, the French in Indochina effectively used the Cold War to secure greater American support of their fight against the communist-led DRV, especially as Mao Zedong lined up the communist bloc, including Stalin, behind Ho Chi Minh in January 1950. Or consider it from another vantage point: Whereas non-communist nationalists in Indonesia like Sukarno were able to attract American sympathy and international support for their war of independence against the Dutch, achieving a negotiated international settlement in 1949, Vietnamese non-communists, now allied with the French against the communists, had less leverage with which to play the Americans against the French. For the Americans in 1950, the need to counter communism now took precedence over supporting anticolonialism. The Franco-American Cold War partnership in Indochina effectively marginalized non-communist anticolonialist nationalists, like the Dai Viet, the VNQDD, and others, who were hoping to follow the Indonesian lead.

Things looked different for communist nationalists closely tracking the Cold War's shift towards East Asia. Contrary to orthodox accounts, Vietnamese communists welcomed Sino-Soviet recognition and the internationalization of the war with the French.[43] It ended their international isolation and provided them with essential aid needed to take the battle to the French in order to win independence on the diplomatic and military battlefields. Alignment with the communist bloc in 1950 also allowed the Vietnamese communists to push through revolutionary social, cultural, agricultural, economic, political, and military change. Vietnamese communists welcomed Sino-Soviet ideas, methods, models, and assistance to help them implement rectification and emulation campaigns, an integral part of the social and communist remodeling of the state and society. Land reform was essential to mobilizing and transforming hundreds of thousands of peasants into soldiers and porters needed to knock out the

---

41. Cited in Chen Jian, 'China and the Indochina Settlement', in Mark Lawrence and Fredrik Logevall, eds., *The First Vietnam War* (Cambridge: Harvard University Press, 2007), pp. 254–255.

42. Devillers, *Histoire du Viêt-Nam*; Mark Atwood Lawrence, *Assuming the Burden: Europe and the American Commitment to War in Vietnam* (Berkeley: University of California Press, 2005); and Pierre Grosser, *La France et l'Indochine (1953–1956). Une « carte de visite » en « peau de chagrin »* (Paris: Institut d'études politiques de Paris, PhD thesis, 2002).

43. See chapters by Christopher Goscha and Tuong Vu in Christopher E. Goscha and Christian Ostermann, eds., *Connecting Histories: Decolonization and the Cold War in Southeast Asia (1945–1962)* (Stanford: Stanford University Press/Woodrow Wilson Center, 2009) and Christopher E. Goscha, 'Courting Diplomatic Disaster? The Difficult Integration of Vietnam into the Internationalist Communist Movement (1945–1950)', *Journal of Vietnamese Studies*, Vol. I, nos. 1–2 (February/August 2006), pp. 59–103.

French.[44] Thus both the DRV Vietnamese and the French found opportunities in the arrival of the Cold War. And by choosing to rely on the Chinese and the Americans, both contributed to the war's internationalization. Neither was a victim; both were actors.

However, the internationalization of the conflagration rapidly made Indochina, like Korea, the theatre of an increasingly deadly conflict. The increased military assistance provided to the belligerents by the Chinese and the Americans augmented its intensity, degree of violence, and the number of casualties, including those of Indochinese civilians.[45] Set piece battles at Cao Bang, Vinh Yen, Dong Trieu, Na San, and Dien Bien Phu cost tens of thousands of lives. Vietnamese statistics confirm that from 1950 artillery and machine gun fire tore up young DRV bodies in frightening numbers and terrible ways, leaving many of those who survived the "face of battle", to borrow John Keegan's famous expression, scarred for life, something that had been relatively rare during the guerrilla phase of the war before 1950.[46] Napalm was used with devastating effect, while the French air force began bombing campaigns of an unprecedented kind, thanks in part to increased American military assistance. Ngo Van Chieu commanded a Viet Minh platoon in northern Vietnam during the battle of Vinh Yen in early 1951. He confided to his diary his unit's first mind-numbing encounter with napalm as follows:

> Be on watch for planes. They will drop bombs and machine gun. Cover yourselves, hide yourselves under bamboo. The planes dived. Then hell opened up before my eyes. It was hell in the form of a big clumsy egg, falling from the first plane ... An immense ball of fire, spreading over hundreds of meters, it seemed to me, sowing terror in the ranks of the soldiers. Napalm. Fire that falls from the sky .... My men ran for cover, and I could not stop them. There is no way you can stay put under this rain of fire that spreads out and burns everything in its path. From everywhere the flames leap up. Joining them was the burst of French machine gun fire, mortars and artillery, transforming into a burning tomb what was only ten minutes earlier a small forest ... His eyes were locked wide open by the horror of the scene he had just witnessed. What was that (the soldier asked)? The atomic bomb? No, napalm.[47]

The level of violence the two sides could generate was real but nevertheless uneven. The DRV had no planes, no napalm, and could not bomb France or French civilians.[48] Their medical services were woefully understaffed and supplied. The internationalization of the war allowed the DRV to produce an army and deploy artillery, mortars, and machine gun fire, but it also put their men at the mercy of some of the deadliest industrial weapons produced during the first half of the twentieth century, unleashed that evening, Ngo Van Chieu wrote, "when darkness never set in". The Viet Minh would only be able to inflict something of this modern destruction on its adversary in

44. See: Benoît de Tréglodé, *Héros et révolution au Viêt Nam* (Paris: L'Harmattan, 2001); Greg Lockhart, *Nation in Arms: The Origins of the People's Army of Vietnam*, (Sydney: Allen & Unwin, 1989); and Bertrand de Hartingh, *Entre le peuple et la nation: La République démocratique du Viet Nam de 1953 à 1957* (Paris: Ecole française d'Extrême Orient, 2003).

45. While the Americans did not provide combat training to the Associated State of Vietnam before 1955, the Chinese most certainly did train thousands of DRV officers and troops, including those in its most important combat divisions.

46. See Christopher Goscha, "Hell in a Very Small Place': Cold War, Decolonization and the Assault on the Vietnamese Body at Dien Bien Phu', special issue, *European Journal of East Asian Studies,* vol. 9, no. 2, (2011), pp. 189–225.

47. Ngo van Chieu, *Journal d'un combatant* (Paris: Editions du Seuil, 1955), (translated by Jacques Despeuch), pp. 154–155.

48. To my knowledge, unlike the FLN during the Algerian War, the Viet Minh never took violence to the colonial metropolis. Nor did Hanoi or its southern allies take the Vietnam War to American cities.

the final days of the battle of Dien Bien Phu, when Soviet-supplied multiple rocket launchers finally arrived on the scene.[49] In all, some 400,000 people died in nine years of war. Of the over 100,000 killed in the French Union forces in the Indochina War, the majority were soldiers of the Associated State of Vietnam, the French African empire, and the Foreign Legion.

Violence also spilled into Laos, the non-Vietnamese highlands, and eventually into eastern Cambodia as Chinese aid allowed the DRV's armed forces to move battalions and even entire divisions across the Indochinese battlefield within a remarkably short period of time. The military expansion of the Vietnamese in western Indochina allowed the DRV/ICP to install associated "resistance governments" (*chinh phu khang chien*) in Laos and Cambodia, the Pathet Lao and the Khmer Issarak. In so doing, Vietnamese communists, thanks to the new international conjuncture and aid, ensured that civil war would come to western Indochina with all its destabilizing effects. By creating national armies for their revolutionary Lao and Cambodian partners, Vietnamese communists also contributed to the widening of the deadly consequences of the war to an Indochinese dimension. (It is no accident that the DRV signed the two Geneva armistices with the French for Laos and Cambodia in July 1954 – not their Lao or Cambodian partners.) In the northern and central highlands, the French, prodded by the Americans, organized autonomous zones for ethnic minorities and manipulated anti-Vietnamese sentiments among them to recruit for their commando operations against the Viet Minh. Indeed, the Americans were the driving force behind the creation of the famous *Groupement de commandos mixtes aéroportés* among the minority ethnic groups in the highlands of central and northern Indochina.[50] Such policies contributed to creating new ethno-nationalist identities and, in so doing, put the ethnic minorities on a collision course with the countervailing Vietnamese ones (both communist and non-communist). In 1953–1954, during powerful northern DRV thrusts southwards and westwards, Cambodians and especially Lao and upland minorities began to die in greater numbers as the war for all of Indochina entered its most decisive phase.

The internationalization of the Indochina War also linked France, Vietnam, Laos, Cambodia, and their ethnic minorities to events occurring around the world. This was certainly the case for the French, who found it increasingly hard to balance the growing costs of the intensifying war in Indochina against concomitant demands for more manpower stemming from their commitments to rearming Europe, partaking in the North Atlantic Treaty Organization, and controlling the course of West German rearmament. All of this cost money and required men. How could the French contribute to the European Defense Community – an idea René Pleven had himself largely devised to check resurging (West) German power – when the French army and its officers remained bogged down in Indochina?

Moreover, the intensification of the Indochina conflict from 1950 only increased the financial burden on the French. As Hugues Tertrais has shown, the final blow to the French did not necessarily occur on the battlefield at Dien Bien Phu in 1954, but rather on the economic front in Europe a year earlier. In 1953, the government finally accepted that it could no longer afford the Indochina War in light of its com-

49. Ngoc An, 'Tieu doan hoa tien 224', *Tap chi lich su quan su*, no. 4 (July August 1997), p. 58. The Soviets delivered 12 rocket launchers to the Vietnamese, meaning that the DRV could have technically launched 72 rockets at one time. Each launcher could project six rockets. The Chinese had used them in Korea and had adapted them to the rough terrain of that country, similar to that of northern Vietnam. The Chinese helped the Vietnamese man some of these rocket launchers just as American pilots flew private supply missions for the French over Dien Bien Phu in the Civil Air Transport (better known during the Vietnam War as "Air America").

50. See the correspondence in 10H266, Service historique de la défense, Château de Vincennes.

mitments in Europe and, increasingly, in North Africa.[51] The war in Indochina had to be stopped. The French may have welcomed the internationalization of the Indochina war in 1949–1950 and recast it as a Cold War imperative in order to obtain American financial backing and prolong the French presence in Vietnam. However, by 1953 one could also argue that the internationalization of the war, especially in light of France's Atlantic linkages and financial commitments to European security (including nervousness about West German rearmament), turned against the French, forcing their colonial hand in Indochina. From September 1953, not unlike the Vietnamese working with their Chinese advisers, the French had to inform the Americans of their operational plans on the Indochina battlefield in exchange for vital assistance.[52] The French also had to make major political concessions to the Associated States of Indochina from 1953. Indeed, before talks opened on ending the war in Geneva in May 1954, these three states had already obtained something very close to full independence. In short, internationalization cut both ways; it never remained static during the nine-year conflict. While the Cold War and trans-Atlantic support may have helped the French to hang on colonially in Indochina after 1948, as Mark Lawrence argues, the picture looked quite different in 1953. Pierre Mendès France seems to have understood this point well when he decided to stake his premiership on reaching a negotiated end of the conflict upon coming to power in 1954.

The further internationalization of the war also forced the Vietnamese communist hand. And here again the year 1953 was a watershed. While international communist support may well have saved the DRV Vietnamese from diplomatic defeat in 1950 and allowed communists to implement radical social revolution, the shift towards peaceful co-existence in Moscow *and* Beijing after Stalin's death in 1953 put the Vietnamese in a very difficult position when a very international conference opened in Geneva in 1954 to deal with the two hot wars in Asia: Korea and Indochina (in Korea a cease-fire had been in effect since mid 1953). Although the Vietnamese may have handed the French an historic military defeat at Dien Bien Phu on 7 May 1954, when the ink dried on the Geneva Accords signed on 21 July 1954, communist nationalists could only control half of the Vietnam that Ho Chi Minh had declared independent on 2 September 1945. Big power politics had once again effectively divided Vietnam, this time at the seventeenth parallel. Although Vietnamese communists signed on at Geneva hoping to prevent the Americans from replacing the French, the Geneva conference was anything but a DRV diplomatic victory. The Americans had every intention of holding the line in Indochina against the expansion of communism further into Asia, something Vietnamese communists had indeed advocated in 1950. By 1954, both French colonialism and Vietnamese communism had suffered setbacks.

Others saw openings in this new level of internationalization. After all, non-communist Vietnamese nationalists in the State of Vietnam were still players in the making of Vietnam, no less determined to use the international dynamics of the Cold War than their communist adversaries allied with Moscow and Beijing. By 1953, Ngo Dinh Diem, like Mendès France, understood that the French no longer had the international leverage of 1948–1950, nor the unflinching support of the Americans. As new research shows, Diem moved to use the Americans as much as the latter would seek

51. Hugues Tertrais, *La piastre et le fusil: Le coût de la guerre d'Indochine, 1945–1954* (Paris: Comité pour l'Histoire Économique et Financière de la France, 2002).

52. The Americans were deeply involved in the crafting of the Navarre Plan, just as the Chinese expected to have a say in Viet Minh operational plans leading up to Dien Bien Phu. Both the French and Viet Minh operational plans for 1953–1954 carried the stamp of approval from their larger backers.

to use him.[53] By losing their international *marge de manoeuvre* in 1953 the French provided Ngo Dinh Diem with an opportunity. Having failed to ratify the European Defense Community, so dear to the Americans during the Geneva Conference, we now know that Mendès France felt obligated to turn over the reins to the Americans in lower Vietnam and he even backed away from recognizing communist China (unlike the British). Whatever the turf wars between the American and French intelligence services in the transitional phase following the Geneva Accords, including the "war of the sects" in 1955, the French could do little as Ngo Dinh Diem consolidated his power and his control over the postcolonial state and eventually pushed the Expeditionary Corps out of Vietnam in 1956.[54] And as Pierre Brocheux reminds us, if Ho Chi Minh had masterminded the exit of the French "colonialists" in the north, Ngo Dinh Diem did the job in the south.[55] French Indochina was dead as of 1956. The French government and its army now focused on another colonial war designed to keep Algeria French. This time, however, a number of ranking veterans of the Indochina War would not accept another humiliation (the loss of France to the Germans in 1940 and the fall of Dien Bien Phu to the Viet Minh in 1954), even if it meant taking civil war to the French mainland. In this sense, the fall of the French Fourth Republic in 1958 cannot be fully understood without situating it within this wider colonial and international context, of which the Indochina War was an essential part.

War certainly influenced the nature of postcolonial Vietnam, communist or noncommunist. Like its Chinese counterpart, the DRV was conceived and forged in war. Many of its economic, monetary, judicial, intelligence, and police structures were formed during the conflict, defined by it, configured to fight it, and continue to influence it to this day. Similar things could be said about the Republic of Vietnam. However, the regrettable lack of scholarship on the birth and evolution of the States of Vietnam, Laos, and Cambodia between 1945 and 1954 prevents one from saying much more at this point.[56] The DRV government ministries and resistance bureaucracy expanded across the country during the Indochina conflict. Although the war state's administration certainly drew upon the colonial state's elites and structures at the outset, by the end of the conflict the DRV had created a new set of civil servants and a bureaucracy that was increasingly subordinate to the communist party's structures and leadership.[57]

---

53. See among others Philip E. Catton, *Diem's Final Failure: Prelude to America's War in Vietnam* (Lawrence: University of Kansas Press, 2002); Edward Miller, 'Vision, Power, and Agency: The Ascent of Ngo Dinh Diem, 1945–1954', *Journal of Southeast Asian Studies* (October 2004), pp. 433–458; Jessica M. Chapman, 'Staging Democracy: South Vietnam's 1955 Referendum to Depose Bao Dai', *Diplomatic History*, vol. 30, no. 4 (September 2006), 671–703; and Kathryn Statler, *Replacing France: The Origins of American Intervention in Vietnam* (Lexington: University of Kentucky Press, 2007).

54. See Pierre Grosser, *La France et l'Indochine (1953–1956).*

55. Nor is it an accident that Sihanouk went on the move in 1953, launching his royal crusade for independence. See my 'Un « *cul de plomb* » et un « *fou génial* »'. Indeed, one could argue that by failing to force the French hand in similar ways in 1953, Bao Dai sealed his fate as a failed nationalist leader, leaving the stage open to the likes of the Diem entourage.

56. Daniel Varga, *La politique française en Indochine (1947–50): Histoire d'une décolonisation manquée,* (Aix-en-Provence: Université Aix-Marseille I, 2004, PhD thesis). However, a truly international history of the Bao Dai "solution" still awaits its historian. The same could be said of the Associated States of Laos and Cambodia.

57. Christopher E. Goscha, *Vietnam: Un Etat né de la guerre* (Paris: Armand Colin, 2011). See also Stein Tønnesson's chapter in Kjeld Erik Brødsgaard and Susan Young, eds, *State Capacity in East Asia: China, Taiwan, Vietnam, and Japan* (Oxford: Oxford University Press, 2000), pp. 236–268.

And while it is not certain that any conflict can technically be labeled a "total war", the Indochina War came close.[58] The conflict allowed the party, as in communist China, to increase its control over the state, army, and civilian populations living in its territories. Mass mobilization drives, rectification campaigns, and land reform are but a few of the revolutionary social changes and methods by which the Vietnamese communists impacted upon civilians and the state in unprecedented ways. And all of these "revolutionary" structures and techniques would serve the DRV well when war, both civil and international, resumed only a few years after the signing of the Geneva Accords. In short, war destroys but it also creates, as Charles Tilly told us long ago. It closes certain historical venues and opens up new ones. The Indochina War was no exception to this rule. I can only hope that the interconnected approach adopted in this dictionary might contribute to a better understanding of the complexity and the significance of this twentieth century conflict.

58. On the problems associated with the idea of "total war", see: Roger Chickering, et al., *A World at Total War: Global Conflict and the Politics of Destruction, 1937–1945* (Washington: Global Historical Institute, 2005) and Hew Strachan, 'Essay and Reflection: On Total War and Modern War', *The International History Review,* vol. 22, no. 2 (June 2000), especially pp. 353–355.

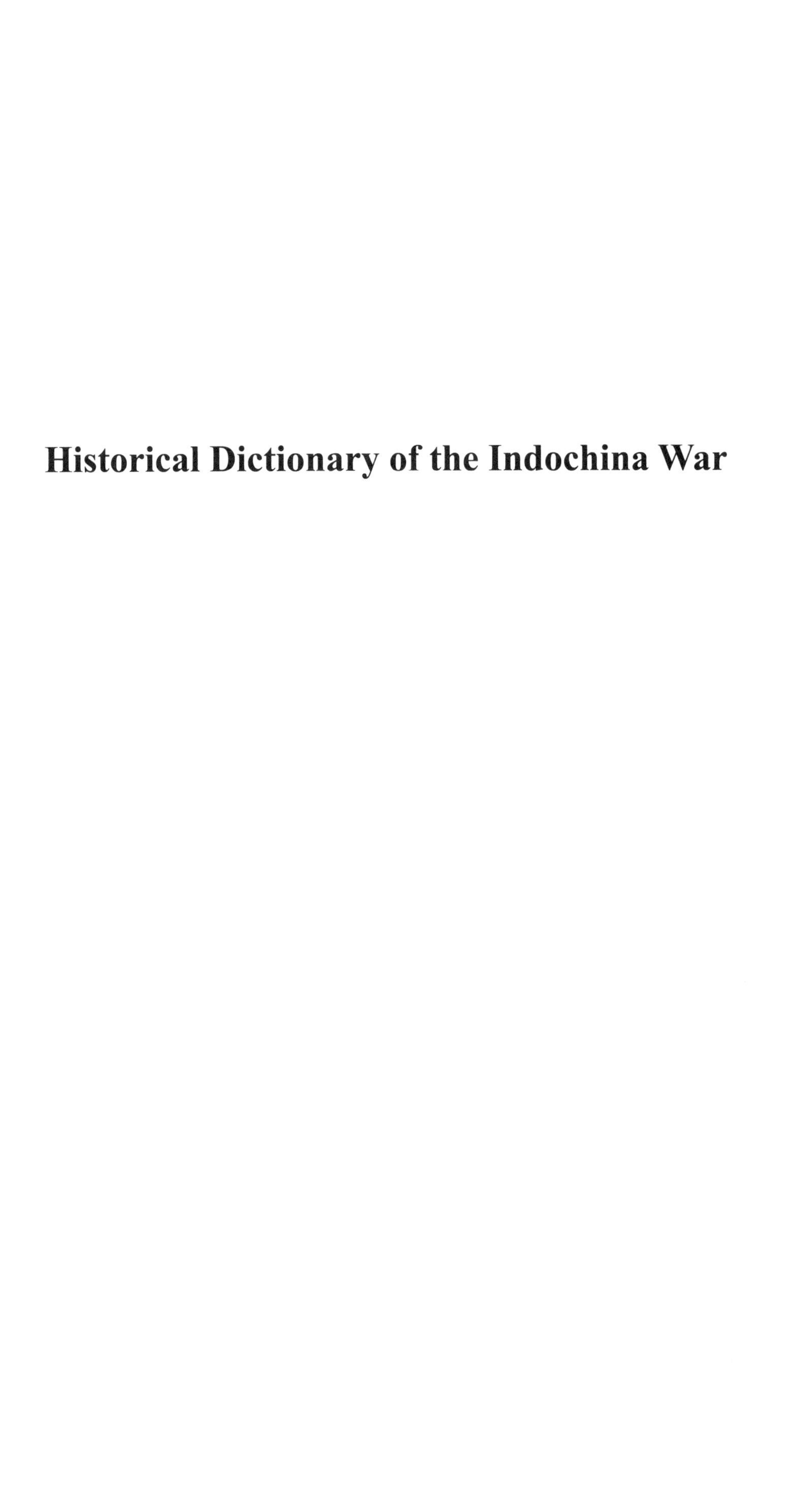

# Historical Dictionary of the Indochina War

# 0–9

**2 SEPTEMBER 1945**. This day marks the official birth of the **Democratic Republic of Vietnam** (DRV). On that day, some 400,000 Vietnamese assembled in Ba Dinh square (formerly Place Puginier) in **Hanoi** to listen to **Ho Chi Minh** celebrate the independence of Vietnam. When the latter stepped up to the microphone and began reading the Vietnamese declaration of independence, he paused and asked his compatriots if they could hear him clearly. Ho's dramatic query was met with a thunderous reply, "Yes!" (*Co!*) In his address, Ho Chi Minh rejected the French division of Vietnam into three parts, insisting on the nation's unity. He condemned French colonial abuses since the 19th century and underscored their failure to "protect" Vietnam against the Japanese during World War II. Two American P-38 Lightning planes passed over the crowd that day. While it was purely accidental, many Vietnamese and French (albeit for opposite reasons) saw in it a symbol of American sympathy for the Vietnamese independence movement. Present at the ceremony was an American intelligence officer, **Archimedes L. Patti**, sympathetic to Vietnamese independence aspirations.

The birth of the DRV on 2 September was also part of a wider shift in the international system as Western decolonization, accelerated by the defeat of Japanese imperialism in August 1945, spread throughout Asia. Further to the south, Indonesian nationalists had also declared their national independence following the Japanese capitulation, as did others. However, unlike the Indians who negotiated their independence with the British, the Indonesians and the Vietnamese had to fight to keep their nation-states alive. The DRV found the road to independence even harder when the **Cold War** arrived in full force in Asia in 1950 and the Americans threw their weight behind the French in order to roll back the communist-led DRV as part of their global containment strategy. When the ink dried on the 1954 **Geneva Accords** ending the Indochina War, only the northern half of the Vietnam Ho Chi Minh had declared independent on 2 September 1945 existed. The other half went to the **Republic of Vietnam**, its noncommunist competitor for postcolonial Vietnam. That changed in 1975, when Vietnamese communists defeated this government and unified all the country under communist control.

In 1976, the DRV was renamed the Socialist Republic of Vietnam (SRV). However, 2 September 1945 is the SRV's official independence day. In 1979, artist Van Tho produced two colorful paintings of the 2 September 1945 Ba Dinh meeting. One is held in the Ministry of Culture, while the other is on display in Hanoi's Museum of History. *See also* AUGUST REVOLUTION.

**23 SEPTEMBER 1945**. On 23 September 1945, the British facilitated a French *coup de force*, ousting forces loyal to or allied with the **Democratic Republic of Vietnam** (DRV) from **Saigon**, marking the first stage of what would become a full-scale war for Vietnam on **19 December 1946** in **Hanoi**. On 25 August 1945, groups pledging allegiance to the DRV had taken control of Saigon following the Allied defeat of the Japanese. They did so in the absence of French forces knocked out of Indochina by the Japanese ***coup de force* of 9 March 1945**. British occupying forces under the command of General **Douglas Gracey** arrived in Saigon in early September to accept the Japanese surrender and maintain order. This was no easy task, however. Tensions were running extremely high between the Vietnamese and French as each side manoeuvred to take control of the city. The French population had been humiliated by Japanese internment and brutalization. They looked to the British not only to deal with the Japanese, but also to put the Vietnamese back in their colonial place. Vietnamese nationalist leaders had no intention of letting such a thing happen. The French had failed to defend Indochina; the colonial pact was over. Reaching a compromise solution in such circumstances would be no easy matter. Worse, confidence plummeted as incidents multiplied. Violence marred celebrations held in Saigon on 2 September 1945 to mark the official declaration of the DRV by **Ho Chi Minh** in Hanoi. And it showed no signs of abating. In a bid to establish order, Douglas Gracey decided to support a French *coup de force* against the Vietnamese, prepared by the recently arrived French Commissioner for the Republic in Cochinchina, **Jean Cédile**. On the evening of 22 September, Gracey declared martial law and allowed **Foreign Legion** troops incarcerated by the Japanese to be re-armed and released. The next day, these unruly troops began to retake the city by force, pushing the representatives of the DRV into the countryside. Heavy-handed treatment of the Vietnamese by these troops and European settlers bent on vengeance reinforced a spiral of violence and instability, as both Cédile and Gracey conceded at the time. On the 24th, unruly Vietnamese elements kidnapped and murdered dozens of Europeans and **Eurasians** in a gruesome **massacre** in the French quarter of Saigon called the *Cité* ***Hérault***. British-led Gurkhas and especially Allied-defeated Japanese troops had to be brought in to help the French establish control over the city and surrounding areas. The war for Vietnam, although limited to areas south of the **16th parallel** until December 1946, had begun in the south, in Saigon, on the 23–24th of September 1945. No one knew at the time that Saigon would also be the scene of the end of the wars for Vietnam thirty years later.

**19 DECEMBER 1946.** The responsibility for, and the exact events, details, and decisions made in the days leading up to the outbreak of full-scale war between the French 4th Republic and the **Democratic Republic of Vietnam** (DRV) on the evening of 19 December 1946 remain unclear and contested on many counts to this day. At the heart of the problem was a clash over two opposing conceptions of who should and would control Vietnam in the wake of the Japanese overthrow of French Indochina in March 1945 and the subsequent Japanese defeat five months later. On the one hand, the French were determined to rebuild a new colonial Indochina of a pentagonal, federal nature, consisting of Cambodia, Laos, **Cochinchina, Annam** and **Tonkin**. On the other hand, Vietnamese nationalists were equally determined to create a unified and eventually independent Vietnamese nation-state. While some in **Ho Chi Minh**'s entourage may have wanted to take up arms early on to make this happen, the DRV's president did not seek a violent clash with the French. In spite of the outbreak of a limited war below the **16th parallel** on **23 September 1945**, Ho Chi Minh appealed to the Chinese, the United States, the Soviet Union, the British, newly independent Asian states, and the **United Nations** to support the Vietnamese case for a negotiated settlement.

For a short time, in mid-1946, just such a deal seemed possible. Under Chinese pressure, Ho Chi Minh and **Jean Sainteny** (representing France) signed the **Accords of 6 March 1946**, agreeing to refer to Vietnam as "a free state" within the French **Indochinese Federation** and **French Union** on the condition that a referendum were held on the unification of Cochinchina with the rest of Vietnam. A military annex to the accord authorized the French to station 15,000 troops in northern Vietnam to replace the withdrawing Chinese troops. However, the French high commissioner for Indochina, Admiral **Georges Thierry d'Argenlieu**, was hostile to the idea of a unitary Vietnam and determined to roll back the DRV's sovereignty in order to create the Indochinese Federation, as instructed by General **Charles de Gaulle**. On 1 June 1946, as Ho was leaving to continue negotiations in France, Thierry d'Argenlieu formally announced the existence of the **Provisional Government of the Republic of Cochinchina** as one of his steps towards the creation of the Indochinese Federation. Despite the French failure to move on the March Accords during the **Fontainebleau Conference** in mid-1946, Ho Chi Minh settled for a ***modus vivendi*** in September, including a cease-fire in southern Vietnam, hoping that this would provide him with much needed time and that a shift to the left in French metropolitan politics would make it possible to achieve an agreement.

Things took a turn for the worse in late 1946, however. Having retaken all of Laos above the 16th parallel in mid-1946 and all Chinese troops now evacuated from northern Indochina by September, French authorities in Indochina intensified their brinksmanship with the DRV. As a result, Franco-Vietnamese relations worsened dramatically in November 1946 when local French officers presented ultimatums to DRV forces during the **Haiphong** and Langson incidents. Not only did Thierry d'Argenlieu support these actions, but his superiors in Paris also covered him and in so doing only emboldened the admiral. Tensions rose further in December as skirmishes broke out, confidence plummeted, and preparations for war began on both sides. While the Vietnamese began evacuating the population, vital ministries, equipment, and personnel from **Hanoi**, Ho Chi Minh tried nonetheless to head off full-scale war, hoping to the last minute that the constitution of a sympathetic government in Paris under the socialist President **Léon Blum** would provide him with a serious interlocutor with whom he could negotiate a way out of what had become a blind alley. However, time was too short, communications were bad, and mutual confidence was at an all time low. Many French authorities in Indochina and Vietnamese in Ho's own entourage wanted a showdown.

On the evening of 19 December 1946, in a still contested and very unclear sequence of events, war broke out in Hanoi, marking what historians consider to be the full-scale outbreak of the Indochina War. At the time, the DRV accused the French of starting the war, while the French claimed the opposite. While it seems well established that it was the Vietnamese who opened the hostilities on 19 December, the jury is still out as to the circumstances in which the attack occurred. To date, French historians **Philippe Devillers** and Frédéric Turpin and Norwegian scholar Stein Tønnesson have provided the hardest, archival evidence showing the degree to which French political and military authorities in Indochina had been preparing since at least April 1946 for the reoccupation of northern Indochina, even if it meant war with the DRV. Such action was in line with de Gaulle's instructions of mid-1945. However, it remains unclear whether the DRV fell into a deliberately set French trap on 19 December, designed to head off negotiations with Léon Blum; whether it was the inability of Ho Chi Minh to control his subordinates in such explosive circumstances; or whether it was the result of a deliberate Vietnamese order to attack. Until more evidence comes to light, one can only conclude that with their backs up against the wall since November, the Vietnamese finally lashed out when militia forces cut the electricity in Hanoi at 20H00.

French commanders in the north were only too happy to respond with force. While **Vo Nguyen Giap** never committed the bulk of his forces to defending the capital, the DRV instructed militia forces and the Capital Brigade to pin down the French in the city in order to allow the government to make it to safe zones. Two months of fierce street fighting ensued, in what the Vietnamese refer to as the battle of Hanoi**.** The French army would not fully reoccupy the capital until late February 1947. The fledgling French 4th Republic was now engaged in a colonial war and the newly born DRV had begun what would turn out to be a 30 year war of national liberation. *See also COUP DE FORCE* OF 9 MARCH 1945; FRANCO-CHINESE ACCORD (28 FEBRUARY 1946).

**16th PARALLEL**. The demarcation line at which the Allies divided former French Indochina into two military operational zones on 2 August 1945. This decision was taken as part of the **Potsdam** Conference (July–August 1945). The French were not present. Given that no one knew the Japanese would capitulate two weeks later, the Allied powers created these two military operational zones as the war effort fully focused on Asia.

Following the Japanese surrender, President Harry Truman approved Order number 1 allowing the British and the Chinese to disarm Japanese troops in Indochina. As a result, **Republic of China** troops were authorized to disarm Japanese forces and to maintain order in northern Indochina above the 16th parallel for the China Theater, while British troops would do the same below that line on behalf of the South East Asia Command.

On 28 August, British General **Douglas Gracey** became chief of the Army Control Commission and commander of Allied Forces for the occupation of French Indochina below the 16th parallel. His main tasks were to maintain law and order, disarm the Japanese, and to locate and repatriate Allied **prisoners of war**. Starting in **Saigon** on 23 September, the British began facilitating the return of the French to the lower half of Indochina, including all of Cambodia, the southern tip of Laos and the lower part of Vietnam (covering all of colonial **Cochinchina** and southern **Annam**).

Because the Chinese occupation forces under the command of General **Lu Han** refused to overthrow the **Democratic Republic of Vietnam** (DRV) or to let the French do it, the Republic of China effectively delayed the return of the French and allowed the DRV to operate free of the French above the 16th parallel while at war with them below that line. This began to change following the signing of the **Franco-Chinese accord** of 28 February and the **6 March Accords of 1946**, allowing the French to relieve the Chinese of their occupation duties by stationing some 15,000 troops above the 16th parallel. It was only when the bulk of the Chinese troops began pulling out of northern Indochina between June and September 1946 that the French intensified their efforts to restore their rule to upper Indochina.

Following the outbreak of full-scale war on **19 December 1946**, the political significance of the

16th parallel largely disappeared. However, the international division of Vietnam was not yet a thing of the past: During the **Geneva Conference** of 1954, it was agreed that Vietnam would be divided provisionally at the **17th parallel**.

**17th PARALLEL.** The demarcation line at which the modern-day nation-state of Vietnam was temporarily divided in accordance with the **Geneva Accords** signed in mid-July 1954. The northern part was attributed to the **Democratic Republic of Vietnam** (DRV), with its capital in **Hanoi**. The southern part remained under the control of the State of Vietnam, which became the **Republic of Vietnam** in October 1955 under the presidency of **Ngo Dinh Diem**. The Republic's capital was located in **Saigon**. The accords held the DRV to withdraw its troops and personnel from southern Indochina and to relocate them to Vietnamese territory north of the 17th parallel, while those of the State of Vietnam and the **French Union** would move to areas below that same line.

The choice of the 17th parallel was only reached after intense negotiations and consultations during the **Geneva Conference**. Moreover, the division of Vietnam into two halves was intended to be a provisional measure pending the organization of elections in 1956 to unite the country peacefully under one sovereign Vietnamese government. Those elections were never held as a fragile peace soon gave way to the resumption of **civil war** and foreign intervention. And as the **Cold War** subsumed the Vietnamese one, the 17th parallel became the *de facto* border between the two Vietnams until the DRV reunified the country in 1975 by military force and declared in 1976 the Socialist Republic of Vietnam as the sovereign state for all of Vietnam. *See also* 16th PARALLEL; INTERNATIONAL COMMISSION FOR SUPERVISION AND CONTROL.

***2ème BUREAU.*** *See DEUXIÈME BUREAU.*

***317ème SECTION.*** French war film on the end of the Indochina War, written and produced by **Pierre Schoendoerffer** in 1965 and based on his novel of the same title (1963). The film focuses on the retreat into Cambodia of four European officers and their Indochinese troops as the faceless soldiers of the **Democratic Republic of Vietnam**'s (DRV) army close in on them from the north. As the European troops are fleeing southwards, they learn of the siege and eventual fall of **Dien Bien Phu** to the enemy. The French platoon, like the French army in Vietnam, was now on its own. Schoendoerffer takes up two of his favorite themes in the film: the daily lives of soldiers at war (he would go on to win an Academy Award for the *Anderson Company*, covering American "grunts" fighting in Vietnam) and the heroic yet tragic trope of the sacrificed French soldier, a theme to which he would return in his films like ***Le crabe tambour*** and ***Dien Bien Phu.*** The *317ème Section* starred Jacques Perrin, Bruno Crémer, Pierre Fabre, Manuel Zarzo, and Boramy Tioulong. The filming took place in Cambodia thanks to the support of Prince **Norodom Sihanouk**. **Raoul Coutard**, who first knew Schoendoerffer during the Indochina War, did the photography for the *317ème Section*, which won the Festival of Cannes prize for best scenario in 1965.

**A.** Code letter used by the **Democratic Republic of Vietnam** strategists to refer secretly to northern Vietnam during the wars for Indochina.

**ABALAN, MICHEL HENRI CHARLES (1920–2000).** French colonial administrator who worked for the Commissioner for the French Republic in **Annam** in 1946 before he transferred to **Tonkin**. There he served in the Political Affairs Section in **Hanoi** and as provincial advisor in **Hoa Binh** between 1946 and 1949.

**ABBOTT, GEORGE MANLOVE (1904–1988).** Upon graduating from the Case School of Applied Science in 1925 and the *Ecole des Ponts et Chaussées* in Paris a year later, Abbott joined the U.S. Foreign Service in 1927. He served in various positions in Calcutta, Oslo, Marseille, and in Manila in December 1941. He returned to the U.S. shortly after the Japanese attack on Pearl Harbor and was re-assigned to France in September 1944 and became 1st Secretary to the U.S. Embassy there in May 1945. In September 1947, he became consul to **Saigon** before being promoted to Consul General in November 1947. He returned to the U.S. in 1950 and was named counselor to Budapest in 1951 and Special Assistant for the **South East Asia Treaty Organization** (SEATO) in 1956.

**ACADEMY, ASSOCIATED STATE OF VIETNAM.** The National Military Academy of the **Republic of Vietnam** opened its doors in December 1948, when the French initiated the School for Regular Officers in Hue. Only two classes graduated before the school transferred to Dalat where **Bao Dai**, the Head of State of the newly created Associated State of Vietnam, now resided. In October 1950, the third class began there. The school remained in Dalat until 1955, although the French changed the name to *École militaire inter-armée* upon moving it from Hue. During this period, the French trained a total of eleven classes (including the two at Hue). Following the French departure, the academy's name was Vietnamized into *Truong Vo Bi Lien Quan*, the equivalent of the former French appellation. The first American military advisors arrived in 1955, referring to the school in English as the Combined Arms School. Much of the core leadership of the State of Vietnam's armed forces followed by that of the **Republic of Vietnam** studied in this school. One of the best-known graduates of the national military academy was **Nguyen Van Thieu**, future president of the Republic of Vietnam. As of May 1974, excluding navy and medical corps officers, of the 80 flag rank officers on active duty roster, half were graduates of the first eleven academy classes and a "supplementary" one held in 1954. Of the 44 provinces chiefs, 17 were academy graduates. *See also* COLONIAL ACADEMY.

**ACCORDS OF 6 MARCH 1946**. Refers to the preliminary accord and subsequent military annex signed by the French and the **Democratic Republic of Vietnam** (DRV). In early 1946, the French and the DRV Vietnamese were increasingly keen to see the Chinese withdraw from northern Indochina, while Republican Chinese leaders such as **Chiang Kai-shek** wanted to transfer their troops in Indochina to northern China where war with Chinese communists loomed large. On 28 February 1946, the **Franco-Chinese Accord** was signed. The Chinese agreed to withdraw their troops from all of Indochina above the **16th parallel**. In exchange, the French gave up their concessions in China and accorded special privileges to the **overseas Chinese** residing in Indochina.

It was agreed that the French would relieve Chinese troops in northern Indochina by 31 March. However, because the tide in the Gulf of Tonkin would only be favorable to a French landing in the northern harbor of Haiphong on 5–6 March, the Commander-in-Chief of French forces General **Philippe Leclerc** dispatched ships from southern Indochina in late February to land some 10,000 troops in Haiphong. Since no formal agreement between the French and the **Democratic Republic of Vietnam** (DRV) had been reached to avoid the possible outbreak of war with the arrival of French troops, local Chinese commanders opposed such a rapid landing.

They were reluctant to get sucked into a possible war between the French and the Vietnamese, as had happened under the British in the south on **23 September 1945**. On the morning of 6 March, Chinese troops opened fire on French ships entering Haiphong harbor. The French returned fire. Chinese negotiators insisted that the Vietnamese and the French sign a compromise agreement before French troops could debark. Since France could not risk an armed confrontation with China, **Jean Sainteny** signed for the French side. **Ho Chi Minh** did so for the DRV while the Chinese must have pressured **Vu Hong Khanh**, leader of the **Vietnamese Nationalist Party** (*Viet Nam Quoc Dan Dang,* VNQDD), to sign off on the document for the Vietnamese non-communists critical of both the French and the DRV.

According to the preliminary accord, the French recognized the DRV as a "free state" (*État libre*) and agreed to hold a referendum in the south on the unification of **Cochinchina** with the DRV in exchange for Vietnam's entry into the **Indochinese Federation** and the **French Union**. The DRV, as a free state, would be able to run its own government, parliament, army, and finances but not its foreign affairs. The subsequent annex accord concerned the stationing of 15,000 French troops in Vietnam above the 16th parallel to replace the withdrawing Chinese forces. The annex stipulated that the French occupying forces in the north would be withdrawn within five years, with a reduction in force levels of 20 percent each year. Sainteny conceded this at the last minute.

This annex accord of 5 years effectively allowed Ho Chi Minh to defend himself against accusations of selling out the nation. It was in this specific context that Ho Chi Minh muttered famously to the French that it was "better to sniff French crap for five years than to have to eat Chinese dung forever!" (*Mieux vaut renifler la crotte française pendant cinq ans que manger la crotte chinoise pour toujours.*) On the French side, according to Stein Tønnesson, the signing of the 6 March Accord had less to do with an expression of French Republican liberalism than with the fact that it was reached in a crisis situation imposed by the Chinese. General Leclerc, Commander of French forces in Indochina, instructed Sainteny to reach an agreement at any cost, "even if this means taking initiatives which could later be disavowed".

While this may have allowed the French to land in northern Vietnam, the result was that the accords suited few on the French side. This was the case for the president of the French Republic, **Georges Bidault**, and the high commissioner in Indochina, **Georges Thierry d'Argenlieu**. Both men were hostile to the idea of having to phase out French troops in the north within such a short time span. Thierry d'Argenlieu was particularly hostile to the DRV's claim to all of Vietnam. He preferred instead to push for Cochinchinese autonomy within an Indochinese Federation, where Cochinchina and "Vietnam" would remain separate entities. On 1 June 1946, he proclaimed the birth of the **Provisional Government of the Republic of Cochinchina**, the first pillar of the pentagonal Federation instructed by **Charles de Gaulle**.

From mid-1946, as the Chinese withdrew the bulk of their troops, the DRV and the French found themselves face to face. It remained to be seen whether decolonization could be negotiated in subsequent Franco-Vietnamese meetings during the **Dalat** and **Fontainebleau Conferences** or whether the two sides would resort to arms.

**ACCORDS OF 8 MARCH 1948.** *See* BAO DAI SOLUTION.

**ACCORDS OF HA LONG BAY.** *See* BAO DAI SOLUTION.

**ACHARD, JACQUES AUGUSTIN (1927–1984).** French colonial administrator in Indochina during the conflict. He briefly served in the cabinet of the high commissioner for Indochina in 1951 before becoming the deputy to the provincial advisor to Mon Cay province in 1952. In 1953, he worked as an administrative delegate in northern Vietnam. In 1954, he served in the Pacification Liaison Office for the Haiphong zone before becoming an advisor to the Royal Lao Government between 1955 and 1956.

**ADMINISTRATIVE OFFICE FOR THE FRONTIER (*Phòng Biên Chính*).** The secret administrative unit through which the **Indochinese Communist Party** (ICP) first directed its affairs in Laos. It was first known in the wake of World War II as the Office for External Affairs (*Phong Ngoai Vu*). In late 1947, the ICP revamped and renamed it the Administrative Office for the Frontier under the leadership of Tran To Chan, a longstanding member of the ICP, fluent in Lao and Thai. The party committee for **Inter-Zone IV**

(*Lien Khu IV*) and its Resistance and Administrative Committee jointly controlled this secret unit in charge of all communist activity in and for Laos and oversaw the secret training of Lao cadres and troops working with the Vietnamese. The Administrative Office for the Frontier created the **Lao Issara Committee for the East** in late 1947, putting **Nūhak Phūmsavan** in charge of it. Like its equivalent in Cambodia, the **Committee for External Affairs** (*Ban Ngoai Vu*), the Administrative Office for the Frontier was the prime mover in the early development of communism in Laos during the Indochina War. *See also* ADVISORY GROUP 100; CAMBODIAN RESISTANCE GOVERNMENT; HOANG VAN HOAN; INDOCHINESE FEDERATION; LAO RESISTANCE GOVERNMENT; NGUYEN KHANG; NGUYEN THANH SON; PARTY AFFAIRS COMMITTEE.

**ADVANCE SOUTHERN UNITS (*Nam Tiến*).** Upon returning to the Sino-Vietnamese frontier in 1941, **Ho Chi Minh** pushed for the creation of Southern Advance Assault Teams (*Doi Xung Phong Nam Tien*). Between February and August 1943, around 20 such teams emerged and participated in low-intensity, agit-prop activities in the north (mainly in the Cao Bang and Lang Son areas) and helped in building up **Viet Minh** bases among populations living along routes running southwards into the Red River Delta. The *Nam Tien* movement was revamped following the birth of the **Democratic Republic of Vietnam** (DRV) in September 1945 and the outbreak of war in the south. Recruiting mainly young men from areas located above the **16th parallel**, the government sent *Nam Tien* units to assist southerners at war against superior French forces and firepower. The southern teams entered into action in October 1945 arriving by boat, train, and on foot. While these young troops ran on high levels of patriotism in the heady days of late 1945 and 1946, they were badly armed and trained. Hundreds even thousands died in battle between 1945 and 1947. *Nam Tien* units nonetheless provided a base from which the Commander-in-Chief of southern forces, **Nguyen Binh** began building, training, and outfitting an army for the DRV upon his arrival in the south in November 1945. *See also* ARMY, FRENCH UNION; EXPEDITIONARY CORPS; PEOPLE'S ARMY OF VIETNAM; SPECIAL FORCES, DEMOCRATIC REPUBLIC OF VIETNAM.

**ADVISORY GROUP 100 (*Đoàn 100*).** Secret Vietnamese political and military delegation dispatched to the Lao regrouping provinces of Phongsaly and Samneua in mid-1954 to help rebuild the **Pathet Lao**. On 28 June 1954, as efforts to reach an agreement for ending the Indochina War intensified at Geneva, General **Vo Nguyen Giap** cabled **Nguyen Khang,** a **Vietnamese Worker's Party's** (VWP) Central Committee member and the head of the **Party's Affairs Committee** for Western Laos (*Ban Can Su Mien Tay*), concerning the need to hold on secretly in Laos. Giap instructed Nguyen Khang that the VWP Central Committee had decided to separate the system of advisors from the volunteer army. This was the crucial first step in the Vietnamese communist decision to maintain a secret advisory presence in Laos. The troops left; hundreds of advisors stayed on. On 16 July 1954, less than five days before the **Geneva Accords** were signed, the Vietnamese High Command signed into being the special advisory group *Doan 100* under the command of political commissar and General **Chu Huy Man**. The VWP instructed group 100 and the Party Affairs Committee to combine their forces in Phongsaly and Samneua to remake the Pathet Lao politically and militarily.

In Laos, more than in Cambodia or even in southern Vietnam, the VWP was going to stay on and they were developing a concrete strategy and transnational project to do so. This meant that the revolutionary struggle would now be carried out in peaceful, political terms and not via direct, armed violence. Group 100 was designed to help the Lao to organize the struggle and defense of the two provinces of Samneau and Phongsaly so that this area would become the revolutionary base for all of Laos. Group 100 also helped Vietnamese communists to build up a Pathet Lao solution capable of standing by their Vietnamese brethren politically, diplomatically, and militarily. *See also* ADMINISTRATIVE OFFICE FOR THE FRONTIER; BAO DAI SOLUTION; INDOCHINESE COMMUNIST PARTY; INDOCHINESE FEDERATION; KHMER ISSARAK; LAO ISSARA COMMITTEE FOR THE EAST; LAO RESISTANCE GOVERNMENT.

***AÉRONAVALE.*** Refers mainly to French fighter planes based on or launched from **navy** aircraft carriers or ground bases for combined land and naval missions. The French used its carrier strike force mainly at the end of the Indochina War, when the enemy knocked out airfields or when the battlefield was located too far from the main French airbases. This was the case during French operations against the forces of the **Democratic Republic of Vietnam** in Laos in 1953, during the battle of **Dien Bien Phu** a year later, and in the highlands of **Inter-Zone V** during the **Atlante** operation of 1954. The French aircraft carrier *L'Arromanches* (named after one of the main Normandy beaches where the Allies landed on D-Day in 1944) was the core of the French strike force. It arrived in Indochina in 1948 and remained there until the end of the war (though it made periodic returns to France for servicing). It participated in the battle of Dien Bien Phu. The French *aéronavale* was also used for surveillance of the coasts against enemy infiltration and trade.

**AESCHLIMANN, CHARLES.** Swiss delegate of the International Committee of the **Red Cross** (ICRC) and member of the French Red Cross during most of the Indochina War. In January 1947, following the **Haiphong** incident and the outbreak of full-scale war in Indochina on **19 December 1946**, he traveled to Vietnam on behalf of the ICRC to establish contact with civilian and military prisoners of war taken by both belligerents. A specialist of Asia and a man of contacts, Aeschlimann quickly entered into negotiations with **Democratic Republic of Vietnam** (DRV) and French authorities, both of whom were reluctant to welcome the Red Cross's presence. While the French argued that this was not a war but an internal security problem, they eventually allowed Aeschlimann to visit their prisons. DRV authorities also allowed him to visit a prisoner camp in Hoa Binh, holding 171 Europeans.

Although Aeschlimann succeeded in gaining the liberation of 29 persons from DRV authorities in 1947, he had little success thereafter. The DRV was wary of the Red Cross' logistical reliance on the French and possible manipulation by them for intelligence purposes. With the intensification of the war in 1950, Aeschlimann's stepped up his overtures to the DRV to allow the Red Cross to contact the increasing number of **French Union** prisoners. His efforts were met largely with silence. In 1954, Aeschlimann failed again to gain access for the ICRC to tend to prisoners taken at **Dien Bien Phu**. Aeschlimann did, however, inspect camps set up for the internment of Chinese nationalist troops fleeing across the Indochinese border in late 1949 and 1950. *See also* RED CROSS; RED CROSS, DEMOCRATIC REPUBLIC OF VIETNAM.

***AFFAIRE BOUDAREL.*** *See* BOUDAREL AFFAIR.

***AFFAIRE DES GÉNÉRAUX.*** In May 1949, the French minister of Defense sent the Chief of Staff of the Army, **Georges Revers**, to Indochina on a fact-finding mission. The latter received orders to provide the government with a fresh and informed view of the actual situation on the ground and policies that could be adopted to improve the French position, diplomatically, and militarily. In mid-1949, Revers traveled to and throughout Indochina before returning to France to make a detailed, pessimistic, and top-secret report on the military situation in Indochina. At the same time, behind the scenes, Revers was intent upon getting General **Charles Mast** named as the new Commander-in-Chief of the armed forces in Indochina as well as High Commissioner.

It was in this dual context that an incident occurred triggering the "affair". On 18 September 1949, a fight broke out between a French soldier and two Vietnamese on a bus platform in Paris. When the French police hauled all of them into the station, they discovered a partial copy of the Revers report in the briefcase of one of the two Vietnamese. His name was Do Dai Phuoc, doctor of law and president of the Vietnamese Students' Association in France. An investigation led investigators to Hoang Van Co, the representative of General **Nguyen Van Xuan** in Paris. Hoang Van Co revealed that he had received the report from Roger Peyré, a periodic and shady agent of the ***Service de documentation extérieure et de contre-espionnage,*** but also a confidant of General Revers. Further investigation also revealed that the report was in the hands of the **Democratic Republic of Vietnam** (DRV) in France and Indochina (although it is to this day unclear how this occurred).

French authorities preferred to quash the incident in order to avoid a full-blown "affair" that could bring with it political fallout. This seemed to be working until the new minister of Defense **René Pleven** fired Revers for his indiscretion, but in so doing drew the attention of the American magazine *Time*. The "affair" went public when this magazine published on 26 December 1949 an article about the divulgation of the report under the provocative title, *Scandal*. On 13 January 1950, the French daily *Le Monde* spoke of *une affaire des généraux*. And thus a major, media scandal was born, as the French papers and politicians jumped on the incident, even though the official commission set up to investigate the "affair" was unable to identify the guilty party.

If much ink has been spilt on who leaked what to whom and when in France, less attention has focused on the impact of the leak of the Revers report to the DRV, how the Vietnamese obtained copies, what they learned from the ultra-secret report, and how they were able to use it in devising or revising their own strategy at a crucial juncture in the Indochina War. As of 2008, a French officer assigned to the military archives of the *Service historique de la Défense* in Vincennes and knowledgeable about this "affair", told this author that the "Revers report" is still classified (*non communicable*).

**AFRICAN TROOPS.** If the French **Expeditionary Corps** that landed in southern Indochina in October 1945 counted few if any black African troops in its ranks at the outset, the inverse would be the case by the end of the Indochina conflict. This was not an accident. In May 1945, General **Charles de Gaulle** prohibited the French Expeditionary Corps from sending Africans to fight in Indochina on the grounds that they would be adversely affected by the nationalist sentiment reigning among the Vietnamese. De Gaulle also feared that such a move would only exacerbate already sharp American anti-colonialist critiques of French colonial policy.

The French quickly reversed this policy, however, when they realized that what they had assumed was going to be a rapid "**pacification**" operation in Indochina was, in fact, becoming a drawn-out and costly colonial war, for which the army would have to find new recruits. Given that the government refused to institute a national draft in the metropole, the French turned to the Empire and began recruiting Africans to fight in Indochina. If the Expeditionary Corps only counted 617 African troops in July 1947, the number peaked at 20,560 in January 1954, accounting for 16.5 percent of the overall total of the Expeditionary troops. By relying on the empire, the French avoided drawing attention to the war in the metropole. The use of colonial troops was also considerably cheaper for a French government increasingly strapped for cash to finance the war. The French army mainly relied upon African troops to serve in the artillery and as infantry soldiers, almost always under European command. Only two battalions of African soldiers entered the elite ranks of the *Groupe mobile*. During the Indochina War, 2,564 African soldiers died and 3,706 were wounded. *See also* ARMY, ASSOCIATED STATE OF VIETNAM; CASUALTIES; FOREIGN LEGION; NORTH AFRICANS.

**AID, AMERICAN.** In April 1949, as Chinese communist forces routed their nationalist opponents and crossed the Yangzi on their way to taking all of China, the French accelerated their overtures to the United States concerning military and financial assistance. It was clear that a Chinese communist victory could provide the French adversary, the **Democratic Republic of Vietnam** (DRV), with a major source of assistance. At the same time, the Western bloc's creation of the **North Atlantic Treaty Organization** in April 1949 obligated France to play a leading military role in the defense of Western Europe. The possible rearmament of West Germany only aggravated the pressure on Paris to invest militarily in Europe instead of Indochina.

Faced with these increasing financial commitments in both Indochina and Europe, the French turned to the Americans for help. On 15 September 1949, the French minister of Foreign Affairs, **Robert Schuman**, asked the American Secretary of State **Dean Acheson** to assist the French financially in the Indochina War. Determined to contain communism, the **Truman** administration viewed such requests favorably. The French and the American governments agreed to a provisional military convention on assistance on 30 December 1949, followed by the Accords of Principles in February 1950. This document established that American assistance would be financial and material. The French fired off their first orders to the American government and in August 1950 the first American ships carrying war material arrived and were unloaded in **Saigon**, sparking off a Vietnamese demonstration opposed to American intervention in the war.

The outbreak of the **Korean War** in June 1950 hardened the American resolve to aid the French in Indochina. On 8 December 1950 an agreement was reached that codified and normalized American aid to the French. General **Jean de Lattre de Tassigny** personally visited Washington to request more American assistance for the outfitting of the new armies of the **Associated**

**States of Indochina** and the modernization of his **Expeditionary Corps**. Between September 1950 and May 1953, the Americans supplied 286,000 tons of material to the Expeditionary Corps. In 1953, the Americans took over the financing of the Associated States of Indochina so that the French could concentrate on military investments in Europe. In 1952, the Americans had assumed around 40 percent of the financial burden of the Indochina War. By 1954, however, this number reached almost 80 percent before American aid ended in July of that year.

As French historian Hugues Tertrais has provocatively put it, the Americans were in effect "buying the war from the French". They were certainly "assuming the burden" as Mark Lawrence has argued. Massive and modern American aid also increased the intensity of the war, especially the use of airpower against what was increasingly becoming a modern DRV army willing to take the battle to the French. *See also* AID, CHINESE COMMUNIST; AID, MALAYSIA; AID, SOVIET; AIR FORCE, FRANCE; ARMY, ASSOCIATED STATE OF CAMBODIA; ARMY, ASSOCIATED STATE OF LAOS; ARMY, ASSOCIATED STATE OF VIETNAM; EXPERIENCE OF WAR; FINANCIAL COST OF INDOCHINA WAR, FRANCE; NAPALM.

**AID, CHINESE COMMUNIST.** According to Vietnamese sources, between May 1950 and June 1954 the **People's Republic of China** provided 21,517 tons of military and economic aid to the **Democratic Republic of Vietnam** (DRV). This aid included weapons, ammunition, and artillery, as well as rice, trucks, and medicines. The nature of this aid breaks down on an annual basis as follows: Between May and December 1950: 3,983 tons; 1951: 6,086 tons; 1952: 2,160 tons; 1953: 4,400 tons; and between January and June 1954: 4,892 tons. Thanks in large part to this assistance, General **Vo Nguyen Giap** built, coordinated, and unleashed a remarkably modern army against the French in a set-piece battle at **Dien Bien Phu** in 1954. Vietnamese troops were also trained and outfitted in southern China in the early 1950s.

Chinese aid also extended into the economic, ideological, intelligence, and health fields. The Vietnamese borrowed and applied Chinese **rectification** methods, allowing them to take hold of the army, the party, and the society they sought mobilize and communize. Between July and September, the DRV received via **Plan Z** 11,546 tons of weapons and equipment and 1,116 motor vehicles of all types. This was the remaining amount that the Chinese and Soviets had budgeted to the DRV, but had not delivered before the Geneva Accords put an end to the war in July 1954. *See also* AID, AMERICAN; AID, MALAYSIA; AID, SOVIET; AIR FORCE, FRANCE; ARMY, ASSOCIATED STATE OF CAMBODIA; ARMY, ASSOCIATED STATE OF LAOS; ARMY, ASSOCIATED STATE OF VIETNAM; FINANCIAL COST OF INDOCHINA WAR, FRANCE.

**AID, MALAYSIA.** In 1947, the Malayan Communist Party, then run by an ethnic Vietnamese named Lai Tec, approved the secret transfer of captured Japanese weapons to the forces of the **Democratic Republic of Vietnam** (DRV) fighting the French in southern Vietnam. The Malayan party assigned this task to **Chan Mun Boy**, who in turn arranged the transfer to the DRV of 150 tons of weapons and equipment by boat. Working closely with **Duong Quang Dong**, in 1947 Chan Mun Boy moved the arms from Malacca to the Thai port town of May Ruot. Vietnamese teams then transported the arms overland across Cambodia to southern Vietnam. After delivering most of the arms successfully to southern Vietnam, Chan Mun Boy joined the Vietnamese resistance, adopted Vietnamese nationality, and ran guns out of Thailand for the DRV until he transferred to Cambodia in 1949. *See also MÉTIS*.

**AID, SOVIET.** Soviet aid to the **Democratic Republic of Vietnam** (DRV) never matched that provided by the Chinese communists, let alone that provided by the Americans to the French. However, many of the arms the Chinese supplied to the Vietnamese were of Soviet origin. There are several reasons explaining the lower level of Soviet assitance to the DRV during the Indochina conflict. For one, **Joseph Stalin** had always been much more focused on Europe than on Asia. This was particularly the case in the immediate aftermath of World War II. Second, following the Chinese communist victory in 1949, the Soviet leader turned over the leadership of the Asian revolutionary front to the Chinese communists led by **Mao Zedong**. Lastly, as Ilya Gaiduk has shown, Stalin did not believe that Asian societies possessed the required conditions to make communism work. Nevertheless, between 1950 and 1954, the Soviet Union did channel some military, medical, economic, and educational assistance to the Vietnamese communists based in northern Vietnam. This aid went overland through the Chinese, however. The Soviets never attempted to challenge the French navy or its American backers during the Indochina War. The exact size of Soviet aid is hard to pin down.

One Vietnamese study of the question confuses Soviet aid with Chinese-supplied Soviet weapons. For example, although the DRV received seventy-six 37 mm Soviet-made anti-aircraft guns, and 12 H6 multitube rocket launchers (Katyusha), K50 submachine guns, and some 700 vehicles (including Molotov trucks), the Chinese, not the Soviets, provided most of them to the Vietnamese from their own stockpiles. The Soviets did provide important though undetermined amounts of antibiotics and quinine (apparently several tons). In July 1951, *Radio Moscow* began a daily broadcast in Vietnamese in favor of the DRV. All of the Soviet assistance provided between 1950 and 1952 was provided free of charge (*khong hoan lai*). On 5 July 1952, DRV authorities signed an agreement with the Soviet Union by which the latter provided an undisclosed loan to the Vietnamese to purchase Soviet goods. Again, the exact nature of the materials provided remains unclear. We do know that from 1952 the Soviets provided cultural assistance via the DRV embassies in Moscow and Beijing. This included the shipment of 308 films, 60 current events films (*bop phim thoi su*), several thousand records, 3,640 cameras, and 24 film projectors. This aid contributed to the development of the DRV's photography branch and to efforts to promote the communization of the state, army, and society. From 1953, the Soviets also reopened the doors of their higher education institutes. Until the end of the Indochina War, over 200 Vietnamese traveled to the Soviet Union to study a wide variety of subjects, including medicine, agricultural development, electrical engineering, chemistry, veterinarian sciences, economics, and construction. Between July and September, the DRV received via **Plan Z** 11,546 tons of weapons and equipment and 1,116 motor vehicles of all types. This was the remaining amount that the Chinese and Soviets had budgeted to the DRV for 1954, but had not delivered before the **Geneva Accords** put an end to the war in July of that year. *See also* AID, AMERICAN; AID, CHINESE COMMUNIST; AID, MALAYSIA.

**AIR AMERICA.** *See* CIVIL AIR TRANSPORT.

**AIR FORCE, DEMOCRATIC REPUBLIC OF VIETNAM (DRV).** The **Democratic Republic of Vietnam** (DRV) attempted to create a national air force during the Indochina War. In 1945, the former Emperor **Bao Dai**, now supreme advisor to **Ho Chi Minh**, donated the first two planes to the DRV's air force. One was a Tiger Moth and the other was a French Morane-Saulnier. Following the outbreak of full-scale war in **Hanoi** on 19 December 1946, the planes were hidden in Chiem Hoa district in the north before being sneaked on to other hideouts. They never posed a threat to the French and never got off the ground except for a few flying lessons. This was no air force.

What concerned DRV air authorities most in the early years of the Indochina War was how best to protect the population and soldiers against French air attacks and bombing and how to shoot down the enemy planes. European **crossovers** with experience in air war gave lessons and translated valuable manuals into Vietnamese or French for use in training classes. During the **Fontainebleau Conference** in mid-1946, **Ta Quang Buu** acquired and brought back a wide range of aviation books and manuals to help train Vietnamese cadres, including aircraft recognition guides and a German manual for shooting down aircraft by deploying concentrated fire by infantry weapons. The German crossover and pilot, **Werner Schulze**, played a particularly important role in translating German aviation materials and instructing Vietnamese air cadres. He helped translate the manual on shooting down enemy aircraft that was printed by the **General Staff** and widely distributed from 1948. By 1949, the Vietnamese claim, the French no longer dared to fly at very low altitudes.

The imminent victory of the Chinese communists in 1949 led DRV strategists to attempt to develop their air force again. In early 1949, **Vo Nguyen Giap**, **Hoang Van Thai**, Phan Phac, and Ho Chi Minh met and decided to create an air task force called the "Air Force Training Unit". On 9 March 1949, as preparations to modernize the Vietnamese army intensified, Vo Nguyen Giap signed a decree creating the Air Force Research Committee (*Ban Nghien Cuu Khong Quan*) that was to work with the Naval Research Committee (*Ban Nghien Cuu Thuy Quan*) and the Bureau of Artillery (*Cuc Phao Binh*). Ta Quang Buu headed up the development of the DRV's aviation, assisted by Schulze and other Japanese and Europeans experienced in aeronautics. However, in the end, the DRV never got pilots or planes off the ground much less in the air. When Chinese communists began providing the Vietnamese with field artillery and anti-aircraft artillery guns, the DRV's Ministry of Defense disbanded the Air Force Research Section and concentrated its personnel and its efforts on operating and developing artillery and anti-aircraft missions against the French **Air Force**.

**AIR FORCE, FRANCE**. At the outset, the French Air Force's role in the war was small compared to that of the ground forces. Part of this was due to the fact that the **Democratic Republic of Vietnam** (DRV) had no air force of which to speak and the **guerrilla** war remained the main concern of the **Expeditionary Corps** until 1950. The paucity of planes in the French Air Force after World War II also explains why French airpower paled compared to that of the ground forces. Most of the planes used in Indochina came from Allied stockpiles from the Pacific War, mainly Spitfires, King Cobras, and C47s.

The Chinese communist victory of 1949 and the enemy's acquisition of a modern army, nurtured by Chinese aid, forced the French Air Force to assume a more active role in what was no longer a guerrilla affair. The French defeat at **Cao Bang** in 1950 had made this clear. In order to integrate and coordinate air support and bombing missions with the ground forces now fighting the DRV army in set piece battles, the French Air Force created three tactical air groupings or ***Groupements aériens tactiques.*** In order to offset the increased financial burden this entailed, the French began receiving large-scale American aid in the form of planes, munitions, fuel, and eventually civilian pilots as part of the **Civil Air Transport** (CAT). Thanks to the U.S. Military Assistance Program, the United States Air Force and Navy provided F6F Hellcats, F8F Bearcats, F4U Corsairs, and B26 Bombers. French and American CAT pilots flew perilous missions to supply besieged troops at **Dien Bien Phu** in 1954. (None of the Americans were active members of the French or American Air Forces; they flew for the CAT.) 10,000 sorties were made and 62 planes were lost during this battle.

In July 1954, when the **Geneva Accords** put an end to the Indochina conflict, the French Air Force had committed 388 planes to the theatre, meaning some 20 percent of the service's total. 10,000 men served in the air force in Indochina or about 7.5 percent of its total personnel. Between 1946 and 1954, the French Air Force lost 434 men, an unknown number of missing in action and 11 wounded.

The core problem for the French Air Force during the Indochina War was one of priorities and money. From the moment the Indochina War intensified with the Chinese communist victory in 1949, French military strategists and politicians at the highest levels had to reconcile two costly but conflicting priorities: maintain a serious air force presence in Indochina and create an equally credible air force as part of the defense of Western Europe, required by the Treaty of Brussels in 1948 and the **North Atlantic Treaty Organization** (NATO) of 1949. From 1953, the air force chiefs of staff made it clear that NATO would have to take precedence over Indochina as the government's main priority. The government explained this to General **Henri Navarre** before sending him to take command in Indochina. That decision coincided with the DRV's acquisition and effective utilization of heavy artillery, ending the French Air Force's unchallenged domination of the skies in the Indochina War. *See also* FINANCIAL COST OF THE INDOCHINA WAR.

**ALBINET, LOUIS CASIMIR HENRI (1898–1991).** Entered the French Military Academy of Saint-Cyr in 1916 and became a second lieutenant in the Colonial Troops in 1919. He served and was wounded on the Western Front in 1917 and twice again in 1918 before the war ended. During the interwar period, he made his career in the colonial army. He served in Morocco (1920–22) and in Indochina (1925–28) before moving on to French Africa during the 1930s. In Indochina, he served in the General Staff of the commanding general of Cochinchina-Cambodia. In the 1930s, he commanded mainly in Senegal. At the head of a Senegalese battalion, he took part in the failed French campaign of 1940. During the Vichy period, he remained in France serving as state secretary for Youth Affairs in late 1942, tending to questions of physical education and sports. His earlier colonial service in Indochina attracted the new French government taking over under General **Charles de Gaulle.** Transferred to the command of the *2ème Brigade coloniale* in November 1944, Albinet joined the **Expeditionary Corps** for the Far East in October 1945 and took command of the *3ème Division d'Infanterie coloniale* in November. Between February and October 1946, he served as deputy to the commanding general of French Troops in Southern Indochina. In October

1946, he assumed direction of the French military command for Cambodia in Phnom Penh until his return to France in March 1948.

**ALCOHOLISM.** If substance abuse posed major problems for the American army during the Vietnam conflict, alcoholism plagued the French army during the Indochina War. Although army medical statistics never established a specific rubric for this pathology, 2,242 repatriations from Indochina for "alcoholism" (*éthylisme*) during nine years of war suggest that there was a problem. Indeed, this number accounts for almost 10 percent of all medical repatriations during the war. Alcohol, such as wine, beer, and *apéritifs* (the *provençal pastis* for example) were in abundant supply to soldiers during the Indochina War. On a number of occasions, the **Air Force** parachuted alcohol to its troops engaged in battle, including those besieged at **Dien Bien Phu**. **Opium** abuse rarely accounted for repatriations during the Indochina War. It was relatively more expensive and harder to prepare, let alone inhale easily while on mission. The **Democratic Republic of Vietnam** and the **Associated States of Indochina** have not published statistics on alcoholism or substance abuse during the war.

**ALESSANDRI, MARCEL JEAN MARIE (1895–1968).** French General who led the famous retreat from Indochina following the Japanese ***coup de force* of 9 March 1945** and returned to command during the Indochina War.

Upon graduating from Saint-Cyr in 1914, he signed up and served during all of World War I, seeing combat during the battles of Verdun and the Somme in 1916. In 1928, Alessandri entered the *École supérieure de guerre* and became battalion commander in 1930. Between 1935 and 1939, he served at this same institution teaching general tactics and rose to the rank of lieutenant colonel in December 1936. In March 1939, he transferred to Indochina where he became deputy then chief of the General Staff of the senior commanding officer. Named full colonel in March 1941, he assumed command of the 5th Foreign Infantry Regiment (*Régiment étranger d'infanterie*) and then that of the 2nd Tonkin Brigade in November 1942. In May 1943, he was promoted to brigadier general, second in command to General Gabriel Sabattier.

Alessandri commanded the Western Task Force of the Red River, when the Japanese *coup de force* occurred in March 1945. Under attack, he and his men retreated towards Laos and then southern China. On 21 March 1945, he was promoted to lieutenant general and in June, he took over as acting senior commanding officer of French Forces in China by a decision of the President of the Provisional French Republic. On 17 August 1945, **Charles de Gaulle** named him interim High Commissioner for Indochina. In September, back in Indochina, Alessandri attended the Allied ceremony in **Hanoi** marking the surrender of the Japanese. However, he walked out when he saw that the French flag was not flown. On 31 October 1945, he became Commissioner of the French Republic and military commander for Cambodia. He signed for the French Republic the Franco-Cambodian *modus vivendi* in January 1946. He also oversaw the early stages of the French reoccupation of Laos above and below the **16th parallel**.

On 23 March 1946, he returned to France after seven years in Asia, but was back in Indochina in June 1948 to serve as the senior commanding officer of French Ground Forces there. On 28 November 1949, he became acting commissioner of the Republic for North Vietnam and commander-in-chief of Ground Forces in North Vietnam, where he argued in favor of the occupation of the northern delta in order to deny the adversary access to vital rice supplies to feed its rapidly expanding army. Alessandri's blockade provoked serious economic problems for the **Democratic Republic of Vietnam** (DRV), but it came too late. By mid-1950, **Chinese aid**, including rice, was reaching the DRV's armed forces. As head of the Operational Zone of Tonkin, Alessandri made plans to take the battle to the adversary in the highlands, but was overruled by the commander-in-chief of French Forces in the Far East, General **Marcel Carpentier**.

Though strongly opposed to the idea, Alessandri was ordered to evacuate Cao Bang, That Ke, and Langson. It was at this point, in the autumn of 1950, that the Vietnamese, supported by the Chinese, attacked the retreating French columns in what became known as the battle of **Cao Bang**. The loss of these frontier posts allowed the Vietnamese to open up crucial supply lines with and accelerate military aid from China. Alessandri's organization of the retreat from Cao Bang was a failure. His underestimation of the adversary's military strength and acumen led to the loss of two entire columns.

In December 1950, he returned to France and was relieved of his duties. In September 1952, he moved to the Ministry in charge of relations with the **Associated States of Indochina** but was stationed in Indochina. As a political and military advisor to **Bao Dai**, he helped organize and train the Vietnamese **Army of the Associated State of Vietnam** between 1952 and 1955. He returned definitively to France in June 1955. *See also COUP DE FORCE* OF 9 MARCH 1945.

**ALGERIAN WAR.** It is well known that the start of the Algerian War on 1 November 1954 followed on the closing of the Indochina War a few months earlier at **Dien Bien Phu** and Geneva. Algerian nationalists at the helm of the *Front de libération nationale* (FLN) were inspired by the Vietnamese military victory over the French at Dien Bien Phu, demonstrating that the colonized could use military force to win independence. Indeed, a FLN delegation visiting Asia met with **Vo Nguyen Giap** in the late 1950s to discuss the Vietnamese experience and how it might be applied in Algeria. The Vietnamese stressed the importance of **guerrilla warfare**, tight organization, and national front work. The Chinese provided similar advice.

Like the Chinese and Vietnamese united fronts, the FLN was designed to build up popular support for the independence movement regardless of sex, creed, or class. FLN leaders created a provisional government and organized guerrilla action in the countryside and in the cities. Indeed, the famous battle of Algiers in 1957 had precedents in the violent urban war **Nguyen Binh** had unleashed in **Saigon** in the late 1940s, to say nothing of the battle of **Hanoi** that had first opened the Indochina conflict between 19 December 1946 and 17 February 1947.

The wars of national liberation led by the **Viet Minh** and the FLN were also carriers of violent civil conflicts. In Vietnam, the **Indochinese Communist Party** went to war with its nationalist competitors as did the FLN's leadership. However, there were also significant differences between the Algerian and Indochinese colonial wars and revolutionary states. For one, the **Democratic Republic of Vietnam** (DRV) was much more successful than its Algerian counterpart in creating a veritable war state during the Indochina conflict, complete with functioning ministries, a bureaucracy, economy, police and health services and so on. Second, the DRV, thanks in part to Chinese communist military aid, successfully transformed a guerrilla army, at least in central and northern Vietnam, into a remarkably modern army. From 1950, Vo Nguyen Giap was commanding six divisions over all of northern Indochina and engaging the French in set-piece battles. The FLN never matched this level of force or wartime modernity in securing Algerian national independence. Whereas the French army suffered a humiliating battle defeat at Dien Bien Phu in 1954, it dominated the FLN on the battlefields in Algeria. Deprived of a jungle-protected rearbase bordering a country like China, the FLN's military force never developed beyond the guerrilla stage.

However, if the FLN lost the war on the battlefield, they were much more successful than the Vietnamese on the diplomatic front. True, the Arab League was unable to match the assistance the international communist bloc led by China provided to the DRV. Nonetheless, like the Indonesian Republicans before them, the FLN leadership was non-communist and anti-colonialist; and this mattered in the international arena. For one, this allowed the Algerian nationalists to play various sides of the **Cold War** more effectively against France. Whereas Washington put its anticolonialism on the backburner in order to support the French in Indochina as part of the wider struggle to contain global communism, in Algeria the Americans were less prone to back the French for a lost colonial cause when it was obvious that the FLN was anything but communist-led. Washington was even less supportive if it meant alienating other Arab countries, such as Egypt, in the increasingly important Middle East region.

Whereas the DRV failed to bring the Vietnamese question before the **United Nations**, the FLN effectively used the decolonization of the international system and the increasing number of "Southern" states entering the General Assembly to push its case against the French on the diplomatic battlefield. Thus, although the DRV pulled off something of a "military revolution" by creating a modern army capable of taking on the French and winning, they were less successful with "diplomatic struggle". The Algerians walked away from the Evian Accords of 1962 with full national independence and territorial integrity. When the ink dried on the **Geneva Accords** of 1954, the contours of the Cold War imposed a diplomatic defeat on the Vietnamese: Ho Chi Minh only obtained half of the Vietnam he had declared independent in 1945.

For many French officers, too, the Indochinese and Algerian wars were also closely intertwined; indeed, both wars of decolonization deeply influenced the nature of the French army, its strategy, tactics, internal cohesion, and especially its politicization. For one, the army's humiliation at Dien Bien Phu, coming on top of the debacle of 1940, left many French officers determined not to lose another war, certainly not in Algeria. *Plus jamais, ça!* and talk of honor could be heard in private conversations among French officers humiliated in Indochina. Rather than walking away from Indochina aware of the reality of decolonization and the power of nationalism, many (not all) French officers left Indochina obsessed with never losing again. Officers arriving in Algeria from Indochina carried other things with them, too. Many officers having fought conventional battles against the DRV in **Tonkin** and **Annam** were deeply frustrated by the absence of such combat in Algeria.

At the same time, a handful of French military officers active in southern Vietnam during the war were convinced that the FLN was engaged in the same type of **guerrilla** tactics and "**revolutionary warfare**" that the Vietnamese communists had used during the Indochina conflict. At the head of these French "theoricians" with experience in southern Vietnam and at the head of the ***Groupements de commandos mixtes aéroportés*** were officers such as **Roger Trinquier, Jacques Hogard**, and of course the godfather to them all, **Charles Lacheroy**. They were soon speaking of "**parallel hierarchies**", **psychological warfare**, and linking the FLN to global communism even though the FLN core leadership was anything but communist. (The FLN never applied communist **rectification, new hero,** and **emulation campaigns** or even Maoist-minded **land reform**.). A handful of these French "centurions" (celebrated by the French film directors **Pierre Schoendoerffer** and **Jean Lartéguy** and military historian **Bernard Fall**) ended up in jail or on the run when they tried to use revolutionary warfare against the French state when **Charles de Gaulle** decided that the decolonization of Algeria was now in France's best interests. In short, France's colonial wars politicized the army and led men such as **Raoul Salan** to refuse to obey orders, even those coming from de Gaulle, on the grounds that it was tantamount to a third humiliating defeat, equal to that of June 1940 and Dien Bien Phu in 1954.

The Indochinese and Algerian wars were also different in that the French army sent to fight in Indochina was a professional one, the **Expeditionary Corps**, whereas the draft was instituted in order to keep Algeria French. Moreover, the settler population in Indochina, some 40,000 ***Français d'Indochine*** in 1945, was much smaller than the one million *Français d'Algérie* living in Algeria in 1954. As a result, many more French soldiers, their families, and European settlers experienced the war, explaining in part why the Algerian War occupies a larger place in the contested French memory of its wars of decolonization. Ironically, thousands of Algerians experienced the Indochina War as soldiers in the multi-ethnic, colonial French Expeditionary Corps.

Significantly, Vietnamese communists maintained their anticolonialist links with Algerians at the helm of the FLN. In 1958, the Vietnam Worker's Party and Ministry of Defense secretly approved and executed the "top secret" delivery of a "large amount" of arms to the FLN to fight the colonizer. The arms, taken from the French during the Indochina War, were shipped successfully by sea to North Africa on a Polish "commercial" ship to be used in this second war of decolonization.

Although the wars and the entities running them were significantly different, the Algerian and Indochina conflicts were clearly linked in a myriad of ways. The supreme irony is perhaps the fact that the man who put an end to the Algerian War in 1962 was the same man who had, in 1945, ordered the French reoccupation of Indochina by force, convinced that Empire was still part of French national identity and a powerful diplomatic lever. His name was Charles de Gaulle. From 1962, he could now steer France down a more independent, assertive course in the international system, often to the dismay of the Americans whom he criticized for embarking on another war in Indochina. *See also ASSOCIATION NATIONALE DES ANCIENS D'INDOCHINE ET DU SOUVENIR INDOCHINOIS*; *ASSOCIATION NATIONALE DES ANCIENS ET AMIS DE L'INDOCHINE ET DU SOUVENIR INDOCHINOIS*; *ASSOCIATION NATIONALE DES ANCIENS PRISONNIERS ET INTERNÉS D'INDOCHINE*; *ASSOCIATION NATIONALE DES COMBATTANTS DE DIEN BIEN PHU*; EXPERIENCE OF WAR; MYTH OF WAR.

**ALL COUNTRY MILITARY MEETING (*Hội Nghị Quân Sự Toàn Quốc*).** On 19 October 1946, the **Indochinese Communist Party** (ICP) held an important military meeting on Nguyen Du Street in **Hanoi**, chaired by the party's acting General Secretary **Truong Chinh.** Attending this meeting were many members of the party's central committee, **Central Party Military Committee** (*Quan Uy*), and important military and political cadres from relevant war zones (but mainly from areas above the **16th parallel**). Delegates at this gathering concluded that sooner or later the French would attack and that the Vietnamese had to be prepared to resist. Orders were given to intensify war preparations, with special attention given to developing armed forces and creating new branches in military supplying, armaments, and medicine. *See also* 23 SEPTEMBER 1945; 19 DECEMBER 1946.

**ALLARD, JACQUES MARIE PAUL (1903–1995).** Son of the Catholic historian Paul Allard, he entered Saint-Cyr in 1923 in the same class as Maurice Challe and **Fernand Gambiez**. Jacques Allard began his military career in French North Africa during the interwar period. During World War II, he participated in the Italian Campaign and the Allied Landing in southern France in August 1944. He was named colonel in 1946. Between late 1949 and 1953, he served as chief of the General Staff of the commander-in-chief of Indochina, General **Jean de Lattre de Tassigny**. After a brief sojourn in Morocco, he returned to Indochina in June 1954 to serve as deputy to the high commissioner and commander-in-chief of the armed forces in Indochina. Allard accompanied **Jean Letourneau** to Washington in June 1952 to discuss increased American military **aid** to the French in Indochina. He would serve in Algeria, determined to keep it French. *See also* ALGERIAN WAR.

**AMERICAN AID.** *See* AID, AMERICAN.

**AMIEL, HENRI (1907–1976).** Made his military career in the colonies and commanded in Cambodia during the latter part of Indochina War. Having refused to honor the armistice of June 1940, Amiel crossed over to Free French forces and fought with Allied forces against the Germans in North Africa. After the war, he took part in the violent "**pacification**" of Madagascar. In 1953, Colonel Amiel became the delegate commanding officer of the garrison of Phnom Penh as well as the commander in charge of the special section for the defense of the same city. He then led the Operational Task Force for the Lower Mekong. In 1955, he was named head of the French Military Mission to Cambodia. He would serve briefly in Algeria before returning to France to finish his military career.

**AN PHÚ XÃ MEETING.** Name of a district in Thu Dau Mot province in southern Vietnam where an important military meeting was held on 20 November 1945 in order to unify the irregular armed forces in the south in the fight against the French. **Nguyen Binh** and **Hoang Dinh Giong** presided over this meeting as the new commander-in-chief of southern armed forces and political commissar, respectively. This meeting organized fighting units, known as detachments or *chi doi*, and placed them under the theoretical command of Nguyen Binh. This meeting marked the first attempt by the **Democratic Republic of Vietnam** to extend its control over what was at this point a very disparate array of southern, armed groups, with no unified leadership.

**ANAI.** *See ASSOCIATION NATIONALE DES ANCIENS D'INDOCHINE ET DU SOUVENIR INDOCHINOIS.*

**ANAPI.** *See ASSOCIATION NATIONALE DES ANCIENS PRISONNIERS ET INTERNÉS D'INDOCHINE.*

**ANDRÉ.** *See* JEAN MARANNE.

**ANDRÉ, MAX (1893–1977).** A member of the ***Mouvement républicain populaire*** (MRP) who headed the French delegations to the Franco-Vietnamese **Dalat Conference** in April–May 1946 and the **Fontainebleau Conference** in July–September 1946. He had lived in Vietnam before World War II.

**ANDRÉ, VALÉRIE (1922–).** First woman named general in France and **helicopter** pilot and medic during the Indochina War. In November 1948, she obtained her medical degree and entered the French **Air Force** with the rank of captain surgeon. She left for Indochina in December 1948 and began work at the military hospital of My Tho in southern Vietnam. Transferred to **Saigon** shortly thereafter, she worked as a chief surgeon for two years at the military hospital Coste, all the while studying to become a helicopter pilot. In September 1950, her hard work paid off: she became a certified civilian pilot and was named head of the helicopter pilots section at the Gia Lam air base in northern Vietnam. This allowed André to become one of the first pilots and doctors to develop and use helicopters in medical evacuation operations. She joined the Female Military Health Corps (*Corps de santé militaire féminin*) in December 1952. During two tours of duty in Indochina, she carried out more than 120 combat missions and evacuated 165 wounded as a pilot. In 1953, she returned to France where she became a certified professional military pilot in December 1954. In February 1958, she entered the *Aviation légère de l'Armée de terre* before landing in Algeria in 1959, where she executed over 360 heli-transport medical evacuation operations. In 1976, this Strasbourg-born officer became surgeon general in the French Air Force, the first woman to hold the rank of general in the French armed forces. *See also* ALGERIAN WAR.

**ANDRIEU, GEORGES (1899–1948).** Commanded the French **Air Force** in Indochina between November 1946 and March 1947.

**ANH BA.** *See* LÊ DUẨN.

**ANH BA.** *See* NGUYỄN BÌNH.

**ANH CẢ.** *See* NGUYỄN LƯƠNG BẰNG.

**ANH SÁU.** *See* LÊ ĐỨC THỌ.

**ANH SÁU.** *See* NGUYỄN CHÍ THANH.

**ANH ÚT.** *See* NGUYỄN VĂN LINH.

**ANH ÚT.** *See* NGUYỄN HỮU THỌ.

**ANIMALS AND WAR.** While modern armies, including the German, French, and Japanese ones, had relied heavily upon animals, horses in particular, at the start of World War II, in the wake of this conflict most Western armies, including their colonial divisions, were largely mechanized. The **French Union** army was no exception. Although the equipment they commanded might not have been state of the art, often coming from Allied war surplus, French troops arriving in Indochina in late 1945 under the command of General **Philippe Leclerc** deployed tanks, trucks, naval vessels, and airplanes. American aid further reinforced the mechanization of the **French Union** forces.

The DRV never possessed this level of modern transportation. The DRV had no **navy** or **air force**. Nor could Chinese **aid** match the modernity of that provided to the French by the Americans. As a result, the Vietnamese war state had to rely heavily on a wide range of animals to ensure vital communications and transport networks as well as to supply troops engaging the French Union soldiers in battle. From the start, packhorses in particular served as a vital means of transportation for the Vietnamese leadership in northern and central Vietnam. Many of the top DRV leadership, including General **Vo Nguyen Giap** and Minister **Le Van Hien,** were at ease on horse-back, moving from one meeting place to another along jungle trails. The government obtained its small horses from local breeders, requisitioned them, or purchased the animals from individual traders. In southern Indochina, the **Viet Minh** often relied on elephants and oxen. Animals were thus an important part of this war of decolonization. This also meant that caring for them became an important priority, symbolized best by the creation of the DRV's first Veterinarian Office in April 1949. While Soviet aid provided the DRV with hundreds of badly needed Molotova trucks, the DRV's needs were such that 500 pack-horses were still used to help supply **Dien Bien Phu** in 1954 and to evacuate wounded soldiers to hospitals in the rear.

The French were well aware of their adversary's reliance on animals and nature. French bombers not only targeted Vietnamese dikes in their attempts to force the DRV hand on the civilian front, but French pilots also intentionally killed hundreds of waterbuffalo in air raids. *See also* AID, AMERICAN; AID, CHINESE; AID, SOVIET; EXPERIENCE OF WAR.

**ANNAM.** This word was first coined by the Chinese to refer to the "Pacified South" (*An Nam*), the ethnic Viet Kingdom situated on the Chinese Middle Kingdom's southern flank. However, under the French, this word acquired several confusing yet geopolitically important meanings. On the one hand, the French borrowed the Chinese term "Annam" to refer to the ethnic Viet Kingdom unified by the Nguyen Dynasty in the early 19th century. On the other hand, by colonizing "Annam" during the second half of the 19th century, the French divided it into three colonial territorial subunits: **Cochinchina** (*Nam Ky*) referred to the French colony consisting of what is roughly southern Vietnam today, **Tonkin** (*Bac Ky*) referred to the protectorate established over the north, while the French used the term Annam (*Trung Ky*) to refer to the protectorate they imposed upon the Nguyen Dynasty and now limited to central Vietnam.

Despite the division of the Nguyen Kingdom into three colonial parts, the French still needed a term with which to refer generally to all of the ethnic Viet people living in Cochinchina, Annam, and Tonkin. They thus continued to use the term "Annam" and "Annamese" to refer, often confusedly, to what today would be considered to be "Vietnam" and the "Vietnamese". However, "Vietnam" did not exist during the colonial period, except in nationalist minds. This began to change following **Bao Dai**'s proclamation of Vietnamese independence on 11 March 1945, made possible by the Japanese overthrow of the French on 9 March 1945. The short-lived Tran Trong Kim government maintained its usage, as did Ho Chi Minh who announced the birth of the **Democratic Republic of Vietnam** on 2 September 1945. Vietnam now referred to an independent and unified territorial unit.

And as the French moved to restore colonial rule, so too did the word "Annam" enter into fierce competition with the national term "Vietnam" whose citizens were now legally defined as "Vietnamese". The Vietnamese also decolonized the colonial terms for the north, the center, and the south, referring to them as *Bac Bo (Tonkin), Trung Bo (Annam),* and *Nam Bo (Cochinchina).*

That words counted in the Indochina War was clear following the outbreak of full-scale war in Vietnam on **19 December 1946**, when the French High Commissioner for Indochina **Georges Thierry d'Argenlieu**, issued secret orders in January 1947 prohibiting his subordinates from using the word "Vietnam". He instructed them to use Cochinchina, Annam, and Tonkin, and "Annamese" or "pays annamites" when referring to all the ethnic Viet living in all three regions (*pays*). *See also* LANGUAGE OF WAR.

**ANTHONIOZ, PIERRE (1913–1996).** Administrator in the French Colonial Ministry and in Vietnam during the Indochina war. In 1937, he accepted a colonial post in Africa before the Germans took him prisoner in France in 1940. He regained his liberty shortly thereafter and immediately joined French Free Forces. Following the war, he transferred to Indochina where he became resident mayor of Dalat and French resident in upper Donnai (Djiring) in 1946 and 1947.

**ANTI-COLONIALISM.** French anti-colonialism during the Indochina conflict was never as militant as it was during the **Algerian War**. French opposition to the colonization of foreign lands found its first advocates in the wake of the European expansion from the 15th century. In France, philosophers such as Voltaire were among the first to criticize publicly the consequences of European domination for the indigenous peoples in the non-Western world, with Voltaire's *Candide (1759)* serving as a model of the genre. Many French spoke out against African slavery, such as Denis Diderot. Economists such as Jean-Baptiste Say opposed colonialism on the liberal grounds advocated by Adam Smith and others. Colonies were monopolies and thus serious obstacles to the development of capitalism, free markets, and their needed exchanges. In the late 20th century, Jacques Marseille went so far as to say that colonies were in fact an economic drain on the development of French capitalism rather than one of its highest forms as Marxists would have it.

In Republican France, at least at the outset, anti-colonialism was found on the left and right. Pierre Loti, the famous writer and journalist for the *Figaro,* wrote damning accounts of the violence the French conquest of Vietnam engendered in the 1880s. And of course Republicans of all political colors contested "Jules Ferry's war" in Tonkin (and Madagascar), not least of all Georges Clémenceau. However, by World War I, the majority of the ruling class had come to accept colonialism as a necessary part of the Republic, believers in France's special mission civilisatrice, the Darwinist and racialist principles underlying it, or convinced that French national identity, international grandeur, and economic expansion depended upon maintaining the second largest empire after the British. Even Republicans critical of colonial absuses during the first half of the 20th century, such as those in the *Ligue des Droits de l'homme,* the ***Section française de l'Internationale ouvrière***, or the **Free Masons** tended to be colonial reformers rather than decolonizers, as Daniel Hémery and **Jacques Dalloz** have shown.

A potent force of anti-colonialism emerged in the wake of the October Revolution in 1917 and the birth of the Soviet Union. Leninism, in particular, provided a powerful theoretical explanation for colonial exploitation. Imperialism, Lenin explained, was the highest stage of capitalism. By linking the plight of the colonial oppressed in Asia and Africa to the wider struggle of the workers in the "North" against capitalist exploitation, Lenin offered a theoretical explanation of colonial domination and way out of it. **Ho Chi Minh** reminded delegates at the historic congress of Tours in 1920 that French socialists had to take into account the plight of the oppressed classes toiling away in Europe as much as the colonized living under colonial rule in the non-Western world. The **French Communist Party** (FCP) became one of the rare voices to speak out and agitate against colonial abuses and at least theoretically support decolonization.

However, French communists were not entirely alone in their denunication of the colonial project in Indochina. Liberal intellectuals associated with the journal ***Esprit*** increasingly took to task the Third Republic's colonial policy. The founder of this progressive, Christian review, Emmanuel Mounier, was on the cutting edge of social Catholicism and anti-colonialism. In 1934, he helped launch the *Manifeste d'intellectuels catholiques pour la justice et la paix*, in which the authors condemned Western colonialism and the idea of a hierarchy of "races" justifying "white" domination. He openly published Andrée Villois's detailed report of colonial abuses in French Indochina and her damning critique of the use of **torture** against Vietnamese who had organized revolts in northern and central Vietnam in 1930 and 1931. After the carnage of World War II, these early, limited critiques of colonialism transformed into wider calls in the pages of *Esprit* for the French Republic to let go of its Empire or at least reform it in ways recognizing the historical reality of Vietnamese nationalism. The debates were lively and often trenchant on Indochina and Algeria.

However, such anti-colonial support had its limits. For example, the FCP cooled its support of the **Indochina Communist Party** when it was necessary to protect its interests in French politics and follow the Soviet line. This was true in the 1930s as Europe moved towards war. It was also true during the Indochina War, most notably at the outset when the FCP leadership balked at supporting Vietnamese communists for fear of jeapordizing their political standing in postwar French elections. That only changed when they entered the opposition and Stalin threw his weight behind Ho Chi Minh in early 1950. From that point, the FCP became the most important militant anti-colonialist voice in France during the Indochina War.

Nonetheless, compared to the Algerian conflict or even the French opposition to the American war in Vietnam, French anti-colonialism remained a relatively minor phenomenon during the Indochina conflict. One searches in vain in French for the equivalent of a George Orwell's *Burmese Days*. André Malraux's *La condition humaine* and his presence and vocal support of Vietnamese nationalism in 1920s Indochina certainly comes close. Yet his extraordinary silence on the Indochina War, Vietnamese nationalism, and decolonization as **Charles de Gaulle's** minister of Information (and later as his minister of Culture) points up the compromises of French anti-colonialism, this time on the right, as France struggled to re-establish its own national identity after German occupation.

The most eloquent and powerful articulations of French anti-colonialism during the Indochina War came from rather unexpected of quarters, from **Jean-Marie Domenach** at *Esprit* and from an erudite "orientalist" raised in Indochina and who directed the entire French Colonial Academy after World War II, **Paul Mus**. In 1949, Mus lost this job training colonial administrators for the Empire, when he published a series of articles in the left-wing Christian paper, ***Témoignage Chrétien***, ostensibly aimed at condemning torture but which essentially amounted to a call for the Republic to recognize the reality of Vietnamese nationalism, end the war, and decolonize Indochina as much as the French colonial mind. Mus went on to teach in the United States, where his work had a decisive impact on the anti-colonial positions adopted by the likes of Frances Fitzgerald. She won the Pulitzer Prize for *Fire in the Lake,* a stinging indictment of the American role in Vietnam and a ringing endorsment of the **Viet Minh's** nationalist cause. She dedicated the book to Mus.

The Vietnam War also contributed to the remobilization of anti-colonialism in the FCP. Two communist intellectuals and journalists for *L'Humanité* in Indochina were particularly important, Charles Fourniau and Alain Ruscio. Both were committed supporters of the **Democratic Republic of Vietnam's** independence cause, its struggle against the Americans, and its ideological orientation. Fourniau created and served as the general secretary of the *Association d'amitié franco-vietnamienne.* He published studies of early Vietnamese anti-colonialism and nationalism, whereas Ruscio focused on the Indochina War. **Like Pierre Schoendoerffer** on the right, Ruscio has been deeply involved on the left in battles over the memory of the Indochina war in particular and that of French colonialism more generally. Instead of heroizing the soldiers, Ruscio has celebrated such Left-wing militants as **Henri Martin** and **Ho Chi Minh**. He also penned the history of the FCP and the Indochina War. *See also* BOUDAREL AFFAIR; EXPERIENCE OF WAR; JEAN CHESNEAUX; MYTH OF WAR.

**ANTI-COMMUNISM.** *See* CIVIL WAR.

**ANZUS.** The Treaty of Mutual Defense signed by Australia, New Zealand, and the United States (ANZUS) on 1 September 1951. Although this treaty was largely designed by the Americans to reassure their allies worried by the American revival of Japan as the centerpiece of Washington's containment in Asia, the Australians and the New Zealanders also closely followed events in Indochina and the possibility of Chinese communist expansion into Southeast Asia. The Eisenhower administration certainly saw ANZUS as important to building a web of security alliances to contain the spread of Sino-Soviet communism into Asia. *See also* GENEVA ACCORDS; NORTH ATLANTIC TREATY ORGANIZATION; SOUTH EAST ASIA TREATY ORGANIZATION.

**APPERT, RAYMOND PAUL ETIENNE MARIE (1925–1973).** Graduate of Saint-Cyr who made his military career in colonial French Africa and served in Indochina in the early days of the war. Early partisan of the French resistance, he led colonial troops during World War II. Named colonel in 1945, he briefly served as the chief of cabinet for the high commissioner, **Georges Thierry d'Argenlieu**. Between 1947 and 1949, he was commander of the Mixed Regiment for Cambodia. He completed his career in French colonial Africa.

**ARGENLIEU (D').** *See* THIERRY D'ARGENLIEU, GEORGES.

**ARMY, ASSOCIATED STATE OF CAMBODIA.** Thanks to the Franco-Cambodian accords of 20 November 1946, Cambodia operated its own army, the *Forces armées royales khmères* (FARK), although the French High Command maintained operational control. With the creation of the Associated State of Cambodia in 1949, Cambodian officers began to replace their French predecessors. Following **Norodom Sihanouk**'s **royal crusade for independence**, in November 1953 the army came under Cambodian national control while Sihanouk took over as commander-in-chief of the armed forces. The Cambodians also assumed its operational control, except for the strategically important area of eastern Cambodia where the French retained operational command over some 6,000 troops. In July 1954, when the **Geneva Accords** put an end to the Indochina War and affirmed Cambodia's full independence, the Cambodian army numbered about 23,000 troops. *See also* ARMY, ASSOCIATED STATE OF LAOS; ARMY, ASSOCIATED STATE OF VIETNAM; EXPEDITIONARY CORPS; PEOPLE'S ARMY OF VIETNAM.

**ARMY, ASSOCIATED STATE OF LAOS.** Between 1946 and 1950, Laos had no national army but rather maintained a *gendarmerie* or police force, while the French army took care of military matters. This changed with the creation of the Associated State of Laos in 1949. Shortly thereafter, on 6 February 1950 a Franco-Lao military convention was signed by which obligatory military service was instituted for Lao men and an army was initiated, though operational control remained under French command. In July 1954, with the end of the war, the Kingdom of Laos' army numbered some 21,000 troops. *See also* ARMY, ASSOCIATED STATE OF CAMBODIA; ARMY, ASSOCIATED STATE OF VIETNAM; EXPEDITIONARY CORPS; PEOPLE'S ARMY OF VIETNAM.

**ARMY, ASSOCIATED STATE OF VIETNAM (*Vệ Binh Quốc Gia*).** Upon the establishment of the Associated State of Vietnam in 1949, the French moved to create an army for it, capable of taking on the forces of the **Democratic Republic of Vietnam** (DRV) in **collaboration** with the French **Expeditionary Corps**. The constitution of an army was allowed for in the Franco-Vietnamese Accords of 1949 and sealed in the Franco-Vietnamese military convention signed on 30 December 1949. Shortly thereafter, a Franco-Vietnamese military committee went to work creating a national army for the Associated State. At the outset, the Associated State's army numbered around 45,000 men. It became a regular army in 1950 and acquired its own General Staff in 1952. The real driving force, however, was General **Jean de Lattre de Tassigny.** He vigorously supported the ***jaunissement*** of the war effort through the creation of a pro-French Vietnamese national army. It would be cost cutting and, with increased American financial and material support, help solve the problem of finding replacement troops. And of course a large Vietnamese army would provide de Lattre with more troops to take on the DRV. Thanks to the inauguration of obligatory military service in 1951, the Associated State's troop level reached some 167,000 troops in 1954 when it became a fully independent state. In March 1952, General **Nguyen Van Hinh** became chief of staff of the Vietnamese army. Militarily, the Associated State of Vietnam was divided into four regions (North, Center, South and the Highlands), with a division theoretically assigned to each of them. Morale in this Vietnamese army was, however, shaky. During the battle of **Dien Bien Phu**, thousands of Vietnamese deserted as the State of Vietnam's army came close to melting down. *See also* ARMY, ASSOCIATED STATE OF CAMBODIA; ARMY, ASSOCIATED STATE OF LAOS; ASSOCIATED STATES OF INDOCHINA; DESERTION; EXPEDITIONARY CORPS; PEOPLE'S ARMY OF VIETNAM.

**ARNAUD, ANDRÉ JEAN LAURENT (1923–).** Colonial administrator active in Indochina during the conflict. He started out as a provincial advisor in Gia Lam in 1948–49 before transferring to Langson to serve in the same capacity between 1949 and 1950. He returned to southern Vietnam where he served as deputy director of the Office of the Press and Information in **Saigon**. He finished his time in Vietnam as deputy director for the Economic and Technical Mission to the **Republic of Vietnam**.

**ARNAUD, GEORGES VICTOR MAURICE (1919–1971).** French colonial administrator who served in **Annam**, first as part of the *Corps de liaison administrative pour l'Extrême Orient* in 1945 then as the head of the "three frontiers" (*trois frontières*) region in Darlac. He finished his time in Indochina as head of the cabinet of the commissioner for the Republic for Southern Vietnam at Nha Trang.

**ARON, RAYMOND CLAUDE FERDINAND (1905–1983).** French philosopher, journalist, and theorist of international relations who supported the French war effort in Indochina. Graduated from the *École normale supérieure*, Aron obtained his *agrégation* in philosophy in 1928 (ranked no. 1) and received his State Doctorate (*doctorat d'État*) in 1933. The outbreak of World War II found him in uniform in 1939 and in the resistance following the French debacle of 1940, when he made his way to London to work with the Free French forces led by **Charles de Gaulle**. After the war, Aron wrote prolifically and regularly in the pages of *Le Figaro*, published widely acclaimed books, and taught at the university level. He was also an *intellectuel engagé*. He joined **Jean-Paul Sartre** in creating *Les temps modernes.*

Aron was a staunch defender of political liberalism and an ardent critique of fascism and increasingly communism. He had gone on the record both during World War II and again following the outbreak of full-scale war in Indochina in **19 December 1946** arguing that the French were in no financial position to reconquer Indochina militarily. The French, he wrote, should respect Vietnamese independence instead of restoring the former colonial regime. He said very little thereafter about the conflict, French colonial policy, or Vietnamese nationalism.

It was through the lenses of the **Cold War** and the **Korean War** that Aron changed tack and supported the French war in Indochina, seeing it as an integral part of the global, Western, American-led fight to prevent communism from making inroads into the decolonizing, politically unstable South. If not, Aron felt, the newly decolonizing states of non-communist Asia would fall like **dominos** to Moscow and Beijing. Aron regretted the American failure to intervene militarily to save the French soldiers fighting at **Dien Bien Phu** in 1954.

Though Aron upset the French right by arguing in favor of decolonization during the Algerian War (*La tragédie algérienne*, 1957), he viewed the Vietnamese nationalist movement and **Ho Chi Minh** in ideological terms as surrogates of Moscow. He later conceded that he had remained too silent about decolonization during the Indochina War. *See* CULTURE; INTELLECTUALS; MYTH OF WAR.

**ARSENEN LAPIN.** *See* KATĀY DŌN SASŌRIT.

**ART, DEMOCRATIC REPUBLIC OF VIETNAM.** Under the **Democratic Republic of Vietnam** (DRV), art had to serve the national independence and, increasingly, the communist cause. The French had first introduced modern art to Vietnam via the creation of the *École des*

*Beaux arts d'Indochine*. While the school did not outlive the Japanese ***coup de force* of 9 March 1945**, it trained some of postcolonial Vietnam's most important artists, several of whom would join the DRV. Vietnamese painter To Ngoc Van, for example, studied and taught at the *École des Beaux arts* between 1939 and 1945. With the advent of the DRV in September 1945, he persuaded many colonially trained artists to put their talents in the service of the nationalist cause. Following the outbreak of full-scale war in **Hanoi** on **19 December 1946,** To Ngoc Van led the way in creating the DRV's School of Fine Arts (*Truong Trung Cap My Thuat*) in the northern hills. It was also known as the "Resistance Class". Artists working there painted for the war effort, the cause of national independence and, increasingly, Marxism-Leninism and social realism. These artists painted scenes depicting the daily life and heroism of the army and its soldiers. Others focused on ethnic minorities, workers, and peasants, all priorities for the communist party. To Ngoc Van was wounded while covering the battle of **Dien Bien Phu** and died shortly thereafter. *See also* CULTURE; INTELLECTUALS; NEW HERO; NOVELS; RECTIFICATION; TRAN DAN; WOMEN.

**ASSOCIATED STATE OF CAMBODIA.** *See* ASSOCIATED STATES OF INDOCHINA.

**ASSOCIATED STATE OF LAOS.** *See* ASSOCIATED STATES OF INDOCHINA.

**ASSOCIATED STATE OF VIETNAM.** *See* ASSOCIATED STATES OF INDOCHINA.

**ASSOCIATED STATES OF INDOCHINA.** The birth of the Associated States of Laos, Cambodia, and Vietnam in 1949 was due to several factors: the French failure to create a viable **Indochinese Federation** after World War II; pressure from non-communist Vietnamese nationalists to unify **Tonkin**, **Annam,** and **Cochinchina** into one national entity; strong resistance from Lao and Cambodian nationalists to the idea of sharing a colonial state of an Indochinese kind with the Vietnamese; international pressure from the United States on the French to accommodate nationalist independence aspirations in order to combat more effectively the communist threat; and the Chinese Red Army's march towards southern China from mid-1948 and the possible Sino-Soviet support for the communist-minded **Democratic Republic of Vietnam** (DRV). In March 1949, following arduous negotiations with the former Emperor **Bao Dai**, an accord was reached creating the Associated State of Vietnam, followed by an accord for Laos on 19 July and another on 8 November for Cambodia doing the same.

As Associated States, Vietnam, Laos, and Cambodia acquired greater internal independence within the **French Union** and some external liberty. However, they still remained legally subordinate to the French via the ministry in charge of relations with the Associated States of Indochina and were subject to other limits on their full national sovereignty, especially in military, diplomatic, and monetary matters. For example, the Associated States were only allowed to establish diplomatic relations with a limited number of foreign capitals, mainly Washington, London, Rome, and Bangkok.

Disappointed by the French, local leaders pushed harder for full independence during the rest of the Indochina conflict. In 1953, for example, **Norodom Sihanouk** launched his famous **royal crusade for Cambodian independence** and won French recognition of Cambodia's independence. In July 1953, under burgeoning financial pressures and commitments to European defense, the **Joseph Laniel** government agreed to "complete" (*parfaire*) the independence of the Associated States and began transferring sovereignty to the three states even before the **Geneva Accords** affirmed the transformation of all the three Associated States into independent nations. The minister in charge of the Associated States was downgraded to state secretary in 1953 before the entire ministry disappeared for good in 1955. *See also* ARMY, ASSOCIATED STATE OF LAOS; ASSOCIATED STATE OF CAMBODIA; ASSOCIATED STATE OF VIETNAM; BAO DAI SOLUTION; CAMBODIAN RESISTANCE GOVERNMENT; LAO RESISTANCE GOVERNMENT.

***ASSOCIATION NATIONALE DES ANCIENS ET AMIS DE L'INDOCHINE ET DU SOUVENIR INDOCHINOIS* (ANAI).** According to the official history of this association, the ANAI was born in 1964 from the merger the *Association métropolitaine des anciens combattants et victimes de la guerre d'Indochine* with the *Association de prévoyance des* ***Français d'Indochine***, both of which had been initially established in 1947 following the outbreak of full-scale war on **19**

**December 1946**. In 1964, two years after the end of the **Algerian War**, the ANAI was designed to play "an important role in the realm of [national] memory". In 1981, the ANAI took over the association of the *Souvenir indochinois* commemorating Indochinese who served and died in France during World War I and tends to their tombs. The ANAI contributed to the repatriation of the **remains** of French Union soldiers killed during the Indochina War and inhumed at the **necropolis** in Fréjus. In 1975, the ANAI initiated the creation of the *Comité national d'entraide franco-vietnamien, franco-cambodgien,* and *franco-laotien.* Until their dissolution in 1992, these committees helped relocate to France and French Guyana some 200,000 Indochinese refugees. The *raison d'être* for the ANAI today is in the making and diffusion of the "memory of Indochina" through its commemorations, publications, exhibitions, seminars, and conferences. *See also* ASSOCIATION OF MOTHERS OF SOLDIERS; CEMETERIES; CULTURE.

***ASSOCIATION NATIONALE DES ANCIENS PRISONNIERS ET INTERNÉS D'INDOCHINE* (ANAPI).** The ANAPI was established in November 1985 with the mission of bringing together and establishing a list of all former "prisoners, internees, and deportees of [French] conflicts in the Far East", meaning deportees of the Japanese between March and August 1945 and French prisoners of war during the Indochina and Korean Wars. The association seeks to promote their "material and moral interests". As of 2008, it counted 1,680 members. The ANAPI was a driving force in getting the French Parliament to vote law No. 89-1013 on 31 December 1989 creating the legal statute of *prisonnier du Viet-Minh*, the initial *raison d'être* of the association. Like the ***Association nationale des anciens et amis de l'Indochine et du souvenir indochinois***, the ANAPI is deeply involved in memory-making in France, organizing conferences, publications, and monuments. The association contributed financially to the construction of the French war memorial at **Dien Bien Phu** and is currently preparing to dedicate a stele in honor of those who died during the battle of **Cao Bang**. *See also ASSOCIATION NATIONALE DES ANCIENS ET AMIS DE L'INDOCHINE ET DU SOUVENIR INDOCHINOIS*; *ASSOCIATION NATIONALE DES ANCIENS D'INDOCHINE ET DU SOUVENIR INDOCHINOIS*; *ASSOCIATION NATIONALE DES COMBATTANTS DE DIEN BIEN PHU;* ASSOCIATION OF MOTHERS OF SOLDIERS; EXPERIENCE OF WAR; MYTH OF WAR; WAR MEMORIAL, DIEN BIEN PHU.

***ASSOCIATION NATIONALE DES COMBATTANTS DE ĐIỆN BIÊN PHỦ*.** From 1955, a number of veterans of the battle of **Dien Bien Phu** decided to gather in different parts of France to commemorate every May the traumatic experience they had survived together. Between 1960 and 1967, several such meetings took place each May among veterans, mainly in Pau and sometimes with the participation of **Marcel Bigeard** or **Pierre Langlais**. In 1968, the year the French government amnestied officers who had turned against the French Republic in Algeria (**Raoul Salan** for example), it was decided that future commemorations would be open to civilians and that a large meeting would be held in 1969 at the *École des troupes aéroportées de Pau*. The association was formalized at this time and was registered as the *Amicale des Anciens de Dien Bien Phu.* On 7 May 1969, the first official meeting of the association took place, complete with a minute of silence, the playing of the *Marseillaise,* and the posing of a wreath of flowers in memory of those who had fallen at Dien Bien Phu or during the Indochina War. In 1979, as the Third Indochina War began, 400 French veterans took part in the 25[th] anniversary of the battle and the Pau chapter of the association launched the organization of a national congress every five years. In 1993, in order to expand the organization, the name was changed to the *Association nationale des combatants de Dien Bien Phu*. *See also ASSOCIATION NATIONALE DES ANCIENS ET AMIS DE L'INDOCHINE ET DU SOUVENIR INDOCHINOIS ; ASSOCIATION NATIONALE DES ANCIENS D'INDOCHINE ET DU SOUVENIR INDOCHINOIS*; *ASSOCIATION NATIONALE DES ANCIENS PRISONNIERS ET INTERNÉS D'INDOCHINE;* ASSOCIATION OF MOTHERS OF SOLDIERS; EXPERIENCE OF WAR; MYTH OF WAR.

**ASSOCIATION OF MOTHERS OF SOLDIERS (*Hội Mẹ Chiến Sĩ*).** The first chapter of this association appeared in June 1947 in Ha Tinh province, when the United Women's Association for Central Vietnam created it (*Hoi Lien Hiep Phu Nu Trung Bo*). The association's main goal was to look after soldiers wounded in battle and to tend to the graves and to the memory of fallen soldiers and martyrs (*Nguoi Hy Sinh*) from the **Democratic**

**Republic of Vietnam**. **Ho Chi Minh** personally thanked the work of the Mothers' Association in tending to and feeding the wounded soldiers and burying the war dead. This was especially the case since the government had little financial means to subsidize the care and feeding of the increasing number of wounded and disabled. The mothers association visited the families of fallen soldiers "in order to comfort them and show them the extent of the state and party's solicitude". Mothers wrote letters to soldiers and adopted them when they passed through villages. In exchange for this state-sponsored consolation, families were expected to recognize the generosity of the party and continue their loyalty to it. As Ngo Van Chieu described this association in his memoirs, the mothers of soldiers were usually elderly women. Once a mother adopted either a soldier or a cadre, the whole family was obligated to protect the "adopted soldier". This could mean tending to his or her wounds. It could also mean protecting him from enemy detection, by making him a member of the family with complete documentation and alibis. These protecting families organized around the "mother" almost always had one or more sons or relatives serving in the DRV army. They were therefore reliable, with the idea being that this "mother of soldiers" association network was taking care of their own loved ones in time of need. This ingenious system created remarkably sure connections for the army and state and served to integrate a wider segment of the population into the DRV's emerging national community. *See also* EXPERIENCE OF WAR; MARTYR; MYTH OF WAR; PENSION, DEMOCRATIC REPUBLIC OF VIETNAM.

**ATLANTE, OPERATION.** The battle of Tay Nguyen (*Chien Dich Tay Nguyen*) or the battle of the Central Highlands as the Vietnamese know it, began in January 1954 and reached a dramatic climax in June 1954, when elements of the Vietnamese 320th Division wiped out much of the elite French *Groupe Mobile 100*. On 20 January 1954, General **Henri Navarre** launched a sea and airborne operation in central Vietnam designed to retake **Inter-Zone V** (*Lien Khu V*) and its population of some two million people living under the control of the **Democratic Republic of Vietnam** (DRV) since 1945. Navarre also felt that this operation would provide needed experience to the Associated State of Vietnam's armed forces; furnish an important piece of territory to the State of Vietnam before diplomatic negotiations opened on ending the war; and prevent the Vietnamese adversary from launching offensive strikes towards southern Indochina from the strategically important highlands. While Navarre had the final say, he authorized his Vietnamese allies to lead the Associated State's troops during this operation. This would show that France's Vietnamese allies could eventually take over from the **Expeditionary Corps** when it began to withdraw.

Navarre claimed that this operation in Inter-Zone V did not disperse or divert needed troop strength away from the building battle for **Dien Bien Phu** to the north. Navarre's adversary, General **Vo Nguyen Giap,** would have disagreed entirely. He welcomed Atlante as an opportunity for the DRV to draw as many French forces as possible away from Dien Bien Phu, so that Giap could isolate and wipe out the French camp in the north before negotiations opened in Geneva on Indochina. Vo Nguyen Giap ordered the 320th division towards the south to disperse and defend Inter-Zone V. Even when Navarre privately conceded to his superiors on 1 January 1954 that the DRV's potential acquisition of artillery would rule out certain victory at Dien Bien Phu, he went ahead with Atlante. By refusing to call off this operation, Navarre turned Dien Bien Phu into a gamble, as **Bernard Fall** has put it. The main target for Vo Nguyen Giap was Dien Bien Phu, which he wiped out on 7 May 1954.

Hardly a month later, as diplomats were locked in difficult negotiations at Geneva to end the war, elements of the 320th decimated much of the elite *Groupe Mobile 100* in the strategically important highlands, in what Fall famously called the *Street without Joy*. It was there where the first battles between the Americans and the North Vietnamese Army occurred in 1965. This was no accident.

***ATTENTISME***. This term refers to an attitude by which one delays making a clear decision until the situation becomes clearer. The word became common in France during World War II, when many had to make difficult choices between supporting political forces allied with Philippe Pétain, **Charles de Gaulle**, the Nazis, or others. The term was widely used during the Indochina War in both French and Vietnamese circles to refer to mainly non-communist Vietnamese nationalists unhappy with or wary of the policies of the French "colonialists" and the Vietnamese "communists" of the **Democratic Republic of Vietnam** (DRV).

At the local level, this term could refer to traders and merchants who refused to come down on one side or the other, preferring to operate in both **French Union** and DRV-controlled zones. It could also refer to patriotic **intellectuals** and professionals who preferred to stay in the cities under French control, but remained unhappy with the French refusal to grant full independence to the Associated State of Vietnam. At another level, it referred to important non-communist leaders such as **Ngo Dinh Diem** or certain **Greater Vietnam Nationalist Party** (*Dai Viet Quoc Dan* or *Dai Viet*) politicians, who refused to join one side or the other. The internationalization of the war in 1950 led a number of Vietnamese non-communist nationalists to climb down from the fence and join the political *mêlée*. This was certainly the case of Ngo Dinh Diem, who saw in the Western recognition of **Bao Dai**'s Associated State of Vietnam the chance to take Vietnam in a new direction. As he wrote in a letter to his brother **Ngo Dinh Nhu** in 1953, *attentisme* was no longer a viable policy. It was time to take action. *See also* COLLABORATION; CROSSOVER; DESERTION.

**AU CHHUEN (1903–1975?).** Prominent politican in numerous Cambodian governments between 1945 and 1954. Born in Battambang province, he received his secondary schooling at the *Lycée Sisowath* in Phnom Penh before studying law at the *Faculté de droit* in **Hanoi**. Upon graduation, he began his career in the colonial bureaucracy in Cambodia. He worked until 1945 as a clerk in the *Résidence supérieure* and served as general secretary then director of the Civil Servants School (*École des Kromokars*). After World War II, he held a wide range of governmental posts. He was state secretary in the Ministry of Religion, Fine Arts and Religious Instruction in the **Sisowath Youtevong** cabinet (December–July 1946); minister of the Interior in the Sisowath Watchayvong cabinet in 1947–48; and counselor to the King in February 1948. He was a founding member of the Progressive Democrat Party, but left it to join the National Union Party of **Khim Tith.** Au Chheun served as minister of Finances in the second cabinet of **Yèm Sambaur** in 1949 and was a delegate to the commission in charge of implementing the Franco-Cambodian Treaty of 1949 creating the Associated State of Cambodia. He then served as minister of Finances in the cabinet of Prince **Sisowath Monipong** in 1950 and assumed the portfolio of Information in the cabinet of Oum Chheang Sun in early 1951. In 1952, with the backing of **Norodom Sihanouk**, he served as general secretary of the Council Presidency (*Présidence du Conseil*) and director of Political Affairs. When Sihanouk reshuffled his government in January 1953, Au Chheun became vice president of the Council and minister of the Interior and Religious Affairs. The new Prime Minister **Penn Nouth** named him deputy prime minister and minister of Foreign Affairs and Religious Affairs in that same month. When Penn Nouth reshuffled his cabinet yet again in July 1953, Au Chheun became minister of Religious Affairs, Fine Arts and Social Action and Labour. In April 1954, Sihanouk named him state minister for Agriculture, Trade, Industrial and Telecommunications. Au Chheun worked as minister of National Economy in the Penn Nouth cabinet formed in April 1954 and was named ambassador to the United Kingdom. He participated in the Cambodian delegation to the **Pau Conference** in 1950.

**AUBOYNEAU, PHILIPPE (1899–1961).** Lieutenant commander and deputy chief of staff of the French Naval Force in the Far East in **Saigon** when war broke out in Europe in 1939. With the French defeat in 1940, Auboyneau crossed over to the French Free Forces in July 1940 and commanded the rearmed warship *Triomphant* in the Pacific. In 1942, he rose to the rank of captain and became chief of staff of Free French Naval Forces and national commissioner to the French Committee of National Liberation. Back in London in 1942 and now a rear admiral, Auboyneau took command of Free French Naval Forces. Following his participation in the Allied landing in Provence in southern France in August 1944, he transferred to Indochina to serve as commander of Naval Forces shortly thereafter known as French Naval Forces in the Far East. In this role, he commanded operations to assist General **Philippe Leclerc**'s troops reoccupy southern **Annam** below the **16th parallel** and oversaw the debarking of French troops in northern Vietnam in 1946 following the **Accords of 6 March 1946**. In early 1947, Admiral **Robert Battet** replaced him. However, Auboyneau returned to Indochina in 1952 and served as commander-in-chief of French Naval Forces in the Far East until 1954.

**AUBRAC, LUCIE (BERNARD, CATHERINE LUCIE, 1912–2007).** French resistance leader during World War II and strong supporter of the **Democratic Republic of Vietnam**'s (DRV) cause during the Indochina War. She grew up in a Catholic wine growing family in the Mâcon region near Lyon. After completing her secondary studies in Lyon, she successfully prepared for the French national exam, the *agrégation*, in Paris in the mid-1930s. During this time, she was drawn to anti-fascist circles and moved to the left politically. She married Raymond Samuel in December 1939 and was working in Lyon when the French capitulated to the Germans in mid-1940. She entered the French resistance in December 1940 and established with MM. d'Astier de la Vigerie, Jean Rochon, and Raymond Samuel among others the internal resistance movement *Libération-Sud*. In 1943, Raymond Samuel adopted the name that would make the couple legendary in resistance circles, Aubrac. Lucie joined her husband in the organization and administration of the *Armée secrète de libération*. In 1943, pregnant with their first child, she organized an audacious jailbreak of major resistance leaders, including her husband. After World War II, Lucie Aubrac returned to teaching, worked for the *Ligue des Droits de l'Homme* and gravitated towards causes supported by the **French Communist Party**. During **Ho Chi Minh**'s visit to France for the **Fontainebleau conference** in mid-1946, the Aubracs became very good friends with him. He became godfather to the Aubracs' daughter. The Aubracs supported the Vietnamese nationalist cause during both the Indochina War and the one that pitted the DRV against the Americans.

**AUBRAC, RAYMOND (SAMUEL, BALMONT RAYMOND, 1914–).** French resistance leader during World War II and strong supporter of the **Democratic Republic of Vietnam**'s (DRV) cause during the Indochina War. Raymond Aubrac and his wife, **Lucie**, joined the resistance in 1940 in Lyon and helped create the *Mouvement Libération-Sud*. Raymond Aubrac was arrested in June 1943 with his close collaborator, Jean Moulin. Aubrac escaped and made his way to London. Upon the liberation of France, **Charles de Gaulle** named him commissioner for the Republic in Marseille in 1944–45. He joined the Ministry of Reconstruction between 1945 and 1948. During **Ho Chi Minh**'s visit to France for the **Fontainebleau conference** in mid-1946, the Aubracs became very good friends with him. Ho became godfather to the Aubracs' daughter. The Aubracs supported the Vietnamese nationalist cause during both the Indochina War and the one that pitted the DRV against the Americans. During the Vietnam War, Raymond Aubrac served as a secret intermediary for the French and Americans to the DRV. *See also* JEAN SAINTENY.

**AUGUST REVOLUTION (*Cách Mạng Tháng Tám 1945*).** Refers to the events of 19 August 1945, when **Viet Minh** forces took power in **Hanoi** and then the rest of the country in the following weeks. The combination of the Japanese ***coup de force* of 9 March 1945** ousting the French from Indochina and the Japanese capitulation on 15 August 1945 provided the Viet Minh with the favorable conditions needed to take power before either the French could return to reassert their colonial control or the Allies could arrive to receive the Japanese surrender. But there was another factor. On the ground, as David Marr has shown, the Viet Minh and the communist leadership behind it were able to ride a ground-swell of popular discontent to power, especially in upper Vietnam where a **famine** had taken around a million lives since 1944. Things were more complicated in southern Vietnam, where the communists were but one voice among several nationalist religious groups. Southern communists had yet to recover from the severe French repression of 1940 and were badly out of touch with the **Indochinese Communist Party**'s new leadership based in the north. On 2 September 1945, thanks to the opening created by the August uprising, **Ho Chi Minh** declared the creation of the **Democratic Republic of Vietnam** in Hanoi. In the existing communist nationalist historiography in Vietnam, the August Revolution is an important source of legitimation, although a number of historians argue that it was more of an insurrection than a revolution. Truong Chinh used the term "revolution" for the first time in a brochure he published marking the one-year anniversary of the new Vietnamese nation-state. By referring to it as the August Revolution, the Vietnamese sought to create a place for it in the history of communist revolutions, alongside that of the October Revolution of 1917.

**AURILLAC, JEAN HONORÉ CHARLES (1903–1967).** Grandson of a naval doctor who served in **Cochinchina** in the 19th century and son of a navy officer, Jean Aurillac began his colonial career in Indochina in 1928. Between 1938 and 1941, he served as head of the cabinet of the *résident supérieur* in Hue. Between 1942 and 1945, he was a cabinet director for Admiral Jean Decoux, governor general of Indochina during the Vichy period. Between March and September 1945, the Japanese held Aurillac prisoner. After working in French Africa, he returned to Indochina in 1950 to serve as a cabinet director to General **Jean de Lattre de Tassigny**, who was High Commissioner for Indochina. Between 1952 and 1956, Aurillac was governor of Overseas France and worked in the Ministry responsible for relations with the **Associated States of Indochina**.

**AURIOL, VINCENT (1884–1966).** Socialist politician involved in major decisions concerning the decolonization of French Indochina as president of the 4th Republic. Auriol began his political career as a lawyer and specialist of financial questions for the ***Section française de l'Internationale ouvrière***. He served as minister of Finances in the **Léon Blum** "Popular Front" government of 1936. Opposed to Vichy and **collaboration** with Germany, he fled to London in 1943. After World War II, he presided over the two constituent assemblies. He became president of the National Assembly on 3 December 1946 and served as president of the 4th Republic between 1947 and 1953. During this time, Auriol presided over the creation of the Associated States of Vietnam, Laos and Cambodia, signing treaties with each State in 1949 as part of the creation of the **Associated States of Indochina**. He received **Bao Dai** in September 1952. *See also* BAO DAI SOLUTION.

**AUSSARESSE, PAUL LOUIS (JEAN SOUAL, 1918–).** Intelligence officer in Indochina attached to the ***Service de Documentation extérieure et de contre-espionnage*** (SDECE). He first distinguished himself in the French resistance during World War II and worked in the resistance intelligence services, the *Bureau central de renseignements et d'action* (BCRA) and the *Direction générale des études et de renseignements* (DGER). On 1 November 1946, he joined the 11th Crack Battalion, a commando team (*11ème bataillon de choc*) he had helped create within the SDECE. In 1948, Aussaresse transferred to Sétif in Algeria, where he became a company commander in the 2nd battalion of the *1er Régiment de chasseurs parachutistes*. He served there as part of a special training program for upcoming service in Indochina, where he and his battalion landed later that year. Upon arriving in Vietnam in 1949, Aussaresse commanded his battalion on diverse missions for the SDECE and the army in northern Vietnam. With the Chinese communist victory in 1949 and the intensification of the war against the **Democratic Republic of Vietnam** (DRV), Aussaresse helped accelerate the SDECE's efforts to develop and use special operations behind enemy lines. From October 1949, he did so as a member of the Operational General Staff's Airborne Base for the North (*État-Major opérationnel de base aéroportée Nord*). This unit was in charge of organizing and preparing airborne intelligence operations in enemy territory, providing maps, photos, and intelligence on the intended targets. Aussaresse was involved in mounting such operations in the lead up to the battle of **Cao Bang**. In 1951, he rejoined his 11th Crack Battalion, which was melded into the newly created ***Groupement des commandos mixtes aéroportés*** in May of that year. He was then sent to southern Vietnam as part of the *Demi-brigade parachutiste du Sud de l'Indochine* (mainly from the 11th Crack Battalion). In July 1951, Aussaresse left Indochina for good. He became the subject of considerable controversy in France for his role in the use of **torture** as an intelligence officer during the Algerian War. Between 1960 and 1963, he taught at Fort Benning in the United States. *See also* CHARLES LACHEROY; COMMANDOS; REVOLUTIONARY WARFARE; ROGER TRINQUIER; *SERVICE ACTION*.

**AXELRAD, ÉDOUARD (1918–).** French colonial administrator, journalist, and author during and after the Indochina War. Axelrad first trained in colonial law. He joined French resistance forces during World War II before being captured and deported to Auschwitz in 1944. He survived the death camp and returned to France. In 1945, he moved to Indochina where he served as Commissioner for the Republic to Hanoi (1945–46) and then as head of Cao Bang province between 1946 and 1950. Between 1951 and 1954, he headed the Office of the Press in **Saigon** before directing the Information Service of the French Embassy in Cambodia (1955–58). He was instrumental in creating the official, illustrated magazine, *Indochine Sud-Est asiatique* and contributed to it regularly. He published a number of semi-fictional novels based upon his colonial and wartime experiences, including *Marie Cassecroûte* on Indochina (1985). He finished his career working in *Parisbas* in Kuala Lumpur, in charge of Southeast Asia. *See also* CULTURE; *MÉTIS*; NOVELS, FRENCH; PSYCHOLOGICAL WARFARE.

**AYROLLES, LÉOPOLD-HENRY.** Parachuted into Laos from Calcutta in early 1945 with other French **commandos** to conduct **guerrilla** and intelligence operations against the Japanese, but forced to retreat to China after the Japanese ***coup de force*** **of 9 March 1945**. He returned to Laos following Japanese capitulation to oppose Vietnamese infiltration into western Indochina. He mobilized anti-**Viet Minh** activities among the Hmong tribes along the Vietnamese-Lao border. In 1948, he published a book on the Japanese ***coup de force*** **of 9 March 1945**, *L'Indochine ne répond plus*.

**BA CỤT.** *See* LÊ QUANG VINH.

**BA DƯƠNG.** *See* DƯƠNG VĂN DƯƠNG.

**BA KHIÊM.** *See* UNG VĂN KHIÊM.

**BÀ MẸ GIO LINH.** *See* MOTHERS OF GIO LINH.

**BẮC BỘ.** *See* TONKIN.

**BẮC KẠN, OPERATION.** *See* LEA, OPERATION.

**BẮC KỲ.** *See* TONKIN.

**BẮC NINH INCIDENT.** On 6 August 1946, Vietnamese forces attacked a French convoy at Bac Ninh, located thirty kilometers from **Hanoi** leading to Langson. Twelve French soldiers died and forty-two were reported wounded in the skirmish. Vietnamese losses were similar if not higher. The French bombed the town later in the day. While the French force had permission to take up their posts in Langson in accordance with Franco-Vietnamese agreements signed in March and April, this "incident" occurred while the **Democratic Republic of Vietnam's** delegation was involved in tense negotiations in France at the **Fontainebleau conference**. It certainly played into the hands of local French authorities who were increasingly intent on rolling back the DRV's national hold in the north. **Vo Nguyen Giap** immediately informed the French that the attack at Bac Ninh had been unauthorized. In any case, the Bac Ninh clash was the first of several incidents which would eventually spin out of control opening the way to the outbreak of full-scale war in Hanoi on **19 December 1946.**

**BAILLET, MARCEL (1914–1957).** Born and raised in colonial Morocco, Baillet served briefly as administrator in southern Indochina during the Indochina War. After graduating from the *École nationale de la France d'Outre-mer* (formerly the **Colonial Academy**), he began a career in French North Africa. In May 1945, he was serving in the *Corps léger d'intervention* in Djidjeli in Algeria. With the victory of the Allies in Europe, the provisional French government transferred him to Sri Lanka. Following the Japanese capitulation and the return of the French to southern Indochina, in December 1945 **Jean Cédile** named him administrator mayor of Saigon-Cholon. He was an ardent supporter of the re-establishment of French colonial control over Indochina. While it is unclear when he left Indochina, he completed the rest of his career in Africa.

**BAILLY, CAMILLE VICTOR (1907–1984).** Career French colonial administrator in Indochina. Between 1930 and 1939, Bailly worked in southern Vietnam as district chief and as an inspector for labor questions. During World War II, he served as the governor general's cabinet director in **Saigon** and director for the Office of the *Résidence supérieure* in Cambodia between 1943 and 1945. With the defeat of the Japanese, he regained his freedom and became provisional director of the Economic Section of the French High Commission for Indochina and briefly the Political Section.

**BALMONT.** *See* RAYMOND AUBRAC.

**BANK OF INDOCHINA.** The French *Banque de l'Indochine* operated throughout both World War II and the Indochina War as a note-issuing entity. Created in 1875, the bank worked closely with the French government underwriting the economic and financial development of the French colonial state in Indochina before expanding its interests throughout Asia, into China, and further. From 1920, **Paul Gannay** ran the bank's operations. Thanks to Vichy's **collaboration** with the Germans and in light of their own interests, the Japanese allowed the bank and its note-issuing *Institut d'émission* to continue functioning in Indochina until the ***coup de force* of 9 March 1945**. From that point, the Japanese turned the *Institut d'émission* over to the *Yokohama Specie Bank*, which proceeded to issue millions of 500 piastres notes. The Japanese refused to cede the bank to the Vietnamese when the **Viet Minh** took power in **Hanoi** in August–September 1945. Faced with Chinese occupation and possible requisition of the Bank, in November 1945 the French successfully and adroitly regained control of the Bank. They used it to finance the Chinese occupation, and in so doing ensured their control of the bank to the detriment of their Vietnamese competitors. The provisional secretary general of the **Indochinese Communist Party**, **Truong Chinh**, later lamented the Vietnamese failure to take the bank by force. Under French control, the *Banque de l'Indochine* immediately stopped the circulation of the 500 piastre notes issued by the Japanese in order to prevent the DRV from using them. It was also a way of demonstrating the re-establishment of French colonial sovereignty. The piastre, as Hugues Tertrais has shown, remained a vital part of the Indochina War until the end. While the appearance of the **Associated States of Indochina** meant that each state would issue its own national notes, rather than the ones issued by the bank's *Institut d'émission*, this never truly occurred until after the ink dried on the **Geneva Accords**. The piastre was the Indochinese currency throughout the conflict and the object of considerable controversy because of its artificial overvaluation compared to the French franc. The Bank of Indochina outlived the French colony by merging with the Banque du Suez in 1974 to create "Indosuez" and is today a part of the *Crédit agricole* group. *See also* CURRENCY, FRENCH INDOCHINA; ECONOMY OF WAR, FRANCE; FINANCIAL COST OF WAR.

**BẢO ĐẠI (NGUYỄN PHÚC VĨNH THỤY, JEAN-ROBERT, 1913–1997).** Last emperor of Vietnam and head of state (*chef d'État*) of the Associated State of Vietnam between 1949 and 1954. Born in Hue, Bao Dai was the only son of Emperor Khai Dinh and Quan Doan Huy Hoang Thai Hau. He was invested as crown prince in 1922. He became king of **Annam** upon the death of his father in 1925 and was crowned as such in January 1926 under the name of Bao Dai, "the great protector". In that same year, Pierre Pasquier and **Albert Sarraut** sent him to France to receive a French education under the direction of the former resident of Annam, Eugène Charles. Bao Dai returned to Annam in 1932 as part of a French strategy to use the monarchy to combat nationalist and communist competitors to French colonial rule. It was the true beginning of the so-called **Bao Dai Solution**.

Bao Dai's formal ascension to the throne was celebrated upon his return in 1932. The young emperor headed, enthusiastically at the outset, a rejuvenated monarchical government, incorporating dynamic Vietnamese nationalists such as **Ngo Dinh Diem**. However, under French heavy-handedness, Ngo Dinh Diem resigned and the success of this first monarchical experiment in colonial counter-revolution ended in failure. In the late 1930s and during the Vichy period in Indochina during World War II, Bao Dai withdrew from political affairs, disappointed by French manipulation of the monarchy. He resisted Vichy's attempts to use him again. He preferred hunting and flying his airplanes. In 1934, he married a wealthy southern Catholic, **Marie-Thérèse Nguyen Huu Thi Lan**, who became the Empress **Nam Phuong**.

With the overthrow of the French following the ***coup de force* of 9 March 1945**, the Japanese kept Bao Dai on to proclaim the independence of Vietnam on 11 March, although his authority only truly covered the protectorates of Annam and **Tonkin.** However, on 14 August, with Japanese permission, he announced the annexation and unification of **Cochinchina** with the rest of "Vietnam" thereby creating a unitary Vietnamese state for the first time since the mid-19th century. Following the Japanese capitulation, Bao Dai publicly abdicated on 30 August in favor of the new government formed in **Hanoi** and subsequently agreed to join it as "supreme advisor" to president **Ho Chi Minh**. He referred to himself as "citizen Vinh Thuy" and handed over the royal sword as the mandate of heaven seemed to shift to the nationalists. Whatever the case, for the first time in centuries, Vietnam no longer had an Emperor.

Shortly before his abdication, he wrote moving letters to the Allied leaders Truman, Stalin, Attlee and also to **Charles de Gaulle,** whom he implored on 20 August to respect Vietnamese independence aspirations: *Je vous prie de comprendre que le seul moyen de sauvegarder les intérêts français et l'influence spirituelle de la France en Indochine est de reconnaître franchement l'indépendance du Vietnam et de renoncer à toute idée de rétablir ici la souveraineté ou une administration française sous quelque forme que ce soit.* De Gaulle would never mention this text; indeed, the French general tried to advance as an alternative to Bao Dai the very king the French had deposed in 1916 for sedition, Duy Tan.

In early 1946, Bao Dai joined the DRV's National Assembly as a deputy from Thanh Hoa province. However, trust between the former Emperor and DRV leaders was fragile. In April 1946, while traveling to China as leader of a failed mission from the DRV government to Chiang Kai-shek, Bao Dai went into exile in Hong Kong. He was residing there when war broke out in all of Vietnam in late 1946. During his time in Hong Kong, French, DRV, and non-communist Vietnamese emissaries approached him in the hope that the ex-Emperor would collaborate with them. The French, led by **Léon Pignon** and flanked by **Jean Cousseau**, were vigorous in their attempts to woo him over to their side. (The disappearance of Duy Tan in a plane wreck left them few royalist options.) To this end, the French government provided Bao Dai with funds to maintain his royal lifestyle.

Getting the former emperor back to Indochina was crucial to making the "*Bao Dai Solution*" work. However, the French government of the socialist **Paul Ramadier** did not immediately sanction a monarchical solution. Instead Ramadier sidelined the major advocates of this idea by deposing **Georges Thierry d'Argenlieu** as high commissioner in early 1947 and dispatching Pignon to serve as commissioner of the Republic to Cambodia. Only with the approach of the **Cold War**, a weakening of the leftist parties' influence in the French government, and the appointment of **Jean Letourneau** (MRP) as minister of Overseas France did the French give up the prospect of reentering negotiations with Ho Chi Minh and resurrect the counter-revolutionary **Bao Dai Solution** of the interwar period and pushed by Pignon since 1946. Under pressure from the Americans and the British, Bao Dai and **Vincent Auriol** signed the Accords of 8 March 1949 creating the Associated State of Vietnam under the presidency of Bao Dai. In April 1949, Bao Dai returned to Vietnam and in May he became head of the Associated State of Vietnam. He did his best to build up a national army capable of taking on the forces of the DRV. The French did not make his task any easier, by refusing to grant his Vietnam real independence to match the nationalist legitimacy of the DRV.

Bao Dai was and remains a controversial figure even after his death in 1997. In the West, many wrote him off as a playboy. Andrew Roth did so in an article published in the *Sunday Tribune* in Singapore in August 1949. **Paul Rivet** followed up in French in 1962 when he wrote of "an emperor of night clubs" (*empereur des boîtes de nuit*). Pulitzer Prize-winning author of *Fire in the Lake* Frances Fitzgerald denied Bao Dai any legitimacy.

Bao Dai returned to France when Prime Minister **Ngo Dinh Diem** replaced him as head of state in 1955. The former emperor died there, after having remarried a French woman in 1972 and converted to Catholicism in 1988. French veterans of the Indochina War participated in his funeral and have made moves to associate the Vietnamese emperor with France's ill-fated colonial war in Indochina. The Socialist Republic of Vietnam sent a bouquet of flowers in homage to the last Emperor. *See also ASSOCIATION NATIONALE DES ANCIENS D'INDOCHINE ET DU SOUVENIR INDOCHINOIS*; *ASSOCIATION NATIONALE DES ANCIENS ET AMIS DE L'INDOCHINE ET DU SOUVENIR INDOCHINOIS*; *ASSOCIATION NATIONALE DES ANCIENS PRISONNIERS ET INTERNÉS D'INDOCHINE*; *ASSOCIATION NATIONALE DES COMBATTANTS DE DIEN BIEN PHU*; MYTH OF WAR.

**BẢO ĐẠI SOLUTION.** The so-called Bao Dai Solution of the late 1940s first began in the wake of World War I, when the former governor general of Indochina, **Albert Sarraut**, then minister of the Colonies, joined hands with the resident of **Annam**, Pierre Pasquier, to use the crown prince **Bao Dai** as the incarnation of Franco-Vietnamese **collaboration** and as a politico-cultural weapon to win over Vietnamese support and combat communists and nationalists contesting colonial rule. After receiving in Paris a French education fit for aristocrats and nobles, Bao Dai returned to Vietnam in 1932 and was dispatched on imperial tours to help calm tensions in areas recently wracked by communist-backed peasant revolts. Under Pasquier's direction, Bao Dai also tried to revive the monarchy and administer a Vietnamese government in accordance with Annam's status as a protectorate. However, the French inability to accord a modicum of autonomy, symbolized by the resignation of **Ngo Dinh Diem** from the government, undermined this first attempt to use Bao Dai and the monarchy for any progressive or counter-revolutionary purposes. Bao Dai withdrew thereafter, uninterested in French efforts to mobilize royalty via his person and disappointed by the French incapacity to provide any real autonomy to the monarchy. Even Vichy's Jean Decoux privately lamented that Bao Dai was no solution.

However, a host of conservative minded colonial officials, both republicans coming out of the French resistance and those who had continued to serve Vichy faithfully in Indochina during the war, joined hands after 1945 to resurrect the Bao Dai project for a third time (Decoux failed during World War II), this time to counter the national threat posed by the emergence of the **Democratic Republic of Vietnam** (DRV). This was particularly true after **Charles de Gaulle's** would-be Vietnamese king, Duy Tan, died in a plane crash in 1945. While Gaullists regretted that Bao Dai had publicly abdicated in August 1945 and become a supreme advisor to the new republic, colonial administrators such as **Charles Bonfils**, **Albert Torel**, **Jean Cousseau**, and **Léon Pignon** had no such qualms. These men all knew each other and the emperor from before the war and were intimately familiar with Sarraut, Pasquier, and Decoux's royalist projects.

Starting in July 1946, as the DRV and French military officers began eliminating the anti-French anti-communist parties, the French began working behind the scenes to woo Bao Dai back home (Bao Dai had left the DRV in April 1946 and chosen exile in Hong Kong). Pignon and Cousseau took the lead. The High Commissioner for Indochina **Georges Thierry d'Argenlieu** supported the idea of finding a Vietnamese "Solution" in order to counter the nationalist one proposed by Ho Chi Minh. Bao Dai did not, however, dutifully return to Vietnam as he had done for the French in 1932. He was well aware of how he had been used since World War I and spoke in derisive terms of the so-called Bao Dai Solution. He remained in Hong Kong hoping to pressure the French to accord him what they had refused **Ho Chi Minh**: national unity and real independence.

In December 1947, following the French decision to exclude the possibility of new talks with Ho Chi Minh's government, Bao Dai met the High Commissioner **Émile Bollaert** in the Bay of Ha Long. A joint declaration was written up and a secret protocol was initialed. Bao Dai agreed to join the "Solution", although the creation of the Associated State of Vietnam was never referred to as such. A future unified Vietnam would remain within the **French Union** as an associated state, the former emperor agreed, and the French would administer much of its military and foreign affairs. However, in exchange, the French had to recognize Vietnamese independence and unification, meaning the transfer of **Cochinchina**. Nationalist leaders, notably Ngo Dinh Diem, refused to accept the secret protocol and moved to the sidelines to wait things out. Bao Dai, under pressure to reach an agreement at a time when the international situation was hostile to the DRV, tried to renegotiate the terms but finally accepted the creation on 26 March 1948 of "a provisional central government" (*un gouvernement central provisoire*) under the leadership of General **Nguyen Van Xuan**. On 25 May 1948, the French agreed to allow this government to represent the former colonial regions of **Tonkin**, Annam and Cochinchina. On 5 June 1948, in the Bay of Ha Long, Bollaert initialed another protocol, in the presence of the emperor, setting the foundation of Franco-Vietnamese relations and agreeing that France would recognize Vietnamese independence. Bao Dai insisted however that the French go all the way and legally transfer Cochinchina to Vietnam and sign a new accord to that effect. Gone was the **Provisional Government of the Republic of Cochinchina** (also known briefly as the *gouvernement provisoire du Sud-Vietnam*). In short, the deteriorating situation in China, increased pressure from the United States, the inability of the French army to defeat the DRV, and the accession of Léon Pignon to the position of high commissioner for Indochina combined to force the French to reach the famous accord of 8 March 1949 between **Vincent Auriol** and Bao Dai. France formally recognized Vietnam's independence, even though it was limited in the diplomatic, economic, and military domains. On 23 April 1949, the Cochinchinese Assembly voted to allow the former French colony of Cochinchina to be attached to the rest of Vietnam.

Bao Dai finally returned to Vietnam after more than four years abroad. However, the French refused to allow the imperial head of state to take up residence in the palace of the high commissioner in **Saigon**. Instead Bao Dai had to set up shop in Dalat. On 2 July 1949, Bao Dai formally oversaw the creation of the Associated State of Vietnam. He became head of state and allowed his prime minister to run a government that was no longer "provisional". On 7 August 1949, the DRV's representative in France, **Tran Ngoc Danh**, unilaterally closed the government's delegation in Paris. (The French could not recognize, even indirectly, two Vietnams.) While the French bowed to British and American pressure to grant increased independence to the Vietnamese in order to take on the wider and more important communist threat triggered by the Chinese communist victory on 1 October 1949, the French, led by Léon Pignon, also recast the colonial Bao Dai Solution as an integral part of the American-led war against global communism. In February 1950, following the Chinese and Soviet diplomatic recognition of Ho Chi Minh's government, the United Kingdom and the United States recognized the Associated State of Vietnam and thus endorsed the Bao Dai Solution dating back to Sarraut's post-World War I strategy.

**BAO KEO.** *See* TRIỆU CÔNG MINH.

**BARBEAU, HENRI.** Worked in the Information Service in Indochina until becoming Economic advisor for the **Provisional Government of the Republic of Cochinchina** in April 1947. In December 1947, he was named advisor on Economic Affairs for Cochinchina. In June 1948, he was described as advisor on Economic Affairs to the high commissioner for Indochina. He was replaced in April 1949.

**BARTLETT, F.P. (?).** Chief of the Economic Section of the United States Embassy in **Saigon** in August 1952, when the press announced that he would direct the Mutual Security Agency Aid programs for the **Associated States of Indochina**.

**BASTID, HÉLÈNE (1907–?).** Bastid lived in Indochina during the interwar period. Her husband worked in the colonial service in the mining sector. She lost her first son in 1947, killed in combat against the **Viet Minh** in Bien Hoa. Marked by the loss, she became deeply involved in tending to wounded soldiers of the **Expeditionary Corps** until the end of the war in 1954, when she returned to France. She remained actively involved with veterans and various patriotic associations, joining the ***Association nationale des anciens d'Indochine*** and becoming its president in 1964. In 1975, she founded the *Comité d'accueil aux réfugiés d'Indochine*, which was integrated into the *Comité national d'entr'aide* led by **Jean Sainteny.** A member of the *Académie des Sciences d'Outre-mer*, Bastid was a member of the *Commission Indochine*, which sponsored a conference and publication advancing the French colonial version of the history of Indochina and its decolonization, entitled *Indochine: Alerte à l'histoire* (1985). *See also* ASSOCIATION OF MOTHERS OF SOLDIERS; MYTH OF WAR; WOMEN.

**BASTID, PAUL (1892–1974).** Member of the French Radical Party (*Parti radical*), deputy and ardent supporter of **Bao Dai** as editor of the newspaper *L'Aurore*. In March 1949, as a deputy for the Seine to the National Assembly, he took part in a fact-finding mission to Indochina to report on the political and military situation there. He returned singing the praises of the High Commissioner in Indochina and the need to support Bao Dai's Vietnam against that of **Ho Chi Minh**. Bastid was convinced that the French had to maintain their prestige in Indochina all the while reinforcing Vietnamese faith in the French commitment to the war. He admitted, however, that the military situation was precarious. *See also* ASSOCIATED STATES OF INDOCHINA; BAO DAI SOLUTION.

**BATAILLON D'INFANTERIE LÉGÈRE D'OUTRE-MER (BILOM).** Because the French government refused to implement national service during the Indochina War, new sources for recruits had to be found elsewhere. The **Foreign Legion** and the Empire were two important reserves. A third one was identified in mid-1948 when the Ministry of Defense approved the ***Mouvement républicain populaire***'s proposal that the French army recruit from among prisoners serving time in France for **collaboration** under Vichy or for having enlisted in the Fascist French *Légion des volontaires français* (LVF) or the German *Waffen SS*. On 1 August 1948, General **Georges Revers**, chief of staff of the army, presided over the creation of the *1er Bataillon d'infanterie légère d'Outre-mer* (BILOM, 1st Overseas Light Infantry Battalion). Officers made recruiting visits to prisons across France. Despite outcries from the Far Left, the government went ahead with the plan and around 4,000 men quickly signed up to serve in Indochina, of whom some 400 soon left to serve in early 1949. Many had served on the Western and Eastern Fronts in Europe before being locked up following the German defeat. Their combat experience and fierce anti-communism, the army figured, made them ideal recruits for Indochina. In exchange for their military service in this colonial conflict, their sentences would be commuted. The first BILOM contingent arrived in **Saigon** on 26 December 1948 and was deployed mainly in the highlands of central Vietnam. The BILOM was dissolved in July 1949, and its troops integrated into the **Expeditionary Corps**. Many of these troops would serve throughout the entire Indochina War before moving on to fight in Algeria. A commemorative plaque dedicated to the men of BILOM who died in Indochina is to be found on the wall of the Galliéni Camp in Fréjus, France, today. *See also* ALGERIAN WAR; CROSSOVERS; DESERTION, DEMOCRATIC REPUBLIC OF VIETNAM; JAPANESE TROOPS, INDOCHINA WAR; REPATRIATION, JAPANESE TROOPS.

**BATTET, ROBERT (1893–1950).** French naval commander during the Indochina War. First distinguished himself during World War I and again at the start of World War II, when he commanded the cruiser *Émile Bertin* and took part in the Norway campaign and the liberation of Corsica as commander of French Naval Forces. After the war, he was assigned to Indochina, where he was put in charge of naval operations in early 1946 in Cam Ranh Bay and Nha Trang. His ships disembarked the **Expeditionary Corps** in Hue and central Vietnam in March 1946. He was appointed vice admiral in 1946. On 18 February 1947, he assumed acting command of French Naval Forces in the Far East from Admiral **Philippe Auboyneau**. In April 1949, Admiral **Paul Ortoli** replaced Battet as commander-in-chief of French Naval Forces in the Far East. In May 1950, Battet was named chief of staff of the **Navy** but died at the end of the same year.

**BAUDET, PHILIPPE (1901–?).** French diplomat who was chief of the Office for Asia-Oceania in the Ministry of Foreign Affairs during the early years of the Indochina War. He was a member of the French delegation to the **Fontainebleau conference** in mid-1946 and a partisan of the **Bao Dai Solution.** In 1954, he served as cabinet director to President **Pierre Mendès France** and advisor on Indochina.

**BẢY CHIẾM.** *See* CAO ĐĂNG CHIẾM.

**BẢY VIỄN.** *See* LÊ VĂN VIỄN.

**BAYEN, MAURICE (1902–1974).** French *normalien*, physics specialist, and dedicated educator during the Indochina War. He was taken prisoner by the Nazis at the outset of World War II, but escaped in 1941 and joined the French resistance. In 1944, he took part in the campaigns to liberate Doubs, Alsace, and then Germany. In 1945, Bayen traveled to Indochina to help reorganize and restart upper level education following the defeat of the Japanese and the return of the French. He worked enthusiastically and tirelessly at his job between 1946 and 1950 as federal commissioner of Education in Indochina. He helped keep the **Albert Sarraut** high school up and running in **Hanoi**. He contributed to the reorganization of the Faculties of Law, Medicine, and Sciences in the Indochina University. He brought to Indochina eminent specialists and instructors, such as Pierre Drach at the Oceanographic Institute in Nha Trang, Jean Filliozat who headed the ***École française d'Extrême-Orient***, as well as René Grousset, Georges Duhamel, Léon Binet, and André Lemaire among others. In Cambodia, he helped reopen the *Lycée de Phnom Penh*. Even the war could not stop him: he personally organized air drops of teaching materials in **Cao Bang** province so that local teachers could keep doing their jobs in spite of the outbreak of intense fighting in this remote, northern region. *See also* COLONIAL ACADEMY; CULTURE; INTELLECTUALS.

**BAZÉ, WILLIAM (1899–1984).** Active French settler and ardent supporter of a continued French presence in Indochina. Bazé was born in **Saigon** to a French planter and a Vietnamese mother. Though orphaned at young age, he went on to become a wealthy planter himself and one of colonial Indochina's most dynamic and colorful personalities. He began his career in 1917 working as an assistant for the *Société des plantations d'hévéas de Xuan Loc* in southern Vietnam. In 1921, on completing his military service, he was named technical director in the same company and would go on to help create 15 plantations in rubber, tea, coffee, and rice. But his interests did not stop there. He was a member of the provincial council of Bien Hoa province between 1931 and 1940 and vice-president then president of the *Société de protection de l'enfance de Cochinchine* between 1922 and 1945. During World War II, he refused to collaborate with the Japanese. He organized a resistance network of his own volition in remote areas on or near his plantations in southern Vietnam. However, Bazé's underground resistance cost him dearly: He was captured, imprisoned, and tortured severely by the Japanese. On his liberation from prison, he had to be carried home on a stretcher. However, he was soon back on his feet, now a staunch Gaullist representing the *Rassemblement du peuple français* in Saigon. In 1947, he became director-general of the *Société des plantations de Xuan Loc* and joined the Company's administrative council in Paris between 1952 and 1970, leading missions to Vietnam every year. He was an active supporter of the interests of the "French Indochinese" or *Français d'Indochine*, serving as honorary president of the *Mutuelle des Français d'Indochine*. He was a member of the *Conseil consultative de Cochinchine* (1945–1946), then the Assembly of **Cochinchina** until 1949, vehemently opposed to the national claims of the **Democratic Republic of Vietnam** on Cochinchina. Virginia Thompson described him as the *éminence grise* of the **Provisional Government of the Republic of Cochinchina**, set in motion by **Jean Cédile** and **Georges Thierry d'Argenlieu** in late 1945. As Bazé said in 1946: "Do not forget that Cochinchina is a part of our national patrimony. By renouncing this, we can create a precedent which Algeria, Madagascar, Black Africa and all our other overseas possessions will not fail to exploit [...]". Bazé expressed his views widely in the Saigon-based newspaper, *Le Populaire*. Between 1949 and 1952, he was an advisor to Bao Dai on Eurasian Affairs. From 1952 to 1958, he was also an advisor to the Assembly of the **French Union** in Paris. Bazé was particularly dedicated to the needs of abandoned Eurasian **children** in Indochina, tending to their schooling, repatriation, and overall care. He and his wife adopted 14 orphans whom they raised to adulthood. In 1945, Bazé became president of the *Fédération des œuvres de l'enfance française d'Indochine*. In mid-1975, he became a founding member of the Administrative Council of the *Comité national d'entraide franco-indochinois* for **refugees** fleeing former French Indochina. He founded the *Conseil supérieur de la chasse aux colonies* and published widely on hunting in Indochina (*Un quart de siècle parmi les éléphants* and *Le tigre d'Indochine*). He held the *Croix de guerre 1939–1945* and many other awards for valor and service during World War II.

**BAZIN, MARCEL MARSHAL (1903–1950).** One of the most redoubtable French police officers in **Saigon** during the Indochina War. A career colonial administrator in French Indochina, he joined the police force there in 1928, holding provincial posts mainly in southern Vietnam. He rose to the rank of police commissioner in 1937. His role in tracking nationalists made him a well-known figure in Vietnamese circles, as did his methods. On 4 April 1937, **Ung Van Khiem** published a stinging indictment of Bazin and his violent methods in *La Lutte* and *Le Travail*. Bazin continued to work for Vichy in **Cochinchina** during World War II, becoming *Chef de police spéciale de l'Est* (PSE) during this time. In early 1945, as the Japanese prepared to overthrow the French, Bazin informed **Tran Van Giau** of his desire to forget the past and to join together secretly with the Vietnamese communists to oppose the Japanese. Bazin personally put the same offer to Huynh Van Nghe. Southern communists apparently refused, although **Truong Chinh** was meeting at the same time with *Gaullistes* in the north to explore similar **collaboration** with the French. In any case, following the Japanese ***coup de force* of 9 March 1945**, the Japanese incarcerated Bazin. Upon his release by the Allies, he remained in Indochina and worked in the French security forces, the ***Sûreté fédérale***, in southern Vietnam. In 1949, he took over the direction of the *Sûreté* for southern Vietnam. He launched a massive and often effective campaign against **Viet Minh** urban **commandos** in Saigon, causing General **Nguyen Binh** and the **Indochinese Communist Party** serious setbacks. Bazin also resumed his use of harsh methods on Vietnamese prisoners. All of this explains why the **Democratic Republic of Vietnam** (DRV) condemned him to death and authorized a Vietnamese assassination squad to kill him. DRV agents shot Bazin dead as he was walking to work in 1950. *See also* NGUYEN VAN TAM; PUBLIC SECURITY SERVICES.

**BCRI.** *See BUREAU CENTRAL DE RENSEIGNEMENTS DE L'INDOCHINE.*

**BD.** *See* COMICS AND WAR; CULTURE; NOVELS.

**BEAUFRÉ, ANDRÉ (1902–1975).** Graduate of Saint-Cyr and career military officer who commanded troops in the Cao Bang area during the Indochina War. Between 1924 and 1938, he served as a second lieutenant in the 5th Regiment of Algerian Colonial Troops (*tirailleurs*). He was sent to Algeria but was imprisoned for his resistance to Vichy rule. In November 1942, Beaufré regained his freedom and took part in the Allied landings in Morocco and Algeria. He passed over to the Free French forces and participated in the Italian, French, and German campaigns, becoming chief of operations of the French First Army. He left for Indochina in March 1947 and joined the command of French Forces in Northern Indochina in May. During this time, he commanded numerous operations in northern Vietnam and helped in taking **Bac Kan** and **Cao Bang** from the **Democratic Republic of Vietnam** (DRV), vital to depriving the adversary of rear bases and access to southern China. In 1948, Beaufré was the deputy to the Commissioner of the Republic in charge of the command of troops in **Cochinchina** and Cambodia. In 1951, he returned to Indochina after serving in Europe. He commanded military operations in northern Vietnam at the head of the *2ème Division de marche* and as operational deputy to General **Jean de Lattre de Tassigny** before taking up another post in 1952. He commanded French troops during the Suez operation in 1956 and would become one of the French army's most important theoreticians in the 1960s on "total war strategy", combining military aspects with psychological, economic, and political ones. In August 1965, Beaufré, now head of the Institute of Strategic Studies in Paris, published a series of articles in *Le Figaro* critical of American air power in Vietnam. *See also* AIR FORCE; CHARLES LACHEROY; REVOLUTIONARY WARFARE.

**BEAUVAIS, ANDRÉ ANTOINE MARCEL (1909–1981).** Graduated from the ***École nationale des langues orientales vivantes***, Beauvais made his career in Indochina as a civil servant. Between 1933 and 1940, he worked in various administrative posts in **Cochinchina** and continued to do so throughout the Vichy period. He worked closely after the war as cabinet director to Vietnamese governments that emerged in southern Vietnam between 1945 and 1950 and were allied with the French.

**BELLEUX, MAURICE (1909–2002).** High ranking French intelligence officer during the Indochina War between December 1947 and April 1956. Graduated from Saint-Cyr in 1931, Belleux simultaneously trained to become a fighter pilot in the French **Air Force**. During World War II, he was deeply involved in intelligence operations against the Germans in France. Until May 1944, he served as a leading member of the "Hunter" network in charge of following German aviation operations on behalf of the *Bureau central de renseignements et d'action* (BCRA). He then transferred briefly to London where he joined the Free French air force. He also entered the *section des études* within the *Direction générale d'études de renseignements* (DGRE) transformed into the ***Service de documentation extérieure et de contre-espionnage*** (SDECE) in November 1944 under the control of the French Council Presidency.

For unclear reasons the SDECE dispatched Belleux to Indochina on a six-month mission. Shortly after his arrival, he became the director of the SDECE's operations in all of Indochina. Named colonel in 1949, he was one of France's top intelligence officers during his eight years in Indochina. Under his direction, the SDECE became particularly effective in intercepting and decrypting many of the **Democratic Republic of Vietnam**'s lower and mid-level radio communications inside and outside Indochina. This allowed the SDECE to provide detailed and highly accurate information on the adversary's troop movements and orders of battle. In the early 1950s, Belleux also played a pivotal role in the creation of the ***Service Action*** and the ***Groupement de commandos mixtes aéroportés***. In 1956, on his return to France, he became head of the French Security Services of the National Defense and Armed Forces. Belleux had bitter enemies and devout servants in official and non-official circles in Indochina. His attempts to interfere in or even control a variety of intelligence operations outside of the SDECE's purview created an adamant enemy in the person of General **Roger Blaizot**, who contested the SDECE's legal right to exist in Indochinese territory – not technically an independent country, he said. Others worshipped the man, not least of all those involved in the SDECE's **commando** and **Service Action** operations. British diplomat and spy, **Trevor-Wilson**, was a frequent guest at the Belleux residence. Far from being the stereotypical spymaster, Belleux was perhaps best immortalized by **Lucien Bodard** in the following terms: "*Au contraire, il est rosé, poupin, les yeux un peu gros, la figure bien ronde, avec une bonne maison, une bonne cave, un jardin exotique, beaucoup de chiens et de serviteurs, et une dame très bien ... Toujours un verre ou un dossier en main, indifférement, ce personnage respire la franchise et la bonne humeur, avec quand meme un air de mystère masquant son importance et son métier ... Tout le monde le soupçonne de tout, mais sans prevue, et il dure*". *See also* EDWARD

LANSDALE; MARCEL BAZIN; OFFICE OF STRATEGIC SERVICES; PIERRE PERRIER; SERVICE ACTION; TRAN QUOC HOAN.

***BELLONE*.** Women's military magazine published by the ***Personnel féminin de l'armée de terre*** (PFAT) during the Indochina War. The magazine began during World War II with the increased feminization of the army. It was initially entitled the *Bulletin du Personnel féminin de l'armée de terre.* Despite a hiatus in the publication of the magazine, the continued feminization of the army during the Indochina War led to the resumption of the magazine in 1948. In December 1952, the name changed to *Bellone, revue des forces féminines françaises* – the only woman's magazine in the French armed forces until its absorption in 1967 by *TAM* (Terre, Air, Mer). While *Bellone* was not a feminist review per se, it promoted the equality of the sexes and contributed significantly to the emergence of a female military identity in the armed forces. *See also* WOMEN.

**BERGOT, ERWAN (1930–1993).** Well-known French veteran of the Indochina War, writer, and supporter of the French military cause in Indochina. In 1951, he volunteered to serve in Indochina, commanding the 1st **Foreign Legion** Airborne Heavy Mortar Company, until he was taken prisoner at **Dien Bien Phu** in May 1954. No sooner had he regained his liberty than he transferred to Algeria in 1955. Wounded in combat there in 1961, he left the army to begin a career as a writer and journalist. In 1962, he became the first editor in chief of the French Army's magazine and published the first of many war **novels**, including his autobiographical one, *Deuxième classe à Dien Bien Phu.* His novels focused on soldiers, camaraderie, and heroism. He received many literary prizes, including the *Prix Claude Farrère* and another from the *Académie française*. Bergot was also instrumental in bringing the plight of the Indochinese veterans to the attention of the French public in the late 1980s and early 1990s. In October 1986, in the French paper, *Le Figaro*, he published an article on the **Democratic Republic of Vietnam**'s (DRV) "death camps" and their heavy toll on the French prisoners. He was also a vocal partisan of the virulent attacks on the French **crossover**, **Georges Boudarel**, who worked in one of the DRV's internment camps for prisoners taken during the battle of Dien Bien Phu. Bergot did much to publicize and politicize the *affaire. See also ASSOCIATION NATIONALE DES ANCIENS D'INDOCHINE ET DU SOUVENIR INDOCHINOIS*; *ASSOCIATION NATIONALE DES ANCIENS ET AMIS DE L'INDOCHINE ET DU SOUVENIR INDOCHINOIS*; *ASSOCIATION NATIONALE DES ANCIENS PRISONNIERS ET INTERNÉS D'INDOCHINE*; *ASSOCIATION NATIONALE DES COMBATTANTS DE DIEN BIEN PHU*; EXPERIENCE OF WAR; INDOCTRINATION; MYTH OF WAR; RECTIFICATION.

**BERLIN CONFERENCE.** *See* GENEVA ACCORDS.

**BERNARD, LUCIE.** *See* LUCIE AUBRAC.

**BERT, MARCEL (1924–).** Served in the political section of the commissioner for the French Republic to Southern **Annam** in 1948 and as deputy chief for the province of Phan Thiet in 1948–49. In 1950, he transferred to Laos to work as the deputy to the provincial advisor of Pakse and then as the delegate for the commissioner for the French Republic in Saravane. Between 1951 and 1953, he worked in the personnel section of the French High Commission for Indochina.

**BERTIN, MAURICE (1870–1968).** Active and dedicated French missionary in Vietnam throughout the Indochina War. After taking part in the Sino-Japanese war of 1895, this young officer discovered his religious calling during a visit to the Church of Notre-Dame-des-Martyrs in Nagasaki. Back in France in 1896, he joined the Franciscan order as a brother and became an ordained priest in 1901. Following the expulsion of his order from France by the Third Republic in 1903, he left for Canada, and then moved on to Japan, Morocco, and Russia. He was called to arms during World War I. In 1920, he returned to Japan to work in the diocese of Nagasaki. In 1928, he left for Indochina and created a community of Franciscans in Hue in 1929 and a convent in Vinh. In 1935, he founded the Franciscan Academy at Thanh Hoa, which was very popular among the Vietnamese. The first ordination of Vietnamese Franciscan priests took place in 1945. Due to the war, in 1946 the Franciscans had to abandon their Academy at Thanh Hoa and ended up residing in Vinh under the control of the **Democratic Republic of Vietnam**. Father Bertin returned to France in 1948 at the age of 78, after spending 17 years in Vietnam. In 1950, he returned to Vietnam as a chaplain and advisor to the Christian Brothers School at Nha Trang. He passed away in Vietnam in 1968.

**BEUCLER, JEAN JACQUES (1923–1999).** Fought in the French Army during the campaigns of Italy, France, and Germany. Beucler arrived in Indochina in 1949 as a lieutenant in the *3e Tabor marocain*. He was taken prisoner during the battle of **Cao Bang** in October 1950 and spent the rest of the war in the **Democratic Republic of Vietnam**'s (DRV) prison camp no. 1. Freed in 1954, he returned to France and became an active politician. In 1977, he served as a state secretary in the Ministry of Defense. During this time he was deeply involved in veteran affairs and an active supporter of former French prisoners who had been held in Vietnamese camps. He served as president of the *Comité d'Entente des Anciens d'Indochine*. To bring the cause of the veterans of the Indochina War to French public attention, in 1977 he published *Quatre ans avec les Viets,* an account of his experiences as a prisoner, and a shorter version entitled *Prisonniers des Viets*, published in 1979 in *Historia*. He was most influential, however, as state secretary for Veterans Affairs. On 13 February 1991, he led the charge against the former **crossover** to the DRV, **Georges Boudarel**, during a conference on Vietnam held in the French Senate. While Beucler had admitted in his memoirs that lack of health care in extremely insalubrious terrain was the main cause for the massive mortality rates in Vietnamese camps, he saw in Boudarel a traitor, a Stalinist, and a communist guilty of "crimes against humanity". Until his death, Beucler dedicated himself to mobilizing public opinion against Boudarel and in favor of the veterans of the Indochina and Algerian wars, France's "forgotten" colonial conflicts. *See also ASSOCIATION NATIONALE DES ANCIENS D'INDOCHINE ET DU SOUVENIR INDOCHINOIS*; *ASSOCIATION NATIONALE DES ANCIENS ET AMIS DE L'INDOCHINE ET DU SOUVENIR INDOCHINOIS*; *ASSOCIATION NATIONALE DES ANCIENS PRISONNIERS ET INTERNÉS D'INDOCHINE*; *ASSOCIATION NATIONALE DES COMBATTANTS DE DIEN BIEN PHU*; BOUDAREL AFFAIR; EXPERIENCE OF WAR; MYTH OF WAR.

**BEVIN, ERNEST (1881–1951).** British labor politician and foreign secretary (1945–1951), who supported European and Asian initiatives to counter the spread of communism. During his long service as foreign secretary, Bevin played a pivotal role in the implementation of the Marshall Plan in 1947 to help rebuild postwar Europe, and in the creation of the **North Atlantic Treaty Organization** in 1949. In Asia, he was instrumental in negotiating the 1951 Colombo Plan. He was also a strong supporter of the French War in Indochina, seeing it as a crucial test to holding the line against communist gains into Southeast Asia, where Britain relied heavily on its colonies to help meet the dollar gap and restart the British economy. His government boldly supported the French **Bao Dai Solution**, granting diplomatic recognition to the Associated State of Vietnam in early 1950. However, to the disappointment of the Americans and the French, Bevin also proceeded to normalize diplomatic relations with the **People's Republic of China** at the same time. *See also* ASSOCIATED STATES OF INDOCHINA; BAO DAI SOLUTION; DOMINO THEORY; SOUTH EAST ASIA TREATY ORGANIZATION.

**BEZIAT, MAÎTRE JOSEPH.** In December 1947, Beziat was re-elected president of the Cochinchina Council and apparently held the post until November 1948. In April 1949, he was elected to the Territorial Assembly of Cochinchina. In January 1949, Nguyen Chan Hai replaced him as president of the parliament of South Vietnam.

**BFDOC.** *See BUREAU FÉDÉRAL DE DOCUMENTATION.*

**BICYCLES.** Unable to match the modern logistics of its French adversary, the **Democratic Republic of Vietnam** (DRV) relied heavily on bicycles and **animals** to meet its transport needs. For example, the DRV postal and communications services used bicycles to carry mail and documents, especially across the lowlands and deltas in secure zones. The **Viet Minh** also imported thousands of bicycles from China and French-controlled zones in order to transport on average 200 kg (440 pounds) of supplies during battles across northern and central Vietnam between 1950 and 1954. Vietnamese authorities deployed civilian porters to push the supply-laden bicycles across rugged territory leading to the battle fronts. During the battle of Dien Bien Phu, for example, bicycle units moved 4,620 tons of petrol products, 1,360 tons of ammunition, 46 tons of spare weapons, and 2,260 tons of foodstuffs (including 1,700 tons of rice) from the Chinese border to troops massing in the valley 600 miles away. In all, the DRV mobilized 20,991 bicycles during the battle of Dien Bien Phu. During the war against the Americans, these bicycle units would be pushed further to the south to supply the war effort, without which there was no **Ho Chi Minh Trail.**

**BIDAULT, GEORGES AUGUSTIN (1899–1983).** French statesman involved in one way or another in virtually every government dealing with the Indochina conflict. Bidault was co-founder of the resistance movement *Combat*, taking over the direction of the National Council upon Jean Moulin's capture. After World War II, he was one of the founding fathers of the ***Mouvement républicain populaire*** and one of its prime movers between 1949 and 1952. He was a member of several of the many French governments emerging out of World War II, serving as prime minister from June to December 1946 and as minister of Foreign Affairs between 1944 and 1948 (except in **Léon Blum**'s transitional cabinet between December 1946 and January 1947).

In 1946, because Bidault did not closely follow the activities of the commission in charge of policy on Indochina, the **Cominindo**, the high commissioner for Indochina, **Georges Thierry d'Argenlieu,** was able to successfully apply an aggressive policy towards the **Democratic Republic of Vietnam** (DRV). Instead of reining in the admiral, Bidault effectively covered him and implicitly backed his tactics, refusing minister of Overseas France **Marius Moutet**'s attempts to get rid of Thierry d'Argenlieu and the Cominindo. Like **Charles de Gaulle**, Bidault was a firm believer in the importance of recovering and maintaining the French Empire, a source of national prestige and of international influence in the wake of France's humiliation in 1940. Bidault refused to make any real concessions to **Ho Chi Minh** during the **Fontainebleau Conference** that could have negotiated a peaceful decolonization of Vietnam. Bidault ordered **Max André**, chief of the French delegation, not to make any concessions to the DRV's wish to run its own foreign affairs. Otherwise, he said, the French would not be able to maintain Vietnam within its colonial embrace.

Like so many French statesmen at the time (and not just on the Right), Bidault feared that concessions to nationalists in Vietnam would trigger a dangerous chain reaction of decolonization elsewhere in the Empire, especially in **North Africa**. War, however, did not solve the political problems. As minister of Foreign Affairs in 1953–54, Bidault was charged with the delicate question of securing an "honorable" end to the Indochina War at the **Geneva Conference** opening in May 1954. Bidault agreed with the Americans that the French should not cut and run in Geneva. While the fall of **Dien Bien Phu** certainly hurt the French position when the conference opened on 8 May, Bidault made it clear that if an acceptable solution were not reached, then the war would be internationalized, meaning the United States would intervene to help the French. Bidault proposed a cease-fire, but refused to talk directly to the DRV and continued to avoid the political side of the problem. Although he eventually agreed to meet DRV delegates and contemplated a provisional, military division of Vietnam, he remained largely intransigent in his negotiating position when his government fell on 12 June 1954. His exit and replacement by **Pierre Mendès France** put an end to his direct involvement in the Indochina War (although he tried to move negotiations along as a caretaker minister).

From the beginning to the end of the Indochina War, Bidault remained a remarkably firm believer in the French Empire. His line on Algeria left no doubt. Indeed, his unflinching support of the maintenance of l'*Algérie française* eventually saw him veer to the far right and support the military-led *Organisation de l'armée secrète*. His affiliation with this illegal entity forced him into exile between 1962 and 1968. Although he was amnestied in 1968, he was banned for life from politics. *See also* ALGERIAN WAR.

**BIER, RENÉ (1923–).** Served as Commissioner for the Republic in **Hanoi** in 1948 then as deputy to the regional counselor for Nam Dinh and then on an interim basis for Hoa Binh in 1949. Between 1951 and 1953, he was commissioner for the Republic to North Vietnam.

**BIỆT ĐỘNG.** *See* SPECIAL FORCES, DEMOCRATIC REPUBLIC OF VIETNAM.

**BIGEARD, MARCEL (BRUNO, 1916–2010).** Undoubtedly France's best-known soldier of its ill-fated colonial wars in Indochina and Algeria. And yet nothing, at the outset, suggested a distinguished military career for this bulldog of a man.

After completing his military service in the army along the Maginot Line (1936–1938), reserve sergeant Bigeard returned to civilian life without much thought. World War II, however, changed all that. He was called back to arms in March 1939 and rejoined the *23ème Régiment d'infanterie de forteresse*. He saw combat for the first time during the German invasion of France in May–June 1940. Though taken prisoner by the Germans during the French debacle, Bigeard finally escaped his captors on a third attempt in November 1941 and made his way to French West Africa (Vichy), where he joined the *Régiment mixte d'infanterie coloniale*. In October 1943, following the Allied liberation of North Africa about a year earlier, he moved to Morocco and volunteered for **commando** training under the British in Algiers in order to conduct clandestine missions into occupied France. He parachuted into France in August 1944 to run and train resistance networks as a specialist in military affairs. He served as an officer in the *Forces françaises de l'intérieur* (FFI). The end of World War II found Bigeard in Germany, a captain in the *23ème Régiment d'infanterie coloniale*.

No sooner was World War II over than France's colonial one in Indochina began. In October 1945, Bigeard participated in the French reoccupation of southern Vietnam under the direction of General **Philippe Leclerc**, still in the *23ème Régiment d'infanterie coloniale* (now *Extrême-Orient*). Bigeard led audacious operations into enemy territory, from which the "Bigeard legend" would spring. "Bruno" was his radio code name. He returned for two more tours of duty. In October 1948, back in France, he was one of a handful of special operations officers involved in creating the *3ème Battaillon colonial de commandos parachutistes* (BCCP). He helped lead it on his second tour of duty in Indochina. He also commanded the *3ème Bataillon Tai* and the *Bataillon de marche indochinois*. In July 1952, on his third tour, he led the *6ème Bataillon de Parachutistes Coloniaux* (BPC) which he would command during the battle at **Dien Bien Phu** in 1954. He was named lieutenant colonel during the battle. Together with **Pierre Langlais**, Bigeard would become legendary for fighting with his men until they were taken prisoner at Dien Bien Phu in early May 1954. He and his men were marched hundreds of kilometers to internment camps where they were held in insalubrious and deadly health conditions until their liberation in 1955. Bigeard would serve again in Algeria at the head of his paratroopers during the battle of Algiers before taking up politics upon his retirement.

Marcel Bigeard published numerous books on politics and France's heroic soldiers of its colonial wars. However, Bigeard also recognized the valor of his Vietnamese adversary. Writing in 1975, as Saigon fell to Vietnamese communist forces, he recalled how he felt following the French colonial debacle at Dien Bien Phu 21 years earlier: "Here I am now a prisoner of these little Vietnamese whom we used to consider in our French army to be good only for working as nurses and drivers. While these men with an extraordinary morale started out with nothing in 1945 but an ideal, irregular armaments and a goal to get rid of the French, in nine years Giap had defeated without a doubt our **Expeditionary Corps**".

France's unlikely soldier was named brigadier general in August 1967. Bigeard remained strangely silent during the **Boudarel affair**. *See also* ALGERIAN WAR; *ASSOCIATION NATIONALE DES ANCIENS D'INDOCHINE ET DU SOUVENIR INDOCHINOIS*; *ASSOCIATION NATIONALE DES ANCIENS ET AMIS DE L'INDOCHINE ET DU SOUVENIR INDOCHINOIS*; *ASSOCIATION NATIONALE DES ANCIENS PRISONNIERS ET INTERNÉS D'INDOCHINE*; *ASSOCIATION NATIONALE DES COMBATTANTS DE DIEN BIEN PHU*; ERWAN BERGET; EXPERIENCE OF WAR; JEAN-JACQUES BEUCLER; MYTH OF WAR.

**BILOM**. *See BATAILLON D'INFANTERIE LÉGÈRE D'OUTRE-MER*.

**BÌNH XUYÊN.** A Vietnamese criminal brotherhood turned paramilitary and political force during the French Indochina War, working first with the **Democratic Republic of Vietnam** (DRV), then with the French but perhaps above all for themselves. The Binh Xuyen got their start in the late 1920s and 1930s in racketeering, petty crime, and river pirating in and around Cholon-Saigon. During World War II, this loosely organized group operated its activities from Binh Xuyen village located on the far side of **Saigon**'s "Y3" bridge. The Binh Xuyen owed their name to that village.

Following the Japanese capitulation in August 1945, the Binh Xuyen put their organization in the patriotic service of the DRV. The independence movement and the war with the French offered financial and political opportunities to these bandits turned patriots. In exchange, at least at the outset, the Binh Xuyen provided the fledgling state with much needed connections and experience in the use of armed violence. In February 1946, the leader of the group, **Ba Duong**, was killed and replaced by **Le Van Vien** (Bay Vien) as supreme commander of the movement. The latter supported the military alliance with the DRV against the returning French. However, serious problems divided the Binh Xuyen from the DRV's military leader in the south, **Nguyen Binh**, who sought to unify southern forces under the government's national control. Like the **Cao Dai** and **Hoa Hoa** politico-religious forces, the Binh Xuyen balked at ceding their local military power to a national army, communist or not. As tensions mounted among the Vietnamese, astute French intelligence officers led by **Antoine Savani** and **Marcel Bazin** launched secret overtures, cut deals, and played on existing Vietnamese disputes in order to splinter the Binh Xuyen from the DRV's armed forces, as they had done in 1947 with much of the Hoa Hoa and Cao Dai forces.

The Binh Xuyen's break with the DRV came in June 1948 when Le Van Vien and forces loyal to him crossed over to the French and their emerging counter-revolutionary government under **Bao Dai**. In exchange for Le Van Vien's **collaboration**, the French and Bao Dai allowed him to resume his underground and lucrative activities in Saigon-Cholon, including the trafficking of **opium** flown in from Hmong areas in northwestern Vietnam. However, once back in his urban stomping grounds, Le Van Vien was no more ready to integrate his 2,000 militia into Bao Dai's national army than he had been in those of the DRV led by **Ho Chi Minh**. Upon assuming leadership of the **Republic of Vietnam** a few years later, **Ngo Dinh Diem** resumed the battle against the "bandit" Binh Xuyen and won, determined as he was to crush any opposition to a national army under his control. *See also* ARMY, ASSOCIATED STATE OF VIETNAM; DAP CHHUON; PEOPLE'S ARMY OF VIETNAM.

**BINOCHE, FRANÇOIS ALPHONSE (1911–1997).** Ranking officer in the **Foreign Legion** who served in Indochina. Arrested by Vichy authorities for his Gaullist activities during World War II, Binoche was imprisoned and judged by the Supreme Court of Gannat but acquitted for lack of proof. He entered the French resistance and the *Forces françaises de l'intérieur*. Seriously wounded, he lost the use of one of his arms. In 1949, after serving in North Africa, he arrived in Indochina to head the 5th Foreign Infantry Regiment. He remained in Indochina until the fall of **Dien Bien Phu**, when he transferred to the Military Cabinet of **Pierre Mendès France**, who was engaged in intense negotiations to end the war at the **Geneva Conference** in 1954. While Binoche would also serve in Algeria, he did not take part in the officer's rebellion initiated there. *See also* ALGERIAN WAR.

**BIROS, CASIMIR (?).** First arrived in Indochina in 1931 and served as provincial chief and directed various mid-level colonial offices. Between 1941 and 1945, he served as *résident de France* in Phan Rang province and was chief of cabinet to the *résident supérieur* in **Annam** before serving as *résident* in Song Cau province. In May 1942, Biros published a pro-Pétainist conference essay in the royalist *La Gazette de Hué*, entitled *Nationalisme et révolution*, in which he condemned the enemies of the National Revolution of Vichy. His article appeared alongside Pham Quynh's essay on Charles Maurras. In 1947, however, the *Commission interministérielle d'enquête pour l'Indochine* cleared him of any wrongdoing. Although the members deplored his participation in such Vichy propaganda, they lauded his patriotism: *C'est un royaliste, un maurrassien. Il garde ses opinions. On ne peut pas lui en faire un grief.* Following the war, he ran political affairs for General Lebris in central Vietnam until October 1948, when he became a cabinet director for the new high commissioner to Indochina, **Léon Pignon**. The two men knew each other from the 1930s. Biros' royalist ideas dovetailed nicely with Pignon's efforts to turn the former Emperor **Bao Dai** against **Ho Chi Minh**'s nationalist Vietnam. In March 1949, Biros visited Malaya with Pignon. A month later, Biros became a level 1 colonial administrator. *See also* ALBERT SARRAUT; ASSOCIATED STATES OF INDOCHINA; BAO DAI SOLUTION.

**BLAIZOT, ROGER (1891–1981).** Named in August 1943 head of the French Military Mission in **India** and designated commander of the French **Expeditionary Forces** in the Far East with the rank of general of the Army Corps. Between October 1944 and June 1945, he served as the head of the French Military Mission attached to the British South-East Asia Command. In April 1948, following General **Jean Valluy**'s recall, Blaizot took over as commander-in-chief of French Armed

Forces in the Far East. He arrived in Indochina in May 1948. In June, he served as acting high commissioner during **Émile Bollaert's** absence. In September 1949, he left Indochina and was replaced by General **Marcel Carpentier**. *See also* MAURICE BELLEUX.

**BLANC, CLÉMENT (1897–1982).** Graduated from the *École polytechnique*, Blanc replaced General **Georges Revers** in December 1949 as chief of staff of the French army and would hold that position until the end of the Indochina War in 1954. During this time, he did his best to provide reinforcements to the armed forces fighting an increasingly modern and intensive war in Indochina; but given France's increasing obligations in Europe he could do little to cure a chronic manpower shortage. Following a visit to the camp of **Dien Bien Phu** in late 1953, he saluted what he saw as the remarkable organization of the camp, but warned of the possible dangers of inclement weather and the difficulties the **air force** would encounter in supplying the camp under enemy fire. In a secret report he made to the government, he emphasized the dire need to negotiate a political solution to the war, for the armed forces in Indochina could not withstand for much longer the war effort that was being asked of them. *See also* EUROPEAN DEFENSE COMMUNITY; FINANCIAL COST OF THE WAR; NORTH ATLANTIC TREATY ORGANIZATION.

**BLIGNIÈRES (DE), HERVÉ LE BARBIER (1914–1989).** Led audacious **commando** raids against the forces of the **Democratic Republic of Vietnam** during the Indochina War. Graduated from Saint-Cyr in 1937, he saw battle against the Germans in Belgium in 1940 and was captured by them. Because of his repeated attempts to escape, the Germans locked him up tightly following his seventh attempt. Liberated in 1945, he studied and taught at the *École militaire de cavalerie* in Saumur. In 1948, he joined the **Foreign Legion** and commanded the squadron of the *1er Régiment étranger de cavalerie* in southern Vietnam until his departure from Indochina in 1950. He and his men became famous for taking the battle to their Vietnamese adversaries by mounting and executing a series of unconventional semi-amphibious attacks in some of the most hostile and swampy territory in the south. They inflicted a number of defeats on General **Nguyen Binh**'s forces in 1948 and 1949. As a colonel in Algeria, Blignières applied many of the same type of operations tested in Indochina. A firm believer in keeping Algeria French, he participated in the failed Putsch of Algiers and served as the chief of staff of the *Organisation de l'armée secrète* in France until his arrest in 1961. *See also* ALGERIAN WAR; CHARLES LACHEROY; DESERTION, DEMOCRATIC REPUBLIC OF VIETNAM; REVOLUTIONARY WARFARE.

**BLOCH-LAINÉ, FRANÇOIS (1912–2002).** Served as financial attaché to the French embassy in China and as financial advisor to the high commissioner to Indochina **Georges Thierry d'Argenlieu** between 1945 and 1946. He became director of the French treasury between 1947 and 1953. Bloch-Lainé was largely responsible for the decision to fix the rate of the Indochinese piastre at 17 francs in late 1945 and organized the exchange of the 500 piastre notes issued in massive quantities by the Japanese after the ***coup de force* of 9 March 1945**. He halted their circulation for they were now falling into the hands of the **Democratic Republic of Vietnam** and the occupying forces of the **Republic of China**. *See also* BANK OF INDOCHINA; CURRENCY, FRENCH INDOCHINA.

**BLUM, LÉON (1872–1950).** Leading French socialist leader unable to head off the outbreak of full-scale war in Indochina in late 1946. A committed Republican, Blum joined the socialist party in 1902 and became a close collaborator of Jean Jaurès. During the Congress of Tours in 1920, Blum warned against a Bolshevik takeover and the dangers of "democratic centralism" for a democracy. He joined the minority that maintained the ***Section française de l'Internationale ouvrière*** (SFIO) while the majority formed what would become the **French Communist Party**. Blum became a pivotal figure in the development of 20th-century socialism. He was best known for presiding over the Popular Front government and its reforms as prime minister between 1936 and 1938. Blum voted against transferring full powers to Philippe Pétain following the fall of France in mid-1940. His ardent republicanism and Jewish ancestry made him a target for Vichy and the Nazis. He was deported to Buchenwald in 1943 and liberated in 1945. After the war, he remained politically active and criticized in the pages of the SFIO's *Le Populaire* the French failure to negotiate an agreement with **Ho Chi Minh**. On 10

December 1946, he published an article warning of the need to avoid war in Indochina. Two days later he was elected by the National Assembly to form France's next government, which he did on the 17th. Hoping to head off war, Ho Chi Minh sent a long telegram to Blum on the 15th, offering to negotiate a peaceful settlement. He asked the French authorities in **Hanoi** to transmit the message. (He had recently accorded an interview to *Paris-Saigon* in which he insisted that he wanted a negotiated solution.) However, local authorities delayed transmission of the president's telegram. Blum received it on the 20th, almost a full day after full-scale war had already broken out in Hanoi. While Blum sent a diplomatic mission headed by **Marius Moutet**, the minister of Overseas France, to investigate the situation, he ended up accepting war. Blum's all-socialist transitional minority government was succeeded by a coalition government under another socialist veteran, **Paul Ramadier**, in late January 1947. During Christmas 1946, Blum commented bitterly about the outbreak of full-scale war under his watch in one short phrase: "I didn't deserve this". *See also* 19 DECEMBER 1946; ACCORDS OF 6 MARCH 1946; HAIPHONG INCIDENT.

**BODARD, LUCIEN (1914–1998).** French journalist, writer, and colorful character working out of **Saigon** during the Indochina War. Born in Chongqing, China, Bodard was the son of the French consul at Shanghai. Between 1947 and 1954, he was the foreign correspondent for *France Soir* in Indochina. Bodard obtained exceptional access to General **Jean de Lattre de Tassigny** and wrote affectionately of him. As one of de Lattre's advisors put it, Bodard was *une sorte de Saint Simon de la cour du Roi Jean*. Bodard knew how to exploit this access in his dispatches, making him one of the best-known reporters covering the Indochina War. He later published with Gallimard a widely read popular history of the Indochina War, divided into three parts: *l'Enlisement*, *l'Humiliation*, and *l'Aventure*. Like **Jean Lartéguy**, he played on the themes of Asian exoticism, the inscrutable Vietnamese communist, and the tragedy and heroism of the abandoned French army and soldier. He contributed greatly to the myth that the **Democratic Republic of Vietnam**'s southern General **Nguyen Binh** was killed by communist leaders jealous of his power and critical of his non-communist past. However, he could also go from discussing high politics and battles to providing some of the most vivid accounts of the war as it was experienced by combatants and everyday people, both the Europeans and the Vietnamese. His exceptional access to influential French authorities such as **Maurice Belleux** and **Jean Cousseau** did not prevent him from making trenchant criticism of the French war effort. His critical gaze also included Vietnamese of all political colors. In June 1955, the non-communist **Republic of Vietnam** expelled Bodard from Vietnam. *See also* CULTURE; EXPERIENCE OF WAR; GRAHAM GREENE; MYTH OF WAR; NOVELS, FRENCH.

**BODET, PIERRE (1902–1987).** Graduated from Saint-Cyr in 1924, he served during the interwar period in colonial North Africa. In 1934, he graduated from the *École supérieure de Guerre* and joined the General Staff of the French **Air Force**. During World War II, Bodet fought with Allied and Free French forces. Between 1947 and 1950, stationed in Indochina, he commanded the French Air Force in the Far East and became lieutenant general. He returned to France in 1950.

**BOLLAERT, ÉMILE (BEAUDOIN, 1890–1978).** Decorated veteran of World War I and a radical socialist, Bollaert distinguished himself again during World War II when, as a deputy of the Third Republic, he refused to vote full powers to Philippe Pétain in 1940 and joined the resistance. In September 1943, Bollaert replaced Jean Moulin as general delegate to occupied France for the French Committee for National Liberation (*Comité français de Libération nationale*). Arrested by the Gestapo in February 1944, he was deported to Buchenwald, Dora, and finally Bergen-Belsen, from which the British army liberated him on 15 April 1945. After the war, he became commissioner for the Republic in Strasbourg before being sent to Indochina to replace **Georges Thierry d'Argenlieu** as high commissioner for Indochina in March 1947. Bollaert refused to exclude the possibility of resuming contact with **Ho Chi Minh**, and for a long time refrained from following up the contacts initiatied by d'Argenlieu's principal advisor **Léon Pignon** with the ex-Emperor **Bao Dai** in Hong Kong. Bollaert dispatched **Paul Mus** to lay down the government's conditions to Ho Chi Minh in May 1947. To no avail. In the autumn of 1947, as France launched **Operation Lea** in a bid to wipe out the **Democratic Republic of Vietnam**, Bollaert resumed work on the **Bao Dai**

**Solution**, holding a highly publicized meeting with the former Emperor in Ha Long Bay at the end of the year. Following a failed attempt on his life in March 1948, Bollaert was replaced by **Léon Pignon** in the fall of 1948.

**BOLLARDIÈRE (DE), JACQUES-PÂRIS (1907–1985).** Born into a Catholic family in Chateaubriant, France, Bollardière was said to be the most decorated French soldier of World War II. A 1930 graduate of France's military academy Saint-Cyr, in 1935 he joined the *1er Régiment de Légion étrangère* in Algeria. In 1940, he transferred to the *13ème demi-brigade de la Légion étrangère* and led his company into battle against the Germans at Narvik in Norway before retreating to England and joining Free French forces there. He took part in the battle of El Alamein. In 1944, two months before the Allied landing in Normandy, he parachuted into the Ardennes as an elite clandestine officer for the British Special Air Service (SAS) and the French *Bureau central de renseignements et d'action* (BCRA). Working in and with the British SAS, he was involved in some of the most audacious and dangerous **commando** operations of World War II in Europe, including the *3ème Régiment de chasseurs parachutistes* jump into the Netherlands on 7 April 1945. In February 1946, he took command of the *Demi Brigade Parachutistes SAS d'Extrême-Orient.* His airborne paratroopers arrived in Indochina in March 1946 and scored a number of important victories over the forces of **Nguyen Binh** until 1948, when Bollardière returned to France. During a second tour of duty in Indochina between 1950 and 1953, he commanded the *Troupes aéroportées d'Indochine* and was a moving force in the creation of the ***Groupement de commandos mixtes aéroportés***. He served in the **Algerian War** and became brigadier general in December 1956. Bollardière ran into serious trouble in Algeria when he objected to the French army's use of **torture** and was one of the rare ranking French officers to speak out against its use at the time. When he broke with his superior, General **Jacques Massu**, over this question, he asked to be relieved of his command in March 1957. His wish was granted, though his troubles continued. After publicly criticizing the army's use of torture, French authorities arrested and imprisoned him in the Fort of Courneuve for 60 days. He later became an active pacifist, supporter of Third World causes, and opponent of nuclear armament. *See also* CHARLES LACHEROY; PAUL AUSSARESSE; REVOLUTIONARY WARFARE; *SERVICE ACTION*; *SERVICE DE DOCUMENTATION EXTERIEURE ET DE CONTRE ESPIONNAGE*.

**BOLLOT, MICHEL (1921–1995).** Career colonial civil servant, who joined the Free French forces and fought in the battle of El Alamein in 1942. After the war, he served as an administrative delegate to **Cochinchina** then in **Tonkin** between 1950 and 1952. Between 1953 and 1954, he was the head of the liaison service working with the military in the "**pacification**" of the western zone of northern Vietnam (Ha Dong, Son Tay and Vinh Yen).

**BONDIS, PAUL-LOUIS (1895–1986).** Lieutenant general in charge of Ground Forces in South Vietnam between 1951 and 1953. Before arriving in Indochina he had served as deputy commanding officer of troops in Tunisia (1946–1949) and commanding officer of the Military Academy of Saint-Cyr (1950–1951). He retired from the army in 1955.

**BONFILS, CHARLES-HENRI (1908–2001).** Ranking career French colonial administrator in Indochina between 1932 and 1950. Graduated from the **Colonial Academy** (*École coloniale*) in 1930, he began his career in Indochina as a deputy to the French resident in Thanh Hoa province between 1932 and 1933 before entering the Head Office for Economic Affairs in the General Government of Indochina (1934–1936). He then served as deputy chief of cabinet for the *résident supérieur* of **Tonkin**. During World War II, he married the daughter of Louis Marty, Indochina's legendary colonial police chief during the interwar years. Bonfils stayed on under Vichy, serving as chief of cabinet for Governor General Admiral Jean Decoux between July 1942 and November 1942. He was resident of Langson province between 1942 and 1944 and chief of cabinet for the French *résident supérieur* for Tonkin from August 1944 until the Japanese ***coup de force* of 9 March 1945**, when he was interned. Following the Japanese defeat, the *Commission d'épuration des fonctionnaires* in **Hanoi** cleared him. Bonfils restarted his colonial career in France working in the *Agence de l'Indochine* (Agindo), which represented High Commissioner **Georges Thierry d'Argenlieu** in Paris. Another *Commission d'épuration* in Paris cleared him a second time in mid-1946, following the investigation of complaints lodged against him by former Gaullist officers in Indochina. They had accused Bonfils of anti-Free French actions along the Sino-Tonkin border and alleged his implication in the Japanese killing of a downed American pilot in 1944. The charges were dismissed. On 28 January 1947, High Commissioner Thierry d'Argenlieu, now at war with the **Democratic Republic of Vietnam**, asked the minister of Overseas France to dispatch Bonfils immediately to help rebuild Indochina. In 1948, Bonfils returned to Indochina to replace **Didier Michel** as the political advisor to the high commissioner of Indochina, **Léon Pignon.** The two knew each other from the interwar period. Pignon considered Bonfils to be "one of the two or three men upon whom one can count to administer the highest positions in the current circumstances". Bonfils served as director of political affairs in **Saigon** between 1947 and 1950. In September 1949, Bonfils presided over a special committee in charge of the problems of the press in Indochina. He also served as a ranking member of the Franco-Vietnamese Commission for the implementation of the March 1949 Bao Dai-Auriol Agreement creating the Associated State of Vietnam. Bonfils left Indochina and his post as political advisor in 1950 to serve as governor of Dahomey (1951–55), Guinea (1955–56), and interim general secretary of Equatorial French Africa (1956–58). *See also* MARCEL BAZIN; PIERRE PERRIER; *SÛRETÉ FÉDÉRALE.*

**BONG SUVANNAVONG (1906–1978).** Teacher and leading non-communist politician in Laos after World War II. Born in Vientiane, Bong Suvannavong studied at the teachers' school in colonial **Hanoi**, graduating as a certified primary school teacher in 1928. He served in educational posts during the rest of the interwar period. During World War II, Bong Suvannavong participated in patriotic activities unleashed by the Vichy regime as the French tried to hold on against the Japanese and the Thais. He presided over the Laotian Artistic and Sports Association. In **collaboration** with Charles Rochet, he promoted patriotic songs, theatrical pieces, and literature. In 1946, with the return of the French, he founded the Party of Lao Unity (*Lao Houam Samphan*) and served as president of the Constituent Assembly of 1947. He was minister of Economy between 1949 and 1950 and deputy from Vientiane between 1951 and 1955.

**BÔNG VĂN DĨA (HAI DĨA, 1905–1983).** Southern Vietnamese who took part in the communist-led Nam Ky uprising of 1940. The French arrested him and packed him off to **Poulo Condor** to serve hard time. There, he met **Le Duan** and other ranking members of the **Indochinese Communist Party** (ICP). Freed in 1945, he returned to southern Vietnam. Shortly thereafter, the **Democratic Republic of Vietnam** sent him to Thailand and Malaysia to buy arms and ammunition for southern troops. During the war against the Americans, Bong Van Dia helped create the maritime **Ho Chi Minh Trail**.

**BONNAFOUS, ROBERT.** French veteran of the Indochina War and former **prisoner of war**. He completed and published his thesis at the Université Paul-Valéry entitled *Les Prisonniers de guerre du corps expéditionnaire français en Extrême-Orient dans les camps viêt minh, 1945–1954*. In 1985, he helped create the ***Association nationale des anciens prisonniers et intérnés d'Indochine*** and played an important role in drafting the law of 1989 creating the statute of "prisoner of the Viet Minh", thereby providing hundreds of former prisoners access to medical benefits in France. Like **Marcel Bigeard**, Bonnafous kept a surprisingly low profile during the **Boudarel affair** in the 1990s. *See also* EXPERIENCE OF WAR; EXPERIENCE OF WAR, DIEN BIEN PHU; MYTH OF WAR; PYSCHOLOGICAL WARFARE.

**BONVISSINI, HENRI (BONVICINI).** Eurasian manager of the virulently anti-**Viet Minh** newspaper in **Saigon**, *Le Populaire*. Like **William Bazé**, Bonvissini was an outspoken anti-communist and supporter of the **Bao Dai Solution** and the Bao Dai-Auriol Agreement creating the Associated State of Vietnam. As Director of the *Saigon Presse,* he was seriously wounded during an assassination attempt on his life in July 1950 by agents of the **Democratic Republic of Vietnam.**

**BÖRCHERS, ERWIN (1906–?).** A German communist who **crossed over** to the **Democratic Republic of Vietnam** (DRV). He took part in anti-fascist activities before the Nazis took power in 1933 when he fled to France. With the outbreak of World War II, he joined the French **Foreign Legion** in 1940 thinking that he would be able to continue fighting fascism in Europe. However, with the disappearance of the Third Republic in June of that year and the emergence of a collaborating French regime under Vichy, Börchers suddenly found himself on a boat sailing to Indochina in 1941 as a Foreign Legion soldier but now taking orders from a French regime collaborating with the very Nazis he so despised, to say nothing of the Japanese occupying Indochina with Vichy's consent. Moreover, as a communist, he was opposed to French colonial domination and sympathetic to Vietnamese communists and their ideological, anti-fascist and liberation goals. In 1943, he began meeting secretly with the ranking underground leaders of the **Indochinese Communist Party** (ICP) in northern Vietnam, including **Truong Chinh**, the acting general secretary of the Party. He also developed contacts with French resistance leaders in Vietnam such as the Socialist **Louis Caput**. Truong Chinh went through Börchers to arrange a meeting in **Hanoi** to discuss cooperation between the Gaullists and the **Viet Minh**. This occurred in December 1944, though little came of it. After the Japanese ***coup de force* of 9 March 1945** overthrowing the French in Indochina, Börchers was imprisoned with the rest of the Legion. Following the defeat of the Japanese and his liberation from prison, he remained within the Foreign Legion, but provided intelligence to Truong Chinh on French military movements and sought to win over supporters for the Vietnamese nationalist cause among other anti-fascist or left-leaning soldiers serving in the French Foreign Legion. In 1944, he became an official member of the ICP. In 1947, with the outbreak of war in all of Indochina, Börchers crossed over to the DRV and was inducted into the Vietnamese army. He adopted the Vietnamese name, *Chien Si* (Fighter or Fighting Soldier) and served as editor of the German and French sections of *Radio Vietnam* (*Dai Phat Thanh Tieng Noi Viet Nam*) and of the government's French-language paper, *La République*, which later became *Le Peuple*. In the army, his work focused on propaganda and proselytizing missions in French and German aimed at winning over the sympathy, support, and/or **desertion** of European troops in the **Expeditionary Corps** (mainly in the Foreign Legion). He was editor in chief of the German-language propaganda paper, *Waffen Bruder* (*Ban Chien Dau* or *Friend of the Soldier*). In 1950, during the third plenum of the ICP, he delivered a speech on the importance of **proselytizing the enemy** (*dich van*) as the war entered a new phase. During the battle of **Dien Bien Phu**, he was in charge of proselytizing operations towards Austrian and German soldiers. He allegedly brought over 123 such troops to the Vietnamese side. In 1955, following the war, he transferred to the Ministry of Culture in the DRV now located in Hanoi, and in 1957 became an official correspondent for the German Democratic Republic's (DDR) Information Service in Hanoi. In 1966 he returned to the DDR. The DRV decorated him for his services during the struggle against the French.

**BORDELS MOBILES DE CAMPAGNE.** Even though the French clamped down on *maisons closes* in metropolitan France at the end of World War II, the army legally administered *Bordels Mobiles de Campagne* (BMC) or Mobile Field Brothels during the entire Indochina War (and again during the **Algerian War**). They were also known as *Bordels Militaires de Campagne* (BMC). The French army first created the BMC's during World War I and again in World War II to tend to the large number of colonial troops fighting for the *Mère patrie*. However, no BMC operated in Indochina during either world war. During the Indochina conflict, the BMC broke the earlier colonial divide, serving both the metropolitan French troops and the different nationalities of what was an ethnically very diverse **Expeditionary Corps**. The French army saw in the operation of the BMCs an effective way of preventing **veneral disease** and of cutting down on desertion, rape, and homosexuality. Two-and-a-half-ton military trucks transported the *bordels* with the troops, sometimes into combat zones. Customers had to pay; so the army's investment was minimal. The women working in the brothels tended to be Vietnamese. However, the diversity of the imperial army in Indochina manifested itself in the bordellos. Well known were the Oulad-Nail women from the Constantine area of Algeria, unmistakable for their richly colored costumes. A BMC was present at **Dien Bien Phu** in 1954 and several Vietnamese and Algerian women died while serving as nurses tending to scores of wounded French Union soldiers. With the fall of the camp to the **Democratic Republic of Vietnam**'s troops on 7 May 1954, around a dozen women of the BMC were marched off with the captured troops. The Algerian women who survived the grueling march and detention were later released; the fate of the Vietnamese women remains unknown to this author. While **Geneviève-Terrauble de Galard** was not the only woman taken prisoner at Dien Bien Phu, Algerian and Vietnamese women never shared the French woman's heroine status. When French officers recommended two female members of the BMC for military citations for acts of heroism demonstrated during heavy fighting during an enemy ambush in Lai Chau province, the establishment refused on the grounds that this would be "inappropriate". *See also PERSONNEL FÉMININ DE L'ARMÉE DE TERRE* (PFAT); WOMEN, DEMOCRATIC REPUBLIC OF VIETNAM; WOMEN, FRENCH ARMED FORCES.

**BORDIER, LOUIS.** A Franco-Hmong officer during the Indochina War. This ***métis*** was married to the eldest daughter of **Deo Van Long**, one of the most powerful Tai families in Laos and upland Vietnam. Bordier was an agricultural official in Indochina during the colonial period and served as a reserve officer in the Indochinese army during World War II. He was apparently among those who took refuge in southern China after the Japanese ***coup de force*** **of 9 March 1945**. During the Indochina war, his links to the Deo family and knowledge of the Tais in northern Vietnam made him an invaluable contact for assisting French military operations in the northwest. Indeed, he became a captain in the ***Groupement de commandos mixtes aéroportés*** active in mounting operations with the Deo family's partisans against the **Democratic Republic of Vietnam** in the Tai region. Bordier was an ardent defender of the Deo Van Long's autonomous **Tai Federation.** *See also* JEAN SASSI; MINORITY ETHNIC GROUPS; PAUL AUSSARESSE; *PAYS MONTAGNARDS DU SUD (*PMS); *SERVICE ACTION; SERVICE DE DOCUMENTATION ET DE CONTRE-ESPIONNAGE.*

**BOUCHER DE CRÈVECOEUR, JEAN MARIE CHARLES (1906–1987).** Graduate of the *École militaire spéciale de Saint-Cyr* in 1924 who was in the same class as Generals **Michel de Brébisson** and **Edmond Jouhaud**. Between 1927 and 1930, 1934 and 1935, and 1936 and 1938, he served as an officer leading colonial troops in Indochina (*21ème Régiment d'infanterie coloniale, tirailleurs cambodgiens*). He was lightly wounded during military operations designed to quell a "Moi" uprising in 1935. In 1940, he was wounded again as a battalion commander during brief but heavy fighting against German forces attacking south of Sédan in France. Following the French defeat, he demobilized. He left France a few months after the Allied landing in North Africa in November 1942 and joined Free French forces in Algeria. In November 1943, he was named commander of the French detachment to **India** (*Commandant le détachement français aux Indes*) and helped create in **collaboration** with the British and lead the first French ***Service Action*** between May 1944 and November 1945. This team was charged with launching clandestine operations into Indochina against the Japanese in collaboration with the British. In December 1945, Boucher de Crèvecoeur became commander of French forces in Laos and played a leading role in the French reoccupation of Laos in 1946. Named colonel in 1946, he returned to France in late 1947, but was back in Indochina in June 1948 as the chief of staff to the commander-in-chief for French Forces in southern Indochina and commander of the Eastern Zone of **Cochinchina** in September 1949. He left Indochina in June 1950 only to return yet again in September 1953, as the commander of French ground forces in Laos. He commanded troops against enemy incursions deep into Laos in 1953 and 1954 and oversaw an audacious if unsuccessful mission to rescue troops fleeing towards Laos during the siege of **Dien Bien Phu**. He left Indochina definitively in October 1955. See also COMMANDOS; JEAN DEUVE; REVOLUTIONARY WARFARE; *SERVICE ACTION.*

**BOUDAREL AFFAIR.** On 13 February 1991, a group of well-organized and motivated French veterans of the Indochina War successfully confronted French scholar and specialist of Vietnam, **Georges Boudarel**, during a conference held in the French Senate on "Vietnam Today". The man who led the charge against Boudarel was **Jean-Jacques Beucleur**, a former prisoner of war in Indochina and now the State Secretary for Veterans Affairs under Valérie Giscard-d'Estaing. Beucleur publicly denounced Boudarel, accusing him of having served as a political commissar in a **Democratic Republic of Vietnam** (DRV) **prisoner of war** camp. Beucler denounced Boudarel for having "blood on his hands". The media picked up on the event. Between February and May 1991, according to Katie Edwards, some 300 articles appeared on the "affaire" in the French press. TV reporters lined up at Boudarel's apartment complex demanding a statement. Boudarel's colleagues, students, and supporters mobilized their troops on the Left as the opposition on the Right did the same.

Boudarel defended his actions on anti-colonialist grounds. He crossed over to the Viet Minh in 1950, he wrote in his *Autobiographie*, disgusted by the colonial war he had witnessed first hand upon arriving in **Saigon** in the late 1940s. While he regretted his role working for the DRV in prisoner of war camps in northern Vietnam, he denied charges that he had killed or tortured, insisting that it was **disease** and a woeful lack of medicine that took the lives of so many French Union prisoners. His detractors cast the war in ideological terms, one in which the French army had fought heroically against communist expansion and in defense of its Vietnamese ally, the Associated State of Vietnam. Men such as Beucleur, **Pierre Guillaume**, and **Déodat Puy-Montbrun** rejected the idea that the Indochina conflict was a colonial one.

In effect, the "Boudarel affair" brought to the fore two contesting memories of the conflict, one anti-colonialist, the other anti-communist. While only time will tell why the Boudarel affair occurred in 1991, several factors were clearly at work. For one, French veteran associations such as the *Association nationale des anciens prisonniers et internés d'Indochine* and the ***Association nationale des anciens et amis de l'Indochine et du souvenir indochinois*** had long been organizing their members, developing political and media networks, and had built an impressive memory making machine by the late 1980s. In 1988, for example, French veterans groups inaugurated the Memorial to the Indochina Wars, the **necropolis** located outside Fréjus. It also contains a mural with the names of the "fallen" soldiers etched on it, based on the American Vietnam War Memorial in Washington, D.C. Indeed, many French veterans were inspired by what they saw happening in the United States in the 1980s under Ronald Reagan: the POW-MIA question had not only served as a political rallying cry for mobilizing memory around a "noble" and "forgotten" cause, but it had also demonstrated to the French side the importance of organization, infrastructure, and the media. In December 1989, reacting to veterans lobbying, the French government created the status of "prisoner of the Viet Minh", granting benefits to aging French veterans and acknowledging the Indochina conflict as a "war". The liberalization of communist Vietnam from 1986 and the crumbling of "world communism" by 1991 also created a favorable context for veteran associations to bring the Indochina War to public attention via the Boudarel affair and to recast the conflict in more anti-communist and heroic terms. The affair even allowed some to begin speaking of the "postive" aspects of French colonialism in Indochina and elsewhere, foreshadowing a decade ahead of time the controversial legislation requiring teachers to discuss the "positive" effects of French colonialism.

The "affaire Boudarel" was less about what happened in the early 1950s in POW camps (a judge threw out the charge against Boudarel of "crimes against humanity") than an indication of an emerging debate in French society, or at least certain political and academic circles, as to how to understand and commemorate the Indochina conflict and French colonialism more widely. However, neither on the Right or Left, was there ideological homogeneity. Socialist Prime Minister Lionel Jospin dismissed Boudarel as a "kapo" (referring to privileged prisoners serving in Nazi prison camps). And if veterans led by Beucleur successfully brought the memory of the Indochina conflict to the fore, there were some very notable exceptions, both of them veterans of the Indochina War and formers POWs – Robert Bonnafous and **Marcel Bigeard**. The Boudarel affair revealed other divergences, too. While historians Pierre Brocheux and Daniel Hémery supported their colleague at Paris VII, they not only rejected the right's anti-communist and nostalgic spin on French colonialism but they also broke with the schematic anti-colonialism and nationalism of many of their colleagues on the Far Left. In 1995, Pierre Brocheux and Daniel Hémery published, in large part as a reaction to the memory battles let loose during the Boudarel affair, their monumental *Indochine, une colonisation ambiguë*. If Bigeard admitted the reality of his former adversary's nationalism, Brocheux and Hémery conceded that colonialism was complex. *See also ASSOCIATION NATIONALE DES ANCIENS D'INDOCHINE ET DU SOUVENIR INDOCHINOIS*; *ASSOCIATION NATIONALE DES ANCIENS ET AMIS DE L'INDOCHINE ET DU SOUVENIR INDOCHINOIS*; *ASSOCIATION NATIONALE DES COMBATTANTS DE DIEN BIEN PHU*; ASSOCIATION OF MOTHERS OF SOLDIERS; EXPERIENCE OF WAR; HISTORY; MYTH OF WAR; WAR MEMORIAL, DIEN BIEN PHU.

**BOUDAREL, GEORGES (1926–2003).** French **crossover** to the **Democratic Republic of Vietnam** (DRV) and highly controversial figure in the politics of memory surrounding the French war in Indochina. Born into a Catholic family in Saint-Étienne, he completed his secondary studies there at the *Institution Notre Dame de Valbenoite* (1944–1945) and obtained his undergraduate degree in Lyon (*licence d'enseignement*) in 1947 certifying him to teach philosophy at the secondary level. It was also during this period that he drifted away from Catholicism and towards communism and anti-colonialism. This became more pronounced following his decision to begin his teaching career in French Indochina. He arrived in **Saigon** on 19 April 1948 to begin work as a student teacher in philosophy at the *Lycées Lalande* and *Yersin* in Dalat (1948), the *Lycée Pavie* in Vientiane (1949), and the *Lycée Marie Curie* in Saigon (1949–1950). During this time, he became involved in the political activities of left-leaning and communist Vietnamese and French **intellectuals** running the *Groupe culturel marxiste* opposed to the Indochina war. Boudarel became increasingly critical of heavy-handed French methods used against the Vietnamese, especially the French crackdown on a Vietnamese student demonstration in 1950, which seems to have been the deciding factor in his decision to cross over to the other side. In December 1950, he secretly left Saigon on the invitation of **Pham Ngoc Thach**, who had him escorted to DRV territory and put to work in propaganda affairs. In January 1951, Boudarel called upon his former students to rally to the Vietnamese nationalist cause led by the DRV. The French army charged him with treason on 15 March 1951. In 1952, as the war intensified in the north, DRV authorities transferred Boudarel to northern Vietnam. There, he was responsible for winning over and indoctrinating **Expeditionary Corps** soldiers taken prisoner by the Vietnamese in increasing large numbers since 1950, many of whom died due to the appalling health conditions, lack of medicine, and poor medical care. Following the end of the Indochina War, Boudarel resided in **Hanoi** and continued working as a propagandist and editor in the official *Radio Viet Nam* until 1958. Between 1959 and 1964, he worked in the Foreign Language Publishing House before leaving for Czechoslovakia and eventually France in 1968, thanks to a French general amnesty (also extended to former French military officers who had turned against the 4th Republic over the decolonization of Algeria). Back in France, between 1968 and 1970, Boudarel put his knowledge of Vietnamese to work as a research scholar in the *Centre national de la recherche scientifique* and in the *Section langues et civilisations orientales* in Paris. Thanks to support from **Jean Chesneaux** and other intellectuals on the Left and Far Left, Boudarel taught at the University of Paris VII from 1970 as a lecturer. Following the end of the Vietnam War in 1975, he became increasingly disillusioned with and critical of Vietnamese communism, publishing a major history of Vietnamese dissent in North Vietnam in the 1950s. This, however, did not prevent politically active veteran associations and survivors of the Vietnamese prisoner camps to launch a (failed) legal battle against Boudarel for "crimes against humanity" during the Indochina War. They were more successful in their media blitz against him, the **Boudarel affair**, effectively forcing him to retire early from his university career. *See also* ALGERIAN WAR; PSYCHOLOGICAL WARFARE; RECTIFICATION; TORTURE.

**BOUDIER, MICHEL (1920–1963).** Famous French **Air Force** pilot during the Indochina War. He joined the Air Force in 1938 and became a fighter pilot in January 1940. Opposed to the armistice, he fled to England in 1940. After further training in the Royal Air Force, he joined the 232nd Squadron of the Royal Air Force in 1941. During the war, he accomplished dozens of missions over France and Belgium, shooting down many enemy planes. Downed himself in July 1944, he was arrested by the Gestapo but passed himself off as a regular soldier and escaped certain execution. Freed by the Allies in April 1945, he returned to flying missions against the Germans briefly before moving on to Indochina, where he joined the 2nd Fighter Squadron in the Far East in February 1947 and then the 4th Fighter Squadron. In 1949 he assumed command of the 1/5 Fighter Squadron. In Indochina, he flew a total of 421 missions against the **Democratic Republic of Vietnam**.

**BOULLE, PIERRE (1912–1994).** After graduating from the *École supérieure d'électricité* in Paris, Boulle became a rubber planter in British Malaya. Although he lived for a while in the bungalow of Henri Fauconnier, winner of the French Goncourt prize for his novel *Malaisie*, Boulle showed few early signs of literary genius. World War II changed this: his wartime experiences served as the subject of his future books. In 1939, as Europe went to war and Japan eyed Southeast Asia from its occupation of coastal China, Boulle reported for military duty in Indochina. Disgusted, he returned to Malaya in 1941 following Vichy's condominium with the Japanese in Indochina. In Singapore, he joined the Free French forces and briefly trained with British commandos before the Japanese took the British crescent. This did not stop him from attempting a high-risk clandestine entry into northern Vietnam via the Black River. Boulle's attempt to link up with resistance forces there ended in failure in 1942, when Vichy authorities arrested him and sentenced him to life imprisonment and hard labor for sedition. In 1944, Boulle escaped to Calcutta, thanks to British support, and returned to a newly liberated France. With the defeat of the Japanese, he returned briefly to Malaya before dedicating himself to a life of writing. With the war and his wartime experiences serving as his subtext, he became famous for the novel David Lean turned into a classic film of the same name, *The Bridge Over the River Kwai* (1952). This novel was based in part on Boulle's time in Vichy's Indochinese prison (Boulle was never a POW in Thailand). Boulle also wrote another famous novel that became something of a cult film, *Planet of the Apes* (1963).

**BOURGOIN, JEAN.** Graduated as a Public Works engineer from the *École polytechnique* in France, he was a member of the French delegation to the **Fontainebleau conference** in mid-1946 and served as an advisor on the Monnet Plan for the reconstruction of France after World War II. For Bourgoin, the colonial and national reconstruction of France went together. In 1948, he went to Indochina as part of wider plans to industrialize Indochina through the development of hydraulic resources and the steel and fertilizing industries. In July 1949, he took part in discussions on war damage claims. *See also* BANK OF INDOCHINA; CURRENCY, FRENCH INDOCHINA; ECONOMY OF WAR, FRANCE; FINANCIAL COST OF WAR.

**BOURGUND, GABRIEL (1898–?).** Career military officer who commanded troops in central Vietnam during the Indochina War. During the interwar period, he served in the colonial army in much of the French Empire. He entered the resistance in 1942 and fled to North Africa. After the war, he volunteered to serve in Indochina and headed the 1st Far East Brigade assembled in Indochina in January 1946. Between June and July 1946, his brigade occupied the highlands of central Vietnam below the **16th parallel.** He was named brigadier general in August 1946 and military commander of **Annam** in January 1947. He led the reoccupation of Hue in 1947. He left Indochina in July 1947, but returned in October 1953 at the head of ground forces for Central Annam. He left Indochina definitively in June 1955. *See also* ETHNIC MINORITIES; *PAYS MONTAGNARDS DU SUD* (PMS).

**BOURLIER, FRANÇOIS (1918–?).** Member of the French Free forces during World War II. Between 1943 and 1945, he worked as an intelligence specialist of Asia in London as part of the *Bureau central de renseignements et d'action* (BCRA). Between 1945 and 1946, he served in **India** as a liaison officer in the *Corps de liaison administrative pour l'Extrême-Orient*. He moved on to Indochina where he was assigned to the high commissioner's delegation for the upland peoples in Ban Me Thuot, working in the military section (1946–1947). He then served as deputy to the commissioner in Darlac and then as district head of Buon Ho and M'Drack between 1947 and 1948. After working as regional advisor to the upper Mekong, he returned to France and was assigned to the Ministry of Overseas France. He helped organize the **Pau Conference** of 1950. *See also* ETHNIC MINORITIES; *PAYS MONTAGNARDS DU SUD* (PMS).

**BOUSSARIE, ARMAND (?–1982).** Graduated from the *École polytechnique* in France in 1930, Boussarie entered the artillery. During the Indochina War, he became a ranking French intelligence officer in the ***Deuxième Bureau***, heading up its office for the *Zone opérationnelle du Tonkin* (ZOT) between January and November 1948. Between June 1950 and April 1953, he ran the *Deuxième Bureau* for the *État-major interarmé des forces terrestres*, probably the single most important intelligence office for the army in Indochina. *See also* ANTOINE SAVANI; INTELLIGENCE SERVICES, ARMY OF THE DEMOCRATIC REPUBLIC OF VIETNAM; MARCEL BAZIN; MAURICE BELLEUX; PIERRE PERRIER; *SERVICE DE DOCUMENTATION ET DE CONTRE-ESPIONNAGE*; *SÛRETÉ FÉDÉRALE*.

**BOUSSARIE, MARCEL MARIE (1920–).** Joined Free French forces on 1 July 1940 before serving in **Brazzaville** in September. He remained there until being transferred to the *École de Cherchell* in October 1943 and then joined General **Philippe Leclerc**'s 2[nd] Armored Division. In January 1952, he transferred to Indochina to the *4[ème] Régiment d'artillerie coloniale* and then in 1953 he was assigned to the general headquarters of French ground forces in North Vietnam.

**BOUTBIEN, LÉON (1915–2001).** French medical doctor and influential politician in the ***Section française de l'Internationale ouvrière*** (SFIO) opposed to the Indochina War. Born into a working-class family, he joined the SFIO at the young age of 15. He completed his secondary studies at the *Lycée Montaigne* then at the prestigious *Lycée Louis-le-Grand*. During the 1930s, he was active in left-wing politics, supported the Republicans during the Spanish **civil war**, and was actively involved in the anti-fascist movement. During World War II, he participated in the resistance movement in France until the Germans deported him in 1943. He ended up in Dachau. After his liberation from this death camp in 1945, he joined the directing committee of the SFIO, located squarely on the left in the Party. He accompanied the socialist minister of Colonies, **Marius Moutet**, on the latter's fact-finding mission to Vietnam following the outbreak of full-scale war in Indochina on **19 December 1946**. Boutbien met with various Vietnamese nationalist elites and called for the resumption of negotiations with the **Democratic Republic of Vietnam**, something the aging and cautious Moutet opposed at this juncture. In 1950, Boutbien published a book on Indochina in which he repeated his opposition to the war. At the same time, he became an advisor to the **French Union**.

**BOYER DE LA TOUR DU MOULIN, PIERRE GEORGES JACQUES MARIE (1896–1976).** Volunteered in 1914 to serve in World War I and emerged four years later a second lieutenant. He spent most of the interwar period in the colonial army in North Africa. During World War II, he led the 2[nd] Moroccan Tabor into battle during the Italian Campaign, the liberation of Corsica, France, and Germany. In July 1947, a brigadier general, he transferred to Indochina where he served as interim then full commander of French troops in southern Indochina from August 1947. In July 1948, he became the acting commissioner for the French Republic to **Cochinchina**. His position became permanent in 1949. During this time, he directed major operations to "pacify" southern Vietnam and defeat the enemy forces led by General **Nguyen Binh**. He was one of the architects of the ***Unités mobiles pour la défense des chrétiens*** designed to take the battle to the enemy among Catholics living in Ben Tre province. He was well known during the Indochina War for creating and installing a sophisticated surveillance system and entrenched positions situated along the major lines of communication in southern Vietnam. It was widely known at the time as the *Plan La Tour*. He left Indochina in October 1949. In November 1950, following the loss of **Cao Bang** to the **Democratic Republic of Vietnam**, he returned to replace General **Marcel Alessandri** as commissioner for the Republic in **Tonkin**. In 1950, de la Tour was also named military advisor to the government of the Associated State of Vietnam and helped it create and organize its own national army. He returned to France upon the arrival of General **Jean de Lattre de Tassigny** in early 1951. De la Tour went on to serve in Algeria and was fiercely opposed to decolonization there. He was close to the *Organisation de l'armée secrète*. In 1962, he published a book entitled: *De l'Indochine à l'Algérie: le martyre de l'armée française*. *See also* ALGERIAN WAR; CHARLES LACHEROY; PARALLEL HIERARCHIES; PSYCHOLOGICAL WARFARE; REVOLUTIONARY WARFARE; ROGER TRINQUIER.

**BOYER, PIERRE JEAN GABRIEL (1888–1980).** Career colonial civil servant in Indochina, trained in law and graduated from the justice section of the **Colonial Academy** (*École coloniale*). He obtained his first colonial post in Indochina in 1914 serving as a substitute judge in Long Xuyen province in southern Vietnam. He volunteered to fight on the Western Front during World War I. He participated in the battle of the Somme in 1916 and was wounded by a gas attack which put him out of service for the rest of the war. He returned to Indochina in 1919 where he pursued a colonial career during the interwar years. He was the first president of the Appellate Courts in Saigon between 1938 and 1950. Although he retired in 1950, he remained a justice advisor to the French high commissioner for Indochina **Jean de Lattre de Tassigny**.

**BRAZZAVILLE CONFERENCE (30 JANUARY–8 FEBRUARY 1944).** French conference organized by the *Comité français de Libération nationale* in early 1944 to define the postwar direction of French colonial policy. World War II had not only transformed the world and France, but it had also unleashed tremendous change throughout European empires. The French one was no exception. Colonial questions were no longer *chasses gardées*. The Americans had been closely following French colonial policy and President Franklin Roosevelt was so critical of French colonialism that he wanted to place Indochina under a trusteeship at the end of the war. All of these factors, combined with preparations to liberate France, explain why **Charles de Gaulle** approved this colonial conference held in Brazzaville in early 1944. Attending the meeting were governor-generals mainly from Africa (Indochina was still occupied by the Japanese and run by Vichy) and the representatives of the Provisional French Consultative Assembly. It was a very French affair, however: No "colonized" person directly participated in the meeting. But Gaullists knew they had to rethink their colonial policy as the war entered its final decisive phase. One of the architects of the conference, **Henri Laurentie**, felt that France had to adopt a "liberal policy" if the French were to maintain their sovereignty against rapidly emerging nationalist elites contesting it from within the Empire. The key concession made at Brazzaville sought to maintain French sovereignty by moving the Empire away from the principle of assimilation and towards federal and liberal ones. Federalism would accord more autonomy to the restless colonized, but would still allow the French remain in charge of the Empire. In July 1944, de Gaulle declared in Washington that colonial federalism was now French policy, adding that the federal idea would be particularly important for Indochina. While Gaullists claimed French colonial policy was "liberal", in the end, as historian Martin Shipway has shown, "the Brazzaville document was hardly innovative, lacking even some of the audacity shown by Vichy colonial decision-makers". The final recommendations issued by the conference ruled out all possibility of decolonization or national independence. Vietnamese nationalists, such as **Ho Chi Minh**, were not impressed by the document. This was especially true following the Japanese overthrow of French colonial rule in Indochina. *See also* CHARLES DE GAULLE; *COUP DE FORCE* OF 9 MARCH 1945; DECLARATION ON INDOCHINA; INDOCHINESE COMMUNIST PARTY; INDOCHINESE FEDERATION; PAUL MUS; LEON PIGNON.

**BRÉBISSON (DE), MICHEL MARIE RENÉ (1905–1991).** Graduated from the *École spéciale militaire de Saint-Cyr* in 1926, in the same class as **Jean Boucher de Crèvecoeur** and **Edmond Jouhaud**. Between 1926 and 1939, de Brébisson served in the Empire, including Indochina between 1937 and 1939. After being taken prisoner during the fall of France in 1940 and then released, he transferred to North Africa and eventually joined Free French forces there. A colonel, he arrived in **Saigon** in early November 1945 and took part in military operations against the **Democratic Republic of Vietnam's** southern forces in Gia Dinh, Go Vap, and areas in central Vietnam all located below the **16th parallel**. He commanded the *Régiment d'infanterie coloniale métropolitaine* in Indochina until he returned to France in early September 1946. There he served in the colonial branch of the General Staff of the National Defense (1947–1949). He returned to Indochina in May 1950 and integrated the 153rd company of the General Headquarters of the General Chiefs of Staff of the French Armed Forces in Indochina. Back in France in September 1951, he served as the personal chief of staff to **Jean Letourneau**, the minister in charge of relations with the **Associated States of Indochina**, and his successor state secretaries **Marc Jacquet** and **Edouard Frédéric-Dupont**. In July 1953, de Brébisson joined the staff of Jacquet, state secretary to the Council Presidency in charge of relations with the Associated States of Indochina. In the early 1950s, de Brébisson made several official trips to the United States concerning, among other things, the war in Indochina. In 1954, he took part in the French delegation to the **Geneva Conference**, working as chief of staff for the state secretary to the Associated States of Indochina. He was said to be one of the "essential architects of the negotiations" at the ground level in Geneva, working closely with his Vietnamese counterparts **Ta Quang Buu** and **Ha Van Lau.** He returned to Saigon for a final tour of duty, serving in the Franco-Vietnamese Delegation for the Central Military Mixed Commission for Vietnam. He was president of the commission. He returned definitively to Paris on 13 June 1955. *See also* DIEN BIEN PHU, BATTLE OF; GENEVA ACCORDS.

**BRINK, FRANCIS GERARD. (1893–1952).** American brigadier general who became the first director of the **Military Assistance Advisory Group** (MAAG) to Indochina on 10 October 1950. A graduate of Cornell University, he joined the army in 1917 and went on to serve extensively in Asia. He was a regimental commander in the Philippines between 1938 and 1941 before joining the China-Burma-India Theatre during World War II and was chief of the Operations Division of the South-East Asia Command between 1944 and 1945. He was promoted to brigadier general in 1944. Brink stayed on in Asia after the war serving at the headquarters of the U.S. army forces in China until 1946. Because of his extensive experience in Asia, he was named the first director of the MAAG in October 1950. He supervised the distribution of military assistance to the French and to a much lesser extent to the **Associated States of Indochina,** because of French efforts to limit his direct contacts with the Indochinese. Brink committed suicide on 24 June 1952 during a conference in Washington, D.C. on American aid to the French in Indochina. Major General **Thomas J. H. Trapnell** replaced him. *See also* AID, AMERICAN.

**BROHON, RAYMOND (1911–2002).** Graduate of Saint-Cyr in 1932 and officer in the French **Air Force** during the Indochina War. Brohon was an officer in the Air Force Chief of Staff between 1940 and 1942. In 1943, he fled by plane to England and joined the Free French forces, participating in the Allied bombing campaign against Germany in 1944 and 1945. Between 1949 and 1953, Brohon served in the French Delegation to the Permanent Group in Washington and followed the meetings on **North Atlantic Treaty Organization**. He also dealt with questions of American military aid to the French war effort in Indochina during this period. From late 1953 to May 1954, he transferred to General **Paul Ely**'s Chief of Staff for the Armed Forces in Indochina. In August 1954, Brohon became personal chief of staff to the state minister in charge of relations with the **Associated States of Indochina**, involved in the discussions on the **South-East Asia Treaty Organization**. He worked in this capacity until July 1955. *See also* AID, AMERICAN.

**BROTHERTON, ALEXANDER (ARCHIBALD, VAN TAN, 1919–).** Australian who served as a liaison for the **Democratic Republic of Vietnam**'s diplomatic mission based in Bangkok after World War II. Brotherton first worked as a printer in the New South Wales Government Printing Office. After serving in the Australian Infantry during World War II, he became involved in anti-colonialist and radical politics in Asia. In 1946, he was a member of the Committee for the Australian-Indonesian Association in Sydney. He worked in the *Vietnamese News Service* in Bangkok, teaching English and helping to run an English-language information service for the **Democratic Republic of Vietnam**. He accompanied **Le Hy** to Shanghai and then on to Moscow in 1948. *See also* AID, SOVIET; HOANG VAN HOAN; JOSEPH STALIN; TRAN NGOC DANH.

**BRUCE, DAVID KIRKPATRICK ESTE (1898–1977).** The son of a U.S. senator, Bruce left Princeton early in order to fight in World War I. The war ended before he could see action, but he stayed on in France to study the language and work for the American Embassy. He returned to the States, where he studied law and became successful in numerous business affairs. With the outbreak of World War II, he joined **William J. Donovan**'s team and participated in the creation of the **Office of Strategic Services** (OSS). From 1943 until the end of the war, he was in charge of OSS operations in Europe and rode with the first French Division when it entered Paris in 1944. In 1949, **Harry S. Truman** appointed him ambassador to France, a post he held until 1952 when he returned to Washington to serve as undersecretary of state. Bruce by his upbringing and service in Europe was much more sympathetic to the French position in the Indochina War. Like his predecessor **Jefferson Caffery**, he argued in favor of supporting the French position in light of American interests in Europe and backed French requests for material and political support from the United States. Bruce was involved in putting a positive spin on the **Bao Dai Solution** so that Washington would accept it. He was also instrumental in sidelining the Southeast Asia Division's attempts to pressure the French to make further concessions on the creation of a truly independent Vietnam capable of equaling the nationalist pull of the **Democratic Republic of Vietnam**. *See also* AID, AMERICAN; ASSOCIATED STATES OF INDOCHINA.

**BRUNET, FÉLIX (1913–1959).** Graduated from the Air Academy in Versailles in 1938 and fought in the brief Battle of France in 1940. In November 1942, he crossed over to the **Air Force** of the Free French forces when the Allies landed in North Africa and quickly distinguished himself as a fighter pilot. In 1945, he signed up for service in Indochina. Between October 1945 and August 1946, he served in the 1st Fighter Squadron in southern Vietnam as head of the Third Section of the General Staff. He joined the 2nd Squadron between August 1946 and September 1947 and yet another in October 1947, the Fighter Group ¼ Dauphiné. Named commander in 1948, he led the ***Groupements aériens tactiques*** for southern Vietnam between 1949 and 1951. Named lieutenant colonel, he assumed leadership in 1951 of the Air Base of Cat Bi in Haiphong. Besides flying combat and support sorties, he also became interested in the use of **helicopters** and their integration into combat and medical operations in Indochina. In northern Vietnam, he flew air and helicopter evacuation missions during the major battles of **Nghia Lo**, Phu Tho, **Vinh Yen**, **Na San,** and **Dien Bien Phu**. In 1954, he left Indochina for Northern Africa where he would play an important role in adapting helicopters to combat and medical evacuation missions during the **Algerian War.**

**BÙ NHÌN.** *See* VIỆT GIAN.

**BUIS, GEORGES PAUL GABRIEL (1912–1998).** Born in **Saigon**, Buis entered Saint-Cyr in 1932 and served in Lebanon until the outbreak of World War II. After distinguished service with Free French forces during World War II, he was named battalion leader and left for Indochina on 17 August 1945 as part of General **Philippe Leclerc**'s Second Armored Division (working in the *3ème Bureau*). Buis arrived in Saigon on 11 September 1945. He simultaneously served as interim head of the *Direction de la Police et de la* ***Sûreté*** *générale* in Saigon in 1945–46 before transferring to Morocco where he directed the Indigenous Affairs Service from August 1946.

**BUNCHHAN MOL (1914–?).** Author of a famous anti-colonial political tract, *Kuk Niyobay* (Political Prison). Little is known about his early life and education before World War II. During the Pacific War, he became politically active and drew the attention of Vichy authorities, who arrested him for his participation in protests demanding the release of Buddhist monks. Bunchhan Mol ended up in the famous colonial prison at **Poulo Condore** where he spent the rest of the war. He regained his freedom following the Japanese ***coup de force of 9 March 1945*** and returned to Cambodia and worked briefly as a bodyguard for **Son Ngoc Thanh** before taking refuge in Thailand. There, he joined **Khmer Issarak** units active in Battambang province. He returned to Cambodia with the signing of the Franco-Khmer accords in 1949 and French moves to accord greater independence to all three of the **Associated States of Indochina**. He joined the **Democrat Party** and was elected deputy to the National Assembly for Kandal province. He was, however, no ally of King **Norodom Sihanouk**. When Sihanouk seized power in 1953, Bunchhan found himself temporarily in prison as the Democrat Party came under fire. *See also* ROYAL CRUSADE FOR INDEPENDENCE.

**BUNUM CHAMPĀSAK (1911–1980).** Prominent Lao nationalist during the Indochina War. Born into the royal family of Champāsak, Bunum studied at the *École de Droit* in Vientiane and entered the Lao administration in 1934. In 1941, when the French ceded the Champāsak territories to the Thais under Japanese pressure, Bunum implored the French to recover this lost Lao territory. In 1943, he became deputy inspector for political affairs for southern Laos. The French let him go in 1944 for unclear reasons. Although he was not initially favorable to the restoration of the French protectorate, he supported the French anti-Japanese guerrillas in 1945 and the French reoccupation of all of Laos in 1946. He backed the signing of a Franco-Lao *modus vivendi* in August 1946, which laid the foundation for the creation of a new and unified Associated State of Laos, covering all of what had, until then, been a politically heterogeneous Laos, and elevating the King of Luang Phrabang to King of all of Laos. In exchange, Bunum Champasak obtained the title of general inspector of the Kingdom of Laos for life and became president of Lao King **Sīsāvangvong**'s Council in 1948. Bunum held the third rank in the protocol hierarchy of the Kingdom. With the creation of the Associated State of Laos in 1949, he became prime minister on 18 March 1949. He played a pivotal role in the dissolution of the **Lao Issara** government-in-exile in Thailand later that year and the return of most of its delegates to Laos. He also pushed for the full French decolonization of Laos via negotiations in the early 1950s. *See also* ASSOCIATED STATES

OF INDOCHINA; BAO DAI SOLUTION; LAO RESISTANCE GOVERNMENT.

**BURCHETT, WILFRED (1911–1983).** Far Left Australian war correspondent whose articles and book on the **Democratic Republic of Vietnam** (DRV), *North of the Seventeenth Parallel* (1956), provided one of the earliest English-language accounts of the "other side". He worked as a foreign correspondent during World War II, providing one of the first Western accounts of the devastation of the Hiroshima nuclear blast. His interest in Asia at war carried into the postwar period. He covered the Panmunjom ceasefire talks in mid-1953 before deciding to visit northern Vietnam in early 1954 in preparation for his assignment to the upcoming **Geneva Conference**. Instead of heading for the French-controlled zones, like most Western correspondents, Burchett made his way to the Sino-Vietnamese border and, thanks at least in part to his politics, crossed into DRV territory in March 1954 just as the Vietnamese began their siege of the French camp at **Dien Bien Phu**. Burchett interviewed scores of Vietnamese leaders, cadres, officers, and even local people. He was one of the first Western journalists to interview **Ho Chi Minh** in the hills of northern Vietnam. Burchett was enamored by what he saw in the Vietnamese struggle against the French and their victory at Dien Bien Phu. He shared their anti-colonialism and hostility to French and American "imperialism". He also shared their view of a revolutionary communist world. Burchett returned to Vietnam in October 1954 when he entered **Hanoi** riding in a DRV military convoy. He would go on to write six books about Vietnam. In *North of the Seventeenth Parallel*, Burchett relied on his interviews to provide readers with one of the first inside accounts of the adversary. Burchett's sympathy for the DRV colored his account of it. Whereas the more anti-communist-minded **Bernard Fall** had no qualms in talking about the excesses committed by the DRV during the **land reform**, Burchett skips over such sensitive matters in his work, even though he was present above the **17th parallel** when sufficiently serious mistakes were committed to lead Ho Chi Minh to issue a public apology to the Vietnamese people a few years later. *See also* BOUDAREL AFFAIR; CINEMA; CROSSOVERS; CULTURE; EMULATION CAMPAIGNS; GEORGES BOUDAREL; HISTORY; INDOCTRINATION; INTELLECTUALS; LUCIEN BODARD; NOVELS; PSYCHOLOGICAL WARFARE; RECTIFICATION.

***BUREAU CENTRAL DE RENSEIGNEMENTS DE L'INDOCHINE* (BCRI)/ CENTRAL INTELLIGENCE OFFICE FOR INDOCHINA.** French intelligence service mainly in charge of counter-espionage activities during the Indochina War. A February 1947 protocol stipulated that this service should concentrate on spying, centralization, local exploitation, and transmission of intelligence to the headquarters of ***Service de documentation extérieure et de contre-espionnage*** and to the office of the French high commissioner in Indochina. The BCRI was particularly concerned with counter-espionage and dealing with foreign interference in Indochina. In 1951, the BCRI became the *Brigade de contre-espionnage opérationnel*. In 1953, this rather effective brigade was renamed *Détachement opérationnel de protection* and would later be redeployed during the **Algerian War.**

***BUREAU DES ARCHIVES TECHNIQUES* (BAT) / OFFICE OF TECHNICAL ARCHIVES.** Indochina-based, French intelligence service in charge of obtaining information of all kinds on foreign countries. It was particularly concerned with following, reporting, and analyzing events occurring in surrounding countries, such as China and Thailand. It integrated parts of the pre-existing *Service de renseignement intercolonial* and received and collated intelligence coming from other French external services on Indochina. The BAT was an organizational part of the ***Service de documentation extérieur et de contre-espionnage*** and was later known as Section 45.

***BUREAU FÉDÉRAL DE DOCUMENTATION* (BFDOC) / FEDERAL BUREAU OF INTELLIGENCE.** Created on 30 July 1946 and based in **Saigon**, the BFDOC was meant to be the main source of intelligence for the French high commissioner for Indochina **Georges Thierry d'Argenlieu**, in the months leading up to the outbreak of full-scale war on **19 December 1946**. The BFDOC was under the control of the director of the high commissioner's cabinet and was designed to centralize all intelligence and information coming from other services of the high commissioner, the commander-in-chief of the French armed forces, and from metropolitan sources such as the ***Service de documentation extérieure et de contre-espionnage***. Thierry d'Argenlieu's close collaborator, **Étienne Schlumberger**, headed up this intelligence service during the crucial period of 1946. Although its local stations were run by French administrators such as **Henri Monthéard** in **Hanoi** from December 1946, the BFDOC relied upon a phalanx of mainly Vietnamese bureaucrats to operate it across all of Indochina. The BFDOC disappeared when its services were officially absorbed by the ***Bureau technique de liaison et de coordination d'Extrême-Orient*** on 29 May 1949, which was a subordinate part of the Ministry of Overseas France's *Bureau technique de liaison et de coordination* created in August 1948.

**BUREAU FOR OVERSEAS CHINESE AFFAIRS FOR NAM BỘ (*Phòng Huê Kiều Vụ Nam Bộ*).** In 1948, the **Democratic Republic of Vietnam** (DRV) applied a new policy towards the large **overseas Chinese** population residing in southern Vietnam, symbolized by the creation of the Bureau for Overseas Chinese Affairs for Nam Bo *(Phong Hue Kieu Vu Nam Bo)* as well as a special committee to mobilize the Chinese population residing there in favor of the Vietnamese independence cause. The bureau and mobilizing committee targeted Chinese students, instructors, and workers. It also had responsibility for the Chinese political refugees fleeing repression in China and Malaya. The **Indochinese Communist Party**'s (ICP) Central Committee dispatched **Pham Dan** to the south to run this new bureau. He began work in 1949 in **collaboration** with the party's Territorial Committee for Nam Bo and its Director **Le Duan**. While the bureau took its administrative cues from the Resistance and Administrative Committee for Nam Bo, in reality the ICP's territorial committee was in charge of it and of policy towards the overseas Chinese in southern Vietnam. *See also* KHMER KROM; MINORITY ETHNIC GROUPS; PEOPLE'S REPUBLIC OF CHINA; REPUBLIC OF CHINA.

***BUREAU TECHNIQUE DE LIAISON ET DE COORDINATION D'EXTRÊME-ORIENT* (BTLCEO) / TECHNICAL OFFICE FOR THE LIAISON AND COORDINATION [OF INTELLIGENCE] IN THE FAR EAST.** Created on 29 May 1949, this French intelligence service effectively replaced the ***Bureau fédéral de documentation***. The BTLCEO was a part of the Ministry of Overseas France's *Bureau technique de liaison et de coordination* (BTLC), created in August 1948 and directed by Colonel Malplatte. The BTLCEO was designed to centralize all intelligence for the High Commissioner's office. It differed from its predecessor in that the high commissioner could now "guide" (*orienter*) and "harmonize" intelligence activities more freely. However, cooperation between the BTLCEO and the ***Service de documentation extérieure et de contre-espionnage*** station in Indochina was not always easy. Nor did the ***Affaire des généraux*** create a better climate for cooperation. While the creation of the ***Direction générale de documentation*** (DGD) in 1950 eclipsed the BTLCEO, the latter did not disappear entirely. Rather it continued to exist as a "research section" of the DGD in charge of centralizing and exploiting intelligence in cooperation with other services concerned with Indochina. The BTLCEO continued to report to the BTLC in the Ministry of Overseas France concerning questions related to metropolitan France and elsewhere in the colonies. However, by the time the Indochina War ended in 1954, it would not be an exaggeration to say that the BTLCEO had for all intents and purposes been absorbed by the DGD. *See also* PUBLIC SECURITY SERVICE; *SÛRETÉ FÉDÉRALE*.

**BURMA.** From the time of its independence from Britain in 1948, the Burmese Union leaders never hid their sympathy for the **Democratic Republic of Vietnam**'s (DRV) struggle for national independence against the French. In 1948, the Burmese government allowed the DRV to form a diplomatic delegation in Rangoon headed by **Tran Van Luan**. This mission became the DRV's most important opening to Asia following the closure of its main operations in Bangkok in 1951. In 1948, the Burmese also secretly dispatched a semi-official delegation to the DRV. It reached **Inter-Zone IV** in central Vietnam, where it delivered weapons and medicines. There were limits, however, to Burmese anti-colonial support, especially as the arrival of the **Cold War** with the **Korean War** in 1950 forced the Burmese government to take into account the communist core of the DRV and its revolutionary Indochinese ambitions in Buddhist oriented Laos and Cambodia. Moreover, like the Indians and the Indonesians, the Burmese leaders were often at odds with the communists in their own country. This conundrum came to a head in 1950 when the Burmese – like and in consultation with the Indians – decided to adopt a "non-aligned" tack by refusing to recognize either **Ho Chi Minh** or **Bao Dai**'s Vietnam. Nevertheless, the Burmese leaned to one side on anti-colonial grounds. In early September 1950, for example, the French ambassador to Rangoon, M. Plion-Bernier, was stunned to learn that the DRV's diplomatic representative to Burma, Tran Van Luan, had been implicitly accorded a kind of limited diplomatic status. On 2 September, during a celebration marking the fifth anniversary of the DRV's independence, Tran Van Luan hosted the Burmese foreign minister, Sao Hkun Hkio; the minister of Health, Myanaung U Tin; the minister of Commerce; and U Kyaw Myint, the permanent secretary of the Burmese Foreign Office among others. The local press related the event with considerable fanfare, including a photo of the foreign minister and Mr. Tran Van Luan together with glasses in their hands, pressed against the DRV flag. When the French ambassador fired off a sharply worded protest to the Burmese foreign minister, asking how Burma could accord such recognition to France's enemy and Bao Dai's competitor, Burma's minister of Internal Affairs explained that the Burmese government sympathized with other people striving for national independence in Southeast Asia. Chinese statesman and diplomat, **Zhou Enlai**, understood the importance of not alienating these newly decolonizing, non-communist yet anti-colonialist states in Asia. During the **Geneva Conference**, he made a point of stopping over in New Delhi and Rangoon, where he met the Burmese leadership. He assured leaders of China's good intentions towards non-communist Southeast Asian nations and expressed his desire to see them refrain from joining the Americans in building a Southeast Asian security organization or alliance in opposition to China. In exchange, the Chinese promised not to try to export communism outside their own borders. Winning over the trust of the Burmese and the Indians was crucial to Zhou Enlai's bid to neutralize parts of non-communist Asia against the Americans at Geneva. The support the Burmese and the Indians accorded to Zhou Enlai at this time also explains how China was able to become a player in non-communist Asian affairs, as the invitation extended to Zhou to the Bandung Conference in 1955 made clear. Without Burmese, Indonesian, and Indian support in 1954 on Indochina, this would never have happened. *See also* INDIA; INDONESIA; NEUTRALIZATION OF INDOCHINA; NEHRU.

**BUTTINGER, JOSEPH A. (1907–1992).** American scholar of Austrian birth who became a leading authority on Vietnamese political history. In his youth, Buttinger served as a leader of Austria's Socialist Youth Movement and secretary of the Social Democratic Party. He opposed the Nazis when they came to power in Germany in 1933, and in 1938 had to flee Austria to Paris with his American wife when Hitler invaded the country and yet again to the United States on the eve of the German conquest of France in mid-1940. During World War II, he ran the International Rescue Committee to assist mainly European refugees fleeing the Nazis. His work with Vietnamese refugees during the 1950s led him into a life-long love affair with Vietnamese history. Not only did he create the *American Friends of Vietnam*, but he also published several books on Vietnam, including *The Smaller Dragon – A Political History* in 1958 and then a two-volume work in 1967 entitled, *Vietnam – A Dragon Embattled*, in which he analyzed Vietnamese history, including the Indochina War period. Together with **Ellen Hammer, Virginia Thompson, Philippe Devillers, Jean Lacouture,** and **Bernard Fall**, he was among the first to introduce modern Vietnam and the Vietnamese to an English-language readership. He was an early supporter of **Ngo Dinh Diem.** *See also* CULTURE; HISTORY; INTELLECTUALS; NOVELS.

**BỬU HỘI.** *See* NGUYỄN-PHƯỚC BỬU HỘI.

**BỬU LỘC**. *See* NGUYỄN-PHƯỚC BỬU LỘC.

**C**. Code letter used by the **Democratic Republic of Vietnam** strategists to refer secretly to Laos during the Indochina Wars.

**CADIÈRE, LÉOPOLD (1869–1955).** French missionary from the *Missions étrangères de Paris* (MEP), who spent most of his life in Vietnam. Born in Aix-en-Provence, he entered the seminary of the MEP in 1890 and was ordained in September 1892. He left for southern Vietnam in October of the same year. He would work there and in Hue for much of his career. He learned to speak Vietnamese flawlessly and published numerous studies on Vietnamese syntax, phonetics, linguistics, and history. Though he never held a university diploma, he was an accomplished and respected ethnographer, anthropologist, indeed one of Indochina's first and foremost scholars of Vietnam. He was also a very modest man. He founded on the eve of World War I the *Association des Amis du Vieux Huê*, and contributed and helped direct its *Bulletin des Amis du Vieux Huê* which would last from 1913 to 1944. Following the Japanese ***coup de force* of 9 March 1945**, he landed up in a Japanese concentration camp at Hue. Following the Japanese defeat, he resumed his work in the area. This did not last long, however. When war broke out between the French and the Vietnamese on **19 December 1946**, the **Democratic Republic of Vietnam** (DRV) took him into custody, along with six other priests, transferred him to Vinh and placed him under house arrest. While he was not intentionally maltreated, he spent over six years as a prisoner of the DRV. He received a personal letter from **Ho Chi Minh** at the start of the war, promising not to harm the priests. Cadière never responded. During his captivity, he wrote his memoirs, *Souvenirs d'un vieil Annamite.* Cadière regained his liberty on 11 June 1953, but refused to return to France. Weakened by his old age and internment, Cadière passed away on 6 July 1955 in Hue. He was buried in the cemetery of the seminary at Phu Xuan in central Vietnam. His passion for Vietnamese culture, customs, beliefs, and language mark his work as they did his life. *See also* CATHOLICS, EXODUS FROM NORTH; CATHOLICS IN VIETNAM AND THE WAR; CHRISTIANS AND OPPOSITION TO THE INDOCHINA WAR; LE HUU TU; PRISONERS OF WAR; VATICAN.

**CAFFERY, THOMAS JEFFERSON (1886–1974).** American career diplomat involved in policy-making towards Indochina during the war. Educated at Tulane University, Caffery joined the Foreign Service in 1910 and served in South America until World War II. Between 1944 and 1949, he served as ambassador to France in Paris, one of the first career diplomats to hold the post. Caffery was convinced that the economic recovery of France was vital to American interests in Europe as the **Cold War** intensified. Caffery, like his successor, **David Bruce**, opposed efforts by the Southeast Asian Division to force the French hand in Indochina. Caffery argued, ultimately successfully, that in light of wider European interests and the global nature of the Cold War, the United States should support the French **Bao Dai Solution.** He was convinced that **Bao Dai** would be able to shore up nationalist support. *See also* AID, AMERICAN; EUROPEAN DEFENSE COMMUNITY; NORTH ATLANTIC TREATY ORGANIZATION.

**CAILLAUD, ROBERT (1921–1995).** Son of a peasant soldier of World War I, Caillaud joined the French resistance in 1942 after graduating from Saint-Cyr (then transferred to Aix-en-Provence). He took part in the Alsace and German Campaigns. In early 1946, he briefly served in Indochina. He returned to Vietnam in January 1949 to serve as an assistant to **Marcel Bigeard**, organizing attacks against the army of the **Democratic Republic of Vietnam** (DRV). In February 1954, he returned to Indochina a third time and was parachuted over **Dien Bien Phu** on 6 April 1954, where he was taken prisoner on 8 May 1954. He regained his freedom in December 1954. *See also* INDOCTRINATION; PRISONER OF WAR; PSYCHOLOGICAL WARFARE.

**CALL TO NATIONAL RESISTANCE (*Lời Kêu Gọi Toàn Quốc Kháng Chiến*).** On 20 December 1946, in the wake of the outbreak of full-scale war between the French and the Vietnamese in **Hanoi** on the evening of the 19th, the president of the **Democratic Republic of Vietnam**, **Ho Chi Minh**, called upon the population to take up arms against the French. This call to arms effectively shifted the government's earlier policy of relying on negotiations, what the **Indochinese Communist Party** had referred to as a policy of "peace in order to advance" (*hoa de tien*), to an armed line. *See also* 19 DECEMBER 1946; BAC NINH; HAIPHONG.

**CAM LY, MASSACRE.** Refers to the French police force's execution of 20 Vietnamese prisoners in reprisal for the **Democratic Republic of Vietnam's** (DRV) killing of a French police officer in Dalat in May 1951. In this month, the DRV's Phan Nhu Thach Commando Unit apparently attempted to capture alive Victor Haasz, a ***métis*** working in the ***Sûreté fédérale*** in Dalat, in order to force the French to release Vietnamese political prisoners in custody there. When Haasz tried to flee, the commando ended up killing him on 11 May 1951. At 19H00, three hours after the shooting, local French authorities transferred 20 Vietnamese political prisoners into a truck and took them to a secret location located deep in the jungle near the Cam Ly creek. Of the 20 prisoners all were executed except for Nguyen Thi Lang, who miraculously survived nine gunshot wounds and wandered out of the woods to safety. This execution sparked an outcry of protest among Vietnamese, including Queen **Nam Phuong** herself, and revealed one of the more savage sides of the Indochina War. **Henri Jumeau**, the acting chief of the police in Dalat, was suspended and briefly jailed on 24 May 1951 for ordering the execution. Also arrested for organizing the mass execution was Tran Dinh Que, the mayor of Dalat. Le Xuan, who would become famous as the future sister-in-law to **Ngo Dinh Diem**, lived in Dalat at the time of the executions. She told the press that the entire affair showed that one Eurasian life equalled twenty Vietnamese lives and had it been a Frenchman, she added, forty Vietnamese would have had to die in exchange. Settler opinion disagreed radically. Europeans living in Dalat and elsewhere in Indochina were largely favorable to Jumeau. Settlers would have agreed, however, with Le Xuan when she noted that Dalat was no longer an "oasis of peace". It will, she concluded, "become a terrorized and unbreathable city like the other ones". One of the Associated State of Vietnam's most zealous anti-terrorist specialists was determined not to let that happen. On 24 June 1951, **Nguyen Vam Tam** personally reorganized the police services in Dalat and arrested the **Viet Minh** squad responsible for Haasz's murder. The **French Communist Party** did much to bring this massacre to the attention of the French public. *See also FRANÇAIS D'INDOCHINE*; HÉRAULT, MASSACRE; MY THUY, MASSACRE; PUBLIC OPINION; TORTURE.

**CAMBODIAN RESISTANCE GOVERNMENT.** As the French accelerated their efforts to create the **Associated States of Indochina** in 1948–1949, the **Democratic Republic of Vietnam** (DRV) countered by moving on their own revolutionary Indochinese state-building projects from April 1949. In April 1950, the Vietnamese presided over the creation of the Cambodian Resistance Government (*Chinh Phu Khang Chien*) and revamped the **Khmer Issarak** national front. With Chinese support now behind them, Vietnamese communists renewed their internationalist commitment to implementing an Indochinese revolution and supporting revolutionary states in opposition to those supported by the French and backed by the West. A ***métis***, **Son Ngoc Minh,** led this Cambodian resistance government. The DRV's attempts to get this Cambodian political entity admitted to the Geneva conference in 1954 met with stiff opposition from the French, British, and Americans as well as the Associated State of Cambodia led by **Norodom Sihanouk**. During the conference, the Chinese also backed away from the DRV's Indochinese pretensions, deciding to recognize the royal governments of Cambodia and Laos as the sole legitimate governments in these two countries. Following the signing of the **Geneva Accords**, the Vietnamese-backed Cambodian resistance government was disbanded and the revolutionary party faded away, leaving the field open to a different generation of Cambodian leaders, such as **Pol Pot** and **Ieng Sary.** *See also* INDOCHINESE COMMUNIST PARTY; INDOCHINESE FEDERATION; LAO RESISTANCE GOVERNMENT.

**CANAC, ANDRÉ (1902–1998).** This French sailor and longtime resident of **Saigon** became an outspoken critic of the French war in Indochina. In

1945, he created the *Groupe culturel marxiste* and founded the short-lived communist paper, *Lendemains*. Like **Louis Caput**, he had excellent relations with Vietnamese nationalist elites, all the while maintaining the respect of French political authorities. This explains why he often served as a useful intermediary for the French and the Vietnamese, especially at the outset of the Indochina War.

**CAO BẰNG, BATTLE OF.** Known as the battle of Le Hong Phong II to the Vietnamese or *Route coloniale 4* to the French, the battle of Cao Bang in October 1950 was linked to the rapidly changing international situation symbolized by the creation of the **People's Republic of China** (PRC) in October 1949. In January 1950, the PRC officially recognized the **Democratic Republic of Vietnam** (DRV). The Soviet Union and the rest of the communist camp followed suit. From May 1950, Chinese military aid and advisors began to cross into DRV territory. This combined Chinese military and diplomatic support effectively internationalized the Franco-Vietnamese war and changed the military nature of the conflict.

For the DRV, it was vital that a large swath of the northern border be opened in order to link the DRV directly to the communist bloc stretching from eastern Europe to southern China. On 7 February 1950, hardly a week after Moscow recognized the DRV, the Vietnamese army began operation Le Hong Phong I in an attempt to take control of Tai regions in northwestern Vietnam, and thereby link up with the Chinese in Yunnan province. It was a failure.

In consultation with Chinese advisors such as **Chen Geng**, General **Vo Nguyen Giap** began preparations to attack the French in the area of **Lang Son** and **Cao Bang** in order to create an opening further to the east. Thanks to the ***affaire des généraux***, Chinese and Vietnamese strategists knew that General **Georges Revers**, chief of the Combined Chiefs of Staff for the French Army, had made a fact-finding mission to Indochina in mid-1949 from which he had concluded that the French should not try to hold the northern border against a potential Chinese attack and should withdraw troops from Cao Bang and Lang Son. Rather than directly attacking French border posts in these two areas, Vo Nguyen Giap decided to wait until the French began withdrawing along vulnerable, narrow roads favorable to a Vietnamese attack.

When the French finally began to withdraw their troops on 3 October 1950 in two separate columns, Vo Nguyen Giap and Chen Geng ordered Vietnamese troops to attack the main French column as it withdrew to the east along *Route Coloniale 4* (RC4). Giap threw artillery and two regiments of the 308th division against the retreating troops. French efforts to relieve the column from Dong Khe and That Khe proved futile given the combination of the inhospitable terrain and the intensity of the Vietnamese attacks. Within two weeks, the DRV scored its first major battle victory over the French. The French lost some 7,000 men in this debacle, most of whom were taken **prisoners** by the Vietnamese army and marched off to camps. From this point, Chinese aid more easily entered DRV territory. The extension of the railway from Nanning to the border at Cao Bang only facilitated this process. This battle victory over the French emboldened the Vietnamese as Vo Nguyen Giap moved on plans for a General Counter Offensive. Within months the Vietnamese general was prepared to attack the delta.

At the international level, the French loss at Cao Bang coincided with the **Korean War** and the entry of Chinese troops into that war. The French and the Americans began to see the wars in Indochina and Korea as part of the same front designed to hold the line against Chinese communist expansion.

While many French strategists would turn to the United States for increased aid, others began to propose alternative solutions for ending the war. During a parliamentary debate on Cao Bang on 19 October 1950, the French Deputy **Pierre Mendès France** argued that the intensification of the Indochina War at Cao Bang had also coincided with the Allied decision to rearm West Germany. The French could not commit the increased numbers of troops and material needed to win in Indochina without undermining its ability to meet its **North Atlantic Treaty Organization** commitments and invest in an army capable of matching that of the West Germans. Mendès France said that either the French renew the draft, increase taxes and decolonize fully the **Associated States of Indochina** in order to win or else they should seek an honorable, negotiated solution to the war. Economically, he argued, the French could not operate on these two fronts simultaneously. The center right government of the time, the ***Mouvement républicain populaire***, preferred to carry on without resolving the problem of financing a war in Indochina and making good on military commitments to the defense of Western Europe.

It would take another three years before Mendès France got his chance to end the war along the lines he set out during the Cao Bang disaster of October 1950. Cao Bang had effectively made it clear that a new more intensive and expensive stage in the war had begun. *See also* AID, AMERICAN; AID, CHINESE; EMILE BOLLAERT; EUROPEAN DEFENSE COMMUNITY; FINANCIAL COST OF INDOCHINA WAR.

**CAO ĐÀI.** The word "Cao Dai" in Vietnamese evokes the supreme or elevated being, which brings peace, harmony, and salvation to the world. The Cao Dai faith is a syncretic, monotheistic religion, combining elements of Taoism, Buddhism, Confucianism, Christianity, and Humanism. The full name of the religion in Vietnamese is *Dai Dao Tam Ky Pho Do*. It is hierarchically structured and based organizationally upon the model of the Roman Catholic Church. A "Pope" (*Ho Phap*) thus leads the Cao Dai Church, with its "Holy" See in Tay Ninh province along the southern Vietnamese-Cambodian border.

The Cao Dai faith emerged in the wake of World War I thanks to the initiative of a group of Vietnamese civil servants, landowners, and, increasingly, peasants attracted by the messianic message of the religion in a time of rapid socio-economic transformation. In 1926, Le Van Trung became leader of the Cao Dai faith. One of the prime movers of the Cao Dai faith, however, was **Pham Cong Tac**. A civil servant in Phnom Penh, he resigned from his post in 1928 and returned to Tay Ninh to help run the rapidly emerging Cao Dai movement with Le Van Trung. Following the death of the latter in 1935, Pham Cong Tac extended his influence and control over the movement's disciples and organization. In 1938, he became the movement's supreme spiritual leader and set it on an increasingly political tack.

At the outset of the Japanese occupation of French Indochina, Pham Cong Tac's suspected links to the Japanese and perceived attempts to create an autonomous religious state and militia led the French to arrest and deport him to Madagascar in 1941. During this time, he rubbed shoulders in colonial cells there with the likes of **Le Gian** and **Tran Hieu**, the future directors of the **Democratic Republic of Vietnam**'s (DRV) security and intelligence services, respectively. The British MI6 secured the release of Le Gian and Tran Hieu to work for Allied secret services against the Japanese, but Pham Cong Tac's ties to the Japanese kept him behind bars throughout the course of the Pacific War. Meanwhile, the Cao Dai leadership in southern Indochina continued to politicize and militarize the movement in its cooperation with the Japanese.

Following the Pacific War, the Cao Dai briefly flirted with the forces of the DRV in a loosely knit anti-colonialist coalition. However, the faith's leaders were wary of the DRV's communist core and above all of the idea of integrating their politico-military forces into the DRV's national fold. Determined to divide the DRV's forces, the French saw an opportunity. They returned Pham Cong Tac from Madagascar to southern Vietnam on 22 August 1946 on the condition that he ally his disciples and their military forces with the French and their non-communist Vietnamese partners. On 8 January 1947, Pham Cong Tac signed an accord with the French along these lines and in April–May 1947, a large part of the Cao Dai forces began crossing over to the French side triggering violent clashes with the DRV's forces. The Commander-in-Chief of the DRV's armed forces in the south, **Nguyen Binh**, would not tolerate what he saw as high treason in a war of national liberation. **Civil war** among Vietnamese had effectively begun within the confines of the colonial conflict.

In contrast to the interwar period, the French actively militarized and politicized this religious movement in order to hold on colonially. That said, relations between the French and the Cao Dai were never smooth. Following a rocky meeting between Pham Cong Tac and General **Jean de Lattre de Tassigny**, who insisted that the Cao Dai leader integrate his forces into the national **army of the Associated State of Vietnam**, Pham Cong Tac terminated his **collaboration** with the French and in March 1952 declared himself supreme commander of a Cao Dai Army. On 19 May 1954, following the French defeat at **Dien Bien Phu**, Pham Cong Tac signed a protocol accepting the integration of the Cao Dai forces into the Associated State's army. However, it was only in 1955, following violent clashes with the national army commanded by **Ngo Dinh Diem**, that the Cao Dai ceded most of their politico-military activities to concentrate on their religious ones.

As the third largest religion in Vietnam today, the Cao Dai faith counts two to three million members inside and outside of Vietnam. *See also* BINH XUYEN; CAO TRIEU PHAT; CATHOLICS IN VIETNAM AND THE WAR;

HOA HAO; LE HUU TU; MINORITY ETHNIC GROUPS; *PAYS MONTAGNARDS DU SUD* (PMS); TRAN QUANG VINH; TRINH MINH THE; VATICAN.

**CAO ĐĂNG CHIẾM (SÁU HOÀNG, BẢY CHIẾM, 1921–2007).** One of the **Democratic Republic of Vietnam**'s (DRV) most important security officials working in southern Vietnam during the Indochina and Vietnam Wars, rising to the rank of a senior lieutenant general. Born into a poor family in My Tho (Tien Giang) province in southern Vietnam, Cao Dang Chiem moved to **Saigon** in search of work and became active in labor politics there by the outset of World War II. In August 1945, he supported communist attempts to take power in Saigon, joined the DRV, and was instrumental in creating the south's first police service, the National Defense Guard (*Quoc Gia Tu Ve Cuoc*). He served as its deputy director, drawing upon his intimate knowledge of Saigon-Cholon. In early 1946, on the orders of the **Indochinese Communist Party**'s (ICP) newly revamped Territorial Committee for Nam Bo (*Xu Uy Nam Bo*), he became director of the newly created **Public Security Services** (*Cong An*) for southern Vietnam. During this time, he worked closely with **Le Duan**, **Nguyen Van Linh**, and especially **Pham Hung** and **Mai Chi Tho** on security matters, including the use of the police in suppressing enemies of the DRV and in consolidating the party's control over the southern population and state. On 12 December 1946, Cao Dang Chiem joined the ICP, and in April 1947 the powerful Party Committee for Saigon (later renamed the Saigon-Gia Dinh special zone). Between 1950 and 1954, he headed the Public Security's southern section in charge of the eastern region. At the end of the Indochina War in 1954, he remained in the south and from December helped run a newly created southern intelligence network designed to follow developments in the south – the southern Party Territorial Committee's Research Branch Responsible for Following the Enemy Situation (*Ban Nghien Cuu Dich Tinh Xu Uy*). He was responsible for providing security to the committee's leadership in general and to that of Le Duan in particular. Together with **Tran Quoc Huong**, he took over as the case officer for the DRV's famous spy **Pham Xuan An**, who provided **Hanoi** with intelligence on the **Republic of Vietnam** throughout the entire American war in Vietnam. *See also* ANTOINE SAVANI; MARCEL BAZIN; NGUYEN VAN TAM; *SÛRETÉ GÉNÉRALE*; TRAN QUOC HOAN.

**CAO PHÁ (NGUYỄN THẾ LƯƠNG, 1920–2006).** Major general in the Vietnamese Army and specialist in clandestine, intelligence operations during the Indochina War. Born into a mandarin family in Quang Nam province, Cao Pha received a colonial primary and secondary education. His father worked in the Indochinese Public Works department in central Vietnam and Cambodia. During World War II, Cao Pha studied at the Faculty of Agriculture at the Indochinese University in **Hanoi**, where he also became involved in nationalist politics. In early 1945, he apparently joined the **Viet Minh**. Following the Japanese ***coup de force* of 9 March 1945** overthrowing the French, Cao Pha joined classmates and enrolled in a new "Front Line Youth School", created in Hue by **Ta Quang Buu**. On 29 August 1945, he helped capture a team of French paratroopers who had landed outside Hue. In September 1945, he was one of two bodyguards who escorted **Bao Dai** to Hanoi to meet **Ho Chi Minh**. He then returned to Hue where he became chief of Special Affairs (*Ban Dac Vu*), meaning intelligence operations, for the Tri Thien Sub Region. Cao Pha was specifically responsible for espionage and counter-espionage activities. In March 1946, he returned to Hanoi and was dispatched to Son Tay to study as a cadre in Class I at the Tran Quoc Tuan Military Academy. He graduated in December 1946 and, following the outbreak of full-scale war on **19 December 1946**, transferred to the Northwest Region and was appointed commander of the 108th Battalion/97th Regiment under the leadership of **Le Trong Tan**. In early 1948, Cao Pha was recalled to the **General Staff** Headquarters in the hills of northern Vietnam, where he served from February 1948 to early 1950. Adopting the code name "Cao Pha", in early 1950 he transferred to work in the Chief of Office 2 or Military Intelligence in the General Staff and became a ranking officer in the new Military Intelligence Department (*Cuc Quan Bao*), created sometime in late 1950 or early 1951. He served as deputy chief of the Military Intelligence Department for a number of major battles, including the battles of **Cao Bang** in 1950 and **Dien Bien Phu** in 1954. Following the signing of the **Geneva Accords** in 1954, he was sent to the Hanoi area to supervise the collection of intelligence on French withdrawal plans and the dispatch of espionage agents and case officers to South Vietnam to infiltrate the new non-communist, postcolonial state emerging there. After serving as deputy director of the General Staff's Military Intelligence Department (also called the Research Department – *Cuc Nghien Cuu*) for many years, in 1967 Cao Pha was appointed as deputy commander of the People's Army's newly-formed Sapper Branch, a position in which he served until the end of the war in 1975.

**CAO THẮNG.** *See* ĐẶNG VĂN SUNG.

**CAO TRIỆU PHÁT (1888–1956).** Born in southern Vietnam, he traveled to France and participated in World War I. Upon his return to French Indochina in 1919, he agitated for greater press freedom and took increased interest in social and political issues. Cao Trieu Phat founded the Worker's Party (*Parti travailliste*) in November 1926 and published two newspapers, *L'Ère nouvelle* then the *Nhut Tan Bao.* In 1928, he joined the **Cao Dai** politico-religious sect. Between 1930 and 1945, he was very active in the development of the Cao Dai faith and social activities, especially in his home province of Bac Lieu. On 23 August 1945, following the Japanese defeat, he helped nationalists take over the province before serving as a member of the Committee for National Liberation in Bac Lieu (*Uy Ban Giai Phong Dan Toc Tinh Bac Lieu*) and as a member of the Provincial Branch of the **Viet Minh** nationalist front in Bac Lieu (*Tinh Bo Mat Tran Viet Minh*). He donated land and money to the Viet Minh cause and urged his followers to support the nationalist cause of the **Democratic Republic of Vietnam** (DRV). In June 1946, the pro-Viet Minh Cao Dai selected him as their deputy to the DRV's National Assembly. Whereas many of the main Cao Dai leaders would break violently with the southern DRV forces in 1947, Cao Trieu Phat continued to work with the government and sent a telegram of support to **Ho Chi Minh** in September 1947 to confirm it publicly. Between 1947 and 1954, Cao Trieu Phat served as an advisor to the Resistance and Administrative Committee for Nam Bo and joined the **Lien Viet** nationalist front. The **Indochinese Communist Party** inducted him into its ranks in 1948 as he became the main leader of the pro-communist Cao Dai forces. In 1954, following the division of Vietnam into two states during the **Geneva Conference**, Cao Trieu Phat relocated to northern Vietnam.

**CAO VĂN KHÁNH (1917–1980).** Senior military officer active in central Vietnam during the Franco-Vietnamese war. He was a teacher of history by profession and apparently relished his work. Cao Van Khanh was an accomplished **scout** during World War II and a dedicated nationalist. This served him well when he joined the Viet Minh in 1945 and enlisted in the **Democratic Republic of Vietnam's** (DRV) fledgling army. Cao Van Khanh received military training in the Front Line Youth Military School (*Truong Quan Su Thanh Nien Tien Tuyen*) in Hue. Thanks to his scouting and military experience, he became vice chairman of the liberation army committee for Hue. Although he was very close to the ranking communist military leaders **Nguyen Chi Thanh** and **Nguyen Chanh**, Cao Van Khanh refused to join the **Indochinese Communist Party**, explaining that his nationalism was sufficient and that he did not want to get involved in politics. In October 1945, he served as platoon leader and led a military delegation from Binh Dinh province. Between December 1946 and November 1948, he was the military commander for **Zone** V (*Khu V*). In late 1948 he transferred to northern Vietnam and played an important role in the creation of the 308th **division**. Until 1954, despite not being a party member, he served as deputy divisional commander of 308th Division taking part in the battles of **Cao Bang** and **Dien Bien Phu** among others. He married **Nguyen Thi Ngoc Toan** days after the guns went silent. The ceremony was held on the battlefield of Dien Bien Phu itself. *See also* EXPERIENCE OF WAR; INTELLIGENCE SERVICE; LOVE AND WAR.

**CAO VĂN THỈNH (1902–1987).** Ranking educator during the war against the French. He studied in the Teacher's Training School in **Saigon** and then in the Higher Teachers' Training School in **Hanoi**, where he became involved in political activities in the 1930s and early 1940s with **Dang Thai Mai** and **Pham Thieu.** In 1945, Cao Van Thinh led the **Vanguard Youth League** (*Thanh Nien Tien Phong*) in Ben Tre and helped take over the province after the Allied defeat of the Japanese in August 1945. In 1946, Cao Van Thinh traveled to Hanoi where he became minister of Education in the **Democratic Republic of Vietnam** (DRV). In 1952, he returned to southern Vietnam and was elected to the Resistance and Administrative Committee for Nam Bo and the Lien Viet Committee for Nam Bo (*Uy Ban Lien Viet Nam Bo*).

He helped develop the educational system during the war in southern zones. One of his main tasks was reducing illiteracy in order to strengthen the efficiency of state institutionalization. At the end of the war, he repatriated to northern Vietnam, where he served in the Department for Southern Vietnam in the DRV's Ministry of Education. He later served as consul general to Cambodia and **Indonesia**.

**CAO VĂN VIÊN (1921–2008).** Born in Laos, Cao Van Vien became a ranking officer in the **army of the Associated State of Vietnam**. He graduated from the *Lycée Pavie* in Vientiane in 1940 as the Japanese entered Indochina. Little is known about his whereabouts during World War II. During the Indochina conflict, he served in the **French Union** forces as a non-commissioned interpreter-translator (French-Vietnamese). In 1949, the French selected him as one of the first NCOs for training as an officer in the emerging Vietnamese national army. He entered the *Centre de perfectionnement de sous-officiers* in Vung Tau. Following graduation, he worked in the army's recruiting office and, in 1950, moved on to work in the press office of the department of Defense in the Associated State of Vietnam. In 1952, Cao Van Vien continued to rise in the army, studying at the **Hanoi** Command and Staff School with the likes of **Nguyen Van Thieu**. He then assumed command of the 10th Battailon and led troops in battles against the **Democratic Republic of Vietnam**. In early 1954, Cao Van Vien served as assistant chief of staff for Intelligence and for Logistics in the 3rd Military Zone before becoming commanding officer of the 56th infantry battalion at the end of the Indochina War.

**CAPA, ROBERT (ENDRE ERNO FRIEDMANN, "BANDI", 1913–1954).** World-renowned Hungarian war photographer killed during the Indochina War. Capa fled from Fascism and anti-Semitism to France in 1933. Thanks to the support of French photographers Henri Cartier-Bresson and André Kertész, Capa became a successful freelance photographer. Léon Trotsky, in exile in Denmark in 1932, had served as the subject of his first published picture. Capa made his name, however, as one of the 20th century's greatest war photographers, covering the Spanish **Civil War**, and both the European and Asian theatres of World War II. He landed with soldiers on the Normandy beaches in 1944 and provided close-up photos of men in the heat of battle. As he put it famously: "If your photographs aren't good enough, you're not close enough." He became a naturalized American citizen in 1946 and changed his name to Robert Capa. In 1947, he joined Cartier-Bresson and others to create the international photo agency *Magnum* in Paris and New York and teamed up with John Steinbeck to write a book on their experiences in the Soviet Union, *A Russian Journal*. In the postwar period, Capa continued to cover major conflicts, such as the first Israeli-Palestinian war of 1948. He traveled to Indochina to cover the violent endgame of French colonial rule in Vietnam for *Life* magazine. He died there in May when he stepped on an antipersonnel mine in the Red River delta. Upon learning of Capa's death, Lieutenant Colonel Jacques Navarre, son of the famous general of the same surname, uttered: *C'est l'Indochine, monsieur*, as he moved by the place where Capa had been resting safely just a few hours earlier. *See also* CINEMA; CULTURE; NOVELS.

**CAPLY, MICHEL.** *See* JEAN DEUVE.

**CAPUT, LOUIS (1895–1954).** Primary school teacher, socialist militant, and ardent supporter of the nationalist cause of the **Democratic Republic of Vietnam** (DRV) during the Indochina War. Caput began teaching in Indochina in the 1930s. He was particularly active in **Hanoi**, where he lived, worked, and created in 1937 the Indochinese branch of the ***Section française de l'Internationale ouvrière*** (SFIO) or the French socialist party. Caput was also an active **Freemason**. He advocated the opening of the SFIO's and Freemasonry's doors to the Vietnamese and was instrumental in admitting **Hoang Minh Giam** – future minister in the DRV – to the SFIO. During the Popular Front period, Caput befriended many Vietnamese nationalists and radicals, including **Truong Chinh**, the future general secretary of the **Indochinese Communist Party** (ICP). During the Vichy period, Caput was widely known to be favorable to the Free French cause, and served a short prison sentence in the early 1940s as a result before Governor General Jean Decoux released him. Caput maintained his links to Vietnamese and French nationalists opposed to the Japanese and served as the go-between for a secret meeting between Free French and Truong Chinh in December 1944 in Hanoi.

While nothing tangible came of the meeting before the Japanese ***coup de force*** **of 9 March 1945** brought down French Indochina, Caput's interwar links to and knowledge of leading Vietnamese nationalists were real. During the Japanese occupation, he also put a number of leftist European soldiers in the **Foreign Legion** such as **Erwin Börchers** in touch with the leaders of the ICP.

By the end of World War II, Caput was clearly favorable to the decolonization of Vietnam and considered one of the most knowledgeable specialists of Vietnamese questions at the time. Like **Paul Mus**, Caput felt that the French could work with the DRV. To this end, he played a behind-the-scenes role in negotiations on the **Accord of 6 March 1946**, working with **Léon Pignon** and **Jean Sainteny**. Caput attended the first **Dalat Conference** held in April 1946 and traveled to Paris to help prepare and participate in the **Fontainebleau conference** designed to follow up on the March accords. During this time, Caput supported Hoang Minh Giam's efforts to create a separate **Vietnamese Socialist Party** as a branch of the SFIO. He lobbied the French Freemason headquarters (*le grand Orient*), urging his listeners in a 17 June 1946 speech to recognize Vietnamese independence aspirations and underscored the need to reach a peaceful entente with the DRV. His attempts to influence the SFIO fell upon deaf ears in France, however. The Socialist minister of Overseas France, **Marius Moutet**, blocked Caput from addressing the Party's congress and prevented him from serving as a negotiator during the Fontainebleau conference. Caput strongly condemned French efforts to create a separate Cochinchinese government and above all to use the former Emperor **Bao Dai** to lead a pro-French, counter-revolutionary government.

By the late 1940s, with the intensification of the war, Caput's views began to win support within the socialist party. In early 1949, the SFIO authorized him to represent the party in southern Vietnam and to establish contact with **Ho Chi Minh** with a view to finding a negotiated settlement to the war. In 1952, Caput regained control of the SFIO's Indochinese branch and successfully imposed his views before returning to France in 1953, where he continued to support a peaceful solution to the war in Indochina. In that year, he published *Pour le rétablissement de la paix en Indochine*.

**CARAVELLE.** The official newspaper of the French **Expeditionary Corps** during the Indochina War.

**CARLE, PIERRE LOUIS JOSEPH (1921–1974).** He tended to Indochinese laborers in France during World War II before being transferred to Indochina after the war to serve as cabinet chief to the political counselor to the high commissioner for Indochina between 1945 and 1947. He worked as a secretary to the **Dalat conference** of 1946.

**CARPENTIER, MARCEL MAURICE (1895–1977).** Graduated from Saint-Cyr in 1913, he saw action during all of World War I. In 1915, at the age of 20, he was the youngest captain in the French army and was wounded several times before the war ended. During the interwar period, he served in Brazil and the Middle East, becoming a commanding officer in 1933. In 1940, Vichy sent him to Algiers. In 1942, with the Allied landing in North Africa, Carpentier crossed over to Free French forces and served in Algiers and Italy as chief of staff for General **Alphonse Juin** and, in 1944, General **Jean de Lattre de Tassigny**. In 1946, Carpentier was promoted to lieutenant general. After serving in Morocco, he landed in Indochina in December 1948 as senior commanding officer of Armed Forces in Indochina. It was a difficult period for him. He was more at ease in North Africa than in Indochina. His reports on the deteriorating military situation in Indochina and requests for increased aid fell upon increasingly deaf ears in Paris. In December 1949, he informed President **Vincent Auriol** that "military victory was no longer possible, only a political solution" could bring the war to an end. Unlike **Marcel Alessandri**, Carpentier did not believe that attacking the forces of the **Democratic Republic of Vietnam** (DRV) on their own terrain was realistic. Like General **Georges Revers** and **Léon Pignon**, he favored pulling troops away from the vulnerable northern border to consolidate positions in the Red River delta from which the French would hold the overwhelming advantage in any battle with the adversary. Carpentier contented himself with continuing "**pacification**" actions. The fiasco of the French retreat during the battle of **Cao Bang** was in part a defeat for Carpentier and his High Command. Thanks to General **Alphonse Juin**, Carpentier was able to avoid humiliation and rapidly transferred out of Indochina in December 1950. Between March and December 1951, he served as one of the deputy chiefs of the General Staff under the direction of General **Dwight D. Eisenhower**, Supreme Commander of Allied Forces in Europe. In August 1950, Carpentier made an official address over *Radio France Asie* in favor of talks on a prisoner exchange with the DRV.

**CASSAIGNE, MARIE PIERRE JEAN, MGR (1895–1973).** French missionary active in Vietnam during the Indochina War. At the outbreak of World War I, he volunteered for military service and witnessed the battle of Verdun. Released from the army in 1919, he entered the Seminary of the *Missions étrangères de Paris* a year later. Ordained in 1925, he left for Indochina shortly thereafter. He first worked in southern Vietnam before transferring to the Highlands in central Vietnam to create a missionary post in Djirling. He proselytized among the minority groups in the area and took care of a leper colony. After spending the 1930s in France, in 1941 he was named Bishop of **Saigon**, much to his surprise. He would remain in Indochina for the next 15 years, organizing aid and providing relief to those imprisoned by the Japanese after their ***coup de force* of 9 March 1945** and to those suffering due to the Indochina War. In 1948, he told an *Associated Press* correspondent that he was against atrocities committed by the French **Expeditionary Corps**, irking French authorities. Suffering from leprosy himself, he was relieved of his duties in 1955 and returned to "his" leper colony in Djirling where he died in 1973 and is buried.

**CASTRIES (DE), CHRISTIAN MARIE FERDINAND DE LA CROIX (1902–1991).** Descending from a long line of military leaders, Christian de Castries is closely associated with the tragic French debacle at **Dien Bien Phu** in 1954. A graduate from the Cavalry Academy of Saumur in 1926, he took part in the failed French campaign of 1940. Taken prisoner by the Germans, he escaped in 1941 and joined the French resistance. As a major in the liberation army, he led troops in the Italian, French, and German campaigns. A squadron leader, he arrived in Indochina in November 1946. Between 1947 and early 1949, he led the *2ème Régiment de marche de spahis marocains d'Extrême-Orient* in southern Vietnam. During this time, he served as commander of the sub-sector of Cai Be, then commander of the sector of Vinh Long in southern Vietnam. He made a second tour of duty in Indochina when he returned to **Saigon** to take command in December 1950 of the *Groupement des Tabors marocains* in the Red River delta. He was wounded in January 1951 during the battle of **Vinh Yen**. On 1 November 1951, he took command of the *Groupe Mobile no.1* until July 1952. Made colonel, he returned to Indochina for a third tour of duty in August 1953 at the head of the *3ème Division militaire territoirale.* On 8 December 1953, he took command of the position of Dien Bien Phu from General **Jean Gilles**. The French sought to block the **Democratic Republic of Vietnam**'s (DRV) attempts to attack Laos through the northwest and welcomed the chance to take on the Vietnamese in a set piece battle, confident that their superior artillery and airpower would crush the enemy. The battle of Dien Bien Phu began on 13 March. A month into the fighting, the French high command made Christian de Castries a brigadier general. On 7 May 1954, the French camp fell to the DRV in a humiliating defeat for the **Expeditionary Corps**. The next day, de Castries was formally taken prisoner and marched off to an enemy prison. He regained his freedom on 4 September 1954. He asked to leave the army in 1959, after commanding the 5th Armored Division in Germany. He died in 1991 at the age of 88. Until his death, he refused to revisit his role in the battle of Dien Bien Phu.

**CASUALTIES, INDOCHINA WAR.** Since the end of the Indochina War, the **Democratic Republic of Vietnam** (DRV), nor its successor since 1976, the Socialist Republic of Vietnam, have ever revealed publicly the total casualies suffered by their armed forces between 1945 and 1954. The French have advanced the rough figure of 500,000 Vietnamese killed during the Indochina War, apparently including civilians.[1] More methodically sound estimations put the number at 300,000.[2] No reliable figures exist for the number of wounded,

1. It would appear that the original source for this widely cited number of 500,000 is Ngo Van Chieu's memoirs, *Journal d'un combatant viet minh,* Paris: Editions du Seuil, 1955, p. 106. How Ngo Van Chieu, an officer in the DRV's army, reached this number is never explained.

2. See Bethany Lacina and Nils Petter Gleditsch, 'Monitoring Trends in Global Combat: A New Dataset of Battle Deaths', *European Journal of Population* 21, no. 2 (2005), 145–166. Michael Clodfelter puts the number of killed at an estimated 175,000 and estimates that 300,000 Vietnamese were wounded during the war. He also suggests that the numbers of civilian "losses" numbered in the "hundreds of thousands". Michael Clodfelter, *Warfare and Armed Conflicts: A Statistical Reference to Casualty and Other Figures, 1618–1991, vol. II (1900–1991),* Jefferson, North Carolina: McFarland & Company, Inc., 1992, p. 1122.

**missing in action**, or deserters on the DRV side. Nor do we have statistics on gender, age, or the social origins of those killed.[3] More reliable statistics exist for **French Union** forces during the Indochina War. Casualty figures were first published in the French Fourth Republic's *Journal officiel* of 12 January 1955 and have been revised by specialists since then. According to the official statistics published in 1955, some 20,700 French nationals ("of all origins", including the "Metropolitan colonial army") died and 22,000 were wounded; **African troops** (coming from French "North Africa" and "Black Africa") accounted for 15,200 deaths and 13,900 wounded; the **Foreign Legion** suffered 11,600 deaths and 7,200 wounded; the "regular indigenous" (*autochtones réguliers* – mainly ethnic Vietnamese) lost 27,700 men and 21,200 wounded; and the indigenous auxiliary troops (*supplétifs*) and the armies of the **Associated States of Indochina** together accounted for 17,600 deaths and 12,100 wounded. In all, according to these 1955 official statistics, the armed forces of the French Union lost 92,800 individuals and 76,400 wounded. According to French military historian Michel Bodin, of the soldiers fighting in the French Union forces who died because of combat and non-combat related reasons, as well as the missing in action, 18,015 were French soldiers coming from the metropole (*troupes métropolitaines*); 10,320 were **North Africans** (coming mainly from Algeria and Morocco); 2,753 Africans (from French colonial Africa); 9,235 Legionnaires; 29,228 indigenous regulars (mainly ethnic Vietnamese); and 42,481 were indigenous auxilaries (*supplétifs*) and soldiers in the armies of the Associated States of Indochina. In all, according to Bodin, the forces of the French Union lost 112,032 individuals. There are problems with all statistics and these are no exception. (Bodin proposes a higher death toll because he counts deaths occurring in enemy camps before and after July 1954, whereas the endpoint for the January 1955 statistics stopped at the armistices signed in mid-1954.) Nonetheless, these numbers provide a broadly accurate account of the casualties inflicted by nine years of war on the French Union forces. From these statistics, for example, one can see that French losses in the war only accounted for 17.5 percent of the total (using Bodin's figures). This lower number can be explained by the French government's refusal to institute the draft combined with the concomitant, ever increasing need to find troops elsewhere – in the Foreign Legion (a 8.2 percent mortality rate); from colonial North Africa (9.2 percent); from colonial "Black" Africa (2.5 percent); from "indigenous" (mainly Vietnamese) regular troops (26 percent); and indigenous auxiliary and troops of the Associated States of Indochina (mainly Vietnamese, 38 percent). Combined, the Vietnamese and non-French troops endured the highest death rates during the war and the ground forces suffered by far the greatest losses, well over 90 percent, followed by the **navy** and the **air force**. In all, the Indochina War took some 400,000 lives.

3. The Vietnamese government has confirmed that it lost 842,405 individuals (apparently including "missing in action") in its armed forces during the Vietnam War and that 484,324 were wounded.

**CATALA, JEAN-MARIE (1897–1970).** French colonial administrator during the Indochina conflict. Born in colonial **Tonkin**, Catala was a former cadet of the Military Preparatory School of Indochina (*École militaire des enfants de troupe de l'Indochine)*. In 1915, he joined the Colonial Artillery and fought on the western front in France. Released from the army, he continued his studies in customs control and returned to Indochina as a colonial civil servant. With degrees in the Chinese and Vietnamese languages, he held the chair of Vietnamese philology at the University of **Hanoi** between 1934 and 1943. In 1946, he transferred to the Ministry of Overseas France as a professor in Vietnamese language and customs at the **Colonial Academy** (*École coloniale*) and at the ***École nationale des langues orientales vivantes.*** In 1949, he returned to Indochina as the prefect for Phan Ray and the deputy prefect for the region of **Saigon**-Cholon and mayor-administrator for the city of Cholon. In 1952, he transferred to the Associated State of Vietnam to serve as cabinet director to **Tran Van Kha**, minister of the Economy and, between 1953 and 1954, to Dr. **Nguyen Van Nhang**, minister of the National Economy. In 1953–54, the Associated State of Vietnam named him general director of Internal and External Commerce. Catala retired in 1955. He contributed to *L'œuvre de la France en Indochine*, published by the Ministry of Overseas France in 1946–47. *See also* CHILDREN.

**CATHERINE**. *See* LUCIE AUBRAC.

**CATHOLICISM**. *See* CATHOLICS, EXODUS FROM NORTH; CATHOLICS IN VIETNAM

AND THE WAR; CHRISTIANS AND FRENCH OPPOSITION TO THE INDOCHINA WAR; LE HUU TU; VATICAN.

**CATHOLICS IN VIETNAM AND THE WAR.** The Indochina War profoundly affected Vietnamese Catholicism, and Vietnamese Catholics influenced the nature of the war.

The Vietnamese first encountered Catholicism when seaborne trading routes brought an increasing number of European Catholic missionaries to Asia. By the late 17th century, some 100,000 Vietnamese had converted to Catholicism for a variety of socio-economic and political reasons. These numbers increased in the following centuries as Catholicism became one of Vietnam's main religions. In 1945, 1.6 million Vietnamese were Catholics.

However, relations between Vietnamese leaders and Catholic missionaries were not without serious problems. Despite the aid provided by the French Bishop Pigneau de Béhaine to Nguyen Phuc Anh (Gia Long) during the latter's unification of Vietnam in 1802, subsequent Nguyen Kings adopted increasingly hostile policies towards Catholic missionaries they suspected of challenging their moral authority and control over populations. Keen on expanding French influence into Asia, the French Catholic Emperor Napoléon III exploited the Nguyen dynasty's persecution of missionaries to justify intervention in and colonization of Cochinchina in the mid-19th century. While secular-minded republican colonial administrators in Indochina were anything but supporters of the Church, they supported European Catholic missions and Vietnamese Catholics, convinced that they were natural colonial allies.

Things were not so clear-cut in practice, however. During the interwar period, Vietnamese Catholicism in particular became more nationally minded, pushing for the Vietnamization of the Church's clergy and leadership in Vietnam. To the consternation of French colonial authorities, the **Vatican** showed itself increasingly supportive of the "indigenization" of the clergies in the non-Western world, including that of Vietnam. The Vatican's postcolonial vision was expressed best in Benedict XV's 1919 apostolic letter *Maximum Illud* and Pius XI's 1926 encyclical *Rerum Ecclesiae*. The colonial (and anti-colonialist) idea according to which the Vatican and Vietnamese Catholics were collaborators is misleading.

Nowhere is this better seen than in the national support Vietnamese Catholics and their leaders pledged to the new nation-state declared by **Ho Chi Minh** in September 1945, the **Democratic Republic of Vietnam** (DRV). On 1 November 1945, one of Vietnam's best-known nationalist Catholics from Phat Diem, **Le Huu Tu**, was ordained archbishop without the interference of French colonial administrators or European missionaries. As Franco-American historian Charles Keith has noted, the "event marked the degree to which Vietnamese bishops had become a locus of growing cultural nationalism in the Vietnamese Catholic community". Hostile to the return of French colonialism, Le Huu Tu accepted Ho Chi Minh's invitation to serve as a supreme advisor to the government. Although Catholic leaders knew that communists were the driving force behind the DRV, between 1945 and 1949, in the absence of a full-blown **Cold War**, Vietnamese religious leaders like Le Huu Tu stressed anti-colonialism and nationalism and did their best to keep Vietnamese Catholics out of the cross-fire following the outbreak of full-scale war between the DRV and the French on **19 December 1946**. Indeed, the two dioceses of Bui Chu and Phat Diem constituted something of an autonomous Catholic national zone in lower **Tonkin**. In the late 1940s, Le Huu Tu was largely successful in keeping the French colonialists and the Vietnamese communists at bay.

From 1950, however, the attempts by both the French and the DRV to take control of autonomous Catholic areas, the radicalization of the DRV stemming from its entry into the communist bloc, the Vatican's condemnation of any **collaboration** with communists, and the emergence of the non-communist Associated State of Vietnam backed by the United States, led religious leaders to lean to the anti-communist side but without abandoning their nationalist and anti-colonialist tack. Catholic autonomy in Phat Diem and Bui Chu finally came to an end in 1951, when the French insisted on taking control of the regions administratively and militarily. Catholic leaders had little choice but to concede.

Nonetheless, the intransigent nationalist position of Catholic Vietnamese leaders led many French strategists to question their loyalty. General **Jean de Lattre de Tassigny** not only blamed Catholics in Phat Diem for the loss of his son, but he also expelled one of Vietnam's most respected Catholic **intellectuals** at the time, **Nguyen Manh**

**Ha**. Despite its condemnation of cooperation with communists, the Vatican continued to support the indigenization and decolonization of Catholicism in Vietnam. Vietnamese took over vicariates in **Hanoi** and Bac Ninh in 1950, Vinh in 1951, Haiphong in 1953, and **Saigon** in 1955. *See also* CAO DAI; CATHOLICS, EXODUS FROM NORTH; CHRISTIANS AND FRENCH OPPOSITION TO THE INDOCHINA WAR; COLLABORATION; HOA HAO.

**CATHOLICS, EXODUS FROM NORTH.** In accordance with the **Geneva Accords** dividing Vietnam provisionally into two states at the **17th parallel** in mid-1954, it was agreed that people living below and above that line would be able to migrate freely from one zone to another within a specified period of time. Around one million Vietnamese decided to leave Vietnam north of the 17th parallel, where the communist-run **Democratic Republic of Vietnam** (DRV) would assume power, in favor of the State of Vietnam in the south. Of this number, around 600,000 Catholics decided to move to the south, meaning about two thirds of the total Catholic population living in the north until mid-1954. 918 Vietnamese priests accompanied their faithful southwards, while some 375 remained among their congregations within the DRV. The famous anti-communist and anti-colonialist nationalist Catholic bishops, **Le Huu Tu** and **Pham Ngoc Chi**, moved to the south in July 1954. This massive number of Vietnamese suddenly choosing to leave the north overwhelmed French logistics. The United States navy stepped in, providing vessels and teams to help transport them from Haiphong to southern Vietnam. Communist authorities would, until very recently, consider these refugees to be **traitors**, while others saw America's **Cold War** hand pushing them to leave the "communist" north for the "free" south. Based on their experiences during the Indochina War, many Catholics feared that the DRV would clamp down on religious expression once in power. Others followed their parish priests, while some saw opportunities to be had in migrating to the south that had nothing to do with religion or ideology. What is sure is that this massive relocation of Vietnamese Catholics to the south would directly affect the nature of post 1954 politics and society in southern Vietnam and even the nature of the American war for Vietnam a few years later. *See also* ASSOCIATED STATES OF INDOCHINA; CATHOLICS IN VIETNAM AND THE WAR; CHRISTIANS AND OPPOSITION TO THE INDOCHINA WAR; NGO DINH DIEM; NGO DINH THUC; REGROUPING TO THE NORTH; VATICAN.

**CÂY MAI MEETING.** Held in Cholon on **23 September 1945**, this meeting between the **Indochinese Communist Party**'s (ICP) Territorial Committee for Cochinchina *(Xu Uy Nam Ky)* and the newly created People's Resistance Committee for Nam Bo approved the decision to take up the fight against the French. On behalf of the ICP's Central Committee, **Hoang Quoc Viet** participated in the meeting. The delegates agreed to begin mobilizing the population against the French via strikes, boycotts, as well as through **guerrilla** and urban warfare.

**CCP.** *See* PEOPLE'S REPUBLIC OF CHINA.

**CÉDILE, JEAN MARIE ARSÈNE (1908–1984).** Ranking French military officer and colonial administrator sent to Indochina to restore French rule after World War II. Graduated at the top of his class at the **Colonial Academy** (*École coloniale*) in 1928 and the holder of a law degree from ***École nationale des langues orientales vivantes,*** Cédile was one of the "best and the brightest" of the French colonial administration. He was also a military man. He served as a reserve officer at Saint-Cyr in 1931 and was named second lieutenant in the *24ème Régiment de tirailleurs sénégalais* stationed in France. Between 1932 and 1940, he worked in the French colonial administration of Cameroon. Mobilized in 1939, he joined Free French forces when General **Philippe Leclerc** arrived in Cameroon. Cédile commanded a company of colonial troops. In 1941 and 1942, he participated in the military campaigns in Libya and Tunisia as part of the *Bataillon de marche no.5*. His unit was present during the battle of El Alamein in October 1942. In July 1943, as a captain, he became cabinet director to **René Pleven** and served as chief of cabinet to the commissioner for the Colonies first in Algiers, then in Paris following the liberation of France. He then moved on to Ceylon (Sri Lanka) in March 1945 as the head of the French Military Mission in South East Asia, linked to the South-East Asia Command led by Lord **Louis Mountbatten**. Cédile closely studied British policy towards **Burma**; he was attached to the staff of British Brigadier Biggons, director of Civil Affairs for Burma. With the defeat of the

Japanese, Cédile became commissioner for the French Republic in **Cochinchina** and Southern **Annam**. He served in this capacity from August 1945 to October 1946. On orders from **Charles de Gaulle** to oversee the restoration of French sovereignty to Indochina as rapidly as possible, Cédile parachuted into southern Vietnam on 24 August 1945, but was captured by the Vietnamese upon his landing and turned over, stripped naked, to the Japanese. Released, Cédile contacted Vietnamese nationalists such as **Tran Van Giau** to discuss the 24 March **Declaration on Indochina** though he did not inform his Vietnamese interlocutors that he was in charge of re-establishing French colonial control over **Saigon** and Cochinchina as a representative of the Provisional Government of the French Republic. With the arrival of British forces in September, Cédile collaborated closely with General **Douglas Gracey**, who allowed Cédile to engineer a *coup de force* on **23 September 1945**. Thanks to **Foreign Legion** troops liberated from Japanese internment, the French were able to push the **Viet Minh** out of Saigon in a chaotic frenzy that effectively initiated hostilities between the French and the Vietnamese below the **16th parallel.** Cédile was a supporter of Cochinchinese separatism and served as advisor to the new High Commissioner **Georges Thierry d'Argenlieu**. Cédile left Indochina in 1947 with the rank of major. In Paris, between 1947 and 1948, he served as director of the *Agence de l'Indochine* before resuming his colonial career in Africa. A decorated officer and colonial administrator, he was elected in 1976 a member of the *Académie des Sciences d'Outre-mer* filling the chair left vacant by **Léon Pignon**.

**CEMETERIES, DEMOCRATIC REPUBLIC OF VIETNAM.** During the Indochina conflict, the **Democratic Republic of Vietnam** (DRV) did its best to finance the establishment of war cemeteries in the territories under its control. Sometime in the late 1940s, the government created cemeteries for soldiers and civilians killed in war, called "*nghia dia*" or "homage to the land". Around 1950, the DRV announced the creation of "martyr cemeteries" (*nghia trang liet si*) in a move designed to bestow a higher level of respect for the sacrifices made by those laid to rest in them. Working through the provincial offices of the ministries of labor and invalids, the government organized investigations to determine who would be admitted to these cemeteries. This meant the careful study of the death certificates signed by administration and combat authorities at the time of the individual's death. For admitted fallen soldiers, the state assumed the funeral costs, thereby relieving the family of an important financial burden. In the early 1950s and again in the wake of the Indochina War, the government tried to transfer the bodies and **remains** of soldiers from individual graves and village cemeteries to larger ones, run by the state. The problem, however, was that Vietnamese burial rituals do not allow for the transfer of the buried body or remains. In order to do so, the authorities organized a special "second" burial ceremony (*cai tang*). In 1957–1958, the DRV exhumed thousands of bodies and reburied them in patriotic cemeteries located in the heart of villages and towns located across central and northern Vietnam in particular. In 1960, the DRV sent special teams to the **Dien Bien Phu** battlefield to exhume the remains of soldiers buried haphazardly during the battle in order to place them in two newly created patriotic cemeteries. In 1961, the Ministry of War Invalids counted 1,975 *nghia trang*, thirteen mid-level cemeteries, and eight funeraries dedicated to major battles during the Indochina War (*nghia trang chien dich lon*). *See also ASSOCIATION NATIONALE DES ANCIENS D'INDOCHINE ET DU SOUVENIR INDOCHINOIS*; *ASSOCIATION NATIONALE DES ANCIENS ET AMIS DE L'INDOCHINE ET DU SOUVENIR INDOCHINOIS*; *ASSOCIATION NATIONALE DES COMBATTANTS DE DIEN BIEN PHU*; ASSOCIATION OF MOTHERS OF SOLDIERS; EXPERIENCE OF WAR; MYTH OF WAR; NECROPOLIS; WAR MEMORIAL, DIEN BIEN PHU.

**CEMETERIES, FRENCH UNION FORCES.** *See* MYTH OF WAR; NECROPOLIS; REMAINS, FRENCH UNION; WAR MEMORIAL, DIEN BIEN PHU.

**CENTRAL INTELLIGENCE AGENCY.** *See* OFFICE OF STRATEGIC SERVICES

**CENTRAL OFFICE FOR THE SOUTHERN REGION (*Trung Ương Cục Miền Nam*).** (Better known to the Americans during the Vietnam War as COSVN or the Central Office for South Vietnam.) The most powerful party organization in the south in charge of southern Vietnam and Cambodia during the latter half of the Indochina conflict. In June 1951, following the **Second**

**Party Congress**, the newly constituted **Vietnamese Worker's Party** (VWP) upgraded the **Indochinese Communist Party**'s Territorial Committee for Nam Bo by transforming it into a party directorate under the control of the VWP's Central Committee. **Le Duan** and his deputy **Le Duc Tho** headed up this new party central office in charge of running the VWP's war and state-consolidation as the Vietnamese prepared to launch a general counter-offensive to take all of Indochina from the French. Joining Le Duan and Le Duc Tho in this central office in the south were **Ha Huy Giap**, **Pham Hung**, Thuong Vu and **Ung Van Khiem**. Following the **Geneva Accords** of 1954 and the relocation of southern troops and cadres to the north, the VWP scaled down its southern operations and revived the Territorial Committee for Nam Bo to run the party's affairs secretly in this new period. The Central Office for the Southern Region was, however, reactivated in the late 1950s, when the war for southern Vietnam intensified again. However, party control in the south was never as strong as in the north, and this well into the "American" war in Vietnam.

**CENTRAL PARTY MILITARY COMMITTEE (*Quân Uỷ Trung Ương*).** Created in January 1946, this military organization was internally known as the Central Party Military Committee (*Dang Uy Quan Su Trung Uong,* or *Quan Uy* for short). Through this committee, the Politburo and the Central Committee's Standing Committee of the **Indochinese Communist Party** ran all military affairs. As in communist China, this increasingly powerful committee devised military strategy, established defense needs, and reported them to the Politburo for approval. **Vo Nguyen Giap** was the official head of the military committee between 1946 and 1977, although his influence was greater during the war against the French than the one against the Americans. *See also* GENERAL STAFF.

**CHABALIER, JEAN-BAPTISTE (1887–1955).** French missionary active in Indochina during the war. He entered the *Missions étrangères de Paris* in 1905. In 1912, he was ordained a priest and dispatched immediately to work in Cambodia. He became father superior for the large Catholic seminary of Phnom Penh in 1929 before being named bishop for this same city in 1937. In 1945, he protected in his diocese more than a hundred French fleeing from the Japanese following the ***coup de force*** **of 9 March 1945**. Despite attacks by irregular **Democratic Republic of Vietnam** forces against his diocese during the Indochina War, the bishop began work on the Phnom Penh Cathedral in October 1952. He passed away before construction was finished, but he was buried in the Cathedral. He was named *Officier de la Légion d'honneur* and *Grand Officier de l'Ordre royal du Cambodge*. *See also* CATHOLICS IN VIETNAM AND THE WAR; CHRISTIANS AND OPPOSITION TO THE INDOCHINA WAR; VATICAN.

**CHALEUN PHOUANGCHAN (1913–?).** Member of the **Pathet Lao** and close collaborator of Prince **Suphānuvong**. Little is known of his activities before 1945, except that he worked in the colonial public works service and was born in Champassak province. Following the Japanese capitulation in August 1945, he joined the **Lao Issara** government and followed it into exile in Thailand following the return of the French in mid-1946. He worked closely with Prince Suphānuvong and travelled with him to Vietnam to join in creating the **Lao Resistance Government** in August 1950. Chaleun Phouangchan pursued advanced political studies in northern Vietnam in the early 1950s before specializing in radio communications. He would go on to be an influential, behind-the-scenes leader of the Pathet Lao. *See also* CAMBODIAN RESISTANCE GOVERNMENT; INDOCHINESE COMMUNIST PARTY; INDOCHINESE FEDERATION.

**CHALIER, PIERRE (1912–1984).** Graduated from the **Colonial Academy** (*École coloniale*) in 1931, he held a language certificate in Khmer from the ***École nationale des langues orientales vivantes***. He served as a colonial civil servant in Cambodia between 1935 and 1951. Fascinated by the country, Chalier mastered the language and studied in depth various aspects of Cambodian society and culture. Little is known about his wartime activities, other than that he apparently distinguished himself during the Franco-Siamese border conflict in 1941. In 1946, he served as a regional colonial advisor in the Cambodian province of Kampot and then in Siemreap in 1948. During this time he was instrumental in winning over **Dap Chhuon**, a ranking leader of the **Khmer Issarak**. In 1947, he served in the cabinets of the Cambodian prime minister and then in that of the French high commissioner for Indochina in 1949. He left Indochina to continue a colonial career in Madagascar and elsewhere. He retired around 1975.

**CHAN MUN BOY (1925–).** Born in Singapore, he joined the Malayan Communist Party (MCP) in 1945. In 1947, the MCP assigned him the task of transporting 150 tons of weapons to Vietnamese fighting the French in southern Indochina. The man who personally selected him for this mission was the general secretary of the MCP and an ethnic Vietnamese, Lai Tec. Chan Mun Boy's duty was to lead five junks laden with Japanese weapons to the Thai coastal town of May Rut from where the **Viet Minh** would transport them to southern Vietnam. Chan Mun Boy collaborated closely with three Vietnamese representatives in the organization of this shipment, Duong Quang Dong, **Bong Van Dia**, and Truong Van Kinh. Together they left Malacca in March 1947 on what they dubbed the Mekong II mission. The weapons were safely unloaded at May Rut, packed on to elephants and horses, and dispatched across Cambodia to southern Vietnam. In late 1947 the Mekong II mission came under French attack. While most of the weapons reached their final destination in interzone IX, Chan Mun Boy and his Khmer companion, **Son Ngoc Minh**, were seriously injured and spent two months recuperating. In 1948, Chan Mun Boy returned to Thailand to resume his work running guns and supplies to the Viet Minh via the sea he knew so well. In 1949, he accompanied Son Ngoc Minh, one of the most important leaders of the **Khmer Issarak**, to Cambodia in order to execute "internationalist tasks". Chan Mun Boy remained there until 1952 when he transferred back to interzone IX. He married a Vietnamese wife in that year, Quan Thi Mai. Besides his "internationalist" work in Cambodia, Chan Mun Boy's fluency in Chinese made him an important link to the large **overseas Chinese** communities the DRV sought to mobilize in the early 1950s. *See also* ANIMALS; CROSSOVERS; METIS.

**CHAN NAK (1892–1954).** Cambodian politician and advisor to **Norodom Sihanouk** from the late 1940s. Born in Phnom Penh, he studied at the *Collège Sisowath* before pursuing advanced law studies in the judicial section of the **Colonial Academy** (*École coloniale*). Upon his return, he began a long career in the Cambodian magistracy and served in the Cambodian Consultative Assembly in the late 1920s. In 1941, he served on the board of the Federal Council of Indochina and became minister of Justice in the Royal Government. Following the Japanese overthrow of the French in the ***coup de force* of 9 March 1945**, he continued to serve as minister of Justice in the Japanese-backed government created on 18 March 1945 and remained at his post under **Son Ngoc Thanh**'s brief premiership. Chan Nak successfully navigated this tricky period in Cambodian politics and Franco-Cambodian relations. Following the return of the French, he joined the French-backed government of Prince Sisowath Monireth on 17 October 1945 to resume his post of minister of Justice. He resigned in December 1946 because of the obstruction of a case he was investigating concerning a member of the Cambodian police force. He joined forces with **Khim Tith** at this time to create the National Union Party. In 1948, he entered the Council for the Kingdom (*Conseil du royaume*) and was reelected to this body in early 1950. Sihanouk kept him on as his minister of Justice in the cabinet created in May 1950, though Chan Nak tendered his resignation following irregularities surrounding the investigation of the assassination of **Ieu Koeus**. Sihanouk refused his resignation. In March 1951, Chan Nak was named a member of the Regency Council (*Conseil de régence*) and became Private Counselor to the Crown on 6 June 1951. Sihanouk made him Council President (*Président du Conseil*) and minister of the Interior on 22 November 1953. Chan Nak resigned from these posts in April 1954.

**CHANG FA-KWEI.** *See* ZHANG FAKUI.

**CHANSON, CHARLES MARIE FERREOL (1902–1951).** One of the more vigorous French generals combating the **Democratic Republic of Vietnam**'s (DRV) southern forces. He entered the *École Polytechnique* in 1922 and the Artillery Academy (*École d'artillerie*) in 1924 before serving in Algeria and Morocco during the interwar period. When World War II began, he entered the *École supérieure de la Guerre* before joining the General Staff of the 6th Army and serving Vichy in Algiers until the Allied landing in North Africa in November 1942. In 1944, a lieutenant colonel, he joined the Free French ground forces' General Staff in England. From October 1945, he commanded the artillery section of the 3rd Colonial Infantry Division. He landed with it in Indochina in late February 1946. Promoted colonel, he held a number of important military positions in southern Vietnam, including ranking commander of troops for the **Saigon**-Cholon sector from March 1946. In southern Vietnam, he adapted his artillery tactics to the **guerrilla** war the **Viet Minh** was pursuing. In October 1947, he was named brigadier general and served as deputy to the commanding general for French forces in southern Indochina from December of that year. In September 1948, he took command of French forces in **Tonkin** but returned to France in early 1949. In October of that same year, he landed again in Indochina to take over from General **Boyer de la Tour du Moulin** as head of ground forces for South Vietnam. In December 1949, he served simultaneously in this position and that of acting commissioner for the Republic in South Vietnam. During this time, he vigorously engaged General **Nguyen Binh**'s troops, handing them a series of crushing defeats. In large part because of his efficiency, the DRV assassinated him on 31 July 1951, together with the Vietnamese governor for the southern part of the Associated State of Vietnam, Thai Lap Thanh. While some in French intelligence thought **Trinh Minh The** was behind this action, **Jean de Lattre de Tassigny** was convinced it was General Nguyen Binh. The French commander-in-chief instructed **Pierre Perrier**, in charge of security in southern Vietnam, to track down Nguyen Binh and "make him pay for Chanson's death".

**CHANTO TRES (1919–?).** Following the Japanese ***coup de force* of 9 March 1945**, Chanto Tres supported **Son Ngoc Thanh** at the head of an independent Japanese-backed government in Cambodia. He fled to Thailand when the French returned to southern Indochina and took Son Ngoc Thanh into custody. Chanto Tres joined the **Khmer Issarak** and was active in Battambang province. He participated in a combined **Viet Minh-Khmer Issarak** attack on Siem Reap in August 1946 in collaboration with forces led by Prince **Norodom Chantaraingsey**. In 1949, the latter put him in charge of the Committee of National Liberation active in western Cambodia. Following the signing of the Franco-Cambodian treaty of 1949 and the creation of the Associated State of Cambodia, Chanto Tres rallied to the Cambodian government and broke his ties with the forces of the **Democratic Republic of Vietnam**. *See also* COLLABORATION; CROSSOVER.

**CHAPUIS.** French **paratrooper** who deserted to the **Democratic Republic of Vietnam** (DRV) around 1950. He subsequently became the head of an effective **commando** unit in northern Vietnam working for the DRV. This made him the avowed enemy of an equally effective French commando leader working on the other side, **Roger Vandenberghe**. Chapuis was captured in mid-1951 by Vandenberghe's forces, but succeeded in escaping after being turned over to military authorities in Nam Dinh. *See also* CROSSOVERS; DESERTION; GEORGES BOUDAREL.

**CHARRET, HENRI ROGER CHARLES (1923–).** Between 1946 and 1948, he served as the head of the French Service for Political, Information and Propaganda Affairs in Indochina. In 1949, he transferred to France to work in the colonial ministry then in the ministry in charge of relations with the **Associated States of Indochina,** mainly in charge of financial and commercial questions.

**CHASSIN, GUILLAUME JEAN MAX (LEJAY-CLER, 1902–1970).** French **Air Force** general, who was deeply influenced by communist tactics during his time in Indochina. Graduated at the top of his class in 1921 at the Naval Academy, he specialized in combined air and sea operations. Following the French defeat in 1940, he remained loyal to the Vichy government led by Philippe Pétain. In 1942, however, when the Allies landed in North Africa, he crossed over to the Free French side. In 1949, he was named lieutenant general and given command of the French Air Force in the Far East on 7 June 1951 before being recalled to France shortly thereafter. In a number of articles published in *Le Monde*, signed under the pseudonym of Lejay-Cler, he expressed his pessimism on the conduct of the war in Indochina. During his time in Indochina, he also became fascinated by **Mao Zedong**'s doctrine on people's war and its application in Vietnam and other parts of the "Third World". Chassin published the first biography in French of Mao Zedong. In early 1951, he penned an influential essay in the *Revue militaire d'information* entitled *La conquête de la Chine par Mao Tsé Toung*. To understand Mao's surprising victory over the **Republic of China**, he argued, one had to understand the strategy of **revolutionary warfare** deployed by the Chinese communists and, by implication, their Vietnamese allies during the Indochina War. *See also* CHARLES LACHEROY; INDOCTRINATION;

PARALLEL HIERARCHIES; PSYCHOLOGICAL WARFARE.

**CHÂTEAU-JOBERT, PIERRE (CONAN, 1912–2005).** Joined Free French forces in England in 1940 using the name "Conan" (referring to the legendary French officer of the same name who served audaciously during World War I). Château-Jobert joined the **Foreign Legion** and participated in battles in Syria and Libya. In September 1942, he joined the paratroopers and led clandestine **commando** missions into occupied France. After the war, he became battalion commander and trained paratroopers in France before landing in Indochina sometime in 1947 at the head of the *Demi-brigade coloniale de commandos parachutistes* (DBCCP). He distinguished himself leading numerous airborne commando raids in Cambodia, **Cochinchina**, and **Annam** between December 1947 and July 1948. After working in France in 1949 and 1950, he returned to Vietnam a lieutenant colonel and resumed the command of the DBCCP and Southern Airborne Troops in operations in northern and southern Vietnam. He also worked closely with **Paul Aussaresse**. In 1952, Château-Jobert left Indochina for Algeria. He took part in the Franco-British landing in Suez in 1956 as the leader of the *11ème Choc*. He opposed the decolonization of Algeria and supported the *Organisation de l'armée secrète*. With an arrest warrant hanging over his head, he fled Algeria and lived underground for seven years in France and abroad. A 1965 death sentence against him was lifted by **Charles de Gaulle**'s general amnesty. *See also* ALGERIAN WAR; *SERVICE ACTION*; *SERVICE DE DOCUMENTATION EXTERIEURE ET DE CONTRE-ESPIONNAGE*.

**CHÂU QUANG LỘ (?–1952).** Opposed to the **Democratic Republic of Vietnam** (DRV), he was the leader of the Hmong in Pha Long in northern Vietnam during much of the Indochina War. He had joined French forces working against the Japanese at the end of World War II before allying his troops with them in the war against the DRV's administrative and military forces. In 1950, he collaborated with French special forces to create an anti-DRV *maquis* in upland Hmong regions east of the Red River. Armed and trained by the ***Groupement de commandos mixtes aéroportés***, he led an uprising against the DRV in mid-1952. He died defending these autonomous, French-backed zones in October 1952. *See also* MINORITY ETHNIC GROUPS; TAI FEDERATION.

**CHAU SEN COCSAL (CHHUM, 1905–2009).** A Cambodian born in the province of Tri Ton in southern Vietnam. He studied at the *Collège Sisowath* and at the *Lycée Chasseloup Laubat*. After a short stint in **Hanoi** at the *École de médecine* he returned to Cambodia and began working in the Cambodian administration. Little is known of his activities during the interwar period other than the fact that he worked in the colonial civil service from 1927 and eventually became governor of the Cambodian province of Kompong Cham. Following the Japanese ***coup de force* of 9 March 1945**, he supported the independence activities of **Son Ngoc Thanh** and served as mayor of Phnom Penh. However, when the French returned and moved to arrest him, he fled to southern Vietnam and joined forces with **Pach Chhoeun** in his native Tri Ton province. He cooperated with the **Democratic Republic of Vietnam** and was elected deputy for Triton in the government's national assembly. His anti-colonial activities were shortlived, however. In February 1946, Chau Sen Cocsal crossed over to the French and the Cambodian royal cause and was named governor of Kandal province in 1947. He became increasingly active in Cambodian politics from this point. He joined **Nhiek Tioulong** and **Lon Nol** in creating the Khmer Renewal Party and assumed the post of director of National Monopolies. He participated in the Cambodian delegation to the **Pau Conference** in 1950 and became *chargé d'affaires* to Thailand in April 1951 and apparently briefly served as ambassador. However, **Norodom Sihanouk** recalled him to Phnom Penh because of supposed contacts between Chau Sen Cocsal's staff and Sihanouk's political enemy Son Ngoc Thanh, who had fled to Thailand in 1952. *See also* COLLABORATION; CROSSOVER.

**CHAUVEL, JEAN (1897–1979).** Close collaborator of **Georges Bidault** and general secretary in the French Ministry of Foreign Affairs between 1944 and 1949. From 1950, he served as French ambassador to the **United Nations** before working as a close advisor to Bidault during the first phase of negotiations during the **Geneva Conference** of 1954. **Pierre Mendès France** retained him as the head of the French delegation to the conference, appreciating the diplomat's "clarity of mind, his boldness in action, and the rigorous principles on which his diplomatic doctrine was founded", as French historians **Philippe Devillers** and **Jean Lacouture** described it.

**CHEA CHINKOC (1904–1975).** Born in Kandal province, Cambodia, he began his career in the colonial civil service in 1924. Little is known of his activites until 1946 when he reappeared on the political scene to help Prince **Norodom Montana** create the Progressive Democratic Party, serving as its general secretary from May 1946. In 1947, he briefly worked as governor of Takeo province and as a chief clerk in the Ministry of National Economy before taking over as minister of Industry and Trade between June 1950 and May 1951 in the Associated State of Cambodia. He briefly served as minister of the Interior in order to run for a seat in the National Assembly elections in Phnom Penh. He lost.

**CHEGARAY, JACQUES.** One if not the first in France to take up publicly the taboo subject of the French army's use of **torture** during the Indochina War. After World War II, he worked as a journalist at *l'Aube*. On 29 July 1949, Chegaray published in the pages of the French Christian newspaper, *Témoignage chrétien*, a front-page article documenting the practice of torture by the French Army (*l'Aube* had refused to run it). The title: « *À côté de la machine à écrire, le mobilier d'un poste comprend une machine à faire parler* ». This frontpage piece provoked a major uproar in the army and on the French Right. In reaction to Chegaray's article, the famous French orientalist and head of the **Colonial Academy** (*École coloniale*), **Paul Mus**, weighed in in the same paper to condemn the use of torture and to break with the French war in Indochina. High Commissioner **Léon Pignon** ordered a full-scale investigation into the question, emphasizing the political dangers the practice of torture could pose for the French mission in Indochina. Unbeknownst to the public at the time, internally the army and security services were investigating another serious incident of torture occurring in the **Hanoi** area. *See also* JULES ROY.

**CHEN GENG (1903–1961).** Born into a wealthy Chinese family in Hunan province, Chen Geng became involved in nationalist politics as a youth and studied military science at the Whampoa Military Academy in Guangzhou (Canton), where he met **Ho Chi Minh** in the mid-1920s. With the advent of the **People's Republic of China** in October 1949, Chen Geng became head of Yunnan province and its military command. Because of his position in southern China and past relationship with Ho Chi Minh, in June 1950 the **Chinese Communist Party** appointed him as the party's representative and commander of the **Chinese Military Advisor Delegation** to Vietnam. He arrived in northern Vietnamese safe zones in July 1950. He immediately went to work making preparations for the Border Campaign at **Cao Bang** in September–October 1950. He played an important advisory role in planning this famous victory, opening the frontier to the **Democratic Republic of Vietnam**, and to large amounts of Chinese aid. On 1 November 1950, following the successful completion of the border campaign, Chen Geng transferred to Korea. General **Wei Guoqing** replaced him. *See also* ARTHUR RADFORD; MAO ZEDONG; PEOPLE'S REPUBLIC OF CHINA; ZHOU ENLAI.

**CHESNEAUX, JEAN (1922–2007).** French specialist of 20th-century Chinese and Vietnamese history and active opponent of the French war in Indochina. Born into a liberal Catholic family, Chesneaux completed his secondary studies at the *Lycées Montaigne* and *Louis-le-Grand* before obtaining his undergraduate degree at the Sorbonne in history in 1941. He joined the resistance movement during World War II and was arrested and incarcerated by the Gestapo in 1943. Upon his liberation in 1944, Chesneaux resumed his studies and his political activism. As the secretary of the Protestant *Entr'aide universitaire international*, Chesneaux went on a fact-finding mission to 12 Asian countries, including Indochina, between November 1946 and August 1948. Following a brief visit to areas controlled by the **Democratic Republic of Vietnam** in the south, Chesneaux was arrested for "treason" by the French authorities. As he later put it, this was his baptism of fire in anti-colonial politics. Upon his liberation from the *Prison centrale de Saigon* and expulsion from Vietnam, he returned to France, joined the **French Communist Party** (FCP) in 1948, and threw himself into the study of modern Chinese history, submitting a thesis (later a book) on the Chinese worker's movement in the 1920s. He was an active opponent of the French war in Indochina and joined like-minded scholars such as **Paul Mus** and **Paul Lévy** to speak out against the war at a conference organized by

Christian activists in Issy-les-Moulineaux in February 1950. In September 1950, he published an enthusiastic account of the DRV in *Action,* coinciding with the publication of **Léo Figuères'** *Je reviens du Vietnam libre* for the FCP. In 1955, Chesneaux published his famous *Contribution à l'histoire de la nation vietnamienne*, adding to the pioneering work on modern Vietnam done by **Paul Mus**, **Philippe Devillers**, **Ellen Hammer,** and **Jean Lacouture.** Although Chesneaux opposed the American war in Vietnam and was the delegate president of the pro-**Hanoi** ***Association d'amitié franco-vietnamienne***, he left the FCP in 1969. In that same year, he played a pivotal role in the creation of the University of Paris VII (Jussieu), where he helped develop a program in non-Western history and recruited young French historians who would pioneer Vietnamese studies and Indochinese colonial history in France, such as Pierre Brocheux, Daniel Hémery, and **Georges Boudarel**. *See also* BOUDAREL AFFAIR; CULTURE; HISTORY; INTELLECTUALS.

**CHEVANCE-BERTIN, MAURICE (1910–1996).** Director of and frequent contributor to the French colonial paper, *Climats,* and advisor to the **French Union**. After returning from a fact-finding trip to Indochina between May and July 1948, he strongly advised against negotiating with the **Democratic Republic of Vietnam** (DRV) on the grounds that it was an international communist organization. As of March 1949, Chevance-Bertin served as president of the Commission of National Defense in the French Union Assembly. In October 1950, he visited Vietnam in his new capacity as military counselor to the head of the Associated State of Vietnam.

**CHEYSSON, CLAUDE (1920–)**. French career diplomat involved in negotiations at the **Geneva Conference**. He obtained the rank of secretary for Foreign Affairs (*secrétaire des Affaires étrangères*) in 1948. In 1952, he was sent to Vietnam where he served as advisor to **Nguyen Van Tam**, the head of the government of the Associated State of Vietnam. Cheysson became deputy then chief of cabinet to **Pierre Mendès France** in mid-1954, in charge of Indochinese Affairs for the French president during negotiations in Geneva.

**CHHEAN VAM (1916–2000).** Cambodian politician and close collaborator with the royal family. Born in Battambang province, little is known of his education and activities before 1945. In April 1946, he helped **Ieu Koeus** and **Sim Var** create the **Democrat Party** and served as its first general secretary. He became minister of Education in the **Sisowath Youtevong** cabinet of December 1946. He kept the same post in the Sisowath Watchayvong government created in August 1947 and became leader of the Democrat Party following the death of Prince Youtevong in 1947. In February 1948, he took over as prime minister and held the post of minister of Education and of National Defense until he was ousted from power in August 1948. He resumed his portfolio as minister of National Defense in the **Penn Nouth** cabinet of August 1948 and held the post until February 1949. In 1948, he accompanied **Norodom Sihanouk** on a trip to France and in 1950 flew with Prince **Sisowath Monipong** to Paris to discuss territorial claims on southern Vietnam and the question of ethnic Khmer minorities residing there. He would retire from political life and go on to become one of Cambodia's most powerful businessmen until 1975.

**CHHUM.** *See* CHAU SEN COCSAL.

**CHHUON MCHHULPICH.** *See* DAP CHHUON.

**CHỊ BA SƯNG RĂNG.** *See* TRIỆU CÔNG MINH.

**CHÍ THUẬN.** *See* NGUYỄN CHÁNH.

**CHỊ TƯ XÓM GÀ.** *See* TRIỆU CÔNG MINH.

**CHIANG KAI-SHEK (JIANG JIESHI, 1887–1975).** Military and political leader of the **Republic of China** whose troops occupied northern Indochina in the wake of World War II. Upon the death of Sun Yat-sen in 1925, Chiang Kai-shek assumed leadership of the Chinese Nationalist Party (the GMD) and adopted an increasingly hostile attitude towards Chinese communists working with nationalists in the First United Front created by Sun Yat-sen in 1923. In 1927, having come to dominate the warlords and begun unifying the country with the help of the **Chinese Communist Party**, Chiang Kai-shek turned on the communists savagely in a bid to take control of China. In so doing, he triggered a **civil war** that would last in one way or another until the Chinese communist victory of 1949. In 1928, he presided over the creation of the Republic of China, based in

Nanjing, and led it until the communists took the mainland in 1949–50 and forced Chiang Kai-shek and the Republic to move to Taiwan.

Until the outbreak of the Sino-Japanese war in 1937, Chiang Kai-shek's interests in Indochina were focused less on the Vietnamese than on renegotiating unequal treaties with the French and obtaining better legal and commercial treatment for the large **overseas Chinese** community residing in Indochina. This changed during World War II, when the French capitulated to the Germans and Vichy collaborated with the Germans. Despite Vichy's reluctance to see the Japanese intervene in Indochina, local French authorities allowed the Japanese to do so.

Based in his wartime capital in the southern city of Chongqing (the Japanese controlled Nanjing and the eastern coast), Chiang Kai-shek and his allies in Yunnan and Guangxi provinces supported Vietnamese nationalists of all political colors against the Japanese and their Vichy collaborators. While there was reluctance to work with the Vietnamese communists (and **Ho Chi Minh** was even incarcerated in China for a long time), Chinese nationalists were willing to support the more effective **Viet Minh** organization as the war progressed. As American President Franklin Roosevelt's most favored Asian ally in the Pacific War, Chiang Kai-shek received American **aid** and participated in major Allied meetings with **Joseph Stalin** and **Winston Churchill**.

With the allied defeat of Germany in Europe and the coming of **Charles de Gaulle** to power in France, Chiang Kai-shek improved relations with the new French government. Above all, he wanted the French to help fight the Japanese. After a long rivalry between Chiang Kai-shek and British Lord Louis Mountbatten over whether French Indochina should belong to one or the other's theatre of operations, a compromise was reached at Potsdam in July 1945, whereby Chiang Kai-shek obtained responsibility for military operations in Indochina north of the **16th parallel** and Mountbatten for south of that line. This resulted, when Japan capitulated a few weeks afterwards, in Chiang Kai-shek becoming responsible for occupying and accepting the Japanese surrender in northern Indochina above the 16th parallel. In September 1945, Chinese forces entered Indochina. On 15 September, Chiang Kai-shek's government issued its occupation policy, summed up in 14 points. Unlike some of his (southern) military leaders in charge of troops in Indochina, such as **Lu Han**, Chiang Kai-shek recognized French sovereignty over Indochina and ordered his officers to stay out of Franco-Vietnamese affairs.

In early 1946, as clashes occurred between nationalist and communist forces in Manchuria, Chiang Kai-shek was increasingly keen on evacuating his troops from Indochina in order to concentrate on his problems with the Chinese communists in northern China. By June 1946, almost all of the Chinese occupying troops had been withdrawn from Indochina and the last remaining contingent left in September. Like the Americans, Chiang Kai-shek thereafter shelved his anti-colonial sympathy for Vietnamese nationalists, as part of the wider struggle against communist expansion, although his diplomats made some attempts to get the British and Americans to intervene when war broke out in **Hanoi** in December 1946.

In 1950, expelled to Taiwan, Chiang Kai-shek's Republic of China recognized the State of Vietnam led by **Bao Dai**. Until the end of the Indochina War, the Republic of China based on Taiwan maintained relations with the French and the **Associated States of Indochina** as part of a wider anti-communist bloc, but also in order to maintain the support of the large overseas Chinese communities living in Indochina against his Chinese adversaries.

**CHILDREN.** Children were not strangers to the face of war in Vietnam. During the Indochina War, **guerrillas** in the countryside and especially in the city employed children as messengers, scouts, and sometimes combatants. The use of children in combat was most prevalent in the early period of the Indochina War leading up to and including the battle of **Hanoi** (December 1946–February 1947). By late 1946, as the French and Vietnamese prepared for a showdown in Hanoi, the Vietnamese armed forces turned to different components of urban society to help them build up their defense of the city, run its communications and logistics, and potentially fight. This led to something of a "total" mobilization of the population of Hanoi, including children.

Nowhere is this better seen than in the creation of a "Children's Guard" (*Ve Ut*). It consisted of 175 children, most of whom were **orphans**. Aged between eight and 14, they had miraculously survived the famine of 1944–1945 and now roamed the underside of Hanoi, begging for food, stealing or working at menial jobs to make ends meet. Homeless, many of these children found a family in the resistance. On the eve of the outbreak of full-scale war on **19 December 1946**, they were enrolled into the famous "Capital Regiment", led by **Vuong Thua Vu,** which remained behind to fight a street war against the better armed **Expeditionary Corps**. While these children were not necessarily recruited to fight per se as combatants, their knowledge of the streets made them invaluable guides, messengers, and scouts. Some ended up with guns in their hands to defend themselves and lobbed grenades against French tanks entering narrow Hanoi streets.

And these orphans had names, too: Vu Trong Phung was ten and Nguyen Van Phuc was eight. Almost all of them were illiterate; instructions were drawn for them in picture forms. Singer Pham Ngoc Truong even composed a song for the children's guard. Two girls became legends in the brigade during the battle of Hanoi. Vu Thi Nhan, 13, and Tran Ngoc Lai, 11, were both orphans and stayed behind to work as messengers during the battle. Having cornered them, French soldiers were apparently stunned by the courage of the two girls and issued orders to bring them in alive. But in war, things do not work out nicely. When the exchange of fire resumed as the French moved to take the building, Tran Ngoc Lai was killed. According to Vietnamese accounts, news of her death set off a frenzied response from the Vietnamese defenders. Her death was transformed immediately into a myth of heroic martyrdom and she entered the legend of the Capital Brigade.

She was not, however, the sole child casualty. When the Capital Brigade withdrew in February 1947, after some 60 days of fighting, only 120 of the 175 children in the guard were still alive. 55 had died. Given that they were almost all orphans, their deaths were problematic for the DRV had no way of knowing who their next of kin was. The army thus buried them as "nameless martyrs" (*Liet Si Vo Danh*). Worse, since they died before having any descendants, there was no one to perform the rituals needed to tend to their wandering souls, which were left to roam between the world of the living and the dead.

The surviving children who could not be returned to their parents or custodians were assigned to army propaganda units in Viet Bac. In early 1948, children in the former Guard older than 15 were transformed into soldiers in the army whereas the remaining 30 under 14 remained in the propaganda unit. In 1950, the last children of the unit were transferred into the army or other positions and the Chidren's Guard was officially dissolved.

The **Vanguard Youth League** and the **scouting** movement provided scores of young recruits to the postcolonial army from 1945. The **Viet Minh** also relied upon children to serve as guides and liaison agents in southern Vietnam. Embracing **Saigon** and Cholon, **zone VII** even organized special paramilitary courses for children.

The French also trained children in the art of war. The **Deuxième Bureau** used children to spy on the adversary. According to one French intelligence officer, Vietnamese children were the best type of intelligence operative, "the surest and most determined". Upon their return in 1946, the French established the *École d'Enfants de Troupe Indochinoise* (EETI) located in the coastal town of Vung Tau (Cap Saint-Jacques at the time). It was open to French, Vietnamese, Cambodian, and Lao children. By 1950, the school counted 200 children (158 Vietnamese, 21 Cambodians, and 21 Lao). Most of them were the sons of officers and soldiers in the armies of the **Associated States of Indochina**. The school also accepted a number of orphans, whose parents were killed during the outbreak of war in 1945–1947. A separate military school existed for Eurasian children, located in Dalat.

Although few studies exist on the topic, war certainly became a part of the mental world for Vietnamese children, in particular those in the **Democratic Republic of Vietnam**. School texts stressed repeatedly the need to fight the foreigner as part of a long Vietnamese heritage. Sports and games for children were militarized, and war games often gave way to the real thing. Military operations repeatedly intruded into village life and with it the violence that left many children orphans and marked by what they had experienced.

We do not know how many Vietnamese children died during the Indochina War, nor do we have an accurate idea of those orphaned by the same conflict. We do know that in 1952 the Vietnamese Worker's Party issued orders to select one thousand children, the sons and daughters of peasant cadres, in order to send them abroad for political training. The Vietnamese also selected 60 Lao and Cambodians for high-level, intensive training in China, the Soviet Union and Eastern Europe. We also know that during the battle of Dien Bien Phu soldiers as young as 16 served on the front lines. With little combat training, they were thrown into the heat of battle. One commander in the 174th regiment later recalled the tragic death of a young, nameless sixteen-year-old from Nghe An in the violent combats on the night of 30 March: "He sacrificed himself on the first night of combat. These youths took part in the war and no one ever had the time to know who they were or to take down their military feats". *See also* ARMY, ASSOCIATED STATE OF VIETNAM; ARMY, ASSOCIATED STATE OF CAMBODIA; ARMY, ASSOCIATED STATE OF LAOS; ASSOCIATION OF MOTHERS OF SOLDIERS; CEMETERIES; *MÉTIS*; RELIGION; WOMEN; YOUTH ASSAULT TEAMS.

**CHÍN.** *See* LÊ DUẨN.

**CHINA.** *See* PEOPLE'S REPUBLIC OF CHINA.

**CHINESE COMMUNIST PARTY.** *See* PEOPLE'S REPUBLIC OF CHINA.

**CHINESE MILITARY ADVISORY DELEGATION.** After assuming power in Beijing in October 1949, the Chinese Communist Party's (CCP) leadership, including **Mao Zedong**, decided to recognize the **Democratic Republic of Vietnam** (DRV) officially on 18 January 1950 and to dispatch both political and military advisory groups to Vietnam to help the Vietnamese win the war against the French, consolidate their party and state, and outfit and train their army. In June 1950, the Chinese Military Advisory Delegation arrived in northern Vietnam under the leadership of **Wei Guoqing**, who answered to the CCP's general-advisor stationed in Vietnam, **Luo Guibo.** The military delegation channeled aid to the Vietnamese army, trained troops and officers in Vietnam and in southern China, and helped the Vietnamese to take the battle to the French **Expeditionary Corps** and win during the battle of **Cao Bang** in September–October 1950. Chinese advisors were attached to the DRV Ministry of Defense, its **General Staff** and its army divisions – even down to the battalion level in some cases. Chinese advisors attached to divisions and regiments played a particularly important role in modernizing operational tactics and developing military intelligence. Chinese advisors provided important input on major battles in the Red River Delta and hills in the early 1950s and were intimately involved in planning for the battle of Cao Bang in 1950 and that of **Dien Bien Phu** in 1954. Chinese advisors actually aimed the firing of the Soviet multiple rocket launcher that arrived at Dien Bien Phu in time to be used for the third wave attack on 1 May. These Chinese advisors paralleled the work of the American **Military Assistance Advisory Group** established in French-controlled Vietnam in September 1950 to help the French and their Vietnamese allies defeat the DRV armed forces as part of a wider global **Cold War** against the Soviets and the Chinese. In all, official Vietnamese sources state, some 2,000 Chinese advisors served in the DRV between 1950 and 1954.

**CHINESE MILITARY INTERVENTION, FRENCH ALLEGATION OF.** Several leading French officers and historians, including the authoritative French military historian **Yves Gras**, claim that on 18 June 1952 Beijing sent an entire division into northwestern Vietnam to help the **Democratic Republic of Vietnam** (DRV) quell an uprising of the Hmong, armed by the French ***Groupement de commandos mixtes aéroportés*** (GCMA). According to these French sources, the insurrection was finally quashed in August after heavy fighting. When military officials such as **Roger Trinquier** and **Edmond Grall** asked to publicize this Chinese communist intervention in order to win over increased American support, the French government allegedly decided to keep it under wraps for fear of an international incident torpedoing their emerging efforts to end the war. **Jean Létourneau** wanted "to avoid any possibility of conflict on the frontier in order to handle the future" (*toute occasion de conflit sur la frontière pour ménager l'avenir*). According to the French, in October 1952 a Chinese commando tracked down and killed the legendary Hmong leader, **Chau Quang Lo**. However, there is no Chinese evidence available in the public domain confirming that Beijing actually sent combat troops into Vietnam during the Indochina War. In 2008, however, a former high ranking Vietnamese diplomat and member of the DRV delegation to the **Geneva Conference** confirmed to this author that Chinese battalions (not divisions) did secretly enter northern Vietnam on several occasions to assist DRV forces. This, he said, occurred in the early 1950s. *See also* MILITARY ASSISTANCE ADVISORY GROUP (MAAG), INDOCHINA; MINORITY ETHNIC GROUPS; *PAYS MONTAGNARDS DU SUD* (PMS); *SERVICE ACTION*; TAI FEDERATION.

**CHINESE POLITICAL ADVISORY DELEGATION.** Following the communist victory of

October 1949, the Chinese Communist Party's leadership, including **Mao Zedong,** decided to recognize the **Democratic Republic of Vietnam** (DRV) officially and to dispatch both political and military advisory groups to Vietnam to help the Vietnamese win the war against the French, strengthen their party and state, and outfit and train their army. The Chinese Political Advisory Delegation arrived in Vietnam in December 1950 and was led by **Luo Guibo**, who was also the advisor-general for the Chinese Advisory Group stationed to Vietnam. The Political Delegation helped the Vietnamese strengthen the communist party and step up its control over the state, its civil servants, and society. Luo Guibo's political delegation played an important role in advising the Vietnamese on reforming the communist party, purging it of undesirable elements, and strengthening its control over and mobilizing the population via reorganized security services, **rectification** and **emulation campaigns**, and intensive ideological training. The political delegation also advised the Vietnamese on implementing numerous economic and banking reforms, and played a pivotal role in the implementation of **land reform** in upper Vietnam from 1953, designed to mobilize the rural population for **Dien Bien Phu** and transforming rural society in revolutionary ways. In all, official Vietnamese sources state, some 2,000 Chinese advisors served in the DRV between 1950 and 1954. *See also* INDOCTRINATION; MILITARY ASSISTANCE ADVISORY GROUP (MAAG), INDOCHINA; NEW HERO; RECTIFICATION.

**CHÍNH HỮU (1928–2007)**. Vietnamese poet from Ha Tinh who worked in propaganda affairs during the Indochina War. In 1946, he entered the **Democratic Republic of Vietnam's** army. Until the end of the conflict, he carried out political propaganda and ideological **indoctrination** courses within the army. Chinh Huu served during this time as a political cadre at the battalion level in units operating in central Vietnam. He took part in the battles of Upper Laos and **Dien Bien Phu**. His most notable works were *The Day I Return* (1947), *Comrade* (1948), and the *Night after Ha Noi* (1949). *See also* CINEMA; CULTURE; INTELLECTUALS; NOVELS, DEMOCRATIC REPUBLIC OF VIETNAM; RECTIFICATION.

**CHRISTIANS AND FRENCH OPPOSITION TO THE WAR**. The Indochina War divided French Christians deeply. If conservative Catholics associated with the center right ***Mouvement républicain populaire*** tended to support the French war in Indochina on nationalist and anti-communist grounds, more liberal-minded French Catholics increasingly objected to the war on anti-colonialist and moral grounds. The rift came into the open in 1949, when the highly influential Christian paper, ***Témoignage Chrétien***, published **Jacques Chegaray**'s denunciation of the French army's use of **torture**, followed by protestant **Paul Mus**'s essays calling on the French to take Vietnamese nationalist demands seriously, and to end what he saw as a senseless colonial war. In February 1950, like-minded Christian opponents of the war organized an informational conference on the Indochina War at Issy-les-Moulineaux. This historic meeting brought together Catholic groups such as the *Jeune république, Christianisme social, La vie nouvelle,* and members of the *Union des chrétiens progressistes* such as the Catholic **Jean Chesneaux** and Joseph Robert, a well-known priest from the left-wing Catholic *Mission ouvrière*. This debate produced a resolution calling on the 4th Republic to reach a negotiated settlement of the war and supported those who "refused to work for the war", meaning communist workers and dockers who were opposed to loading war material on boats headed to Indochina. The Issy meeting was significant in that it opened the way for French *Chrétiens progressistes* to collaborate increasingly with the working class allied with the **French Communist Party** and contributed to an emerging sense of public opposition to the Indochina War. In early June 1954, *Le Monde* published an anti-war Catholic text calling upon the government not to fail in its efforts at the **Geneva Conference** to find a peaceful end to the war, insisting that the Indochina conflict could not be considered to constitute a "just war". *See also* CATHOLICS, EXODUS FROM NORTH; CATHOLICS IN VIETNAM AND THE WAR; LE HUU TU; PUBLIC OPINION; VATICAN.

**CHU BÁ PHƯƠNG.** Non-communist Vietnamese nationalist born in northern Vietnam. In 1945, he was a member of the **Vietnamese Nationalist Party** (*Viet Nam Quoc Dan Dang,* VNQDD). In March 1946, he became minister of the National Economy in the **Democratic Republic of Vietnam** (DRV), a post he still held when he served as a member of the Vietnamese delegation to the **Fontainebleau Conference** in mid-1946. During this time, the French and the DRV armies attacked and drove the VNQDD and the Revolutionary Alliance Party (*Dong Minh Hoi*) from Vietnam into southern China. Chu Ba Phuong remained loyal to the DRV, leading what was called the "reformed", pro-governmental VNQDD. In October 1946, he remained in the revamped National Assembly serving as minister of Social Welfare. He was reappointed to this post in July 1947. He remained in the DRV government into the 1950s, holding figurehead positions of little real power. *See also* CIVIL WAR; NGUYEN TUONG TAM; POULO CONDOR; TRUONG TU ANH; VU HONG KHANH.

**CHU HUY MÂN (CHU VĂN ĐIỀU, HAI MẠNH, 1913–2006).** High-ranking military leader in the **Democratic Republic of Vietnam** (DRV), born in Nghe An province. He joined the revolutionary movement in Vietnam in 1929 and became a member of the **Indochinese Communist Party** about a year later. He was incarcerated on numerous occasions. In 1940, the French transferred him to a prison in the highlands of Kontum. In 1943, Chu Huy Man escaped and helped take control of Quang Nam province following the Japanese defeat in August 1945. He became deputy secretary for the Provincial Committee of Quang Nam and a political commissar in the Detachment (*Chi Doi*) Quang Nam. Between 1945 and 1951, he served as the president of the Politico-Military Committee for **Zone** C (*Ban Quan Chinh Khu C*) located in central Vietnam and as a political cadre in the Route 9 Front before becoming regimental chief and political commissar in **Inter-Zone IV** (*Lien Khu IV*). Between 1951 and 1954, he was the deputy political commissar then the political commissar for the 316th **Division**. He served in this capacity during the battle of **Dien Bien Phu**. In mid-1954, in spite of the **Geneva Accords** directing all foreign troops and personnel to leave Laos, he transferred secretly to eastern Laos where he presided over the creation of the **Pathet Lao**'s army and headed up **Advisory Group 100.** *See also* ADMINISTRATIVE OFFICE FOR THE FRONTIER; COMMITTEE FOR EXTERNAL AFFAIRS; COMMITTEE FOR THE EAST, LAO ISSARA; INDOCHINESE COMMUNIST PARTY; INDOCHINESE FEDERATION; KAISÔN PHOMVIHĂN; LAO RESISTANCE GOVERNMENT; PARTY AFFAIRS COMMITTEE.

**CHU VĂN ĐIỀU.** *See* CHU HUY MÂN.

**CHU VĂN TẤN (TÂN HỒNG, 1910–1984).** Longstanding communist member and ranking military officer of Nung origin, born in Bac Thai province in northern Vietnam. Chu Van Tan joined the **Indochinese Communist Party** (ICP) in northern Vietnam in 1934 and was active in his native Vo Nha and Bac Son areas. In February 1941, he became a member of the ICP's Regional Committee of **Tonkin** (*Xu Uy Bac Ky*) and participated in leading revolts in Bac Son in that year. He was also one of the founding fathers of the **People's Army of Vietnam** (*Quan Doi Nhan Dan Viet Nam*), called the **National Salvation Army** (*Cuu Quoc Quan*) in 1941. In September of that year, he served at the head of a platoon in the 2nd National Salvation Army (C*uu Quoc Quan 2*) and in 1944 he commanded the 3rd National Salvation Army (*Cuu Quoc Quan 3*) in the northern Vietnamese military zone called Hoang Hoa Tham. After the Japanese defeat in August 1945, he served as the minister of Defense in the first Provisional Government of the **Democratic Republic of Vietnam** in 1945. He held the post until March 1946, at which time he was named head of Region 4 and then transferred to run war **Zone** I (*Chien Khu I*). Between 1949 and 1954, he led the Inter-zone for the North (*Lien Khu Viet Bac*) as well as being in charge of the Army's Military Tribunal for this region.

**CHUAN KEM PIKET.** *See* DAP CHHUON.

**CHUITON (LE), RAYMOND (1892–?).** Entered the French Naval Academy in 1911 and joined the French resistance during World War II. After the war, he went to Indochina where he served as a cabinet secretary to Admiral **Georges Thierry d'Argenlieu** between September 1945 and September 1946. He retired in late 1946.

**CHUON KEMPHETCHR.** *See* DAP CHHUON.

**CHURCHILL, WINSTON S. (1874–1965).** Until March 1945, he vetoed any British initiative to ask President Franklin Roosevelt to revise his Indochina policy in a pro-French direction, since he knew how strong Roosevelt's hostility to French rule in Indochina was. However, after the Japanese coup against the French on 9 March 1945, Churchill authorized a message to Roosevelt, pleading the cause of the French. The American President died before be could answer his British counterpart. Defeated in elections in

July 1945, Sir Winston Churchill returned to the premiership in 1951 and held it until 1955. During the battle of **Dien Bien Phu**, he refused **Joseph Laniel**'s government's requests that the British intervene militarily in order to save the French camp. On 27 April 1954, Churchill made it clear that such an intervention would torpedo the **Geneva Conference** and the chances of reaching an accord on Korea and Indochina. In the wake of **Joseph Stalin's** death in 1953, Churchill wanted to reduce global tensions concentrated in Asia, not increase them. He fully approved foreign minister **Anthony Eden**'s attempts to reach an accord at Geneva. *See also* JOHN FOSTER DULLES; GENEVA ACCORDS; VAUTOUR.

**CIA.** *See* OFFICE OF STRATEGIC SERVICES.

**CINEMA, DEMOCRATIC REPUBLIC OF VIETNAM.** The cinema had always been popular in French Indochina before World War II – 52 cinemas operated in colonial Vietnam in 1932. Cinema in the **Democratic Republic of Vietnam** (DRV) first appeared in southern Vietnam in 1948, when a number of propaganda reports were filmed in chaotic and difficult conditions, such as *The Capture of the Moc Hoa Post*, *The Battle of Tra Vinh*, or the *Production of Soap in Warzone IX*. **Khuong Me** was one of the best-known southern film-makers in the DRV at this time. In 1950, the north also took to cinema with the filming of the capture of Dong Khe during the battle of **Cao Bang**. The film was hurried off to Beijing where it was developed, then shipped on to Berlin by the Trans-Siberian Railway to be shown during the World Youth Festival. The Vietnamese delegation returned from East Germany with cinematographic material and, with the assistance of Chinese filmmakers, they produced in 1952 the film *Vietnam in Combat*. It was shown at the Karlovy Vary International Film Festival in then-communist Czechoslovakia. In 1953, DRV Vietnamese filmmakers shot their own film, a long documentary entitled the *Victory of the Northwest*. Even if it was no work of art, the film's authors, Mai Loc and Tran Loi, succeeded in obtaining clear images from the shadow of a thick jungle canopy, and this in a time of war. This filmmaking experience served the Vietnamese well at the time of the battle of **Dien Bien Phu**, when the Vietnamese team joined forces with the Soviet filmmaker **Roman Karmen** to produce a reconstitution of the historic battle. They spliced the parts together in **Hanoi** after the return of the DRV to Hanoi in late 1954/1955 to make a propaganda documentary of the historic battle. In the early 1950s, the DRV projected Chinese communist films in base camps for propaganda purposes. Ngo Van Chieu recalled the showing of a film praising the heroic victory of Chinese communists over **Chiang Kai-shek**'s troops: "At the end of the film, we discussed it while a commissar delivered a speech on the struggle we were leading and the achievements of the socialist countries". Little is known of cinema in the **Associated States of Indochina** or the **French Union** forces. *See also* CINEMA, FRANCE; CULTURE; EMULATION CAMPAIGN; INDOCTRINATION; NEW HERO; NOVELS; PSYCHOLOGICAL WARFARE; RECTIFICATION.

**CINEMA, FRANCE.** Unlike its American counterpart's interest in the Vietnam War, French cinema has paid comparatively little attention to the Indochina War. The reasons for this are hard to pin down. The fact that the Indochina War was fought by a professional army, the **Expeditionary Corps**, and not a draft one, lowered its impact upon French society and intellectual debates. Somewhat fewer Frenchmen died in Indochina than in Algeria between 1945 and 1962. The fact that the European settler population living in Indochina was so small also gave it much less salience than the many *pied noirs* in Algeria. About one million Europeans lived in Algeria in 1954 and most moved to France when the war ended in 1962, thus driving its impact home much more directly.

In 1957, some three years after the end of the Indochina War, two films on the conflict nevertheless appeared on the big screen in France: *Patrouille de choc* and *Mort en fraude*. Claude Bernard-Aubert's *Patrouille de Choc* focuses on the last stand of a small group of French soldiers, holed up in an isolated post, as they came under hard Vietnamese attack. In order to head off the censors, Bernard-Aubert had to rewrite the ending so that his soldiers could be offered the chance to escape annihilation (the first title of the film was *Patrouille sans espoir*). While Bernard-Aubert is focused on French soldiers fighting valiantly, Marcel Camus adopted Jean Hougron's novel, *Mort en fraude* (released in English as *Fugitive in Saigon*) to examine how the protagonist, a young Frenchman, tried to understand the Vietnamese and the reasons why they fought. By having the main character live with Vietnamese villagers and eventually die in a massacre let loose by the French army, Camus was one of the rare French directors to critique French colonialism and the war in Indochina through the cinema. Despite the fact that he took up the question of atrocities committed by the **Democratic Republic of Vietnam** (DRV), the French government banned this film in its colonies.

Few other directors were ever as critical or as daring. Most have tended to celebrate the heroism of the French soldiers fighting on when the government abandoned the army it sent in to do the job. A veteran of the Indochina War and an official photographer for the army, **Pierre Schoendoerffer**, is the bestknown example. He produced the ***317ème Section*** in 1965 as American troops headed into southern Vietnam to fight. Like Bernard-Aubert, Schoendoerffer follows a French platoon as it flees the rapidly advancing Vietnamese army at the very moment that the DRV's troops were overruning **Dien Bien Phu**. Tragedy is Schoendoerffer's favorite trope, but military honor and nationalism drive his films. This certainly comes through in his other films flashing back to Indochina through the **Algerian War**, like *L'honneur d'un capitaine* or ***Le crabe tambour***. In 1992, he returned to the heroism of the lost French army in **Dien Bien Phu** just as Bernard-Aubert had also returned to the theme of the tragic French soldiers in *Le facteur s'en va-t-en guerre* (1966). The latter follows them this time to their capture and dispatch to re-education camps before they escape. Schoendoerffer also latched on to the camps. In his *Là-haut, un roi au-dessus des nuages* he has a veteran of the Indochina War go back into Vietnam in search of a Vietnamese comrade and officer escaping from a communist Vietnamese re-education camp. Henri Decoins' *Les parias de la gloire* (1964) stars **Roger Delpey**, author of the novel on which the film is based and a veteran of the Indochina War. *Le fort du fou* (1963) deals with Vietnamese **Catholics** and French soldiers resisting the communist onslaught while *Transit à Saigon* (1963) is based on a drug trafficking scandal. Other French films based on or evoking the Indochina War include: *Ils étaient cinq, Les tripes au soleil, Match contre la mort, Les lâches vivent d'espoir, Charlie Bravo, Ramuntcho, Ascenseur pour l'échafaud* and *Le souffle au cœur. See also* ART; COMICS AND WAR; CULTURE; INDOCTRINATION; INTELLECTUALS; NOVELS; PYSCHOLOGICAL WARFARE.

**CITY AT WAR.** *See* HANOI; SAIGON.

**CIVIL AIR TRANSPORT (CAT).** Private American air company used by the Central Intelligence Agency (CIA) to help the French **Air Force** during the latter part of the Indochina War. The CAT emerged in the wake of the Pacific War when General Claire Chennault teamed up with veterans of his famous Flying Tigers in China to create the Civil Air Transport (CAT). Between 1946 and 1949, its main task was to assist **Chiang Kai-shek**'s nationalist forces in their fight against Chinese communists. With the defeat of the nationalists in 1949 and faced with bankruptcy due to the loss of operations on the mainland, CAT leaders looked to other markets and financial sources in order to keep their company afloat.

The arrival of the **Cold War** in Asia, the intensification of the Indochina War, and the increased American commitment to holding the line against communism there worked in CAT's favor in two ways. First, the intensity of the battles between the French and the forces of **Democratic Republic of Vietnam** (DRV) in Indochina increased the French demand for air and firepower. However, because of commitments in Europe, the French government found it difficult to commit sufficient air forces to Indochina. Second, American Cold-War commitments in Asia led Washington to approve and to finance the CIA's purchase of the CAT for running clandestine operations throughout the region. In August 1950, the American intelligence service purchased the CAT for less than one million dollars. The CAT continued, however, to function as a private company; only its highest-ranking directors, such as Claire Chennault, knew of the company's new relationship with the CIA and the covert nature of some of its missions.

However, CAT's attempts to penetrate the Indochina war market between 1950 and 1952 encountered considerable resistance from French political authorities suspicious of American political and commercial motivations. It was only in 1953, when the intensity of military operations on the battlefield and the inability of the French Air Force to respond adequately, that General **Henri Navarre** pushed through a deal with the CAT. President **Dwight D. Eisenhower** signed off on the project in March 1953, authorizing the company to provide pilots to fly 12 new C-119's ("Flying Boxcars"). During operation Squaw I, CAT pilots helped supply French troops during the battle of **Na San** in Laos in 1952, and played an important role in supplying the besieged French camp at **Dien Bien Phu** in 1954 during operation Squaw II. Between 13 March and 6 May 1954, American pilots in the CAT flew some 682 missions over the valley of Dien Bien Phu, but not without suffering losses. On 6 May, enemy fire brought down a CAT-piloted C-119 in Laos, killing the legendary American pilot **James McGovern**.

While Squaw II's mission officially ended in July 1954, CAT's activities in Indochina did not. Following the signing of the **Geneva Accords** dividing Vietnam provisionally into a communist state in the north and a non-communist one in the south, CAT pilots helped transport some 20,000 Vietnamese civilians leaving the north as part of *Opération Cognac*. In May 1959, as the DRV reactivitated the **Ho Chi Minh Trail** passing through Laos, CAT was renamed Air America and would help the CIA operate clandestine missions in Laos in particular. See also *GROUPEMENT DE COMMANDOS MIXTES AEROPORTES; SERVICE ACTION*.

**CIVIL WAR.** Wars of decolonization almost always spawn civil violence at some level as different groups vie for control over the postcolonial state and its ideological soul. The civil violence of the colonial conflict was most prominent in eastern Indochina, where communism had divided Vietnamese nationalists since the 1920s.

The roots of this conflict reached back to the revolts led by the **Vietnamese Nationalist Party** (known better as the VNQDD) and the **Indochinese Communist Party** (ICP) in central and upper Vietnam in the early 1930s. Crushed by the French, nationalists from both groups took refuge mainly in southern China. There, violent ideological breaks occurred between leaders of both sides, divided as to the type of political regime and social program that would be instituted in Vietnam upon its future liberation from French colonialism. Similar divergences occurred behind the bars of the colonial prison on **Poulo Condor** island, when nationalists and communists suddenly found themselves arguing, even fighting, over the future of Vietnam. **Tran Huy Lieu**, for example, crossed over to the communist side in this prison reflection of Vietnamese politics.

The matter was put on hold until the Japanese brought down French Indochina in March 1945. Then, the question as to who would rule the new nation-state following the Japanese defeat suddenly became very real. The low-scale political violence confined to Poulo Condor cells and southern Chinese backstreets rapidly transformed into a civil war when communists and nationalists returned to Vietnam in mid-1945, armed, and determined to impose their vision of the national future, even it meant using force against other Vietnamese. The colonial war breaking out between the French and the DRV in 1945–46 was thus doubled by a civil conflict with roots in the interwar period. In mid-1946, with the Chinese out of the way and **Ho Chi Minh** in Paris, **Vo Nguyen Giap** successfully attacked non-communist nationalist parties hostile to the communists, pushing most of them back into southern China.

While some French officers had initially supported Vo Nguyen Giap's destruction of the nationalist forces, local political leaders, above all **Léon Pignon**, regretted that the French now found themselves face-to-face with the **Viet Minh**. As early as January 1947, Pignon had advised his superiors secretly that the French war with the DRV had to "be transposed" to a Vietnamese playing field, using the Viet Minh's adversaries to do the fighting. French-backed civil war now emerged in force. The French turned to the former Emperor Bao Dai, now living in exile in China and apparently unhappy with the DRV, in order to build a counter-revolutionary state, around which non-communist nationalists would rally. In 1947–1948, the French rallied religious groups in the south, most notably the **Cao Dai, Hoa Hao** and **Binh Xuyen**, to their cause, aggravating the spread of civil violence across all of Vietnam.

Meanwhile, Vietnamese non-communists such as the VNQDD and the **Greater Vietnam Party** hoped that their anti-communism and the Cold War would force Paris to accord them the independence the French had denied to the DRV and to them in 1945–1946. They would be disappointed. Although the French convinced Bao Dai to return to Vietnam and although an Associated State of Vietnam emerged in 1949 under American pressure, the French only slowly granted non-communist nationalists sovereignty. And yet this did not prevent the French from pushing the Associated State of Vietnam to increase the number of Vietnamese fighting against the DRV. From 1950, as the Cold War bore down upon Indochina, tens of thousands of Vietnamese began fighting in the French Union forces against the Vietnamese forces of the DRV.

By "Vietnamizing" the war from 1950 (what the French called ***jaunissement,*** or "yellowing"), the French exacerbated an already intense civil war among the Vietnamese. Colonialism, communism, nationalism, and anti-communism thus made for a deadly combination in Indochina. Violence also spilled into Laos, the non-Vietnamese highlands and eventually into eastern Cambodia, as Chinese aid allowed the DRV's armed forces to move troops across the Indochinese battlefield. The expansion of DRV troops into western Indochina also allowed the DRV/ICP to install associated "**resistance governments**" (*chinh phu khang chien*) in Laos and Cambodia, the **Pathet Lao** and the **Khmer Issarak**. By creating national armies, states, and revolutionary parties for their revolutionary Lao and Cambodian partners, Vietnamese communists also contributed to the widening of the deadly consequences of civil war to an Indochinese dimension. *See also* ADMINISTRATIVE OFFICE FOR THE FRONTIER; COMMITTEE FOR EXTERNAL AFFAIRS; COMMITTEE FOR THE EAST, LAO ISSARA; PARTY AFFAIRS COMMITTEE.

**CLARAC, ACHILLE MARIE (1903–1999).** Career French diplomat who served in Indochina as the French restored their colonial order in 1945–1946. Clarac worked in various diplomatic posts in the United States and the Middle East before joining Free French forces in North Africa following the Allied landing there in November 1942. From late 1945, he served as diplomatic advisor to the French High Commissioner **Georges Thierry d'Argenlieu**. He was involved in negotiations with the **Republic of China** and the Kingdom of **Thailand** concerning the withdrawal of Chinese troops from northern Indochina and the retrocession of territories ceded to the Thais under Japanese duress during World War II. He left his diplomatic post in Indochina in 1947, following the outbreak of war on **19 December 1946** and the departure of Thierry d'Argenlieu. Between 1954 and 1955, he was the cabinet director to Minister Guy La Chambre, in charge of relations with the **Associated States of Indochina**. In 1959, Clarac became ambassador to the Kingdom of Thailand.

**CLARK, MARK WAYNE (1896–1984).** Influential American general involved in providing aid to the French during the Indochina War. Graduated from the United States Military Academy at West Point, he first saw battle as second lieutenant in World War I. In 1942, Clark became chief of staff of the Army Ground Forces and deputy commander-in-chief of the Allied Forces in the North African theatre. He served as deputy to **Dwight D. Eisenhower**. Clark persuaded French Admiral Jean Louis Darlan to break with Vichy and end French resistance to Allied forces landing in North Africa. In 1943, he led the Fifth Army and played a leading role in the liberation of Europe, freeing Rome in June 1944. In May 1952, **Harry Truman** appointed Clark commander-in-chief of the **United Nations** forces in Korea and Clark signed the Korean armistice in July 1953. In 1952, he visited Indochina, meeting with **Jean Letourneau**, **Bao Dai**, and Generals **Raoul Salan** and **Nguyen Van Hinh**. He oversaw American military **aid** to the French in Indochina and was convinced that the French were capable of conducting the war without American officers interfering, much to the relief of French officials worried by the growing American presence. Meanwhile, Clark reported to the American Joint Chiefs of Staff that the **Democratic Republic of Vietnam** was under the complete control of communist China. *See also* AID, AMERICAN; AID, CHINESE; AID, SOVIET.

**CLÉMENTIN, JEAN MANAN (1924–).** Considered to be one of the best informed Western journalists covering the Indochina War at the time. He left for Indochina as a soldier in the French army, but soon switched to journalism. He wrote first for the army before moving on to the *Associated Press* where he made his name (often under the pseudonym of *Tante Sojha*). Sometime in the late 1940s, he wrote a series of highly critical articles about French policy in Indochina in the military paper, *Combat*. He returned to France in 1950 and went on to play an important role in the development of the famous French investigative and satirical newspaper, *Le Canard Enchaîné*.

**CLOS, MAX (1925–2002).** French journalist during the Indochina War for the *Associated Press* and then *Le Monde*. In 1952, he conducted interviews with returning French prisoners and wrote a series of stories on Vietnamese prisoner-of-war camps. He was the chief editor of the French paper *Le Figaro* between 1970 and 1990. In 1955, the government of **Ngo Dinh Diem** expelled him, together with **Lucien Bodard**, from southern Vietnam.

**COCHINCHINA.** Term originally coined by Portuguese travelers to describe the southern Nguyen dynasty. The French used the term to describe the colony they carved out of present day southern Vietnam by the mid-1860s, *la Cochinchine*. In Vietnamese, this French geopolitical term translated as *Nam Ky*. Following the Japanese ***coup de force* of 9 March 1945** ousting the French from Indochina, the **Tran Trong Kim** government adopted the term southern section or *Nam Phan* in the Official Gazette to replace the colonial terms *Cochinchine/Nam Ky*. The **Democratic Republic of Vietnam** followed suit but dropped *Phan* in favour of *Bo* to come up with the term, *Nam Bo*, or southern region. Upon returning to Indochina after World War II, the French would revive the colonial term, "Cochinchina", as part of a wider battle over the control of the south and its political status: would it be colonial (Cochinchina/Indochinese Federation) or national (Nam Bo/Vietnam)? With the failure of the **Indochinese Federation** in 1947 and of Cochinchinese autonomy, from 1948 the French backed away from the idea of a separate southern entity and allowed **Bao Dai** to unify the country under the national name of Vietnam with the southern part referred to in Vietnamese as *Nam Viet*. Cochinchina as a legal, geopolitical colonial reality ceased to exist. *See also* 23 SEPTEMBER 1945; 19 DECEMBER 1946; ACCORDS OF 6 MARCH 1946; ANNAM; BAO DAI SOLUTION; COCHINCHINESE CIVIL GUARD; GEORGES THIERRY D'ARGENLIEU; INDOCHINESE FEDERATION; JEAN CEDILE; LANGUAGE OF WAR; NGUYEN VAN THINH; PROVISIONAL GOVERNMENT OF THE REPUBLIC OF COCHINCHINA; TONKIN.

**COCHINCHINESE CIVIL GUARD**. The civil guard for Cochinchina was first created on 19 September 1909 in charge of maintaining internal security in the southern colony. It played an important role in smashing the communist revolt in Cochinchina in 1940. In 1944, the French rebaptized it the *Garde civile indochinoise* and increased its size and personnel. The Japanese, however, disbanded it in March 1945 when they overthrew the French in Indochina. Upon returning to southern Indochina, General **Jean Valluy** reconstituted it in late August or October 1946 in order to ensure local security while the **Expeditionary Corps** concentrated on more pressing military matters. In March 1947, it officially became the *Garde républicaine cochinchinoise* and was attached to the **Provisional Government of the Republic of Cochinchina**. With the failure of Cochinchinese autonomy and the unification of Vietnam under **Bao Dai** from June 1948, it was increasingly nationalized and renamed the *Garde du Viet Nam Sud* (*Doi Thanh Ve Binh Nam Viet*). The name changed yet again in April 1949 to become the Vietnamese Republican National Guard (*Ve Binh Quoc Gia Viet Nam*). Until 1949, European officers mainly commanded the 8,000 to 10,000 man strong civil guard. *See also* ARMY, ASSOCIATED STATE OF VIETNAM; PEOPLE'S ARMY OF VIETNAM.

**COGNY, RENÉ JULES LUCIEN (1904–1968).** Ranking French officer during the Indochina War. Graduated from the *École polytechnique* in 1925, he entered the army as an artillery officer. He was captured by the Germans in June 1940, but was allowed to return to France where he continued working in the army. He crossed over to the Resistance in 1942, when the Germans occupied southern France. In October 1943, Cogny was arrested and deported to Germany. Following World War II, he taught in the *École supérieure de Guerre*. In March 1950, he became brigadier general and in December 1950 arrived in **Saigon** to serve as the director of the Military Cabinet of General **Jean de Lattre de Tassigny** then serving as high commissioner and commander-in-chief of French Armed Forces in Indochina. Upon the latter's death, Cogny briefly worked for General **Raoul Salan** but differences between the two men led Cogny to take up the command of the *2ème Division de marche du Tonkin* for the eastern sector in March 1952. In May 1953, he became lieutenant general and assumed command of the ground forces in North Vietnam, at the helm when **Dien Bien Phu** fell to the DRV in May 1954. He stayed on in Indochina, serving as *Délégué général pour le nord Vietnam* between December 1954 and May 1955. His command of the ground forces for North Vietnam also ended in May 1955, when he returned to France.

**COLD WAR.** The Indochina War was one of the hottest and deadliest battlegrounds of the Cold War. The opposition between the East and the West, between the Soviet bloc and the Western bloc, first made itself felt shortly after the Pacific War ended.

American President **Harry Truman** abandoned his predecessor's hostility towards the French in Indochina and distanced himself from Franklin Roosevelt's belief in the Grand Alliance as a basis for building the postwar international system. By early 1947, Truman was determined to "contain" Soviet expansionism. To do this, he needed French support in Europe and he was not going to put it at risk by forcing them to decolonize rapidly in Indochina. **Ho Chi Minh**'s letters and overtures to the Americans between 1945 and 1947 went unanswered. In contrast to the pressure the Americans put on the Dutch to end the war with non-communist nationalists in **Indonesia** in 1949, the French were able to prolong their colonial presence in Indochina and to implicate the United States in that process on anticommunist grounds.

The fact that the Soviets balked at supporting the **Democratic Republic of Vietnam** (DRV) only reinforced the French hand. Like Truman, Stalin was much more interested in maintaining good relations with the French in the hopes that they would distance themselves from the Americans, especially in light of the electoral success of the **French Communist Party** in France after the war. Stalin was not going to jeopardize his relations with the French after World War II by pushing the French too hard on Indochina. Like Truman, Stalin refused to answer Ho Chi Minh's letters. And if Truman suspected Ho Chi Minh of being Moscow's man in Asia, Stalin feared that Ho Chi Minh was not sufficiently internationalist and might follow Tito's example by adopting a neutralist line in international affairs at a crucial juncture.

For the DRV, the Chinese communist victory of October 1949 shifted the Cold War to Asia and in so doing saved the DRV from diplomatic defeat. In January 1950, the Chinese persuaded Stalin to recognize the DRV, bringing with him the entire communist bloc. The Americans responded within weeks by recognizing the Associated State of Vietnam, bringing with them most of the Western alliance. However, non-communist Asian states, with the exceptions of Thailand and the Republics of China and of Korea, refused to choose between the two Vietnams, knowing that behind this choice lay the seeds of a major conflagration, as **Jawaharlal Nehru** put it.

Many ranking Vietnamese communists welcomed the arrival of the Cold War and were ready to assume their place as frontline soldiers in the global battle for Southeast Asia. **Truong Chinh**, acting general secretary of the **Indochinese Communist Party**, put it that way at the time. He promised to push revolution in all of Indochina in order to serve as the communist bloc's bulwark in Southeast Asia against the West. The Cold War also allowed Vietnamese communists to begin transforming Vietnamese society in radical ways. The party began to increase its control over society, purge itself of socially unfit members, and launch land reform before the war against the colonizer had even finished.

The Cold War also complicated the DRV's quest for power. Nowhere was this clearer than during the **Geneva Conference** of 1954. Despite the fact that the DRV had used military force to inflict an extraordinary defeat upon the colonizer at **Dien Bien Phu**, the DRV only obtained half of the Vietnam that Ho Chi Minh had declared independent in September 1945. Following Stalin's death in April 1953, the Chinese and the Soviets had decided to seek a thaw in relations with the West by ending the Korean and Indochinese wars, even if it meant dividing Vietnam provisionally. They accepted a divided Korea in 1953; they did it again in Vietnam a year later. *See also* NEUTRALIZATION OF INDOCHINA.

**COLLABORATION.** The creation and operation of empires have always depended upon the support of the conquered local elites and populations. The expansion of Japanese and German empires across much of Europe and Asia during World War II infused the word "collaboration" with highly charged political, cultural, and social meanings that legitimated acts of violence at the end of the war against those who had worked with the foreign occupiers. It also allowed the postwar leaders distributing justice to set the agenda for the future and legitimate their own new nation-states. For Europeans, the names of Hacha, Pavelic, Quisling, and Pétain are well known. China has its Wang Jingwei, Puyi and, for the Chinese communists, there is **Chiang Kai-shek**.

The Indochina War has its own set of "collaborators", referred to as *giac/bandits*, *bu nhin/puppets* or *nguy/quislings*. The **Democratic Republic of Vietnam** held in particular contempt the persons of **Bao Dai** and **Ngo Dinh Diem** for collaborating with the "foreign invaders", the French and the American "colonialists" and "imperialists", respectively. Meanwhile, the Associated State of Vietnam followed by the State and Republic of Vietnam stigmatized the communist leadership led by **Ho Chi Minh** for selling out the nation to Chinese and Soviet communists.

"Collaboration" is of course a complex historical phenomenon. Domination elicits a series of shifting strategies of association, accommodation, and resistance. The superiority of the occupier's power over the occupied or the probability or improbability of outside intervention determine levels and types of collaboration. Ideology can drive collaboration. This was true in many parts of German-occupied Europe during World War II. Elites in the Hitler's Europe often saw new possibilities, even revolutionary ones, in working with the occupiers. As Jan T. Gross defines it, collaboration is "occupier-driven" but it implicates the history of both the occupied and the occupiers: "Collaboration – its logic, its appeal or self-justification, its social base – emerges in each country precisely at the intersection between the occupier's intent and the occupied's perception about the range of options at their disposal". This could mean cooperating with the occupier in order to survive difficult indeed life-threatening situations in high-politics and everyday life. And the level of cooperation could change in one direction or another in terms of a decline or an increase in the occupier's strength. The collapse of an *ancien régime* or the rise of a new one, even a foreign-backed one, could also provide opportunities for those opposed to the old order or seeking to push revolutionary change.

Collaboration had been a vital part of European colonial expansion. In Indochina, the French even developed a specific policy of collaboration. This emerged in the wake of World War I when **Albert Sarraut**, then Governor General of Indochina and leading Republican colonial thinker of the time, announced to Vietnamese elites in **Hanoi** a new policy of Franco-Vietnamese collaboration – *la politique de collaboration franco-annamite*. As Agathe Larcher has shown, this new colonial strategy initiated in 1919 was designed to legitimate colonial rule, to associate moderate, pro-French Vietnamese elites with the French and to head off emerging nationalist, communist, and foreign threats to French rule over Indochina. During World War I, the famous anti-colonialist Phan Boi Chau and even the Vietnamese King, Duy Tan, tried to foment a revolt against the French. Sarraut promised reforms, a political charter, and even evoked independence to win over Vietnamese essential to running the colonial state. The French would be liberal with those who worked with them to build Indochina; but they would brook no opposition to the colonial right to rule. Sarraut was behind the creation of the redoubtable ***Sûrete.***

While this *politique de collaboration* turned out to be a failure by 1930, as colonial reformism foundered and a new round of nationalist revolts shook Indochina, it was not without its successes. In the early 1920s, Phan Boi Chau rallied to the "Franco-Vietnamese policy of collaboration", worried by the rise of Japan after the Great War and convinced that the French were sincere in their efforts to reform. Other nationalists saw colonial occupation as an opportunity to push through radical measures that would have been impossible under the old order. Phan Chu Trinh, not unlike some Koreans working under the Japanese, joined the French convinced that they were the best allies for promoting a socio-cultural revolution in Vietnam and sidelining the monarchy in favor of some sort of colonial democracy. Both Phans were ultimately disappointed, but neither knew the outcome of the colonial story at the time.

World War II also generated a new series of collaborative relationships. Staring in 1940, the Japanese occupation of Indochina gave rise to a particularly complex situation and set of power dynamics. Whereas the Japanese overthrew Western colonial regimes across Southeast Asia, incorporating them into their own Asian empire, the fall of France in June 1940 and Pétain's decision in October 1940 to pursue a policy of collaboration with Nazi Germany prevented the Japanese from overthrowing the French in Indochina. As a result, until early 1945 two colonial empires ruled Indochina, a French one located within a wider Japanese one. Both the Japanese and the French competed for the hearts and minds of their Vietnamese subjects. Both sides pitched the advantages of their colonial project. But neither could go too far in this strange colonial condominium. The Japanese needed the French and the French needed to work with the Japanese to hold on to Indochina.

Things changed as Japanese fortunes worsened in the war and the Allied liberation of France in 1944 brought a new French government to power under the leadership of General **Charles de Gaulle**. On 9 March 1945, convinced that the French in Indochina were shifting their loyalties to the Allies, the Japanese overthrew the rudderless post Vichy authorities and in so doing brought down the Indochinese colonial house with it. While Decoux saw himself as a hero for having successfully preserved Indochina as long as possible, de Gaulle viewed him as a "collaborator" to be purged. And many a Gaullist official arriving in Indochina in mid-1945 viewed much of the former Vichy colonial authorities as well as European settler community with suspicion if not outright disdain. De Gaulle himself designated a new admiral to lead Indochina, **Georges Thierry d'Argenlieu**, with strict orders to rebuild a French colonial state in the form of an **Indochinese Federation**. Meanwhile, leaders of the **Cao Dai** and **Hoa Hao** had relied on the Japanese during the war to push their projects forward. Several Vietnamese nationalists saw revolution in fascist ideas promoted by the Germans and their Japanese allies.

However, the collapse of the French and Japanese colonial hold on Indochina changed power relationships profoundly in mid-1945. Taking advantage of this, the **Viet Minh** took power in August 1945 and created a new nation-state, the **Democratic Republic of Vietnam** (DRV). Within no time, two new nation-states born out of World War II, one French led by Charles de Gaulle, the other Vietnamese under Ho Chi Minh, began competiting for the loyalties and cooperation of the Vietnamese people. Viet Minh authorities immediately went to work arresting Vietnamese who had collaborated with the Japanese and the French (and, in their view, risked doing so again). Two of Sarraut's colonial partners, Pham Quynh and Bui Quang Chieu, were executed. However, in an extraordinary move, the Emperor **Bao Dai** broke with the policy of Franco-Vietnamese collaboration, abdicated, and angered the French by joining the DRV as "supreme advisor". Added to this were non-communist nationalist parties led by the **Vietnamese Nationalist Party** and the Dai Viet, each of which urged Vietnamese not to collaborate with the French "colonialists" or the Viet Minh "communists". Loyalty thus became an extremely complex and contested notion at the time. The DRV made it clear via its security services that it would deal harshly with those who collaborated with the French and posed a national security threat to the new nation-state. The criminalization of collaboration was reinforced in law and through propaganda drives.

In the south, power relations changed again on **23 September 1945**, when the French, now backed by the British, drove the Viet Minh out of **Saigon** and, with the arrival of the Expeditionary Corps a few weeks later, began to reoccupy Indochina below the **16th parallel**. This "second" French occupation changed the dynamics of collaboration yet again, leading a handful of southern elites such as **Nguyen Van Thinh** and **Le Van Hoach** to join the French in restoring order and creating the **Provisional Government of the Republic of Cochinchina**. The DRV's military commander in the south, **Nguyen Binh**, issued death warrants against such "collaborators" and "traitors".

Vietnamese elites opposed to colonialism and communism found themselves in a particularly difficult situation. Their fierce **anti-colonialism** had alienated them from the French as possible collaborators, while their anti-communism had led them into opposition or **civil war** with the Viet Minh/ICP. By the late 1940s, many of these non-communist nationalists in the VNQDD and Dai Viet parties chose to support the French counter-revolutionary state led by Bao Dai, backed increasingly from 1950 by the United States, as the lesser of two evils. Anticommunist Vietnamese elites also saw in the **Bao Dai solution** and the **Cold War** the chance to force the French hand and to oppose the rise of what appeared to be a communist-driven DRV. The latter did its best to counter Franco-Associated State of Vietnam moves, alternating between persuasion and violence all the while casting itself as the true nationalist state and portraying those working with the French and Americans as "quislings", "puppets", and "bandits". Some, including **Ngo Dinh Diem**, refused to collaborate with either side, preferring to pursue a policy of ***attentisme***.

This wide range of strategies reflected not only the number of options available, but it also points up the degree to which the Indochina War gave rise to new power centers and changing power relations. The internationalization of the war, symbolized by the support provided by the Americans and the Chinese from 1950 to each of the main belligerents also generated new relationships and shifted old ones. However, none of these groups ever imposed or enjoyed unwavering loyalty during nine years of war. Control over territories and their populations shifted from one group to another. From 1947, the DRV only controlled remotes parts of Vietnam. The French security and military forces held the deltas, the cities, and the bulk of the population. This led to particularly complex strategies of association for hundreds of thousands of civilians living in these areas as they tried to conduct their everyday lives without getting caught in the crossfire of competing sovereignties and demands on their loyalty, labor, assets, and sons and daughters. Things became even more complex in 1949, when the Associated State of Vietnam came to life, backed with its own security services, army, and propaganda machines.

The internationalization of the war and the need to mobilize civilians and troops for major battles saw the communist leadership impose national service and a series of revolutionary methods designed to more effectively control the population – **emulation campaigns, rectification,** education, and policing. Many embraced this revolution let loose in wartime. Land reform certainly won the cooperation of thousands of peasants. However, the communization of the state and the society led many others to flee DRV zones, and not just "the rich".

**COLLET, FRANÇOIS (1922–1994).** One of the French army's best **commando** officers during the Indochina War. He began his military career on the eve of World War II as a naval officer and crossed over to the Allied side during the war. In 1945, he left for Indochina as part of the commando paratroopers. He led the *Monfort* commando section during the entire Indochina war. After the conflict, he transferred to the **Republic of Vietnam**'s Naval Training Group and served as second in command of an ocean dredger in Can Tho in 1955. In 1956, Collet was part of the Franco-British commando team that landed at Port Said during the Suez Crisis.

**COLLINS, JOSEPH LAWTON (1896–1987).** Graduated from West Point in 1917, Collins taught in several American military academies and served in the American General Staff of the Philippine Division between 1933 and 1936. During World War II, he led the 25th Division in heavy fighting in Guadalcanal in 1943. He then transferred to the European theater where he helped in the planning of the D-Day landing at Normandy in 1944. His VII Corps landed on Utah beach and took Cherbourg before fighting all the way into Germany. After the war, Collins rose to army chief of staff to General Omar Bradley at the head of the Joint Chiefs of Staff. Collins was involved in the army's integration into the **North Atlantic Treaty Organization** and was a supporter of the **Korean War** (though he opposed Douglas MacArthur's attempts to expand the conflict northwards into China against **Harry Truman**'s will). **Dwight D. Eisenhower** appointed Collins to serve as the president's special envoy to Vietnam between November 1954 and May 1955, holding the rank of ambassador and charged with coordinating all American activities there in consultation with his old friend, French General **Paul Ely**. Concerning the **Republic of Vietnam**, Collins tended to a variety of important matters for the White House, including the question of refugee resettlement, political democracy, economic development, land reform, and the establishment and training of an all-Vietnamese army. In line with the **Ely-Collins agreement** of 13 December 1954, on 12 February 1955, the United States took over the training of the Vietnamese armed forces while the French withdrew their instructors. Collins reported back favorably on the emerging Republic of Vietnam and recommended providing American assistance to it. However, like many French officials, including Ely, he advised against supporting **Ngo Dinh Diem.** In the end, however, Eisenhower opted to support the Vietnamese leader given the absence of any other viable option and under pressure from congressional leaders. Collins retired from the army in 1956.

**COLONIAL ACADEMY.** The origins of the French *École coloniale* or Colonial Academy can be traced to the creation of the *École cambodgienne* by Auguste Pavie in 1885 to train Cambodian elites. However, with the rapid expansion of the French empire under the Third Republic, a decision was quickly made to transform the Cambodian school into a *bona fide* Academy designed to train young French civil servants to serve in all the Empire. In 1889, Eugène Étienne officially rebaptized the Cambodian school as the French *École coloniale* or Colonial Academy. A handful of non-French colonial subject elites continued to train in the Academy. The Lao nationalist Prince **Phetxarāt** was one; even the future **Ho Chi Minh** unsuccessfully applied to study there. However, the "indigenous" section of the Academy was rapidly dwarfed in size and quality by what became a republican *grande école* for training French colonial administrators to run the Empire. The Academy's class of 1912 counted 32 students, increasing to 118 in 1930 and 428 in 1938. Some of the main French political actors in the Indochina War graduated from the Academy in the 1920s and 1930s, including **Léon Pignon**, **Charles Bonfils**, **Pierre Messmer**, and **Jean Cédile,** to name but a few. Students studied colonial law, administration, and economics, as well as the history and languages of the country to which they were assigned (proficiency requirements in a foreign language were much better at the outset than during the interwar period). Graduation from the Academy offered its French students entry into the upper echelons of the Empire. In 1936, with the advent of the Popular Front in France, the Academy was renamed the *École nationale de la France d'Outre-mer*. After World War II, the French specialist of Asian history and cultures, **Paul Mus**, assumed the direction of the school. However, his sympathy for Vietnamese nationalism, his public critique of the army's use of **torture** in Indochina, and his increasingly vocal calls for decolonization cost him his job there. In 1959, as decolonization accelerated and the French fought another colonial war in Algeria, the school was renamed yet again as the *Institut des hautes études d'Outre-mer*. In 2002, the vestiges of the Colonial Academy were fused into the *École nationale d'administration* (ENA).

**COLONNA, CÔME DAMIEN (1904–?).** French civil servant who made his career in Indochina. After serving for 10 years in Laos, in 1943 he became provincial chief of Chau Doc (1943–44) and Ha Tien (1945–47) in Vietnam. In 1948, he worked as the chief of cabinet for the minister of Labour in the provisional southern Vietnamese government. Between 1949 and 1950, he was director of the Office of Tourism in Indochina before taking a position in the economics section in the High Commissioner's Office for Indochina between 1951 and 1952.

**COLONS.** *See* FRANÇAIS D'INDOCHINE.

**COMBAT.** *See* CASUALTIES; CEMETERIES; EXPERIENCE OF WAR; MYTH OF WAR.

**COMICS AND WAR.** Better known in French as the BD or *bande dessinée* (drawn strip), a number of Francophone artitists and writers have used the comic strip as an original way of taking up the Indochina War, exploring the question of French colonialism, and examining contested issues in the politics of French memory-making. Two Belgian artists, Jan Bucquoy and Erwin Sels, were among the first to do so in *Une épopée française* (1990). Through the personnage of a young French lieutenant, Bucquoy and Sels paint a damning portrait of French colonialism and of the atrocities committed by the **Expeditionary Corps** during the conflict, complete with severed heads and portrayals of **torture**. At the same time, the French duo Lax and Giroud published the first of a two part series on the Indochina War, entitled *Les oubliés d'Annam* (1990, complete edition 2000). Like their Belgian counterparts, Lax and Giroud provide a pointed critique of the French conduct of the Indochina War in particular and of French colonialism more generally. In *Les oubliés d'Annam*, the reader follows a young French officer in Indochina as he confronts colonial atrocities, discovers Vietnamese nationalism (through a Vietnamese woman as in *Une épopée française*) before finally, after much soul searching, deserting to the **Viet Minh**.

What makes these early BDs on the Indochina War so remarkable is the extent to which their publication coincided with, if not participated in a wider French battle over the memory of colonialism and the failed wars of decolonization in Indochina and Algeria. Indeed, as these comics came off the press, the **Boudarel affair** exploded and set off a sustained, sometimes violent and always passionate debate in the media. **Georges Boudarel** had joined the Viet Minh as a young man; the French Right singled him out in the early 1990s as a war criminal. Significantly, shortly before the Boudarel affair began, Lax and Giroud had relied upon Jacques Doyon's *Les soldats blancs de Ho Chi Minh*, and at least to some extent the person of Georges Boudarel described in Doyon's book, to construct the main character in *Les oubliés d'Annam*. More recently, in 2003 Stanislas and Rullier have returned to the Indochina War with *La vie de Victor Levallois*: *Trafic en Indochine*, and *La route de Cao Bang*. Lax and Giroud produced something of a colonial sequel to the *Oubliés d'Annam* on the **Algerian War**, entitled *Azrayen*. *See also* CINEMA; CULTURE; HISTORY; INTELLECTUALS; NOVELS.

**COMININDO.** Officially known as the *Comité interministériel de l'Indochine*. **Charles de Gaulle** created this powerful inter-ministerial committee for Indochina on 21 February 1945 in order to oversee the reoccupation of Indochina and centralize policy-making under the president of the Provisional Government of the Republic of France, instead of, as before, the Ministry of Colonies. Members of this committee included the ministers of Colonies, Economy and Finance, War, Foreign Affairs and the head of Intelligence (at that time the *Direction générale des études et recherches*). All correspondence with the high commissioner for Indochina went through this office, making its general secretary the single most informed person in the government on the state of affairs in Indochina. **François de Langlade** was one of its first general secretaries. Following de Gaulle's lead, **Félix Gouin** and **Georges Bidault** maintained the Comindo. While not always in agreement, the Cominindo's leaders tended to back **Georges Thierry d'Argenlieu**'s increasingly aggressive actions towards the **Democratic Republic of Vietnam** until the outbreak of war on **19 December 1946**. In January 1947, as the battle for **Hanoi** raged, **Léon Blum**'s government succeeded in getting rid of the Cominindo and put the Ministry of Overseas France back in charge of Indochinese affairs.

***COMITÉ INTERMINISTÉRIEL DE L'INDOCHINE.*** *See* COMININDO.

**COMMANDO**. According to **Edmond Grall**, commander of the ***Groupement des commandos mixtes aéroportés*** (GCMA) between 1951 and 1953, the French meaning of the word "commando" during the Indochina War referred to punctual, localized operations using sudden action to surprise and jolt the enemy. Theoretically, such operations were not to be confused with "Action" or "***Service Action***" missions, which were designed to build up secret *maquis* to use against the enemy. However, "action" operations could deploy commando means to attain their goals and in practice the line between the two concepts was blurred. **Roger Vandenberghe**, for example, executed commando operations to jolt the enemy, whereas Grall's GCMA executed "action" to build up maquis behind enemy lines. *See also* CHARLES LACHEROY; REVOLUTIONARY WARFARE.

**COMMITTEE FOR EXTERNAL AFFAIRS (*Ban Ngoại Vụ*)**. The secret administrative unit through which the **Indochinese Communist Party** (ICP) first directed its affairs in Cambodia during the Indochina War. This entity first emerged as the Committee for Overseas Affairs (*Ban Hai Ngoai*) in 1947. In August 1948, the veteran communist **Nguyen Thanh Son** took charge of this committee under the new name of the Committee for External Affairs (*Ban Ngoai Vu*); it answered directly to the ICP's Territorial Committee for Nam Bo (*Xu Uy Nam Bo*) run by **Le Duan**. The Committee for External Affairs was based in the Vietnamese border province of Ha Tien in **Zone IX** (*Khu IX*) and officially began operations on 7 December 1948. Adminstratively and militarily, this committee led all the liberation zones into which the ICP had divided Cambodia: the Southeast, Southwest, and Northeast, and the Phnom Penh special region. (The Overseas **Party Affairs Committee** in Thailand, led by **Hoang Van Hoan**, administered the northwestern zone.) To carry out his work, Nguyen Thanh Son also relied upon the National Salvation League of Overseas Vietnamese in Cambodia (*Lien Doan Viet Kieu Cuu Quoc Cao Mien*). The Committee for External Affairs was the main conduit through which the Vietnamese introduced communism into Cambodia during the Indochina War. *See also* ADMINISTRATIVE OFFICE FOR THE FRONTIER; ADVISORY GROUP 100; CHU HUY MAN; COMMITTEE FOR THE EAST, LAO ISSARA; INDOCHINESE FEDERATION; NGUYEN KHANH.

**COMMITTEE FOR THE EAST, LAO ISSARA**. Founded by the **Indochinese Commuist Party** (ICP) in late 1947 and run by **Inter-Zone IV** (*Lien Khu IV*), the **Lao Issara** Committee for the East operated from Con Cuong, located on the Vietnamese-Lao border. Although the committee was theoretically a part of the Lao Issara government-in-exile in Thailand, its location on Inter-Zone IV's western border allowed the ICP to use it as an opening into a Lao Issara nationalist movement largely suspicious of communism and the Vietnamese. The Eastern committee counted among its Lao members **Ōkham Anurak**, **Nūhak Phūmsavan**, Som Phommachanh, and **Kaisôn Phomvihān**, all future allies of Vietnamese communists. The Lao Issara Committee for the East allowed the Vietnamese to keep close tabs on the development of the Lao Issara movement and, upon its dissolution in 1949, be in a position to rebuild a new Lao nationalist movement under the supervision of the ICP (with the creation of Party Affairs Committees for Laos) and in **collaboration** with the **Democratic Republic of Vietnam**'s military goal to retake all of Indochina from the French. The committee for the east worked in close collaboration with the ICP's **Administrative Office for the Frontier** operating simultaneously in the same area. *See also* ADVISORY GROUP 100; CHU HUY MAN; COMMITTEE FOR EXTERNAL AFFAIRS; INDOCHINESE FEDERATION; NGUYEN KHANH; NGUYEN THANH SON.

**COMPAIN, JACQUES MARIE JULIEN (1912–1984).** A behind-the-scenes, ranking colonial administrator during the entire Indochina War. Compain was a graduate of the **Colonial Academy** (*École coloniale*) and began his career as a colonial civil servant in French Indochina. Between 1936 and 1939, he was deputy head of the provinces of Ha Dong, Phuc Yen, Vinh Yen and Nam Dinh. He served Vichy faithfully in Indochina, working between 1941 and 1943 as the deputy chief of cabinet to the *résident supérieur au* ***Tonkin*** in **Hanoi** and then in the same capacity for the *résident supérieur en* ***Annam*** (1943–44). He had briefly served as *résident* for the province of Hoa Binh until the Japanese ***coup de force*** **of 9 March 1945** landed him in prison. Following the Japanese defeat, he resumed his work in Indochina, serving in late 1945 as chief of cabinet to the commissioner for the Republic in Hanoi under **Jean Sainteny**. In 1946–47, he headed the political affairs section in the high commissioner's office for Indochina in **Saigon** and served under **Léon Pignon** in 1947. Between 1947 and 1949, he was advisor for the *Région Sud Mékong*. He attended the **Pau Conference** in 1950 as the deputy general secretary for the French side and became in that same year inspector for Political and Administrative Affairs and then advisor to the commissioner for the Republic to Cambodia. He apparently held both posts until 1953. In March 1954, he was designated general delegate to North Vietnam, to serve again under Jean Sainteny. After the Indochina War, he became the director of the French Information Services and general advisor to the commander-in-chief until the French army's withdrawal from Indochina in 1955. He was an observer to the Bandung Conference that same year before continuing his colonial career in New Caledonia and Djibouti.

**CONEIN, LUCIEN E. (1919–1998).** Franco-American intelligence officer involved in secret operations in Vietnam at the start and end of the Indochina War. Born in Paris, Conein was sent to live with his aunt in the United States following the death of his father in 1924. He grew up speaking French and English fluently but dropped out of high school early and took a job working as a typesetter and printer in Kansas City, Kansas. During the 1930s, he put in four years with the Kansas National Guard. World War II changed his life forever. Upon the outbreak of the war in Europe in 1939, he immediately joined the French army at the French consulate in Chicago. Following the French defeat of 1940, he returned to the USA in 1941 and joined the U.S. army, serving one and a half years in the Field Artillery. In August 1942, he was naturalized as an American citizen. This allowed him to enter Officer Candidate School later that year. His fluency in French and earlier combat experience in France landed him in the **Office of Strategic Services** (OSS) in July 1943 and eventually back in France, where he was dropped into Nazi-occupied areas in the south in order to deliver weapons to resistance forces. Conein was a member of the legendary Jedburgh commandos, rubbing shoulders with the likes of William E. Colby, Aaron Bank, and John K. Singlaub (all of whom would go on to play important intelligence roles in the Vietnam War).

Following the end of the war in Europe, Conein transferred to an OSS unit in China organizing raids against Japanese targets in northern Vietnam. In mid-1945, he was busy training French troops in southern China along the Vietnamese border. He arrived in **Hanoi** a few days after **Archimedes Patti** in August 1945. Unlike Patti, Conein was anything but impressed by what he saw during Vietnamese independence demonstrations on 2 September 1945. In 1947, Conein joined the OSS's successor, the Central Intelligence Agency (CIA) and became the stuff of legends in the intelligence community. In mid-1954, as the **Geneva Accords** put an end to the Indochina War and divided the country into two provisional states at the **17th parallel**, Conein joined **Edward Lansdale's Saigon**-based military mission, from which he organized "stay-behinds" or anti-communist **commandos**, intelligence posts, and propaganda in northern Vietnam. Such activities had little if any success inside North Vietnam. He was, however, an important go-between for the U.S. embassy in Saigon and military officers in the **Republic of Vietnam** plotting against **Ngo Dinh Diem** in 1963. He is buried in Arlington Cemetery in Washington, D.C.

**CÔNG AN.** *See* PUBLIC SECURITY SERVICES, DEMOCRATIC REPUBLIC OF VIETNAM.

**CONGREGATIONS.** *See GROUPEMENTS ADMINISTRATIFS CHINOIS RÉGIONAUX* (G.A.C.R)/ADMINISTRATIVE CHINESE REGIONAL GROUPINGS.

**CORNEVIN, ROBERT (1919–1988).** He graduated from the **Colonial Academy** on the eve of World War II. His activities during the war are unknown. He joined the *Corps léger d'intervention* in 1945, landing in **Saigon** in October of that year. Transferred to Cambodia, he worked in the colonial administration as a human resources director, advisor for sports and youth affairs in Cambodia, and various other administrative roles. He was particularly involved in developing the **scouting** movement in Cambodia. He left Indochina in 1948. Between 1971 and 1988, he served as secretary of the *Académie des Sciences d'Outre-mer.*

***CORPS EXPÉDITIONNAIRE.*** *See* EXPEDITIONARY CORPS.

**COSTE-FLORET, PAUL (1911–1979).** French politician involved in policy-making towards the Indochina War. In 1937, he studied law in France and became professor of law at the University of Algiers. During World War II, he joined the Allies and entered the French resistance in North Africa, where he was secretly involved in the Anglo-American landing in November 1942. In 1945, he served as one of the prosecutors at the Nuremberg trials. A member of the ***Mouvement républicain populaire***, he served as a deputy to the National Assembly between 1946 and 1967, minister of War in 1947 and Overseas France between 1947 and 1949. In May 1947, following the destructive battle of **Hanoi**, Coste-Floret announced that there "was no longer any military problem in Indochina". As minister of War, he was deeply involved in promoting the **Bao Dai Solution**, playing a pivotal role in negotiations leading to the signing of the Ha Long Bay Accords on 5 June 1948. He conducted a fact-finding mission to Indochina in August 1949. When **Pierre Mendès France** called for a negotiated settlement to the Indochina War on financial grounds, Coste-Floret countered that the French could rely upon the Americans and avoid instituting the draft in France by developing the Indochinese armies. By 1952, however, with the Chinese communists behind the **Democratic Republic of Vietnam**, Coste-Floret had changed his mind and advocated an "international settlement" of the war in Indochina. *See also* GENEVA ACCORDS; *JAUNISSEMENT*.

**COSVN.** *See* CENTRAL OFFICE FOR THE SOUTHERN REGION.

***COUP DE FORCE* OF 9 MARCH 1945.** Because of Vichy France's collaboration with Nazi Germany, Japan's axis ally in World War II, the Japanese occupied all of colonial Indochina during most of World War II but did not overthrow the French administration. Rather the Japanese allowed Vichy to continue operating the colony and supplying the Japanese war machine in its war in the Pacific. Things changed, however, following the Allied liberation of France in 1944, the disappearance of Vichy, and the shift of the Allied war effort to Asia. Fearful of a possible Allied landing in Indochina and the likely defection of the local French to the enemy camp in such a scenario, at 18H00 on 9 March 1945 the Japanese ambassador to French Indochina presented an ultimatum to the governor general, Admiral Jean Decoux, requiring that the French place all of their military and police forces under Japanese control. The Japanese did not wait for a reply. The army quickly interned most of the French colonial army and administrators, replacing the large majority of them with Vietnamese, Lao, and Khmer. French troops in **Tonkin** put up stubborn resistance in some areas before being captured, killed, or forced to flee towards the Chinese border. In a matter of days, the Japanese had brought down colonial French Indochina. French treaties were abrogated and nationalists in Laos, Cambodia, and Vietnam declared the independence of their new states, some more sincere about it than others. The effects of the Japanese coup were immense. For one, the rapidity with which the Japanese defeated the French made it clear to Vietnamese nationalists in particular that the French were not invincible. Second, whatever the contradictions, the Japanese took the lid off nationalist aspirations that had been growing rapidly since the 1920s, the winds of which had even been fanned by Vichy and Japan's competiting patriotic drives. During a secret mission to **Hanoi**, **Paul Mus** witnessed the coup with his own eyes as he escaped from the city. He reported to his superiors that the coup had marked the "profound evolution of a mentality which can only be called national". And of course the overthrow of the French, followed by the defeat of the Japanese in August 1945, created the favourable conditions thanks to which the **Viet Minh** took power in all of Vietnam's main power centres during the second half of August 1945. *See also* AUGUST REVOLUTION; CIVIL WAR; COLLABORATION; DEMOCRATIC REPUBLIC OF VIETNAM; VIET MINH.

**COURT MARTIAL, DEMOCRATIC REPUBLIC OF VIETNAM.** One of the few known cases of a court martial in the **Democratic Republic of Vietnam** (DRV) occurred during the battle of **Dien Bien Phu**. It became known as the "T59" or "Kilometer or Station (*tram*) 59" affair. Dr. **Nguyen Thi Ngoc Toan**, who was directly involved in the events leading to the trial of three military medics, revealed in 2007 that she transferred to station 59 in charge of treating seriously wounded soldiers arriving from the battlefield. She replaced an individual who had been disciplined for failing to protect corpses from being stripped of their personal belongings by passing porters in need of good clothing. Meanwhile, due to heavy rain and the increasing flow of incoming wounded, a backlog of wounded soldiers soon overwhelmed the medical staff working in this station. Instead of tending to the capacity of 100 wounded, the medics were faced with caring for 300. Food, water, medicines, and clothing soon became scarce. The chaos was such that the ranking political cadre in charge of the station began disciplinary action to restore order and to set an example. He summoned Nguyen Thi Ngoc Toan and informed her that she and two others were guilty of negligence in their care of the wounded soldiers complaining of their plight. The court martial of each of the three was held in the compound for the wounded. Supported by the wounded soldiers present at this surrealistic scene, Nguyen Thi Ngoc Toan successfully defended herself, escaped indictment, and transferred to another medical unit. Her two other co-workers had already been convicted of negligence for having eaten when the soldiers went hungry. Nguyen Thi Ngoc Toan disagreed strongly with the court's verdict against these two men. In light of their strenuous work transporting the wounded and dead, they had to eat in order to carry on, she insisted. To no avail. She then spoke out publicly in their defense saying that the party was wrong to have court martialed them. One of the men court martialed was a war veteran who had lost his arm in battle. In 1991, in one furtive sentence, the Ministry of Defense's official medical history of the Indochina War confirmed that the "disciplinary case T59" (*vu ky luat T59*) did indeed occur but provides no other details than confirming that food, water, and care were lacking until this disciplinary action happened.

Recently released DRV sources confirm that other cases of insubordination occurred during the battle of Dien Bien Phu, especially after the second wave attack. In mid-April, general **Vo Nguyen Giap** singled out for severe criticism and punishment growing cases of insubordination, cowardice, and lack of morale among other weaknesses. He pinpointed cases of soldiers, officers and cadres failing to enter into combat or to use their weapons. To fix these "rightist problems", the Politburo dispatched dozens of political cadres, who organized study sessions, propaganda drives, and mini **rectification** campaigns to raise morale and return as many men to their combat units as possible. For those who refused to carry on, military discipline was de rigueur. Executions for insubordination or cowardice occurred. General Vo Nguyen Giap signed orders authorizing court martials and disciplinary actions *pour l'exemple* (*nham muc dich giao duc*). A military court tried a battalion leader of the 102nd regiment of the 308th division for cowardice. *See also* COURT MARTIAL, FRENCH UNION; CROSSOVERS; DESERTION; INDOCTRINATION.

**COURT MARTIAL, FRENCH UNION.** One of the rare known instances when a French commanding officer attempted to court martial **French Union** troops for alleged mutiny occurred during the battle of **Dien Bien Phu** in 1954. According to French military historian **Bernard Fall**, this event took place when Algerian troops failed to attack an enemy strongpoint held by the **Democratic Republic of Vietnam** at an intense moment in the battle. Worried that such insubordination could spread, Colonel **André Lalande** decided to set an example: execution for cowardice. Lalande ordered the Algerian platoon commanders to select two men, each of whom would be tried and executed by firing squad at 18H00. While the court martial proceedings were organized and apparently were conducted during the battle, French, French Union, and Algerian opposition to Lalande's orders became intense, threatening to undermine morale in an even worse way. The commanding officer eventually backed down when an acceptable alternative was proposed to him before the camp was overrun on 7 May 1954. *See also* COURT MARTIAL, DEMOCRATIC REPUBLIC OF VIETNAM; CROSSOVERS; DESERTION; RECTIFICATION.

**COUSSEAU, JEAN GERMAIN NOËL BERNARD (1901–?).** One of the most influential behind-the-scenes French colonial officials to have ever served in Indochina. Born and raised in northern Vietnam, Cousseau learned to love the country, its culture, and above all its language. Though he held a diploma in Vietnamese from the ***École nationale des langues orientales vivantes*** in Paris, he learned the intricacies of the language on the ground in Vietnam. If there is one thing upon which Cousseau's colonial superiors and communist opponents agreed entirely, it was the fact that he spoke flawless Vietnamese. Cousseau also studied Chinese and apparently expressed himself well in English.

Between 1927 and 1940, he worked in a variety colonial administrative positions in northern Vietnam (Moncay, Tuyen Quang, Quang Yen, and Hon Cay) before becoming the interim *résident* of **Son La** province between February 1940 and April 1943. He had also been initiated into the world of colonial intelligence during the interwar period. In 1932, the director of Political Affairs and Security for Indochina, Louis Marty, had dispatched him secretly to Yunnan to set up a "special intelligence service", a mission which, Marty wrote, he executed perfectly. In Son La, Cousseau closely monitored the activities of Vietnamese communist prisoners held in the famous colonial prison located there. He apparently engaged them in debates over a wide range of cultural, literary, and political issues. Ranking Vietnamese communists incarcerated there who came to know Cousseau in one way or another included **Le Gian**, **Tran Dang Ninh** and **Le Duc Tho**. Vietnamese sources mention Cousseau's Vietnamese wife at this time; French sources do not.

Between April 1943 and the Japanese ***coup de force*** **of 9 March 1945**, Cousseau headed the Local Information Office for Propaganda and the Press in **Tonkin** (*Service local de l'information de la propagande et de la presse du Tonkin*). Between December 1944 and March 1945, he also headed the Bureau of Annamese Affairs (*Service des affaires annamites*) in the *Résidence supérieure* for Tonkin. (The famous Vietnamese novelist of the 1930s, **Nguyen Cong Hoan,** occupied Cousseau's position as official censor during the Democratic Republic of Vietnam's administration of **Hanoi** until **19 December 1946**.) Upon his release from Japanese internment, Cousseau remained in Indochina and put his knowledge of Vietnamese and Vietnamese politics in the service of 4th Republic's colonial return to Indochina. In October 1945, he was working as the chief of the Office of Political Affairs for the commissioner for the Republic to Northern Indochina and became a close, behind-the-scenes collaborator with the French high commissioner for Indochina **Georges Thierry d'Argenlieu,** in 1946. He also advised **Léon Pignon**, political advisor in northern Indochina. The two men had known each other in the 1930s.

Following the outbreak of war in 1946, the new High Commissioner **Émile Bollaert** sent Cousseau to Hong Kong to open secret contacts with **Bao Dai**. Cousseau conducted three behind-the-scenes missions to persuade the former Emperor to join forces with the French (missions of February 1947, September 1947, and June–September 1948). Cousseau personally escorted Bao Dai to Ha Long Bay to conduct talks with Émile Bollaert in December 1947. Together with Léon Pignon, Cousseau was one of the masterminds of the **Bao Dai Solution**. However, Cousseau also conceded privately to the French journalist **Jean Clémentin** that all the "good" Vietnamese "elements" were supporting **Ho Chi Minh**.

In October 1948, Cousseau transferred to the Paris office of the high commissioner for France in Indochina. In March 1949, back in Vietnam, he ran the high commissioner's service in charge of the *Population montagnardes du Sud indochinois*. Following his trip to France with Bao Dai in late 1950, Cousseau faded from the political scene with the creation of the Associated State of Vietnam. However, "France's mystery man", as American Ambassador **Donald Heath** put it privately in July 1954, continued to operate discreetly until **Ngo Dinh Diem** assumed the leadership of the State of Vietnam in 1954, and turned it into the **Republic of Vietnam** in 1955. The French decided it best not to allow Cousseau to return to Vietnam under Republican rule, precisely because of Cousseau's close association with Bao Dai, who had been deposed by Ngo Dinh Diem. It is not certain whether Cousseau ever returned to his native Vietnam. His former communist competitors now established in Hanoi by 1955 knew him only too well, as did Ngo Dinh Diem. As one high commissioner privately wrote of Cousseau, *il n'est pas l'homme du « service courant »; mais bien utilisé, il peut rendre les plus précieux services »*. To this day, historians still know few of the actual details of those "precious services".

**COUTARD, RAOUL (1924–).** Famous French *nouvelle vague* director of photography and war photographer during the Indochina War. In 1945, he signed up in the **Expeditionary Corps** to fight the Japanese, but ended up in Indochina where he remained for a decade covering the war against the **Democratic Republic of Vietnam** as a photographer. During this time, he spent some five years working as an official photographer for the French army and another five years as a freelancer for *Life, Paris Match, Indochine Sud-Est Asiatique,* and *Radar*. In 1953–54, he produced a short documentary in and on Laos for the French Ministry of Information, entitled *La section d'action psychologique*. With Jean-Michel de Kermadec he made another documentary on the Chinese city of Cholon near **Saigon**. In 1958, he became a director of film photography without ever having used a movie camera. **Pierre Schoendoerffer**, another veteran of the Indochina War and official photographer during the war, asked him to direct the photography for *La passe du diable*. From there, Coutard went on to become an active member of the *nouvelle vague* in French cinema. He was director of photography for 17 Godard and four Truffaut films (including *À bout de souffle* and *Tirez sur le pianiste*). He collaborated with Pierre Schoendoerffer on the *Le* ***crabe tambour***. Indeed, he shared the latter's heroization of the abandoned soldier and anti-communism (which made for apparently lively but friendly exchanges with Godard and Truffaut). Coutard directed his own film on the American war in Vietnam, entitled *Hoa Binh* (1970). Instead of focusing on the lost soldiers preoccupying Schoendoerffer's films, Coutard examined the effects of war on the forgotten children at the local level. The film won the Jean Vigo prize and received an Academy Award nomination for best foreign-language film in 1971, as the war for Vietnam continued. *See also* CINEMA; COMICS AND WAR; CULTURE; NOVELS; PYSCHOLOGICAL WARFARE.

**CRABE TAMBOUR, LE.** In 1977, **Pierre Schoendorffer**, a veteran of the Indochina War and a prominent French film-maker, adapted his novel *Le crabe tambour* for the big screen. The main protagonist of the film is based on the real life experiences of a French navy captain, **Pierre Guillaume**. The latter distinguished himself in combat in the Mekong Delta during the Indochina War and received the *Légion d'honneur* for his military feats at the age of 25. When Guillaume's brother perished in combat in Algeria, Pierre replaced him and ended up joining in the officers' Putsch designed to keep Algeria French and to prevent the army from losing another war. Guillaume spent eight years in a French prison for his actions in the *Organisation de l'armée secrète*. Schoendorffer uses Guillaume's tragic yet heroic itinerary as the trope for his film's reflection on the destiny of the French army in some 30 years of mainly colonial war. Through a series of flashbacks, Schoendorffer tells the story of forsaken French soldiers and officers, this time through the now aged and dying sailor representing Guillaume, as he makes his last mission through the foggy waters of the North Sea with painful, shrouded memories of the Indochina and **Algerian Wars**. **Raoul Coutard**, a close friend of Schoendorffer and a veteran of the Indochina War too, collaborated on the film's photography and received a *César* in 1978 for it. Jean Rochefort, Jacques Perrin, and Claude Rich starred in the film. Rochefort received a *César* for best actor. *Le crabe tambour* remains something of a cult film in France, and not just for those located on the Right of the French political spectrum. *See also* 317ème SECTION; CINEMA; COMICS AND WAR; NOVELS.

**CRÉPIN, JEAN ALBERT ÉMILE (1908–1996).** One of the rare French army officers who recognized the reality of Vietnamese nationalism and the importance of negotiating with **Ho Chi Minh**. He graduated from the *École Polytechnique* in France in 1928. In 1930, he entered the army as a second lieutenant, serving in China and French Cameroon during the interwar years. In August 1940, he joined Free French forces and in 1943, he assumed the command of the artillery for the 2nd Free French Division, which became the 2nd Armored Division (*Division blindée*) led by General **Philippe Leclerc**. Named colonel in 1944, Crépin took part in the liberation of Paris. In August 1945, he joined the French **Expeditionary Corps** and arrived in **Saigon** on 4 December to command the artillery section for the Expeditionary Corps in the Far East. Between January and early March 1946, he took part in the French mission negotiating the **Franco-Chinese Accords** in late February. From 10 April 1946, he served as deputy to General **Jean Valluy** in charge of French ground troops in northern Indochina and the 9th Colonial Infantry Division (*9ème DIC*). In the summer of 1946, during Valluy's absence, Crépin also became acting commissioner for **Tonkin** and North **Annam**. During this time, he did little to prevent General **Vo Nguyen Giap** from eliminating non-communist political parties opposed to Ho Chi Minh and the return of the French, especially the anti-French **Vietnamese**

**Nationalist Party** and the Dong Minh Hoi. Crepin's actions were, however, not appreciated by his superiors hostile to the **Democratic Republic of Vietnam** (DRV). The architect of the **Bao Dai Solution**, **Léon Pignon**, was particularly outraged by the elimination of the non-communist parties on Crépin's watch, despite their anti-French attitude. To Pignon's chagrin, their elimination left the French face to face with the DRV. Crepin left his position on 11 October 1946 and returned to France on 8 January 1947. He and his successor in **Hanoi**, General Morlière, were two of the very rare ranking French military officers to warn against the dangers of trying to oppose Vietnamese nationalism by military force. Crépin would serve the government loyally in Algeria before going on to hold top posts in the French army in Europe and in the aero-space industry.

**CRIME.** War always opens up opportunities for those involved in illegal activities. The Indochina conflict was no exception. Armed violence generated a breakdown in law and order as colonial and nationalist groups moved to take or retake power. In southern Vietnam during the interwar period, "social banditry" developed in the context of the economic depression. The emergence of the **Binh Xuyen** and men such as **Le Van Vien** and especially **Duong Van Duong** is a case in point. In the 1930s, the latter became known as something of a local "Robin Hood" (*vo hiep giang ho*) for sharing the spoils of his illicit trade with the poor. Duong Van Duong's notoriety brought him to the attention of communists as well as the leaders of the emerging Binh Xuyen movement. He commanded the respect of communists he met in prison while serving time there on two occasions in 1941. In August 1945, following the overthrow of the French and the defeat of the Japanese a few months later, Duong Van Duong served in the Binh Xuyen forces that helped to take power in **Saigon** and he supported the **Viet Minh**, as did the leader of the Binh Xuyen, Le Van Vien, a former convict. However, such relationships had their limits as the **Democratic Republic of Vietnam** learned when Le Van Vien crossed over to the French in mid-1948. *See also* CAO DAI; CIVIL WAR; COLLABORATION; CROSSOVERS; HOA HAO.

**CROSSOVERS.** Refers to those people who switched their allegiance or loyalty from one group to another during the Indochina War. Oftentimes the crossovers were deserters from the **French Union** forces or those of the **Associated States of Indochina**. Just as often they came from the ranks of the **Democratic Republic of Vietnam** (DRV), described as *ralliés* or *transfuges* by the French at the time.

At the outset, the DRV welcomed crossovers into its ranks, especially those with expertise which they could transmit to the emerging Vietnamese army and state. In exchange for their services, the DRV accorded them Vietnamese nationality, referring to them as *Viet Nam Moi* or "New Vietnamese". The DRV employed hundreds of Japanese officers and soldiers to teach military science in newly created military academies, train troops, and even command combat units against the French. Japanese instructors also helped develop and run the DRV's nascent intelligence services, while others worked in the medical and banking services. One Japanese crossover, **Ishii Takuo**, worked directly with General **Nguyen Son**, while French speaking European crossovers such as **Erwin Börchers**, **Ernst Frey**, and **Rudy Schröder** joined **Vo Nguyen Giap** to help him take on the French following the outbreak of war on **19 December 1946**. European crossovers, however, were soon moved into propaganda roles in prisoner camps as the war intensified and the number of Europeans captured multiplied. The DRV also used crossovers to penetrate behind French lines. In 1948, for example, **Ha Van Lau** and **Tran Quy Hai** used two German deserters to attack a French post in Thua Thien. As Europeans, they were able to fool the enemy into thinking that they were on the French side, thereby allowing them to penetrate the post and wipe it out in a surprise attack. On another occasion, a **commando** unit led by an Austrian **Foreign Legion** deserter known in Vietnamese as "Kemen" (Carmen?) was sent into Hue to assassinate a close advisor to **Bao Dai**, **Phan Van Giao.** However, he mistakenly identified his target and ended up killing the uncle of Ha Van Lau.

However, crossovers did not simply move in one direction, towards the DRV. From the start, many non-communist nationalists and religious leaders left the DRV, most notably the leaders of the **Binh Xuyen** and the **Cao Dai, Le Van Vien** and **Pham Cong Tac.** Although many nationalists supported the independence cause of the DRV in the early years of war, thousands left the same state in the early 1950s, as the communist core at its helm asserted its power and began communizing the DRV, allying it with the communist bloc, and defining revolutionary identity along class lines instead of national ones. **Land reform, rectification,** and obligatory **indoctrination** courses only reinforced this exodus. Famous non-communist nationalists like **Hoang Van Chi** and **Pham Duy** left the DRV in the early 1950s, upset with the shift in the DRV's priorities from a united front to the implementation of a communist-guided social revolution. Even sympathetic intellectuals like **Nguyen Manh Ha** and **Hoang Xuan Han** refused to cross over to the DRV upon the DRV's return to **Hanoi** in late 1954. Meanwhile, thousands of DRV soldiers, civil servants, and even cadres crossed over to the French Union forces and the Associated State of Vietnam. *See also* COLLABORATION; DESERTION, DEMOCRATIC REPUBLIC OF VIETNAM; DESERTION, FRENCH UNION FORCES; DESERTION, JAPANESE; GEORGES BOUDAREL.

**CULTURE, DEMOCRATIC REPUBLIC OF VIETNAM.** Culture was a weapon of war and part of the **Democratic Republic of Vietnam**'s (DRV) national and social project throughout the Indochina conflict. Betting that World War II would provide them with the propitious moment to take power and opposed to Japan and Vichy's patriotic propaganda and youth drives on the cultural front, communist leaders of the **Viet Minh** began developing their own cultural strategy before the new nation-state had even materialized. Most importantly, DRV culture would be a national as well as a communist driven one. Spearheading this project was the acting general secretary of the **Indochinese Communist Party** (ICP), **Truong Chinh**. In 1943, in a landmark document, he developed an Outline Cultural Program for Vietnam (*De Cuong Van Hoa Viet Nam*). This master plan served as the foundation for the ICP's nationalist and communist culture. Culture had to serve the Party; it could not exist independently, even if the party was willing to remain flexible in order to maintain the support of non-party **intellectuals** in the bid for national independence.

With the advent of the new Vietnamese nation-state in September 1945, Vietnamese cultural strategists placed the emphasis on building the nation, promoting independence, and opposing the restoration of French colonialism. The outbreak of war in southern Vietnam in September 1945 meant that from the outset the DRV's cultural policies had to serve above all the national resistance rather than stress radical social revolution that could undermine internal social cohesion at such a crucial point in time. In November 1946, Truong Chinh presided over the ICP's "First All-Country Cultural Congress", reminding his party listeners that "culture had to lead the people to reach independence, self strength, and reliance". In 1945–1946, cultural national salvation associations and papers appeared to rally artists, singers, and intellectuals around the independence cause, many of whom were not necessarily party members.

The ICP's cultural policy began to adopt a more communist orientation in 1948. While the exact reasons for the timing of this shift remain unclear, it was no doubt related to the intensification of the **Cold War** (Jdanov's 1947 division of the world into two opposing ideological camps for example) and the ICP/DRV's renewed attempts to obtain support from the communist camp. In any case, during the Second All-Country Cultural Congress held in July 1948, Truong Chinh announced the party's new cultural line, entitled *Marxism and Vietnamese Culture*. Besides stressing the continued importance of building national culture, he added that it was now time to begin developing a culture opposed to "outlooks and tendencies of a colonial, feudal, and reactionary bourgeois type" and to use Marxism-Leninism as the new cultural "compass" (*kim chi*). Truong Chinh also looked to Chinese communist cultural policies for guidance, announcing that the ICP had recently dispatched a cultural fact-finding mission to China, led by **Nguyen Khanh Toan** and **Ly Ban** among others. They were "to study Chinese experiences" in the cultural domain. Truong Chinh explained that the Vietnamese would also rely on the experiences of the Soviet Union, having recently received Soviet documents via China. The general secretary announced that the ICP was moving to create a "Research Committee on History, Geography, and Letters" to spearhead such revolutionary cultural transformations. On 2 December 1953, as the French and the Vietnamese prepared for a showdown at **Dien Bien Phu**, the ICP finally established the Research Commission for History, Geography, and Letters (*Ban Nghien Cuu Lich Su, Dia Ly, Van Hoc*). **Tran Huy Lieu** became its first director in 1953, joined by Ton Quang Phiet and the philosopher, **Tran Duc Thao**. The new commission was designed "to raise the patriotic and internationalist proletarian spirit of our people" (*Gop Phan Nang Cao Tinh Than Yeu Nuoc Va

*Tinh Than Quoc Te Vo San Cua Nhan Dan Ta*). During the Indochina War, the DRV's cultural project was as nationalist as it was communist.

**CUNG ĐINH QUỲ (1901–?).** Graduated at the top of his class from the *École supérieure d'agriculture et de sylviculture* in 1923 and began work in this sector in Hue and **Hanoi** during the interwar period. He became head of the Office of Water and Forests during this time. After the Japanese ***coup de force* of 9 March 1945**, he took up politics within the **Vietnamese Nationalist Party** (*Viet Nam Quoc Dan Dang,* VNQDD). He became deputy for this non-communist party in the March 1946 government reshuffle of the **Democratic Republic of Vietnam** and vice president of the National Assembly. He was one of the ranking opposition leaders there, voting against the National Constitution in 1946. He miraculously survived the combined French and Vietnamese communist attacks on the non-communist parties in mid-1946 and reappeared in the new Vietnamese government formed in October 1946. He escaped from Hanoi to Bac Ninh following the outbreak of full-scale war on **19 December 1946** before making his way to French-controlled Hanoi in May 1947 where he resumed his work as a civil servant in the water and forest office. He remained nonetheless an active member of the Vietnamese Nationalist Party. In August 1947, he was named general secretary of the "Nationalist Popular Movement" (*Phong Trao Quoc Gia Binh Dan*), which had been created in order to prepare for the return of **Bao Dai**. In 1951, he refused **Tran Van Huu**'s invitation to become governor of North Vietnam in the Associated State of Vietnam. In early 1952, he joined the Central Committee of the Vietnamese Nationalist Party. He was named minister of Agriculture in the **Nguyen Van Tam** government created on 6 June 1952. *See also* BAO DAI SOLUTION.

**CURRENCY, ASSOCIATED STATES OF INDOCHINA.** Despite the emergence of the Associated States of Vietnam, Laos, and Cambodia in 1949 along national lines, all three states remained financially interconnected to France and to each other via the *piastre indochinoise,* issued by the *Institut d'émission des États du Cambodge, du Laos et du Vietnam*. Only in 1953 did the **Associated States of Indochina** acquire their separate national currencies – the *dong* in Vietnam, the *riel* in Cambodia and the *kip* in Laos. While the *riel* and the *kip* circulated rather rapidly throughout all Cambodia and Laos, respectively, the Associated State of Vietnam's *dong* was limited to areas under its control, mainly in the cities. Meanwhile, the **Democratic Republic of Vietnam** (DRV) had been issuing its own national currency since 1945, also called the *dong*, in territories under its control. The DRV's allies in Laos and Cambodia, the **Pathet Lao** and the **Khmer Issarak**, never issued their own currencies during the Indochina War. In 1955, fully decolonized currencies were issued by the newly created national banks of the Kingdom of Cambodia, of Laos, and of the **Republic of Vietnam**. *See also* BANK OF INDOCHINA; CURRENCY, FRENCH INDOCHINA; ECONOMY OF WAR; FINANCIAL COST OF WAR.

**CURRENCY, DEMOCRATIC REPUBLIC OF VIETNAM.** The Vietnamese currency, the *dong*, was first introduced at the outset of the Indochina War by the **Democratic Republic of Vietnam** (DRV). From September 1945, DRV leaders printed the name of the government over colonial Vichy bills. They also began printing *Cu Ho* or "venerable Ho Chi Minh" bills on a printing press purchased from the French owner of the *Imprimerie Taupin*. The DRV government printed its own money throughout the war. Despite high levels of inflation and its vulnerability to stronger currencies, the existence of an independent currency was considered to be vital to the national legitimacy of the DRV in its fight against the French. During the war, the French attacked the DRV economy by producing and introducing false *dong* in a bid to aggravate inflation in the DRV zones and thereby undermine its attractiveness and legitimacy. Because of the chronic weakness of the *dong,* the DRV authorities also carefully controlled and used the French *piastre indochinoise* to conduct their exchanges. *See also* CURRENCY, FRENCH INDOCHINA; ECONOMY OF WAR; FINANCIAL COST OF WAR.

**CURRENCY, FRENCH INDOCHINA.** As the French moved to consolidate the Indochinese Union in 1887, they simultaneously created a common currency for the emerging colonial state, the Indochinese piastre or *piastre indochinoise*. In 1885, the governor general of Indochina approved a decree officially making the *piastre de commerce* legal tender for Indochina, pegging the piastre at one Mexican dollar (24.4935g silver). In

1895, the colonial government reduced the silver content to block the export of piastre coins and the colonial currency was from this point referred to simply as the piastre. In 1920, the piastre was pegged to the French franc but regained convertibility between 1921 and 1930, when the **Bank of Indochina** pegged the piastre to the franc (1 piastre = 10 French francs). This remained the case until World War II, though Indochina ended pegging its exchange rate to gold following the French abandoning the gold standard in 1936. However, the rate of 1 piastre to 10 French francs continued, at least nominally, until the Japanese overthrew French Indochina during the ***coup de force* of 9 March 1945**, took control of the Bank of Indochina and the *Institut d'émission*, and began printing massive quantities of 500-piastre notes (triggering equally high levels of inflation). Following the Japanese defeat in August 1945, the colonial piastre was no longer the unrivalled currency. When **Ho Chi Minh** declared the creation of the **Democratic Republic of Vietnam** (DRV) on 2 September 1945, he also created a Vietnamese national currency, the *dong*. Two currencies, one colonial, one national, competed with each other from this point as the French moved to reimpose their state, currency, and economic control. On 17 November 1945, the French high commissioner for Indochina, based in **Saigon**, issued a currency confiscation order to reduce inflation and to deny colonial currency to the DRV based in **Hanoi**. The massive number of 500-piastres notes issued by the Japanese after 9 March 1945 were prohibited and demonetized, with very little compensation. The French required that the other notes be deposited and were blocked until 20 September 1946. On 26 December 1945, the high commissioner's office, led by the financial advisor **François Bloch-Lainé**, revalued the piastre from 1 piastre = 10 French francs to 1 piastre = 17 French francs, based on the questionable assumption that Indochina had fared better than France during the war. This move was also designed to increase French exports to the colony. The piastre remained pegged to 17 francs until May 1953, when the French unilaterally devalued the piastre to its prewar parity of 10 francs, but without consulting the **Associated States of Indochina**. This unilateral decision angered local leaders and only reinforced the desire of all three states to obtain their full independence rapidly, especially in the financial domain. During the Indochina War, the overvalued exchange rate between the French franc and the Indochinese piastre gave rise to the "piastre affair". By purchasing the piastre at the market price of ten francs and then presenting the same piastre to the *Office Indochinois des changes* – legally obligated to buy the piastre at 17 francs – speculators made a tidy profit of seven francs for every piastre, all at the expense of the French taxpayer. Soldiers paid in francs also benefited from this overvaluation. The French government tolerated this practice until the French daily *Le Monde* exposed its workings in a November 1952 article that caused the biggest scandal of the war since the **affaires des généraux**. The source of this report was a former employee of the *Office des Changes* in Saigon, Jacques Despuech. With documents in hand, Despuech published a book on the subject, *Le Trafic des piastres*, and implicated some of the highest-ranking leaders in Vietnam and France. Under such scrutiny, the French government decided on 11 May 1953 to devaluate the piastre to 10 francs. The Associated States demanded and obtained fuller independence from this point. *See also* CURRENCY, DEMOCRATIC REPUBLIC OF VIETNAM; ECONOMY OF WAR; FINANCIAL COST OF WAR; NORODOM SIHANOUK; ROYAL CRUSADE FOR INDEPENDENCE.

**D.** Code letter used by the **Democratic Republic of Vietnam** to refer secretly to Cambodia during the Indochina Wars. It was later changed to "K" for Kampuchea at an unknown date.

**ĐẠI VIỆT.** *See* GREATER VIETNAM NATIONALIST PARTY.

**D'ARGENLIEU.** *See*: THIERRY D'ARGENLIEU.

**DALAT CONFERENCE (FIRST MEETING, APRIL–MAY 1946).** The first of two Franco-Vietnamese conferences held between 17 April and 11 May 1946 to follow up on the **Accords of 6 March 1946**. In late March 1946, **Ho Chi Minh**, as president of the **Democratic Republic of Vietnam** (DRV), and **Georges Thierry d'Argenlieu**, French high commissioner for Indochina, met in the bay of Ha Long to hammer out how and where subsequent negotiations would take place. The Vietnamese president wanted to by-pass the high commissioner in order to negotiate directly with the French government and in France. Thierry d'Argenlieu, on the other hand, wanted to ensure the meeting occurred in Indochina and not in France. In the end, Ho Chi Minh accepted the high commissioner's proposal that a "preparatory conference" be held in the colonial hill station of Dalat, preparing the way for a larger conference to occur in France in late May during which the "preliminary accord" signed on 6 March would be completed and finalized.

Both sides agreed that three main issues remained on the negotiating table: 1. Vietnam's diplomatic relations with third countries; 2. the future status of the Indochinese Federation and Vietnam's place within it; and 3. French cultural and economic interests in Vietnam. The divisive point boiled down to two very different visions of the **Indochinese Federation** and the DRV's place within it. Thierry d'Argenlieu saw the Indochinese Federation as a collection of "free states" (*États libres*). While each would enjoy considerable autonomy within the federal structure, they would not be independent; they would exist rather as part of a wider Indochinese colonial state, subordinate to the high commissioner, and part of the **French Union** under metropolitan leadership. The DRV, on the other side, sought to increase the autonomy of Vietnam within the Federation, and by a "Vietnamese free state" Ho Chi Minh meant the unification of **Tonkin**/Bac bo, **Annam**/Trung Bo and **Cochinchina**/Nam Bo into one territorial entity, that of the DRV. More than anything else, the Vietnamese insistence on the reunification of Cochinchina/Nam Bo with the rest of Vietnam (the DRV) and Thierry d'Argenlieu's determination to keep Cochinchina as a separate "free state" (in the Indochinese Federation) produced two very different conceptions of political space and sovereignty. For the Vietnamese, it was a national question, one that triggered heated debates comparing Vietnam's "Cochinchina" to France's "Alsace-Lorraine". Even in the cultural domain, the Vietnamese refused to return to the French higher learning establishments such as the ***École Française d'Extrême-Orient***, though the Pasteur Institute and a number of hospitals were turned over.

In the end, little progress was achieved during the first Dalat Conference. No agreement was reached on the referendum called for in the 6 March Accords. As British historian Martin Shipway has observed, Thierry d'Argenlieu placed his hopes in the Dalat conference, while the DRV leadership placed all its bets for reaching a negotiated settlement on the upcoming **Fontainebleau Conference** in July in France. *See also* 23 SEPTEMBER 1945; CHARLES DE GAULLE; DALAT CONFERENCE (SECOND MEETING).

**DALAT CONFERENCE (SECOND MEETING, AUGUST 1946).** The failure of the first Dalat Conference did not deter the French high commissioner for Indochina, **Georges Thierry d'Argenlieu**, from organizing a second conference in order to move forward on his **Indochinese Federation** and validate the existence of a separate Cochinchinese state within it. The second conference in Dalat began on 1 August 1946 and this time the high commissioner did not receive any representatives of the **Democratic Republic of**

**Vietnam** (DRV), but instead invited participants representing the other Indochinese states, including Laos, Cambodia and the **Provisional Government of the Republic of Cochinchina**, which he had officially announced on 1 June 1946. The timing of the second conference was intentionally designed to coincide with the negotiations occurring at Fontainebleau between the DRV and the French government over the future status of **Cochinchina**/Nam Bo. Delegates at the second conference began studying the federal institutions Thierry d'Argenlieu was determined to put in place (police, currency, customs, etc.). The leader of the DRV's delegation to the **Fontainebleau Conference**, which had begun on 6 July, **Pham Van Dong**, strongly denounced the holding of the second Dalat conference and on 1 August broke off the negotiations at Fontainebleau in protest, resuming them on 24 August.

**DALLOZ, JACQUES (1943–2005).** Eminent French historian of the Indochina War. Jacques Dalloz successfully passed the French *agrégation* certifying him to teach history and geography at the high school level. In 1969, he began work at this level before accepting a position in the early 1970s teaching history in the *classes préparatoires* at the military academy of Saint Cyr. There he remained until his retirement in 2003. He also taught simultaneously for more than a decade as a *maître de conférence d'histoire contemporaine* at the *Institut d'études politiques* in Paris. Dalloz loved history, that of the French 4th Republic in general and of the Indochina War in particular. In 1987, he produced what may be the best interpretive synthesis of the Indochina War to date, *La guerre d'Indochine, 1945–1954* (published in English translation in 1990). He followed it up in 2006 with a historical dictionary of the Indochina War. He also published dozens of high quality research articles on political and intellectual aspects of the conflict. In 1994, he obtained his doctorate in history. *See also* BERNARD FALL; PAUL MUS; PHILIPPE DEVILLERS.

**ĐÀM NGỌC LƯU.** *See* ĐÀM QUANG TRUNG.

**ĐÀM QUANG TRUNG (ĐÀM NGỌC LƯU, 1921–1995).** Veteran Vietnamese military officer of Tai origin active in Cao Bang province during the Indochina War. He became a member of the **Indochinese Communist Party** in 1939. In 1940, the French captured him. Though he walked free shortly thereafter, he remained under police surveillance. In September 1944, he began secretly building resistance bases and **guerrilla** training camps along the Sino-Vietnamese border. In December 1944, he joined the Vietnamese Propaganda and Liberation Army (*Doi Viet Nam Tuyen Truyen Giai Phong Quan*). In August 1945, he commanded a company in the Liberation Army and helped take over the province of Thai Nguyen following the Japanese defeat. In late 1945, he served as a company leader in Detachment 4 (*Chi Doi 4*) and as the chief of the special zone of **Hanoi**. Between December 1946 and 1950, he was a deputy commander of **Inter-Zone V** (*Lien Khu V*) and commanded the zone's main force regiment. Between 1953 and 1954, he served as deputy commander of the 312th Division. *See also* MINORITY ETHNIC GROUPS; TAI FEDERATION.

**ĐÀM VĂN MÔNG.** *See* LÊ QUẢNG BA.

**ĐẶNG CHÂN LIỆU (1918?–?).** Son of a Confucian scholar and mandarin in the Nguyen court in Hue. After finishing his secondary education at the *Lycée Albert Sarraut* in **Hanoi**, Dang Chan Lieu traveled to France where he completed his undergraduate studies, studying political science and international relations in a bid to enter the French diplomatic corps. This apparently failed. He rejected an offer to serve Vichy during World War II and took up residence in England. He soon spoke English as fluently as French. He joined the **Viet Minh** as World War II came to a close. In March 1947, he wrote an article in the American journal, *Pacific Affairs,* entitled *Annamese Nationalism*. He was part of the Vietnamese delegation to the **Fontainebleau Conference** in mid-1946. He remained in Paris and served as the press attaché in the diplomatic delegation of the **Democratic Republic of Vietnam** in the French capital. He left France with the closure of the delegation in 1949 and worked in (unofficial) Vietnamese diplomatic posts in Rangoon and Jakarta. He apparently returned to northern Vietnam in the early 1950s and may have been in some sort of political trouble like **Tran Ngoc Danh** and **Le Hy**. *See also* BURMA; INDIA; INDONESIA.

**ĐẶNG HOÁN BỔN (1901–1991).** Chinese businessman born in Hainan and raised in Cholon who supported the cause of the **Democratic Republic of Vietnam** during the Indochina War. Dang Hoan

Bon arrived with his family in Cholon when he was very young. The family grew wealthy and became a big landholder in southern Vietnam during the colonial period. Dang studied law at Shanghai University, where he became politically active. He returned to Vietnam in 1936 to help tend to family properties and the operation of a number of industrial projects in Cholon. In mid-1945, he transferred much of his possessions in Cholon and his land in Ben Tre to the Vietnamese resistance movement. He helped the Vietnamese government mobilize the **overseas Chinese** in southern Vietnam during the war and created a Vietnamese Chinese Friendship Association (*Hoi Huu Nghi Viet Trung*). After the division of Vietnam into two states during the **Geneva Conference** in 1954, Dang Hoan Bon was relocated to northern Vietnam where he served as the vice president of the Federated Overseas Chinese Association in **Hanoi** and directed the Sino-Vietnamese hospital in Hanoi.

**ĐẶNG HỮU CHÍ (1903–?).** Born in Hai Duong province in northern Vietnam and educated in medicine at the Faculty of Medicine in **Hanoi**. He served in the Indochinese colonial army during the interwar period. Little is known of his activities during the Vichy period. Between 1948–1949, he served as the minister of Health in the provisional government of **Cochinchina**/Vietnam of **Nguyen Van Xuan**. In 1949, he was said to be mayor of Haiphong. In January 1951, he was named governor of North Vietnam and assumed his functions in April of that year. He was instrumental in bringing the famous writer and non-communist politician, **Nguyen Tuong Tam**, back to Vietnam.

**ĐẶNG KIM GIANG (ĐẶNG RAO, 1910–1983).** Born in Thai Binh province in northern Vietnam, Dang Kim Giang became active in nationalist politics in the late 1920s and joined the **Indochinese Communist Party** (ICP) in 1930. He rose quickly in the party, joining the regional committee for Tonkin before the French arrested and incarcerated him in **Son La** and other prisons during World War II. He escaped around 1945 and helped the ICP take power in Ha Dong province, serving as president of this province's newly created people's committee as well as the party's deputy. He was elected to the **Democratic Republic of Vietnam**'s first National Assembly. During the Indochina War, Dang Kim Giang served as president of the Resistance and Administrative Committee for **zone** II, and as deputy director for the party's committee for that same zone. In 1951, he transferred to work in the army as the deputy director of the General Supply Bureau (*Tong cuc cung cap*) within the larger logistics bureau. In this role, he participated in supplying the battles of **Cao Bang**, **Laos**, **Hoa Binh**, and in the northwest. During the battle of Dien Bien Phu, he replaced **Tran Dang Ninh** at the head of the supply office. After the Geneva Accords were signed and Vietnam provisionally divided into two states, he rose to the rank of major general in 1958. However, a few years later, he was stripped of his power and many of his titles when he was accused of being pro-Soviet, when the Vietnamese communist party split over the best strategy for fighting the war against the Americans and the **Republic of Vietnam.**

**ĐẶNG MINH TRỨ (1900–1981).** Vietnamese professor born into a peasant family in My Tho province, who became a leading figure in the postcolonial Vietnamese education system. He received his secondary education at *Lycée Chasseloup Laubat* in Saigon. Thanks to a government scholarship, he pursued his studies at the University of Montpellier in France. Upon his return to Vietnam, he taught at the Pétrus Truong Vinh Ky School in Saigon. In the heady days following the defeat of the Japanese in mid-1945, he mobilized **intellectuals** and scholars to support the newly formed Vietnamese national government, the **Democratic Republic of Vietnam** (DRV) and the resistance against the restoration of colonial rule. Dang Minh Tru, together with **Nguyen Van Huong** and **Luu Van Lang**, privately met with High Commissioner **Émile Bollaert** to present him with a petition calling upon the French to negotiate with **Ho Chi Minh**. Bollaert refused. Although Dang Minh Tru was not a member of the communist party, sometime in late 1947 or 1948 he crossed over to DRV zones to live and work. He was appointed president of the Resistance and Administrative Committee for Saigon-Cholon. In 1949, he served as head of the Educational Service for Nam Bo (*So Giao Duc Nam Bo*). In 1950, he was elected to serve as the president of the Resistance and Administrative Committee for Can Tho and he held this post until he was relocated to North Vietnam following the division of Vietnam into two states during the **Geneva Conference** of 1954.

**ĐẶNG NGỌC CHÂN (1894–?).** Vietnamese primary school teacher born in Chau Doc province in southern Vietnam. After completing his secondary studies at the *Lycée Chasseloup Laubat* in **Saigon**, he began working as a primary school teacher in 1913. He became a secretary-interpreter in 1915. Between 1917 and 1920, he attended the *École supérieure de droit et d'admnistration* at the Indochinese University in **Hanoi**. He entered the civil service in **Cochinchina** in 1924 and served as a delegate to the International Colonial Exhibition in Vincennes in 1931. Until 1945, he worked in the colonial administration in central and southern Vietnam, especially in Cholon. After World War II, he cooperated with the French in their bid to promote a separate Cochinchinese political identity. He was minister without portfolio in the **Provisional Government of the Republic of Cochinchina**, created by **Georges Thierry d'Argenlieu**. In March and April 1947, he represented the French-backed governments in Indochina during the Asian Relations Conference in New Delhi, much to the disappointment of his DRV adversaries there. *See also* COLLABORATION; INDIA.

**ĐẶNG PHÚC THÔNG (1904–1951/52).** Brother to **Dang Chan Lieu** and well-known French-educated mining specialist and supporter of the **Democratic Republic of Vietnam** (DRV). He left for France in 1935, where he studied at the *École supérieure des mines*. In March 1946, he was named minister of Communications in the DRV and held this post until 1949. In 1946, he also became chairman of the Planning Board and president of the Pedagogical School in **Hanoi**. He also directed the government railroads. During the outbreak of war in Hanoi in December 1946, the French arrested him and offered him important positions in exchange for his **collaboration**. He refused. In March 1947, Dang Phuc Thong met privately but separately with **Léon Pignon** and **Paul Mus** concerning French colonial plans for Indochina and for the **French Union**. In both meetings, he made his commitment to the Vietnamese national cause clear and then made good on it: In August 1947, Dang Phuc Thong left French-controlled Vietnam to return to work for the DRV, this time in government zones in upper central Vietnam – **Inter-Zone IV** (*Lien Khu IV*). In September 1949, he became a vice minister of Public Works and Communications in the government and director of Inter-Zone IV's Technical School. He also oversaw the zone's Railroads and Public Works from 1949. He passed away in 1951 or early 1952 for unknown reasons.

**ĐẶNG THAI MAI (1902–1984).** One of Vietnam's best known **intellectuals** during the colonial period living in the culturally vibrant **Inter-Zone IV** (*Lien Khu IV*) during the Indochina War. Dang Thai Mai was born and raised in Nghe Tinh province in upper central Vietnam. He served as a professor at the *Collège Quoc Hoc* in Hue between 1928 and 1930 and then moved to **Hanoi** where he taught at the Gia Long School in 1932. He helped launch the famous *Thang Long* Academy in Hanoi in 1933, where he taught and helped out a number of the future leaders of the **Democratic Republic of Vietnam** (DRV), including **Vo Nguyen Giap** and **Hoang Minh Giam**, and met **Pham Van Dong**. While he apparently did not join the **Indochinese Communist Party** (ICP) in the 1930s, he was actively involved in social and leftist political debates and causes. He was a frequent contributor to left-wing Vietnamese papers unshackled during the Popular Front period, such as *Le Travail, Notre Voix, Ban,* and *Rassemblement*. He took a keen interest in Vietnamese literature about which he published a number of works. He also closely followed cultural changes in revolutionary China. During World War II, he wrote for the *Thanh Nghi* magazine.

Following the defeat of the Japanese in 1945, he joined the DRV, serving as minister of National Education in the Provisional Government from September 1945 to March 1946. He allegedly joined the ICP sometime in 1945. In any case, he was a member of the **Democratic Party** and president of the Cultural Association for National Salvation (*Hoi Van Hoa Cuu Quoc*) from this point. After the outbreak of war in all of Vietnam in December 1946, he moved to government areas located in Inter-Zone IV in upper central Vietnam. There he served as Chairman of the Resistance and Administrative Committee of Thanh Hoa province between 1947 and 1948. Between 1948 and 1949, he was president of the Vietnam Cultural Association. He worked as dean of the Literature College for Inter-Zone IV in 1950 as well as director of the Educational Service for this same zone until the end of the Indochina War. He was a deputy to the DRV's first five National Assemblies. During his time in Inter-Zone IV, he was deeply involved in discussing if not debating cultural questions with General **Nguyen Son** and others. Indeed, Dang Thai Mai enjoyed the respect of the core leaders of the ICP and Army. He became **Vo Nguyen Giap**'s father-in-law when his daughter, Dang Bich Ha, married the famous general in 1947. **Le Duan** and Pham Van Dong attended his funeral.

**ĐẶNG TÍNH (ĐẶNG VĂN TĨ, 1920–1973).** Ranking Vietnamese military leader in northern Vietnam and member of the military delegation attending the **Geneva Conference** of 1954. He joined the **Indochinese Communist Party** in 1945, as French colonial Indochina crumbled following the Japanese ***coup de force* of 9 March 1945**. He led an armed propaganda unit in northern Vietnam before serving in 1945 and 1946 as a district then provincial representative for the **Democratic Republic of Vietnam** in Hai Duong. He joined the army in 1946. Between 1947 and 1949, he was a political cadre in a self-defense unit and the provincial head of Hai Duong before becoming a member of **Inter-Zone III** (*Lien Khu III*). Between 1950 and 1951, he served as a political cadre for the Route 5 Front and as president of the Resistance and Administrative Committee for the province of Thai Binh. Between April 1951 and 1953, he worked as a political cadre in Inter-Zone III and then in the Command for the Left Bank of the Red River Zone. Between October 1953 and the end of the war in mid-1954, he became a deputy to the head of the Bureau of the People's Militia (*Cuc Dan Quan*) before taking charge of the Tactical Office in the General Chiefs of Staff in the Vietnamese army. During the **Geneva Conference**, he was a delegate in the Military Representative Delegation. Between August 1954 and February 1955, he headed the **People's Army of Vietnam** Representative Delegation to the Joint Committee on the Cease Fire in Laos.

**ĐẶNG VĂN NGỮ (1910–1967).** Vietnamese doctor who helped develop a vaccination against cholera for soldiers during the Indochina War. Graduated from the School of Pharmacy attached to the Indochinese University, he travelled to Japan during World War II. There, he continued to study medicine in Tokyo. In 1949, he returned to Vietnam and clandestinely made his way to the *maquis* where he joined doctors of the **Democratic Republic of Vietnam** (DRV) working in Chiem Hoa. He brought with him from Japan two types of mushrooms that were crucial to developing penicillin and streptomycin in resistance zones in northern Vietnam, badly needed as the war against the French entered a more intensive and deadly phase. He lost his wife to disease during the Indochina War and was a brother-in-law to **Nguyen Thi Ngoc Toan**. He perished in 1967 during an American B-52 air strike while working in the Thua Thien war zone. He had been sent there to prepare to make a vaccine against malaria for soldiers fighting the Americans and the Republic of Vietnam.

**ĐẶNG VĂN QUANG (1929–?).** Born in southern Vietnam, Dang Van Quang studied at the Catholic *École Taberd*. While he was not born a Catholic, he converted as an adult. Little else is known of his early life. In 1948, he entered the first class of the French-backed National Military Academy and graduated in June 1949 as the Associated State of Vietnam emerged. He was commissioned as a second lieutenant and led a platoon in southern Vietnam. Soon thereafter he entered the Advanced Infantry School in Coetquidan, France. Joining him there was one of his former classmates, **Nguyen Van Thieu**. The French saw in Dang Van Quang a promising leader for the new Vietnamese national army. In 1951, Dang Van Quang returned to Vietnam and served as a company commander in his home province of Soc Trang and was actively involved in French military operations in the south to defeat the **Viet Minh**. Around 1951, he traveled to **Hanoi** to study in the Tactical Course at the Command and Staff School. His classmates there were: Nguyen Van Thieu, Nguyen Khanh, and **Cao Van Vien** among others. Upon graduation, Dang Van Quang became Commander of the 55th Infantry Battalion in 1953 in the Nam Dinh area southeast of Hanoi. In 1954, he attended the General Staff Course in Hanoi. He converted to Catholicism while serving in Hue as **Ngo Dinh Diem** assumed control of what remained of the State of Vietnam below the **17th parallel**. An in-law of the Ngo family was his sponsor at baptism. His loyalty to the Diem family helped him make a meteoric rise in the army, but his dexterity was such that his career survived the coup against and assassination of Diem in 1963.

**ĐẶNG VĂN SUNG (CAO THẮNG, 1915–1998).** Vietnamese doctor and non-communist nationalist politician during the Franco-Vietnamese War. Born into a family of mandarins in Nghe An province, he studied medicine to become a doctor during the colonial period. After World War II, he served as a deputy for the **Greater Vietnam Nationalist Party** (*Dai Viet Quoc Dan Dang*) in the National Assembly of the **Democratic Republic of Vietnam**. After the outbreak of full-scale war on **19 December 1946** and faced with communist persecution, he fled to southern China in 1947. He helped forge an alliance between the **Vietnamese Nationalist Party** and the Greater Vietnam Nationalist Party in 1948. After the **Geneva Conference** provisionally divided Vietnam into a communist north and a non-communist south, he led a failed undercover espionage infiltration operation into northern Vietnam composed of Greater Vietnam Nationalist Party members. He directed the newspaper *Chinh Luan* in **Saigon** in the 1960s.

**ĐẶNG VĂN TĨ.** *See* ĐẶNG TÍNH.

**ĐẶNG VĂN VIỆT (1920–).** Vietnamese colonel who participated in the battle of **Cao Bang** in 1950 and wrote a book on the subject. Born into an aristocratic family in Hue, he studied medicine in **Hanoi** until 1945, when he joined the Youth of the Front Lines (*Thanh Nien Tien Tuyen*). In 1945, he entered the armed forces of the **Democratic Republic of Vietnam** (DRV). Between 1945 and 1947, he served as a platoon leader before becoming the head of the Committee for Research and Tactics in the army General Chief of Staff. In 1948 and 1949, he was the deputy regimental leader and then head of the 28th Regiment. In 1948, he joined the **Indochinese Communist Party**. From 1949 to 1953, he led the 174th Regiment (which became part of the 316th Division when it was formed in early 1951). During this time, he was active in numerous encounters with the French and commanded the 174th regiment to victory during the famous 1950 battle of Cao Bang which helped open the Chinese frontier to the DRV. In 1952, he commanded the same regiment in the battle of the Northwest (*Chien Dich Tay Bac*). However, despite his military exploits and membership of the party during the Indochina conflict, the DRV refused to promote him and his father fell victim to the excesses of the **land reform**.

**ĐẶNG VŨ LẠC (1902–1948).** Leader of the **Greater Vietnam Nationalist Party** (*Dai Viet Quoc Dan Dang*). Born into a family of scholar patriots from Nam Dinh, he obtained his degree in medicine and opened his first practice in **Hanoi** in 1932. In 1935, he joined the City Council of Hanoi. He was also increasingly involved in nationalist activities, publishing secretly a non-communist nationalist newspaper called *Unity* (*Thong Nhat*). He joined the Vietnamese Section of the ***Section française de l'Internationale ouvrière*** and entered the Greater Vietnam Nationalist-Socialist Party (*Dang Dai Viet Dan Xa*) in 1941. In 1945, he joined forces with the non-communist nationalist forces, and helped resurrect the Greater Vietnam Nationalist Party in 1947–1948 after it had been badly mauled by the **Viet Minh** nationalist front led by the **Indochinese Communist Party**. Forces of the **Democratic Republic of Vietnam** assassinated his son.

**ĐẢNG XÃ HỘI VIỆT NAM**. *See* VIETNAMESE SOCIALIST PARTY.

**ĐẶNG XUÂN KHU.** *See* TRƯỜNG CHINH.

**DANNAUD, JEAN-PIERRE (1921–1995).** Writer and dashing spokesman for General **Jean de Lattre de Tassigny** during the Indochina War. Graduated first in his class from the *École normale supérieure* with an *aggrégation* in philosophy, Dannaud joined the French resistance in 1942 and served as a young lieutenant under de Lattre during World War II, leading a French company in Italy and southern France, before moving to Indochina as part of General **Philippe Leclerc**'s 2nd Armored Division. In **Saigon**, Dannaud went to work as an aide-de-camp for **Jean Cédile**, commissioner for the Republic to **Cochinchina** and Southern **Annam**, serving as director of the French Information Service (*Directeur des services français d'information*). One American diplomat wrote that "he has a brilliant mind and much tact". In 1946, Dannaud was involved in the French re-occupation of Laos and was apparently slightly wounded during the battle of **Thakhek** in mid-1946. When de Lattre arrived in Indochina in 1950 as high commissioner and commander-in-chief, Dannaud became an advisor, spokesman, and speech-writer for his former boss until the latter's death in 1952. During this time, Dannaud was one of the prime movers of the government's *Revue Indochine Sud-est asiatique*. Like **Jean Lartéguy** and **Pierre Schoendoerffer**, in his writings Dannaud celebrated the heroism of the **French Union** soldiers fighting against all odds, and without recognition in the metropole. No sooner had the war ended than he published a commemorative photo album of the war, entitled:

*Guerre morte... Il y avait une guerre d'Indochine*. As his preface explains, the book was conceived as a homage to the soldiers who had "fallen for France" there. Largely absent in Dannaud's writing is any mention of the other side, and there is nothing on his secret meeting in a jail cell in 1946 with one of Vietnam's most brilliant French-trained intellectuals of the time, Dr. **Pham Ngoc Thach**. Dannaud had been sent to reason with the **Democratic Republic of Vietnam's** diplomat whom the French had jailed when Thach had showed up unannounced for the first **Dalat Conference**. Dannaud failed to win over Thach to the French colonial cause. Dannaud remained above all an ardent defender of the French cause and in particular of de Lattre, popularizing the expression *le roi Jean* in several hagiographic writings (*Historia*, 1972). *See also* CINEMA; CULTURE; NOVELS, FRANCE.

**ĐÀO DUY ANH (1904–1988).** One of modern Vietnam's greatest lexicographers, cultural luminaries, and supporters of the nationalist cause of the **Democratic Republic of Vietnam** (DRV). Born in Thanh Hoa province in upper central Vietnam, he studied Chinese as a youngster before entering the *Collège Quoc Hoc* in Hue and the *Lycée Dong Hoi* in Quang Binh province. He also became active in nationalist politics and joined the New Vietnam Party (*Tan Viet*) in 1927 all the while assisting **Huynh Thuc Khang** to produce his famous newspaper, *Tieng Dan*. Following his liberation from a jail sentence for political activities in 1929, Dao Duy Anh concentrated his efforts on the cultural scene during the 1930s, producing famous Chinese-Vietnamese and French-Vietnamese dictionaries in 1932 and 1936 respectively, and published a landmark essay in 1938 on Vietnamese **culture.** Like **Hoang Xuan Han**, Dao Duy Anh was one of the first nationalist historians of modern Vietnam. As he wrote in his memoirs much later: "My karma, it's the **history** of Viet Nam. If I am known, that's only by national history – if one condemns me, that's only by national history". He would go on to publish several major works on Vietnamese national history including the *The Vietnamese Land through History* (1964) and a *Dictionary of Kieu* (1974), Vietnam's national heroine par excellence. He also put history and culture in the service of the national cause of the DRV during the Indochina War. From late 1945, he was member of the Executive Committee of the National Salvation Cultural Association for Trung Bo and briefly taught at the University of **Hanoi** until the outbreak of full-scale war on **19 December 1946** sent him to **Inter-Zone IV** (*Lien Khu IV*) in central Vietnam. There he taught in resistance schools and pursued his research interests as best he could until the end of the war in 1954. During the Indochina War, he trained many of the DRV's first generation of national historians. *See also* INTELLECTUALS.

**ĐÀO PHÚC LỘC.** *See* HOÀNG MINH ĐÀO.

**ĐÀO XUÂN MAI.** While details are scarce, Dao Xuan Mai was apparently a former student from central Vietnam in the *Collège de Vinh* who was expelled in 1927 with **Nguyen Duy Trinh** for taking part in nation-wide student strikes following the death of Phan Chu Trinh. Dao Xuan Mai and Nguyen Duy Trinh were involved in the rue Barbier affair and were arrested and sentenced in 1929 for their participation in it. After World War II, Dao Xuan Mai returned to northern Vietnam where he briefly became chief of the North Vietnamese security services before turning the job over to **Le Gian**. *See also* PUBLIC SECURITY SERVICES.

**DAP CHHUON (CHUAN KEM PIKET, CHUON KEMPHETCHR, CHHUON MCHHULPICH, 1912–1959).** Prominent Cambodian warlord-patriot who ruled a fiefdom in Siemreap province before **crossing over** to the Associated State of Cambodia in 1949. He began his career in the Indochinese colonial army. In 1943, he held the rank of sergeant in the *Garde indigène* in Cambodia, serving as the accountant for his unit. In 1944, according to French sources, he deserted and made off with some 20,000 piastres for Thailand. There, he joined the Thai-backed **Khmer Issarak** movement located along the Thai-Cambodian border and opposed French rule in Cambodia. He took part in an attack against French forces in Siem Reap in August 1946. From this point, he also began collaborating with the forces of the **Democratic Republic of Vietnam** (DRV) active along the Thai-Cambodian border and became president of the DRV-backed Committee for the Liberation of the Cambodian People in 1948. Following the signing of the Franco-Cambodian accords of 1949, the French and **Norodom Sihanouk** intensified their efforts to win over Dap Chhuon to the Associated State of Cambodia and succeeded to some extent. In a spectacular event staged at Angkor Wat on 10 October 1949, Dap

Chhuon formally pledged his allegiance to King Sihanouk. In exchange, Dap Chhuon received the command of the "autonomous military sector of Siemreap", his longtime stomping ground. He became battalion leader and his militia was integrated with the Franco-Khmer troops. While he was tempted to join the anti-royalist activities of **Son Ngoc Thanh** and the **Democrat Party** in 1952, Dap Chhuon remained loyal to Sihanouk. In 1953, he supported Sihanouk's **royal crusade for independence** and was named colonel in exchange for his fidelity. Though ambitious, Dap Chhuon was also prudent and careful. He ruled his fiefdom in the west, imposing taxes and raising troops, until the end of the Indochina War. He was one of Sihanouk's most reliable military and political supporters. In 1954, he participated in the **Geneva Conference**. *See also* COLLABORATION; CRIME; DESERTION.

**DARCOURT, PIERRE (1926–).** Born in southern Vietnam, Pierre Darcourt grew up in colonial Indochina, attending in the 1940s the *Lycée Chasseloup-Laubat* in Saigon and its equivalent in Hanoi, the *Lycée* ***Albert Sarraut***. Darcourt joined the French resistance in Indochina towards the end of World War II and fled to southern China with retreating French forces following the Japanese **coup de force of 9 March 1945**. He returned to Indochina a soldier and was wounded twice during the Indochina conflict. He worked as a security officer for General **Jean de Lattre de Tassigny**, to whom he dedicated a hagiographic book in 1965 entitled *De Lattre au Vietnam: une année de victoires*. After the war, Darcourt became a journalist and writer. He worked until 1998 for *Le Figaro*. He published a detailed biography of the famous leader of the **Binh Xuyen**, **Le Van Vien** and another entitled, *Vietnam, qu'as-tu fait de tes fils?*

**DARIDAN, JEAN HENRI (1906–2002).** Career French diplomat involved in dealing with the Thais and the **Lao Issara** concerning the future of Indochina during the Indochina War. He worked in various diplomatic posts prior to World War II before joining Free French forces in 1943. In 1945, with the end of the war, he was named diplomatic advisor in Shanghai and then Nanjing. Between 1945 and 1947, he was *chargé* to the French Legation in Bangkok, where he was involved in negotiations with the Thais over the retrocession of territories ceded to them by the French under Japanese duress at the start of World War II. Daridan was also instrumental in persuading most of the Lao Issara leaders to return to Laos with the creation of an Associated State of Laos in 1949. In 1954, he became deputy general commissioner in Indochina, charged with implementing the **Geneva Accords.**

**DAVÉE, ROBERT (1900(?)–?).** Little-known, behind-the-scenes French colonial administrator and negotiator during the early stages of the Indochina War. Born and educated in France, he traveled widely in Spain in his childhood and obtained his university degree at the Sorbonne. He taught Spanish for many years at the *École normale supérieure* in Paris. While he became a recognized expert on Latin America in France, Davée also developed an increasing interest in Indochina during the 1930s, publishing a number of articles in *L'Illustration* and *France-Indochine*. His expertise somehow came to the attention of Admiral **Georges Thierry d'Argenlieu**, high commissioner of Indochina in 1945–1946, who made Davée his director of the Office for Information and the Press in **Saigon**. Davée held this position in late 1945 and early 1946 before becoming an economic delegate assigned (apparently) to the **Democratic Republic of Vietnam** (DRV) in November 1946. He advocated negotiating a way out the Franco-Vietnamese impasse of mid-1946. Virginia Thompson described him as one of Thierry d'Argenlieu's liberal aides who resigned in protest at the admiral's hostile policy towards the DRV in September. In April 1949, he was chairman of the French delegation in charge of negotiations with the Cambodians. In August 1949, he became secretary of the French delegation for implementing the Agreements of March 1949 to create the Associated State of Cambodia. Having survived an airplane crash in Bahrain, in October 1950 he represented **Albert Sarraut** as host to the Lao delegation visiting the French town of Dinan to participate in a memorial ceremony commemorating Auguste Pavie, the famous French explorer and colonizer of Laos at the turn of the 20th century.

**ĐÁY, BATTLE OF (*Chiến Dịch Quang Trung*, 28 MAY 1951–20 JUNE 1951).** The battle of Day began on the night of 28–29 May 1951, when the **Democratic Republic of Vietnam**'s (DRV) high command sent elements of the 304th, 308th, and 320th divisions against French positions in the area running from Phu Ly to Yen Mo, located along the Day River in the rice-rich areas of the southwestern part of the Red River delta. These larger units were supported by simultaneous **guerrilla** action within the delta. The DRV's main strategic goals were to seize rice in the area, recruit more men, step up guerrilla activites in the delta and win over Catholic support there. While General **Jean de Lattre de Tassigny** and his second in command General **François Gonzalez de Linarès** successfully stopped the brunt of the Vietnamese advance, the DRV was not looking to engage in a set-piece battle, content to have achieved their goals of creating guerrilla instability and gaining access to rice. The battle ended in early June to all intents and purposes. During the early stages of the battle of Day, however, Catholic leaders in the strategically important areas of Phat Diem and Bui Chu, such as the Bishop **Le Huu Tu**, refused to take a position in favor of the French, and even allowed the DRV's forces to traverse their territories without reporting it. This enraged de Lattre, who held the Catholics responsible for the death of his son, **Bernard de Lattre de Tassigny**, killed during this battle. As a result, the elder de Lattre moved to end effective Catholic autonomy and assumed the defense of Phat Diem and Bui Chu on the same terms as other provinces in the Associated State of Vietnam. *See also* BINH XUYEN; CAO DAI; CATHOLICS IN VIETNAM AND THE WAR; HOA HAO; VATICAN.

**DE GAULLE, CHARLES (1890–1970).** Political and military leader of Free French forces and government during World War II who was determined to restore French colonial sovereignty over Indochina by force if need be. De Gaulle served as president of the Provisional Government of the French Republic between 1944 and 20 January 1946. To de Gaulle, the maintenance of the French colonial empire was vital to restoring national prestige and ensuring France's place in the postwar international system. Without the colonies, de Gaulle declared, France was but a second-tier country. Following the Japanese overthrow of French Indochina, on 24 March 1945 de Gaulle issued the **Declaration on Indochina**. While this document promised liberal reforms and greater **collaboration** with the colonized, it was not a plan for decolonization. Following the Japanese capitulation in August 1945, General de Gaulle issued instructions to Admiral **Georges Thierry d'Argenlieu,** his new high commissioner for Indochina, to recover and restore French colonial sovereignty to Indochina in accordance with the March Declaration and the government's federal model of empire. As Frédéric Turpin has shown, even though de Gaulle left the political scene in January 1946 and retired to his residence in Colombey Les Deux Églises, he remained in close touch with Thierry d'Argenlieu and General Philippe Leclerc, and supported the admiral's aggressive line towards the **Democratic Republic of Vietnam**. De Gaulle remained a firm believer in the need to restore French colonial rule to Indochina and France's prestige in the world and his views weighed heavily in Gaullist circles during the Indochina War, making it harder for those seeking to adopt a more conciliatory attitude towards decolonization. When the war in Algeria entered a critical phase, de Gaulle returned to power in 1958, but he increasingly adopted a more realistic attitude towards decolonization and its importance for France's position and prestige in an increasingly postcolonial international system. This was in marked contrast to his position on Indochina in 1945. *See also* ALGERIAN WAR; UNITED NATIONS.

**DE LA TOUR PLAN.** In 1948, General **Pierre-Georges Boyer de la Tour** embarked upon a major "**pacification**" effort based on the creation of a system of inter-linked posts protecting the economy and the major lines of communications in the Mekong Delta. By September 1949, de la Tour had installed some 3,000 fortified posts, surrounded by barbed wire, and mobilized some 70,000 men to run it. In 1949–1950, General **Nguyen Binh** tried to break de la Tour's hold on the delta, especially with a view to obtaining rice. However, Nguyen Binh's decision to send main force battalions against these posts ended in a stinging defeat for the Vietnamese general. Without their own artillery and adequate logistics, the Vietnamese forces were vulnerable to French artillery and airpower. *See also* PARALLEL HIERARCHIES; PSYCHOLOGICAL WARFARE; REVOLUTIONARY WARFARE; *SERVICE ACTION*.

**DE LATTRE DE TASSIGNY, BERNARD (1928–1951).** Son of the famous Marshal of the same name and the youngest soldier in the French army in 1944, when Charles de Gaulle authorized his induction. Bernard de Lattre participated in the liberation of southern France and Germany (taking part in intensive fighting at Karlsruhe and Constance). Following the war, he underwent officer training at Coëtquidan and Saumer. Named second lieutenant in late 1946, he left for Indochina in December 1948 to lead a squadron of the *1^er^ régiment des chasseurs*. He commanded posts at Yen My and Hung Yen near territories controlled by the Democratic Republic of Vietnam. During this time, he organized and launched a series of audacious operations against and sometimes behind enemy lines. His commitment was even greater when his father took over military and political command of all of Indochina in 1950. Determined to show his mettle, in March 1951 he transferred to the more risky *1^er^ Bataillon de marche du régiment des chasseurs*. In late May 1951, on a mission to halt an enemy offensive against Catholic areas in Ninh Binh, his unit was attacked by the adversary and Bernard de Lattre was killed by an artillery shell. He was 23.

**DE LATTRE DE TASSIGNY, JEAN JOSEPH MARIE GABRIEL (LE ROI JEAN, 1889–1952)**. Marshal de Lattre de Tassigny's name is intimately associated with the French war in Indochina. Known to some as the *roi* or King Jean for his legendary love of pomp, circumstance, and a dash of *panache*, de Lattre graduated from Saint-Cyr in 1911. He fought in World War I, seeing combat at Verdun and the Chemin des Dames. He was wounded four times. There was mettle behind the pomp. During the interwar period, he commanded a battalion in the 5th Infantry Regiment (1928–1931) and took part in the Rif War in Morocco. He led the 151st Infantry Regiment between 1935 and 1937. He was promoted general in 1939, the youngest at the time. After the Germans invaded southern France (Vichy's free zone) in November 1942, following the Allied landings in North Africa, de Lattre was one of the very few to order his troops to resist this second German invasion of France. He was arrested, accused of treason, and sentenced to 10 years in prison by Vichy authorities. He escaped to Algiers via London the following year, joined the Free French forces and took part in the Allied liberation of France and Germany. On 9 May 1945, on behalf of the French provisional government, he accepted the German capitulation in Berlin. Between 1945 and 1950, he served as chief of staff of the Defense, general inspector of the Army, and then as both general inspector of the Armed Forces and senior commander of Ground Forces in Europe.

The French government turned to him to save the deteriorating military situation in Indochina, hoping that his reputation and vigorous actions would raise morale after the **Cao Bang** disaster in 1950. De Lattre only accepted the Indochinese command on the condition that he held both military and civilian powers in Indochina. His wish was granted. On 6 December 1950, he became high commissioner for Indochina and commander-in-chief of French Forces in the Far East.

From December 1950, de Lattre intensified efforts to create a modern army for the newly born counter-revolutionary Associated State of Vietnam presided over by **Bao Dai**. He played a pivotal role in recasting the Indochina War as a vital part of the **Cold War**, crucial to gaining American support for the war effort. The Vietnamization of the fighting and the Americanization of its financing went hand-in-hand for de Lattre. In March 1952, he attended the Conference of Singapore which brought together the military representatives of the United States, France, and Great Britain to discuss the defense of Southeast Asia against a possible Chinese communist attack. De Lattre argued forcefully that Indochina was the vital bulkwark for containing communism in Asia.

It was also in this dual context that de Lattre made his famous speech to high school youth at the *Lycée Chasseloup-Laubat* in **Saigon** in 1951, declaring: *« Soyez des hommes, c'est-à-dire, si vous êtes communistes, rejoignez le* ***Viet Minh****, il y a là des individus qui se battent bien pour une cause mauvaise. Mais, si vous êtes des patriotes, combattez pour votre patrie, car cette guerre est la vôtre ... Cette guerre, que vous l'ayez voulue ou non est la guerre du Vietnam pour le Vietnam. Et la France ne la fera pour vous que si vous la faites avec elle".*

De Lattre scored a number of victories in the battlefield against the **Democratic Republic of Vietnam**, notably at **Vinh Yen**, in his bid to fortify the delta against a possible Sino-Vietnamese attack from the North. On 11 January 1952, after losing his only son in Indochina, he died of cancer. He was named posthumously (four days later) Marshal of France and was buried in *Les Invalides* in Paris.

**DEBÈS, PIERRE LOUIS (1900–1947).** French colonel in command of French forces in Haiphong and the main executor of the violent military conquest of Haiphong on 23–24 November 1946. Upon graduating from Saint-Cyr, he spent the interwar years leading colonial troops, including a tour of duty in French Indochina between 1931 and 1934. During World War II, he took part in the French and German Campaigns before returning to Indochina in late 1945 to take part in the French reoccupation of **Cochinchina**. He commanded the *23ème Régiment d'infanterie coloniale*. Following the signing of the **Accords of 6 March 1946**, he was named commander of the French military sector for **Haiphong**. His ultimatums to the **Democratic Republic of Vietnam** (DRV) in November 1946 led to the bloody reoccupation of the city by French naval and land forces, killing thousands of Vietnamese civilians remaining in the city or fleeing to nearby Kien An. In February 1947, he succeeded General **Louis Morlière** as interim commander of French troops in Northern Indochina until General **Raoul Salan** arrived. During this time, he completed the violent reoccupation of Hanoi by mid-February 1947. Debès died in an airplane accident in Tonkin later that year. Together with General **Jean Valluy** and High Commissioner **Georges Thierry d'Argenlieu**, Debès was among the most aggressive in dealing with the representatives of the DRV.

**DECLARATION ON INDOCHINA.** On 24 March 1945, hardly two weeks after the Japanese overthrew the French in Indochina, the Provisional Government of the French Republic led by **Charles de Gaulle** issued its first major public statement on its policy towards Indochina in particular and towards the rest of the Empire in general. In effect, the declaration on Indochina mentioned officially for the first time the term "**French Union**" and served to outline in broad terms the nature of the French Union which would replace the "Empire". Based on the federal ideas developed during the **Brazzaville Conference**, and in particular the thinking of **Henri Laurentie** and **Léon Pignon**, the declaration of March 1945 called for the creation of a pentagonal **Indochinese Federation** regrouping **Tonkin**, **Annam**, **Cochinchina**, Laos, and Cambodia. Although the federal structure was designed to give each state a greater level of autonomy, ultimate sovereignty resided with the French, who would rule through a high commissioner (the new name for the governor general). The Indochinese Federation would in turn be linked to the other French colonial states via its membership in the French Union. The problem was that the text had already been overtaken by events in Asia: the Japanese overthrow of the French in colonial Indochina on 9 March and **Bao Dai**'s declaration of Vietnam's independence shortly thereafter. The Indochina declaration made no mention of the independence or the unification of Vietnam, much to the dissatisfaction of Vietnamese nationalists of many political colors. *See also* ACCORDS OF 6 MARCH 1946; *COUP DE FORCE* OF 9 MARCH 1945; DALAT CONFERENCE.

**DEFFERRE, GASTON PAUL CHARLES (1910–1986).** French socialist who came to oppose the Indochina War. Educated in Nîmes, Defferre studied law in Aix-en-Provence and practiced it between 1931 and 1951. During World War II, he was a member of the clandestine ***Section française de l'Internationale ouvrière*** (SFIO) Executive Bureau. In October 1945, he was elected deputy of the National Assembly from the Bouches-du-Rhône department and served as under-secretary of state in the Ministry of Overseas France during the **Léon Blum** government between December 1946 and January 1947. He closely followed the Indochina question within the SFIO and became a staunch critic of the war in the party and the National Assembly. When the socialists entered the opposition, he strongly supported the party's refusal to approve the continued financing of the war. He was convinced that the only solution to the war was a negotiated one. *See also* FRENCH COMMUNIST PARTY; LOUIS CAPUT; PUBLIC OPINION, FRENCH.

**DEJEAN, MAURICE (1899–1982).** French diplomat during the Indochina War, who served in 1953 and 1954 as general commissioner in **Saigon**. Dejean supported General **Henri Navarre**'s decision to defend Laos in mid-1953 by taking a stand at **Dien Bien Phu**. Dejean also played a pivotal role in obtaining American air support for the battle of Dien Bien Phu, including the use of **napalm**.

**DELPEY, ROGER (1926–2007).** French veteran of the Indochina War, Delpey became known for his implication in a political affair during the Valéry Giscard d'Estaing period that landed Delpey in jail. He was also well known for his popular fictional series on French soldiers fighting in the Indochina War, *Soldats de la boue*, in which he celebrates the heroic, forgotten soldiers of the **French Union** forces. *See also* CINEMA; CULTURE; EXPERIENCE OF WAR; MYTH OF WAR; NOVELS.

**DELTEIL, HENRI NOËL BARTHÉLEMY (1903–1980).** Veteran French officer of the Indochina War. Graduated from Saint-Cyr in 1924, he made his career in the colonies during the interwar period, first in North Africa and then in Indochina (1936–1938). He joined Free French forces in 1941 and took part in the liberation of France with the *21ème Régiment d'infanterie coloniale*. Promoted colonel in 1945, he returned to Indochina in December of that year and commanded the *21ème Régiment d'infanterie coloniale* during the French reoccupation of southern Vietnam. He returned a third time to serve as a deputy to the French commander of ground forces in South Vietnam between 1953 and 1955. Named brigadier general in 1954, he was a member of the French delegation to the **Geneva Conference**, headed up the joint military commission with **Ta Quang Buu**, and co-signed on 21 July 1954 the military agreements of the **Geneva Accords** with his Vietnamese counterpart concerning the conditions of the cease-fire and the regrouping zones for Laos and Vietnam. When Ta Quang Buu had initialed the military conventions, he invited Delteil to share a glass of champagne to celebrate the end of the war, to which Delteil replied: "Please understand that I cannot accept".

**DELVERT, JEAN (1921–2005).** French specialist of Cambodia who first worked in Indochina as an adjunct professor at the *Institut des lettres* in **Saigon** between 1948 and 1949. He then served as principal of the *Lycée Sisowath* in Phnom Penh and advisor to the Cambodian national education system between 1949 and 1950 before working as the principal of the *Lycée Descartes* in Phnom Penh until 1954, when he became cultural advisor and head of the French cultural mission in postcolonial Cambodia (1954–1959). He published a number of scholarly works on Cambodian history, economy, and demographics.

**DEMOCRAT PARTY, CAMBODIA.** The Democrat Party emerged in the wake of World War II, marked by the Japanese overthrow of the French in March 1945 and the emergence of Cambodian nationalists determined to play a greater role in Cambodian politics. In January 1946, as the French moved to reoccupy southern Indochina and come to a *modus vivendi* restoring Cambodia to the Indochinese colonial state, **Ieu Koeus, Chhen Vam,** and **Sim Var** presided over the creation of the Democrat party. Cambodian democrats accepted the return of French colonial rule, but were determined to push for greater political autonomy and, eventually, independence. The party's political platform also sought to curb the power of the King, calling for the establishment of a constitutional monarchy, and the creation of a single legislature from which a government would be formed and to which the monarchy would be subordinate. In the Assembly elections held in September 1946, the Democrats won 70% of the vote and 50 of the 62 seats for which they competed. They obtained a majority in the Assembly; the Democrat party was thus a force with which to be reckoned. Ieu Koeus assumed leadership of the organization following the death of Prince Youtévong in 1947. However, by 1950, serious splits had occurred within the Democrat party as a number of ranking leaders defected to form competing parties and platforms. In January 1950, unknown assailants gunned down the leader of the Democrats, Ieu Koeus, further weakening the party. Nonetheless, between 1947 and 1951, the Democrats continued to win the majority of seats in the Assembly and thus led the Council of Ministers at the head of the government. However, during this time, King **Norodom Sihanouk,** determined not to be sidelined, reasserted himself politically, exploited the Democrat Party's internal weaknesses, dissolved the Assembly and launched his **royal crusade for the independence** of Cambodia in early 1953. Not only did he force the French hand on the issue of independence, but he successfully transformed himself into a nationalist monarch, despite his colonial origins. Sihanouk was now in a position to sideline the Democrats, something that would turn violent after the Indochina War ended in 1954 and postcolonial Cambodia's leaders renewed their struggles for the control of Cambodia's political future. *See also* CIVIL WAR.

**DEMOCRATIC REPUBLIC OF VIETNAM (DRV).** On 2 September 1945, **Ho Chi Minh** announced the formation of the Democratic Republic of Vietnam (DRV) in **Hanoi**, complete with a Declaration of Independence and the creation of a provisional government which would rule until elections could be held and a National Assembly could meet to constitute a new government (this occurred in March 1946). The DRV sought to unite under its national control the three colonial entities into which the Kingdom of Dai Nam had been divided since French conquest began in the mid-19th century: **Tonkin**, **Annam,**

and **Cochinchina**. The DRV referred to these new territories, respectively, as Bac Bo, Trung Bo, and Nam Bo. Despite the outbreak of war in the south in September 1945, the DRV continued to operate from its capital in Hanoi until 19 December 1946, when full-scale war pushed the central government into the hills of northern Vietnam. The DRV led the fight against the French during the entire Indochina War. Not only was it born in a state of war, but it developed during the Indochina conflict as a state of war. Nevertheless, when the **Geneva Accords** put an end to the Indochina War in mid-1954, the DRV could only claim half of the Vietnam Ho Chi Minh had declared independent in September 1945. The portion positioned below the **17th parallel** was assigned to non-communist Vietnamese nationalists running the State of Vietnam until elections could be held in 1956 to unite the country peacefully. That never happened. In April 1975, after a second war, the DRV took the south by force, unified the country and, in 1976, renamed it all the Socialist Republic of Vietnam. The Vietnamese Communist Party was in charge. *See also* ASSOCIATED STATES OF INDOCHINA; BAO DAI SOLUTION; CIVIL WAR; COLD WAR; INDOCHINESE COMMUNIST PARTY; REPUBLIC OF VIETNAM.

**DENING, MABERLY ESLER.** British diplomat, former chief of Special Operations Executive in the South East Asia Command and chief political advisor to the Supreme Allied Commander South East Asia, **Louis Mountbatten**, at the outset of the Indochina War. Dening tended to support French interests in Indochina, knowing that a strong French presence there would work to protect British interests in Singapore and Malaya. Like **Albert Torel**, Dening felt that the Vietnamese "would undoubtedly welcome the return of the European". However, he felt the French should make concessions in favor of Vietnamese nationalism and autonomy if they wanted to hold on in Indochina in the long term. In 1946, Dening took over the Foreign Office's Southeast Asia division and advised that the British should cultivate its relationships with Western powers in Asia, but that they should also develop a "general partnership" with independent or soon to be independent "Asian peoples". Dening refused a French proposal to create a Franco-British-Dutch "colonial charter", but he urged his government to support efforts to pressure Asian leaders to support Western efforts to prop up **Bao Dai** as a way of containing communism in Asia. *See also* ASSOCIATED STATES OF INDOCHINA; BAO DAI SOLUTION; BURMA; INDIA; INDONESIA.

**ĐÈO VĂN LONG.** White Tai and president of the **Tai Federation** created by the French during the Indochina War and based in Lai Chau in northwestern Vietnam. Although he had been a member of the **Vietnam Nationalist Party** (*Viet Nam Quoc Dan Dang*, VNQDD), with the arrival of the Chinese communists on Vietnam's northern border in 1950 and the strengthening of the forces of the **Democratic Republic of Vietnam** (DRV), Deo Van Long joined the French ***Groupement de commandos mixtes aéroportés*** and participated in numerous **commando** operations designed to deny the DRV access to upland minority regions and harass enemy supply lines and communications. In December 1954, Generals **René Cogny** and **Jean Gilles** traveled to Lai Chau to inform Deo Van Long that the French were pulling out of northern Vietnam in accordance with the **Geneva Accords**. On 8 December 1954, Deo Van Long left Lai Chau on a C-47 transport plane bound for **Hanoi** and ultimately France, where he lived in exile. *See also* MINORITY ETHNIC GROUPS; *PAYS MONTAGNARDS DU SUD* (PMS).

**DEPARTMENT OF OVERSEAS CHINESE AFFAIRS (*Hoa Kiều Vụ*).** The **Democratic Republic of Vietnam** created this department in early 1946 to administer several thousand overseas Chinese residing in Vietnam above the **16th parallel**, mainly in the cities. Fluent in Chinese and a ranking communist leader, **Ly Ban** directed this department for the government at the outset. This was not an easy task given that Chinese Republican forces were occupying northern Indochina and were pursuing their own policies towards the large **overseas Chinese** populations in Indochina. This department seems to have remained intact and theoretically extended its administration to all of the Chinese living in DRV Vietnam during the Indochina War. *See also* FRANCO-CHINESE ACCORD; JACQUES DEQUEKER; MINORITY ETHNIC GROUPS; *PAYS MONTAGNARDS DU SUD* (PMS); REPUBLIC OF CHINA.

**DEQUEKER, JACQUES (1920–1986).** French career colonial administrator in charge of Indochinese workers in France between 1941 and 1945 before being attached to the French mission to the

Far East based in **India** then in southern China. He arrived in Vietnam in late 1945 and served as deputy chief of cabinet to the high commissioner for Indochina **Georges Thierry d'Argenlieu**. In 1948, after short stints as the French delegate to Haiphong (1945–46) and Mon Cay (1946–47), he became bureau chief of Chinese Affairs in **Hanoi** for the high commissioner. After a brief absence, he returned to the same post now based in **Saigon**, where he worked in 1949–50. *See also* DEPARTMENT OF OVERSEAS CHINESE AFFAIRS; MINORITY ETHNIC GROUPS; *PAYS MONTAGNARDS DU SUD* (PMS).

**DESCOEUVRES, DR.** Sent to Indochina in 1947 as delegate of the International **Red Cross** to dispense medical treatment and, if possible, help free European hostages taken by Vietnamese forces following the outbreak of full-scale war in Indochina on **19 December 1946**. After four months of efforts, he left Indochina empty-handed and strongly criticized the **Democratic Republic of Vietnam**.

**DESERTION, DEMOCRATIC REPUBLIC OF VIETNAM.** The **Democratic Republic of Vietnam** (DRV) never produced statistics on the number of desertions occurring in its military and administrative ranks. However, French and captured DRV documents confirm that the phenomenon existed and the numbers were high. According to Jean-Marc Le Page, French statistics for the sole sector of Bien Hoa confirm that for 1952 alone there were on average 400 to 500 desertations (*ralliés*) to the French Union side. For all of Indochina, during the first ten months of 1952, total desertions numbered 4,906 individuals and another 40,000 refugees. Two thirds of these desertions occurred in southern Vietnam, where the DRV's control was weakest and the French military operations were most successful, especially after 1950. Many of these desertions consisted of common soldiers and bureaucrats trying to flee poverty, the French blockade, and famine in many DRV territories. Another motivating factor was Vietnamese Workers' Party's decision to communize the state and increase its control over civilians, bureaucrats, and soldiers. Deserters, the French said, included regular troops, military and political commissars, and civil servants (doctors, tax collectors, administrators, etc). The French did not count peasants or non-military or low-level administrative employees in the DRV as deserters, but rather as refugees entering the Franco-State of Vietnam zones. While it would be dangerous to extrapolate from the 1952 statistics, it is clear that even a very conservative estimate for the entire war or even the more intense 1950–54 period would produce desertions numbering in the tens of thousands, similar to those experienced by the State of Vietnam. *See also* COLLABORATION; CROSSOVERS; DESERTION, FRENCH UNION FORCES; DESERTION, JAPANESE.

**DESERTION, FRENCH UNION FORCES.** According to official French statistics released in early 1955, the total number of desertions within the ranks of the **French Union** forces during the Indochina War totalled 71,443, with the majority of the defections occurring within the ranks of the Associated State of Vietnam and this occurring in the latter stages of the war. In the rubric "French Forces" – the Army, **Air Force**, **Navy**, **North Africans**, Africans, **Foreign Legion** and Indigenous Regular troops – 16,550 desertions are on record. Of this number, the biggest defections occurred during the first six months of 1954 among the "indigenous", mainly Vietnamese regulars in the French **Expeditionary Corps**. The number of desertions for this group jumped from 1,156 in 1953 to 11,705 during the first half of 1954. Foreign Legion desertions increased from 128 to 363 for the same period, while that of **African troops** increased from 5 to 21 in 1954 and even less for North Africans and metropolitan French soldiers. However, the armies of the **Associated States of Indochina** registered high levels of desertion, reaching a total of 38,717 by the end of the war, jumping from 2,187 desertions in 1953 to 32,336 during the first six months of 1954. Such high rates of desertion suggest that morale was low. Other reasons for desertion, especially among the Foreign Legion and the Expeditionary Corps, were due to crimes, drunkenness, fights, mistreatment or perceptions of mistreatment by commanding officers. Anti-colonialism only accounted for a very small minority of desertions. The **Viet Minh** welcomed hundreds of **crossovers** into its ranks, especially European and African ones, in order to use them for propaganda and, in some cases, military purposes. *See also* ARMY, ASSOCIATED STATE OF VIETNAM; COLLABORATION; DESERTION, DEMOCRATIC REPUBLIC OF VIETNAM; DESERTION, JAPANESE; INDOCTRINATION.

**DESERTION, JAPANESE.** It is difficult to establish the exact number of Japanese desertions in Indochina at the end of the Pacific War on 2 September 1945. A French report based on captured **Democratic Republic of Vietnam** (DRV) documents and the declarations of returned Japanese deserters suggests that there were around 4,000 Japanese desertions in **Tonkin** and **Annam** north of the **16th parallel** by December 1946. Not all of them joined the DRV. A maximum of 1,000 to 2,000 Japanese were effectively in the service of the DRV army and state between 1945 and 1950. There were 500–600 deserters in Vietnam below the 16th parallel at the end of 1946 and no more than 300 deserters remaining there after 1948, because of a rather successful repatriation operation led by **Hiroo Saito** at the head of the *Service des déserteurs japonais*. These Japanese deserters assisted the Vietnamese in medical, economic, military, and intelligence activities. In exchange for their services, the DRV accorded them Vietnamese citizenship, referring to them as "New Vietnamese" (***Viet Nam Moi***). Even five Taiwanese agricultural engineers working in the Japanese army were allowed to join the DRV (Japanese authorities had refused to repatriate them to Japan, because they were not "Japanese"). From 1950, as a new group of Asian advisors arrived in Vietnam, the communist Chinese, Japanese **crossovers** had to give up their positions. Some returned to French-controlled zones in order to be repatriated to Japan in the early 1950s and again in the wake of the **Geneva Accords** of July 1954. Between 1954 and 1960, arrangements were made with the DRV to return some 100 former imperial soldiers to Japan. According to recent Vietnamese security publications, between late October 1953 and late 1954, the DRV returned more than 100 hundred of the Japanese soldiers remaining in its ranks. However, the DRV apparently prohibited them from taking their Vietnamese families with them, something which divided families and created great hardship for Vietnamese mothers left to run their households all alone. According to one recent Vietnamese account, the "majority" of Japanese crossovers who did not return after the Geneva Accords had died in battle during the war or succumbed to disease in insalubrious areas of Vietnam without access to proper healthcare. In the 1990s, as Vietnam opened up to the world and the **Cold War** faded away, children born of Japanese-Vietnamese marriages could visit Japan and on some occasions renew contact with their fathers, whom they had not seen since their early childhood some four decades earlier. *See also* COLLABORATION; DESERTION, DEMOCRATIC REPUBLIC OF VIETNAM; DESERTION, FRENCH UNION; VIETNAMESE IN JAPAN.

**DETACHMENT TRẦN PHÚ (*Chi Đội Trần Phú*).** One of four detachments the General Directorate or the **Tong Bo Viet Minh** raised in 1946 from among **overseas Vietnamese** populations in Thailand and Laos. Numbering 426 troops at the outset, the Tran Phu detachment left northeast Thailand in December 1946 and arrived in Tay Ninh in February 1947, where it operated along the Cambodian border. In 1949, it was incorporated into the 109th Regiment in southern Vietnam. **Nguyen Chanh** served as the detachment's first commander, with the Vietnamese-Cambodian **Son Ngoc Minh** working as his political advisor.

**DEUVE, JEAN (MICHEL CAPLY, 1918–2008).** French intelligence officer who played a pivotal role in the creation of the police and intelligence forces of the Royal Lao Government during the entire Indochina War. An officer in the French army, he participated in and was wounded during the battle of France in 1940. Having recovered, he transferred to French West Africa to work in the Cartographic Office for French West Africa. In 1943, now part of Free French forces, he was sent to **India** where he joined British Force 136 in charge of conducting special operations in Japanese-occupied Asia. Following intensive **guerrilla** and intelligence training by the British in Calcutta, allied forces parachuted Deuve and nine other members of Force 136 into the Lao hills around Paksane in January 1945. Deuve and his counterparts conducted clandestine operations against and gathered intelligence on the Japanese. Following the return of the French to Laos in mid-1946, he served as head of the French ***Deuxième Bureau*** for French Forces in Laos (*Forces du Laos*) between 1946 and 1949. With the emergence of the Associated State of Laos in 1949, he became director of the Lao Police, a position he held until 1954. Between 1954 and 1964, he served as counselor to the prime minister and helped the Royal Lao Government build its intelligence services and organize covert operations and **psychological warfare** against the government's communist adversaries. Following his retirement from French intelligence, he went on to become a foremost authority on Lao political, military, and intelligence history, writing under the *nom de plume* of Michel Caply. He wrote a number of erudite books, including *Le Royaume du Laos 1949–1965, Le Laos 1945–1949,* and *Guérilla au Laos.*

**DEUX CENTS BOUGIES.** *See* LÊ DUẨN.

***DEUXIÈME BUREAU* (*2ème BUREAU*).** Refers to the intelligence section of the French armed forces, the "2nd Office" or G2 for Americans. It was present in the different echelons of all the General Staffs operating in the French **Navy**, **Air Force,** and Ground Forces. The French 2ème Bureau was re-established in Indochina in October 1945 with the arrival of French re-occupying forces to the south and was extended northwards following the Chinese withdrawal in 1946. Organizationally and theoretically, the 2ème Bureau covered all of Indochina down to the sectorial level and sometimes even lower. However, in reality, there were vast zones of Vietnam, especially in northern and in central Vietnam, that escaped close scrutiny by this military intelligence service. According to a ranking member of the *Deuxième Bureau* during the Indochina War, Marcel Boussarie, the main objective of this intelligence service was "to make the enemy seen". Each bureau consisted of a "*section étrangère*" and a "*section Indochine*", with the latter by far the most important and largest in staff. The Indochina section gathered intelligence mainly on political, military, and economic developments in the enemy zone as well as the enemy's depots, routes, and lines of communications. A third section was added during the war, mainly in the south, the **Psychological Warfare** Unit. The main territorial *Deuxième Bureau* offices usually numbered 15 officers and relied on a much larger number of mainly Vietnamese interpreters. But as Boussarie conceded, compared to the equivalent British and American intelligence services in Asia at the time, the French *Deuxième Bureau* in Indochina was by far the smallest.

**DEVAUX, MAX ALEXANDRE HENRI (1912–?).** Born in Nam Dinh province, Devaux made his colonial career in Laos, where he worked in various posts between 1936 and 1945. Following the Japanese ***coup de force* of 9 March 1945**, he fled to China. He returned to Luang Prabang following the French reoccupation of Laos in mid-1946 and became delegate for the commissioner for the French Republic to Luang Prabang in 1950. Between 1951 and 1961, he worked in various capacities for the Associated State of Laos, then the Royal Lao Government.

**DEVILLERS, PHILIPPE (né MULLENDER, 1920–).** French journalist and historian who covered the events leading up to the outbreak of the Indochina War on **19 December 1946**. Devillers' Indochinese experience was something of an accident. When a former classmate asked him if he wanted to join the press service of the French **Expeditionary Corps** leaving for Indochina, Devillers said yes. Traveling with him on the boat to Asia was another future Indochina hand and grand reporter, **Jean Lacouture**. Bunked together, they were both part of General **Philippe Leclerc**'s Press Service (then called the 5th Bureau). During his stay in Indochina between November 1945 and October 1946, Devillers reported on Franco-Vietnamese negotiations for *Le Monde* and wrote for the Expeditionary Corps's weekly *Caravelle* (with Lacouture). During this time, Devillers conducted scores of interviews with missionaries, intelligence officers, and Vietnamese and French luminaries, and collected materials for his path-breaking study of the history of contemporary Vietnam published in 1952, *Histoire du Vietnam de 1940 à 1952.* In December 1945, he joined forces with Jean Lacouture and others to create the weekly *Paris-Saigon.* This paper was designed to provide the **Saigon** population with news of France and the world and to promote a sincere debate on Indochina in favor of finding a political solution to the Franco-Vietnamese crisis that was hitting hardest in the south at this time.

Whereas Devillers supported the restoration of French colonial order to Indochina upon arriving in Saigon, he soon became one of the staunchest defenders of Vietnamese nationalism and decolonization following his year in Vietnam and research into modern Vietnamese history. "No Vietnamese government", he wrote, "that appears to be playing the French game rather than that of Vietnam will ever enjoy real authority, never command the trust of the people".

On 1 November 1948, Devillers entered the French government as head of cabinet to the deputy for the general secretary of the government (the French equivalent at the time of the Prime Minister's Office). Between 1950 and 1952, he was responsible for diplomatic affairs and had access to important diplomatic cables concerning the outbreak of the war in 1945–46. It was in this context that he began to suspect that the local French authorities had provoked the Vietnamese into a war in late 1946. The revelations of French **torture** in the pages of *Témoignage Chrétien* radicalized Devillers' critique of the French refusal to take Vietnamese independence demands seriously. The publication of such ideas in his *History of Vietnam* led him to resign from Matignon three days before the book went to press on 28 April 1952. Thanks to the support of **Jean Marie Domenach**, director of ***Esprit***, Devillers published his book with the anticolonialist-minded *Éditions du Seuil*.

Devillers, along with Jean Lacouture, **Paul Mus** and **Jean Chesneaux**, were among the first in France to write on modern Vietnam and to introduce to a wider reading public Vietnamese nationalism, political parties, and the nature of the Franco-Vietnamese war. Indeed, Devillers replaced Paul Mus at the *Collège libre des sciences sociales et économiques*, teaching the first course in France on contemporary Vietnamese history. At the heart of Devillers's research, however, was the argument that French authorities in Indochina had provoked the **Democratic Republic of Vietnam** into war in 1946. In 1988, he made his case by publishing a collection of internal French documents on the outbreak of the war, entitled *Paris-Saigon-Hanoi.* He was, however, no communist fellow traveler. Indeed, **Ngo Dinh Nhu**, the brother of **Ngo Dinh Diem**, initiated the young Frenchman to Vietnamese nationalist history. In the end, Devillers was something of an early Gaullist decolonizer.

**DEVINAT, PAUL (1890–1980).** French Radical Socialist opposed to the **Democratic Republic of Vietnam** and influential policy-maker on colonial questions from 1945. In October 1952, he was elected to head the National Assembly's Sub-committee for Overseas Territories and in this position he closely followed events in and policy-making for Indochina. He supported the **Bao Dai Solution**, convinced that **Ho Chi Minh's** forces could be defeated politically and militarily. In 1953, he actively solicited American military aid and was among those who were determined to transform France's colonial war in Indochina into an integral part of the American-led **Cold War** against communism.

**DEWEY, ALBERT PETER (1916–1945).** Dewey was America's first casualty in the wars for Vietnam. Born in Chicago and the son of a prominent congressman, Dewey was educated in Switzerland and Great Britain before studying French history at Yale and law at the University of Virginia. At ease in French, he worked as a journalist in Paris during the lead-up to the German invasion of France and joined Polish forces fighting in France until Paris capitulated in mid-1940. Back in the United States, Dewey joined the United States Army in 1942 and then the **Office of Strategic Services** (OSS), which parachuted him and his team into France in 1944. He ran intelligence operations in support of the Allied liberation of Europe.

In July 1945, the OSS selected him to lead a team to **Saigon** after the Japanese surrender. The code name of the operation was *Embankment*. Dewey's mission was to recover 214 Americans taken prisoner by the Japanese during the war, gather intelligence on southern Indochina, and protect American property. Dewey arrived in Saigon on 4 September and was met by members of the Japanese High Command and representatives of various Vietnamese nationalist groups, including the **Viet Minh**. Until 12 September, Dewey's OSS team was the only Allied presence in Saigon. Dewey met with southern Viet Minh leaders such as **Pham Van Bach** and **Pham Ngoc Thach** and even acted as a go-between for the Vietnamese and the French. Meanwhile, the British and the French closely monitored his activities. On 23 September, when **Jean Cédile** authorized interned French troops to take control of Saigon as British General **Douglas Gracey** looked the other way, Dewey informed Gracey of the need to take control of the situation and put an end to increasing violence between the French and the Vietnamese. The next day, Gracey declared Dewey *persona non grata* and ordered him to leave Indochina. Like the French, Gracey suspected Dewey of harboring pro-Viet Minh or anti-colonialist views. What is sure is that Dewey was not optimistic about the chances for peace: "**Cochinchina** is burning", he wrote, "the French and British are finished here, and we ought to clear out of Southeast Asia".

On 26 September, the day he was scheduled to leave, unknown assailants opened fire on Dewey's jeep, apparently mistaking the French-speaking American for a French officer. He was killed instantly. His body was never recovered, making him the first American **missing in action** in the Indochina War. Pham Ngoc Thach wrote a personal letter of condolence to Dewey's father, saying that his son had been an "illuminating light that came with the spirit of chivalry". However, the American State Department refused to transmit the father's reply to Pham Ngoc Thach on the grounds that it would lead to "misunderstanding and recrimination". A memorial plaque dedicated to Dewey and his service to France during World War II can be viewed to this day in the cathedral of Bayeux in Normandy, France.

**DIASPORA, VIETNAMESE IN FRANCE**. *See* OVERSEAS VIETNAMESE IN FRANCE.

**DIASPORA, VIETNAMESE IN JAPAN**. *See* OVERSEAS VIETNAMESE IN JAPAN.

**DIASPORA, VIETNAMESE IN THAILAND**. *See* OVERSEAS VIETNAMESE IN THAILAND.

**ĐỊCH VẬN**. *See* PROSELYTIZING THE ENEMY.

**ĐIỆN BIÊN PHỦ, BATTLE OF (13 March–7 May 1954)**. One of the most important battles of the 20th century, during which the colonized engaged the colonizer in a violent set-piece battle and won. Drawing upon the experiences gathered from the French victory at **Na San**, in late 1953 General **Henri Navarre** ordered the creation of an even bigger and more solidly entrenched camp in the valley of Dien Bien Phu. As at Na San, work on an airstrip began immediately. Located far in the hills of northwestern Vietnam, not far from the Lao border, this airstrip would serve as the vital lifeline for supplying some 15,000 **French Union** troops in Dien Bien Phu. Many high-ranking French and American military officials and politicians agreed with Navarre that the camp could hold and break the back of the enemy's main forces. French artillery, air power, and resistance positions, each of which was given a feminine name from A to H (Béatrice, for example), would mow down the attacking enemy soldiers, destroy General **Vo Nguyen Giap**'s core divisions, and thus hand the Vietnamese an even worse defeat than the one they had suffered at Na San in 1952. The French stationed twelve battle-hardened battalions to execute this task. As Robert Guillain reported on the eve of the battle, from the multinational grunts to the French officers, the French Union soldiers were spoiling for a fight, confident that Dien Bien Phu was the perfect place to break the adversary once and for all. Many were actually worried that the Vietnamese would not attack, mirroring paradoxically Vo Nguyen Giap's fear that the French would pull out before he could *casser du français*.

Although Navarre received intelligence in early January 1954 suggesting that the **Democratic Republic of Vietnam** (DRV) was indeed determined and able to bring artillery into position in order to attack the French and knock out the airstrip, something which Vo Nguyen Giap had failed to do at Na San, it was too late for the French general to pull out by air or via Laos without risking a replay of the **Cao Bang** debacle. Nevertheless, Giap's fixation on Dien Bien Phu did not prevent his opponent from launching his cherished operation ***Atlante*** against the enemy's positions in central Vietnam. This operation began on 29 January.

Relieved by Navarre's double decision to dig in at Dien Bien Phu on the one hand and to go ahead with *Atlante* in central Vietnam on the other, Vo Nguyen Giap concentrated his elite divisions – the 308th, 312th, 316th and 304th – around Dien Bien Phu with instructions to encircle, strike, strangulate, and annihilate the camp. Meanwhile, the 351st Heavy Artillery Division was moved into place with 12,37mm cannons, anti-aircraft guns (equipped with 12,37mm cannons), and two air defense machine battalions. Grueling though it was, the DRV ensured that its troops received arms, rice, and medicines. The logistical services mobilized hundreds of **animals,** 128 trucks, 11,000 boats and rafts, and more than 20,000 **bicycles** to deliver 27,400 tons of rice. Motivated by the **land reform** approved in December 1953, more than 200,000 Vietnamese porters from northern and central Vietnam set the logistics into motion in order to supply over 50,000 troops.

On 13 March, the Vietnamese let loose their artillery with deadly accuracy. They quickly knocked out a number of unprotected French artillery guns and blasted the airstrip as they moved to sever the camp's lifeline to the outside. Giap's intelligence officers had meticulously studied what had gone wrong at Na San. This time, they had every intention of taking out the airstrip from the outset by turning artillery shells on the French. And they were largely successful. Indeed, French artillery specialists were shocked by the enemy's use of artillery, above all its precision, and equally frustrated by their inability to locate the DRV's guns camouflaged in the surrounding hills.

The Vietnamese had knocked out the French airstrip by 17 March. However, that did not mean the battle was over. Like their adversaries, French Union soldiers were going to fight. The Vietnamese had launched their first massive, powerful, and costly attack on the 13th as troops moved under heavy French artillery and machine gun fire, submerging the advance posts of Béatrice and Gabrielle. While planes continued to make supply drops to French Union forces facing advancing DRV troops, inclement weather and low cloud cover rendered them vulnerable to DRV artillery and machine gun fire.

Moreover, the battle was not a simple carbon copy of Chinese **wave tactics** applied in Korea; Dien Bien Phu strangely resembled the trench warfare of World War I. Some spoke of Verdun. What differentiated the DRV's use of trenches in 1954 from those at Verdun was that the Vietnamese ones were mobile, expanding slowly to surround the enemy camp instead of forming a straight line. Like the trench warfare of WWI, however, young Vietnamese boys sent over the top suffered terrible casualties when they ran into intense machine gun and artillery fire, as did French Union forces counter-attacking. For both sides, torrential rains quickly filled the trenches with mud, water, disease, and blood, as soldiers often had to make their way around rotting corpses. While American pilots flew supply missions over Dien Bien Phu, Washington refused to save the camp by launching operation **Vautour**. As a result, no U.S. bombers arrived from the Philippines to blast DRV positions around Dien Bien Phu. The French Union soldiers were on their own as the DRV's army launched two more wave attacks, extending their trenches meter by meter, strangling the enemy, until the camp finally fell on 7 May 1954 at 17H00, at the cost of around 4,000 DRV lives. *See also* CIVIL AIR TRANSPORT; DIEN BIEN PHU, BATTLE PREPARATION AND CONTEXT; DIEN BIEN PHU, CANCELLATION OF FIRST ATTACK; DIEN BIEN PHU, EXPERIENCE OF BATTLE; DIEN BIEN PHU, FILM; DIEN BIEN PHU, SIGNIFICANCE OF.

**ĐIỆN BIÊN PHỦ, BATTLE PREPARATION AND CONTEXT**. One cannot understand the full significance of the battle of Dien Bien Phu without situating it in its Franco-Vietnamese, international, and military dimensions. First the French side. French Prime Minister **René Mayer** was a strong believer in strengthening France's role in Europe and the Atlantic community. Fighting a major war in Indochina prevented him from doing this effectively; meanwhile the Allies were pushing to rearm West Germany in order to better contain the Soviet Union in Europe. Financially, France could not afford to undertake a war in Indochina and contribute to European defense at the same time. An "honorable end" (*une sortie honorable*) to the conflict had to be found.

In this context, on 8 May 1953, Mayer named General **Henri Navarre** commander-in-chief of the armed forces in Indochina. The government instructed Navarre to create the necessary military conditions on the battlefield so that French diplomats could reach a favorable solution at the negotiating table. Navarre came up with a two-pronged plan. For 1953–1954, the army would avoid large-scale battles with the enemy in order to rebuild **French Union** forces and then, in 1954–55, deliver a decisive military blow to the army of the **Democratic Republic of Vietnam** (DRV) in order to force the adversary to the negotiating table on terms favorable to the French. Upon his arrival in Indochina in mid-1953, Navarre focused his attention less on the northern delta than on areas in central Vietnam controlled by the DRV since the start of the war. One of Navarre's main offensives, operation ***Atlante***, was designed to retake southern central Vietnam from the DRV, known as **Inter-Zone V** (*Lien Khu V*). While Navarre was eager to break his adversary, he had no intention at the outset of fighting a major battle in the valley of Dien Bien Phu. Nor did his adversary, General **Vo Nguyen Giap**.

To understand how this battle occurred, one must of course factor in the DRV side. First, the **Vietnamese Worker's Party** adopted key decisions in early 1953 that would affect the direction of the road leading to the battle of Dien Bien Phu. In January 1953, the party accelerated preparations to implement **land reform**. The timing was not an accident. Besides its social, economic, and ideological significance, land reform was also designed to mobilize tens of thousands of Vietnamese peasants in favor of the war effort. By providing them with a piece of land, they would participate more enthusiastically and actively in the resistance and above all in the logistics that the DRV's army would need to take the battle to the French. Vietnamese porters would be crucial to bringing artillery, medicines, and above all rice to tens of thousands of troops fighting French Union forces. Second, the party leadership also decided in early 1953 that not only did the army have to develop its own artillery and anti-air defense forces in order to take out the entrenched French positions in any future battle, but the army simultaneously had to devise a strategy to disperse the **Expeditionary Corp**'s troops across Indochina. These two things went hand in hand in the DRV strategic mind. Moreover, no one in the DRV's **General Staff** had forgotten the terrible defeat suffered at **Na San** in 1952. Indeed, Vo Nguyen Giap's General Staff and military intelligence closely studied the lessons of Na San in developing their strategy for 1953–54. Throughout 1953, the DRV reorganized its Artillery Regiment (75mm), created a new artillery regiment of 105mm guns, and constituted its first 37mm anti-air battalion. Lastly, the Vietnamese needed to score a major battle victory: the death of **Joseph Stalin** and the armistice in Korea by mid-1953 had opened up the possibility that things would change at the international level for Korea as well as for Indochina, the two hotspots in the international system.

All of this was underway on the Vietnamese side, when the French adopted the **Navarre Plan** in July 1953. Vietnamese sources now reveal that their intelligence services were initially in the dark as to what Navarre planned to do. By mid-September 1953, however, the DRV's services "acquired a good understanding of the basic elements of the Navarre Plan". The Vietnamese army has recently revealed that communist Chinese intelligence services helped them obtain important details of the plan in early September. This allowed the Vietnamese Politburo to better devise its own strategy, what would become the 1953–1954 Winter Spring Campaign. Vietnamese leaders decided that because Navarre was "massing his forces to occupy and hold the **Tonkin** lowlands, we will force him to disperse his forces out to other sectors so that we can annihilate them". Rather than trying to attack the Delta, where the French would easily concentrate their artillery and air power on any attacking force, the Politburo decided to try to draw the French away from the delta by attacking towards Lai Chau in northwestern Vietnam and Phongsaly in Laos, then towards central and southern Laos and even as far as northeast Cambodia. In mid-November 1953, the Vietnamese Politburo approved its Winter Spring Plan and issued mission orders to its divisions. On 19 November, Vo Nguyen Giap informed his military intelligence officers of the politburo Plan.

Thinking that the Vietnamese were out to take Luang Prabang if not all of Laos, General Navarre decided to commit troops to Dien Bien Phu in order to protect Luang Prabang. This was never the DRV's main strategic intention. On 20 November, the French began parachuting six battalions into Dien Bien Phu. The commander of this airborne force was none other than General **Jean Gilles**, the same man who had handed the DRV the stinging defeat at Na San and who had commanded its elaborate defensive complex. Surprised, the DRV General Staff immediately instructed its intelligence service to explain what the French were up to. Vo Nguyen Giap's two main questions to his intelligence people were: "Is the enemy going to withdraw?" and "How are they deployed?"

Navarre's decision to send French Union troops towards southern central Vietnam (operation Atlante), Laos, and Lai Chau and then to take a simultaneous stand at Dien Bien Phu unexpectedly presented the Vietnamese high command and politburo with exactly the type of battle that they wanted to fight in order to create favorable military conditions for their own diplomatic negotiations.

The changing international context was now of great importance for all those concerned. The disappearance of Stalin in April 1953 and the signing of a cease-fire in Korea in July convinced Soviet and Chinese leaders that the other hot spot in Asia, Indochina, could be solved diplomatically, too. British and French leaders tended to agree. Soviet and Chinese leaders wanted to end tensions at the international level in order to focus on pressing domestic matters. The Soviets also hoped that by taking a conciliatory line on Indochina, they would be able to woo the French away from the creation a **European Defense Community** and the rearmament of West Germany. On 28 September 1953, Moscow sent a note to France, Great Britain, and the United States proposing to hold an international conference to ease international tensions. This conference, the Soviets argued, should include the **People's Republic of China**, which was involved in both Asian wars. On 8 October, **Zhou Enlai** expressed his support for the Soviet proposal. In early 1954, during the four-power conference in Berlin, the Soviet plan was endorsed and preparations began for holding a major international conference in Geneva on the two Asian hotspots in the international system.

The Soviets and Chinese had informed the Vietnamese of their desire to reach a negotiated settlement to the Indochina War and this directly influenced the way the Vietnamese Politburo conceived its strategy for winning a decisive battle at Dien Bien Phu within the context of the Fall-Winter campaign. DRV military intelligence immediately returned to the abandoned Na San camp to study the French complex there, knowing that they would be up against a "super Na San" at Dien Bien Phu. The question remained, however: would Navarre stay put in Dien Bien Phu or would he pull his troops out at the last minute, thereby denying the Vietnamese the showdown they now so badly wanted? The answer came on 3 December when DRV military intelligence informed Giap that Navarre had committed his side to battle.

With the international context firmly in mind, the Politburo issued orders instructing the army to surround the camp and wipe it out entirely, all the while continuing the three other campaigns designed to disperse the French forces as far across Indochina as possible. On 6 December, the Politburo and high command decided to commit all 35,000 men to Dien Bien Phu for a battle lasting some 45 days. Massive mobilization began as tens of thousands of peasants began to transport rice, weapons, and artillery to the hills surrounding the camp. Land reform was officially approved in December 1953 and implemented in upper central and northern Vietnam. Meanwhile, on 17 December 1953, the Politburo approved a resolution approving the policy of negotiating and fighting. For the Vietnamese, the local and international conditions had combined to create conditions to win at Dien Bien Phu and to open negotiations favorable to them at the negotiating table. However, all of this meant that losing the battle of Dien Bien Phu was simply not an option. Victory had to be achieved at "one-hundred-percent", as the Politburo put it. This is why the DRV cancelled its initial attack against Dien Bien Phu, planned for 25 January 1954.

However, Navarre refused to cancel operation Atlante. On 29 January, he launched the operation against lower central Vietnam all the while digging in at Dien Bien Phu in the far northwest. Relieved by Navarre's actions, the Vietnamese continued to concentrate their best divisions on wiping out Dien Bien Phu and focused on solving their final logistic problems. For Navarre the battle would be a short one; the Vietnamese would be unable to bring in sufficient artillery to bear on the fortified camp. Besides the French Union soldiers waiting to mow down enemy attackers with machine guns, the camp was also protected by heavy artillery and airpower. So sure of his ability to knock out enemy guns, the French artillery commander for the battle, Colonel Piroth, refused to protect his own guns from possible attack. All of this despite the fact that French intelligence services had informed the high command that the Vietnamese were bringing in artillery and massing their forces around Dien Bien Phu. Based on this, even Navarre conceded in early January that if the Vietnamese succeeded in delivering their artillery to the battlefield, he would not be able to guarantee victory. The problem was that preparations, operations, and morale were so advanced that it was too late to pull out of Dien Bien Phu in mid-January by air or via Laos without repeating the Cao Bang debacle or handing the adversary a de facto victory at a key point in international negotiations related to Indochina (the Berlin conference met between 25 January and 18 February). Thus, while Giap cancelled his January attack on the grounds that it was premature, Navarre kept his men in the valley, convinced that it was too late to annul the showdown.

On 13 March 1954, with their logistics and artillery now in place, the Vietnamese launched their first attack in a fury. French confidence cracked in the first days of the battle when the camp began taking direct hits from well-coordinated Vietnamese artillery fire, and French cannons and planes failed to knock out enemy positions hidden in the surrounding hills. Only a few days after the battle had begun, Piroth committed suicide for having underestimated the enemy. And yet no one in early or mid-1953 knew that a showdown would occur at Dien Bien Phu. As a former ranking military intelligence officer working for Vo Nguyen Giap at the time later recalled: "Dien Bien Phu became a battle that neither the enemy nor our side had originally anticipated in our plans. We were concerned that the enemy would retreat and abandon the area, while the enemy was afraid that we would not dare to attack". Both sides got what they wanted; but the DRV Vietnamese won the epic showdown. *See also* DIEN BIEN PHU, BATTLE OF; DIEN BIEN PHU, CANCELLATION OF FIRST ATTACK; DIEN BIEN PHU, EXPERIENCE OF BATTLE; DIEN BIEN PHU, FILM; DIEN BIEN PHU, SIGNIFICANCE OF; EUROPEAN DEFENSE COMMUNITY; FINANCIAL COST OF WAR; LAOS, BATTLES OF; NORTH ATLANTIC TREATY ORGANIZATION.

**ĐIỆN BIÊN PHỦ, CANCELLATION OF FIRST ATTACK.** On 5 January 1954, General

**Vo Nguyen Giap** went to the hills overlooking the valley of Dien Bien Phu in the company of his main Chinese advisor, **Wei Guoqing**, in order to make final preparations before launching the attack on **French Union** Forces entrenched in the valley below him. **Ho Chi Minh** had told his commanding general that the battle of Dien Bien Phu had to be won at all costs; defeat was not an option. If there was any doubt that it could not be a 100 percent victory, then Vo Nguyen Giap had orders from the Politburo to postpone the attack. As of 14 January, all in the General Staff were still agreed to attack swiftly in order to wipe out entirely the French encampment. The Vietnamese attack on Dien Bien Phu was set for 25 January at 17H00, as dusk set in.

However, on 24 January, a Vietnamese soldier of the 312th Division fell into French hands, allowing military intelligence to learn of the exact time and date of the imminent attack. The **Viet Minh** intercepted French radio communications indicating that the French were now aware of the attack time. The Army's Security Department (*Cuc Bao Ve Quan Doi*) informed Vo Nguyen Giap of this and the attack was postponed for 24 hours. Those 24 hours were fateful. Vo Nguyen Giap was under pressure from his Chinese advisors, his own mobilized troops and officers, and some of his General Staff to attack resolutely – and now. They argued that everything was in place and that a cancellation of the attack would seed dissension among the troops and the tens of thousands of exhausted porters. Vo Nguyen Giap, however, was not sure that the Vietnamese could win at 100 percent. For him – and apparently for Ho Chi Minh as well – that was enough to call off the January attack. And that is what he did.

Vo Nguyen Giap later cited the three main reasons for his fateful decision. First, the Vietnamese army had never taken on such a huge position, manned by so many French Union battalions and protected by tanks, heavy artillery, and air power (the Vietnamese had suffered a stinging defeat at **Na San** in 1952). Second, this would have been the first time that Vietnamese artillery would have to execute coordinated calibration and firing on a grand scale from protected but unfavourable aiming sites. He was worried by the fact that one artillery regiment commander had recently admitted that he did not know how to use his cannon. Third, Vietnamese soldiers had never attacked in waves in broad daylight over what would be an extended period of time. The French camp at Dien Bien Phu stretched over 15 km in length and 6–7 km in width. Accurate and coordinated artillery fire would thus be crucial to knocking out French positions and allowing Vietnamese troops to attack. Not all of the Vietnamese artillery had arrived in place by the January attack date; and in the meantime the French had considerably reinforced their fortifications in the valley. The stakes were even higher as the Berlin Conference opened at the same time, on 25 January; military defeat would have had catastrophic consequences for the DRV at the diplomatic table. Vo Nguyen Giap cancelled the attack, switching the plan to "attack surely and advance surely" (*Danh Chac, Tien Chac*). His Chinese advisor, **Wei Guoqing**, agreed.

In March, Vo Nguyen Giap threw his best divisions against the French Union hunkered down in Dien Bien Phu and won in a set-piece battle. *See also* DIEN BIEN PHU, BATTLE OF; DIEN BIEN PHU, BATTLE PREPARATION AND CONTEXT; DIEN BIEN PHU, EXPERIENCE OF BATTLE; DIEN BIEN PHU, FILM; DIEN BIEN PHU, SIGNIFICANCE OF.

**ĐIỆN BIÊN PHỦ, EXPERIENCE OF BATTLE.** The fighting was at times ferocious at Dien Bien Phu during the three Vietnamese attacks occurring between 13 March and 7 May 1954. Artillery explosions obliterated the small Tai border town and churned the surrounding green fields into craters, surrounded by mounds of black dirt and rubble. Those who recall the valley floor after the battle spoke of Verdun. Attacking soldiers going over the top encountered deadly machine gun fire while French planes tried to bomb as closely as possible to the perimeter protecting their besieged troops all the while combing the surrounding cliffs for signs of enemy movements, including the porters and troops slowly lugging weapons up the jungle hills. Heavy, seemingly incessant rain in April filled the trenches with knee deep mud, breeding disease and infections as un-evacuated corpses on both sides rotted away, giving rise to an indescribable stench matched only by the sights of the decomposing cadavers. Swarms of yellow flies descended upon the corpses and the infected wounds leaving their larvae to turn into maggots, terrifying young soldiers on both sides of the trenches. Towards the end, a major dysentery epidemic broke out on the Vietnamese side. Similar things occurred on the French Union side.

Internal studies reveal that the **Democratic Republic of Vietnam's** (DRV) medical services treated 10,130 wounded Vietnamese during the battle of Dien Bien Phu, including minor (flesh wounds), medium (bone fractures), and seriously wounded (requiring surgery). Getting them out of the line of fire and to the hospitals behind the lines was an arduous task given the gruelling conditions. Rains flooded the trenches and seeped into field hospitals. Only 34% of the DRV men wounded during the first wave attack could be transported to a medical station of any type in under six hours albeit by the third attack 63% were being transported to safety within that period of time. Within days of the first attack, however, field hospitals were overwhelmed with wounded. A medical student in Surgical Unit No. 2 during the battle, **Nguyen Thi Ngoc Toan,** recalled decades later "that it was very scary at night".

The extraordinary mobilization of upper Vietnam for the battle of Dien Bien Phu reached beyond the soldiers. The 261,451 men and women civilian porters (and 500 pack horses) were as much a part of this battle as the soldiers. Besides the weapons they lugged, they also hauled tons of rice and medicines to feed and heal the soldiers. This also made them some of the prime targets for French bombers as the line between civilian porters and combatants blurred. The violence of the Battle of Dien Bien Phu thus extended beyond the valley floor, running across all of upper Vietnam and even into northern Laos.

But violence was most concentrated on the battlefield and the Vietnamese soldier took the direct hits. Vietnamese troops at Dien Bien Phu suffered a killed-in-action rate of 32% during the first wave attack, 25% during the second, while with the third it dropped to 20%. Artillery fire accounted for 86.3% of the wounds inflicted on DRV bodies at Dien Bien Phu. Precise statistics are such that one can map this assault as follows: (1) head, face and neck injuries, 23.7%, (2) upper limb wounds, 32.5%, (3) lower limb wounds, 27%, (4) chest and back injuries, 11%, (5) stomach injuries, 2.6%, and (6) bone and organ injuries in the pelvic area, 2.7%. Of the soldiers suffering severe head and back injuries, hundreds of them would never walk again, being disabled (*tan phe*), paralyzed (*te liet*), or worse.

The battle of Dien Bien Phu was the single most intense battle of the entire Indochina War both for the **French Union** and **Viet Minh** armies. It may well have been the single most violent showdown of 20th-century wars of decolonization. By mid-April, after the second wave, morale dipped dangerously on the DRV side. According to official statistics, the DRV suffered 13,930 casualties of whom 4,020 died because of battle wounds. French military intelligence estimated that the DRV lost around 20,000 men in this two-month battle of the trenches. 10,000 would seem a more accurate estimation. Over 2,000 French Union forces died defending the entrenched camp at Dien Bien Phu. *See also* COURT MARTIAL, DEMOCRATIC REPUBLIC OF VIETNAM; DESERTION; DIEN BIEN PHU, BATTLE OF; DIEN BIEN PHU, BATTLE PREPARATION AND CONTEXT; DIEN BIEN PHU, CANCELLATION OF FIRST ATTACK; DIEN BIEN PHU, FILM; DIEN BIEN PHU, SIGNIFICANCE OF.

**ĐIỆN BIÊN PHỦ, FILM.** Film directed by **Pierre Schoendoerffer** in 1991, celebrating the tragic heroism of forsaken French soldiers fighting the lost battle at **Dien Bien Phu** in 1954. Although he had vowed he would never go back to Vietnam following his own capture there in 1954, with the 40th anniversary of Dien Bien Phu upon him Schoendoerffer returned to communist Vietnam to make this Franco-Vietnamese production. He dedicated his film to the **French Union** soldiers who had fought against all odds for France at Dien Bien Phu in 1954. As in his earlier films, Schoendoeffer celebrates the heroism of the "forgotten" soldiers and portrays the war through the eyes of those who fought it for the French side. *See also 317ème SECTION*; CINEMA, DEMOCRATIC REPUBLIC OF VIETNAM; CINEMA, FRANCE; CRABE TAMBOUR, LE; DIEN BIEN PHU, BATTLE OF; DIEN BIEN PHU, BATTLE PREPARATION AND CONTEXT; DIEN BIEN PHU, CANCELLATION OF FIRST ATTACK; DIEN BIEN PHU, EXPERIENCE OF BATTLE; DIEN BIEN PHU, SIGNIFICANCE OF; MYTH OF WAR; PRISONERS OF WAR.

**ĐIỆN BIÊN PHỦ, SIGNIFICANCE OF.** The significance of the battle of **Dien Bien Phu** manifests itself in many ways. First, it was a modern military engagement, a set-piece battle, and a victory for what had only a few years earlier been the **guerrilla** army of the **Democratic Republic of Vietnam** (DRV). It was not so much that the French **Expeditionary Corps** was weak in 1954 – indeed, the Americans had almost been overrun in Korea by Chinese and North Korean **wave tactics** – but rather that the DRV had put together a professional army and succeeded in executing a modern battle, using artillery and anti-aircraft weapons in a coordinated fashion. The DRV case sheds light on how a war state makes the transition from a guerrilla force to a modern army. It also shows how a Western colonial power's own "colonized" enemy borrowed foreign military knowledge and aid from abroad to defeat that power in a classic military battle. In this sense, the DRV's defeat of the French at Dien Bien Phu in 1954 is as important as the Japanese defeat of the Russians at Tsushima in 1905.

The DRV victory at Dien Bien Phu also resonated far and wide in the global South, providing hope and inspiration to other colonized peoples fighting colonial domination. The message seemed to be clear: the colonized could develop modern "military force" and use it against the colonizer to achieve national independence. On 1 November 1954, hardly three months after the **Geneva Accords** had been signed on Indochina, the *Front de libération national* (FLN) began their own independence struggle for control of Algeria. At the military level, Dien Bien Phu is a case study in the dangers of underestimating a non-Western adversary, whatever its origin, and its capacity to battle with lethal force. General **Henri Navarre** was not the only one to commit this error.

However, the DRV's military victory at Dien Bien Phu did not ensure diplomatic success at Geneva. Unlike the Indonesians and the Algerians, the communist core of the DRV prevented the **Viet Minh** from playing the Americans against the colonial power on the diplomatic front. What worried the American strategists most at Dien Bien Phu was the fear that Sino-Soviet communism would spread throughout the region if the West did not take a stand. As the battle raged at Dien Bien Phu in April 1954, President **Dwight D. Eisenhower** announced the **domino theory** and the American desire to stop the spread of communism into Asia at the Indochinese pass. The DRV may have won the battle at Dien Bien Phu but they did not win diplomatically at the negotiating table in Geneva. In July 1954, the DRV only obtained half of the Vietnam declared independent by **Ho Chi Minh** in September 1945, as the Americans threw their weight behind the State of Vietnam led by **Ngo Dinh Diem**.

Lastly, the battle of Dien Bien Phu was not just a "French" battle, but rather a multi-national, imperial and international mobilization of manpower and resources. Almost 70% of the troops fighting the Viet Minh at Dien Bien Phu were not French. They were Legionnaires, Africans, North Africans, and most importantly Vietnamese, who accounted for 33% of the total number of troops. And while the Americans and the Chinese did not send combat troops into Indochina as in Korea, each of them was directly involved in the planning and financing of this epic battle. The end of the French empire in Indochina in mid-1954 was a profoundly international affair, both militarily and diplomatically. *See also* ALGERIAN WAR; DIEN BIEN PHU, BATTLE OF; DIEN BIEN PHU, BATTLE PREPARATION AND CONTEXT; DIEN BIEN PHU, CANCELLATION OF FIRST ATTACK; DIEN BIEN PHU, EXPERIENCE OF BATTLE; DIEN BIEN PHU, FILM.

**DIỆP BA (1916–1967).** Vietnamese lawyer born in My Tho province in southern Vietnam, who served in the **Democratic Republic of Vietnam**'s (DRV) security services. He studied law at the Indochinese University in **Hanoi** and apparently joined the French bar. With the advent of the DRV, he served as vice president of the Resistance and Administrative Committee for My Tho province and represented it in the first National Assembly session. From January 1948, he served as chief of the southern security forces until he was relocated to northern Vietnam following the end of the war and the provisional division of Vietnam into two different states in 1954.

**DIỆP TƯ (1916–1976).** Southern resistance leader from My Tho province in southern Vietnam and specialist in militia organization. He was the twin brother of **Diep Ba**, head of southern security services during much of the Indochina War. In 1945, Diep Tu joined the **Vanguard Youth League** (*Thanh Nien Tien Phong*) and helped nationalists take power in My Tho following the Japanese capitulation in August 1945. Between 1946 and 1947, he ran the Secretariat of the Resistance Committee for Southeastern Vietnam (*Uy Ban Khanh Chien Mien Nam Dong*), which was first based in central Vietnam because of the rapid French reoccupation of Indochina below the **16th parallel**. He also served as a political cadre in the Southern Movement Troops (*Bo Doi Nam Tien*) sent to fight the French in 1946. Between 1948 and 1951, he was the head of the Bureau of the Militia in the war **Zone VIII**'s High Command. In 1952, he ran the Political Office of the High Command in western Nam Bo (*Truong Phong Chinh Tri Bo Tu Lenh Mien Tay Nam Bo*). Between 1952 and 1954, he served as deputy political cadre in Can Tho province. Finally, in 1954, following the provisional division of Vietnam into two states during the **Geneva Conference**, he relocated to northern Vietnam. Discharged from the army, he joined the University of **Hanoi** as a vice dean.

**DIETHELM, ANDRÉ (1896–1954).** Graduated from the *École normale* (rue d'Ulm) in 1914, André Diethelm joined the army and saw combat during World War I. During the interwar period, he was involved in Indochinese financial affairs and had been briefly stationed there before becoming cabinet director for Georges Mandel between 1938 and 1940. Following the 1940 French defeat, Diethelm joined the Free French forces under General **Charles de Gaulle** and served as minister of War until November 1945. An ardent Gaullist, he served as deputy for Seine-et-Oise at the head of the *Rassemblement du peuple français* (RPF). He was a firm supporter of de Gaulle's Indochinese policy and an equally committed believer in the French Empire. In May 1949, he sought to block the Assembly's move to amend the legal status of **Cochinchina** on the grounds that the government had "neither the will to fight **Ho Chi Minh**, nor to support **Bao Dai**". He made a fact-finding trip to Indochina in late 1949. In February 1950, following the Sino-Soviet communist recognition of the **Democratic Republic of Vietnam**, he approved the bill to ratifiy the French accords with the **Associated States of Indochina** in order to demonstrate "our unbreakable will to maintain France and the French Union". He advised against applying such a policy elsewhere in the empire, arguing that the colonized there were "less evolved". But the French, he added, had "to remain in Indochina". Diethelm was implicated in the **piastre affair** and was a strong defender of French naturalized Vietnamese and **métis.** *See also* CURRENCY, FRENCH INDOCHINA; WILLIAM BAZÉ.

**DIGO, YVES (1897–1974).** He first served in Indochina during the interwar period as a civil servant until Vichy relieved him of his post in 1941. He then crossed over to the Free French forces. He returned to Indochina in 1947, serving as an advisor to the new high commissioner **Émile Bollaert**. In December 1947, he became commissioner for the Republic to **Tonkin**, a position he held until 1950.

**DILLON, C. DOUGLAS**. (1909–2003). He came from an affluent American family and graduated from Harvard. He had made his name in financial affairs in the private and public sectors before serving as an officer in the United States Navy during World War II. After the war, he returned to public service. A Republican, he served as President **Dwight D. Eisenhower's** ambassador to France between 1953 and 1957. He was deeply involved in negotiations with the French over the Indochina War and the **Geneva Accords**.

**DINASSAUT.** *See DIVISION NAVALE D'ASSAUT.*

**ĐINH NGỌC LIÊN (1911–1991)**. Vietnamese singer in the army during the two wars for Vietnam (1945–1975). During the interwar period, he was a soldier in the *tirailleurs indochinois*. Although a non-communist, in 1945 he joined the national resistance against the French and entered the **Democratic Republic of Vietnam**'s fledgling armed forces. He led the Vietnamese Army Musical Group (*Doan Quan Nhac Viet Nam*) from its inception in August 1945. Between 1945 and 1954, he ran musical affairs for the army. In 1989, he was named the First Artist of the **People's Army of Vietman** (*Quan Doi Nhan Dan Viet Nam*). It is unclear if or when he joined the communist party. *See also* CINEMA; CULTURE; INDOCTRINATION; NOVELS; RECTIFICATION.

**ĐINH THỊ CẨN (1920–).** Vietnamese political cadre from Nghe An province in charge of the mobilization of women during the Indochina War. Increasingly involved in radical nationalist politics during the 1930s, she joined the **Indochinese Communist Party** in 1940. She was incarcerated for her political activities between 1941 and August 1945. Between 1945 and 1946, she served as a member of the Standing Committee of the **Viet Minh** national front in Vinh and was secretary of the Committee for the Mobilization of Women. Between 1946 and 1947, she worked on the Standing Committee of the Committee for the Mobilization of Women in central Vietnam. Between 1947 and 1959, she was the deputy secretary of the Central Government's Women's Mobilization Committee (*Ban Phu Van Trung Uong*). *See also* WOMEN.

**ĐINH XUÂN QUANG (1922–).** Vietnamese judge and nationalist politician from Quang Binh province. He completed his secondary studies at the *Lycée Albert Sarraut* in **Hanoi** and obtained the American equivalent of a Bachelor's degree in Law (*licence*) in the Faculty of Law at the Indochinese University. In 1936, he joined the Judicial Service in Indochina and was ranked first for the entrance examination for the much sought after legal clerkships. He became a judicial clerk in 1937 and served in the Appellate Court in Hanoi until 1945 (following a brief transfer to Vinh). After the Japanese ***coup de force* of 9 March 1945**, he supported the eviction of French judges in favor of Vietnamese ones; the political circumstances of mid-1945 facilitated this process. The Japanese-backed government of **Tran Trong Kim** named him on 15 August 1945 3rd Level Judge at the Court of Hanoi. On 23 March 1946, the **Democratic Republic of Vietnam** made him a prosecutor. He resigned, however, on 1 April 1946 and joined **Bao Dai** in southern China or Hong Kong where he served as legal counsel to the former Emperor. In January 1950, Dinh Xuan Quang was designated under secretary of state in the Presidency of the government led by **Nguyen Phan Long**. He became state secretary for the Budget in the second cabinet of **Tran Van Huu**, created on 18 February 1951, and served also as acting minister of Health. On 8 March 1952, he was named secretary of state in the Presidency of the third government led by Tran Van Huu. In September 1952, he was named by decree the president of the Administrative Court of the Associated State of Vietnam and in February 1953 he was advisor to the National Appellate Court in **Saigon**. He briefly served as deputy minister in the government formed by Prince **Buu Loc** on 11 January 1954.

**ĐINH XUÂN TIN.** *See* **LÊ TRỌNG NGHĨA.**

**DIO, LOUIS JOSEPH MARIE (1908–1994).** French military commander in Cambodia during the Indochina War. Graduated from Saint-Cyr in 1928, he served in the colonial army in French Africa in the 1930s. In 1940, he joined General **Philippe Leclerc** in North Africa, participating in many of the 2nd Armored Division's exploits, including the battle of France and Germany. In June 1945, he replaced Leclerc at the head of the 2nd Armored Division. In June 1950, he arrived in Indochina and took command of the *Forces du Cambodge* and then in May 1951 the *Forces terrestres du Cambodge*. In October 1951, he served as high commissioner of the Republic in Cambodia and continued as the commander-in-chief of its armed forces. He returned to France in July 1952.

**DIRECTION GÉNÉRALE DE LA DOCUMENTATION (DGD).** On 6 February 1950, as the **Cold War** intensified the fighting in the Indochinese battlefields and internationalized the war on the diplomatic front, the French created this new centralizing intelligence agency for the high commissioner in Indochina. The DGD's main goal was "to control, coordinate and guide" intelligence activities in Indochina and Southeast Asia. Though answerable to the high commissioner, the general director of the DGD enjoyed greater powers than his predecessors in the ***Bureau technique de liaison et de coordination d'Extrême-Orient***. The DGD's director was authorized not only to centralize intelligence coming from different sources, but to oversee the orientation and operation of intelligence strategy and collaboration, including counter-espionage and electronic interceptions. The director was also authorized to oversee collaboration between military and civil intelligence services and to collaborate with foreign, friendly intelligence services. The head of the DGD was also expected to collaborate effectively with the ***Service de documentation extérieure et de contre-espionnage*** in choosing where to set up intelligence posts in Southeast Asia. Despite attempts by General **Jean de Lattre de Tassigny** to sideline the DGD, it remained active until the end of the Indochina War. In March 1954, the DGD was assigned the additional intelligence tasks of monitoring political and economic questions pertaining to Indochina. *See also DEUXIEME BUREAU*; JEAN COUSSEAU; MARCEL BAZIN; MAURICE BELLEUX; PUBLIC SECURITY SERVICE.

**DIRTY WAR.** *See SALE GUERRE.*

**DISEASE, DEMOCRATIC REPUBLIC OF VIETNAM.** Before young **Democratic Republic of Vietnam** (DRV) soldiers went into battle, they had to be fit enough to fight. Cholera, malaria, dysentery, and typhoid could be as lethal as flying bullets and artillery fire. And if disease did not kill instantly, it often incapacitated scores of able-bodied men for weeks, indeed months, sometimes spreading from one unit to another before moving on indiscriminately. The DRV's soldier's body was no more immune to tropical diseases than the colonial one. The problem was that the DRV's medical services lacked quality medicines in sufficient quantities. In a special meeting of the military medical service held in May 1947, **Vo Nguyen Giap** had emphasized the importance of fighting cholera in all of its forms. In 1948, **Ho Chi Minh** had to remind military medical staff that a chronic lack of medicine and a failure to carefully preserve medicines in their possession meant that too many soldiers remained sick. For the period between 1945 and 1950, disease and sickness probably exacted a heavier toll on the Vietnamese soldier's health than the **French Union** armed forces did. Many combat units, even regiments, often operated at 50% manpower because of debilitating and sometimes lethal diseases. The French Union army never had to confront this problem on this scale. Although local innovations helped combat sickness, modern communist bloc aid was essential to reducing the high levels of sickness in DRV combat units. Between 1952 and 1954, Sino-Soviet medical **aid** amounted to 110 tons and 46 trunks of medicines, consisting mainly of vaccines, antibiotics, and anti malaria pills, as well as medical instruments. Thanks to these medicines, the DRV supplied and required its main force troops to take anti-cholera pills for eight months in northern Vietnam and three months in less infected areas in central Vietnam. Also contributing to this decline were the military medical corps' stepped-up propaganda drives among the soldiers, stressing the importance of good hygiene, clean drinking water, and regular bathing. Special preventive disease clinics appeared within the army ranks, while political cadres ensured that the rules were followed. Between 1950 and 1954, the overall number of the sick among the troops fell from an astounding high of 51.2% in 1950 to 31.2% in 1954, with cholera being the enemy no. 1. The level of cholera afflictions in the army dropped from 31% in 1951 to 27.9% in 1952. By the time of Dien Bien Phu, DRV divisions were judged to be on average 90% healthy. When viewed from the vantage point of the combatant's health, there was more to winning on the battlefield than providing troops with big guns. *See also* EXPERIENCE OF WAR.

**DISSOLUTION OF THE INDOCHINESE COMMUNIST PARTY.** In late 1945, Vietnamese communists came under enormous pressure as they tried to keep the **Democratic Republic of Vietnam** (DRV) afloat against internal and external threats. Inside Vietnam, anti-communist nationalist parties such as the **Vietnamese Nationalist Party** (*Viet Nam Quoc Dan Dang*, VNQDD), the **Greater Vietnam Nationalist Party** (*Dai Viet Quoc Dan Dang*) and the Alliance League (*Dong Minh Hoi*) launched intense anti-communist propaganda drives portraying **Ho Chi Minh** as a communist ready to sell out the country to the French. These nationalist parties also called upon the occupying Chinese republican troops to support them against the Vietnamese communists. **Indochinese Communist Party** (ICP) leaders also worried that the overt presence of the communist party could alienate important non-communist international sympathy for the DRV's cause, coming from the **Republic of China**, the United States, and newly emerging independent states in Asia. It was in this context that Ho Chi Minh and at least part of the communist leadership present at that time made the decision to dissolve the ICP on 11 November 1945. Members were invited to join a newly created "Marxist Study Group". The ICP's daily paper, *Liberation Flag* (*Co Giai Phong*) turned into the *Truth* (*Su That*) paper. Significantly, the announcement of the party's dissolution generated doubts within the French, Chinese, and Soviet communist parties about the real ideological colors and loyalty of the Vietnamese communists and of Ho Chi Minh in particular. However, the communist party was never really disbanded. Rather it went underground (*rut vao bi mat*). It officially resurfaced in early 1951 as the **Vietnamese Worker's Party**. *See also* FRENCH COMMUNIST PARTY.

***DIVISION NAVALE D'ASSAUT*** **(DINASSAUT).** Small, mobile yet heavily armed and armoured French flotillas deployed during the Indochina War for executing amphibious operations against enemy forces using Vietnam's long craggy coasts and numerous inlets, rivers, and streams. Dinassaut forces often followed the waterways deep inside the country, where conventional naval forces could not venture. This also allowed them to operate in tandem with overland military operations. The average dinassaut possessed some 12 vessels, including an armoured Landing Ship Support, Large (LSSL), two Landing Craft, Material (LCM) and about six other LCM. The Dinassaut no. 3 in the Red River delta grew to about 20 vessels and even included its own Landing Craft, Tank (LCT)-borne armoured vehicles. The Dinassaut played a pivotal role in the battle of **Hoa Binh**, engaging in a ferocious battle against the **Democratic Republic of Vietnam** on the Black River around Notre Dame Rock and elsewhere in the Red River delta tributaries.

**DIVISIONS, ASSOCATED STATE OF VIETNAM.** *See* ARMY OF THE ASSOCIATED STATE OF VIETNAM; FRENCH UNION.

**DIVISIONS, DEMOCRATIC REPUBLIC OF VIETNAM**. During the second half of the Indochina War, the Vietnamese army created, outfitted, and ran seven divisions against the French. In 1949, the **Democratic Republic of Vietnam** organized its first main force division, the 308th. Thanks to Chinese weapons and training, in 1950–51 the army formed the 304th, 312th, 316th, 320th, 325th, and 351st divisions. From 1950, the French army was no longer only engaged in low-intensity, counter-insurgency, **guerrilla** or "**pacification**" operations. It now faced an increasingly modern and effective Vietnamese fighting force. Chinese outfitting and training was one reason for this. But the Vietnamese ability to organize, coordinate, and run modern divisions across almost all of Indochina left no doubt that the "colonized" were now able to take the battle to the "colonizers" in modern and intense set-piece battles. The colonial war ending in 1954 was no longer as asymmetric as it had been at the start in 1945. *See also* ALGERIAN WAR.

**ĐỖ ĐỨC LIÊM.** *See* VŨ LANG.

**ĐỖ MƯỜI (1917–).** Vietnamese communist nationalist born in **Hanoi** and former general secretary of the Vietnamese Communist Party. He became politically active in nationalist and communist politics during the Popular Front period, joining the **Indochinese Communist Party** in 1939. In 1941, the French police arrested him on political grounds and incarcerated him in Hoa Lo prison in Hanoi until his release in March 1945 following the Japanese ***coup de force* of 9 March 1945**. In August of 1945, he helped the **Viet Minh** take power in Hanoi and joined the **Democratic Republic of Vietnam**. Between 1945 and 1955, he served in a variety of politico-administrative positions: provincial party secretary of Ha Dong, secretary of the party Provincial Committee of Ha Nam, secretary of the party Provincial Committee of Nam Dinh, as well as president of the Resistance and Administrative Committee of the same province. From around 1950, he served as deputy party secretary for **Inter-Zone III** (*Lien Khu III*) as well as the vice president of the Resistance and Administrative Committee of the same zone. He was political commissar in Inter-Zone III's military command. Sometime before the end of the war, he served as the president of the Resistance and Administrative Committee and political commissar for the High Command of the zone for the Right Bank of the Red River. With the end of the war, as party secretary and president of the Administrative Committee of Haiphong, he presided over the evacuation of French troops from the port city in late 1954 and 1955.

**ĐỖ VĂN NĂNG (1915–1950).** Born in Vinh Long province in southern Vietnam, he joined the colonial administration, working as a secretary in the *résidence* in Kompong Chnang in Cambodia between 1935 and 1943 and then in a colonial mining office until the Japanese overthrew the French in March 1945. Do Van Nang then briefly worked in the Japanese police in the south. A non-communist nationalist, he joined the **Greater Vietnam Nationalist Party** (*Dai Viet Quoc Dan Dang*) and was editor of the paper *Thanh Nien* (Youth). He was also associated with the local chapter of the ***Section française de l'Internationale ouvrière,*** writing articles for its newspaper, *La Justice*. After collaborating briefly with the **Democratic Republic of Vietnam**'s (DRV) forces in the south against the French reoccupation, he broke with the government over its communist core. His opposition to the communists cost him his life in March 1950, when agents of the DRV assassinated him.

**ĐỖ XUÂN HỢP (1906–1985).** Vietnamese surgeon graduated from the *École supérieure de pharmacie* in 1929 and the *Faculté de médecine* in **Hanoi** in 1935, where he lectured between 1932 and 1945. After working in Lao Cai, Do Xuan Hop returned to Hanoi in 1932 and began working as an assistant doctor to the French Dr. **Pierre Huard** in the surgical clinic at the *Faculté de médecine.* Under Huard, he interned in surgery at the Phu Doan (de Lannessan) hospital and then began teaching in the surgical clinic in the medical school. During this time, Huard and Do Xuan Hop continued working together. In 1942, the two men published the results of their collaborative work, *Morphologie humaine et anatomie artis-*

*tique*. Do Xuan Hop was a member of the *Institut indochinois pour l'étude de l'homme*.

Following the defeat of the Japanese, he supported the nationalist cause of the **Democratic Republic of Vietnam** (DRV). He and his wife helped create, train, and lead the fledgling Vietnamese **Red Cross** in Hanoi in 1945–46. He was also one of the founding members of the **Vietnamese Socialist Party** (*Dang Xa Hoi*). With the outbreak of full-scale war on **19 December 1946**, he and his wife left their urban lifestyles behind to take to the jungles of northern Vietnam. In 1947, Do Xuan Hop ran the Military Hospital of Zone X, tending to soldiers wounded in the battle for Hanoi. With the intensification of the war in 1949–50, the government assigned him the task of training more doctors to deal with the rapidly increasing number of wounded. He taught and eventually ran the DRV's Military Medical School (*Truong Dai Hoc Quan Y*) in Tuyen Quang province. He also taught at the Chiem Hoa Medical School run by Drs. **Ho Dac Di** and **Ton That Tung**. Do Xuan Hop translated scores of medical terms, manuals, and articles into Vietnamese in order to train new doctors being sent to tend to wounded soldiers. He was instrumental in creating in November 1948 the Vietnamese Army Medical journal, *Xay Dung* (Construction).

In 1949, during a break from teaching at the DRV medical school in the jungles of northern Vietnam, a French radio broadcast informed Do Xuan Hop that the French *Académie nationale de médecine* had awarded him and Huard the prestigious Testus prize for *Morphologie humaine*. When Hop looked at his wife to see her reaction to the news and the French request that they return to Hanoi and fly to Paris to accept it, she just kept on working in silence and didn't look up. Four decades later, during an official visit to Vietnam, French President François Mitterand would present the prize in person to his wife (Do Xuan Hop passed away in 1985). *See also* DISEASE; PAUL GRAUWIN; TON THAT TUNG.

**ĐOÀN 100.** *See* ADVISORY GROUP 100.

**ĐOÀN KHUÊ (1923–1999).** Vietnamese general from Quang Tri who served during all three Indochinese wars between 1945 and 1991 (in Cambodia). He became active in nationalist and communist politics in the late 1930s in the Quang Tri region. In late 1940, the colonial police picked him up and incarcerated him in Quang Tri before transferring him to the main prison in Buan Me Thuot. In May 1945, following the Japanese ***coup de force* of 9 March 1945**, he walked free and immediately returned to Quang Tri to help take power there, serving as a military delegate on the newly formed Provisional Committee for the Province of Quang Tri. In June 1945, he joined the **Indochinese Communist Party**. From August 1945, he served as a political cadre and helped develop local armed forces. He served as the Party's secretary to the Quang Ngai Military Academy, opened to train Vietnamese officers and soldiers to take on the French returning in force to Indochina below the **16th parallel.** From April 1947, he served as a political cadre in "regiments" 69, 73, 78, 126, and 84. He rapidly became a ranking communist and military leader in **Inter-Zone V** (*Lien Khu V*). He served as the secretary of the Party's Committee in several regiments. From May 1953, he was a political commissar in the 108th regiment and the secretary of the Party's Committee and deputy commissar in the 305th **Division**. When the 305th Division was formed in the Binh Dinh regroupment area in September 1954 in preparation for the troop regroupment to North Vietnam, Doan Khue served as secretary of the Party Committee and deputy commissar in the 305th Division. *See also* REGROUPING TO THE NORTH; SALOTH SAR.

**ĐOÀN QUÂN TẤN (1895–1970).** Colonial civil servant and national educator born in Long Xuyen province in southern Vietnam. He began his career in the Indochinese Customs Service in 1917 before entering the *École supérieure de droit et d'administration de Hanoi* (which soon became the Faculty of Law at the Indochinese University). He continued his studies in law in Paris. Upon his return, he joined the **Bank of Indochina** in 1932. Little is known about his activities during World War II. Between 1948 and 1949, however, he served as minister of Education in the French-backed provisional government of South Vietnam (**Cochinchina**). Between 1952 and 1954, he was director of the Vietnamese Information Service for the Associated State of Vietnam and then ran the National Library of the **Republic of Vietnam** between 1954 and 1957. He was a specialist in French and Vietnamese theatre.

**DOMENACH, JEAN-MARIE (1922–1997).** French **intellectual** and humanist opposed to the Indochina War. Domenach joined the resistance at the University of Lyon before joining the French *maquis* in August 1943 in the Vercors region. Following the war, he joined the progressive Christian review ***Esprit***, founded by Emmanuel Mounier, serving as its secretary between 1946 and 1957 and its director between 1957 and 1976. Anti-colonialist, Domenach opposed the Indochina War in the pages of *Esprit* from 1947 and recognized, like his friend **Paul Mus**, the historical reality of decolonization and the need for France to take it seriously now rather than later. He participated in the historic French meeting on opposing the Indochina War, organized by Christian groups, at Issy-les-Moulineaux in February 1950 and contributed to the writing of the final motion. Like **Jean-Paul Sartre**, he supported the liberation of **Henri Martin**. He was also active within the *Comité d'étude et d'action pour le règlement pacifique de la guerre du Vietnam.* He maintained his convictions during the **Algerian War** and supported **Charles de Gaulle**'s policy of ending the war there. In 1971, he created with Michel Foucault and Pierre Vidal-Naquet the *Groupe d'information sur les prisons*. And in 1975, he joined both Jean-Paul Sartre and **Raymond Aron** in supporting the Vietnamese "boat people" fleeing many of the same communist leaders for whom Domenach had agitated during the Indochina War. *See also* CHRISTIANS AND FRENCH OPPOSITION TO THE INDOCHINA WAR; PUBLIC OPINION.

**DOMINO THEORY.** This famous theory is widely attributed to President **Dwight D. Eisenhower**. When asked during a press conference on 7 April 1954 to explain Indochina's "strategic importance" to the United States, the president explained that economic interests (tin, tungsten, rubber) were as much at stake for the United States as the human ones (450 million people who could fall under "Communist dictatorship"). He then continued: "Finally, you have broader considerations that might follow what you would call the 'falling domino' principle. You have a row of dominoes set up, you knock over the first one, and what will happen to the last one is the certainty that it will go over very quickly. So you could have a beginning of a disintegration that would have the most profound influences". And this, he added, would have "incalculable" consequences for the "free world". Subsequent Americans presidents invoked this theory to justify continued American commitment to and involvement in Vietnam. However, the domino theory probably did not appear *ex nihilo*. For example, in order to win over American support of the French fighting on the **Cold War**'s Southeast Asian front, French General **Jean de Lattre de Tassigny** (and others) had been fond of speaking in such terms. In September 1951, he argued that once **Tonkin** was lost to the communists, "there would be no wall before Suez" capable of stopping communist advances in the South. *See also* NSC 5405; NSC 64.

**ĐỒNG SĨ HUA (1916–).** Vietnamese civil servant during the colonial period who returned to Vietnam from New Caledonia in 1945. Born to a wealthy family in Thua Thien province, he studied in Hue and became a colonial secretary in the office of the French Resident in Dalat. In 1936 he transferred to Port Villa in the New Hebrides and then to New Caledonia. After the end of the Pacific War, in 1947, he returned to Vietnam and worked briefly in Hue before crossing over to the **Democratic Republic of Vietnam**. There, he worked in the labor movement in **Inter-Zone IV** (*Lien Khu IV*) in upper central Vietnam.

**ĐỒNG SĨ NGUYÊN (NGUYỄN HỮU VŨ, NGUYỄN VĂN ĐỒNG, 1923–).** Vietnamese general during the two Vietnam Wars. Born in Quang Binh province, Dong Si Nguyen became politically active during the Popular Front period and joined the **Indochinese Communist Party** in 1939. After the Japanese overthrew the French in Indochina during the ***coup de force* of 9 March 1945**, he was active in his home province where he helped form the Party Cadre Committee for Quang Binh. During the war, he served as a member of the party's standing committee for the province. Between 1945 and 1948, he was a political commissar as well as the provincial head of Quang Binh. He was deeply involved in developing the control of the party in the army. He participated in the battles of **Dong Trieu** and Tran Hung Dao and served as a party delegate to the High Command during the invasion of central Laos in 1953. He was the head of the delegation in charge of monitoring the supplying of the front (from central Vietnam) during the battle of **Dien Bien Phu**. He was also one of those in charge of the exchange of prisoners in 1954 and 1955 and the reception of soldiers and cadres being repatriated from the south.

**ĐÔNG TRIỀU, BATTLE OF (*Hoàng Hoa Thám*, 23 MARCH–7 APRIL 1951).** General **Vo Nguyen Giap**'s failure to take **Vinh Yen** in the Red River valley in January 1951 did not deter him from striking against Dong Trieu, located in the northeastern part of the delta. Beginning on 23 March 1951, Giap sent elements of the 308th and 312th divisions to destroy French posts there and to develop **guerrilla** activities. However, Vietnamese troops suffered heavy losses from French artillery and airpower and Vo Nguyen Giap ended the battle on 7 April. The official Vietnamese military version of this battle concedes in no uncertain terms a Vietnamese failure.

**ĐỒNG.** *See* CURRENCY, DEMOCRATIC REPUBLIC OF VIETNAM.

**DONOVAN, WILLIAM JOSEPH ("WILD BILL", 1883–1959).** A law graduate from Columbia University (1907), William Donovan distinguished himself in battle during World War I serving in the American Expeditionary force in France. Because of his battle exploits, he was the first to receive the four highest decorations for valor in the United States. During the interwar period, he returned to practicing law. The outbreak of World War II changed all that. Upon the recommendation of Britain's intelligence chief in New York, William S. Stephenson, Franklin Roosevelt named him director of the **Office of Strategic Services** (OSS) in June 1942, subordinate to the Joint Chiefs of Staff. As early as the autumn of 1941 Donovan had spoken of the possibility of sending secret American teams behind enemy lines in China, Mongolia, and Indochina. He left the OSS at the end of the Pacific War and the army a year later. President **Dwight D. Eisenhower** asked him to serve as ambassador to the Kingdom of Thailand, which he did between 1953 and 1954, and played an important role in developing American policy during the closing years of the French Indochina War and preparing the way for greater American involvement in Indochina in particular and Southeast Asia in general.

**DOOLEY, THOMAS (1927–1961).** Born into a Catholic family in Saint Louis, Missouri, in the United States, Dooley became a doctor of medicine and served in the Navy during World War II as a medical corpsman between 1944 and 1946. He left the armed forces that year. He encountered Vietnam in 1954, when he helped transport Vietnamese Catholic refugees from North to South Vietnam following the division of the country in accordance with the **Geneva Accords**. His participation in this evacuation operation known as *Passage to Freedom* marked him profoundly. His was staunchly anti-communist and a proponent of supporting Southeast Asians against the communist threat. He worked in the port of Haiphong as a medical officer and interpreter (he had studied French) dealing with refugee matters until the **Democratic Republic of Vietnam** took over officially in May 1955. Upon his return to the United States, he wrote his first book, based on his experiences in Vietnam. Entitled *Deliver Us From Evil,* it became a best seller and was published in a shortened form in *Reader's Digest* before being reprinted in 11 foreign languages. Dooley was charismatic, gay, at ease speaking publicly, but he was also very sure of himself and his mission in Indochina. As one of his colleagues put it: "Upon meeting Tom, he was a man you either loved, or hated, but never forgot". *See also* CATHOLICS, EXODUS FROM NORTH; CATHOLICS IN VIETNAM AND THE WAR; CHRISTIANS AND OPPOSITION TO THE INDOCHINA WAR; LE HUU TU; VATICAN.

**DRAFT, ASSOCIATED STATE OF VIETNAM.** *See* ARMY, ASSOCIATED STATE OF VIETNAM.

**DRAFT, DEMOCRATIC REPUBLIC OF VIETNAM.** Upon coming to power in September 1945, the **Democratic Republic of Vietnam** (DRV) did not instaure mandatory national service. The one exception to this was in the medical field. In 1946, the government issued legislation allowing it to draft badly needed doctors, physicians, and pharmacists. Military service was voluntary until 4 November 1949, when the government issued a decree implementing mandatory wartime military service, although it could only be enforced in territories it effectively controlled. The military draft only applied to men, though it is not clear which age range exactly. On 12 February 1950, hardly a month after the communist bloc recognized the DRV diplomatically, the Vietnamese government issued a decree authorizing the general mobilization (*tong dong vien*) of manpower, materials, and resources. In short, having made the decision to take the war to the French on the battlefield as part of their General Counter Offensive strategy, Vietnamese communists needed direct access to more troops, manpower, and materials, and fast (preparations for a frontier battle were already underway in early 1950). While legislation passed in the early days of the DRV allowed the government to confiscate materials, the 1950 "general mobilization" decree went far beyond it by according the government special legal powers to confiscate goods, food, require obligatory military service and recruit the civilian manpower (*dan cong*) needed to win the war in this vital, intensive phase of the war in central and northern Vietnam. The government obtained the power to recruit Vietnamese citizens between 18 and 50, regardless of sex, to serve as the civilian porters constituting the army's logistics until the battle of **Dien Bien Phu.**

**DRAPIER, ANTONIN-FERNAND, MGR. (1891–1967).** Influential French Bishop in Indochina during the war. Ordained Bishop in 1929, he was appointed by the **Vatican** and served as its Apostolic Delegate to Indochina between 1936 and 1950. He was the Principal Consecrator of **Pierre Martin Ngo Dinh Thuc**. In 1948, Drapier refused to recognize the **Democratic Republic of Vietnam**'s Catholic Union (*Lien Doan Cong Giao*) on the grounds that it was independent of Vatican authority. This led to tensions between the new Vietnamese government and the Vatican. In April 1950, before leaving for Rome, he traveled to Dalat to meet with **Bao Dai**, head of the newly created non-communist Associated State of Vietnam, concerning the exchange of diplomatic representatives with the Vatican. *See also* CATHOLICS, EXODUS FROM NORTH; CATHOLICS IN VIETNAM AND THE WAR; CHRISTIANS AND OPPOSITION TO THE INDOCHINA WAR; LE HUU TU; VATICAN.

**DRONNE, RAYMOND (1908–1991).** French politician who joined the Free French forces in August 1940 and served in the Second Armored Division under General **Philippe Leclerc** during the liberation of France in 1944. He followed Leclerc to Indochina, commanding a battalion in the Second Armored Division during the French reoccupation of southern Vietnam below the **16th parallel**. Dronne left the army in 1947 for unclear reasons, but stated that he had been disgusted by what he saw (it is not clear to what precisely he was referring). He began a long career in politics in the Gaullist *Rassemblement du peuple français*. Dronne was an ardent defender of the French colonial empire and insisted that Indochina had to remain within the **French Union**. As a deputy for Sarthe, he severely criticized a wide range of governments for their faulty policies on Indochina, although he never accepted the idea of decolonizing Indochina. His position and critiques never faltered, not even during the Battle of **Dien Bien Phu** and the **Geneva Conference**. He remained opposed to any sort of abandonment of French Indochina.

**DUCLOS, JACQUES (1896–1975).** Number two in the **French Communist Party** (FCP) during the Indochina War. Taken prisoner during World War I, he turned to politics after the conflict, joined the FCP, and rose rapidly in its ranks thanks to his work in the Comintern and support from **Joseph Stalin**'s ally and head of the FCP, **Maurice Thorez**. After World War II, Duclos was sympathetic to the independence aspirations of the **Democratic Republic of Vietnam**, led by another communist who had been a part of the Comintern's networks during the interwar period, **Ho Chi Minh**. However, Duclos and others in the FCP disappointed their Vietnamese counterparts in the **Indochinese Communist Party** with their tepid support for the DRV's nationalist cause at the outset of the Indochina War. **Ho Chi Minh**'s diplomat abroad, **Pham Ngoc Thach**, reported as much to his Soviet interlocutor in late 1947.

**DUFOUR, ROBERT**. Head of the Office for Indigenous Affairs in **Cochinchina** until the Japanese ***coup de force* of 9 March 1945**. He remained in Indochina to serve in 1947 as commissioner for the Republic in Cochinchina. After a brief absence, he returned in 1948 to take over as a special advisor on Social Affairs to the high commissioner for Indochina. In 1949, he worked as a political advisor to **Léon Pignon**.

**DUGARDIER, ROBERT.** After serving as French Consul in Shanghai, he moved to Indochina where he worked in 1949–50 as the diplomatic advisor to the French high commissioner for Indochina, **Léon Pignon**. Dugardier held the rank of minister plenipotentiary. He accompanied Pignon to Malaya in March 1949.

**DULAC, LÉON HIPPOLYTE GUILLAUME ANDRÉ (1907–1992).** Graduated from the *École spéciale militiare de Saint-Cyr* in 1925 (in the same class as **Charles Lacheroy**), Dulac served in the colonial army during the interwar period and in intelligence for the resistance during World War II. At the head of the *41ème Régiment d'infanterie*, he served in Indochina from 1951working as chief of staff for the *Forces terrestres du Nord Vietnam* and commanding officer of *Groupe mobile no. 1.*

**DULLES, JOHN FOSTER (1888–1959).** Graduating at the top of his class at Princeton University, Dulles pursued graduate studies at the Sorbonne where he studied with the nobel prize-winning philosopher, Henri Bergson. Dulles practised law briefly before joining the American Foreign Service, serving as chief legal advisor on the reparations commission at the Versailles Conference. He had studied with Woodrow Wilson at Princeton and shared his internationalism despite Dulles' Republican Party affiliation. Dulles returned to his law practice during most of the interwar period. During World War II, he was involved in efforts to reform the international system along the lines set out by Wilson's 14 points, but the outbreak of the **Cold War** set limits on such a grand strategy.

After World War II, Dulles was pivotal in negotiations ending the American occupation of Japan, supported the **North Atlantic Treaty Oganization**, and was an ardent anti-communist opponent of the Soviet Union. Impressed, **Dwight D. Eisenhower** appointed Dulles his secretary of state. In this capacity, Dulles became well known for his ideas on "massive retaliation" and "brinksmanship" as a way of deterring communist expansionism. Dulles threatened to use atomic weapons in order to force through armistice negotiations to stop the fighting in Korea and again during the Taiwan crisis of 1954. However, when the French requested that the United States intervene directly in the Indochina War to save besieged soldiers at **Dien Bien Phu**, Dulles advised against such a move. He participated in and closely followed the **Geneva Conference** and its subsequent accords. His agreement to let the French negotiate an end to the war in Indochina at the diplomatic table was linked at least to some degree to his need to win over French ratification of the **European Defense Community**. But well aware of Republican hostility towards communist China and Joseph McCarthy's attacks on diplomats having "lost China" to the communists, Dulles refused to shake the hand of Premier **Zhou Enlai** at Geneva. In the end, Dulles acquiesced to the division of Vietnam at the **17th parallel**.

With the French out of the way, the statesman sought to contain communism more effectively by supporting an anti-communist, fully decolonized Vietnamese **Republic of Vietnam** led by **Ngo Dinh Diem**. Dulles doubled his Vietnamese strategy at the regional level by overseeing the creation of a **South East Asia Treaty Organization** (SEATO), part of a larger web of security alliances designed to contain communist expansion across the globe. SEATO was also designed in part to thwart Zhou Enlai's attempts to neutralize non-communist Asia against the United States at Geneva and to deny the communists victory in Southeast Asia beyond **Tonkin**. SEATO came to life in September 1954 a few weeks after the ink had dried on the **Geneva Accords.** *See also* NEUTRALIZATION OF INDOCHINA.

**DƯƠNG BÁ LỘC**. *See* JEAN MOREAU.

**DƯƠNG BẠCH MAI (BOUROV, 1905–1964)**. Vietnamese **intellectual** and communist nationalist who studied in Moscow prior to World War II and was incarcerated by the French during the Indochina War. Born in Ba Ria province in southern Vietnam, he completed his secondary education in **Saigon** at the *Lycée Chasseloup Laubat* in 1922 before moving to **Hanoi** to study at the *École de Commerce*. In 1925, he left for France where he lived and agitated politically. In the fall of 1929, he continued on to Moscow on a Chinese passport. There he enrolled in the **Stalin** School for Workers of the East. He studied with the likes of **Tran Ngoc Danh** and **Ha Huy Giap**. He returned to southern Vietnam in 1931, where he was active in local politics and journalism and collaborated with a variety of nationalist intellectuals. During the Popular Front period he was elected to the City Council of Saigon. In 1939, he was arrested and sent to **Poulo Condor** together with Le Hong Phong, **Le Duan** and Nguyen An Ninh. In 1943, he was liberated but placed under surveillance in Bien Hoa province in southern Vietnam. Following the advent of the **Viet Minh**, he served briefly as head of the police in southern Vietnam for the **Democratic Republic of Vietnam** (DRV). Married to a French woman, he helped calm anti-French tensions among the Vietnamese in early September 1945 and gained the release of several French nationals taken prisoner by Vietnamese forces. After the British-backed French *coup de force* of **23 September 1945**, he fled to eastern parts of southern Vietnam where he became general inspector for political affairs for the eastern provinces in the Resistance Committee for the south. In 1946, he took part in the **Fontainebleau Conference**. He stayed in France and, with his longtime classmate **Tran Ngoc Danh**, helped establish and run the representational office of the DRV in Paris. In March 1947, at the request of Paul Reynaud, the French arrested him on the grounds that he had been the architect of "terrorist" acts against French nationals during his time as inspector in eastern southern Vietnam. He was transferred to Djibouti where he remained under *résidence surveillée* until he was finally transferred to Chi Hoa prison in Saigon. When the French Permanent Military Tribunal failed to convict him, French local authorities placed him under a fairly liberal *résidence surveillée* in Kontum in the central highlands. **Léon Pignon**, then high commissioner, was not surprised to learn of his escape shortly thereafter to Viet Minh zones.

**DƯƠNG ĐỨC HIỀN (1916–1963).** Vietnamese lawyer and politician in the **Democratic Republic of Vietnam** (DRV). Graduated from the Faculty of Law in **Hanoi** in 1940, he worked as a lecturer and helped create the **Vietnamese Democratic Party** (*Dang Dan Chu Viet Nam*) in June 1944, which joined the **Viet Minh** national front in September 1945. Although a non-communist, Duong Duc Hien supported the Viet Minh's anti-colonialist program. He served as minister of Youth in the Provisional Government of the DRV. He later became the general secretary and the vice president of the Central Committee of the **Lien Viet** Front (which replaced the Viet Minh). He would be pushed aside when the **Indochinese Communist Party** began to assert itself and its domination of the government and the state from the early 1950s.

**DƯƠNG QUỐC CHÍNH (LÊ HIẾN MAI, 1918–1992).** Vietnamese military commander who served the **Democratic Republic of Vietnam** in northern and southern Vietnam during the Indochina War. Born in Ha Tay province near **Hanoi**, he became politically active in the late 1930s. In 1940, he joined the **Indochinese Communist Party** (ICP) and began mobilizing Vietnamese youth in the Son Tay area. The French police arrested and incarcerated him in several colonial prisons until his escape in August 1944. He joined the **National Salvation Army** (*Cuu Quoc Quan*) in May 1945, served as a delegate of the **Viet Minh**'s General Directorate or ***Tong Bo***, and was then sent to northern Laos in late 1945 to serve as a political delegate to Vietnamese forces operating in Sam Neau and Xieng Khouang provinces. In March 1946, he returned to Vietnam to serve in **Zone II** as head of the **General Staff**, political commissar and chief of the Party's military committee. From February 1947, he directed from Zone II the Western Front bordering Laos against a possible French attack. In 1948, he was named major general and political commissar for **Inter-Zone I** (*Lien Khu I*) before being dispatched to southern Vietnam. In June 1949, he served as political commissar to the High Command for the south under the direction of General **Nguyen Binh** and acted briefly as the deputy secretary to the ICP's Territorial Committee for Nam Bo. Between 1950 and 1952, he was deputy commander of the High Command for the south as well as the deputy commander and party member of the **Inter-Zone for Eastern Nam Bo**. In 1953, he took command of the **Inter-Zone for Western Nam Bo** and as secretary of the corresponding and controlling Party parallel structure.

**DƯƠNG TẤN TÀI (1896–?).** Colonial civil servant and leading non-communist nationalist. Born in the southern province of Go Cong, he graduated from the *École supérieure de droit et d'administration* in 1921. He began his civil service career as a mandarin in southern Vietnam in 1921, reaching the level of district chief in 1939. In 1934, he obtained French citizenship and was thus able to join the French Provincial Council of Go Cong in 1938. In 1941, he joined the Municipal Council of Saigon. Little is known about his activities during World War II. He played a role in French efforts to build a counter revolutionary government in the person of **Bao Dai**. Duong Tan Tai was under secretary of state for Finances in the government presided over by the ex-emperor on 1 July 1949 and became minister of Finances on 17 October 1949. He maintained his portfolio in the government led by **Tran Van Huu** from May 1950. He was a member of the Vietnamese delegation to the **Pau Conference** in 1950 and was minister of Public Service in the second cabinet of Tran Van Huu created on 18 February 1951, but was excluded from the new government Tran Van Huu constituted in March 1952. Duong Tan Tai returned as minister of Finances in the government Prince **Buu Loc** formed on 11 January 1954.

**DƯƠNG VĂN DƯƠNG (BA DƯƠNG, 1894–1946).** Leader of the **Binh Xuyen** armed forces that fought with the **Viet Minh** against the French reoccupation in 1945–1946. Duong Van Duong was born into a poor southern family in the present-day area of Thu Duc. His father was a member of a secret society and the young Duong grew up in that world. He also became very involved in Vietnamese boxing (*vo*) and began giving courses in traditional and modern boxing to support himself after the death of his father in 1936. During this time, he became known as something of a local "Robin Hood" (*vo hiep giang ho*), using his martial arts skills to "take from the rich to give to the poor" as a sympathetic Vietnamese account recently put it.

By the start of World War II, his local notoriety brought him to the attention of communists as well as the leaders of the emerging Binh Xuyen movement, which always paid close attention to the traditional martial arts and the *demi-monde* they shared. Duong Van Duong joined the Binh Xuyen in the Nha Be area sometime in the late 1930s, but he also commanded the respect of communists he met in prison while serving time there on two occasions in 1941. These connections were such that in 1945 Duong Van Duong put his martial arts skills in the service of **Pham Ngoc Thach**'s **Vanguard Youth Movement** in mid-1945. In August 1945, following the overthrow of the French and the defeat of the Japanese a few months later, Duong Van Duong served in Binh Xuyen forces that helped take power in **Saigon**. He maintained his contacts with communists and shared their desire to prevent the return of the French. He helped win over Vietnamese colonial troops to the resistance, negotiated with local Japanese the transfer of small arms and ammunition, and created and led his own paramilitary force, known as the "adventurers of the *demi-monde*" (*giang ho tu chieng*). At the outset, the Binh Xuyen collaborated with the Viet Minh in opposing the French reoccupation of southern Vietnam. Duong Van Duong received the task of amassing weapons and teaching martial arts to young recruits. He saw combat against the French in September and October 1945. In mid-December 1945, with the arrival of **Nguyen Binh**, Duong Van Duong served briefly as his deputy regional director for **zone VII** and commander of the Inter-Military Detachments (*Lien Chi Doi*) 2, 3, and 4. He led his troops into some of the fiercest battles against the French during the reoccupation. He was killed during a French airstrike in early 1946 in southern Vietnam.

In early 1948, on Nguyen Binh's recommendation, the DRV posthumously named Duong Van Duong major general, although this did not prevent the break between the DRV and the Binh Xuyen later that year. *See also* CAO DAI; COLLABORATION; CRIME; HOA HAO; LE VAN HIEN.

**DƯƠNG VĂN MINH (1916–2001).** Educated at the *Lycée Chasseloup-Laubat* in **Saigon**, he joined the French army in 1940. He was promoted to the rank of major in 1952 and graduated from the War College (*École de guerre*) in Paris in 1953. Following the division of Vietnam into two states during the **Geneva Conference** in 1954, Duong Van Minh, joined the armed forces of the State of Vietnam which became the **Republic of Vietnam** in 1955. In late 1954, he was the deputy commander of the 1st Military Region. In 1955, a colonel, he commanded the Saigon-Cholon Zone and played a pivotal role in suppressing **Binh Xuyen** and **Hoa Hao** forces contesting **Ngo Dinh Diem**'s power. He was rose to the rank of major general at the end of the year. *See also* ARMY, ASSOCIATED STATE OF VIETNAM; EXPEDITIONARY CORPS; LE VAN HIEN; NGUYEN VAN THIEU.

**DUPIN, ROGER ÉMILE LUCIEN (1919–).** French colonial administrator who served as provincial head of Haut Donnai in Djirling between 1948 and 1950.

**DUPONT D'ISIGNY, PAULE.** Member of the *Infirmières parachutistes secouristes de l'Air* and a certified pilot and paratrooper during the Indochina War. She flew some 4,200 hours and executed 30 combat missions during her military career.

**DURAND, MAURICE (1914–1966).** Born of a French father and a Vietnamese mother, Maurice Durand was one of the finest specialists of Vietnamese culture, language, and history of his time. His father was professor of Chinese at the Indochinese University in **Hanoi** and worked in the Office of Translations in the city's Justice Hall. The young Durand excelled in his studies, graduating from both the *Lycée Albert Sarraut* in Hanoi and the elite school *Louis le Grand* in Paris. He volunteered to fight in World War II, ended up in North Africa, and saw combat with the Allies in the liberation of Tunisia. Upon being discharged from the army in 1946, he became a member of the ***École française d'Extrême-Orient***, working there between 1947 and 1957. Between 1954 and 1957, following the signature of the **Geneva Accords** and the French evacuation from northern Vietnam, he directed the *École*'s scaled-down center in Hanoi. In 1957, he returned to France and was named Professor (*directeur d'études*) at the *École pratique des hautes études* at the Sorbonne, where he taught Vietnamese history and culture. He published a large number of books and articles on Vietnamese history, literature, culture, grammar, including *Connaissance du Vietnam*, published in 1954. *See also* METIS.

**EA SICHAU (1920–1959).** Born in Cambodia's Kampong Cham province, he collaborated closely with **Son Ngoc Thanh**'s government following the Japanese ***coup de force* of 9 March 1945**. However, the rapid return of the French and the arrest of Son Ngoc Thanh changed Ea Sichau's political itinerary notably. Between May 1946 and December 1950, he studied at the *École des hautes études commerciales* in Paris, where he also served as the president of the Cambodian Students' Association. During this time, he became increasingly involved in left-wing politics, taking part in a Cambodian Marxist study group. He returned to Cambodia in 1951 and worked in the Foreign Ministry of the newly created Associated State of Cambodia. During this time, he helped Son Ngoc Thanh publish the novel *Khmer Krauk* (Khmers Awake!). In January 1952, he was named director of customs. In March, he briefly served as interim general secretary to **Huy Kanthoul**, then president of the Council of Ministers. Throughout this period, Ea Sichau remained a staunch supporter of Son Ngoc Thanh and fled with the latter to the Thai-Cambodian border in March 1952. There they would form the *Khmer Serei* (Free Khmer) movement in opposition to **Norodom Sihanouk**. However, in 1954, as French Indochina began to crumble at **Dien Bien Phu**, he broke ranks and returned to Phnom Penh and joined the **Democrat Party** now led by Norodom Phurissara.

**ÉCARLAT, PIERRE EUGÈNE (1905–1992).** French colonial administrator who made his career in Indochina. Between 1929 and 1939, he served in a variety of administrative positions in Tonkin and did the same for Vichy along the Sino-Vietnamese frontier during World War II. Following the Japanese defeat, he was named regional advisor for the Tai countries (1947–1948). Between 1948 and 1952, he was in charge of the administrative affairs for the city of **Hanoi**. *See also* MINORITY ETHNIC GROUPS; THAI FEDERATION.

***ÉCOLE COLONIALE.*** *See* COLONIAL ACADEMY.

***ÉCOLE D'ENFANTS DE TROUPE INDOCHINOISE.*** *See* CHILDREN.

***ÉCOLE FRANÇAISE D'EXTRÊME-ORIENT* (EFEO).** Created at the turn of the 20th century, scholars of this French research institute specialized in archeology, philology, and the history of the "Far East" or *Extrême-orient*. The creation of the *École* was linked to the French state's need to know better the people over whom it was now ruling in Indochina. Indeed, the *École* had first assumed its form and location thanks to a decree issued by the architect of modern French Indochina, Governor General Paul Doumer. The EFEO followed in the tradition of the *École française de Rome* (1875) and the *École française d'Athènes* (1846). Founded in **Saigon** in 1898, three years later the EFEO moved to **Hanoi**, where the colonial government for Indochina was headquartered.

While the EFEO was designed to be an instrument of the colonial state, from 1920 it became administratively autonomous. Although it financed the school in part, the colonial state did not systematically set the EFEO's research priorities; its members, working in tandem with metropolitan scholars, did. Most of the EFEO's scholars immersed themselves in the local cultures and languages they had come to know and appreciate. A handful of Vietnamese scholars, such as **Nguyen Van To**, also worked with French scholars at the *École*. **Collaboration** between the school's scholars and the colonial state certainly occurred. However, some of the EFEO's scholars would advocate decolonization after World War II. The renowned scholars **Paul Mus** and **Paul Lévy** were the most notable. Mus supported the nationalist cause of the **Democratic Republic of Vietnam**. He wrote some of the first Western language texts on colonial and postcolonial Vietnam and contributed to the building of Vietnamese studies in the United States, where he taught at Yale University until his death in 1969.

Following the Japanese overthrow of the French in the ***coup de force* of 9 March 1945**, the DRV assumed control of the *École* in Hanoi until the outbreak of war on **19 December 1946**.

After retaking the city, the French resumed their administration of the institution; however, the war prevented the EFEO from regaining its prewar momentum. In 1957, following the end of the Indochina War and the provisional division of Vietnam into two states, the *École* pulled out of Hanoi and then out of Cambodia in 1972. The EFEO now operates from Paris, whither its headquarters were transferred in 1968. Since the end of the **Cold War**, the opening of Vietnam, and the regeneration of Cambodia, the *École* is once again active in the region in promoting scholarship and exchanges. The EFEO currently operates offices in Vietnam, Laos, and Cambodia. *See also* COLONIAL ACADEMY; *ÉCOLE NATIONALE DES LANGUES ORIENTALES VIVANTES.*

***ÉCOLE NATIONALE DES LANGUES ORIENTALES VIVANTES* (ENLOV).** The ENLOV trained scores of colonial administrators in the languages and civilisations of the countries to where they were to be dispatched. The origins of the ENLOV date to the reign of Louis XIV, when, in 1669, Colbert created this institution to train interpreters being dispatched to the Middle East. Despite the tumultuous events of the French revolution, Republicans maintained the school and transformed it into the *École spéciale des langues orientales* to teach mainly Middle and Near Eastern languages. In 1914, the term *nationale* replaced *spéciale* to become the *École nationale des langues orientales vivantes* or "*Langues O*" for short. By this time, the school provided instruction in the civilizations and languages of most of the non-Western world. In 1971, the school was rebaptized as the *Institut national des langues et civilisations orientales* (INALCO), and attached to the University of Paris III. During its lifetime, the ENLOV helped train scores of colonial administrators for work in Indochina, including **Léon Pignon**, high commissioner for Indochina during the Indochina War and the mastermind of the **Bao Dai Solution**.

**ECONOMY OF WAR, FRANCE.** War and the instability it generated adversely affected the economic value of Indochina for the French. In 1940, Indochina attracted 46% of all private French assets invested in the empire, down from 55% on the eve of World War I. The great depression and the slump in the rubber industry in the 1930s accounted for part of this drop. Private capital fled at an even faster rate during the Indochina conflict, falling 30% annually in 1947, 1948 and again in 1951. In real terms, Laurent Césari tells us, total private assets in Indochina fell by two-thirds between 1943 and 1954 while public assets declined by a third. The majority of this colonial investment was transferred to colonial North and West Africa. French investments in Africa increased from 127 million francs in 1945 to 137 in 1948 to 229 million in 1953. The vagaries of war increased production, transportation, and labor costs for operating plantations and industries in Indochina. The development of synthetic rubber further depressed the postwar rubber industry there. Importers preferred to buy cheaper rice on the Southeast Asian market and even turned to growing it in the Camargue region in southern France. Plans to industrialize Indochina also failed during the conflict. However, Indochinese imports from the metropole were second only to Algeria, rising from 56,9% of the value of all Indochinese imports in 1947 to 78% in 1951 and again in 1953. The French achieved this quasi monopoly by denying import licenses to those wishing to do business in Indochina from countries outside the *zone franc*. However, with the end of the war in 1954, the French lost the right to issue such licenses and with it the monopoly. French goods may have accounted for 52,4% of the State of Vietnam's total imports in 1955 but that number rapidly declined to 24,7% in 1956 and only 19,4% in 1959. Moreover, as Césari points out, Indochinese exports to France only covered half of the war related expenditures allocated in the French budget. In short, the conflict was a serious drain on French finances. The United States helped ease the burden by covering on averge 41,9% of war expenditures between 1952 and 1954. To make matters worse, French rearmament in Europe accounted for a greater investment than that put in the Indochina conflict. Military spending as a percentage of French gross national product soon matched the high levels registered by the Americans as they moved to contain the communist bloc globally. *See also* EUROPEAN DEFENSE COMMUNITY; KOREAN WAR.

**EDEN, ANTHONY (1897–1977).** British statesman and diplomat who played an important role as the "honest broker" during the **Geneva Conference** designed to negotiate an end to the Indochina conflict in 1954. After serving on the Western Front during World War I, he was elected to the British House of Commons in 1923. Although named foreign secretary in 1935, he resigned in 1938 in protest at the appeasement of Hitler over Czechoslovakia. He served **Winston Churchill** as foreign secretary during World War II and again between 1951 and 1955. In March 1945, as French forces defended themselves against the Japanese onslaught in Indochina, Eden insisted that Churchill approach U.S. President Franklin Roosevelt to garner U.S. support for the French struggle. After Churchill and Eden had returned to power in 1951, their government supported the armistice ending the shooting in Korea in mid-1953, and shared Moscow's and Beijing's desire to find a peaceful settlement to the Indochina War at Geneva in mid-1954. Besides being a talented and seasoned diplomat, Eden's effectiveness at Geneva was strengthened by his government's diplomatic relations with communist China and Commonwealth links to **India** and **Burma**, not to mention a longstanding working relationship with the Americans and president **Dwight D. Eisenhower** in particular. Anthony Eden served as "co-president" of the Geneva Conference together with **Viatcheslav Molotov** of the Soviet Union. The two diplomats presided alternately over the conference's sessions.

**EIJI WAJIMA**. Head of the Far East Department in the Japanese Ministry of Foreign Affairs. He arrived in **Saigon** on 29 January 1953 to confer with **Nguyen Van Tam** and General **Raoul Salan** among others about the establishment of a Japanese diplomatic mission to the Associated State of Vietnam and the payment of reparations for damages incurred during World War II.

**EISENHOWER, DWIGHT D. (1890–1969).** American president who increasingly considered Indochina to be a crucial testing ground for containing communism in Asia. Raised in Kansas from the age of two, Eisenhower graduated from West Point in 1919. Promoted to general in 1941, he commanded the Allied landing in North Africa in 1942 before going on to lead Allied forces in Europe. Elected president in 1952, he helped bring an end to the **Korean War** by threatening a nuclear one. His administration increased American military **aid** to the French in Indochina in order to hold the line against the perceived expansion of Sino-Soviet communism into Southeast Asia via Indochina. His government thus continued **Harry Truman**'s policy of supporting the French-backed Associated States of Vietnam, Laos, and Cambodia. In April 1954, as the battle of **Dien Bien Phu** raged, he spoke for the first time of a "**domino theory**". According to this thinking, if Vietnam were allowed to fall to the communists, then the rest of Southeast Asia would follow suit. While Eisenhower considered authorizing the American Air Force to defend the French camp at Dien Bien Phu in operation **Vautour**, in the end he was unwilling to risk escalating the war and committing American troops. Led by his secretary of state, **John Foster Dulles**, Eisenhower's administration initially took a hard line during the **Geneva Conference**, but ultimately acquiesced in the provisional division of Vietnam at the **17^th^ parallel**. Eisenhower's administration took note of the final declaration and the armistices ending the fighting in Laos, Cambodia, and Vietnam. With the French now gone and with them allegations of American backing of French colonialism dissipated, the Eisenhower administration backed the non-communist Vietnamese nationalist, **Ngo Dinh Diem**, as a more effective way of containing communism. In September 1954, to further strengthen the American hand, Eisenhower expanded his global web of security alliances with the creation in September 1954 of the **South East Asia Treaty Organization**. For Eisenhower's team, Vietnam was the crucial Southeast Asian link in Washington's global **Cold War** grand strategy to contain the Sino-Soviet powers dominating the Eurasian landmass.

**ELY, PAUL HENRI ROMUALD (1897–1975).** Last commander-in-chief of French forces during the Indochina War. In 1915, he signed up, served in, and was wounded during World War I. Ely entered Saint-Cyr in 1919. He was wounded again during the battle of France in 1940. He crossed over to the French resistance when German troops occupied southern France in 1942 and as Allied troops invaded French North Africa. In February 1944, he made his way to London and worked with General **Charles de Gaulle**. Promoted general in 1945, he served as the secretary of the Military Cabinet in the Ministry of Defense before becoming chief of staff for General **Jean de Lattre de Tassigny**. In October 1953, he was named chief of staff of the French Armed Forces and oversaw General **Henri Navarre**'s plans to engage the **Democratic Republic of Vietnam** (DRV) and develop the armed forces of the **Associated States of Indochina**. In response to Navarre's plea for more troops, Ely wrote in

November 1953 that this was hardly possible, since "the flower of the army is to be found in Indochina" (*la fleur de l'armée se trouve en Indochine*). Between 9 and 28 February 1954, he conducted an inspection tour of **Dien Bien Phu** with the minister of Defense **René Pleven**, during which both were impressed by what they saw. Ely worried, however, that the **air force** might encounter trouble supplying the valley. Between 20 and 27 March 1954, the government sent Ely to Washington to request American air support in the event that the Chinese intervened. American Admiral **Arthur Radford** was sensitive to Ely's needs and even prepared plans to intervene in Dien Bien Bien from airbases in the Philippines. Little came of this plan, the **Vautour** operation, and the French camp fell to the DRV's troops on 7 May 1954. Ely returned to Indochina between 16 and 25 May in order to take stock of the changed military situation. In early June 1954, he replaced Navarre as general commissar and commander-in-chief of French Armed Forces in Indochina. Unlike Navarre, Ely pulled the army back from the highlands. He launched operation *Auvergne* to consolidate the French army's control in the delta surrounding **Hanoi**. This operation caught the adversary by surprise and was instrumental in facilitating the evacuation of the remaining Vietnamese **Catholic** leadership in the Bui Chu area south of Hanoi. During the **Geneva Conference**, **Pierre Mendès France** consulted Ely on the delays needed to evacuate the north and where to establish the demarcation line between the north and the south. Mendès France asked that Ely sign on to the military and political clauses of the Geneva agreements. Ely agreed. On 21 July, General **Henri Delteil** signed the accords on behalf of Commander-in-Chief General Ely. Until 6 June 1955, Ely served as Indochina's last high commissioner and oversaw the departure of most French armed forces from all of Vietnam. He was instrumental in assigning **Jean Sainteny** to Hanoi as the French government's general delegate to the DRV. Ely's relations with **Ngo Dinh Diem**, the head of the **Republic of Vietnam**, were however strained. On 2 June 1955, as Ngo Dinh Diem consolidated his power over the postcolonial state, Ely left former French Indochina for good. *See also* ELY – COLLINS AGREEMENT.

**ELY–COLLINS AGREEMENT.** Accord signed on 13 December 1954 between Generals **Paul Ely** on the French side and **Lawton Collins** on the American side. This agreement set out the terms for Franco-American cooperation in the training of the national army of the **Republic of Vietnam**. This document allowed for the Americans as of 1 January 1955 to assist the "government of Vietnam" in the organization and training of its armed forces "under the supreme authority of the French commander-in-chief", General Ely. The terms of this agreement announced first the reduction of the armed forces from 270,000 to 90,000 men. Second, the French would by 1 July 1955 accord complete autonomy to this army.

**EMIRY, OLIVIER JEAN (1911–1998).** Career French colonial administrator who served between 1942 and 1950 in a variety of posts dealing with the highland peoples of southern central Vietnam. He was chief of cabinet to the French high commissioner's delegate to the highland populations of southern Indochina (*populations montagnardes du sud de l'Indochine*) between 1948 and 1949 and provincial head of Darlac (1949–1950). In 1951, he served as the delegate to Danang for the commissioner for the French Republic for Central Vietnam. Between 1952 and 1954, he worked as an advisor to the Associated State of Vietnam.

**EMULATION CAMPAIGN.** Known in Vietnamese as *phong trao thi dua ai quoc*, "patriotic emulation campaigns" began in earnest in 1948 as the French moved to create a counter-revolutionary state under Bao Dai, potentially capable of drawing popular support away from the **Democratic Republic of Vietnam** (DRV) in the countryside. The start of DRV emulation campaigns in 1948 was also linked to the adoption of a more internationalist line by the **Indochinese Communist Party** (ICP) following the announcement of the Jdanov line in September 1947 opposing an American-led capitalist bloc to the Moscow-led communist one. In the late 1940s, Vietnamese communists used emulation campaigns to mobilize manpower and to generate support for their beleaguered war state. The ICP approved the launching of the first emulation campaign in the spring of 1948. By obligating the people under its military control to participate in these campaigns, the ICP created patriotic competitions (*thi dua*) in order to encourage the populations to produce more, to support the resistance financially, to associate them with the party's "just cause" and its mass organizations, to eradicate illiteracy, and to disseminate the debuts of revolutionary ideology. Such patriotic competitions reached down, though not without difficulty, to the district and village levels. They were much more common in northern and central Vietnam, where DRV military control was greater, than in the south where the French military and anti-communist Vietnamese nationalist and religious forces were stronger. During campaigns lasting anywhere from a few weeks to several months, cadres fanned out into villages. Relying upon local mass organizations, such as peasant, women, or youth organizations, they began organizing patriotic competitions. This could include recruiting drives for the local militia or longer lasting campaigns to clear new land and increase agricultural production. However, these early campaigns only produced limited results. In 1952, inspired by Sino-Soviet models and the need to mobilize large numbers of people for modern war, the ICP revamped and relaunched its emulation campaigns in central and northern DRV zones. It was also at this point that class became a major theme in these drives rather than just broad appeals to Vietnamese nationalism. **Hoang Dao Thuy**, who headed the Vietnamese **scouting** movement during World War II, was on the central government's patriotic emulation committee at the outset. *See also* CHARLES LACHEROY; LAND REFORM; NEW HERO; PSYCHOLGICAL WARFARE; RECTIFICATION; REVOLUTIONARY WARFARE.

**ERSKINE, GRAVES G.** *See* MELBY–ERSKINE MISSION.

***ESPRIT*.** Intellectuals associated with the French review *Esprit* (Spirit) were among the first to criticize the Third Republic's colonial policy before World War II and to oppose the French war in Indochina from the outset. The founder of this liberal, Catholic forum, Emmanuel Mounier, is best known for his ideas on "personalism", many of which were later borrowed by **Ngo Dinh Diem** and his brothers during the Indochina War. Mounier was also on the cutting edge of Catholic anti-colonialism. In 1934, he helped launch the *Manifeste d'intellectuels catholiques pour la justice et la paix*, in which the authors condemned Western colonialism (the Italian version in this case) and the idea of a hierarchy of "races" justifying "white" domination. He openly published Andrée Villois's detailed report of French colonial abuses in French Indochina and her damning critique of the French use of **torture** against Vietnamese who had organized revolts in northern and central Vietnam in 1930 and 1931. After the carnage of World War II, these early, limited critiques of colonialism transformed into wider calls in the pages of *Esprit* for the French Republic to let go of its Empire or at least reform it in ways recognizing the historical reality of Vietnamese nationalism. The debates were lively and often trenchant on Indochina and Algeria. Bertrand d'Astorg wrote a particulary important critique of the French war in Indochina in February 1947, as did **Paul Mus**, **Jean-Marie Domenach**, and others. The review also opened its columns to the Vietnamese and other "colonized", including an essay signed by Ho Huu Tuong, the father of Harvard historian of modern Vietnam, Hue-Tam Ho-Tai. *See also* CATHOLICS, EXODUS FROM NORTH; CHRISTIANS AND FRENCH OPPOSITION TO THE WAR; PUBLIC OPINION, FRENCH; *TÉMOIGNAGE CHRÉTIEN*.

**EURASIANS.** *See MÉTIS*.

**EUROPEAN DEFENSE COMMUNITY (EDC).** Following the outbreak of the **Korean War** in 1950, Western leaders feared that the Soviets would take advantage of the war in Asia in order to strike deep into Western Europe. In September 1950, American leaders began to push hard for a greater degree of Western European and Atlantic military cooperation, integration, and rearmament. They introduced changes to make the **North Atlantic Treaty Organization** (NATO) more effective militarily; they also supported the rearming of the Federal Republic of Germany and advocated its membership in NATO.

Moscow viewed with alarm the potential rearming and integration of West Germany into the Atlantic Alliance. And so did the French, having gone to war with Germany three times since the late 19th century. In an attempt to use a European supranational framework to control the (West) Germans better, French minister of Defense **René Pleven** proposed the creation of the European Defense Community (EDC). By incorporating smaller German military forces into this institutional military framework, the French could control German military power more effectively, all the while presenting the Soviet threat to Western Europe with a unified European military force. In 1952, the signing of the Treaty of Paris created the EDC. It was now up to each member state to ratify it. This was easier said than done.

Under increasing pressure from the Americans, from 1953 Western European parliaments began ratifying the treaty.

Ratification by the French National Assembly, however, was a problem since a growing number of senators on the Left and the Right was opposed to the EDC, fearful of rearming Germany or reluctant to submit national interests to a supranational body (or both). While there is no evidence of a *marchandage planétaire* or a global deal between the French and the Soviets by which the Soviets would pressure the **Democratic Republic of Vietnam** to negotiate an end to the Indochina War at Geneva in exchange for the French torpedoing of the EDC, it is clear, as Laurent Césari has noted, that the EDC strengthened indirectly the French position at Geneva. On the one hand, **John Foster Dulles** probably would have never accepted in Berlin putting Indochina on the conference agenda for Geneva or dispatching the high ranking diplomat **Walter Bedell Smith** to attend the closing of the Geneva conference if the Treaty of Paris had already been ratified (or rejected) by the French National Assembly in early 1954. On the other hand, the possibility that the French might break with Washington and vote against the treaty, and hence undermine Western attempts to integrate and rearm Western Germany, could only have inclined the Soviets to take a more accommodating position towards French positions on Indochina. Hardly a month after the ink had dried on the **Geneva Accords**, the French National Assembly voted against ratifying the treaty, much to the consternation of the Americans. However, a new way was found to rearm the Federal Republic of Germany and integrate it into the Western alliance.

What did not change was the pressure on the French to end the costly war in Indochina and to transfer much needed French troops and officers to Europe, so as not to let the other nations, including West Germany, diminish French influence there. American anger with the French over the EDC was such that **Pierre Mendès France** was willing to let the Americans take the lead in southern Vietnam following the signing of the Geneva Accords. The French leader also duly joined the **South East Asia Treaty Organization** spearheaded by the Americans. Nor did Mendès France dare to recognize communist China as the British had already done. The international connections between Europe and the Indochina War were real, even after the armistice ending the Indochina conflict was achieved.

**EXECUTIONS.** All the belligerents carried out executions during the Indochina War. According to historian David Marr, several thousand enemies of the **Viet Minh** "failed to survive abductions" in the wake of the August insurrection of 1945. In southern Vietnam, the **Democratic Republic of Vietnam's** (DRV) **Nguyen Binh** authorized on numerous occasions the execution of Vietnamese individuals judged to be enemies or traitors, not least of all the leader of the Hoa Hao **Huynh Phu So** in 1947. Anti-communist nationalist opposition parties and politico-religious militias were also involved in executions in 1945–1946. During the DRV's Chinese inspired land reform, the state executed hundreds of "class" enemies, including many who had been supporters of the independence cause. One of the more controversial "class based" executions in mid-1953 was that of a well-known woman supporter of the anti-colonial cause who was also a landowner, Nguyen Thi Nam. The French were no strangers to executions either. In 1955, an internal French report conceded that the number of Vietnamese war prisoners who died or were executed during their detainment in French custody exceeded 9,000. For unknown reasons, this document notes that a "large number of executions" occurred in 1952–1953. Of the 9,000 dead, only 2,080 of their tombs could be identified as of 1955. The bodies of the rest were apparently rarely if ever recovered.

**EXPEDITIONARY CORPS.** The Empire held an important place in **Charles de Gaulle**'s strategic thinking and the Free French army reflected it. De Gaulle's government-in-exile, the *Comité français de Libération nationale* (CFLN), first came to life in Algeria following the Allied liberation of North Africa in 1942. From there, Free French forces drew upon the colonies to build a new army. In September 1943, the CFLN created the *Corps Expéditionnaire d'Extrême-Orient* and confided its command to General **Roger Blaizot**. De Gaulle was equally determined to liberate Indochina from Vichy and the Japanese. However, it was only after the liberation of France in mid-1944 that the French could begin work on creating a real Expeditionary Corps for the Far East. They did so by combining the *2ème Division blindée* under the command of **Jacques Massu**, the *9ème Division d'infanterie coloniale* (*9ème DIC*) led by **Jean Valluy**, and the *3ème Division d'Infanterie coloniale* (*3ème DIC*). General **Philippe Leclerc** replaced Blaizot as commander of the Expeditionary Corps for the Far East, which debarked in **Saigon** in early October 1945. The size of the Expeditionary Corps (excluding auxiliary troops or "*supplétifs*") grew from around 53,000 in January 1946 to 110,245 on 31 March 1948 before increasing to 204,000 on 1 January 1954.[4]

The Expeditionary Corps was a professional or volunteer army. Unlike for the **Algerian War**, there was no national draft in France for the Indochina War, although **Pierre Mendès France** threatened to introduce one if a negotiated settlement to the conflict were not reached. Moreover, budget constraints and military commitments to Europe and elsewhere made the question of providing troops to the Expeditionary Corps a permanent problem. As French military historian Michel Bodin has shown, throughout the entire war, almost two thirds of the soldiers of the Expeditionary Corps were *not* French nationals. The army drew instead on a wide variety of men from French North Africa (Algeria, Morocco, Tunisia), French Africa (mainly Senegal), the French **Foreign Legion** (many but not exclusively from the former German Third Reich), and above all Indochina (from Vietnam first then secondly from Cambodia and Laos).

In 1948, with the war anything but over, the French army decided to create mixed units and to step up the "***jaunissement***" or "Vietnamization" (literally, "yellowing") of the Expeditionary Corps in order to make up for the lack of French and European troops as the war entered its most intensive phase. Even the Foreign Legion and the elite French paratroopers were forced to create "mixed battalions" to remain operational. If French and Vietnamese troops fought together during the Indochina War, more so than the Americans did with their South Vietnamese counterparts in the 1960s, it was mainly because French nationals were such a relative minority in the French Expeditionary Corps. In all, 1,609,980 men served in the Expeditionary Corps in Indochina between November 1945 and July 1954.

In accordance with the **Geneva Accords** signed in July 1954, the French stationed the Expeditionary Corps in the provisional state located below the **17th parallel**, then known as the State of Vietnam. The Expeditionary Corps was to implement the Geneva agreements. As Pierre Grosser has pointed out, the French Expeditionary Corps also served an important symbolic role for the French in the wake of the Indochina War – proof that the French army had not been truly defeated (an obsession for many officers) and that by remaining in southern Vietnam, in Asia, the French thus remained a world power in the eyes of the Americans and British. However, despite the French desire to maintain its army in non-communist Indochina, Paris no longer had the financial wherewithal or the political will to do so. Moreover, the European commitments that had long burdened the French army and the outbreak of the **Algerian War** hardly allowed for such overextension. As François Mitterand put it in 1952, the French had to concentrate their energies on Africa and Europe. And **Ngo Dinh Diem,** president of the **Republic of Vietnam** from 1955, was only too happy to get the French out of the way. In April 1956, the French withdrew their army from Indochina, ending one hundred years of a French military presence in Vietnam. *See also* ARMY, ASSOCIATED STATE OF VIETNAM, LAOS, CAMBODIA; FINANCIAL COST OF THE WAR; SOUTH EAST ASIA TREATY ORGANIZATION.

**EXPERIENCE OF WAR.** By providing large amounts of military **aid** to the French and the **Democratic Republic of Vietnam** (DRV), the Americans and the Chinese respectively intensified the level of violence soldiers encountered on northern and central Vietnamese battlefields between 1950, starting at **Cao Bang**, and culminating in the historic battle of **Dien Bien Phu** in 1954. Both the French and the DRV actively sollicited this aid in the hope of defeating the other on the battlefield. As a result, the Indochina conflict was no longer a simple low-intensity **guerrilla** conflagration. Set-piece battles raged from the northern border to the highlands in lower central Vietnam. Vietnamese and French Union troops clashed violently in the Red River delta at **Vinh Yen. Viet Minh** soldiers were mowed down in the hills at Na San when they attacked the French camp in waves. Evacuating and transporting soldiers from the battlefields remained a chronic problem for the Viet Minh. Unlike the French and the Americans, and this during almost three decades of war, the DRV was never able to evacuate its wounded with helicopters. True, the Vietnamese used Soviet-supplied trucks to transport wounded during the battle of Nghia Lo and again at Dien Bien Phu,

4. In March 1968, the American army in Vietnam numbered 510,000 troops and the army of the **Republic of Vietnam** 800,000 men, meaning some 1.3 million troops just for southern Vietnam.

and it did matter. But for most battles, the DRV had to mobilize human porters and animals to get the wounded out of the line of fire and to medical stations behind the lines. Distances were long and the terrain was harsh, hilly, often lined with cliffs, marshes, and thick jungles. Carrying hundreds of wounded across treacherous locations for distances of twenty or more kilometres was gruelling, physically exhausting, time consuming, and no doubt psychologically disturbing work. It took two full days before porters could evacuate 67% of the wounded to divisional field hospitals during the battle of the Day River. Internal communist studies confirm that the death rate for soldiers experiencing battle between 1950 and 1954 was high. It reached 28% at Vinh Yen, 25% for the battle of Hoang Hoa Tham, 24% for Quang Trung, 26% at Ly Thuong Kiet, and 26% at **Nghia Lo**. During the brutal delta battle of Vinh Yen in early 1951, of the 1,166 wounded soldiers on record, the main causes of their wounds were due to artillery fire (21%), mortar shells (16.8%), grenades (9.3%), machine gunfire (30.5%), aerial bombing (14.6%), and concussions (4.8%). Artillery guns accounted for 63% of the wounds inflicted during the battle of Vinh Yen, with the number reaching 68% at Dong Trieu, 77% at Nghia Lo, and an "atrocious" (*ac liet*) 90% at Tu Vu during the battle of **Hoa Binh**. These high rates of death by artillery fire and mortars only confirm that modern war had now worked its way into the Indochina War. Behind these cold, impersonal statistics hide gruesome, traumatic combat experiences: thousands of young Vietnamese bodies were quite literally being pulverized as they tried to storm entrenched enemy positions in wave attacks. Hand-to-hand combat accounted for very few battlefield deaths. Artillery shells did. The DRV's fledgling and problem-ridden medical services were overwhelmed with major trauma related wounds. Although the Vietnamese soldier was as human as his colonial opponent, the chances of him dying because of his wounds, even from less than severe ones, were significantly higher than his colonial counterpart. In spite of the DRV's clearly committed medical services, victory on the battlefield, when it occurred, was often achieved from 1950 at the cost of high casualties. *See also* DIEN BIEN PHU, EXPERIENCE OF BATTLE; MYTH OF WAR.

**FAGET, JEAN.** Director of the *Courrier de Saigon* in the late 1930s. He published the only French newspaper in Indochina following the Japanese overthrow of the French in the ***coup de force* of 9 March 1945**, the *Opinion partiale*. During the Indochina War, he continued to run a number of newspapers, including the *Journal de Saigon* which later became the *Journal d'Extrême-Orient*.

**FAIDĀNG LÔBLIAYAO (1907–1989).** Hmong leader of the Lor clan from Xieng Khouang province in Laos and active in the **Pathet Lao.** Opposed to the return of the French after World War II, he worked against the Japanese in mid-1945 before joining the **Lao Issara**. He was also a vowed enemy of **Touby Faidang**, who supported the French return to Indochina. This made Lôbliayao a natural target for the Vietnamese communists to recruit to their side and they did. In the late 1940s, Lôbliayao served as a member of the Lao Issara's **Committee for the East,** collaborating closely with the Vietnamese located on the border of central Vietnam. In August 1950, he attended the congress that created the **Lao Resistance Government** and Pathet Lao national front. He was minister without portfolio while serving as the representative of the Hmong. During the rest of the Indochina War, he was active in **guerrilla** operations in Xieng Khouang province.

**FALL, BERNARD (1926–1967).** Bernard Fall was born into a Jewish merchant family in Vienna, Austria. In 1937, as Hitler eyed Austria, the Fall family hustled their 11-year-old son and his younger sister off to France. Bernard was placed in a Parisian elementary school, where he soon learned to speak and write French as fluently as his native German. In mid-1940, the entire family fled to the *zone libre* in the south. Fall grew up fast during the conflict. He had just turned 16 when the Germans occupied all of France in late 1942. Most scarring of all was the Nazi murder of his parents. In August 1942, his mother was arrested and sent to the infamous French concentration camp in Drancy before being shipped off to Auschwitz. She never returned. On 27 November 1943, the Gestapo arrested Bernard's father and tortured him to death. Bernard himself secretly joined the French underground resistance on 8 November 1942 – the very day the Allies landed in North Africa.

Like the **Viet Minh** he would later study, Fall got his first taste as a French *maquisard* of what it meant to fight a **guerrilla** war against a militarily superior occupying power. He first joined the *Forces françaises de l'intérieur* (FFI) before moving into the *Groupes francs de la Résistance* in the Alps, and then finally landed in the *Groupement FFI Haute-Savoie*. During the liberation of France, he served as a sergeant in the 1st French Army under the command of General **Jean de Lattre de Tassigny**. While he saw some real combat at this time, his perfect knowledge of German landed him quickly in the French Army's Intelligence Service, where he worked until his demobilization in March 1946. He then worked as a translator for the American General Staff between 1946 and 1948. In 1946, thanks to his fluency in German and no doubt his contacts with the Americans, he joined a research team working for the War Crimes for the International Court of Nuremberg. In 1949, he transferred to the *Service International de Recherche des Nations Unies,* where he worked until 1950. In 1950–1951, he completed a degree in Political Science at the American University in the Allied Zone in Germany and in 1951 he obtained a Franco-American study scholarship that allowed him to travel to the United States for the first time. In 1952, he completed his Masters Degree in Political Science at Syracuse University in New York and then began his PhD on the **Democratic Republic of Vietnam** (DRV).

The topic dovetailed perfectly with the growing U.S. interest in Vietnam, both the French and the Vietnamese sides. The conjuncture was perfect for the making of an expert. In 1953, he spent six fruitful months conducting research in war-torn Vietnam. In Indochina, his personality, his time in the French resistance, his fluency in French, and his sensitivity to the fighting soldier and sympathy for "centurion" officers carrying on against all odds, opened doors to him through which few of his peers could have entered. Back in the US, Fall submitted his PhD in 1954 on the birth and the evolution of the **Viet Minh** between 1945 and 1954. It provided the first serious study in any Western language of the nature of the "enemy". Fall examined the DRV's organization, the construction of the revolutionary state, its economy, ideology, propaganda, and armed forces. He would also write a famous account of the battle of **Dien Bien Phu**, *Hell in a Very Small Place.* Like **Philippe Devillers** and **Paul Mus**, few could rival him as a Vietnamese scholar and writer. Fall wasted no time putting himself on the map of Vietnamese and Vietnam war studies in the United States, publishing scores of articles and books, and was on the move until the day he died, accompanying U.S. marines on a patrol north of Hue in 1967.

**FAMINE.** Increased population pressure, falling paddy output, poor weather and cultivation methods, and a shift to industrial crops all converged to greatly reduce the 1944 rice crop in Tonkin and in the north-central provinces of Thanh Hoa and Nghe An, thereby triggering one of the worst famines in Vietnamese history. During World War II, the French and the Japanese refused to reduce taxes on farmers, thereby increasing the burden placed upon them without getting them to produce more. Meanwhile, the French and the Japanese stockpiled rice for their own needs. As the supply of rice fell, its price skyrocketed on the blackmarket, greatly exceeding the officially set price. Farmers hoarded rice in order to meet their own needs rather than sell it on the markets. The only way to head off mass famine was to transport rice from the south. However, Allied bombers had severed the north-south railway and destroyed bridges, while submarines kept coastal shipping to a minimum. Junks and parts of the railway could have been used, but French and Japanese officials were more concerned with the war in the Pacific now that the Allies were on their way to victory in Europe. From December 1944 until about May 1945, famine swooped across **Tonkin** and upper **Annam,** killing an estimated one million Vietnamese. As David Marr notes: "about 10 percent of the population of the region affected perished in a five month period". While the Japanese overthrow of the French in March 1945 and the Allied defeat of the Japanese a few months later opened the way for the **Viet Minh** to take power, to a large extent the famine created a wave of popular discontent, on which the Viet Minh rode to power in mid-1945, as David Marr and Gabriel Kolko have argued.

**FARGUE, JEAN-PAUL (1924–1984).** Colonial administrator during the Indochina War. Graduated from the **Colonial Academy** (*École coloniale*), Fargue worked in northern Vietnam between February 1948 and August 1954. Between February and June 1948, he served as a provincial advisor in Hai Duong province, then as chief of the Bureau of Political Affairs in **Hanoi** between July and December 1948. He was provincial advisor at Langson and then private secretary to the commissar of the Republic for **Tonkin** in the late 1940s. Between 1950 and 1951, he worked as a colonial administrator in Tien Yen and Lai Chau provinces before serving as deputy director to the French Bureau of Information in North Vietnam. He left Indochina in 1954 to finish his colonial career in French Africa before retiring in 1961.

**FARINAUD, MARIE-ÉTIENNE (1896–1983).** French medical doctor and biologist who made his career in French Indochina. He first arrived in the colony in 1925, where he worked in the Pasteur Institute in **Saigon** (1930–1931 and 1935–1939) and in **Hanoi** (1931–1934). After World War II, he returned to Indochina as part of the Anti-Malaria Bureau for the French Troops in the Far East. In 1947 and 1948 he served as director of the Pasteur Institute in Hanoi. In early 1947, he wrote a lengthy report on the Vietnamese attack on the Institute's premises on **19 December 1946**. *See also* DISEASE, DEMOCRATIC REPUBLIC OF VIETNAM.

**FAUGERE, FERNAND-DOMINIQUE.** Controller general of the ***Sûreté fédérale*** in **Saigon** in 1950. A ***métis***, Faugère was fluent in Vietnamese. He joined the colonial police in 1931 or 1932 and rose rapidly in its ranks over the next decade. He served as a deputy to Jacques-Robert Debord and Paul Pujol during the Vichy period. This high-level, behind-the-scenes French security official remained active after World War II and was deeply involved in secret political operations, including the **Bao Dai Solution**. Unfortunately, we know little about the nature of those activities. *See also* ALBERT SARRAUT; ALBERT TOREL; JEAN COUSSEAU; LEON PIGNON.

**FAURE, EDGAR (1908–1988).** French deputy from Jura and member of the radical party. He served as minister of Finance in **Joseph Laniel**'s government. In this capacity, Faure was deeply involved in financial questions related to the war and participated in negotiations with the Americans to obtain their financial assistance in the French war effort. *See also* FINANCIAL COST OF WAR; ECONOMY OF WAR, FRANCE.

**FAY, PIERRE JOSEPH ARMAND LEON (1899–1971).** Graduated from Saint-Cyr in 1917 and named second lieutenant in 1919. Fay entered the French **Air Force** in 1921 and became a fighter pilot. In September 1939, he rose to the rank of lieutenant colonel, joined General Weygand's general staff, and witnessed France's defeat at the hands of the Germans in mid-1940. Vichy transferred him to North Africa. He joined Free French forces following the Allied landing there in late 1942. In March 1945, Fay left for Kandy where on 15 August 1945 he was named commander of the French Air Force in Indochina. He served in this capacity in Indochina until April 1946, when he returned to France for medical reasons. Upon his return, Fay met often with his close friend, **Pierre Mendès France**, advising him on the situation in Indochina. In April 1953, Fay became deputy chief of staff for the Air Force and then chief of staff in August 1953. In this position, Fay concluded that the Air Force could not afford to rearm in Europe and fight the Indochina War at the same time. Such thinking undoubtedly rubbed off on Mendès France who was already concerned about the **financial cost of the war** and France's inability to assume it in light of its growing European commitments. During the battle of **Dien Bien Phu**, Fay participated in the meetings on the operation **Vautour** and the possible use of American bombers to save Dien Bien Phu. General Fay was, however, one of the rare officers to have inspected Dien Bien Phu before the battle and to have dissented from the idea that the camp was impregnable. Standing within the perimeter in late 1953, he went on record in front of **René Pleven**, **Paul Ely**, and **John W. O'Daniel** saying: "I shall advise General **Navarre** to take advantage of the respite available to him and the fact he can still use his two airfields, to evacuate all the men he can, for he is done for. That's all". *See also* EUROPEAN DEFENSE COMMUNITY; NORTH ATLANTIC TREATY ORGANIZATION; SOUTH EAST ASIA TREATY ORGANIZATION.

***FÉDÉRATION INDOCHINOISE.*** *See* INDOCHINESE FEDERATION.

**FENN, CHARLES.** Born in London, Fenn emigrated to the United States where he became an American citizen. He served in World War II as a Marine Corps officer and was assigned to the **Office of Strategic Services** (OSS) and sent to China as a member of the Air Ground Services, in charge of rescuing downed Allied pilots and conducting intelligence operations in French Indochina under Japanese occupation. One of his most important Vietnamese sources of information and contacts for rescuing downed pilots over Indochina was none other than **Ho Chi Minh,** about whom he later wrote a short biography.

**FERRANDI, JEAN (1920–1989).** One of the best French intelligence officers active during the Indochina War. He was named second lieutenant in the Colonial Infantry upon his graduation from the Cadet Officers Training Academy in Cherchell in 1943 before crossing over to the Allied cause. He took part in the campaigns to liberate France and Germany within the 9th Colonial Infantry Division. With the war over, he transferred to Indochina where he joined the 2nd Battalion of the *23ème Régiment d'Infanterie Coloniale* in the *9ème Division d'infanterie coloniale* (DIC) under General **Jean Valluy**. Ferrandi was stationed to southern Vietnam where he participated in the French re-occupation of the Mekong Delta. Following the signing of the **Accords of 6 March 1946,** his regiment landed in **Haiphong** where he took part in the violent French occupation of the city in November 1946. In 1947, he returned to France for specialized studies in Asian affairs before being sent back to Indochina in May 1950 to work in the Section for General Research in the ***Deuxième Bureau*** for the Operational Zone of **Tonkin** (*Zone opérationnelle du Tonkin*). Ferrandi became an experienced intelligence officer and wrote in-depth studies of the adversary as the war moved into its most intensive phase. Ferrandi's intelligence work was of great value during the battles of **Vinh Yen**, Mao Khe, and Nam Dinh. In November 1951, relying on Ferrandi's *Deuxième Bureau*, General **Jean de Lattre de Tassigny** agreed to occupy **Hoa Binh**. General **Raoul Salan** turned to Ferrandi for a number of audacious military manoeuvres, including the battle of **Na San** in late 1952. In 1954, Ferrandi witnessed the debacle at **Dien Bien Phu** while serving between

June and October as chief of Staff to General Salan, who returned briefly to help General **Paul Ely** as the new commander-in-chief of French armed forces in Indochina. Ferrandi would rejoin Salan in Algeria and was condemned to death for his participation in the Putsch of 1961 (the sentence was later commuted). *See also* ALGERIAN WAR; PARALLEL HIERARCHIES; REVOLUTIONARY WARFARE.

**FERRARI, PIERRE (1924–).** French war photographer during the Indochina War. At the age of 19, Ferrari joined the French resistance in Auvergne and joined General **Jean de Lattre de Tassigny**'s forces in 1944. In 1952, he joined the *Service Cinéma des Armées* (SCA) and began work as a war photographer in Indochina for the army. *See also* CINEMA; NOVELS; PIERRE SCHOENDORFFER.

**FIGUÈRES, LÉOPOLD (LÉO) (1918–).** Ranking French communist sympathetic to the **Indochinese Communist Party** (ICP) during and after the Indochina War. He joined the Communist Youth Party in 1932 and the **French Communist Party** (FCP) in 1934. He was a member of the FCP's Central Committee between 1945 and 1976. Between 1935 and 1937, he studied at the International Leninist School in Moscow. He organized the recruiting and transfer of volunteers to fight in Spain from his base in the Pyrénées in France. During World War II, he directed the activities of the Communist Youth movement in the Southern Zone of France and became in 1945 the National Director of the Communist Youth Movement which became the *Union de la Jeunesse républicaine de France*. In 1945–1946, he was a communist deputy from the Pyrénées. In 1949–1950, the FCP sent him on an important fact-finding mission to the newly founded **People's Republic of China** in Beijing and the **Democratic Republic of Vietnam** in the mountains of northern Vietnam. He met Liu Shaoqi and **Zhou Enlai** in Beijing before meeting **Ho Chi Minh**, **Truong Chinh**, **Ha Huy Tap,** and other ranking communist leaders of the ICP in northern Vietnam. Figuères had been instructed by a doubtful FCP to determine the communist mettle of Indochinese communists and of Ho Chi Minh himself. Ho's role in the **dissolution of the Indochinese Communist Party** in November 1945 had raised doubts about the ideological orientation of the Vietnamese communist core. Following his visit, however, Figuères wrote a well-publicized book (200,000 copies were printed), *Je reviens du Vietnam libre*, in which he praised the Vietnamese cause and confirmed the ICP's ideological loyalty to the internationalist communist movement led by the Soviet Union. Figuères's mission helped restore better ideological confidence between the ICP and the FCP and erased doubts in the internationalist communist movement about Ho Chi Minh's ideological wavering and possible Titoist inclinations. The French government, however, issued an arrest warrant against him forcing Figuères into semi-clandestinity for years.

**FINANCIAL COST OF INDOCHINA WAR, FRANCE.** If most studies of the Indochina War focus on its political, military, and diplomatic aspects, the increasing cost of the war was one of the main reasons explaining why the French government finally decided to end the war at a negotiating table in Geneva in 1954. **Pierre Mendès France**, the French prime minister who would force through a deal at Geneva, summed it up nicely: "While all problems may not be financial [at the outset], they become so one day. This [was] the case of the Indochinese affair: if it was badly run on the political, military, and moral levels, things were even worse in budgetary terms". According to French specialist Hugues Tertrais, the overall cost of the war for the French was three billion francs[5] (3,000 *milliards*) between 1945 and 1955, of which the French paid around 70 percent of the total (2–2.4 billion francs), with the Americans picking up most of the rest of the tab.

Until the **Cold War**'s internationalization of the Indochina War in 1950, the financial weight of the war oscillated between 100 and 130 million francs annually. However, the arrival of Chinese aid allowed the **Democratic Republic of Vietnam** (DRV) to modernize their army and to take the battle to the French, increasing the intensity, size, and cost of the battles. Between 1950 and 1951, following the battle of **Cao Bang**, the French spending on military matters in Indochina grew by 47 percent. At the same time, the Berlin Crisis and the French commitment to the **North Atlantic Treaty Organization** (NATO) placed greater pressures on the French to allocate more of their budget to European defense and rearmament, something which President **René Pleven** himself proposed in the form of the **European Defense Community**. The French had to triple

5. Calcuated at the French franc rate of 1953.

their military budget between 1948 and 1952 in order to keep pace with their expanding military commitments to both Europe and Indochina.

To lower the financial burden, the French stepped up the "indigenization" or ***jaunissement*** of the army in Indochina by creating national forces for the Associated States. The French also redoubled their requests to the United States to assume a greater cost of the Indochina War as an essential part of containing communism in Asia. Other measures were taken on the economic front. On 10 May 1953, for example, **René Mayer** unilaterally devalued the Indochinese piastre to 10 francs in order to improve the French financial position. In August 1953, the French government asked the Americans to help finance the Associated States of Indochina by increasing the American contribution to the war for 1954 to 80 percent.

It was thus in this context of severe financial pressure in 1953 that the government assigned General **Henri Navarre** the difficult task of strengthening France's position on the battlefield in order to reach a negotiated, political solution to the war, but without increasing the costs of the war. In short, from 1953, the French could no longer afford the Indochina War. Nor could they afford to send more troops to Indochina to fight. *See also* CURRENCY, FRENCH INDOCHINA; ECONOMY OF WAR; ROYAL CRUSADE FOR INDEPENDENCE.

**FLAG, DEMOCRATIC REPUBLIC OF VIETNAM.** The national flag adopted by the **Democratic Republic of Vietnam** (DRV) upon its creation in 1945 had first been used in a 23 November 1940 meeting in the south, during which communists prepared to launch an insurrection in Cochinchina. While it remains unclear who exactly designed the flag, what is sure is that it was a southern initiative. In October 1945, the provisional National Assembly in **Hanoi** approved the model as the government's official flag, the same one which flies over all of Vietnam since the DRV defeated the **Republic of Vietnam** in 1975 and unified the country under its communist rule shortly thereafter. *See also* CURRENCY, DEMOCRATIC REPUBLIC OF VIETNAM.

**FLEURQUIN, PIERRE ALBÉRIE GABRIEL (1905–1971).** Deputy chief of staff to the French high commissioner in Indochina, **Georges Thierry D'Argenlieu**, between 1945 and 1947. A pilot in the French **Air Force** since 1925, he served in 1953–1954 as the tactical assistant to the commanding general of the 1er ***Groupement aérien tactique***.

**FOCCART, JACQUES (1913–1997).** After serving in the French resistance during World War II, this dedicated Gaullist became something of a specialist in colonial affairs for the *Rassemblement du peuple français* (RPF). In 1950, he served as an advisor to the French Union and was in charge of overseas territories for the RPF. He was strongly opposed to negotiating with the **Democratic Republic of Vietnam** and condemned the **French Communist Party**'s support of Vietnamese independence aspirations. He returned from a fact-finding trip to Indochina in late 1952 to write that France had "to remain in Indochina and continue [its] work" there. The Gaullists could not and should not negotiate with **Ho Chi Minh**, he insisted. *See also* CHARLES DE GAULLE.

**FONDE, JULIEN ROGER JEAN PIERRE (1908–1983).** French liaison officer to the **Democratic Republic of Vietnam** in the months leading up to the outbreak of full-scale war on **19 December 1946**. Fonde signed up for the army in 1927 and decided to make a career of it. During the interwar period, he served mainly in French Senegal. He crossed over to Free French forces in July 1943 and became an officer in **Philippe Leclerc**'s famous 2nd Armored Division during campaigns in Africa and Europe before following Leclerc to Indochina in October 1945, where he participated in the French re-occupation of Tay Ninh province. On 11 March 1946, Fonde was appointed head of the French team assigned to the Franco-Vietnamese Mixed Liaison and Control Committee for **Tonkin** and Northern **Annam**, located in **Hanoi**. This entity was put into place following the return of French troops to northern Vietnam according to the **Accords of 6 March 1946** and its military convention. On 20 December 1946, as war fighting raged in Hanoi, he joined the cabinet of the commanding general of French Troops in North Vietnam and in March 1947 he entered the cabinet of the commanding general for French Troops in the Far East. He returned to France in April 1947 but was back in Indochina in December 1953 working for the head of the French Military Mission to the Associated State of Vietnam, then the commanding general of Ground Forces in the Highlands, and finally in the command of Ground Forces in North Vietnam in April

1954. He led Groupe Mobile 4 between April and September 1954, when it was dissolved. He ended his service in Indochina as part of Ground Troops in South Vietnam. In March 1955, he transferred to the general staff of the commanding general of Indochina before returning to France in January 1956. Fonde insisted later that Leclerc did not want war, a thesis he advanced in a book he wrote in 1971, entitled *Traitez à tout prix*.

**FONG SITTHITHAM (1907–?).** An influential Thai politician of ethnic Lao origin sympathetic to obtaining greater autonomy for the ethnic Lao part of north-eastern Thailand during the Indochina War. Born in Ubon province, he became politically active in the 1930s and was elected deputy to the Thai National Assembly for Ubon. He held this post until 1951. During World War II, he was an active leader in the Free Thai movement and supported the **Lao Issara** and the **Democratic Republic of Vietnam** against the restoration of French colonial rule after the Japanese defeat. Between 1946 and 1948, he was minister of Education in the Thai government. His dream of creating a greater Laos of trans-Mekong grandeur remained illusory. Following a failed attempt to overthrow **Pibun Songgram** in 1951, he withdrew from Thai political life.

**FONTAINEBLEAU CONFERENCE (6 July–13 September 1946).** On 6 July 1946, negotiators of the French 4th Republic and the **Democratic Republic of Vietnam** (DRV) met in Fontainebleau, France, to take up unresolved questions stemming from the **6 March Accords of 1946**. **Max André** led the French delegation. **Pham Van Dong** was the chief negotiator in the talks for the DRV. The negotiations began in a tense atmosphere. In his opening remarks, Pham Van Dong condemned **Georges Thierry d'Argenlieu**'s creation of a separate Cochinchinese state, the **Provisional Government of the Republic of Cochinchina.**

Five main issues were to be discussed during the conference: the DRV's position in the emerging **French Union** and its diplomatic relations with foreign countries; the creation of an **Indochinese Federation**; the status of **Cochinchina**; economic problems; and the drafting of a new Franco-Vietnamese treaty. While progress was made on certain points, the major stumbling block remained the political status of Cochinchina/Nam Bo. The 6 March Accords had called for the organization of a referendum to determine the future status of the former French colony with respect to the emergence of the new Vietnamese "free state", the DRV, and a new colonial one, the Indochinese Federation. When the high commissioner for Indochina, Thierry d'Argenlieu, organized a separate conference on 1 August, the second **Dalat conference**, to move on the Indochinese Federation, the DRV delegation suspended negotiations, asking who was in charge, **Saigon** or Paris. Talks resumed on 25 August, when the French government agreed to reach an accord on the referendum, but linked it to the re-establishment of order in southern Vietnam.

The Fontainebleau conference ultimately broke down when the French refused to set a date for a referendum in and on Cochinchina. On 13 September, Pham Van Dong and the rest of the DRV delegation packed their bags and left for **Hanoi**. Determined to avoid war, Ho Chi Minh remained to plead with his French interlocutors to give him something he could take home to appease hawks in his camp calling for an end to negotiations with the French. As he put it to **Jean Sainteny**: "Don't let me leave like this, arm me against those who seek to cast me aside; you will not regret it". During the early hours of 14 September 1946, Ho Chi Minh convinced **Marius Moutet** to sign a provisional **modus vivendi**. The main idea was that a cease-fire would be instituted in southern Vietnam and, once order restored, negotiations on the elections in Cochinchina could resume. At the heart of the failure of the Fontainebleau conference and the modus vivendi was the problem of Cochinchina. As one French delegate wrote of the conference at the time, "everything depends on the Cochinchina question: Franco-Vietnamese friendship, peace and order in Vietnam, the future of our relations. We must settle this affair as quickly as possible".

**FOREIGN LEGION.** The French *Légion étrangère* refers to the branch of the French army that recruits, inducts, and uses non-French nationals as soldiers. In exchange for their military service, these foreign soldiers can eventually receive French nationality. The birth and the evolution of the Foreign Legion are closely related to the history of the French colonial empire. Faced with a shortage of manpower, the French created the legion in 1831 in order to help them conquer Algeria. This double theme in the Foreign Legion's conception – French colonial conquest and a chronic need for troops – remained valid when the French moved to reconquer Indochina between 1945 and 1954 and to keep Algeria French between 1954 and 1962. For both wars of decolonization, the 4th Republic turned to the Foreign Legion. In 1945, some 16,000 troops from the Foreign Legion were in Indochina. In 1953, the number reached 36,312. Nationalities in the Legion in Indochina included Germans, Poles, Soviets, Ukranians, Greeks, and even Americans. In all, during the Indochina war, 72,833 *légionnaires* served in Indochina, present in all the major battles, including **Cao Bang** and **Dien Bien Phu**. 8,508 *légionnaires* died during the war and 9,234 were wounded. Hundreds served time in Vietnamese prison camps in central and northern Vietnam. The last Foreign Legion unit left Vietnam in April 1956. The non-French character of the Foreign Legion helped the French government reduce the impact of the war on French society and public opinion and allowed the 4th Republic to avoid instituting the draft. That said, the **French Communist Party** was able to exploit the presence of former Nazis in the Foreign Legion in their propaganda drives against the war. But the idea that the French Foreign Legion was crawling with Nazis from World War II is off the mark. *See also BATAILLON D'INFANTERIE LÉGÈRE D'OUTRE-MER*; CROSSOVERS; DESERTION; ERNST FREY; RUDY SCHRÖDER.

**FOSSEY-FRANÇOIS, ALBERT (1909–1958).** He was mobilized during the French debacle of June 1940 and joined the resistance in 1943, serving as chief of the department of Creuse for the *Forces françaises de l'intérieur* in 1944 and obtained the rank of lieutenant colonel. With the end of the war, he joined the newly reconstituted French national army as a battalion leader. Between 1947 and 1951, he made three tours of duty in Indochina as head of the 3rd battalion of the *1er Régiment de chasseurs parachutistes* (1er RCP). From March 1953, he directed the *Bureau de guerre psychologique*. *See also* CHARLES LACHEROY; INDOCTRINATION; PACIFICATION; PSYCHOLOGICAL WARFARE; REVOLUTIONARY WARFARE; *SERVICE ACTION*.

***FRANÇAIS D'INDOCHINE.*** On the eve of World War II, the European population of Indochina numbered around 35–40,000 civilians, consisting mainly of French citizens but also of a smattering of Europeans, French-naturalized Vietnamese, Indians, and ***métis***. The majority of the European population was concentrated in urban centres, mainly in **Hanoi** and **Saigon**. About 40 percent of the European population worked in the colonial administration, while the others took to commerce, banking and, to a lesser extent, ran sugar and rubber plantations. As a colony, **Cochinchina**'s French citizens could elect a deputy to the French Assembly and had their own Cochinchinese Assembly. Some 600 European missionaries also lived and worked in Indochina, although not all of them were French citizens nor were they posted to the big cities. The European community ran its own associations, sporting clubs, and chambers of commerce.

While some Europeans mingled with the native Vietnamese, such as Ernest Babut and the **Paul Mus** family, most tended to live and work in separate worlds. Over time, the Europeans born and raised in Indochina came to think of themselves in Indochinese terms, increasingly using the term *Français d'Indochine* or even "*Indochinois*" in a semantic move to distinguish themselves from metropolitan French (not unlike the Europeans who considered themselves to be "Algerians" or "Americans"). **William Bazé**, for example, was a very active supporter of such an identity and of settler interests, serving as honorary president of the *Mutuelle des Français d'Indochine*. His Saigon-based newspaper, *Le Populaire*, was one of the most important settler papers of the time.

For most of World War II the political condominium between Vichy France and the Japanese spared the European population in Indochina from the tragic fate of other European communities in Southeast Asia, such as the Dutch in **Indonesia** and the British in **Burma** and Malaya. This changed dramatically during the four and half months following the Japanese overthrow of the French in Indochina in the ***coup de force* of 9 March 1945**. During this period, the Japanese incarcerated an estimated 756 French individuals (242 in Hanoi, 82 in Hue, 150 in Saigon, 150 in Haiphong and 59 in Phnom Penh). According to the French archives, the Japanese killed 400 French civilians and 1,800 French military personnel. The large majority of French working the Indochinese administration were replaced by Vietnamese, Lao, or Khmers. The Japanese *coup d'état* also had the effect of concentrating even more of the European population in the cities and towns by forcing (through incarceration) or frightening French settlers in the countryside to move. By their very presence as occupiers of Indochina, the Japanese humiliated the European population and this was not lost upon the Vietnamese, Lao, and Cambodians.

The end of World War II did not re-establish the prewar daily life of the *Français d'Indochine*. Most settlers keen on protecting their earlier colonial status and interests viewed with fear the emergence of a new Vietnamese nation-state, the **Democratic Republic of Vietnam** (DRV). Numbering some 5,000 in Hanoi in late 1945, few supported Vietnamese nationalist aspirations or French decolonization of Indochina. The settlers overwhelming turned to and often joined French forces sent to re-establish French colonial rule. Tensions between the Vietnamese and the French community in Saigon turned ugly and lethal in early September 1945, when violent altercations occurred in the streets. When the French moved to retake Saigon and its suburbs by force on **23 September 1945**, many (not all) Europeans exacted vengeance on the Vietnamese during the reoccupation. On 23–24 September, Vietnamese groups committed a **massacre** in the Hérault quarter of Saigon, taking hundreds of European hostages and killing many of them in terrible circumstances, especially Franco-Vietnamese *métis* considered to be **traitors** to the new Vietnamese nation. Similar violence occurred between Vietnamese and Europeans living in Hanoi following the outbreak of full-scale war in Hanoi on **19 December 1946**.

While the French army retook the main colonial cities during the Indochina War, things would never be the same. Many European settlers left Indochina in 1945 and 1946. Others, like William Bazé, stayed on, putting their hopes in the **Bao Dai Solution**. When the **Geneva Accords** formalized the decolonization of Indochina and divided Vietnam provisionally into a two states, a communist one in the north and a non-communist one in the south, the overwhelming majority of the Europeans still remaining in the north either left Indochina for good or migrated to southern Vietnam where a handful remained until the victory of the DRV in 1975 forced them to pack their bags and leave again. The French estimated that 6,500 French civilians lived and worked in Hanoi before the Geneva Accords were signed in July 1954. Of that number, only 114 remained in mid-November. *See also* COLLABORATION; HÉRAULT MASSACRE.

**FRANCÈS, ROBERT (1921–).** Graduated from the Colonial Academy (*École coloniale*) in 1942, he left France and joined Free French forces in July 1943 before making his way to North Africa. Francès took part in the liberation of France and was badly wounded by a mine explosion. During the Indochina War, he was a colonial administrator appointed in June 1947 to head the *Surêté* in **Cochinchina**. Little else is known about him.

**FRANCO-CHINESE ACCORD (28 FEBRUARY 1946).** The Franco-Chinese accord cleared the way for the withdrawal of Chinese troops from Indochina above the **16th parallel**. In accordance with the **Potsdam conference**, the **Republic of China**'s troops accepted the Japanese surrender in and occupied Indochina above the 16th parallel, whereas the British did the same below that line. Unlike the British, local Chinese commanders refused to facilitate the French return to the north. In order to reoccupy northern Indochina, the French were thus determined to negotiate the rapid withdrawal of the Chinese and their replacement by the French. Despite the reluctance of some of his commanders in Indochina, **Chiang Kai-shek** was increasingly amenable to such a withdrawal, something which would allow him to concentrate on problems with communists in northern China. The Accords signed on 28 February 1946 included a "Franco-Chinese Treaty on the Renunciation of Extra-territoriality and Related Rights" and an "Accord on Sino-Indochinese Relations". The French agreed to renounce their concessions in China, including Shanghai, to return Guangzhouwan to the Republic of China, and to improve the legal status and privileges of the **overseas Chinese** living in Indochina among other things. In exchange, the Chinese agreed to pull their troops out of northern Indochina before 31 March 1946. Although the Chinese government had verbally accepted the principle that French troops would replace Chinese ones, the procedure for doing so was not spelled out clearly in the Accords and Chinese officers in Indochina were not necessarily amenable to a rapid French reoccupation on their watch, as the events leading up to the **Accords of 6 March** made clear.

**FRÉDÉRIC-DUPONT, ÉDOUARD (1902–1995).** French politician and strong defender of keeping Indochina French. A lawyer by profession, he entered politics in the 1920s and was elected a city councillor in 1933 as a "national republican", a very conservative one. A few years later, he became councillor for the city of Paris. He was a staunch opponent of the Popular Front. In 1940 he voted full powers to Marshal Philippe Pétain and served Vichy on the city council of Paris. At the same time, he provided intelligence to the French resistance movement from inside the city council and helped Jews escape from German-occupied France. This saved his career from almost certain doom. He returned to politics in 1945, when he was elected deputy for the first district of the Seine and eventually was briefly accepted by the Gaullists in 1951 in the *Rassemblement du peuple français* but was excluded a year later. He joined the *Action républicaine et sociale* led by Antoine Pinay and was elected again to the city council of Paris. He was a devoted believer in the French Empire and its maintenance in Indochina and North Africa. He briefly served as minister in charge of Relations with the Associated States for a few days in June 1954 during the **Geneva Conference**. He voted against the **Geneva Accords** in the French Assembly on 23 July 1954, seeing it as a sell-out of French interests.

**FREEMASONS**. Freemasonry began as a fraternal organization in Great Britain before spreading across much of the globe. The fraternity of brothers is divided into Grand Lodges, often called Orients, which administer smaller lodges at the grassroots level. In France, Freemasonry acquired an anti-clerical Republican hue under the Third Republic. The French *Grand Orient* is located in Paris and administered its lodges in the colonies from there.

Freemasons in Indochina counted among their ranks leading colonial administrators and **intellectuals**, including Auguste Pavie and Paul Doumer. While Freemasons critiqued the excesses of colonial repression, few supported decolonization, favoring a much milder form of colonial reformism. Indeed, most remained believers in the Third Republic's colonial mission and played an influential role in the creation of the **Colonial Academy** *(École coloniale)*. The Freemasons created a number of lodges in Indochina, including *La Fraternité tonkinoise* (1887), *L'Étoile du Tonkin* (1892), and the *Les Écossais du Tonkin* (1912) in **Hanoi**, *L'Avenir khmer* (1906) in Phnom Penh, and *La Ruche d'Orient* (1908) in **Saigon**. At the outset, these lodges balked at admitting Vietnamese, Lao, and Khmer to their ranks. Freemasonary remained a French and very male-oriented society. Following World War I, however, pressure to admit Vietnamese grew and northern lodges were particularly open to this trend (for unclear reasons). Two Vietnamese lodges emerged during the interwar period, the lodges of *Confucius* and *Khong Phu Tseu*. The French intellectual and leader of the ***Section française de l'Internationale ouvrière***'s branch in Indochina, **Louis Caput**, was also a Freemason, an emerging anti-colonialist, and an active supporter of admitting Vietnamese to the Freemasonry movement. He supported the initiation of **Hoang Minh Giam**, future minister to **Ho Chi Minh**, to the fraternity in the 1930s. According to French historian **Jacques Dalloz**, the famous diplomat and personal doctor to Ho Chi Minh, **Pham Ngoc Thach**, also joined a Freemason lodge in the 1930s.

During Vichy, Decoux unleashed the *Révolution Nationale*, forcing the Freemasonry movement underground and weakening it greatly over the long term in Indochina. With the Japanese overthrow of the French in the ***coup de force* of 9 March 1945**, most Vietnamese Freemasons withdrew, were killed (Bui Quang Chieu and Duong Van Giao for example), or crossed over to the nationalist cause of the **Democratic Republic of Vietnam** (DRV) (Pham Ngoc Thach and Hoang Minh Giam). Upon returning to Indochina, the French encouraged local masons to re-establish their lodges in Indochina, rebuilding *Le Réveil de l'Orient* in Saigon and *La Fraternité tonkinoise* in Hanoi. However, these lodges attracted very few Vietnamese members and French freemasons remained deeply divided over the question of decolonization and Vietnamese independence in particular. Louis Caput pushed increasingly for the recognition of Vietnamese nationalism. Conservative-minded Freemasons in Saigon, such as Maurice Weil, however, supported Cochinchinese separatism and even wrote off Vietnamese nationalists aligned with **Bao Dai** as "anti-French". This blind conservatism only eroded an already faltering French Freemason organization in Indochina after World War II, something from which it never recovered. This author is unaware of what became of Freemasons in postcolonial Vietnam, either in the DRV or the **Republic of Vietnam**. *See also* CAO DAI; CATHOLICS, EXODUS FROM NORTH; CATHOLICS IN VIETNAM AND THE WAR; CHRISTIANS AND OPPOSITION TO THE INDOCHINA WAR; LE HUU TU; PRISONERS OF WAR; HOA HAO; VATICAN.

**FRÉJUS.** *See* NECROPOLIS.

**FRENCH COMMUNIST PARTY.** Created in 1920 during the Congress of Tours, the French Communist Party (FCP) was one of the rare political groups to support Vietnamese anti-colonialism during the interwar period. That support continued after World War II, but it was marred by the FCP's reluctance to jeopardize its majority position in the postwar French coalition government and the potential chance to lead it by supporting too overtly the independence cause of the **Democratic Republic of Vietnam** (DRV). In November 1946, the FCP became the biggest political party in France, winning 28 percent of the vote and electing 170 deputies to the National Assembly. This made it a major partner in the coalition government led by a socialist. Support for the DRV was ambiguous. On 22 March 1947, when President **Paul Ramadier** asked for a vote of confidence on approving money for the Indochina War, communist deputies were absent and the communist ministers voted with the government. Even the communist representative to the **Cominindo**, Charles Tillon, remained taciturn during the coalition period, as was another influential communist, **Henri Lozeray**. In 1946–1947, supporting French national unity trumped communist internationalism and anti-colonialism. French conservatives even thanked their leftist counterparts and the Soviet Union for not interfering in the war in Indochina in early 1947.

The party's policy on Vietnam changed when it entered into the opposition in May 1947. However, doubts remained between the FCP and their Vietnamese communist counterparts. Certain French communist leaders questioned **Ho Chi Minh**'s decision to dissolve the **Indochinese Communist Party** in November 1945, while the Vietnamese complained privately of the FCP's lack of support for a brother party and the anti-colonial struggle. As **Pham Ngoc Thach** explained to a Soviet diplomat in Switzerland in September 1947, the FCP had provided little tangible help to the Vietnamese communist movement. From early 1949, as the **Cold War** intensified in Europe, the FCP organized its first mass campaign in France against the "***sale guerre***" or dirty war in Indochina and, with the support of the *Confédération Générale du Travail*, launched worker's strikes demanding "peace in Vietnam" and "bringing home the **Expeditionary Corps**". This mobilization opened the way for increased worker agitation, including the refusal of dockers in 1950 to load war material on to ships in Marseilles, Dunkirk, La Rochelle, and elsewhere en route to Indochina. The party also launched an effective, highly public campaign to free **Henri Martin**, arrested by the French security services for his role in the docker strikes of 1950. External factors also explain the increase in French communist support for the Vietnamese. Moscow and Beijing's decision to recognize the DRV in January 1950 aligned the communist bloc squarely behind the DRV.

Upon his return from a visit to DRV areas in northern Vietnam, the FCP emissary **Léopold Figuères** reported favourably on the Vietnamese communist movement, its struggle for national liberation, and its ideological reliability. While the Chinese took the lead in assisting the Vietnamese communists, the FCP immediately sent two ranking delegates to help the DRV in propaganda and **proselytizing** overtures towards French troops in the Expeditionary Corps. The first was named André, who adopted the Vietnamese name Le Chinh and became a secretary of a party provincial committee. The second was comrade Roland who took the Vietnamese name Lang but left Vietnam soon thereafter, allegedly unable to adjust to the harsh living conditions. André was none other than **Jean Marrane**. Upon the latter's suggestion, the DRV began releasing prisoners as part of a wider strategy to influence French public opinion positively by stressing "peace and repatriation" of the soldiers. Marrane also helped the DRV to target better enemy French soldiers in their proselytizing and propaganda missions. Elsewhere in Indochina the FCP had little real influence, neither in the army nor in the *Groupe culturel marxiste* that operated in **Saigon** between 1945 and 1950. It was in France where the FCP played the leading mobilizing role in turning **public opinion** against the Indochina War, casting it as a "shameful" event rather than a heroic one. *See also* BOUDAREL AFFAIR; GEORGES BOUDAREL; INTELLECTUALS; MYTH OF WAR; *SECTION FRANÇAISE DE L'INTERNATIONALE OUVRIÈRE*.

**FRENCH UNION.** The idea for creating a new colonial entity after World War II was linked to the French desire to hold on to its colonial empire, considered to be an integral part of its national identity and international standing. As the head of the Free French provisional government based in Algiers, **Charles de Gaulle** organized an important conference at **Brazzaville** in early 1944 to study colonial reforms. While de Gaulle refused to embark upon a policy of decolonization, his colonial specialists, such as **Henri Laurentie**, sought to provide the colonies with greater local autonomy within the context of a wider French Union, discussed in detail during this conference. This autonomy would be accorded through a Union based on a federal system. As historians Martin Shipway and Daniel Hémery have shown, Indochina was to be the litmus test for the French Union, crucial in determining its political shape and defining the future course of "France's relations with the emerging forces of colonial nationalism". The 24 March **Declaration on Indochina** marked the first official French use of the term *Union française*. The 4th Republic's constitution of 1946 announced its formal creation, comprising metropolitan France, French overseas departments, territories, settlements, and **United Nations** trusteeships. The former French colonies became departments whereas protectorates were accorded greater autonomy. The French **Indochinese Federation** – not Vietnam – would thus be an important Asian component of the French Union. In the **Accords of 6 March 1946**, the French and the Vietnamese agreed to recognize the **Democratic Republic of Vietnam** as a "free state" within the Indochinese Federation, itself in turn part of the French Union. The outbreak of full-scale war put an end to such compromises between the two belligerants. But war also struck a severe blow to the viability of the French Union. In 1954, with the war over, the **Associated States of Indochina** all withdrew from the French Union, followed by Morocco and Tunisia two years later. In 1958, the French Union had to be recast as the French Community as the historical reality of decolonization began to sink in to official French colonial minds. *See also* ALGERIAN WAR; ANTICOLONIALISM; *ESPRIT*; CHARLES DE GAULLE; PAUL MUS.

**FREY, ERNST (NGUYỄN DÂN, 1915–?).** Austrian **crossover** to the **Democratic Republic of Vietnam** (DRV) during the Indochina War. Born into a Jewish family in Austria, he joined the Communist Youth League following Hitler's accession to power in 1933. Like other anti-fascist militants, he fled to France as Hitler annexed Austria in 1938 and joined the French **Foreign Legion** to carry on the fight as part of the Third Republic. However, following the French defeat of 1940 and Vichy's collaboration with Germany, Frey found himself from July 1941 posted to the Foreign Legion in colonial Indochina, run jointly by Vichy and the Japanese (Germany's Asian ally). During the war, Frey, **Erwin Börchers,** and other left-leaning soldiers in the Foreign Legion met often with **Louis Caput**, head of the ***Section française de l'Internationale ouvrière*** in Indochina, and even **Truong Chinh** in late 1944, the provisional general secretary of the **Indochinese Communist Party** (ICP) based outside **Hanoi**. Truong Chinh advised Frey and others to mobilize support among likeminded soldiers in the Legion.

Following the Japanese overthrow of the French in the ***coup de force* of 9 March 1945**, Frey was interned with the rest of the Foreign Legion. Upon his liberation following the Japanese defeat in August, he renewed his contacts with those Vietnamese who were now at the head of the newly created DRV. He openly supported the Vietnamese nationalist cause, adopting the Vietnamese name of Nguyen Dan. Like Börchers, Frey's work was developing anti-colonialist propaganda aimed mainly at the French Foreign Legion. However, Frey's military training in the Legion made him attractive to the DRV. He worked with the Chinese-trained **Vuong Thua Vu** instructing young troops and officers in military science. As the French **Expeditionary Corps** began to retake southern Vietnam below the **16th parallel**, Frey was sent to work with **Nguyen Son**. Frey directed real battles against the French at An Khe, something which gained him the confidence of the Vietnamese who named him "colonel" (*dai ta*) in exchange for his services. He then returned to the north to work directly with **Vo Nguyen Giap** and played a role in Giap's nascent **General Staff**, helped plan ambushes against the French, and led some **Viet Minh** soldiers in battle, becoming the official leader of a small military zone in **Viet Bac**.

Despite difficulties in Frey's relations with the ICP, **Truong Chinh** backed him until mid-1950. This trust was such that Frey was one of the few Europeans to address the important 3rd all-Party plenum of 1950. There were, however, problems. Frey resented bitterly what he saw as serious military and political errors committed by the ICP. Following a failed attempt to inform the **Chinese Communist Party** independently of these matters, he was recalled and repatriated rapidly to Eastern Europe via China. He eventually made his way back to Austria, where he lost the communist faith and became a fervent Catholic before apparently giving up on universal faiths altogether. In 1982, in what has to be one of the strangest meetings of minds in the memory-making of the Indochina War, the right-wing French *Front National* leader, former Foreign Legion paratrooper and member of the *OAS*, **Pierre Sergent** published a fascinating, sympathetic biography of his former enemy, entitled *Un étrange Monsieur Frey.* Foreign Legion soldiers in the French army and internationalist combatants in the DRV's ranks make for strange parallels.

**FRIANG, BRIGITTE (1924–).** One of the few women war correspondents covering the Indochina War. Friang was a French resistant during World War II. Captured by the Gestapo at the age of 19, she was imprisoned, deported, and tortured. A tattooed serial number on her forearm left no doubt as to where she had been. Upon liberation, she began a long career in journalism. Between 1947 and 1951, she was *attachée de presse* to André Malraux. From 1951, she covered the Indochina War for the French Information Service and trained as a certified French paratrooper. She often accompanied troops into combat, including the audacious jump she made with the 6th Colonial Paratrooper Battalion at Tu Le. Many of her articles appeared in *Indochine Sud-est Asiatique*. Another famous war correspondent, **Bernard Fall**, described her as "one of a kind". "Brigitte Friang looked like any girl should look", he recalled, "except for her gray blue eyes. No matter how gay the conversation, how relaxed the evening, Brigitte's eyes never seemed quite reconciled to smiling." She returned to France in 1954. She published two books on her experiences: *Regarde toi qui meurs* (1970) on her experiences during World War II and *Les fleurs du ciel* (1955). In 1976, she published a damning account of the communist-led **Democratic Republic of Vietnam**, now in charge of all of Vietnam, *La mousson de la liberté Vietnam: du colonialisme au stalinisme.* Friang was the inspiration for Malraux's chapter on deportation in his *Antimémoires. See also* EXPERIENCE OF WAR; NOVELS; MYTH OF WAR.

**G.A.C.R.** *See GROUPEMENTS ADMINISTRATIFS CHINOIS RÉGIONAUX* (G.A.C.R) / ADMINISTRATIVE CHINESE REGIONAL GROUPINGS.

**GABARRE, MARCEL ANTOINE HENRI (1913–1975)**. French colonial administrator who made his career in Indochina. Between 1936 and 1943, he held a variety of administrative posts in **Cochinchina**. Little is known of his whereabouts or activities between 1943 and 1947, when he reappeared as deputy to the director of the Political Affairs Section for **Tonkin** and Northern **Annam**. Between 1947 and 1950, he served as head of the Political Affairs Section in **Hanoi** before transferring to the section dealing with litigation matters. He left Indochina in 1953.

**GABRILLAGUES, FERNAND FRÉDÉRIC (1918–1982).** French colonial administrator who was in charge of organizing the investigation into Japanese war criminals in Indochina during World War II (1946–1947). He was a provincial advisor in the Tai area of northern Vietnam in 1949, attached to the personnel section of the high commissioner's office in 1950–1951, and a delegate for the commissioner for the French Republic to Sam Neua province in Laos between 1951 and 1952.

**GALARD (DE), GENEVIÈVE-TERRAUBE (1925–).** French nurse who tended the wounded during the battle of **Dien Bien Phu**. She joined the French **Air Force** in January 1953 and arrived in Indochina in May of that year. After a short transfer to Algeria, she returned to Indochina in January 1954. There, she joined the French Air Medics, *Infirmières pilotes secouristes de l'air*, to treat battle wounded troops. Galard volunteered to serve during the battle of Dien Bien Phu and flew into the camp despite heavy enemy artillery fire. On 27 March, she made her last flight into the besieged camp and was taken prisoner when the Vietnamese won the battle on 7 May 1954. Surprised to find this French woman among their prisoners, the **Democratic Republic of Vietnam** (DRV) authorities liberated her on 24 May 1954. She returned to Indochina to work between May and July 1955. She was not, however, the only woman present during the battle of Dien Bien Phu, nor was she the only woman taken prisoner by the DRV. *See also BORDELS MOBILES DE CAMPAGNE*; NORTH AFRICANS; *PERSONNEL FÉMININ DE L'ARMÉE DE TERRE* (PFAT); WOMEN, FRENCH ARMED FORCES.

**GALLAGHER, PHILIP E. (1897–1976).** During World War II, he served as brigadier general attached to the First War Area, Chinese Combat Command. In August 1945, he became advisor to the commander of the Chinese Occupation Force for Indochina above the **16th parallel**. He was also the American liaison officer with Chinese General **Lu Han**.

**GAMBIEZ, FERNAND CHARLES LOUIS (1903–1989).** French officer determined to deny the adversary access to strategically important Catholic parts of central Vietnam during the Indochina War. Graduated from the *École spéciale militaire de Saint-Cyr* in 1925, he served in North Africa where he participated in "**pacification**" operations in Tunisia and Morocco. He remained in France after the debacle of 1940, but crossed over to Free French Forces in 1942 and returned to North Africa. In 1943, he was one of the architects of the first French *Bataillons de choc* for use in special missions and operations behind enemy lines. Gambiez and his assault troops successfully landed in Sicily and Corsica to help prepare the Allied landing in southern France. Gambiez applied these **guerrilla** methods in the Indochina War between 1949 and 1953. He took a particular interest in preventing the enemy from taking control of Catholic parts of Vietnam, especially at Phat Diem and Bui Chu. Between December 1949 and October 1950, he commanded the zone for the northern delta in **Tonkin** before becoming chief of staff for French Ground Forces in North Vietnam and in the Operational Zone of Tonkin (October 1950–January 1951). In January 1951, he became head of the Southern Delta Zone in North Vietnam. In November, he assumed acting leadership of the *Division de marche du Tonkin*. Despite taking sick leave in France in 1952, he returned to Indochina in 1953 as chief of the Combined Chiefs of Staff in Indochina and commanding officer of the *2ème Division nord africaine*. In June 1954, he was deputy to the commander-in-chief of French Ground Forces in South Vietnam and oversaw the coordination of French assistance to Vietnamese refugees leaving northern Vietnam following the signature of the **Geneva Accords** and the installation of the **Democratic Republic of Vietnam (DRV)** above the **17th parallel**. On 23 March 1954, he lost his son, Second Lieutenant Alain Gambiez at **Dien Bien Phu** and a nephew succumbed in a DRV prisoner camp shortly thereafter.

**GANNAY, PAUL.** General inspector for the **Bank of Indochina** and director of its **Saigon** branch from 1920.

**GARDET, ROGER (1900–1989).** French officer in southern Vietnam during the last stages of the Indochina War. After volunteering for the army in 1919, Gardet landed in Haiphong in 1922 and stayed in Vietnam until 1924. In 1940, he joined Free French forces in Africa and led a colonial light battalion. He took part in the liberation of France. Between 1952 and 1953, he was deputy to the commanding general of French Ground Forces in South Vietnam before taking command of Ground Forces in Laos and then those in South Vietnam in 1953–1954.

**GAUDART, JOSEPH FRANK (1902–1948).** French colonial administrator during the Indochina War. Graduated from the **Colonial Academy** (*École coloniale*) in 1926, Gaudart made his career in Indochina. During the interwar period, he worked in Quang Tri province before administering the province of Vinh during the Japanese occupation. Arrested by the Japanese following the ***coup de force*** **of 9 March 1945**, he returned to France upon his liberation a few months later. In 1947, he was back in Indochina as the political advisor for northern **Annam**, charged with facilitating the French reoccupation of territories held by the **Democratic Republic of Vietnam** since 1945. In 1948, he was killed during an ambush in central Vietnam.

**GAULTIER DE LA FERRIÈRE, JACQUES MARIE GEORGES (1923–).** Served in the Commissariat for the Republic in Cambodia between 1946 and 1950 before working as the bureau chief of Cultural Affairs for the high commissioner's office in **Saigon** between 1950 and 1953. Between 1955 and 1957, he served in the Political Affairs section in the French Ministry of Foreign Affairs in charge of relations with Vietnam, Laos, and Cambodia.

**GENERAL POLITICAL BUREAU (*Tổng Cục Chính Trị*).** First started as the Political Bureau (*Cuc Chinh Tri*), created in September 1945 and led by **Van Tien Dung**. It became the General Political Bureau on 11 July 1950, as the **Democratic Republic of Vietnam** prepared to launch the General Counter Offensive to take the war to the French at **Cao Bang** and elsewhere. **Nguyen Chi Thanh** served as its leader from 1950 to 1961. Through the General Political Bureau, the communist party ensured the political indoctrination of the armed forces and reinforced communist control over the armed forces. The General Political Bureau answered directly to the **Central Party Military Committee** (*Quan Uy Trung Uong*) led by **Vo Nguyen Giap**, subordinate to the Politburo.

**GENERAL STAFF, DEMOCRATIC REPUBLIC OF VIETNAM.** On 7 September 1945, the **Indochinese Communist Party** (ICP) Central Committee authorized **Vo Nguyen Giap** to establish the first office of the General Staff. **Hoang Van Thai** led this office, working in tandem with Vo Nguyen Giap as the head of the Ministry of Interior and minister of Defense. The **Democratic Republic of Vietnam** government ran the Ministry of Defense whereas the ICP created the General Staff in order to command all the armed forces in Vietnam. It would be the instrument by which the Party would maintain its control over military affairs, no matter who controlled the Ministry of Defense. This was particularly important in 1945–1946 when non-communist politicians entered the DRV government. The General Staff was in charge of commanding operations, organizational matters, training of the army, and intelligence.

**GENERALS AFFAIR.** *See AFFAIRE DES GÉNÉRAUX.*

**GENEVA ACCORDS.** The Geneva conference of 1954 ranks as one of the most important international gatherings in the history of the post-World War II international system.

The death of **Joseph Stalin** in March 1953 and the end of the shooting in Korea a few months later opened the way for a thaw in what had until then been very tense East–West relations spanning much of the globe. The outbreak of the **Korean War** in June 1950 pitted American-led **United Nations** troops against Soviet-backed Chinese and Korean ones. Since 1950, the Chinese and to a lesser extent the Soviets had supported the **Democratic Republic of Vietnam**'s (DRV) forces against those of the **French Union**, backed by the Americans. With Stalin gone and the guns silent in Korea, the new leadership emerging in Moscow made it clear that it wanted to reduce tensions in both Europe and Asia in order to focus on internal economic matters. A détente would facilitate this process. Their Chinese allies shared this view. The Korean War had proved a heavy drain for Beijing in terms of materials and manpower. The revolutionary restructuring of the economy and the society along communist lines, including radical **land reform**, had exhausted the country. Having been isolated by the United States diplomatically, Chinese leaders also felt that a great power conference on Asia would allow them finally to join the international concert of nations. The Soviets concurred.

The French and the British agreed that the time was ripe to ease tensions in the international system. In 1953, French president **Joseph Laniel** understood that the French could no longer afford the Indochina War in light of its building military commitments to Western European defense. In mid-1953, Laniel sent **Henri Navarre** to Indochina to create the necessary military conditions for reaching an honorable end to the Indochina War at the negotiating table. Easing tensions over Germany was first on the list of topics to discuss, when French, British, Soviet, and American foreign ministers convened in Berlin in early 1954. However, it was decided at Berlin that the next meeting, to be held in the Swiss capital of Geneva, would discuss the two major global hotspots in the international system, in Asia – Korea and Indochina.

Like the Americans, the Chinese were deeply involved in both conflicts, and thus expected to play an important role in their resolution. The Soviets supported the Chinese bid and the British, who had formally recognized communist China, tended to agree. The Americans, however, continued in their refusal to recognize the **People's Republic of China** (PRC), blocking its entry into the United Nation's Security Council and its attempt to serve as the fifth power hosting the upcoming Geneva talks dealing with Asia. If the Soviet Union failed to get communist China recognized as one of the official powers at Geneva, the Americans agreed that the four main powers could invite delegations of their choosing. This allowed the Chinese to take part in their first major international conference, while the Americans could avoid recognizing the reality of the PRC. Nonetheless, despite the thaw in East–West relations in 1953–1954, the Sino-American split cast a long shadow over the conference and its negotiations from beginning to end, as Laurent Césari has demonstrated. American secretary of state **John Foster Dulles** instructed his diplomats to refrain from sitting at the same table as the Chinese, nor were they to shake the adversary's hands (McCarthyism was building to a crescendo by mid-1954). The Chinese foreign minister, **Zhou Enlai**, never forgot Dulles's refusal to shake his outstretched hand during the Geneva Conference.

Dulles had agreed in Berlin to put Indochina on the agenda for two main reasons. First, he wanted to avoid seeing the hawkish French government led by **Joseph Laniel** and **Georges Bidault** replaced by a dovish one, capable of caving into communist demands or having elections that could end in a "peaceful" communist take-over at the negotiating table. Dulles also agreed to let the Geneva Conference take up Indochina in the hope that he could get the Laniel government to push forward the ratification of the **European Defense Community** (EDC), a top concern for the American's in their containment of the Soviet Union in Europe. Besides the "four powers plus China", the conference included the main Indochinese parties concerned with the war: the Associated States of Vietnam, Laos, Cambodia, and the Democratic Republic of Vietnam. The DRV failed in its attempts to get its associated states in Laos and Cambodia accepted at Geneva. **India** also participated unofficially in the person of **Krishna Menon**, India's specialist on Indochina and a close confidant of **Jawaharlal Nehru**.

The Soviets and the British, co-presidents of the conference, tacitly agreed not to let the Sino-American break spin out of control during the negotiations. As for Zhou Enlai, he wanted a solution to the Indochina War in order to keep the United States from replacing the French on China's southern flank, worried by Eisenhower's expanding web of alliances, and aware of the fact that the Korean problem was not going to be solved and that the Americans would not leave South Korea any time soon. Zhou had already begun developing a policy of "peaceful co-existence" with non-communist countries in Asia in order to neutralize Indochina and non-communist postcolonial Asia against American attempts to bring these states into collective security alliances aimed at containing and perhaps even "rolling back" communist China. Shortly before arriving in Geneva, the Chinese statesman had signed an agreement with Nehru over Tibet, contributing to a major thaw in relations between the two Asian giants. In a series of negotiations held with the Indians between December 1953 and June 1954, the Chinese reassured the Indians and other non-communist, newly decolonized neighbors of China's peaceful intentions in the form of the "five principles of peaceful co-existence" or *Panchseel*.

The Soviet Union was also keen on easing tensions in Asia in order to achieve a détente with the non-communist anti-colonialist states emerging in the South as decolonization moved its way westward on a South-South axis and into the **United Nations** General Assembly. Providing Paris with an honourable way out of the Indochina War could also help the Soviets pressure the French into torpedoing the EDC and opposing the rearmament of Germany, which was of much greater geopolitical importance to the Kremlin than Indochina. The British also wanted to reduce tensions and the threat of world war, one which would have placed Britain – more than the United States – in the nuclear line of fire of the Soviet Union. **Winston Churchill** even hoped that the Geneva Conference could prepare the ground for a great power summit to create a "new treaty of Locarno".

The DRV, at war with the French over Indochina since 1945–1946, was represented by **Pham Van Dong**. Despite their military victory at **Dien Bien Phu** on 7 May, Vietnamese communists agreed to concentrate their efforts now on the diplomatic front, in concert with the Soviets and the Chinese. Almost a decade of war had taken its toll on the Vietnamese people and army, and the DRV leaders knew it. The Vietnamese had won a major battle victory at Dien Bien Phu, but not necessarily the war. They also worried, like the Chinese, that the Americans would replace the French if an accord were not reached.

On 8 May, the day after Dien Bien Phu fell, the conference took up the question of Indochina. Unsurprisingly, the French and DRV adopted hard-line opening positions. With a green light from the Soviets to take the lead in solving this prickly Asian problem, Zhou Enlai immediately went to work bringing the two sides together in view of reaching an acceptable political solution. He started by getting both belligerents to sit down together in private on 17 May to discuss the issue of recovering wounded soldiers at Dien Bien Phu. On that same day, Soviet foreign minister **Viatcheslav Molotov** proposed the debut of negotiations on the armistice.

In a concession designed to advance negotiations, Zhou Enlai announced on 20 May that the situation in Laos and Cambodia was different than that of Vietnam. In short, the Chinese premier did not support the DRV's revolutionary associated states of Indochina and would eventually agree that DRV troops in western Indochina were as foreign as the French ones and would have to go. Not only did this respond to Western demands, but it was also part of Zhou's plan to win over Indian support and neutralize the region. Rolling back Vietnamese communist claims to Indochina allowed Zhou to show to his Indian counterpart that the communists were no longer trying to export communism beyond Vietnam's borders. The second concession was the communist agreement to partition Vietnam at the 13th, 14th, or **16th parallels**. On 10 June, working through the joint military commission, **Ta Quang Buu** informed his French counterparts that the DRV would be open to the idea of dividing Vietnam provisionally until general elections could be held to unify the country.

However, the negotiations hardly advanced beyond that. And when the conference on Korea broke down in mid-June, things looked equally bleak for Indochina, where an armistice had not even been reached. To head off a diplomatic impasse, on 16 June Zhou Enlai informed **Anthony Eden** that he would be able to get Pham Van Dong to agree to pull DRV troops out of Laos and Cambodia. This coincided with the fall of the Laniel government on 13 June and Laniel's replacement by **Pierre Mendès France**, determined, like Zhou Enlai, to reach a settlement. Not only did Mendès France up the ante by announcing that he would personally negotiate at Geneva and resign in one month's time if an agreement were not reached, but he also threatened to institute the draft and bring in the US in order to put added pressure on his communist counterparts to negotiate further. John Foster Dulles's hawkish comments about American action seemed to add credence to Mendès France's words. Bluff or not, this the Chinese, the Soviets, and the DRV did not want. The communist partners began preparing concessions to make sure a deal could be reached.

Outstanding issues included determining the line of partition for Vietnam and setting a date for general elections. Mendès France wanted to draw a line at the **17th parallel** to provide Laos with an outlet to the sea via route no. 9. He also wanted to avoid setting a precise timetable for the elections, hoping to buy time so that the State of Vietnam could regroup, consolidate, and compete with the DRV in the future national elections. The French were opposed to according regrouping zones to the **Pathet Lao** and **Khmer Issarak**. As for the DRV, its leadership was opposed to accepting the 17th parallel as the demarcation line, since it would surrender to the enemy vast territories the DRV had ruled since 1945, including those of **Inter-Zone V** for which Pham Van Dong had been responsible during a good part of the Indochina conflict.

On 23 June, Zhou Enlai informed Mendès France that the questions of elections and partition would have to be negotiated one way or another to reach an agreement. He then left the conference to consult his government, regional neighbors, and the DRV. In Asia, Zhou Enlai stopped over in New Delhi, where he reassured Nehru of communist China's peaceful intentions in exchange for the implicit neutrality of non-communist Asia. Zhou Enlai informed Nehru that the kingdoms of Laos and Cambodia would be neutral, part of what he and Nehru called "Southeast Nations of a New Type", that is "non-aligned", non-communist postcolonial Asian states. Zhou then made his way to the southern Chinese city of **Liuzhou**, where he held a crucial meeting with **Ho Chi Minh**, **Vo Nguyen Giap,** and **Hoang Van Hoan** on the final negotiating strategy to be adopted at Geneva to reach a final agreement. Between 3 and 5 July 1954, Zhou argued to Ho that direct American intervention was possible, even likely, in the event that the Geneva talks failed. Such a scenario, the Chinese statesman stressed, would greatly complicate the DRV's battle, not to mention China's own security. Ho concurred and both sides agreed to coordinate their policies so as to reach an agreement with Mendès France, their best last chance. It was agreed that the 16th parallel could serve as the temporary dividing line for Vietnam; a non-communist political solution was accepted for Cambodia; the Chinese and Vietnamese would negotiate strongly to acquire concentration zones for the Pathet Lao in Samneua and Phongsaly provinces in Laos. Upon his return home, Ho Chi Minh argued successfully to the **Vietnam Worker's Party** that all these concessions, including the division of Vietnam at the 16th parallel, were vital to obtaining an accord and preventing the Americans from intervening directly as they had in Korea in 1950. Vietnamese communists also backed away from their right to speak for all of Indochina. As Zhou reported to the Chinese government in August 1954 on the Liuzhou meeting, Ho Chi Minh "expressed the opinion that the five principles [of co-existence] were completely applicable to the consolidation and development of friendly relations among Vietnam, Laos and Cambodia".

Meanwhile, Anthony Eden had traveled to Washington between 25 and 28 June, during which time he agreed to the American project to create a Southeast Asian Treaty of Defense, the future **South East Asia Treaty Organization** (SEATO). The signatories of this treaty would guarantee the final solution reached at the Geneva Conference. However, in the event that an armistice were violated, the signatories could respond militarily, even individually if the coalition was not of the same mind. While Eden had hoped to turn the Southeast Asian idea into something of an Asian Locarno agreement covering the security of both communist and anti-communist states in the region, Dulles and Republicans in the United States refused. The future SEATO was open to neutral states like India, but not to communist ones. SEATO, for Dulles, was at least to some extent a response to Zhou's attempts to neutralize non-communist Asia against the Americans, thus explaining Dulles's anger at **India, Burma**, and **Indonesia**'s neutral tack. One cannot grasp the historical significance of Geneva without placing it within this wider global dimension.

Back in Geneva, Zhou, Eden, Molotov, and Mendès France accelerated their efforts to reach an agreement before Mendès France had to face his rapidly approaching 20 July deadline. Under intense pressure, the DRV finally agreed to pull its troops out of Laos and Cambodia and, far from its initial proposition, accepted the partition of Vietnam at the 17th parallel, with the DRV taking charge of the territory north of that line and **French Union** forces the south. DRV troops and personnel in Cambodia, Laos and southern Vietnam would be regrouped to northern Vietnam, whereas those of the Associated State of Vietnam and French Union forces would regroup to the south. Khmer Issarak forces laid down their arms and were reintegrated into the royalist forces or returned to civilian life. In Laos, two regrouping zones were created for the Pathet Lao in Phongsaly and Samneau provinces.

The Conference approved the creation of the **International Commission for Supervision and Control** (usually referred to as the ICC) for Vietnam, Laos, and Cambodia. Its leadership reflected the **Cold War** of the time: Poland, Canada, and India. The ICC was designed to supervise the armistice, the regrouping of cadres and soldiers, and help organize the general elections. On this point, elections were scheduled to be held in mid-1956 in all of Vietnam in order to decide under which Vietnam, the DRV or the emerging **Republic of Vietnam** (until October 1955 the State of Vietnam), the country would be unified (technically both states claimed territorial legitimacy over all of Vietnam). In the early hours of 21 July 1954, the French and the DRV initialized the armistice ending the fighting in Vietnam, followed by separate agreements for Laos and Cambodia. The first Indochina war had come to an end.

The Agreement on the Cessation of Hostilities consisted of six chapters, 47 articles, and an annex. The Geneva cessation agreement was signed on July 21 by General **Henri Delteil** for the French Union forces and Vice Defense Minister Ta Quang Buu for the DRV. The agreement came into force on 22 July 1954. On 21 July, a "final declaration" consisting of 13 articles was issued that "noted the accords that put an end to hostilities in Cambodia, Laos, and Vietnam and that organized the international control and surveillance of the disposition of these accords". Among other things, the articles called for elections to be held in July 1955 in Laos and Cambodia and in July 1956 in Vietnam in order to create governments of national unity. Article 4 ruled out the entry of foreign troops, personnel, and arms into Vietnam, while Article 5 ruled out the establishment of foreign military bases there. Article 6 repeated that the 17th parallel was only provisional in nature. In no way was it to constitute a political or territorial border.

The State of Vietnam, led by **Bao Dai** and **Ngo Dinh Diem**, was adamantly opposed to the partition and the obligation to hold elections in 1956. On 21 July 1954, the delegate of the State of Vietnam deposed a formal declaration protesting against the French decision to agree to the holding of elections in 1956 and insisted that the **United Nations** implement the armistice. The State of Vietnam also indicated that it "reserved its full freedom of action in order to safeguard the sacred right of the Vietnamese people to territorial unity, national independence, and liberty". The Americans also issued a separate declaration in which they took note of the accords and recognized Articles 1 to 12. Significantly, Dulles's diplomat at Geneva, **Walter Bedell Smith** – who was sent to Geneva in the hope of prodding the French to move on the EDC – abstained from taking note of Article 13 of the declaration, which held that Washington should participate in follow-up consultations to ensure the application of the agreements. Moreover, he stated that concerning Article 7, the United States, like the State of Vietnam, only approved of the holding of elections under United Nations control, not under that of the ICC. As Laurent Césari has noted, the American refusal to recognize Article 13 made it clear that the Americans were as hostile to holding elections as the State of Vietnam.

While the conference members at the time referred to the 13 articles of the "final declaration" as the "accords", technically speaking there were no legally binding "accords" other than the three armistices or ceasefires signed on 21 July. In their haste to reach an agreement, the architects of the Geneva accords produced a flawed peace. The ICC had little if any power for implementing much less enforcing the declaration's articles on the ground. The communist bloc, including the DRV, had bet on elections and a political solution, but nothing legally bound the State of Vietnam to participate. The Americans now were determined to build up a truly postcolonial, non-communist Vietnam under the leadership of Ngo Dinh Diem. To back up this nation-building project at the international level, in September 1954 Dulles succeeded in creating SEATO and extending its protection to the three former states of French Indochina. *See also* GENEVA ACCORDS, CAMBODIA; GENEVA ACCORDS, LAOS; NEUTRALIZATION OF INDOCHINA.

**GENEVA ACCORDS, CAMBODIA (1954).** The Cambodian delegate to the **Geneva Conference**,

General **Nhiek Tioulong**, almost derailed the signing of an accord when he insisted on the right of his country to maintain foreign military relations if it so desired. In a last-minute compromise, Article 7 contained a Cambodian declaration ruling out foreign military alliances or bases. Determined to reach an agreement, the communist side went ahead and signed an armistice agreement for Vietnam in the early hours of 21 July 1954. Nhiek Tioulong signed a cease-fire agreement with **Ta Quang Buu** later in the afternoon. Two days later, on 23 July, in accordance with the Agreement on the cessation of hostilities, a cease-fire came into effect in Cambodia at 8H00 Beijing time. This agreement required the French to pull out all union forces and the **Democratic Republic of Vietnam** (DRV) to withdraw its armed units. In addition, **Khmer Issarak** and Cambodian communist allies of the DRV had to withdraw to northern Vietnam or lay down their arms in favor of those of the Associated State of Cambodia's army. The military clauses of the Geneva accords on Cambodia were largely completed by the end of 1954. Between 12 and 18 October, some 2,400 DRV troops and 1,000 Khmer Issarak withdrew to northern Vietnam thanks to the help of the **International Commission for Supervision and Control**. *See also* NEUTRALIZATION OF INDOCHINA.

**GENEVA ACCORDS, LAOS (1954).** The Agreement on the Cessation of Hostilities in Laos was signed on 22 July 1954 by **Ta Quang Buu** for the **Democratic Republic of Vietnam** (DRV) and French General **Henri Delteil.** This agreement required the French and the DRV to withdraw their forces and honor the cease-fire. The accords on Laos excluded all foreign bases in Laos except the French base at Séno and prohibited the introduction of foreign military personel into Laos, the sole exception being the maintenance of a French military training mission limited to 1,500 men. Unlike the situation in Cambodia, pressure from the Vietnamese and the Chinese succeeded in gaining provisional regrouping zones for the DRV's Lao allies, the **Pathet Lao**. According to Article 14, Pathet Lao forces were allowed to be "concentrated in the provisional assembly areas" in the provinces of Phongsaly and Samneua "pending a political settlement". Most **French Union** and DRV forces were evacuated from Laos by mid-November 1954, although the **International Commission for Supervision and Control** complained that the lack of cooperation from both sides made it hard for them to supervise the withdrawal. The exact political status of the two regrouping provinces "pending a political settlement" was left unclear in the accords and this proved to be a major point of contention among the Lao, regional, and international actors as civil and Cold wars broke out in Laos over the next few years. Did the two territories fall under the national territorial sovereignty of the Royal Lao Government? Or were they to be administered by the Pathet Lao as some sort of sub sovereign entity until a political settlement could be reached? The Royal Lao Government was convinced of its right to integrate the provinces into the national body whereas the Pathet Lao, backed by the DRV, eventually rejected this interpretation. *See also* ADVISORY GROUP 100; CHU HUY MAN; NGUYEN KHANG; NEUTRALIZATION OF INDOCHINA.

**GENEVA CONFERENCE.** *See* GENEVA ACCORDS.

**GENTIL, PIERRE ARISTIDE MARIE GASTON (1919–2002).** French colonial administrator who served in a variety of posts in Laos between 1946 and 1948. Between 1948 and 1949, he was head of the Civil Affairs Cabinet of the commissioner for the Republic to Laos and provincial advisor for Tranninh and Luang Prabang. He published a novel on his experiences in Laos, entitled *Remous du Mékong* (1950).

**GEYRE, GEORGES (1925–).** He served in Indochina between 1949 and 1952 as chief secretary to the diplomatic counselor of the French High Commission in Indochina, and the private secretary to the commissioner for the French Republic for Laos and chief deputy in the high commissioner's Information Service. Between 1952 and 1955, he was head of the Political Affairs Section of the high commissioner for Indochina and head of the French Information Service in Cambodia.

**GIAO GIẲNG.** *See* VŨ HỒNG KHANH.

**GILLES, JEAN MARCELLIN JOSEPH CALIXTE ("LE CYCLOPE", 1904–1961).** One of the Indochina War's legendary French officers, Gilles was a massively built man. His heavy accent gave away his native Catalan origins. Graduated from Saint-Cyr and made a captain in 1939, he first served in the General Staff of the 7th Colonial

Infantry Division. During the interwar period, he commanded troops in colonial Vietnam between 1928 and 1929 at the head of the *51ème Régiment de tirailleurs indochinois*. He joined fighting French Forces following the Allied liberation of North Africa in November 1942 and participated in the campaigns to liberate France and Germany. He was assigned to Indochina between October 1945 and January 1947, taking part in the French reoccupation of **Cochinchina** and the city of **Haiphong**. He was a very meticulous, organizational type of officer. It was said that he never advanced unless he was sure of the ground before him. He headed up the 3rd Bureau for General **Philippe Leclerc** as deputy chief of operations. In 1946, he was named colonel. In 1947, he left Indochina, but returned in November 1951 to work in the operations bureau during the battles of **Hoa Binh**, **Na San**, and **Dien Bien Phu** among others. Never to be outdone, he obtained his paratrooper certificate at the age of 44 and in 1953 he became brigadier general. He parachuted into Dien Bien Phu on 20 November 1953 in order to take command of the camp and begin preparations for the famous battle against the **Democratic Republic of Vietnam**. However, he advised his superiors of the vulnerability of the camp to enemy artillery attacks before transferring to another position. In June 1954, he led airborne troops in Indochina before taking command in early August of the *25ème Division d'infanterie aéroportée*. In November 1954, he was sent to Algeria to help repress the nationalist uprising there and rejoined one of his closest collaborators from Indochina, General **Raoul Salan**. *See also* ALGERIAN WAR.

**GIMBERT, ROBERT (1919–1982).** In 1945, he served as a French delegate for the province of Cholon and ran the **Poulo Condor** penitentiary in 1946. Between 1948 and 1951, he served in various administrative posts in northern Vietnam.

**GMD.** *See* REPUBLIC OF CHINA.

**GODARD, YVES (1911–1975).** French officer involved in developing special operations during the Indochina War. Graduated from Saint-Cyr in 1932, Godard fought with the Polish army when war broke out in Europe in 1939. On his return to France, he fought on the Maginot Line until the Germans captured him. He escaped his captors and joined the *Forces françaises de l'intérieur*. In the resistance, he formed special **commando** and assault troops to carry out special operations behind enemy lines. Following the war, he was promoted to battalion leader and in May 1948 took command of the *11ème Battaillon de parachutistes de choc* or the famous *11ème Choc*. His task was to reorganize the battalion to make it an elite special forces unit. He did and several such units were shipped off to Indochina. In 1952, he asked to transfer to Indochina. In the spring of 1954, he commanded a special force unit called "*Crèvecoeur*", designed to evacuate French forces escaping from the Vietnamese siege of **Dien Bien Phu**. After the signature of the **Geneva Accords**, Godard served as chief of staff to General **Jacques Massu** during the Suez Crisis in 1956 and joined many of his former officer comrades in the **Algerian War**, participating in the *Organisation armée secrète* and the officer's Putsch against the French government itself. He died in exile in Belgium in 1975.

**GOLD WEEK.** Between 17 and 24 September 1945, the leaders of the provisional government of the **Democratic Republic of Vietnam** (DRV) organized a "gold week" (*tuan le vang*). **Ho Chi Minh** called on the population, and especially the middle class and the rich, to make contributions to help finance the newly created state and its defense forces. The DRV was badly in need of funds, given the outbreak of war in the south on 23 September, the high costs incurred by the Chinese occupation, the failure of the government to take over the **Bank of Indochina**, and popular pressure against the continuation of colonial taxes. According to Vietnamese statistics, the government collected 370 kg of gold and 20 million Indochinese piastres. *See also* CURRENCY, DEMOCRATIC REPUBLIC OF VIETNAM; FINANCIAL COST OF INDOCHINA WAR.

**GONÇALVÈS-CAMINHA, PEDRO MARIO (1919–).** Member of the *Comité interministériel de l'Indochine* or the **COMININDO** in 1945. He joined **Georges Thierry d'Argenlieu**'s cabinet in the High Commissioner's Office in Indochina in 1946. Between 1947 and 1949, he was deputy then head of cabinet for the commissioner for the French Republic in **Tonkin**.

**GONZALEZ DE LINARÈS, FRANÇOIS JEAN ANTONIN MARIE AMÉDÉE (1897–1955).** Graduated from Saint-Cyr in 1914, de Linarès fought on the Western Front during all of World

War I. He was wounded on several occasions. During the interwar period, he taught at Saint-Cyr and served in the colonial army in North Africa. He served Vichy until the Allied liberation of North Africa, when he joined Free French forces, served in the French military mission to London and took part in the Italian Campaign. He became brigadier general in 1944. In January 1951, General **Jean de Lattre de Tassigny** asked him to come to Indochina to replace General **Pierre-Georges Boyer de la Tour** as commissioner for the Republic in North Vietnam and in charge of French Forces in North Vietnam and the *Zone opérationnelle du **Tonkin***. De Linarès assumed his functions in January–February 1951. Between July and September 1952, during the absence of General **Raoul Salan**, he served as acting commander-in-chief of all French ground, air and naval forces in Indochina. De Linarès oversaw the evacuation of troops during the battle of **Hoa Binh** in 1952. In May 1953, he relinquished his command of ground troops in northern Vietnam. In June, he returned to France and passed away due to illness in 1955.

**GORCE, PIERRE MARIE MARTIAL (1917–).** In 1946–1947, he served as chief of cabinet to the federal commissioner for Political Affairs in the high commissioner's office. Between 1947 and 1948, he was chief of cabinet to the commissioner for the French Republic to Cambodia. In 1948, Gorce returned to work as cabinet chief for the high commissioner until 1950. Between 1951 and 1961, he served in Cambodia as an advisor to the high commissioner there in 1953, then as high commissioner to Cambodia himself between 1954 and 1955. He stayed on as ambassador to Cambodia between 1956 and 1961. From 1986, he served as vice president of the *Association des anciens et amis de l'Indochine*.

**GOUROU, PIERRE (1900–1999).** French geographer during the colonial period and supporter of the French **Indochinese Federation** during the Indochina War. Gourou was born in the Empire, grew up in it, and worked in it throughout its decolonization. Although he was born in Tunisia, he was always fascinated by the Far East and the linkage between their dense populations and the development of their civilizations. He completed his undergraduate studies in Lyon in 1923, successfully obtained the *aggrégation* in history and geography and landed a position in 1926 teaching at the *Lycée Albert Sarraut* in **Hanoi**. Gourou's research focused on the northern delta, its population, and historical geography. In 1936, the ***École française d'Extrême-Orient*** published his state thesis, *Les paysans du Delta tonkinois, étude de Géographie humaine*. In 1940, he published *L'utilisation du sol en Indochine française*. Like **Paul Mus,** Gourou was largely oblivious to the historical significance of the developing nationalism in the colonies in the 1930s. He wrote favourably of the positive contributions of French colonialism, ignoring peasant revolts in central Vietnam and nationalist ones in the north in 1930–1931. He worked as a technical advisor to the colonial state, involving himself in the government's efforts to develop the deltas of the Red River and the Mekong. He returned to Europe in 1936. Although he was mobilized for war in 1939, the French defeat in 1940 returned him to civil life at the *Faculté des lettres de Bordeaux*. At the end of World War II, he was vice president of the Liberation Committee for Gironde. In December 1944, he travelled to the United States to participate in meetings on Asia and its future. In 1947, he was named Professor to the *Collège de France*, holding the chair *Étude du monde tropical*. Like his colleague at the same institution, Paul Mus, Gourou also worked as an advisor to the French government as it moved to retake the Indochinese colony it had lost to the Japanese and also advised the **Democratic Republic of Vietnam** (DRV) in 1945. In April 1946, the government named Gourou to the French delegation that held talks with the DRV during the first **Dalat Conference**. In June 1947, as war raged between the French and the Vietnamese, Gourou published an essay in favor of the French government's **Indochinese Federation**, entitled *L'avenir de l'Indochine***.** A condensed English-language version of this essay appeared in *Pacific Affairs*. Unlike Mus, however, Gourou remained largely silent on the Indochina War. Although he ended up working for the government, he was happiest with his research and particularly his work on the tropics. *See also* ANTICOLONIALISM; *ESPRIT; TEMOIGNAGE CHRETIEN*.

**GRACEY, DOUGLAS DAVID (SIR) (1894–1964).** Commander-in-chief of Allied Land Forces French Indo-China 1945–1946. Born in Gorakhpur, **India**, and the son of a British civil servant there, Gracey attended Sandhurst and joined the British Indian Army in 1914. He served in World

War I in the 1st Battalion of the 1st King George's Own Gurkha Rifles, and he accompanied them to **Saigon** in 1945 as World War II ended in Asia. Between 1942 and 1946, Gracey served as general officer commanding the 20th Indian Division. In September 1945, in accordance with agreements reached at the **Potsdam conference**, Gracey led 20,000 troops of his 20th Division to accept the Japanese surrender below the **16th parallel** in former French Indochina, while Chinese nationalist troops occupied northern Indochina above that line. He arrived in Saigon on 13 September 1945. His mission was to disarm all Japanese forces in lower Indochina, maintain law and order, and locate and evacuate Allied **prisoners of war**. He was faced with a volatile situation in Saigon. Tensions were rising between the Vietnamese and the French as to who would control southern Vietnam. On 22 September 1945, Gracey agreed to allow French authorities led by French Colonel **Jean Cédile** to unlock troops imprisoned by the Japanese during the ***coup de force* of 9 March 1945** and use them to take control of Saigon and outlying areas. In the early hours of 23 September, French forces moved to dislodge the Vietnamese in a *coup de force*. Fighting was intense, forcing Gracey to use Japanese troops to restore order in addition to his Indian ones. On 9 October 1945, the British officially recognized the French as the sole civil administration in Indochina below the 16th parallel. On 28 January 1946, Gracey left Saigon. Nonetheless, the outbreak of violence on **23 September 1945** marked the beginning of armed hostilities in Vietnam between the French and nationalist groups allied with the **Democratic Republic of Vietnam**. It occurred while Gracey was on watch, although full-scale war would not engulf all of Vietnam until **19 December 1946**, some six months after the Chinese withdrawal from northern Indochina.

**GRACIEUX, JEAN (1908–1974).** Graduated from Saint-Cyr in 1929, he pursued his military career during the interwar period in colonial Africa. Gracieux fought with Free French forces in Algiers and took part in the landing in southern France in 1944. Named lieutenant colonel in 1945, he served as deputy director of Colonial Troops. In 1948, he arrived in Indochina, where he was named deputy head of the chief of staff for operations within the General Staff of the **Expeditionary Corps** for the Far East. From late 1950 to May 1953, he was 1st deputy chief of staff, in charge of operations at the Combined General Staff and Ground Forces in Indochina under General **Jacques Allard**. He would take part in the airborne operation in Suez in 1956.

**GRALL, EDMOND.** Commanded the ***Groupement des commandos mixtes aéroportés*** from its creation in 1951 until his repatriation to France in May 1953. Little else is known about this special forces specialist.

**GRAS, YVES (1921–).** Renowned French military historian of the Indochina War, Yves Gras served with Free French forces during World War II and during France's two wars of decolonization in Indochina and Algeria. He served in Indochina as a young officer between 1950 and 1953. He is best known for his pathbreaking military history of the Indochina war, *Histoire de la guerre d'Indochine* (1979). It remains to date the single best military history of the conflict. *See also* BERNARD FALL; PHILIPPE DEVILLERS.

**GRAUWIN, PAUL, M.D.** Legendary French doctor who operated on the wounded throughout the battle of **Dien Bien Phu**. He had served as a reserve officer in Indochina since the outset of the war. This baldless doctor, as **Bernard Fall** memorialized him, "looked like a roman emperor with rimless glasses". Grauwin ran the French mobile surgical detachment 29, which possessed enough personnel to run a small field hospital and to execute the main functions of a surgery room. He tried to run just such an operation during the battle of Dien Bien Phu, but was overwhelmed by the large number of casualties and the lack of supplies from the outside when the enemy knocked out the airstrip. Working day and night, Grauwin performed surgery until the day the Vietnamese victors walked into his makeshift surgery room. As a ranking enemy medical officer told him that day, "we have seen, as we passed through, your bunkers crammed with wounded. We recognized that odor. We understand what you must have gone through, but there is nothing we could do about it. That's all I can tell you". Grauwin was struck by the humanity of this man, but less so by the political cadres who set this French doctor on a gruelling POW trek across the insalubrious terrain of northern Vietnam before deciding to send him back home a few weeks later. Grauwin stayed on in Asia to run a private hospital in Phnom Penh after the war. *See also* DISEASE; DO XUAN

HOP; EXPERIENCE OF WAR; EXPERIENCE OF BATTLE, DIEN BIEN PHU; HO DAC DI; PRISONER OF WAR; TON THAT TUNG.

**GREATER VIETNAM NATIONALIST PARTY (*Đại Việt Quốc Dân* OR *Đại Việt*).** This nationalist party was made up of a number of earlier non-communist splinter groups that emerged after the French repression of the **Vietnamese Nationalist Party** (*Viet Nam Quoc Dan Dang*, VNQDD) in 1930. The most famous of them, the Greater Vietnamese Nationalist Party (*Dai Viet Quoc Dan Dang* or DVQDD), better known as *Dai Viet* from the late 1940s, was created by a nationalist-minded student named **Truong Tu Anh**. This party came into the open in early 1939, complete with a political program. The second, called the Greater Vietnamese National-Socialist Party (*Dai Viet Quoc Xa*) came to life in 1936, but would not be active until after the Japanese ***coup de force* of 9 March 1945**. The third, the Greater Vietnamese Humanist Party (*Dai Viet Duy Dan*), was created in 1937 by Ly Dong A before he took refuge in China. Lastly, the Greater Vietnamese Authentic People's Party (*Dai Viet Dan Chinh*) was created in 1938 under the leadership of the famous northern **intellectual**, **Nguyen Tuong Tam**, better known by his *nom de plume,* Nhat Linh.

Following the Japanese overthrow of the French in March 1945, *Dai Viet* groups supported the Japanese-backed Vietnamese government led by **Tran Trong Kim**. With the defeat of the Japanese and the advent of the **Democratic Republic of Vietnam** (DRV), *Dai Viet* members joined forces with non-communist nationalists returning from decades of exile in China with occupying Chinese republican troops, above all the Vietnamese Nationalist Party. A rejuvenated *Dai Viet* party emerged in late 1945 under the leadership of Truong Tu Anh and joined forces with the VNQDD. This *Dai Viet*-VNQDD alliance was fiercely anti-colonialist and anti-communist, based mainly in central and northern Vietnam. It came under combined DRV and French fire in mid-1946 for its opposition to both the Vietnamese communists and French colonialists. Truong Tu Anh disappeared in **Hanoi** on the day full-scale war broke out in Vietnam on **19 December 1946**. The circumstances surrounding his death remain unclear.

Despite their **anti-colonialism**, most *Dai Viet* members remained in French controlled zones after the outbreak of war and hoped to use anti-communism and ***attentisme*** to pressure the French to support their non-communist nationalist project against the communist-led DRV, especially with the arrival of the **Cold War**. The French deeply disappointed them on both counts. By refusing to grant full-scale independence to Vietnam, the French undermined the nationalist credentials of what was already a very faction-plagued socio-political movement. *Dai Viet* leaders supported the **Bao Dai Solution** and occupied important cabinet and provincial positions in the Associated State of Vietnam. Yet prominent nationalist leaders, such as **Phan Huy Quat**, continued to criticize the French for their failure to decolonize fully the Associated State in the face of the communist threat and the DRV's nationalist pull. *See also* ASSOCIATED STATES OF INDOCHINA; CIVIL WAR; COLLABORATION; NGO DINH DIEM; POULO CONDOR.

**GREENE, GRAHAM (1904–1991).** British war correspondent and author of the famous **novel** on the Indochina War, *The Quiet American*. Graduated from Oxford University, Greene pursued his career in journalism at *The Times* and the *Spectator* until World War II broke out. In 1941, he joined the British Intelligence Service serving in Africa and Europe. He left intelligence in 1944 and returned to writing. In the 1950s, he traveled widely in British Malaya and French Indochina as a correspondent for *Life* and *The New Republic*. **Saigon** at war in the early 1950s provided him with the setting for his bestselling novel, *A Quiet American* (1956). Greene knew Indochina particularly well. Not only did he travel there often, but he met with ranking French military and civilian authorities, including General **Raoul Salan**. In 1951, the director of the French Security Service for Indochina and General **Jean de Lattre de Tassigny** asked Greene to leave Indochina on the grounds that he was still working for the British Intelligence Service. Salan, however, authorized Greene to remain and allowed him to travel widely in southern Vietnam. Salan was clearly fond of Greene and his take on the war, as the French general revealed in his memoirs written years later. *See also* CINEMA; CULTURE.

**GRIFFIN MISSION.** *See* ROBERT ALLEN GRIFFIN.

**GRIFFIN, ROBERT ALLEN (1893–1981).** Led the U.S. Economic Cooperation Administration mission to Southeast Asia in 1950 to determine the size, type, and best ways of providing increased aid to Southeast Asian countries to support democracy in the region and thereby thwart communist expansion. The Griffin mission arrived in Indochina on 23 February 1950 in the wake of American diplomatic recognitation of the Associated State of Vietnam and as ships of the Seventh Fleet were paying a courtesy call to **Saigon** at the behest of the State Department and the French. American strategists considered Southeast Asia to constitute an important geopolitical and economic linchpin in the containment of global communism. With Moscow and Beijing now behind the Democratic Republic of Vietnam, supporting the French and the Associated States took on added importance. On his return from Southeast Asia, Griffin urged the government to provide large-scale aid to Indochina. He added that such American backing would convince non-communist Vietnamese nationalists sitting on the fence to support the **Bao Dai Solution**. Griffin also warned that if the United States did not aid the French, then they might well cut their losses and pull out of Indochina completely. *See also* AID, AMERICAN; *ATTENTISME*.

**GROUP 100.** *See* ADVISORY GROUP 100.

***GROUPEMENT DE COMMANDOS MIXTES AÉROPORTÉS* (GCMA).** The history of this highly secret **commando** unit is complicated and its importance remains controversial. The conceptual origins of the GCMA are to be found in World War II, in Allied commando operations run against German and Japanese occupied territories. The main idea was to send commando teams behind enemy lines to work with local partisans in gathering intelligence on the enemy, winning over popular support, and organizing and executing commando operations to harass the enemy (sabotage, assassinations, etc) or to rally the *maquis* to the Allied cause during a major military offensive (similar to the Jedburgh commandos working in occupied France during the Normandy landing in 1944). Many of those recruited to operate the GCMA had worked behind Japanese lines in Laos in early 1945, men such as **Jean Sassi**. However, between 1945 and 1950, most commanding French officers in Indochina had little interest in and often disdained such clandestine operations. Paradoxically, the push for creating the GCMA came from the Americans as the **Cold War** spread to Asia with the Chinese communist victory in October 1949 and the outbreak of the **Korean War** in June 1950. The Americans hoped to draw upon earlier commando experiences in Europe and Asia to create a ***Service Action*** in Indochina to work in tandem with the French and with similar teams in Korea to help contain Sino-Soviet communist expansion at the global level. Like the Jedburghs operating in German-occupied Europe during World War II, commando forces in Asia would operate behind enemy lines among minority ethnic groups in the highlands of Indochina to harass Vietnamese and Chinese communists. In early or mid-1950, the Central Intelligence Agency (CIA) dispatched officers to Indochina led by Colonel Chester to meet with the high commissioner for Indochina, **Léon Pignon**, about the need to create just such a clandestine service. Drawing upon earlier experiences, the Americans were convinced that such a *Service Action* could work effectively among the upland ethnic minorities populating much of the highlands of upper Indochina and southern China. The CIA's Thibault de Saint Phall further discussed such plans with the French and **Bao Dai** before taking up the question directly with the CIA's natural counterpart in Paris and Indochina, the ***Service de documentation extérieure et de contre espionage*** (SDECE). The Americans eventually proposed that a commando school should be located in Vung Tau. Funded by the Americans, this school would be in charge of training ethnic minority commandos to operate behind **Viet Minh** lines in northern and central Vietnam. The head of SDECE, **Maurice Belleux**, objected to letting the Americans operate such a highly sensitive operation on their own. The newly arrived commander-in-chief and high commissioner for Indochina, General **Jean de Lattre de Tassigny,** shared this opinion and braked the CIA's ambitions. Nevertheless, the French recognized the importance of expanding cooperation with the CIA on this matter in light of the globalization of the Cold War into Asia and its relevance to their war in Indochina. And there was always the growing **financial cost of the war**. Between 1951 and 1952, the French reached agreements with the Americans by which the CIA and the SDECE established formal cooperation, including the development of a *Service Action* in Indochina to work with the American equivalent in Korea. The American overtures had effectively forced the French to create their own *Service Action* (SA). As a result, SDECE headquarters assigned officers from its metropolitan SA and the ***Direction générale de documentation*** (DGD) to compile dossiers on the **Democratic Republic of Vietnam** (DRV), the ethnic minorities, and areas where such operations could be developed. A commando school in Dalat began recruiting and training Hmong, Moi, and other ethnic minority soldiers who would serve as the vital guides and conduits to French officers sent to work behind lines. The Americans helped finance the French SA in Indochina. In exchange for this support, de Lattre allowed a special American liaison team headed by Helwin Hall to remain in Indochina, working in collaboration with the SDECE, on this project. On 7 April 1951, de Lattre officially approved the creation of a SA for Indochina, which came to life three days later and was jointly run by the SDECE-DGD. Given the sensitive nature of this project, in 1952 it was decided to create a camouflage unit to house the *Service Action*; it would be attached to a mixed paratrooper unit. The name chosen was: *Groupement de commandos mixtes aéroportés* (GCMA) and placed under the command of **Edmond Grall**. It was an organizational part of the SDECE/Indochina, known internally as Section 49. The GCMA was designed to build up French **guerrilla** activity behind enemy lines and develop a *maquis* among upland peoples, who, with Franco-American support, would harass the enemy and work in coordination with the French army to hinder enemy movements in the strategically important highlands, especially in the Hmong and Tai areas of northwestern Vietnam (near southern China). In January 1952, **Roger Trinquier** began running a *maquis* there to create a permanent state of insecurity in DRV territory. He commanded the GCMA from mid-1953 (when it was renamed *Groupement mixte d'intervention* or GMI). Upon taking command of the armed forces in Indochina, General **Henri Navarre** supported the GCMA/GMI, instructing it to "create, maintain, and generalize the indigenous resistance by exploiting methodically minority tendencies of a religious, ethnic and political nature". However, in the end, the military and political effectiveness of the GCMA was limited. While Trinquier may have garnered thousands of Hmong supporters by 1954, his *maquis* could do little if anything to stop the DRV's army from marching on **Dien Bien Phu** or blocking their logistics and supply lines. Following the signing of the **Geneva Accords**, the French would leave behind thousands of their ethnic minority allies and their families to the mercy of the DRV. On 20 July 1954, hours before the signing of the Geneva Accords, it was decided that the GCMA/GMI would cease all activities in the *maquis* (*la mise en sommeil des maquis*). As of 31 August, the GCMA, the Service Action created by SDECE, and pushed by the CIA, formally ceased to exist.[6] The Americans would resurrect this project in another form during the Vietnam War. However, it got its start during the Indochina War in the context of the globalization of the Cold War, if not during World War II. *See also* CHINESE MILITARY INTERVENTION, FRENCH ALLEGATION OF; OFFICE OF STRATEGIC SERVICES; *PAYS MONTAGNARDS DU SUD* (PMS); TAI FEDERATION.

***GROUPEMENT DES CONTRÔLES RADIO-ÉLECTRIQUES*** **(GCR).** Part of the General Commissariat for Indochina, the Groupement des contrôles radio-électriques was probably the most important military network of mobile listening stations located throughout Indochina, operating 24 hours a day, 7 days a week, year round. The GCR first got its start in the metropole on 15 March 1945, taking over Vichy's infrastructure. It was directly subordinate to the *président du conseil*. The Japanese occupation and their overthrow of the French greatly weakend French listening posts. On 26 January 1946, the High Commissioner **Georges Thierry d'Argenlieu** created a provisional service called the *Groupement d'écoutes radioélectriques de l'Indochine* (GERI). On 8 November 1946, it became the *Direction régionale du Groupement des controles radioélectriques* and was directly integrated and subordinated to the GCR based out of France. In Indochina, the GCR served (not without creating some tension) both the High Commissioner's office and the operational needs of the **Deuxième Bureau** for French Ground Forces in the Far East. The GCR network was in charge of intercepting **Democratic Republic of Vietnam** and Chinese radio communications, propaganda emissions, and international press traffic. According to **Armand Boussarie**, a ranking intelligence officer during the Indochina War and a specialist on the question, the GCR provided "extremely rich" signals intelligence during the conflict.

6. This entry is based on the original sources held in 10H266, Service historique de la défense, Vincennes, France.

***GROUPEMENTS ADMINISTRATIFS CHINOIS RÉGIONAUX***

**(G.A.C.R)/ADMINISTRATIVE CHINESE REGIONAL GROUPINGS.** Following negotiations with the **Republic of China**, in August 1948 the French agreed to rename the *congrégations* (*bangs*) they had used since the late 19th century to regroup and administer the five different Chinese groups living in Indochina under a new name: Administrative Chinese Regional Groupings (*Groupements administratifs chinois régionaux*). The French allowed Chinese consulates in Indochina to have a say in the election of local Chinese headmen to lead the five different groupings – Guangzhou (Canton), Fujian, Chaozhou, Hainan and the Hakka. As for the **Associated States of Indochina**, their national control over the Chinese populations living within their emerging national states remained limited. In 1951, the Associated State of Vietnam gained some increased control over the nomination of the Chinese headmen directing the regional groupings. However, real power remained in French colonial hands when it came to deciding prickly questions concerning Chinese immigration, expulsions, and legal jurisdiction. The divisive question of the "naturalization" or "Vietnamisation" of the **overseas Chinese** and the end of their separate legal status was put on hold until the French were forced to let go of Indochina in mid-1954. When **Ngo Dinh Diem** took charge of the Republic of Vietnam in 1955, he put an end to the congregations and required the oveseas Chinese to either become Vietnamese nationals or choose between one of the two Chinas, the **Peoples Republic of China** on the mainland or the **Republic of China** now based in Taiwan. The majority chose to become Vietnamese. The **Democratic Republic of Vietnam**, however, did not obligate Chinese to become Vietnamese, at least not at the outset. Internationalism, not nationalism, theoretically guided their notion of nationality, at least until relations soured between the two in the 1970s. *See also* MINORITY ETHNIC GROUPS; OVERSEAS VIETNAMESE IN FRANCE; OVERSEAS VIETNAMESE IN THAILAND.

***GROUPEMENTS AÉRIENS TACTIQUES* (GATAC).** Until 1950, the **guerrilla** nature of the Indochina War prevented the **Air Force** from undertaking major operations. The arrival of the **Cold War** in 1950, including large-scale Chinese and American **aid** to the belligerants, changed all this. Airpower was now needed to supply and support ground troops engaging the enemy across much of the Indochinese theatre. To this end, in 1950, the Aerial Tactical Commands for Indochina was created, consisting of three subcommands known as the *Groupement aériens tactiques* (GATAC): the GATAC North responsible for northern Vietnam and Laos, the GATAC South covering **Cochinchina**, Cambodia and southern central Vietnam, and GATAC Center in charge of operations in Central Vietnam and southern Laos. During the **Democratic Republic of Vietnam**'s invasions of Laos in 1953–1954, a GATAC Laos briefly came to life. GATAC North provided air support during the battles of **Hoa Binh**, **Na San,** and **Dien Bien Phu.** All of this increased the financial burden on the French and the Americans. *See also* FINANCIAL COST OF THE WAR.

**GUERRE RÉVOLUTIONNAIRE.** *See* REVOLUTIONARY WARFARE.

**GUERRILLA.** "Guerrilla" is the Spanish word meaning "small war". Guerrilla warfare was first practiced by small-armed Spanish groups resisting Napoléon Bonaparte's invasion and occupation of Spain in the early 19th century. Since then, the word has been used to refer to small-scale groups of combatants fighting an unconventional war on their territory or among a sympathetic population against a militarily stronger adversary. The term was further popularized and theorized during the wars of the 20th century. In 1937, at war against the invading Japanese army, Chinese communist leader **Mao Zedong** published his influential *On Guerrilla War*. He divided guerrilla war into three phases. The first phase required guerrillas to win over the support of the local population. Phase two called for increasing attacks against the enemy state's institutions and military forces. The last phase mixes guerrilla hit and run tactics with the use of conventional warfare in order to overthrow the enemy and take control of the country, including the cities. This work and many other Chinese and Maoist texts were imported, translated, and applied by the **Democratic Republic of Vietnam** (DRV) in its battle against the French during the Indochina War. From the late 1930s, Vietnamese communists had access to many of Mao's major works in Chinese and Vietnamese translation, including *On Guerrilla War* (1937) and *On Protracted War* (1938).

Like the Chinese, the Vietnamese focused on building up a wide nationalist front, mobilizing the populations under their control, and operating hit-run-operations to bog down the enemy. In 1947, **Truong Chinh** (*Long March*) identified three phases in **revolutionary warfare**. The first level was the guerrilla, the second was a combination of guerrilla and conventional forces, while the third phase set the main battle forces against the enemy in the General Counter Offensive. For General **Vo Nguyen Giap**, guerrilla warfare obligated the Vietnamese to avoid the enemy's forces when they were strong, attacking them when they were weak. The guerrilla army never attacked its foe directly, but rather harassed it, dispersed it, and tried to exhaust it. However, following the Chinese communist victory of 1949, both Generals **Nguyen Binh** in the south and Vo Nguyen Giap in the north overestimated their chances of winning the General Counter Offensive and were forced to resume guerrilla operations when they suffered serious setbacks at the hands of the **Expeditionary Corps** in the Red and Mekong river deltas.

The Chinese and the Vietnamese were not the only ones to practice guerrilla warfare, however. Many officers in the French army in Indochina had used such tactics during the French resistance against the German occupation of France during World War II. Based on this experience and confronted by the Sino-Vietnamese guerrilla model, some of them began to promote the idea of changing French military practices in favor of developing guerrilla ones in order to take the battle to the Vietnamese on their own terms. In August 1949, Colonel **Maurice Redon**, former ranking leader of the *Forces françaises de l'intérieur* in France and now in charge in southern Vietnam, sent a report to the army command in France arguing in favor of teaching a new type of warfare, that of guerrilla tactics, to young officers being sent to command troops in Indochina. General **Marcel Carpentier** agreed, asking that guerrilla tactics be used against the **Democratic Republic of Vietnam** in order to break its "fluidity" and force the adversary into the open so that the army could attack and destroy them more easily with conventional forces. In short, the French guerrilla experience from World War II and the growing desire to imitate their Vietnamese adversary in using such a strategy during the Indochina War laid the theoretical groundwork for the creation of ***Service Action*** groups and the ***Groupement de commandos mixtes aéroportés***. It also led French military science into a new type of "**revolutionary warfare**". The British and the Americans were also well acquainted with it from World War II and especially the **Korean War**. Counter-intersurgency was by no means a French invention, although the French became its leading specialists for much of the 1950s. *See also* ALGERIAN WAR; CHARLES LACHEROY; EDWARD LANSDALE; INDOCTRINATION; PARALLEL HIERARCHIES; PSYCHOLOGICAL WARFARE.

**GUILLAUME, PIERRE (1925–2002).** The real-life French **navy** captain and veteran of the Indochina War upon whom **Pierre Schoendorffer** based his cult film, ***Le crabe tambour.*** Graduated from the French Naval Academy in 1945, Guillaume chose to serve in Indochina where he was duly assigned to lead a River Flotilla. He served three tours of duty during the Indochina War, executing numerous **commando** operations. He then moved on to Algeria, where he wanted to replace his brother killed in combat. He led his own commando group. Implicated in the Army Putsch in Algeria in 1961, he spent almost eight years in a French prison. Amnestied in 1968, he left in his boat in search of new horizons, and memories of former ones, enshrouded in fog, the subject of *Le crabe tambour. See also* ALGERIAN WAR; MYTH OF WAR.

**GUILLERMAZ, JACQUES (1911–1998).** French intelligence officer and specialist of modern China who advised the French government on Asian affairs during the **Geneva Conference**. Graduated from Saint-Cyr in 1937, Guillermaz began his military career working as a deputy military attaché in the French embassy to the **Republic of China** based first in Beijing then in Chongqing with the outbreak of the Pacific War. He held this post until 1943, when he left for Algiers and took part in the liberation of France. At the end of World War II, he returned to China where he served as military attaché to the French Embassy to the Republic of China now based in Nanjing. During this time, he renewed and expanded his impressive contacts with Chinese nationalists and communists. In 1949, he witnessed the Chinese communist victory before being assigned to the French Embassy in Bangkok in 1950 where he worked as a military attaché and intelligence officer. During this time, he became an astute analyst of Southeast Asian affairs in general and of the Indochina War in particular. In 1954, he served as an advisor to the French delegation during the Geneva Conference. He played a pivotal, behind-the-scenes role in organizing and conducting negotiations with the Chinese, especially **Huang Hua** and **Wang Bingnan**, in a bid to reach an agreement in Geneva to end the war. Guillermaz was also a strong advocate of the need to develop French scholarship and understanding of modern China. To this end, in 1958, he founded the *Centre de recherches et de documentation sur la Chine contemporaine* and directed it between 1958 and 1975. He published some of the first French studies on modern China, including *La Chine populaire* (1959) and *Histoire du Parti communiste chinois: 1921–1949* (1968). His memoirs appeared in 1989, *Une vie pour la Chine: mémoires (1937–1989).*

**GUIRIEC, HYACINTHE ANTOINE JULES (1898–?).** Career colonial civil servant in Indochina. After seeing combat in World War I, Guiriec joined the colonial civil service in Indochina in 1924. During the interwar period, he served in a variety of administrative posts in Tonkin, as deputy then full *résident* at the provincial level. He was administrative mayor for **Hanoi** between October 1942 and October 1943, then inspector for Administrative Affairs for Tonkin until the Japanese ***coup de force* of 9 March 1945**. Between April 1947 and July 1948, he served as director of the General Administration of Indochina and advisor to the high commissioner of Indochina for Social Affairs, helping to devise a new labor code for Indochina. Between July 1948 and April 1950, he worked as the high commissioner's delegate to what became the Associated State of Vietnam. In September 1949, Guiriec presided over the 2nd meeting of the Commission for the Application of the 1949 Franco-Vietnamese agreements designed to create this Vietnamese state. *See also* ASSOCIATED STATES OF INDOCHINA.

**GULLION, EDMUND ASHBURY (1913–1998).** American consul general in **Saigon** during the second half of the Indochina War. Graduated from Princeton in 1935, he entered the foreign service in July 1937. He served in Marseilles, Salonika, London, and was on temporary assignment to Algiers in 1942 before returning to London. He returned to the State Department in 1945 and worked on special assignment for the under secretary until 1947. In December 1949, fluent in French, he became American consul to Saigon and consul general there in February 1950. In March of that year, he was also named counselor to Saigon, a diplomatic title in addition to his consular title. He was dean of the Fletcher School of Diplomacy at Tufts between 1964 and 1978. *See also* AID, AMERICAN.

**GUOMINDANG.** *See* REPUBLIC OF CHINA.

**H122 AFFAIR.** In March 1948, the **Democratic Republic of Vietnam**'s (DRV) Bureau of Intelligence in the Ministry of Defense obtained an enemy document entitled: "Report by the Agent Code-name H122". Not only did the French report focus on the DRV's own military plans for the upcoming autumn/winter offensive, but it was clear that the spy who provided this report had to be in the upper levels of the **Inter-Zone Viet Bac** (*Lien Khu Viet Bac*) military High Command. Arrests and interrogations multiplied as intelligence officers moved to flush out the agent. Within one month, "several hundred military cadres and officers at the regimental level were arrested and interrogated". To make matters worse, the DRV used **torture** liberally to locate the spy and his/her network. Some 200 cadres, military personnel, and 103 civilians were interrogated. Under physical pressure, many admitted to being in the pay of the French ***Deuxième Bureau*** and/or members of anti-communist nationalist parties, such as the **Vietnam Nationalist Party** (*Viet Nam Quoc Dan Dang* or VNQDD) and the **Greater Vietnam Nationalist Party** (*Dai Viet Quoc Dan Dang*). To prevent a meltdown, the **Indochinese Communist Party**'s (ICP) Central Committee brought in their top intelligence official, **Tran Dang Ninh**, who scrupulously investigated the affair, interviewing scores of prisoners and comparing and analyzing their confessions. He also put a brake on the use of torture. He concluded that this was a French-mounted deception operation designed to sow precisely the sort of paranoia and internal divisions afflicting the party and army over the spy codenamed "H122", who, he concluded, did not exist. One Vietnamese official present at the time later told **Georges Boudarel** that this French operation provoked remarkable "panic" in the ICP and the army and the deception had been "easily believed by us". That said, there is no French confirmation that they undertook this deception operation. *See also* INTELLIGENCE SERVICES, DEMOCRATIC REPUBLIC OF VIETNAM; PUBLIC SECURITY FORCES.

**HÀ BÁ CANG.** *See* HOÀNG QUỐC VIỆT.

**HÀ HUY GIÁP (1907–1995).** Leading Vietnamese communist theoretician during the Indochinese War. Born in Ha Tinh province, he pursued his secondary studies in the *Lycée du Protectorat (Truong Buoi)*. He studied with **Hoang Xuan Han** and **Nguyen Xien** and befriended **Pham Van Dong** and **Dang Thai Mai**. In 1926, he took part in the general student strikes triggered by the death of Phan Chu Trinh. He was designated to leave for Canton with Tran Phu and Ton Quang Phiet for training in **Ho Chi Minh**'s Revolutionary Youth League. However, French surveillance prevented him from leaving. He thus remained in the south and became secretary of the Revolutionary Youth League in **Cochinchina** in 1926 before joining the Annamese Communist Party in late 1930. A year later, the French arrested and incarcerated him until 1936. The French freed him from **Poulo Condor** that year, but placed him under house arrest. In August 1945, Ha Huy Giap attended the Tan Trao Conference of the **Indochinese Communist Party** (ICP) on behalf of the southern Territorial Committee of the *Tien Phong* communist group. In September 1945, he returned to **Saigon** and served in propaganda and national front work. He cooperated secretly with the Marxist Cultural Group in Saigon. In 1947, he returned to the *maquis* and joined the delegation traveling to northern Vietnam to participate in the upcoming Second Party Congress. When the congress was postponed, however, he remained in the north and was named deputy to the Committee of the ICP's Central Committee for the Implementation of Political Propaganda and Ideological Education (*Ban Tuyen Huan Tuyen Truyen Va Huan Luyen*). He served also as deputy director of the Nguyen Ai Quoc Academy. During the Second Party Congress, held in early 1951, he was elected an alternate member to the Central Committee before returning to southern Vietnam. From that point until the signing of the **Geneva Accords** ending the war in 1954, he served on the Party's Central Bureau for the South (*Cuc Trung Uong Mien Nam*), responsible for propaganda, ideological training, and front work. He became the director of the **Truong Chinh Academy**, the southern Party cadres' equivalent of the Nguyen Ai Quoc Academy.

**HÀ KẾ TẤN (1914–?).** Born in Ha Tay province in northern Vietnam, Ha Ke Tan became politically active during the Popular Front period and joined the **Indochinese Communist Party** (ICP) in 1937. In 1940, the French arrested him and incarcerated him in several prisons in northern Vietnam. In August 1944, he escaped and resumed work for the Party in **Tonkin**. In April 1945, he joined the ICP's Tonkin Territorial Committee (*Xu Uy Bac Ky*), in charge of the provinces of Nam Dinh and Ha Nam, where he helped the **Viet Minh** take power following the Japanese defeat in August 1945. He joined the army in 1945 and assumed the military command of the three provinces of Ha Nam, Nam Dinh, and Ninh Binh. In 1949, he was a political commissar in the Route 4 Front and then served in the same capacity in the Northeastern Front. In October 1954, he was in charge of the 350th division responsible for taking over from withdrawing French forces.

**HÀ VĂN LÂU (1918–).** Colonel in the **People's Army of Vietnam** (*Quan Doi Nhan Dan Viet Nam*) and military delegate to the **Geneva Conference** of 1954. Born into a bourgeois Vietnamese family, he became involved in nationalist politics during the 1930s and participated in the **scouting** movement all the while working as a colonial civil servant. In September 1945, he joined the forces of the **Democratic Republic of Vietnam** on nationalist grounds. He apparently never became a member of the communist party. After commanding **Viet Minh** forces on the Nha Trang front when the French returned to Indochina in 1945, in late 1946 he moved up to Hue to command a "regiment". By 1950 he was serving as the commander of the Binh Tri Thien Front. In 1951, the government summoned him to the north where he was put to work in the **General Staff** of the High Command in the tactical office. He worked closely during this period with General **Hoang Van Thai**, chief of staff of the armed forces under **Vo Nguyen Giap**. In March 1954, **Pham Van Dong** asked him to serve in the Vietnamese delegation to the Geneva Conference. Ha Van Lau attended to military questions for the delegation, assisting **Ta Quang Buu,** and developed a particularly effective working relationship with his French counterpart **Michel de Brébisson**, against whom Ha Van Lau had fought during the war in central Vietnam in 1945–1947. Ha Van Lau became a military liaison officer to the **International Control and Supervisory Commission**. His uncle, who worked for **Phan Van Giao** (a close advisor to **Bao Dai**), was mistakenly killed in the late 1940s by a **Viet Minh** commando unit led by the Austrian **Foreign Legion crossover**, Kemen (Carmen?). Ha Van Lau accepted that this had been a terrible accident, but it no doubt explains his transfer to northern Vietnam.

**HAAS, ÉMILE AUGUSTE (1905–1960).** Served as the head of the Financial Service of the commissioner for the Republic for Southern Annam in 1946–1947 and deputy to the administrator of Dalat in 1947–1948. In 1949, he was head of the Financial Services for the highland peoples in southern Indochina (*populations montagnardes de l'Indochine du Sud*).

**HAI HÙNG**. *See* PHẠM HÙNG.

**HAI LONG.** *See* VŨ NGỌC NHẠ PIERRE.

**HAIPHONG INCIDENT (20–23 NOVEMBER 1946).** Following the Japanese overthrow of the French in Indochina on 9 March 1945, the northern Vietnamese colonial city of Haiphong fell under Japanese control before being transferred to the nationalist control of the **Democratic Republic of Vietnam** (DRV) upon the Japanese defeat in August 1945. On 6 March 1946, French forces established a military presence there in line with the **Franco-Chinese Accord** and that of the **Accords of 6 March 1946**. The DRV continued to administer the port, its taxes and duties, as part of what it considered to be its territorial sovereignty. The French contested this nationalist interpretation on colonial grounds, but were prevented from doing anything about it as long as the Chinese republican troops occupying Vietnam north of the **16th parallel** remained there. With the withdrawal of the last remaining Chinese troops by 18 September 1946, local French authorities in Indochina led by High Commissioner **Georges Thierry d'Argenlieu** pushed a more aggressive line towards the DRV, rolling back its authority in order to advance the restoration of colonial sovereignty. As long as a negotiated settlement remained elusive, a clash between the French and the Viet Minh always remained a real possibility. And that it is what happened in the strategically important northern Vietnamese port of Haiphong when the question arose as to who exercised control of customs there.

The "Haiphong incident" began on 20 November 1946, when French officials challenged the jurisdiction of the DRV's port authorities to intercept a Chinese junk carrying petrol in the harbor. When the French began to unload the cargo, Vietnamese customs officials, soldiers, and police intervened to stop them on the grounds that this was a sovereign DRV matter – and not a colonial or federal one. While the French and Vietnamese versions diverge from this point as to who escalated this local incident into a violent clash two days later, at the heart of the matter was again a contested interpretation of sovereignty. Admiral Georges Thierry d'Argenlieu and his allies on the ground, especially Colonel **Jean Debès**, had no desire to negotiate the question. When a French vehicle came under fire in Haiphong, Debès used this as a pretext to advance French control of the entire city of Haiphong. **Ho Chi Minh** did not want to risk escalating the incident into a *causis belli*, knowing full well that the DRV was not yet in a position to take on the French militarily.

Debès's superior, General **Louis Morlière,** opposed his subordinate's aggressive line in Haiphong and rushed a liaison team to calm things down. A cease-fire agreement was signed on 21 November 1946. However, when General **Jean Valluy**, Morlière's own superior and an ally of Thierry d'Argenlieu, learned of it, he instructed Debès as follows: "The time has come to teach a harsh lesson to those who attacked us like traitors. By all the means at your disposal, you are to take complete control of Haiphong and bring the Vietnamese government and army to recognize its error". Paris was informed of the situation, but indecision allowed these local officials to transform the incident into something tipping dangerously close to war above the 16th parallel. On 22 November Morlière caved in, although he warned Valluy that such action would destroy the **Accords of 6 March** and make full-scale war with the DRV almost inevitable.

Valluy ordered Debès to administer the "lesson". Debès delivered an ultimatum to the Vietnamese on 23 November, demanding that they turn over control of the city. Debès only left his Vietnamese interlocutors three hours in which to respond. When he failed to receive an answer, he began a general attack on the city, using heavy artillery provided by French warships anchored in the harbor. While the DRV had already evacuated most of the civilians, many remained and were often indistinguishable from local militia forces. Others perished while fleeing to nearby Kien An. **Paul Mus**, citing French Vice Admiral **Robert Battet**, claimed that 6,000 people died that day. However, as far as we know, Battet was not there at the time. American Vice Consul **James O'Sullivan**, relying on an interview with the French chief of the ***Deuxième Bureau***, estimated deaths to range between 1,500 and 2,000. **Léon Pignon**, one of Thierry d'Argenlieu's supporters, claimed that the number killed in the Haiphong battle numbered "certainly in the thousands" (*se chiffrent certainement par milliers*). Whatever the precise number of casualties, the French attack on the city was brutal. Even **Jean Sainteny** described Debès's attack as "very brilliant but also very brutal".

It remains unclear who was at fault for the initial escalation following the French seizure of the Chinese vessel on 20 November. What is sure is that the wider historical battle over national versus colonial sovereignty was the principle cause of this break and adumbrated the violent rupture between the two sides a month later in **Hanoi**. What is also clear is that the French, especially Valluy and Debès, were responsible for breaking the cease-fire in order to transform a local incident into a major military action costing the lives of thousands of Vietnamese and effectively putting the DRV's back against the wall. More than anything else, the violent conquest of Haiphong convinced DRV leaders that they had to prepare for war. Stein Tonnesson makes the point that the Haiphong incident must also be understood in the context of Thierry d'Argenlieu's decision to adopt a more aggressive line towards the DRV in the north following Dr. **Nguyen Van Thinh**'s suicide in the south on 10 November. Paris, however, had never approved this shift in policy. *See also* 23 SEPTEMBER 1945; 19 DECEMBER 1946; MASSACRES.

**HAK MONG SHENG (1915–1969).** Cambodian politician in the **Democrat Party** during the Indochina War. Born in Kamong Trabek, Hak Mon Sheng worked in the colonial protectorate as a district headman in Kampong Cham. Following World War II and the return of the French, he served as governor of Stung Treng province in 1946. He joined the Democrat Party during this time and served as secretary to the Ministry of Finances in the **Sisowath Youtevong** government between

December 1946 and July 1947. He won a seat in 1947 in the National Assembly representing the province of Kompong Cham. He also headed up the Democrat Party's parliamentary group and served as secretary to the National Assembly. In 1950, he joined the Democrat Party Steering Committee, but he lost his National Assembly seat in 1951.

**HAMMER, ELLEN (1922–2001).** Graduated from Barnard College in 1941, Ellen Hammer obtained her PhD in public law and government at Columbia University. She became deeply interested in colonial Indochina and the Indochina War. In 1954, the year French Indochina crumbled at **Dien Bien Phu**, she published *The Struggle for Indochina,* which appeared in a revised edition in 1966 as *The Struggle for Indochina: Vietnam and the French Experience* (1940–1955). She was one of the very first Americans to write on colonial Indochina and the war. She was highly critical of the French and well disposed towards non-communist nationalists. She knew **Ngo Dinh Diem** during the Indochina War and became a supporter. Her work, together with that of the likes of **Paul Mus**, **Philippe Devillers**, **Jean Lacouture,** and **Bernard Fall**, was required reading for those seeking to understand contemporary Vietnam, especially for Americans readers and policy makers as the United States became involved in the Vietnam War.

**HÁN THƯ.** *See* NGUYỄN TIẾN LÃNG.

**HANOI.** Hanoi served as the political capital of French colonial Indochina between the end of the 19th century and the **Japanese coup de force of 9 March 1945** that brought it down. Following the Allied defeat of the Japanese in mid-August 1945, the **Viet Minh** came to power and on 2 September 1945 **Ho Chi Minh** announced the creation of the **Democratic Republic of Vietnam** (DRV), with its capital based in Hanoi. Within a few weeks tens of thousands of Chinese troops fanned out across the country, including Hanoi, to disarm the Japanese and maintain order. They brought with them non-communist Vietnamese nationalist parties, such as the **Vietnamese Nationalist Party** and the Alliance party of the *Dong Minh Hoi*, hostile to the Viet Minh and its hold on power. Against this backdrop a severe famine was on its way to killing some one million Vietnamese, filling the city with emaciated souls searching for food and the cadavers of those who died trying. It was in Hanoi the the DRV government led by president Ho Chi Minh operated until the outbreak of full-scale war on 19 December 1946 pushed it deep into the northern hills. In 1943, Hanoi's population was about 120,000 though the famine must have increased the number greatly between 1944 and 1945.

Having moved to retake southern Vietnam since the outbreak of hostilities in **Saigon** on 23 September 1945, the French negotiated an accord with the Chinese in late February 1946 and the Accords of 6 March 1946 with the Vietnamese, allowing for the stationing of 15,000 French troops in northern Indochina, including Hanoi. With the withdrawal of the last Chinese troops in September 1946, tensions rapidly increased as French authorities led by Admiral **Georges Thierry d'Argenlieu** adopted a more aggressive policy towards the DRV and challenged its sovereignty in Haiphong and then in Hanoi, leading to the outbreak of war. However, in order to allow the government to make it to the countryside, the DRV high command decided to take a stand in Hanoi, giving rise to the first and only true urban battle of the Indochina conflict.

The task of fighting the French in Hanoi fell to the Capitol Regiment led by **Vuong Thua Vu** and a motley crew of militia forces. The government ordered the evacuation of the city and the barricading of streets in order to bog down the French. In all, some 2,000 militia men and women, including 200 **children** working as guides and scouts, stayed on in the city to fight for two months. The battle for the city turned out to be a violent one, forcing French troops to take the city street by street, often house by house. As in **Haiphong** a month earlier, colonel **Jean Debès** received authorization from General **Jean Valluy** to shell and bomb militia strongholds in the Hanoi old quarter. On 17 February, the capitol regiment withdrew from the city leaving much of it in rubble.

The destruction and continued insecurity were such that much of the civilian population remained reluctant to return. As late as 1948–1949, according to William Turley, the population of inner Hanoi may have still been as low as 10,000. During this time, the DRV created something of an "underground" city. Indeed, no sooner had the battle of Hanoi ended in February 1947 than the DRV police forces returned to the city to maintain an eye on the French, their military movements, and political actions. The security services were responsible for tracking down and on some occasions assassinating those Vietnamese who would collaborate with the French.

However, this did not stop people from returning to Hanoi from 1949–50, as the **Bao Dai solution** got off the ground and the growing French military presence gave rise to a boom in commercial, administrative, and service functions. By 1951, the estimated population of Hanoi numbered 217,000 of whom 80,000 lived in the inner city. The French and the State of Vietnam maintained their hold on the capital. From 1950, the police and the armed forces drove much of the DRV's "underground city" out of the capital or into hiding. French armed forces controlled much of the Red River delta. And by defeating **Vo Nguyen Giap** during the battle of **Vinh Yen** in 1951, General **Jean de Lattre de Tassigny** made it clear that the DRV would not be taking Hanoi from the French any time soon. Nor would the Viet Minh be able to encircle and starve the city into submission as **Mao Zedong's** troops were often doing in China.

During the second half of the Indochina War, increased security, the surge in the French military presence, the growth of the Associated State of Vietnam's administration, and the augmentation of the civilian population led to the development of small-scale industries and retailers. By the time the war ended in mid-1954, some 40,000 market stallkeepers, shop owners, peddelers and hawkers served an urban Hanoi population of 400,000. Part of this increase came from the countryside. As the war intensified in its violence from 1950, many rural families sent their loved ones to live with friends or relatives in the city. Moreover, as the DRV embarked upon a revolutionary agenda that shifted from national union to one based on class struggle many land owners and traders flooded into the capital city. **Land reform** and the violence accompanying it also sent thousands into Hanoi in 1953 and early 1954. While many of the Europeans left Hanoi for the south at the end of the conflict (around 2,000 Europeans resided in Hanoi following World War II), the overall population did not decline that noticeably. However, the war left the returning DRV authorities with a city of divided loyalities, some of whom welcomed the return of the nationalist government but many of whom feared its revolutionary agenda. The war also left the DRV authorities with 15,000 prostitutes and 19,000 abandoned or orphaned children. *See also* COLLABORATION; CROSSOVER; DESERTION.

**HARTEMANN, ANDRÉ (1899–1951).** French **Air Force** pilot during the Indochina War. He entered the French army during World War I and made his career in the colonies during the interwar period. In 1934, he left the Army in Algiers to join the Air Force. After the French debacle of June 1940, Vichy sent him to Algiers where he crossed over to Free French forces following the allied landing in North Africa in November 1942. In April 1950, he was named commander of the French Air Force in the Far East. He gained the confidence of General **Jean de Lattre de Tassigny** by his ability to supply ground troops effectively from the air during battles, in particular during the battle of **Vinh Yen** in 1951. In 1950, Hartemann was promoted to lieutenant general. In May 1951, he perished when the **Democratic Republic of Vietnam** shot down his plane in the highlands of northern Vietnam. His body was never recovered.

**HEATH, DONALD R. (1894–1981).** American career foreign service officer and strong supporter of the **Associated States of Indochina**. He entered the diplomatic corps in 1920 after serving two years as White House correspondent for *United Press* and worked in several posts in Europe and the Americas. He arrived in **Saigon** in October 1950 having been named the first American minister to the French-backed Associated States of Vietnam, Laos, and Cambodia. In 1951, he stated that the situation in Vietnam was improving. In July 1952, with the up-grade from legation to embassy status, he became the American ambassador to the Associated States of Vietnam and Cambodia. Heath believed that the key to success in Indochina lay in a partnership between France and the United States. He advised against trying to oust the French from Indochina, given the limits on the American ability to take over effectively. He also tried to calm what he saw as misinformed perceptions held by French and American officials and journalists reporting on the war. During the battle of **Dien Bien Phu**, Heath was in favor of some sort of American intervention to save the besieged camp. He ran into problems, however, when his increasing lack of faith in **Ngo Dinh Diem** diverged from the administration's support of the Vietnamese leader. He left Saigon in November 1954.

**HÉBERT, RENÉ.** French special operations officer during the Indochina War. In 1931, he joined the **Foreign Legion** and participated in the continued "**pacification**" of Morocco. He entered the resistance during World War II, was taken prisoner but escaped to make his way to Algeria. There, he joined in 1943 the *Bureau central de renseignements et d'action* (BCRA) and became a trained paratrooper under American instruction. In Indochina, he continued to work in special **commando** operations. In January 1947, he was seriously wounded and lost part of his left leg. This did not stop him from returning to Indochina in 1952 in the *1^er^ Régiment de chasseurs parachutistes*. His long experience in commando operations made him a natural recruit for the ***Groupement de commandos mixtes aéroportés***. He went to work developing a *maquis* among the Hmong in the highlands of northern Vietnam as part of a wider strategy of harassing Vietnamese supply lines and military movements. He worked in the Na San region with the regional representative of North Vietnam and set up a Hmong *maquis* in 1953 in the Song Ma valley and along route 41 in an attempt to harass adversary supply lines running into upper Laos and northwest Vietnam. In many ways, Hébert was one of the French army's first "political cadres", sent into hostile territory to win over local support. *See also* MINORITY ETHNIC GROUPS.

**HELICOPTERS.** Helicopters were certainly not as present in the French war in Indochina as they would be during the **Algerian War** or for the Americans in Vietnam in the 1960s. During the Indochina War, the French used helicopters almost exclusively for medical evacuation purposes. The French purchased their first helicopters (mainly Hiller H23 and Sikorsky) from the United States in 1949, to be used by the army's medical service (*Service de santé*). Between 1950 and 1954, French ground forces in Indochina possessed 42 machines, although less than half of them were operational on a daily basis. The medical service relied increasingly on helicopters as the war intensified from 1950 and as did the number of war related casualties. Between 1950 and 1954, the medical service transported almost 12,000 men including almost 1,000 during the early days of the battle of **Dien Bien Phu**. Helicopters were used to rescue 38 downed pilots and 80 escapees from the same battle in May 1954.

**HENTIC, PIERRE (1917–?).** French captain who became legendary in Indochina for mounting and executing **commando** raids against the **Democratic Republic of Vietnam** (DRV) in central Vietnam using highland minority groups. He saw combat as a non-commissioned officer in the *Chasseurs alpins* at Narvik and served as the head of the Boa-Bom network in the French resistance and was apparently deported by the Germans. Upon his liberation after World War II, he served as an intelligence officer in the French army and led the revolt of the Hres against the DRV in the early 1950s. After the war, he was sent to Algeria to apply the same methods. Little else is known about this behind-the-scenes special operations officer. *See also* ALGERIAN WAR; MINORITY ETHNIC GROUPS.

**HÉRAULT, MASSACRE.** The exact details of the events leading up to the Vietnamese massacre of dozens of French civilians in a mixed quarter of colonial **Saigon** on the 24–25 of September 1945 may never be fully known. The violence that occurred during the early hours of that morning must nonetheless be situated within the wider context of the Japanese overthrow of the French in Indochina in the ***coup de force* of 9 March 1945**, Vietnamese attempts to create a new nation-state in the wake of the Japanese defeat by the Allies in mid-August 1945, the humiliation this triggered among the European settler population, and the chaos, uncertainty, and insecurity that occurs in the midst of such rapid, deep change.

Until March 1945, the European population in French Indochina lived in relative peace thanks to the condominium between France, Germany, and by extension Germany's ally, Japan. That changed, however, with the liberation of France in 1944 and **Charles de Gaulle**'s determination to fight the Japanese and eliminate Vichy authorities there in order to legitimate his government's national claim to Indochina. On 9 March 1945, worried that leaderless Vichy authorities would rally to Gaullists, the Japanese overthrew the French in Indochina. For some five months, around 40,000 European settlers lived in precarious, humiliating, and often very dangerous circumstances. Things became even more complicated when the Allies defeated the Japanese. This allowed Vietnamese allied with the **Viet Minh** to take charge of Saigon by late August. For about three weeks, the French community living in Saigon found the tables turned on them as the former colonized sought to assert national control over the colonial city. The Japanese mainly looked on as they awaited the arrival of British forces sent to disarm them below the **16th parallel** in Indochina. The Japanese refused to free the colonial and foreign legion troops they had incarcerated.

Despite their efforts, local **Democratic Republic of Vietnam** (DRV) leaders had a hard time preventing Vietnamese from humiliating and attacking the vulnerable European community. On 2 September 1945, for example, Vietnamese mobs attacked the French in Saigon during festivities organized to celebrate the declaration of Vietnam's independence by **Ho Chi Minh**. A French Catholic priest sympathetic to the Vietnamese, Father Tricoire, was gunned down in front of the cathedral steps. Rumors of a French counter attack spread quickly; confidence between the two sides fell as Vietnamese authorities began arresting French while Vietnamese looters attacked French and Chinese shops. The local colonial press spoke of a "massacre"; "Black Sunday" some christened it. Local reports of 100 Europeans dead contrasted however with internal Japanese reports of four or five French dead and 14 Vietnamese casualties.

Whatever the exact number, the chances of heading off a wider confrontation in the south plummeted on this day. Many French promised to take revenge once they re-took control of the city. That day came on **23 September** when British forces under General **Douglas Gracey** backed a French *coup d'état* to oust the Vietnamese, using colonial forces incarcerated by the Japanese, many of whom had been taunted by the Vietnamese during the 2 September incidents. Tensions were high. The French coup unleashed months of pent-up fears and frustrations among many in the European community and the newly freed colonial troops. Some took out their anger on any Vietnamese they could find. Many brought in Vietnamese prisoners on leashes, their hands bound. Others set to attacking and beating Vietnamese in the streets, many of them innocent bystanders. **Pham Ngoc Thach**'s French wife's teeth were punched in that day, presumably because of her "traitorous" marriage to the southern leader of the Viet Minh. British and French officials like Gracey and **Jean Cédile** were appalled by this behaviour and Gracey even ordered the unruly colonial troops back to their barracks in order to restore order. Although the DRV authorities had been driven from the city, Gracey was worried that the French might not be able to avoid anarchy any better than the Vietnamese. Curfew, he hoped, would restore a semblance of order. He was wrong.

During the night of 24–25, Vietnamese attackers entered the French-Eurasian-Vietnamese district of Hérault, in the Tan Dinh and Dakao suburbs of Saigon, and perpetrated one of the most gruesome massacres of the entire Indochina War. In the early hours of the 24th, dozens of assailants took some three hundred European and Eurasian civilians as hostages, including women and children. Many of the hostages, especially the ***métis***, were horribly mutilated, tortured, beaten, raped, and killed.

Some French officials would try to pin the massacre on the DRV/**Viet Minh** in an attempt to discredit the adversary. The problem, however, was that their own intelligence services and those of the British knew that the Viet Minh was unable to direct such hotheaded elements. One British officer went so far as to say that the Viet Minh was "not an identity" during the massacre. Jean Cédile himself ruled out direct DRV involvement. French, British, and American investigations concurred that the **Binh Xuyen** were the most likely perpetrators of the attacks and killings. Recent publications in Vietnam reveal that the DRV's internal investigation came to the same conclusion. When **Nguyen Binh**, the new commander-in-chief of the armed forces in the south, arrived in November 1945, he ordered his men to track down and bring to him those who had perpetrated the massacre at Hérault. A few weeks later, Ba Nho (Le Van Khoi) appeared before the one-eyed chief of the DRV's southern forces. The hastily arranged military court tried this member of the Binh Xuyen and summarily sentenced him to death. Nguyen Binh walked up to him, handed him a pistol, looked him in the face and told Ba Nho to kill himself on the spot. He did.

The exact number killed during the massacre is still a matter of contention. The total almost certainly did not exceed 100. As Cédile later admitted, his estimates at the time put the number of killed between 30 and 90. When pushed, he said that the "reality was around 40". It was already too many. *See also* CAM LY, MASSACRE; EXPERIENCE OF WAR; *FRANÇAIS D'INDOCHINE*; MY THUY, MASSACRE; MYTH OF WAR.

**HERCKEL, RAOUL (1898–1978).** French military officer who first served in Indochina in the 1930s. Thanks to the support of **Georges Thierry d'Argenlieu**, he returned to Indochina in mid-

1946 to serve as the commander of the sector of **Hanoi**, a position he held when full-scale war broke out on **19 December 1946**. He signed the accord with **Hoang Huu Nam** on 21 November 1946 to end the clashes that the violent French reoccupation of the city of **Haiphong** had initiated. In 1948, Herckel served as the personal secretary to General **Pierre Boyer de la Tour** and headed the French Military Mission assigned to the Provisional Government of Vietnam based in **Saigon**. He left Indochina in early 1951.

**HERMITTE (L'), RENÉ (1918–2005).** French journalist who closely followed and criticized the French government's war in Indochina. Hermitte was a linguist and specialist of Slavic languages who left academia to join the French resistance during World War II. He was on the staff of the French communist paper *L'Humanité* at this time and began an adventurous life as an international correspondent. In Indochina, he interviewed **Ho Chi Minh** and supported the peaceful decolonization of the French Empire and the end of the war in Indochina. *See also* ANTICOLONIALISM; FRENCH COMMUNIST PARTY.

**HERO.** *See* NEW HERO.

***HIÉRARCHIES PARALLÈLES.*** *See* PARALLEL HIERARCHIES.

**HIROO SAITO**. Japanese colonel who remained in Indochina after World War II to extricate Japanese soldiers and officers who had crossed over to the **Democratic Republic of Vietnam** and others following the Japanese capitulation in August 1945. Having lived in France during the interwar period, he spoke excellent French and maintained close working relations with French officers, especially **Antoine Savani**, head of the ***Deuxième Bureau*** in South Vietnam in the late 1940s. In the 1930s, Hiroo Saito studied in the most prestigious intelligence schools of the Japanese army before serving as an officer in the General Staff of the 55th Division in **Burma** during most of World War II. Following the Japanese capitulation, he set up and ran, in collaboration with Savani, the *Service des déserteurs japonais* (SDJ). Relying on a wide range of Vietnamese agents and connections, he entered into contact with dozens of Japanese officers who had left their units upon the Japanese defeat in August 1945. By 1948, Saito had succeeded in returning some 350 Japanese deserters. Due to this success, he was later sent to the North to mount a similar mission, but with less success. *See also* CROSSOVERS; DESERTION, JAPANESE.

**HISTORY, DEMOCRATIC REPUBLIC OF VIETNAM.** Vietnamese nationalist and communist history was forged and professionalized during the Indochina War. For the **Democratic Republic of Vietnam** (DRV), history was a powerful weapon to be used against French and Vietnamese opponents. It was needed to legitimate and justify the war among the leadership, in propaganda drives, and in resistance classrooms. In a meeting presided over by **Truong Chinh** in **Hanoi** in late 1945, the provisional general secretary of the **Indochinese Communist Party** (ICP) called upon the likes of Nguyen Dinh Thi, **Xuan Dieu,** and **Luu Van Loi** to prepare a "black book" (*sach den*) containing all the crimes committed by the colonialists over some 80 years. From the outset history served to discredit the colonial *mission civilisatrice* positing that the French had improved the well being of the colonized through schools and hospitals and thus deserved to remain in charge. History simultaneously served to promote the national idea the new nationalist leadership was set on creating and diffusing among those living within this new territory referred to as "Vietnam".

Having taken over the colony's printing presses, the DRV began publishing scores of papers and books promoting a new nationalist history. The cultural and educational services produced books, articles, reviews, and manuals condemning French colonial crimes and glorifying the Vietnamese of the past, present, and future. Ancient heroes – the Tay Son brothers and the Trung sisters – came back to life, re-armed, and were mobilized as part of the wider war effort. Resistance schools taught a national history that had never been permitted during the colonial period. Colonial heros of the 19th century became villains. Those Vietnamese who had resisted the French conquest now found a heroic place in nationalist textbooks.

However, much of what was produced during the Indochina War was not necessarily tightly controlled by the party, which did not exercise "total" control over farway zones. Things began to change in central and northern DRV areas in 1950 when the ICP rejoined the international communist movement and the party began to consolidate its control over the state, including educational and cultural services. In 1949, for example, **Ho Chi**

**Minh** instructed cultural cadres in the party to begin preparing an official history of the nationalist resistance movement to be used for educational purposes. The party congress of early 1951 underscored the importance of preparing a history of the party (*Quyen Dang Su*). However, nothing materialized until September 1953, when the **Vietnamese Worker's Party** issued a decree creating a Historical Research Center led by **Tran Huy Lieu**.

A number of famous **intellectuals** contributed directly to teaching and preparing national and party histories during the Indochina War, including Tran Huy Lieu, **Tran Van Giau**, **Dao Duy Anh**, **Nguyen Khanh Toan**, Ton Quang Phiet, Van Tan, Nguyen Luong Bich, Vu Ngoc Phan, **Dang Thai Mai**, **Pham Thieu**, **Tran Duc Thao**. The main organizations and institutions involved in historical production during the war ranged from the Marxist Research Association (*Hoi Nghien Cuu Chu nghia Mac*), the government's Cultural Department (*Vu Van Hoc*), the Central Committee's Commission for Indoctrination and Cadre Training, and the Historical Section of the Ministry of Education (*Ban Su Cua Bo Quoc Gia Giao Du*c), not to mention a plethora of cultural associations located at the **Inter-Zones** and local levels. Vietnam's modern nationalist historiography did not emerge ex nihilo in 1954 with the return of the DRV to Hanoi following the signing of the **Geneva Accords**. It had already begun during the war itself. Indeed, history was an essential part of the making of the DRV during the Indochina conflict. *See also* EMULATION CAMPAIGNS; NEW HEROS; RECTIFICATION.

**HMONG**. *See* MINORITY ETHNIC GROUPS.

**HỒ CHÍ MINH (1890–1969).** President of the **Democratic Republic of Vietnam** (DRV) during the entire Indochina War. Born in Nghe An province in upper central Vietnam, Nguyen Tat Thanh, as Ho Chi Minh was first known, studied at the *Quoc Hoc* college in Hue. The son of a mandarin, he studied Chinese and French and was something of bridge between the generation of patriots and reformers such as Phan Boi Chau and Phan Chu Trinh and that of a younger, more radical and nationalist minded generation that came of age in the 1920s and filled the ranks of the future Vietnamese communist movement.

From an early age, Ho was determined to do something for his country. After failing to gain admission to the French **colonial academy**, he decided to strike out on his own in 1911 heading for the West as a cook on a French ocean liner. In 1917, he settled down in Paris and entered into contact with reformist-minded nationalists such as Phan Chu Trinh now living in France. Attracted, like so many other colonized at the time, by American President Woodrow Wilson's talk of self determination, Ho addressed a petition to the leaders meeting at Versailles, asking them to take into account the nationalist and reformist aspirations of the Vietnamese and other colonized, especially since many of them had shed their blood for the *mère patrie* during World War I. His pleas went unanswered.

Disappointed, Nguyen Ai Quoc or Nguyen the Patriot, as he now called himself, looked to another emerging power calling into question European colonialism, the Soviet Union. Moreover, Lenin's theses on capitalism and imperialism provided an historical explanation of Western domination of much of the world, including Vietnam, and offered a way out of what had seemed to be a Social Darwinian dead end. The Soviets seemed to make good on their promise to aid the colonized when they formed the Comintern in 1919 and shifted their attention to southern China with the creation of the **Chinese Communist Party** (CCP) in Shanghai in 1921. Ho Chi Minh was still in France at this time. In 1920, shortly after the Versailles Conference had closed, he attended the socialist congress of Tours, during which he chose to become a member of the **French Communist Party** on anti-colonialist grounds.

Having made the cut, in late 1924 he left for Moscow where he underwent training and was quickly sent on to Guangzhou (Canton) in southern China. There, he rubbed shoulders with Chinese communists and nationalists working in a United Front, helped Soviet advisors stationed in the south to assist Chinese nationalists against the warlords, and, most importantly, began winning over patriotic Vietnamese immigrants and exiles in China to his cause. It was also during this time that Ho Chi Minh collaborated with some of the future leaders of the CCP, including **Zhou Enlai** (whom he had first met briefly in France). In 1925, Ho Chi Minh presided over the creation of the Vietnamese Revolutionary Youth League in Guangzhou, filling its ranks with young Vietnamese radicals fleeing Vietnam following student strikes and police crackdowns inside Indochina. The outbreak of the Chinese **civil war** in 1927, however, forced him to return to Europe by way of

Moscow. But he was soon back in Asia, working this time for the Comintern, among the **overseas Vietnamese** in Thailand, and collaborating with Chinese communists and **overseas Chinese** to create embryonic communist parties for Thailand, Laos, and Malaya.

It was also in this regional and global context that he created the Vietnamese Communist Party, with the help of the CCP and the Comintern. When young Vietnamese internationalists took him to task for his use of "Vietnam" instead of "Indochina", considered to be the correct territorial model for taking on the colonialists, the party was renamed the "**Indochinese Communist Party**" (ICP) later that year. In 1931, the British arrested him but released him in 1933. He then took refuge in the Soviet Union before returning to southern China via Yan'an as World War II spread from China into Southeast Asia via Indochina. In 1941, back in Vietnam for the first time in some thirty years, he presided over the creation of the **Viet Minh** nationalist front (*Viet Nam Doc Lap Dong Minh*). He downplayed class struggle and radical social reform in favor of building up a broad nationalist front, which could, once the moment arrived, help the communists take power.

That moment came in 1945, first in March when the Japanese overthrew the French and then a few months later when the Allies defeated the Japanese. Riding a famine-driven wave of popular unrest to power, the Viet Minh took control of major towns of Vietnam from mid-August moving from the north to the south. On 2 September 1945, Ho Chi Minh formally declared the creation of the DRV before thousands of cheering Vietnamese. When he asked his compatriots if they could hear him (*Dong bao co nghe ro khong?*), the crowd roared back with a resounding "yes" (*Co!*).

During the tense years of 1945–1946, as the DRV tried to hold on against all odds, Ho Chi Minh was the most important Vietnamese statesman and diplomat for the country. Besides leading complicated negotiations with the French as war was already underway in the south, he also dealt directly with occupying Chinese forces and even took the unprecedented decision to dissolve the ICP in order to hold on against competing anti-communist nationalist parties backed by the Republic of China's troops. In early March 1946, under extraordinary pressure from the Chinese to sign a political accord before the French debarked via Haiphong, Ho Chi Minh signed the **Accord of 6 March 1946** with **Jean Sainteny** and **Vu Hong Khanh**. While the French agreed that the DRV was a "free state" and that a referendum would be held to decide the unification of **Cochinchina** with the rest of "Vietnam", Ho Chi Minh also settled for less than full recognition of national independence. The DRV would remain in the Indochinese Federation and the **French Union** as a "free state" or a local one within the wider colonial federation.

Despite the critiques from opposition leaders, his ability to project himself as the father or defender of the Vietnamese nation survived the accord. Indeed, it was from this crucial period that he called himself "Ho Chi Minh", or roughly the "one who enlightens", and was increasingly referred to as "Uncle" or *Bac* in Vietnamese. Unlike hotter heads in his party and government, and especially among the anti-communist Vietnamese opposition and French authorities in Indochina, Ho Chi Minh went to extraordinary lengths to negotiate a deal with the French to avoid full-scale war. When the **Fontainebleau Conference** of mid-1946 failed, he succeeded in obtaining a last minute **modus vivendi**, hoping that the coming to power of a Leftist government could help him avoid a violent meltdown in Indochina where High Commissionner **Georges Thierry d'Argenlieu** was determined to apply to the letter **Charles de Gaulle**'s instructions for retaking all of Indochina. Ho Chi Minh held his troops in line, even during the violent incidents at **Lang Son** and **Haiphong** in November 1946. But this was a harder act to pull off in December, as violent incidents increased between the French and the Vietnamese. Still, Ho Chi Minh held out the hope that the arrival of the socialist and liberal minded **Léon Blum** would provide the chance to reach a peaceful settlement. The Vietnamese president would be disappointed. On the evening of **19 December 1946**, with their backs against the wall, the Vietnamese lashed out. It was full-scale war and Ho, though he certainly regretted it, was determined to fight.

From his headquarters in northern Vietnam, he played a leading role in building and leading the government and planning military and diplomatic strategy. He was consulted on major policies both within the government and party. He also played a crucial role in foreign affairs. In late 1949, for example, he left for China and the Soviet Union. Thanks in particular to Chinese support, in January 1950 communist China, the Soviet Union and the rest of the communist bloc recognized the DRV and supported the Vietnamese military struggle against the French Union forces. In exchange for this support, however, **Stalin** and **Mao Zedong** expected Ho Chi Minh, whose internationalist fidelity had been called into question with his **dissolution of the Indochinese Communist Party** in November 1945 and failure to carry out land reform, to implement communist **land reform** and assert the party's control over the state, the society, and the war. Ho returned to Beijing and Moscow in 1952 and agreed to begin preparations to implement land reform.

In 1954, Ho yet again played a crucial role in making the decision to negotiate at the **Geneva Conference** and agreed with his longtime friend Zhou Enlai during the **Liuzhou Conference** in early July 1954 that the Vietnamese should agree to a partition of the country and to the idea of holding elections in order to unify the country peacefully. He also agreed to neutralize Laos and Cambodia by putting on hold Vietnamese communist claims to run all of revolutionary Indochina. While some leading communists supported the decision to reach a settlement at Geneva, agreeing that the Americans would replace the French otherwise, some, like **Le Duan,** regretted the decision to abandon the south and would not hesitate to reactivate the southern resistance when it became clear that the general elections set out in the **Geneva Accords** would never be held. *See also* NEUTRALIZATION OF INDOCHINA.

**HO CHI MINH TRAIL**. The **Ho Chi Minh** Trail did not begin during the American War in Vietnam; it came to life during the French Indochina War. Moreover, at the outset, the trail was not an overland but rather a maritime or coastal route. This North-South supply route running between **Inter-Zones IV** and **V** to **Zones VII, VIII** and **IX** in the south had been secretly called the Ho Chi Minh liaison road (*Duong lien lac Ho Chi Minh*) since at least 1947. Besides arms and supplies, this route also moved important cadres back and forth (including **Le Duan**), ensured vital communications, transferred money and gold, and strengthened the leadership of the northern-based central committee over the southern resistance.

With the arrival of the **Cold War** in 1950 and the military and diplomatic intensification of the Indochina War, the Vietnamese were forced to "push" the maritime trail inwards into Indochina as the French Navy increased its surveillance of the coastline and sea. Indeed, since 1949, the **Democratic Republic of Vietnam** had begun plans to create on overland route to link southern Indochina to its northern half in order to spread Chinese aid southwards via overland trails. In his report to the Ministry of Defense in 1951, General **Nguyen Binh**, commander-in-chief of southern armed forces, explained in detail preparations underway to create an overland "route crossing all of Indochina" from Inter-Zone IV via southern Laos and north eastern Cambodia in order to supply southern Vietnam "once the Ho Chi Minh [maritime] liaison route presently doubling route no.1 is blocked".

The shifting of the Ho Chi Minh Trail towards the spine of Indochina was thus a direct result of the Chinese communist victory, the outbreak of the **Korean War**, and the real threat of increased U.S. intervention in Indochina by sea and overland from Thailand. Nguyen Binh predicted that if the war widened and the United States entered it against the Chinese and Vietnamese, then the weight of the conflict would shift rapidly to southern Vietnam. In such a scenario, a secret supply trail would be needed to keep the southern resistance alive. The famous Ho Chi Minh *overland* trail – allegedly created in 1959 – got its start, at least conceptually, a decade earlier, at the Cold War conjuncture of 1949–50. *See also* HOA BINH, BATTLE OF.

**HỒ CHÍ TOÁN.** *See* STEFAN KUBIAK.

**HỒ ĐẮC DI (1901–1984).** Vietnamese surgeon in the **Democratic Republic of Vietnam** (DRV) during the Indochina War. Born in Ha Tinh province, he was the son of Ho Dac Trung, a prominent minister in the late 19th-century Nguyen Court, and brother to Ho Dac Khai and **Ho Dac Diem**. Graduated a medical doctor from the Faculty of Medicine of the University of Paris, Ho Dac Di specialized in surgery and interned as an assistant in several French hospitals. He lived in France between 1918 and 1933. An accomplished violinist, Ho Dac Di often joined Eve Curie, a pianist, to play music at her parents' home. Eve was the daughter of the French scientists, Pierre and Marie Curie. She later became the wife of **Pierre Mendès France**. On his return to Vietnam, Ho Dac Di lectured in the Faculty of Medicine at the Indochinese University and was a surgeon at the *Hôpital du Protectorat* (Phu Doan) in **Hanoi**. While he claimed that he was first won over to the nationalist cause upon reading **Ho Chi Minh**'s open letter to the Versailles Conference, of equal importance was the humiliation and anger he repeatedly felt upon returning to a colonial society in which he could not assume leadership responsibilities commensurate with his training or even with his experiences in the metropolis. In any case, he joined the DRV in 1945 and dedicated the rest of his life to developing Vietnam's post-colonial medical institutions and independence. He made the inaugural speech during the opening of the University of Vietnam (ex Indochinese University) in 1946 and served as the dean of the Faculty of Medicine. Following the outbreak of full-scale war on **19 December 1946**, he moved to **Inter-Zone IV** (*Lien Khu IV*), where he was named to the permanent Committee of Sciences and Technology and continued training Vietnamese doctors. In November 1948, he was instrumental in creating the first medical journal of the DRV, *Xay Dung* (Construction). He published widely in French and Vietnamese medical journals. *See also* DISEASE; EXPERIENCE OF BATTLE, DIEN BIEN PHU; PAUL GRAUWIN.

**HỒ ĐẮC DIỀM (1899–1986).** Vietnamese lawyer in the **Democratic Republic of Vietnam** (DRV) during the Indochina War. He was the son of Ho Dac Trung, prominent minister in the late 19th-century Nguyen Court, and brother to **Ho Dac Di** and Ho Dac Lien. He studied law in France where he earned his doctorate degree. Upon his return to Vietnam, he worked for the Nguyen Dynasty as chief of the Private Secretariat and then as assessor to the Ministry of Justice in the Royal Government between 1924 and 1929. In 1929, he joined the civil service in the Protectorate of **Tonkin** working as a provincial administrator, an examining magistrate (*juge d'instruction*), and as a deputy in the Presidency of the Provincial Tribunal. In 1941, he took charge of the province of Ha Dong, one of the highest posts a "native" could occupy in the Indochinese colonial administration. Nevertheless, in 1945, he crossed over to the DRV on nationalist grounds. In October 1949, he was reported to be working as a chief justice in the **Inter-Zone IV**'s (*Lien Khu IV*) Court of Appeals and joined the Propaganda Committee for the Creation of a Scientific Workers' Union.

**HỒ NAM.** *See* TRẦN VĂN GIÀU.

**HỒ THANH BIỂN (1890–1976).** Vietnamese Catholic priest who supported the nationalist cause of the **Democratic Republic of Vietnam** (DRV). Born in Long Xuyen province, he was ordained a priest on 21 September 1921 in Phnom Penh. He served congregations in Tra Long, Hoa Hung, and My Luong during the interwar period. He was also part of a wider nationalist awakening among the Vietnamese Catholic clergy in the 1920s and 1930s. With the outbreak of the Franco-Vietnamese war, he chose the **Viet Minh** and supported the cause of the DRV. In 1948, Ho Thanh Bien was head of the Catholic Resistance Association of the province of Soc Trang, the vice president of the local **Lien Viet** Front for the same province, and deputy head of the Catholic Resistance Association of Nam Bo. On 19 September 1954, following the division of Vietnam into two states during the **Geneva Conference**, Ho Thanh Bien along with Fathers Vo Thanh Trinh and Tran Quang Nghiem relocated to northern Vietnam while thousands of northern Vietnamese Catholics took refuge in the south. *See also* CATHOLICS IN VIETNAM AND THE WAR; REFUGEES, FRANCE.

**HỒ THỊ BI (HỒ THỊ SÁU, HỒ THỊ HOA, NĂM BI, 1916–?).** Vietnamese woman political cadre in the army during the war against the French. She was born in **Saigon** and became politically active during the 1930s, taking part in the Indochinese Congress of 1936. She joined the **Indochinese Communist Party** in 1945 and became a cadre in the army in charge of mobilizing women and running special undercover missions into the city to supply the resistance. In 1947, she led special contact unit 12 (*Ban Cong Tac 12*) on clandestine operations between Saigon and the surrounding area. Between 1949 and 1951, she contributed to the building of the Duong Minh Chau war zone and the creation of a commercial base for the resistance in Tanot in Cambodia. *See also* WOMEN.

**HỒ THỊ HOA.** *See* HỒ THỊ BI.

**HỒ THỊ SÁU.** *See* HỒ THỊ BI.

**HỒ TÙNG MẬU (1896–1951).** Communist leader who played an important, early role in the administration of **Inter-Zone IV** (*Lien Khu IV*) during the Indochina War. Born and raised in Nghe Anh province, he left for southern China after failing the mandarin examination of 1915. There, he collaborated with Phan Boi Chau then **Ho Chi Minh** in the creation of the Vietnamese Revolutionary Youth League. Ho Tung Mau joined the **Chinese**

**Communist Party** and contributed to the creation of the **Indochinese Communist Party** (ICP) in 1930. Arrested in 1931, he was forcibly returned to Indochina and incarcerated in various prisons there for almost fifteen years. Liberated in 1945 thanks to the Japanese, he rejoined the Nghe An – Ha Tinh region where he was elected president of the Resistance and Administrative Committee for Inter-Zone IV and member of the ICP for the same zone. He was elected an alternate member to the party's Central Committee in 1951. He was killed during a French air raid on the market of Cong located between Thanh Hoa and Vinh in late 1951.

**HỒ VĂN HUÊ (1917–1976).** Vietnamese doctor who worked for the **Democratic Republic of Vietnam** (DRV) during the Indochina War. Born in Long An province in southern Vietnam, he graduated from the Faculty of Medicine in the Indochinese University in 1944. He also became active in nationalist politics during this time. In 1945, with the overthrow of the French and the defeat of the Japanese, he joined the **Viet Minh** front and worked for the DRV. He first served as the president of the People's Committee of Quang Loi in Binh Long province. Between 1945 and 1946, as war raged in southern Vietnam, he ran the Military Medical Branch for Thuan Loi in Bien Hoa province. Between 1946 and 1951, he directed the Military Medical branch for the Lac An war zone and served as the head of the Military Medicine Department of **Inter-Zone** VII (*Lien Khu VII*). During this time, he worked with a team of southern Vietnamese doctors, who together trained dozens of Vietnamese medics to tend to the wounded in the battlefields. He also oversaw the (clandestine) importation from **Saigon** and the manufacture in Inter-Zone VII of much needed medicines and vaccinations (against cholera). Between 1951 and 1952, he was head of the Bureau of Military Medicine for Nam Bo (*Truong Phong Quan Y Nam Bo*). Between 1952 and 1955, he headed the Medical Service for the newly created **Inter-Zone for Eastern Nam Bo** (*Phan Lien Khu Mien Dong Nam Bo*). In March 1950, he joined the **Indochinese Communist Party**. In 1955, according to the stipulations of the **Geneva Accords**, Ho Van Hue relocated to northern Vietnam where he worked in the DRV's Military Medical Branch.

**HOÀ BÌNH, BATTLE OF (10 DECEMBER 1951–25 FEBRUARY 1952).** Following major defeats in the northern delta in 1951, the **Democratic Republic of Vietnam**'s (DRV) High Command began work to push a strategic route southwards along the hilly western periphery of the delta in order to supply central and southern zones. Controlling Hoa Binh and areas along the Black River was crucial to the extension of this trans-Indochinese route. The DRV had retaken Hoa Binh in 1950, turning it into a major interchange in its logistics and communications with the rest of Indochina. The French were not dupes, however: in November 1951, General **Jean de Lattre de Tassigny** recovered Hoa Binh in order to thwart the development of just such an Indochinese supply route, to prevent the DRV from infiltrating troops into the delta via the south, to reassure **minority ethnic groups** in Hoa Binh of French resolve, and to demonstrate the French will to take on the Vietnamese, especially to the Americans and the emerging Associated State of Vietnam.

General **Vo Nguyen Giap** was determined to take it back and saw an advantage in attacking the French posts there given the craggy, mountainous terrain (similar to the terrain he exploited successfully during the **Cao Bang** battle). On 10 December 1951, Vo Nguyen Giap sent battle-hardened elements of the 304$^{th}$, 308$^{th}$, 312$^{th}$, and 351$^{st}$ against French positions. Attacking at night in order to avoid the full brunt of French airpower, Giap threw waves of men against the **French Union** forces in a bid to encircle, overwhelm, and destroy the camp. The French had five infantry battalions, an artillery group, and mobile groups waiting for them and paratroopers were already harassing Vo Nguyen Giap's lines of communications. Fighting at Hoa Binh was intense, with French artillery inflicting heavy losses on the DRV's troops attempting frontal assaults. During the battle, the French **Air Force** lost its first plane to the adversary's still rudimentary but operational anti-aircraft battery as the DRV's troops expanded their control in the Hoa Binh–Black River area. On 22–23 February, as the Vietnamese massed for a final knock-out punch, General **Raoul Salan** decided to pull his troops out of Hoa Binh, preventing Giap from scoring the decisive victory he wanted.

The battle cost the lives of some 10,000 killed and wounded for the DRV and about a 1,000 for the **Expeditionary Corps**. Although neither side scored a clear victory, it was clear from this point that the DRV's army was operating in a modern fashion, that its commanders were quite capable of coordinating and operating a battle over a large area, and that they were keen on taking the battle to the French using Chinese-inspired **wave tactics**. By taking Hoa Binh, the DRV also began work pushing an overland **Ho Chi Minh Trail** southwards to supply **Inter-Zone V** (*Lien Khu V*) and lower Indochina. As Yves Gras aptly summed up the significance of the battle: "The truth is that the Viet Minh, very fluid and mobile, was moving with great speed and knew how to concentrate its efforts at the opportune moment". The problem for the Vietnamese high command, however, was that the French were very good at pulling out their forces, thereby denying Vo Nguyen Giap a decisive victory he increasingly had to score.

**HÒA HẢO**. The word "Hoa Hao" in Vietnamese means "conciliation" or "concord". The Hoa Hao faith emerged in the late 1930s in the Mekong Delta. The messianic leader of the movement, **Huynh Phu So**, drew heavily on local Buddhist beliefs and the southern popularity of Maitreya Buddha, the Saviour, to build this millenarian religious movement. Huynh Phu So attracted a large peasant following, many of whom were looking for a saviour and the promise of a better world to help them make it through the difficult economic times of the 1930s. By the time the Japanese started moving into northern Indochina in 1940, Huynh Phu So had thousands of followers located in large swaths of the Mekong delta running up the river into Cambodia. The Hoa Hao faith was particularly strong in the Vietnamese provinces of Tan Chau, Chau Doc and Long Xuyen. During World War II, the Japanese backed Huynh Phu So and pressured the French to release him from captivity. Upon the defeat of the Japanese in August 1945, Huynh Phu So temporarily aligned his followers with the nationalist cause of the **Democratic Republic of Vietnam** (DRV). That collaboration, however, did not last long. Confidence was lacking on both sides. By 1947, the French ***Deuxième Bureau*** in southern Vietnam intensified its contacts with members of the Hoa Hao in an effort to lure them from the DRV. In April 1947, attacks between the Hoa Hao and the DRV led to a violent break when the DRV's forces assassinated Huynh Phu So in order to consolidate their hold over the military forces in the south and block French attempts to turn the Hoa Hao and others against them, both politically and militarily. The Hoa Hao, **Cao Dai,** and eventually the **Binh Xuyen** would cross over to the French and their counter-revolutionary state led by **Bao Dai**. However, Hoa Hao collaboration was always precarious at best. Leaders, such as **Le Quang Vinh** and **Tran Van Soai,** moved back and forth among the DRV, the French, Bao Dai, and later **Ngo Dinh Diem** forces. *See also* HUYNH VAN TRI; NGUYEN GIAC NGO.

**HOÀNG.** *See* TRẦN VĂN GIÀU.

**HOÀNG ANH KIỆT.** *See* HOÀNG NAM HÙNG.

**HOÀNG CHUNG (DZIM).** Ethnic Nung from Muong Khuong who joined forces with the French and **Ly Seo Nung** in 1946 and 1947 against the efforts of the **Democratic Republic of Vietnam** (DRV) to control ethnic non-Viet regions of upland northern Vietnam (mainly Tai and Nung territories). Hoang Chung joined the ***Groupement de commandos mixtes aéroportés*** upon its creation in 1950 in a bid to deny the DRV access to the strategically important Tai region. He was involved in numerous **commando** operations until the end of the war in 1954, when he successfully made his way to Laos. He and his Nung comrades were involved in some of the most ferocious, up-close fighting of the Indochina War. He continued to work on special missions in Laos until the French ***Service de documentation extérieure et de contre-espionnage*** relocated him to France where he served out the rest of his military career in the *11ème Bataillon de choc.*

**HOÀNG ĐẠO THÚY (1900–1994).** Vietnamese scout who became one of the **Democratic Republic of Vietnam**'s (DRV) most important military communications and information specialists. He became involved in nationalist politics during the 1930s as a journalist, promoter of the Vietnamese language, and above all as the general commissioner of Vietnam's **scouting** movement during World War II. He secretly worked with **Truong Chinh** to bring over the scouts to the revolutionary cause as World War II drew to a close. Hoang Dao Thuy attended the Tan Trao Conference of the **Indochinese Communist Party** in mid-August 1945. On his return to **Hanoi**, he immediately began to rally the scouts to the **Viet Minh** and then to the DRV. He joined the army that same year. Hoang Dao Thuy helped win over **Ta Quang Buu**'s collaboration; the latter was head of the scouting movement in central Vietnam. Hoang Dao Thuy also put his scouting knowledge of communications in the service of the armed forces of the DRV. On 9 September 1945, he became the first director of the army's Bureau of Communications and Liaisons (*Phong Thong tin lien lac*) attached to the General Staff. He helped launch what became a functional and vital radio and telephone transmission system for the army in particular and the DRV in general. In April 1946, he left this position to run the first and third classes (khoa I and III) of the **Tran Quoc Tuan Military Academy** (*Truong Vo Bi Tran Quoc Tuan*), serving in between as the head of the Army-Engineer Communications (*Giao thong cong binh*). On 18 June 1949, Ho Chi Minh named him director of the Bureau of Information and Liaison (*Cuc Thong tin lien lac*) attached to the Vietnamese High Command under General **Vo Nguyen Giap**. Hoang Dao Thuy created the government and military's first radio codes and encryptions, and telegram dispatching system, and began teaching the first courses to a new generation of Vietnamese communications, radio, and intelligence specialists. In November 1949, he issued a telegraphic message as the former general commissioner of the Vietnamese Scouts, calling on Vietnamese scouts to "stand up … to be ready to kill the enemy and liberate the whole of Vietnamese territory". In the late 1940s, he also served as head of the Bureau for politico-military training (*Cuc truong Quan huan*) within the army's General Staff. He was the chief commander for communications and liaisons during the battle of **Dien Bien Phu** in 1954, working from within the special Battle Unit 3 (*Ban ba chien dich*).

**HOÀNG ĐÌNH GIỌNG (VŨ ĐỨC, 1904–1947).** Vietnamese communist and **commando** parachuted into Vietnam by the British during World War II. Born in **Cao Bang** province in northern Vietnam, Hoang Dinh Giong was of ethnic Tai origin. He studied Chinese characters before completing his primary education in a Franco-Vietnamese school. He traveled to **Hanoi** for his secondary studies at the *Lycée Bach Nghe* where he studied with Hoang Van Thu. During the general student strikes triggered by Phan Chu Trinh's death in 1926, he was expelled from school. In November 1927, he left Vietnam for southern China where he joined **Ho Chi Minh**'s Vietnam Revolutionary Youth League in Canton and underwent training there. He was one of the early members of the **Indochinese Communist Party** (ICP) and was a member of the Party's Overseas Committee in China led by Le Hong Phong. In 1935, Hoang Dinh Giong attended the first congress of the party in Macao and joined the Executive Committee of the ICP before being sent back to northern Vietnam to build up bases. In February 1936, the French arrested him in Haiphong and sentenced him to five years in prison. He was sent to Hoa Lo prison in Hanoi, then to **Son La,** and on to Madagascar in May 1941. In July 1942, the British occupied the island, allowing Free French forces under **Charles de Gaulle's** leadership to replace the Vichy administration. The British and French agreed to free a number of the Vietnamese prisoners in order to use them in commando and intelligence missions in Vichy-Japanese-occupied Indochina. Around 1944, the Allies parachuted Hoang Dinh Giong and a number of other former political prisoners into Indochina where Hoang Dinh Giong immediately resumed his activities in Cao Bang province. In 1945, the ICP put him in charge of taking power in Cao Bang province. On 1 October 1945, Ho Chi Minh and the ICP named Hoang Dinh Giong the commander of the Southern Movement Troops (*Bo Doi Nam Tien*) under the *nom de guerre* of Vu Duc. In November 1945, these troops took part in battles against the French in the **Saigon** Gia Dinh region. From December 1945, Hoang Dinh Giong became head of **Zone IX** (*Khu IX*) in southwestern Vietnam. He was recalled to northern Vietnam in November 1946 to undertake a new mission; but he never made it. On 17 March 1947, he was killed in battle. *See also* LE GIAN; MINORITY ETHNIC GROUPS; PHAM CONG TAC; TAI FEDERATION; TRAN HIEU.

**HOÀNG ĐÌNH TÙNG.** Japanese **crossover** to the **Democratic Republic of Vietnam** (DRV), who had served as the former director of the local branch of the Bank of Yokohama in **Hanoi**. After the Japanese defeat in 1945, he rallied to the DRV and served as an advisor to the "National Bank of Vietnam" (*Quoc Gia Ngan Hang Viet Nam*). According to **Le Van Hien**, Tung played an influential role in the making of Vietnam's early "banking policy". His true Japanese name is unknown to this writer.

**HOÀNG ĐỨC NHÃ.** *See* VŨ NGỌC NHẠ, PIERRE.

**HOÀNG HAI ĐÌNH.** *See* HOÀNG NAM HÙNG.

**HOÀNG HOA THÁM.** *See* DONG TRIEU, BATTLE OF.

**HOÀNG HỮU NAM (PHAN BÔI, 1911–1947).** Minister in the **Democratic Republic of Vietnam** (DRV) during the run up to the Indochina War. Born in Quang Nam province in central Vietnam, he studied at the *Collège Quoc Hoc* in Hue. He took part in the student strikes triggered by the arrest of Phan Boi Chau. Expelled, he went to **Hanoi** to work in a printing house and became involved in nationalist and communist politics. In 1929, he traveled to **Saigon** and joined the **Indochinese Communist Party** (ICP) around 1930, when the French arrested him and sent him to **Poulo Condor**. In 1936, thanks to the Popular Front, he left prison and returned to Hanoi where he participated in the Indochinese Congress of 1936 and joined the Editorial Committee of the ICP's paper, *Tin Tuc*. In 1939, French authorities arrested him again and locked him up in Bac Me in Ha Giang before deporting him to Madagascar in June 1940. In 1943, following the British occupation of the French island until then under Vichy control, Hoang Huu Nam and a number of other Vietnamese political prisoners in Madagascar such as **Le Gian** and **Hoang Dinh Giong**, were incorporated into British **commando** teams and sent to **India**. Hoang Huu Nam parachuted into Indochina in 1944 to conduct intelligence and **guerrilla** activities against the Japanese. Back in Vietnam, he entered into contact with the Party in the north. After the creation of the DRV, he served in military and diplomatic positions. In late 1945, he was under-secretary of the Interior and chairman of the Supreme Committee for National Defense. In 1946, he served as the Ministry of Defense's delegate to the Franco-Vietnamese Mixed Commission. He negotiated directly with colonel **Pierre Lami** and **Raoul Herckel** during the intense events leading to the **Haiphong Incident** in November 1946. He was a deputy in the First National Assembly elected in March of that year. He evacuated to northern Vietnam after the outbreak of full-scale war on **19 December 1946**. He drowned while crossing a river in Tuyen Quang in 1947.

**HOÀNG LUNG.** In charge of the creation and operation of special missions, psychological operations against the enemy, and rescue operations in northern upland Tai regions during the second half of the Indochina War. *See also* ETHNIC MINORITIES; *PAYS MONTAGNARDS DU SUD* (PMS); TAI FEDERATION.

**HOÀNG MINH CHÍNH (TRẦN NGỌC NGHIÊM, LÊ HỒNG, 1922–2008).** Vietnamese **intellectual** committed to the **Democratic Republic of Vietnam** during the Indochina War. Born in Nam Ha, he became active in radical politics in the 1930s and joined the **Indochinese Communist Party** in 1939. During the war, he served in the army in northern Vietnam. He led the audacious attack on the French military airbase at Gia Lam on 8 March 1954 in an effort to sabotage planes supplying the soon-to-be besieged **French Union** troops at **Dien Bien Phu**. In 1957, he joined the staff of the **Ho Chi Minh** Academy for training cadres and he left to study in the Soviet Union. Upon his return to **Hanoi** in 1961, he became rector of the Institute of Philosophy. He was also the victim of a divisive dispute within the party over the strategy to use during the Tet Offensive of early 1968 and the related question of which side of the Sino-Soviet dispute to support. He was accused of being "pro-Soviet", a "revisionist", and purged. Between 1967 and 1973, he lived in confinement and underwent "reform" (*cai tao*). Between 1973 and 1976, he lived in Son Tay province under *résidence surveillée* (*quan che*). *See also* NGUYEN HUU DANG; VU DINH HUYNH.

**HOÀNG MINH ĐẠO (ĐÀO PHÚC LỘC, HOÀNG MINH PHỤNG, NĂM THU, NĂM ĐẠO, NĂM ĐỜI, 1923–1969).** One of the founding architects of the **Democratic Republic of Vietnam**'s (DRV) military intelligence service. At ease in Chinese, he became active in nationalist politics in Haiphong during the heady years of the Popular Front period, joining the **Indochinese Communist Party** in 1939. In 1940, the French arrested and sentenced him to two years of prison. Upon his release in early 1943, he remained under police surveillance in his hometown of Mongcai. He quickly evaded his handlers and returned to his political activies in Moncai and Haiphong, in charge of secretly transporting cadres and materials between northern Vietnam and southern China. He also worked briefly in the Haiphong area with the future general of the south, **Nguyen Binh**. At one point, Hoang Minh Dao made his way to southern China, where Chinese nationalists fighting the Japanese and opposed to Vichy France taught him the intelligence trade.

He began his long espionage career in Vietnam in 1945 with the creation of the DRV. In that year, he played a pivotal role in creating the DRV's intelligence branch for the **General Staff**. He also took charge of the Office of Intelligence for the Military Committee (*Phong Tinh Bao Quan Uy Hoi*) under the Ministry of National Defense. Hoang Minh Dao's main tasks were to assemble an operating intelligence service and staff, capable of providing intelligence and analysis to the government's decision-makers and general staff faced with the increasing likelihood of war in 1946. With the outbreak of war on **19 December 1946**, Hoang Minh Dao transferred his intelligence service to Tuyen Quang province.

In 1948, **Vo Nguyen Giap** and **Hoang Van Thai** sent him south where he directed the Military Intelligence Branch for Nam Bo (*Truong Ban Quan Bao Nam Bo*) under the commander-in-chief for the south, General Nguyen Binh, with whom Hoang Minh Dao had worked in 1945 in northern Vietnam. During Hoang Minh Dao's time in the south, he resolved a particularly sensitive case implicating 34 mainly party members at the district and provincial levels in eastern Nam Bo in an alleged enemy spy ring. After careful study, Hoang Minh Dao's internal investigation concluded that they had been victims of injustice and regained their former positions. Hoang Minh Dao would remain in the south after the **Geneva Accords** were signed in July 1954, provisionally dividing Vietnam into two states. From December 1954, he helped run a newly created southern espionage network designed to follow developments in the south, the southern Party Commission's Research Branch Responsible for Following the Enemy Situation (*Ban Nghien Cuu Dich Tinh Xu Uy*). Hoang Minh Dao continued his work in espionage operations in the **Republic of Vietnam** until he was unmasked and killed in an ambush in Vam Co Dong in 1969. *See also* H122 AFFAIR; PHAM NGOC THAO; PUBLIC SECURITY SERVICES; TRAN DANG NINH; TRAN QUOC HOAN.

**HOÀNG MINH GIÁM (CHU THIÊN, 1904–1995).** One of the **Democratic Republic of Vietnam**'s (DRV) pivotal diplomats during the early years of the Indochina War. Born into a scholarly family in Ha Dong near **Hanoi**, he graduated from the *École supérieure de Hanoi* in 1926. He briefly taught at the *Collège Sisowath* in Phnom Penh in 1926–27 before returning to Hanoi to tutor and pursue a career in journalism. In 1934, he was instrumental in founding the famous private high school in Hanoi, *Thang Long*. He served as director of the school and became close friends with **Vo Nguyen Giap** (who joined Giam's tutorial staff at the school). In the 1930s, Hoang Minh Giam became an active Vietnamese member of the ***Section française de l'Internationale ouvrière***'s Indochina branch and befriended its leader, **Louis Caput**. Giam wrote periodically in the *Annam Nouveau* and other papers. In 1945, with the overthrow of the French and the defeat of the Japanese, he joined the **Viet Minh** and the DRV and became director of the cabinet for the Ministry of the Interior (headed by Vo Nguyen Giap) and then became vice minister of the Interior. Giam was elected deputy to the National Assembly in January 1946 and was involved in the negotiations leading to the **Accords of 6 March 1946**. In June and July 1946, he participated in the Vietnamese delegation to the **Fontainebleau Conference** in France and served as a pivotal go-between for **Ho Chi Minh** in meetings with French socialists and possibly with **Freemasons** in the metropolis. Hoang Minh Giam remained in France to help create and run the government diplomatic delegation in Paris. While in France he also supported the creation of a new **Vietnamese Socialist Party**; however, the French government declared his presence *inopportune* in October 1946. On his return to Hanoi on 25 November, he became under-secretary of state for Foreign Affairs. In 1947, he was named minister of Foreign Affairs, a post he held until August 1954 when he resigned citing health reasons. During the First Congress of the Vietnamese Socialist Party, held in northern Vietnam in July 1947, he was elected to the Central Committee. In March 1951, following the communist party's 2nd Congress, he was elected to the Permanent Committee of the **Lien Viet**. He was a non-communist.

**HOÀNG MINH PHỤNG.** *See* HOÀNG MINH ĐÀO.

**HOÀNG MINH THẢO (TẠ THÁI AN, 1921–2008).** Commander of the 304th Division during the Indochina War. Born in Hai Hung province in northern Vietnam, he became politically active during the Popular Front period. In 1941, he joined the **Viet Minh** and underwent military training in southern China. From late 1944, he helped build up political bases and **guerrilla** activities in

Lang Son province along the border with China. He joined the army in 1944. In 1945, he was part of a special committee that oversaw the border operations of the Viet Minh's General Directorate or ***Tong Bo*** with southern China. He joined the **Indochinese Communist Party** in March 1945 and between 1945 and 1949 served as the Ministry of Defense's special delegate for the maritime provinces on the right bank of the Red River. He also served as head of war **Zone** III and then deputy head of **Inter-Zone III**'s (*Lien Khu III*) military command. In late 1949, he transferred to **Inter-Zone IV** (*Lien Khu* IV) where he briefly served as the commander-in-chief of ground forces there. Between 1950 and 1953, he commanded the 304$^{th}$ Division. He was named major general in 1950.

**HOÀNG MỸ.** *See* TRẦN HIỆU.

**HOÀNG NAM HỒNG.** *See* HOÀNG NAM HÙNG.

**HOÀNG NAM HÙNG (HOÀNG HAI ĐÌNH, HOÀNG ANH KIỆT, HOÀNG NAM HỒNG, NGUYỄN NAM HÙNG, 1889–?).** Long-time Vietnamese anti-colonialist in China who transferred his loyalty to **Bao Dai** in the late 1940s. Born in northern Vietnam, he immigrated to China during World War I and became an officer in the Chinese nationalist army. In China, he joined non-communist Vietnamese nationalists in promoting Vietnamese independence from abroad and collaborated closely with the exiled Prince Cuong De based in Japan. In 1939, Hoang Nam Hung helped create the League for the National Restoration of Vietnam (*Viet Nam Phuc Quoc Dong Minh Hoi*) in Guangzhou (Canton) under the nominal leadership of Cuong De. His activities during World War II remain unclear. After the war, in October 1947, Hoang Nam Hung met with Bao Dai in Hong Kong and reorganized and led the League for the National Restoration of Vietnam from February 1948. He also joined another non-communist nationalist party, the National Unity Party (*Viet Nam Quoc Gia Lien Hiep*). In August 1948, under attack in the League for the National Restoration of Vietnam, he resigned from the Presidency and the Directing Committee. In December 1949, as the Chinese Red Army approached the Indochinese border, he returned to Vietnam on 5 January 1950 after decades of living in exile. Bao Dai asked him to work towards the unification of the various non-communist nationalist parties. In February 1950, Hoang Nam Hung met with the leaders of the pro-French **Cao Dai** in southern Vietnam and promised to collaborate with them. In April 1950, Bao Dai named him general secretary of the Study Committee for the Unification of National Armed Forces and member of the Assistance Committee to Returning Nationalists created in October 1950. Upon the death of Cuong De in Japan, Hoang Nam Hung organized a memorial service for the exiled prince held on 22 April 1951 with the authorization of Bao Dai and later wrote the biography of the exiled prince. In 1952, Hoang Nam Hung became state secretary for the "Returnees and the **Pacification**" in the **Nguyen Van Tam** government, created on 6 June 1952.

**HOÀNG QUÂN BÌNH.** *See* NGUYỄN ĐÌNH LUYỆN.

**HOÀNG QUỐC VIỆT (HẠ BÁ CANG, 1905– 1992).** One of the ranking members of the **Indochinese Communist Party** (ICP) during the Indochinese War. Born of a working-class family in Bac Ninh province, in 1922 Hoang Quoc Viet entered the *École pratique d'industrie de Haiphong*, but was expelled in 1925 for his participation in general students' strikes triggered by the trial of Phan Boi Chau. He then went to work as a miner in Thai Nguyen, Quang Yen, and Haiphong provinces in the north. In 1928, he joined the Vietnamese Revolutionary Youth League and two years later the ICP, serving as an alternate on the Executive Committee of the Central Committee. He was arrested by the French that same year and ended up in **Poulo Condor**. There he worked closely with **Pham Van Dong** and **Le Duan**. He was released in November 1936 thanks to the clemency of the Popular Front government in France. He immediately returned to radical politics. He was instrumental in organizing the 1937 strikes among miners in Hon Gay and mobilizing workers there. In 1937, he was also elected general secretary of the ICP's Territorial Committee for **Tonkin** (*Xu Uy Bac Ky*).

In 1941, he was among those who welcomed **Ho Chi Minh** back to Vietnam. He participated in the 8$^{th}$ Plenum of the Executive Committee of the ICP's Central Committee which created the **Viet Minh**, became a member of the Standing Committee of the Central Committee, and was put in charge of the General Directorate or ***Tong Bo*** running the Viet Minh nationalist front. Working from outside **Hanoi** with **Truong Chinh**, he remained at the head of the Territorial Committee of Tonkin and helped organize the jailbreaks of several communist leaders until the end of the war. Between the fall of 1945 and August 1946, he supported the unification of Vietnamese unions into the party-controlled Federated Vietnamese Worker's Union (*Viet Nam Tong Lien Doan Lao Dong*). In late August 1945, he led an important party delegation as leader of the Viet Minh to southern Vietnam in order to establish communications between northern and southern communists who had long been out of touch and was charged with placing the nationalist uprisings in central and southern Vietnam under the direct control of the Party and the **Democratic Republic of Vietnam**. He informed **Tran Van Giau** of his recall to the north and put Le Duan in charge of the ICP in the south as the head of the Territorial Committee of Nam Bo (*Xu Uy Nam Bo*). As of 1948, Hoang Quoc Viet still directed the Viet Minh's General Directorate. He became president of the Federation of Vietnamese Unions in 1950, was re-elected to the ICP's Central Committee in early 1951, and joined the **Vietnamese Worker's Party**'s Politburo.

**HOÀNG SÂM (TRẦN VĂN KỲ, 1915–1968).** Senior communist leader in the Vietnamese army during the Indochinese War, fluent in Chinese. Born in Quang Binh province, he joined the **Indochinese Communist Party** (ICP) in 1933. Between 1934 and 1939, he was in and out of prison for his political activities. Between 1937 and 1939, he was a member of the ICP's Provincial Committee for Cao Bang in charge of communications with cadres in Yunnan and Guangxi provinces in China. He headed up the armed propaganda unit in the **Viet Minh Tong Bo** between 1941 and 1943, ensuring the security of the 8th Plenum held in 1941. In December 1944, he was one of the first leaders of the newly created Vietnamese Propaganda and Liberation Army (*Viet Nam Tuyen Truyen Gia Phong Quan*). He led **guerrilla** operations that helped the Viet Minh expand its influence in northern Vietnamese provinces. Between 1946 and 1950, he served as head of war **Zone** II and commanded the Western Advance Front, before assuming the military command of **Inter-Zone III** (*Lien Khu III*). In 1951, the Ministry of Defense named him its special delegate overseeing the operation of the 312th and 304th Divisions in battle. His fluency in Chinese undoubtedly made him a crucial go-between with Chinese advisors attached to these units. In 1953–1954, Hoang Sam led the 304th Division, leading it into battle in central Laos during the winter offensive designed to draw French forces away from **Dien Bien Phu**.

**HOÀNG THỊ NGHỊ (NAM HÀ, 1929–).** Effective member of the **Democratic Republic of Vietnam**'s (DRV) efforts to rally enemy soldiers to its side. She joined the **Indochinese Communist Party** in 1947 and the army in 1948. Between September 1945 and January 1948, Hoang Thi Nghi worked mobilizing women in the Kien Thuy region. Between 1948 and 1954, she worked as a cadre in the **Proselytizing the Enemy** (*dich van*) operations, successfully rallying to the DRV's cause 100 Vietnamese from the Associated State of Vietnam's army and a section of African troops near Do Son. After the 1954 partition of Vietnam into two halves, she received instructions sending her secretly south in order to put her mobilizing talents to work deep inside enemy territory.

**HOÀNG TÍCH TRÍ (1903–1958).** Vietnamese medical doctor and minister of Health for the **Democratic Republic of Vietnam** (DRV) during the Indochina conflict. After beginning his medical studies at the *Faculté de médecine de Hanoi*, he traveled to France in 1932 and graduated from the *Faculté de médecine de Paris* in 1935 and specialized thereafter in microbiology at the Pasteur Institute in Paris. Between 1938 and 1945, he directed the Pasteur Institute's laboratory in **Hanoi** and was a distinguished member of the French microbiology association, several Indochinese medical associations, as well as deputy director of the *Amicale des médecins et pharmaciens indochinois*. Between November 1946 and 1958, he was the DRV's Health minister and put his experience in the Pasteur Institute in the service of the government's microbiology unit (*Vi Trung Hoc*). He also taught at the DRV's medical school in Hanoi in 1946 and continued to do so following its transfer to northern Vietnam.

**HOÀNG TÙNG (TRẦN KHÁNH THỌ, 1920–2010).** Influential behind-the-scenes leader in the Vietnamese communist hierarchy and close ally of **Le Duc Tho** and admirer of **Truong Chinh**. Born in Ha Nam province, Hoang Tung became politically active in Vietnam during the 1930s working as a journalist. In 1937, he joined the Democratic Youth Group (*Doan Thanh Nien Dan

*Chu*). During this time, he worked with the likes of **Nguyen Duy Trinh** and **Nguyen Co Thach** and was particularly close to Le Duc Tho, who ran the book shop Phan Khai in **Hanoi**. The police arrested Hoang Tung in 1940 and incarcerated him in **Son La** until his release in late 1944 or early 1945 through negotiations with the French *résident* of the province (almost certainly **Jean Cousseau**). Hoang Tung apparently joined the **Indochinese Communist Party** (ICP) in prison in 1943. Upon his release, he resumed his collaboration with Le Duc Tho and joined other senior communist members in preparing political bases with a view to taking power following the Japanese defeat. To this end, he ran the ICP's "**Secure Zone**" (*An Toan Khu*), located just outside of Hanoi and from where the communist leadership under Truong Chinh and Le Duc Tho operated clandestinely. Hoang Tung secretly escorted **Ho Chi Minh** to Hanoi, installing him in the former Governor General's Palace, following the defeat of the Japanese and the creation of the **Democratic Republic of Vietnam**. In 1945, Hoang Tung served on the ICP's Territorial Committee for **Tonkin** (*Xu Uy Bac Ky*), the party Committee for the City of Hanoi, and headed war Zone III. In 1948, he was named deputy director of the powerful Organizational Department of the ICP, serving under its director and his longtime friend, Le Duc Tho. The two of them worked closely together to become powerful members of the Vietnamese Communist Party well into the 1980s.

**HOÀNG VĂN CHÍ (1913–1988).** Vietnamese non-communist nationalist who left the **Democratic Republic of Vietnam** (DRV) at the end of the war. He studied at the *Lycée Albert Sarraut* and the Indochinese University in **Hanoi** in the 1930s, taking a degree in science. He also became politically active during the Popular Front period, joining the Indochinese section of the ***Section française de l'Internationale ouvrière***. In 1945, he supported the independence cause of the newly created DRV, helping to design and produce the new national money, the *dong*, and making weapons for the war effort. Following the outbreak of full-scale war on **19 December 1946**, he went to work in war **Inter-Zone IV** in upper central Vietnam. There, he rubbed shoulders with the likes of General **Nguyen Son**. While he admired and supported the anti-colonial cause of the DRV, he increasingly objected to the communisation of the resistance and the state he witnessed from 1950. He objected particularly to the importation and application of Chinese methods of "**rectification**" in Inter-zone IV and dogmatic **land reform**. He would leave the DRV following the **Geneva Accords** of 1954 and joined the **Republic of Vietnam** in the south. He wrote a number of essays and books increasingly hostile to Vietnamese communism and the DRV which he had once served. *See also* COLLABORATION; DESERTION, DEMOCRATIC REPUBLIC OF VIETNAM.

**HOÀNG VĂN HOAN (PHÓNG, THÁI LƯƠNG NAM, 1905–1991).** Powerful Vietnamese communist diplomat in Thailand and China during the Indochinese War. Born and raised in Nghe Tinh province, he began his revolutionary career in Guangdong (Canton), where he joined **Ho Chi Minh**'s Vietnamese Revolutionary Youth League and studied at the Chinese Military Academy at Whampoa. Fluent in Chinese, he joined the **Chinese Communist Party** at this time. In 1928, following the outbreak of the Chinese **civil war**, he moved to Thailand where he was an active member of the **Indochinese Communist Party**'s (ICP) bases along the Mekong River and in Bangkok. He was also fluent in Thai. He returned to southern China in 1935. In both countries, he was a close collaborator with Ho Chi Minh. His knowledge of southern Chinese politics and the Chinese language made him a crucial go-between with the Chinese of all political stripes. He helped form an "early" **Viet Minh** in southern China in the 1930s and joined the General Directorate (***Tong Bo***) of the "real" Viet Minh in 1941. He returned to Vietnam for the first time in decades at this time. With the creation of the **Democratic Republic of Vietnam** (DRV) in 1945, he joined the ICP's Central Committee and was named vice minister in the Ministry of Defense. In March 1946, he was elected deputy and named a member of the Permanent Committee of the National Assembly. Following the outbreak of full-scale war on **19 December 1946**, in 1947 he was designated a governmental delegate to war **Zone** IV (*Khu Chien IV*) in upper central Vietnam. In 1948, he returned to northeast Thailand and Bangkok where he served as the head of the ICP's "Overseas Cadres Committee" (*Ban Can Su Hai Ngoai*) in charge of governmental and party foreign policy not only in Asia but in the world. One of his tasks was to make contact with and win over the support of major communist parties and governments, above all the Chinese Communist Party and that of the Soviet Union. In December 1950, following Beijing's diplomatic recognition of Ho Chi Minh's Vietnam, Hoang Van Hoan became the DRV's plenipotentiary minister to the **People's Republic of China**. In October 1952, he obtained the rank of ambassador, Vietnam's first to China. He was a crucial link between the Vietnamese and the Chinese during the Indochinese War, facilitating the delivery of Chinese military, economic, and diplomatic aid. He was a member of the DRV's delegation to the **Geneva Conference** and accompanied Ho Chi Minh to **Liuzhou** to meet with **Zhou Enlai** in early July 1954 concerning concessions to be made at Geneva in order to reach an agreement.

**HOÀNG VĂN THÁI (HOÀNG VĂN XIÊM, 1915–1986).** Chief of staff of the Vietnamese army until 1953 and close collaborator with **Vo Nguyen Giap**. Born in Thai Binh province in northern Vietnam, he became involved in radical nationalist politics during the Popular Front period. In 1938, he joined the **Indochinese Communist Party**. Tracked by the French police, he fled to China in 1941 where he entered a Chinese nationalist military academy in Kweilin. He returned to Vietnam in 1944 and participated in the creation of the Propaganda Brigade of the Vietnamese Liberation Army, put in charge of intelligence matters. In April 1945, he was responsible for running the Politico-Military Academy for the Resistance to the Japanese in Tan Trao. In September 1945, he oversaw the creation of a **General Staff** for the fledgling Vietnamese army. In December, he became chief of staff in the Vietnamese army and was named major general in 1948. He directed the General Staff during the battle of **Cao Bang** in 1950 before ceding his position to General **Van Tien Dung** in 1953 for unclear reasons, as the battle of **Dien Bien Phu** shaped up.

**HOÀNG VĂN XIÊM.** *See* HOÀNG VĂN THÁI.

**HOÀNG XUÂN BÌNH (?–2000).** Born in Ha Tinh province in upper central Vietnam, Hoang Xuan Binh was the younger brother of the famous Vietnamese intellectual, **Hoang Xuan Han**. Unlike his brother, Hoang Xuan Binh crossed over early as a student to **Viet Minh** forces, helping them to take power in Hue. He joined the nascent army of the **Democratic Republic of Vietnam** (DRV), and participated in Emperor **Bao Dai**'s abdication in Hue in August 1945. In early 1946, on orders from the Ministry of Defense, Hoang Xuan Binh accompanied Lao Prince **Suphānuvong** to Laos, where he served as one of the prince's body-guards until the French reoccupation of Laos forced them into exile in Thailand. There, Hoang Xuan Binh helped negotiate arms deals for the DRV and recruited a combat unit from **overseas Vietnamese** in Thailand, which he led back to southern Vietnam in 1947 under the name of Quang Trung III. His unit came under French attack and Hoang Xuan Binh was captured by the French **Deuxième Bureau**. In May 1948, a French military tribunal tried Hoang Xuan Binh for treason. Binh's lawyer, **Nguyen Huu Tho**, argued that this was absurd since his client did not have French nationality, but was rather a Vietnamese patriot. The court sentenced him to three years of prison nonetheless. Upon his release, Hoang Xuan Binh returned to the *maquis*. Some forty years later, Binh's captor, French intelligence officer Léon Fallon, returned Hoang Xuan Binh's private documents and diary. The two officers had discreetly become friends and exchanged letters during Binh's incarceration in the late 1940s.

**HOÀNG XUÂN HÃN (1909–1996).** Born in Ha Tinh province, Hoang Xuan Han became one of Vietnam's best known **intellectuals**. He completed his primary and part of his secondary studies in Vinh and Thanh Hoa between 1917 and 1926 before moving on to **Hanoi** to study at the *Lycée Albert Sarraut*, from which he graduated in mathematics in 1928. He obtained a scholarship to study in France and attended the prestigious preparatory school, *Lycée Saint Louis*, until 1930, specializing in mathematics. From this point he studied at the most prestigious French learning institutions of the time: the *École polytechnique* (1930–32), the *École nationale des ponts et chaussées* (1932–1934), and the *École normale supérieure* (1935–1936), rue d'Ulm, where he became a certified instructor of mathematics. Upon his return to Indochina shortly thereafter, he taught at the *Lycée du Protectorat*, the *École d'agriculture et de sylviculture*, and the *Agents techniques des travaux publics*.

Though always discreet and no political militant, Hoang Xuan Han was nonetheless increasingly attracted to nationalist politics, especially during the heady days of the Popular Front period in Indochina. He joined the Association for the vulgarization of *quoc ngu* at this time. He also put his knowledge of Chinese characters and the Sino-Vietnamese script, *chu nom*, in the service of unearthing Vietnam's national history, heritage, and heroes. When the *Lycée du Protectorat* was moved to Thanh Hoa, he studied inscriptions of the ancient Vietnamese General Ly Thuong Kiet and wrote on other military heroes of the past, such as the Tay Son brothers.

Following the Japanese overthrow of the French in the ***coup de force* of 9 March 1945**, Hoang Xuan Han became the minister of Education and the Arts in the short-lived **Tran Trong Kim** government. He met with **Bao Dai** on several occasions during this time to discuss the future of Vietnam. As minister of Education, he oversaw the use of Vietnamese in the Vietnamese education program instead of French.

While Hoang Xuan Han was sympathetic to the nationalist cause of the **Democratic Republic of Vietnam** (DRV), he never held a governmental position. He did, however, accept **Ho Chi Minh**'s invitation to take part in the DRV delegation to the **Dalat Conference** in 1946. He remained in French-controlled Hanoi after the outbreak of war on **19 December 1946**, dedicating himself to teaching and researching one of the greatest national works of Vietnam, the *Tale of Kieu* (*Truyen Kieu*) and publishing an heroic biography of Ly Thuong Kiet in 1949. Indeed, Hoang Xuan Han made his contribution to the anti-colonial cause as something of a nationalist historian during the Indochina War. However, this did not keep him in Vietnam. In the early 1950s, he moved to France and helped develop the Vietnamese holdings in the *Bibliothèque nationale de France*, as well as in libraries in Italy and at the **Vatican**. He was present at the **Geneva Conference**, upon the invitation of **Phan Anh** and **Nguyen Manh Ha**. He died in France. *See also ATTENTISME*; COLLABORATION; HISTORY, DEMOCRATIC REPUBLIC OF VIETNAM.

**HOÀNG XUÂN NHỊ (WILLY, 1914–1991).** Vietnamese **intellectual** who supported the **Democratic Republic of Vietnam** (DRV) and worked in **Proselytizing the Enemy** (*dich van*) services during the Indochina War. Born in Ha Tinh province, Hoang Xuan Nhi traveled in Europe and lived in France during much of the interwar period. He remained there under German-occupied Vichy France. It was during this time that he worked with Germans and learned to speak the language effectively. In 1945, he was one of many Vietnamese residing in France who supported the DRV's cause. Following the failure of the **Fontainebleau Conference** in 1946, he heeded **Ho Chi Minh**'s call to return home to support the national struggle. He returned to Vietnam via **Saigon** where he helped create and served as editor-in-chief of southern Vietnam's first foreign language resistance newspaper *Tieng Noi Bung Bien* (The Voice of the *Maquis*). When more and more **Foreign Legion** troops began crossing over to the Vietnamese side, the government created an "International Brigade" in war **Zone VIII** (*Chien Khu VIII*), composed mainly of Germans. Because Hoang Xuan Nhi spoke French, German, and English, he became a political cadre in this brigade. His job was to convert his mainly European **crossovers** to the DRV cause through propaganda and political indoctrination courses. In 1947, he served as the director of the Educational Service for Nam Bo. He joined the **Indochinese Communist Party** at about the same time, serving on the Party's Executive Committee for war **Zone IX** (*Khu IX*). Until the end of the war, he was in charge of building up and administering the propaganda and education systems in the south. In 1954, with the division of Vietnam during the **Geneva Conference**, he repatriated to northern Vietnam where he would continue to work in educational and political indoctrination matters. *See also* DESERTION, FRENCH UNION; DESERTION, DEMOCRATIC REPUBLIC OF VIETNAM.

**HOGARD, JACQUES CLAUDE ÉMILE MICHEL (1918–1999).** Son of a general, Hogard graduated from Saint-Cyr in October 1939 and joined the *4ème Division d'Infanterie Coloniale*. During the German invasion of France in mid-1940, he was taken prisoner and would not regain his liberty until the end of the war. Between 1945 and 1953, Hogard served almost continuously in Indochina. Until 1949, he commanded troops in the **Expeditionary Corps**. After a brief return to France, in July 1950 he was back in Indochina where he joined the *Mission française d'instruction militaire au Cambodge* as a deputy to the chief of staff. He also commanded a battalion of the Associated State of Cambodia's army, notably the *4ème Bataillon des chasseurs cambodgiens*. While in Cambodia, he became increasingly interested in counter-insurgency theories, techniques, and operations, what the French came to call "**revolutionary warfare**" or *guerre révolutionnaire*. Influenced too by the British experiences in Malaya, Hogard and others began attempting to separate the peasants from the **guerrillas**, moving towards the creation of protected "strategic" hamlets in Cambodia. While he did not know it at the time, a unit of his Cambodian battalion eliminated the legendary Vietnamese General **Nguyen Binh** in the jungles of northeastern Cambodia in September 1951. Hogard would serve in Algeria in order to keep it "French". In 1956, he wrote an influential essay on revolutionary warfare, *Guerre révolutionnaire ou révolution dans l'art de la guerre*, in which he claimed that the "revolutionary warfare" practiced by the DRV for control of the civilian population "has become permanent, universal, and truly global". *See also* ALGERIAN WAR.

**HỒNG LĨNH.** *See* NGUYỄN KHÁNH TOÀN.

**HOPPENOT, HENRI (1891–1977).** Entered the French diplomatic corps in 1914 and served in posts across the globe during the interwar period. He joined the Free French forces in 1942. In 1945, he became ambassador to Switzerland until 1952, when he became the Permanent Representative for France to the Security Council of the **United Nations**. In 1955, he was named *Ambassadeur en mission extraordinaire* to Southeast Asia as well as the French high commissioner to the Republic of Vietnam, replacing General **Paul Ely**.

**HUANG HUA (1913–2010).** Chinese diplomat who was part of the Chinese delegation to the **Geneva Conference** of 1954 on Indochina and Korea. He joined the **Chinese Communist Party** (CCP) in 1936 and introduced American journalists such as Edgar Snow to Soviet areas run by the Chinese communists in Yan'an. During World War II, Huang Hua served as political secretary to general Zhu De and, from 1941, he worked as the secretary of the Overseas Affairs Committee for the Central Committee. From 1944, he ran the Foreign Affairs Liaison Section of the CCP's Central Committee. He continued to hold important foreign affairs positions during the Chinese **civil war** (1946–1949). Following the communist victory in 1949, he met with the American Ambassador to the **Republic of China**, John Leighton Stuart, to discuss the future of Sino-American relations. Huang Hua directed the Foreign Affairs Office in the communist Municipal Military Control Commission in Nanjing. The talks went nowhere as **Mao Zedong** aligned China with the Soviet Union and the **Korean War** opposed the Chinese and the Americans on the battlefield. A confirmed diplomat, Huang Hua returned to the international scene in 1953 as a ranking official involved in political talks on the truce during the Korean War and became director of the Foreign ministry's Department of Western European and African Affairs. In 1954, he accompanied **Zhou Enlai** to Geneva as part of the Chinese delegation negotiating an end to the wars in Korea and Indochina. He was officially listed as an advisor from the Ministry of Foreign Affairs. However, thanks to his mastery of English (he had translated for Edgar Snow in the late 1930s), he was also the delegation's English language translator at Geneva and the official spokesman for the Chinese during the conference. In 1976, he became minister of Foreign Affairs. He held this position during the events leading to the third Indochinese War in 1979, pitting Chinese and Vietnamese communists against each other.

**HUARD, PAUL MARIE LÉON (1903–1994).** French general who oversaw the restoration of French rule to Cambodia after World War II. He served in Vietnam during the interwar period, commanding colonial troops in the *9ème Régiment d'infanterie coloniale* and as chief of the *Bataillon de tirailleurs montagnards du Sud* ***Annam***. During World War II, he left Algiers to join the **Expeditionary Corps** for the Far East taking form under General **Roger Blaizot** in **India**. Huard arrived in Kandy on 22 October 1944 to work with Blaizot in the South East Asia Command. In April 1945, he flew to China to tend to French troops fleeing Indochina following the Japanese ***coup de force*** **of 9 March 1945**. Huard arrived in **Saigon** on 3 October 1945 and served as acting commissioner for the French Republic to Cambodia between 12 October and 15 November 1945. During this time, he restored French rule to Cambodia and hustled off **Son Ngoc Thanh** to a colonial jail in Saigon.

**HUARD, PIERRE (1901–1983).** French surgeon-general in the Naval Medical Corps active during the Indochina War. Graduated from the Naval Medical School in Bordeaux in 1920, he served in the colonial army during the interwar period. In 1933, he began a long career in colonial Indochina where he was posted to **Hanoi**. During this time, he practiced medicine and became a respected surgeon. He was also greatly interested in Sino-Vietnamese medicine and practices. From 1940, he taught medicine in the Faculty of Medicine in the Indochinese University in Hanoi. During the Indochina War, he cared for **French Union** troops and did his best to promote a rapprochement between the French and the Vietnamese. He also became dean of the Faculty of Medicine at the University of Hanoi around 1947. He gave discreet courses to intelligence officers in the **Deuxième Bureau** during the Indochina War on such subjects such as *De la psychologie, de la mentalité de l'Annamite*. Between 1950 and 1952, he was the Red Cross's delegate to northern Vietnam. Thanks to his prewar contacts with medical personnel now working in the **Democratic Republic of Vietnam** (DRV), he personally negotiated following the **Cao Bang** battle an accord allowing the safe evacuation of some 200 wounded men of the **French Union** forces. However, upon arriving in Indochina, General **Jean de Lattre de Tassigny** was suspicious of Huard's contacts with the enemy and successfully forced Huard to resign from his position. In 1954, after the fall of **Dien Bien Phu** and the imprisonment of thousands of French Union soldiers, he was named delegate for the French High Command as well as the International **Red Cross** to negotiate with the his counterparts in the DRV. He was charged with improving the sanitary and living conditions of the French Union soldiers held in captivity. He succeeded in obtaining the immediate return of more than 500 wounded and sick soldiers. He administered the French Hospital in Hanoi until December 1955 when he returned to France. He went on to pursue an illustrious University career in medicine and founded French Universities in the Ivory Coast and Benin. During the colonial period, he trained many of the leading doctors working in the DRV.

**HUNT, PIERRE (1925–).** A career colonial administrator, he worked in the Commission for southern **Annam** between 1946 and 1949. Between 1950 and 1951, he was attached to the high commissioner's office in Cambodia. Between 1951 and 1956, he was in charge of the information services in **Hanoi** (1951–1953) and **Saigon** (1953–1956).

**HUNTER, WILLIAM H.** Behind-the-scenes, American intelligence officer based in Bangkok following the Indochina War as an assistant naval attaché at the United States Legation. While details are scarce, he was one of the best informed American intelligence officers at the time on Indochinese military and political affairs, having access to the highest levels of the French Indochinese military, political, and intelligence services. He also met on numerous occasions in Bangkok with representatives of the **Democratic Republic of Vietnam**, the **Lao Issara**, the **Khmer Issarak,** and even the Soviet Legation in Bangkok. He left Indochina "precipitously" in November 1949. While French intelligence officers worked with him during his frequent visits to Indochina, they were also highly suspicious of him. Little else is known about this man or his activities other than he had the support of his Legation in Bangkok. *See also DEUXIEME BUREAU*; OFFICE OF STRATEGIC SERVICES; *SERVICE DE DOCUMENTATION EXTERIEURE ET DE CONTRE-ESPIONNAGE*; *SÛRETÉ FÉDÉRALE*.

**HỮU MAI (TRẦN HỮU MAI, TRẦN MAI NAM, 1926–2007).** Novelist in the armed forces of the **Democratic Republic of Vietnam**. Born in Nam Dinh province, Huu Mai joined the Vietnamese army in 1946. He worked as editor of the military paper *Quan Tien Phong* in the 308th division. He witnessed many of the biggest battles of the Indochina War. After the war, he helped run the army's cultural journal, *Van Nghe Quan Doi*. He wrote some of the first novels and reportages on battles of the first Indochina War, including *Nhung Ngay Bao Tap* (1957) and *Cao Diem Cuoi Cung* (1961).

**HUY CẬN (1919–2005).** Born and raised in a Confucian family in the Nghe An-Ha Tinh region of Vietnam, Huy Can was educated in the *Lycée Khai Dinh* and then in the *École supérieure des eaux et forêts*, from which he graduated a forestry engineer in the early 1940s. During this time, he befriended his partner and close friend, the poet **Xuan Dieu**. Like the latter, Huy Can had become a leading figure in the New Poetry movement, writing famous poems such as *Sacred Flame*. He was also active in nationalist politics. He was one of ten Vietnamese who created the **Vietnamese Democratic Party** (*Viet Nam Dan Chu Dang*) and sympathized with the communist movement. In August 1945, he represented the Democratic Party during the Tan Trao Conference in mid-August 1945 and played an instrumental role in integrating the Democratic Party into the **Viet Minh** nationalist front. He and **Tran Huy Lieu** organized the abdication ceremony of **Bao Dai** in Hue on 30 August 1945. Huy Can was named minister without portfolio in the Provisional Government of the **Democratic Republic of Vietnam** between September 1945 and March 1946. In March 1946, he became minister of Agriculture. In 1947, he replaced **Pham Van Dong** as vice minister of the National Economy. While communist authorities frowned upon his homosexual relationship with Xuan Dieu, they never stopped him from serving on the cultural front during the Indochina War and long after.

**HUY KANTHOUL (1909–1991).** Prominent Cambodian nationalist opposed to **Norodom Sihanouk**'s consolidation of power in the early 1950s. Born in Phnom Penh, he completed his primary and secondary studies at the *Collège Sisowath* and at the *École supérieure de Pédagogie* in **Hanoi**. He returned to Phnom Penh and taught at the *Collège Sisowath*. In 1937, he studied in France for five months. He became a member of the **Democrat Party** in 1946 and served as minister of Information and Propaganda in the **Sisowath Youtevong** cabinet of December 1946, and maintained the post in the newly formed Sisowath Watchayvong cabinet of July 1947. In 1948, he became minister of Rites and Fine Arts in the All Democrat Cabinet formed in February. He was minister of Education and Youth in the **Sisowath Monipong** cabinet of December 1950; however, he refused to accept the post in the Oum Chheang Sun cabinet of March 1951. He was general secretary of the Democrat Party when he became prime minister in October 1951, following the electoral victory of the democrats in September. He served simultaneously as minister of Social Action. In June 1952, Sihanouk dismissed him when the king moved against a royal ally, **Yèm Sambaur**. Sihanouk dissolved the Assembly and government in June 1952 and moved to consolidate his control over Cambodian politics in early 1953. Huy Kanthoul was forced into exile in France.

**HUY MONG (1902–1975).** Prominent Cambodian **Democrat Party** leader during the Indochina War. Between 1926 and 1945, he worked as a clerk in the Indochinese colonial administration in Cambodia. Little is known of his activities during World War II. After the war, he joined the Democrat Party and became state secretary in the Ministry of National Defense in the all Democrat Cabinet led by **Chhean Vam** in February 1948. **Yèm Sambaur** named him minister of Defense in his cabinet in Feburary 1949, but was dropped in the second cabinet formed in September of that year. In September 1950, he replaced **Tep Phan** as the royal delegate to the province of Siemreap. In 1952, Huy Mong left his post in Siemreap to become director of the Ministry of Information in the Associated State of Cambodia.

**HUỲNH CƯỜNG (1923–).** Ethnic Khmer from southern Vietnam who supported the **Democratic Republic of Vietnam** (DRV) in the south during the Indochina War. During World War II, Huynh Cuong graduated from the *École supérieure des études bouddhiques* in Phnom Penh. He returned to southern Vietnam to teach and joined the Cambodian Buddhist Association in **Cochinchina**. He played a pivotal role in ending violent incidents between Khmer and Viet populations in southern Vietnam in 1945–1946. He supported the efforts of the DRV to create "greater solidarity" between the two races living in the new nation-state of Vietnam and worked for the government among the Khmer population living in southern Vietnam during the Indochina War. He was also a strong defender of Cambodian culture and language in southern Vietnam. He would become an active member of the Buddhist opposition movement to **Ngo Dinh Diem** after 1954, when he became general secretary of the Khmer Buddhist Institute in the **Republic of Vietnam**. *See also* KHMER KROM.

**HUỲNH ĐẮC HƯƠNG (1921–).** Influential political leader in central Vietnam during the Franco-Vietnamese conflict. He became involved in radical politics in the 1930s and joined the **Indochinese Communist Party** (ICP) in 1942. Upon liberation from prison in March 1945, he returned to Quang Nam province and helped nationalists take over there after World War II. In October 1945, besides serving as a ranking communist in the region, he became head of the Political-Military Academy of Quang Nam and then a regimental political commissar. Between 1948 and 1949, he was deputy director of the Political Office of **Inter-Zone V** (*Lien Khu V*). In March 1952, he served as a special ICP delegate for that region. A year later, he resumed his tasks in Inter-Zone V, where he remained until the end of the war.

**HUỲNH PHAN HỘ (PHAN TRỌNG HỘ, 1911–1947).** Behind-the-scenes communist leader in southern Vietnam in the 1940s. Born in Soc Trang, he studied at the Can Tho high school. There he joined general student strikes triggered by the funeral of Phan Chu Trinh. Until 1945, he worked on a large colonial plantation in Can Tho. During World War II, he became increasingly involved in communist politics in this province where he was won over by a senior southern communist, **Ung Van Khiem**. Huynh Phan Ho used his work on the plantation to cover Ung Van Khiem's communist activities and to help southern leaders rebuild after the devastating repression of the failed communist uprising of 1940. Huynh Phan Ho entered the **Indochinese Communist Party** (ICP) around 1945. At the end of World War II, he helped nationalists take power in Can Tho and became a member of the Resistance Committee in Hau Giang provinces where he was in charge of nationalist front work. In September 1945, the ICP put him in charge of the Republican Guards in Can Tho. When the French returned militarily, he participated in numerous battles in late 1945 and all of 1946. In early 1947, the Ministry of Defense named him head of war **Zone IX** (*Khu Chien IX*). He died in combat in July 1947.

**HUỲNH PHÚ SỔ (1920–1947).** Founder of the Vietnamese religious movement, the **Hoa Hao,** who was assassinated by the forces of the **Democratic Republic of Vietnam** (DRV). Born in Chau Doc province in southern Vietnam, he studied in a Franco-Vietnamese elementary school before dedicating himself to the creation of a new syncretic Buddhist sect, the Hoa Hao, announced in 1939. His influence spread across western Nam Bo and eventually led the French to arrest him. During World War II, the Japanese developed contacts with the Hoa Hao and freed Huynh Phu So from French incarceration in 1942 in **Saigon**. In 1945, with the defeat of the Japanese, Huynh Phu So temporarily aligned his followers with the nationalist cause of the DRV. That collaboration, however, did not last long. By 1947, the French Army's ***Deuxième Bureau*** was able to intensify its contacts with members of the Hoa Hoa in an effort to break them off from the **Viet Minh**. Confidence was already lacking between the DRV and a variety of politico-religious groups in the south. In June 1946, Huynh Phu So created a separate political party called the Vietnamese National-Socialist Party (*Dang Viet Nam Dan Chu Xa Hoi*, or *Dang Dan Xa* for short) and appointed himself leader. In April 1947, attacks between the Hoa Hao and the Viet Minh, exacerbated by shrewd moves by French intelligence officers, such as **Antoine Savani**, led to a violent break when the DRV's forces assassinated Huynh Phu So in order to consolidate their hold over the military forces in the south and block French attempts to turn the Hoa Hoa and others against them, politically and militarily. The Hoa Hoa, **Cao Dai,** and eventually the **Binh Xuyen** would transfer their allegiance to the French and their counter-revolutionary state under construction thanks to **Bao Dai**'s **collaboration**. French journalist **Jean Lacouture** came away from an interview with Huynh Phu So, whom the French called the "mad monk" (*le bonze fou*) in 1945, struck by "*son visage de visionnaire, d'une tension et d'une beauté saisissante était de ceux que l'on ne peut oublier*".

**HUỲNH TẤN PHÁT (SÁU PHÁT, TAM CHÍ, 1913–1989).** Born in My Tho province in southern Vietnam, Huynh Tan Phat graduated from the *École supérieure des beaux-arts* in **Hanoi** in 1938. He became politically active during the heady Popular Front days lasting between 1936 and 1939. He took part in the Indochinese General Students Association (*Tong Hoi Sinh Vien Dong Duong*) and the Student Friendship Association in **Cochinchina** (*Hoi Ai Huu Sinh Vien Nam Ky*). He was the director of the Youth (*Thanh Nien*) newspaper in 1943. He joined the **Indochinese Communist Party** shortly after the Japanese ***coup de force*** **of 9 March 1945** and helped nationalists take power in **Saigon** a few months later. With the birth of the **Democratic Republic of Vietnam**, he served briefly as deputy director of the Bureau of Information and Press in the south (*So Thong Tin Bao Chi*). In early 1946, he was arrested by the French, but was released in 1947. He continued to work underground in Saigon and joined the **Vietnamese Democratic Party** (*Dang Dan Chu*). Sometime around 1949, he left Saigon for the *maquis* where he became a member on the **Resistance and Administrative Committee** of Nam Bo and director of the Bureau of Information for Nam Bo (*So Thong Tin Nam Bo*). Between 1950 and 1954, he served on the board of the Resistance and Administrative Committee for the Special Zone of Saigon-Cholon. He directed the paper *Dai Tieng Noi Sai Gon – Cho Lon Tu Do* (from the secret **War Zone D** located just outside the city) until the end of the war. After Vietnam was divided provisionally into two states in 1954, he remained in the south and in 1957 was elected a member of the Party's Secret Committee for the Conglomerate of Saigon-Cholon.

**HUỲNH THÚC KHÁNG (MINH VIÊN, 1876–1947).** Vietnamese nationalist during the first half of the 20th century and supporter of the **Democratic Republic of Vietnam** (DRV). He passed the traditional examination system to become a doctor in 1904. Born into a modest scholarly family in Quang Nam province, Huynh Thuc Khang was an early nationalist reformer, influenced by Chinese texts arriving via the **overseas Chinese** active in the port of Hoi An. While he knew Phan Boi Chau, he preferred the reformist ideas of Phan Chu Trinh and was an early Vietnamese supporter of the French League for the Defense of Human Rights or the *Ligue des droits de l'Homme*. In 1908, following local tax revolts, he was arrested, sentenced by the Court of Hue to "perpetual deportation", and incarcerated in the colonial prison at **Poulo Condor**. He was liberated in 1925. Thanks to his patriotism, he was elected to the Consultative Chamber of **Annam**, but resigned in 1928 convinced that the French were not willing to reform. He turned to journalism and edited the central Vietnamese nationalist paper, *Tieng Dan*. After the Japanese overthrow of the French on 9 March 1945, he refused to join the Japanese-backed **Tran Trong Kim** government. However, **Ho Chi Minh** won him over to the nationalist cause of the DRV. On 2 March 1946, Huynh Thuc Khang became a deputy in the Vietnamese National Assembly and was named minister of the Interior. He worked closely with **Vo Nguyen Giap**, whom he had known from the colonial period. In late 1946, Huynh Thuc Khang was sent as a special government delegate to war **Zone** V (*Khu Chien V*) to try to solve problems concerning local pre–1945 officials who balked at collaborating with the new government. During the summer of 1946, he served as acting president of the DRV during Ho Chi Minh's absence from June to October. He passed away in Quang Ngai in early 1947, having been sent to work there with **Pham Van Dong**.

**HUỲNH VĂN NGHỆ (TAM NGẠI, 1914–1977).** Ranking leader of **Inter-Zone VII** (*Lien Khu VII*) in eastern Nam Bo during the Indochina War. Born in southern Vietnam, Huynh Van Nghe studied in the Petrus Ky high school and became politically active during the 1930s. Because of his support for the 1940 communist-backed uprising in **Cochinchina**, he finally had to flee to Thailand in 1942. In 1944, he secretly returned to **Saigon** where he helped nationalists take power following the Japanese defeat in August 1945. He participated in combat against the return of the French to southern Vietnam in 1945 and 1946. He played an important role in setting up what would become a famous clandestine base – **War Zone D**, located in Bien Hoa province near Saigon-Cholon. In January 1948, he was named deputy director of war **Zone VII** (*Khu VII*) in eastern Nam Bo. In 1953, he was called to northern Vietnam where he was put in charge of the Bureau of Army Politico-Military Training in the **General Staff** of the Armed Forces (*Cuc Quan Huan Bo Tong Tham Muu*).

**HUỲNH VĂN TRÌ (MƯỜI TRÌ, 1909–1979).** Leader of **Hoa Hao** forces largely loyal to the **Democratic Republic of Vietnam** (DRV) during the Indochina War. He was born into a rural family in Gia Dinh province near **Saigon**. Little is known about his activities during the interwar period, except that he was sufficiently active between 1930 and 1945 to land himself in colonial prison four times – each time at **Poulo Condor** (from which he apparently escaped four times). During his time there, this adept of the **Hoa Hao** Buddhist sect rubbed shoulders with **Pham Hung**, a southern senior communist who would head up the DRV's security forces during the Indochina War. Huynh Van Tri's last jailbreak put him in southern Vietnam in time to help nationalists take power there. In 1947, he took over the leadership of Detachment 4 (*Chi Doi 4*) before becoming the head of the 304th regiment. In March 1947, **Nguyen Binh** sent him to negotiate with Hoa Hoa leaders suspicious of the **Viet Minh**, but to no avail. Despite the violent break between the Hoa Hao and the DRV's southern forces in 1947, Huynh Van Tri remained loyal to the government, with his prison ties to the communists undoubtedly coming into play. He was responsible for rebuilding cooperation with the Hoa Hoa in the Long Chau Ha region and he ran the **Indochina Communist Party**'s Provincial Committee for Long Chau Ha province between 1950 and 1954 (meaning that he must have joined the party early on). With the division of Vietnam into two provisional states during the **Geneva Conference** in 1954, he relocated to northern Vietnam where he would hold ranking posts in the army during the Vietnam War.

# I

**ICC.** *See* INTERNATIONAL COMMISSION FOR SUPERVISION AND CONTROL IN VIETNAM.

**IEHLÉ, PIERRE (1914–1984).** Graduated from the French Naval Academy in the mid-1930s, Iehlé crossed over to Free French forces in December 1940 and made his way to Dakar. He saw combat in Syria in 1941 and fought at El Alamein a year later. Following World War II, he transferred to Indochina where he served as chief of cabinet to the high commissioner for Indochina between 1945 and 1947, **Georges Thierry d'Argenlieu**. After a short return to France, Iehlé was back in Indochina in 1948 to work in the General Staff of the commanding general of French Ground Troops in **Tonkin**. For nine months in 1950, he commanded the French naval post at Ream, Cambodia, in the Gulf of Thailand before returning to France at the end of the year.

**IENG SARY (KIM TRANG, 1929–).** Early Cambodian communist and future Khmer Rouge leader. Born in the province of Vinh Binh in colonial southern Vietnam, Ieng Sary grew up in Cambodia where he obtained a scholarship to study at the *Lycée Sisowath* in Phnom Penh. He met **Saloth Sar**, the future Pol Pot, in 1947 and both supported the newly created Cambodian **Democrat Party**. Although Ieng Sary helped organize an anti-colonialist student demonstration at the *Lycée Sisowath* in 1949, this did not prevent him from obtaining a government scholarship to study in France, which he did between 1950 and 1953. He enrolled in a commercial school in Paris before transferring briefly in 1953 to the *Institut d'études politiques*, better known as *SciencesPo*. During his time in France, he became involved in radical politics with Saloth Sar and others. He is alleged to have joined the **French Communist Party**. Upon his return to Cambodia, he at first played an insignificant role in the Cambodian communist movement dominated by Cambodians allied with Vietnamese communists. *See also* ADVISORY GROUP 100; CAMBODIAN RESISTANCE GOVERNMENT; COLLABORATION; COMMITTEE FOR EXTERNAL AFFAIRS; HOANG VAN HOAN; INDOCHINESE COMMUNIST PARTY; INDOCHINESE FEDERATION; KHMER KROM; NGUYEN KHANG; NGUYEN THANH SON; PARTY AFFAIRS COMMITTEE; LAO RESISTANCE GOVERNMENT.

**IEU KOEUS (1905–1950).** Leading Cambodian politician and leader of the **Democrat Party,** assassinated in 1950. Born in Battambang province, he completed his early studies in the main pagoda school of Kandal province and in the primary school in the provincial capital of Battambang. He pursued his secondary studies at the *Lycée Sisowath* in Phnom Penh before studying at the *École de commerce* in **Hanoi**, from which he graduated at the top of his class in 1927. He returned to Cambodia to work for a rubber plantation and as an entrepreneur on major public works projects in Battambang. He also became involved in nationalist politics in the 1930s, collaborating with **Son Ngoc Thanh** and others linked to the Buddhist Institute under the patronage of Suzanne Karpelès of the ***École française d'Extrême-Orient***. One of Cambodia's early nationalists, Ieu Koeus participated in creating the first Khmer-language typewriter and published a Khmer grammar book. In 1940, he became a member of the *Chambres des représentants du peuple* in Cambodia. Little is known of his activities during World War II other than the fact that he served as deputy minister of the Economy in the shortlived Son Ngoc Thanh government backed by the Japanese in mid-1945. After the Pacific War, however, he played a pivotal role in the creation of the Democrat Party in 1946 and was named provisional president of the National Assembly in charge of elaborating a national constitution. In 1947, he took over as leader of the Democrat Party. Between 20 and 28 September 1949, he was president of the council and minister of the Interior. In 1949, the King sent him to France for the signing of the Franco-Cambodian Accord. He was assassinated on 14 January 1950 by a grenade attack in the Democrat Party headquarters in Phnom Penh. The perpetrators have never been positively identified. *See also*

NORODOM SIHANOUK; ROYAL CRUSADE FOR INDEPENDENCE.

**IMFELD, HANS (1902–1947).** French citizen of Swiss origin who served as commissioner to Laos following World War II. Imfeld entered the French army in 1925 and became a second lieutenant in 1930. He left for Indochina in 1932, where he was named lieutenant that same year. He commanded in the colonial army in **Tonkin** before returning briefly to France in 1936. There he studied intensively geography and topography before rejoining the colonial army in Indochina in 1937. In October 1943, during the Japanese occupation, he joined the Free French Military Mission based in southern China and was condemned to death by a Vichy military court in **Hanoi** for **desertion**. He became a major in 1944 in the forces of the French Provisional Republic led by **Charles de Gaulle**. In July 1944, he joined the French advance party in **India**, the *détachement français des Indes,* working with and trained by British special forces. The British parachuted Imfeld secretly into Indochina in February 1945. He narrowly escaped capture during the Japanese ***coup de force* of 9 March 1945**. As part of a larger **guerrilla** operation in Laos, Imfeld ran a network in the northern part of the country. On 2 September 1945, he became French Commissioner for the Republic in Laos. However, unable to gain the support of the Chinese forces sent to accept the Japanese surrender in Laos above the **16th parallel**, in January 1946 he pulled back into Thailand before returning to Indochina to conduct covert operations in the Tai territories of northern Vietnam. Besides being an important and effective intelligence officer, he also served as Commissioner (interim) for Laos between March 1946 and April 1946. On 11 October 1947, an agent of the **Democratic Republic of Vietnam** working undercover as a barber assassinated Imfeld in his hotel room at the *Hôtel des Nations* in **Saigon**. However, it was later learned that the DRV assassin had mistaken Imfeld for **Jean Cédile.**

**INALCO.** *See ÉCOLE NATIONALE DES LANGUES ORIENTALES VIVANTES.*

**INDIA.** The Indians, like the Thais, Burmese, and Indonesians, were widely sympathetic to the **Democratic Republic of Vietnam**'s (DRV) struggle for national independence, but not its communist agenda for Indochina. None of this was lost on **Viet Minh** leaders upon coming to power.

In 1946, when India gained her independence, the DRV made overtures to **Jawaharlal Nehru** in the hope of securing the support of one of Asia's "awakening giants", and a vocally anti-colonialist one at that. In March 1946, a DRV editorial lauded Nehru's plans for building an Asian Union, one which would uplift the "small and weak nations" in Asia. A year later, keen to tap into the Indian leader's pan-Asianism, the DRV sent representatives to the Inter-Relations Conference organized and hosted by him. Nehru's opposition to the landing of French warships and planes in Indian ports impressed the Vietnamese, as did his critique of the British use of **Indian** soldiers to crush the nationalist insurrection in southern Vietnam. However, in the end, all that Pandit Nehru would offer the Vietnamese nationalist movement during the Indochina War was "moral" support. He refused to accord military aid, for fear of jeopardizing Indian negotiations with the French over Pondicherry and widening the conflict in Indochina and Asia. He tried to steer a neutral path. For example, Nehru allowed the French high commissioner for Indochina, **Georges Thierry d'Argenlieu**, to send the delegate of the **Provisional Government of the Republic of Cochinchina** to the Asian Relations Conference in 1947, much to the DRV's disappointment. Nor did Nehru bring up the Vietnamese question effectively in the **United Nations**, despite just such a request from the DRV's diplomat-at-large **Pham Ngoc Thach** in 1948.

Nehru's direct involvement in pushing the Dutch to end the war in Indonesia stood in contrast to his refusal to take concrete measures to help the DRV. There are several reasons for this. The arrival of the **Cold War** in Asia in force in 1950, symbolized by the outbreak of the **Korean War**, saw the West increase pressure upon India to choose between one of the two Vietnams – either the Associated State of Vietnam led by **Bao Dai** or **Ho Chi Minh**'s DRV, which had been recognized by the communist bloc in early 1950. As a major non-communist post-colonial Asian state, India became the scene of intense diplomatic pressure. Backed by the French, Bao Dai sent his first emissaries to New Delhi in 1949 to try to convince the Indian government to recognize the State of Vietnam. Fluent in English and one of the DRV's future top diplomats, Ngo Dien left for New Delhi to do the same. To no avail. Nehru refused to recognize either of the two Vietnams. In a press conference on 6 January 1950, even before the

Sino-Soviet recognition of the DRV, he explained that his government would not align itself with any side in the building Cold War: "India's policy is to give no official recognition in Indo-China to any government, as authority there is divided. For the present we are just to watch developments there and let the people of Indo-China decide".

There was more to it than that, however. At odds with communists inside India and upset by communist China's hard line on Tibet since 1950 and its criticism of Indian non-communist leaders, the Indians had their own reasons for wanting to see communism contained at the Indochinese pass. Indians such as Nehru were suspicious of the DRV's revolutionary ambitions in Laos and Cambodia, which were considered to share a common cultural heritage with India.

Chinese statesman and diplomat, **Zhou Enlai,** clearly understood that improving relations with India was vital to implementing his policy of peaceful co-existence as the Korean War came to an end in 1953 and negotiations to end the Indochina War intensified. In April 1954, the Indians and Chinese reached an agreement to remove Tibet as a point of contention between the two sides and the Chinese promised that they would not export communism outside their borders. During a trip to New Delhi during the Geneva negotiations, Zhou Enlai reiterated China's peaceful intentions and its refusal to export communism outside its borders. Zhou also reassured Nehru that he did not support the Vietnamese communist attempts to push an Indochinese revolution on the Lao and Cambodians. Neutrality is what Zhou wanted. To this end, he agreed with Nehru that the royal governments of Laos and Cambodia were legitimate, and not the resistance governments of the **Pathet Lao** and the **Khmer Issarak**. This meeting with Nehru and the joint communiqué issued at its closure allowed Zhou Enlai to move negotiations forward at Geneva and to "neutralize" non-communist Asian states such as India, Indonesia, and Burma against the Americans. This *détente* with China also explains why Nehru was willing to invite Zhou Enlai to take part in the Bandung Conference of 1955. *See also* GENEVA ACCORDS; INDIANS, INDOCHINA WAR; NEUTRALIZATION OF INDOCHINA.

**INDIANS, INDOCHINA WAR.** The French were not the only ones to rely on their colonies to fight their wars and occupy large swaths of Asia following the defeat of imperial Japan in mid-1945. In September 1945, in accordance with agreements reached during the **Potsdam conference**, Sir Douglas Gracey led 20,000 troops of his 20th (mainly) Indian division to accept the Japanese surrender below the **16th parallel** in former French Indochina, while Chinese nationalist troops occupied northern Indochina above that line. These Indian troops helped disarm all Japanese forces in lower Indochina, maintain law and order, locate and evacuate Allied **prisoners of war**, and, following the outbreak of war in southern Vietnam on **23 September 1945**, engage **Viet Minh** forces in battle. The outbreak of violence that day led to a strange Euro-Asian coalition operating against the Viet Minh comprised of Indian colonial troops and Japanese imperial ones. Vietnamese resentment, as Christopher Bayly and Tim Harper have noted, bubbled up, resulting in the killing of half a dozen local Indians living in **Saigon** in 1945. Similar things happened in **Hanoi** during the outbreak of full-scale war on **19 December 1946**. Vietnamese nationalists were not the only ones to decry the British use of Indian troops. **Nehru** also condemned the use of Asian troops against other Asians fighting for their national independence. In late October 1945, Lord Wavell, the British Viceroy of India, urged the rapid withdrawal of Indian forces from Indochina. However, the damage was done. No longer would the British dare to use their colonial Asian troops in operations against other nationalist movements in Asia. Indians, however, were no strangers to Vietnam or Southeast Asia, having lived, worked, and traded there long before the arrival of the French and the British. While the Indian community in Indochina, numbering some 2,000 individuals, never matched that of the **overseas Chinese**, they occupied positions in local banking and trading networks and worked in garment businesses and in the colonial administration in Hanoi, Phnom Penh, and Saigon. However, many of these Indians returned to India because of the unrest generated during the Indochina War. *See also* CROSSOVERS; MINORITY ETHNIC GROUPS; JAPANESE TROOPS, INDOCHINA WAR; REPATRIATION, JAPANESE TROOPS.

**INDOCHINESE COMMUNIST PARTY (ICP).** The Indochinese Communist Party (ICP) played the leading role in the war of national liberation against the French between 1945 and 1954 and in the establishment of a single-party communist state during the conflict, above the **17th parallel** from 1954, and in all of Vietnam from 1975.

**Ho Chi Minh** played a vital role in grafting communism to Vietnamese nationalism, to borrow Huynh Kim Khanh's analogy, in the late 1920s. This began when Ho Chi Minh created the Revolutionary Youth League in Guangzhou (Canton) in 1925 before fusing it with other self-proclaimed communist parties inside Vietnam to create the Vietnamese Communist Party in Hong Kong in February 1930, with the help of the Comintern and the **Chinese Communist Party**. However, younger Vietnamese communists such as Tran Phu contested Ho's ideological mettle. Tran criticized Ho's narrow nationalism and weak internationalism. Upon the request of the Comintern, the party changed its name from the *Vietnamese* to the *Indochinese* Communist Party in late 1930. In 1931, the Comintern recognized the ICP as an official section of the Soviet-led communist movement.

Ho Chi Minh returned to the scene as war broke out across the globe in the late 1930s. In May 1941, he played a pivotal role in getting the **Viet Minh** off the ground during the 8th Plenum of the ICP's Central Committee, even though he was not general secretary of the party. Indeed, the party had suffered greatly inside Vietnam, first in the early 1930s when the French crushed communist-backed peasant revolts in central Vietnam and again in **Cochinchina** when the French smashed a communist-led uprising in 1940. This colonial repression effectively shifted the center of gravity of Vietnamese communism to the north, with the establishment of a core group of communists working under the leadership of **Truong Chinh** in the Red River delta. A second group emerged along the Sino-Vietnamese border with the return of Ho Chi Minh to southern China. Both groups worked to build up national front organizations. For a period of four years, while most communist cadres were still locked up in colonial prisons, these two groups positioned the ICP-led Viet Minh to take power at the propitious moment.

Following the Japanese overthrow of the French in March 1945, the release of dozens of communists strengthened the party ranks. In August, however, while the main communist leaders were gathered at Tan Trao to prepare for an uprising to converge with the coming Allied invasion, the Japanese suddenly capitulated in the wake of the nuclear attacks on Nagasaki and Hiroshima. This prevented the communists from leading the **August Revolution** as directly as its leaders would later claim. Rather the party rode a groundswell of famine-driven discontent to power, with local, second-rank communists acting as the main organizers, as David Marr has shown. Even after 1945, the ICP was never as omnipresent as its official historians and anti-communist detractors would have us believe. The party was particularly weak in southern Vietnam, due to the failed communist uprising of 1940, division among party factions, and serious competition from non-communist nationalist, religious, and patriotic bandit groups – the **Hoa Hao, Cao Dai** and **Binh Xuyen**. Indeed, until around 1951, the ICP had to create a number of different nationalist alliances and front associations, take control of the army and security forces, and eliminate rival parties before it could truly claim to direct the state and society. Even then, the party's hold on the state was never "total", nor was its control of Vietnamese territory.

International pressures also complicated the party's operation. In a move designed to allay American, Chinese, and oppositional anti-communism, the communist leadership in the north went so far as to declare publicly the **dissolution of the Indochinese Communist Party.** In reality, the party never truly disbanded, preferring to operate from behind the scenes. The dissolution of the party nonetheless raised doubts among the French, Chinese, and especially Soviet communists as to the ideological commitment of the ICP in general and the ideological mettle of Ho Chi Minh in particular. In 1949 and early 1950, **Tran Ngoc Danh**, the younger brother of Tran Phu, reiterated his brother's earlier criticism of Ho Chi Minh's narrow nationalist deviationism. Chinese communists, not least of all **Mao Zedong**, backed Ho Chi Minh against his detractors in the communist world. And the ICP returned in force from 1950, thanks to the Sino-Soviet diplomatic recognition of the **Democratic Republic of Vietnam** and the arrival of Chinese military, technical, economic, and ideological **aid**.

In order to demonstrate its fidelity to the international movement, the ICP changed its name to become the **Vietnamese Workers' Party** (VWP) and agreed to begin the communization of the state, the army, and society in areas under DRV control. In 1953, the VWP officially began implementing **land reform** in order to mobilize the society for the war, break the traditional social structures in the countryside, prepare the economy for communist transformation, and allay international communist fears that the ICP was not sufficiently communist. The party's name was changed back to "Vietnam", on the grounds that the revolutionary tide was more advanced in the eastern part of former French Indochina and in light of the simultaneous French decision to transform colonial Indochina into three associated states – Laos, Cambodia, and Vietnam. However, like the French, this did not mean that Vietnamese communists abandoned their Indochinese tack. From 1950, the Vietnamese communists helped their allies in Laos and Cambodia to create "resistance governments", proto-communist parties, and national fronts in order to take on the French **Associated States of Indochina**. The Indochinese internationalist model imposed in 1930 remained valid throughout the entire Indochina War. For Vietnamese communists, communism was both nationalist and internationalist. *See also* ASSOCIATED STATES OF INDOCHINA; CAMBODIAN RESISTANCE GOVERNMENT; CIVIL WAR; COMMITTEE OF EXTERNAL AFFAIRS; GREATER VIETNAMESE NATIONALIST PARTY; INDOCHINESE FEDERATION; JOSEPH STALIN; LAO RESISTANCE GOVERNMENT; MAO ZEDONG; PARTY CADRES COMMITTEE; PEOPLE'S REPUBLIC OF CHINA; RECTIFICATION.

**INDOCHINESE FEDERATION.** The provisional French government led by **Charles de Gaulle** formally announced its plans to create an Indochinese Federation in the **Declaration on Indochina** of 23 March 1945, some two weeks after the Japanese ***coup de force* of 9 March 1945** had brought down French Indochina. During the **Brazzaville Conference** in 1944, de Gaulle's colonial specialists had agreed that a **French Union** predicated on colonial federalism, especially in Indochina, would announce the implementation of a liberal French colonial policy. Federalism would allow the French to allay American critiques of French colonial policy and neutralize nationalist sentiment in the Empire let loose by World War II and France's defeat in 1940. But federalism was not an association or a commonwealth allowing for the emergence of independent nation-states. As one of the main architects of the Federation, **Léon Pignon**, put it: "the ultimate aim of our policy is nonetheless and above all to keep Indochina French".

According to this French plan, Indochina would be transformed into a colonial Federation composed of five territories: **Tonkin**, **Annam**, **Cochinchina**, Laos, and Cambodia. An Indochinese Assembly would be elected to write legislation, giving deputies the right to vote on taxes and the budget. Indochinese and French Union citizenship would be bestowed upon the non-French inhabitants of the new colonial state and freedom of the press, of religion, and of association would be accorded and workers rights respected. The French planned to industrialize eastern Indochina in light of growing demographic problems. In exchange, the French expected to stay at the helm. The Federation's ministers and upper house would be subordinate to a French governor general, appointed by the French government. France would represent Indochina diplomatically and the federation's armed forces would fall under French supervision as part of those of the wider French Union.

The problem was that events in Indochina had already outpaced the 23 March declaration in which the French officially announced their vision of the Indochinese Federation. The Japanese had just brought down colonial Indochina and had granted the local states an independence as hollow as it might have been in practice. The **Viet Minh** was thinking in terms of national independence and no longer colonial reform. Worse, the Indochinese Federation was based upon a pentagonal structure, one which divided the national idea of Vietnam into three continued colonial parts, stirring the nationalist ire of the majority of communists and non-communists alike. Indeed, the French designed the Federation in part to check Vietnamese domination of it and to counteract Vietnamese nationalism.

Upon arriving in Indochina in 1945, the French High Commissioner **Georges Thierry d'Argenlieu** followed Charles de Gaulle's instructions to the letter by retaking the lost colony piece by piece in order to recast it in the federal form. On 1 June 1946, he countered the **Democratic Republic of Vietnam**'s (DRV) attempts to reunify Cochinchina with the rest of Vietnam by announcing the creation of a separate Cochinchinese "free state" (*état libre*).

The DRV leadership was not necessarily opposed to the idea of joining the Federation, as **Ho Chi Minh**'s signing of the **Accords of 6 March 1946** made clear. However, the Vietnamese were determined to realize the unification of Vietnam and ensure its eventual independence. The Indochinese Federation thus meant different things to the French and the Vietnamese. As Ho Chi Minh put it, his government would agree to take part in a Federation of a mainly economic nature, "but was determined to block the re-emergence of the prewar governor general in the disguise of the

Federation". To an increasing number of Vietnamese nationalists, French colonialism, federal or not, could not continue indefinitely. Vietnamese nationalists, and not just the communists, claimed the right to rule themselves. *See also* INDOCHINESE COMMUNIST PARTY; VIETNAMESE NATIONALIST PARTY.

**INDOCHINESE TRAIL.** *See* HO CHI MINH TRAIL.

**INDOCTRINATION.** Both the French Fourth Republic and the **Democratic Republic of Vietnam** (DRV) organized the re-education and the indoctrination of their respective prisoners. And both drew upon the experiences of World War II in doing so. The Allies had organized special "democracy" classes for their prisoners while the Soviets provided communist re-education for many of their captured. The French and the Vietnamese were well aware of these models and adopted, adapted, and applied them during the Indochina War to varying degrees. With the creation of **Deuxième Bureau**'s **psychological warfare** operations in the early 1950s, the French army allocated a sizeable amount of money to the re-education of Vietnamese prisoners. This meant the organization of special political classes during which French and Vietnamese propagandist specialists dispensed an anti-communist, pro-Western program. On several occasions, once re-education was sufficiently attained, the French integrated the soldiers into its fighting forces or used them as agents in its various intelligence services. The DRV carefully organized the indoctrination of thousands of its **French Union prisoners of war** taken in the early 1950s. They often drew upon Sino-Soviet communist models. In elaborate re-education classes, political cadres, even leftist European **crossovers** like **Rudy Schroeder** and **Georges Boudarel**, indoctrinated French Union prisoners about the just cause of the DRV's war of national independence, the crimes of French colonialism in Indochina, and the advantages of communist civilization. The most important communist method of indoctrination was the process of **rectification**, designed to instill a new ideological way of thinking among cadres, soldiers, and bureaucrats in the DRV. *See also* EMULATION CAMPAIGN, NEW HERO.

**INDONESIA.** Indonesians, like the Burmese and Indians, were widely sympathetic to the **Democratic Republic of Vietnam**'s (DRV) struggle for national independence. However, the DRV's communist core posed problems for these non-communist states, especially Indonesian Republicans who were often at odds with communists in their own ranks or fearful of being labelled communists by the Dutch or the United States. As Indonesian statesman Sutan Sjahrir put it privately in late 1945 concerning his reluctance to respond to early Vietnamese calls to create an anti-colonial Southeast Asian bloc: "**Ho Chi Minh** is facing the French who will resist him for a very long time. Ho is also dependent on the support of the Communists, who are very powerful in the independence movement, which is not the case with us [...] If we ally ourselves with Ho Chi Minh, we will weaken ourselves and delay independence". Moreover, whereas Vietnamese communists would attack their non-communist nationalist competitors in Vietnam in 1946, forcing them to work with the French, the Indonesian Republicans smashed their communist competitors in 1948 during the Madiun revolt. Two very different postcolonial states and outcomes were thus at work.

The arrival of the **Cold War** in full force in 1950 put the Indonesians in a difficult position, as the West pressured them to recognize the Associated State of Vietnam led by **Bao Dai** instead of the DRV (which had been recognized by the communist bloc in January 1950). In March 1950, Prime Minister Muhammad Hatta informed the British that his government was closely studying the Vietnamese question. In fact, Indonesia came surprisingly close to recognizing the DRV diplomatically on anticolonial grounds. In early June, a motion to recognize the DRV came before the Indonesian parliament. Dr. Sakirman of the *Partai Sosialis* had submitted this motion. The House had already debated it; a vote on it was imminent. The Sakirman motion was very anti-colonialist, something which made it hard for any nationalist leader, including Hatta, to oppose. But Hatta did not want to take sides over Vietnam, agreeing with **Jawaharlal Nehru** that behind this choice between two Vietnam's lay the seeds of a major conflict. To avoid recognizing the DRV, the government enlisted Mr. Natsir, a member of the Muslim Masjumi party, to submit a watered-down counter motion, stopping short of diplomatic recognition but still sufficiently anti-colonialist in tone and content. Mr. Natsir's motion urged the government to study the Vietnam question in greater detail before extending recognition. "We have to bring the **Viet Minh** question", Natsir said, "on to an international level", arguing that the "Viet Minh's struggle for freedom runs parallel with Indonesia's struggle, but if we support the Viet Minh's struggle we must give such assistance as will benefit the Viet Minh without weakening Indonesia's positions". When the debate resumed, the Socialists continued to push for diplomatic recognition of the DRV as part of the fight against imperialism. They insisted that Indonesia should not allow its foreign policy to be dictated by foreign loan conditions and Western pressure. In the end, both motions were presented together, with each member being left the right to vote for the motion of his or her choice. To the relief of the Hatta government, to say nothing of the Americans, British, and French, the Natsir motion won over the Sakirman one by a vote of 49 to 38. The question of Indonesian diplomatic recognition of the DRV was thus shelved for the time being, and a potential crisis in Indonesian-American relations averted. *See also* CIVIL WAR; VIETNAMESE NATIONALIST PARTY.

**INDUSTRIALIZATION.** *See* ECONOMY OF WAR, FRANCE.

**INSTRUCTIONS FOR "PEOPLE'S TOTAL RESISTANCE" (*Chỉ Thị "Toàn Dân Kháng Chiến"*).** On 22 December 1946, in the wake of the outbreak of full-scale war in all of Vietnam on **19 December 1946**, the Standing Committee of the **Indochinese Communist Party** issued a policy directive calling for armed resistance against the French. The Vietnamese struggle was to be a "total" (*toan dien*) war, both in terms of the fighting against the French and in terms of building the state (*vua khang chien vua kien quoc*). *See also* DISEASE; EXPEDITIONARY CORPS; EXPERIENCE OF WAR; PEOPLE'S ARMY OF VIETNAM.

**INTELLECTUALS, FRENCH.** If the **Algerian War** mobilized scores of French intellectuals, ranging from **Jean Paul Sartre** to **Raymond Aron**, what is most striking about the Indochina War is the relative silence of the French intellectual class during and about France's first war of decolonization. There were exceptions to be sure. For example, intellectuals associated with the reviews ***Esprit*** and ***Témoignage Chrétien*** published penetrating articles on colonialism and nationalism in Indochina. Indeed, *Esprit* was one of the rare reviews to have published articles condemning the French use of **torture** in Vietnam in the early 1930s. Under **Jean-Marie Domenach's** guidance, this review continued to speak out against the war in Indochina after World War II. Incisive essays appeared on the dangers of French colonial policy and the need to take colonial nationalism seriously in the global South.

In 1949, the French scholar and director of the **Colonial Academy**, **Paul Mus**, dropped a bombshell when he published a series of articles condemning the French army's use of torture, using this as a way of criticizing the failure of the French to recognize the historical reality of Vietnamese nationalism and humanity. While Mus's essays irked the Right and Far Right, the question of torture never provoked intellectuals into a full-blown debate on the colonial question or the righteousness of the war, much less public demonstrations against the conflict. This is in contrast to the situation during the Algerian War, when the question of torture in particular coalesced French intellectuals led by Vidal Naquet into a driving force. Part of this was due to the fact that Indochina was far away and the use of a professional, colonial army there meant that French society itself was much less affected by the violence than during the Algerian one, when national service was in effect.

Intellectuals in the **French Communist Party** (FPC) were certainly among the first to speak out against colonialism, and long before World War II. They organized demonstrations against the Indochina War – strikes among dockers loading munitions for Indochina and demands for the release of **Henri Martin**, jailed for his opposition to the war. In so doing so, communist activists helped bring the Indochina conflict to the attention of the French public by the early 1950s. But at the outset of the war, even communists could go strangely silent in light of the FCP's desire to maintain its favorable position in the government coalition. During the Indochina War, with a few notable exceptions, French novelists, artists, musicians, poets, and screenwriters were relatively uninterested in the conflict. That the head of the colonial academy itself became arguably the most vocal and famous critic of the war says something about the wider intellectual uninterest in the Indochina War. *See also* BORIS VIAN; CHRISTIANS AND FRENCH OPPOSITION TO THE WAR;

CINEMA; NOVELS; PIERRE SCHOENDOERFFER; PUBLIC OPINION.

**INTELLECTUALS, DEMOCRATIC REPUBLIC OF VIETNAM.** At the outset, the independence cause of the **Democratic Republic of Vietnam** (DRV) attracted among the best and the brightest of the Vietnamese intellectual class. The DRV certainly needed them. Not only were the intellectuals an important source of legitimation for the young government, but their technical, legal, administrative, engineering, and medical talents were in great demand for building the new postcolonial state. Some of the best known names of those joining the DRV include **Pham Ngoc Thach**, Nguyen Manh Tuong, **Ton That Tung**, **Kha Vang Can**, **Nguyen Van Huong**, **Ca Van Thinh**, **Pham Thieu**, **Tran Dai Nghia**, **Pham Duy**, **Pham Ngoc Thao,** and **Tran Duc Thao.** Even former Emperor **Bao Dai** and Catholic Bishop **Le Huu Tu** supported the DRV cause at the outset, making it easier for a wide range of Vietnamese to join the **Viet Minh.**

Almost all of these young intellectuals were French-trained, more often than not admirers of French culture and language. Some had studied in France and were married to French women. Albeit anti-colonialist and nationalist, few, if any were *anti-français*. Dr. **Ho Dac Di** trained as a surgeon in France and played music with the daughter of Pierre and Marie Curie (who later married **Pierre Mendès France**). Ho Chi Minh made a point of assigning these illustrious French-trained Vietnamese to his (large) delegations sent to negotiate with the French during the **Dalat** and **Fontainebleau Conferences**. Many Vietnamese elites in France returned to Vietnam to work in the resistance government following the outbreak of full-scale war. The case of **Tran Dai Nghia** certainly comes to mind. A number of sympathetic Vietnamese intellectuals remained in the French-occupied cities, such as **Nguyen Manh Ha** and **Hoang Xuan Han**. Their refusal to collaborate with the French continued to serve the DRV cause as did their petitions and mediatized critiques of the war.

However, many of the best and brightest nationalists did not cross over to the DRV and those who did could change their minds. Why? Because of the communization of the new nation-state from 1950. The Chinese communist recognition of and military aid to the DRV led the **Indochinese Communist Party** to tighten its grip on the state and on its ideological control of civil servants, officiers, soldiers, and intellectuals. Party **rectification** and emulation campaigns sought to mobilize, control, and homogenize – and not to promote individual thought. Moreover, the new emphasis on "workers" and "peasants" ensured that mainly urban, "bourgeois" intellectuals found themselves in the wrong "class". If supporting the nationalist cause was not a problem, many "bourgeois" intellectuals balked at the idea of accepting the party's limits on freedom of expression and the politization of art, culture, and even medicine.

Desertions multiplied during the second half of the Indochina War because of the DRV's communization of the state, party, and society within the territories it controlled. Singer **Pham Duy**'s defection to the Associated State of Vietnam in the early 1950s was a common case, as was that of **Hoang Van Chi** and **Le Huu Tu**. Several threw in their lot with the communist party like Dr. **Ton That Tung**, while many retreated into the isolation of their villages or decided to live abroad. Even most of the sympathetic Vietnamese intellectuals living in **Hanoi**, who had refused to collaborate with the French and the Associated State of Vietnam, packed their bags and moved to **Saigon** or France rather than live under communist rule after the signing of the **Geneva Accords**. These people had closely followed the communization of the DRV, especially the **land reform** begun in 1953. *See also ATTENTISME*; CATHOLICS, EXODUS FROM NORTH; CATHOLICS IN VIETNAM AND THE WAR; CHRISTIANS AND OPPOSITION TO THE INDOCHINA WAR; CIVIL WAR; COLLABORATION; CROSSOVERS; DESERTION; NGUYEN MANH HA; POULO CONDOR; REFUGEES, FRANCE; VATICAN.

**INTELLIGENCE SERVICES, ARMY OF THE DEMOCRATIC REPUBLIC OF VIETNAM.** Upon creating the **Democratic Republic of Vietnam's** (DRV) **General Staff** on 7 September 1945, the Ministry of Defense authorized **Hoang Minh Dao** to lead a new military intelligence bureau, called *Phong 2*, a rough equivalent of the French ***Deuxième Bureau*** or 2[nd] Office (G2). This rudimentary military intelligence service followed as best it could enemy military movements in Vietnam above the **16[th] parallel,** especially in DRV **Inter-Zones IV** and **V** (*Lien Khu IV/V*). Below that line, the Vietnamese were largely on their own. Military intelligence received a boost on 25 March 1946, when **Ho Chi Minh** signed into law decree 34, which consolidated within the Ministry of Defense a separate Bureau of Intelligence (*Tình Bao Cuc*). In May 1947, the president signed a second piece of legislation creating a new High Command, consisting of a revamped Bureau of Intelligence (*Cuc Tinh Bao*). Until June 1948, **Tran Hieu** headed the Bureau of Intelligence for the High Command in the Ministry of Defense.

In central and especially northern Vietnam, this military intelligence service established offices at the provincial and district levels, though things never worked smoothly at the lower levels. Until 1949, it was mainly concerned with sabotage, commando operations, assassination missions, and local espionage. The Ministry of Defense's Bureau of Intelligence was extended to southern Vietnam in 1948.

The internationalization of the Franco-Vietnamese war from 1950 put added pressure on military intelligence to improve its work in order to take the war to the French. In 1950, a new Bureau of Military Intelligence (*Cuc Quan Bao*) emerged within the General Staff under the direction of **Le Trong Nghia**. This change was designed to meet the increasing needs of the army as it moved to engage the French in more modern warfare and set-piece battles. In early 1955, the DRV created a new intelligence service to run clandestine networks in the south, the southern Party Commission's Research Branch Responsible for Following the Enemy Situation (*Ban Nghien Cuu Dich Tinh Xu Uy*). *See also* LE GIAN; MAURICE BELLEUX; PHAM NGOC THAO; PUBLIC SECURITY SERVICES; *SERVICE DE DOCUMENTATION EXTERIEURE ET DE CONTRE-ESPIONAGE*; *SÛRETÉ FÉDÉRALE*; TRAN DANG NINH.

**INTERNATIONAL COMMISSION FOR SUPERVISION AND CONTROL IN VIETNAM (ICSC usually abbreviated ICC).** The **Geneva Accords** of July 1954 approved the creation of this international commission in order to oversee the implementation of the accords to end the Indochina War. The ICC was designed among other things to supervise the application of the cease-fire, the disarming of the belligerents, the withdrawal and regrouping of troops, and the care of **prisoners of war** and wounded. The selection of the three commission members – Canada, Poland, and **India** – was implicitly designed to reflect the power alignments of the **Cold War** at the time. Canada was considered to be pro-Western, Poland represented the communist bloc interests, while India embodied emerging "non-aligned" sentiments and thus served as the chairman for the commission. Created as of 11 August 1954, decisions taken by the commission had to obtain a two-thirds majority to pass. The ICC operated in the four states recognized in the Geneva Accords of 1954: the **Democratic Republic of Vietnam**, the State of Vietnam/**Republic of Vietnam**, the State of Laos/Royal Lao, and the State of Cambodia/Royal Cambodia. The weakness of the commission, however, was its lack of any sort of power or mechanism to enforce its decisions. The ICC submitted its recommendations to the Geneva powers (via the chair countries of 1954, Great Britain and the Soviet Union) for their study. Because the belligerents were not obligated to respect the ICC's decisions, it soon became clear how difficult it would be to enforce the armistice much less the elections projected for mid-1956. The peace signed at Geneva in July 1954 thus remained a fragile one and local actors in Indochina and international ones above often stymied the ICC's work on the ground.

**INTER-ZONE (*Liên Khu*).** A combined military and administrative unit established by the **Democratic Republic of Vietnam** (DRV). Each DRV Inter-Zone had its own Resistance and Administrative Committee and Military Command (*Bo Tu Lenh*). The DRV began creating Inter-Zones in January 1948 by regrouping smaller "regional" **Zones** (*Khu*) created in late 1945 and 1946. Decree 120-SL of 1948 created the following Inter-Zones, overwhelmingly concentrated in central and northern Vietnam: **Inter-Zones I**, **III**, X, **IV**, **V**. In 1951, southern zones were combined to form the **Inter-Zone for Eastern Nam Bo** (*Phan Lien Khu Mien Dong*) and the **Inter-Zone for Western Nam Bo** (*Phan Lien Khu Mien Tay*). In 1957, the Inter-Zone system was replaced by a more military one called "military regions" (*Quan Khu*).

**INTER-ZONE FOR EASTERN NAM BO (*Phân Liên Khu Miền Đông*).** This **Inter-Zone** emerged in May 1951 as the **Vietnamese Worker's Party** (VWP) moved to consolidate and expand its control over the south and its political and military forces there. This Inter-Zone, the first in the south, replaced the eastern half of war **Zones VII**, **VIII** and **IX** and was responsible for the military and political administration of the eastern half of southern Vietnam for the **Democratic Republic**

**of Vietnam**. This Inter-Zone consisted of the provinces of Gia Dinh, Tay Ninh, Thu Dau Mot, Bien Hoa, Ba Ria, Cho Lon, My Tho, Dong Thap, Tan An, Go Cong, Long Xuyen, parts of Chau Doc, and the special urban zone of **Saigon**. The high command for the south administered this new and more powerful Inter-Zone. **Tran Van Tra** served as its first military commander; **Pham Hung** was the political commissar. With the recall and death of General **Nguyen Binh** in September 1951, former head of war Zone VII and head of all armed forces in the south, the VWP was finally in a position to take control of administrative and military forces that had escaped its direct control since late 1945.

**INTER-ZONE FOR WESTERN NAM BO** (***Phân Liên Khu Miền Tây***). This **Inter-Zone** emerged in May 1951 as the **Vietnamese Worker's Party** moved to consolidate and expand its control over the south. It replaced the western parts of **Zones VII**, **VIII** and **IX** and was responsible for the military and political administration of the western half of southern Vietnam for the **Democratic Republic of Vietnam**. It consisted of the provinces of Vinh Long, Tra Vinh, Ben Tre, Can Tho, Soc Trang, Bac Lieu, and parts of Long Xuyen, Chau Doc, and Ha Tien. It was directly subordinate to the commander-in-chief for Nam Bo, **Tran Van Tra.** Its first military commander was **Phan Trong Tue**; the political commissar was **Nguyen Van Vinh**.

**INTER-ZONE I** (***Liên Khu I***). Created by decree 120-SL on 25 January 1948, this zone consisted of ten provinces: Cao Bang, Bac Can, Lang Son, Thai Nguyen, Bac Giang, Bac Ninh, Phuc Yen, Quang Yen, Hon Gai, and Hai Ninh. It shared a northern border with China, a southern one with **Inter-Zone III**, a western one with Inter-Zone X and to the east lay the Gulf of **Tonkin**. In early 1948, this zone allegedly held seven regiments and three infantry battalions. Inter-Zone I was combined with Inter-Zone X on 4 November 1949 to create **Inter-Zone Viet Bac** under the military command of **Chu Van Tan** and the political leadership of Commissar **Le Hien Mai.**

**INTER-ZONE III** (***Liên Khu III***). Created by decree 120-SL on 25 January 1948 by the **Democratic Republic of Vietnam**. Located in the northern delta, this zone combined **Zones** II, III and XI and consisted of the following provinces: Hai Phong, Kien An, Thai Binh, Hung Yen, Hai Duong, **Hanoi**, Ha Dong, Son Tay, Ha Nam, Nam Dinh, Ninh Binh, and Hoa Binh. It bordered **Inter-Zone Viet Bac** to the north and west, **Inter-Zone IV** to the southwest, and the sea to the east and southeast. As of April 1954, this zone consisted of four regiments, nine battalions and 58 platoons. Inter-Zone III's first commander-in-chief was **Hoang Sam** while **Le Quang Hoa**, and then **Do Muoi** (the future general secretary of the Vietnamese Communist Party) served as its ranking political commissars.

**INTER-ZONE IV** (***Liên Khu IV***). Created by decree 120-SL on 25 January 1948, this zone of the **Democratic Republic of Vietnam** (DRV) consisted of the following provinces in upper central Vietnam: Thanh Hoa, Nghe An, Ha Tinh, Quang Binh, Quang Tri, and Thua Thien. It was grafted on to a prexisting war **Zone** IV (*Khu*). To the north, **Inter-Zone** IV bordered **Inter-Zones Viet Bac** and **III**, to the south lay **Inter-Zone V**, to the east was the South China Sea and Laos was situated to the west. Inter-Zone IV was unique in that most of it remained in the hands of DRV during the Indochina War (the city of Hue was under French control). However, LK IV operated without direct control from DRV or party headquarters in northern Vietnam. In 1950, the provinces of Quang Binh, Quang Tri, and Thua Thien were organized into a separate military zone, the *Binh Tri Thien Front* with it own separate military command. Inter-Zone IV consisted of six regiments and one battalion. Its first commander-in-chief was **Nguyen Son**, while **Tran Van Quang** served as the ranking political commissar for this Inter-Zone.

**INTER-ZONE V** (***Liên Khu V***). Created on 20 October 1948 by the **Democratic Republic of Vietnam**, this zone combined the previous **Zones** (*Khu*) V, VI and XV. It consisted of the following provinces: Quang Nam, Quang Ngai, Binh Dinh, Phu Yen, Khanh Hoa, Ninh Thuan, Binh Thuan, Kon Tum, Gia Lai, Dac Lac, Lam Vien, and Dong Nai Thuong (Lam Dong). To the north, it bordered **Inter-Zone IV**, to the east lay the sea, while to the west was Cambodia and Laos. In April 1948, **Inter-Zone** V consisted of seven regiments and one battalion. The first commander-in-chief of this Inter-Zone was **Nguyen The Lam**, while **Nguyen Chanh** served as the ranking political commissar.

**INTER-ZONE VIET BAC (*Liên Khu Viêt Bắc*).** Created by decree 127-SL on 4 November 1949 by the **Democratic Republic of Vietnam**, this new zone combined **Zones** X and I. It bordered China to the north and Laos to the west and the sea to the east. It was one of the biggest zones in Vietnam, covering most of the northern Delta – the northwest, the north and the northeast. In July 1952, the provinces of Yen Bai, Lao Cai, Son La, and Lai Chau were detached from it in order to create the Northwestern Zone (*Khu Tay Bac*). As of April 1954, it consisted of one regiment, 15 battalions, and 81 platoons. It was dissolved in June 1957. The first commander-in-chief was **Le Quang Ba** and the political commissar was **Chu Van Tan**.

**ISAACS, HAROLD (1910–1986).** American journalist who covered Asian affairs for *Newsweek* and other news organizations. Isaacs's Asian intellectual odyssey began in China in the early 1930s, when he wrote critically of the **Republic of China** led by **Chiang Kai-shek**, captured best in the publication of *The Tragedy of the Chinese Revolution*. He returned to the United States, joined *Newsweek*, and launched his career with this magazine covering the Pacific War. His critique of the Chinese nationalists kept him out of China until the communists overthrew Chiang Kai-shek on the continent in 1949. Isaacs's sympathetic view of Asian revolution was matched by a fierce opposition to European colonialism. This was particularly evident in his support of **Ho Chi Minh**'s **Democratic Republic of Vietnam**. (Isaacs had allegedly first met Ho Chi Minh in China in 1932.) Isaacs covered the tumultuous events of Vietnam in 1945, relating them in lively prose in *No Peace for Asia*. He returned often to Vietnam for *Newsweek* and provided some particularly incisive journalism. He was also an *intellectuel engagé*. He told the State Department's diplomat in charge of Southeast Asia, **Charlton Ogburn**, that it was folly for the Americans to support **Bao Dai** and the **Bao Dai Solution**. The former emperor had no nationalist legitimacy compared to Ho Chi Minh, Isaacs insisted. *See also* INTELLECTUALS.

**ISHII TAKUO (1917–?).** Perhaps the most important Japanese officer to **crossover** to and work in the **Democratic Republic of Vietnam** (DRV) during the early stages of the Indochina War. At the time of the Japanese capitulation in Indochina in August 1945, Ishii was 27 years old. As a major, he was allegedly the youngest commanding officer in the Japanese army at the time. Colonel **Hiroo Saito**, in charge of repatriating Japanese deserters for the French after World War II, had been his commanding officer in the General Staff of the 55th Division in **Burma** during the Pacific War. Ishii Takuo had first been trained at the Nakano Academy, an elite officers' training school. He was well versed in the most modern Japanese methods of war and the finer methods of clandestine warfare. He had even commanded from within the General Staff of the 55th Division in Burma, and had taken part in the difficult battle of Rangoon.

For military reasons above all, Colonel Saito believed this taciturn, bearded, and chain-smoking man to be an extremely dangerous "weapon" in the hands of the DRV. And he was. Ishii deserted his demobilized Japanese unit on 17 December 1945 in Banam in Cambodia. He brought with him other veterans of Nakano and the 55th Division. Once won over to the DRV, he traded in his passable English to learn Vietnamese. In exchange for his military **collaboration**, the **Viet Minh** named him a "colonel". Thus began his career as a military instructor for the DRV. In May 1946, he left Baria for Quang Ngai in the company of **Pham Van Bach**, president of the Resistance Committee of Nam Bo. There, he taught Vietnamese officers in the Military Academy of Quang Ngai. He placed other Japanese officers whom he had known before in this school. In late 1946, Ishii allegedly became "chief advisor" for troops in the south. In August 1946, **Nguyen Son** sent him to Tuy Hoa to found another military school. In 1947, he offered elite training to 130 Vietnamese officer candidates and in late June 1948 he provided military training to cadres of **Zones VII**, **VIII** and **IX** located further south. He also participated in combat against the French. It is unclear what became of him. *See also* DESERTION, JAPANESE; JAPANESE TROOPS, INDOCHINA WAR.

**ITH SEAM (1910–?).** Prominent Cambodian politician and entrepreneur. Born in Prey Veng province, he studied at the pagoda school of his native village there. He received his primary school education at the *École Doudart de Lagrée* in Phnom Penh before completing his secondary studies at the *Lycée Sisowath* in 1928. He thereafter worked in the colonial bureaucracy in Cambodia, serving as a secretary for the French residents of Kandal and Kampong Cham between 1928 and 1936. In 1939, he left the colonial civil service and devoted himself entirely to business activities in logging and related construction projects. After World War II, he became a member of the **Democrat Party** and in 1947 he was elected deputy to the National Assembly for Kampong Cham. He was named minister of Commerce, Industry, and Provisions in the all-Democrat Party Cabinet of February–August 1948. He slowly withdrew from politics from the early 1950s in order to concentrate on his business interests.

# J

**JACQ, BISHOP, O. P. (?–1960).** French missionary active in northern Vietnam during the Indochina War. A member of the Order of the Preachers (Dominicans), he first arrived in **Tonkin** in January 1937, charged with creating a mission near the northern frontier town of **Cao Bang**. He remained there until the Japanese ***coup de force* of 9 March 1945**. After a short stint in France in 1946, he returned to Indochina in charge of the Cao Bang diocese. In July 1948, he became bishop co-adjutor of the Apostolic Vicar of Langson and Cao Bang. Jacq remained in this position until 1958, even after Cao Bang fell to the **Democratic Republic of Vietnam** (DRV) in 1950 and all of northern Vietnam in 1954. In October 1958, the DRV authorities finally expelled him from northern Vietnam.

**JACQUET, MARC (1913–1983).** Having served in the French resistance during World War II, he became a dedicated Gaullist, member of the *Rassemblement du peuple français*, and served as deputy between 1951 and 1955. He entered the government of **Joseph Laniel** in 1953 and accepted the portfolio of state secretary responsible for relations with the **Associated States of Indochina**. In 1954, he made a fact-finding trip to Indochina for the minister of Defense, **René Pleven**. He was a member of the top secret "war committee" during the preparations for Operation **Vautour** in early 1954. Jacquet, however, differed from Pleven in that he more ardently supported negotiations with the **Democratic Republic of Vietnam** in order to end the conflict. As a result, Pleven moved him out of his inner circle during the **Geneva Conference** negotiations. Jacquet lost his job in late May 1954, falsely accused of having leaked secret information to *L'Express*.

**JAHAN, PIERRE (1929/1930–1954).** A French paratrooper who debarked in Indochina in 1952 and briefly worked as a photographer for the French Press Information Service until about 1953, when he transferred back to his paratrooper unit. He died in hand-to-hand combat during the Battle of **Dien Bien Phu.**

**JAQUIN, HENRI.** Officer in the French **Foreign Legion** who had in all some fifteen years of active service in Asia as a platoon, company, and battalion leader. He was head of the ***Deuxième Bureau*** for **Tonkin** when the Japanese ***coup de force* of 9 March 1945** brought down French Indochina. He returned to work in the *Deuxième Bureau* under General Jean de Lattre de Tassigny and **Raoul Salan**. Little else is known of his activities.

**JAPANESE TROOPS, INDOCHINA WAR.** Tokyo's capitulation in mid-August 1945 did not mean that Japanese troops did not take part in the Indochina War. They did. Indeed, vanquished Japanese soldiers helped both the Vietnamese and the French sides. This was particularly the case in southern Vietnam at the outset of the conflict, when Franco-Vietnamese tensions and disorder led the British under General **Douglas Gracey** to maintain Japanese troops in place to ensure order instead of concentrating and disarming them right away. Japanese officers agreed to help the British maintain order, especially following the chaotic situation created by the outbreak of war below the **16th parallel** between the French and the Vietnamese on **23 September 1945**. The French inability to maintain order after launching their coup that day only reinforced Franco-British reliance on the Japanese troops to restore French colonial order. For example, the French used Japanese soldiers to fight Vietnamese forces in battle in Nha Trang. As Peter Dunn wrote: "The important part played by the Japanese troops at this stage [late 1945] cannot be over-emphasized. They were doing most of the dirty work in clearing roadblocks, patrolling and investigating, and rounding up wanted Vietnamese. After a slow start they were now taking a more active role in anti-**Viet Minh** operations, but their distaste for this activity remained undiminished." On 3 March 1946, the British Combined Chiefs of Staff authorized **Louis Mountbatten** to transfer responsibilities for the Japanese in southern Indochina to the French. According to French archival records, approximately 30,500 Japanese located in northern Indochina were repatriated to Japan through the port of Haiphong from 29 April 1946.

By 8H00 on 14 May 1946, the remaining 68,084 Japanese in Indochina below the **16th parallel** had been shipped off. The British turned over 1,596 Japanese prisoners to the French, including 427 wanted for war crimes. Of the 2,700 **Democratic Republic of Vietnam** (DRV) troops killed during the British occupation, only some 600 were killed by combined British **Indian** Troops. The remaining 2,000 lives were taken by combined Japanese and French forces battling the Vietnamese for control of southern Vietnam. Japanese historian Masaya Shiraishi has concluded that the Japanese lost 109 men in battles against the DRV's forces during this period, and had 132 wounded and 72 missing in action. The DRV also relied upon hundreds of Japanese soldiers who crossed over to help the Vietnamese fight the French. *See also* CROSSOVERS; DESERTION; REPATRIATION, JAPANESE TROOPS.

**JARAI.** *See* MINORITY ETHNIC GROUPS; *PAYS MONTAGNARDS DU SUD* (PMS).

***JAUNISSEMENT.*** French term that became increasingly popular from the early 1950s to refer to what Americans would later call the "Vietnamization" of the war. In French, "*jaunissement*" literally means "yellowing". By the end of the Indochina conflict, ethnic Vietnamese troops and auxiliaries (*supplétifs*) of the Associated State of Vietnam constituted the largest ethnic group of soldiers serving in the French Union army. While ethnic French troops accounted for 88% of **French Union** losses in 1946, in 1953 the number had dropped to 17%. Vietnamese casualties, the vast majority of which occurred between 1949 and 1954, were the highest by 1954. As French historian **Jacques Dalloz** pointed out, "from the point of view of deaths at least, the vietnamization (of French Union forces) had made good progress".

**JESSUP, PHILIP (1897–1986).** American legal expert, scholar, and diplomat-at-large working in international organizations and with an interest in decolonization. He served as the American ambassador-at-large to Southeast Asia between 1948 and 1952 and was one of the main architects of American policy towards the French Associated States of Vietnam, Laos, and Cambodia during this period. In 1950, he made a fact-finding trip around the region, meeting with European and Asian leaders, including **Léon Pignon** and **Bao Dai** in Indochina. He became a staunch supporter of **Bao Dai**, the **Bao Dai Solution**, and the **Associated States of Indochina**, advising Washington to pressure the French to accord fuller independence to these states. He published his experiences of decolonization in *The Birth of Nations* (1974).

**JIANG JIESHI.** *See* CHIANG KAI-SHEK.

**JOINT CHIEFS OF STAFF, DEMOCRATIC REPUBLIC OF VIETNAM (*Bộ Tổng Tham Mưu*).** **Ho Chi Minh** signed the chiefs of staff into law on 7 September 1945. It was designed to study and elaborate strategic, tactical, and military policies on the one hand and to organize, train, and lead the government's armed forces on the other. General **Hoang Van Thai** headed the staff between 1945 and 1953. For unclear reasons, **Van Tien Dung** replaced him in 1954, serving in that same position until 1978.

**JOUHAUD, EDMOND (1905–1995).** Born in Oran in Algeria, Jouhaud completed his secondary studies in Algeria before entering Saint-Cyr in 1924. His classmates included **Jean Boucher de Crèvecoeur** and **Michel de Brébisson**. During World War II, Jouhaud became an important military leader in the *Forces françaises de l'intérieur* in the Bordeaux region. Named colonel at the end of the war, he became deputy chief then chief of staff to the **Air Force** in Tunisia in 1948. He then went to Indochina where he became in 1954 commander-in-chief of the Air Force there. He would later serve in the **Algerian War,** determined to keep it French, and participated in the *Organisation armée secrète* (OAS) until his arrest in his hometown of Oran.

**JUBELIN, ANDRÉ (1906–1986).** Graduated from the French Naval Academy, he served in France and North Africa during the interwar period. He joined Free French forces at the start of World War II in Singapore, as chief of the artillery on the cruiser *Lamotte-Picquet*, and then attended to maritime liaisons between Algiers and the European mainland. After the war, he took command of the light cruiser *Triomphant* and debarked French troops in **Saigon** and Nha Trang in 1945–1946. He remained in Indochina until 1948, working on the aircraft carrier *Arromanches*. In 1950, he returned to France.

**JUGLAS, J. J. (1904–1982).** French Deputy after World War II and member of the French delegation to the **Fontainebleau conference** in July 1946. In 1947, he served as president of the National Assembly's Commission for Overseas Territories. As part of a parlimentary enquiry committee into the use of military credits for Indochina, he traveled to Indochina on a fact-finding mission in early 1949.

**JUIN, ALPHONSE PIERRE (1888–1967).** Born in Algeria, Juin completed his secondary studies in Constantine before studying at Saint-Cyr from which he graduated in 1912 in the same class as **Charles de Gaulle**. Fascinated by Morocco, he joined the colonial army there and participated in "**pacification**" operations and led his Moroccan troops into combat in the *Chemin des Dames* during World War I. After the war, he resumed his military career in the colonies, mainly in North Africa and Syria, where he participated in the Rif War and served on Marshal Louis Hubert Lyautey's private staff. During the Battle of France, he led the *15ème division d'infanterie motorisée* covering the withdrawal of the 1st French Army via Dunkirk. The Germans took Juin prisoner and enclosed him in the Koenigstein fort, but Vichy obtained his release in June 1941, made him a general, and sent him to command colonial troops in North Africa in November 1941. Juin joined Free French forces after the allied landing in North Africa in November 1942. Vichy then revoked his French nationality. In that same month, Juin assumed command of Free French forces in Tunisia and was named general. Put in charge of the French Expeditionary Corps in August 1943, he took part in the liberation of Italy and France before dealing with the Algerian revolt in Sétif in May 1945 as Chief of Staff of National Defense. In April 1946, the government dispatched him to the Far East to negotiate the withdrawal of Chinese Nationalist troops from northern Indochina above the **16th parallel**. Juin was an ardent believer in the French Empire and its maintenance. As head of the French Chiefs of Staff during the Franco-Vietnamese crisis in November–December 1946, he intervened to prevent his deputy, Admiral Barjot, from asking critical questions concerning the actions of High Commissioner **Georges Thierry d'Argenlieu** and the commander of French forces in Indochina, General **Jean Valluy**, during the violent occupation of Haiphong. In October 1950, in the midst of the **Cao Bang** debacle, the government sent Juin back to Indochina to raise morale and put the army back on a war footing. He transferred to Europe in 1951 and named *Maréchal de France* in May 1952.

**JUMEAU, HENRI**. As a lieutenant, Henri Jumeau was involved in the altercations that triggered the **Haiphong Incident** in November 1946. The Vietnamese arrested him when he tried to intervene in what the **Democratic Republic of Vietnam** (DRV) considered to be an internal matter. Jumeau also belonged to a secret "military security" group located within the Haiphong branch of the **Bureau fédéral de documenation** reporting to High Commissioner **Georges Thierry d'Argenlieu** in 1946. Jumeau later transferred to the Indochinese police force. He was the acting chief of police in Dalat when he was suspended and jailed on 24 May 1951 for ordering the execution of 20 Vietnamese prisoners, in reprisal for the killing of a French police officer, Victor Haaz, by **commando** forces of the DRV. Indeed, a few days earlier, the Phan Nhu Thach suicide squad had apprehended and then killed the Dalat *Sûreté* officer when he tried to escape. The execution of the 20 Vietnamese prisoners caused an outcry in Vietnamese papers throughout the country. *See also* CAM LY, MASSACRE; EXPERIENCE OF WAR; HÉRAULT, MASSACRE; MY THUY, MASSACRE; MYTH OF WAR.

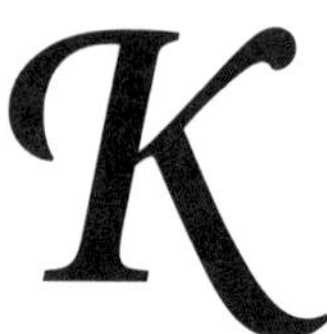

**K.** *See* D.

**KAISÔN PHOMVIHĀN (NGUYỄN QUỐC TRỊ, ANH BẢY, 1920–2002).** The most powerful Lao communist by the end of the Indochina War as well as communist Vietnam's most trusted ally. The son of a Vietnamese civil servant and a Lao mother, Kaisôn spoke Vietnamese nearly as fluently as his native Lao. Born in Savannakhet province, he pursued his secondary studies at the *Lycée du Protectorat* in **Hanoi** during the 1930s and stayed on during World War II, when he may have enrolled at the *Faculté de droit* in Hanoi under the name of Nguyen Quoc Tri (Nguyen of a National Mind).

Like so many Vietnamese at the time, he became active in nationalist politics during the Popular Front and Vichy periods. He joined the **Lao Issara** in Savannakhet when French Indochina crumbled in mid-1945, serving in the National Salvation Association of Lao Youth and then in Prince **Suphānuvong**'s Committee for an Independent Laos. In late 1945, he returned to Hanoi with a group of Lao recruits for training in Vietnam. In early 1946, **Ho Chi Minh** called upon him to join a secret Lao-Viet Contact Liaison Group (*Ban Cong Tac Lao-Viet*). It marked the beginning of a long and close partnership with Vietnamese communists.

When full-scale war broke out on **19 December 1946**, he followed the central government of the **Democratic Republic of Vietnam** into the northern hills of Vietnam. There he worked in political propaganda teams active along the Lao border. In February 1948, the **Indochinese Communist Party** (ICP) created the Northern Lao Assault Team (*Doi Xung Phong Lao Bac*) to conduct political propaganda, create local armed forces and expand the revolution into northern Laos. Kaisôn was the team's Lao leader. In early 1949, thanks to this propaganda work and due to the personal support of **Vo Nguyen Giap**, **Song Hao,** and **Le Tan Trong**, the northern Lao assault team was transformed into the Lao revolutionary army known as *Latsavong*. Kaisôn sealed his revolutionary credentials in July 1949, when he officially joined the ICP. In mid-1950, he entered the **Lao Resistance Government** as National Defense minister and commander-in-chief of the army. He was also elected to the central committee of the newly formed national front. In February 1951, he attended the ICP's Second Party Congress in northern Vietnam as chief of the party's Lao Regional Committee (*Xu Uy Lao*).

Given the decision at that congress to reorganize the ICP into three national parties, the Vietnamese assigned him the task of forming a separate but associated Lao Communist Party. Kaisôn became the most important Lao communist from this point and communist Vietnam's most valuable ally in running revolutionary Laos. Vietnamese communists referred to him as *Anh Bay* or Brother number seven. *See also* ADMINISTRATIVE OFFICE FOR THE FRONTIER; ADVISORY GROUP 100; CAMBODIAN RESISTANCE GOVERNMENT; COMMITTEE FOR EXTERNAL AFFAIRS; COMMITTEE FOR THE EAST, LAO ISSARA; HOANG VAN HOAN; INDOCHINESE FEDERATION; LAO RESISTANCE GOVERNMENT; *MÉTIS*; NGUYEN KHANG; NGUYEN THANH SON; NUHAK PHUMSAVAN; PARTY AFFAIRS COMMITTEE.

**KAMATH, MELLO.** Served as the 1st Secretary in the **Indian** Embassy in the United States before being named in August 1949 to run the Indian Consulate General in **Saigon**. He was close to **Nehru**, sharing his sympathy for **Ho Chi Minh**'s nationalist cause and hostility to the French **Bao Dai Solution.** *See also* GENEVA ACCORDS; DOUGLAS GRACEY; INDIA; SOUTH EAST ASIA TREATY ORGANIZATION.

**KARMEN, ROMAN LAZAREVITCH (1906–1978).** Soviet photographer, film maker, and propagandist who covered the Spanish Civil War, the Sino-Japanese War, World War II, the Soviet taking of Berlin, and the Vietnamese capture of the French camp at **Dien Bien Phu**. Karmen produced the famous picture of the Soviet hammer and sickle floating over the Reichstag. It was also

Karmen who provided the famous photo of the column of French prisoners being marched away in the form of an S after the battle of Dien Bien Phu. It was a re-enactment, based on a similar *mise-en-scène* ordered by Karmen with German prisoners taken during the battle of Stalingrad. *See also* CINEMA; CULTURE; INDOCTRINATION; MYTH OF WAR; NOVELS; PRISONERS OF WAR; PSYCHOLOGICAL WARFARE.

**KATĀY DŌN SASŌRIT (WILLIAM KATĀY "WILLIAM THE RABBIT", ARSENEN LAPIN, 1904–1959).** Prominent Lao nationalist who was opposed both to French colonialism and to Vietnamese and Lao communism. Born in Champāsak province of a Vietnamese father and a Lao mother, he studied at the *École supérieure de droit et d'administration* in **Hanoi** and entered the Indochinese colonial bureaucracy upon graduation. He worked as a colonial assessor in the Superior Court of Appeals and Nullification in Laos. He was active in numerous associations. He served as president of the Association of Lao Civil Servants, the Lao Association of Art and Sports, and was general secretary of the Lao Scouting Association. During World War II, he helped create and run the Lao Renovation Movement. In 1943, he headed the Office of Economic Affairs at the French *Résidence supérieure* in Laos. Following the Japanese ***coup de force* of 9 March 1945**, he worked with the Japanese until their defeat in August. Katāy then joined the newly proclaimed **Lao Issara** government of 12 October 1945, serving as minister of Finance. He fled to Thailand following the French military reoccupation of Laos in mid-1946 and continued to serve as minister of Finance in the Lao Issara government-in-exile there. He returned to Laos in 1949, with the dissolution of the Lao Issara and the emergence of the Associated State of Laos. Between 1951 and 1954, he was minister of Finance and National Economy in the latter government. In November 1954, he became prime minister and held the post until 1956. He also became leader of the Progressive Party in 1954. He was strongly anti-communist and opposed to dealing with the Vietnamese-backed **Pathet Lao**. *See also* ASSOCIATED STATES OF INDOCHINA; GENEVA ACCORDS; INDOCHINESE FEDERATION; LAO RESISTANCE GOVERNMENT.

**KELLER, RENÉ PAUL LEON JULES (1909–1975).** After graduating from *École spéciale militaire* at Saint-Cyr in 1929, he served in the colonial army in Africa during most of the 1930s. He led colonial troops in France during the Battle of France. Following the French debacle, Vichy transferred him to Dakar in 1941. After the Allied liberation of North Africa in late 1942, he chose the Free French forces, joining the *9ème Division d'Infanterie coloniale* (DIC) in late 1943. He landed with the *9ème DIC* in France in August 1944 and distinguished himself as an intelligence officer for that division in Alsace and Germany. In June 1945, he transferred to the **Expeditionary Corps** for the Far East and debarked in **Saigon** in November 1945. He was actively involved in the French reoccupation of southern Indochina, taking part in the "**pacification**" of Tan An, Dong Nai, and Cap St. Jacques. A few months later, with the French reoccupation of Indochina above the **16th parallel** underway, Keller moved to Haiphong, where he served as chief of the ***Deuxième Bureau*** for the Chief of Staff to the commander-in-chief of French armed forces in Indochina. He held this position until his return to France in February 1949. He returned to Indochina at lieutenant colonel in late 1953 and resumed his intelligence work in the operational zone of French ground troops in northern Vietnam. He transferred to southern Vietnam in March 1954. Following the war, he advised the Associated State of Vietnam on military matters before returning to France in December 1954.

**KENNEDY, JOHN F. (1917–1963).** Although much ink has been spilled on Kennedy's role in the American war in Vietnam, his initiation to the country and its troubles occurred during the Indochina conflict, as Fredrik Logevall has shown. Kennedy first arrived in **Saigon** in 1951, a young congressman seeking to bolster his foreign policy credentials for an upcoming senate race. The Vietnam visit was part of a wider, seven-week trip to Asia and the Middle East. Accompanying him among others was his brother, Robert. While they remarked upon the bustling shops and pleasant restaurants lining the famous *rue Catinat* in downtown Saigon, they also noticed that anti-grenade netting suggested that all was not well. The outbreak of small-arms fire only reinforced their apprehensions. "Cannot go outside city because of guerrillas", Robert confided to his diary. "Could hear shooting as evening wore on". The Kennedy brothers met **Bao Dai** and **Edmund Gullion**, the chargé d'affaires of the American legation. Unlike the American minister, **Donald Heath**, who supported the French cause, Gullion painted a different, more sobering picture of the war and French policies in Indochina. He advocated greater independence for the Associated State of Vietnam. In his meeting with General **Jean de Lattre de Tassigny** Kennedy expressed such doubts about French policy, asking de Lattre why he should expect the Vietnamese troops to sign up enthusiastically in order to keep Vietnam part of the French Empire. De Lattre was unimpressed and later sent a formal letter of complaint to Heath. Kennedy wrote in his trip diary: "We are more and more becoming colonialists in the minds of the people. Because everyone believes that we control the U.N. [and] because our wealth is supposedly inexhaustible, we will be damned if we don't do what they [the emerging nations] want". Kennedy felt that it would be better to combat communism by fighting Third World "poverty and want", "sickness and disease", and "injustice and inequality". In a speech he delivered before the Boston Chamber of Commerce upon his return, he continued: "In Indochina we have allied ourselves to the desperate effort of the French regime to hang on to the remnants of an empire. There is no broad general support of the native Vietnam Government among the people of that area", concluding that if a free election were held, it "would go in favor of Ho and his Communists". *See also* ARMY, ASSOCIATED STATE OF VIETNAM; ASSOCIATED STATES OF INDOCHINA; BAO DAI SOLUTION; DOMINO THEORY; *JAUNISSEMENT*.

**KHÁ VĂN CẨN (1908–1982).** Southern engineer and economic specialist in the service of the **Democratic Republic of Vietnam** (DRV) during the Indochina War. Born in Cholon, he studied between 1930 and 1933 at the *École nationale des arts et métiers* in Aix-en-Provence, from which he received an engineering degree. Between 1934 and 1939, he worked in the Renault car factories in Billancourt near Paris as a designer, technical agent, and engineer. He made several trips to Indochina during this time to oversee the delivery of Renault equipment for the construction of the Indochinese railways and the training of Indochinese railway personnel on its use and maintenance. In 1939, he resigned from Renault and returned to Vietnam to become directing manager of the *Fonderies et ateliers de constructions mécaniques et métalliques* in **Cochinchina**. In 1944, he was a member of the Administrative Council for Cochinchina. Following the Japanese overthrow of the French in the ***coup de force* of 9 March 1945**, he became the head of physical education, sports, and youth activities for Cochinchina. He continued to serve as vice president of the Council of Cochinchina. Following the Japanese defeat in August 1945, he joined the forces of the DRV and was named advisor in economic affairs for the Resistance and Administrative Committee of Nam Bo. He supported the wartime economic policy of trying to blockade the French-held areas. He was also a member of the Special Minting Committee for Nam Bo.

**KHÁI HƯNG (TRẦN KHÁNH GIƯ, 1896–1947).** One of Vietnam's best-known 20th-century novelists and non-communist nationalists. Khai Hung was born into a family of mandarins in Hai Duong province, of which his father was governor. He completed his secondary education in a French high school in **Hanoi** before entering the private school of *Thang Long* in 1931 where he met **Nguyen Tuong Tam** (Nhat Linh), with whom he would join literary and political forces. Both played pivotal roles in the Self Strengthening Group (*Tu Luc Van Doan*) in the 1930s and in the development of modern Vietnamese literature and journalism. Khai Hung penned scores of articles in the group's journals and published a number of novels. He also became politically active during the Popular Front period (1936–39) and World War II. In 1941, Vichy authorities incarcerated him on political grounds. Following the Japanese overthrow of the French in March 1945, he returned to the political scene. He and Nguyen Tuong Tam joined the revived **Vietnamese Nationalist Party** (*Viet Nam Quoc Dan Dang*, VNQDD) in opposition to the **Indochinese Communist Party** (ICP) and its nationalist front, the **Viet Minh**. They turned their journalistic and literary skills against the communists thanks to the creation of an oppositional paper, *Viet Nam*. Their relations with the communist nationalists deteriorated greatly in late 1945 and 1946 as a **civil war** emerged within a colonial one. Sometime in 1947, DRV provincial forces assassinated Khai Hung. However, it is not clear whether they were acting on orders from the ICP or independently of the center.

**KHAMFEUANE TOUNAROM (1920–?).** Behind-the-scenes leader of the **Pathet Lao** in the early 1950s. Born in Xieng Khouang province, he served in the colonial bureaucracy in Phongsaly and Luang Prabang as World War II came to a close. Opposed to the return of the French, he joined the **Lao Issara** at Luang Prabang and entered its secret **Committee for the East**. He worked closely with the Vietnamese along the Lao-**Democratic Republic of Vietnam** border. In August 1950, he was present at the creation of the **Lao Resistance Government** and national front. He served as a deputy to **Phūmī Vongvichit** and then as minister of the Interior in the new government. He attended the **Geneva Conference** in 1954 as a private advisor to Prince **Suphānuvong**.

**KHAMMAO VILAI (XIANG, MAO, 1892?–1965).** Important non-communist Lao leader opposed to the restoration of French colonialism and Vietnamese-backed Indochinese communism. Born into a wealthy family, he studied at the *Collège Sisowath* in Phnom Penh and then in France at the *École Pratique de Commerce* in Dijon between 1911 and 1916. He returned to Indochina in 1917 and worked as a colonial clerk and interpreter in the Judiciary Service in Vientiane for almost twenty years. He was widely respected for his legal knowledge and integrity. In 1922, he returned to France as the interpreter for the Lao delegation to the colonial exposition held in Marseilles. On his return, he served as president of the Indigenous Tribunal in Vientiane and as provincial governor of Vientiane. Following the overthrow of the French and the Allied defeat of the Japanese, he played a decisive role in creating the **Lao Issara** government in October 1945 and served as its first prime minister. In April 1946, he fled to Thailand following the French reoccupation of Laos and continued to work as the head of the Lao Issara government-in-exile in Bangkok. When the French created the Associated State of Laos in 1949, he dissolved the Lao Issara by decree on 24 October 1949 and returned to Laos, where the King named him minister of Justice and of Public Health in the **Phuy Xananikôn** government. On 19 October 1949, he issued the communiqué dismissing Prince **Phetxarāt** from his position as "acting head" of the now defunct Lao Issara and called upon all Lao to return home. In 1950, he helped found the Progressive Party with **Suvanna Phūmā**, regrouping most of the returned Lao Issara within it. *See also* ASSOCIATED STATES OF INDOCHINA; COLLABORATION.

**KHAMTAI SĪPHANDÔN (1924–).** Important southern leader of the **Pathet Lao** during the Indochina War. Born in Pakse province, Khamtai got his start working in the colonial civil service. With the French advance on Laos in early 1946, he fled his position at the Post Office at Savannakhet and crossed into northeastern Thailand. There, he joined forces with another southerner, **Sīthon Kommadam**. Vietnamese communist delegates based in Ubon won him over to the anticolonialist cause. Following the dissolution of the **Lao Issara** in 1949, he remained in Thailand. Prince **Phetxarāt** put him at the head of the Resistance Committee for Southern Laos. Throughout this time, Khamtai Sīphandôn continued to work closely with Sīthon Kommadam and the Vietnamese communists based in Ubon. In August 1950, he took part in the creation of the **Lao Resistance Government** in northern Vietnam as a representative for southern Laos where he returned at this time. Between 1951 and 1953, he was active in southern Laos before joining **Kaisôn Phomvihān**'s staff in the Ministry of Defense, where he worked for the rest of the war. *See also* ADMINISTRATIVE OFFICE FOR THE FRONTIER; ADVISORY GROUP 100; CAMBODIAN RESISTANCE GOVERNMENT; INDOCHINESE FEDERATION; COMMITTEE FOR EXTERNAL AFFAIRS; HOANG VAN HOAN; NGUYEN KHANG; NGUYEN THANH SON; NUHAK PHUMSAVAN; PARTY AFFAIRS COMMITTEE.

**KHIM TITH (1896–1975?).** Born in Phnom Penh, he completed his primary studies at the *École Francis Garnier* in Phnom Penh before volunteering in 1916 to serve in World War I. After failing the physical the first time, he tried again a year later and succeeded. He apparently saw action on the Western front and certainly participated in the occupation of Germany in 1919. He returned to Cambodia in 1920 with the rank of sergeant and began work as a schoolteacher. He also studied at the *École d'administration cambodgienne* from which he graduated at the head of his class in 1924 and entered the colonial bureaucracy. He worked as a district and provincial head in numerous Cambodian provinces during the interwar period. He maintained excellent relations with the Buddhist community and, during World War II, was one of the main organizers of the youth movement, *Yuvan*. The French assigned him a tough post in Siemreap province when relations with Thailand deteriorated in 1940–41. Following the Japanese overthrow of the French in the ***coup de force* of 9 March 1945**, he sheltered a number of endangered Europeans. He also joined the Japanese-backed government of **Son Ngoc Thanh**, serving as minister of National Defense. Though opposed to any alliance with the **Democratic Republic of Vietnam** (DRV) and an ardent supporter of Cambodian independence, he entered into contact with the British in **Saigon** as well as with **Jean Cédile** and General **Philippe Leclerc**. As minister of Defense, Khim Tit helped the latter to arrange the arrest of Son Ngoc Thanh in October 1945. Khim Tit became minister of Public Works, Health, and Communications in the French-backed cabinet of Prince Monireth in late 1945 and joined the National Union Party in 1947, and soon served as its general secretary. In January 1948, he was elected an advisor to the Kingdom in charge of the provinces of Kratie and Stung Treng. In December 1948, he began publishing the paper *Sachak Pardamean* (The Truth) on behalf of a group of royal advisors and moderate nationalists. In October 1949, following **Norodom Sihanouk**'s dissolution of the National Assembly, he resigned his post as president of the Commission of National Defense, the Interior, and Foreign Affairs within the Council for the Kingdom (*conseil du royaume*). Khim Tit resumed his work as president in early 1951. On 19 January 1951, he signed a document sent to Sihanouk calling for the restoration of the National Assembly. He then became minister of Public Works and Communications in the first cabinet of Oum Chheng Sun, constituted on 23 March 1951, and was appointed governor of Kandal province shortly thereafter. As governor, he helped win over **Puth Chhay** to the Franco-Cambodian side. He became minister of National Defense in the cabinet set up by Sihanouk on 20 November 1953 and led by **Chan Nak**. Khim Tith was virulently opposed to Vietnamese support of the **Khmer Issarak** and supported Sihanouk's opposition to the intervention of the DRV's army in eastern Cambodia in early 1954. Khim Tith was minister of the Interior in charge of local defense in the newly formed cabinet of Sihanouk on 6 April 1954 and maintained this post in the **Penn Nouth** cabinet created on 17 April 1954. In March 1955, he joined Sam Sary and Penn Nouth as a member of the High Council for the Crown (*Haut conseil de la courronne*).

**KHMER ISSARAK.** The "Free Cambodia" movement first came to life in Bangkok on 20 December 1940, when the Thai government, at odds with the French over western Indochina, allowed a Cambodian nationalist-minded monk, Phra Phiset Panich or **Poc Khun** to create the Khmer Independence Party (*Phak Khmer Issarak*). Chaovalit and **Khuang Aphaiwong**, Thai politicians with ancient family links to western Cambodia, were strong supporters of the Khmer Issarak movement. This support continued into the Indochina War, as the Thais tried to hold on to Cambodia's western provinces of Battambang and Siemreap, which the Japanese had helped them obtain from the French in 1941. Their efforts came to naught, however, when the Thai government, under U.S. pressure, retroceded the territories to the French in November 1946 and the Conciliation Commission designed to hear Thai desiderata closed in early September 1947.

Shortly thereafter, the French High Commissioner to Indochina, **Émile Bollaert**, sent a report to Paris explaining the importance of putting an end to the Khmer Issarak and **Lao Issara** independence movements in Thailand, both of which undermined French efforts to build up and legitimize pro-French states in Laos and Cambodia. In mid-1947, the French moved to rally these "dissident elements" to the French cause in Indochina. The French Commissioner in Cambodia **Léon Pignon**, entered into contact with Poc Khun (and Prince **Phetxarāt**) in the hope of wooing him away from the Thais. Pignon promised a total amnesty to the Khmer Issarak partisans if they returned to Cambodia. While Poc Khun stayed put, many Khmer Issarak returned to Cambodia.

Meanwhile, Vietnamese communists, like their French adversaries, were keen on attracting the Khmer Issarak movement to their cause. In early 1948, the **Indochinese Communist Party** (ICP) revived its Indochinese revolutionary vision and moved to create a new Cambodian nationalist front, based in Cambodia and allied with the Vietnamese, called the "Committee for the Liberation of Kampuchea". The Vietnamese explained that this committee would serve as a "provisional government" in opposition to the one the French were creating. The Vietnamese-backed Cambodian Committee would later constitute a National Assembly and thereby establish a permanent government. In charge of this revolutionary state-building project was **Nguyen Thanh Son**, the ICP's most important official in charge of Vietnamese activities in

Cambodia. Thanks to his efforts, the Committee came to life in the Dangrek hills in mid-August 1948, led by **Dap Chhuon** and seconded by Poc Khun.

However, as in Laos, it was the arrival of the Cold War in 1949–50 and French moves to create the **Associated States of Indochina** in Laos and Cambodia that led the ICP to create a revolutionary party and resistance government for Cambodia. The defection of Dap Chhuon in 1949, like much of the Lao Issara in that same year, caused a crisis for the ICP. As a result, the ICP assigned the task of creating a new government and party for Cambodia to Nguyen Thanh Son, head of the **Committee for External Affairs** (*Ban Ngoai Vu*) and **Hoang Van Hoan**, chief of the all-powerful Overseas Party Affairs Committee (*Ban Can Su Hai Ngoai*) based in Thailand. After a meeting in Bangkok in 1949, Nguyen Thanh Son returned to Indochina and created the **Party Affairs Committee** for all of Cambodia (*Ban Can Su Toan Mien*), the single most powerful revolutionary organization in all of Cambodia and run by the ICP.

In March 1950, as in Laos a few months later, the ICP organized a Cadres Congress for Cambodia bringing together Issaraks from across the country to create a new national front, provisional government, and revolutionary party. During this meeting held in Ha Tien, Vietnam, the delegates outlined the future **Cambodian Resistance Government** and its revolutionary tack. In April, the Representative Assembly for all of Cambodia (*Cuoc Dai Bieu Hoi Nghi Toan Mien/Moho Sannibat Tamnang I'sara' Nokor Khmaer*) formed a new "Unifed National Front of the Khmer Issarak" (*Mat Tran Issarak Thong Nhut Toan Quoc* or *Sammakum Khmaer I'sara* in Cambodian) and created a Provisional Central Committee of National Liberation (*Uy Ban Giai Phong Dan Toc Trung Uong Lam Thoi* or *Kana' Cheat Mukkakeaha Mochchhoem Nokor Khmaer* in Cambodia), based on the **Viet Minh** model. **Son Ngoc Minh** and other Cambodian luminaries were present. However, creating a revolutionary party for Cambodia was much harder. It was only in mid-1951 that the Party Affairs Committee for Cambodia finally created the People's Revolutionary Party for Cambodia with **Son Ngoc Minh** at its helm. **Nguyen Thanh Son**, backed by **Le Duc Tho** and **Le Duan**, was its caretaker. *See also* ADMINISTRATIVE OFFICE FOR THE FRONTIER; COMMITTEE FOR THE EAST, LAO ISSARA; *MÉTIS*.

**KHMER KROM.** This term refers to ethnic Khmers living in the "lower" Mekong region (*krom* or *duoi* meaning "below" in Khmer and Vietnamese respectively), now a part of the nation state of the Socialist Republic of Vietnam.

Ethnic Khmers first inhabited the lower Mekong before the Vietnamese began consolidating their hold over the delta from the 17th century. Vietnamese conquest left hundreds of thousands of Khmers living under the rule of the Nguyen dynasty when the French began colonizing the Mekong delta in 1859 in the form of a Cochinchinese colony based out of **Saigon**. The French Second Empire followed this up a few years later by establishing a protectorate over all of Cambodia.

By creating colonial **Cochinchina,** the French established a precise and internationally recognized legal border separating this southern colony and its inhabitants from the Cambodian protectorate, even though both territories were part of the Indochinese Union created in 1887. This had the effect of placing ethnic Khmers living within Cochinchinese borders under the sovereignty of French Cochinchina, and not under the jurisdiction of Cambodian "protected" authorities. In other words, Khmer Krom, in legal terms, became colonial Cochinchinese subjects. Meanwhile, during the colonial period, Khmer Krom concentrated in Cochinchinese provinces such as Tra Vinh and Tri Ton continued to come into contact with the ever-increasing numbers of ethnic Vietnamese living in and moving into the area. Many Khmer Krom learned Vietnamese and intermarried, including future nationalists such as **Dap Chhuon**. Moreover, Khmer Krom produced some of Cambodia's best-known nationalists, including **Son Ngoc Thanh**. However, there were also tensions between ethnic Khmer and Vietnamese living in southern Vietnam, as increased Vietnamese immigration put greater pressure on local Khmer lands, opportunities, and identities.

The crumbling of colonial Indochina following the Japanese ***coup de force* of 9 March 1945** and the concomitant surge in Vietnamese nationalism did not ensure the peaceful resolution of such problems. Nor did French efforts to turn the Khmers against the Vietnamese during the Indochina War. Between 1945 and 1947, for example, ethnic violence escalated between ethnic Khmers and Vietnamese in the lower Mekong, resulting in a number of massacres setting Khmers against Vietnamese. While the French were at first content to fan Khmer hostility in order to contain Vietnamese nationalism, they found themselves backtracking as their own **Bao Dai solution** obligated them to transfer their cherished Cochinchinese colony to the Associated State of Vietnam. Cochinchina, meaning its colonially established borders and the populations residing within them, became part of a territorially unprecedented Vietnamese nation-state, the Associated State of Vietnam.

The Cambodian government, led by **Norodom Sihanouk**, opposed the incorporation of territories and populations considered to have been "Cambodian" before the French carved out colonial Cochinchina. For Cambodian nationalists, "Kampuchea Krom" or Lower Cambodia along with its ethnic Khmers had to be transferred to the nation-state represented by the Associated State of Cambodia. However, by signing accords with the Vietnamese creating the Associated State of Vietnam in 1949, the French effectively acquiesced to the transformation of precolonial Kampuchea Krom territories and Khmer Khrom colonial subjects into Vietnamese national ones, much to the anger of the Cambodian governments and Cambodian nationalists to this day. Some three hundred thousand ethnic Khmers are thought to live in southern Vietnam today. *See also* CAO DAI; CAM LY, MASSACRE; HÉRAULT, MASSACRE; HOA HAO; MINORITY ETHNIC GROUPS; MY THUY, MASSACRE; OVERSEAS CHINESE; OVERSEAS VIETNAMESE IN THAILAND; *PAYS MONTAGNARDS DU SUD*; TAI FEDERATION.

**KHUANG APHAIWONG (LUANG KOVIT APHAIWONG, 1902–1968).** Important Thai politician with ties to western Cambodia and supporter of Indochinese resistance movements against the French. The Aphaiwong family was originally of ethnic Khmer origin, having ruled over vast parts of western Cambodia under Thai control until Battambang and Siemreap provinces were ceded to the French at the turn of the 19th century. The Aphaiwong family nonetheless maintained economic, family, and political links to Battambang province in particular. Khuang Aphaiwong completed his primary education at the *Assumption College* in Bangkok and studied engineering at the École centrale de Lyon in France. After his return to Thailand he worked in the telegraph department and eventually became its director. Besides Thai and Khmer, Khuang Aphaiwong was also at ease in English and French. He was fascinated by cinema and travelled to Hollywood after World War I to study the seventh art. 20th-Century Fox employed him at one point and he made a film for this American company in 1924 about the Cambodian jungle. Khuang Aphaiwong became an important Thai politician in the 1930s and supported the creation of a constitutional monarchy in 1932. During World War II he served as prime minister in 1944 and 1945. He helped found the Democratic Party in Thailand in 1946 and headed it up at the outset. He became prime minister in 1946 and again in 1947–48 before leaving the government to lead the opposition party against the returning **Pibun Songgram**. During World War II and until entering into opposition in 1948, Aphaiwong supported Lao, Cambodian, and Vietnamese resistance groups opposed to French rule in Indochina, a goal shared by most Thai officials at the time. He was particularly interested in helping the first **Khmer Issarak** groups located along the Thai-French Indochinese border during and after World War II. He was heavily involved in trading activities, and helped supply representatives of the **Democratic Republic of Vietnam** stationed in Thailand during the first half of the Indochina War with arms and supplies.

**KHƯƠNG MỄ (1916–2004).** Prominent Vietnamese war photographer during the Indochinese conflict. Born in the Mekong Delta province of An Giang, he dabbled in photography before taking it seriously with the outbreak of the war in southern Vietnam. In 1946, he joined the **Democratic Republic of Vietnam**'s independence struggle as a war photographer and, with a group of colleagues, created the Film-makers Group for **Zone** VIII. In spite of wartime shortages and the damaging humidity of the south, his team managed to produce its first film, *The Battle of Moc Hoa* in 1948. This one was followed by others, including *Tran La Bang, Chien Dich Tra Vinh*, and *Chien Dich Cau Ke*. Designed to support the government's war effort, these films glorified the Vietnamese nationalist cause and the heroism of the soldiers. In 1954, with the end of the war, he moved to northern Vietnam and continued to put his photography and film-making in the service of the official war cause. Perhaps his best-known film was *Co Nghip* (Ms. Nghip), dedicated to the liberation of **Saigon** and filmed in 1976 just after the unification of Vietnam under communist leadership. *See also* CINEMA; INDOCTRINATION; NOVELS; PIERRE SCHOENDOERFFER; PSYCHOLOGICAL WARFARE.

**KINDAVONG, Prince (1900–1951).** Member of the Lao royal family who joined Allied forces against the Japanese during World War II. He worked in the Indochinese colonial administration during the interwar period, serving as chief of Meuang Kasy in 1945. Following the Japanese ***coup de force* of 9 March 1945**, he joined in the resistance against the Japanese and secretly aided the Allies and Free French. Prince Kindavong supported the return of the French. In March 1945, King **Sīsāvangvong** named him royal delegate to Upper Laos and royal representative to the Provisional Government of the French Republic. On 27 August 1945, Kindavong sent a telegram to **Charles de Gaulle**, expressing Laos's "respectful fidelity". Between 1946 and 1947, Kindavong was minister in the government of the Kingdom of Laos. He died of illness in Paris in 1951.

**KINIM PHOSĒNĀ (1916–1963).** Lao non-communist nationalist who played an increasingly important role in Lao politics after World War II. Born of a Lao father and a Chinese mother, Kinim Phosēnā was educated in colonial Indochina and began his career working for the colonial bureaucracy in 1938. He joined French **commandos** resisting the Japanese towards the end of the Pacific War and refused to collaborate with the **Lao Issara** national government created in October 1945. He held numerous administrative posts and became a successful entrepreneur. He was elected deputy for Sam Neau province in 1951. Between 1953 and 1955, he served as vice president of the National Assembly of the Associated State of Laos. Politically, he moved towards neutralism and in 1955 he founded the Peace through Neutrality Party. He was assassinated in 1963, while serving as foreign minister of the Royal Lao government.

**KMT.** *See* REPUBLIC OF CHINA.

**KNOWLAND, WILLIAM FIFE (1908–1974).** American senator favorable to supporting non-communist states in Indochina during the Franco-Vietnamese war. Born into a Republican political family, Knowland was elected to the California Senate in 1934 and joined the Republican National Committee in 1938. After working as a staff writer in the army in Europe during World War II, he returned to the United States in 1945 to serve as a United States senator. He became increasingly conservative in his views and criticized both **Harry S. Truman** and **Dwight D. Eisenhower**'s policies towards Asia. He was staunchly opposed to recognizing the **People's Republic of China**'s entry into the **United Nations** and supported Joseph McCarthy's anti-communist crusade in the early 1950s. In the wake of the French defeat at **Dien Bien Phu**, Knowland said during a television interview that if the Chinese communists intervened in Indochina, he would favor the dispatch of American troops there. He and Michael Mansfield urged non-communist Asian countries to form an Asian defense pact.

**KOENIG, MARIE PIERRE (1898–1970).** French general and committed Gaullist during the Indochina War. Koenig served in the 13 Demi Brigade of the French **Foreign Legion** in Norway before joining **Charles de Gaulle**'s Free French forces in Africa and the Middle East during World War II. He became major general in 1943 and was named assistant chief of staff of French ground forces in North Africa before transferring to the United Kingdom in April 1944, where he became commander-in-chief of French forces and French Forces of the Interior. A staunch defender of the maintenance of the **French Union**, in June 1951 Koenig called for the introduction of the national draft in order to win the war in Indochina once and for all. To no avail. In December 1952, he told a French paper that the Indochinese countries were not sufficiently committed to fighting the war. They do not "fight the war in the way Clemenceau understood it and we are perhaps in the year 1917 of the Indochina War". When, in the wake of the **Dien Bien Phu** disaster, the French government asked Koenig if he would take over in Indochina, he said only on the condition that the government institute the draft. When the government refused, he replied: "Don't count on me". Although **Pierre Mendès France** successfully sidelined Koenig during the negotiation of the **Geneva accords** in mid-1954, the French president's threat to reinstate the draft if an agreement were not reached by 20 July echoed Koenig's repeated calls for just such action. *See also* EXPEDITIONARY CORPS.

**KOMAKI OOMIYA.** Educated in France in the 1920s, Oomiya worked in Indochina in the 1930s as a specialist in mining, banking, and legal questions. He was at ease in French. During World War II, he collaborated secretly with Vietnamese nationalists opposed to the French. This collaboration came into the open following the Japanese defeat in August 1945 and the advent of the **Democratic Republic of Vietnam**. After his release from an internment camp, Oomiya began working as an intermediary between the Vietnamese, French, Chinese, and Soviet delegates, allegedly playing some sort of role in the negotiations leading to the **Accords of 6 March 1946.** *See also* CROSSOVERS; DESERTION; JAPANESE TROOPS, INDOCHINA WAR; REPATRIATION, JAPANESE TROOPS.

**KOREAN WAR**. The outbreak of the Korean War in June 1950 extended the heat of the **Cold War** from Europe to Asia, and this directly affected the course of the Indochina War. For one, upon the outbreak of the Korean conflict, American President **Harry S. Truman** declared on 27 July that the United States would not only send troops to protect the Republic of Korea against communist aggression, but that it would also step up its military aid to Taiwan and to the French fighting communists in Indochina as part of a wider containment strategy in Asia. Second, the French saw in the Korean War the chance to recast the Indochina War as a vital part of the global American Cold War to contain Sino-Soviet communism to its Eurasian limits. To this end, the French sent a regiment to fight alongside American forces in Korea, *le régiment de Corée*. American aid began flowing to the French in earnest following the outbreak of the Korean War, symbolized nicely by the creation of the American **Military Advisory and Assistance Group** in **Saigon** in September 1950. Third, not unlike the French, Vietnamese communists also saw in the Korean War a chance to link their movement more closely to the communist revolutionary one. Just as the Chinese were fighting the American "imperialists" in Korea, the Vietnamese were taking on the French "colonialists" in Indochina as part of the wider internationalist battle against the "capitalist camp" in Asia. The **Democratic Republic of Vietnam** (DRV) recognized the North Korean government and dispatched delegates there during the Indochina conflict.

Hence, for both the French and the Vietnamese, the Korean War allowed them in varying degrees to link colonial and national liberation wars to the wider global struggles inherent in the Cold War. The DRV's propaganda strongly supported the North Koreans and blamed the outbreak of the war in Korea on the United States. French propaganda reflected the opposing view of course. The linkage between the Korean and Indochina Wars continued to the end. When an armistice stopped the fighting in Korea in mid-1953, French leaders seeking to find an "honorable end" to the Indochina conflict announced that it "would be hard to conceive that a true peace could be instituted in the Far East as long as war continued in other parts of Asia", meaning Indochina. Similar things were occurring on the Vietnamese side, as the Soviets and the Chinese began to emphasize the importance of negotiations both in Korea and Indochina. The key decisions leading to both the battle of **Dien Bien Phu** and the **Geneva Conference** began in 1953, with the signing of the armistice on Korea constituting a major factor. North Korean pilots would later fly MIGs to protect the DRV against the Americans during the Vietnam War. *See also* DIEN BIEN PHU, BATTLE PREPARATION AND CONTEXT.

**KOSAL (1904–?).** Career magistrate and Cambodian politician. Born in Chau Doc province in southern Vietnam, he completed his secondary studies at the *Lycée Sisowath* and then at the *Lycée Chasseloup Laubat* in **Saigon** before going on to study at the teachers' college in **Hanoi** from which he graduated as a certified primary school teacher in 1928. In 1929, he changed tack and went to work as an advisor in the Cambodian Chamber of Indictments (*Sala Kromchot* or *Chambre de mises en accusation*). In 1933, he was named advisor to the final court of appeals (*Sala Vinichay* or *cour de cassation*) and remained in that post until 1939. In 1940, he became president of the court of first instance (*Sala Dambaung* or the *tribunal de première instance*) in Takeo. Little is known of his activities during World War II or immediately thereafter. In February 1949, however, he was appointed minister of Justice in the **Yèm Sambaur** cabinet and held the position until 1950. Hostile to the **Democrat Party**, he helped Yèm Sambaur create the National Recovery Party and acted as its general secretary. He lost, however, in the National Assembly elections of 1951.

**KOSHIRO IWAI (NGUYỄN VĂN SÁU, SÁU NHẬT, 1921–).** Japanese soldier who crossed over to the **Democratic Republic of Vietnam** (DRV) in the wake of World War II. He was inducted into and served in the Vietnamese army between 1945 and 1955. In 1947, he led troops into battle around Lang Son and conducted special operations behind enemy lines. By 1949, he had become a battalion deputy commander in the DRV's army. He was most appreciated, however, for the technical training he provided in **General Staff** work, battle preparations, and military intelligence. The Vietnamese army no longer hides the important advisory and intelligence role Koshiro Iwai played during the frontier battles against the French in 1950 as a member of the 174th regiment. He also solved problems that allowed the Vietnamese to employ their newly acquired Chinese artillery more effectively against French positions during the battle of **Cao Bang**. His contributions and loyalty were sufficiently important for him to be admitted to the **Vietnamese Worker's Party** in 1952. He was also a member of the Japanese Communist Party. He returned to Japan in 1955, where he established with Nakahara Minh Ngoc the Japan-Vietnam Friendship Association. *See also* CROSSOVERS; DESERTION; JAPANESE TROOPS, INDOCHINA WAR; REPATRIATION, JAPANESE TROOPS.

**KOWAL, GEORGES (?–1952).** War photographer for the *Service cinématographique des armées* during the Indochina War. Little is known about his family background other than the fact that he and his brother were orphaned at a young age and grew up in a public orphanage in France. Georges Kowal arrived in Indochina in December 1948 to work as a non-commissioned officer in the **Air Force**, in charge of cinematography, before transferring to the information service of the high commissioner for Indochina. He produced a number of reports taking him across all of Indochina until 1951, when he left the military and became a civilian film-maker working on a contract basis for the army. From the start in 1951 Kowal made his name as one of Indochina's leading war photographers, covering major battles occurring in and around the **Tonkin** delta. He jumped with paratroopers during the battle of Thai Nguyen and again at **Hoa Binh**. This was his last jump, however. He was killed in battle there in 1952. His brother continued to serve in Indochina in the **Foreign Legion**. *See also* CINEMA; CULTURE; NOVELS; PIERRE SCHOENDOERFFER; PSYCHOLOGICAL WARFARE.

**KRULL, GERMAINE (1897–1985).** Born in Germany, Krull was on the cutting edge of modern photography and art by the 1920s and one of the architects of what came to be known as New Vision Photography. She was also a politically engaged intellectual, sympathetic to national liberation movements in Asia and Africa. She worked with the French resistance in **Brazzaville** in 1944 and covered the French invasion of southern France. She then reported the end of World War II in **India**, **Indonesia**, and Vietnam, working as a journalist and a photographer. She was present in **Saigon** when war broke out between the French and the Vietnamese on **23 September 1945**, and was aghast at what she saw. She wrote a damning account of French actions in the *coup de force* of 23 September. She continued to cover Southeast Asia in the following years, making Bangkok her home base. She knew **Jim Thompson** well and met often with leading Vietnamese, Lao, and Cambodian nationalists working out of or passing through Bangkok, including **Oun Sananikone**. *See also* CINEMA; CULTURE; HERAULT, MASSACRE; INTELLECTUALS; NOVELS.

**KU APHAI (1892–1964).** Lao non-communist politician and royalist. Born in southern Laos, he studied in colonial **Saigon** and Phnom Penh before pursuing advanced studies in France. He returned to Indochina on the eve of World War I and began his career in the colonial civil service. Between 1915 and 1929, he worked in the office of the *résident supérieur* in Laos and was local leader of Khong district between 1929 and 1941. When the French had to cede large parts of southern Laos to the Thais under Japanese pressure, he became governor of Pakse in 1941, a post he held in one form or another until 1947. Between 1947 and 1949, he served as minister of Education and Health and then president of the Royal Council.

**KU VÔRAVONG (1914–1954).** Leading Lao non-communist politician during the Indochina War. The son of a school teacher, Ku Vôravong was born in Savannakhet and attended the *Collège Pavie* in Laos and the *Lycée Albert Sarraut* in **Hanoi** before going on to France to complete his secondary studies in a high school in Montpellier. He then studied law at the University of Montpellier. Back in Indochina, between 1933 and 1935, he studied and graduated from the *École de droit et d'administration* in Laos. He worked between 1935 and 1938 as a secretary in the *Résidence supérieure* in Laos and then as a secretary in the *Inspection des affaires administratives et du travail* in Laos until 1941, when he became district chief (*chaomuong*). In that same year, in *An*

*Appeal to the Youth,* he exhorted the patriotic feelings of his Lao listeners and expressed hostility to continued Vietnamese immigration and civil servants in Laos. In 1941, he was named general secretary of the Royal Palace in Luang Prabang. Following the Japanese ***coup de force*** **of 9 March 1945**, he joined French **guerrillas** parachuted into Laos working against the Japanese. He refused to join the **Lao Issara** and was virulently opposed to **Viet Minh** interference in Lao affairs. Following the French reoccupation of Laos in mid-1946, he became minister of Justice and Religious Affairs in the first constitutional government of the Royal Lao government between late 1947 and early 1949. He was minister of the Economy and of the Interior (March 1949–February 1950) in the newly created Associated State of Laos, and minister of Religious Affairs, Sports, and Youth in 1950. He was elected deputy of Thakhek in 1947 and was co-founder of the Lao Union Party (*Lao Rouam Sampan*). In 1948, he created his own political party, Democracy, favorable to a constitutional monarchy. In 1954, when Vietnamese communist forces invaded Lao territory, Prime Minister **Suvanna Phūmā** designated him minister of Defense. On 18 September 1954, he was assassinated in Vientiane, contributing to the fall of Suvanna Phūmā's government.

**KUBIAK, STEFAN (HỒ CHÍ TOÁN, 1923–1963).** Polish **crossover** to the **Democratic Republic of Vietnam** (DRV) during the Indochina War. Born in Lodz, Kubiak was the son of a poor weaver. While in uniform in the Polish Army, he fell into German hands during World War II and ended up in a labor camp in Germany in 1940. In 1943, he escaped and joined the Soviet army in 1944 in the offensive against the Nazis before re-joining the Polish Army at the end of the war. For unclear reasons, he deserted and made his way to Western Europe where he joined the French **Foreign Legion** and eventually ended up in Indochina in December 1946. In April 1947, he deserted yet again, this time the Foreign Legion at Nam Dinh, and crossed over to the ranks of the DRV, where he went to work in the army's propaganda and **proselytizing the enemy** (*dich van*) offices. Between 1948 and 1954, he participated in 10 battles and scores of minor operations, distinguishing himself during the battles of **Hoa Binh** and **Dien Bien Phu**. He was an official member of the **People's Army of Vietnam** between 1947 and 1963, taking the Vietnamese name of Ho Chi Toan. Between 1955 and 1957, he served as a chief of staff for a DRV artillery regiment. He was named captain in the Vietnamese army in 1958. Between 1957 and 1963, he was on the staff of the **People's Army newspaper**. He died in 1963 in **Hanoi**. *See also* DESERTION.

**KUOMINTANG.** *See* REPUBLIC OF CHINA.

# L

**LA CHAMBRE, GUY (1898–1975).** French politician and minister of the **Air Force** between January 1938 and March 1940. He was the French minister responsible for relations with the **Associated States of Indochina** between September 1954 and February 1955 in the cabinet of **Pierre Mendès France**.

**LÃ VĨNH LỢI (LÊ HI, LÊ HY, TỪ LÂM, HỒNG LỆ, ANH LINH, DR. LEE, 1913–1994).** During the Popular Front period, he became involved in nationalist and communist politics, working under **Truong Chinh** in the **Hanoi** bureau of *Tin Tuc* newspaper. In 1939, Le Vinh Loi joined the **Indochinese Communist Party** (ICP) before the French arrested and incarcerated him at **Poulo Condor** shortly thereafter. He was heavily involved in prison politics and rubbed shoulders there with the likes of **Tran Ngoc Danh, Ton Duc Thang,** and **Pham Hung**. He regained his liberty in September 1945 and helped run the southern resistance newspaper, *Cuu Quoc*. At ease in French and English, Le Hy arrived in Bangkok in early 1946 to promote the Vietnamese nationalist cause to the region and the world. He helped establish and run the **Democratic Republic of Vietnam**'s (DRV) information bureau there (*Thong Tan Xa Viet Nam* or the Vietnam News Service) between 1945 and 1948. He also met regularly with American and other diplomats stationed in Southeast Asia. He accompanied **Pham Ngoc Thach** to Rangoon in April 1948 on a diplomatic mission. Later that year, he left for Prague via Shanghai and Moscow in the company of an Australian communist, **Alexander Brotherton**, to create a new Bureau of Information in Prague for the DRV. He arrived in Moscow in August 1948. However, neither the DRV nor the ICP had authorized his "mission". In Moscow, he nonetheless attempted to establish direct contact with the Soviet government and communist party, hoping to obtain military, diplomatic, and financial aid. To this end, he also collaborated with **Tran Ngoc Danh**, who had also contacted the Soviets without authorization and criticized the ideological mettle of the ICP in general and that of **Ho Chi Minh** in particular. Both were expelled from the party on their return to northern Vietnam in late 1950. La Vinh Loi apparently got into trouble again in the 1960s when he was accused of being a pro-Soviet "revisionist".

**LABROUQUÈRE, ANDRÉ**. General secretary of the **Cominindo** in the first half of 1946 before serving as the private secretary to the minister of Overseas France, **Maurice Moutet.** He was the author of *La Justice en Indochine* (1938).

**LACHARRIÈRE (DE), LADREIT.** Served as Legal advisor to the high commissioner for Indochina **Georges Thierry d'Argenlieu** from late 1945 and was named commissioner for Legal Affairs in October 1946.

**LACHEROY, CHARLES (1906–2005).** One of the best-known French theoreticians of "**revolutionary warfare**", who got his start during the Indochina War. Lacheroy joined the *École spéciale militaire* at Saint-Cyr in 1925. In 1927, he transferred to the colonial infantry, serving in the Upper Volta in a regiment of Senegalese *tirailleurs* between 1928 and 1930. He subsequently moved on to Syria, where he learned of the exploits of Lawrence of Arabia and concluded that victory in **guerrilla** war depended on "psychology". He was arrested in Rabat in December 1940 for assisting French resistance agents. Though the charges were unfounded, he ended up in jail in Clermont-Ferrand, sharing a cell with none other than **Pierre Mendès France**. Released for lack of incriminating evidence, Lacheroy returned to Vichy North Africa before joining Free French forces upon the Allied landing there in 1942. He took part in the liberation of Italy under General **Alphonse Juin**, and then served under General **Jean de Lattre de Tassigny** in the 1st French Army taking part in the liberation of France and Germany.

In February 1951, after working in the Ivory Coast, he landed in southern Vietnam where he took command of the Bien Hoa Zone. It was also there that he began studying in detail the **Viet Minh**'s guerrilla tactics and developing his ideas on counter-insurgency, thanks to the archives of the **Deuxième Bureau** in charge of southern Vietnam. In 1952, he ran an internal conference for officers in his sector on the organizational and psychological nature of the Viet Minh's warfare, entitled *Une arme du Viet Minh: les hiérarchies parallèles*. He emphasized how the communists effectively organized and controlled the populations as a weapon and he popularized the idea of **parallel hierarchies** in French military science. Lacheroy also discovered the military writings of **Mao Zedong** on "revolutionary war".

All this launched something of a new career for him as theoretician and instructor in what he (and others) would call *guerre révolutionnaire*. He returned to France in mid-1953 to teach such subjects at the Centre of Asian and African Studies within the Colonial Army headquarters. An excellent speaker, he propounded his ideas on counter-insurgency and **psychological warfare** and began to attract the interest and attention of high-ranking army strategists, theorists, and leaders facing similar wars in the Empire. Indeed, his understanding of Vietnamese communism and the adversary's organization, adaptation, and use of guerrilla, communist and psychological strategies would serve as a model for counter-insurgency fighting during the Algerian War and elsewhere. In 1955, Lacheroy ran a pivotal conference bringing together his ideas (and those of others) on counter-insurgency, entitled *Action Viet Minh et communiste en Indochine ou une leçon de "guerre révolutionnaire"*. In 2003, he published his memoirs, entitled *De Saint-Cyr à l'action psychologique*. *See also* ANTOINE SAVANI; *GROUPEMENT DE COMMANDOS MIXTES AÉROPORTÉS* (GCMA); ROGER TRINQUIER; *SERVICE ACTION*.

**LACOUTURE, JEAN (1921–).** Jean Lacouture left for Indochina in October 1945 as part of General **Philippe Leclerc**'s *service de presse*. Lacouture shared a cabin on the same boat with **Philippe Devillers**. They would discover Vietnam together in 1945–1946 and go on to co-author a number of major works on the wars for Indochina. Like Devillers, Lacouture wrote for the **Expeditionary Corps**'s paper, *Caravelle,* and helped found the weekly paper *Paris-Saigon*, which sought to inform the French in Indochina of world events and promote a peaceful solution to a war which had already begun with the Vietnamese in the south on **23 September 1945**. During his time in Indochina, Lacouture interviewed **Ho Chi Minh, Vo Nguyen Giap**, **Bao Dai**, and other Vietnamese political leaders. This French correspondent also met and interviewed ranking French officials before returning to France on 18 December 1946. Like Devillers, Lacouture was struck by the force of Vietnamese nationalism as represented by the leaders of the **Democratic Republic of Vietnam**, in particular Ho Chi Minh. It was vain for France to try to maintain its colonial rule in Indochina, he concluded. The key to the war resided in recognizing Vietnamese independence. After spending several years in Morocco and Egypt, he became a journalist in Paris. He returned to Indochina in 1953 for *Le Monde* and published a series of articles on different aspects of the conflagration. Jean Lacouture together with Philippe Devillers, **Bernard Fall**, **Paul Mus,** and **Ellen Hammer** were among the first journalists-historians to provide detailed accounts and analyses of contemporary Vietnamese history and the Indochina War.

**LALANDE, ANDRÉ (1913–1995).** French officer taken prisoner during the battle of **Dien Bien Phu**. Graduated from Saint-Cyr in 1933, he participated in the Allied expedition against the Nazis at Narvik, Norway. He fled to Great Britain on 20 June 1940 and immediately joined the emerging Free French forces under the command of General **Charles de Gaulle**. Lalande worked in the General Staff of French Ground Forces in Great Britain from June 1941. Two years later he was named major and took part in all the major Free French military campaigns in Egypt, Libya, Tunisia, Italy, and France, usually in the 13th Half Brigade of the **Foreign Legion**. In 1946, he graduated at the head of his class from Saint-Cyr before taking a job with the **North Atlantic Treaty Organization**. In 1953, Lalande volunteered for service in Indochina, where he commanded a regiment of the Foreign Legion (*3ème Régiment étranger d'infanterie, REI*) and Mobile Group 6. He commanded troops during the battle of Dien Bien Phu and was named colonel as the battle raged. He led the famous strongpoint of Isabelle which put up a ferocious fight against the adversary until Lalande and his remaining men were taken prisoner on 8 May 1954. He was liberated in September and returned to France in October 1954. He would go on to serve in the **Algerian War**.

**LÂM THÀNH NGUYÊN (1909–?).** Leading **Hoa Hao** figure, who crossed over to the French in the early years of the Indochina War. Born in Can Tho, Lam Thanh Nguyen converted to the Hoa Hoa Buddhist faith in 1941. During World War II, his **collaboration** with the Japanese landed him in a French colonial jail. He walked free following the Japanese ***coup de force* of 9 March 1945**. After the Allied defeat of the Japanese a few months later, he joined the ranks of the **Democratic Republic of Vietnam** in 1946, serving as a deputy to **Tran Van Soai**. In March 1947, the French thought they had won him over as violence with the **Viet Minh** nationalist front in the south escalated; however, he returned to the *maquis* shortly after opening talks with his former enemies. In January 1948, he broke with Tran Van Soai in order to maintain his independence and control of his troops. At the same time, his relations with the Viet Minh deteriorated to the point that he crossed over definitively to the French on 14 February 1949 and agreed to serve as deputy to General Tran Van Soai with the rank of colonel. He broke yet again with the latter in July 1950, but was considered by the French still to be "pro French". The latter needed him and his men in order to build an army for the Associated State of Vietnam. In August 1953, the French estimated his forces to number 3,306 men.

**LAMI, PIERRE (1909–1994).** French colonel in 1946 and director of Political and Administrative Affairs in **Tonkin** and North **Annam**. Graduated from the **Colonial Academy** (*École coloniale*), he served in Chad where he joined Free French forces in 1940. After World War II, he resumed his colonial career in Indochina. From 1 October 1946, he served as General **Louis Morlière**'s chief political advisor. During the **Haiphong** incident of November 1946, he helped both sides reach a cease-fire on the afternoon of 20 November 1946. When **Pierre Debès**, under instructions from **Jean Valluy,** broke it in order to take Haiphong from the **Democratic Republic of Vietnam** and to teach the Vietnamese a "severe lesson", Lami did his best to dissuade them, but to no avail. Lami met on several friendly occasions with Vietnamese nationalist **Pham Khac Hoe**, arrested by the French during the outbreak of war in **Hanoi** on **19 December 1946** and placed under surveillance. Lami later transferred to Dalat, but it is unclear when or why he left Indochina.

**LAND REFORM**. The communist leadership of the **Democratic Republic of Vietnam** (DRV) officially began land reform in December 1953 – at the height of the Indochina War. Vietnamese communists adopted this radical measure in order to transform both society and state into the communist mold, enter the internationalist communist bloc, and mobilize peasants in the war against the French for national independence.

In 1945, more than 80% of the population lived in the countryside, precisely where the government and army had been operating since 1947. Until 1950, however, Vietnamese communists had stressed national unity over social revolution. **Ho Chi Minh** had been central to this shift in policy when he presided over the creation of the **Viet Minh** in 1941. And whatever the internal, theoretical credo, the **Indochinese Communist Party** leadership continued to stress national solidarity throughout the first half of the war. The party had already confiscated and distributed enemy land in its possession. It had also approved rent and interest rate reductions. Following Sino-Soviet diplomatic recognition of the DRV in January 1950, Vietnamese communists adopted more communist-minded policies in social, state, intellectual, and diplomatic affairs.

Most ranking Vietnamese communists saw the implementation of land reform in 1953 as a powerful source for mobilizing the countryside against the French (peasants would serve more ardently in exchange for land) and indispensable to breaking the hold of the landlord class in order to promote eventual communist revolution such as agricultural collectivization. Adopting land reform would also be an important part of joining the internationalist communist movement led by **Joseph Stalin** at the top and **Mao Zedong** in Asia. No sooner had they taken power than Chinese communists began sending specialists to Vietnam to help the **Vietnamese Worker's Party** (VWP) devise and implement land reform based largely upon the Chinese model (which the Chinese themselves were enthusiastically applying on a national basis between 1950 and 1953).

Although the VWP officially implemented land reform in December 1953, preparations had been underway since early 1953 following Ho Chi Minh's return from Beijing and Moscow in 1952. Full-scale land reform was limited mainly to areas in northern and central Vietnam under DRV control. Little occurred in southern DRV areas. The VWP organized special land reform cadre teams, which investigated and classified the population as landlords, rich peasants, middle peasants, poor peasants, or agricultural laborers. These teams penetrated villages and, with the backing of the police and the military, organized mobilization and hate sessions against landlords and rich peasants, and tried many of them in hastily convened "people's courts", before proceeding to expropriate and redistribute their land as the Chinese were doing to the north. This social revolution in the countryside continued until 1956, when its disastrous results finally forced the party to end it and apologize publicly for its excesses, errors, and **executions**. Ho Chi Minh replaced **Truong Chinh** as general secretary of the party.

While the exact numbers killed because of the land reform remain contested, hundreds of Vietnamese perished during this time, many of whom had supported the DRV's nationalist cause since the outset of the Indochina War. Many "bourgeois" nationalists also left the DRV at this point. The start of land reform in late 1953 was also connected to the need to mobilize the peasant population in favor of modern war and set-piece battles requiring unprecedented levels of manpower both for fighting and running logistics. By promising to distribute land to the peasants, the party sought to mobilize the manpower vital to ensuring victory at **Dien Bien Phu** as negotiations began at the international level to end the war diplomatically. *See also* DIEN BIEN PHU, BATTLE PREPARATION AND CONTEXT.

**LẠNG SƠN INCIDENT.** This "incident" occurred in late November 1946 in a Vietnamese provincial capital located near the Chinese border. Like the preceding **Haiphong incident** (without which the Lang Son incident would not have occurred), the Lang Son clash between French and **Democratic Republic of Vietnam** (DRV) forces can be explained at two levels. On the one hand, it marked the failure of the French and the Vietnamese to negotiate a peaceful solution to the future of Vietnam's political status. On another level, the Lang Son incident pointed up the degree to which local French authorities were willing to act independently of their superiors.

French troops arrived in the border town on 8 July 1946, in accordance with the **Accords of 6 March 1946** and the related April military convention authorizing 15,000 French troops to take over from the Chinese now leaving Indochina above the **16th parallel**. While the DRV accepted the stationing of French troops in Lang Son and worked with them via a Franco-Vietnamese liaison committee, relations became increasingly strained as High Commissioner **Georges Thierry d'Argenlieu** and General **Jean Valluy** adopted a more aggressive line towards the DRV.

As in the port of Haiphong, the month of November was particularly tense in the inland border town of Lang Son. On 20 November, the French exhumed the cadavers of individuals killed by the Japanese in 1945 near the Lang Son citadel, but in doing so they destroyed DRV defenses obstructing their work. The Vietnamese rebuilt their defenses and mined them in a bid to ensure their protection and assert their government's sovereignty. When two French men were killed in unclear circumstances on the morning of 21 November, the French forces opened fire on the Vietnamese positions facing them. A cease-fire was reached in order to prevent the incident from escalating out of control. However, this did not last long as local French troops led by Colonel Sizaire decided to destroy the DRV citadel. Like **Pierre Debès** in Haiphong, Sizaire issued an ultimatum to the Vietnamese side ordering its leaders to free two French prisoners and 10 Chinese. The DRV released the two French men, but not the Chinese (considered to be subject to Vietnamese law). On 25 November, Sizaire attacked and took the citadel at Lang Son from the Vietnamese. On 30 November, Valluy ordered General **Louis Morlière** to extend French military control over the strategically important region lying between Lang Son and the sea.

Although the responsibility for the initial incident remains unclear, local French officers deliberately chose to escalate the incident in order to retake Lang Son and to extend military and colonial control over the strategically important northern frontier and coastline. The leaders of the DRV held back their troops in the hope of reaching a negotiated solution. *See also* 19 DECEMBER 1946; OVERSEAS CHINESE.

**LANGLADE (DE), FRANÇOIS GIRON (LUTÈCE).** Gaullist resistance leader involved in Indochinese affairs, who had been a rubber planter in British Malaya for almost two decades. In 1941, **Charles de Gaulle** sent him to **India** where de Langlade joined the French Indochina section of Force 136 and was deeply involved in its resistance plans for Indochina. In mid-1944, with the liberation of France underway, de Gaulle named Colonel de Langlade his "political delegate" and sent him on a secret mission to Indochina to contact the Vichy Governor General Admiral Jean Decoux, in order to win over local French authorities to the Free French cause. In July 1944, the British parachuted de Langlade (code name *Lutèce*) into **Tonkin**, where he entered into contact with General Eugène Mordant at the head of the Indochinese colonial army. Mordant had secretly entered into contact with the Free French in late 1942 and had been designated in 1944 to lead resistance operations there. Mordant, however, was not keen on taking up arms and prevented de Langlade from meeting Decoux. The mission was a failure. No sooner had de Langlade returned to liberated Paris in August 1944 and made his report to de Gaulle than the latter told him to "go back" to **Hanoi** to make direct contact with Decoux. In late November 1944, de Langlade reached Hanoi and met personally with Decoux, Mordant, Aymé, and Sabattier. Decoux recognized the legitimacy of the Provisional Government of de Gaulle, but insisted on remaining in control of Indochinese affairs and *au courant* of resistance activities, contrary to de Gaulle's orders to the admiral. De Langlade could not make such assurances and the mission was a limited success. De Gaulle, however, was exasperated by the lack of fighting spirit demonstrated by French authorities in Indochina. De Langlade became a close confidant to de Gaulle on Indochina policy. In the wake of the Pacific War, de Langlade served as de Gaulle's trusted advisor on Indochinese affairs, appointed general secretary of de Gaulle's newly created **Cominindo** in charge of Indochinese policy. The former rubber planter and *résistant* was nonetheless unable to prevent his boss from naming **Georges Thierry d'Argenlieu** high commissioner to Indochina. Thierry d'Argenlieu was, de Langlade later told British historian Peter Dunn, "a bit of a disaster. But that was de Gaulle. The man didn't matter – what was important was the job, and any man should have been able to fill it". *See also* COLLABORATION.

**LANGLADE (DE), PAUL ANNET JOSEPH ALEXANDRE GIROT (1894–1980).** Distinguished himself in combat in World War I and was seriously injured in 1915. In 1916, he became a pilot and served in the French Air Force. During the interwar period, he returned to the cavalry and served in French North Africa until World War II saw him join forces with Free French and Allied forces in Tunisia following the Allied landing in November 1942. It was at this time that he joined General Philippe Leclerc's 2nd Armored Division and took part in the liberation of Europe. De Langlade served after World War II as military governor of Strasbourg in 1946–47 and commander of the *École d'application de l'arme blindée cavalerie* between 1947 and 1950. Between 1952 and 1953, he was commanding officer of Ground Troops in Cambodia and deputy commander-in-chief for Ground Troops in Indochina in 1953 and 1954. He became lieutenant general in 1948.

**LANGLAIS, PIERRE CHARLES ALBERT MARIE (1909–1988).** French officer who commanded hundreds of **French Union** soldiers during the battle of **Dien Bien Phu**. Born in Brittany, Langlais graduated from Saint-Cyr and made a career in the army. During World War II, he saw combat in Italy, France, and Germany, before transferring to Indochina in October 1945 as part of the 9th Colonial Infantry Division. He participated in the French reoccupation of southern Vietnam before transferring to the north where he took part in the street fighting in **Hanoi** following the outbreak of full-scale war on **19 December 1946**. In 1949, he returned to Indochina for a second tour of duty and witnessed from the northern border the Chinese communist decimation of their nationalist rivals. He also served in central Vietnam and northern Laos before returning to France where he took over from **Jean Gilles** at the head of the 1st Colonial Half-Brigade of Paratrooper **Commandos**. This also meant that Langlais had to become a paratrooper himself, which he did. Around 1953, he returned to Indochina for a third tour of duty and found himself commanding not just his paratroopers at Dien Bien Phu, but hundreds of other soldiers who looked to him for leadership as the battle turned into a defeat. He provided it until the camp went down on 7 May 1954.

Langlais was famous for his temper and no-holds-barred directness. He was also unique among French officers for his capacity after the war to recognize the extraordinary feat which the adversary had achieved at Dien Bien Phu. Unlike so many left bitter by defeat, especially in the army, Langlais credited the Vietnamese, communist or not, for what they had done in 1954. He also refused to blame others for French mistakes. He reserved a particularly harsh criticism for the likes of **Charles Lacheroy** and the proponents of "**revolutionary warfare**". The problem with Lacheroy and the anti-communist ideas his acolytes would apply in the **Algerian War**, Langlais concluded, was that they failed to understand the reality and the power of another ideology, modern nationalism: *La guerre d'Indochine fut une guerre d'indépendance contre la France et si l'outil de combat fut forgé par des méthodes marxistes, il n'en reste pas moins vrai que le soldat Viet Minh qui montait, et avec quel courage, à l'assaut des positions de Dien Bien Phu, luttait pour nous mettre à la porte de chez lui où nous n'étions pas chez nous*. *See also* AID, CHINESE; EXPERIENCE OF WAR, DIEN BIEN PHU; MARCEL BIGEARD; MYTH OF WAR.

**LANGUAGE AND WAR.** War always affects the nature of language. The Indochina War was no exception. In French and Vietnamese, for example, a host of words entered each vocabulary to identify, denigrate, and even dehumanize the other. Members of the French army shortened **Viet Minh** to **les Viet** early on in the conflagration to refer to their adversaries in the **Democratic Republic of Vietnam** (DRV). French officers and **French Union** soldiers used it widely in daily conversations, reports, and later in the war literature some of them produced. Many in the European settler community, the **Français d'Indochine**, did the same. Authors such as **Roger Delpey** popularized *les Viet* in *Soldats de la boue*. Memoirs published in the 1980s by **Marcel Bigeard** and others gave it a new lease on life in French and in the heat of the **Boudarel affair.**

But such use of language was not an exclusively French affair. **Civil war** witnessed Vietnamese coin and use words to refer to each other in similarly dehumanizing ways. Anti-communist Vietnamese nationalists referred to their opponents with the derogatory term ***Viet Cong***, meaning Vietnamese communist but conveying something less than human. Communist nationalists shot back with couplets such as *Viet gian, bu nhin,* and *nguy* ("traitor", "lackey", and "puppet"). The idea in using all of these epithets was to try to deny legitimacy and oftentimes humanity to the other in what was a civil as much as a colonial war. Early on in the war, Vietnamese nationalists of all political colors opposed to the return of the French resurrected the term *giac*, meaning "pirate" or "bandit", to refer to the "foreigners" attempting to steal or pillage the country. The Vietnamese had used this term to refer to the French during the conquest of the 19th century. Communist nationalists would use it to refer increasingly to the American "imperialists" intervening in the war from 1950 whereas non-communists directed it towards Chinese "communists" (*trung cong*) interfering on behalf of their Vietnamese allies.

With the communization of the DRV, communist Vietnamese cadres introduced more class-oriented terms to refer to their French, American, and Vietnamese enemies, including of course "imperialists", "capitalists", and "bourgeois". Different social categories for the peasants emerged in DRV zones in central and northern Vietnam. Via the army, the school, newspapers, and scores of mass mobilization and propaganda campaigns, the DRV introduced a panolpy of revolutionary terms, few of which had ever been used in the Vietnamese countryside where the government was now based. Shortly after arriving in **Hanoi** in early 1951, one famous DRV operative, **Nguyen Bac**, had a real scare, when, during a visit to the local barber, the latter asked him if he were not from the *maquis*. Terrified, Bac asked him why he would think such a thing. The barber told him to take a look at the poor quality of his clothes, the buttons, and above all "your way of speaking". As he later reminisced in his memoirs: "We, the party cadres, no longer spoke like ordinary people. We said "solidarity" for mutual assistance, "**emulation**" for an everyday rivalry, "revolutionary enthusiasm" instead of village celebrations … In any case this incident served as a lesson for me. It taught me to be on guard against myself and to rediscover my normal diction".

War forced the DRV and the Associated State of Vietnam to rely heavily on the Vietnamese national language, *quoc ngu*. For both sides, literacy was vital to their ability to educate populations, train bureaucrats, cadres, and officers, in short operate a sustained and effective nation-state. War reinforced the use and spread of the Vietnamese language in other ways, too. Because the number of elites at ease in French was never sufficient to meet the needs of the war-state, the DRV promoted the Vietnamization of all types of knowledge. Specialists translated into Vietnamese scores of technical texts on radio transmissions, encryption, and decrypting.

War even led to a "re-indigenization" of Vietnamese medicine and its French-trained doctors. As the conflict intensified from 1950, the number of serious, combat-related casualties skyrocketed, increasing the DRV's needs for medical personnel, doctors, and pharmacists as well as nurses, assistants, and medics. The DRV's medical services had no choice but to recruit students from the countryside, where Vietnamese knowledge of French had always been weakest. As a result, in the middle of a full-blown war, the Vietnamese medical corps embarked upon the extraordinary project of translating scores of French medical textbooks, manuals, and lectures into Vietnamese, bringing French-trained intellectuals into closer touch with their own language and identity.

Lastly, the DRV, the French, and the **Associated States of Indochina** all sought out and recruited translators, interpreters, and bi- or multi-lingual people at all levels of society. Intelligence services in particular turned to the large **overseas Chinese** communities in Vietnam to serve as spies and sources of information. Vietnamese and French turned to ***métis*** to help them to navigate safely wide yet vital cultural divides. Bi-lingualism was a *sine qua non.*

**LANIEL, JOSEPH (1889–1975).** French president who presided over the opening of the **Geneva Conference** and the fall of **Dien Bien Phu**. Deputy for Calvados, he served as under secretary of state for Finances in the Paul Reynaud government in March 1940 and voted full powers to Philippe Pétain ending the 3rd Republic. However, he joined the resistance in 1941 and helped establish the *Conseil national de la Résistance.* After World War II, he was re-elected deputy for Calvados and founded the center-right *Parti républicain de la liberté.* After serving as minister in several governments in the 4th Republic, he became *Président du Conseil* in June 1953. His government would last but one year, racked by strikes and the questions of the **European Defense Community** and decolonization. To help negotiate an end to the war in Indochina, Laniel relied on two men who had been directly involved in the failure to head off war in 1945–1946 – **Georges Bidault** in charge of Foreign Affairs and **René Pleven** as minister of Defense. Financially burdened and under pressure to focus on Europe, Laniel's government's strategy was nonetheless more realistic than its conservative predecessors. The main goal was to try to negotiate an "honorable way out" (*sortie honorable*) of the war. To do this, the government approved the **Navarre plan**. It was designed to strengthen the French military position in Indochina in order to open negotiations on favorable terms with the adversary. However, things did not work out as planned when the **Democratic Republic of Vietnam's** (DRV) army besieged the French camp at Dien Bien Phu. Despite the Laniel government's hope that the American Air Force would intervene through operation **Vautour**, it never happened. On 7 May 1954 Dien Bien Phu fell to the DRV's armed forces. Although Laniel's government went ahead with the Geneva Conference, his cabinet fell on 12 June, allowing **Pierre Mendès France** to take over the negotiations and end the war. It was also the Laniel government that was forced, in a declaration on Indochina on 3 July 1953, to grant much fuller independence (*parfaire*) to the **Associated States of Indochina**, especially following **Norodom Sihanouk**'s **royal crusade for independence** and the unilateral devaluation of the piastre. Laniel wrote a book about all these events, entitled *Le drame indochinois. De Dien Bien Phu au pari de Genève. See also* CURRENCY, FRENCH INDOCHINA; FINANCIAL COST OF THE INDOCHINA WAR.

**LANSDALE, EDWARD GEARY. (1908–1987).** Prominent American intelligence officer in the **Office of Strategic Services** (OSS) and the Central Intelligence Agency (CIA) active in Southeast Asia during the Indochina War. Born in Detroit, Michigan, he served in the European theatre in the OSS during World War II. In 1945, he transferred to the Philippines with the rank of major and was appointed chief of the Intelligence Division in the Headquarters Air Forces Western Pacific. Until 1948, he helped resolve cases of US soldiers missing in action and collaborated with the Filipino military in rebuilding their intelligence services. He returned to the Philippines in 1950 on the personal request of President Elpidio Quirino and joined the Joint United States Military Assistance Group there. He helped Filipino Defense Minister Ramon Magsaysay stamp out a communist insurgency, the Huks, and developed Filipino psychological operations in order to combat this new type of war. Lansdale was named colonel in 1951.

In light of his counter-insurgency experience, the CIA dispatched Lansdale to Vietnam in 1953 to help the Associated State of Vietnam led by **Bao Dai**. Lansdale worked again in Indochina between 1954 and 1956. During this time, he served in **Saigon** training and advising on counter-insurgency techniques, engineering anti-communist propaganda, and entering into contact with militia groups and religious groups in the south, such as the **Cao Dai** and **Trinh Minh The**. After the **Geneva Conference** confirmed the withdrawal of the French, Lansdale threw his weight behind the **Republic of Vietnam** and its new leader, **Ngo Dinh Diem**. He also trained **Pham Xuan An**, who had recently gone to work as a mole for the DRV secret services. Lansdale's autobiography is entitled *In the Midst of Wars: An American's Mission to Southeast Asia* (1972). *See also* ANTOINE SAVANI; *GROUPEMENT DE COMMANDOS MIXTES AÉROPORTÉS* (GCMA); MARCEL BAZIN; MAURICE BELLEUX; NOVELS, FRENCH, INDOCHINA WAR; *SERVICE ACTION*; *SERVICE DE DOCUMENTATION EXTERIEURE ET DE CONTRE-ESPIONNAGE*.

**LAO ISSARA.** Also known as the "Promoters" (*Khana Kokan*), the Lao Issara leadership consisted of patriotic civil servants who had worked in the French colonial administration and a group of Lao patriots like Thao Oun who had been in Thailand during World War II as exiles or in the service of the Bangkok government. A number of them had worked directly with the Seri Thai or Free Thai movement run by **Pridi Phanomyong** and dominated by ethnic Lao from Isan such as **Tieng Serikhan** and **Thongin Phuriphat**. Others came from the Lao offshoot known as the Lao Pen Lao (Laos for the Lao).

Whatever its weaknesses, the Lao Issara government took the first steps to create a postcolonial nation-state in Laos in the wake of World War II. On 8 October, its spokesman informed King **Sisavang Vong** that its leaders intended to establish a constitutional monarchy. The King refused. On 12 October, the Issara held a ceremony in Vientiane to proclaim the independence and unity of Laos under its national authority. The new government promulgated the nation's first constitution and on 15 October presented its programme to the provisional National Assembly. On 19 November, the Lao Issara deposed the king.

As was the case in Vietnam, the presence of Chinese troops in Laos did not last for long. In February 1946, the geopolitical situation changed significantly when French and Chinese authorities signed an accord allowing French troops to replace their counterparts above the **16th parallel**. On 21 March, the French re-occupied **Thakhek** in a bloody attack and moved northwards to retake all of Laos by May. They restored Sisavang Vong to his pre-March 1945 positions. In the spring of 1946, Phetsarath and the Lao Issara government crossed the Mekong for exile in Thailand. Under the continued premiership of Khammao, the Lao Issara now operated out of Bangkok, where it was based, and Northeastern Thailand, where its soldiers and guerrillas were stationed. While militarily the Issara never posed a threat on the other side of the Mekong, the presence of many of the best and brightest of the French-trained elite in exile undermined French attempts to legitimate their post-war colonial project in Laos. Throughout the late 1940s, Lao Issara representatives did their best to use Thailand to build regional and international contacts and recognition. Issara delegates met with Thai, American, Vietnamese, and British officials to discuss the course of events in Indochina. As for the French, their main concern was to dissolve the Lao Issara as quickly as possible, bring its members back to Laos, and thereby legitimate their own political project.

The coming of the **Cold War**, marked by Chinese communist victories and increasing American pressure on the French to decolonize, modified the thrust of this policy. The changing international context effectively pushed the French to sign conventions with each monarchy in 1949, recognizing their national independence within the confines of the **French Union**. Political strategists led by High Commissioner **Léon Pignon** used the creation of these Associated States to remove the raison d'être of the Lao Issara (and the **Khmer Issarak**) and thereby bring its leaders back to Laos. The Franco-Lao convention as signed in Paris on 19 July 1949 followed the one signed with Bao Dai and preceded another one with **Norodom Sihanouk**.

No sooner had the ink dried on the convention than the French turned to dissolving the Lao Issara. In a remarkable operation, the French opened secret meetings with Issara members that successfully neutralized the movement in Thailand and brought most of its leaders back to Laos. This operation was facilitated by the fact that the Franco-Lao convention creating the Associated State of Laos satisfied the desires of most of the Issara nationalists who had been in Thailand since 1946. On 24 October 1949, three weeks after the proclamation of the People's Republic of China, the prime minister of the Provisional Government of Laos, Khammao, proclaimed the official dissolution of the Lao Issara government and movement. Guaranteed amnesty and often posts in the Associated State of Laos, almost all of the major leaders of the movement and government returned to Laos in late 1949 and 1950. The two revealing exceptions were **Phetsarath** and his half-brother

Prince **Suphānuvong.** *See also* ADMINISTRATIVE OFFICE FOR THE FRONTIER; ASSOCIATED STATES OF INDOCHINA; COMMITTEE FOR EXTERNAL AFFAIRS; COMMITTEE FOR THE EAST, LAO ISSARA; INDOCHINESE COMMUNIST PARTY; INDOCHINESE FEDERATION; KAISÔN PHOMVIHĀN; LAO RESISTANCE GOVERNMENT; PARTY AFFAIRS COMMITTEE.

**LAO RESISTANCE GOVERNMENT.** As the French accelerated their efforts to create the Associated States of Vietnam, Laos, and Cambodia in 1948–1949, the **Democratic Republic of Vietnam** (DRV) countered from April 1949 by developing their own revolutionary Indochinese alliance. In August 1950, the Vietnamese presided over the creation of the **Lao Resistance Government** (*Chinh Phu Khang Chien Lao*) and the **Pathet Lao** national front, replacing the now defunct **Lao Issara** movement. With Chinese support now behind them, Vietnamese communists reaffirmed their internationalist commitment to an Indochinese revolution and to Indochinese associated states in opposition to those supported by the French and backed by the West. Prince **Suphānuvong** led this Laos resistance government aligned with the DRV. *See also* ADMINISTRATIVE OFFICE FOR THE FRONTIER; ADVISORY GROUP 100; ASSOCIATED STATES OF INDOCHINA; COMMITTEE FOR EXTERNAL AFFAIRS; COMMITTEE FOR THE EAST, LAO ISSARA; INDOCHINESE COMMUNIST PARTY; INDOCHINESE FEDERATION; KAISÔN PHOMVIHĀN; LAO RESISTANCE GOVERNMENT; NGUYEN THANH SON; PARTY AFFAIRS COMMITTEE.

**LAOS, FIRST BATTLE OF (13 April–18 May 1953).** The **Democratic Republic of Vietnam**'s (DRV) High Command launched a major attack into northern Laos in April and May 1953 in a bid to open a land route to supply **Inter-Zones IV** and **V** and to boost the **Lao Resistance Government** as part of its wider Indochinese ambitions. As General **Vo Nguyen Giap** put it at the time: "Our strategic aim is to take all of Indochina, that is Vietnam, Laos and Cambodia…" Elements of the 308th, 312th and 316th divisions attacked upper Laos from mid-April, moving into Sam Neua and Xieng Khouang before threatening to move on Luang Prabang. Whereas the French pulled out of the first two places, they held solid in Luang Prabang and counter-attacked from 9 May, retaking Xieng Khouang. While the battle ended for the Vietnamese on 18 May, the DRV's army occupied Sam Neau and large parts of Xieng Khouang and Phongsaly. The Vietnamese installed the **Pathet Lao** in these areas. Thanks to the DRV, Prince **Suphānuvong** established his resistance capital in Sam Neua.

At the international level, the spectacular Vietnamese invasion of Laos set off warning bells in Washington. Many American strategists worried that the DRV's Indochinese ambitions hid wider Southeast Asian ones. The Americans were also increasingly disappointed by General **Raoul Salan**'s defensive strategy, urging him to take the initiative in the battlefield instead of letting the Vietnamese do it for him. Even voices in the French public took notice of the Vietnamese invasion into Laos and the fact that the DRV was not a simple hit-and-run **guerrilla** movement but a remarkably modern army, now on the move in western Indochina. French leaders had also been caught off guard by the DRV's threat to Luang Prabang, an ally whose defense the French were now obligated to defend by treaty commitments. This concern influenced the French decision to occupy and hold **Dien Bien Phu** in order to prevent the DRV from moving on Laos again in 1954. Lastly, the DRV's Indochina strategy had forced the French to commit and disperse more troops to defend western Indochina and the highlands.

Although this does not appear to have been one of the goals of the spring 1953 attack on upper Laos, DRV strategists understood the significance of what they had done and identified drawing the French into the highlands and across Indochina as one of the main aims of their 1953–1954 campaign leading to the victory at Dien Bien Phu. *See also* DIEN BIEN PHU, BATTLE PREPARATION AND CONTEXT; LAOS, SECOND BATTLE OF.

**LAOS, SECOND BATTLE OF (15 December 1953–May 1954).** In mid-September 1953, the intelligence services of the **Democratic Republic of Vietnam** (DRV) "acquired a good understanding of the basic elements of the **Navarre Plan**" and used this in their preparations for the 1953–1954 Winter Spring Campaign. The Vietnamese Politburo and High Command concluded that General **Henri Navarre** was massing his forces to occupy and hold the **Tonkin** lowlands. Vietnamese strategists concluded that it was imperative to force

Navarre "to disperse his forces out to other sectors so that we can annihilate them". Rather than trying to attack the delta, where the French could concentrate their artillery and air power easily on the attacking forces, the Politburo decided to try to disperse the French, taking advantage of the rougher terrain in northwest Vietnam and Laos. This was the context in which the second battle of Laos was conceived and launched weeks after the Politburo approved the winter 1953–spring 1954 military plan in November 1953.

On 20 December, the DRV sent elements of three divisions into central Laos and briefly occupied the Lao town of **Thakhek** and threatened briefly the French military base at Séno. When Navarre decided to dig in at **Dien Bien Phu**, the Vietnamese maintained the pressure on central Laos and pushed troops even further into northeastern Cambodia and the highlands of **Inter-Zone V** (*Lien Khu V*). It was now vital to draw as many French forces as possible away from the main battlefield at Dien Bien Phu. Meanwhile, following the cancellation of the first attack on Dien Bien Phu in January 1954, General **Vo Nguyen Giap** pulled his famous 308th division away from the battlefield and sent it into northern Laos in a bid to further divert the French from Dien Bien Phu so that final preparations for the March attack could be made (when Giap then recalled the 308th to let it loose on Dien Bien Phu). Both attacks on Laos (in the center and the north) revealed yet again the capacity of the DRV to operate militarily on an Indochinese level and this explains to a large extent why the DRV and its Lao allies were in a stronger position in Laos when negotiations opened in Geneva the day Dien Bien Phu fell to the DRV. *See also* DIEN BIEN PHU, CANCELLATION OF FIRST ATTACK; GENEVA CONFERENCE; PATHET LAO.

**LAPIERRE, HENRI GUSTAVE LEON (1895–1985).** Longtime military officer serving in Indochina. Graduated from Saint-Cyr in 1914, Lapierre served throughout World War I, being wounded at the Somme in 1915. He served in the colonies during the interwar period, mainly in Africa. However, in 1937 he transferred to Indochina, where he would remain in one way or another until 1947. As lieutenant colonel he was the head of the General Staff of the Colonial Division of **Tonkin**, second in command in the 10th Colonial Infantry Regiment based in Hue and then head of the 1st Regiment of Tonkinese *Tirailleurs* in **Hanoi**. Vichy named him colonel in September of 1941. During the Japanese ***coup de force* of 9 March 1945**, his troops were overwhelmed by the adversary and those who survived were imprisoned until Allied liberation. Lapierre remained in Indochina after the Japanese capitulation. In late 1945, with the arrival of the French **Expeditionary Corps**, General **Philippe Leclerc** assigned him the command of the Northern Cochinchinese Zone. Lapierre left Indochina in December 1946. In early 1953, he led a mission to study the use of colonial troops in the Indochina War.

**LARTÉGUY, JEAN (JEAN PIERRE LUCIEN OASTY, 1920–?).** Volunteered to fight at the start of World War II and joined the Free French forces in 1942, conducting **commando** operations in France. After the war, he became a correspondent during the **Korean War** and a prolific writer on decolonization, nationalist movements in the South, and on France's forgotten soldiers, the "centurions" as he liked to put it. He dedicated several novels to Indochina, including *La ville étranglée* (1955), *Les âmes errantes* (1956), *Les centurions* (1960), and *Le mal jaune* (1962). *See also* CINEMA; EXPERIENCE OF WAR; LANGUAGE OF WAR; MYTH OF WAR; NOVELS.

**LAURENTIE, HENRI (1901–1984).** High-ranking colonial administrator and principal architect of Gaullist colonial policy during World War II and that of the early French 4th Republic. Trained in law and a graduate of the ***École nationale des langues orientales vivantes***, Laurentie began a long career in the colonial civil service in 1922. In 1924, he served as deputy director of Indigenous Affairs in Cameroon, rising rapidly in the colonial hierarchy. In 1927, he became an administrator of the colonies and moved into the Bureau of Political Affairs in Cameroon. Between 1930 and 1934, he served as high commissioner for the Levant in Damas. In August 1940, in Chad, Laurentie helped win over the colony to Free French forces and became general secretary of Chad then part of French Equatorial Africa.

Named governor of the colonies in 1942, Laurentie played a leading role in the preparation of the **Brazzaville Conference** and the 24 March 1945 **Declaration on Indochina**. **René Pleven** named him *directeur des Affaires politiques au Commissariat aux Colonies* in Algiers. There Laurentie worked closely with **Léon Pignon** on formulating a new colonial policy for Indochina.

With the end of World War II, this bureau moved to Paris and was renamed the Ministry of Overseas France, in which Laurentie served as director of Political Affairs until 1947. He thereafter worked as deputy delegate for France to the **United Nations**.

According to British historian Martin Shipway, Laurentie was something of a "colonial liberal", ready to take up the question of Vietnamese independence which the 24 March Declaration on Indochina refused to do. For Laurentie, the March declaration could have been a point of departure for a new colonial policy. However, like **Paul Mus**, Laurentie had to accept that **Charles de Gaulle** was opposed to making any serious concessions to Vietnamese nationalism. As Laurentie wrote to the director of *Combat* in September 1945: "I can, in a private capacity, tell you this: the Annamese national sentiment, or even the Lao and Cambodian national ones, constitutes an undeniable fact and French policy would do well to satisfy it". In October 1945, Laurentie went through the **Cominindo** in an attempt to warn against what he saw as High Commissioner **Georges Thierry d'Argenlieu's** and Commander-in-Chief of the Armed Forces **Philippe Leclerc**'s dangerous underestimation of Vietnamese nationalism. He was called back into line but not before exhorting the French to demonstrate "their liberal intentions and publicly admit the principle of conversation with (legitimate) elements representing Annamese nationalism".

While he would salute the signing of the **Accords of 6 March 1946** as a sign of French liberalism, he would be profoundly disappointed by what followed, not just the Cochinchinese separatism supported by Thierry d'Argenlieu but also by what he saw as the **Democratic Republic of Vietnam**'s (DRV) preference for war from November 1946. In late 1946, he argued against making any more concessions to the DRV. On 12 June 1947, he resigned from his position in the Ministry of Colonies.

**LE CHINH.** *See* JEAN MARRANE.

**LÊ CỘNG TRINH (MARCEL, 1916–?).** Vietnamese pilot and general director of the Associated State of Vietnam's *Air Vietnam*. Born in Go Cong province in southern Vietnam, Le Cong Trinh held French citizenship. In 1939, he was called to arms in France and trained to fly observation planes in the French **Air Force**. Following the French defeat, he returned to Indochina in February 1941 and was stationed at the Tan Son Nhut air base. In March 1943, he transferred to a bomber squadron at the colonial airbase in Tong in northern Vietnam, but left the air force a few months later. Between 1943 and March 1945, he worked as a secretary in the commercial office of the *Brasserie et glacières d'Indochine* (BGI) and became in 1945 deputy director then director of the BGI in Can Tho province. Following the overthrow of the French and the advent of the **Democratic Republic of Vietnam** (DRV), he became president of the People's Committee in Can Tho and remained in charge of the BGI, simultaneously providing military training to youth groups. In October 1945, he joined the resistance against the French and took the BGI's funds with him. In November 1945, he created one of the first Vietnamese weapons repair factories. However, for unclear reasons, he returned to the French zone in March 1946 and resumed his work at the Tan Son Nhut airbase as a deputy commander there. In August 1949, the British invited him to participate in an air show in Singapore. Between 1951 and 1954, he served as general director of the Associated State of Vietnam's first airline company, *Air Vietnam*. On 16 June 1954, president **Buu Loc** made him *Chevalier de l'ordre national du Vietnam*.

**LÊ ĐÌNH CHI (1912–1949).** Lawyer instrumental in the creation of the **Democratic Republic of Vietnam**'s (DRV) judicial branch during the Indochina War. He completed his secondary education in northern Vietnam and studied law at the *Faculté de droit* in **Hanoi**, obtaining his degree in 1935. He was also deeply involved in radical politics. He joined the Vietnam Revolutionary Youth League in the late 1920s and was a classmate of **Truong Chinh**. Le Dinh Chi left Hanoi for **Saigon** in the 1930s, where he worked as a lawyer in the Saigon Municipal Court (some sources say the Criminal Court). He took part in the Indochinese Congress during the Popular Front period. With the advent of the DRV in 1945, Le Dinh Chi sold some of his possessions in order to buy weapons for troops opposing the return of the French and supported detachment 11 (*chi doi 11*) in Tay Ninh province. In early 1946, he headed up the Board of Military Justice for war **Zone VII** (*Ban Quan Phap Khu VII*). He played a role in persuading reluctant **intellectuals**, bureaucrats, and professionals in Saigon-Cholon to join or at least support clandestinely the national resistance movement led by the DRV. In early 1946, working with the lawyer **Nguyen Thanh Vinh**, Le Dinh Chi organized the secret visit to Saigon-Cholon of **Nguyen Binh**, the head of war Zone VII (*Khu VII*) and the commander-in-chief of the southern Armed Forces. In 1948–1949, Le Dinh Chinh ran the Bureau of Military Justice for the Nam Bo High Command (*Phong Quan Phap Bo Tu Lenh Nam Bo*) before becoming the director of the Military Justice Service of the Military High Command of Nam Bo (*Nha Quan Phap Thuoc Bo Tu Lenh Nam Bo*). He helped develop the DRV's justice system in the south, producing legal texts on a wide range of socio-political matters. He also oversaw the training of the DRV's first lawyers in southern Vietnam. In 1949, he perished in a French air raid.

**LÊ DUẨN (ANH BA, CHÍN, DEUX CENTS BOUGIES, 1907–1986).** The most powerful communist leader in southern Vietnam during the Indochina War. Born in Quang Tri province in central Vietnam, Le Duan grew up in a working-class family. In 1928, he joined the Vietnam Revolutionary Youth League and then the **Indochinese Communist Party** (ICP) in 1930. In 1931, he was a member of the Committee for Political Propaganda and Ideological Indoctrination within the ICP's Territorial Committee for **Tonkin** (*Xu Uy Bac Ky*). He was arrested in that same year in Haiphong and sentenced to 20 years in prison and shipped off to the French maximum security prison in **Poulo Condor**. Thanks to the liberal policies of the Popular Front government, however, he regained his freedom in 1936 and resumed his political activities for the party in the central Vietnamese provinces. He played an active role in the creation of an Indochinese Democratic Front and Congress during the Popular Front period. In 1937, he became secretary of the Party's Territorial Committee for **Annam** (*Xu Uy Trung Ky*). In 1939, he joined the ICP's Standing Committee of the Central Committee. In 1940, the French colonial police arrested him in **Saigon** and sent him back to Poulo Condor. He was very active in communist politics while serving time and forged crucial and long-lasting relationships with communist and non-communist nationalists, including **Pham Hung, Nguyen Van Linh,** and **Pham Van Dong**.

Le Duan returned to the Vietnamese mainland on **23 September 1945,** the very day war with the French broke out in southern Vietnam. But once in Vietnam, he lost no time asserting his authority over party and security affairs in the south. With **Tran Van Giau** recalled to the north, in October 1945 a plenum of the Executive Committee of the ICP's Territorial Committee for **Cochinchina** (*Xu Uy Nam Ky*) named him its new leader. From that point until the end of the war in 1954, Le Duan was the highest-ranking communist leader in southern Vietnam. In 1946, he traveled to **Hanoi** where he met with **Ho Chi Minh** and other senior ICP members about the policies to adopt in Vietnam in general and in the south in particular. In late 1946, the Central Committee sent him back to the south to reassert the party's control and rebuild its bases, membership, and activities. He arrived in the south in early 1947.

Shortly thereafter, Le Duan became secretary of the party's Territorial Committee for Nam Bo (*Xu Uy Nam Bo*) as well as the head of the Bureau of Nam Bo Militia (*Phong Dan Quan Nam Bo*). His deputy in the Territorial Committee was another powerful communist, **Le Duc Tho**. In 1951, the Territorial Committee of Nam Bo transformed into an even more powerful ICP organization in charge of both southern Vietnam and Cambodia – the Bureau of the [ICP's] **Central Office for the Southern Region** (*Trung Uong Cuc Mien Nam*, better known by its American acronym, COSVN). Le Duan served as its secretary; his deputy was Le Duc Tho. During the ICP's Second Party Congress of early 1951, Le Duan was elected to the Party's Executive Committee for the Central Committee and the Politburo (he remained in the south). In 1951, with the disappearance of **Nguyen Binh**, Le Duan's team transformed the politico-military organization of Nam Bo into two new regions, the **Eastern** and **Western Inter-zonal Sections** (*Phan Lien Khu Mien Dong* and *Phan Lien Khu Mien Tay)* in a clear move to consolidate the ICP's control over military matters. Le Duan was secretary of the eastern party section, while Le Duc Tho took over the western section.

In late 1952, Le Duan returned to the north where he worked closely with the party leadership in Thai Nguyen province until early 1954. One conclusion he reached was the need to create main force military units in the south capable of keeping pace with expanding military developments and military strength in the north. He also called for a strengthening of the ICP's network and control over the **Democratic Republic of Vietnam**'s administration in southern Vietnam. In June 1953, he made a brief trip to Beijing to recover from illness, during which time he met Liu Shaoqi. Le Duan returned to Vietnam in September. In early 1954, he left for the south with the rank of Politburo member and as secretary of the ICP's Territorial Committee for Nam Bo. He stopped over in Quang Ngai province to organize political training of mid-and upper-level communist cadres for lower-central and southern Vietnam. He finally returned to the south in early September 1954, following the signing of the **Geneva Accords** in July.

Although he was not happy with the party's decision to accept the provisional division of the country at Geneva, or to agree to elections, he nonetheless accepted the difficult task of persuading southern cadres and fighters to lay down their arms and relocate to northern Vietnam. Le Duan, however, remained in the south to set up an ultra-secret communist network in former **Zone IX** (*Khu IX*). He simultaneously worked undercover in Saigon in 1955 and 1956, with his friend from Poulo Condor, now secretary of the Party's City Committee for Saigon-Cholon, **Nguyen Van Linh**. The Bureau of the Central Committee for the Southern Region reverted to the Territorial Committee of Nam Bo whose headquarters was secretly located in Saigon itself. **Ngo Dinh Diem**'s intelligence services were aware that Le Duan had stayed behind, and worked vigorously to prevent the communists from creating sleeper cells and infiltrating the emerging **Republic of Vietnam**. Le Duan returned to the north in 1957 via Hong Kong and Guangzhou (Canton), thanks to **overseas Chinese** working in the government's **Bureau for Overseas Chinese Affairs in Nam Bo**. He went on to become general secretary of the communist party shortly thereafter.

**LÊ ĐỨC ANH (1920–).** Senior Vietnamese military and communist cadre during the Indochina War. Born in central Vietnam, he became politically active during the Popular Front period and joined the **Indochinese Communist Party** (ICP) in 1938. He participated in the **Vanguard Youth League** (*Thanh Nien Tien Phong*) that helped nationalists take power in southern Vietnam in August 1945. He joined the army in that same month and became a member of the ICP Standing Committee for the Provincial Committee in Thu Dau Mot. Between August 1945 and April 1947, he was a platoon leader before becoming a battalion political commissar. Between May 1947 and August 1948, he served as political commissar in Detachment 1 (*chi doi 1*) before carrying out the same task in the 301st Regiment. Between October 1948 and 1950, he was on the General Staff of the Military Command of **Inter-Zone VII** (*Lien Khu VII*) and then **Inter-Zone VIII** (*Lien Khu VIII*). Between 1951 and 1954, following the disappearance of **Nguyen Binh**, he became deputy chief of staff then chief of staff for the High Command of Nam Bo. He worked closely with **Le Duan, Pham Hung, Nguyen Van Linh,** and **Le Duc Tho** during the entire war and well after.

**LÊ ĐỨC THỌ (PHAN ĐÌNH KHAI, SÁU BÚA, ANH SÁU, 1911–1990).** One of the most powerful leaders in the Vietnamese communist movement, both in the Politburo and in southern Vietnam during the Indochina War. Born into a mandarin family in Nam Dinh, Le Duc Tho became politically active in the 1920s. He took part in the general student strikes triggered by Phan Chu Trinh's death in 1926; joined in 1928 the student association of Nam Dinh, run by the Vietnam Revolutionary Youth League; and became a member of the **Indochinese Communist Party** (ICP) in 1930. The French colonial police arrested him in November 1930 and imprisoned him in **Poulo Condor** where he became an important communist leader. Thanks to the more liberal-minded Popular Front, in 1936 he walked free and returned to his political activities as a journalist and party organizer in northern Vietnam, mainly in his home province of Nam Dinh. In 1939, the French arrested him again and incarcerated him in prisons in **Hanoi**, Hoa Binh and **Son La** under the direction of **Jean Cousseau**, then interim *résident* for this northern province. Little is known about Le Duc Tho's activities in prison during this time, although he must have rubbed shoulders with other communists who would go on to hold high positions in the **Democratic Republic of Vietnam** (DRV) – **Le Gian** and **Tran Quoc Hoan** among others.

Upon his release in September 1944, the ICP assigned him important tasks in the Hanoi area as preparations accelerated to launch an insurrection in conjunction with an expected Allied invasion. Le Duc Tho was one of the leaders in charge of running the party's **Secure Zone** (*An Toan Khu*) set up near the northern capital. He was also in charge of important organizational work and the training of reliable communist cadres. In October 1944, his influence was such that he became a member of the ICP's Central Committee and was directly responsible for running the powerful party Territorial Committee for **Tonkin** (*Xu Uy Bac Ky*). He worked closely during this period with the provisional general secretary of the party, **Truong Chinh**. In August 1945, during the Tan Trao Conference, Le Duc Tho joined the ICP's Standing Committee and became responsible for the internal organizational operations of the party, a powerful position that he would retain throughout both Indochina wars.

In 1948, the Central Committee decided to send him to southern Vietnam as its special delegate to strengthen contacts, transmit directives, and help revamp and expand the party's organization in the south. He arrived in 1949, with a letter from Truong Chinh designating him to run the party's affairs in the south. For unclear reasons, he ended up deferring to **Le Duan**, to which the ICP leadership agreed. Despite clashing at the outset, the two men developed a close working relationship that would last well into the 1980s. In 1949, Le Duc Tho became the deputy secretary of the party's Territorial Committee for Nam Bo. In early 1951, during the Second Party Congress, he joined the Executive Committee of the ICP's Central Committee and seconded Le Duan on the ICP's newly created **Central Office for the Southern Region** (*Trung Uong Cuc Mien Nam*, better known by its American acronym, COSVN). Le Duc Tho also headed its "Organizational Board" (*Ban To Chuc*).

In 1954, following the division of Vietnam during the **Geneva Conference**, Le Duc Tho repatriated to northern Vietnam and joined the Politburo in 1955. In late 1956, in keeping with his earlier organizational work for the party, he became head of the Organization Board of the party's Central Committee. Together, Le Duc Tho and Le Duan were the two single most powerful party leaders in southern Vietnam during the Indochina War and eventually in the entire **Vietnamese Worker's Party** during the Vietnam War.

**LÊ DUY NGHĨA**. *See* TRẦN NGỌC DANH.

**LÊ GIẢN (TÔ GĨ).** One of the founders of the **Democratic Republic of Vietnam**'s (DRV) **Public Security Services**. He became politically active in the 1920s and joined in the general student strikes triggered by the death of Phan Chu Trinh in 1926. He joined the **Indochinese Communist Party** (ICP) in the 1930s. In April 1940, the French arrested and incarcerated him at **Son La**, then administered by the interim *Résident* **Jean Cousseau**. Le Gian was then deported to Madagascar in June 1941 where he served time with **Tran Hieu**, **Hoang Huu Nam**, and **Hoang Dinh Giong. Cao Dai** leader **Pham Cong Tac** later joined them. With the Allied occupation of Madagascar in 1943, the British recruited Le Gian and the other communist nationalists to work in Allied propaganda and intelligence operations against the Japanese in Indochina. Le Gian's knowledge of English, anti-fascist credentials and willingness to fight the Japanese trumped his communist affiliation. The British transferred him to **India** and trained him in **guerrilla** warfare, radio operations, and espionage. Despite initial hesitations, Le Gian agreed to work in the Allied intelligence operations, providing information on the Japanese and helping to free downed Allied pilots. In August 1944, the British or Americans parachuted him into northern Vietnam, where he immediately went to work providing intelligence on the Japanese to the Allies, all the while entering into contact with the ICP whose leaders were eager to assist the Allied war effort while preparing to launch an uprising in conjunction with an Allied invasion of Indochina. In February 1946, the DRV created the Public Security Department (*Viet Nam Cong An Vu*) with Le Gian serving as its general director. He held this post under one title or another until **Tran Quoc Hoan** replaced him in 1953. Le Gian played a particularly important role in helping to eliminate non-communist nationalist parties in northern Vietnam in 1946. *See also* CIVIL WAR; H122 AFFAIR; VIETNAMESE NATIONALIST PARTY.

**LÊ HIẾN MAI.** *See* DƯƠNG QUỐC CHÍNH.

**LÊ HỒNG.** *See* HOÀNG MINH CHÍNH.

**LÊ HỮU TỪ (1897–1967)**. One of the most influential Catholic nationalist priests during the Indochina War, opposed both to Vietnamese communism and French colonialism. Born in Quang Tri province in 1897, he was ordained a priest of the Order of Cistercians in December 1928. He became vicar apostolic of Phat Diem in June 1945 and was ordained archbishop on 1 November 1945. As Charles Keith has noted, this "was the first ordination in independent Vietnam and the first ordination of a Vietnamese bishop to take place without a single European bishop or missionary present. The event marked the degree to which Vietnamese bishops had become a locus of growing cultural nationalism in the Vietnamese Catholic community". Hostile to the return of French colonialism to Vietnam, Le Huu Tu accepted **Ho Chi Minh**'s invitation to serve as a supreme advisor to the government, like **Bao Dai**.

Following the outbreak of full-scale war on **19 December 1946**, Le Huu Tu did his best to keep his large Catholic diocese out of the line of fire. The two dioceses of Bui Chu and Phat Diem constituted a sort of autonomous Catholic zone in upper central Vietnam. Until the **Cold War** intensified the war, Le Huu Tu was largely successful in keeping the French colonialists and the Vietnamese communists at bay. He was also perhaps the only priest at the time in Vietnam to head his own private "army", a Catholic militia numbering some 6,000 individuals as of 1951. However, as the **Democratic Republic of Vietnam** (DRV) moved to control this strategically important area in the early 1950s, the French responded in kind, drawing Le Huu Tu and his followers inexorably into the conflagration. Despite the DRV propaganda attacks against him, Le Huu Tu remained ardently anti-colonialist and continued to repel French efforts to bring him and his disciples over to their side. His hostility towards the French was such that General **Jean de Lattre de Tassigny** met privately with the Pope in Rome in 1951 in an attempt to rein in this independent-minded priest.

Caught in the middle, Le Huu Tu eventually agreed to work with the emerging Vietnamese state led by the former emperor, Bao Dai. In April 1951, the bishops of Bui Chu and Phat Diem joined the Associated State of Vietnam. However, Le Huu Tu's hostility to French colonialism remained. In 1953, he advised Bao Dai to take refuge in the United States rather than cooperate with the French. Le Huu Tu met personally with the American consulate general in **Hanoi** and tried to negotiate directly with them rather than going through the French. He commanded a loyal following among Vietnamese Catholics and his nationalism even earned him the respect of Ho Chi Minh and the communists. One of the **Indochinese Communist Party's** top officials, **Tran Dang Ninh**, met with this independent-minded priest in a bid to keep him on the DRV's side. To no avail. Following the division of Vietnam into two states in mid-1954, Le Huu Tu moved to southern Vietnam where he died in April 1967. *See also* CATHOLICS, EXODUS FROM NORTH; CATHOLICS IN VIETNAM AND THE WAR; CHRISTIANS AND OPPOSITION TO THE INDOCHINA WAR; VATICAN.

**LÊ HY.** *See* LÃ VĨNH LỢI.

**LÊ LIÊM (TRỊNH ĐÌNH HUẤN, 1922–1985).** Senior Vietnamese military leader during the Indochina War. Born in Ha Dong province in the north, between 1936 and 1938 he studied at the famous private high school *Thang Long*, where he rubbed shoulders with **Vo Nguyen Giap** and other future nationalist leaders. He became active in nationalist politics during the Popular Front period and joined the **Indochinese Communist Party** (ICP) during this time. In 1940, the French arrested and incarcerated him in the **Son La** colonial prison. Released in 1943, he resumed his political activities in areas around **Hanoi** where he served as a member of the Standing Committee of the party's Territorial Committee for **Tonkin** (*Xu Uy Bac Ky*). With the advent of the **Democratic Republic of Vietnam** in 1945, he served as the ICP's secretary for war **Zone** III (*Khu Chien III*) near Hanoi as well as the president of the Resistance and Administrative Committee for the same zone. Following the outbreak of full-scale war on **19 December 1946**, he led the Bureau of the People's Militia (*Cuc Dan Quan*). He served in the political section of the General Political Bureau (*Tong Cuc Chinh Tri*) and eventually became the deputy director of this powerful military organization. He participated in the army's major military operations in the north between 1950 and 1954. During the battle of **Dien Bien Phu**, he was in charge of all political questions at the front.

**LE PULOCH, LOUIS (1904–1976).** Served in the colonial army in Indochina during the interwar period (1925–1929, 1935–39), commanding troops mainly in the regiment of the *Tirailleurs tonkinois*. The Germans took him prisoner during the Battle of France in mid-1940. Upon his release in 1941, he transferred to French Vichy Africa and then crossed over to Free French forces following the Allied Landing in North Africa in November 1942. He took part in the liberation of France and Germany. After World War II, now a colonel, Le Puloch headed up the colonial section in the general staff of the National Defense ministry and returned to Indochina in August 1946 to serve as the head of cabinet to High Commissioner **Georges Thierry d'Argenlieu**. In December, interim high commissioner for Indochina, General **Jean Val-**

**luy**, dispatched Le Puloch to Paris in an attempt to convince the French government that a total break with the **Democratic Republic of Vietnam** was necessary. Le Puloch stayed on in Indochina after the Thierry d'Argenlieu's removal in early 1947, although little is known about his activities until October 1949 when he left.

**LÊ QUẢNG BA (ĐÀM VĂN MÔNG, 1914–1988).** Senior Vietnamese military commander in the north during the war against the French. Born in Cao Bang province along the Chinese border, he was of ethnic Tai origin. In the 1930s, he became active in communist and nationalist politics. In 1936, he joined the **Indochinese Communist Party** and directed **guerrilla** operations in the Cao Bang region from 1941. In 1944, he joined the **Viet Minh** and the fledgling army. Between November 1945 and 1947, he served as a deputy commander of war **Zone** I (*Khu Chien 1*), then commander of the **Hanoi** zone before directing war Zone XII (*Khu Chien XII*). Between 1948 and 1949, he was deputy commander of Front 2 (the northeastern part of Vietnam) before being named commander of the Front for the Maritime Provinces in the northeast and along the Chinese border. In December 1949, he became commander-in-chief of the **Inter-Zone Viet Bac** (*Lien Khu Viet Bac*) and the first commander of the 316th Division.

**LÊ QUANG ĐẠO (NGUYỄN ĐỨC NGUYÊN, 1921–1999).** Influential Vietnamese communist leader in northern Vietnam, Haiphong, and **Hanoi** during the Indochina War. Born in Bac Ninh province in the North, he became politically active during the Popular Front period and joined the **Indochinese Communist Party** (ICP) in 1940. He rose quickly in the northern communist organization. By late 1942, he had become a member of the Party's Territorial Committee for **Tonkin** (*Xu Uy Bac Ky*). Between 1943 and 1945, he served as secretary for the party's powerful Cadres Committee for the city of Hanoi, a member of the Standing Committee of the Territorial Committee for Tonkin, an editor for the **Viet Minh**'s mouthpiece, *Cuu Quoc*, and the ICP's *Co Giai Phong*. Between August 1945 and 1946, he was a political commissar in the armed forces in Bac Giang province and then secretary of the party's Urban Committee for Haiphong. Between 1946 and 1949, he was a member of the ICP's Territorial Committee for Tonkin and secretary of the party's City Committee for Hanoi before becoming the deputy secretary of the party's Special Committee for the Hanoi Zone. In 1949, he was the deputy head of the Committee for Political Propaganda and Ideological Training for the party's Central Committee and a member of the Standing Committee of **Inter-Zone III**'s (*Lien Khu III*) party committee. He served in this post during the battle of **Cao Bang**. Between 1950 and 1954, he headed the Bureau for Political Propaganda and Ideological Training within the army's General Political Directorate (*Tong Cuc Chinh Tri*). In 1954–1955, he was a delegate to the Mixed Central Armistice Commission of Hanoi.

**LÊ QUANG HÒA (LÊ THÀNH KIM, 1914–1993).** Political commissar in the armed forces of the **Democratic Republic of Vietnam** (DRV) in northern Vietnam during the Indochina War. Born in Hai Hung province in northern Vietnam, he joined the **Indochinese Communist Party** in 1939 before the French arrested and sentenced him to five years in prison that same year. In March 1945, thanks to the Japanese *coup de force*, he regained his freedom and began building up party bases in Son Tay province and helped the **Viet Minh** take power there in mid-1945. He entered the DRV army in 1945. Between November 1945 and 1949, he worked as a political commissar in **Inter-Zone III** (*Lien Khu III*), serving there as a secretary of the party's Military Committee at the inter-zonal level. He was also a member of the Standing Committee of the zone's regional party committee. Between 1950 and 1955, he was the deputy then the head of the army's General Staff Bureau for Politico-Military Training. *See also* CENTRAL PARTY MILITARY COMMITTEE.

**LÊ QUANG HUY (1909–?).** Well-known nationalist politician in the Associated State of Vietnam. Born in Sa Dec province in southern Vietnam, Le Quang Huy was educated in France, graduating in the early 1930s as an engineer from the *École centrale des arts et manufactures* in Paris. In April 1930, he presented a petition to the minister of the Colonies and the president of the Republic protesting the French condemnations of the Vietnamese perpetrators of the Yen Bay uprising earlier that year. Back in Indochina, he joined the public works division as a contractual inspector for the colonial railways. Between 1938 and early 1946, he was chief of material and tractions in the 1st District of the Indochinese Railroad in

**Tonkin** and Northern **Annam**. With the outbreak of war on **19 December 1946**, he left Vietnam in February 1946 to reside in France. Between 1946 and 1950, he worked as chief of the Office for the Planning of Materials at the Central Railway Office for Overseas France in Paris. He returned to **Saigon** in February 1950 to work for the newly created Associated State of Vietnam. In early 1950, he became the minister of Public Works and Reconstruction in the **Nguyen Phan Long** government. He also served as a member of the Vietnamese delegation to the **Pau Conference** in June of that same year. He became minister of Public Works, Transportations, and Telecommunications in the second cabinet of **Tran Van Huu**, constituted on 18 February 1951. Le Quang Huy maintained this post in the government of Prince **Buu Loc**, constituted on 11 January 1954.

**LÊ QUANG VINH (BA CỤT, c. 1920–1955).** A supporter of the **Hoa Hao** Buddhist faith during the Indochina war. This former buffalo keeper from Long Xuyen in southern Vietnam switched from one side to another during the conflict. In 1945–1946, he collaborated militarily with the nationalist forces of the **Democratic Republic of Vietnam** (DRV) against the French before joining the Hoa Hao when relations with the **Viet Minh** soured during the first half of 1947. In June of that year, he crossed over to the French side for the first of four times, his final "act of submission" occurring in November 1953. The French saw in him and his men a force to be used against the DRV in the southwestern part of the country. But Ba Cut did not just have enemies among the Viet Minh. In 1956, forces loyal to **Ngo Dinh Diem** had him executed. *See also* CIVIL WAR; COLLABORATION; DESERTION; VIETNAMESE NATIONALIST PARTY.

**LÊ QUỐC LỘC (1916–1987).** Painter in the **Democratic Republic of Vietnam**'s Propaganda Office during wars against the French and the Americans. Educated in colonial Indochina in the arts, he put his artistic talents in the service of the nationalist cause after 1945. He worked in the Painting Section of the Bureau of Propaganda in war **Zone** III (*Khu Chien III*) in the **Hanoi** area. In this capacity, he trained painters in the liberated zone and in the French-occupied ones to implement the government's propaganda needs. He designed scores of posters during the Indochina War. Two of his works, *Everything for the Front* and *Help Pay Agriculture Taxes*, won him prizes from the government in 1951 as the resistance entered the more intensive phase of the General Counter Offensive and **land reform**. *See also* CINEMA; CULTURE; INTELLECTUALS; NOVELS.

**LÊ QUỐC SẢN (1920–2000).** Vietnamese military commander in southern Vietnam during the war against the French. Born in Nam Ha province, he joined the Vietnamese army in April 1945 and the **Indochinese Communist Party** that same year. In August, he commanded the Liberation Forces of the **overseas Vietnamese** in Savannakhet. He sought refuge in Thailand following the violent French reoccupation of Laos in mid-1946. In December of that year, he became the deputy commander of the Tran Phu Detachment (*Chi Doi Tran Phu*) that delivered weapons from Thailand to southern Vietnam. From that point until his repatriation to northern Vietnam after the **Geneva Conference** of 1954, he was deputy regimental commander, regimental commander, inter-regimental commander then military head of the province of Vinh Tra for the DRV. *See also* THAKHEK.

**LÊ SỸ QUỲ.** *See* THIẾU SƠN.

**LÊ TẤN NAM (1899–?).** Strong partisan of the French and non-communist politician in the Associated State of Vietnam in the early 1950s. Born in Sa Dec province in southern Vietnam, Le Tan Nam completed his secondary education at the *Lycée Chasseloup Laubat* in **Saigon** before graduating in 1921 from the *École supérieure de droit et d'administration* in **Hanoi**. Between 1921 and 1924, he worked in the colonial civil service as an assistant in the *Résidence supérieure* in Phnom Penh. Between 1924 and 1927, he pushed paper in the colonial offices of Cholon before serving in a variety of similar posts in southern Vietnam. In August 1938, he traveled to France to take up a year-long training course in the Ministry of the Colonies, where he worked as an attaché in the Cabinet of Georges Mandel until September 1939. In that same year, he chose to be naturalized as a French citizen. In October 1939, he transferred to the Cabinet of the Governor of **Cochinchina**. During World War II, he continued his work under the Vichy regime. Following the Japanese ***coup de force* of 9 March 1945**, he was demoted by the Japanese for his pro-French sentiments. However, despite holding French citizenship, he kept his job as an administrator in My Tho province. The **Democratic Republic of Vietnam** (DRV) relieved him of all of his duties because of his pro-French attitude. Le Tan Nam subsequently kept a low profile in Saigon until the return of the French in force in October 1945. Between 14 November 1945 and 7 September 1947, with French support, he became head of the province of Tan An in southern Vietnam. His collaboration with the French earned him the wrath of nationalists. On 15 April 1946, the DRV's courts condemned him to death *in absentia*. **Nguyen Binh** personally ordered his execution for **collaboration** with the enemy. Following the French failure to create an **Indochinese Federation**, on 8 October 1947 Le Tan Nam became under-secretary of state for the Interior in the **Nguyen Van Xuan** government. He maintained this post until July 1949 when he became advisor to the government and an expert on the commission for the implementation of the recently signed Franco-Vietnamese Accords of March 1949 to create the Associated State of Vietnam. In February 1951, he became prefect of the Saigon-Cholon region and minister of Justice in the government of **Nguyen Van Tam**, created on 6 June 1952, a position he maintained until January 1954. This author is unaware of his subsequent activities. *See also* CIVIL WAR.

**LÊ THẮNG (LÊ VANG THẮNG, 1903–?).** Vietnamese journalist, French-trained lawyer, and non-communist nationalist politician. Born in Phuc Yen in northern Vietnam, he was a popular public speaker in his Masonic Lodge of Confucius during the interwar period and one of the directors of the Vietnamese newspaper, *L'Annam Nouveau,* founded by his friend Nguyen Van Vinh. Le Thang was affiliated with the ***Section française de l'Internationale ouvrière*** in the 1930s and a member of the French League of Human Rights (the *Ligue des Droits de l'Homme, section "tonkinoise"*). He was married to a French woman, Diane Beccari. In 1934, he was the secretary for the Office of the Chamber of Representatives for **Tonkin** and served in that post until 1940 as its delegate to the Grand Council of Financial and Economic Interests for Indochina. In May 1935, he became municipal counselor for **Hanoi**. Little is known of his activities during World War II. On coming to power in September 1945, the **Democratic Republic of Vietnam** held him in great suspicion. Following the outbreak of war on **19 December 1946**, Le Thang returned to Hanoi and joined the **Greater Vietnam Nationalist Party** (*Dai Viet Quoc Dan Dang*). On 1 October 1948, he assumed the leadership of the party following the death of Dr. **Dang Vu Lac**. Between July 1949 and January 1950, Le Thang served as under-secretary of state in the Ministry of Foreign Affairs for the **Bao Dai** government and maintained the same post in the subsequent government formed by **Nguyen Phan Long**. Le Thang supported a number of non-communist nationalist political groups in northern Vietnam and ran the Vietnamese-language paper, *Quoc Dan*, the mouthpiece of the National People's Movement (*Phong Trao Quoc Gia Dinh Dan*, founded in March 1951). He also remained an active entrepreneur. In June 1952, he joined the **Nguyen Van Tam** government as minister for Social Action and Labour, a post he maintained until January 1954. He became minister of Information in the government of Prince **Buu Loc**, constituted on 11 January 1954. *See also* FREEMASONS.

**LÊ THÀNH KIM.** *See* LÊ QUANG HOÀ.

**LÊ THANH NGHỊ (NGUYỄN KHẮC XỨNG, 1911–1989).** Senior Vietnamese communist and military official in the Red River Delta and **Hanoi** during the Indochina War. Born in Hai Duong province in northern Vietnam, he worked in the coal mines as an electrician before World War II. He became a political activist among the miners and, in 1930, joined the **Indochinese Communist Party** (ICP). In that same year, the French arrested him, sentenced him to forced labor for life, and shipped him off to **Poulo Condor**. Thanks to the liberal policies implemented by the Popular Front government, however, he recovered his freedom in 1936 and resumed his political activities among the working classes of Hanoi where he was a member of the ICP's branch for the capital. In late 1937, he returned to his native Hai Duong to organize workers there. In late 1939, he joined the ICP's Territorial Committee for **Tonkin** (*Xu Uy Bac Ky*), before being arrested by the French in early 1940, who sentenced him to a term of five years and dispatched him this time to the **Son La** prison. In early 1945, he left prison and rejoined the ICP's Territorial Committee of Tonkin, directing military affairs in the Hoang Hoa Tham Military Zone. In August 1945, he served as the Territorial Committee of Tonkin's representative to the maritime region and joined its Standing Committee in 1946. In 1948, he ran the secretariat of the ICP's Central Committee. Until 1954, he served as the secretary for the party's Committee for **Inter-Zone III** (*Lien Khu III*), president of the Resistance and Administrative Committee of Inter-Zone III, and political commissar for the same region. Between 1951 and 1986, he was a member of the Executive Committee of the Party's Central Committee. From 1952, he served as the secretary of the party's branch for Hanoi.

**LÊ THỊ XUYỀN.** Former teacher at the *Collège de jeunes filles de Dong Khanh* in Hue, she supported the nationalist cause of the **Democratic Republic of Vietnam**. Around 1946, she helped create the Women's Association for National Salvation in **collaboration** with counterparts who had taught in other girls' schools in upper Vietnam, such as Nguyen Thi Thuc Vien, Phan Thi Anh, and **Nguyen Xien**. She married **Le Van Hien**, minister of Economy and ranking member of the **Indochinese Communist Party**.

**LÊ THIẾT HÙNG (LÊ VĂN SỬU, LÊ VĂN NGHIỆM, LÊ QUỐC VỌNG, 1908–1986).** One of the major architects of the **Democratic Republic of Vietnam**'s (DRV) army. Born in Nghe An province in upper central Vietnam, he left for Thailand in 1923 before moving on to Guangzhou (Canton) in late 1924, where **Ho Chi Minh** inducted him into the Vietnam Revolutionary Youth League in 1925, told him to learn Chinese fast, and enrolled him in the Whampoa Military Academy to study modern military science. Working in these Sino-Vietnamese networks, Le Thiet Hung became a member of the Chinese Nationalist Party (*Guomindang*) and an officer in the Chinese nationalist army. He also secretly became a member of the **Indochinese Communist Party** (ICP) in 1930. During the 1930s, he served as a mole for the Vietnamese and Chinese communist parties, providing important intelligence on the final nationalist attacks **Chiang Kai-shek** launched against the Jiangxi communist soviets. In 1941, Ho Chi Minh instructed Le Thiet Hung to help create what became the Vietnamese national army. In mid-1945, Le Thiet Hung served as the first director of the Cao Bang Military Academy and helped the **Viet Minh** take power in the Cao Bang region. With the creation of the DRV, he returned to upper central Vietnam to command what became known as military **Inter-Zone IV** (*Lien Khu IV*). In late 1945, he served as chief of this zone. Following the signing of the **Accords of 6 March 1946**, the ICP recalled him to **Hanoi** to represent the government in a joint military commission with the French to oversee the withdrawal of Chinese nationalist troops by their French counterparts. This task required a Vietnamese officer with the rank of general. In 1946, Le Thiet Hung received this honor, when he was named major general (though it appears to have only been officially bestowed in 1948). Between 1947 and 1950, Le Thiet Hung was the first general inspector of the Army, commander of the Bac Kan front, and headmaster of the Politico-Military Middle-Level Refresher Academy. Between 1950 and 1954, he served as the headmaster of the Vietnamese Infantry Academy as well as chief of the Bureau for Politico Military Training. In 1950, he traveled to Yunnan province in southern China to run the army's military academy (*Truong luc quan*) in collaboration with **Tran Tu Binh**. In tandem with the Chinese, he oversaw the training and politicization of thousands of Vietnamese officers and soldiers in this academy. He was also on watch when 4,000 soldiers undergoing **rectification** in China in 1952 "admitted" under heavy questioning to working for enemy intelligence services in order to placate their accusers. *See also* INDOCTRINATION; TORTURE.

**LÊ TRỌNG NGHĨA (ĐOÀN XUÂN TÍN, LÊ NGỌC) (1922–).** Member of the **Vietnamese Democratic Party** (*Dang Dan Chu Viet Nam*) who helped the **Viet Minh** take power during the August insurrection in **Hanoi** in 1945. A trusted communist, he was a member of the **Indochinese Communist Party**'s (ICP) territorial committee for **Tonkin**. In the late 1930s or early 1940s, the French incarcerated him in Hoa Lo prison. He regained his liberty around May 1945. In that month, **Le Duc Tho** assigned him to work in the ICP's **Party Affairs Committee** inside the Vietnamese Democratic Party. In this capacity, Le Trong Nghia helped win over its intellectuals, notables, students, and government officials to the Viet Minh cause. He was a member of the Hanoi Revolutionary Military Committee before joining the Northern Region Revolutionary People's Committee, responsible for liaison with the Japanese. Little is known about his activities until 1950, when he became head of the Army's Bureau of Military Intelligence (*Cuc Quan Bao*), chief of the General Staff's Military Intelligence Department, and head of intelligence for the **Dien Bien Phu** campaign in 1954. He was clearly a very important communist party member in order to hold such an essential position at the head of military intelligence.

**LÊ TRỌNG TẤN (LÊ TRỌNG TỐ, 1914–1986).** Led the famous 312th **Division** into battle at **Dien Bien Phu** in 1954. Born in Ha Tay province in northern Vietnam, he became politically active in 1944 and joined the **Indochinese Communist Party** in 1945. He helped the **Viet Minh** take power in his native Ha Dong province in August 1945 as a military cadre. Between late 1945 and 1950, he was a deputy then a regimental commander, as well as a political commissar in the army. He led the 209th regiment and served as its deputy commander during the battle of **Cao Bang** in 1950. Between December 1950 and the end of the war, he was the first commander of the newly constituted 312th Division and commanded it to victory during the battle of Dien Bien Phu.

**LÊ TRỌNG TỐ**. *See* LÊ TRỌNG TẤN.

**LÊ VĂN CHI (1907–1993).** One of the early architects of the educational system of the **Democratic Republic of Vietnam** (DRV) in southern Vietnam. Born in Tien Giang province in southern Vietnam, he graduated from the Pedagogical Secondary School in **Saigon** in 1927 as a primary school teacher. He then moved to **Hanoi** to study in the Higher Pedagogical School. After graduation, he taught in the My Tho High School and served as a primary school inspector in Can Tho before taking up a teaching position in the Pétrus Truong Vinh Ky School in Saigon. Little else is know about him before 1945. Following the Japanese ***coup de force* of 9 March 1945**, he became a member of the **Vanguard Youth League** (*Thanh Nien Tien Phong*). Although he remained in Saigon after war broke out in southern Vietnam on **23 September 1945**, he was sympathetic to the DRV. In late 1947, upset by the French refusal to take decolonization seriously, he left the city for the resistance zones. He worked in the Educational Service for Nam Bo (*So Giao Duc Nam Bo*) in **Inter-Zone** IX (*Lien Khu IX*). He played a pivotal role in obtaining and developing teaching materials for secondary schools, for both teachers and students. From 1948, he helped create Resistance Teacher Training Schools and secondary schools in the south. Besides teaching himself, he also served as the principal of the south's major resistance secondary schools: **Nguyen Van To**, **Thai Van Lung**, and **Huynh Phan Ho**. In 1954, with the signing of the **Geneva Accords** dividing the country into two states, he returned to Saigon to live and work.

**LÊ VĂN HIẾN (1904–?).** Ranking Vietnamese communist who served as minister of Finances during the Indochina War. Born in central Vietnam, he began his career in the colonial postal service before becoming involved in radical politics in the late 1920s. In 1928, he joined the Vietnam Revolutionary Youth League and was arrested three years later on a charge of sedition. In 1933, upon his release, he opened a bookshop in Da Nang, joined the **Indochinese Communist Party** in 1935, and agitated during the Popular Front period. In 1940, he was arrested again and remained in jail until the end of World War II. Upon his release, he joined the **Democratic Republic of Vietnam** government in September 1945, serving first as minister of Labor then, from March 1946, as minister of Finances. He held this post until 1958. In 1946, he entered the Vietnamese National Assembly. During the war years, he was deeply involved in high-level decision-making on important economic, financial, and political questions for the party and the government. In 1995, he published his wartime memoirs in two volumes, *Nhat ky mot bo truong* or *Diary of a Minister.*

**LÊ VĂN HOẠCH (1896?–1978).** Non-communist Cochinchinese politician active in the late 1940s in creating a counter-revolutionary Vietnamese government allied with the French. Born in Can Tho province in southern Vietnam, he completed his secondary studies at the *Lycée Chasseloup Laubat* in **Saigon** and then graduated as a doctor in medicine from the *École de médecine* in **Hanoi**. For eight years, he worked in the *Hôpital Lalung Bonnaire*, where he specialized in opthalmology, before setting up his own private practice in Can Tho as an opthalmologist and general practitioner. He maintained a number of contacts with the Japanese during World War II and was named, after the Japanese ***coup de force* of 9 March 1945**, Police Commissioner for the Municipality of Can Tho. He resigned in July of that same year. This did not prevent him from intervening on several occasions to save the lives of French and Vietnamese threatened by the Japanese because of their relations with the French. After the Japanese defeat, Le Van Hoach kept a low profile as Vietnamese groups hostile to the restoration of French colonial rule took control of the south. However, when the French returned in late 1945, he offered his cooperation and was named delegate for the province of Can Tho within the Cochinchinese Council. He actively participated in the creation of the **Provisional Government of the Republic of Cochinchina**, officially announced by Admiral **Georges Thierry d'Argenlieu** on 1 June 1946. In July, Le Van Hoach was elected vice president of its Assembly. On 29 November 1946, he replaced Dr. Nguyen Van Thinh as president of the Cochinchinese Republic following the latter's suicide. Le Van Hoach ran the Republic until September 1947. He was also involved in the French-inspired **Bao Dai Solution**. He accompanied **Pham Cong Tac** to meet with **Bao Dai** in April 1948 and was one of the signatories of the Ha Long Bay accords in May 1948. Le Van Hoach turned to the noncommunist religious sects in order to build up support for a counter-revolutionary government led by Bao Dai, the Associated State of Vietnam. To this end, he created the *Rassemblement national du Sud Vietnam*, with the support of some **Cao Dai** and **Hoa Hao** forces. On 8 March 1952, he was named minister of Agriculture in the third government presided by **Tran Van Huu**. He was named minister of Health in the **Nguyen Van Tam** government formed on 6 June 1952. However, his failure to obtain more important ministerial posts provoked dissensions with his Cao Dai allies, as did his failure to consult with them. On 13 June 1952, Hoach lost the support of Cao Dai leader Pham Cong Tac. During a shake-up of the government, on 9 January 1953, Le Van Hoach became vice premier and minister of Information and **Psychological Warfare**. Le Van Hoach was an avid hunter, traveler, and amateur pilot.

**LÊ VĂN LẠC.** *See* TRẦN MAI.

**LÊ VĂN LƯƠNG (NGUYỄN CÔNG MIỀU, PHẠM VĂN KHƯƠNG, 1912–1995).** Powerful behind-the-scenes Vietnamese communist who rose within the party during the Indochina War. Born in Hung Yen province in northern Vietnam, in 1927 he joined the Vietnam Revolutionary Youth League. In 1930 or 1931, he became a member of the **Indochinese Communist Party** (ICP). The French arrested him in March 1931 and incarcerated him at **Poulo Condor**. He remained there until 1945. During those 14 years, he became part of the party's inner circle in Poulo Condor, together with **Le Duan**, **Pham Hung**, and several others. Those links also ensured him an important place in the party after the **Democratic Republic of Vietnam** came to life in September 1945. On returning to southern Vietnam around this time, he became an alternate member on the Party's Territorial Committee for Nam Bo (*Xu Uy Nam Bo*). In January 1946, he traveled to **Hanoi** where he helped **Truong Chinh** direct the Party's review, *Su That*, and its publishing house of the same name. He did so until May 1947, when he was selected to run the ICP's Central Committee's secretariat. He also became an alternate member on the ICP's Executive Committee for the Central Committee and in 1948 he headed the Organizational Board for the Central Committee. During the Second Party Congress held in early 1951, he was elected to the Executive Committee of the Central Committee and named an alternate Politburo member. Sometime shortly thereafter, he became a full Politburo member and was responsible for internal party organizational matters, a powerful position. He was also involved in developing and applying the **land reform** program. In 1954, he became vice minister of the Interior. He was the younger brother of the famous writer, **Nguyen Cong Hoan.** In 1956, as punishment for his errors during the land reform, Le Van Luong was stripped of his ranking positions, removed from the Politburo, and downgraded from a full to alternate member in the Central Committee.

**LÊ VĂN NGHIỆM.** *See* LÊ THIẾT HÙNG.

**LÊ VĂN SỬU.** *See* LÊ THIẾT HÙNG.

**LÊ VĂN THẮNG.** *See* TRẦN VĂN KHA.

**LÊ VĂN VIỄN (BẢY VIỄN, 1904–1972).** Best known leader of the **Binh Xuyen** who defected from the armed forces of the **Democratic Republic of Vietnam** (DRV) to those of **Bao Dai** and the French. Born in Cholon, he grew up streetwise, learning to box, frequenting secret societies, and increasingly on the wrong side of the law. On 14 May 1921, he was sentenced to 20 days in prison for theft. He was 17. Between 1921 and 1940, he was sentenced at least five more times for burglary, unauthorized possession of weapons, and "bad company" (*associations de malfaiteurs*). The French shipped him off to **Poulo Condor**. He succeeded in escaping only to be arrested again in December 1939. He was apparently released from jail in the early 1940s. During World War II, he joined a band of brigands and outlaws active in the village of Binh Xuyen south of **Saigon**, whence the name.

Following the overthrow of the French and the advent of the DRV, Le Van Vien and the Binh Xuyen supported the nationalist cause against the French. He briefly served as the commander in chief of Saigon-Cholon until the French forced the Viet Minh out of Saigon on **23 September 1945**. In February 1946, the leader of the Binh Xuyen, **Ba Duong**, died in a firefight with the French and Le Van Vien was chosen to take over the movement as its supreme commander and head of its armed forces. For about two years, Le Van Vien allied the Binh Xuyen with the DRV and its army under the direction of **Nguyen Binh**. As the movement's spokesman put it at the time, "From now on the Binh Xuyen bids farewell to its adventurous past and is now ready to swear its loyalty to the government and to sacrifice itself for the country". Despite differences with Nguyen Binh and the DRV's desire to create a unified, national army, in July 1946 Le Van Vien served as his deputy in war **Zone VII** (*Khu Chien VII*). However, serious problems continued to divide the two men. And the communist core at the helm of the DRV did little to assuage Binh Xuyen worries.

The final break occurred in June 1948, when Le Van Vien and forces loyal to him decided to **cross-over** to the French-backed Vietnamese government. To formalize his new loyalty, Le Van Vien was received by General **Pierre Boyer de la Tour** and **Bao Dai**. On 10 September 1948, the French formalized his *ralliement*. Documents were signed integrating his armed forces into those of the **French Union**, in which he obtained the rank of colonel. In January 1949, Le Van Vien established his operations in the Saigon-Cholon area as the French authorities looked the other way. The latter needed his political and military support to build a counter-revolutionary alternative to the DRV. In November 1950, Bao Dai received Le Van Vien in a private audience in Dalat. The latter promised to support the Associated State of Vietnam and to collaborate militarily with the **Cao Dai** forces. In 1952, Le Van Vien obtained the right to run a variety of gambling operations in Saigon-Cholon in exchange for a tax paid to the government. He was deeply involved in the operations of the famous colonial gambling center, *Le Grand Monde*. He also successfully placed Binh Xuyen men in the Ministry of Interior and the **Public Security Services** of the Associated State of Vietnam. In order to build a national army along the lines set out by General **Jean de Lattre de Tassigny**, Bao Dai named Le Van Vien brigadier general on 7 April 1952. The truck driver and common criminal of the 1930s had come a long way. In exchange, Le Van Vien signed an agreement with the Cao Dai and **Hoa Hao** to support Bao Dai. Le Van Vien instigated the creation in May 1954 of the National Salvation Front (*Mat Tran Quoc Gia Cuu Quoc*) allying the Binh Xuyen, Cao Dai, Hoa Hao, and some **Catholic** groups. He was a member of its presidium. On 14 January 1953, he also became president of the Automobile Club of Vietnam.

After the signing of the **Geneva Accords** in 1954 provisionally dividing Vietnam into two states, Le Van Vien entered into conflict with the new Prime Minister **Ngo Dinh Diem**. When Le Van Vien refused on 15 March 1955 to respond to Diem's desire to meet, violence broke out at the end of the month between Binh Xuyen militia and State of Vietnam paratroopers. The latter won. Le Van Vien fled to France where he lived out the rest of his life. He was laid to rest in 1972 in a Parisian cemetery.

**LÊ VANG SANG.** *See* TRẦN VĂN SOÁI.

**LÊ VANG THẮNG.** *See* LÊ THẮNG.

**LÉA, OPÉRATION.** On 29 January 1947, a month after the outbreak of full scale war in Indochina, High Commissioner **Georges Thierry d'Argenlieu** issued secret orders to begin military preparations to capture the headquarters of the **Democratic Republic of Vietnam** (DRV) located in northern Vietnam. He followed this up on 17 February instructing military planners to use paratroopers and **commandos** to capture the enemy leadership by early March. The new high commissioner for Indochina **Émile Bollaert** maintained this operation, issuing directives on 19 May 1947 authorizing a commando operation to be launched against the north from September 1947 in order to harass the DRV and to cut its supply routes running to southern China. These were in effect the two main goals of what became known to the French as *opération Léa* or *Bac Kan* to the Vietnamese.

Opération Léa began on 7 October 1947, when Lieutenant Colonel **Henri Sauvagnac** landed with his paratroopers at the frontier village of Bac Kan while other commando groups parachuted into adjoining regions in a move to encircle the DRV's leaders. The French operation numbered some 1,000 men at the outset and it almost succeeded in apprehending much of the Vietnamese leadership located there. Indeed, the DRV intelligence services were caught badly off guard by the French attack and the leadership only barely escaped capture. Some did not: paratroopers killed the well-known scholar and minister **Nguyen Van To** as he tried to escape. In the next ten days, the French would bring in some 10,000 men to take control of strategic points along the frontier running to Cao Bang. Though the French had failed to capture **Ho Chi Minh**, General **Raoul Salan** was happy to have deprived the DRV of its trading routes to southern China. The DRV would not regain access to China until 1950, when they inflicted a defeat on the French at **Cao Bang**. The French also launched *Léa* to "pacify" **Tonkin**. The operation ended in early November 1947.

**Pacification**, however, proved illusory as the DRV's troops melted into the jungle, before reactivating a **guerrilla** war that would keep them alive until the arrival of Chinese military **aid** changed the nature of the war. The French high command, led by General **Jean Valluy**, had failed to wipe out the leadership and end the war in one final operation. *See also* AID, CHINESE COMMUNIST.

**LEBRIS.** Former inspector of Public Instruction in Indochina before World War II and a general in the reserve forces in the colonial army. At ease in Vietnamese, he served as commissioner of the French Republic for Central **Annam** in 1947. He participated in **Émile Bollaert**'s negotiations with **Bao Dai** in the Bay of Ha Long in December 1947. A member of the **Democratic Republic of Vietnam** considered him to be "a [colonial] diehard, one of the most intelligent and dangerous of our adversaries", though little is known of his activities other than that he returned to France in August 1949.

**LECLERC, PHILIPPE MARIE DE HAUTECLOQUE (1902–1947).** One of France's most illustrious generals during World War II and in the early stages of the Indochina War. In 1924, Leclerc graduated from Saint-Cyr and was promoted major in the Cavalry. During the interwar period, he worked as an instructor at Saint-Cyr and served in posts in Germany and Africa. In late May 1940, during the Battle of France, he was taken prisoner along with the rest of the General Staff of the 4th Infantry Division. He escaped, took up arms, was wounded, and sent back to prison. On 17 June he escaped again and made his way to London where he joined General **Charles de Gaulle** adopting the pseudonym of "Leclerc". In August 1940, de Gaulle dispatched him to French Equatorial Africa where Leclerc helped win over the colony to the Free French cause. In November 1940, he became a colonel and the designated military commander for Chad. He commanded troops in major campaigns at the head of the 2nd Armored Division. He landed at Normandy in August 1944 and led the liberation of Paris.

With the war over, he took command of the French **Expeditionary Corps** on 16 August 1945 and was charged with re-establishing French sovereignty over Indochina. He traveled first to Tokyo to sign the Japanese act of surrender on **2 September 1945.** In command of the 2nd Armored Division, he landed in **Saigon** on 5 October 1945 and asserted control of the major cities, routes, and bridges in most of Indochina below the **16th parallel**. Following the **Accords of 6 March 1946** and the concomitant military convention signed in early April 1946, 15,000 French troops were authorized to land in northern Indochina above the 16th parallel to replace the withdrawing Chinese troops. Leclerc entered **Hanoi** on 18 March to a cheering French population and a wary Vietnamese one. He also met on several occasions with **Ho Chi Minh**.

While Leclerc was aware of the reality of Vietnamese nationalism and was not adverse to dialogue with the **Democratic Republic of Vietnam** (DRV), he was also committed to re-establishing French sovereignty over all of Indochina as de Gaulle had instructed him to do. If he made concessions during the 6 March Accords, it was largely because he was faced with combined Vietnamese and Chinese opposition to a *coup de force* against the north. Like **Georges Thierry d'Argenlieu**, in mid-1946 Leclerc scolded General **Jean Crépin** for not showing the Vietnamese government "that we are stronger" (*nous sommes les plus forts*), "the only way to obtain a reconciliatory attitude from their representatives in Paris". Leclerc left Indochina on 18 July 1946. He was named general (*général d'armée*) and general inspector of Land Forces in North Africa, having refused to replace Thierry d'Argenlieu as high commissioner for Indochina in early 1947. On 28 November 1947, Leclerc died in a plane crash in Algeria. He is buried in the *Invalides* and was posthumously named *Maréchal de France* (Field Marshal). One of his sons died in a DRV **prisoner of war** camp.

**LECUIR, HENRI.** Career colonial civil servant in Indochina. He first served during the interwar period as police commissioner in **Saigon**-Cholon. Following the Japanese ***coup de force* of 9 March 1945**, he was incarcerated and tortured by the Japanese. After his liberation by the Allies, he worked as head police chief in charge of the 2nd Quarter of Saigon. In February 1949, he became head of the Central Commissariat of Cholon. He was described as acting police chief for Saigon when on 25 March 1950 **Nguyen Tan Cuong** replaced him on behalf of the newly created Associated State of Vietnam.

**LÉGER, PAUL-ALAIN (1922–1999).** French special operations officer during the Indochina War. In April 1942, he joined the *1er Régiment de zouaves* and transferred to the third regiment of the same name. In that unit, he conducted intelligence operations for the French resistance before going to the United Kingdom where he studied at Ringway to become a paratrooper. In July 1944, he parachuted into France where he was active until his return to England in February 1945. After the war, he returned to France and volunteered to serve in Indochina. He landed in **Saigon** in February 1946 and joined the *1er bataillon S.A.S* which became the *Demi-brigade S.A.S.* He left Indochina around October 1947 and was involved in training and leading **commandos** in France and French Equatorial Africa. He returned to Indochina for a second tour of duty in April 1953 and was assigned to the ***Groupement de commandos mixtes aéroportés*** and instructed commandos at Cap St. Jacques. In Indochina, he specialized in counter-insurgency, ***Service Action***, and deception operations against the forces of the **Democratic Republic of Vietnam** in central Vietnam. During his time in Indochina, he also worked closely with the ***Service de documentation et de contre-espionage***. He led troops into action at the Cu Lao Ré base in central Vietnam until December 1954, when he returned to France to direct the *Centre d'études asiatiques et africaines*. During the **Algerian war**, he played a pivotal role in mounting the famous *Bleuïte* operation before his participation in the Officer's Putsch ended his service there and military career. *See also* H122 AFFAIR.

**LÉGION ÉTRANGÈRE**. *See* FOREIGN LEGION.

**LEJAY-CLER.** *See* GUILLAUME CHASSIN.

**LEROY, JEAN (1915–?).** Born in the southern Vietnamese province of Ben Tre of a Vietnamese mother and a French father, Leroy was one of the best known ***métis*** in the French army. While the details of his early life are hard to come by, he was in the *Garde indochinoise* between 1942 and 1944. In 1947 he worked as an administrative delegate in Ben Tre province. A Catholic, in 1947 he began organizing and arming southern Catholic villages with French approval against the influence of the **Democratic Republic of Vietnam** (DRV). As the war intensified, he drew upon Catholic communities to create "self-defense units" and "voluntary brigades" which he transformed into the ***Unités mobiles de défense des Chrétiens*** (UMDC) or Mobile Defensive Units for Christian Outposts consisting of some 1,000 troops. He created 94 first aid posts in territory under his control. With the support of the French, in August 1950 the UMDC numbered between 3,000 and 4,000 mainly Catholic militia men and women who ensured the security of the Ben Tre area. The French promoted him to lieutenant colonel in recognition of his work. With the creation of the Associated State of Vietnam, Leroy joined the emerging non-communist, French-backed national army. Although he supported **Bao Dai** on anti-communist grounds, he refused to integrate his militia troops into the new army. His refusal led President **Tran Van Huu** in 1952 to ask General **Raoul Salan** to remove Leroy. Salan refused.

British novelist **Graham Greene**, who wrote the preface for Leroy's memoirs, was fascinated by this Franco-Vietnamese commando officer who was also an avid reader of Proudhon, Montesquieu, and Pascal. But the reality was perhaps less glorious. There were relatively few Catholics in Ben Tre province at the time. And the Vietnamese Catholic leadership in Vietnam refused to allow Leroy to refer to his troops as "Catholics", while others saw in Leroy's actions a strategy designed to turn Ben Tre province into his personal fiefdom – free of the control of the DRV and the Associated State of Vietnam. Others questioned his methods. French war correspondent **Lucien**

**Bodard** painted a much darker picture of Leroy than his admirers. Following the Indochina War, Leroy's opposition to **Ngo Dinh Diem** led him to join the French army rather than submit to the national pretensions of the **Republic of Vietnam.**

***LES VIET.*** Disparaging term used within the French army during the Indochina War to refer to the Vietnamese soldiers and by the end of the conflict the civilians associated with the **Democratic Republic of Vietnam**. While "*Viet*" refers to the Vietnamese word referring to the majority Viet ethnic group living in today's Vietnam, it appears to have begun in French as a derivative of the term **Viet Minh.** By the end of the conflit, *les Viet* could refer in French, especially in Indochina, to the Vietnamese in general, regardless of political affiliation or location. The word is still used by some in French today to refer to the Viet Minh, although not always with a pejorative intention in mind. *See also* CIVIL WAR; COLLABORATION; *FRANÇAIS D'INDOCHINE*; LANGUAGE OF WAR; *VIET CONG*; VIET GIAN; *VIET QUOC*.

**LESSEPS (DE), LOUIS (1914–1971).** French intelligence officer during the Indochina War. Lesseps was a trained lawyer and a member of the French resistance during World War II. In September 1944, he was assigned to work in intelligence in the French Military Mission under the command of **Jean Sainteny** in Kunming. Lesseps thereafter served in intelligence-gathering for the rest of the conflict in **Saigon**, then in Laos. He participated in the audacious rescue mission mounted by General **Jean Boucher de Crèvecoeur** to pick up soldiers fleeing the besieged French camp at **Dien Bien Phu** before moving on to Algeria. He wrote several novels about his life as a soldier in Indochina and Algeria (e.g. *Soldats de la pluie*, 1966).

**LETOURNEAU, JEAN (1907–1986).** Pivotal figure in the French 4th Republic and in its colonial policy in Indochina. In the late 1930s, Letourneau became a member and then director of the *Parti démocrate populaire*, the ancestor of the ***Mouvement républicain populaire*** (MRP). During World War II, he joined the French resistance and worked closely with **Georges Bidault**. In 1944, Letourneau became director of the press in the provisional Republic's Ministry of Information and joined the Directing Committee of the MRP. He became deputy of the 1st National Assembly of the 4th Republic for the department of Sarthe, where he served until 1956. He was the minister of Posts and Telegraphs until December 1946 and in 1947 he became minister of Commerce, then minister for Reconstruction and Urbanism. Between 1949 and 1953, he served as the minister of Overseas France and state minister in charge of relations with the **Associated States of Indochina**.

Upon the death of General **Jean de Lattre de Tassigny** in January 1952, he was named high commissioner for Indochina and moved to **Saigon**. Letourneau was opposed to real negotiations with the **Democratic Republic of Vietnam** and was determined to make the Associated States of Indochina work in order to maintain French influence in the Far East and contain communism. In May 1953, Letourneau withdrew from the Indochinese scene to concentrate upon Africa. He served as an advisor to the **French Union** between 1956 and 1958. He was a member of the *Académie des Sciences d'Outre-mer* and president of the association *Amitié France-Vietnam*. Despite his earlier opposition to negotiating with the enemy, he praised the results obtained by **Pierre Mendès France** in the **Geneva Accords**.

**LEUAM INSĪXIANGMAI (1917–).** Ranking non-communist politician in Laos and brother-in-law to Prince **Bunum**. Born in Savannakhet province, Leuam completed his primary education in Vientiane and his secondary studies at the *Lycée Sisowath* in Phnom Penh. He began his career in the Lao level of the colonial administration in 1937, serving as a district chief (*chaomuang)* until 1945. He served as secretary to the prime minister of the Kingdom of Luang Prabang between 1942 and 1944. With the return of the French, he became governor (*chaokhouang*) of Savannakhet in late 1945 and a member of the Constituent Assembly created in 1947. He was hostile to the **Lao Issara** and openly supportive of the French cause, volunteering to join the French army in June 1947. Between December 1947 and February 1949, he served as minister of Finances in the **Suvannarāt** government. Between March 1949 and February 1950, he was minister of the Interior and of Justice in the Bunum government. In 1950, he was elected deputy of Savannakhet for the Independent Party and was named minister of the National Economy. He became minister of Health in 1953 in the Associated State of Laos.

**LEUBA, JEANNE (1882–1979).** French writer in Indochina imprisoned by the Japanese after the ***coup de force* of 9 March 1945**. Upon liberation, she worked in the newly constructed colonial radio service in Phnom Penh, thanks to her knowledge of music and literature. She remained there until 1950. She also wrote a number of colonial novels, including *Le **métis** ensorcelé* (1941). She was married to Henri Parmentier, head of the Archeological Service of the ***École française d'Extrême-Orient***.

**LEVAIN, MARCEL (?–1989).** Worked in **Hanoi** during World War II for the Intercolonial Intelligence Service (*Service de renseignement intercolonial*) during which time he began organizing resistance cells against the Japanese. As early as 1940, he had begun creating a resistance intelligence network in Indochina with his Chinese nationalist counterparts and established the first covert operations units in that same year. He later worked secretly with the French Military Mission in Kunming under the direction of **Jean Sainteny** and helped run its covert operations into Indochina. Levain helped organize the two secret missions of **François de Langlade** into Indochina during the War. After the Japanese ***coup de force* of 9 March 1945**, he was sent to a concentration camp in Hoa Binh, but escaped to make his way to China to continue working for Sainteny. Little is known of his activities until 1953, when he was serving as chief of the ***Deuxième Bureau*** for French Ground Forces in North Vietnam (*Forces terrestres du Nord Vietnam*). He held that post from 1 March 1953 until the end of the Indochina War.

**LÉVY, PAUL (1909–1998).** Director of the ***École française d'Extrême-Orient*** (EFEO), who opposed the French war in Indochina. Born in **Saigon**, Paul Lévy obtained his undergraduate degree from the *Institut d'ethnologie* in Paris in 1934 before becoming a member of the EFEO in 1937. He worked on archeological digs in Laos and Cambodia before studying ethnic groups in northern and central Vietnam. He contributed to the development of colonial museums throughout Indochina and was named in 1938 conservator of the ethnology and prehistory department of the *Musée Louis Finot* in **Hanoi**. He co-founded with Pierre Huard the *Institut indochinois pour l'étude de l'homme,* working together with Vietnamese scholars during the Pacific War. He also taught history, ethnology, and archeology at the Indochinese University during the war. Following the outbreak of full-scale war between the French and the Vietnamese on **19 December 1946**, the French took back control of the EFEO's headquarters in Hanoi. Between 1947 and 1950, Lévy served as director of the EFEO in Hanoi at a difficult time. In 1950, he accepted a post at the *École pratique des hautes etudes* (4th section) in Paris. No longer attached to the EFEO, Lévy felt free to express his opposition to the French war in Indochina. As a specialist of Vietnam, he took part in the February 1950 informational meeting on the Indochina War organized by Christian activists at Issy-les-Moulineaux. He ended his address to this meeting by criticizing a war that sowed only "ruin, hate, and bloodshed". He joined the *Comité d'étude et d'action pour le règlement pacifique de la guerre du Vietnam*, called on the French government for a settlement to the conflict, and would later speak out against the American war in Vietnam. *See also* CHRISTIANS AND FRENCH OPPOSITION TO THE WAR; INTELLECTUALS; PUBLIC OPINION.

**LI BISHAN.** *See* LÝ BAN.

**LI PEIWEN.** *See* LÝ BAN.

**LI YING.** *See* LÝ BAN.

***LIBERATION FLAG* (*Cờ Giải Phóng*).** In 1941, the provisional general secretary of the **Indochinese Communist Party** (ICP), **Truong Chinh**, began publishing what he called the new series of the *Liberation* newspaper on behalf of the ICP. It was considered a "new" series because the party's Territorial Committee for **Tonkin** (*Xu Uy Bac Ky*) under **Hoang Van Thu** had already been publishing an earlier version of *Liberation*. On 10 October 1942, the standing committee of the ICP's central committee began publishing *Liberation Flag* (*Co Giai Phong*), from then on referred to as the propaganda mouthpiece for the central committee of the ICP. Truong Chinh was directly responsible for its publication. Contributors included **Hoang Quoc Viet,** Hoang Van Thu, **Le Quang Dao**, and **Le Liem** among many others. Following the advent of the **Democratic Republic of Vietnam**, Truong Chinh published the paper in **Hanoi**. On 12 September 1945, the first open edition of the paper appeared. Following the **dissolution of the ICP** in November 1945, the daily *Liberation*

*Flag* became the monthly review, *Truth* (*Su That*), published for internal party distribution only.

**LIÊN KHU**. *See* INTER-ZONE.

**LIÊN VIỆT (*Hội Liên Hiệp Quốc Dân Việt Nam*).** In May 1946, as armed clashes broke out between the forces of the **Democratic Republic of Vietnam** (DRV) and the **Indochinese Communist Party** on the one hand and the anti-communist nationalist parties on the other, the DRV created a new national front called the Association of United Vietnamese People (*Hoi Lien Hiep Quoc Dan Viet Nam*) or Lien Viet for short. **Ho Chi Minh** was honorary president of this new association which regrouped all patriotic individuals who had not yet joined the **Viet Minh** front. **Huynh Thuc Khang** was elected its chairman, seconded by **Ton Duc Thang**. Given that the opposition parties (and the French) had been quite successful in portraying the Viet Minh as a communist-run entity, the DRV needed to attract non-communist groups in order to isolate the anti-communist parties and broaden its popular base and legitimacy. The Lien Viet remained a classic Leninist front organization designed to increase national support for the DRV and isolate the opposition. As **Truong Chinh** said, "all persons worthy of being called Vietnamese must become members". The main idea was for the anti-communist parties to either accept the front and submit or face **civil war** with the DRV. See also LANGUAGE OF WAR; *VIET QUOC; VIET CONG.*

**LIUZHOU CONFERENCE.** At a crucial juncture of the **Geneva Conference**, between 3 and 5 July 1954, **Ho Chi Minh** and **Zhou Enlai** met in the Chinese border town of Liuzhou to discuss and align their negotiating strategies. Much had changed during the course of the negotiations on Indochina since early May. Accompanying Ho Chi Minh were **Hoang Van Hoan** and **Vo Nguyen Giap**. Zhou Enlai had recently returned from a meeting with Pandit **Jawaharlal Nehru** in New Delhi, concerning the need to neutralize Southeast Asia in order to keep the Americans from intervening in the region in general and in Indochina in particular. Zhou Enlai argued convincingly to Ho Chi Minh that direct American intervention was possible; an accord thus had to be reached at Geneva by all possible means in order to prevent this. American intervention, Zhou Enlai stressed, would greatly complicate the DRV's battle, not to mention China's security. Ho Chi Minh agreed and both sides decided to coordinate their policies so as to reach an accord with the French. To this end, it was agreed that: the **16th parallel** could serve as the temporary dividing line for Vietnam; elections to create a coalition government for all of Vietnam would occur; a non-communist political solution was accepted for Cambodia; the Chinese and Vietnamese would negotiate strongly to acquire concentration zones for the **Pathet Lao** in Samneua and Phongsaly provinces in Laos. Significantly, the Vietnamese also agreed that the Pathet Lao would no longer be considered as a competing national government, but rather as a political entity which could eventually participate in general elections to form a coalition government and a neutral Laos.

Ho Chi Minh returned to Vietnam and argued successfully to the **Vietnamese Workers' Party** that all these concessions, including the provisional division of Vietnam pending elections, were vital to obtaining an accord with the French and preventing the Americans from intervening directly. Zhou Enlai also revealed in the Liuzhou talks that he had come to understand that "Indochina" was not a nation, but rather a colonial state which now consisted of three "national states" – Vietnam, Laos, and Cambodia. While Zhou Enlai accepted that Indochina had been one battlefield during the war against the French, he argued in favor of recognizing the national legitimacy of the Royal Governments in Laos and Cambodia. Ho Chi Minh agreed to this at Liuzhou. As Zhou reported to the Chinese government in August 1954 on the Liuzhou meeting, Ho Chi Minh "expressed the opinion that the five principles [of co-existence] were completely applicable to the consolidation and development of friendly relations among Vietnam, Laos, and Cambodia". *See also* ASSOCIATED STATES OF INDOCHINA; BAO DAI SOLUTION; INDOCHINESE FEDERATION.

**LON NOL (1913–1985).** Influential Cambodian politician and military officer during the Indochina War. He completed his primary studies at the *École Doudart de Lagrée* in Phnom Penh and his secondary studies in **Saigon** at the *Lycée Chasseloup Laubat* (1928–1934), where he also became politically active and studied with the likes of **Sirik Matak Sisowath**. He returned to Cambodia in 1934 and worked in the colonial administration in Siem Reap as a judge before transferring to become a police officer in Kompong Cham province. According to Nasir Carime-Abdoul, between 1939 and 1944 Lon Nol rose in the administrative ranks of Kompong Cham province (1939, deputy to the district chief of Kompong Siem; 1939, the same post in Prey Chhor district; 1940, deputy to the governor of Kompong Cham; 1940–1942, district chief of Kassutin; and 1942–1944, district chief of Tbaung Khmum).

Following the Japanese ***coup de force* of 9 March 1945**, he accepted a Japanese invitation to serve as governor of Kratié province and then work as chief of the Cambodian police force. This was shortlived, however. When the French returned to Cambodia in October, they overthrew the **Son Ngoc Thanh** government installed by the Japanese. Lon Nol nevertheless navigated the period deftly and became governor of Battambang province in 1947 after the Thais returned it to Franco-Cambodian control in late 1946. He joined forces with **Nhiek Tioulong** in September 1947 to create the *Parti de la Rénovation khmère*. His attempts to get elected to the National Assembly as a member of this party failed, however. In 1949, Lon Nol headed the investigation into the assassination of **Democrat Party** leader, **Ieu Koeus**. The Democrat government led by **Huy Kanthoul** briefly arrested Lon Nol, triggering the ire of **Norodom Sihanouk**. In December 1952, Sihanouk put Lon Nol in charge of fighting partisans of Son Ngoc Thanh in Battambang province and promoted him to the rank of colonel a year later. During Sihanouk's crusade for independence, Lon Nol was an important supporter and became governor and commander of Battambang province. In 1954, following the signing of the **Geneva Accords**, he presided over the mixed commission that worked with the **International Commission for Supervision and Control** to oversee the withdrawal of the **Democratic Republic of Vietnam**'s personnel from Cambodia.

**LONGEAUX, LOUIS (1908–1996).** Graduated from the *École polytechnique* and *Ponts-et-Chaussées*, Longeaux began his colonial career in Indochina in 1935 working as a mining engineer in **Tonkin**. A **Freemason**, he joined the French resistance inside Indochina, working as a deputy to the commander-in-chief of Armed Forces in Indochina Aymé Mordant. Longeaux fled to southern China with General Sabbatier after the Japanese ***coup de force* of 9 March 1945**. Longeaux then made his way to Calcutta before returning to France, where he contacted one of his resistance confidants from Indochina, now in charge of **Charles de Gaulle**'s **Cominindo**, **François de Langlade**. The latter introduced him to de Gaulle's new high commissioner for Indochina, **Georges Thierry d'Argenlieu**, who took Longeaux on as his chief of civilian cabinet. The two got on well and Longeaux entered Thierry d'Argenlieu's close circle of advisors involved in devising policy in Indochina, especially towards the **Democratic Republic of Vietnam**. Following the departure of Thierry d'Argenlieu, Longeaux remained in Indochina working as *chef des personnels des administrations*.

**LORILLOT, HENRI AUGUSTIN (1901–1985).** French officer serving in central Vietnam during the Indochina War. Graduated from Saint-Cyr in 1921, Lorillot made his career in colonial Africa during the interwar period. He served in the 1920s in the Bureau of Indigenous Affairs in Morocco and took part in the "**pacification**" of revolts there. In 1935, he entered the *École supérieure de guerre* in France and studied and worked there until 1937. Following the French capitulation in 1940, Lorillot served in the French Delegation to the German Armistice Commission before returning to French North Africa. There, he crossed over to Free French forces following the Allied invasion of North Africa in November 1942. He worked as a liaison officer to the British 1st Army and then transferred to join the French General Staff in Great Britain in 1944. On 1 August 1945, he became head of the RMLE/EO, renamed the 2nd Foreign Legion Infantry Regiment (*2ème Régiment étranger d'infanterie*) in January 1946. Promoted to colonel, he arrived in Nha Trang in February 1946 at the head of the 2nd Foreign Legion Infantry Regiment in charge of the French reoccupation of central Vietnam below the **16th parallel**. His activities were both military and political. From 1946, he held the combined functions of commissioner for the Republic to Southern **Annam** (below the 16th parallel) and military commander for the same region. In June 1947, he was promoted to brigadier general. He left Indochina in June 1948, but returned in 1949 to serve simultaneously as commissioner for the Republic in Central Vietnam and commander of French Forces in the same region. In 1951 he returned to France before shipping off to participate in the **Algerian War**.

**LOUBET, LUCIEN VINCENT.** Longtime colonial administrator in Cambodia, Loubet served between 1929 and 1938 as deputy administrator for various provinces in Cambodia, before becoming *résident* of Kompong Cham between 1938 and 1939. In 1939, he was named delegate for the French protectorate to the Cambodian government. In 1941, he served as general secretary of the Phnom Penh Courthouse and political commissioner in charge of relations with the Japanese. He ran into problems during the war, however, because of his membership of the **Freemasonry** movement and was suspected of being a Gaullist by Vichy hardliners. In 1942, he transferred to Laos as the new *résident* of Savannakhet, then as *résident* mayor of Vientiane. Between 1945 and 1947, he served as advisor to the prime minister of Cambodia. Between 1947 and 1948, he was inspector of Political Affairs for Cambodia and in 1948, director of the Office of the commissioner for the Republic to Cambodia. Between May 1948 and February 1949, he was commissioner for the Republic to Cambodia, replacing **Léon Pignon**. In February 1949, Loubet was severely injured in an airplane accident and transferred to the office in charge of personnel and financial affairs for the general commissioner for France in Indochina where he worked between 1950 and 1956. Loubet was a member of the Franco-Cambodian delegation dispatched to Washington to solve the border dispute with Thailand in 1946.

**LOVE AND WAR.** Little if anything has been written about the question of love and war during the Indochina conflict. And yet love made itself felt at various levels. Like any war, love manifested itself in scores of letters written by parents to their **children** in the **French Union**, **Democratic Republic of Vietnam** (DRV) and **Associated State of Indochina's** armies. The archives in France hold letters from mothers trying to locate their sons **missing in action**. The same could be said of lovers and husbands and wives. Following skirmishes and battles, soldiers often found love letters on the dead addressed to girlfriends and photographs of children they would never see in this world. French Union veterans or their descendents hold many such documents and no doubt Vietnamese veterans possess similar things. Some forty years after the war ended, French intelligence officer Léon Fallon returned the private documents and diary of **Hoang Xuan Binh** to his family in Vietnam. To this day, former French Union and Vietnamese families of all sides of the conflagration are still trying to find the **remains** of their loved ones lost in the conflict, submitting themselves to DNA testing and traveling to sites around the country hoping to reach some kind of closure.

Despite the propaganda to which they were subjected, soldiers often went into battle and endured not for the "empire", not for ideologies such as nationalism or communism, but because of the intimate bonds of love they had created with their fellow combatants.

However, love was not without its manipulations during the Indochina War. While control was never "total", the communist party closely controlled marriages among ranking cadres, ensuring that match-making was done in the best interest of the Party and in line with the new communist morality. Although the high-ranking couple **Nguyen Thi Ngoc Toan** and **Cao Van Khanh** clearly loved each other from their school days in Hue and did not exactly have perfect class *résumés*, their nationalist credentials and loyalty to the Party right through the heat of the battle of **Dien Bien Phu** made them an exemplary couple. No sooner had the battle ended than the party arranged their marriage on the war-torn battlefield, even though Toan would have preferred to organize a traditional marriage in their native Hue, "an important, solemn occasion" with family and friends. The Party thought otherwise and prevailed. The chief of the army's General Political Department, Tran Luong, personally officiated at this marriage ceremony held on 22 May 1954 at Dien Bien Phu. Theirs was one of several, hastily arranged, politically motivated marriages. As for the wedding gifts, Toan later recalled that "we got two medallions, one was an Uncle Ho medallion and the other was an Uncle Mao medallion ... Then Tran Luong told us to kiss, and everyone sang".

The DRV, like the French, also manipulated gender and sexuality in order to obtain intelligence on the enemy via "love brigades". And despite its claims to moral superiority, the communist leadership could also look the other way. We now know that **Le Duan**, who spent years in the south away from his first wife, had a second one in the south. He was not the only male leader to enjoy polygamy.

**LOZERAY, RODOLPHE HENRI (1898–1952).** Important member of the **French Communist Party** who supported the independence cause of the **Democratic Republic of Vietnam** (DRV). Following the liberation of France in 1945, he became a member of the constituent Assemblies of 1945–46 and deputy to the National Assembly between 1946 and 1951. As a specialist on colonial questions, he served as a vice-president of the National Assembly's Commission for Overseas Territories between 1945 and 1950, and as an advisor to the **French Union**. He was also a member of the French delegation to the **Fontainebleau Conference**. While Lozeray sympathized with the need to find a negotiated settlement with the DRV, he preferred not to push the Vietnamese case too hard for fear of hurting the communist party's national appeal as elections approached in France. In March 1947, however, with war now raging in Indochina, he delivered a speech to the National Assembly calling upon the government to negotiate with **Ho Chi Minh.**

**LU HAN (c. 1894–1974).** Born in Yunnan province in southern China, Lu Han graduated from the Military Academy of the same province (like Vietnamese General **Vuong Thua Vu**) and from 1932 served as chief of the Military Council Bureau of the Nanjing-based **Republic of China**. Lu Han commanded the First Group Army in the Ninth War Area in the early 1940s and was in charge of relations with the **Vietnamese Nationalist Party** (*Viet Nam Quoc Dan Dang* or VNQDD) active in Yunnan province. In August 1945, with the defeat of the Japanese, **Chiang Kai-shek** appointed him leader of the Allied Occupation Force for Indochina. Lu Han accepted the Japanese surrender in **Hanoi**; however, he refused to fly the French flag during the Japanese capitulation ceremony for lack of orders. Chiang Kai-shek later appointed him governor of Yunnan province, replacing Lung Yun, who had been deposed by Chiang Kai-shek while Lu Han and his Yunnanese troops were in Indochina.

**LUANG KOVIT APHAIWONG.** *See* KHUANG APHAIWONG.

**LUO GUIBO (1907–1995).** Served as the top-ranking communist Chinese advisor directing and coordinating the military and political parts of China's assistance to the **Democratic Republic of Vietnam** (DRV) during the latter half of the Indochina War. In 1924, Luo Guibo entered the Jiangxi Provincial Teacher's College in Guanzhou before returning to his native Nankang to teach in a primary school. During this time, he became involved in left-wing politics and joined the **Chinese Communist Party** (CCP) in 1926 and began work mobilizing students in the province. He rapidly rose in the provincial party ranks and, with the outbreak of the Chinese civil war a year later, he distinguished himself as a competent military leader. In 1930, he joined the Red Army as a political commissar where he remained until the Chinese communist victory in 1949. In 1949, General Zhu De, commander-in-chief of the army, assigned him to the 7th Corps in Beijing where he also became bureau chief of the CCP's Central Military Commission.

When the CCP decided to provide diplomatic, military, and economic aid to the DRV, Luo Guibo was selected to go to Vietnam to represent the CCP and to carry out a three-month tour to evaluate the DRV's needs. He arrived in Vietnam on 16 February 1950 and reported to the Central Committee of the **Indochinese Communist Party** (ICP) on 10 March. Based largely on Luo's reports from Vietnam and requests from the Vietnamese, the CCP decided in March 1950 to send a **Chinese Military Advisory Delegation** to Vietnam under the leadership of **Wei Guoqing**. This military delegation answered to Luo Guibo, who also officially headed the **Chinese Political Advisory Delegation** which arrived in Vietnam in December 1950. He was thus the highest ranking Chinese leader in DRV Vietnam, in charge of both the military and political delegations. In late 1950, he was officially referred to as China's advisor-general to the DRV. During this time, he met with the highest ranking leaders of the ICP to discuss **Chinese aid,** the military strategy against the French, the new policies the DRV/ICP would adopt in this new stage of the war, and socialist transformation. After the **Geneva Conference** ended the Indochina War in 1954, Luo Guibo served as China's first ambassador to the DRV.

**LƯU ĐOÀN HUYNH (1929–2010).** Born in Laos, the son of a non-commissioned Vietnamese officer in the *Garde indochinoise* stationed there and a half Lao, half Vietnamese mother, Luu Doan Huynh attended the *Lycée Auguste Pavie* in Vientiane. In mid-1945, following the Japanese overthrow of the French in March and the Allied victory over the Japanese a few months later, Luu Doan Huynh joined a **Viet Minh** fighting unit in Savannakhet in October, and suffered injuries during the violent French return there in April 1946.

Huynh was taken to a hospital in Thailand where he slowly recovered. Once better, he went to work in Thailand monitoring regional and international radio broadcasts and preparing reports on current events for the **Democratic Republic of Vietnam's** (DRV) delegation in Bangkok. In 1948, he helped escort a Burmese government delegation to **Inter-Zone IV** (*Lien Khu IV*), including an important arms delivery. When the DRV's mission in Bangkok closed in 1951, Huynh returned to northern Vietnam by way of Rangoon. He entered the Ministry of Foreign Affairs before being sent, in 1952, with his boss **Nguyen Duc Quy**, to work in the government's new Embassy in Moscow led by Ambassador **Nguyen Luong Bang**. Luu Doan Huynh was part of the first generation of postcolonial diplomats of modern Vietnam and a specialist in Asian and Western affairs, as the rest of his diplomatic career would make clear.

**LƯU ĐỨC PHÓ.** *See* NGUYỄN DUY TRINH.

**LƯU VĂN LANG (1880–1969).** One of a number of southern **intellectuals** in **Saigon** who supported the **Democratic Republic of Vietnam** (DRV) during the late 1940s. After having completed his secondary studies at the *Lycée Chasseloup Laubat* in Saigon, he obtained a scholarship to pursue his studies in France where he specialized in engineering at the *École centrale* in Paris. On his return to Vietnam, he was sent to Yunnan province in southern China to work on the Yunnan railway line being built by the French between Kunming and **Hanoi**. Between 1909 and 1940, he worked in the colonial civil service in Saigon as a civil engineer. He was also active in intellectual, social, and patriotic politics. He was one of the founders of the *Hoi Khai Tri Tien Duc* in Hanoi and the *Hoi Samipic* in Saigon. He was actively involved in finding scholarships to help poor students obtain an education. Little is known about his activities during World War II. In September 1945, when the French moved to retake southern Vietnam, Luu Van Lang refused to collaborate with them. He actively called upon the French to accept the national reality of the DRV and to negotiate with **Ho Chi Minh**. Luu Van Lang worked with a number of other non-communist intellectuals to prepare and submit to the French authorities a declaration calling on the French to negotiate with the Vietnamese government. They presented the document and their demands in person to High Commissioner **Émile Bollaert,** but in vain. In 1949, Luu Van Lang signed a second declaration opposing the **Bao Dai Solution** and called upon the French once again to negotiate with the government represented by Ho Chi Minh. *See also ATTENTISME.*

**LƯU VĂN LỢI (1913–).** Leading propagandist for the **Democratic Republic of Vietnam** (DRV) during the Indochina War. Trained in law, Luu Van Loi put his knowledge of French in the service of the new Republic. Between 1945 and December 1946, he worked in **Hanoi** on the editorial team of the government's first two French-language newspapers, *La République* and *Le Peuple*. In 1947, he joined the army and continued to work in journalism and propaganda. In 1947, he headed the army's first Bureau for the **Proselytizing of the Enemy** or *dich van* (*Truong Phong Dich Van*) and from 1949 he directed the proselytizing office of the army political bureau (*Cuc chinh tri*). He led Vietnamese propaganda efforts to promote desertions among soldiers in the French **Expeditionary Corps**, to win them over to the Vietnamese cause, and to indoctrinate and use them as propaganda weapons in the conflict. Until the end of the war in 1954, he worked closely with the **French Communist Party**'s official delegate to the Vietnamese party, **Jean Marrane** ("André"). Together they devised more effective propaganda and proselytizing methods for rallying French deserters and stimulating the anti-war movement in the army and in France. They edited the French-language paper, *Paix et repatriement*, to attract **desertions** and oversaw the release of a number of French prisoners of war "to stimulate the anti-war movement in France". Luu Van Loi also worked closely with Marouf, the delegate of the Moroccan Communist Party dispatched to Vietnam to help proselytize among **North African** troops in the **French Union** Army. In 1950 and 1951, Luu Van Loi also served as the editor-in-chief of the **People's Army Newspaper** (*Bao Quan Doi Nhan Dan*). He was a member of the DRV's delegation charged with the implementation of the **Geneva Accords** of 1954 and was a member of the team sent to negotiate with the French on the exchange of **prisoners of war**. Luu Van Loi later served on the Vietnamese team dispatched to Paris in the late 1960s to negotiate with the Americans, and has published his memoirs on these matters.

**LÝ ANH TƯ.** *See* NGUYỄN SƠN.

**LÝ BÁ PHẨM (1923–2008).** Born in southern Vietnam, Ly Ba Pham attended primary school in Can Tho between 1930 and 1940 before completing his secondary schooling in **Saigon** in 1942. Little is known of his activities until 1949, when he joined the second class of the National Military Academy in Hue. In 1950, now an officer in the **army of the Associated State of Vietnam**, he participated in combat operations in upper Vietnam against the **Democratic Republic of Vietnam** until 1953. In that year, he also became an instructor and, for a short time, Chief of the Instruction Section of the National Military Academy. In 1955, he attended the French Command and General Staff College in Paris. He was allegedly affiliated with the **Hoa Hao** faith.

**LÝ BAN (LI BISHAN, LI PEIWEN, LI PING, LI YING, 1912–1982?).** A powerful if little known Vietnamese communist of Chinese origin. Born in Long An province in southern Vietnam, he grew up in an **overseas Chinese** family and was introduced to communist ideas via overseas Chinese revolutionary networks. In 1933, he left Vietnam secretly for China where he became active in revolutionary politics and joined the **Chinese Communist Party** (CCP). He studied in the Chinese Soviets in Ruijin province and underwent intensive ideological training there. He fled these areas when Chinese nationalists forced Chinese communists to make the famous Long March, but had to drop out because of sickness. Ly Ban fell into the hands of the Chinese nationalist forces, but regained his liberty soon thereafter for lack of incriminating evidence. He then returned to Shantou. Using the alias of Li Ying, he resumed undercover communist activities with the approval of the party. He was active in the anti-Japanese resistance and helped the CCP rebuild its clandestine networks in southern China. During World War II, he was active in the Fujian–Guangdong–Jiangxi border area. In all, Ly Ban was active in China for some ten years.

As World War II came to an end, he requested authorization from the CCP to return to Vietnam to support the cause of the newly founded **Democratic Republic of Vietnam** and duly returned to Vietnam in July 1946. The **Indochinese Communist Party** put him in charge of its **Bureau for Overseas Chinese Affairs** (*Hoa Kieu Vu*). In 1948, he led the Committee for the Mobilization of the Overseas Chinese. He also worked in the Ministry of Defense taking care of important political matters relating to Chinese aid and was involved in establishing closer relations with the CCP in the late 1940s. He was also something of an ardent Maoist advocate of radical social change and **land reform** in the early 1950s. *See also* AID, CHINESE; INDOCTRINATION; NEW HERO; RECTIFICATION.

**LY SEO NUNG (1914–1982).** Lieutenant in the French army and intermediary between the French ***Groupement de commandos mixtes aéroportés*** (GCMA) and upland ethnic non-Viet minority groups. An ethnic Nung himself, Ly Seo Nung was a non-commissioned officer in the *Bataillon de tirailleurs tonkinois* in 1939 and joined the French resistance to the Japanese after the ***coup de force* of 9 March 1945**, before following them into southern China shortly thereafter. He returned to Vietnam and helped retake areas east of Lao Cai from Chinese occupying forces and then Vietnamese nationalist forces. Opposed to the **Democratic Republic of Vietnam** (DRV), in early 1951 he volunteered to work in the French GCMA and helped develop an anti-DRV *maquis* around the Red River near **Nghia Lo**. However, the DRV's entry into this area and the **Geneva accords** of 1954 put an end to the GCMA and their aid to Ly Seo Nung and other ethnic minorities. Tracked by the DRV's forces, Ly Seo Nung barely escaped to Laos, from where the French evacuated him to New Caledonia. He obtained French nationality in 1962, became a battalion leader in the French army, and apparently died in Nouméa. See also CIVIL WAR; COLLABORATION; MINORITY ETHNIC GROUPS; TAI FEDERATION.

**LÝ THƯỜNG KIỆT, BATTLE OF.** *See* NGHIA LO, BATTLE OF.

**MĀ KHAIKHAMPHITHŪN (1904–?).** Behind-the-scenes leader of the **Pathet Lao**, closely allied with the **Democratic Republic of Vietnam** (DRV). An ethnic Phu Tai born in Savannakhet province, Mā Khaikhamphithūn joined the **Lao Issara** after World War II. In 1946, he became a member of the highly secret Lao Issara **Committee for the East**, which collaborated closely with Vietnamese communists in central Vietnam. In August 1950, he took part in the creation of the **Lao Resistance Government** and national front, the Pathet Lao. He served as a special delegate of the Pathet Lao to the DRV in **Inter-Zone V**, where he met regularly with **Pham Van Dong**. Mā Khaikhamphithūn joined the **Indochinese Communist Party** during this time and was in charge of training new Lao politico-military cadres. In 1953, he became president of the Administrative Committee of the Pathet Lao for Sam Neau province. He was a member of the Pathet Lao delegation to the **Geneva Conference**.

**MACDONALD, MALCOLM (1901–1981**). British Commissioner General for South East Asia who strongly advocated the **Bao Dai Solution**. Educated at Queen's College, Oxford, he began his political career as a Labour Member of Parliament between 1929 and 1931. He then became involved in colonial matters, serving as parliamentary under-secretary to the British Dominions Office between 1931 and 1935 before becoming secretary of state for the Dominions between 1935 and 1938 and then for the Colonies until 1940. Between 1941 and 1946, he was British commissioner for Canada and then governor general of the Malayan Union and Singapore, a post he assumed in May 1946. In 1949, as the **Cold War** spread with full force into Asia, MacDonald became the British commissioner general for Southeast Asia. During this time, he closely collaborated with the French in Indochina to protect the region from the threat of communism. He visited Indochina on several occasions and made a point of supporting the French bid to create a viable, counter-revolutionary Associated State of Vietnam, capable of taking on the **Democratic Republic of Vietnam**. He met often with **Léon Pignon** and relentlessly supported French efforts to use the former Vietnamese emperor to create a government capable of containing communism at the Indochinese pass. During meetings with General **Jean de Lattre de Tassigny** in Singapore on the defense of Southeast Asia, MacDonald stated that the "line of defense for Malaysia went through **Tonkin**". MacDonald also played an important role in the transformation of the British Empire in Asia. He served as high commissioner in **India** between 1955 and 1960 and headed the British delegation at the second **Geneva Conference** on Laos in 1961–1962. *See also* NEUTRALIZATION OF INDOCHINA.

**MAI CHÍ THỌ (NĂM XUÂN, NGUYỄN XUÂN MAI, 1922– 2007).** Senior communist leader and behind-the-scenes organizer of the **Democratic Republic of Vietnam's** security forces. He became involved in radical politics during the Popular Front period in the late 1930s, when he was a high school student at the *Lycée Khai Dinh* in central Vietnam (formerly known as the *Collège Quoc Hoc*). In the early 1940s, he was allegedly arrested and tortured by the French. He landed at **Poulo Condor** where he agitated behind bars with **Le Duan**, **Pham Hung,** and **Nguyen Van Linh**. They all returned to southern Vietnam on 23 September 1945, where Mai Chi Tho played an important role in the creation and administration of the **Public Security Services** (*Cong An*). He was the younger brother to another powerful communist leader, **Le Duc Tho**. Following the division of Vietnam during the **Geneva Conference** of 1954, Mai Chi Tho remained in southern Vietnam with Le Duan to set up secret intelligence and counter-espionage networks on the direct orders of the **Vietnamese Workers' Party**. From December 1954, Mai Chi Tho helped run the Party's southern Territorial Committee's Research Branch Responsible for Following the Enemy Situation (*Ban Nghien Cuu Dich Tinh Xu Uy*). He returned temporarily to the north in 1955. *See also* ANTOINE SAVANI; JEAN COUSSEAU; LE GIAN; MAI HUU XUAN; MAR-

CEL BAZIN; MAURICE BELLEUX; PIERRE PERRIER; *SERVICE DE DOCUMENTATION EXTÉRIEURE ET DE CONTRE-ESPIONNAGE*; *SÛRETÉ FÉDÉRALE*; TRAN HIEU.

**MAI HỮU XUÂN.** French-trained police agent who ran the Associated State of Vietnam's security services until 1954. Little is known of his education and early career. He learned the police and spying trade from one of the French colonial administration's security czars, **Marcel Bazin**. Under Bazin, Mai Huu Xuan served in the highly secret and often very efficient *Police spéciale de l'Est*, in charge of tracking and eliminating the **Democratic Republic of Vietnam**'s (DRV) underground urban-based party and military forces. When Bazin was assassinated by agents of the DRV in April 1951, Mai Huu Xuan stepped in to become the leading security person in the newly created Associated State of Vietnam. In August 1950, he assumed the direction of the southern Vietnamese security forces. Before the end of the Indochina war, he had replaced **Tran Van Don** at the head of Military Security. Following the provisional division of Vietnam during the **Geneva Conference** in 1954, **Bao Dai** tried to shift control of the police to the **Binh Xuyen** led by **Le Van Vien**. Not to be sidelined, Mai Huu Xuan created his own military security service to take on the Binh Xuyen. This earned him the support of the new Prime Minister **Ngo Dinh Diem**, at least for the time being. *See also* JEAN COUSSEAU; MAURICE BELLEUX; *SERVICE DE DOCUMENTATION EXTÉRIEURE ET DE CONTRE-ESPIONNAGE*; *SÛRETÉ FÉDÉRALE*.

**MAI LÂM.** One of the first diplomats trained by the **Democratic Republic of Vietnam**'s diplomatic services and trusted by the communist party to run sensitive missions on the outside. He left with Hoang Nguyen in 1948 to work in Southeast Asia. He started in **Burma** but was then transferred to Thailand to administer to the revamping of the **Indochinese Communist Party**'s relations with the Lao and Cambodian resistance and budding communist movements. He carried out particularly important tasks in Cambodia in the late 1940s and again following the overthrow of the *Khmer Rouge* after 1975. Mai Lam spearheaded the Vietnamese transformation of Tuol Seng prison in Phnom Penh into a museum of the *Khmer Rouge*'s atrocities. *See also* ADVISORY GROUP 100; CAMBODIAN RESISTANCE GOVERNMENT; COMMITTEE FOR EXTERNAL AFFAIRS; HOANG VAN HOAN; INDOCHINESE COMMUNIST PARTY; INDOCHINESE FEDERATION; NGUYEN KHANG; NGUYEN THANH SON; PARTY AFFAIRS COMMITTEE; LAO RESISTANCE GOVERNMENT.

**MAI THẾ CHÂU (CHÂU LƯƠNG).** Stranded in Madagascar in 1940 at the outbreak of war in France, and fluent in French and English, Mai The Chau accepted a British offer to work in the Vietnamese section of the British Information Service based in Calcutta. He was also a committed nationalist. In August 1945, with the Pacific War over, he left for New Delhi where he became the unofficial diplomatic representative for the **Democratic Republic of Vietnam** (DRV) in **India**. He contacted Indian statesmen, including **Jawaharlal Nehru**, to plead for diplomatic and military assistance for the Vietnamese fighting the return of French colonialism. He met with Indian journalists and radio broadcasters in a bid to turn Indian public opinion, already hostile to colonial domination, against the French. He represented the DRV at the Inter-Asian Relations Conference in New Delhi in 1947. In 1951, when the DRV opened its first Embassy in Beijing, he transferred there to work with **Hoang Van Hoan**.

**MAI VĂN HIẾN** (1923–2006). Artist in the Vietnamese army during the Indochina War. He became politically active in 1945 when he supported the nationalist cause of the **Democratic Republic of Vietnam** (DRV). He joined the army in 1947 and the **Indochinese Communist Party** two years later. He was a graduate of the *École française des Beaux-arts* in **Hanoi** and is considered to be one of the founding fathers of contemporary Vietnamese painting. From the outset, he put his painting in the service of the war effort and nation-making. In late 1945, he painted the first official banknote for the DRV with **Ho Chi Minh**'s portrait on it. He began working for the armed forces in 1946. Throughout the conflict, he painted and drew heroic Vietnamese fighting men and women. He was present during the battles of **Cao Bang**, Upper Laos, and **Dien Bien Phu**. In 1954, he received a national award for his painting entitled *The Meeting (Gap nhau)*.

**MAISONNEUVE, REGIS BOUVET.** French captain and head of the Bureau for Chinese Affairs in **Tonkin** in the late 1940s.

**MALLERET, LOUIS (1901–1970).** French archeologist at the head of the **Hanoi**-based ***École française d'Extrême-Orient*** (EFEO) during the latter part of the Indochina War. Malleret was a specialist in Indochinese literature, history, and archeology. He served as director of the EFEO between 1950 and 1956, playing a pivotal role in moving the school from its colonial to postcolonial context. He transferred the EFEO to France at the end of the war, but bequeathed much to research institutes of the **Democratic Republic of Vietnam** and the **Republic of Vietnam**. At the EFEO, Malleret created research centers in Laos and Cambodia and promoted major archeological digs in Angkor. He returned to France in 1957 and published several erudite studies on Indochina, including a seven volume series on the Archeology of the Mekong Delta published between 1959 and 1963. *See also* CULTURE; HISTORY; INTELLECTUALS.

**MANSFIELD, MICHAEL JOSEPH (1903–2001).** Democratic congressman who opposed direct American intervention in the Indochina War. In the 1930s, Mansfield left his work as a miner to obtain his undergraduate and master's degrees at the Montana State University, specializing in Asian affairs. In 1942, he was elected U.S. congress representative of the 1st Montana District, a post he held until 1952 and during which time he served on the Foreign Relations Committee. In 1952, he was elected to the U.S. Senate. His specialization in foreign affairs and Asia in particular led him to take an active interest in the war in Indochina. On 8 February 1954, as the battle of **Dien Bien Phu** shaped up, Mansfield asked the Senate whether it was ready to send American troops to Indochina if the French and Associated State of Vietnam forces faltered. On 16 May, in the wake of the French debacle at Dien Bien Phu, Mansfield announced his opposition to American military intervention in the war. The Americans should support Asians opposing communism, but the U.S. could not fight their battles for them. In August and September 1954, Mansfield made a fact-finding mission to Southeast Asia. Upon his return, on 15 October 1954, he declared his support for **Ngo Dinh Diem** and his government, as the sole leader capable of leading a non-communist Vietnam. Any attempt to replace him would be a mistake, Mansfield argued. The latter was an old acquaintance of Ngo Dinh Diem. *See also* AID, AMERICAN.

**MAO ZEDONG (1893–1976).** President of the **People's Republic of China** between 1949 and 1976 and the driving force in the Chinese Communist Party (CCP) until his death. Unlike **Zhou Enlai**, Mao never left China before 1949. Instead he played a pivotal role in the making of Chinese communism as it was forced out of the coastal cities of Shanghai and Guangzhou (Canton) by **civil war** and into the peasant world of the Chinese interior. Mao consolidated his power and leadership at the head of the Party during the Long March and especially at Yan'an during the Sino-Japanese war, advocating the importance of ruralizing Chinese communism and rectifying the Party and army.

The displacement of the CCP towards the north, the expansion of the Chinese civil war, and the outbreak of World War II made it harder for Chinese and Vietnamese communists to maintain their earlier **collaboration** in southern China. It is not known whether Mao Zedong ever knew **Ho Chi Minh** in Guangzhou during the First United Front period (1923–1927). Nor do we know whether Mao met Ho during the latter's return to Vietnam from the Soviet Union by way of Yan'an in the late 1930s. Contact was always difficult. The resumption of the Chinese civil war in 1946 further isolated the Chinese communists from their Vietnamese counterparts. This changed, however, in 1949 when the Chinese communists led by Mao Zedong defeated the Chinese Republicans and established a new communist state in China, sharing a long border with Indochina.

Impressed by the Chinese victory and convinced that the prospects for revolution were better in Asia than in Europe, **Joseph Stalin** ceded to Mao the task of running internationalist communist affairs in Asia, most notably with regard to Korea and Vietnam. Mao Zedong, Chinese historians Chen Jian and Qiang Zhai tell us, was a dedicated internationalist. While security was an important factor in Mao's decision to support Ho Chi Minh's struggle against the French, the Chinese helmsman also believed in the importance of supporting communist revolutions on the move. The Vietnamese version was one such case. In January 1950, Chinese communists led by Mao not only recognized the Democratic Republic of Vietnam diplomatically, but Mao personally persuaded Stalin to forget the past and support Ho Chi Minh and the Vietnamese communist movement. Stalin agreed. During the rest of the Indochina War, Mao Zedong took a personal interest in the course of the Indochina War, providing advice to his advisors working with the Vietnamese in political, economic, and above all military matters. He closely followed preparations for and operations during the battle of **Dien Bien Phu** and during the **Geneva Conference.**

**MARCHAL, LÉON (1900–1956).** Between May 1949 and March 1951, Marchal served as French plenipotentiary ambassador to Bangkok. He was involved in negotiations with the Thais leading to Bangkok's diplomatic recognition of the **Associated States of Indochina** in early 1950. He also played an important role in negotiating the return of the majority of **Lao Issara** leaders based in Thailand following the signing of accords to create an Associated State of Laos.

**MARION, ROGER FRANÇOIS MARIE MAURICE (1917–1971).** French colonial administrator who made his career in Indochina. Upon his liberation from a Japanese prisoner camp in 1945, he took part in the restoration of French control over lower Vietnam. Between 1946 and 1950, he worked in administrative posts in Cambodia. Between 1951 and 1952, he was head of the province of Haut Donnai before moving on to Laos. Between 1952 and 1956, he served as cabinet chief to the French high representative to Laos (1952–1953), as the French representative to the King of Laos (1953–54), and then as the French representative to upper and middle Laos between 1956 and 1957.

**MARNEFFE, HUBERT (1901–1970).** French specialist in tropical diseases who taught at the Faculty of Medicine at the Indochinese University. In April 1946, he became director of the Pasteur Institute in **Saigon** and then general director for all the Pasteur centers in Indochina between 1949 and 1955. During this time, he studied and published widely on typhus, leprosy, and rabies. With the end of the French colonial presence in Vietnam in 1954, Marneffe was able to negotiate an agreement with the new national governments based in **Hanoi** and Saigon by which the French were allowed to maintain 50 percent control over the Pasteur Institutes in Vietnam for 10 years in Saigon, Hanoi, Dalat, and Nha Trang.

**MARRANE, JEAN (LE CHINH, ANDRE, 1923–).** A lifetime member of the **French Communist Party** (FCP), Jean Marrane first met **Ho Chi Minh** in Moscow during the winter of 1934–1935. Marrane's mother worked in the secretariat of the Third Communist International in the Soviet capital. In December 1950, the FCP dispatched him to the **Democratic Republic of Vietnam** (DRV) as one of its two special delegates assigned to work with the Vietnamese communists. This followed upon the diplomatic recognition of the DRV by Moscow and Beijing in early 1950 and the return of Vietnamese communists to the internationalist fold with which they had lost touch at the outbreak of World War II. His dispatch also followed upon the return of the FCP's **Léo Figuères,** who confirmed that the Vietnamese communist party was now on the right internationalist track. Marrane arrived in northern Vietnam in time to take part in the second party congress, held in early 1951, giving birth to the **Vietnam Worker's Party**. He remained in northern Vietnam until January 1953. During his two years working in the DRV, he collaborated closely with **Luu Van Loi** in organizing propaganda campaigns towards the French **Expeditionary Corps** and prisoners in DRV hands. Jean Marrane is the nephew of the French communist leader, Georges Marrane (whose daughter married the Catholic nationalist intellectual, **Nguyen Manh Ha**). Jean Marrane contributed to the making of the documentary film, *Le silence des rizières*, on French soldiers serving in the DRV, insisting that French **prisoners of war** taken by the Vietnamese were never mistreated. *See also* BOUDAREL AFFAIR; CROSSOVERS; DESERTION; INDOCTRINATION; INTELLECTUALS; PRISONERS OF WAR; PUBLIC OPINION.

**MARSON, PAUL (1906–1987).** French special operations officer who served during the Indochina War. He joined Free French forces during his service in Chad in August 1940 and led colonial troops into combat in North African battles and the liberation of Europe in 1944–45 as part of General **Philippe Leclerc**'s 2nd Armored Division. In September 1945, Marson followed the 2nd Armored Division to Indochina where he took part in the French reoccupation of Indochina below the **16th parallel** between October 1945 and February 1946. Following the signing of the **Accords of 6 March 1946**, he landed in **Haiphong** as part of the limited French contingent transferred to northern Indochina to replace the withdrawing Chinese. He participated in the violent French reoccupation of **Hanoi** between December 1946 and February 1947. He then transferred to the 5th and later the

3rd Colonial Battalion of Paratroopers as a captain. He served several tours of duty in Indochina in this capacity between 1948 and 1952. Between April 1952 and June 1954, he led the *Groupement mixte d'intervention aéroportée régional* for Laos. Between 1956 and March 1960, he worked on the French military base at Séno in Laos.

**MARTIN, HENRI (1927–).** French communist activist opposed to the French Indochina War whose arrest and incarceration set off a national outcry in France in 1950. Martin grew up in a communist and Catholic family. He joined the French resistance during World War II and participated in the liberation of France within a company of the communist-oriented *Francs tireurs partisans* (FTP). He was a member of the **French Communist Party** (FCP). In 1945, he signed up with the French **Navy** on a five year contract thinking he was going to fight the Japanese in Asia. He ended up taking part in military operations against the communist-led **Democratic Republic of Vietnam** (DRV) and witnessed the violent take-over of **Haiphong** in November 1946. He requested to be repatriated and returned to France in 1947. Back in the metropolis, but still in the army, he secretly agitated against the colonial conflagration among his comrades. In July 1949, stationed at the naval dockyard in Toulon, he began distributing political tracts to new recruits urging them to oppose the conflict in Indochina. Military authorities arrested him in March 1950 because of his actions. The FCP rallied behind Martin and his cause in order to mobilize **public opinion** against the war. Militants organized propaganda campaigns, petitions, and songs. Pablo Picasso painted his portrait. In October, Martin appeared before a military court, was tried on charges of demoralizing the army, and was sentenced to five years in prison. **Vincent Auriol** had him discreetly released on 2 August 1953, as the FCP continued to rally behind him and the anti-colonial cause. The French philosopher **Jean-Paul Sartre** also threw his intellectual weight behind Martin's cause, publishing in late 1953 *L'affaire Henri Martin*. Alain Rusico, a leading French specialist of modern Vietnam favorable to the DRV and a longtime member of the FCP, has more recently kept the memory of Henri Martin alive. To this day, Vietnamese official communist historiography judges Henri Martin to be a "friend" (*ban*) of the DRV, for having "stepped up the struggle of the French people against the invading war in Vietnam". The *affaire Henri Martin* certainly caught the attention of French public opinion, until then little interested in the war in Indochina, and contributed to mobilizing public opinion against the war. *See also* ANTICOLONIALISM; JEAN MARANNE; NEW HERO; INDOCTRINATION; INTELLECTUALS; MAURICE THOREZ; MYTH OF WAR; RECTIFICATION.

**MARTINET, ANDRÉ (1905–1964).** French naval officer who served in General **Philippe Leclerc**'s General Staff during World War II and headed the French Liaison Committee with the South East Asia Command under the leadership of General **Louis Mountbatten**, charged with disarming defeated Japanese troops stationed below the **16th parallel**. In 1946–1947, Martinet became naval commander and led an Armored Regiment of Naval Fusiliers during the reoccupation of northern Indochina. In 1947 and 1948, he headed the Combined Operation Section in the General Staff of the French Navy in Indochina. In 1948 and 1949, he commanded the vessel *Paul Goffeny* and then served as chief of General Studies in the Naval General Staff. Promoted to colonel (*capitaine de vaisseau*) in 1951, he commanded River Forces in South Vietnam and Cambodia between 1952 and 1953. In 1954, he served as the naval expert for the French delegation to the **Geneva Conference,** and between 1958 and 1959 he was a military advisor and French naval delegate to the **South East Asia Treaty Organization**.

**MARTINI, FRANÇOIS JOSEPH (1895–1965).** Franco-Cambodian scholar who came to oppose the French war in Indochina. Born in Can Tho in southern Vietnam to a Corsican father and a Cambodian mother, Martini studied law and philosophy before taking up arms during World War I. In one battle on the Western Front, an artillery barrage buried him until his comrades pulled him out of the pulverized ground in a coma. He survived the war and returned to his studies. Aware of his interest in languages, Sylvain Lévi persuaded him to study Sanskrit, Thai, and Khmer and thus began the scholarly career of François Martini. He studied these languages at the ***École nationale des langues orientales vivantes*** and was heavily influenced by the famous linguist André Martinet at the *École pratique des hautes études*. Between 1941 and 1946, Martini was professor at the **Colonial Academy** (*École coloniale*) and at the *École pratique des hautes études* between 1940 and 1944. In 1945, he debarked in Indochina as an administrative liaison officer and apparently rendered important services to the ***École française d'Extrême-Orient*** (EFEO) during this time. He arrived in Cambodia with the French **Expeditionary Corps** in 1946 with the rank of colonel. He was named advisor to the Cambodian minister of the Fine Arts and Religion and, with the support of the EFEO and the commissioner for the Republic to Cambodia, became general secretary of the Buddhist Institute in Phnom Penh in 1947. He also became an associate member of the EFEO in that same year, responsible for the conservation of the monuments of Cambodia. He returned to France in 1950 to take up the position of professor which he had already acquired in 1947 at the *École nationale des langues orientales vivantes*. He was also one of the few colonially trained scholars who publicly advocated decolonization. *See also* ANTICOLONIALISM; LOUIS MALLERET; PAUL MUS.

**MARTINOFF, RAYMOND (1926–1954).** He arrived in Indochina in 1947 and served as a sergeant with the Moroccan infantry sharpshooters. A volunteer, he made three tours of duty during the conflict. In 1953, he obtained a Rolleiflex camera and a chance to cover the war for the French Press Information Service. As a photographer, he accompanied troops into battle. An artillery shell killed him as he was photographing planes evacuating wounded troops during the battle of **Dien Bien Phu**.

**MARTYR.** Vietnamese communists at the helm of the **Democratic Republic of Vietnam** defined, codified, and categorized their 'chosen' fallen soldiers of the Indochina War according to a system of martyrs (*liet si*). This patriotic elite, as Benoit de Tréglodé has shown, provided an important source of legitimacy for the party and the state it ran. In order for families to receive a posthumous certificate recognizing the entry of their deceased into the realm of the martyrs, surviving members had to demonstrate that the former soldier or resistance bureaucrat had died as the result of a direct confrontation with the enemy or as a result of bombing or imprisonment, including **torture**. In July 1956, the government defined five groups of people who could qualify for "national martrydom" as cadres and bureaucrats of the revolution: those of the **land reform** campaign; members of the people's army; those of the Viet Minh's pre-**August Revolution** guerillas; workers engaged in national defense; and youth who died in the defense of the nation. Although the law of 1956 theoretically excluded class, religion, and ethnicity as criteria for choosing martyrs, in practice the communist-minded DRV made selections based on such ideological factors. In 1962, the DRV had on file 11,290 "martyr families" (*gia dinh liet si*). Such a legal status entailed more than honor for the families. It also entitled widows, parents, and children of the deceased to state privileges and financial support. For the DRV leadership, control of the heroic dead allowed it to reinforce its legitimacy, control the meaning of the war from which its legitimacy derived, and keep **pension** costs manageable. *See also* CEMETERIES; EXPERIENCE OF WAR; MYTH OF WAR.

**MASSACRES.** *See* CAM LY, MASSACRE; EXPERIENCE OF WAR; HÉRAULT, MASSACRE; KHMER KROM; MY THUY, MASSACRE; MYTH OF WAR; THAKHEK, BATTLE OF.

**MASSU, JACQUES ÉMILE CHARLES MARIE (1908–2002).** French paratrooper and officer during the Indochina War. Graduated from the *École spéciale militaire de Saint-Cyr* in 1930, Massu served in France and in the colonial army in Africa in the 1930s. He was an avowed admirer of Marshal Louis Hubert Lyautey. He crossed over to Free French forces in Chad and in 1942 was battalion leader, commanding the *Bataillon de marche no.1*. In August 1944, he joined the famous 2nd Armored Division led by General **Philippe Leclerc** and distinguished himself during the French and German campaigns. In September 1945, handpicked by Leclerc, Massu left for Indochina at the head of the *Groupement de Marche* of the 2nd Armored Division (*groupement Massu*) and landed in Indochina on 19 October 1945. He participated in the reoccupation of Indochina below the **16th parallel**, leading *opération Moussac* the day after his arrival, and debarked with his section in **Haiphong** after the signing of the **Accords of 6 March 1946**. He became colonel in March 1946. His section retired in September 1946 and he left Indochina in November of that year (though he made a brief trip there between 25 December 1946 and 15 February 1947 for unclear reasons). Back in France, he trained intensively as a paratrooper in the *École des troupes aéroportées de Pau* and created a center for the training of paratroopers in Brittany for deployment to Indochina. It was called the *1ère Demi Brigade coloniale de* ***commandos*** *parachutistes* (1/2 B.C.C.P). He took command of this special force on 1 October 1947. In two years, he trained six battalions in paratrooper commando operations. He returned briefly to Indochina in June and July 1948 as part of a fact-finding mission related to his training program. In 1949, he transferred to Africa and was promoted to brigadier general in 1955. He commanded French paratroopers during the Suez invasion of 1956. He led the army rebellion in Algiers in 1958 against the French government, which led to the fall of the 4th Republic and the return of **Charles de Gaulle** to power in that year. He became famous during the battle of Algiers and controversial because of the army's use of **torture** during the **Algerian War.**

**MAST, CHARLES (1889–1977).** French general graduated from the ***École nationale des langues orientales vivantes*** with a specialization in Japanese civilization and language. He joined the infantry in 1907 and graduated from Saint-Cyr before World War I. He made his career in Japan during the interwar years, where he served in the Embassy as a specialist on Japanese military matters. He became brigadier general in May 1940, when he fell into German hands during the Battle of France. He was released upon the request of Vichy and dispatched to Algeria where he headed the Division of Algiers for Philippe Pétain. Mast crossed over to the Free French side following the Allied invasion of North Africa in November 1942. In 1943, General **Charles de Gaulle** named him *résident général* for France in Tunisia, a post he held until 1947 when he was promoted to the rank of general (*général d'armée*). His name was tainted, however, by the "**Generals Affair**". Mast was identified as having committed the indiscretion of allowing the **Democratic Republic of Vietnam** to obtain a copy of the sensitive report by General **Georges Revers** on the troubled situation in Indochina. Following a Parliamentary investigation, Mast "retired" on 5 October 1949 and resigned from the Army (together with General Revers).

**MATHIVET DE LA VILLE DE MIRMONT, PIERRE ANTOINE (1914–1998).** Between 1945 and 1947, he served on the **Comité interminisériel de l'Indochine** before being dispatched to Cambodia where he worked as a private advisor to King **Norodom Sihanouk** between 1947 and 1950. Between 1951 and 1954, Mathivet was the French representative to lower Laos and was an advisor to the French high commissioner to Cambodia, then to the French Embassy replacing it, between 1955 and 1958.

**MAYER, RENÉ (1895–1972).** French premier between January and May 1953. He joined Free French forces during World War II and served as minister in several governments in the 4th Republic. Mayer was a strong supporter of the **European Defense Community** (EDC). While the French government had signed the treaty to create the EDC, the National Assembly had not yet ratified it. Upon becoming premier in January 1953, Mayer continued to support the ratification of the treaty. However, he understood that in order to do so he would have to find a way to wind down the war in Indochina. This would allow him to appease deputies opposed to such heavy military and financial commitments in Asia and Europe at the same time. For Mayer, Europe took priority over Indochina. He thus began to seek a "*sortie honorable*" from the Indochina War. It was in this context that he named **Henri Navarre** commander-in-chief of the Armed Forces in Indochina, instructing him to create the necessary conditions on the battlefield to strengthen the French hand at the negotiating table. *See also* GENEVA ACCORDS.

**MCGOVERN, JAMES B., JR. (EARTHQUAKE MCGOON, ?–1954).** Captain in the United States Air Force and a Central Intelligence Agency (CIA) operative. McGovern made a name for himself during World War II as a fighter pilot serving in the 14th Air Force in China under the command of General Claire Chennault, who founded the *Flying Tigers* in southern China. Chennault also founded the civilian airline known as **Civil Air Transport** (CAT) to supply Chinese Republican forces during the civil war against their communist adversaries. An imposing figure, McGovern flew C-119s for the CAT operations in China and elsewhere in Asia before moving on in 1953 to help French forces and their allies in Indochina fighting the **Democratic Republic of Vietnam** (DRV). On 6 May 1954, while attempting to drop a howitzer to the besieged French garrison at **Dien Bien Phu**, McGovern's plane came under enemy fire and crashed 75 miles to the west in Laos. Dien Bien Phu fell to the DRV the next day. It was only in 2006 that American forensic experts positively identified his skeletal remains and returned them to his family in the United States.

**MEDICAL EVACUATIONS, FRENCH.** Of the 50,377 individuals repatriated to France until 1953 for medical reasons during the Indochina War, almost a third was due to serious wounds suffered in combat. The remaining evacuations were due to disease (tuberculosis, paludism, etc.) and "severe psychic troubles", according to official French medical records. *See also* CASUALTIES; EXPERIENCE OF WAR; EXPERIENCE OF WAR, DIEN BIEN PHU; HELICOPTERS.

**MEDICAL TREATMENT, FRENCH UNION.** 551,257 French, **North African,** African and **Foreign Legion** troops were treated for medical reasons related to the war during the Indochina War, as well as 142,866 "Indochinese". *See also* CASUALTIES; DISEASE; EXPERIENCE OF WAR; DIEN BIEN PHU, EXPERIENCE OF WAR.

**MEHTA, A. N.** Indian major attached to the Indian Agency General in Chongqing during World War II. On 26 November 1946, he was appointed first Indian vice consul for Indochina in **Saigon**. He worked closely with Dr. **Charles Aeschlimann** and John Embree and was favorable to the anticolonial cause of the **Democratic Republic of Vietnam**. He was also a trusted confidant of **Jawaharlal Nehru** and apparently related to the latter's family by marriage. *See also* DOUGLAS GRACEY; INDIA; INDIANS.

**MEI JIASHENG.** Chinese officer who arrived in Vietnam as the deputy commander of the **Chinese Military Advisor Delegation**, under the leadership of **Wei Guoqing**, and took full command of the delegation shortly thereafter. Mei Jiasheng worked directly with **Vo Nguyen Giap** and his chief of staff until 1953, **Hoang Van Thai**. He was directly involved in devising military strategy and tactics to be deployed against the French. Most importantly, he introduced Chinese **wave tactics** being used in Korea against the Americans. In January 1954, when Vo Nguyen Giap decided to delay the attack on **Dien Bien Phu,** Mei Jiasheng agreed with his Vietnamese counterpart that the attack was premature.

**MEIKLEREID, ERNEST WILLIAM (1899–?).** British diplomat and political advisor to General **Douglas Gracey** in southern Indochina after World War II. Educated at Monkton Combe School and Emmanuel College, Cambridge, he began his diplomatic career as a student interpreter in the Siam (later Thailand) Consular Service in 1923 and was named vice consul (Grade 2) in April 1925. Between 1927 and 1928, he was in charge of the **Saigon** Consulate-General and became vice consul in 1928 before being sent to Batavia (Jakarta) later that year. He then alternated between Siam and the Dutch Indies (**Indonesia**) until being made acting consul general at Saigon in May 1941. Following a brief transfer to Dakar, he was promoted to Foreign Service officer and appointed consul general at Saigon in October 1945 before leaving for good in November 1947. He also served in late 1945 and early 1946 as political advisor to General Gracey during the British occupation of southern Indochina below the **16th parallel**. He deftly advised Gracey on political matters. During his time in southern Vietnam, he also met with southern representatives of the **Democratic Republic of Vietnam** and the French concerning the question of hostages and survivors of the massacre at the *Cité* ***Hérault***. Meiklereid was highly critical of what he saw as the shocking behaviour of the local French population and soldiers towards the Vietnamese in Saigon during the days leading up to **23 September 1945**; however, he also took the Vietnamese nationalists to task for demanding too much, too fast. Gracey nominated Meiklereid for the 1946 King's Birthday Honors List, in light of his "tactful determination to steer the political ship out of what promised to be very troubled waters" in Vietnam. *See also* ARTHUR GEOFFREY TREVOR-WILSON.

**MELBY–ERSKINE MISSION.** This joint survey team arrived in **Saigon** on 15 July 1950 following the American decision to accord increased military aid to the French fighting in Indochina. The mission consisted of officials from the State and Defense Departments. John F. Melby of the State Department led the mission; Major General Graves B. Erksine of the U.S. Marine Corps was in charge of military matters. The Melby–Erskine mission was responsible for determining the long-term French needs and nature of American aid and how best to go about providing it. During its three weeks in Indochina, the team observed French military operations and installations. While Erskine in particular had little good to say about the French army, the team leaders seemed to agree that solving the war was a political problem, one which depended upon the French granting full independence as quickly as possible to the Associated State of Vietnam. Melby concluded at one point that "the political interests of France and the Associated States are not only different, they are mutually exclusive". In the end, however, what mattered most was holding the line against possible Chinese communist intervention, something that the French could not do at the current level of American military aid. The Melby–Erskine mission thus recommended that a U.S. military assistance advisory group for Indochina be established rapidly. This mirrored a move by the Chinese to set up a remarkably similar advisory group in Vietnam to help the **Democratic Republic of Vietnam**. The French, however, were opposed to the American mission's recommendation, worried that it would send the wrong signal to their Vietnamese allies, who would wonder who was really in charge, the French or the Americans, thereby allowing them to play the Americans against the French. *See also* AID, AMERICAN; AID, CHINESE.

**MELBY, JOHN F.** *See* MELBY–ERSKINE MISSION.

**MEMORIAL, CAO BẰNG.** In 2001, the ***Association nationale des anciens prisonniers internés d'Indochine*** (ANAPI) submitted a project to the French President Jacques Chirac to construct a stele along the former colonial Route no.4 in memory of French soldiers who died not only during battles in **Cao Bang** between 1944–1945 and 1947–1950, but also those who perished in prisoner of war camps run by the **Democratic Republic of Vietnam**. While the current Vietnamese authorities appear open to the memorial project, French funding has not been accorded as of early 2011. This memorial is designed to complement the one the ANAPI helped create at **Dien Bien Phu** and which is funded and officially recognized by the French state. *See also ASSOCIATION NATIONALE DES ANCIENS D'INDOCHINE ET DU SOUVENIR INDOCHINOIS*; *ASSOCIATION NATIONALE DES ANCIENS ET AMIS DE L'INDOCHINE ET DU SOUVENIR INDOCHINOIS*; *ASSOCIATION NATIONALE DES ANCIENS PRISONNIERS ET INTERNÉS D'INDOCHINE*; *ASSOCIATION NATIONALE DES COMBATTANTS DE DIEN BIEN PHU*; ASSOCIATION OF MOTHERS OF SOLDIERS; BOUDAREL AFFAIR; EXPERIENCE OF WAR; EXPERIENCE OF WAR, DIEN BIEN PHU; MARTYRS; MYTH OF WAR; WAR MEMORIAL, DIEN BIEN PHU.

**MEMORIAL, FRANCE.** *See* NECROPOLIS, FRÉJUS.

**MEMORIAL DAY, INDOCHINA WAR.** In response to the 2004 request of several associations representing veterans of the Indochina War, the French government approved by decree on 26 May 2005 the creation of an official memorial day for the Indochina War (*journée du souvenir de la Guerre d'Indochine*). The associations selected 8 June, for it corresponds to the day in 1980 when the remains of the "unknown soldier of Indochina" (*soldat inconnu d'Indochine*) were interred in the national **necropolis** of Notre-Dame de Lorette in the department of Pas-de-Calais. Notre-Dame de Lorette is home to the French National Military Cemetery, site of a major battle of World War I, and the final resting place of the unknown soldiers of that war, World War II, and the Algerian War. On 8 June 2005, Michèle Alliot-Marie, then minister of Defense, and Hamlaoui Mekachera, then deputy minister of Veteran Affairs, attended the first commemoration of the Indochina Memorial Day. On that day, Mme Alliot-Marie addressed the coffin containing the remains of the unknown soldier of the Indochina War. She said: "Through him, it is the totality of his comrades to whom we pay tribute today". This unknown soldier had "fallen" during the battle of Dien Bien Phu. His remains were discovered in Vietnam in December 2004 and were later inhumed at the necropolis in Fréjus, where the official ceremony for Indochina Memorial Day is now held. The life of the dead carries on. *See also ASSOCIATION NATIONALE DES ANCIENS D'INDOCHINE ET DU SOUVENIR INDOCHINOIS*; *ASSOCIATION NATIONALE DES ANCIENS ET AMIS DE L'INDOCHINE ET DU SOUVENIR INDOCHINOIS*; *ASSOCIATION NATIONALE DES ANCIENS PRISONNIERS ET INTERNÉS D'INDOCHINE*; *ASSOCIATION NATIONALE DES COMBATTANTS DE DIEN BIEN PHU*; ASSOCIATION OF MOTHERS OF SOLDIERS; BOUDAREL AFFAIR; CEMETERY; EXPERIENCE OF WAR; EXPERIENCE OF WAR, DIEN BIEN PHU; MARTYRS; MYTH OF WAR; WAR MEMORIAL, DIEN BIEN PHU.

***MÉMORIAL DES GUERRES EN INDOCHINE DE FRÉJUS.*** *See* NECROPOLIS, FRÉJUS.

**MENDÈS FRANCE, PIERRE ISAAC ISIDORE (1907–1982).** French statesman instrumental in bringing an end to the Indochina War during the **Geneva Conference**. Pierre Mendès France studied law at the *École libre des sciences politiques* and became heavily involved in socialist politics as a member of the *Parti radical*. He supported the left-wing Popular Front in the late 1930s and was in uniform in North Africa when World War II broke out. Following the fall of France in 1940, the Vichy government arrested this Jewish statesman, sentenced him to six years in prison for trying to escape to North Africa, and put him behind bars in Clermont-Ferrand (where he rubbed shoulders with the father of French **revolutionary warfare** in Indochina, **Charles Lacheroy**). Mendès France's famous escape shortly thereafter allowed him to make his way to London where he joined **Charles de Gaulle** and the Free French movement. De Gaulle made him commissioner and then minister of National Economy in the provisional government in waiting. Following the liberation of France in 1944, Mendès France resigned from this position and was re-elected deputy of Eure in 1945.

He had first publicly criticized the government's conduct of the Indochina war in 1950, following the French failure to hold the frontier town of **Cao Bang** (thus allowing Chinese communist **aid** to flow directly to the **Viet Minh**) and in light of the financial burden of the war. He called for the opening of negotiations to reach a political solution to the conflict or for the institution of the draft in order to fight the war correctly on the ground.

Four years later, as Vietnamese communist forces scored an even more stunning victory over the French army at **Dien Bien Phu**, Mendès France risked his position as head of the government to find a diplomatic solution to the conflagration. On the day of his investiture, he announced he would resign one month later, on 20 July, if a cease-fire were not reached in negotiations already underway in Geneva. To make sure it happened, he personally assumed the portfolio of minister of Foreign Affairs. His strategy sought to neutralize Laos and Cambodia and to divide Vietnam so that a non-communist state could survive in the south. He was largely successful in this endeavor thanks to the willingness of Chinese Prime Minister **Zhou Enlai** to accept the neutralization of Laos and Cambodia and the division of Vietnam in order to keep the Americans from taking over the war from the French on China's southern flank. In the early hours of 21 July 1954, the **Geneva Accords** on Indochina were signed.

**MENON, KRISHNA VENGALIL KRISHNAN (1897–1974). Indian** diplomat who represented **Jawaharlal Nehru** during the **Geneva Conference** of 1954. Educated at the Presidency College in Madras, Menon joined the Theosophical Society and was active in the home rule movement. He graduated from the London School of Economics, where he studied law in the 1920s. In 1927, he became the general secretary of the **India** League in Britain and through it developed a lifelong friendship with Nehru in the Indian nationalist movement. Following independence, Prime Minister Nehru appointed him first high commissioner to the United Kingdom. Menon was instrumental in keeping India within the British Commonwealth. He served as a member of the Indian parliament between 1952 and 1967.

Keen on promoting a peaceful solution to the Indochina War, Nehru sent Menon, now Indian ambassador to Moscow and delegate to the **United Nations**, to Geneva to work with **Anthony Eden** as a commonwealth member and independently in order to facilitate contacts among the various parties in order to reach a negotiated solution. Menon arrived in the Swiss capital on 24 May 1954 and quickly went to work meeting with the Chinese diplomat **Zhou Enlai** and his American counterpart **Walter Bedell Smith** among others. One Geneva delegate went so far as to describe Menon as a "germ carrier" at Geneva – peace germs for some, germs of discord for others.

What is clear is that through Menon, Nehru made it clear to Zhou Enlai and **Viatcheslav Molotov** that the **Democratic Republic of Vietnam**'s (DRV) refusal to pull out of Laos and Cambodia and desire to impose "resistance governments" there threatened to jeopardize Chinese and Soviet relations with non-communist South and Southeast Asian countries such as India, **Indonesia**, and **Burma**. Menon's arguments had a real influence on Zhou and his decision to distance himself from the DRV's Indochinese ambitions. One month later, on 24 June, Zhou Enlai made his historic trip to New Delhi to talk to Nehru about the course of the Geneva negotiations, conceding that the royal governments of Laos and Cambodia were legitimate on the condition that they remained neutral in the **Cold War**. Menon had helped facilitate this important inter-Asian contact. He also negotiated India's role as president of the **International Commission for Supervision and Control**. *See also* CAMBODIAN RESISTANCE GOVERNMENT; INDONESIA; LAO RESISTANCE GOVERNMENT; NEUTRALIZATION OF INDOCHINA.

**MEO.** *See* MINORITY ETHNIC GROUPS.

**MERCY TEAM, HANOI.** With the defeat of the Japanese, the American **Office of Strategic Services** moved on its plans to drop rescue teams into Japanese POW camps in Asia to protect prisoners and return them to Allied control. One such team was sent to **Hanoi** to tend to several thousands Allied POWs held there. **Archimedes Patti** headed up the Hanoi Mercy Team, arriving in late August 1945.

**MÉRIC, ÉDOUARD (1901–1973).** French colonial administrator in Indochina during the conflict. Graduated from Saint-Cyr in 1923, he made his career in colonial Morocco during the interwar years. He joined Free French forces during World War II and distinguished himself as a commander. Between 1946 and 1949, he served as a lieutenant colonel in Indochina at the head of the 3rd Foreign Infantry Regiment (*3e REI*) and commander of the Eastern Zone of **Cochinchina**. He returned to Indochina as a colonel in the late 1940s to serve as chief of staff to General **Pierre-Georges Boyer de la Tour**.

**MESSMER, PIERRE AUGUSTE JOSEPH (1916–2007).** French colonial administrator deeply involved in the troubled decolonization of Indochina. Graduating from the **Colonial Academy** (*École coloniale*) in 1934, Messmer held a doctoral degree in law from the ***École nationale des langues orientales vivantes***. He began his military service in Senegal in 1937. Following the French defeat in 1940, he joined Free French forces in London in July and was sent to North Africa in the **Foreign Legion**, where he participated in numerous battles, including Bir Hakeim and El Alamein. He landed in Normandy in August 1944 and entered Paris as part of the liberating army. He was named major in the French army in January 1945 and dispatched to Calcutta to create a French Administrative Liaison Military Mission (*Mission militaire de liaison administrative*) in the capacity of acting colonial commissioner for the Republic. He parachuted into **Tonkin** on 25 August 1945 charged with re-establishing French sovereignty to Indochina as commissioner for the Republic in Tonkin and North **Annam**. However, on 27 August, he fell into the hands of **Viet Minh** forces. Some two months later, he escaped captivity and joined the French Mission under **Jean Sainteny,** now based in **Hanoi**, and served as the commissioner for the Republic in Tonkin and North Annam. Messmer entered high-level colonial affairs in 1946, when he became general secretary of the ***Comité interministériel de l'Indochine***. He participated in the first **Dalat Conference** in April – May 1946, during which he stood up to High Commissioner **Georges Thierry d'Argenlieu** by stating that Vietnam was a single nation and that separating it from **Cochinchina** was a dangerous policy. He was also instrumental in warning against any further French military action against the **Democratic Republic of Vietnam** after the **Haiphong** and **Langson** clashes in November–December 1946. Messmer accompanied **Maurice Moutet** on his mission to Indochina in late December 1946. Between 1947 and 1948, he served as personal secretary to **Émile Bollaert**, the new high commissioner to Indochina, before returning to France to become chief administrator for Overseas France (*Administrateur en chef de la France d'Outre-mer*). He held numerous colonial posts in French Africa (governor of Mauritania and the Ivory Coast) and served as minister of Defense at the time of the **Algerian War**. He also served as French prime minister between 1972 and 1974. In 1998, looking back over his colonial career and the decolonization of the French Empire, he published *Les Blancs s'en vont, récits de décolonisation.*

***MÉTIS.*** The French term referring to **children** of ethnically mixed marriages. The Vietnamese use the term *tay lai;* the Lao say *luk khrung*. Mixed Franco-Indochinese unions were not uncommon during the colonial period, but by no means as common as those occurring in colonial **Indonesia.** *Métis* or Eurasians in Indochina only numbered a few thousand at any given time during the colonial period. French men, usually colonial administrators, officers, and traders, often married "Indochinese" women. Given that the 35–40,000 Europeans living in Indochina on the eve of World War II were concentrated in eastern Indochina and in the lowland cities, they tended to marry Vietnamese women. Many European settlers and soldiers also had concubines. Of these relationships hundreds of Franco-Vietnamese children were born.

During the early colonial period, European colonial society tended to shun *métis* children and discouraged mixed marriages for fear of "contaminating" French "blood". The fact that the majority of Eurasians were born out of wedlock, sometimes of an unknown father, also meant that they could not legally obtain French nationality. This often made their integration in French colonial society all the more difficult. During the colonial period, private Eurasian welfare societies tried to change this and scoured the countryside for Eurasian children abandoned by their fathers. Opposed to the idea of these *métis* living among the Vietnamese, these civilian societies took the children, sometimes by force, from their mothers and placed them in orphanages.

Eurasians born to legal unions were in a better situation. Indeed, a number of such *métis* became important figures in colonial and postcolonial Indochina, such as **William Bazé** and Henri de La Chevrotière. French women also married Vietnamese men and had *métis* children. The future diplomat-at-large for the **Democratic Republic of Vietnam** (DRV), Dr. **Pham Ngoc Thach**, married a French woman, Marie Louise Jeandot, while **Nguyen Manh Ha** married the daughter of Georges Marranne, a senior leader in the **French Communist Party** and deputy in the National Assembly. Neither woman came from the French colonial society in Indochina. The couples met in the metropolis.

While the social and legal status of abandoned Eurasian children improved by the late 1930s, the *métis* always occupied something of a grey area in colonial society, one that became dangerous with the outbreak of the Indochina War. Upon its creation, the DRV passed legislation requiring Eurasians to adopt Vietnamese nationality. For some xenophobic Vietnamese nationalists, *métis* were the living symbol of illicit **collaboration** with the enemy, the colonizer. Eurasians sometimes found themselves in the crossfire when French and Vietnamese took to arms to determine who would rule Vietnam. In **Saigon**, during the massacre in the mixed quarter of **Hérault**, Vietnamese attackers singled out *métis* in their raids, kidnapping and killing dozens of them in horrendous circumstances. During the war, the French ***Sûreté*** and ***Deuxième Bureau*** recruited *métis* into their ranks, in light of their mastery of both languages and ability to penetrate into Vietnamese circles much more easily than their French counterparts. **Fernand Faugère** served **Léon Pignon** faithfully as a trusted advisor in the *Sûreté* and secret go-between with Vietnamese of all political colors. In **Hanoi**, the Franco-Vietnamese **Charles Petit**, inspector for the *Sûreté*, secretly infiltrated the forces of the DRV in late 1946. He tipped the French off about the planned Vietnamese attack for the night of the **19 December 1946**. The DRV took his family hostage in reprisal.

The DRV also relied upon *tay lai* during the conflict, one of the best examples being **Jean Moreau** who handled sensitive military and intelligence missions. Ngo Van Chieu dedicates an entire chapter in his memoirs to the DRV's reliance on a loyal *métis* in the army, who "chose his mother's country (Vietnam) and proved it".

However, Eurasians were not the only *métis* touched by the Indochina War. Inter-Asian couples and their *métis* children were just as notable and much more important numerically than the Franco-Indochinese ones. Sino-Vietnamese marriages and children are a case in point. In 1921, Cochinchina was home to 64,500 *Minh Huong*, the Vietnamese term referring to the *métis* children of Sino-Vietnamese unions. A decade later the number had risen to 73,000. During the Indochina War, the nationalist-minded Viet Minh had no problems recruiting these bilingual and bi-cultural Asian *métis* into its ranks, especially to help maintain good relations with the Chinese populations, to translate increasingly large amounts of political and technical information coming from communist China, to help run commercial affairs inside and outside Vietnam, and even to work in intelligence. Vietnamese did not just marry Europeans coming from the metropolis. Not only was the Vietnamese General **Nguyen Son** a ranking member of the Chinese and Vietnamese communist parties, but he had also married a Chinese woman during his time in China.

Of the thousands of mainly male Vietnamese cadres sent to work in western Indochina many married local women in Laos and Cambodia. Unsurprisingly, the DRV cultivated close relationships with *métis* born of Lao–Vietnamese and Cambodian–Vietnamese mixed marriages. Again, these children, now adults, spoke both languages and provided the DRV with an entry into western Indochinese politics, societies, and cultures. Two of the DRV's most important allies in Laos and Cambodia were Vietnamese–Lao and Vietnamese–Khmer *métis*: **Kaisôn Phomvihān** and **Son Ngoc Minh**. The "Red Prince" **Suphānuvong**, close ally to Vietnamese communists during 30 years of war, married a Vietnamese woman from a prominent Dalat family. Their *luk khrung* children hold high-ranking positions in Laos to this day. *See also* KHMER KROM; LANGUAGE OF WAR; LOVE AND WAR; HERAULT, MASSACRE.

**MICHAUDEL, MAURICE MARIE AUGUSTE (1901–1975).** Lao specialist and colonial official who made his career in Indochina. Graduated from the ***École nationale des langues orientales vivantes*** with a degree in law, Michaudel first served in Cambodia in 1926–1927 as an attaché in the *résident supérieur*'s cabinet and as a deputy to the head of the province of Kompong Cham. He dedicated the rest of his career to Laos. Indeed, he was something of an admirer of all things Lao. He spoke the language fluently and lived with a Lao woman, with whom he had three children. Between 1927 and 1933, he served in Vientiane (1927–1929), Pakse (1930–1931), and then worked on administrative and legislative questions in the *Résidence supérieure* until 1933. Between 1934 and 1942, Michaudel moved around much of Laos working as provincial chief in the Upper Mekong (1934), *résident* to Thakhek (1935), Saravane (1936–1938), and Savannakhet (1939–1942). He served Vichy Indochina in Vientiane as chief of the office of the Lao *résident supérieur* (1942–1944), then head of the *Service local de l'information, de la propagande et de la presse* (1944 – March 1945). Michaudel was a close collaborator of Charles Rochet, and helped edit and publish *Nouveau Laos, Lao Nhay*, and *Tin Lao* in French, Lao, and Vietnamese, respectively. On 2 June 1945, the Japanese placed Michaudel under "*internement spécial*". Following the Japanese defeat, the *Commission d'épuration* in Indochina cleared him of charges of "collaboration with the enemy". He was back at work in December 1945 at the head of the Office for Laotian Affairs operating from **Saigon**, a job he held until August 1946. With the French reoccupation of Laos in mid-1946, Michaudel returned to Laos and worked as the chief of the "General Administration" for the Commissioner for the Republic to Laos (1946–1947) and then as Commissioner for the Republic in Laos on an interim basis (July 1947 – March 1948). In 1948, he took leave in France. He returned to Indochina in 1950 to work as the head of the Diplomatic Services in the high commissioner's office for Indochina. It is unclear when he left Indochina definitively.

**MICHEL, ÉTIENNE DIDIER (1916–1950).** During the Battle of France, the Germans took him prisoner. Michel escaped captivity in late 1943 and made his way to North Africa where he joined the French resistance and was wounded during the Alsace campaign. Between 1946 and 1948, he worked in Indochina as the director of Information in **Cochinchina**, then as deputy to the political advisor to the French high commissioner in Indochina and finally as political advisor to the high commissioner. He accompanied High Commissioner **Émile Bollaert** during negotiations with **Bao Dai** in the Bay of Ha Long in December 1947. He left Indochina in 1949.

**MIGRATION.** *See* DESERTION; HANOI; SAIGON.

**MILITARY ASSISTANCE ADVISORY GROUP (MAAG), INDOCHINA.** Following Chinese and Soviet diplomatic recognition of the **Democratic Republic of Vietnam** (DRV) in January 1950 and the outbreak of the **Korean War** in June of that year, in September American President **Harry S. Truman** authorized and dispatched the Military Assistance Advisory Group (MAAG) to Vietnam to assist the French in using American **aid** to fight the DRV. The **Griffin** and **Melby–Erskine** missions had prepared the way earlier in the year for the implementation of such military assistance, albeit that much remained to be ironed out. The American contingent arrived in September 1950 and was eventually placed under the leadership of General **Francis G. Brink**. MAAG was up and working as of 17 September 1950. Like their Chinese adversaries assisting the DRV, the Americans were responsible for providing military and economic aid to the French and advising on military strategy and tactics. Brink presided over a team of sixty, working in five branches: Aid Supply, Transport, Technical Services, Logistics, and Operations. In December 1950, the French, the Americans, and the three **Associated States of Indochina** signed the Pentalateral Mutual Defense Assistance Pact establishing the rules by which military assistance would be provided. However, the combination of the ambiguous wording of certain clauses concerning the supervision of military assistance, the small size of the advisory group, French reluctance to allow the Americans to become too directly involved in internal military questions and operations, and problems of language greatly limited the effectiveness of

American attempts to oversee and inspect the utilization of their military aid. In addition to the army, MAAG Air Force and Navy teams also provided aid to the French. Brink personally flew to Tokyo in 1951 to obtain crucial supplies from the Far East Command Headquarters for the French and he made another trip there during the battle for Phat Diem. Despite such assistance, General **Jean de Lattre de Tassigny** complained that MAAG was responsible for turning down French requests for aid. Brink's investigation of this matter turned up no evidence substantiating such an allegation. The French were particularly opposed to American and non-communist Vietnamese desires to bypass the French in order to channel military aid directly to the national armies of the Associated States of Indochina. As American historian Georges Herring has pointed out, whatever the talk of a "Western alliance against communism", relations between the French and the MAAG officers were often stormy. MAAG officers visited the battlefields in 1953 and early 1954, although the French had refused to consult MAAG before the operation began in November. Between 1950 and 1954, American military aid to the French exceeded 2.6 billion dollars. The MAAG remained operational following the signing of the **Geneva Accords**, allowing the Americans to continue to provide aid and training to the armed forces of the **Republic of Vietnam** (The Geneva accords recognized the on-going validity of the pre-existing agreements.). In January 1962, MAAG was subordinated to the newly created Military Assistance Command, Vietnam (MACV). In 1964, when it became clear that a new war for Vietnam was in the making, MAAG was phased out. *See also* AID, AMERICAN; AID, CHINESE COMMUNIST; AID, SOVIET; FINANCIAL COST OF INDOCHINA WAR, FRANCE.

**MILITARY REGIONS, ASSOCIATED STATE OF VIETNAM.** In July 1952, the French and the Associated State of Vietnam authorities officially divided Vietnam into four major military regions. The 1st military region included southern Vietnam, the 2nd covered central Vietnam, the 3rd incorporated northern Vietnam, including the mountain areas, while the 4th military region referred specifically to the central highlands (*vung cao nguyen mien nam*). **Bao Dai** signed into law the decree creating these zones. In March 1954, a new decree amended the 2nd military region to include that portion of Vietnam running "from the northern border of Quang Ngai province 'up'", probably meaning to the border with the 3rd military region. It also modified the 4th military region to include the central highlands and central Vietnam from the northern border of Quang Ngai down, meaning to region 1 in southern Vietnam. In 1956, when it became increasingly clear that Vietnam would not be unified, the **Republic of Vietnam** redefined the pre-existing zones to cover areas below the **17th parallel.** *See also* INTERZONE; ZONE.

**MINH VIÊN.** *See* HUỲNH THÚC KHÁNG.

**MINORITY ETHNIC GROUPS.** Ethnic minority groups in former French Indochina were caught in the crossfire in the war mainly between the **Democratic Republic of Vietnam** (DRV) and Franco-Vietnamese forces between 1945 and 1954.

The ethno-linguistic make-up of Laos, Cambodia, and Vietnam was and remains very heterogeneous. A colonial census of 1938 recorded 16.7 million ethnic Vietnamese, 2.9 million Khmer and almost 800,000 Lao. Colonial authorities also counted sizeable "minority" populations, including some 600,000 Tai and Tho, 214,000 Man and Hmong, 1 million "Moi", including Bahnar, Sedang, Stieng, Jarai, and Rhadé located mainly in the central Vietnamese highlands.

During the Indochina conflict, the French adopted the well-known strategy of "divide and rule". The army recruited from among the different ethnic minorities in Indochina, convinced that it could turn their supposed anti-Vietnamese animosities against the DRV in strategically important upland areas. Of particular importance were the Tai, Nung, and Hmong populations located behind DRV lines in the highlands of northwestern Vietnam as well as those located in the central highlands, what the French referred to as the ***Pays montagnards du sud*** (PMS) since 1946.

Pushed by the Americans, the French ***Groupement de commandos mixtes aéroportés*** relied heavily on upland peoples to harass the DRV in its own territory. Notable allies for the French among the ethnic minorites were **Deo Van Long**, president of the **Tai Federation** created by the French in 1948, and **Chau Quang Lo**, an ethnic Hmong. The French army even created distinct batallions based along these ethnic minority lines, some of which were present during the battle of **Dien Bien Phu**, itself located in Tai-Lao lands.

French support for the creation of new ethnic minority armies, communities, and identities worked against the efforts of the DRV and the Associated State of Vietnam to incorporate them into a Vietnamese citizenship.

With the end of the war in mid-1954 and the division of Vietnam into two provisional states at the **17th parallel**, the French could do little to help their partisans who now fell squarely under the national control of the DRV in the north and that of the **Republic of Vietnam** in the south. The French evacuated a small number of minority ethnic allies and their families to southern Vietnam and France following the **Geneva Accords**, while some escaped by foot to Laos. However, most remained behind and some paid with their lives for their **collaboration** with the French. In areas below the 17th parallel, the minority ethnic troops returned to their homes but they too soon came under the tighter national control of the Republic of Vietnam led by **Ngo Dinh Diem**. As for the leaders of the DRV, they countered French efforts to turn the minority groups against them in military and political ways. In exchange for their cooperation, communist authorities granted them greater degrees of autonomy. Vietnamese communists also counted among their own ranks ethnic minority leaders such as **Hoang Dinh Giong** of Tai origin and **Chu Van Tan** from the Nung. *See also* KHMER KROM; OVERSEAS CHINESE; OVERSEAS VIETNAMESE.

**MISSING IN ACTION.** The **Democratic Republic of Vietnam** has never released the official statistics revealing how many men and women went missing in action (*mat tich*) between 1945 and 1954. In 1962, however, Bac Ninh provincial authorities officially identified 262 families, including 80 "missing in action families". The total number of "absentees, missing or unreturned" (*absents, disparus ou non rentrés*) from the military forces of the French Union numbered 20,661 as of 17 October 1954. The number for the armed forces of the Associated States was about 9,000. *See also* CASUALTIES, INDOCHINA WAR; CEMETERIES; MARTYRS; MEMORIAL DAY, INDOCHINA WAR; MYTH OF WAR.

**MISSOFFE, FRANÇOIS (1919–2003).** Diplomat, politician, and Asian specialist for the French government during the Indochina War. The son of a navy admiral, he joined the French resistance at the outset of World War II and was captured by the Japanese in Indochina. Upon liberation around September 1945, he joined **Jean Sainteny**'s mission in **Hanoi** where he administered financial questions related to the re-establishment of French sovereignty to Indochina. He was and remained virulently hostile to what he saw as American interference in French internal matters in Indochina. He resented above all American Major **Archimedes Patti**'s activities in Hanoi in late 1945. Missoffe returned to France in 1946 to pursue a career in business and politics. He served as French ambassador to Japan between 1964 and 1966. In 1977, he published a book on Asia, including his activities in Indochina, entitled *Duel rouge*. He loved jazz and in his youth had even created a jazz orchestra with none other than **Boris Vian**. *See also* BANK OF INDOCHINA; CURRENCY, FRENCH INDOCHINA; FINANCIAL COST OF THE WAR.

**MISTRAL, JEAN ÉDOUARD (1922–1995).** French colonial civil servant. Between 1945 and 1949, he served as the head of the district of Mdrack in the central Vietnamese highlands and was chief of cabinet to the high commissioner for Indochina for the upland populations of southern Indochina (*Les populations montagnardes du Sud-Indochine*) in Ban Me Thuot. *See also* MINORITY ETHINIC GROUPS; *PAYS MONTAGNARDS DU SUD* (PMS).

**MIXED MARRIAGE.** *See* LOVE AND WAR; *MÉTIS*.

**MOBILE FIELD BROTHEL.** *See BORDELS MOBILES DE CAMPAGNE*.

***MODUS VIVENDI*, FRANCO-CAMBODIAN.** Because the British facilitated the return of the French to Indochina below the **16th parallel** in September 1945, the French were able to reoccupy Cambodia rapidly. On 15 October 1945, General **Philippe Leclerc** had **Son Ngoc Thanh** arrested and opened negotiations with the Cambodian royal family to re-establish the status of this former protectorate and its place within the emerging **French Union** and its component **Indochinese Federation**. On 7 January 1946, the two sides signed a *modus vivendi* allowing for the internal autonomy of the Kingdom but placing it within an Indochinese Federation and the French Union. Faced with increasing Khmer calls for liberal reforms, **Norodom Sihanouk** and the French agreed to promulgate a constitution, guaranteeing political freedoms and universal male suffrage. In May 1946, direct, universal male suffrage was established. Sihanouk created a provisional National Assembly to deliberate the drafting of a constitution as set out in the Franco-Khmer talks. Elections occurred on 1 September 1946, giving the **Democrat Party** a victory. The majority democrat leadership declared itself a Constituent Assembly and called for the right to lead the government as the majority party. At the second **Dalat Conference** in August 1946, Lao and Cambodian delegates accepted the French proposals to create an Indochinese Federation and signed a document denouncing the **Democratic Republic of Vietnam**'s alleged claim to represent all of Indochina.

***MODUS VIVENDI*, FRANCO-VIETNAMESE.** Before giving up on the **Fontainebleau Conference**, the delegation of the **Democratic Republic of Vietnam** (DRV) sought to obtain a *modus vivendi* in order to hold the French to respecting the latter's promise to allow a referendum on the unification of **Cochinchina** with Vietnam. However, the head of the Vietnamese delegation, **Pham Van Dong**, refused to sign the document when it was presented to him on 10 September 1946, since the French had still refused to set a date for such a referendum. The Fontainebleau Conference thus ended in failure. Determined to avoid war, however, **Ho Chi Minh** stayed behind and pleaded with his French interlocutors to give him something he could take home to appease those calling for an end to negotiations with the French. As he put it to **Jean Sainteny**, "Don't let me leave like this, arm me against those who seek to cast me aside; you will not regret it". During the early hours of 15 September 1946, Ho Chi Minh persuaded **Marius Moutet**, socialist minister of the Colonies, to sign a provisional modus vivendi, prepared by **Léon Pignon** and dated 14 September. The main idea was that a cease-fire would be instituted in southern Vietnam (Article 9) and once calm was restored then negotiations on the holding of a referendum in and on **Cochinchina** could resume (Article 10). Negotiations on reaching a definitive agreement were to be held before 1 February 1947.

**MOFFAT, ABBOT LOW (1901–1996).** American diplomat involved in negotiations between the French and Vietnamese and between the French and the Thais in 1946 over the retrocession of Cambodian and Lao provinces annexed by Thailand in 1941.

Born into a prominent Manhattan family and graduated from Harvard University in 1923, Moffat obtained his law degree from Columbia University before serving as a prominent lawyer and Republican politician in New York. In 1943, he resigned his state seat and joined the United States Department of State, where he served as head of the Philippine and Southeast Asian Division between 1944 and 1947. He headed a mission to **Saigon** and **Hanoi** in early December 1946, during which time he received French thanks for his role in obtaining the Thai retrocession of Cambodian provinces. During his trip to Hanoi, he also met with **Hoang Minh Giam**, **Hoang Huu Nam,** and **Vo Nguyen Giap**. If Moffat was at ease with the two Hoangs, he was repelled by Giap, whom he characterized in 1946 as the "typical commie, the cartoon commie". Against the wishes of **Jean Sainteny**, Moffat also met with president **Ho Chi Minh** in December of that year.

Although Dean Acheson had warned Moffat to "keep in mind Ho's clear record as [an] agent [of] international communism", in his reports Moffat underscored the historical reality and force of nationalism in Vietnam and was sympathetic to the anti-colonial cause of the **Democratic Republic of Vietnam**. He had also warned against supporting what he saw as the corrupt government of **Chiang Kai-shek** against the Chinese communists. His views did nothing to prevent the outbreak of war in Indochina in late 1946. They did, however, attract the attention of Joseph McCarthy, who wrote Moffat off as a "pro-communist".

Moffat regretted the shift in American Asian policy towards what he saw as blind anti-communism, asserting at one point that it seemed as if things had regressed "right back in[to] the wars of religion". He felt that the support of viable nationalist aims was the best way for the US to head off the communist threat. He deplored French reluctance to decolonize in Indochina and argued that such a policy was pushing Vietnam into the arms of the communists. He became an open critic of subsequent American involvement in Vietnam. Speaking to the Fulbright committee in 1972, Moffat criticized the absence of instructions from the State Department after World War II, since "it seemed Ho was hoping that I would have some message for him and I was miserable not to be able to say anything".

While Moffat was right to say that he had no instructions as to dealing with Ho Chi Minh upon his departure for Hanoi in December 1946, they were waiting for him on his return to Saigon. They were that he should avoid giving the impression that the United States would interfere with French policy with regards to Indochina. *See also* AID, AMERICAN; COLD WAR; OFFICE OF STRATEGIC SERVICES.

**MOLOTOV, VIATCHESLAV SKRIABINE (1890–1986).** Soviet diplomat and foreign minister who played a pivotal role in reaching an agreement on Indochina at the **Geneva Conference** of 1954. He joined the communist party at 16 and became one of **Joseph Stalin**'s loyal collaborators. He became commissar for Foreign Affairs in May 1939 and was involved in negotiating the German – Soviet Pact of that year. He held this post until 1949, when he became vice president of the Council of Ministers. In 1953, following the death of Stalin, he took over the direction of Soviet foreign policy. During the Berlin conference in early 1954, he strongly supported the participation of the **People's Republic of China** in the upcoming conference on the Korean and Indochina Wars at Geneva. He promoted just such a meeting in order to "diminish tension in international relations". As co-president with Britain's **Anthony Eden**, Molotov played a pivotal role in preparing and reaching an agreement to end the Indochina War during the Geneva Conference of 1954. His relationship with Stalin's successor, Nikita Khrushchev, was however an increasingly rocky one. Molotov would lose his post at the head of the Ministry of Foreign Affairs in 1956 and would be expelled from the party between 1962 and 1984. *See also* AID, SOVIET.

**MONEGLIA, VINCENT.** French military officer in charge of the Vietnamese Military Academy in **Hanoi**, created in the early 1950s to train a modern Vietnamese officer corps for the Associated State of Vietnam. He headed a delegation of French and Vietnamese (Associated State) officers to the front lines in Korea to study American methods of troop training and to coordinate them with those being used in Indochina as part of a wider front against communist forces in Asia. *See also* AID, CHINESE; AID, SOVIET; ARMY, ASSOCIATED STATE OF VIETNAM; COLD WAR; DOMINO THEORY; KOREAN WAR.

**MONTHÉARD, HENRI DENIS ALFRED (1911–1961).** Born in **Hanoi**, Monthéard was a career colonial administrator in French Indochina. Between 1935 and 1945, he served in various posts in northern Vietnam and Hanoi. Between 1945 and 1947, he was in charge of the service for repatriations and secretary of the commission for purging (*épuration*) Vichy's Indochinese administration. He also oversaw the early intelligence operations of the ***Bureau fédéral de documentation***'s Hanoi base. Between 1948 and 1954, he held ranking administrative positions close to the political advisor for the French high commissioner to Indochina (1948–1951) and to the deputy diplomatic advisor (1952–1953). In 1954, he became advisor to the Liaison for Pacification working with the commander-in-chief of the armed forces. Following the signing of the **Geneva Accords** of 1954, he returned to France to serve in the ministry in charge of relations with the Associated States for Vietnam, Laos, and Cambodia.

**MOREAU, JEAN (DƯƠNG BÁ LỘC, 1925–).** Born in central Vietnam to a French colonial civil servant and a Vietnamese–Italian mother, Moreau grew up in Phu Yen where his father was stationed. He completed his primary and secondary studies in Hue. Following the Japanese ***coup de force* of 9 March 1945** and the emergence of the **Democratic Republic of Vietnam** (DRV), Moreau had to choose his nationality if not his national identity. More at ease in the Vietnamese culture and language, and sympathetic to the Vietnamese quest for independence, he opted to become a citizen of the DRV in 1945, adopting the Vietnamese name of Duong Ba Loc. He participated in the **August Revolution** in Phu Yen province before joining the Vietnamese army. He joined the **Indochinese Communist Party** in 1947.

During the Indochina War, Moreau worked in intelligence operations in the French-occupied city of Nha Trang and as a military intelligence cadre in the Tay Nguyen military region. He ran a number of sensitive and dangerous covert operations for the DRV. Thanks to his bilingualism, he also served as a cultural and political instructor in the Vietnamese army. After the **Geneva Accords**, Moreau relocated to northern Vietnam. French officers who encountered him during his transfer to the north were astonished by his refusal to return to France. For Moreau, there was no question, however: he was Vietnamese. He nonetheless played the roles of French and American officers in a number of DRV propaganda films, including *The* ***17th Parallel*** *Night and Day* (*Vi Tuyen 17 Ngay Va Dem*) and *There Is Only One Person Left Alive* (*Chi Mot Nguoi Con Song*) among many others. As of early 2011, he lives in Vietnam with his family. *See also* CROSSOVERS; CULTURE; LANGUAGE OF WAR; LOVE AND WAR; *MÉTIS*; NOVELS.

**MOREAU, LOUIS GUY MARLE (?).** Graduated from the **Colonial Academy** (*École coloniale*) in 1947, he was assigned to the commissioner for the Republic in Hue between 1948 and 1949. Between 1951 and 1954, he was provincial chief of Pleiku. He returned to France at the end of the Indochina War and joined the section in charge of the former Associated States of Vietnam, Laos, and Cambodia in the French Ministry of Foreign Affairs. In 1955, he was named the representative to Haiphong of the French general delegate before transferring to the General Delegation of the French government in **Hanoi** between 1955 and 1958. *See also* MINORITY ETHNIC GROUPS; *PAYS MONTAGNARDS DU SUD* (PMS).

**MOREL, ANDRÉ (1916–1979).** A naval officer in 1940, Morel joined resistance forces in June of that year. He also signed up to serve in the French Naval Fusiliers. He saw combat at Bir-Hakeim in June 1942 and participated in major battles in North Africa and in the liberation of Europe in Italy and France. Following World War II, he left for Indochina with the 1st Regiment of Naval Fusiliers. Admiral **Georges Thierry d'Argenlieu** awarded him in **Saigon** the *Croix de la libération* on 11 November 1946. Morel faithfully served Thierry d'Argenlieu in 1945–1946. He left his regiment in July 1947. While he apparently remained in Indochina, the details of Morel's precise activities remain unclear.

**MORET, ANDRÉ.** Head of the **Tonkin** Section of the *Direction de la Police et de la Sûreté générale* and in northern **Annam** between December 1945 and November 1948. Little else is known of his activities in Indochina. *See also SÛRETÉ FÉDÉRALE.*

**MORLIÈRE, LOUIS CONSTANT (1897–1980).** One of the few ranking French military officers opposed to the road leading to full-scale war in 1946. Morlière fought in World War I in the 2nd Colonial Infantry Regiment and graduated from Saint-Cyr shortly thereafter. During the interwar period, he fulfilled four missions to Indochina. Though deeply involved in colonial and military affairs, he demonstrated a real interest in the country and people. Between 1938 and 1940, he was deputy then chief of staff for Georges Mandel, then minister of Colonies. During World War II, Vichy assigned him to North Africa, where he crossed over to Free French forces when the Allies landed there in late 1942. He fought with the Americans against the Germans in North Africa. Named brigadier general, he landed in southern France in 1944 with the 9th Colonial Infantry Division and took part in the French and German campaigns. During the liberation of France, Morlière was replaced at the head of the 9th Colonial Infantry Division by the younger **Jean Valluy**. This had implications for the course of events in Vietnam in 1946.

In 1946, Morlière was sent to Indochina as commanding officer of French Forces in Northern Vietnam, where he would also serve as acting commissioner of the Republic for **Tonkin** and North **Annam** while Jean Sainteny was away in France. During this time, he did his best to respect the **Accords of 6 March 1946** in order to avoid war. Between August and December 1946, he did not prevent the **Democratic Republic of Vietnam**'s (DRV) efforts to shut down the anti-French non-communist parties, such as the **Vietnamese Nationalist Party** and the Dong Minh Hoi. Morlière increasingly found himself in disagreement with his superior in **Saigon**, Jean Valluy and his subordinate and chief of staff, Colonel **Pierre Debès**. The latter and Valluy shared **Georges Thierry d'Argenlieu's** open hostility for the DRV. Friction came into the open when Morlière tried to prevent Debès's hard-handed occupation of **Haiphong** in November 1946. The latter, however, had acted in Haiphong upon direct orders from Valluy.

Morlière's desire to reach a peaceful settlement displeased Valluy, Debès, and Thierry d'Argenlieu, all of whom increasingly sidelined Morlière in their plans and contacts with the Vietnamese. When colonel **Julien Fonde** reported on **Ho Chi Minh** and **Vo Nguyen Giap**'s refusal to accept any more ultimatums in December 1946, Morlière responded regretfully: "Yes, we are now headed for the irreparable. I have said it. I have written it. You know it full well… Alas! They [the DRV Vietnamese] are now resolved [to fight], I feel. They will persevere and fortify their blockade. And blood will cement their unity [of purpose]". On the basis of a recommendation signed by General **Philippe Leclerc**, Morlière left Indochina in February 1947, with a full-blown colonial war now underway. Between November and January, he wrote several reports on the Franco-Vietnamese crisis, some of which were leaked to the French press.

***MORT EN FRAUDE.*** Rare French film critical of the war in Indochina made by Marcel Camus. Adapted from Jean Hougron's novel of the same name, *Mort en Fraude* tells the story of a young Frenchman who debarks in Indochina around 1950 only to fall victim to a smuggler's scheme before realizing that his suffering is nothing compared to that of the Vietnamese who have long been victimized by colonialism. The Frenchman throws in his lot with the local resistance, discovers Vietnamese nationalism, and, in so doing, himself. Camus became much better known in France and abroad for his next film, *Black Orpheus*. *See also* CINEMA, DEMOCRATIC REPUBLIC OF VIETNAM; CINEMA, FRANCE; CULTURE; NOVELS.

**MOTAIS DE NARBONNE, LÉON (1906–1971).** Career colonial civil servant in Indochina. He first studied law in Aix-en-Provence before specializing in colonial law in the **Colonial Academy** (*École coloniale*) in Paris. He arrived in **Saigon** in 1932, where he made his career in the Indochinese colonial administration. Little is known of his activities during World War II. After the war, he remained in Indochina where he served as general delegate for the **Red Cross**. In 1948, he became advisor to the **French Union** for the **Associated States of Indochina**. In 1952, he represented the interests of the French *résident* within the Council of the French Republic. Motais was an ardent believer in the French Union and supporter of the Associated States of Indochina in collaboration with the French. However, the meltdown of the French presence in Indochina following the debacle at **Dien Bien Phu** left him bitter and disenchanted, although he continued to represent in France the interests of French residents in the Far East. *See also FRANÇAIS D'INDOCHINE.*

**MOTHERS OF GIO LINH.** Upon returning to Vietnam in 2005, the Vietnamese singer and song writer, **Pham Duy**, travelled to central Vietnam to retrace the steps that had first led him to compose one of his most powerful songs on the violence and sorrow of the Indochina War – *The Mothers of Gio Linh*. The song tells the true story of Vietnamese mothers whose sons – the commune head Nguyen Duc Ky and teacher Nguyen Phi – were beheaded by French Union soldiers in August 1948. Their severed heads were displayed along public roads to strike fear into other villagers tempted to support the **Viet Minh**. Both men were from Gio Linh village. During his service in the **Democratic Republic of Vietnam**, Pham Duy allowed this song to be used for propaganda purposes. However, the song continues to be sung to this day both in Vietnam and among overseas Vietnamese. *See also* ANTICOLONIALISM; BORIS VIAN; CAM LY, MASSACRE; EXPERIENCE OF WAR; MARTYR; MY THUY, MASSACRE; MYTH OF WAR; TORTURE.

**MOUNTBATTEN, LOUIS, LORD (1900–1979).** Served as the head of the British South East Asia Command responsible for accepting the Japanese surrender in much of Southeast Asia and in charge of occupying the southern half of former French Indochina below the **16th parallel** in accordance with decisions made at the **Potsdam conference.** Son of the German Prince Louis de Battenberg, Mountbatten was the Anglicization of the family name. Mountbatten began his career as a naval officer in 1916 during World War I. In 1939, he received his first important command, the destroyer *Kelly*, which was sunk off the coast of Crete in 1941. Churchill named him chief of Combined Operations in the Armed Forces in 1941. Mountbatten organized the disastrous raid on Dieppe in August 1942, but would apply the lessons learned from this experience to the planning of the successful Allied Landing at Normandy in 1944. In September 1943, he was named supreme commander of Allied Forces in South East Asia. He was in charge of British troops sent to accept the Japanese capitulation in former French Indochina below the 16th parallel from September 1945 to early March 1946. He absolved himself of any further responsibility at this date upon learning that the French General **Philippe Leclerc** was preparing an imminent invasion of northern Indochina by shipping forces from the south to the north. Mountbatten played a pivotal role in negotiating the independence of **India** in 1947, as well as that of **Burma**. *See also* 23 SEPTEMBER 1945; 19 DECEMBER 1946; DOUGLAS GRACEY; JEAN CÉDILE.

**MOUTET, MARIUS (1876–1968).** Ranking leader of the ***Section française de l'Internationale ouvrière*** in France, a defender of human rights, but also one of the most dedicated colonial minds of the 3rd and 4th Republics. He founded the first section of the *Ligue des droits de l'homme* in Lyon in 1914 and fought for more political rights for the "indigenous" in Algeria and dreamed of a "democratic colonization". He served as minister of the Colonies in 1936–1938. During this time, he implemented many reformist measures in the colonies, outlawing forced labor, freeing scores of political prisoners in Indochina, and even naming the first black man as colonial governor of Guadeloupe, Félix Eboué. In 1940, following the German defeat of the French, Moutet was one of 84 deputies who refused to vote in favor of according "full powers" to Philippe Pétain. As a result, Moutet was sidelined from the Vichy regime. After World War II, he served as minister of Overseas France in several governments. During this time, he met with **Ho Chi Minh** in an attempt to head off war, but to no avail. During his fact-finding mission to Indochina on behalf of **Léon Blum** in late December 1946 and January 1947, **Georges Thierry d'Argenlieu** prevented the **Democratic Republic of Vietnam** (DRV) from presenting to Moutet their side of the story behind the outbreak of war on **19 December 1946**. And now at war, Moutet was not particularly determined to sound out the Vietnamese. The renewal of talks would have to wait. He supported military operations. *See also* 23 SEPTEMBER 1945; 19 DECEMBER 1946; ACCORDS OF 6 MARCH 1946; *MODUS VIVENDI*.

***MOUVEMENT RÉPUBLICAIN POPULAIRE* (MRP).** In 1945–1946, the MRP participated in a French coalition government (with the socialists and communists). The MRP strongly opposed the decolonization of Indochina, supported the maintenance of the Empire, and backed Admiral **Georges Thierry d'Argenlieu**'s heavy-handed policies in Vietnam in 1945–1946 to re-establish colonial authority over Indochina, lost after the Japanese ***coup de force* of 9 March 1945**.

**Georges Bidault** was its most important leader during the Indochina War, serving as president and minister of Foreign Affairs during the crucial period between June and December 1946. Like **Charles de Gaulle**, Bidault was convinced that the Empire had and would continue to make France "grande", leading Bidault to adopt a hard line during the **Fontainebleau Conference** that ended in failure in September 1946. If the French were to let go in Vietnam, he reasoned, then they would soon be forced to do so in the rest of the Empire. The MRP supported colonial federalism with the French at the helm, but not decolonization along national lines, not even within a commonwealth. However, by owing so much to the person of Charles de Gaulle, Bidault and others found it hard to reverse or to adjust the former's orders to restore French colonial rule over Vietnam for fear of undermining their fragile domestic base and nationalist credentials.

The MRP's support of the aggressive High Commissioner Thierry d'Argenlieu in Indochina, the party's inability to grasp the historical reality of decolonization, and its hardline reactions to **Ho Chi Minh**'s attempts to negotiate a peaceful solution in 1946 all contributed to the outbreak of full-scale war on **19 December 1946**. The MRP continued to adopt a tough position on the war throughout the duration of the conflict. Rather than resuming negotiations with Ho Chi Minh, the party's leadership supported the **Bao Dai Solution**, granting to the former emperor what had been refused to Ho Chi Minh: national unity and independence. The problem, however, was that this French party was also opposed to granting real independence to the Associated State of Vietnam, something which further compromised the possibility of reaching a viable non-communist nationalist solution. *See also* ASSOCIATED STATES OF INDOCHINA; GENEVA ACCORDS.

**MUNE.** Collaborator with Prince **Phetxarāt** in Thailand who joined Prince **Suphānuvong** and his Vietnamese backers following the dissolution of the **Lao Issara** in 1949. Born in the Ban Keun region of Vientiane province, Mune began his career in the colonial bureaucracy in the *Garde des eaux et forêts* during the interwar period. Little is known about his activities during World War II. He joined the **Lao Issara** government in October 1945 and followed the government into exile in Thailand following the return of the French in mid-1946. He collaborated closely with Prince Phetxarāt in Thailand, but crossed over to Prince Suphānuvong's entourage upon the dissolution of the Lao Issara in 1949. He followed Suphānuvong to northern Vietnam to rebuild a new Lao Issara movement in association with the Vietnamese. In August 1950, Mune participated in the congress that created the **Lao Resistance Government** and a new national front. Between 1950 and 1954, he was apparently active in the area west of Vientiane. *See also* COLLABORATION; CROSSOVER.

**MƯỜI CÚC.** *See* NGUYỄN VĂN LINH.

**MƯỜI HƯƠNG.** *See* TRẦN QUỐC HƯƠNG.

**MUS, PAUL (CAILLE, 1902–1969).** French specialist in Asian cultures and one of the few **intellectuals** to speak out against the war in Indochina at the time. The son of a school teacher and colonial educator in Indochina, Mus grew up and worked in Vietnam until World War II. After graduating from the *Lycée Albert Sarraut* in **Hanoi**, he completed his studies in France under the French philosopher, pacificist, and his godfather, Alain. Mus's father was a **Freemason** and Mus may well have been one, too. Between 1921 and 1925, Mus obtained his undergraduate degree in philosophy and then began a career in Asian studies at the *École pratique des hautes études* and joined the *École française d'Extrême-Orient* as a permanent member in 1929. His subjects of research were as wide ranging as his interdisciplinary approach. He published a monumental study of *Borobudur* in 1935, analyzed the meaning of temples at Angkor, and traveled into Cham territories in central Vietnam. Mobilized in 1939, he saw brief but intense combat in France in 1940. Following the armistice, Vichy named him in 1941 Director of Education for French West Africa, a post he held until 1943.

Following the Allied landing in North Africa, Free French forces made him a lieutenant and sent him to Asia in light of his knowledge of Vietnamese and Indochina. He arrived in **India** under the code name *caille* (quail) and served in a **commando** unit preparing to be dropped into Indochina under **François de Langlade**, a representative of **Charles de Gaulle** in the Far East. In January 1945, Mus parachuted into southern Laos and made his way to Hanoi as head of a **psychological warfare** unit for the French resistance in Indochina. His mission was to make contact with Vietnamese elites to strengthen the internal resistance in Indochina. He met Admiral Jean Decoux but hardly had time to build up resistance networks before the Japanese struck. Indeed, Mus barely escaped from Hanoi during the Japanese ***coup de force* of 9 March 1945**.

As he was making his way into the countryside, he was deeply moved by the outpouring of Vietnamese nationalism he witnessed. It marked a turning in his thinking. While he remained a colonial humanist, he began to factor the reality of Vietnamese nationalism into his thinking. Back in Paris, he became political advisor to General **Philippe Leclerc** and accompanied him during the French reoccupation of southern Vietnam. In 1946, Mus returned to Paris and began warning French politicians of the dangers of not taking Vietnamese nationalism seriously. But de Gaulle brushed him away saying that "We will return to Indochina because we are stronger". Between 1946 and 1950, Mus served as director of the *École nationale de la France d'Outre-mer*, the former **Colonial Academy** (*École coloniale*). In December 1946, he joined the prestigious *Collège de France*, holding the Chair in *Civilisation d'Extrême-Orient*. In April 1947, **Émile Bollaert** charged Mus with delivering what amounted to an ultimatum to **Ho Chi Minh**. Mus traveled to the remote headquarters of the **Democratic Republic of Vietnam** (DRV) in the hills of **Tonkin**. Ho Chi Minh refused the French demands, telling Mus on 11 May: "*si nous acceptions cela, nous serions des lâches. Dans l'Union française, il n'y a pas de place pour les lâches*".

During the late 1940s, Mus became increasingly frustrated by and critical of French policy towards Vietnam. The breaking point came between August 1949 and January 1950 when he wrote a series of essays critical of French colonial policy and the use of torture in Indochina in the pages of the progressive Christian paper, ***Témoignage Chrétien.*** This cost him his job at the colonial academy and coincided with his decision to take up a teaching position in Southeast Asian studies at Yale University, where he alternated with teaching at the *Collège de France*. In 1952, he published his classic study of the (mainly DRV) Vietnamese and their revolution, *Viêt-Nam: Sociologie d'une guerre* and followed it up with a little-known book on the French colonial mind, entitled *Le destin de l'Union française: de l'Indochine à l'Afrique*, published in 1954 as the French colonial empire in Indochina came tumbling down.

His impact upon the American anti-war movement during the Vietnam War would turn out to be greater than his influence in France during the Indochina War. Frances Fitzgerald's *Fire in the Lake* was inspired by Mus's work. She dedicated her Pulitzer Prize-winning book to the former head of the French Colonial Academy. Together with **Philippe Devillers**, Mus was one of the first to write and teach about contemporary Vietnamese history in France and the United States in the wake of World War II. Mus, however, had little to say about the communist core driving the DRV; nationalism and colonialism were his post World War II research subjects. *See also* ALGERIAN WAR; ANTICOLONIALISM; BERNARD FALL; *ESPRIT*; JEAN CHESNEAUX; PAUL LEVY; PUBLIC OPINION.

**MUTINY.** *See* COURT MARTIAL.

**MỸ THỦY, MASSACRE.** According to Vietnamese sources and direct witnesses, in early 1948, **French Union** ground and naval forces opened fire on and bombed the village of My Thuy located on the coast of Quang Tri province, killing a total of 562 villagers, including women and children. French Union paratroopers then went on a shooting rampage in the village while naval assault forces used heavy cannons to flatten much of what was left of the village. It remained largely abandoned until 1975. As at My Lai during the American War, the scale of the massacre left an indelible scar on the village and poses enormous existential problems to this day for the survivors and their families. After 1975, with the end of the second Indochina War, villagers decided to build a small temple and altar in memory of those who had perished in My Thuy. It also serves as a sacred place to perform rituals to soothe the spirits of those who had been killed but whose souls continue to roam the land. While apparently reluctant at first to support such religious activities, Vietnamese communist authorities have since realized the importance of patronizing such important local initiatives for the sake of their own political legitimacy. In 2001, the Ministry of Culture and Information officially recognized My Thuy village as a national monument and in 2005 the government invested 500 million *dong* to create a temple on the site where the massacre occurred. This temple allows those who lost loved ones to perform the needed religious rituals of ancestor worship. It also serves as a powerful local site of memory symbolizing the sorrow generated by the Indochina War. *See also* CAM LY, MASSACRE; CASUALTIES; CEMETERIES; EXPERIENCE OF WAR; HÉRAULT, MASSACRE; MARTYR; MYTH OF WAR; NECROPOLIS, FRÉJUS; TORTURE.

**MYTH OF WAR, DEMOCRATIC REPUBLIC OF VIETNAM.** To this day, communist party accounts of the Indochina war focus on the heroism of the combatants and the glorious victory that they achieved on the battlefields leading to **Dien Bien Phu** on 7 May 1954. For the **Democratic Republic of Vietnam**, the victory of Dien Bien Phu is a vital chapter in the party's inevitable march towards complete victory in 1975 (*nhat dinh thang loi*) and an integral part of its nationalist legitimacy.

With almost a million and a half dead by 1975, the party has confirmed George Mosse's myth of the experience of war by creating an elaborate national cult in honour of its "fallen soldiers", complete with shrines for **martyrs,** war **cemeteries,** and monuments. Through an array of official publications, school textbooks, and documentaries, the party not only defines but also controls the meaning of the war.

To challenge the heroic myth of war in communist Vietnam is thus to invite the wrath of the leadership. And yet a veteran of the Vietnam War, Bao Ninh, did just that in 1991, when he dared to write of the "sorrow" of war and the indescribable suffering it inflicted upon soldiers and civilians. Instead of speaking of heroism, Bao Ninh spoke of the ugliness of war, the bloody dismemberment of comrades hit by American shells. He even questioned whether the party's wars were worth it all in the end as communism gave way to capitalism in the early 1990s. Caught off guard by one of its own soldiers, the party lashed out, aghast that this heroic soldier could speak of such things, but worried that his account could undermine the leadership's control over the meaning of the war. Thirty years earlier, another veteran, **Tran Dan**, had tried to describe something of the "reality" of the battle violence he had witnessed as a soldier-artist at Dien Bien Phu. With an eye on the competing Vietnam taking form in the south after the **Geneva Accords**, the party made sure that his account of Dien Bien Phu, published in 1955, stayed on nationalist cue. When he began to stray, the party shut him down for thirty years.

Until very recently, to write about the "real" face of war in Vietnam, above all that of the historic battle of Dien Bien Phu, is to challenge the most powerful myth of the regime – heroic, sacred, patriotic resistance (*cuoc khang chien than thanh*). *See also* CAO BANG; EXPERIENCE OF WAR, DIEN BIEN PHU; MYTH OF WAR, FRANCE; NASAN.

**MYTH OF WAR, FRANCE.** In France, veterans of the Indochina War and veteran associations and their families have been actively involved in defining the meaning of the Indochina War. No sooner had the Indochina conflict ended in 1954 than a small but highly influential group of veterans adopted the themes of "tragedy" and "abandonment" by the government in order to sacralize the soldier and by extension the army's "heroic" and "noble" role in the Indochina War. Writers, most notably **Jean Lartéguy**, had developed the idea of "*les centurions*", the title of one of his legendary semi-fictional novels, who soldiered on nobly against all hope in France's long wars of decolonization. **Roger Delpey** popularized the idea further in *Soldats de la boue*, a series of *romans de gares* in which he celebrated France's heroic, forgotten soldiers. Other authors never hesitated to evoke the idea of a government stab in the back.

No one man has contributed more to popularizing the "noble" meaning of the army's role in France's colonial wars than **Pierre Schoendoerffer**, novelist, film producer, "Indo" veteran, and a former member of the army's official photographic service during the conflict. To Schoendoerffer, the soldiers of France's colonial wars were unsung heroes, who had been sacrificed by inept politicians and abandoned. Heroic tragedy is Schoendoerffer's favorite theme. When asked what he felt about the Indochina debacle, he replied: *La honte. La rage d'avoir été abandonné par la France*. This message comes through clearly in the *317ème section*; the entire film is focused on a lone combat unit desperately trying to escape annihilation as its French commanders learn of the fall of **Dien Bien Phu**. Anti-communist, Schoendoerffer declared in 1984 that he would never return to Vietnam because of what happened. He did, however, in order to film *Dien Bien Phu* in 1992, yet another heroic commemoration of the besieged French men fighting on during the battle of Dien Bien Phu. At the heart of his reflection, however, is an ardent desire to legtimate military defeat and erase humiliation by recasting it in national terms as a sacred sacrifice.

A variety of veteran associations share his point of view and Schoendoerffer's efforts to cast the Indochina War in tragic yet purifying terms. As the latter put it to the *Association nationale des anciens d'Indochine* on the meaning of Dien Bien Phu and his film on it 40 years later: "*tout était donc perdu. Alors, dans un ultime sursaut, des centaines et des centaines d'hommes obscurs et ordinaires vinrent, non pour redresser une situation désormais sans espoir, mais pour maintenir jusqu'au bout et le plus haut possible quelque chose qui ressemblait à une certaine idée de la France*".

It is this "certain idea of France", an all too obvious allusion to **Charles de Gaulle**'s nationalist justification to fight on in 1940 for the "real France", that provides the nationalist source for this mythic reading of the Indochina War. In the 1980s, as the American government stepped up its search for the missing in action and Ronald Reagan led the charge to recast the American commitment to Vietnam as a noble effort, veteran associations in France mobilized, multiplied, and pushed for wider official and public recognition of their cause and its positive role in the French nation. Monuments emerged in France and even in communist Vietnam honoring the sacrifice of the army. These veterans associations latched on to the **Boudarel affair** in the early 1990s in order to make their case and advance their cause, not without considerable success. Leading the charge against **Georges Boudarel** was **Erwan Bergot**, a novelist, nationalist, and veteran of the Indochina War. Like the Vietnamese myth of war, this French one does not seek to question or understand the reasons for the French involvement in the Indochina or **Algerian Wars**. That is not what myths are designed to do. *See also* ANTI-COLONIALISM; *ASSOCIATION NATIONALE DES ANCIENS D'INDOCHINE ET DU SOUVENIR INDOCHINOIS*; *ASSOCIATION NATIONALE DES ANCIENS ET AMIS DE L'INDOCHINE ET DU SOUVENIR INDOCHINOIS*; *ASSOCIATION NATIONALE DES ANCIENS PRISONNIERS ET INTERNÉS D'INDOCHINE*; *ASSOCIATION NATIONALE DES COMBATTANTS DE DIEN BIEN PHU*; ASSOCIATION OF MOTHERS OF SOLDIERS; COMICS AND WAR; EXPERIENCE OF WAR; MARCEL BIGEARD; MISSING IN ACTION; REMAINS; PIERRE LANGLAIS; WAR MEMORIAL, DIEN BIEN PHU.

# N

**NA SAN, BATTLE OF.** In late 1952, in a bid to block the advance of the **Democratic Republic of Vietnam**'s (DRV) army into northwestern Vietnam and Laos, General **Raoul Salan** transformed Na San, a small upland village located along the Lao border, into a major entrenched position. Some 20,000 men were transferred to Na San to turn it into a "*usine de guerre fabuleuse pour l'époque*". At the height of the work, Dakota planes were landing or taking off every 15 minutes. The French dug trenches, installed heavy artillery, and built an airbase to supply the camp from afar. A defensive fortress, supplied by air, was thus waiting for the Vietnamese when they attacked.

General **Vo Nguyen Giap** was confident that he could take the isolated camp and consolidate his hold over strategically important Tai regions in northwestern Vietnam and northern Laos. He had taken **Nghia Lo** from the French earlier that year; he counted on doing the same at Na San. However, his intelligence services failed to provide him with accurate information on the new type of defensive war Salan was preparing for him in Na San. On 30 November, Vo Nguyen Giap sent waves of his troops from the 308th and 312th divisions against the camp. He was shocked by the ferocity of the French reponse. Enemy artillery and aerial bombing decimated his men attacking under the cover of night. Indeed, French artillery fired 5,600 mortars alone during the night of 30 November–1 December. No sooner had the battle started than Giap had to call it off on 2 December 1952. The Vietnamese lacked the artillery they needed to knock out such a fortified position. Nor did they have the logistical capacities to transport large quantities of such artillery to the battlefield. Vo Nguyen Giap also realized that his inability to take out the airstrip meant that the French could continue to supply the camp. Instead of taking Na San, the Vietnamese simply decided to go around it and a few months later Salan pulled his troops out of Na San.

While Na San was a crushing defeat, the DRV also learned precious lessons. Vo Nguyen Giap sent intelligence teams back to the battlefield to study the fortified camp carefully. Indeed, the lessons of Na San served the DRV well when the French decided, in the following year, to set up "a super Na San" not too far away, in a valley named **Dien Bien Phu**. What General **Henri Navarre** (and others) did not anticipate was that the Vietnamese would deliver their artillery to Dien Bien Phu and knock out the French airstrip early on. For both the French and the Vietnamese, Na San and Dien Bien Phu were thus closely intertwined. As one French analyst has correctly described French strategy: "*Dien Bien Phu est inscrit dans Na San*". No Vietnamese military historian worth his mettle would disagree. For Na San was an integral part of DRV preparations for Dien Bien Phu.

**NAISON SICHAN.** *See* NGÔ THẤT SƠN.

**NAM.** *See* TÔ KÝ.

**NĂM BI.** *See* HỒ THỊ BI.

**NAM BỘ.** *See* COCHINCHINA.

**NAM CAO (1919–1951).** Vietnamese **intellectual** who ardently defended the cause of the **Democratic Republic of Vietnam** during the Indochina War. Nam Cao distinguished himself in the 1940s for his realist and psychologically nuanced descriptions of the daily life and world of the Vietnamese peasants and local teachers in northern Vietnam. He also became a militant communist during this time and put his cultural and literary talents in the service of the **Indochinese Communist Party** and the fight against the French. While he continued to write works of literary value, he also took an active part in the war on the propaganda front. While on a mission to mobilize populations behind enemy lines in 1951, he died during an enemy ambush.

**NĂM ĐẠO.** *See* HOÀNG MINH ĐÀO.

**NĂM ĐỜI.** *See* HOÀNG MINH ĐÀO.

**NAM HÙNG.** *See* NGUYỄN CHÍ THANH.

**NAM KỲ**. *See* COCHINCHINA.

**NĂM LỬA.** *See* TRẦN VĂN SOÁI.

**NAM PHƯƠNG (1914–1963).** Wife of **Bao Dai** and Empress of Vietnam until 1945. A French national and Catholic, her full name was Marie-Thérèse Nguyen Huu Thi Lan. Born in Go Cong province in southern Vietnam, she studied at the *Couvent des Oiseaux* in Dalat. In 1934, she married Bao Dai and adopted the dynastic name of Nam Phuong (the Southern Direction). The couple had five children: Crown Prince Bao Long, Phuong Mai, Phuong Lien, Phuong Dung, and Bao Thang. In 1939, despite the Vatican's opposition to her marriage with a non-Catholic, she visited Rome and met the pope in an official audience. With the advent of the **Democratic Republic of Vietnam**, she and her husband initially supported the new Vietnamese government when Bao Dai abdicated. In early 1946, when Admiral **Georges Thierry d'Argenlieu** offered to restore the monarchy in exchange for their **collaboration**, she apparently sent his emissaries packing. In January 1947, she escaped with her children from Hue, as war between the French and the DRV engulfed the imperial capital. They went to live in Dalat before rejoining Bao Dai in Hong Kong. Later in 1947, she and the children moved to *Chateau Thorenz* near Cannes. In 1963, she died of a heart attack in Cabrignac, France.

**NĂM THU.** *See* HOÀNG MINH ĐÀO.

**NAM TIẾN.** *See* ADVANCE SOUTHERN UNITS.

**NAM XUÂN.** *See* MAI CHÍ THỌ.

**NAPALM.** Derived from the combination of the words "naphthene" and "palmitate", napalm is a highly incendiary jelly which the Americans developed and began to deliver by air as incendiary bombs during World War II. From 1950, thanks to supplies from the Americans, the French **Air Force** began using napalm bombs in Indochina against the armed forces of the **Democratic Republic of Vietnam**, though civilians were often victims of its use. Napalm not only burns its targets, but it also deoxygenates the area within its zone, often causing death to humans and **animals** by asphyxiation. Vietnamese sources have long revealed that the French use of napalm was a horrifying experience. As Ngo Van Chieu described his platoon's first experience with it in early 1951: "Hell first came in the form of ovide containers dropped by the first and then by a second plane. Then, in an instant, an immense wall of fire running for hundred of meters terrorized my men. That's napalm! Fire that falls from the sky… Was that an atomic bomb, asked one of my men, his pupils dilated by fear. No, it's napalm!" During the battle of **Dien Bien Phu**, the French used American-supplied "Flying Boxcar" C-119s to drop more than six tons of napalm on enemy communication lines and targets located around the battlefield.

**NATIONAL ANTHEM, DEMOCRATIC REPUBLIC OF VIETNAM.** Nguyen Van Cao first wrote what became the **Democratic Republic of Vietnam**'s (DRV) national anthem in 1944 in a secret hideout in the north. He refined it and published it in the **Viet Minh**'s clandestine newspaper, *Doc Lap*, as *Tien Quan Ca (March to the Front)*. It was used during the **August Revolution** in **Hanoi** in 1945, became the official national anthem of the DRV in 1946, and was used in government **Inter-Zones** throughout the Indochina War. *Tien Quan Ca* became the national anthem for all of Vietnam following the DRV's reunification of the country under Hanoi's communist rule in 1976.

**NATIONAL ANTHEM, REPUBLIC OF VIETNAM.** The origins of the national anthem of the **Republic of Vietnam** are to be found in the marching song *Appeal to the Youth* (*Tieng Goi Thanh Nien),* composed by Luu Huu Phuoc. The **Tran Trong Kim** government declared independent by the Japanese after the overthrow of the French in March 1945 first used it as its national anthem. Even though Luu Huu Phuoc went on to become a member of the **Viet Minh** and the **Vietnamese Worker's Party**, the Republic of Vietnam decided in 1955 to keep the song as its national anthem on the grounds that it remained a national asset and that Luu Huu Phuoc was not a communist when he first composed the song.

***NATIONAL DEFENSE REVIEW* (*Quốc Phòng Toàn Dân*).** The official military review of the **People's Army of Vietnam** under the control of the Ministry of Defense and the **Central Party Military Committee** (*Quan Uy*). It first came to life in April 1948 under the name *Quan Su Tap San* and then *Quan Chinh Tap San*. In August 1957, it became officially known as the *Vietnamese Army Review* (*Tap Chi Quan Doi Nhan Dan*). It kept that name until April 1988, when it became *Quoc Phong Toan Dan*.

**NATIONAL MILITARY ACADEMY, ASSOCIATED STATE OF VIETNAM.** *See* ACADEMY, ASSOCIATED STATE OF VIETNAM.

**NATIONAL SALVATION ARMY (*Cứu Quốc Quân*).** This small militia came to life in 1941 after the failed Bac Son uprising in northern Vietnam. Under the leadership of the **Indochinese Communist Party** (ICP), it operated at the squadron level and was more involved in protecting party leaders and obtaining food from villagers than in conducting serious military manoeuvres. **Chu Van Tan** was the driving force behind the National Salvation Army.

**NATIONAL SALVATION NEWSPAPER (*Báo Cứu Quốc*).** On 21 January 1942, this paper became the official mouthpiece for the General Directorate of the **Viet Minh** (*Tong Bo Viet Minh*) for which the provisional general secretary of the **Indochinese Communist Party**, **Truong Chinh**, was directly responsible. At the outset, it was secretly published in Ha Dong in the office of the Party's Territorial Committee for Tonkin (*Xu Uy Bac Ky*). With the advent of the **Democratic Republic of Vietnam** in September 1945, it was published in **Hanoi**. **Xuan Thuy** replaced Truong Chinh to run the paper from this point. Other members of the editorial team included **Tran Huy Lieu,** Nhu Phong, **Xuan Dieu** and Pham Van Hao.

**NAVARRE, HENRI EUGÈNE (1898–1983).** French general who made the decision to fight at **Dien Bien Phu**. Graduated from Saint-Cyr in 1917, Navarre served on the Western Front during World War I. He made his career as a specialist of Germany in the intelligence services and in the colonial army in Africa. In 1940, he worked as head of the 2nd Office for General Weygand in North Africa before crossing over to Free French forces under General **Jean de Lattre de Tassigny**. Navarre was named colonel in March 1944 and commanded French occupation forces in Germany between 1945 and 1948. Transferred to Algeria, he commanded the Division of Constantine between 1948 and 1949. Named major general in 1950, he returned to Germany in 1952 as deputy commander of French Forces. In 1952, he was named lieutenant general and ran the General Staff for Marshal **Alphonse Juin** in charge of Allied Forces in Central Europe.

When French authorities began to look for a younger, more dynamic officer to replace General **Raoul Salan** in Indochina, premier **René Mayer** selected Navarre for the job. In May 1953, Navarre became commander of French armed forces in Indochina. Navarre devised a plan, approved by the government, to create the necessary military conditions in Indochina to allow the government to negotiate an end to the war from a position of strength. At the heart of **Navarre's plan** was operation **Atlante**, designed to retake much of central Vietnam from the adversary. However, when the **Democratic Republic of Vietnam**'s forces seemed determined to take Laos, Navarre decided to block them by digging in at Dien Bien Phu. While Dien Bien Phu was second in importance to central Vietnam for Navarre, he remained nonetheless determined to use the valley to break the Vietnamese army if it dared to attack the entrenched camp as had happened during the battle of **Na San**.

Navarre erred badly by underestimating his enemy and by overestimating his own tactics and strategy. It cost him the battle when the Vietnamese, supported by the Chinese, delivered the artillery to positions surrounding Dien Bien Phu, calibrated it with devastating effectiveness, and took out the vital airstrip. On 7 May 1954, the French camp fell to the Vietnamese. In June 1954, Navarre lost his job in Indochina when General **Paul Ely** replaced him. Navarre returned to France in June 1954 and retired from the army in 1956, humiliated and bitter. He published a defense of his actions in *Agonie de l'Indochine*. *See also* DIEN BIEN PHU, BATTLE PREPARATION AND CONTEXT; GENEVA ACCORDS; NAVARRE PLAN.

**NAVARRE PLAN**. The Navarre Plan owes its name to **Henri Navarre**, the general the **Joseph Laniel** government selected to take over in Indochina until an acceptable negotiated settlement could be reached to end the war in Indochina. Laniel's Prime Minister **René Mayer** was a strong believer in strengthening France's role in Europe and the Atlantic community; the Indochina War had diverted France's attention from this priority. Financially, France could no longer afford to undertake a war in Indochina and contribute to European defense at the same time. An "honorable end" (*une sortie honorable*) to the Indochina War thus had to be reached. With this in mind, on 8 May 1953, the Laniel government named Navarre commander-in-chief of the armed forces in Indochina. The government instructed Navarre to create the necessary military conditions for an acceptable political solution to the war.

In this context, Navarre devised a plan for 1953–1954 designed to avoid large-scale battles with the enemy in order to rebuild **French Union** forces. In 1954–1955, the army would deliver decisive military blows to the army of the **Democratic Republic of Vietnam** (DRV) in order to force the enemy to the negotiating table on terms favorable to the French. During the period of 1953–1954, Navarre decided to adopt a defensive posture in the north and avoid engaging the DRV's main divisions, while moving much more aggressively against weaker forces in southern and especially central Vietnam, which had been under enemy control since the start of the war in 1945–1946. The Americans were involved in the making of the plan and paid most of its bill, hoping to keep the French in the war and containment alive without having to commit troops themselves. In July 1953, the French government approved the "Navarre Plan". Upon arriving in Indochina, Navarre focused his attention on the Red River Delta and prepared his main offensive, operation **Atlante**, against DRV positions in **Inter-Zone V** (*Lien Khu V*).

In September 1953, thanks in part to the Chinese, the DRV's intelligence services acquired a good understanding of the basic elements of the Navarre Plan and the **General Staff** used it in preparing the 1953–1954 Winter Spring Campaign. **Ho Chi Minh** concluded from this that Navarre was "massing his forces to occupy and hold the **Tonkin** lowlands, so we will force him to disperse his forces out to other sectors so that we can annihilate them". Indeed, rather than trying to attack the delta, where the French could concentrate their artillery and air power easily on the attacking forces, the Politburo decided to disperse the French, taking advantage of the rougher terrain in northwest Tonkin and Laos. The idea was to disperse the French as much as possible by attacking towards the northwest at Lai Chau and Phongsaly in Laos, then towards central and southern Laos, even as far as northeast Cambodia. The third move would be to mobilize **guerrillas** behind enemy lines.

It was in this context that Navarre surprised the Vietnamese, when he decided to commit to a battle in remote **Dien Bien Phu** in order to block the DRV from taking Laos although that was never the latter's strategic intention. Nor had Navarre's decision to occupy Dien Bien Phu been a part of his initial "plan". His main objective was and remained operation Atlante against Inter-Zone V. What reassured **Vo Nguyen Giap** was Navarre's decision to deviate from his own initial plan to take on the Vietnamese at Dien Bien Phu and his simultaneous commitment to executing operation Atlante. In the Politburo's view, operation Atlante only contributed to dispersing French forces away from what now became the DRV's growing fixation on winning at Dien Bien Phu. Vo Nguyen Giap was now determined to knock out the airbase, bring in the artillery needed to make it happen, and create the logistics needed to inflict a major battle defeat on the French at Dien Bien Phu before opening negotiations in Geneva. The Politburo and National Assembly officially approved **land reform** in December 1953, vital to mobilizing the troops and manpower to supply the battlefield for this showdown.

On 13 May, hours after learning by radio that the French were attacking in central Vietnam, Vo Nguyen Giap launched his attack. On 7 May 1954, the French camp at Dien Bien Phu fell to DRV forces, while Navarre's attempt to take back central Vietnam ended in failure. The Navarre plan never got a second chance. The **Geneva Accords** put a political end to the war on 21 July 1954.

**NAVY, ASSOCIATED STATE OF VIETNAM.** Like the army, the French **Navy** came under budgetary pressure to increase the number of Lao, Cambodians, and especially Vietnamese in its ranks. With the creation of the Associated State of Vietnam in 1949, the French were in a position to push for the creation of a Vietnamese navy capable of working with them. In 1951, the French established a naval training center in Nha Trang with the goal of training a Vietnamese river police force and coast guard. In 1952, the French initiated a naval academy to train Vietnamese officers in Nha Trang, while other candidates trained at the Naval Academy in France. In 1954, the Associated State of Vietnam's navy counted 22 naval officers and 750 sailors, not a particularly large number compared to the some 10,000 French navy men serving in Indochina. French naval officers continued to oversee the Associated State's fledgling navy until the end of the war. The real take-off in the Vietnamese navy occurred under the **Republic of Vietnam** during the Vietnam War.

**NAVY, DEMOCRATIC REPUBLIC OF VIETNAM.** On 5 September 1949, the **General Staff** of the **Democratic Republic of Vietnam** (DRV) established a "Naval Studies Section" to begin work on creating a navy. The government instructed this section to begin training officers in coastal and astronomical navigation and developing maritime supply routes between southeastern China and eastern Vietnam. A special naval unit called "Company 71" traveled to south-eastern China in 1950–1951 to undergo intensive training. However, Chinese communist knowledge of modern naval techniques was spotty at best and had never been a priority for Chinese communists based since the 1930s deep inside China. The **People's Republic of China** thus provided little modern naval training at this point. Nor did the Soviet Union. Back in Vietnam, Company 71 nonetheless initiated efforts to open water routes between southern China and Hainan and the bay of Ha Long and central Vietnam. The results were very limited, however. The main Chinese supply lines going to Vietnam remained overland ones. In the end, naval operations remained rudimentary and focused on using Vietnam's myriad of rivers and estuaries. The DRV Navy had no modern war vessels at this time, and the French **Navy**, backed increasingly by the US from 1950, monitored effectively the South China Sea and the Gulf of Siam. However, during the battle of **Dien Bien Phu**, the DRV mobilized hundreds of river crafts to transport rice, men, weapons, artillery and even trucks to the frontlines. *See also* HO CHI MINH TRAIL.

**NAVY, FRENCH.** The French naval force in Indochina was referred to as the *Forces maritimes d'Extrême Orient* (FMEO). It was at first represented in Indochina by the aircraft carrier *Arromanches*, carrying the 3rd Carrier Assault Squadron equipped with SB2C Helldivers and the 11th Carrier Fighter Squadron equipped with F6F Hellcats. The French navy also deployed six heavy Privateer Bombers of Squadron 28F. During the Indochina War, some 10,000 French Navy men served mainly in Vietnam and by the end of the conflict in 1954 1,038 men had been killed or were missing in action. Because the **Democratic Republic of Vietnam** had no real navy of which to speak and because neither the Soviets nor the Chinese communists supported their Vietnamese ally by sea, the FMEO was never engaged in classic naval battles during the entire Indochina conflict. Instead, the navy focused on coastal surveillance and transport, moving both by sea and up Vietnam's long coastlines or penetrating into its myriad of rivers, canals, and coves. The coastal surveillance operation, known as SURMAR (*surveillance maritime*), patrolled the Indochinese coast from Thai waters in the Gulf of Siam to the Gulf of **Tonkin** bordering southern China. Its main goal was to stop the enemy's clandestine, inter-zonal traffic especially active from departure points in the central **Inter-Zones IV** and **V**. Between 1948 and 1952, SURMAR's vessels inspected some 30,000 junks and sampans and destroyed or confiscated more than 17,000 of them, taking 4,000 tons of rice, 2,500 tons of salt, 284 tons sugar as well as weapons and medicines. The French Navy played a pivotal role in debarking French troops in central and northern Vietnam in 1946 as well as during the battle of **Dien Bien Phu**. Of the 10,400 air missions operated during the battle between 20 November 1953 and 8 May 1954, 1,267 were flown by the French Navy. In April 1954, as the battle raged at Dien Bien Phu, the Americans loaned the *Belleau Wood* aircraft carrier to the French, manned by French personnel. The French navy also helped transport tens of thousands of Vietnamese leaving northern Vietnam for the south following the signing of the **Geneva Accords** ending the war in July 1954. On 15 May 1955, the French navy evacuated the last **French Union** troops from northern Vietnam.

**NECROPOLIS, FRÉJUS.** In 1986, the French and Vietnamese governments signed a protocol for the repatriation of the remains of **French Union** soldiers killed in Vietnam between 1940 and 1954. On 10 October 1986, Jacques Chirac, then prime minister, received at Roissy airport the first coffins carrying the remains of French Union Forces killed during the Indochina War. In all, some thirty thousand remains were returned over the next year or so. As a result, the French government decided to create a necropolis in Fréjus to receive, inhume, and memorialize many of these soldiers *morts pour la France*, as well as a select number of civilians killed during the conflict. Officials ended up selecting the southern town of Fréjus because of its colonial past, having served as the principle camp through which thousands of French troops had passed on their way to the colonies since the 19th century. Fréjus was also home to the *Musée des troupes de la Marine*. In 1993, socialist President François Mitterand inaugurated the National Necropolis at Fréjus. It is currently home to the remains of 17,250 soldiers of diverse nationalities of the former French Union. The remains of over 3,000 "unknown victims" rest in the crypt inside the necropolis. The memorial belongs to the French state and is administered by the state secretary to the Ministry of Defense in charge of veteran's affairs. The local chapter of the veteran affairs in Marseille manages the site. The final addition to the necropolis was the memorial wall, *Mur du souvenir*. Inscribed on it are the names of the some 34,000 *morts pour la France* whose bodies are not held in the necropolis. This "wall of memory" was inspired by Maya Lin's Vietnam memorial in the United States. *See also ASSOCIATION NATIONALE DES ANCIENS D'INDOCHINE ET DU SOUVENIR INDOCHINOIS*; *ASSOCIATION NATIONALE DES ANCIENS ET AMIS DE L'INDOCHINE ET DU SOUVENIR INDOCHINOIS*; *ASSOCIATION NATIONALE DES ANCIENS PRISONNIERS ET INTERNÉS D'INDOCHINE*; *ASSOCIATION NATIONALE DES COMBATTANTS DE DIEN BIEN PHU*; ASSOCIATION OF MOTHERS OF SOLDIERS; CEMETERIES; COMICS AND WAR; EXPERIENCE OF WAR; MISSING IN ACTION; MYTH OF WAR; REMAINS; WAR MEMORIAL, DIEN BIEN PHU.

**NEHRU, JAWAHARLAL (1889–1964). Indian** statesman and supporter of a peaceful solution to the Indochina War. Educated at Harrow School and at Trinity College, Cambridge, Nehru became a lawyer in colonial **India** and worked in a colonial high court. In 1918, he joined the Indian National Congress and, together with Mahatma Gandhi, transformed it into a major Indian independence party. During the interwar period, he met a number of Vietnamese leaders, including the constitutionalists Bui Quang Chieu and Duong Van Giao. The British arrested and imprisoned Nehru on numerous occasions for his nationalist activities. Following World War II, he negotiated India's independence with the British and, after partition and creation of Pakistan, became India's first prime minister in 1947, a post he held until 1964. As decolonization moved through the region, Nehru sought to position India at the center of a new Asian era. He even dreamed of creating and leading an Asian Union. To this effect, he organized the Inter-Asian Conference in New Delhi in 1947 and another a few years later.

Of particular concern to him were Dutch and French attempts to restore their colonial control over Indochina and **Indonesia**. In both cases, Nehru expressed his sympathy for the Vietnamese and Indonesian nationalist movements. He was also distraught at the idea that the spread of the **Cold War** into the region, especially with the emergence of two Vietnams in January–February 1950 and the outbreak of the **Korean War** a few months later, would allow other non-Asian powers to interfere in what he felt should be a purely Asian, postcolonial affair.

Significantly, he took a much more active role in support for the Indonesian war than he did for the **Democratic Republic of Vietnam** (DRV). Despite the DRV's plea for concrete Indian aid against the French, Nehru would only concede "moral" support. He even made a point of allowing the French-backed Indochinese governments to send delegates to the conferences he organized, thereby according them the same treatment as the DRV. Part of the problem was that Nehru did not want to undermine his negotiations with the French over the return of Pondicherry. Part of the problem was also the communist core running the DRV, unlike the Indonesian Republicans fighting the Dutch. Nowhere was this clearer than in Nehru's refusal to recognize diplomatically in 1950 either of the two Vietnams led by **Ho Chi Minh** and **Bao Dai**. This allowed Nehru to renew his calls for a peaceful settlement of the wars in Korea and in Indochina.

Indeed, during the **Geneva Conference**, Nehru agreed to play an increasingly important role in ensuring peace. During the conference, he met privately with **Zhou Enlai** at a crucial meeting in late June to support China's move to neutralize non-communist Asia against the Americans in exchange for a Chinese promise not to export communism outside their borders and to recognize the royal governments of Laos and Cambodia. Nehru also agreed that India would be willing to join a commission to control a cease-fire. Consequently, India joined Poland and Canada as the three members of the **International Commission for Supervision and Control in Vietnam**. In part because of the Indochinese question, Nehru intensified his efforts with others in the region to carve out a "non-aligned" course of action. In 1955, he co-organized with Indonesian President Sukarno the Bandung Conference. It was no accident that this historic meeting occurred less than a year after the signing of the Geneva Accords. On 17 October 1954, Nehru visited **Hanoi** for the first time. *See also* BURMA; NEUTRALIZATION OF INDOCHINA.

**NER, MARCEL.** French educator in Indochina who became a vocal critic of the French war in Vietnam. Graduated a certified educator in philosophy (*agrégé*) in 1925, he began teaching this subject in Indochina in August 1926 at the *Lycée Albert Sarraut*. The future Vietnamese General **Vo Nguyen Giap** was one of his pupils in the 1930s; the two remained in contact during the difficult times of 1945–1946. In the early 1930s, Ner closely followed Vietnamese socio-political debates, published articles to this effect in *France-Indochine*, and transmitted a political petition (*cahier de voeux*) written by Pham Quynh and Pham Huy Luc to the colonial government in 1931. Like Pham Quynh and Pham Huy Luc, Ner was also a **Freemason**. His research focused on upland peoples in Indochina and he thrived on his **collaboration** with scholars at the ***École française d'Extrême-Orient*** in the 1930s, including **Paul Mus**.

During the Japanese ***coup de force* of 9 March 1945**, Ner escaped from Tam Dao with a dozen of his students before they made their way to southern China and eventually back to France via Calcutta in July 1945, thanks to the support of the French Ambassador to the **Republic of China**. Ner returned to Indochina in September 1945 and was named in October advisor *par interim* to the high commissioner on educational matters. Between April 1946 and August 1947, he served as director of Education in Indochina. He participated in preparations for the **Dalat Conference** in April 1946 and **Ho Chi Minh**'s trip to France for negotiations at **Fontainebleau** a few months later.

Like Paul Mus, Ner understood that Vietnamese nationalism was an historical reality that could not be ignored and he ended up supporting Vietnamese claims to independence. His views became more pronounced as the war dragged on. He participated in a special issue published by **Jean-Paul Sartre**'s *Les Temps Modernes* (August – September 1953) supporting Vietnamese independence and critical of French colonial policies. He met with the DRV delegation in Geneva in mid-1954. During this time, he continued to work as a respected ethnologist, publishing works on the Cham in central Vietnam.

**NEUTRALIZATION OF INDOCHINA.** To different degrees, the Chinese, Soviets, British, Indians, and the French were the biggest defenders of the "neutralization" of Indochina during the **Geneva Conference** of 1954. Since 1950, the leaders of **India**, **Indonesia**, and **Burma** had refused to recognize diplomatically either of the two Vietnams led by **Ho Chi Minh** and **Bao Dai**. All were wary of allying themselves in the **Cold War** now making its way violently into the region via Korea and northern Vietnam. Chinese and Vietnamese communist talk of spreading revolution further into the region did little to reassure Indians, Burmese, and Indonesians, nor did American pressure on them to join with the West to "contain" communism.

By 1953, however, Chinese strategists had begun to revise their hostile attitude to these non-communist Asian states. The reluctance of the latter to throw in their lot with the West held out the hope that the Chinese could tap into decolonization and anti-colonialism in order to improve relations with these states, and thereby thwart American attempts to turn them against Beijing on anti-communist grounds. Chinese negotiators arriving in Geneva were particularly determined to reach an accord on Indochina that would prevent the United States from replacing the French and creating a Southeast Asian anti-communist security pact. Talk was in the air of just such a grand strategy and of course the Chinese did not need to be reminded of the importance of Japan, Taiwan and South Korea as beachheads in American containment in the Far East.

Just weeks before the opening of the Geneva conference, Zhou Enlai reached an agreement with **Jawaharlal Nehru** over Tibet, allowing the two Asian giants to normalize their relations for the first time and embrace the five principles of co-existence of *Pansheela*. At a crucial juncture in the Geneva negotiations, Zhou Enlai personally travelled to New Delhi in late June 1954 to meet Pandit Nehru, promising him that Beijing would not export communism to the region and that China's Vietnamese allies would not try to make all of Indochina communist. Zhou Enlai made good on his pledge when he recognized the reality of the royal governments in Cambodia and Laos. Zhou Enlai made a similar trip to **Burma** before meeting with Ho Chi Minh at **Liuzhou** in early

July 1954. During this important meeting, Zhou Enlai informed Ho Chi Minh that the Chinese supported the emergence of Southeast Asian Nations of a "New Type", referring to non-communist, neutral countries such as India, Burma, and Indonesia. Zhou also informed the Vietnamese that the Chinese were scaling back their support for the Indochinese revolutionary ambitions of the Vietnamese communists in Laos and Cambodia. A Vietnamese revolution, yes; an Indochinese one, no, or at least not now. The Indians in particular insisted upon this concession as a sign of Sino-Vietnamese communist good intentions towards the region. The Vietnamese agreed.

With the division of Vietnam into two provisional states at Geneva in July 1954, the north and the south were prohibited from hosting foreign military bases and from joining any type of military alliance, nor could arms be increased beyond those needed to replace outdated ones. While the Cambodian government reserved the right to solicit outside military aid, it privately promised not to allow the installation of foreign military bases on its territory. In Laos, the French were allowed to maintain two bases and a limited number of personnel, on the understanding that they too were agreed to keeping Laos neutral.

The extent of Zhou Enlai's success in neutralizing Indochina and Southeast Asia against the Americans is still open to debate. The Americans were certainly aware of what Zhou Enlai was trying to do and the American creation of the **South East Asia Treaty Organization** can be seen to a large extent as a challenge to Zhou Enlai's Asian strategy of neutralization. In the end, such neutrality was extremely fragile and would be hard to maintain as local, regional, and international actors moved to sway Indochina or parts of it towards their camp, first in Laos, then in southern Vietnam. *See also* GENEVA ACCORDS; JOHN FOSTER DULLES; PLAN Z.

**NEW HERO.** Refers to the "exemplary" men and women exalted by the communist leadership of the **Democratic Republic of Vietnam** (DRV) during the Indochina War. However, the Vietnamese communist party's "new hero" (*anh hung moi*) was not quite as revolutionary as we may think. For one, Vietnamese communists drew upon a long tradition of hero worship and martyr veneration in Sino-Vietnamese political culture, one in which the state singled out men and women of virtue (*dao duc*) whom society should strive to emulate.

Vietnamese anti-colonialists opposing French colonial domination at the turn of the 19th century recast ancient hero veneration in nationalist ways by inventing a new pantheon of heroic nationalists and martyrs to be emulated by young Vietnamese patriots. Vietnam's first modern nationalist, Phan Boi Chau, was the main architect of this new generation of heroes.

While Vietnamese communists continued to promote new patriotic heroes as part of their own struggle to gain Vietnam's national independence, they went further by adding a new socialist man to the heroic, emulative repertoire. This layer, however, drew its inspiration from Sino-Soviet communist models that arrived in northern Vietnam in full force following the entry of the DRV into the international communist bloc in early 1950. It was also linked to the decision taken by Vietnamese communists to begin transforming Vietnamese society in patently communist ways.

The creation of the "new hero" and the "new (communist) man" was an instrument by which the Vietnamese communist party sought to take hold of, control, and remake Vietnamese society in truly revolutionary ways, as Benoit de Tréglodé has shown. Under the close supervision of the communist party, cadres carefully selected heroes from among the peasants and soldiers who were considered to represent the "new" men and women. These exemplary people were to serve as models to follow in setting the foundation of the new communist society. Whereas **land reform** was designed in part to begin the restructuring of Vietnamese rural society, the dissemination of "new heros" throughout the DRV via massive propaganda drives and **emulation campaigns** allowed the party to align itself with the peasantry, the workers, soldiers, women, and petty traders. Bourgeois individuals, patriotic or not, were not to be emulated. Hero worship was also a powerful tool by which the party began to inculcate a new range of virtues and values openly identified with communism and the wider international world of which the DRV was now a part.

In May 1952, the **Vietnamese Worker's Party** officially began its revolutionary heroization project in earnest. Besides being patriotic, the "new heroes" had to embody unflagging loyalty to the party. As Truong Chinh characterized the new hero in 1952, "The hero has a strong class sentiment. He knows how to distinguish the good from the bad, the friend from the enemy. He knows himself and has a responsible outlook towards the leadership and the masses. It is not personal interest that guides him in the war or in work production but rather the collective good". While the Chinese advisors working closely with the Vietnamese communist leadership certainly provided advice and experiences, it was the Vietnamese leadership that chose to undertake this "heroic" emulation campaign. *See also* COLD WAR; CULTURE; HISTORY; INDOCTRINATION; LANGUAGE OF WAR; MARTYRS; LOVE AND WAR; RECTIFICATION.

**NEW MAN.** *See* NEW HERO; RECTIFICATION.

**NEW VIETNAMESE.** *See* NEW HERO; RECTIFICATION; VIET NAM MOI.

**NGHĨA LỘ, BATTLE OF (29 September–10 October 1951).** Having suffered defeats in the Red River Delta earlier in the year, the Vietnamese high command shifted its attention to the northwest highlands. On 29 September, the **Democratic Republic of Vietnam** (DRV) opened what it called the Ly Thuong Kiet campaign by sending elements mainly from the 312th division against the French position at Nghia Lo. The main goals of this campaign were to destroy French attempts to strengthen the **Tai Federation** against the DRV, to develop **guerrilla** operations in the area, and to attack the French on more favorable terrain than in the open delta. This battle was also designed to help open a corridor to central and southern Indochina running down the western, hilly and forested side of the delta. Using **wave tactics** and attacking by night, the Vietnamese overran the rather small camp in early October and handed General **Raoul Salan** a defeat. Salan responded by ordering his men to regroup and reinforce greatly the French post at **Na San** in order to stop the Vietnamese march in the Tai territories and on to Laos. When the Vietnamese moved on Na San in 1952, Salan confronted them with a full-blown entrenched camp, supplied by air, and outfitted with heavy artillery. Indeed, the defeat suffered at Nghia Lo led Salan to develop his famous strategy of entrenched camps, *les hérissons*. As Salan put it in the wake of his loss at Nghia Lo: "We have absorbed the shock, the loss of the Nghia Lo sector is a painful one. But it's not a decisive one [...] The game has only just begun". Indeed, the Vietnamese victory at Nghia Lo would turn into a defeat for **Vo Nguyen Giap** at Na San. But the final match of this shift of the battle from the delta to the highlands would be played out at **Dien Bien Phu** in 1953–1954.

**NGHIÊM KẾ TỔ.** Prominent member of the **Vietnamese Nationalist Party** (*Viet Nam Quoc Dan Dang*, VNQDD) who virulently opposed the communist leadership of the **Democratic Republic of Vietnam** (DRV). Following the failed nationalist uprising at Yen Bay in 1930, he took refuge in southern China where he joined the overseas branch of the VNQDD. Fluent in Chinese, he returned to Vietnam with Chinese occupying forces after World War II. Although he served as under-secretary to the Ministry of Foreign Affairs (or possibly acting minister of Foreign Affairs) in the DRV between March and November 1946, he remained an adamant opponent of the **Indochinese Communist Party**, many of whose leaders he had known since the 1930s in southern China. He accompanied **Bao Dai** to China in April 1946 and, after returning, lost his position in the government. In October, Nghiem Ke To went underground in **Hanoi**, with a Chinese passport. However, the French kept him under surveillance and, shortly after the outbreak of hostilities in Hanoi on 19 December 1946, brought him in. Following his release, he returned to southern China to lead the VNQDD, once again from exile in southern China.

**NGHIÊM VĂN TRỊ (1907–1993).** Vietnamese non-communist politician and minister in the Associated State of Vietnam. Born in Nam Dinh province, he left Vietnam in 1921 to pursue his studies in France. In 1932, he graduated as an engineer from the *École centrale des arts et manufactures* in Paris. In July of that year, he was also naturalized as a French citizen and married a French or Swiss national. In 1933, he completed his military service in Metz as a reserve captain in the artillery. He returned to Vietnam in December 1933 and, between 1934 and 1945, worked in the Indochinese railway service. Following the Japanese ***coup de force* of 9 March 1945**, he refused to collaborate with the Japanese and asked to be treated the same as his fellow French compatriots. He received the French *Croix de guerre* at the end of World War II for his courage. He supported the French return to Indochina and French colonial policy. In November 1947, he began a political career as the personal advisor to General **Nguyen Van Xuan** at the head of the French-created and -backed **Provisional Government of the Repub-**

lic of Cochinchina. In November 1947, Nguyen Van Xuan sent him on a special mission to meet with **Bao Dai** in Hong Kong. In 1948, Nghiem Van Tri served as an aide to Bao Dai. In June 1952, he became minister of Defense in the government of **Nguyen Van Tam**, but resigned from the post in December of that year following differences with General **Nguyen Van Hinh**, chief of staff of the Vietnamese Army Forces.

**NGHIÊM XUÂN YỂM (1913–2000).** Minister of Agriculture in the **Democratic Republic of Vietnam** (DRV). Born in Ha Dong province in northern Vietnam, he graduated with a degree in agronomy from the *École supérieure de l'agriculture et des forêts* in **Hanoi**. In 1944, he joined the **Vietnamese Democratic Party** (*Dang Dan Chu Viet Nam*) and the **Viet Minh** shortly thereafter. Nghiem Xuan Yem took part in relief efforts to help victims of the devastating famine of 1944–1945. Between 1947 and 1953, he served as under-secretary for Agriculture in the DRV, minister of Agriculture between 1953 and 1960, and member of the Executive Committee of the Central Committee of the Vietnamese Democratic Party between 1950 and 1958.

**NGÔ ĐÌNH DIỆM, JEAN-BAPTISTE (1901–1963).** One of Vietnam's best-known non-communist nationalist leaders. Born in Quang Binh province in central Vietnam, Ngo Dinh Diem grew up in a patriotic and influential **Catholic** family. His father, Ngo Dinh Kha, was the mandarin former minister of rituals in the court of Thanh Thai and close confidant of Nguyen Huu Bai, an influential mandarin in the service of King Khai Dinh and his son, **Bao Dai**. Ngo Dinh Diem started his career as a provincial chief in central Vietnam. When the French sidelined Nguyen Huu Bai in an imperial "reform" in 1933, his protégé Ngo Dinh Diem was named minister of the Interior in an attempt to appease his mentor and lend nationalist legitimacy to Governor General Pierre Pasquier's attempt to energize the monarchy against internal and external threats. This first **Bao Dai Solution** failed. Diem resigned with great fanfare a few months later, though he remained involved in Catholic intrigues at the court.

When a number of Catholic priests in upper central Vietnam and ranking mandarins began to support a possible "Diem solution" as Vichy tried to hold on in Indochina, Admiral Jean Decoux had Bao Dai sign an "order of expulsion" against Ngo Dinh Diem. Apprised secretly of the news, Diem fled to **Saigon** and took refuge in the offices of the Japanese General Staff until the Japanese ***coup de force* of 9 March 1945**. During the war, he secretly worked with **Cao Dai** leaders and dispatched an envoy to Cuong De concerning possible **collaboration.** However, when the Japanese offered him the premiership after overthrowing the French, Ngo Dinh Diem declined. He also refused to support the newly born **Democratic Republic of Vietnam** (DRV) following the Japanese capitulation and local **Viet Minh** forces arrested him in mid-1945. However, **Ho Chi Minh** personally ordered Ngo Dinh Diem to be released in light of his impeccable nationalist credentials. Executing him would have alienated important parts of the fragile nationalist coalition Ho hoped to turn against the French.

Following the outbreak of war in late 1946, French authorities and Ngo Dinh Diem remained in touch; however, Ngo Dinh Diem balked at supporting the French revival of the **Bao Dai solution**, unless the French granted Vietnam real independence. Following a brief stay in the St-Paul Clinic in **Hanoi**, Ngo Dinh Diem moved into the Redemptorist mission in northern Vietnam. In 1947 and 1948, he made a number of trips to southern and central Vietnam, as well as to Hong Kong where he visited Bao Dai. In May 1949, Bao Dai asked him to form a government, but Ngo Dinh Diem declined again on grounds that French concessions in the Accords of 8 March 1949 remained insufficient. Diem insisted on real and total independence. The French refused to budge. During this time, Ngo Dinh Diem continued to travel around the country meeting nationalists of all ideological colors, called upon the international community to pressure the French to give up their colonial obsession in Indochina, and yet kept channels open to the French and the DRV in the hope that his ***attentisme*** could win him concessions by playing one side against the other.

In early 1950, however, Ngo Dinh Diem realized that, with the arrival of the **Cold War** and the Americans on the scene, he could no longer sit; he had to act. In late June 1950, he formed a nationalist grouping called the Extremist Nationalist Movement (*Phong Trao Quoc Gia Qua Khich*) to struggle against Vietnamese communism. The DRV responded in kind to his shift in tack in July 1950 by condemning him to death *in absentia*. In August 1950, Ngo Dinh Diem left for Japan where he renewed contacts with Prince Cuong De concerning the need to create an anti-communist nationalist government in Vietnam (apparently hoping to tap into the legitimist branch of the Nguyen dynasty that Cuong De represented). Ngo Dinh Diem then left for the United States in September in a bid to win over American support for his plans and meet with influential American leaders of the time. He would continue to network inside and outside Vietnam with his brothers in order to realize a non-communist and fully independent Vietnam. As he wrote in a letter to his brother **Ngo Dinh Nhu** in 1953: "*L'attentisme qui était légitime autrefois est devenu maintenant criminel*". In the fall of 1953, Ngo Dinh Nhu organized an anti-communist congress in Saigon and launched an intense propaganda drive in his brother's favor among non-communist groups.

On 16 June 1954, the Associated State of Vietnam issued Decree no. 38-CT authorizing Ngo Dinh Diem to create a new government to take over from Prince **Buu Loc**. While many in Washington were happy to learn of this change of leadership as American diplomats adopted a hard-line position at the **Geneva Conference**, this does not mean that they masterminded Ngo Dinh Diem's rise to power. Internal, local dynamics were also at work. On 19 June 1954, Ngo Dinh Diem became president of Council thanks to ordinance no. 15 and created his cabinet on 6 July 1954. He held the presidency of Council and served as minister of the Interior and of Defense. Like Bao Dai and others, he opposed the **Geneva Accord**'s division of Vietnam into two halves and refused to sign the accords as prime minister of the Associated State of Vietnam, implement them in 1955 as president of the **Republic of Vietnam**, or organize elections to be held in 1956 to reunite the country. He was determined to create a fully independent, modern, and anti-communist nation-state, and not just in what became known as "South Vietnam". However, his detractors became increasingly numerous, and not just among the communists. Ngo Dinh Diem perished in a *coup d'état* on 2 November 1963, which had the support of the Americans. *See also* BINH XUYEN; CAO DAI; HOA HAO.

**NGÔ ĐÌNH NHU, JACOB (1910–1963).** Vietnamese historian and archivist and non-communist nationalist. Born in Thua Thien province in central Vietnam, Ngo Dinh Nhu was the son of a well-known mandarin in the service of the Nguyen court, Ngo Dinh Kha, and younger brother of the non-communist nationalist, **Ngo Dinh Diem**. Ngo Dinh Nhu travelled to France in late 1931 to study history at the *Faculté des lettres de Paris*. He shone in the subject. He was also the first Vietnamese to graduate from the elite French school for archivists – *L'École des Chartes*. He ranked number six upon his entry into this prestigious school in 1935 and graduated number three in 1938 as an archivist – paleographer. His thesis was entitled *Mœurs et coutumes des Tonkinois aux XVIIe et XVIIIe siècles d'après les voyageurs et missionnaires*. He also received his degree in letters (history) in 1938.

On his return to Vietnam, he was named deputy curator of the Archives and Libraries of Indochina. After World War II, he was actively involved in nationalist politics and shared his brother's revulsion for both French colonialism and Vietnamese communism. In May 1949, for example, he met with **Bao Dai** and **Buu Loc** to discuss the recently signed Accords of 8 March 1949 with the French. However, like his brother, he insisted that the French had to concede real independence. He dedicated himself to supporting his brother's leadership of a non-communist, anti-colonialist political alternative to Bao Dai, **Ho Chi Minh**, and the French.

Ngo Dinh Nhu was very interested in political, economic, and social change as well as the notion of personalism, one of the pillars of Ngo Dinh Diem's political philosophy. In the late 1940s, Ngo Dinh Nhu organized a study group, *Xa Hoi* (Society), to discuss such ideas and published in the early 1950s a modest review of the same name. At the same time, he reached out to other non-communist, like-minded nationalist groups, such as **Saigon intellectuals**, Buddhists, Tran Quoc Buu's Vietnamese Confederation of Labor, and **Nguyen Ton Hoan** of the **Dai Viet**. Ngo Dinh Nhu and his brother then brought many of these groups together to form the *Dang Can Lao Nhan Vi* in 1952 or 1953. While this party was a rather loose coalition during the Indochina War, the Ngo brothers would turn it into one of the building blocks of Ngo Dinh Diem's rule between 1955 and 1963. Ngo Dinh Nhu perished with his brother in a *coup d'état* in Saigon on 2 November 1963, carried out with the backing of the Americans. *See also* ANTI-COLONIALISM; *ESPRIT*.

**NGÔ ĐÌNH THỤC, PIERRE MARTIN (1897–1994).** One of Vietnam's most important **Catholic** and nationalist leaders. Born in central Vietnam into a Catholic family, Ngo Dinh Thuc was the son of the powerful mandarin and minister of rituals at the Nguyen Court, Ngo Dinh Kha, and elder brother of the nationalist leader **Ngo Dinh Diem** and of the historian **Ngo Dinh Nhu**. He entered the seminary of An Ninh at age 12 and spent eight years there before studying philosophy and theology in Rome. He was ordained a priest in December 1925. He then left for Paris, where he studied canon law and obtained his undergraduate degree (*licence*) in letters in France in 1929. Like his brother Ngo Dinh Diem, Ngo Dinh Thuc was close to Nguyen Huu Bai's faction at the Hue court, which is why French colonial authorities were wary of him and his rise in the Catholic Church in Vietnam. In January 1938, Ngo Dinh Thuc was named Vicar Apostolic of Vinh Long province in southern Vietnam and then ordained bishop later that year, despite resistance from colonial authorities. He was the third Vietnamese to obtain the rank of bishop.

Like his brothers, he was a Vietnamese patriot and supported efforts to put an end to French colonialism. While he was strongly anti-communist, he was careful not to antagonize the **Democratic Republic of Vietnam**'s authorities in Vinh Long province where he lived and worked. In 1946, he petitioned the Pope and Christians in Britain and the United States to stop the Indochina War and to support full Vietnamese independence of a non-communist kind. During Ngo Dinh Diem's travels in the West, Ngo Dinh Thuc often accompanied his brother and used his Catholic networks and youth associations to mobilize support for him. The **Vatican** named Ngo Dinh Thuc Archbishop of Hue in 1960. He was in Rome in November 1963 when his brothers Diem and Nhu were killed in a *coup d'état*, backed by the Americans.

**NGÔ GIA KHẢM (1912–1990).** One of the architects of the **Democratic Republic of Vietnam**'s arms-manufacturing industry during the Indochina War. Born in Bac Ninh province in northern Vietnam, he joined the **Indochinese Communist Party** in 1936. The French arrested and jailed him in the colonial prison of **Son La**. Upon his release in 1944, Ngo Gia Kham played a decisive role in creating one of the first military weapons-producing factories in northern Vietnam. He helped set up and run explosive-making workshops for making and distributing mines, grenades, and ammunition throughout the **Inter-Zone Viet Bac** (*Lien Khu Viet Bac*). He also served as one of the DRV's first **new heroes.** *See also* EMULATION CAMPAIGN; RECTIFICATION.

**NGÔ MẠNH GƯƠNG.** *See* NGÔ THẤT SƠN.

**NGÔ THẤT SƠN (TRỊNH NGỌC ÁNH, NGÔ MẠNH GƯƠNG, NAISƠN SICHĂN, CHOEUN, 1919–1952).** Charismatic Vietnamese who led combined **Khmer Issarak** and **Viet Minh** troops in Cambodia during the Indochina War. Born in Chau Doc province in southern Vietnam, Ngo That Son completed his secondary education at the *Lycée Sisowath* and the *École normale* in Phnom Penh, during which time he learned to speak flawless Khmer. He joined the colonial bureaucracy in Cambodia as a primary school teacher and specialized in physical education. In 1940, he studied sports in Phan Thiet province at the then Vichy-backed *École supérieure d'éducation physique d'Indochine en Cochinchine* (Esepic). In 1944, Vichy certified him as a physical education instructor.

On 1 September 1945, he quit his job teaching in order to join the Viet Minh in southern Vietnam. He led an advance propaganda team designed to stop attacks by Khmer populations against their Vietnamese neighbors in **Cochinchina**. On 8 December 1945, no doubt because of his training in physical education, he was sent to study military science at the new military academy run by the **Democratic Republic of Vietnam** in the northern province of Son Tay. After a crash course, he was sent back to the south in early 1946, but had to take refuge in Thailand. There he organized Overseas Troops No. 1, made up of recruits from the Vietnamese populations in Thailand. He served as their deputy commander and returned with them to southern Vietnam in September 1946. He then worked along the Vietnamese–Cambodian border, winning over Cambodians to the Vietnamese cause, including the large Khmer populations in southern Vietnam. He also developed military operations against the French with Khmer Issarak forces situated along the southern Vietnamese border.

In March 1948, he became deputy commander of the 305$^{th}$ Regiment, which would be better known as the *Sivotha* Troop, consisting of Vietnamese and Cambodian soldiers mainly active in Kompong Cham province. His perfect knowledge of Khmer and his charismatic personality made him popular among his Khmer troops. In May 1949, during a battle with Franco-Cambodian troops, he was wounded and taken prisoner in the province of Svay Rieng. French authorities and even **Norodom Sihanouk** urged Ngo That Son to switch sides, relying on one of his classmates from his high school days, **Nhiek Tioulong**, to win him over. Harsher methods were apparently also used, but to no avail. While the idea of exchanging Ngo That Son for the French colonels Charton and Lepage, captured during the battle of **Cao Bang**, was considered, it came to naught. Ngo That Son and Huynh Ba Nung died of gunshot wounds sometime in the early 1950s in what remain mysterious circumstances. *See* KHMER KROM.

**NGUYỄN ÁI QUỐC**. *See* HỒ CHÍ MINH.

**NGUYỄN BÁ SANG (MICHEL SANG, 1915–?).** Vietnamese **Catholic** priest and staunch defender of the nationalist cause of the **Democratic Republic of Vietnam** (DRV) during the Indochina War. Born in Tan An province in southern Vietnam, Nguyen Ba Sang was opposed to the return of French rule to Vietnam. He and his brother, Nguyen Ba Luat (also a priest), were active in the southern section of the Association of Vietnamese Catholics for National Salvation. In August 1946, French authorities condemned Nguyen Ba Sang to a suspended sentence of a year for his political activities. Upon his release, he immediately took to the *maquis* to work for the DRV in southern Vietnam. There, he served as an advisor to the Administrative and Executive Committee for Nam Bo on Catholic affairs. In November 1946, he and his brother helped create the General Union of Vietnamese Catholics in southern Vietnam. He was arrested in November 1947 and interned by French military authorities in the camp Virigile, in **Saigon**. As of August 1951, he was still being held there.

**NGUYỄN BẮC (1922–).** Vietnamese security operative, who remained undercover in **Hanoi** following the outbreak of war on **19 December 1946** and tried to mobilize **intellectuals** and students against the war. Born into a poor mandarin family in Hai Duong province in northern Vietnam, Nguyen Bac studied at the *Lycée du Protectorat* and then the Indochina Teachers' School in Hanoi. During the late 1930s and early 1940s, he became increasingly involved in nationalist politics and joined the **Viet Minh** upon the Japanese capitulation in August 1945. He was elected the first chairman of Kinh Mon district in Hai Duong province at this time. For unclear reasons, he was transferred by the **Democratic Republic of Vietnam**'s (DRV) Security Services to work undercover in Hanoi under **Tran Quoc Hoan** from 1951 to the end of the war. He was in charge of recruiting secret agents, building undercover party organizations, and winning over the support of the intellectuals and students in Hanoi to the nationalist cause. He worked underground in Hanoi for the entire Indochina War, relying on the nationalist sympathy of intellectuals such as **Hoang Xuan Han**, Pham Khac Quang, and Vu Van Hien to spread the DRV's message. Nguyen Bac played the pivotal role in devising the Petition for the Restoration of Peace in Indochina and getting it signed by leading intellectuals in northern Vietnam in the propaganda drive against the French. After the Indochina War, he served as director of the Hanoi City Bureau of Culture and Information (*So Van Hoa Thong Tin Ha Noi*) between 1954 and 1979. In the 1990s, he published his memoirs entitled *Into the Occupied City*. *See also* LANGUAGE OF WAR.

**NGUYỄN BÌNH (NGUYỄN PHƯƠNG THẢO, LE BORGNE, ANH BA, 1904–1951).** Commander-in-chief of the **Democratic Republic of Vietnam**'s (DRV) armed forces in southern Vietnam between November 1945 and September 1951. Born in Hai Hung province in northern Vietnam, **Nguyen Binh** came from a poor family. After finishing his primary schooling, he moved to Haiphong and then made his way to **Cochinchina** where he worked as a laundry boy and frequented the docks of **Saigon**. He also became increasingly involved in nationalist politics. It was during this time that he befriended an influential **intellectual** and journalist, **Tran Huy Lieu**, who introduced him into the **Vietnamese Nationalist Party** (*Viet Nam Quoc Dan Dang*, VNQDD) in 1928. In 1930, the French sentenced Nguyen Binh to hard labor in **Poulo Condor** for his political activities. However, while Tran Huy Lieu crossed over to the **Indochinese Communist Party** (ICP) while doing hard time, Nguyen Binh did not. He left the island on 12 October 1934, and the nature of his activities during the rest of the 1930s remains a mystery.

During World War II, he reappeared in Haiphong, organizing anti-Japanese and then anti-French activities in cooperation with communists working in the Red River Delta, including his long time friend Tran Huy Lieu. Following the Japanese overthrow of the French, Nguyen Binh began organizing his own local armed forces in the coastal areas of northeastern Vietnam, in what was known as the Tran Hung Dao war zone. With the emergence of the DRV in September 1945, **Ho Chi Minh** and other communist leaders were impressed by Nguyen Binh's initiative in these areas. They brought him into the government and turned this independent-minded nationalist into their military commander-in-chief for a southern Vietnam already at war.

Nguyen Binh arrived in the south in November 1945 and began unifying bandit groups, sects, and religious forces as best he could into an organized armed force to fight the French forces of General **Philippe Leclerc**. In December 1945, Nguyen Binh became chief of war **Zone VII** (*Bo Tu Lenh Khu VII*) in eastern Nam Bo, including the colonial city of Saigon-Cholon. When all the best French forces transferred to the north in March 1946, he was able to strengthen his guerrilla activities considerably in the south. In June 1946, Nguyuen Binh joined the ICP. Later that year, he urged **Hanoi**-based leaders to forget about negotiating with the French and to prepare instead for full-scale war, including the leveling of Hanoi. Indeed, he ran an angry urban war against the French and their Vietnamese allies in the streets and back alleys of Saigon-Cholon throughout the rest of the 1940s. On several occasions, Nguyen Binh made his way secretly into Saigon to organize sabotage and assassination squads.

In early 1947, as the French began to break off the **Cao Dai** and **Hoa Hao** from Nguyen Binh's united front, he took a hard line towards the defecting religious leaders. The result was civil war between Nguyen Binh's army and the forces of the Hoa Hao and Cao Dai, leading to the Viet Minh's assassination of **Huynh Phu So**. In 1948, the leader of the **Binh Xuyen**, **Le Van Vien**, broke with Nguyen Binh and defected to the French side. In January 1948, Nguyen Binh was named major general in the DRV army, second only to General **Vo Nguyen Giap**.

In 1949, as the Vietnamese prepared for the "general counter-offensive", Ho Chi Minh named him commander of the armed forces in the south. Nguyen Binh began building in earnest a modern army, organized in battalions and briefly as regiments. In 1949 and 1950, apparently on orders from the north, he launched head-on attacks against French posts across southern Vietnam. Thanks to superior artillery and air power, the French handed him one of his worst setbacks in his life while powerful communists began to criticize his tactics. Nonetheless, Nguyen Binh had demonstrated that not only could southerners fight an urban war, but they could also move towards creating a modern army as in the north, and this without a Chinese rear-guard and large-scale foreign **aid**.

In 1951, following important changes occurring at the international level and within the ICP, the DRV summoned Nguyen Binh to the north for further training and consultations in preparation for the wider war against the French, including the creation of a trans-Indochinese supply trail running from the north to the south. While crossing through northeastern Cambodia, Nguyen Binh perished in an ambush in September 1951 laid by the 4th *Bataillon de chasseurs cambodgiens* under **Jacques Hogard**. General Nguyen Binh's remains were returned to Vietnam from Cambodia in 2000. *See also* ANTOINE SAVANI; COLLABORATION; HO CHI MINH TRAIL; MARCEL BAZIN.

**NGUYỄN CẨM GIANG**. *See* NGUYỄN HẢI THẦN.

**NGUYỄN CAO KỲ (1930–).** Vietnamese officer in the armed forces of the Associated State of Vietnam and later politician in the **Republic of Vietnam**. Born in Son Tay province in northern Vietnam, Nguyen Cao Ky grew up the son of a school teacher. He completed his secondary education in the *Lycée Chu Van An* in **Hanoi** in 1948 and then entered the Nam Dinh Reserve Officers' School, created by the French to build an army for what became the Associated State of Vietnam. Upon graduation, he was named first lieutenant. In 1953–1954, he studied to be a fighter pilot in France and North Africa. He graduated from the Marrakech Aviation School in Morocco. After completing his studies at the Saint Avold Aviation School in France in September 1954, he became a transport pilot in the French **Air Force** and briefly served as a pilot in the French Air Force during the **Algerian War**. In December 1954, he returned to join the armed forces of what would soon become the Republic of Vietnam under **Ngo Dinh Diem**. Not long after the latter's death, Nguyen Cao Ky served as prime minister of the Republic between 1965 and 1967 and vice president between 1967 and 1971. With the communist victory in 1975, he went into exile in the United States.

**NGUYỄN CHẤN.** *See* TRẦN VĂN TRÀ.

**NGUYỄN CHÁNH (1917–2001).** Ranking military commander in southern Vietnam during the Indochina War. Born in Binh Dinh province in lower central Vietnam, he joined the **Indochinese Communist Party** in 1946. Between July 1945 and late 1946, he served at the head of an **overseas Vietnamese** combat unit in Thakhek, Laos. Following the French reoccupation of Laos, he fled to Thailand. In December 1946, he helped to constitute the Tran Phu Detachment (*Chi Doi Tran Phu*) in Thailand and to escort it to southern Vietnam in order to provide arms and troops for the resistance. In 1948, he became the chief of war **Zone VIII** (*Khu Chien VIII*). Between 1949 and 1953, he was the chief of the **General Staff** for the High Command in southern Vietnam and served as the military commander of **Inter-Zone IX** (*Lien Khu IX*) before becoming deputy commander as well as chief of the General Staff of the newly formed **Inter-Zone for Western Nam Bo**. In July 1954, he became a special delegate of the Vietnamese High Command in the south in charge of overseeing the repatriation of southern cadres and military personnel to the north following the provisional division of Vietnam in 1954 at the **17th parallel**.

**NGUYỄN CHÁNH (CHÍ THUẬN, 1914–1957).** Powerful poltico-military cadre in central Vietnam during the Indochina War. Born in Quang Ngai province in lower central Vietnam, Nguyen Chanh joined the Vietnamese Revolutionary Youth Party in 1929 and became a member of the **Indochinese Communist Party** (ICP) in 1931. Despite going in and out of prison, he remained politically active during the Popular Front period. His activities during World War II are unknown. With the advent of the **Democratic Republic of Vietnam** in 1945, he served as the party secretary for the province of Quang Ngai; held the same post for the Interprovincial Party Committee of Quang Ngai and Binh Dinh; and helped local communists take power in Quang Ngai in August and September 1945. Between late 1945 and 1948, he was the Ministry of Defense's delegate to lower central Vietnam and deputy secretary for the ICP's Provincial Party Committee in war **Zone** V (*Khu Chien V*). From 1948, he served as political commissar for **Inter-Zone V** (*Lien Khu V*) and was the deputy secretary for its Party Committee. Between 1951 and 1954, he worked as the secretary of the Party Committee for Inter-Zone V and political commissar and military commander of the same entity. He commanded the battle of Northern Tay Nguyen in 1954. Between 1954 and 1956, he was involved in repatriating troops in Inter-Zone V to northern Vietnam in accordance with the **Geneva Accords** provisionally dividing Vietnam into two halves at the **17th parallel**. Nguyen Chanh's wife was **Pham Kiet's** little sister.

**NGUYỄN CHÍ THANH (TRƯỜNG SƠN, ANH SÁU, SƯ RĨ, NAM HÙNG, 1914–1967).** Powerful poltico-military cadre who rose rapidly in the army and the Party during the Indochina War. Born into a peasant family in Thua Thien province in lower central Vietnam, he became politically active during the Popular Front period, joining the **Indochinese Communist Party** (ICP) in July 1937. In 1938, he became secretary of the Party's Provincial Committee for Thua Thien. Later that year, the French arrested but released him shortly thereafter. He continued to serve as the secretary of the Party's Thua Thien Provincial Committee until he was arrested again in mid-1939 and sent to prisons in Hue, Lao Bao, and finally Ban Me Thuat. In 1941, he escaped and returned to building Party bases in Thua Thien. He was arrested a third time in 1943, but regained his liberty following the Japanese overthrow of the French in the ***coup de force* of 9 March 1945**. He returned to lower central Vietnam to help the Party take power. In August 1945, he attended the Party's Conference in Tan Trao and became a member of the Executive Committee of the ICP's Central Committee. He assumed the post of secretary in the Party's Territorial Committee for **Annam** (*Xu Uy Trung Ky*). He also joined the **Viet Minh**'s General Directorate or ***Tong Bo***. In 1947, he became secretary of the Party's Provincial Committee for Thua Thien and later the secretary of the Party Committee for the "Sectorial Zone" (*Phan Khu*) for Binh-Tri-Thien (Quang Binh, Quang Tri and Thua Thien). From late 1948 to 1950, he was the secretary of the Party's Committee for **Inter-Zone IV** (*Lien Khu IV*). In late 1950, his influence grew considerably when he became the director of the General Political Directorate of the **People's Army of Vietnam** (*Tong Cuc Chinh Tri Quan Doi Nhan Dan*) as well as the deputy secretary of the ICP's powerful General Military Committee (*Tong Quan Uy*). He served in this latter post until 1961. During the Second Party Congress held in early 1951, he was elected to the Executive Committee of the Central Committee and the Politburo. Besides being a very powerful man, Nguyen

Chi Thanh was also a very out-going, jovial, and popular figure in the army. He died of a heart attack in the 108th Military Hospital in **Hanoi** while involved in tense discussions within the Politburo on planning for the upcoming 1968 Tet Offensive. *See also* CENTRAL PARTY MILITARY COMMITTEE.

**NGUYỄN CƠ THẠCH (PHẠM VĂN CƯƠNG, 1921–1998).** Born in Nam Dinh province in northern Vietnam, Nguyen Co Thach became politically active during the Popular Front period in French Indochina in the 1930s. In 1940, the French arrested and sentenced him to five years of prison in jails in Nam Dinh, **Son La,** and Hoa Binh. In 1943, he joined the **Indochinese Communist Party** (ICP) in Son La prison, where ranking party leaders such as **Le Duc Tho** and **Tran Quoc Hoan** were held. Released from jail following the Japanese ***coup de force* of 9 March 1945**, Nguyen Co Thach's prison record served him well in the **Democratic Republic of Vietnam** (DRV). In September 1945, he went to work in the Ministry of Defense as a personal secretary to **Vo Nguyen Giap**. In 1947, he became secretary of the powerful Military Committee (*Quan Uy*). In 1949, he was deputy then secretary of the ICP's Provincial Committee for Ha Dong; he also served as president of its **Resistance and Administrative Committee**. In 1951, he became a member of **Inter-Zone III**'s (*Lien Khu III*) party delegation and a member of its Resistance and Administrative Committee. In 1954, Nguyen Co Thach transferred to the Ministry of Foreign Affairs where he worked in the secretariat. In 1956, he became the DRV's consul general to **India** and headed the Vietnamese delegation to the second international conference on Geneva on Laos (1961–1962). *See also* CENTRAL PARTY MILITARY COMMITTEE; VO VAN KIET.

**NGUYỄN CÔNG HOAN (1903–1977).** Vietnamese writer and supporter of the **Democratic Republic of Vietnam** (DRV). He graduated from the Pedagogical School in **Hanoi** and worked as a school teacher during the interwar period. He distinguished himself as a writer in the 1930s. During the Popular Front period, he published perhaps his best-known novel, *Dead End* (*Buoc Duong Cung*), which was banned by the colonial authorities. Following the overthrow of the French and the defeat of the Japanese in 1945, he joined the ranks of the **Viet Minh** and replaced his colonial predecessor, **Jean Cousseau**, as censor for the DRV, all the while serving as director of the Northern Propaganda Department. Following the outbreak of full-scale war on **19 December 1946**, Nguyen Cong Hoan joined the army and edited the paper, *Ve Quoc Quan* (National Defense Forces) and served as director of the army's cultural school. For the rest of the war, he dedicated himself to developing educational and cultural programs for the resistance government. His writing glorified the nationalist cause and the heroic struggle of the Vietnamese people against the French.

**NGUYỄN CÔNG MIỀU.** *See* LÊ VĂN LƯƠNG.

**NGUYỄN ĐỆ (1900–1992).** Non-communist Catholic nationalist active during the Indochina War. Born in **Hanoi**, he was educated at the *Collège Paul Bert* and then in the *Lycée Albert Sarraut* in Hanoi before graduating from the *École supérieure de droit et d'administration*. Between 1923 and 1926, Nguyen De worked in the colonial administration until he joined the **Bank of Indochina** in 1926. Following commercial training in France, he returned to Hanoi in 1928 and became the first Vietnamese *agent courtier* for the Bank in Indochina (a post held only by Chinese until then). In 1931, he was a member of the Consultative Council of Jurisprudence for **Tonkin**. He also joined **Bao Dai**'s imperial cabinet as a head clerk. However, he lost his position in the imperial cabinet in August 1933 along with one of his close allies, **Ngo Dinh Diem**. His problems were such that the French wanted to expel him from **Annam** to Tonkin. Nguyen De returned to Tonkin in 1935 and resumed his business career.

During World War II, he refused to collaborate with the Japanese and the French, taking refuge in southern Vietnam. Following the war, he briefly served in the **Democratic Republic of Vietnam** as an advisor in the Vietnamese delegation to the **Fontainebleau** negotiations in mid-1946. He remained in the north after the outbreak of the Indochina War on **19 December 1946**, but refused to join the French-created government led by General **Nguyen Van Xuan**. In October 1948, he was a member of the non-communist National Unity Party (*Quoc Gia Lien Hiep*). He returned to the political scene with the birth of the Associated State of Vietnam. He also renewed his ties to the royal family. In June 1950, he became director of the Imperial Cabinet and traveled with Bao Dai to France between June and October 1950.

He served as one of Bao Dai's closest and most powerful advisors. For **Lucien Bodard**, Nguyen De was "ferociousness" incarnate. All the while, Nguyen De continued to develop his business interests in Vietnam and Europe, creating two new trading houses, one in Paris, the other in London. He tried to bring over the Catholic nationalists to Bao Dai's cause by winning over the support of Ngo Dinh Diem, but to no avail. In April 1952, he served as the director of both the Civilian and Military cabinets for Bao Dai. He was named state minister and imperial delegate for the Upland Peoples of Vietnam in the **Buu Loc** government created in January 1954. He eventually moved to France where he died in 1992.

**NGUYỄN ĐÌNH LUYỆN (NGUYỄN VĂN LUYỆN, HOÀNG QUANG BÌNH, 1896–?).** Leading member of the **Greater Vietnam Nationalist Party** (*Dai Viet Quoc Dan Dang*) in the 1940s. Trained as a doctor, he worked as a surgeon in a hospital in Baria in southern Vietnam. During the 1930s, he became involved in nationalist politics and found his way to the north where he founded the Vietnamese-language newspaper, *Tin Moi*. Following the Japanese ***coup de force* of 9 March 1945**, he served in the government of **Tran Trong Kim** before becoming a deputy in the National Assembly of the **Democratic Republic of Vietnam** (DRV). He took part in the Vietnamese delegation to the **Dalat Conference** in April 1946. However, as a member of the Greater Vietnam Nationalist Party, he became increasingly wary of communist control of the DRV. He remained in **Hanoi** after the outbreak of war on **19 December 1946** and served as the permanent general secretary of the Greater Vietnam Nationalist Party for (French-controlled) northern Vietnam in 1949.

**NGUYỄN ĐÌNH ƯU** (1918–2002). War photographer in the **People's Army of Vietnam** during the Indochina War. Born in Hai Phong province in northeastern Vietnam, he joined the armed forces of the **Democratic Republic of Vietnam** in 1946 and the **Indochinese Communist Party** in 1949. He covered Vietnamese men and women in battle between 1948 and 1978. Some of his work includes *Nu Dan Quan*, *Dien Bien Hom Nay*, *Bo Doi Ve Lang*, and *Du kich Bac Kan*.

**NGUYỄN ĐÔN (1918–**). Important military leader in **Inter-Zone V** (*Lien Khu V*) during the Indochina War. Born in Quang Ngai province in lower central Vietnam, Nguyen Don became involved in radical politics during the Popular Front period in colonial Indochina, joining the **Indochinese Communist Party** (ICP) in 1938. His political activities landed him in jail. Between 1939 and 1945, he served time in a French colonial prison in central Vietnam. Following the Japanese overthrow of the French in the ***coup de force* of 9 March 1945**, he regained his freedom and helped create the ICP's Provisional Provincial Committee for Quang Ngai. On 14 August 1945, he became a member of the Standing Committee of the Party's Provincial Committee for Quang Ngai and helped the communists take power there. In September 1945, he became deputy commander of the Politico-Military Committee for the Lower Section of Central Vietnam located below the **16th parallel**, in charge of areas between Phu Yen and Binh Thuan. From 1946, he served as a political commissar in the Quang Ngai 2nd Detachment (*Chi Doi 2*) and then in the 94th and 68th regiments (though much smaller in reality). In 1948, he served as the chief of the organizational and control offices for Inter-Zone V as well as the political commissar for its weapons-producing committee. He was political commissar in the 210th regiment (later the 108th). In 1950, he worked as the political commissar and the military commander of the southern Tay Nguyen front. Between 1951 and 1954, he was the military chief of staff of Inter-Zone V as well as the deputy commander of the same zone. He took part in the bloody battle of An Khe in 1953 and fought against the French operation **Atlante** in 1954. He became divisional commander and political commissar for the 324th division in 1955.

**NGUYỄN ĐỨC NGUYÊN.** *See* LÊ QUANG ĐẠO.

**NGUYỄN ĐỨC QUỲ (c. 1918–?).** During World War II, Nguyen Duc Quy abandoned his studies to take up journalism and became involved in nationalist politics. In 1942, he joined the **Indochinese Communist Party** and was serving as secretary to **Vo Nguyen Giap** in secure zones in northern Vietnam by the end of the war. During this time, he helped locate and extricate downed American pilots. Following the creation of the **Democratic Republic of Vietnam** (DRV), he worked in the Ministry of Defense. In late 1945, he accompanied **Pham Ngoc Thach** to Bangkok to serve as a diplomatic secretary there. The government sent Quy back to Thailand in 1946 as the head the government's diplomatic delegation in Bangkok in charge of relations with South and Southeast Asia. He arrived there in 1946, as tensions mounted with the French in Indochina and negotiations stalled in France. During his time in Bangkok, Nguyen Duc Quy met with both American and Soviet representatives and served as the point man in the government's relations with much of Asia and the world. He spoke fluent Thai and maintained relationships with both the Seri Thai led by **Pridi Banomyong** and his adversary **Pibun Songgram**. Nguyen Duc Quy was particularly close to **Thongin Phuriphat**, who was pivotal in the opening of the DRV's diplomatic mission in 1946. The coming of the **Cold War** made it harder for the Vietnamese to maintain their diplomatic office, however. Nguyen Duc Quy was finally forced to leave Thailand in 1951 following the Thai recognition of the Associated State of Vietnam led by **Bao Dai**, under increasing American pressure. In February 1952, the DRV transferred Nguyen Duc Quy to Moscow where he served as the first secretary to its newly formed Embassy in the Soviet Union. *See also* LE HY; TRAN NGOC DANH.

**NGUYỄN ĐỨC THỤY.** One of the **Democratic Republic of Vietnam**'s (DRV) most important China specialists during the early stages of the Indochina War. He spoke Chinese fluently and had probably lived in southern China before World War II. In 1945, he headed up the DRV's **Bureau for Overseas Chinese Affairs** and its Office for Foreign Trade in northern Vietnam. He led a commercial delegation to southern China in early 1947 in order to obtain aid and to develop border trade with China. French intelligence services were aware of these attempts and the French offensive against Bac Kan in September and October 1947 was designed in large part to deny the DRV commercial access to southern China. *See also* LEA, OPERATION.

**NGUYỄN ĐỨC VIỆT.** *See* WERNER SCHULZE.

**NGUYỄN DUY THANH (1909–?).** Military officer who defected from the armed forces of the **Democratic Republic of Vietnam** (DRV) in 1950. Born in Bac Ninh province in northern Vietnam, he graduated in 1933 as an electrical engineer from the *École supérieure de mécanique et d'électricité* in Paris. He worked in a variety of colonial engineering posts between 1933 and 1944. Between September 1945 and April 1946, he joined the DRV at the head of the *Société indochinoise d'électricité* in **Hanoi** and served as an advisor to the government's delegation to the **Dalat Conference**. Between August and November 1946, Nguyen Duy Thanh worked as director of military engineering in the DRV's Ministry of Defense. On 18 December 1946, he evacuated Hanoi and transferred to Vinh to continue working as an engineer in **Inter-Zone IV** (*Lien khu IV*) until April 1950, when he defected to the French-backed Associated State of Vietnam led by **Bao Dai**, for fear of the increasing communist hold over the DRV. In May 1950, Bao Dai asked him to join the **Tran Van Huu** government. Though Nguyen Duy Thanh declined the offer, he agreed to become minister of Planning and Reconstruction in the second cabinet of Tran Van Huu. In August 1950, Bao Dai appointed him as his goodwill envoy to **India**, responsible for winning over Indian sympathy and possible diplomatic recognition of the Associated State of Vietnam. In July 1952, Bao Dai named him as one of the Vietnamese delegates to the Assembly of the **French Union**. Nguyen Duy Thanh later joined the **Republic of Vietnam**. See also COLLABORATION; DESERTION.

**NGUYỄN DUY TRINH (LƯU ĐỨC PHO, 1910–1985).** Powerful communist leader in central Vietnam during the Indochina War. Born in Nghe An province in upper central Vietnam, Nguyen Duy Trinh joined the New Vietnam Party (*Dang Tan Viet*) and then the **Indochinese Communist Party** (ICP) in 1930. In 1931, colonial authorities arrested and condemned him to 13 years of hard labor. In 1935, he landed in **Poulo Condor** and was then interned in 1942 in a concentration camp in the Kontum highlands. During this time, he was active in communist politics in prison. Between 1936 and 1941, for example, he was secretary of the ICP's special party cell for the Poulo Condor prison. Following the Japanese overthrow of the French in the ***coup de force* of 9 March 1945**, he regained his liberty and resumed his work in central Vietnam where he helped the Party take power in Vinh and Hue. He rapidly became one of the most important communist leaders in central Vietnam. He joined the Standing Committee of the Party's Territorial Committee for Central Vietnam (*Xu Uy Trung Bo*) and became vice president of the Resistance and Administrative Committee for Central Vietnam. He was elected a deputy in the National Assembly of 1946. Between 1946 and 1954, he served as the secretary of the Party's Committee in charge of **Inter-Zone V** (*Lien Khu V*) and was the president of the Resistance and Administrative Committee for Southern Central Vietnam. In 1951, he was elected to the Central Committee of the newly formed **Vietnamese Worker's Party** and joined the Politburo in 1956. After the **Geneva Accords** divided Vietnam provisionally in two in 1954, he moved to northern Vietnam where he obtained a vice ministerial post in the President's Office.

**NGUYỄN GIÁC NGỘ (1897–?).** One of the leaders of the **Hoa Hao** forces who broke with the **Democratic Republic of Vietnam** (DRV) in the late 1940s. Born in Long Xuyen province in southern Vietnam, Nguyen Giac Ngo was a non-commissioned officer in the **Cochinchinese Civil Guard** between 1923 and 1943. Sometime in the early 1940s, he joined the Hoa Hao Buddhist faith. In 1943, the French interned and then deported him to **Poulo Condor**. He regained his freedom following the Japanese ***coup de force* of 9 March 1945**. Faced with the return of the French in late 1945, he allied his men with the army being put together under the leadership of the DRV's **Nguyen Binh**. However, when the rift between the Hoa Hao and the **Viet Minh** came into the open in 1947, Nguyen Giac Ngo tried to work independently of the Viet Minh and the French. The French failed to get him to defect in September 1948. Instead Nguyen Giac Ngo became the leader of some three Hoa Hao dissidents now making up the Vietnamese National-Socialist Party (*Dang Viet Nam Dan Chu Xa Hoi*, or *Dang Dan Xa* for short). He enjoyed considerable popularity in the western reaches of southern Vietnam. In February 1950, as the **Cold War** intensified the Indochinese conflict, Nguyen Giac Ngo crossed over to the Associated State of Vietnam led by **Bao Dai** and swore loyalty to the former emperor in March. He was one of the rare dissident leaders at the time to agree to incorporate his forces into the national army under construction. *See also* BINH XUYEN; DESERTION.

**NGUYỄN HẢI THẦN (NGUYỄN VĂN THẮNG, NGUYỄN CẨM GIANG, VŨ HẢI THU, 1879–1955).** One of the best-known non-communist Vietnamese nationalists opposed to French colonialism and Vietnamese communism. Born in Ha Dong province, he grew up in an anti-colonial and patriotic milieu marked by the violent French conquest of upper Vietnam in the late 19th century. He left for Japan in 1905 as part of Phan Boi Chau's Go East movement (*Dong Du*) before making his way to southern China where he would organize anti-colonial activities until 1945. In 1912, Phan Boi Chau put him in charge of a suicide squadron designated to assassinate the then Governor General **Albert Sarraut** in 1913. It failed but the French condemned Nguyen Hai Than to death *in absentia* for trying. In 1924, Nguyen Hai Than helped Phan Boi Chau create a nationalist party in southern China based on the Chinese Nationalist Party (*Guomindang*).

Nguyen Hai Than was virulently opposed to communism and its emergence in Vietnam (and China). He joined forces with the **Vietnamese Nationalist Party** (*Viet Nam Quoc Dan Dang*, VNQDD) led by **Vu Hong Khanh** and others to win over Chinese nationalist support during World War II. To this end, Nguyen Hai Than presided over the creation in 1942 of the Vietnamese Alliance Party (*Viet Nam Cach Mang Dong Minh Hoi* or *Dong Minh Hoi* for short). He returned to Vietnam in September 1945 with the Chinese army sent to accept the Japanese surrender.

While Nguyen Hai Than had counted on the Chinese to remove the communists from the newly formed **Democratic Republic of Vietnam** (DRV) and help non-communist nationalists rise to power in **Hanoi**, he found himself in the uncomfortable position of having to deal with **Ho Chi Minh** since local Chinese officers did not want to risk greater chaos by overthrowing the DRV as the British had done in the south. The Chinese nonetheless pressured Ho to allow for a greater non-communist presence in the government. On 22 December 1945, thanks to Chinese pressure, the *Dong Minh Hoi* obtained 20 seats in the National Assembly that was elected on 6 January 1946. Nguyen Hai Than was also invited to become vice president of the DRV. This was confirmed on 24 February 1946 by an accord and approved by the National Assembly in early March.

However, when the the French returned in force to northern Vietnam following the **Franco-Chinese Accords of February 1946** and the **Accords of 6 March 1946**, and the Chinese army began to withdraw from Indochina, Nguyen Hai Than decided to do the same. He had no real army of which to speak and no real political support upon which to rely inside Vietnam. He took refuge in Guangxi then in Guangzhou (Canton), where he received a Chinese pension. He collaborated briefly with **Bao Dai** in Hong Kong in 1947, but ended up fading away in China, sidelined by both Bao Dai and the Chinese communists. *See also* CHIANG KAI-SHEK; CIVIL WAR; REPUBLIC OF CHINA.

**NGUYỄN HOÀI THANH.** *See* NGUYỄN VĂN THANH.

**NGUYỄN HỮU ĐANG (1913–2007).** Prominent Vietnamese cultural figure in the **Democratic Republic of Vietnam** (DRV) during and after the Indochina War. Born in Thai Binh province in northern Vietnam, he became affiliated with the Vietnamese Revolutionary Youth League in 1929 before being arrested and placed under *résidence surveillée* by the French. Upon his release, he studied at the Pedagogical School in **Hanoi** between 1932 and 1936 before resuming his political activities during the Popular Front period. Nguyen Huu Dang contributed regularly to party papers such as *Tin Tuc* and *Doi Nay*, and worked with the likes of **Truong Chinh**, **Tran Huy Lieu**, and others. In 1943, he joined the **Indochinese Communist Party** and remained particularly close to Truong Chinh, the provisional general secretary of the party. Nguyen Huu Dang was one of the main organizers of the independence ceremony held in Ba Dinh square on 2 September 1945 during which **Ho Chi Minh** announced the formal creation of the DRV. Nguyen Huu Dang served as minister of Propaganda then as minister of Youth in the DRV. Following the outbreak of full-scale war on **19 December 1946**, he dedicated himself to the organization and implementation of major propaganda and mobilization campaigns for the government, mainly on the journalistic and educational fronts. Following the Indochina War, his fortune took a turn for the worse when he fell from official favor for his role in the *Nhan Van Giai Pham* movement. In 1958, DRV authorities arrested him for serving as an alleged French spy and in 1967 communist authorities sentenced him to 15 years in prison on the grounds that he was "opposed to the Party" (*Xet Lai Chong Dang*). *See also* HOANG MINH CHINH; VU DINH HUYNH.

**NGUYỄN HỮU THỊ LAN, MARIE-THERESE.** *See* NAM PHƯƠNG.

**NGUYỄN HỮU THỌ (ANH ÚT, 1910–1996).** Leading southern **intellectual** who agitated against the French during the Indochina War. Born in Cholon, the son of a rubber plantation manager, he left for France in 1921 where he studied law. He returned to Vietnam in 1933 and joined the Cochinchinese Bar the following year. In April 1932, he requested French citizenship but his application was apparently refused. We know little about his activities in the 1930s and during World War II.

While he supported the **Democratic Republic of Vietnam** (DRV), serving in late 1945 as the president of the Tribunal of Can Tho, he was also one of the supporters of the *Mouvement populaire cochinchinois*. Such activities apparently landed him in hot water for DRV forces arrested him on 7 July 1947 and put him under house arrest until his liberation on 12 September 1947. In June 1949, he returned to the political scene when he helped create the anti-war newspaper, *Pour la Paix*, in association with French leftists in the ***Groupe culturel marxiste*** in **Saigon**. Nguyen Huu Tho is said to have joined the **Indochinese Communist Party** at that time.

On 19 March 1950, he participated in student demonstrations against the visit of an American warship to Saigon in particular and against stepped-up American intervention in the Indochina War in general. The **Public Security Services** of the Associated State of Vietnam arrested him for this. He was provisionally released on 27 March 1950 on bail, but was arrested again on 15 April 1950 for handing out political pamphlets. In August 1950, French and Vietnamese authorities exiled him to a remote village in Lai Chau province in northern Vietnam and then placed him under house arrest in Son Tay in June 1951, when DRV agents attempted to contact him. An amnesty granted in 1952 allowed him to walk free. He returned to Saigon and in April 1954 helped create the *Mouvement pour la défense de la paix* and was a vocal supporter of the implementation of the **Geneva Accords** and the holding of elections in 1956. He served as one of the movement's vice presidents. Vietnamese communists would renew their collaboration with him during the Vietnam War, making him chairman of the southern National Liberation Front in 1960. *See also* ATTENTISME; COLLABORATION; CROSSOVERS.

**NGUYỄN HỮU TRÍ (1905–1954).** Born in Thai Binh province in northern Vietnam, he completed his primary and secondary studies at the *Collège du Protectorat* and at the *Lycée Albert Sarraut* in **Hanoi**. He then graduated from the *École des hautes études indochinoises* in Hanoi and joined the mandarinate in Thai Binh province. He became a magistrate in Ha Dong province and assumed the post of president of the Tribunal at Nam Dinh, then Hung Yen. When the **Viet Minh** took power in mid-August 1945, he resigned his position as provincial governor of Thai Binh, which he had held since the Japanese ***coup de force* of 9 March 1945**. He was hostile to French attempts to rebuild their colonial state in Indochina but distrustful of Vietnamese communist intentions in the **Democratic Republic of Vietnam** (DRV). Though he briefly served as director of the cabinet of the minister of the Interior in the DRV in late 1945, he was a member of the **Greater Vietnam Nationalist Party** (*Dai Viet Quoc Dan Dang*). He refused to take part in the **Bao Dai Solution**, disappointed by the French refusal to grant real independence to non-communist Vietnamese. He agreed, however, to serve as governor of North Vietnam on two occasions as part of the emerging Associated State of Vietnam (between July 1949 and April 1951 and again between November 1952 and July 1954). He accepted the post of minister of Defense in the second cabinet of **Tran Van Huu**, constituted on 18 February 1951. He was an energetic and capable administrator, non-communist, and no French stooge.

**NGUYỄN HỮU VŨ.** *See* ĐỒNG SĨ NGUYÊN.

**NGUYỄN HUY LAI (1908–?).** Leading non-communist Vietnamese nationalist and Catholic active in politics during the Indochina War. Born in **Hanoi**, he left for France to complete his studies. He obtained his doctorate in law at the *Faculté de droit* in Paris as well as a degree from the *Institut de criminologie* at the University of Paris. He met his French wife during this time, Jeanne Cartier. Nguyen Huy Lai had returned to Indochina by the early 1930s and begun work as a lawyer at the Appellate Court in Hanoi. In 1934, he became president of the anti-communist *Comité du groupement de l'action sociale indochinoise*. He was the founder and president of the *Cercle d'études sociales catholiques* in Hanoi and involved in work to re-educate delinquents. Little is known about his activities during World War II. He was an ardent supporter of a non-communist, independent Vietnam, but one allied with the French. In January 1950, **Bao Dai** named him a representative of the Associated State of Vietnam to the **French Union**. He was, however, critical of the mediocre nationalist credentials of many of the politicians chosen by Bao Dai to serve in the government, "unknown to the masses" he said. Nguyen Huy Lai became minister of Finances and National Economy in the **Nguyen Van Tam** government of 6 June 1952.

**NGUYỄN KEN.** *See* NGUYỄN THẾ LAM.

**NGUYỄN KHẮC VỆ (1896–?).** Non-communist judge in the Associated State of Vietnam. Born in Tra Vinh province in southern Vietnam, he left for France at the age of 12. He completed his secondary studies at the *Lycée de Pau* in 1916, obtained his bachelor's degree in law at the *Faculté de droit* in Paris in 1919, and his doctorate in law in 1922. While in France, he was apparently naturalized as a French citizen. He married one of the daughters of the constitutionalist Bui Quang Chieu, and was the uncle of the colonial lawyer and future president of the Resistance and Administrative Committee for Nam Bo, **Pham Van Bach**. In 1921, Nguyen Khac Ve was the secretary of the *Association mutuelle des Indochinois* of Paris. He was a member of the Vietnamese delegation sent to the Colonial Exhibition in Marseilles in 1922. Upon his definitive return to Vietnam in 1923, he worked as a judge in **Saigon** until 1945. During the tumultuous events of 1945, both the Japanese and the **Democratic Republic of Vietnam** kept him on. In early 1946, he returned to French-controlled Saigon with his family and served as an advisor to the Appellate Court in Saigon as of August 1947. He became minister of Justice on 8 October 1947 in the cabinet of General **Nguyen Van Xuan**, and was appointed again on 23 May 1948, 1 July 1949, and 18 February 1951 in the Associated State of Vietnam. In March 1953, he became ambassador for the Associated State of Vietnam to Great Britain. He was author of *La naturalisation française en Indochine* (1921) and in 1947 he wrote and published an essay on the *Franco-Vietnamese problem*.

**NGUYỄN KHẮC VIỆN (1913–1997).** Journalist, writer, propagandist, pediatrician, and spokesman for the **Democratic Republic of Vietnam**. Born in Ha Tinh province, he obtained his bachelor's degree in philosophy and lived in France in the 1940s. In 1952, he began actively agitating in France against the war in Indochina. He wrote widely in defense of Vietnamese culture and nationalism, and in opposition to the Indochina War in the pages of the influential French review, *La pensée*. With the end of the Indochina War in 1954, he returned to **Hanoi** and directed the French-language section of the government's cultural publications, *Études vietnamiennes* and the *Courrier du Vietnam*. He was an ardent defender of the French *francophonie* project and received in 1992 the *Grand prix de la francophonie* for services rendered to the cause. *See also* CULTURE; HISTORY; INDOCTRINATION.

**NGUYỄN KHẮC XỨNG.** *See* LÊ THANH NGHỊ.

**NGUYỄN KHẢI (NGUYỄN MẠNH KHẢI, 1930–2008).** Vietnamese **intellectual** and writer working in the army of the **Democratic Republic of Vietnam** during the Indochina War. Born in Nam Dinh province, Nguyen Khai joined the army in the heady days of 1947. He was 17. A year later, he entered the **Indochinese Communist Party**. For the next 30 years, he wrote prolifically on the daily life and the mettle of the Vietnamese soldiers and their heroic victories over the French and the Americans. In 1951–1952, he received a prize from the Association of Vietnamese writers for his book *Construction* (*Xay Dung*). *See also* CINEMA; CULTURE; INTELLECTUALS; MYTH OF WAR; NOVELS; TRAN DAN.

**NGUYỄN KHANG (NGUYEN VAN DE).** One of the most important and influential Vietnamese cadres working in **Laos** during both wars for Indochina. Fluent in Lao, he helped recruit and train **Kaisôn Phomvihān** during the Indochina War. He initiated the first efforts to create a genuine Lao party in 1953 and was in charge of political and party affairs "for *all* of Laos" (*ca nuoc*) before and after the signing of the **Geneva Accords** in mid-1954. He was, with General **Chu Huy Man**, instrumental in the transnational remaking of the **Pathet Lao** from mid-1954 until 1957. This full member of the Central Committee was the **Vietnamese Worker's Party**'s most important behind-the-scenes player in Laos from the late 1940s well into the 1970s. *See also* ADMINISTRATIVE OFFICE FOR THE FRONTIER; ADVISORY GROUP 100; COMMITTEE FOR EXTERNAL AFFAIRS; COMMITTEE FOR THE EAST, LAO ISSARA; HOANG VAN HOAN; NGUYEN THANH SON; PARTY AFFAIRS COMMITTEE.

**NGUYỄN KHÁNH (1927–).** Born in southern Vietnam, Nguyen Khanh completed his primary studies in Tra Vinh and **Saigon** between 1931 and 1937. Between 1938 and 1944, he attended secondary school in Cambodia (and perhaps in Saigon, too). Despite growing up in a very Francophile family (he may have had French citizenship), he joined the **Viet Minh** in 1945 and fought the French for over a year. For unclear reasons, he crossed over to French Union forces in 1947. In July of that year, he graduated from the first and only class of the *École militaire d'Extrême-Orient* in Dalat and was commissioned to the 1st Regiment of the South Vietnamese National Guard. In late 1947, he travelled to France to attend the French Army's Infantry School in Auvours. He completed his coursework there in 1948 before studying at the Airborne School in Pau. In July 1948, he became a first lieutenant. Having finished his airborne training in mid-1949, he became an aide de camp to the minister of National Defense for the newly created Associated State of Vietnam. In May 1950, Nguyen Khanh became chief of the security section at the Imperial Palace in **Hanoi**. In February 1951, he took command of the 1st Vietnamese Parachute Company and fought the Viet Minh. In March 1952, he moved up to command the 22nd Vietnamese Battalion. Between June 1952 and June 1953, he attended the French Staff School in Hanoi, rubbing shoulders with **Nguyen Van Thieu** and **Cao Van Vien**. Promoted major in July 1953, he took command of the 13th Vietnamese Battalion and later in the year commanded the 11th *Groupe Mobile* operating in the highlands of central Vietnam. His unit was involved in combat operations against the **Democratic Republic of Vietnam**'s forces as the Indochina War drew to a close in June 1954. *See also* CROSSOVER; DESERTION.

**NGUYỄN KHÁNH TOÀN (HỒNG LĨNH, 1905–1993).** Vietnamese communist trained in Moscow in the 1930s and educator in the **Democratic Republic of Vietnam** (DRV). Born in Vinh in central Vietnam, Nguyen Khanh Toan became increasingly radicalized during student strikes in support of Phan Boi Chau and in memory of Phan Chu Trinh. In 1926, he left **Hanoi** for **Saigon** where he was editor of *L'Annam*. Faced with possible incarceration, he left for France in 1928 before moving on to study in the Soviet Union. He returned to Vietnam sometime around 1939 and made his way to Yan'an, capital of the

**Chinese Communist Party** during World War II, and stayed there until the war's end in 1945, when he returned to Vietnam with **Nguyen Son** in late 1945. The Party put him to work with **Luu Van Loi** running its French-language government newspaper, *La République*, then *Le Peuple.* Nguyen Khanh Toan wrote in the party's internal journal, *Su That*, under the pen name of Hong Linh or Red Soldier. He played a pivotal role in developing the DRV's educational system in northern Vietnam during the Indochina conflict. *See also* CULTURE; HISTORY.

**NGUYỄN KINH CHI (1899–1986).** Doctor in the medical corps of the **People's Army of Vietnam**. Born in Ha Tinh province in upper central Vietnam, Nguyen Kinh Chi studied pharmacology between 1918 and 1922 at the Indochinese University in **Hanoi**. Between 1922 and 1943, he worked in hospitals in Quang Binh, Buon Me Thuat, Kontum, and Qui Nhon. Between 1944 and 1945, he was active in a secret **Viet Minh** cell operated by **Ton Quang Phiet**. Nguyen Kinh Chi joined the **Indochinese Communist Party** sometime shortly thereafter. In August 1945, he became the director of the Medical Service for Trung Bo (*Nha Y Te Trung Bo*) for the **Democratic Republic of Vietnam**. Between 1947 and 1952, he was minister of Health as well as director of the **Inter-Zone IV**'s (*Lien Khu IV*) medical service. Between 1953 and 1956, he worked as the head of the health service for the province of Nghe An. *See also* DISEASE; EXPERIENCE OF WAR; TON THAT TUNG.

**NGUYỄN LƯƠNG BẰNG (SAO ĐỎ, ANH CẢ, 1904–1979).** First Vietnamese ambassador to the Soviet Union and general director of the Vietnamese National Bank for the **Democratic Republic of Vietnam** (DRV). Born in the northern province of Hai Duong, he worked as a sailor and joined the Vietnamese Revolutionary Youth League in southern China. He returned to Vietnam to build the organization, especially among workers in the ports of Haiphong and **Saigon**-Cholon. He joined the **Indochinese Communist Party** (ICP) in the early 1930s. The French arrested him, repatriated him to Vietnam, and sentenced him to 20 years of hard labor. He escaped from prison in 1932, but fell into French hands again in 1933. Colonial authorities incarcerated him in **Son La** prison where he remained until 1943 when he escaped a third time. In that year, he was designated an alternate member of the ICP's Central Committee in charge of the Party's finances and propaganda towards enemy soldiers. He also held a powerful position in the **Viet Minh**, in charge of its financial section. During the Tan Trao Conference in August 1945, he joined the ICP's Central Committee and became a ranking member of the Viet Minh's General Directorate or ***Tong Bo***. He played a decisive role in the organization of the famous "**gold week**" in upper Vietnam in late 1945 and continued to garner funds for the party and the government during the war. In June 1951, he became general director of the DRV's National Bank and in 1952 was named Vietnam's first ambassador to the Soviet Union, a post he held until December 1956. He also served on the ICP's Investigative Bureau for the Government.

**NGUYỄN MẠNH HÀ (1913–1992).** Leading **Catholic** politician in the **Democratic Republic of Vietnam** (DRV) in the early years of the Indochina War. He was educated in France, a graduate of the *Institut des Sciences politiques* (Sciences Po). He held a doctorate in law. His father was a naturalized French citizen and so was he. He never joined the communist party, even though his French wife (Renée) was the daughter of Georges Marrane, a senior leader in and deputy for the **French Communist Party**. Nguyen Manh Ha returned to Vietnam in 1938 and became active in the Catholic Action associations in northern Vietnam. During World War II, he worked in the labor department of the Haiphong Municipal Council.

A committed nationalist, he joined the DRV, serving as minister of the National Economy between September 1945 and March 1946. He was part of the Vietnamese delegation attending the **Fontainebleau Conference** in mid-1946. He was described at this time as under-secretary for the National Economy. He became chairman of the *Association Vietnam – France* in that same year and was a member of the *Jeunesse ouvrière chrétienne* formed in northern Vietnam in 1942 (He had founded its Haiphong chapter). He remained, however, in French-controlled **Hanoi** following the outbreak of war on **19 December 1946**. During this time, he promoted a peaceful resolution to the Franco-Vietnamese conflict. He refused, however, French offers to cross over to their side. To their intense irritation and that of their Vienamese allies, Nguyen Manh Ha preferred ***attentisme.*** He was opposed to French colonialism, but he was also wary of the DRV's communist core. He served as news editor of *Cong Luan*, shut down by the French in 1948 for its allegedly subversive ideas. He was critical of the forced labor camps the French set up in central and southern Vietnam and maintained secret contacts with leaders of the DRV during the entire Indochina War. He refused Prince **Buu Loc**'s offer of a government position in May 1949. In 1951, General **Jean de Lattre de Tassigny** expelled him from Indochina. Nguyen Manh Ha's hope was to create something of a "Third Force" to bring peace to an increasingly divided Vietnam. *See also* ANTICOLONIALISM; CATHOLICS, EXODUS FROM NORTH; CATHOLICS IN VIETNAM AND THE WAR; CHRISTIANS AND OPPOSITION TO THE INDOCHINA WAR; COLLABORATION; CROSSOVERS; HOANG XUAN HAN; LE HUU TU; VATICAN.

**NGUYỄN MẠNH KHẢI.** *See* NGUYỄN KHẢI.

**NGUYỄN NAM HÙNG.** *See* HOÀNG NAM HÙNG.

**NGUYỄN NGỌC NHỨT (1918–1952).** Engineer and **Cao Dai** disciple who supported the **Democratic Republic of Vietnam** (DRV). In 1937, he left France to pursue his studies and returned to Vietnam in December 1946 with an engineering degree from the *École centrale des arts et manufactures* in Paris and a French wife. Following the end of World War II, the outpouring of patriotic fervor among the **overseas Vietnamese in France**, especially during **Ho Chi Minh**'s visit to France for the **Fontainebleau Conference** in mid-1946, deeply impacted upon him. He apparently met the new president of the DRV at this point. Nguyen Ngoc Nhut's brother, Nguyen Ngoc Bich, had already joined the **Viet Minh** in southern Vietnam and urged his brother to support the resistance. In late 1946, Nguyen Ngoc Nhut returned home to southern Vietnam determined to fight for the nationalist cause. On 16 February 1947, he joined DRV zones in the south and began working in a weapons-manufacturing workshop war in **Zone VIII** (*Khu VIII*). In May 1947, he started organizing demolition and sabotage squadrons. He also represented **intellectuals** within the Resistance and Administrative Committee of the same zone. He called on intellectuals in **Saigon** to cross over to the Vietnamese nationalist cause led by the Viet Minh. Following the violent break between southern government forces and the Cao Dai, the DRV asked him to serve from November 1947 as the vice president of the Central Committee of the Unified National Salvation Cao Dai movement led by **Cao Trieu Phat**. In January 1948, Nguyen Ngoc Nhut was elected Commissioner for Social Affairs in Nam Bo, responsible for organizing relief and help for the indigent, refugees, and war wounded and their families. He also tended to questions of hygiene in cooperation with the government's health services. In June 1949, during a French military operation, he was taken prisoner. Despite intensive French, Vietnamese, and family efforts to win over this Vietnamese nationalist to the cause of **Bao Dai**'s Associated State of Vietnam, Nguyen Ngoc Nhut refused to switch sides. Even the application of **torture** failed to persuade him to reconsider. Although he was finally released in 1952, he died shortly thereafter at the age of 34 in unclear circumstances. Albeit unconfirmed, one recent Vietnamese account of Nguyen Ngoc Nhut claims that he was "disposed of secretly" (*thu tieu*). *See also* COLLABORATION; DESERTION; DISEASE; OVERSEAS VIETNAMESE IN THAILAND.

**NGUYỄN NGỌC VỸ (1911–?).** Active on the propaganda and diplomatic fronts for the **Democratic Republic of Vietnam** (DRV) during the Indochina conflict. During the interwar period, he worked in a French trading house in Indochina and apparently traveled throughout Asia on business. World War II found him working as a radio announcer for the Vietnamese-language section of the Far Eastern Service of the BBC, based in New Delhi. Following the Japanese defeat in August 1945, he put his broadcasting experience in the service of the nationalist cause of the DRV. In 1947, he served as the DRV's delegate to Singapore where he created the Association of overseas Vietnamese there. In 1948, he helped run the government's Information Service there. He seems to have remained active in one way or another in Singapore until the end of the war in 1954. *See also* LE HY; MAI LAM; MAI THE CHAU; OVERSEAS VIETNAMESE IN FRANCE; OVERSEAS VIETNAMESE IN THAILAND.

**NGUYỄN PHAN LONG (1889–1960).** Prominent Vietnamese non-communist nationalist politician during the colonial period and the Indochina War. He was a leading figure in the Constitutionalist Party formed in 1923. Though he was born in northern Vietnam, he considered himself "southern" and lived and worked there all his life. He was editor-in-chief of the well-known newspaper, *L'Écho Annamite*. Following World War II, he refused to serve the **Democratic Republic of Vietnam**, but demanded that the French accept the national unity and inevitable decolonization of Vietnam. He rejected the idea of creating an **Indochinese Federation** and initially felt that the French had to negotiate with **Ho Chi Minh**, though he switched to support **Bao Dai**'s efforts to create what became the Associated State of Vietnam. Following the Accords of 8 March 1949, Nguyen Phan Long agreed to serve as Foreign minister in Bao Dai's government of July 1949. In August of that year, he chaired the Vietnamese delegation in charge of the application of the March accords. He became prime minister in January 1950. His increasingly close relations with the Americans led to problems with the French, who pressured him to resign in April 1950. Part of the problem was that Nguyen Phan Long insisted that American **aid** flow directly to the Vietnamese without going through the French. But the French were determined to continue running the show. *See also* COLLABORATION.

**NGUYỄN PHÚC VĨNH THỤY.** *See* BẢO ĐẠI.

**NGUYỄN PHƯƠNG THẢO.** *See* NGUYỄN BÌNH.

**NGUYỄN QUỐC TRỊ.** *See* KAISÔN PHOMVIHĀN.

**NGUYỄN QUYẾT (NGUYỄN TIẾN VĂN, 1922–).** Born in Hung Yen in northern Vietnam, Nguyen Quyet joined the **Indochinese Communist Party** in 1940 and the armed forces of the **Democratic Republic of Vietnam** in August 1945. Between 1943 and 1945, he was active in building Party cells in and around **Hanoi**, serving as the secretary to the Party's urban cell for Hanoi. In January 1946, he joined the *Go South* or ***Nam Tien*** movement in order to oppose returning French forces. Between 1947 and 1952, he worked as a political commissar in the Quang Nam-Da Nang Front and served as a military delegate to the Resistance and Administrative Committee for the **Inter-Zone** of Quang Nam and Da Nang. In 1953, he served as the political chief of the Party for **Inter-Zone V** (*Lien Khu V*). Between December 1954 and 1955, he was the deputy chief political commissar for the 305th Division.

**NGUYỄN SƠN (VŨ NGUYÊN BÁC, LÝ ANH TỰ, VŨ HỒNG THỦY, 1908–1956).** A general in both the Chinese and Vietnamese communist armies and a dynamic military leader in central Vietnam during the first half of the Indochina conflict. Born in the **Hanoi** area, Nguyen Son studied at the pedagogical school in Hanoi in the early 1920s, where he first met **Pham Van Dong** and became involved in nationalist politics. Nguyen Son left Vietnam for southern China around 1925. In Guangzhou (Canton), **Ho Chi Minh** inducted him into the Vietnamese Revolutionary Youth League, put him to work studying Chinese, and enrolled him in the Whampoa Political-Military Academy located outside Guangzhou (Canton) to study modern military science among other things. During this time, Nguyen Son worked with Pham Van Dong and **Hoang Van Hoan**. The young Nguyen Son also joined the Chinese Nationalist Party (*Guomindang*).

In December 1927, with **civil war** erupting between Chinese nationalists and communists, and the Vietnamese youth league on the run, Nguyen Son crossed over to the **Chinese Communist Party** (CCP) before fleeing to northeast Thailand to escape arrest. In 1929, at the request of the CCP, Nguyen Son returned to southern China, to Fujian province, where he became a political commissar in the 34th division of the Chinese Red Army's 12th army and rose rapidly to become a high-ranking political cadre in the liberation army. He adopted a new Chinese name, Hong Thuy or Red Flood, and actively participated in mass mobilization, propaganda, rectification, and propaganda affairs. In 1931, he was head of the propaganda unit and a political and cultural instructor in the Central Military Political School in the army in Jiangxi. He became a full member of the CCP's Executive Central Committee before making the "Long March" with **Mao Zedong**, **Zhou Enlai**, and General Zhu De in 1934. Despite being expelled several times from the party on charges of being an "international spy", he regained the support of the Maoists. Once at Yan'an, he continued to work as an influential political commissar in the army, wrote in internal Chinese politico-military journals, became a master political organizer and propagandist for the 8th Route Army, and married a Chinese CCP cadre. His Chinese was reportedly flawless. He also became a student at the Red Army University in Wa Yaobao in Shaanbei. His teachers included Mao Zedong and Zhou Enlai, lecturing on Maoist strategy and politics. In 1943, he underwent a special **rectification** course, a Maoist speciality. Nguyen Son's fluency in Chinese and rank within the Chinese communist party was such that he trained Chinese cadres and exhorted the Chinese "masses" to fight the Japanese.

With the approval of the CCP, he returned to Hanoi in late 1945 with **Nguyen Khanh Toan**. Upon his arrival in Vietnam, he adopted the name Nguyen Son and became president of the newly formed Resistance Committee for Southern Vietnam (*Uy Ban Khang Chien Mien Nam Viet Nam*). In 1946, he transferred to Quang Ngai to serve as the director of the Quang Ngai Military School (*Truong Luc Quan Trung Hoc Quang Ngai*). In January 1947, because of his experience in the Chinese Red Army, he was assigned to work as the Head of the Bureau for Military and Political Indoctrination in the Army's **General Staff** (*Cuc Truong Cuc Quan Huan Bo Tong Tham Muu*). In July 1947, he was named military commander as well as political commissar for **Inter-Zone IV** (*Lien Khu IV*) in upper central Vietnam. In 1948, Ho Chi Minh dispatched **Pham Ngoc Thach** to Inter-Zone IV to bestow upon Nguyen Son the rank of major general in the Vietnamese army. During this time, Nguyen son also translated numerous Chinese communist and Maoist texts into Vietnamese for training purposes, including Mao's treatise on ***Revolutionary War*** and the *Issue of Strategy*.

In October 1950, as the Chinese entered the **Korean War**, Nguyen Son returned to China to work as an ideological and political instructor in the Chinese Red Army. In 1955, Mao Zedong named him a major general in the Chinese army in recognition of his services. In August 1956, Nguyen Son returned to Hanoi where he died of stomach cancer shortly after his arrival. During his time as commander of Inter-Zone IV, Nguyen Son allowed remarkably lively cultural exchanges and debates to occur. However, he was also one of the first Vietnamese communists to introduce Chinese methods of "rectification" (*chinh huan*). *See also* CINEMA; CROSSOVERS; CULTURE; EMULATION CAMPAIGN; HISTORY; INDOCTRINATION; METIS; LE THIET HUNG; NEW HERO; NGUYEN THANH SON; NGUYEN TIEN LANG; NOVELS; VUONG THUA VU.

**NGUYỄN TẤN CƯỜNG.** Little is known of his early life and activities. After World War II, Nguyen Tan Cuong joined in French efforts to build a separate southern state in **Cochinchina**. In 1946 and 1947, he was under-secretary and then minister for Youth and Sports in the **Provisional Government of the Republic of Cochinchina**. He was also under-secretary of state for the Security of the Capital in the same government in 1946. In January 1948 and again in January 1949, he was elected to lead the Cochinchina Front Party. He wrote often in *Le Populaire* in favor of southern autonomy. He also worked in developing the security services of the emerging Associated State of Vietnam. In April 1950, he took over as the new director of the security forces for this state, though he was only formally in charge of the **Saigon**-Cholon Municipal Police, a post he held until 1951.

**NGUYỄN THANH GIƯNG, HENRI (1894–?).** Non-communist southern Vietnamese politician who served in the **Provisional Government of the Republic of Cochinchina**. He completed his secondary studies at the *Lycée Chasseloup Laubat* in **Saigon** and then in France from 1914. He received his bachelor's degree from the *Faculté des sciences* in Marseilles. In 1926, he became a naturalized French citizen. Nguyen Thanh Giung returned definitively to southern Vietnam in April 1924 to teach in Saigon at the Pedagogical School, the *Lycée Chasseloup Laubat,* and the *Lycée Pétrus Ky*. Between 1941 and 1945, he served as director of the My Tho elementary school. He supported French efforts to create a Provisional Government of the Republic of Cochinchina, serving in the first cabinet led by Dr. **Nguyen Van Thinh** as minister of National Education. In 1951, Nguyen Thanh Giung became vice rector of the University of **Hanoi** and minister of National Education and Youth in the third government led by **Tran Van Huu**, constituted on 8 March 1952. He maintained this position under **Nguyen Van Tam** until 1953.

**NGUYỄN THÀNH LẬP.** Minister of Finance in the **Provisional Government of the Republic of Cochinchina** created on 1 June 1946. The **Democratic Republic of Vietnam**'s **special forces** assassinated him shortly thereafter. *See also* NGUYEN BINH; SAIGON.

**NGUYỄN THANH SƠN (NGUYỄN VĂN TÂY, 1910–1996).** Born in Can Tho province in southern Vietnam, he became involved in radical politics in the 1920s and left Vietnam for Guangzhou (Canton), where he met **Ho Chi Minh** and entered the Whampoa Politico-Military Academy. He returned to southern Vietnam around 1930, fluent in Chinese, and joined the **Indochina Communist Party** (ICP). The French arrested him in that same year and incarcerated him at **Poulo Condor**. He regained his freedom in 1936, thanks to the liberal policies of the Popular Front. Little is know about his activities during World War II.

In 1945, he joined the ICP's Territorial Committee for **Cochinchina** (*Xu Uy Nam Ky*) and briefly served as vice president of the Resistance and Administrative Committee for Nam Bo. He was called to **Hanoi** in early 1946 and assigned the tasks of supplying the southern resistance from Thailand and of developing a Khmer resistance movement capable of collaborating with the **Democratic Republic of Vietnam** (DRV) against the French and their Indochinese allies. In 1948, Nguyen Thanh Son took command of the powerful **Committee for External Affairs** in charge of administering the ICP's policies in Cambodia and running supply missions across mainland Southeast Asia. From this point, he became the ICP/DRV's single most important Cambodian specialist and the main architect of early Cambodian communism of an Indochinese kind. From 1949, he was in charge of the entire "Cambodian Front", in cooperation with **Vu Huu Binh** in Thailand. Nguyen Thanh Son was allegedly named general in 1952 and led the DRV's commission in charge of implementing the **Geneva Accords** in Cambodia. For unknown reasons, he never rose to higher positions following the end of the Indochina War. *See also* ADMINISTRATIVE OFFICE FOR THE FRONTIER; ADVISORY GROUP 100; CHU HUY MAN; COMMITTEE FOR THE EAST, LAO ISSARA; HOANG VAN HOAN; INDOCHINESE FEDERATION; *METIS;* NGUYEN KHANH; PARTY AFFAIRS COMMITTEE; SON NGOC MINH.

**NGUYỄN THẾ LÂM (NGUYỄN KÈN, 1918–).** Born in Binh Thuan province in central Vietnam, Nguyen The Lam joined the army in 1945 and the **Indochinese Communist Party** in 1946. In August 1945, he was a member of the Executive Committee of the **Viet Minh** front and a military representative to the province of Thua Thien. In October 1945, he led a platoon in the Go South or ***Nam Tien*** combat units sent to fight the French below the **16th parallel**. Between 1946 and 1947, he commanded the 81st "regiment" in what became **Inter-Zone V** (*Lien Khu V*). Between 1948 and 1949, he was the deputy then commander of war **Zone** VI (*Khu VI*). Between 1949 and 1950, he served as commander-in-chief of Inter-Zone V's troops. In 1952, he became deputy then commander of the 320th division.

**NGUYỄN THẾ LƯƠNG.** *See* CAO PHÁ.

**NGUYỄN THỊ BA (1917–).** Born in Long An province in southern Vietnam, Nguyen Thi Ba became politically active in the 1930s and became a liaison agent for the **Indochinese Communist Party** during the 1940 uprising in southern Vietnam. Between 1940 and 1945, she served as a secret liaison for the party and its cells in **Saigon**-Cholon. During the Indochina War, she was a finance agent and mobilized women in the province of Long An. Her work during this period in Saigon-Cholon later made her an important intelligence agent during the war against the Americans. *See also* OVERSEAS CHINESE; WOMEN.

**NGUYỄN THỊ BÌNH (NGUYỄN THỊ CHÂU SA, 1927–).** Southern Vietnamese militant opposed to increasing American involvement in the Indochina War. Born in **Saigon**, she was the granddaughter of the Vietnamese reformer, Phan Chu Trinh. She became politically active during the Indochina War, joining the Association of Progressive Women in 1950 and mobilized students and **intellectuals** for the nationalist cause during the Tran Van On demonstrations. In 1950, she cooperated with **Nguyen Huu Tho** in organizing a large demonstration of students and intellectuals against the visit of an American warship to Saigon and against increasing American involvement in the Indochina conflagration. French authorities arrested and jailed her. She regained her freedom following the signature of the **Geneva Accords** in 1954. The two main leaders of this anti-American demonstration in 1950, Nguyen Thi Binh and Nguyen Huu Tho, later played leading roles in the National Liberation Front during the Vietnam War. *See also* WOMEN.

**NGUYỄN THỊ ĐỊNH (BA ĐỊNH, 1920–1992).** One of the **Democratic Republic of Vietnam**'s most active women mobilizers during the Indochina War. Born in Ben Tre in southern Vietnam, she joined the **Indochinese Communist Party** in 1938 and took part in the Indochinese Congress organized during the Popular Front period. In

1940, during the communist uprising in **Cochinchina**, the French arrested and jailed her in Ba Ra (reserved mainly for common criminals) until 1943, when she resumed her political activities and helped the Party take power in Ben Tre province in 1945. In that same year, she joined the Executive Committee of the Women's Salvation Association for Ben Tre and began mobilizing women for the **Viet Minh** cause. In 1946, she traveled to northern Vietnam by boat to report to the Party Central Committee on the situation in the south since 1940 and to procure arms for the southern resistance. She arranged an important shipment of arms to war **Zone VIII** (*Khu Chien VIII*) at this time. She returned to the south a year later and joined the Party's Provincial Committee for Ben Tre. In 1948, she became the head of the province's National Salvation Women's Section. Her activities during the rest of the Indochina War remain obscure. She served as an important political and military leader in the National Liberation Front during the war against the Americans and was later named general. *See also* NGUYEN HUU THO; NGUYEN THI BINH; WOMEN.

**NGUYEN THI NGOC TOAN (1930–).** Her father was Ton That Dan, a member of the Nguyen imperial family and minister in Emperor Bao Dai's government until a government shuffle excluded him from power. Nguyen Thi Ngoc Toan studied at the *Dong Khanh* secondary school in Hue. With the advent of the **Democratic Republic of Vietnam** (DRV) in 1945, she joined the **Viet Minh** and served in the army as a nurse and medic. Between 1947 and 1949, she returned undercover to Hue to work in propaganda activities, something which landed her in prison on several occasions. Thanks to her imperial connections and fluency in French, she regained her liberty. She left the French-controlled zone in 1949 to make her way to the north where she joined the **Indochinese Communist Party** and entered the DRV's Medical School. She studied under **Ho Dac Dy** and became the sister-in-law of Dr. **Dang Van Ngu**. Still a medical student, she tended to wounded during the Battle of **Dien Bien Phu**. During the battle, she landed in hot water when she contested the organization of a **court martial**, in which she was on trial with two others, on the grounds that it was politically motivated and deceitful. In the wake of the battle and in the desolate landscape it had left behind, she married **Cao Van Khanh** on 22 May 1954, at the time the Deputy Commander of the 308th Division. After the war, she completed her medical studies and became a doctor. She became deeply involved in Agent Orange research after her husband died of liver cancer, allegedly a result of the American use of the herbicide. She also lost a son to liver disease. *See also* EXPERIENCE OF WAR, DIEN BIEN PHU; LANGUAGE OF WAR; LOVE AND WAR; NGUYEN THI BINH; NGUYEN THI THAP; WOMEN.

**NGUYỄN THỊ NGỌC TỐT.** *See* NGUYỄN THỊ THẬP.

**NGUYỄN THỊ THẬP (NGUYỄN THỊ NGỌC TỐT, 1908–1996).** Veteran communist leader and woman mobilizer in southern Vietnam. Born in My Tho province, she became politically active in the late 1920s. She joined the **Indochinese Communist Party** (ICP) in 1931 and in 1935 became a member of the Party's Territorial Committee for **Cochinchina** (*Xu Uy Nam Ky*). The French arrested her that same year but released her soon thereafter. In 1940, she played an active role in the Party's failed uprising in Cochinchina. Despite this setback, she remained politically active and tried to rebuild bases in Bac Lieu and Vinh Long provinces. She rejoined the party's resurrected Territorial Committee and traveled to the north to participate in the ICP's Conference in Tan Trao in mid-1945, although it is unclear whether she arrived in time. She was elected a deputy in the **Democratic Republic of Vietnam**'s National Assembly in 1946. During the Indochina War, she served as the secretary of the Party's Women's National Salvation Association for Nam Bo (*Doan Phu Nu Cuu Quoc Nam Bo*). She distinguished herself in the mobilization of women. In 1952, she returned to northern Vietnam to work with the party's Central Committee. Upon returning to southern Vietnam in 1954, she was among those charged with ensuring the application of the **Geneva Accords**, in particular the organization of elections in 1956. *See also* NGUYEN HUU THO; NGUYEN THI BINH; NGUYEN THI DINH; WOMEN.

**NGUYỄN TIẾN LÃNG (HÁN THU, THƯỢNG UYỂN, 1909–1976).** Non-communist Vietnamese journalist, politician, and prisoner of the **Democratic Republic of Vietnam** (DRV) during the first half of the Indochina conflict. Born in Ha Dong province near **Hanoi**, he completed his secondary studies at the *Lycée Albert Sarraut* in Hanoi and then at the *Faculté de droit* at the University of Hanoi before pursuing higher studies at the *École pratique des hautes études* in Paris. From 1929, he made his career working in the mandarinate in northern Vietnam, all the while pursuing literary, journalistic, and political interests. He wrote for a wide variety of Vietnamese papers, including *An Nam Tap Chi, Nam Phong*, and the royalist-minded *Gazette de Hué*. Between 1932 and 1934, he worked in the information service of the *Résident Supérieur* of **Tonkin** René Robin. Between 1936 and 1940, Nguyen Tien Lang was director of the Archives, Research, Translations and Press for the Imperial Palace in Hue. He directed **Bao Dai**'s Cabinet during this period. He transferred to Hoi An in 1944 and became provincial governor of Dalat, where he was arrested by forces loyal to the DRV. He was moved to **Inter-Zone IV** (*Lien Khu IV*). In December 1946, a DRV military tribunal in Thanh Hoa condemned him as a "Vietnamese traitor" or ***Viet Gian*** and revoked his civic rights. He was not jailed but, rather surprisingly, assigned to work as a personal secretary to General **Nguyen Son** in Thanh Hoa. Nguyen Tien Lang also taught literature and culture in Inter-Zone IV's schools. He left the DRV in 1951 and accepted a job as a private secretary to Empress **Nam Phuong**, now residing in Cannes. He held that post between 1952 and 1955. In 1954, he wrote an absorbing account of his time in Inter-Zone IV, entitled *Les chemins de la révolte*. *See also* CIVIL WAR; COLLABORATION.

**NGUYỄN TÔN HOÀN (1917–2001).** Born in Tay Ninh province, he enrolled in the *Faculté de médecine* in **Hanoi**, but soon dropped out and became involved in nationalist politics. He joined the **Greater Vietnam Nationalist Party** (*Dai Viet Quoc Dan Dang*) sometime in the late 1930s or early 1940s. He was active in non-communist nationalist activities following the Japanese defeat and the advent of the **Democratic Republic of Vietnam** (DRV) in 1945. At odds with the DRV's forces, he fled to China in 1946 to escape repression. **Bao Dai** dispatched him to **Saigon** in August 1947 as one of his delegates in charge of sizing up the non-communist nationalist situation inside the country. From 1948, Nguyen Ton Hoan led the Greater Vietnam Party in southern Vietnam. He was critical of the French refusal to grant full independence to a non-communist, nationalist Vietnam in order to take on the DRV. He also collaborated with **Ngo Dinh Diem** at this time. In July 1949, the French suspended the publication of Nguyen Ton Hoan's paper, *Duoc Viet*. He served as state secretary and minister of Youth and Sports in several cabinets of the Associated State of Vietnam. He was one of the first to introduce ping-pong to Vietnam.

**NGUYỄN TRỌNG CẢNH.** *See* TRẦN QUỐC HOÀN.

**NGUYỄN TRỌNG VINH (1916–).** Born in Thanh Hoa province, Nguyen Trong Vinh became politically active during the Popular Front period in the mid-1930s. He joined the **Indochinese Communist Party** (ICP) in 1939. Colonial authorities arrested and imprisoned him about a year later. In February 1945, he regained his freedom and immediately set to helping the ICP seize power in August 1945. In November 1945, he served as the Party's provincial secretary for Phuc Yen. A year later, on the eve of the outbreak of full-scale war, he assumed the Party and administrative direction of Thai Binh province. In February 1947, at war, the **Democratic Republic of Vietnam** made him the political commissar for **Zone** I and assigned him to the party's Standing Committee for this zone. In February 1948, he joined the army's newly created Political Bureau (*Cuc Chinh Tri*) in charge of training cadres. In 1950, he served as deputy director of the Political Bureau. Later in his career, he served as ambassador to China between 1974 and 1989.

**NGUYỄN TRUNG VỊNH (1901–?).** Prominent, non-communist nationalist during the Indochina War. Born in Chau Doc province in southern Vietnam, he studied in Hong Kong and held a bachelor's degree in English. He was also a graduate of the *École des hautes études commerciales* in France. During the interwar period, he worked in colonial Indochina as a specialist in commerce and agriculture. His activities during World War II are unknown. He was an active supporter of Franco-Vietnamese cooperation and very hostile to the **Democratic Republic of Vietnam**. He held French citizenship. He was named under-secretary of the National Economy for the provisional South Vietnam government in April 1948. In 1950, he served as the president of the Vietnamese delegation to the **Pau Conference** in France. In February 1951, he became minister of Finance in the second cabinet of **Tran Van Huu**; minister of Foreign Affairs in the third Tran Van Huu cabinet of 8 March 1952; and appointed by decree advisor to the Assembly of the **French Union** in June 1952. In January 1954, he became vice president of Council and minister of Agriculture and **Land Reform** in the new government led by Prince **Buu Loc**.

**NGUYỄN TÚ MINH.** *See* NGUYỄN VĂN THANH.

**NGUYỄN TƯỜNG TAM (NHẤT LINH, 1910– 1963).** Vietnamese journalist, novelist, and anti-communist nationalist. He completed his secondary studies in 1923 at the *Lycée du Protectorat* in **Hanoi** and worked in the colonial administration as a civil servant. By the 1930s, he had become one of Vietnam's best-known writers and founded the literary group, *Tu Luc Van Doan* (Self Reliance Group). He left his job in the civil service and dedicated himself full-time to writing and journalism. He also studied at the *École supérieure des beaux-arts* in Hanoi and then studied journalism in France between 1927 and 1930. Besides his cultural interests, Nguyen Tuong Tam also became increasingly involved in nationalist politics in the 1930s. In 1939, he founded the Greater Viet Nam People's Party (*Dai Viet Dan Chinh*) before fleeing to China to avoid French arrest.

He returned to northern Vietnam following the formation of the **Democratic Republic of Vietnam** (DRV) and joined forces with the **Vietnamese Nationalist Party** (*Viet Nam Quoc Dan Dang*, VNQDD) and the **Greater Vietnam Nationalist Party** (*Dai Viet Quoc Dan Dang*) in opposition to the **Indochinese Communist Party**. He briefly served as the DRV's minister of Foreign Affairs between March and November 1946. In April 1946, he led the Vietnamese delegation in negotiations with the French during the **Dalat Conference** but was overshadowed by others. He refused to take part in the **Fontainebleau** negotiations in mid-1946 in France and left Vietnam for China shortly thereafter. He was Foreign Minister in name only. In 1947, together with other exiled nationalist leaders, he participated in the formation of the United National Front, which urged **Bao Dai** (he was also in China) to act as its spokesman in creating an anti-communist alternative to the DRV. Nguyen Tuong Tam withdrew from politics in October 1947 and returned to Hanoi in 1951 before moving to **Saigon** after the **Geneva Accords** provisionally divided Vietnam in 1954. He committed suicide in Saigon in 1963. *See also* CIVIL WAR; CULTURE; KHAI HUNG.

**NGUYỄN VĂN BAN.** *See* NGUYỄN XUÂN HOÀNG.

**NGUYỄN VĂN CHÍ (1903–1989).** Worked as an educator in the **Democratic Republic of Vietnam** (DRV) during the war. Born in My Tho province in southern Vietnam, Nguyen Van Chi completed his secondary studies at the *Lycée Chasseloup Laubat* in **Saigon** before continuing his studies at the *École supérieure de pédagogie de **Hanoi*** where he studied with **Dang Thai Mai**, **Cao Van Thinh,** and Ton Quang Phiet. Nguyen Van Chi graduated from there in 1928 and taught in a number of secondary schools, including the *Lycée Pétrus Truong Vinh Ky* in Saigon. After World War II, he became increasingly involved in nationalist politics. In early 1946, such activities landed him in jail, although he was released shortly thereafter. He refused to cooperate with the colonial authorities and stopped teaching in French-backed schools. In early 1947, he left Saigon with **Dang Minh Tru** to work in the DRV's rudimentary educational system. He soon found himself director of the Educational Service in the south, where he helped create a number of resistance schools (**Nguyen Van To**, Thai Van Lung, **Huynh Phan Ho**, etc.). Following the end of the war, he remained in the south to work.

**NGUYỄN VĂN CHÍ (1906–1980).** Spokesman for the **Democratic Republic of Vietnam** (DRV) during the Indochina War. In 1924, he entered the *École normale d'instituteurs* in **Saigon** before continuing his studies in Lyon, France. He obtained his high school diploma there and then studied at the *Faculté des lettres* in Lyon. In 1930, following the crushing of the Yen Bay revolt, Nguyen Van Chi participated in Vietnamese student demonstrations against colonial repression. He met his wife, Juliette Baccot there (better known as Françoise Corrèze in the French Resistance) and became friends with **Pham Van Bach**. In 1937, 15 days before taking the prestigious French national exam (*agrégation*), Nguyen Van Chi was refused the right to do so on the grounds that he was not a French citizen and that his legal status of *sujet français* was not sufficient to reverse this decision, a discriminatory experience that marked him profoundly. In 1938, he was elected president of the *Association des étudiants* *coloniaux de France* and crossed paths with the likes of L. S. Senghor. Despite Nguyen Van Chi's status of *sujet français*, he joined and was accepted into the French army to fight the Nazis and, following the early French defeat in 1940, he joined the French Resistance. In 1941, the Nazis executed his cousin, Huynh Khuong An, at Chateaubriant and deported Nguyen Van Chi's wife.[7] In 1946, thanks to his wartime service, Nguyen Van Chi was finally naturalized as a French citizen; but this did not prevent him from supporting the nationalist cause of the DRV. In 1947, on the request of **Pham Van Dong**, Nguyen Van Chi moved to Paris to help the Vietnamese diplomatic delegation there broadcast the Vietnamese cause to the French people and the world. He became an advisor to **Tran Ngoc Danh**, head of the delegation. Even after the expulsion of Tran Ngoc Danh in 1949, Nguyen Van Chi continued to work as the DRV's Paris press attaché. He attended the **Geneva Conference** of 1954 and wrote numerous articles in ***Esprit, Témoignage chrétien*** and *Le Monde* in favor of French decolonization and Vietnamese independence. *See also* ANTICOLONIALISM; COLLABORATION; DESERTION.

**NGUYỄN VĂN CÚC.** *See* NGUYỄN VĂN LINH.

**NGUYEN VAN DE.** *See* NGUYEN KHANG.

**NGUYỄN VĂN ĐÔI.** *See* VƯƠNG THỪA VŨ.

**NGUYỄN VĂN ĐỒNG.** *See* ĐỒNG SĨ NGUYÊN.

**NGUYỄN VĂN HÌNH (1915–2004).** Prominent non-communist politician and military officer in the Associated State of Vietnam. Like his father Nguyen Van Tam, Hinh enjoyed French nationality. He completed his secondary studies at the *Lycée Chasseloup-Laubat* before traveling to France to study mathematics at the *Lycée Saint Louis*. In 1938, he graduated as a pilot from the French *École de l'air* and served in a bomber squadron in the French **Air Force**. During the fall of France in 1940, Nguyen Van Hinh received the *Croix de guerre*. He later joined Free French forces, commanding a bomber group based in Algeria. He participated in the French occupation of Germany. In 1947, he held the rank of lieutenant colonel in the French armed forces. In that year, he joined the French General Staff of the Air as Assistant to the Chief of the Signals Section. In 1948, he returned to Algeria to command an air group again.

In 1949, he returned to Vietnam with his squadron. In October 1949, he was named chief of operations (3ème bureau) in the French Far East Air Command (*Commandement Air en Extrême-Orient*). In May 1950, the new prime minister to **Bao Dai, Tran Van Huu,** appointed Nguyen Van Hinh's father chief of the security forces. The prime minister also asked the son to help create the armed forces for the Associated State of Vietnam in 1949. Nguyen Van Hinh agreed and was detached from the French Air Command and appointed secretary general of the Ministry of National Defense in the Tran Van Huu government. In November 1950, Nguyen Van Hinh also assumed the duty of serving as chief of Bao Dai's military cabinet. The new French commander-in-chief, general **Jean de Lattre de Tassigny**, was a mobilizing force in creating an effective Vietnamese national army and looked to Nguyen Van Hinh to play a leading role as one of the most experienced Vietnamese officers of the time. In 1951, Nguyen Van Hinh became a colonel. He was a firm believer in the need to create uniquely Vietnamese "**commando** battalions" to take the battle to the adversary. Bao Dai and the French supported him in this endeavor. In March 1952, Nguyen Van Hinh was promoted to brigadier general and became the first chief of staff of the Vietnamese national army. In February 1953, the Franco-Vietnamese High Command adopted his commando project. In that year, he visited the United States to observe training instruction and methods and pressed the Americans to help make up for the lag in French assistance.

As the war reached its climax at **Dien Bien Phu** in 1953–1954, Nguyen Van Hinh, as chief of staff, was directly involved in planning operation **Atlante** (along with **Nguyen Van Thieu** and Nguyen Van Vy). Nguyen Van Hinh served as chief of the Joint Chiefs of Staff of the armed forces of the Associated State of Vietnam until **Ngo Dinh Diem** fired him on 11 September 1954. Reluctant to take on Diem, Nguyen Van Hinh returned to France and rejoined the French Air Force. He served in the **Algerian War** at Colomb-Béchar before becoming deputy commandant in the French Air Force in May 1962 and deputy chief of the Joint Chiefs of Staff. He retired from the French Air Force in late 1969. Two of his

7. One can visit the memorial dedicated to Huynh Khuong An and others in the French Cemetery Père Lachaise in Paris.

brothers were killed by **Democratic Republic of Vietnam**'s forces in 1945.

**NGUYỄN VĂN HƯƠNG (1906–?).** Military surgeon in the **Democratic Republic of Vietnam** (DRV) during the Indochina War. Born in Long Xuyen province in southern Vietnam, in 1927 he entered the *Faculté de médecine* at the Indochinese University and continued his studies in France between 1931 and 1933. He graduated from the *Faculté de médecine* in Paris. Between 1934 and 1945, he practiced medicine in **Saigon**. On 6 January 1946, he was elected to the DRV's National Assembly for the province of Long Xuyen. In 1947, he became a member of the Resistance and Administrative Committee for Nam Bo and simultaneously served as the director of the Medical Service for the Militia in Nam Bo (*So Y Te Quan Dan Y Nam Bo*) during the Indochina War. In 1954, following the division of Vietnam, he repatriated to northern Vietnam and worked there as the director of the 303rd military hospital. *See also* DISEASE; EXPERIENCE OF WAR, DIEN BIEN PHU.

**NGUYỄN VĂN HUYÊN (1905–1975).** One of modern Vietnam's cultural and educational luminaries. Born in **Hanoi**, Nguyen Van Huyen was orphaned at a young age. However, this did not stop him from becoming highly educated. Between 1926 and 1935, he studied in France where he received his bachelor's degree in letters in 1929 and in law in 1931. Between 1931 and 1935, he taught at the ***École nationale des langues orientales vivantes***. In 1934, he was the first Vietnamese to submit to the Sorbonne both a doctoral thesis (*Les chants alternés des garçons et des filles en* ***Annam***) and a complementary thesis (*L'habitat sur pilotis en Asie du Sud-Est*). Both works were published. He returned to Vietnam in 1935 and taught at the *École du Protectorat* until 1938, when he began working in the ***École française d'Extrême-Orient***, becoming a permanent member in 1940. Between 1941 and 1945, he took part in the *Comité de recherches scientifiques de l'Indochine* (1941–1945). During the Japanese occupation, he was a member of the Indochinese Federal Council. With the advent of the **Democratic Republic of Vietnam** in 1945, he took over the direction of the *École française d'Extrême-Orient* and became director of the Department of University Studies (*Dai Hoc Hoc Vu*) when it was opened in November 1945. He served as an advisor to the Vietnamese delegation during the **Dalat Conference** in April 1946 and was a member of the Vietnamese delegation to the **Fontainebleau Conference** in mid-1946. In October 1946, he became minister of Public Instruction. He held that post for the next 29 years even though he never became a member of the communist party.

**NGUYỄN VĂN KHƯƠNG.** *See* SONG HÀO.

**NGUYỄN VĂN KỈNH (TRUNG NAM, 1916–1981).** Powerful, behind-the-scenes communist leader in the south during the Indochina War. Born in **Saigon**, Nguyen Van Kinh grew up in a francophile intellectual family. He became politically active during the Popular Front period. Between 1935 and 1937, he was a member of the Communist Youth League. In 1938, he joined the **Indochinese Communist Party** (ICP), was active in the organization of the Indochinese Congress during the Popular Front, and wrote in several communist papers such as *Le Peuple*. The French arrested and incarcerated him in 1941. He walked out of prison in April 1945 following the Japanese overthrow of the French. In October 1945, Nguyen Van Kinh joined with other communists, including **Le Duan**, at a secret conference in My Tho province in the south to create the revamped and unified ICP Territorial Committee for Nam Bo (*Xu Uy Nam Bo*). He became a member of this new Party committee. In January 1946, he was elected to the **Democratic Republic of Vietnam** National Assembly. Between 1948 and 1951, he was deputy to Le Duan on the Territorial Committee, making him one of the most powerful behind-the-scenes communists running the war and the Party in the south. During the Second Party Congress in early 1951, Nguyen Van Kinh became an alternate member on the Executive Committee of the Central Committee. When the Territorial Committee was replaced by the Party's new **Central Office for the Southern Region** (*Trung Uong Cuc Mien Nam*, better known by its American acronym as COSVN) in June 1951, he served on its Standing Committee until the end of the war using the nom de guerre of Trung Nam. In 1952, he was president of the Federation of Students of Nam Bo. After the **Geneva Accords** divided Vietnam into two provisional halves in mid-1954, Nguyen Van Kinh repatriated to the north where he worked in the party's Central Committee and served later as ambassador to the Soviet Union.

**NGUYỄN VĂN LẬP.** *See* KOSTAS SARANTIDIS.

**NGUYỄN VĂN LINH (NGUYỄN VĂN CÚC, MƯỜI CÚC, ANH ÚT, 1915–1998).** One of the ranking communist leaders in southern Vietnam who worked closely with **Le Duan** and **Le Duc Tho** during the Indochina War. Born in Hung Yen province in northern Vietnam, Nguyen Van Linh became involved in radical politics in the late 1920s. In 1930, colonial authorities arrested and shipped him off to prison at **Poulo Condor**. In 1936, with the advent of the Popular Front period, Nguyen Van Linh regained his freedom, joined the **Indochinese Communist Party**, and began mobilizing workers in the Haiphong area. In 1939, the Party sent him to southern and central Vietnam to help rebuild networks there. In late 1939, he helped reorganize the Party's Territorial Committee for **Annam** (*Xu Uy Trung Ky*). In early 1941, the French arrested him in Vinh and sent him back to Poulo Condor. Nguyen Van Linh returned to southern Vietnam on **23 September 1945**, together with Le Duan and **Pham Hung**, and helped rebuild the Party's leadership in the south. He played a particularly important role in running the Party's networks and the war from **Saigon**-Cholon, where he became in August 1946 secretary of the Party's city branch, organizing workers and unions from behind the scenes. In 1947, he joined the Party's powerful Territorial Committee for Nam Bo (*Xu Uy Nam Bo*) and in July 1948 he entered its Standing Committee. In 1950, he presided over the Party's Special Region for Saigon-Cholon (*Dac Khu Saigon-Cholon*). In 1953, he was called to the north to head up the "Board for Political Propaganda and Ideological Education" (*Ban Tuyen Huan*) in the Party's Central Committee. In mid-1954, the Politburo directed Le Duan and a number of other high-ranking communists, including Nguyen Van Linh, to return to work secretly in southern Vietnam after the war. The bonds formed with Le Duan during the Indochina War helped Nguyen Van Linh become one of the most powerful communists in Vietnam. He would serve as general secretary of the Vietnamese Communist Party between 1986 and 1991.

**NGUYỄN VĂN LONG.** A southern communist trained in Thailand who carried out important clandestine missions in Southeast Asia during the Indochina War. Although he worked for the Japanese secret services in Thailand during World War II, he successfully camouflaged his communist affiliation. He knew personally Thai statesmen **Pibun Songgram** and **Pridi Banomyong**. After the war, Nguyen Van Long collaborated closely with Vietnamese communists working out of Thailand. In the late 1940s, he traveled to northern **Burma** to establish new logistical links with northern Vietnam and helped recruit disgruntled **Lao Issara** troops to the **Democratic Republic of Vietnam**'s cause. He was particularly close to Lao Prince **Suphānuvong**. *See also* OVERSEAS VIETNAMESE IN THAILAND.

**NGUYỄN VĂN LUYỆN.** *See* NGUYỄN ĐÌNH LUYỆN.

**NGUYỄN VĂN SÂM (?–1947).** Following the Japanese overthrow of the French in the ***coup de force* of 9 March 1945**, he founded the Vietnamese National Independence Party (*Viet Nam Quoc Gia Doc Lap Dang*). He served as the imperial delegate of **Bao Dai** in Cochinchina and played a role in obtaining Japan's permission, in August, to unify the French colony of Cochinchina with the rest of Vietnam. He resigned, however, with the advent of the **Democratic Republic of Vietnam** (DRV) and the abdication of the emperor. He later supported non-communist efforts to set up a national front with Bao Dai at its head in order to compete with the DRV. The DRV and the **Indochinese Communist Party** judged his activities sufficiently dangerous for having him assassinated on 10 October 1947. *See also* CIVIL WAR; VIETNAMESE NATIONALIST PARTY.

**NGUYỄN VĂN TÂM (1895–1990).** Prominent non-communist nationalist strongly opposed to the **Democratic Republic of Vietnam** (DRV) during the Indochina War. Born in Tay Ninh province in southern Vietnam, **Nguyen Van Tam** began his career as a school teacher, but shifted into the colonial administration where he rose to the rank of provincial governor. He was an ardent French supporter and obtained French nationality in 1927. He was instrumental in the effective repression of the communist uprising in **Cochinchina** in 1940. His harsh tactics, especially in My Tho province, in the 1930s led people to refer to him widely as the "Tiger of Cai Lay" (the birthplace of **Cao Dang Chiem**). One of his sons, **Nguyen Van Hinh**, became a pilot in the French **Air Force** and served in the Battle of France in 1940.

Following the Japanese overthrow of the French in March 1945, Nguyen Van Tam was arrested and tortured. Upon the advent of the DRV, he found himself behind bars again. Forces loyal to the DRV killed two of his other sons, something which Nguyen Van Tam never forgot or forgave. On 1 June 1946, he joined the French-conceived **Provisional Government of the Republic of Cochinchina** as under-secretary of state for Internal Security. He then became minister of Defense in the cabinet of **Le Van Hoach** following the suicide of **Nguyen Van Thinh** in November 1946.

Nguyen Van Tam supported the political autonomy of Cochinchina. He was an advisor to the Provisional Committee of the *Rassemblement autonomiste cochinchinois* and, on 11 March 1950, became its general secretary. However, he put his separatist ideas on hold in order to support the anti-communist Associated State of Vietnam, led by **Bao Dai**.

Nguyen Van Tam concentrated on developing the new state's policing and security forces. On 12 June 1950, he began serving as general director of the National Police and Security in the first cabinet of **Tran Van Huu**, putting an end to the DRV's urban war on **Saigon** in 1950. He became minister of Public Security in the second cabinet of Tran Van Huu, created on 18 February 1951. He was said to be "tough and hard-working and an expert in dealing with the terrorist movements in Saìgon". General **Jean de Lattre de Tassigny** made him *Officier de la Légion d'honneur* on 8 May 1951 in recognition of his counter-terrorist activities and had him promoted to commander in March 1952.

In June 1951, Nguyen Van Tam was put in charge of the reorganization and "**pacification**" of "liberated" zones in northern Vietnam and obtained "special powers" from the government to achieve these ends. In August 1951, he became acting minister of National Defense during the absence of Tran Van Huu. On 16 November 1951, because of his effective "pacification" activities, the government asked him to serve temporarily as the governor of northern Vietnam. On 2 December 1951, Bao Dai issued a decree making him imperial delegate for the territory of the *Populations montagnardes du Nord*. In 1952, Nguyen Van Tam became minister of the Interior in the third government of Tran Van Huu, created on 8 March 1952. On 6 June 1952, Bao Dai asked him to form and lead a new government, maintaining his portfolio as minister of the Interior.

While there is no doubt that Nguyen Van Tam's destiny and choices were closely tied to those of the French, even this stalwart partner became disillusioned by the colonizers, announcing in a public radio broadcast that it was "important that we no longer remain in this Union as tenants of a house built without us". Nguyen Van Tam played a pivotal role in shutting down the DRV's urban war in Saigon-Cholon and elsewhere. He also did not mince his words or his actions. He advised **Jawaharlal Nehru** to settle his own problems before trying to arbitrate those of his neighbors. And as for Vietnamese communism, he said that "One does not come to terms with the **Indochinese Communist Party**. One beats it down, or it beats you down". He died in France in 1990.

**NGUYỄN VĂN TẠO (1908–1970).** Born in Cholon in southern Vietnam and orphaned at a young age, Nguyen Van Tao was raised by a rich property owner who financed his studies. In 1923, he entered the *Lycée Chasseloup Laubat* in **Saigon**, where he shone until his expulsion in 1926 for taking part in the student strikes sweeping Vietnam following the death of Phan Chu Trinh. Nguyen Van Tao secretly left for France in August 1926, where he continued his studies at the *Lycée Mignet* in Aix-en-Provence between October 1926 and April 1927. During his time in France, he also made a leftward journey leading him to the **French Communist Party** (FCP), which he joined in 1927. Nguyen Van Tao organized the Indochinese communist "group" in Paris in April 1928 and was active in the FCP's Colonial Section. Between 1928 and 1931, he was a member of the FCP's Central Committee and contributed to the communist paper, *L'Humanité*. He was expelled from France in 1931 because of his participation in the organization of an "anti-Exhibition" at the *Exposition coloniale* held outside Paris, in which he highlighted the evils of French colonialism.

Back in southern Vietnam, he was active in politics during the more liberal Popular Front period, helping to organize the Indochinese Congress. This did not stop colonial authorities from arresting and incarcerating him in 1936, though he regained his freedom about a year later. The French arrested Nguyen Van Tao again in 1940 and sent him to **Poulo Condor** before transferring in 1943 to Ba Ria. Upon his release from this particularly rough place in 1944, he was placed under house arrest in Rach Gia province. He ardently supported the **Democratic Republic of Vietnam** and traveled to the north in 1946 to take part in the National Assembly. He became minister of Labor in that same year. In 1947, Nguyen Van Tao joined the Central Committee of the **Indochinese Communist Party**. Surprisingly little, however, is known about his activities thereafter.

**NGUYỄN VĂN TÂY.** *See* NGUYỄN THANH SƠN.

**NGUYỄN VĂN THẮNG.** *See* NGUYỄN HẢI THẦN.

**NGUYỄN VĂN THANH (NGUYỄN HOÀI THANH, SÁU THANH, NGUYỄN TÚ MINH, 1915–?).** Military leader of the **Cao Dai** movement during much of the Indochina War. Born in Tay Ninh province in southern Vietnam, Nguyen Van Thanh helped construct the Cao Dai's holy temple in Tay Ninh in 1935. In 1941, according to the French police, he entered the service of the Japanese and collaborated with another leading Cao Dai figure, **Tran Quang Vinh**. Nguyen Van Thanh became something of a military leader following the outbreak of war between the **Democratic Republic of Vietnam** (DRV) and the French in September 1945. He collaborated militarily with the DRV until the leading Cao Dai forces defected to the French in mid-1946. Nguyen Van Thanh returned to the Cao Dai holy center in Tay Ninh in late 1946 and began collaborating discreetly with French armed forces against the DRV in southern Vietnam. He was designated commander-in-chief of Cao Dai troops in June 1951 and elected president of the Central Committee of the Vietnamese Restoration Party (*Viet Nam Phuc Quoc Hoi*) at the same time. He resigned his command in March 1953 because of pressures within the Cao Dai movement. He then left for France where he briefly studied at the *École de guerre*, thanks to the support of French General **Paul-Louis Bondis**. Nguyen Van Thanh returned again to France in July 1953. *See also* COLLABORATION; DESERTION.

**NGUYỄN VĂN THÍCH, JEAN-MARIE (1889–?).** An ardent **Catholic** supporter of Vietnamese independence and the nationalist cause of the **Democratic Republic of Vietnam** (DRV). Born in Thua Thien province in central Vietnam, he studied in the Catholic school Pellerin in Hue to become a school teacher. He graduated in 1912 and began teaching in Hue then elsewhere in central Vietnam. In 1918, he converted to Catholicism, despite the opposition of his father, and entered the Grand Seminary in Hue. He was ordained a priest in 1926 and began teaching at the *Institut des petits frères du Sacré Cœur* in Truong An. In 1927, Fr. Nguyen Van Thich published what may be the first developed critique of communism written by a Vietnamese author, *Van De Cong San* or the Problem of Communism. In 1934, he returned to teach at the Small Seminary in An Ninh. He was also deeply involved in the nationalization of Vietnamese Catholicism during the interwar period. In 1936, he founded and edited the bi-monthly literary review, *Vi Chua* (For God). He was a strong supporter of **scouting** and the supreme advisor for the League of Catholics of Vietnam. He wrote frequently in Vietnamese Catholic papers *Lien Doan* and *To Quoc*.

His nationalism was such that he became an early Catholic supporter of the DRV's independence cause. He addressed a large meeting of Vietnamese Catholics in the *Stade olympique* in Hue on 23 September 1945 during which he called upon the faithful to support the independence of Vietnam and its spokesman, **Ho Chi Minh**. Following the outbreak of full-scale war on **19 December 1946**, he appears to have remained in Hue, but refused to take part in French-backed governments. In 1946, he was named chaplain at the *École Pellerin* and priest for the Kim Long area in central Vietnam. On 7 May 1950, he became president of the central Vietnamese chapter of the Association for the Assistance of War Refugees. He was also a professor at the *Lycée Khai Dinh* in Hue. His activities thereafter remain unclear.

**NGUYỄN VĂN THIỆU (1923/24?–2001).** Noncommunist Vietnamese nationalist and President of the **Republic of Vietnam** (1967–1975). Born in Phan Rang in central Vietnam in 1924, he grew up in a fishing and rice-cultivating family. He changed his original date of birth from 1924 to 1923 on the advice of an astrologer and studied at the Catholic Pellerin School in Hue. With the overthrow of the French in March 1945 and the defeat of the Japanese, he briefly joined the **Democratic Republic of Vietnam** (DRV) and became a district chief. He converted to Catholicism in order to marry Christine-Hélène Nguyen Van Nhi (Nguyen Thi Mai Anh). Nguyen Van Thieu was hostile to the communists and their plans for Vietnam. He left the DRV to enter the French Merchant Marine Academy. In December

1948, he entered the School for Regular Officers from which he graduated in June 1949. In 1949, he also attended the French Infantry School in Coetquidan, France, and studied in the Staff College in **Hanoi** in 1952. He participated in several operations against the DRV, including encounters near his home village during Operation **Atlante**. At the end of the war, he was serving in Hung Yen in the north as battalion commander. *See also* COLLABORATION; CROSSOVER; DESERTION; VIETNAMESE NATIONALIST PARTY.

**NGUYỄN VĂN THỊNH (1888–1946).** Vietnamese non-communist politician who led the French-created **Provisional Government of the Republic of Cochinchina** until his death on 10 November 1946. Born in Cholon in southern Vietnam, he graduated as a doctor from the Pasteur Institute and the *Institut de médecine coloniale* in Paris, where he wrote his thesis on beriberi. He acquired French citizenship, became a member of the Indochinese Constitutionalist Party in 1926, and served as a federal counselor during the Vichy period. He was a delegate to the Indochinese Economic Conference in Tokyo in 1942. He was also the owner of large rice fields in southern Vietnam and was at one time the president of the Rice Growers' Union.

Following the Japanese overthrow of the French in the ***coup de force*** **of 9 March 1945**, he became president of the National Relief Commission. With the Japanese defeat a few months later, he refused to collaborate with the newly created **Democratic Republic of Vietnam** in order to serve as the first president of the Provisional Government of the Republic of Cochinchina from 7 May 1946, though formally announced by High Commissioners **Georges Thierry d'Argenlieu** on 1 June 1946. Nguyen Van Thinh was *président du Conseil* (prime minister) and minister of the Interior of the new government. As a French citizen, he largely enjoyed the support of the French settler community. He held his post until 10 November 1946.

Disillusioned by the course of events, he hung himself, dealing a severe blow to French colonial efforts to build up **Cochinchina** against nationalist pressure to incorporate it into Vietnam. His suicide sparked a crisis among French decision-makers fearful of losing Cochinchina to the DRV and led in part to the adoption of a much harder line in French relations with the DRV based in **Hanoi**. French attention increasingly turned to resurrecting the **Bao Dai Solution** of the early 1930s. In the suicide note he left behind, Nguyen Van Thinh explained that the leaders of Vietnam had to act: *Si la masse de notre peuple ne m'a pas compris, je veux que vous, mes amis, les intellectuels Trung, Nam, Bac, vous qui avez la charge du destin de la patrie, ne vous cantonnez plus dans une expectative criminelle. Vous devez réagir. See also ATTENTISME*; COLLABORATION; *FRANÇAIS D'INDOCHINE*.

**NGUYỄN VĂN THỌ.** *See* VŨ TÙNG.

**NGUYỄN VĂN TỐ (ỨNG HOÈ, 1889–1947).** One of modern Vietnam's most illustrious **intellectuals** killed by the French during a paratrooper raid on Bac Kan in October 1947. Born in **Hanoi**, he studied at the College of Interpreters and the *École de droit* in Hanoi. During the interwar period, he joined the ranks of the ***École Française d'Extrême-Orient***, where he worked with the likes of **Paul Mus** and Georges Coedès. During World War II, Nguyen Van To served as acting head of the administrative secretariat and conducted research into Vietnamese customs and literature. He was also active in Vietnamese nationalist activities. He served as president of the *Société d'enseignement mutuel de l'association pour la diffusion du Quoc Ngu,* was a regular contributor to the nationalist journal, *Tri Tan*, vice president of the *Société annamite d'encouragement à l'art et à l'industire*, municipal advisor for Hanoi, and held the rank of *Chevalier de la Légion d'Honneur*. He was well known in Hanoi for wearing a traditional Vietnamese tunic with a black turban.

With the overthrow of the French and the end of World War II, he became a dedicated supporter of the independence of Vietnam. He joined the **Democratic Republic of Vietnam** (DRV), serving as the minister of Social Affairs in the provisional government between September 1945 and March 1946. He was chairman of the government's first First National Assembly in 1946 and was appointed minister without portfolio in the government of November 1946. During this time, he continued to write moving and powerful essays on nationalism and colonialism in the government's French-language paper, *Le Peuple*, including some of the first indictments of the French use of **torture**. Following the outbreak of full-scale war on **19 December 1946**, he continued to serve the government in the hills of northern Vietnam. Albeit a non-communist, he was a fierce anti-colonialist. As he confided to a friend in 1947 on what he saw as the obsessive French desire to recreate colonial Indochina: "*Cette résistance sera très longue à cause de la stupidité des colonialistes français. Ils feront souffrir notre peuple, mais jamais ils ne parviendront à rétablir leur protectorat*". He was killed in 1947 when French paratroopers landed in Bac Kan in an effort to eliminate the DRV's leadership. As of early 2011, his body had never been recovered. *See also* LÉA, OPERATION.

**NGUYỄN VĂN VỊNH (1918–1978).** Born in Nam Dinh province in northern Vietnam, he became involved in nationalist politics in the late 1930s. Colonial authorities arrested and incarcerated him 1937. He regained his freedom in 1940 and moved between Haiphong and southern Vietnam before returning to the north where he entered into contact with **Truong Chinh**. He was arrested again in 1943, sentenced to 20 years of hard labor, and shipped off to **Poulo Condor**. Upon his release at the end of World War II, he joined the armed forces of the **Democratic Republic of Vietnam**. He had apparently joined the **Indochinese Communist Party** (ICP) by 1947, when he became a member Party's Territorial Committee for Nam Bo. Nguyen Van Vinh served on the committee until 1949. His real task was in helping the ICP keep tabs on military affairs in southern Vietnam. Between 1946 and 1950, he was a political commissar to the High Command of war **Zone VIII** (*Khu Chien VIII*) in southern Vietnam, the ICP's secretary for the zone, and a member of the Party's territorial committee for the south. His relationship with Truong Chinh and no doubt the time he shared with ranking communists behind bars at Poulo Condor explain his meteoric rise in the Party's southern politico-military organizations. He worked closely with **Tran Van Tra** in building, consolidating, and leading war Zone VIII. With the death of **Nguyen Binh** in 1951, Nguyen Van Vinh and Tran Van Tra assumed more important tasks in running the Party's Military Affairs in southern Vietnam. In 1952, Nguyen Van Vinh became the secretary for the Party's Military Zone Committee and political commissar to the High Command for the **Inter-Zone for Western Nam Bo** (*Phan Lien Khu Mien Tay Nam Bo*). Between 1953 and 1954, he joined the Party's Standing Committee for this same section, and became deputy commander for the **Inter-Zone for Eastern Nam Bo** (*Phan Lien Khu Mien Dong Nam Bo*). He also played a pivotal role in developing zone VIII's photographic section. Following the division of Vietnam into two provisional halves at Geneva in mid-1954, he repatriated to the north.

**NGUYỄN VĂN VỸ (1916–?).** Born in **Hanoi**, Nguyen Van Vy completed his secondary studies at the *Lycée Albert Sarraut* between 1930 and 1937 before studying law at the *Faculté de droit* between 1937 and 1939. In 1940, he joined the French colonial army and attended the military academy at Tong. Upon graduation, he was commissioned in the French army in which he served between 1940 and 1948 as an Infantry Unit Commander. In 1948, he studied in the French Army's Airborne School in Pau before returning to Vietnam in September to command two new Vietnamese airborne units. In 1950, the French dropped Nguyen Van Vy into the dissident Catholic area of Phat Diem. After a few shots were allegedly fired, Vy helped broker a deal between the armed, anti-colonialist Catholics led by **Le Huu Tu** and the emerging Associated State of Vietnam led by **Bao Dai.** In May 1950, **Nguyen Van Hinh**, secretary general of the Ministry of National defense, selected Nguyen Van Vy to attend the French Army's General Staff School at the *École supérieure de Guerre* in Paris. Vy studied with the likes of **Tran Van Don.** Upon his return to Vietnam, Nguyen Van Vy replaced Nguyen Van Hinh as director of Bao Dai's military cabinet. In 1952, Nguyen Van Vy attained the rank of full colonel in the Associated State of Vietnam and brigadier general in July 1954. He was named a military advisor to the Vietnamese delegation to the **Geneva Conference** led by Tran Van Do.

**NGUYỄN VĂN VỸ, MICHEL (1895–1976).** Southern Vietnamese **intellectual** who supported the independence cause of the **Democratic Republic of Vietnam** (DRV). Born in Sa Dec province, he studied in France were he graduated from the *École supérieure du commerce*. He also acquired French citizenship and married the daughter of a French banker. He returned to French Indochina in the 1920s and worked as a deputy director in the *Banque franco-chinoise*. He was an active intellectual during the interwar period, member of the **Vietnamese Democratic Party** (*Dang Dan Chu*), and served on the directing Committee of the Association for the Promotion of Quoc Ngu (*Hôi Truyen Ba Quôc Ngu*). While he remained in **Saigon** during the Indochina War and never joined the communist party, he was among southern intellectuals who submitted a petition to the

French in 1947 calling on them to negotiate with **Ho Chi Minh**'s government. In August 1954, he participated in the Movement for the Defense of Peace led by **Nguyen Huu Tho** aimed at unifying Vietnam through elections in accordance with the **Geneva Accords** of 1954. *See also* NGUYEN THI BINH; NGUYEN THI DINH.

**NGUYỄN VĂN XUÂN (1892–1989?).** Leading non-communist politician and military officer in the **Provisional Government of the Republic of Cochinchina.** Born in Gia Dinh province, he studied in France and was the first Vietnamese to enter the *École polytechnique*. He fought on the Western Front during World War I and received the French *Croix de guerre* with palms for bravery. General Philippe Pétain personally cited him for the bravery he demonstrated during the battle of Verdun. Nguyen Van Xuan obtained French citizenship and married a French woman. He apparently remained in the French army, serving in Indochina during the interwar period. In 1939, he was vice director of artillery for Cochinchina and Cambodia. Later in that year, he also worked in Paris in the Ministry of the colonies' military division in charge of equipping the French Empire for defense. He then returned to Indochina.

When the Japanese overthrew the French in the ***coup de force* of 9 March 1945**, he refused to collaborate and joined his wife who had been incarcerated in the Citadel in **Hanoi** by the Japanese. When the French returned to southern Vietnam, he returned to **Saigon** to serve as vice president of the Cochinchinese Council. He held the rank of colonel in the French army. In July–August 1946, he served as president of the delegation of the Provisional Government of the Republic of Cochinchina to the second **Dalat Conference**. Between June and December 1946, he was minister of Defense and vice president of the Provisional Government. By 1947, he held the rank of general in the French army. He took over from **Le Van Hoach** as the president of the Cochinchinese Republic in October 1947, assuming simultaneously the portfolios of Defense and the Interior. In April 1948, he returned to the premiership and served simultaneously as minister of Defense and the Interior. He was instrumental in efforts to bring **Bao Dai** back to lead a non-communist Vietnamese state against the **Democratic Republic of Vietnam** (DRV). On 20 May 1948, he became president of the provisional government of South Vietnam. A month later, a DRV military court sentenced him to death *in absentia* for treason. In May 1949, Nguyen Van Xuan attained the rank of general of division, although it is unclear whether it was in the French army or that of the emerging Associated State of Vietnam. His government resigned in June 1949 upon the return of Bao Dai to Vietnam. In July 1949, he assumed the post of vice president and minister of Defense in Bao Dai's new government. He later moved to France where he apparently died in 1989. *See also* ASSOCIATED STATES OF INDOCHINA; BAO DAI SOLUTION.

**NGUYỄN XIỂN (1907–1997).** Senior Vietnamese administrator and educator in the **Democratic Republic of Vietnam** (DRV). Born in Nghe An province, he became involved in nationalist politics during patriotic demonstrations following the death of Phan Chu Trinh. He completed his high school education in **Hanoi** in 1928 and left for France to pursue studies in engineering. Following his return to Vietnam in 1932, he worked in the Indochinese meteorological service. He became good friends with Lao Prince **Suphānuvong** during their studies in Paris. With the advent of the DRV in September 1945, Nguyen Xien served as the first president of the Administrative Committee for Northern Vietnam (*Uy Ban Hanh Chinh Bac Bo*) and director of the government's meteorological and hydraulic service. He was elected deputy in 1946 and in 1947 became deputy to the general secretary of the **Vietnamese Socialist Party**. Following the outbreak of full-scale war on **19 December 1946**, he helped create and lectured at the University of Basic Sciences and Higher Learning (*Truong Dai Hoc Khoa Hoc Co Ban va Su Pham Cao Cap*) where he developed the curriculum in mathematics in the hills of northern Vietnam. In 1951 and 1952, he taught at the Vietnamese School in Nanning in China.

**NGUYỄN XUÂN HOÀNG (NGUYỄN VĂN BAN, 1918–1987).** Born in Thai Binh province, Nguyen Xuan Hoang became involved in radical politics during the Popular Front period. He joined the **Indochinese Communist Party** in 1938 and served time in colonial prisons in Hoa Lo and **Poulo Condor** between 1942 and 1945. Upon his release in September 1945, he worked in southern Vietnam training political cadres for the Party in the southern war **Zone IX** (*Chien Khu IX*). In 1946–1947, he was responsible for the press in this same zone and in September 1948 he was running the political bureau there. Between June 1950 and July 1954, he transferred to northwestern Cambodia, where he served as head of the zone's political office and became deputy military commander and then commander-in-chief and political commissar for Vietnamese Volunteer Troops in all of Cambodia. In 1978, he was selected to lead the special working group B68 in charge of creating a new "revolution" and administration in and for Cambodia as **Hanoi** prepared to overthrow **Pol Pot**'s Democratic Kampuchea.

**NGUYỄN XUÂN MAI.** *See* MAI CHÍ THỌ.

**NGUYỄN-PHƯỚC BỬU HỘI (1915–1972).** French biochemist and prince in the Nguyen dynasty. After completing his secondary studies in colonial Indochina, he obtained his doctorate at the University of Paris (Sorbonne) in chemistry and lectured at the *École Polytechnique* in Paris between 1947 and 1949. He then served as director general in the Office of Atomic Energy until 1963. He was a French national, married to the American-born journalist and historian of modern Vietnam, **Ellen Hammer**.

**NGUYỄN-PHƯỚC BỬU LỘC (1914–1990).** Lawyer, politician, and prince in the Nguyen dynasty. After having completed his secondary and undergraduate studies at the *Lycée Albert Sarraut* and the *Faculté de droit* in **Hanoi**, Buu Loc left for France in 1939 to pursue his doctorate in Political Science and Economics and joined the French Bar at the Appellate Court of Paris. He defended and later published his thesis on *L'usure chez les paysans au Viet Nam* and received the *prix d'Empire* for it. After World War II, he returned to Vietnam and began a political career thanks to the emergence of a non-communist Vietnam led by the former Emperor **Bao Dai**. Buu Loc was a cousin. The latter served between October 1948 and late 1950 as cabinet director to Bao Dai in Dalat. As head of the Vietnamese delegation, Buu Loc helped negotiate the Franco-Vietnamese Accords of 8 March 1949 laying the foundation for the birth of the non-communist Associated State of Vietnam. He also monitored the debates and the ratification of new legislation in the government's National Assembly in 1950. In early 1951, he travelled to France to serve as the State of Vietnam's diplomatic representative. In May 1952, he became high commissioner for Vietnam in France, with the rank of ambassador. That same year he was elected non-resident member of the French *Académie des sciences coloniales*. Frustrated by France's unwillingness to grant full independence, he became increasingly critical of French colonial thinking, which, he claimed, undermined the legitimacy of a non-communist Vietnam competing with the **Democratic Republic of Vietnam**. On 17 December 1953, Bao Dai asked his cousin to form a new government following the resignation of President **Nguyen Van Tam**. Buu Loc agreed and announced a new government in **Saigon** on 11 January 1954. He advocated a policy of "enlightened" autocracy. However, his government garnered little more popular support than any of its predecessors, despite the fact that he had obtained a treaty promising greater independence. His April 1954 decision to integrate the armed forces of the sects into the **army of the Associated State of Vietnam** elicited strong opposition from **Cao Dai** leaders. Buu Loc was both president and minister of the Interior until **Ngo Dinh Diem** replaced him during the **Geneva Conference** in mid-June 1954. The prince served again as high commissioner to France between 1954 and 1955.

**NHIEK TIOULONG (1908–1996).** Leading Cambodian nationalist and politician. Born in Phnom Penh, Nhiek Tioulong came from an affluent and influential Cambodian family. He completed his elementary schooling at the *Collège Sisowath* and his secondary education at the *Lycée Chausseloup Laubat* in **Saigon**. Upon graduation, he was named 2nd class *anouc montrey* or notable in 1932 in the Cambodian level of the French Indochinese colonial service. He subsequently went on to hold important posts as deputy governor of the province of Prey Vang, district chief at Prey Vang, and provincial governor in Pursat and Kompong Cham, where he was working when the Japanese overthrew the French during the ***coup de force* of 9 March 1945**. The Japanese named him governor of the city of Phnom Penh. Nhiek Tioulong also served as minister of Education in the short-lived **Son Ngoc Thanh** cabinet. He nonetheless successfully negotiated the return of the French to Cambodia in late 1945, joining in October 1945 the cabinet of Prince Norodom Monireth as minister of Finances all the while continuing to run the city of Phnom Penh until February 1946.

Nhiek Tioulong headed the Cambodian delegation to the 2nd **Dalat conference** in July 1946. In dicussions there and elsewhere, he frankly expressed his hostility to the Vietnamese and French conception of an **Indochinese Federation**, which allowed the Vietnamese, in his view, to dominate Laos and Cambodia. He was anti-communist and hostile to Vietnamese meddling in Cambodian internal affairs.

In December 1946, following the resignation of Prince Monireth, Nhiek Tioulong became state minister in charge of the territories retroceded by the Thais in that month. He held this position until January 1947. In 1947, Tioulong joined forces with his ally, **Lon Nol**, to create the Khmer Renewal Party. In April 1948, he was appointed the Cambodian government's delegate to the high commissioner for France in Indochina as well as its delegate to the Superior Council of the **French Union**, where he began working in France in August 1948. Upon his return to Cambodia in November 1949, King **Norodom Sihanouk** conferred upon him the rank of colonel in the emerging Khmer Royal Army (*Armée royale khmère*) and chief of staff. Nhiek Tioulong held this position until December 1949, when he was reassigned as delegate to the French high commissioner's office. In May 1950, he became a royal delegate to the province of Battambang with the rank of minister. In the 2nd Monivong cabinet (January–March 1951), he served briefly as minister of Finance. He held the same position in the Oum Chheng Sun cabinet, constituted in March 1951. In May 1951, Nhiek Tioulong became minister of Information when Chheng Sun reshuffled the cabinet.

Nhiek Tioulong played a pivotal role in the departure of Norodom Sihanouk to Thailand in June 1953 and supported Sihanouk's **royal crusade for independence**. In July 1953, Nhiek Tioulong became minister of Public Works and Telecommunications in the reshuffled cabinet of **Penn Nouth**. In April 1954, Sihanouk made Nhiek Tioulong state minister in charge of Foreign Affairs. When Sihanouk turned over power to Penn Nouth, Nhiek Tioulong became minister of National Defense and commander-in-chief of the army in the new cabinet. *See also* DEMOCRAT PARTY.

**NIXON, RICHARD MILHOUS (1913–1994).** American vice president to **Dwight D. Eisenhower** who traveled to Indochina in 1953 to urge the French and their **Associated States of Indochina** to hold the line against communist expansion into the region. During his high-level visit to the Associated States of Vietnam, Laos, and Cambodia, Nixon met with French civilian and military leaders such as **Henri Navarre**, **René Cogny**, and **Maurice Dejean** as well as **Norodom Sihanouk**, **Bao Dai**, and **Suvanna Phūmā**. While Nixon was sensitive to nationalist demands, he urged the Associated States not to press the French too hard given the wider need to fight communist expansion into Southeast Asia. On 16 April 1954, as the **Democratic Republic of Vietnam** tightened the noose around the French camp at **Dien Bien Phu**, Nixon backed away from his heretofore bellicose statements to say that the United States should be careful not to get involved in the conflict and that it should pursue a "peaceful and honorable solution" to the war during the upcoming **Geneva Conference**. He repeated a few days later the need to reach a "negotiated peace" on the condition that it was "honorable".

**NONG KIMNY (1912–?).** Cambodian diplomat and politician. Nong Kimny completed his secondary studies at the *Lycée Chasseloup Laubat* in **Saigon** before joining the Cambodian level of the colonial civil service as a notable (*anouc montrey*). He soon rose to the rank of provincial governor of Kompong Speu. In 1941, he became King **Norodom Sihanouk's** private secretary and the following year head of the royal cabinet. Nong Kimny was wounded seriously during the Japanese ***coup de force* of 9 March 1945** that ended French rule of Indochina. He apparently joined the Japanese-backed **Son Ngoc Thanh** cabinet before returning to the French side during the Indochina War. In February 1948, Nong Kimny became first secretary of the French Legation in Bangkok, considered to be the first "Indochinese" to enter the French diplomatic corps. In February 1951, he was named chief of the Cambodian diplomatic mission to Washington D.C. with the rank of minister, representing the Associated State of Cambodia created in 1949. In 1952, he became Cambodia's first ambassador to the United States. He was a member of the delegation that signed the Japanese Peace Treaty in San Francisco in September 1951.

**NORDLINGER, STEPHEN.** American officer sent to **Hanoi** on 28 August 1945 to locate and protect Allied **prisoners of war**. A fluent French speaker, he provided important medical assistance to the 4,500 French POWs under Japanese custody at the citadel and, with the support of **Ho Chi Minh**, did the same for the large French community in Hanoi, saving hundreds of lives. Thanks to Nordlinger, the **Democratic Republic of Vietnam** allowed French civilian medical personnel to resume their work in hospitals in northern Vietnam. While some American officers felt that Nordlinger was too Francophile in his outlook, he agreed to Vietnamese demands that the French tricolor be removed from the citadel. And it was. Nordlinger also resisted French efforts to rearm troops in the citadel and delivered a letter from Ho Chi Minh to the Secretary of State in Washington. *See also* AID, AMERICAN; COLD WAR; OFFICE OF STRATEGIC SERVICES; ARCHIMEDES PATTI.

**NORODOM CHANTARAINGSEY (1924–1975).** Cambodian royalist who broke with the French, the **Democratic Republic of Vietnam** (DRV), and **Norodom Sihanouk** to run his own fiefdom during the Indochina War. Chantaraingsey was born in Phnom Penh of royal lineage, although we know little about his education and early career during the colonial period. In August 1945, he joined a military contingent headed by Thioum Muong and backed by the Japanese. He held the rank of sergeant. The Japanese hoped to use this military contingent to support **Son Ngoc Thanh**. However, the rapid return of the French to Cambodia and the arrest of Son Ngoc Thanh following the Japanese capitulation put an end to this militia. Chantaraingsey was demoted and transferred into the newly formed National Guard (formerly the *Garde indigène*). Frustrated, he deserted and fled to Thailand on 9 December 1945. There, he began grouping an array of followers, numbering some 150 men at the outset, to oppose the French from areas along the western Cambodian border. He took part in the August 1946 attack on Siem Reap, together with **Dap Chhuon** and forces of the DRV. Though Chantaraingsey was distrustful of the DRV-backed Committee for Cambodian Liberation active in western Cambodia, in April 1949 he replaced Dap Chhuon at its head. However, from 1950, as the war intensified with the arrival of the **Cold War** and the French and the Vietnamese redoubled their efforts to win over non-communist anti-colonialists, tensions emerged between Chantaraingsey and the Vietnamese, and the prince became increasingly attracted by French and Royal Cambodian offers to grant him clemency if he abandoned his dissidence. In 1952, Chantaraingsey left the DRV-backed Committee for Cambodian Liberation and in early 1954 he crossed over to the Associated State of Cambodia in exchange for the right to maintain his fiefdom. His wish was granted. *See also* COLLABORATION; CROSSOVER; DESERTION.

**NORODOM MONTANA (1902–1975).** He completed his elementary studies at the *Collège Sisowath* in Phonm Penh and worked in the colonial bureaucracy at the Indochinese and Cambodian level. He served as provincial governor and minister of Religion, Fine Arts, and Economy in the Royal Government of Cambodia. He urged **Norodom Sihanouk** not to abdicate during the Japanese ***coup de force* of 9 March 1945** although he himself served as minister of Agriculture in the **Son Ngoc Thanh** government. Between early 1948 and February 1952, Norodom Montana was elected counsellor, vice president then president of the Council for the Kingdom (*conseil du Royaume*). He was a strong political supporter of Sihanouk's consolidation of power. In November 1953, he was named minister of Public Education. He served as minister of Religion, Social Action, and Labor in the cabinet Sihanouk formed on 6 April 1954 and held the same post in the government **Penn Nouth** created on 17 April 1954. *See also* ROYAL CRUSADE FOR INDEPENDENCE.

**NORODOM SIHANOUK (1922–).** Cambodia's most important historical figure of the 20th century and an influential actor in Cambodia during the entire Indochina War. Born in Phnom Penh to Prince Norodom Suramarit and Princess Kossaman Nearirak, Sihanouk received his primary education at the *École François Baudoin* in Phnom Penh in the early 1930s before pursuing his secondary studies at the *Lycée Chasseloup Laubat* in **Saigon**, where he specialized in Greek and Latin rhetoric. His real passion during this time, however, was for modern sports – football (soccer), cycling, and horse-riding. In 1941, he acceded to the throne when the French Governor General Jean Decoux crowned him king in October of that year. During the Vichy regime, Decoux mobilized the Indochinese monarchies in order to hold on against the occupying Japanese and their Thai allies determined to take large swaths of western Indochina. Backed by the French, Sihanouk left the royal palace and began to move about the country and towards the "people" for the first time. Sihanouk supported Cambodia's national independence in alliance with **Son Ngoc Thanh** after the Japanese ***coup de force* of 9 March 1945** removed the French. Upon the defeat of the Japanese in August, Sihanouk then welcomed the French back. While he conceded some of his power by allowing the promulgation of a new constitution, he had Prince Norodom Monireth appointed as prime minister. This allowed him, between July and October 1947, to make a Buddhist religious retreat, marking the first time a reigning king had ever done so. During this time, he also pursued military studies in Saumur, France, at the *École d'application de l'arme blindée et cavalerie*.

Sihanouk returned to the political scene with the creation of the **Associated States of Indochina** in 1949, increasingly worried that the **Democrat Party** would eclipse him and the monarchy for good. Sihanouk exercised his power as president of the Council of Ministers between 2 and 31 May 1950 and again between 16 June 1952 and 23 January 1953. He launched his **royal crusade for independence** in 1952–1953, when he supported the removal of the **Huy Kanthoul** government, dominated by the rival Democrat Party, traveled to Thailand, France, and North America to plead his nationalist cause, and threatened to mobilize the Khmer against the French if they failed to decolonize on his terms. He simultaneously condemned the **Democratic Republic of Vietnam**'s (DRV) support of the **Khmer Issarak** and their combined military intervention in eastern Cambodia in early 1954. He successfully exploited local and international situations to force the French to grant full independence to Cambodia on 9 November 1953.

Because the amended constitution of 1954 precluded the king from playing an active role in national politics, Sihanouk abdicated in favor of his father, Norodom Suramarit, in March 1955. However, he would return to the political scene and would go on to play one of the most important roles in Cambodian politics during the Vietnam War. He returned a final time to the Cambodian throne between 1993 and 2004. *See also* ASSOCIATED STATES OF INDOCHINA; BAO DAI; BAO DAI SOLUTION; PHETXARĀT RATTANAVONGSĀ; SĪSĀVANGVONG; SUPHĀNUVONG.

**NORTH AFRICANS.** At first the French balked at sending North Africans[8] to fight for them in Indochina, fearful that they would be "contaminated" by Vietnamese nationalism, but this policy changed significantly over the course of the war. For one, the 4th Republic's refusal to institute a national draft in France quickly made this policy untenable as the demand for new troops quickly out-stripped the metropolitan volunteer supply. Second, the Indochina War was no simple police operation. It was going to be a long, drawn-out affair. In 1947, General **Philippe Leclerc** reversed orders prohibiting the use of North African troops in Indochina. As a result, between 1947 and 1952, the number of North Africans serving in the **French Union** forces in Indochina jumped from 8,300 to 34,700. In 1953, at its highpoint, 38,024 North Africans served in the **Expeditionary Corps**, representing 31 percent of its non-metropolitan troops (excluding the Indochinese troops). Most North Africans enlisted in the Expeditionary Corps for financial reasons. As a rule, they did not operate in high risk combat zones. The French preferred to put them in charge of **pacification** duties or working behind the lines. However, with the intensification of the war from 1950, an increasing number of North African troops saw combat and many were taken prisoner at **Dien Bien Phu** in mid-1954. In all, 9,451 North Africans were killed or listed as **missing in action** during the Indochina War. 11,407 were wounded. Mahommed Oufki became one of the rare North African officers commanding troops in the Expeditionary Corps, whereas Mohammed Ben Aomar (Maaroud) became one of the most famous Algerian **crossovers** to the forces of the **Democratic Republic of Vietnam**, known as Anh Ma. In 1948, the DRV created a special propaganda unit (DINA) consisting of some twenty North African crossovers from Algeria, Tunisia, and Morocco. In 1950, with the arrival of Chinese advisors and communist support, the DRV disbanded this unit.

**NORTH ATLANTIC TREATY ORGANIZATION (NATO).** Following the communist-engineered *coup d'état* in Prague in February 1948, Western European governments worried by possible Soviet aggression further west signed the Treaty of Brussels in March. The Americans were, however, reluctant to commit themselves by a treaty to the military defense of Europe, preferring to mobilize economic resources via the Marshall Plan to contain the Soviets. The Berlin Crisis of 1948–1949 changed all this, however, leading the United States to reconsider Western European requests for it to join a trans-Atlantic collective security arrangement. Washington agreed. In April 1949, the North Atlantic Treaty was signed. It included the states of the United Kingdom, France, Luxembourg, the Netherlands, Belgium

8. From the then French territories of Algeria, Tunisia, and Morocco.

(the Treaty of Brussels signatories), the United States, Canada, Iceland, Denmark, Italy, Norway, and Portugal. In 1952, Greece and Turkey joined the North Atlantic Treaty Organization (NATO). West Germany did so in 1955.

For France, membership of NATO had repercussions for its conduct of the war in Indochina. For example, the creation of NATO in 1949 shortly preceded the internationalization and the intensification of the Indochina War as the Chinese communists began supporting the **Democratic Republic of Vietnam** and entered the **Korean War** in 1950. French military strategists and politicians thus had to reconcile two costly but conflicting priorities: maintain a serious air and infantry presence in Indochina in view of possible Chinese intervention in Southeast Asia, and do the same for the defense of Western Europe in line with its NATO commitments against possible Soviet attack. Which was more important, many asked, "the defense of Europe or the defense of Indochina"? From 1953, it was clear in metropolitan circles that NATO and European questions had to take precedence, as General **Henri Navarre** knew when he was sent to Indochina that summer. As for the Americans, Eisenhower built on NATO by spinning a web of global security alliances designed to contain communism along its Eurasian axis, including the **South East Asia Treaty Organization** and the Baghdad Pact (CENTO) in 1954 and 1955, respectively.

**NOVELS, FRENCH.** If the Vietnam War gave rise to a number of pathbreaking novels in English on the conflict, the men who fought it, and the government, policies, and national cultures that sent them there, one searches in vain for the equivalent in French of Michael Herr's *Dispatches* or Tim O'Brien's *The Things They Carried.* There is certainly no French equivalent to the powerful Vietnamese account of the brutality of war written by Bao Ninh in 1991, *The Sorrow of War*. Like many of the war films made by **Pierre Schoendoerffer**, French novelists have tended to celebrate the army's values, heroism, and "a certain idea" of French nationalism, as Schoendoerffer put it. **Jean Lartéguy**, veteran of World War II and journalist during the **Korean War**, churned out a number of books on soldiers at war in Indochina in one way or another, including *La ville étranglée* (1955), *Les âmes errantes* (1956), *Les centurions* (1960), *Le mal jaune* (1962), and *Le saltimbanque*. In *Le mal jaune*, he paints a nostalgic, exotic, and, in the end, stereotyped view of Indochina and its inhabitants as seen by veterans who had fought there. In *Les centurions*, he traces the heroic if tragic itinerary of mainly French soldiers in the **Expeditionary Corps** as they move from one war to another, from Indochina to Algeria by way of Suez. The heroic, abandoned soldiers also serve as the trope for Pierre Schoendoerffer's novel the ***317ème Section***, as they flee faceless Vietnamese communist forces closing in on them as Dien Bien Phu falls. **Édouard Axelrad**, a former colonial official turned journalist during the war, wrote a novel entitled *Marie Casse-Croûte* in which he traces the life of the daughter of a Vietnamese nationalist turned prostitute who becomes a Madame herself and supports the French war effort, to the point of sending a couple of dozen of her "girls" to the besieged camp at **Dien Bien Phu**. They ended up saving lives heroically as makeshift nurses as the battle closed in on them. Another type of novel takes up the question of **prisoners of war** in the communist prisoner camps of the **Democratic Republic of Vietnam**. Gérard Avelane's account of a Vietnamese prisoner camp, *L'enfer du camp 13* (1965) is a case in point. British author **Graham Greene** wrote perhaps the most sophisticated novel on the Indochina War. In *The Quiet American*, he takes on a myriad of complex issues with finesse, not least of all the entry of the Americans into the war as French colonialism waned and the British looked on, perplexed. *See also* CINEMA; CULTURE; EXPERIENCE OF WAR; MYTH OF WAR: NOVELS, VIETNAMESE; TRAN DAN.

**NOVELS, VIETNAMESE.** Bao Ninh's penetrating account of the Vietnam War, *The Sorrow of War*, published in 1991, has no equivalent for the Indochina conflict. A dozen or so war novels on the Indochina War have been published in the communist-run **Democratic Republic of Vietnam** (DRV) since 1954. They tend to follow the Communist Party line, focusing on the heroism of the Vietnamese soldier, the infallibility of the Communist Party, and the righteousness of the Vietnamese nationalist cause. Social realism is *de rigueur*, as even Pham Thanh Tam's diary *Drawing Under Fire* confirms. The adversary is faceless, one-dimensional, and brutal. Despite the difficulties of escaping communist censure, there are important exceptions. Le Kham's *On the Other Side of the Border (Ben kia bien gioi)* and *Before the Battle Starts (Truoc gio no)* were among the few novels to treat combat in fairly realistic, less propagandistic terms. In *Men after Men, Wave after Wave* (*Nguoi nguoi lop lop*), Tran Dan recounts his experiences at the front lines during the battle of **Dien Bien Phu**. Published in 1955, during a brief liberal opening in the Party's control over literature and the arts, Tran Dan goes beyond communist heroic stereotypes to provide a moving portrait of men at war, humanizing them and their experiences. While he certainly followed the Party's heroic line, not unlike **Pierre Schoendoerffer** on the other side (they both worked in army propaganda units), Tran Dan provided one of the rare accounts of the heavy price paid by the soldiers fighting this war. He even spoke of the terrible machine-gun fire that mowed so many of them down as they tried to take the entrenched enemy camp. Tran Dan's desire to give more realistic accounts of battle apparently landed him in hot water shortly after the publication of his book. As the DRV prepared to fight another war, there was no room for such nuanced, realist, and above all independent accounts of men at war. Such war literature only emerged following the end of the **Cold War** in 1989 with communist Vietnam's opening to the world. Tran Dan's work on the war reappeared in print in 1991, coinciding with the publication of Bao Ninh's *The Sorrow of War*. This author is unaware of any equivalent novel portraying the war from the point of view of the soldiers of the **Associated States of Indochina**. *See also* CINEMA; CULTURE; EXPERIENCE OF WAR; EXPERIENCE OF WAR, DIEN BIEN PHU; HISTORY; MYTH OF WAR; NOVELS, FRENCH.

**NSC-5405.** Issued on 14 January 1954, National Security Council memorandum 5405 stated that the defense of **Tonkin** was essential to the containment of communism for Southeast Asia. This American document ruled out the division of Vietnam into a communist north and a noncommunist south; the line had to be held along the Sino-Vietnamese frontier. The document even rejected the creation of a coalition government with the participation of the **Democratic Republic of Vietnam**. *See also* COLD WAR; DOMINO THEORY; GENEVA ACCORDS; SOUTH EAST ASIA TREATY ORGANIZATION.

**NSC-64.** This National Security Council memorandum, approved by U.S. President **Harry S. Truman** in March 1950, was one of the first to deal directly with Indochina, by placing its defense within the wider American strategy of defending geopolitical and economic interests in Southeast Asia and containing the expansion of global communism. The approval of this document came in the wake of the Chinese communist victory in October 1949 and especially Beijing and Moscow's decision to recognize diplomatically and support the **Democratic Republic of Vietnam** in the Indochina War. If Indochina fell to the communists, this American policy document argued, the rest of "Southeast Asia would then be in grave hazard": "It is important to United States' security interests that all practicable measures be taken to prevent further communist expansion in Southeast Asia. Indochina is a key area of Southeast Asia and is under immediate threat". NSC-64 was one of the pillars of what became known as the **domino theory**, underpinning American policy towards Indochina well into the 1960s. *See also* AID, AMERICAN; COLD WAR; KOREAN WAR; NSC 5405; NORTH ATLANTIC TREATY ORGANIZATION.

**NŪHAK PHŪMSAVAN (1916–2008).** One of the main architects of the Lao communist movement. Born into a family of modest means in Mukdaharn province in northeast Thailand, he began his career as a truck driver in a Chinese-run transport company operating from the Mekong River area to eastern Vietnam. His fluency in Vietnamese and Thai facilitated his work. He was married twice, first to a Lao and then to a Vietnamese. Between 1941 and 1945, he set up his own transport business crossing the Annamese Chain. His life changed directions in Da Nang in the heady days of mid-1945. While on business there, representatives of the **Democratic Republic of Vietnam** (DRV) won him over to the nationalist cause and Nūhak suddenly found himself in **Hanoi** discussing revolutionary business for perhaps the first time in his life. In September or October 1945, he returned to Savannakhet and teamed up with Prince **Suphānuvong**, who was building the Committee for an Independent Laos there. Nūhak joined the **Lao Issara** and the prince sent him back to Hanoi, where his knowledge of Vietnamese and communications between Vietnam and Laos made him an excellent go-between. By 1947, he had returned to central Laos and become president of the Lao Issara **Committee for the East**. He worked closely with ranking Vietnamese leaders in **Inter-Zone IV** (*Lien Khu IV*) and became a member of the **Indochinese Communist Party** in 1947. He participated in the **Lao Resistance Government** and **Pathet Lao** national front. He served as minister of Economy and Finance in the new government. In 1953, as Vietnamese armed forces struck deep into Laos, Nūhak moved to Sam Neau with other government leaders to administer the resistance government on Lao territory. In 1954, he travelled on a DRV passport to serve as the Pathet Lao's delegate to the **Geneva Conference**. However, international opposition was such that the Chinese and even the Vietnamese dropped their request. Nūhak observed the conference from the sidelines. *See also* INDOCHINESE FEDERATION; ADMINISTRATIVE OFFICE FOR THE FRONTIER; ADVISORY GROUP 100; CAMBODIAN RESISTANCE GOVERNMENT; COMMITTEE FOR EXTERNAL AFFAIRS; HOANG VAN HOAN; KAISON PHOUMVIHANE; *METIS*; NGUYEN KHANG; NGUYEN THANH SON; PARTY AFFAIRS COMMITTEE.

**NÙNG.** *See* MINORITY ETHNIC GROUPS.

**NYIAVEU LÔBLIAYAO (1912–1999).** Hmong leader who fought with the Vietnamese against the French during the Indochina War. Born in Nong Het district in Xieng Khuang, Nyiaveu welcomed the Japanese overthrow of the French in March 1945. His hostility towards the French attracted the interest of Vietnamese communists, who recruited him to their anti-colonialist cause in November 1945. Between 1946 and 1949, he served as a member of the **Lao Issara**'s **Committee for the East**, working closely with the Vietnamese in **Inter-Zone IV** (*Lien Khu IV*). He participated in the **Lao Resistance Government** created in mid-1950 and was a Central Committee member of the **Pathet Lao** national front. During the Vietnamese invasion of Laos in 1953–54, he served as a guide.

**NYO, GEORGES YVES (1895–1980).** Graduated from Saint-Cyr in 1914, Nyo led a company on the western front during all of World War I. During the interwar period, he made his career in the colonial army, serving in Morocco and French West Africa before transferring to Indochina. There, he served as battalion leader between 1933 and 1935, mainly in the highlands of central Vietnam. In 1936, Nyo played a pivotal role in crushing the revolt led by Kommadam, the father of the future Lao communist leader **Sīthon Kommadam**. The French army decorated Nyo for "destroying the authority of this rebel leader". Nyo was named lieutenant colonel in that same year. Following the fall of France in 1940, Nyo worked in French West Africa until his return to France in 1942. In 1943, he joined Free French forces in Casablanca. Promoted to brigadier general in October of that year, he was charged with creating the 1st Colonial Division for the Far East that then became the 3rd Colonial Infantry Division of which he took command on 16 August 1945. Between February 1946 and July 1947, he served as commander of French Forces in **Cochinchina** and southern **Annam** (below the **16th parallel**). He became major general in August 1946. On 1 November 1946, he headed the French military delegation sent to **Hanoi** to discuss with his counterparts in the **Democratic Republic of Vietnam** (DRV) the military clauses concerning southern Vietnam contained in the ***modus vivendi*** signed in September in Paris. While negotiations broke down over the question of the DRV's representation in southern Vietnam, Nyo's troops created a network of military posts there to protect the local administration and economic resources of the region. In 1947, following the outbreak of full-scale war, he commanded 38,000 troops in the south (around 40 percent of the **Expeditionary Corps**'s troops at the time) and 6,000 Cochinchinese Guards. But Nyo conceded that his tactics and numbers had not succeeded in "pacifying" the south. It is not clear when he left Indochina or why. *See also* PACIFICATION.

**NYŪY APHAI (1909–1963).** Born in 1909 in Khong and educated in colonial Indochina and France, where he completed his studies. He began his career as a civil servant in 1933. In that year, he held the rank of provincial governor (*chaomuong)* and worked in the Bureau of Political and Administrative Affairs in the *Résidence supérieure* in Laos. In 1937, he left the colonial civil service to teach and was one of the founders of the Lao Renovation Movement during World War II. During this time, he published a wide variety of cultural and historical essays on Laos. Following World War II, he joined the **Lao Issara** serving as minister of Education. He fled to Thailand following the French return in mid-1946, but returned to Laos in 1947 and was named an advisor to the king in 1948. Upon the creation of the Associated State of Laos in 1949, he became minister of Education, Rites, Health, and Information in **Bunum**'s cabinet of 19 March 1949. Nyuy Aphai was a delegate to the signing of the Franco-Lao accords of 1950 and to the **Pau Conference** of 1950. Between 1951 and 1954, he was Prime Minister **Suvanna Phūmā**'s minister of Foreign Affairs.

**OCCUPATION, CHINESE.** The Chinese occupation of northern Indochina above the **16th parallel** between September 1945 and April 1946 was an onerous one. According to French financial records cited by historian Hugues Tertrais, eight months of Chinese occupation in the north cost the French between 425 and 427 million piasters or 4.25 to 4.27 billion francs. This amounted to more than two times the normal fiscal revenue for all of Indochina during an equivalent period of time. During the occupation, the Chinese currency was artificially overvalued, causing severe difficulties for the already financially strapped **Democratic Republic of Vietnam** (DRV) and this in the aftermath of the terrible **famine** that had claimed some one million Vietnamese lives. Leaders of the **Indochinese Communist Party** also feared that the anti-communist minded **Republic of China** might overthrow the fledgling Vietnamese government led by **Ho Chi Minh**. Indeed, the latter went out of his way in late 1945 to win over the support of local Chinese authorities, such as **Lou Han** and **Siao Wen**.

However costly the Chinese occupation was for the Vietnamese, the triple Chinese decision not to allow French forces to return immediately to the north, not to rearm the French troops incarcerated in the north since March 1945, and not to remove the Vietnamese provisional government led by Ho Chi Minh effectively allowed the DRV to operate freely above the 16th parallel for over a year, consolidating its power and developing its armed forces. Chinese nationalists also played a decisive role in persuading the DRV and France to sign the **Accords of 6 March 1946** so that the imminent arrival of French troops in the north would not trigger war as it had done for the British a few months earlier in the south. Most Chinese troops had withdrawn from northern Indochina by mid-June 1946. In September 1946, the last remaining personnel withdrew from northern Indochina, allowing local French authorities to push a more aggressive line against the **Hanoi**-based DRV government. *See also* 19 DECEMEBER 1946; FRANCO-CHINESE ACCORD (28 FEBRUARY 1946); OVERSEAS CHINESE.

**O'CONNELL, MADELEINE (?–1947**). Born to a family of Irish immigrants who made a new life in French Indochina at the turn of the 19th century working in the colonial administration. Madeleine O'Connell was educated at the *Couvent des oiseaux* in Dalat and took over the family plantation in Tay Ninh province in southern Indochina as well as a successful dairy farm there. She ran charities in and around her plantation, taking in abandoned children and raising them as best she could. During World War II, she maintained secret links with the French resistance and stashed arms on its behalf.

Prior to the Japanese ***coup de force*** **of 9 March 1945**, the Japanese sent a team of four men to arrest her on charges of collaborating with the French resistance or allied intelligence operatives. She killed all four men. She paid dearly for this when the Japanese finally brought her in alive and began torturing her in order to flush out the whereabouts of resistants and theirs arms caches. She refused to talk. The Japanese then decided to stage her mock execution, hoping that she would break. While the Japanese executioners were ordered to shoot away from her and did, local populations claimed that the Black Virgin of Tay Ninh had placed her hand in front of O'Connell to deflect the bullets. Whatever the truth, a legend was born.

No sooner had the Japanese capitulated than the Franco-Vietnamese war began below the **16th parallel**. The O'Connell family took up arms against **Viet Minh** agents trying to infiltrate their plantation, politicize their workers, and control this strategic area. The Viet Minh named her "*Madame Canon*", since she was always heavily armed, and put a price on her head. In late 1947, the Viet Minh prepared an ambush while she was traveling by car. After a fierce firefight, she was hit by a bullet and died of her wound on Christmas Eve. The Viet Minh considered her death to be an important blow to the morale of the European settlers still living in the countryside. The O'Connell family remained in southern Vietnam until the 1970s, but resided mainly in **Saigon**. *See also* 23 SEPTEMBER 1945; *FRANÇAIS D'INDOCHINE*; HERAULT, MASSACRE; TORTURE.

**O'DANIEL, JOHN W. ("IRON MIKE", 1894–1975).** Served for the U.S. in France during World War I as a sergeant, where he gained the nickname of "Iron Mike" and won the Distinguished Service Cross and Purple Heart. During the interwar period, he became an officer and rose rapidly in the army. He graduated in 1939 from the Command and Staff School at Fort Leavenworth, Kansas. During World War II, he was named colonel in 1941 and became assistant chief of staff for operations in the Third Army. In July 1942, now a general, he was attached to Allied Force Headquarters in Europe where he served as commander of the American Invasion Training School in the United Kingdom and led the 168th Infantry Regiment in the Allied invasion of North Africa in November 1942. He led the unit that occupied Algiers. In June 1943, he became deputy commander of the Third Infantry Division which landed in Sicily and after fierce fighting took Rome. He then led troops debarking in Provence, at the head of the Third Division as it crossed the Rhine on its way to Berlin. After the war, he became the commander of the Infantry School at Fort Benning. He commanded troops in the **Korean War** in 1951 before becoming chief of the **Military Assistance Advisory Group** (MAAG) for Indochina in April 1954, at the request of President **Dwight D. Eisenhower**. O'Daniel shared Eisenhower's determination to hold the line in Vietnam against perceived Sino-Soviet communist expansion into Southeast Asia.

In May 1953, the French **René Mayer** invited the Americans to send a military mission to Indochina as part of the French president's decision to name a new general, **Henri Navarre**, and to devise a new military strategy to bring the war to a successful end. The Americans selected O'Daniel, the Commander of the U.S. Army, Pacific, who arrived in Indochina in June 1953 one month after Navarre assumed his command. O'Daniel knew Navarre well and became an ardent supporter of the **Navarre plan**. According to American historian Ronald Spector, O'Daniel helped put aggressive mettle into Navarre's strategy and plan. O'Daniel informed his superiors that the French were now determined "to see this war through to success at an early date". He returned to Indochina for a second visit in November 1953 as Navarre's men prepared the entrenched camp at **Dien Bien Phu**. Thanks to the friendly working relationship between the two men, Navarre agreed to O'Daniel's suggestion that four American officers be assigned to Navarre's staff. Navarre also agreed to an increase in the size of the MAAG. Again, O'Daniel counseled increased support of the French: "We should fully support General Navarre, in whose success we have such a large stake". Indeed, on 2 Feburary 1954, as then commander of U.S. Army forces in the Pacific, O'Daniel visited the camp at Dien Bien Phu with a retinue of American officers who had served in Korea against Chinese ground and artillery assaults. He and his team expressed their support of Navarre's decision to take on the **Democratic Republic of Vietnam** there. On 1 January 1955, O'Daniel assumed full responsibility for assisting the State of Vietnam in the organization and training of its armed forces, under the supreme authority of the French Commander-in-Chief General **Paul Ely.** O'Daniel also had good working relations with **Ngo Dinh Diem**, prime minister of the Associated State of Vietnam and president of its successor state, the **Republic of Vietnam**. "I still believe this country can be saved", he said, "I have not even begun to think of writing it off". *See also* AID, AMERICAN; ARMY, ASSOCIATED STATE OF VIETNAM; COLD WAR; EXPEDITIONARY CORPS; GENEVA ACCORDS.

**O'DANIEL MISSIONS.** *See* JOHN W. O'DANIEL.

**OFFICE FOR NAM BỘ (*Phòng Nam Bộ*).** In October or November 1945, the **Democratic Republic of Vietnam** created a special office designed to gather information and expertise on the south in order to help policymakers with devising and implementing decisions at this key time in negotiations with the French. This office was also responsible for diffusing propaganda in favor of the resistance in the south. Nguyen Van Cai headed the office. His deputy was Hai Soc.

**OFFICE OF STRATEGIC SERVICES (OSS).** American external intelligence agency that came to life by presidential order in June 1942 as World War II raged across Europe and Asia. Now at war across much of Eurasia, President Franklin Roosevelt felt he needed a centralized intelligence agency to provide strategic information of the highest possible quality. He put Major General **William Donovan** at the head of this new agency, subordinate to the Joint Chiefs of Staff. The OSS was divided into three main operational branches: intelligence, special operations, and operational groups. Europe and Asia were obviously the two major geographical areas of interest to the OSS in the global war against the Axis powers, Germany and Japan. In Asia, the OSS was active in southern China, where it worked closely with the **Republic of China** and was in contact with Chinese communists. In order to obtain intelligence on Japanese troop movements and to rescue downed Allied pilots, it also cooperated with groups linked to the French in Indochina and, after these networks went dead on 9 March 1945, with **Ho Chi Minh** and his communist-led **Viet Minh**. OSS teams even provided a small amount of weapons and military training to future General **Vo Nguyen Giap**'s still rag-tag military forces during the summer of 1945. Further south, the Allies provided similar aid to communists fighting the Japanese in Malaya. Following the Japanese capitulation in August 1945, various OSS teams arrived in Indochina to tend to **prisoners of war** and gather intelligence, including **Archimedes Patti** in **Hanoi** and **A. Peter Dewey** in **Saigon**.

The OSS was phased out with the end of the Pacific War; but, with the start of the **Cold War**, it would re-emerge in 1947 as the Central Intelligence Agency (CIA). The phase-out of the OSS was prolonged, however, since the follow-up Strategic Services Unit continued to provide intelligence reports on the situation in Vietnam into 1946. With the withdrawal of the OSS, the Americans relied upon their consulates in Hanoi and Saigon to provide information and analysis on Indochina. The Americans also turned to their presence in Thailand to collect information on French Indochina. Colonel **William Hunter** worked out of Bangkok as naval attaché providing intelligence and analysis on Indochina until 1949.

If the globalizing effects of World War II had pushed American intelligence operations into Indochina in the fight against the Japanese, the rapid spread of the Cold War into Asia in 1949–1950 renewed American interest in Indochina as part of Washington's efforts to contain the spread of Eurasian communism. In 1950, the CIA dispatched delegates to meet with the French about exchanging intelligence and developing joint clandestine operations. The CIA's Colonel Chester and M. de Saint Phall first met with the high commissioner for Indochina, **Léon Pignon,** about such matters. While there was some confusion at the outset as to with whom the CIA should work, in the end negotiations in Paris, Washington, and between the CIA and its real counterpart ***Service de documentation et de contre-espionnage*** (SDECE), led to the establishment in May and June 1951 of an accord allowing the CIA to operate in Indochina via the United States Embassy in Saigon. This accord received final approval in Washington from the heads of the CIA and the SDECE. The CIA agreed to provide the SDECE in Indochina with one hundred radio posts.

The two sides also accepted to exchange ***Service Action*** missions in Indochina and Korea, pointing up the extent to which the Americans were thinking in global terms about unconventional containment strategies. An American liaison officer of the CIA was attached to the SDECE, while two SDECE officers joined the corresponding CIA service in Korea. The CIA had first tried to develop a *Service Action* in Indochina following their initial meetings with Léon Pignon in 1950, but ran into opposition from **Maurice Belleux** at the head of the SDECE and General **Jean de Lattre de Tassigny**, who balked at letting the Americans run the show. Nevertheless, the 1951 accord improved cooperation between the two intelligence services. From 1952, cooperation between the CIA and the SDECE was such that the two sides were exchanging intelligence on a weekly basis on military matters and communism in the region. The Americans also helped finance the creation of the French *Service Action* in Indochina and the ***Groupement de commandos mixtes aéroportés***.

**OFFROY, RAYMOND (1909–2003).** Career French diplomat who served as director of the Information Services for the high commissioner's office in Indochina until March 1952, when he became diplomatic advisor to the high commissioner. In 1953, he was named deputy to the general commissioner for France in Indochina. Between 1954 and December 1957, he served as ambassador to the Kingdom of Thailand in Bangkok. He accompanied **Jean Letourneau** to Washington D.C. in June 1952 and was a member of the French diplomatic delegation to the **Geneva Conference** of 1954. Based in Bangkok, he became the French permanent representative to the **South East Asia Treaty Organization** between 1955 and 1957.

**OGBURN, CHARLTON (1911–1998).** American diplomat in the Far Eastern Section of the Department of State involved in American policy-making towards Vietnam in the wake of World War II. Raised in New York and graduated from Harvard in 1932, Ogburn traveled, reviewed books, and published his own. During World War

II, he moved from being a private to a captain in military intelligence, mainly active in Asia. He drew upon this experience when he entered the State Department to serve as a diplomat in Far and Middle Eastern Affairs. In 1947, he was part of the **United Nations**'s Security Council's Committee of Good Offices charged with solving the Dutch–Indonesian war. In the Division of Southeast Asian Affairs, he closely followed developments in Indochina. He emphasized the importance of Vietnamese nationalism and the dangers of supporting a French colonial return to Indochina. In April 1949, he warned against rushing to recognize the Associated State of Vietnam unless the French made greater political concessions on Vietnamese independence and **Bao Dai** proved himself more attractive nationally than **Chiang Kai-shek** had been in China. Ogburn and others were overruled. In January 1950, Washington diplomatically recognized the Associated State of Vietnam. Bitter, Ogburn warned: "I think we are heading into a very bad mess in the policy we are now following toward Indochina". In 1957, his cover story on *Merrill's Marauders* in *Harper's* landed him an attractive advance for a book. He jumped at the chance, and retired from the Department of State, and resumed an already successful writing career.

**ŌKHAM ANURAK (1916–).** A behind-the-scenes leader of the **Pathet Lao**. He worked during the interwar period in a French mining company in Laos and then followed in his father's footsteps to become a *chaomuong* (provincial governor). Little is known of his activities during World War II. Following the overthrow of the French in March and the Japanese surrender in August in 1945, he joined the **Lao Issara** and served as a military commander in southern Laos. He fled to central Vietnam following the return of the French in mid-1946 and began a long partnership with the Vietnamese communists. In 1946, **Ho Chi Minh** welcomed him in **Hanoi** and put him in touch with **Kaisôn Phomvihān** and **Nūhak Phūmsavan**. Anurak joined them and Vietnamese communists in creating the **Lao Issara's Committee for the East** and ran **guerrilla** activities along Route 9, located near his home province of Sepone. However, in spite of his close collaboration with the Vietnamese and Lao communists, he rallied to the Associated State of Laos in the early 1950s and retired from politics for the rest of the Indochina War. *See also* ADMINISTRATIVE OFFICE FOR THE FRONTIER; ADVISORY GROUP 100; CAMBODIAN RESISTANCE GOVERNMENT; COLLABORATION; COMMITTEE FOR EXTERNAL AFFAIRS; CROSSOVERS; HOANG VAN HOAN; INDOCHINESE FEDERATION; LAO RESISTANCE GOVERNMENT; NGUYEN KHANG; NGUYEN THANH SON; PARTY AFFAIRS COMMITTEE.

**OPIUM.** For centuries, opium has been grown throughout areas of southern China and upper South and Southeast Asia. Opium has traditionally been used for medicinal, ritual, social, and leisure purposes in Asia. And for centuries, Asians and Europeans traded in the opium commerce running from **India** to China via maritime port cities and across the mountains dividing northern Southeast Asian from southern China, especially via Yunnan province bordering upper Laos and northwestern Vietnam. In upper Indochina and southern China, the Hmong were heavily involved in this form of agriculture, one that was strictly controlled by the French during the colonial period. A monopoly, opium became one of the colonial state's most important sources of revenue. The French administered the opium monopoly until 1945, when the Japanese *coup de force* in March brought down colonial Indochina.

While the authorities of the **Democratic Republic of Vietnam** (DRV) may have outlawed the purchase and use of opium upon taking power later that year, they sought to tap into this trade since it provided them with a highly valuable export, one which they could sell in order to buy arms, munitions, and medicines, and one which they could transport easily and secretly.

In the early 1950s, as the forces of the DRV moved into opium-producing Hmong and Tai regions in northwestern Vietnam, the French countered by infiltrating their newly created ***Groupement de commandos mixtes aéroportés*** (GCMA) into these zones. There, the GCMA entered into contact with anti-DRV Tai and Hmong leaders in order to create a clandestine *maquis* among the minorities from which the French could harass the DRV military operations in the northwest. One of the leaders of the GCMA in this area, **Roger Trinquier**, contacted the Hmong leader, **Tūbī Līfung**, in order to obtain his support for the GCMA fighting the DRV. In exchange for his **collaboration**, however, Tūbī Līfung insisted that the French provide him with the means to sell his opium crop each year. Given that the French state could not and would not buy the opium as in the past, the GCMA was secretly authorized to transport the harvest by air to **Saigon**, where Tūbī found a buyer in the person of **Le Van Vien**, the head of the **Binh Xuyen,** himself deeply involved in the entertainment and drug business in Saigon-Cholon.

Recognizing the importance of countering the enemy by every means possible in this decisive phase of the war, during the spring of 1953, General **Henri Navarre** authorized Trinquier and Tūbī to find a way to transport the opium to Saigon. From this emerged "operation X". In short, Trinquier organized the transport of stocks of 800 kg of raw opium on DC3s, which his agents flew to the Binh Xuyen's representatives at a secret GCMA base near Dalat. From there, the opium traveled by truck to Saigon. A few days later, Tūbī would fly into Dalat to be paid.

Given the budgetary constraints under which the French army was operating in Indochina by 1953, it is clear that the attraction of the opium trade was strong for GCMA leaders. For one, the French army gained the support of Tūbī's Hmong fighters in a strategically important zone where the DRV was expanding its politico-military movements. Second, after each opium deal was sealed, Tūbī deposited 50,000 francs in the coffers of the cash-strapped GCMA. The GCMA's *maquis* operations in the northwest were virtually "self-financed" thanks to this opium trade. However, despite the important sums generated by this traffick, the idea that the battle of **Dien Bien Phu** in 1954 was fought over the control of the opium market is an exaggeration. *See also* ALCOHOLISM; DIEN BIEN PHU, BATTLE PREPARATION AND CONTEXT; ECONOMY OF WAR; FINANCIAL COST OF THE WAR, FRANCE.

**OPPOSITION TO THE WAR.** *See* ANTICOLONIALISM; BOUDAREL AFFAIR; CHRISTIANS AND OPPOSITION TO THE INDOCHINA WAR; CIVIL WAR; *ESPRIT*; FRENCH COMMUNIST PARTY; HENRI MARTIN; JEAN CHESNEAUX; PAUL MUS; *TÉMOIGNAGE CHRÉTIEN*.

**ORPHANS.** Young Vietnamese orphans sometimes found themselves caught up in the violence of the Indochina conflict. During the colonial period, the Bao Anh orphanage in **Hanoi** (now the center for the blind on 135 Nguyen Thai Hoc street) cared for dozens of parentless, whose numbers increased significantly due to the terrible **famine** that struck northern Vietnam between 1944 and 1945. During World War II, patriotic **intellectuals**, in particular members of the Association for the Promotion of Quoc Ngu, taught Vietnamese orphans at the Bao Anh center to read and write.

Young though they were, many of these orphans followed their nationalist-minded teachers into the ranks of the **Democratic Republic of Vietnam** after the Japanese defeat in August 1945. Nguyen Khac Ky was one such teacher to bring a number of the Bao Anh orphans with him and eventually into military preparations to defend Hanoi against French reoccupation in late 1946. The **Viet Minh** employed these orphans as messengers and liaison agents (*Lien Lac Vien*) in the **Children**'s Guard (*ve ut*) and apparently agreed to integrate this unit into the capital brigade led by **Vuong Thua Vu**. One of the youngest orphans to join the brigade as a part of the Children's Guard was only eight years old. During the battle of Hanoi, several of these orphans ran highly dangerous liaison missions; some even took up arms and several were killed in battle. After the evacuation of the city, the Vietnamese army incorporated these orphans into artistic youth groups and moved them out of the line of fire. Vietnamese orphans were also active in the south, working as messengers and liaison agents in the urban battle for **Saigon** in particular. Nguyen Hong Phuoc, for example, worked for **Zone VII**'s Military Medical Service as a liaison agent. He was killed before he turned 15. *See also* CASUALTIES; EXPERIENCE OF WAR; MYTH OF WAR.

**ORTOLI, PAUL (1900–1979).** French naval officer during the Indochina War. He was with Free French naval forces during World War II and the Allied Landing in Provence in 1944. In November 1946, he became rear admiral. In 1949 he took command of the Naval Forces in the Far East (*Forces maritimes d'Extrême-Orient*) and oversaw a number of operations in the Mekong Delta mainly against smugglers and clandestine **Democratic Republic of Vietnam** trading operations. He returned to France in 1952, replaced by Rear Admiral **Philippe Auboyneau**. In 1955, Ortoli served as a military advisor to the **South East Asia Treaty Organisation** and was promoted to admiral in the French **Navy**.

**OSS.** *See* OFFICE OF STRATEGIC SERVICES.

**O'SULLIVAN, JAMES O. (1916–).** American diplomat posted in **Hanoi** when war broke out in all of Indochina on **19 December 1946**. Upon graduation from Yale Law School, he joined the Foreign Service in February 1942. At ease in French, he first served in Montreal, Cayenne, and Martinique before becoming vice consul in Chongqing in China. He was then dispatched to **Saigon** to serve as deputy to **Charles Reed**, the American consul in Saigon. In March 1946, Reed dispatched O'Sullivan to **Hanoi** where the State Department authorized him to remain on a temporary basis in order to report on the complex situation in northern Vietnam under Chinese occupation. In July 1946, O'Sullivan became vice consul in Hanoi. With a green light from the French, he and Reed went on to set up a full-fledged American Consulate in Hanoi by 9 January 1947 (though the Quai d'Orsay had not yet recognized O'Sullivan officially as vice consul in Hanoi). In May 1947, the State Department promoted him to Foreign Service officer class 5, officially making him a full consul. O'Sullivan was sympathetic to Vietnamese nationalist aspirations and critical of the French determination to re-establish colonial order. Following the outbreak of full-scale war in Hanoi on **19 December 1946**, O'Sullivan helped facilitate the safe passage of thousands of people from the capital. He later served in Jakarta. *See also* ARTHUR GOEFFREY TREVOR-WILSON.

**OUROT SUVANNAVONG (1908–?).** Non-communist, pro-French Lao leader and French citizen. He began his career in the Lao administration in 1936. He became president of the provincial tribunal for Vientiane and was in charge of tourism for Laos. He continued working in the colonial judiciary service under Vichy and remained pro-French throughout the war. In 1946, he was an acting justice of the peace. A year later, he became legal advisor to the Royal Lao government and president of the High Court of Appeals and Annulments. The French sent him as a delegate to the Asian Relations Conference in April 1947 held in New Delhi. In July 1948, he left for France to represent Laos in the Assembly of the French Union and was still a counsellor of the French Union when he attended the **Pau Conference** in June 1950.

**OVERSEAS CHINESE.** As elsewhere in Southeast Asia, Vietnam is home to a large Chinese population. Chinese immigrants had long traded in Vietnamese ports such as Haiphong, Hoi An, and **Saigon**-Cholon. Chinese immigration was most concentrated in southern Vietnam, where the Chinese contributed to urban and agricultural development and foreign trade. To administer the Chinese, the Nguyen dynasty had divided the Chinese population into *bangs* or congregations according to their place of origin, mainly in southern China. In all, there were five *bangs* for the Chinese originating from Guangdong, Chaozhou, Fujian, Hainan, and one for the Hakka.

The French maintained this system and accelerated Chinese immigration in order to develop their colonial economy and industry. In 1879, there were some 45,000 Chinese living in **Cochinchina**. In 1921, the French counted around 156,000. Over the next 30 years, Chinese immigration increased significantly in French Indochina. According to French statistics from 1950, some 600,000 Chinese resided permanently in southern Vietnam, mainly in the city of Saigon-Cholon. Some 70,000 Chinese lived in **Tonkin**, mainly along the Sino-Vietnamese border and in the port of Haiphong. Cambodia had between 150,000 and 200,000 Chinese and a few thousand Chinese lived in Laos.

Most but not all of the Chinese remained in or moved to the cities during the war. It is hard to determine the exact number of Chinese residing in **zones** controlled by the **Democratic Republic of Vietnam** (DRV) during the Indochina War at any one time. The DRV probably administered directly some 20,000 to 40,000 Chinese, mainly in the south and in areas located along the Sino-Vietnamese border in the north. These overseas Chinese fell theoretically under the direction of the Bureau of Chinese Affairs in the DRV's Ministry of the Interior. On the regional level, by the late 1940s, the provincial Resistance and Administrative Commitees had begun to organize the overseas Chinese in the south via the **Bureau of Overseas Chinese Affairs** (*Phong Hoa Kieu Vu Nam Bo*).

With the communist victory in China in 1949, the DRV intensified its efforts from 1950 to win over the support of the overseas Chinese and organize them more firmly under the DRV's control. On orders from the north, southern Vietnamese communists issued directives calling for closer **collaboration** with the local Chinese in the war against the French. In 1950, the head of the **People's Republic of China**'s overseas Chinese affairs called on the Chinese in Southeast Asia "to unite closely with all the revolutionary peoples" and to aid the local national liberation movements of the countries in which they resided. On the ground, though, the results were mixed at best. The DRV had trouble finding cadres capable of speaking the various Chinese dialects. These local Chinese populations, often living in semi-autonomous *bangs*, were not always keen on cooperating with the DRV in the war against the French. In many cases, the **Republic of China** consulates in **Hanoi** and Saigon had a much stronger presence among Chinese congregations than the DRV and sometimes the French.

On 4 December 1950, following high-level discussions with the Chinese communists, the **Indochinese Communist Party** (ICP) issued guidelines concerning the "overseas Chinese question" (*ve van de Hoa Kieu o Viet Nam*). This document accorded equal rights to overseas Chinese living in Vietnamese territories. Although the ICP spoke of all of Vietnam, the new policy would apply to overseas Chinese living in DRV territories, meaning but a small proportion of the overall populations concentrated in Hanoi, Haiphong and above all Saigon-Cholon, all under Franco-Associated State of Vietnam control. The ICP did not require the overseas Chinese to become national citizens of the DRV. Chinese living in Vietnam also received authorization to create and run their own schools, use their own language, and publish their own newspapers in Chinese. Most important was mobilizing the Chinese in Vietnam, especially in the enemy zones where they were most numerous, against the French.

In July 1950, the DRV created a special administrative organization for the Chinese, called the General Association of the Liberation of the Overseas Chinese of Nam Bo (*Tong Hoi Giai Lien Nam Bo Hoa Kieu*). In 1952, Vietnamese communists issued follow up guidelines to the 1950 ones. It reiterated the government's commitment to guaranteeing in legal terms the rights of Chinese living in Vietnamese territories on the same level as Vietnamese citizens. This document also repeated the government's commitment to allowing Chinese living in DRV territories to take part in Vietnamese politics and state administration. The problem was that many Chinese feared that by joining DRV associations they would lose pre-existing Chinese associations and would be eventually required to adopt DRV citizenship. The 1952 document reiterated the party and government's commitment to respecting their Chinese citizenship (to the People's Republic of China). This document also targeted for the first time the need to mobilize the Chinese working class in colonial Vietnamese cities. Lastly, Chinese traders were important commercial intermediaries for the DRV's war economy, essential to trading clandestinely with the rice markets of Saigon-Cholon. The Sino-Viet Minh rice trade was particularly profitable from 1946 to 1948. In 1948 alone, the **Viet Minh** in the south earned 500 million piastres from their rice exports from the Transbassac region, sold mainly through Saigon-Cholon markets thanks to Chinese go-betweens. Chinese traders also helped the Viet Minh import needed goods from the French zones and even as far away as Hong Kong. In 1952, DRV agents in Cambodia generated a minimum of 12 million piastres from the pepper trade in Kampot Province – run almost exclusively by the Chinese for centuries. *See also GROUPEMENTS ADMINISTRATIFS CHINOIS RÉGIONAUX*; KHMER KROM; MINORITY ETHNIC GROUPS; OVERSEAS VIETNAMESE IN THAILAND; *PAYS MONTAGNARD DU SUD* (PMS); PHẠM ĐÀN.

**OVERSEAS VIETNAMESE IN FRANCE.** The French colonization of Vietnam during the second half of the 19th century opened the way for the birth a Vietnamese diaspora in France. Mobilization of manpower during World War I led to the recruitment of some 50,000 mainly Vietnamese who served as workers and soldiers (*linh tho*) in France. Several thousand stayed on following the armistice to work in textile and automobile plants as well as on the construction of railways in northern France. Joining them were several hundred Vietnamese sailors, cooks, and servants, who worked on French and European ships serving Indochina and elsewhere. During the interwar period, several thousand mainly students lived and studied in France, though many returned. On the eve of World War II, the French government requisitioned some 20,000 Vietnamese to move to France as part of the program of *Main-d'oeuvre indigène* (MOI) or Indigenous Manpower. No sooner had they arrived in early 1940 than the Germans defeated the French and occupied the country. Later that year around 4,500 of the MOI returned to Indochina. According to Pierre Daum, at the end of World War II, some 25,000 Vietnamese resided in France – 14,000 workers, 7,000 tirailleurs, and some 4,000 students and others. Between 1946 and 1952, the majority of the workers and soldiers repatriated to Vietnam.

During the Indochina War, many well-to-do families in the Associated State of Vietnam sent their sons to France as students rather than see them enlisted into the army. The Associated State of Vietnam approved the draft in mid-1951. Educational exchanges with France also continued during the conflict. Several hundreds Vietnamese students continued to study in the metropole. According to the French security services, as of 1954, 27,350 Vietnamese were residing in France or had been since 1945 (the periodization is not clear).

Until the Associated State of Vietnam got off the ground in 1949 and established its diplomatic and cultural offices in France, the **Democratic Republic of Vietnam** had little competition when it came to working among the Vietnamese communities in Paris, Marseille, and elsewhere. In 1946, during his trip to France, **Ho Chi Minh** personally appealed to the Vietnamese in France to support the new government and its nationalist cause and to pressure the French to negotiate in good faith. The DRV operated a diplomatic delegation in Paris until 1949 (when the Associated State of Vietnam came into being). One of its main tasks was to win over and mobilize the overseas Vietnamese in favor the DRV's war effort. This meant arranging demonstrations, promoting propaganda drives, contacting patriotic intellectuals, lobbying politicians, organizing students and workers, and so on. The Vietnamese in France also helped the DRV obtain much needed materials, especially hi-tech equipment and books needed inside Vietnam for building the cryptographic office or the medical school. The Vietnamese in France were often precious conduits between the "inside" and the "outside" for the embattled DRV. Overseas Vietnamese also returned to Vietnam and enlisted in the DRV's ranks. *See also* OVERSEAS VIETNAMESE IN JAPAN; OVERSEAS VIETNAMESE IN THAILAND; NGUYEN NGOC NHUT; TRAN DAI NGHIA.

**OVERSEAS VIETNAMESE IN JAPAN**. During the repatriation of Japanese **crossovers** in the **Democratic Republic of Vietnam** (DRV) to Japan between 1954 and 1960, only 20 families were able to leave Vietnam with their Japanese fathers. Given that the DRV prohibited this, one can assume that these families probably left from areas below the **17th parallel**, controlled by the Associated State of Vietnam in the wake of the signing of the **Geneva Accords** of 1954 and over which the DRV lost control. These families mainly relocated to the big cities of Osaka and Tokyo. The shift to life in postwar, urban Japan was often not easy for returning Japanese soldiers who had lived in the jungle for more than ten years and had continued their combat career well beyond the Japanese defeat in 1945. Life was even harder for the Vietnamese wives who did not know Japanese or Japanese culture. Finding work was hard for both husband and wife. And to make matters worse, these mixed couples often could not escape the eye of the **Cold War**. Their affiliation with the communist-run DRV led the Japanese police to tail many families well into the 1960s. Le Thi Hue followed her husband to Japan in 1959 and later recalled in an interview that it was an "extremely hard" period in her life. While other Vietnamese had lived and studied in Japan since the turn of the 20th century, this was for all intents and purposes the beginning of a Vietnamese diaspora in Japan. *See also* DESERTION; LOVE AND WAR; OVERSEAS CHINESE; OVERSEAS VIETNAMESE IN FRANCE; OVERSEAS VIETNAMESE IN THAILAND.

**OVERSEAS VIETNAMESE IN THAILAND.** The Indochina War directly affected the 50,000 Vietnamese residing in Thailand. Since the 17th century, Vietnamese from northern, central, and southern Vietnam had settled in areas of eastern Thailand running from Nakhon Phanom along the Mekong River to Chantaburi in the Gulf of Thailand. Several thousand also lived in Bangkok. These Vietnamese immigrants were fluent in Thai and many had supported Vietnamese anti-colonialists ranging from Phan Boi Chau to **Ho Chi Minh**. With the advent of the **Democratic Republic of Vietnam** (DRV) in September 1945, the new government dispatched delegates to Thailand to rally the large Vietnamese population to the nationalist cause. Not only were these overseas Vietnamese strategically located near Indochina, but Thai leaders were also opposed to the return of French colonialism. As in southern China, where thousands of Vietnamese émigrés also lived, the DRV turned to the Vietnamese in Thailand to help it establish a diplomatic delegation for Southeast Asia in 1946 and to operate commercial activities in the area until 1951.

Fluent in Vietnamese and Thai, the overseas Vietnamese were invaluable cultural and linguistic intermediaries for the DRV delegates arriving in Thailand to work. Several hundred were involved negotiating deals and transporting arms and supplies to central and southern Vietnam. A Buddhist monk named Bao An who immigrated to Bangkok from Cambodia during the colonial period is a case in point. His religious fervor as well as his fluency in Khmer and in Thai helped him to become a highly respected monk in Bangkok. His anti-colonial politics also earned him the sympathy of Thai officialdom and DRV agents keen on preventing the French return to Indochina after World War II. Bao An also used his contacts and influence in the service of the Vietnamese nationalist movement, becoming one of the five most powerful delegates of the DRV's delegation in Bangkok.

The DRV also turned to the overseas Vietnamese to recruit troops to fight in southern Vietnam in the early years of the war. Between late 1945 and 1948, several thousand overseas Vietnamese youth signed up to fight the French in southern Vietnam and Cambodia. The **Indochinese Communist Party** also ran some of its most secret and important external activities out of Thailand and anchored among the overseas Vietnamese. In 1948, for example, **Hoang Van Hoan** arrived in northeast Thailand to run the party's external cadres affairs committee responsible for all relations with the outside. Hoang Van Hoan knew Thailand well. He had worked and lived there for years during the interwar years. He spoke Thai fluently. The ICP relied upon its revolutionary networks in Thailand to foster and administer the development of communism in Laos and Cambodia.

The Thai government turned a blind eye to these activities during the first half of the Indochina conflict. What counted most for Bangkok leaders, even for Phibun Songgkram upon his return to power in 1948, was opposing French claims on territories taken by the Thais during World War II in western Laos and Cambodia. This changed, however, in 1950, when the Chinese communist victory to the north ushered in the Cold War to Southeast Asia. Under American pressure but also in a move designed to reinforce his internal power, **Pibun Songgram** closed the Vietnamese diplomatic delegation in 1951 and adopted measures hostile to the overseas Vietnamese populations in Thailand and their support of what was now considered to be a communist-driven DRV, hostile to Thai security. While overseas Vietnamese party cells would continue to support the government and party, the center of the ICP's external networks shifted to southern China from 1950 as Chinese communists began channeling large amounts of aid to the DRV. As in France, from 1950 the Associated State of Vietnam began to operate in Thailand and among the overseas Vietnamese. *See also* CAMBODIAN RESISTANCE GOVERNMENT; EXTERNAL AFFAIRS COMMITTEE; INDOCHINESE FEDERATION; LAO RESISTANCE GOVERNMENT; NGO THAT SON; NGUYEN DUC QUY; NGUYEN KHANG; NGUYEN THANH SON; OVERSEAS CHINESE; OVERSEAS VIETNAMESE IN FRANCE; OVERSEAS VIETNAMESE IN JAPAN; PARTY AFFAIRS COMMITTEE; PHAM NGOC THACH; PRIDI PHANOMYONG; TIENG SERIKHAN; TRAN VAN GIAU.

**PACH CHHOEUN (1896–1971).** Prominent Cambodian nationalist and active member of the **Democrat Party** during the Indochina War. After working as an interpreter in the colonial army during World War I, he returned to Indochina where he trained as an archivist in **Hanoi**. In 1925, he went to Phnom Penh to join the colonial civil service there. By the 1930s, he had become increasingly involved in nationalist politics and joined forces with **Son Ngoc Thanh** to serve as managing director of the nationalist newspaper *Nagaravatta* between 1936 and 1942, when his involvement in a Buddhist demonstration landed him in the colonial prison on **Poulo Condor** island. There, he rubbed shoulders with some of the most important Vietnamese communists of the time. Following the Japanese overthrow of the French in the ***coup de force* of 9 March 1945**, Pach Chhoeun regained his freedom and returned to Phnom Penh to assume a post as minister of the National Economy and Recovery in the shortlived Japanese-backed Son Ngoc Thanh cabinet between August and October 1945. When the French returned to Cambodia, he fled to southern Vietnam where he briefly collaborated with forces allied with the **Democratic Republic of Vietnam**. He crossed over to the French in April 1946 and was sent to live in France until 1950. Pach Choeunn returned to Cambodia in November 1950, thanks to a French presidential pardon, and supported the **Democrat Party** from 1951. He simultaneously served as director of the Royal Library in Phnom Penh. **Huy Kanthoul** named him state minister of Information between October 1951 and June 1952. He thereafter withdrew from politics to concentrate on his evolving business interests. *See also* COLLABORATION; CROSSOVER; DESERTION.

**PACIFICATION.** For colonizers, conquest and pacification are often two sides of the same coin. Once a territory and its population have been conquered, the conquering power must then secure its control over that territory and its population through a process of "pacification". The term became increasingly used in France in the 19th century when the French had to pacify the peoples they had conquered violently in Algeria and Indochina. However, the French did not invent the term "pacification". Other European colonial powers were using it, too. 19th-century French architects of colonial "pacification" programs in Asia and Africa, such as Joseph Galliéni and Hubert Lyautey, looked to the Roman Empire for models. In the French case, "pacification" came to mean, in the 19th century and again in the "re-pacification" of Indochina in 1945, the use of military and/or police forces to control a precise territory by dividing it into contiguous compartments or squares. During the Indochina War, this process was referred to as the *quadrillage* or *carroyage* of a territorial space, in short its "sectoring off". Many French officers involved in pacification in Indochina had gained first hand experience of its methods during the interwar period in North Africa, especially during the Rif War in Morocco. General **Jean de Lattre de Tassigny** is a case in point. Several had worked under Lyautey or were inspired by him, such as **Georges Spillmann**, **Alphonse Juin**, and **Jacques Massu**.

The basic blueprint for pacification used during the Indochina war was the following. First, the delimiting of the space to be pacified was centered on main lines of communications and their intersections, controlled of course by the conquering power's military forces. At the intersections of the spatial sectors, the French created small but fortified military posts, each of which theoretically possessed radios, ran agents, and interacted with surrounding villages in their respective sectors. The idea was to create an overall military *quadrillage* of the conquered territory in which all contiguous squares or compartments, usually no more than four or five kilometers square, were as closely linked together as possible. This skeleton (*ossature*) was for the French army the foundation upon which "pacification" rested. The French then organized self-defense militias (*milices d'auto-défense*) in the villages they controlled in order to prevent the "rebels" from penetrating their network of control. The French referred to these forces as the "conjunctive tissue" (*tissu *conjonctif*) of the larger pacified body, linked to the skeleton via the French-controlled posts. The French drew upon their pacification experiences in the deserts of Algeria to deploy mobile troops across this *quadrillage* to attack "rebel" forces inside their territory. Together with the High Command, these reserves acted as the "nervous system", as one major French pacification theorist explained it during the Indochina conflict. Indeed, once the **Expeditionary Corps** had re-conquered most of the cities and lines of communication in southern Vietnam in 1945–1946, they then began to apply this model to their re-pacification of **Cochinchina** and elsewhere.

However, during the Indochina War, the **Democratic Republic of Vietnam** (DRV) and the **Indochinese Communist Party** developed and extended their own territorial state and party administration and means of controlling the population and space, something which anti-colonialists of the 19th century had never truly been able to do. The DRV also infiltrated the French network through agents, propaganda, its own police forces, and then full-scale battle. By 1953, General **Fernand Gambiez** conceded that the French army needed one battalion to ensure the defense of 500–800 km² and ever-increasing amounts of concrete to build the needed look-out posts. In all, the **Expeditionary Corps** had to commit 30–40 battalions to "territorial missions", that is, maintaining continued pacification and its supporting structures and personnel. And this is why when the DRV intensified its classic military operations, obliging the French to transfer battalions to engage them on the battlefield in the north, the DRV was simultaneously able to expand its guerrilla operations into the French "pacification network" in the Red River and Mekong Deltas. *See also GROUPEMENT DE COMMANDOS MIXTES AÉROPORTÉS*; PARALLEL HIERARCHIES; RENÉ HÉBERT; REVOLUTIONARY WARFARE; *SERVICE ACTION*.

**PAGNIEZ, YVONNE (1896–1981).** Certified (*agrégée*) philosophy teacher and journalist during the Indochina War. During World War II, she was an early *résistante* to German occupation and was eventually captured and deported to Germany. She survived and received the *Croix de guerre* among other medals for her work. After the war, she left for Indochina as a correspondent and published scores of articles on the conflict in the *Journal de Genève* and the *Revue des Deux Mondes*. She also wrote a number of books on Indochina at war: *Français d'Indochine*, *Choses vues au Viêt-nam*, and *Le Viêt-Minh et la guerre psychologique*. Together with **Brigitte Friang**, she was one of the rare women correspondents covering the Indochina War. *See also* GENEVIÈVE-TERRAUBLE DE GALARD; *PERSONNEL FÉMININ DE L'ARMÉE DE TERRE* (PFAT); WOMEN, DEMOCRATIC REPUBLIC OF VIETNAM; WOMEN, FRENCH ARMED FORCES.

**PANIKKAR, KAVALAM MADHAVA (1895–1963).** Indian diplomat educated at the University of Oxford. Upon his return to **India** following World War I, he lectured at Aligarh and Calcutta Universities. In 1925, he went into journalism and became the editor of the *Hindustan Times*. From there, he launched his political career serving as the foreign minister for the local princely state of Patiala, then as foreign then chief minister to the state of Bikaner (1944–1947). After India gained its independence in 1947, he served as the country's first ambassador to China (1948–1952) before going on to hold the same position in Egypt and France. During his time in Beijing, Panikkar supported **Jawaharlal Nehru**'s policy of improving relations with the Chinese. He also met with the **Democratic Republic of Vietnam**'s (DRV) new ambassador to China, **Hoang Van Hoan**. In 1952, the latter pressed the Indians to recognize the DRV instead of the Associated State of Vietnam led by **Bao Dai**. Why, Hoang Van Hoan asked in one meeting, did New Delhi refuse to recognize the DRV? Panikkar explained that the Indians were waiting to see how things turned out, but he also pressed Hoang Van Hoan to confirm whether Vietnamese communists planned to export communism to Laos and Cambodia, something which worried the Indians greatly, as the **Geneva Conference** would show. Panikkar wrote a number of books, including *Asia and Western Dominance* (1953) and *In Two Chinas* (1955). *See also* INDIANS.

**PARALLEL HIERARCHIES.** Term attributed to **Charles Lacheroy,** used by him publicly for the first time at a conference in southern Vietnam in 1952. According to Lacheroy, the system of parallel hierarchies referred to the structures by which the Vietnamese communists organized and controlled the populations in their **zones**. Each member of society is subject to two hierarchies. The first is the administrative, territorial one, running from the village to the provincial and zonal levels. The second hierarchy is composed of state-sponsored mass associations for peasants, workers, youth, women, etc., all of which are organized within the national front, the **Lien Viet**. The communist party controls both hierarchies. Political commissars, working through party cells, connect both pillars midway, thereby ensuring secret party control at each level of the parallel hierarchies. In reality, intelligence analysts in the ***Deuxième Bureau*** in southern Vietnam had already developed such ideas before Lacheroy arrived upon the scene. However, Lacheroy would transform the "parallel hierarchies" into something of a "theory", one which would catch on in the French Army and would be applied to varying degrees in the **Algerian War**. In a famous scene from Gillo Pontecorvo's film on the Algerian War, *La Battaglia di Algeri,* a French paratrooper called in to maintain order explains methodically on a blackboard the intricacies of "parallel hierarchies" and how they can be dismantled. That the Algerian nationalist movement, the *Front de libération nationale* (FLN), was not led by a communist party and did not have any ties to Sino-Vietnamese communist models did not prevent French theoricians from promoting their theory there. *See also* BERNARD FALL; GUERRILLA; PACIFICATION; REVOLUTIONARY WARFARE; *SERVICE ACTION*; SPECIAL AIR SERVICE (SAS).

**PARATROOPERS.** *See* SPECIAL AIR SERVICE (SAS).

**PARISOT, JEAN-PAUL.** Career civil servant in French Indochina. Between 1925 and 1945, he served in diverse administrative posts in Laos and **Cochinchina**. Between 1945 and 1946, he served as commissioner for the Republic to Middle and Lower Laos, and as provincial advisor for the provinces of Savannakhet and Pakse. Between 1948 and 1949, he was cabinet chief for the commissioner to the Republic for Cochinchina.

**PARIS–SAIGON.** Local **Saigon** paper created after World War II by Marc Planchon, later joined by **Philippe Devillers** and **Jean Lacouture**, to inform the French population in southern Vietnam about world events and to promote a peaceful settlement to the war already underway with the Vietnamese in **Cochinchina** since **23 September 1945**. It ceased publication in 1947. *See also* ANTICOLONIALISM; CINEMA; CULTURE; *ESPRIT*; INTELLECTUALS; *TÉMOIGNAGE CHRÉTIEN*.

**PARTY AFFAIRS COMMITTEE (*Ban Cán Sự*).** Term used by the **Indochinese Communist Party** (ICP) to refer to its directing, administrative committees operating in newly opened **zones**, the first structural step in creating creating local or regional-provincial communist committees (*Xu Uy* or *Dang Bo*). Besides forming them in the Vietnamese countryside, the ICP also operated secret Party Affairs Committees in Laos, Cambodia, and upland non-Viet areas during the Indochina War. The Affairs Committees for Laos and Cambodia were the single most powerful administrative unit through which the ICP worked in western Indochina during the conflict. These committees served as the foundations upon which Lao and Cambodian communism emerged. In 1949, the ICP assigned the task of creating a new revolutionary government and party for Cambodia to **Nguyen Thanh Son**, head of the **Committee for External Affairs** (*Ban Ngoai Vu*) and **Hoang Van Hoan**, chief of the all-powerful Overseas Party Affairs Committee (*Ban Can Su Hai Ngoai*) based in Thailand. After a meeting in Bangkok in 1949, Nguyen Thanh Son returned to Indochina and created the Party Affairs Committee for all of Cambodia (*Ban Can Su Toan Mien*), the single most powerful revolutionary organization in all of Cambodia and run by the ICP. In March 1950, as in Laos a few months later, the ICP organized a Cadres Congress for Cambodia bringing together **Khmer Issaraks** from across the country to create a new national front, provisional government, and revolutionary party. Separate party affairs sub-committees existed for the regional section into which the ICP had divided Cambodia. The ICP administered Laos in the same manner. The Western Party Cadres Committee for Laos (*Ban Can Su mien Tay*) was the clearing-house for communist affairs in Laos and the man in charge was **Nguyen Khang**. While the ICP gave way to the Vietnamese Workers Party in 1951, Vietnamese communists kept their trans-national Indochinese revolution alive via these powerful cadres committees. *See also* ADMINISTRATIVE OFFICE FOR THE FRONTIER; ADVISORY GROUP 100; CAMBODIAN RESISTANCE GOVERNMENT; COLLABORATION; COMMITTEE FOR THE EAST, LAO ISSARA; IENG SARY; INDOCHINESE FEDERATION; KAISON

PHOUMVIHAN; LAO RESISTANCE GOVERNMENT; PATHET LAO; POL POT.

**PATHET LAO.** Following the dissolution of the **Lao Issara** in October 1949 and faced with the emergence of the Associated State of Laos, Vietnamese and Lao leaders opposed to the French met in **Democratic Republic of Vietnam** (DRV) controlled territory in Vietnam in August 1950 to create the **Lao Resistance Government** and a new national front, the *Pathet Lao* or Lao Nation. Like the **Viet Minh**, the Pathet Lao was designed to gather support from all different parts of Lao society, regardless of class, ethnicity, or gender. The Pathet Lao, like the **Khmer Issarak**, worked closely with the DRV and the **Lien Viet** national front during the rest of the Indochina War. *See also* ADMINISTRATIVE OFFICE FOR THE FRONTIER; ADVISORY GROUP 100; ASSOCIATED STATES OF INDOCHINA; COMMITTEE FOR EXTERNAL AFFAIRS; COMMITTEE FOR THE EAST, LAO ISSARA; INDOCHINESE COMMUNIST PARTY; INDOCHINESE FEDERATION; KAISÔN PHOMVIHĀN; LAO RESISTANCE GOVERNMENT; PARTY AFFAIRS COMMITTEE.

**PATTI, ARCHIMEDES L. A. (1914–1998).** A native of New York, Patti joined the United States army in 1941, serving as an infantry officer in Europe during World War II and in military intelligence in the **Office of Strategic Services** (OSS) in the China Theater at the end of the Pacific War. He headed the OSS team sent to **Hanoi** to tend to Allied POWs and European internees and to maintain order as best as possible. He arrived in Hanoi by plane on 22 August at the head of the **Mercy** team, bringing with him **Jean Sainteny**'s five-man team. Athough he was under orders to maintain strict neutrality in the Franco-Vietnamese dispute, he quickly became involved in political matters, forwarding messages from **Ho Chi Minh** to President **Harry Truman** for example. Patti was fully aware of Ho Chi Minh's communist résumé, but tended to sympathize with Vietnamese independence aspirations, something which gained him few friends among French officials such as Jean Sainteny. Patti reported on Vietnamese nationalist aspirations and the dangers a French colonial return would spark. However, many at OSS headquarters felt that he had not remained neutral in his role. Following his retirement in 1957, Patti worked for 13 years as a crisis management specialist in the Office of Emergency Planning in Washington D.C. In 1982, he published *Why Vietnam? Prelude to America's Albatross*, in which he revealed in detail his intelligence work in southern China and northern Vietnam at the closing of the Pacific War. He is buried in Arlington cemetery. *See also* A. PETER DEWEY.

**PAU CONFERENCE.** Held in November 1950, this conference in the French town of Pau was designed to celebrate the creation of the **Associated States of Indochina** in 1949 and to iron out a number of problems concerning relations among the Lao, Cambodians, and Vietnamese. Above all, what would be the nature of the continued Indochinese "association"? Despite **Albert Sarraut**'s praise of the historic Indochinese past of the Associated States, heated debates at Pau among the leaders of the three states revealed just how contested the idea of a continued "Indochinese" association was. Of particular concern was the prickly question of an Indochinese monetary and customs union for all three countries. Even Vietnamese delegates spoke in favor of creating national currencies instead of maintaining the colonial-era piastre. Echoing arguments from the 1930s, the Lao and the Cambodians feared that the Vietnamese would dominate such a union and dug in their heals. By the end of the conference, it was clear that such joint services would fail to overcome national oppositions coming from the Lao and Cambodians. Unlike the French colonizers and their communist competitors, few non-communist Lao, Cambodian, or even Vietnamese nationalists believed in "Indochina". For them, the idea only served to preserve French monetary interference and control. Although the organization of the *Institut d'émission* and the administration of the port of **Saigon** operated according to an Indochinese model, many services, including customs and the treasuries, transferred to the local governments in the wake of the Pau conference. The Associated State of Vietnam's leaders also succeeded in freeing themselves of the obligation to take part in any conflict into which the French might enter. In short, Pau pointed up the degree to which the Associated States of Indochina had every intention of realizing their full national independence in opposition to the colonial Indochinese model. In September 1951, for example, **Tran Van Huu** attended the San Francisco conference with a view to signing a peace treaty with Japan. During this visit to the United States, the Vietnamese prime minister met with **Harry Truman** and Clement Attlee, symbolizing the increasing autonomy of the Associated State of Vietnam at the international level. The Pau conference also coincided with communist Vietnamese efforts to build up their own policy of Indochinese association via the creation of the **Pathet Lao** and **Khmer Issarak** national fronts, resistance governments, and **party affairs committees.** *See also* CAMBODIAN RESISTANCE GOVERNMENT; GENEVA ACCORDS; LAO RESISTANCE GOVERNMENT; NEUTRALIZATION OF INDOCHINA.

**PAUL-BONCOUR, JEAN LOUIS (1898–1973).** Career French diplomat who held a number of positions in Europe and North America during the interwar period. He worked as *chargé d'affaires* in Chongqing between 1941 and 1943, after which Vichy removed him of his functions. In 1948, he was the French delegate to the first **United Nations** Commission in Korea. Between 1951 and 1953, he served as ambassador to Thailand and collaborated closely with French political and military authorities in Indochina. In 1954, he served as the general secretary of the debates on Korea and Indochina during the **Geneva Conference** before representing France at the United Nations. *See also* JACQUES GUILLERMAZ.

***PAYS MONTAGNARDS DU SUD* (PMS).** Following the outbreak of full-scale war with the **Democratic Republic of Vietnam** (DRV) on 19 December 1946, the French assigned increasing geopolitical importance to controlling the central highlands in northern **Cochinchina** and much of **Annam**, as they did to turning the **minority ethnic groups** living there against the **Viet Minh** operating from the lowlands.

However, as Oscar Salemink has shown, this policy of divide and rule adopted by the likes of High Commissioner **Georges Thierry d'Argenlieu** had its roots in the colonial past. In the late 19th century, as the French moved to consolidate their hold over Indochina, they paid particular attention to the strategic location of the highlands, especially as they moved to roll back the influence of Siam (today's Thailand). Having consolidated colonial Indochina, French attention subsequently focused on the highlands as a way of controlling anti-colonial insurrections among the Vietnamese concentrated in the lowlands. French administrators in the highlands, such as the legendary Léopold Sabatier, contributed to the making of a separate non-Vietnamese identity for upland peoples by opposing Vietnamese immigration to the plateaux. He emphasized a separate ethnic identity for the *montagnards*, and even created a customary law code for the Rhadé. Administrators, military officers, and ethnographers contributed to this ethnicization by classifying four major "tribes" in the central highlands by the 1930s – the Bahnar, Sedang, Rhadé, and Jarai. Soon French colonial specialists of the central highlands were speaking of an "essential cultural unity" emerging from historical tribal diversity. And many French increasingly defined this identity in terms of its "historic" opposition to all that was Vietnamese. Military strategists worried by Vietnamese revolts further emphasized the importance of the highlands and the need "to save this race, to disentangle it from all harmful foreign influences through a direct administration, and to tie these tribes to us … These proud peoples with their spirit of independence will provide us with elite troops, (serve) as safety valves in case of internal insurgency, and (act) as powerful combat units in case of external war".

French strategists returning to rebuild colonial Indochina after World War II built upon this preexisting French montagnard policy, extending it now to other ethnic minority areas in the highlands of Indochina, especially among the Tai and the Nung in northwestern Vietnam. In May 1946, faced with the DRV's territorial claim to all of Vietnam (Cochinchina, Annam, and **Tonkin**), the French high commissioner for Indochina Georges Thierry d'Argenlieu issued a decree making the central highlands a "Special Administrative Circumscription", better known as the autonomous region for the *Populations montagnardes du Sud-Indochinois* or PMSI. Administered by a special French delegate, it consisted of the five upland provinces in Annam but excluded montagnard populations in the lower part of the territory as well as in Cochinchina, Cambodia, and Laos. Thierry d'Argenlieu's strategy was to contain and if possible roll back the DRV. The same was true in the south.

Four days after establishing the PMSI, on 1 June 1946 Thierry d'Argenlieu announced the creation of the **Provisional Government of the Republic of Cochinchina**. The high commissioner had no trouble incorporating ethnic minority highland peoples into this new "Cochinchinese" entity given its alignment on the French. Engaged in intense negotiations at **Fontainebleau**, DRV officials protested vigorously against both French creations. To no avail. As one French spokesman countered the DRV's national claim to the highlands: "neither geographically, historically nor ethnically, can the highlands be considered a part of Vietnam". DRV delegates reminded the French of Alsace-Lorraine. On 21 June, French troops received the order to retake the highlands from the DRV below the **16$^{th}$ parallel**.

Significantly, the French were no more willing to cede the upland regions to the counterrevolutionary Vietnamese government that they began to push in the form of the **Bao Dai solution**. Colonel **Jacques Massu** even proposed, and Thierry d'Argenlieu approved, a plan to allow retired French veterans to establish plantations in the central highlands with the goal of maintaining French control and promoting a separate identity to check Vietnamese nationalism. Results were limited, however. With the Chinese communists on their way to victory in the north in 1949, the French finally allowed Bao Dai's government to assert its "eminent rights" over the highlands. However, this French Associated State of Vietnam had to recognize the "free evolution of these populations in relation to their traditions and customs".

Things changed again in early 1950, when the **Cold War** saw the American-led bloc recognize **Bao Dai's** Vietnam and pressure the French to decolonize further in Vietnam in order to better contain the nationalist attraction of communist Vietnam. For example, two decrees in 1950 "attached to Bao Dai personally all provinces and territories inhabited by non-Vietnamese populations traditionally under the court of Hue", meaning the five provinces of Annam. The Crown Domain of the Southern Higlander Country (*Domaine de la couronne du pays montagnards du Sud*) or PMS was thus born. Although the French nominally recognized Vietnamese sovereignty over the highlands in the form of this crown domain, they maintained a *statut particulier* for the highlands because of "special French obligations" and continued to direct the PMS through their special delegate, a Frenchman, not a Vietnamese representative of the Associated State. In May 1951, Bao Dai signed a law promulgating the creation of a "special regulation" designed to provide more highlander participation in local affairs all the while reaffirming the "eminent rights" of Vietnam over this territory. However, Vietnamese national control over the central highlands remained incomplete until the end of the conflict in 1954.

While the montagnards had to navigate at least one French colonial and two Vietnamese national projects during nine years of war, the conflict also gave rise to profound changes. For one, the French and the Associated State of Vietnam promoted efforts to produce an educated anti-Viet Minh elite. Hundreds of young men coming from across the highlands met each other in the classrooms of the *Collège Sabbatier* in Ban Me Thuot, studied what became a common upland language, Rhadé, accepted administrative positions outside their native lands, and in so doing developed long-lasting and often unprecedented relationships extending across the hills. Marriage across clan lines often resulted. Similar things happened in the combat units created by the Franco-Vietnamese forces to fight the DRV forces. In short, the Indochina War gave rise to a new common "highlander" sociopolitical identity, one that would assume national goals within a short period of time. In 1953, the State of Vietnam counted an estimated 500,000 highland people in the Crown Domain (excluding parts of former Cochinchina). *See also* TAI FEDERATION.

**PEACE IN ORDER TO ADVANCE INSTRUCTIONS (*Hoà Để Tiến*).** On 9 March 1946, in the immediate aftermath of the signing of the **Accords of 6 March 1946**, the Standing Committee of the Central Committee of the **Indochinese Communist Party** issued this document to explain to cadres the reasons for the signing of the accords and the party's decision to pursue a path of negotiations with the French. One of the main arguments was the need to accelerate the withdrawal of the Chinese from the north in order to make fewer the **Democratic Republic of Vietnam**'s enemies, and thereby buy time to strengthen the state and its armed forces in the event the "peaceful path" failed and full-scale war broke out. *See also* 19 DECEMBER 1946; FRANCO-CHINESE ACCORDS; OCCUPATION, CHINESE.

**PECHKOFF, ZINOVI (1884–1966).** The adopted son of the Russian writer Maxim Gorky (A. M. Peshkov) who became a French citizen and a diplomat in Asia. In 1914, Pechkoff arrived in France and joined the **Foreign Legion**. He lost one of his arms in combat in World War I. Between 1918 and 1920, he carried out a number of diplomatic missions to Russia and Asia before returning to his Foreign Legion unit stationed in Morocco between 1921 and 1926. In 1923, he was naturalized a French citizen *par le sang versé*. In 1941, at the head of the Foreign Legion in Morocco, he joined Free French forces. Because of his knowledge of the Far East, he was between 1943 and 1945 the delegate then the ambassador to the **Republic of China** led by **Chiang Kai-shek**. Between 1946 and 1949, he headed the French Mission to Japan and became ambassador. During this time, he worked closely with French military and political authorities in Indochina. He helped organize the repatriation of Japanese soldiers from Indochina to Japan, prosecute Japanese war criminals in Indochina, and return Japanese **crossovers** who wanted to leave the **Democratic Republic of Vietnam**.

**PENAVAIRE, ROMAIN VICTOR JOSEPH (1904–1968).** French colonial administrator in Indochina. He began his career as the chief of the intelligence service in colonial Kouang Tcheouwan (today's Zhanjiang) before transferring to Cambodia in 1934. Until 1941, he served in diverse administrative positions across Cambodia working in **Cochinchina** and **Annam** under Vichy. Following the Japanese defeat, Penavaire returned to Cambodian affairs as president of the Franco-Cambodian Study Commission in 1945–1946, then as interim commissioner for the Republic to Cambodia, a job he acquired officially in December 1946. He participated in the Franco-Siamese reconciliation committee of 1947, following the Thai return of Indochinese territories acquired during World War II. In 1948, he was part of a diplomatic mission sent to the United States to plead the case for Franco-Cambodian and Franco-Lao efforts in the Indochina War. Between 1949 and 1951, Penavaire worked in the high commissioner's office in **Saigon** as director of personnel and as advisor on economic affairs. He attended the **Pau Conference** in June 1950 and joined the Board of Directors of the Institute of Currency Circulation for the **Associated States of Indochina** when it emerged in May 1951. *See also* BANK OF INDOCHINA; CURRENCY, FRENCH INDOCHINA.

**PENN NOUTH (1906–1985).** Prominent Cambodian politician during the Indochina War. Born in Phnom Penh, he completed his primary studies at the *Collège Sisowath* and entered the colonial administration working as a secretary in the *Résidence supérieure* in Cambodia before attaining the rank of *anouc montrey* or notable in 1935 in the Cambodian administration. He served as a district chief and deputy governor in the 1930s. In 1938, he completed a training course in France in the Ministry of the Colonies. Upon his return, he was appointed head of the office of the Ministry of the Palace, Finance and Fine Arts, playing a pivotal role in the reorganization and modernization of the monarchy in the person of **Norodom Sihanouk**. He would go on to become the king's main advisor and confidant.

Following the Japanese overthrow of the French in the ***coup de force* of 9 March 1945**, he worked as deputy minister of Finance and held this post until the return of the French in October 1945, when he became governor of Kompong Cham province, a position he held until February 1946. He then worked as mayor of Phnom Penh as well as state minister in the **Sisowath Youtevong** cabinet between December 1946 and July 1947. He attended the **Dalat Conference** in 1946. Norodom Sihanouk asked him to form a new government in August 1948 in which he served as prime minister and minister of the Interior and of Information. He resigned in January 1949 when the opposition, the **Democrat Party**, took over the National Assembly. Though he was sympathetic to many of the Democrat projects, he remained a loyal supporter of Sihanouk. He became a member of the Council of the Regency (*Conseil de régence*) in July 1949 and Sihanouk put him in charge of the implementation of the Franco-Khmer Treaty signed on 8 November 1949 (he was in charge of economic, financial, and planning questions). In May 1950, Penn Nouth became state minister in charge of National Defense thanks to the support of Sihanouk. He was a member of the Cambodian delegation to the **Pau conference** in 1950. In June 1951, he became Private Counselor to the Crown. In January 1953, he served briefly as prime minister and minister for Sports and Youth.

During Sihanouk's **royal crusade for independence**, Penn Nouth played the pivotal, behind the scenes role of negotiating Cambodia's decolonization with the French. He enjoyed the full support and authorization of Sihanouk, who had set up camp in northwestern Cambodia to force the French hand. Penn Nouth briefly served as Sihanouk's delegate prime minister and minister of Economic and Financial Affairs in the cabinet formed on 6 April 1954. One week later, he agreed to take over as prime minister of a reshuffled cabinet announced on 17 April 1954 and which lasted until 31 July 1954. He resumed as prime minister on 1 August 1954, as the ink dried on the **Geneva Accords** on Indochina.

**PENSION, DEMOCRATIC REPUBLIC OF VIETNAM.** In February 1947, following the outbreak of full-scale war on **19 December 1946**, the **Democratic Republic of Vietnam** instituted an official pension for its war disabled and **martyr** families. In 1956 and again in 1959 the government fulfilled this by decreeing that the state would provide pensions to martyr families, those of fallen soldiers, cadres, workers, and other patriots who had died or had gone **missing in action** since 19 August 1945. Only those families whose deceased had served a minimum of three years in his or her wartime capacity could receive permanent pension benefits. Budget concerns guided the state's issuances of pensions. The government took into account the economic situation of the family and only provided pensions after a thorough investigation and certification of the deceased's case. In 1962, the maximum a family could receive, even if it had lost more than one member to the war, was thirty *dongs* a month per family. *See also* EXPERIENCE OF WAR; MYTH OF WAR.

**PEOPLE'S ARMY NEWSPAPER (*Báo Quân Đội Nhân Dân Việt Nam*).** Created on 20 October 1950 out of the merger of the pre-existing *Ve Quoc Quan* and the *Quan Du Kich* publications, this new army paper served as the official mouthpiece for the **People's Army of Vietnam** and was widely distributed within the army for training purposes. It operated under the control of the **Central Party Military Committee** (*Quan Uy*) and the Ministry of Defense.

**PEOPLE'S ARMY OF CAMBODIA.** Backed by the **Democratic Republic of Vietnam**, the People's Army of Cambodia emerged at the **Cold War** conjuncture of 1950–51. This "revolutionary" army came to life officially on 19 June 1951 in Kampot province, about a year after the creation of the People's Revolutionary Party of Cambodia and the **Cambodian Resistance Government** in 1950. Based on the Sino-Vietnamese model, the Cambodian army numbered several thousand troops by the end of the war in 1954 and, thanks to the military support of the Vietnamese in 1953–1954, controlled large swaths of territory in northeastern Cambodia. In accordance with the **Geneva Accords** signed in July 1954, its troops were demobilized, integrated into the Associated State of Cambodia's national army, or relocated to northern Vietnam. *See also* ADMINISTRATIVE OFFICE FOR THE FRONTIER; ARMY, ASSOCIATED STATE OF CAMBODIA; COMMITTEE FOR EXTERNAL AFFAIRS; COMMITTEE FOR THE EAST, LAO ISSARA; HOANG VAN HOAN; INDOCHINESE COMMUNIST PARTY; NGUYEN THANH SON; PARTY AFFAIRS COMMITTEE.

**PEOPLE'S ARMY OF LAOS.** The origins of the People's Army of Laos can be traced to the activites of **Kaisôn Phomvihān** and his Vietnamese communist allies operating in northwestern Vietnam in the late 1940s. In February 1948, the **Indochinese Communist Party** created the Northern Lao Assault Team (*Doi Xung Phong Lao Bac*) to conduct political propaganda, create local armed groups, and expand the resistance into northern Laos. Kaisôn was the team's Lao leader. In January 1949, thanks to this propaganda work and the personal support of **Vo Nguyen Giap**, **Song Hao**, and **Le Tan Trong**, the northern Lao assault team became the embryonic Lao armed force known as *Latsavong*. However, it was not until **Advisory Group 100** arrived in September 1954 in the regrouping zones for the **Pathet Lao** in Phongsaly and Samneau that a true Pathet Lao army emerged following the signing of the **Geneva Accords.** *See also* ADMINISTRATIVE OFFICE FOR THE FRONTIER; ARMY, ASSOCIATED STATE OF LAOS; COMMITTEE FOR EXTERNAL AFFAIRS; COMMITTEE FOR THE EAST, LAO ISSARA; HOANG VAN HOAN; NGUYEN KHANG; NGUYEN THANH SON; PARTY AFFAIRS COMMITTEE.

**PEOPLE'S ARMY OF VIETNAM (*Quân Đội Nhân Dân Việt Nam*).** The official founding date of the People's Army of Vietnam is 22 December 1944, when the **Indochinese Communist Party** (ICP) leaders founded the Armed Propaganda Brigade for the Liberation of Vietnam (*Doi Viet Nam Tuyen Truyen Gia Phong Quan*) along the Sino-Vietnamese border in **Cao Bang** province. **Vo Nguyen Giap** served as its first commander and led mobilization campaigns among populations in remote areas of northern Vietnam and initiated some small-scale **guerrilla** operations against Japanese troops. This proto-army consisted of some 30 individuals at the outset. In May 1945, following the Japanese overthrow of the French, the ICP combined the Armed Propaganda Brigade for the Liberation of Vietnam with the Salvation Army (*Cuu Quoc Quan*) to create the Vietnamese Liberation Army (*Viet Nam Giai Phong Quan*) in Thai Nguyen province. It helped take power in the wake of the Japanese defeat in August in northern and central Vietnam. Following the establishment of the **Democratic Republic of Vietnam** (DRV) on 2 September 1945, the government transformed the Vietnamese Liberation Army into the National Defense Force (*Ve Quoc Doan*) in November 1945. In May 1946, **Ho Chi Minh** signed a decree changing this entity into the Vietnamese National Army (*Quan Doi Quoc Gia*) which became the People's Army of Vietnam in 1950 (*Quan Doi Nhan Dan Viet Nam*). In 1948, Vo Nguyen Giap was named general (*Dai Tuong*) and placed officially at the head of all the DRV's armed forces. *See also* AID, CHINESE; AID, SOVIET; ARMY OF THE ASSOCIATED STATE OF VIETNAM; NGUYEN BINH; NGUYEN SON; PEOPLE'S ARMY OF CAMBODIA; PEOPLE'S ARMY OF LAOS.

**PEOPLE'S ARMY PUBLISHING HOUSE (*Nhà Xuất Bản Quân Đội Nhân Dân*).** Created in July 1950 as the official publishing house of the Ministry of Defense and the **Central Party Military Committee** (*Quan Uy*). Its main tasks consisted of producing the history of the people's army and the resistance, as well as publishing military memoirs (*hoi ky*). The thematic emphasis was on patriotism, the leadership of the party, and the heroic deeds of the armed forces. The People's Army Publishing House was also designed to provide educational materials and manuals to be used in the training of the armed forces.

**PEOPLE'S PAPER (*Nhân Dân*).** Official mouthpiece of the **Vietnamese Worker's Party**, it came to life on 11 March 1951 during the **Indochinese Communist Party's** second party conference. *Nhan Dan* replaced *Su That* (*The Truth*) which had served as the party's mouthpiece since late 1945. *Nhan Dan* was based in northern Vietnam during the Indochina War before transferring to **Hanoi** in late 1954 or early 1955. It became a daily on 20 October 1954.

**PEOPLE'S REPUBLIC OF CHINA.** The People's Republic of China was from its advent on 1 October 1949 the **Democratic Republic of Vietnam**'s (DRV) most important ally in the region and the world until the signing of the **Geneva Accords** in 1954. Personal ties between Chinese and Vietnamese communist leaders reached back to the 1920s. **Ho Chi Minh** had first brushed shoulders with **Zhou Enlai** in Paris following World War I and rejoined him in Guangzhou (Canton) in the mid-1920s at the Whampoa Politico-Military Academy. These longstanding friendships and the Chinese Communist Party's desire to promote revolution elsewhere in Asia after coming to power in October 1949 saw the Chinese support the Vietnamese case for diplomatic recognition, in contrast to a remarkably reluctant **Joseph Stalin**. Indeed, the Chinese led the way by recognizing the DRV officially on 17 January 1950, followed shortly thereafter by Moscow and the rest of the communist bloc. The Chinese provided vital economic and military aid and training to the Vietnamese army during the First Indochina War, allowing the DRV to go beyond **guerrilla** warfare to take the battle to the French **Expeditionary Corps** in set-piece battles. **Mao Zedong** personally followed major Vietnamese military operations, including the battle of **Dien Bien Phu**. A **Chinese Military Advisory Delegation** arrived in northern Vietnam in 1950 to help the Vietnamese in the further communisation of their party, economy, and cadres. However, the adoption of the Chinese-modelled **land reform** provoked disastrous results in northern Vietnam. That did not prevent both sides from cooperating closely during international negotiations seeking to end the Indochina conflict during the **Geneva Conference**. *See also* AID, CHINESE; GENEVA ACCORDS.

**PEOPLE'S REVOLUTIONARY PARTY OF CAMBODIA.** *See* INDOCHINESE COMMUNIST PARTY; KHMER ISSARAK.

**PERAUD, JEAN (1923–1954).** Peraud joined the French army in January 1945 and landed in Indochina as part of the *1^er^ BCP*. He worked in the army as a war photographer in the *Service de presse et d'information militaires des forces terrestres en Extrême-Orient*, covering major battles of the Indochina War between 1950 and 1954. During this time, he followed troops into battle and provided photographs of intense combat between **French Union** and **Democratic Republic of Vietnam** (DRV) forces. On 18 March 1954, he parachuted into **Dien Bien Phu** and went down with the camp in the 71[st] Headquarters Company, to which he was attached. The DRV army took him prisoner on 8 May 1954 and sent off to a prison camp in the company of **Pierre Schoendoerffer** and **Daniel Camus**. Having been tortured and locked up by the Nazis in Buchenwald in 1944, Peraud told his companions that he had no desire to repeat the communist version it: "I've just got to get out of this. I can't do it twice. This time I'm sure I won't come out of it alive". He bolted with Schoendoerffer at a sharp turn in the road. The Vietnamese guards captured the latter. Peraud never made it out of the jungle and was declared *mort pour la France* in July 1954. *See also* CASUALTIES; EXPERIENCE OF WAR; MYTH OF WAR; PRISONER OF WAR.

**PEREYRA (DE), MIGUEL-JOAQUIN (1903–?).** A graduate of SciencesPo in Paris, he joined the colonial administration in Indochina in 1927. He worked in the Head Office of Political Affairs (*Direction du cabinet des affaires politiques*) until early 1930, when he transferred briefly to the Ministry of Foreign Affairs to work in Kunming between March and November 1930. Between 1933 and March 1945, he worked in a variety of colonial posts, including that of *résident* of Ha Nam, Ninh Binh, Nam Dinh, and *résident* mayor in **Hanoi**. In February 1947, he was named the delegate for the high commissioner to **Tonkin** and North **Annam** before transferring to Laos to serve as the commissioner for the Republic to Laos from December 1949 and then the high commissioner for the Republic to Laos in April 1953, a post he held until April 1954, when he was assigned to Madagascar. In June 1948, he briefly filled in as the acting diplomatic advisor to **Émile Bollaert**.

**PERRIER, PIERRE. (1906–?).** One of France's top civilian security chiefs during the Indochina War. He joined the French resistance during World War II and received the *croix de guerre, 39–45*. After World War II, he served in the metropolitan police force before landing in Indochina as a 1st rank administrator in the *Corps de liaison administrative pour l'Extrême-Orient*. He began work officially for the high commissioner on 12 January 1946. At an unknown date but sometime in the late 1940s, Perrier became director of the Security Services for Indochina. Unfortunately, little else is known of his activities.

***PERSONNEL FÉMININ DE L'ARMÉE DE TERRE* (PFAT).** The number of women serving in the French **Expeditionary Corps**'s *Personnel féminin de l'armée de terre* grew to more than 2,000 by the end of the Indochina War, not counting an additional 30 women serving in the **Navy** and 120 in the **Air Force**. Around 500 women were recruited locally into the PFAT from the wives of civilian or military personnel working in Indochina. While many filled positions as secretaries, French women in the armed forces in Indochina were doing more than just pushing pencils for the General Staffs. Some served in combat zones. Indeed, over 100 women in the PFAT were killed during the war. Aged between 25 and 35, these mainly French women were ambulance drivers, nurses, **helicopter** pilots, and surgeons. Helicopter pilot Captain **Valérie André**, for example, evacuated wounded soldiers from high risk combat zones and provided them with vital first aid. Having survived a Nazi death camp, **Paule Dupont d'Isigny** joined the PFAT and became a member of the *Infirmières parachutistes secourites de l'Air*. She flew more than 4,000 hours as a pilot during the Indochina war, including more than 30 combat missions to rescue wounded soldiers in battle zones. Aline Lerouge was well known at the time for her audacious missions to rescue soldiers in her American-made ambulance. She died serving the army in it. Scores of other women were involved in the essential work of rigging parachutes for airborne units, especially before and during the battle of **Dien Bien Phu**. However, the French army did not allow women to serve in regular combat units. They remained confined mainly to this special women's unit tending to the wounded. *See also* WOMEN, DEMOCRATIC REPUBLIC OF VIETNAM.

***PERSONNELS INTERNÉS MILITAIRES* (PIM).** *See* PRISONERS OF WAR, DEMOCRATIC REPUBLIC OF VIETNAM.

**PETIT, CHARLES EUGÈNE FERNAND (1908–?).** ***Métis*** inspector for the French *Sûreté* in Indochina who secretly infiltrated the forces of the **Democratic Republic of Vietnam** (DRV) in late 1946 and tipped off the French about a planned Vietnamese attack for the night of the 19th of December. Born to a French father and a Vietnamese mother, Petit was raised in colonial **Hanoi**. Before returning there in late 1945 or 1946, he had worked in Paris and in Marseilles, in charge of a French counter-espionage unit working among the Vietnamese in France. Under cover, he was able to win over the confidence of representatives of the DRV in France without them being aware of his role as a French-employed agent. Thanks to letters of introduction from Vietnamese leaders in France, Petit was then able to enter into the services of the DRV and joined the ranks of one of the local militia *(Tu Ve)* in his neighborhood in Hanoi. Petit played a minor role in reporting on Vietnamese preparations for war in mid-December 1946. During the day of the 19th, he learned that orders had been given to attack the French at 20H00 that evening. When he asked permission from the head of his militia unit to take leave for a few minutes, he was warned that if he did not return, his family "would suffer the consequences". He immediately informed Colonel **Pierre Lami**, Commissioner Lanèque and Major **André Moret** of the imminent attack. Details of his subsequent activites are unknown.

**PHẠM CÔNG TẮC (1890[9]–1959).** Religious leader of the **Cao Dai** religious movement and adversary of the **Democratic Republic of Vietnam** (DRV) during the Indochina War. Born in Tan An province in southern Vietnam, he began his career in 1910 working in the colonial customs service where he rose to the rank of third class secretary by the mid-1920s. In 1927, the French transferred him to Phnom Penh in order to remove him from his emerging religious activities in **Saigon** and Tay Ninh province. However, he resigned from his post in the civil service that same year, left Phnom Penh on 6 January 1928, and returned to Tay Ninh to rejoin the rapidly growing Cao Dai religious movement led by Le Van Trung. Following the death of the latter in 1935, Pham Cong Tac extended his influence and control over the movement's disciples and organization. In 1938, he took control of the movement when he became the supreme spiritual leader of the Cao Dai. His suspected links to the Japanese and perceived attempts to create an autonomous religious state and militia outside of colonial control led the French to arrest and deport him to Madagascar in 1941. There, he served time with the future heads of the DRV's secret services, **Le Gian** and **Tran Hieu**. The French brought him back to southern Vietnam on 22 August 1946 on the condition that he collaborate with them against the **Viet Minh**. On 8 January 1947, he signed an accord with the French General Staff to align Cao Dai armed forces with the French and their Vietnamese allies. On 17 April 1947, he stated his support for the return of **Bao Dai** to Vietnam. From this point, his break with the forces of the DRV was for intents and purposes inevitable. In 1947, a large part of the Cao Dai forces left the Viet Minh front and armed forces, and began crossing over to the French side and the Associated State of Vietnam state they were constructing with Bao Dai. With the creation of the Associated State in 1949, Pham Cong Tac met with the ex-emperor to discuss the integration of Cao Dai forces into the new State of Vietnam army. Following a very rocky meeting with General **Jean de Lattre de Tassigny**, who insisted that Pham Cong Tac integrate his forces into the national army, Tac put an end to his collaboration with the French and in March 1952 declared himself supreme commander of the Cao Dai Army. On 19 May 1954, following the French defeat at **Dien Bien Phu**, Pham Cong Tac signed a protocol accepting the integration of the Cao Dai forces into the Armed Forces of the Associated State of Vietnam. *See also* BINH XUYEN; COLLABORATION; CROSSOVER; DESERTION; HOA HAO; HUYNH PHU XO; LE VAN VIEN.

**PHẠM ĐÀN (TRƯƠNG LAI)**. Important communist leader in charge of the **overseas Chinese** for the **Democratic Republic of Vietnam** in the south. In 1948, the **Indochinese Communist Party** (ICP) Central Committee dispatched him to southern Vietnam. In 1949, with the approval of **Le Duan**, he began working from Dong Thap Muoi at the head of the Committee for the Mobilization of the Overseas Chinese and in charge of the **Bureau for Overseas Chinese Affairs in Nam Bo**. With the Chinese communists aiding the Vietnamese in the north, the Vietnamese attached increased importance to garnering the support of the large Chinese population living in southern Vietnam. This was Pham Dan's main task. To this end, he helped publish resistance papers in Chinese and Vietnamese, disseminated a wide range of propaganda, and urged the Chinese in Vietnam to join Sino-Vietnamese friendship associations, clubs, and fronts. He also oversaw accelerated efforts to set up departments for the overseas Chinese in every southern province under the secret control of the ICP. Pham Dan returned to northern Vietnam around 1951.

**PHẠM ĐANG CAO (1914–1987).** Graduated from the French ***École nationale des langues***

9. One internal French record reports that Pham Cong Tac was born in 1893.

***orientales vivantes***, he became a career colonial administrator and held the French *Croix de guerre*. Between 1946 and 1954, he served in a variety of colonial posts including the Police Service for **Saigon**-Cholon (1946–1947), the Department of Economic Affairs in **Cochinchina** (1947–1948), and as provincial chief of Ben Tre (1948–1949) and Can Tho (1950–1954) provinces. He went on to serve in French colonial Africa before taking his retirement in France where he passed away. He was a naturalized French citizen.

**PHẠM DUY (PHẠM DUY CẦN, 1921–).** One of modern Vietnam's greatest musicians and singers. Born in **Hanoi**, Pham Duy grew up with the arts; his father and brothers were well known for their cultural achievements. Pham Duy entered the private *Lycée Thang Long* in Hanoi in 1936 and became involved in nationalist politics there during the Popular Front period, brushing shoulders with the likes of future General **Vo Nguyen Giap**. During World War II, while studying the fine arts in Hanoi, Pham Duy wrote his first major song *Co Hai Mo*. Thanks to this hit and others, he soon embarked upon a singing tour of Indochina as a member of the Duc Huy musical troupe. He even performed on *Radio Indochine* in 1943–1944.

The famine of 1945 and the outbreak of war between the French and the **Democratic Republic of Vietnam** (DRV) changed all this. Pham Duy joined the resistance and put his singing talents in the service of the nationalist independence movement in **Inter-Zone IV** (*Lien Khu IV*). He participated in the DRV's arts and propaganda campaigns in the early days of the resistance war; he wrote songs in favor of the struggle and the armed forces, critical of French colonialism. He befriended another resistance artist, Van Cao, and the two became close friends. Pham Duy also came to respect the arts-minded Maoist general running the zone, **Nguyen Son**. Pham Duy wrote songs such as *The Warrior Without a Name (Chien Si Vo Danh), The Debt of Bones and Blood (No Xuong Mau), Competing in Patriotism (Thi Dua Ai Quoc),* and *Music of the Years of Youth (Nhac Tuoi Xanh)* among many others. All these songs dovetailed nicely with the party's belief that all art should serve the war, the revolution, and the mobilization of the "masses". He also discovered the brutality of war while on missions that provided him with new material for his songwriting. He wrote a particularly powerful song called ***Mothers of Gio Linh*** *(Ba Me Gio Linh)*, in which he recounted the true story and the profound sorrow of mothers whose sons – a teacher Nguyen Phi and a commune chief Nguyen Duc Ky – were beheaded by French soldiers in Mai Xa village, Gio Linh district in Quang Tri. Returning to the village in 2005, Pham Duy still remembered "crying like a child after writing the song" during the Indochina conflict.

If such songs certainly pleased the DRV's leaders at the time, Pham Duy was less enamored of communist ideology and its politicization of art, culture, and music. From 1950, he objected to the increasing communization of the state and the resistance movement to the detriment of non-communist nationalists such as himself. And he could not stand the party's limits on independent thought and artistic freedom. He refused an invitation to join the party and undergo cultural training in Moscow. Instead, in the early 1950s, he left the ranks of the DRV and returned to the French-controlled urban zones, hoping that the Associated State of Vietnam could provide a better nationalist alternative than the one promised by the communists. He was among hundreds of **crossovers** to do so. Upon his defection, the DRV immediately banned his songs in resistance-controlled zones and dismissed the importance of his art. His *oeuvre* would, however, attract continued admiration and fans in the **Republic of Vietnam** until 1975 and among the Vietnamese overseas community to this day. Since the end of the **Cold War** and Vietnam's capitalist transformation he has reconquered airwaves and fans in the Socialist Republic of Vietnam. Indeed, in 2005, Pham Duy left California, where he had resided since 1975, to live in **Saigon**. His music was officially approved to hit the airwaves in July of 2005. *See also* BORIS VIAN; CAM LY, MASSACRE; COLLABORATION; EXPERIENCE OF WAR; HÉRAULT, MASSACRE; MY THUY, MASSACRE; MYTH OF WAR; NEW HERO; RECTIFICATION.

**PHẠM HÙNG (PHẠM VĂN THIỆN, HAI HÙNG, 1912–1988).** One of the leading architects of the **Democratic Republic of Vietnam**'s (DRV) security forces in southern Vietnam during the Indochina War. Born in Vinh Long province in southern Vietnam, Pham Hung started his studies at the *Collège de My Tho*. He became politically active during patriotic student strikes in the mid-1920s. He studied and agitated with the likes of **Nguyen Thanh Son** (Nguyen Van Tay) and **Ung Van Khiem**. In 1930, he joined the **Indochinese**

**Communist Party** (ICP) and was active in My Tho province until his arrest in 1931 with **Le Van Luong** and deportation to **Poulo Condor** in 1934. Pham Hung was sentenced to death for the killing of a My Tho landlord (later reduced to life imprisonment). He was amnestied in 1936 thanks to the clemency of the Popular Front, but rearrested in 1939 and returned to Poulo Condor. Like **Nguyen Binh**, Pham Hung knew how to take care of himself in the rough and tumble world of the colonial prison. He protected weaker ICP members from assault and handled sensitive contacts with gang leaders and wardens. He remained at Poulo Condor until 23 September 1945, when he set foot in southern Vietnam with **Le Duan**, **Nguyen Van Linh**, and **Mai Chi Tho**. He had forged close ties to these increasingly powerful men in prison and the communist movement, and would continue to work with them in southern Vietnam and the communist party well into the 1980s. In November 1945, Pham Hung joined the party's Territorial Committee for Nam Bo (*Xu Uy Nam Bo*) and soon became deputy secretary to Le Duan. Pham Hung took over building the DRV/ICP's security services in the south and served as deputy director of the **Public Security Services** for Nam Bo from 1946. In reality, he was the driving force behind the southern security services. In 1951, during the Party's second congress he was elected to the Executive Committee of the Central Committee of the **Vietnam Worker's Party**. Between 1952 and 1954, he joined the party's **Central Office for the Southern Region** (*Trung Uong Cuc Mien Nam*, better known by its American acronym as COSVN) and served as its deputy director until the end of the Indochina War. He was also the president of the Resistance and Administrative Committee for the **Inter-Zone for Eastern Nam Bo** (*Phan Lien Khu Mien Dong*) as well as its controlling party committee. In this position, he worked closely with Le Duan and **Le Duc Tho**. With the signing of the **Geneva Accords** in July 1954, Pham Hung regrouped to **Hanoi**. However in late 1954 or early 1955, he returned to **Saigon** where he worked as the head of the **People's Army of Vietnam**'s High Command Liaison Mission to the **International Commission for Supervision and Control.** He was one of the most powerful communists in Vietnam until his death in 1988.

**PHẠM HUY THÔNG (1916–1988).** Vietnamese supporter of the **Democratic Republic of Vietnam** (DRV) active in France during the Indochina War. Born in Hai Hung province, he received his bachelor's degree in law in 1937 from the *Faculté de droit* at the University of Indochina and was a member of the Students Association in the north (*Tong Hoi Sinh Vien*). In France in 1942, he obtained his doctorate in law, and between 1944 and 1950, worked in the *Centre national de recherche scientifique* (CNRS). During this time, he was active among the Vietnamese community living in France. Between 1940 and 1942, he ran the Overseas Vietnamese Association in Toulouse before joining the Vietnamese Cultural and Friendship center in Paris in 1943. During his trip to France in mid-1946, **Ho Chi Minh** selected Pham Huy Thong to serve as a personal secretary in light of his contacts among the large Vietnamese community living in France. Favorable to the nationalist cause led by Ho Chi Minh, Pham Huy Thong led the independence battle on the French front, especially in his mobilization of the **overseas Vietnamese in France.** Between 1948 and 1952, he served as general secretary of the *Union culturelle de France* (*Lien Hiep Van Hoa tai Phap*) for the Vietnamese living in France and elsewhere abroad. He published an essay on the nature of Vietnamese literature in October 1947 in this association's bulletin. He also led the French section of the **Lien Viet** nationalist front. In 1949, Pham Huy Thong became a member of the **French Communist Party** and helped organize anti-war demonstrations and information campaigns in the metropolis shortly thereafter. In 1952, these activities led French authorities to repatriate him to Vietnam where he was placed under surveillance by the Associated State of Vietnam authorities. He refused offers to work in the Associated State and remained a firm supporter of the DRV. On 4 May 1958, he wrote an article critical of **Tran Duc Thao** and the liberal-minded *Nhan Van Giai Pham* literary group based in **Hanoi**. Loyal to the Vietnamese communist line, his essay appeared in the party's mouthpiece in Hanoi, *Nhan Dan*.

**PHẠM KHẮC HOÈ (1902–1995).** In August 1945, he served as a secretary to **Bao Dai** and was a cousin of the Vietnamese intellectual, **Hoang Xuan Han**. Through his links to Ton Quang Phiet, he secretly contacted the **Viet Minh** in the weeks leading up to the **August Revolution**. He personally helped Bao Dai draft his abdication statement and helped direct him to the **Democratic Republic of Vietnam** (DRV) as a simple citizen.

In July 1946, Pham Khac Hoe served as the general secretary to the DRV's delegation to the **Fontainebleau Conference.** Back in Vietnam, the French arrested him on 21 December 1946, immediately following the outbreak of full-scale war in **Hanoi**. In August 1949, he crossed into DRV-administered territory.

**PHẠM KIỆT (PHẠM QUANG KHÁNH, 1912–1975).** Powerful behind-the-scenes communist leader in central Vietnam during the Indochina War. Born in Quang Ngai province, he became politically active during the student strikes of the mid-1920s. He joined the Viet Nam Revolutionary Youth League in 1929 and then the **Indochinese Communist Party** in 1931. He was arrested by the French that same year and imprisoned at Buon Me Thuot, but was apparently released shortly thereafter. In 1943, he commanded the first clandestine **guerrilla** unit in the Ba To area in Quang Ngai province. On 11 March 1945, following the Japanese overthrow of the French two days earlier, his unit took part in the "uprising" at the Ba To plantation, in the district of the same name, and eventually in all the province when the Japanese had capitulated in August. During the war against the French, he remained in **Inter-Zone V** (*Lien Khu V*) in the Quang Ngai area where the party assigned him important military missions. He took part in the battle of **Hoa Binh** in 1950 and **Dien Bien Phu** in 1954 as the delegate for the army's powerful Security Department (*Cuc Bao Ve Quan Doi*). Pham Kiet's wife was **Nguyen Chanh**'s younger sister.

**PHẠM NGỌC CHI, PIERRE-MARIE (1909–1988).** Influential Vietnamese **Catholic** priest who first collaborated then broke with the **Democratic Republic of Vietnam**. He was ordained a priest in 1933 and served as director of the Great Seminary in Phat Diem. He was a close ally of the powerful Vietnamese bishop **Le Huu Tu**. On 3 February 1950, Pham Ngoc Chi was appointed Vicar Apostolic and Bishop of Bui Chu in lower **Tonkin** thanks to the influence of Le Huu Tu in Vatican circles. Although Pham Ngoc Chi was an ardent Vietnamese nationalist, he had little faith in the communists. The Pope received him in 1950 as Pham Ngoc Chi was increasingly leaning towards the Associated State of Vietnam on anti-communist grounds. *See also* CATHOLICS, EXODUS FROM NORTH; CATHOLICS IN VIETNAM AND THE WAR; CHRISTIANS AND OPPOSITION TO THE INDOCHINA WAR; COLLABORATION; VATICAN.

**PHẠM NGỌC MẬU (PHẠM NGỌC QUYẾT, 1919–1993).** Political commissar in northern Vietnam during the Indochina War. Born in Thai Binh province, he joined the **Indochinese Communist Party** in 1939 before being arrested and incarcerated by the French at **Son La** until his release in March 1945. He helped rebuild the party's bases in Son Tay province and assisted nationalists in taking power there in August 1945 when he became vice president of the province's Military Committee. In December 1945, he was deputy director of **Zone** II (*Khu II*). A year later, in December 1946, he transferred to Zone I (*Khu I*) as a political commissar. In September 1948, he became political commissar for the 121st Regiment and then for the 246th Regiment in 1949. In May 1951, he was appointed deputy then in 1953 commanding political commissar for the 351st Division.

**PHẠM NGỌC QUYẾT.** *See* PHẠM NGỌC MẬU.

**PHẠM NGỌC THẠCH (1909–1968).** One of the **Democratic Republic of Vietnam**'s (DRV) most eminent diplomats and behind-the-scenes leaders during the Indochina War. Born in Binh Dinh province in central Vietnam, he was the son of a wealthy school principal; his mother was of royal blood. Around 1909, while teaching in Qui Nhon, his father helped the future **Ho Chi Minh** prepare his exams to become a teacher. This early link between the two families might explain why Pham Ngoc Thach, anything but a hardcore communist in the 1930s, later served as a personal and trusted advisor to the president of the DRV, Ho Chi Minh. Pham Ngoc Thach completed his secondary education in **Hanoi** at the *Lycée Albert Sarraut* before entering the *Faculté de médecine* in Hanoi, where he shone. He continued his medical studies in France, where he was awarded his doctorate of medicine in 1934 and named assistant at the *Faculté de médecine de Paris* before taking a similar post in the *Sanatorium de l'Albarine*. He worked closely with the doctors Monod and Lelong, renowned specialists in tuberculosis. It was also at this time that he married a French nurse working there, Marie Louise Jeandot. They moved to **Saigon** in 1936 where Pham Ngoc Thach opened his own private practice. According to **Jacques Dalloz**, he also became a **Freemason** during this time. In 1942, Pham Ngoc Thach and his friends, such as **Kha Van Can** and Thai Van Lung, began to use the **scouting** movement to promote their nationalist politics. It became the driving force of the **Vanguard Youth Movement** (*Thanh Nien Tien Phong*), in which Pham Ngoc Thach played the leading role in 1945, with a green light from the Japanese.

Sometime before the end of World War II, Pham Ngoc Thach became a member of the **Indochinese Communist Party**. He enthusiastically supported the DRV's nationalist cause and mobilized the youth movement in its favor in the south. He became minister of Public Health in the newly created government and served as Ho Chi Minh's private physician. In September 1945, he was named commissar for External Affairs for Nam Bo and helped run the "Bureau for Nam Bo" created in Hanoi before returning secretly to southern Vietnam shortly thereafter. To the anger of the high commissioner for Indochina, **Georges Thierry d'Argenlieu**, Pham Ngoc Thach successfully made his way to the **Dalat Conference** of April 1946, entering the Lang Bian Palace as the DRV's delegate from the south. Borrowing the expression from **Vo Nguyen Giap**, French journalist **Georges Chaffard** wrote: "*Voilà qui est plus fort que la bombe atomique*". Thach insisted that southern Vietnam was an integral part of the Vietnamese nation led by the DRV and that any attempt to break off **Cochinchina**, as Thierry d'Argenlieu sought to do, was doomed to failure. The French saw this as a provocation, arrested, and incarcerated him. When the dashing young **Jean-Pierre Dannaud**, an advisor to **Jean Cédile**, arrived in his cell confident he could win over Thach to the French cause, Pham Ngoc Thach sent him packing on nationalist grounds. Disappointed, the French finally expelled Pham Ngoc Thach to Hanoi.

During a ministerial shake-up on 3 November 1946, Pham Ngoc Thach was named undersecretary of state in the Presidency of the Council led by Ho Chi Minh. The latter saw in Thach a trustworthy and sophisticated individual vital to building and leading the government's nascent diplomacy. Between 1945 and 1948, Pham Ngoc Thach traveled the globe to win support for the new Vietnamese nation-state, meeting leaders from Asia, Europe, France, and the United States. In 1947, he made a secret trip to Europe apparently on Ho Chi Minh's personal behest in a bid to win over support from the French and Soviet communist parties. The results were disappointing. Upon his return to northern Vietnam in 1948, he ceded his position to **Hoang Van Hoan**.

However, Thach continued to carry out a number of important missions for the government. In 1948, he was referred to in the Vietnamese press as president of the Council, a post that Ho Chi Minh had held. Noting this, the French political advisor to the high commissioner for Indochina wrote privately of Pham Ngoc Thach as follows: "*Intelligent, quoique utopiste, nationaliste passionné, ennemi irréductible – non de la France – mais de ses représentants en Indochine – Thach, dans son nouveau poste qu'il soit réel ou fictif, ne peut être que le partisan d'une politique de lutte à outrance*". Between 1950 and early 1953, he served as president of the Resistance and Administrative Committee for the Special Zone of Saigon-Cholon and the government's delegate to the southern resistance administration. It was also during this time that he began an offensive to win over southern **intellectuals** in the cities to the DRV nationalist cause. He met with journalists, artists, intellectuals, teachers, and students. He liaised with leftist and sympathetic European intellectuals, such as **Georges Boudarel** and those of the *Groupe marxiste culturel* in Saigon. As the Indochina War drew to an end, his urban connections and networks allowed him to recruit one of the DRV's most famous southern spies, **Pham Xuan An**. As one Vietnamese described Dr. Thach: "No matter how much he walked he never tired; and the enthusiasm he invested in his work was equal to that of three persons" (*Di bo khong biet met va lam viec hang hai bang ba nguoi*).

**PHẠM NGỌC THẢO, ALBERT (1922–1965).** Vietnamese **Catholic** intelligence officer in the service of the **Democratic Republic of Vietnam** (DRV). Pham Ngoc Thao was the ninth child in a wealthy Catholic family of 12. Born in **Saigon**, he had French nationality from birth (his grandfather had been naturalized in 1888). Pham Ngoc Thao completed his secondary studies in the Catholic *Lycée Taberd* in Saigon and then entered the public works service in colonial Indochina. In 1945, when the French moved to retake Vietnam by force, he renounced his French citizenship, took to the *maquis* to join the **Viet Minh**, and became a Vietnamese citizen in the DRV. In 1946, he was selected for advanced military training at the **Tran Quoc Tuan Military Academy** (*Truong Vo Bi Tran Quoc Tuan*) in Son Tay province in northern Vietnam. Graduated from the 1st Class, he traveled to lower central Vietnam to serve as a liaison agent in the army, moving ranking cadres between North and South Vietnam. When he successfully escorted **Le Duan**, the head of the party Regional Committee for Nam Bo, to the south, the latter decided to move Pham Ngoc Thao into intelligence and espionage operations. Pham Ngoc Thao also had close ties to **Nguyen Binh**, serving as the head of the military's secret affairs unit or *Phong Mat Vu Ban Quan Su Nam Bo* based in Saigon-Cholon from 1946. He stayed on as chief of the military intelligence office until this special unit was transformed into the Intelligence Service for the Southern High Command (*Ban Quan bao Bo Tu Lenh Nam Bo*). In 1948, **Hoang Minh Dao** replaced him at the head of southern military intelligence. Pham Ngoc Thao became battalion leader of the 410th in **Zone IX** (*Khu IX*). Between 1952 and 1953, he served as the commander of the 307th battalion in war Zone IX (*Chien Khu IX*). Pham Ngoc Thao was the son-in-law of the powerful southern leader, **Pham Thieu**, and brother of **Pham Ngoc Thuan**, who worked in the Resistance and Administration for Nam Bo. Despite holding important and sensitive posts, Pham Ngoc Thao never became a communist party member.

Following the **Geneva Accords** of 1954 ending the war and dividing Vietnam provisionally into two states, he remained in the south on instructions from Le Duan. As Vo Van Kiet recalled it: "Anh Ba Duan had great confidence in Pham Ngoc Thao and assigned him a very special task". Thanks to a powerful Catholic connection in the person of **Ngo Dinh Thuc**, Pham Ngoc Thao gained the trust of the latter's brother, **Ngo Dinh Diem**. One of the communist party's master spy handlers, **Tran Quoc Huong**, took over as his case officer and oversaw Thao's infiltration of the **Republic of Vietnam** for the DRV. It remains unclear to this author how Pham Ngoc Thao could win over the trust of the Ngo family. Ranking intelligence and counter espionage officers in the Republic of Vietnam were well aware of his intelligence work for the DRV during the Indochina War. They also knew that his brother Pham Ngoc Thuan was the DRV's ambassador to East Germany. In any event, things eventually spun out of control. Pham Ngoc Thao became "too impulsive" and "imprudent", leading to his "tragic end", is how DRV General **Tran Van Tra** later explained it to **Georges Boudarel**. That tragic end came in 1965 when Pham Ngoc Thao was arrested and apparently tortured to death.

**PHẠM NGỌC THUẦN, GASTON (1914–2002).** Prominent non-communist **Catholic** leader of the **Democratic Republic of Vietnam**'s (DRV) Resistance and Administrative Committee for Nam Bo. Born into a wealthy family of 12 in the southern province of Ben Tre, Pham Ngoc Thuan studied law and became a successful lawyer and member of the **Saigon** Bar during the interwar period. He was born a French citizen (his grandfather had been naturalized in 1888) and trained in French Catholic schools. He married Bui Thi Cam (niece of Bui Quang Chieu and Vietnam's first female lawyer). He was a remarkable orator in French, even winning a prize for his French eloquence in his student days. He volunteered to fight in 1939 and was mobilized in France during the debacle of 1940. He left the French army and returned to Indochina in 1941 to resume his work as a lawyer. The Japanese appointed him public prosecutor at the Saigon Court of Appeals following their ***coup de force* on 9 March 1945**.

Like his brother **Pham Ngoc Thao**, he was an ardent nationalist. He joined the **Vanguard Youth League** (*Thanh Nien Tien Phong*) in mid-1945, led by **Pham Ngoc Thach**. For Pham Ngoc Thuan, Vietnam would only obtain its independence through armed struggle. On 23 September, when the French began retaking Saigon by force, he took to the *maquis*. On 14 July 1946, he joined the **Indochinese Communist Party** (ICP) and in so doing crossed a political line his brother, Pham Ngoc Thao, apparently refused to do. A few weeks earlier, Pham Ngoc Thuan had signed a moving and powerful eulogy for his close friend **Thai Van Lung**, who had been tortured to death by the French in prison. The two events were undoubtedly linked. In any case, Pham Ngoc Thuan immediately put his military experience from France to work helping to train young nationalist recruits in My Tho province. In September 1946, he joined the DRV's Resistance and Administrative Committee for the south. His party credentials and above all his friendship with **Le Duan** allowed him to serve as a political commissar in the armed forces for southern Vietnam. In 1949, he became vice president of the southern Resistance and Administrative Committee and served as acting president in 1950 during the absence of **Pham Van Bach**. He also founded and published the **Viet Minh** newspaper *Tieng Noi Bung Bien (Voix du Maquis)*.

With the end of the war in 1954, he rejoined his wife (who had also become a member of the ICP) and relocated to northern Vietnam. He later became ambassador to East Germany (1958–1963), witnessed the construction of the Berlin Wall, and represented Vietnam during the burial of the founder of the German Communist Party, Walter Ulbricht. He died in exile in France, having become increasingly critical of the Vietnamese Party's inability to reform itself. *See also* TORTURE.

**PHẠM QUANG KHÁNH.** *See* PHẠM KIỆT.

**PHẠM QUANG LỄ.** *See* TRẦN ĐẠI NGHĨA.

**PHẠM THIỀU (1904–1986).** Vietnamese **intellectual** and resistance administrator in southern Vietnam during the Indochina War. Born in Nghe An province, he graduated in 1927 as a teacher from the Higher Teacher's School in **Hanoi** (*École supérieure pédagogique de Hanoi*). He taught at the *Lycée Pétrus Ky* in **Cochinchina** and elsewhere. He apparently helped **Louis Malleret** during the latter's archeological digs in the Mekong Delta during World War II and became increasingly active in nationalist politics, serving as vice president of the Association for the Promotion of [the language] *Quoc Ngu* in **Saigon** and participating in the **Vanguard Youth League** (*Thanh Nien Tien Phong*) led by **Pham Ngoc Thach**. In 1945, Pham Thieu joined the **Democratic Republic of Vietnam** (DRV) in southern Vietnam. He was the director of the Politico-Military School at Bien Hoa, chief of the Political Bureau of the High Command for **Inter-Zone** VII (*Lien Khu VII*), and ran the resistance paper, *Tien Dao*. Between 1946 and 1949, he was a member of the Resistance and Administrative Committee for Nam Bo, director of the Committee of Propaganda for Nam Bo, and director of the Radio Service for the south. Because of his knowledge of the Chinese language and Chinese culture, he also worked as head of the **Bureau for Overseas Chinese Affairs in Nam Bo**. To hold such posts, he must have joined the communist party at some point, but the details are lacking. After the **Geneva Accords** ended the war in 1954 by dividing Vietnam provisionally into two halves, he relocated to the north. Pham Thieu was also the father-in-law of one of the DRV's top spies, **Pham Ngoc Thao**.

**PHẠM THƯ.** *See* TRẦN DUY HƯNG.

**PHẠM VĂN BẠCH (1910–1987).** Southern Vietnamese lawyer and politician at the head of the Resistance and Administrative Committee for Nam Bo during most of the Indochina War. Born in Ben Tre province, he studied law and literature in France, where he obtained his law degree. He returned to Vietnam in 1936 and taught in a Can Tho high school. Both in France and Vietnam he became increasingly involved in nationalist and communist politics. In France, he had frequented the French Communist Youth Group. During the Popular Front period in Indochina, he collaborated with Vietnamese communists although he apparently never joined the party himself. This made him an important non-communist ally when the **Democratic Republic of Vietnam** (DRV) came to power in September 1945. Following the recall of **Tran Van Giau** to **Hanoi** in late 1945, Pham Van Bach took over as president of the Provisional Executive Committee of the People's Committee for Nam Bo (*Uy Ban Nhan Dan Nam Bo*). In February 1946, he arrived in Hanoi as a representative of the government from the south. It was also at this time that **Truong Chinh** introduced him to **Ho Chi Minh**. Pham Van Bach joined the **Indochinese Communist Party** in June 1946 on the introduction of **Pham Ngoc Thach** and Ngo Tan Nhon. Pham Van Bach returned to southern Vietnam after the outbreak of full-scale war on **19 December 1946**, where he served as president of the Resistance and Administrative Committee for Nam Bo. With the end of the war, he relocated to northern Vietnam and worked in the People's Superior Court in the DRV.

**PHẠM VĂN BÌNH (1901–?).** Non-communist nationalist politician active in the Associated State of Vietnam. Born in Thai Binh province in northern Vietnam, his family had served the Nguyen court in the 19th century. He completed his secondary studies at the *Lycée Albert Sarraut* in **Hanoi**, then studied at the *École supérieure de commerce* there. He was an accomplished tennis player in colonial Indochina. In 1929, he became director of the Thai Binh branch of the *Banque agricole*, but resigned to run the land he had inherited from his father. He also worked in the colonial civil service as chief of cabinet to the French *résident* in Nam Dinh between 1930 and 1931, as peasant revolts spread throughout this region. In 1937, he moved to Hanoi where he collaborated with **Nguyen Tuong Tam** on the literary front and helped create the socially conscious League of Light (*Anh Sang*) during the Popular Front period. Following the Japanese ***coup de force* of 9 March 1945**, he became increasingly involved in nationalist politics during the **Tran Trong Kim** government. With the advent of the **Democratic Republic of Vietnam** (DRV), he served as chief of cabinet to his friend, Nguyen Tuong Tam, who was minister of Foreign Affairs in 1946. The DRV dispatched Pham Van Binh to Chongqing to contact **Bao Dai**, who had taken refuge in China in early 1946. Bao Dai sent him back to Hanoi to ask the government to let the royal family join him in China. DRV authorities placed Pham Van Binh under house arrest in Hanoi and then transferred him to northern Vietnam following the outbreak of full-scale war on **19 December 1946**. The French freed him during their paratrooper raid on Bac Kan in October 1947. Following the signing of the Franco-Vietnamese Accords of 8 March 1949, Pham Van Binh worked closely for Bao Dai as a private secretary and representative in Paris. In January 1950, the former emperor named him an Associated State of Vietnam's representative to the Assembly of the **French Union**. Pham Van Binh served as state secretary in the ministry for Sports and Youth in the second cabinet of **Tran Van Huu** of February 1951. *See also* LEA, OPERATION.

**PHẠM VĂN CƯƠNG.** *See* NGUYỄN CƠ THẠCH.

**PHẠM VĂN ĐỒNG (TỐ, 1906–2000).** A leader of the **Democratic Republic of Vietnam** (DRV) and chief negotiator during the **Fontainebleau** and **Geneva Conferences**. He was born into a mandarin family in Quang Ngai province in lower central Vietnam. His father was a private secretary to the Emperor Duy Tan. Pham Van Dong became politically active during the student movements of 1925–1926, triggered by the death of Phan Chu Trinh and the arrest and trial of Phan Boi Chau. In 1926, Pham Van Dong left Vietnam for southern China where he joined **Ho Chi Minh**'s Viet Nam Youth League in Guangzhou (Canton). He returned to Vietnam in late 1927 to build up revolutionary activities in southern Vietnam. In 1929 he became a member of the Youth League's **Cochinchina** branch and then joined the General Directorate of the organization. In July 1929, the French arrested him in **Saigon** and gave him a ten year prison term before shipping him off to **Poulo Condor**. Pham Van Dong apparently joined the **Indochinese Communist Party** (ICP) in prison. In July 1936, thanks to the Popular Front government, he regained his freedom and resumed his political activities openly, serving as editor of the *La Volonté indochinoise*. In May 1940, with World War II underway, he returned to southern China where he renewed contact with Ho Chi Minh and helped create the nationalist front, the **Viet Minh**, in northern Vietnam in early 1941. In August 1945, he attended the Tan Trao Conference. With the birth of the DRV in September 1945, he served in the provisional government as minister of National Economy. In January 1946, he was elected to the National Assembly. During the summer of 1946, Pham Van Dong led the Vietnamese delegation in negotiations with the French during the Fontainebleau conference. This marked the beginning of a long career as one of the government's most active and important diplomats. During the cabinet shuffle of November 1946, he became under-secretary in the Ministry of National Economy. In late 1946, the ICP appointed him as the government and Party's special delegate to lower central Vietnam in **Inter-Zone V** (*Lien Khu V*) and served as the general secretary of the same zone's Party committee (*Bi Thu Khu Uy Khu V*). In 1947, he became an alternate member of the Executive Committee of the ICP's Central Committee and an official member in 1949. In August of that year, he became deputy prime minister of the DRV and president of the Supreme Defense Council. During the Second Party Congress held in early 1951, he joined the Politburo. In 1954, Pham Van Dong headed the government's delegation to the Geneva Conference and was chief of the Party Central Committee's powerful External Affairs Committee (*Ban Doi Ngoai*). Although his exact role is unclear, Pham Van Dong was involved in implementing the **land reform** policies initiated in 1953.

**PHAM VAN HUA.** *See* SONG NGOC MINH.

**PHẠM VĂN KHOA (1914–1992).** Vietnamese war photographer during the Indochina War. Born in Hai Phong province in northern Vietnam, he became politically active during the Popular Front period. In 1937, he took part in efforts to promote the use of *Quoc Ngu* as the Vietnamese national language. He joined the **Indochinese Communist Party** in 1942. Following the birth of the **Democratic Republic of Vietnam**, he helped **Truong Chinh** run the party's newspaper, *Su That* (*The Truth*). He was active in developing Vietnamese propaganda via the performing arts and followed Vietnamese troops into battle as a war photographer. He served as the first director of the National State Run Enterprise of Filmmakers and Photographers in 1953.

**PHẠM VĂN KHƯƠNG.** *See* LÊ VĂN LƯƠNG.

**PHẠM VĂN PHU.** *See* TRẦN TỬ BÌNH.

**PHẠM VĂN THIỆN.** *See* PHẠM VĂN HÙNG.

**PHẠM XUÂN ẨN (TRẦN VĂN TRUNG, HAI TRUNG, 1927–2006).** One of the **Democratic Republic of Vietnam**'s legendary spies during the Vietnam War. Born in Bien Hoa province in southern Vietnam, Pham Xuan An was the son of a colonial civil servant. He became involved in nationalist politics during World War II. In 1945, he dropped out of the *Collège de Can Tho* and signed up for a **Viet Minh** crash course in military training. In 1947, however, Pham Xuan An left the *maquis* and returned to French-controlled **Saigon** in order to finish his secondary education in 1948 and take care of his ailing father. During this time, he also returned to nationalist politics and participated in several student protests against French policy and American intervention, including the large protest against the visit by two American warships to Saigon in 1950. In order to support his ill father, he took a job as a secretary with the Caltex oil company until 1950, when he passed the exam to become a government customs clerk. In mid-1951, he planned to re-join the resistance; however, **Pham Ngoc Thach** persuaded him to remain in the city to report on events and personalities there. In early 1952, Pham Ngoc Thach personally recruited Pham Xuan An into the newly emerging strategic intelligence service, and in 1953 Pham Xuan An was secretly inducted into the **Vietnamese Worker's Party** in a ceremony presided over by **Le Duc Tho**. In early 1954, Pham Xuan An began working as a mole in the French army in the lower levels of the **Psychological Warfare** Section in the General Staff, thanks to an introduction from his cousin, Captain Pham Xuan Giai. The French never unmasked Pham Xuan An. Following the division of Vietnam into two halves during the **Geneva Conference**, Pham Xuan An would go on to spy for **Hanoi** against the **Republic of Vietnam** and the Americans. He worked for **Edward Lansdale** of the CIA and Rufus Phillips, and collaborated with a host of largely unsuspecting and eminent Western journalists. His cover? He worked as a correspondent for *Time Magazine*. **Tran Quoc Huong** was his new case officer. Like the French, the Americans never unmasked Pham Xuan An.

**PHAN ANH (1912–1990).** Born in Ha Tinh province in upper central Vietnam, Phan Anh graduated as a lawyer from the *Faculté de droit* at the Indochinese University in 1936 or 1937. He traveled to France to pursue his law studies, but the outbreak of World War II in Europe in 1939 forced him to return to Indochina. He was politically active in the 1930s, serving as the president of the General Association of Students. Besides working as a lawyer in **Hanoi** during World War II, he also taught at the eminent private school *Thang Long* (where **Pham Duy** and **Vo Nguyen Giap** also studied in the 1930s). Phan Anh published in the intellectual review, *Thanh Nghi*. Following the Japanese overthrow of the French in the ***coup de force* of 9 March 1945**, Phan Anh briefly served as minister of Youth in the short-lived **Tran Trong Kim** government and began work on a constitution for an independent Vietnam in May 1945. He was a non-communist, a jovial man, favorable to the nationalist cause of the **Democratic Republic of Vietnam** (DRV). He served as minister of Defense between March and November 1946, when his long-time friend, Vo Nguyen Giap, replaced him. He was also a member of the Vietnamese delegation to the **Fontainebleau Conference** in mid-1946. He remained in Hanoi after the outbreak of war on **19 December 1946**. Pro-**Bao Dai** representatives tried to win him over to their side but to no avail. He returned to the *maquis* shortly thereafter. In July 1947, during a cabinet reshuffle, he became minister of National Economy in the DRV. In 1949, he was a member of the Supreme Defense Council, which included such powerful figures as Vo Nguyen Giap and **Pham Van Dong**. In July 1954, Phan Anh joined the diplomatic delegation sent to negotiate at the **Geneva Conference**. He also served in the government as minister of Industry and Commerce.

**PHAN BỘI.** *See* HOÀNG HỮU NAM.

**PHAN ĐÌNH KHẢI.** *See* LÊ ĐỨC THỌ.

**PHAN HUY DÂN (PHAN QUANG DÂN, 1918–?).** Non-communist nationalist and diplomat during the Indochina War. Born in Vinh in upper central Vietnam, Phan Huy Dan completed his primary studies at the Catholic school Pellerin in Hue. After obtaining his secondary diploma in **Hanoi** in 1937, he entered the *Faculté de médecine* at the Indochinese University that same year and graduated as a doctor in 1942. He practiced medicine in Hanoi until the Japanese overthrew the French in the ***coup de force* of 9 March 1945**. During the famine of 1945, he helped to feed the poor, bury the dead, and maintain sanitary services. He was a socially committed doctor and intellectual. But he was no communist. Indeed, rather than join the **Viet Minh** in 1945, he entered the ranks of the **Vietnamese Nationalist Party** (*Viet Nam Quoc Dan Dang*, VNQDD) and the **Greater Vietnam Nationalist Party** (*Dai Viet Quoc Dan*). He helped run anti-communist, nationalist newspapers such as *Binh Minh* and *Thiet Thuc*. He supported the creation of a coalition government with **Bao Dai** playing a unifying role. On 21 February 1946, he organized a demonstration in Hanoi to demand the return of Bao Dai to power. With the rupture between the communist and anti-communist nationalists intensifying, he fled to China in April 1946 and joined Bao Dai's entourage as it made its way to Hong Kong. He accompanied Bao Dai to Europe in late 1947 before returning to Vietnam in February 1948 in order to prepare the constitution for a new Vietnamese government in which he would serve as minister of Information briefly. His relations with Bao Dai were difficult and despite his efforts to create a "third force", his influence quickly dissipated. *See also* ATTENTISME.

**PHAN HUY QUÁT (1911–1979).** Non-communist nationalist politician in the **Democratic Republic of Vietnam** (DRV) who crossed over to the Associated State of Vietnam. Born in the central province of Ha Tinh, he completed his primary education at the Catholic school Pellerin in Hue and then at the *Lycée du Protectorat* in **Hanoi** before entering the *Faculté de Médecine* in Hanoi, from which he graduated a doctor of medicine in 1936. Until the end of World War II, he operated his own private medical practice in Hanoi. Phan Huy Quat was a member of the *Société commerciale du Nord* and the *Société cinématographique du Vietnam*. He also became politically active during the Popular Front period in the late 1930s. He joined the **Greater Vietnam Nationalist Party** (*Dai Viet Quoc Dan Dang*) whose leader, **Dang Van Sung**, was his cousin. Phan Huy Quat was an ardent nationalist.

In 1945 following the overthrow of the French and the defeat of the Japanese, he supported the independence cause of the DRV. He briefly served as the president of the **People's Administrative Committee for Trung Bo**. However, wary of the communist core of the **Viet Minh**, he joined efforts to create a non-communist nation-state under the leadership of **Bao Dai**. The latter named him under secretary of state for National Education in the first government of the Associated State of Vietnam created in 1949. He became minister of Defense in the short-lived government presided over by **Nguyen Phan Long** in January 1950. In February 1951, he was named minister of Education in the second government of **Tran Van Huu**, but resigned soon after. He called upon the French to grant full and real independence to the Vietnamese. He criticized leaders such as Tran Van Huu and **Nguyen Van Hinh** who, in his view, had no real nationalist support or pull. Phan Huy Quat did his best to ease General Nguyen Van Hinh out of the army of the Associated State of Vietnam in a bid to delink this new state from its colonial conception. Phan Huy Quat served as the deputy general secretary of the Popular National Movement (*Phong Trao Quoc Gia Binh Dan*), linked to the Greater Vietnam Nationalist Party. He saw in the **Cold War**'s internationalization of the Indochina War the chance to pressure the French and their Vietnamese allies to move towards real independence. He declared in a speech to Greater Vietnam members in Hanoi in May 1952 that "the Vietnamese question has become today one of an international order. We must consider a problem of such great importance according to this international conjuncture and in all its aspects". In June 1953, **Nguyen Van Tam** named him vice minister of National Defense in his government and Phan Huy Quat continued to hold this post in the government presided over by prince **Buu Loc** on 11 January 1954. Phan Huy Quat died in a communist prison in Chi Hoa in 1979. *See also* CROSSOVERS; DESERTION; PRISONERS OF WAR.

**PHAN KẾ TOẠI (1892–1992).** Prominent non-communist nationalist who joined the ranks of the **Democratic Republic of Vietnam** (DRV) during the Indochina War. Born in the former Ha Tay province in upper central Vietnam, Phan Ke Toai graduated from the **Colonial Academy** (*École coloniale*) in 1914 and worked as a district mandarin and became a provincial governor (*Tong Doc*) for Thai Binh in 1942. Following the Japanese overthrow of the French in the ***coup de force* of 9 March 1945**, the Japanese-backed Vietnamese government led by **Tran Trong Kim** appointed Phan Ke Toai as **Bao Dai**'s imperial commissioner for **Tonkin** (*Kham Sai Bac Ky*). Phan Ke Toai was sympathetic to the **Viet Minh** and their preparations to take power (he knew his own son Phan Ke An was involved in the movement). He resigned his post as imperial delegate on 17 August and helped clear the way for a peaceful take-over of power by the Viet Minh in the following days in **Hanoi**. Following the outbreak of war in all of Vietnam on **19 December 1946**, Phan Ke Toai was residing in Son Tay province. He responded favorably to an invitation from **Ho Chi Minh** to join the DRV. In 1947, he became minister of the Interior and on 19 August 1948 he became a member of the Supreme National Defense Commission (*Hoi Dong Quoc Phong Toi Cao*) led by Ho Chi Minh. In 1951, Phan Ke Toai resumed his post as minister of the Interior.

**PHAN KHẮC HY (1927–).** Political cadre in the army in central Vietnam and Laos during the Indochina War. Born in Quang Binh province, he completed his secondary studies in Vinh. With the advent of the **Democratic Republic of Vietnam**, he joined the **Indochinese Communist Party** and was named secretary of the Party's Committee for Dong Hoi. In June 1949, Phan Khac Hy joined the Party's Provincial Committee for Quang Binh and rose to become deputy secretary of the Provincial Committee as well as the provincial military leader. In early 1952, in preparation for the General Counter Offensive, he was named deputy political commissar then political commissar for the 18th Regiment active on the Binh Tri Thien front as well as in central Laos along route 9. He was involved in military operations coordinated with the battle of **Dien Bien Phu** during the winter spring of 1953–1954. Following the end of the war, he and his regiment relocated to the north.

**PHAN KHẮC SỬU (1905–1970).** A French-trained agronomist, he became active in nationalist politics in the late 1930s. His **anticolonialism**, however, landed him in a French colonial jail at the start of World War II. He received a sentence of eight years of prison and shipped off to **Poulo Condor**. Following the Japanese overthrow of the French in the ***coup de force* of 9 March 1945**, Phan Khac Suu regained his liberty but kept a low profile in the Mekong Delta as the French went to war with the **Democratic Republic of Vietnam**. In 1948 he returned to **Saigon** and in 1949 became minister of Agriculture, Social Action and Labor in the first **Bao Dai** government. He resigned after two months. He was affiliated with religious movements in the Mekong delta. *See also* CROSSOVER; DESERTION.

**PHAN TRỌNG HỘ.** *See* HUỲNH PHAN HỘ.

**PHAN TRỌNG TUỆ (1917–1991).** Behind-the-scenes but powerful communist leader in southern Vietnam during the Indochina War. Born in Vientiane, he joined the **Indochinese Communist Party** (ICP) in that Lao city in 1934. A year later, his family was expelled from Laos and returned to their original district in Son Tay province in northern Vietnam. Phan Trong Tue continued to work for the ICP there, becoming the Party's underground provincial chief. In 1943, he was arrested by the French and deported to **Poulo Condor**. Between June 1943 and September 1945, he was politically active in communist cells in the prison where he must have met the likes of **Nguyen Van Linh** and **Le Duan**, for they all returned to southern Vietnam on **23 September 1945** – the day war broke out in southern Vietnam. In late 1945, he was a member of the Party's Interprovincial Committee for Western Nam Bo (*Lien Tinh Uy Mien Tay Nam Bo*). In 1946, he served as a political commissar to the High Command of war **Zone IX** (*Chien Khu IX*), headed the Party's Regional Committee for this same zone, and served on the Standing Committee of the Party's Regional Committee for Western Nam Bo. In 1947, he entered the all-powerful Southern Communist Territorial Committee for Nam Bo under the leadership of Le Duan. In December 1948, he was assigned to war **Zone VII** (*Chien Khu VII*) as a political commissar. In 1949, the Party designated him political commissar to the Military Command for the Special Zone of **Saigon**-Cholon. He also served as the Party's secretary for this special zone and joined the Resistance and Administrative Committee for Saigon-Cholon. In late 1950, he was a member of the southern delegation sent to attend the Second Party Congress in early 1951. In 1951, he returned to the south to run the High Command for war

Zone IX and when this zone was dissolved he became deputy political commissar and deputy commander of the new **Inter-Zone for Western Nam Bo** (*Phan Lien Khu Mien Tay Nam Bo*). Between 1952 and 1953, he was commander-in-chief of this zone. With the signing of the **Geneva Accords** in 1954 dividing Vietnam provisionally into two states, Phan Trong Tue served as a deputy chief in the **People's Army of Vietnam**'s (*Quan Doi Nhan Dan Viet Nam*) delegation to the **International Commission for Supervision and Control** set up to implement the cease-fire in Indochina. He seconded **Pham Hung**. Phan Trong Tue then relocated to northern Vietnam and helped run the continued implementation of the cease fire there.

**PHAN VĂN GIÁO (1901–1965).** Advisor and dedicated partisan of the **Bao Dai Solution** following the outbreak of the Indochina War. Born in Thanh Hoa province in upper central Vietnam, he completed his primary education at the Catholic schools of Taberd in **Saigon** and Pellerin in Hue. In 1918, he entered the *École supérieure de pharmacie* in **Hanoi**, graduating in 1922. Between 1922 and 1928, he worked as a pharmacist in the Medical Assistance Service for **Annam** (*Assistance médicale de l'Annam*). He then ran his own pharmacy in Thanh Hoa. He was also politically active, serving as a provincial counselor for Thanh Hoa, member of the Chamber of Agriculture and Commerce for Northern Annam, and member of the *Grand conseil des intérêts économiques et financiers de l'Indochine*. During World War II, he was a provincial counselor of Thanh Hoa province.

After the ***coup de force* of 9 March 1945** ousting the French, the Japanese held him in custody. And his confinement did not stop there. On coming to power, the forces of the **Democratic Republic of Vietnam** (DRV) arrested him around September 1945. In February 1946, the Revolutionary Tribunal of Vinh sentenced him to six years of forced labor and confiscated his possessions. After 15 months of detention, he regained his liberty and returned to Hanoi in November 1946 and then to Saigon. Phan Van Giao was a Catholic and a monarchist as well as an ardent supporter of creating a non-communist independent Vietnamese nation-state. In March 1947, he traveled to Hong Kong to meet with **Bao Dai** and helped persuade the ex-emperor to oppose the communists on the political front. In May 1948, General **Nguyen Van Xuan** named Phan Van Giao state minister and regional governor of central Vietnam. The latter continued to serve as governor in the governments of Bao Dai (1949) and **Nguyen Phan Long** (1950). In April 1950, upon the orders of Bao Dai, Phan Van Giao became general inspector of the Vietnamese National Armed Forces, all the while remaining governor of central Vietnam. In May 1950, he was promoted to lieutenant general. From this point, he worked to create a viable and effective national army and united political front against the DRV. To this end, he met with leaders of the **Binh Xuyen**, **Cao Dai**, **Catholics**, and the **Greater Vietnam Nationalist Party** (*Dai Viet Quoc Dan Dang*). In July 1951, he resigned his post as governor of central Vietnam due to a fall-out with Bao Dai. He was named vice president of the Council and minister of Information and Propaganda in the **Nguyen Van Tam** government constituted on 6 June 1952. In 1954, General **Henri Navarre** entrusted him with the joint command of operation **Atlante** in order to retake large swaths of central Vietnam from the DRV. Following the end of the war and the ascension of **Ngo Dinh Diem**, Phan Van Giao took refuge in Cannes. He died in France in 1965. *See also* INTER-ZONE V.

**PHAO PANYA.** *See* PHOUY PANYA.

**PHETXARĀT RATTANAVONGSĀ, (1890–1959).** One of the most important Lao nationalists of the 20th century and an ardent opponent of the restoration of French colonialism to Laos after World War II. Phetxarāt was born into the royal family of the Kingdom of Luang Prabang, the son of the Viceroy Boun Khong. He completed his secondary studies at the *Lycée Chasseloup Laubat* in **Saigon** before moving on to Paris in 1905 to study at the **Colonial Academy** (*École coloniale*) and at the Parisian *Lycées* of *Lavoisier* and *Louis Le Grand*. As one of the best educated Indochinese at the time, Prince Phetxarāt returned to Laos in 1912 keen on playing an important role in the administration and modernization of his country. In 1914, he joined the colonial civil service as a clerk in the *Direction des finances du royaume de Luang Prabang* and then in the *Bureau de la Résidence supérieure au Laos*. In 1919, he was appointed to the cabinet of the *résident supérieur* of Laos and put in charge of "questions related to the indigenous administration". In 1923, he was promoted to the post of *Inspecteur indigène des*

*Affaires politiques et administratives du Laos*, the highest post held by a Lao in the colonial administration at the time. His activities were considerable. Between 1919 and 1930 he served on the *Conseil de gouvernement*, and on the *Grand conseil des intérêts économiques et financiers de l'Indochine* in 1932 and 1933. By royal decree, in 1941 the King of Luang Prabang bestowed upon him the title of *Tiao Maha Oupahat*, the equivalent of viceroy. In 1941, Phetxarāt became prime minister of the Royal Government of Luang Prabang and served as minister of Interior.

However, his relations with the King of Luang Prabang, **Sīsāvangvong**, and the latter's French backers, became increasingly strained during the war and differences came into the open following the Japanese overthrow of the French in March 1945. Phetxarāt once remarked in private that though the King may reign, it was he who "ran the place" (*c'est moi qui fait marcher la boîte*). With the French gone, Phetxarāt asserted his influence in political matters, abrogating unilaterally the French protectorate and proclaiming the unity of Laos in September. As a result, the King of Luang Prabang stripped him of his titles and functions on 10 October.

Phetxarāt now broke openly with the King and the French by lending his name to the **Lao Issara** government, serving as its president of honor. On 19 November, with Phetxarāt's backing, the Lao Issara deposed King Sīsāvangvong. In mid-1946, following the French reoccupation of all of Laos, Phetxarāt followed the Lao Issara into exile in Thailand and agreed on 1 December to serve as supreme counselor to the provisional Lao Issara government now based in Bangkok. He effectively served as the acting chief of the government. Phetxarāt was well connected in Thai royal, political, and police circles. Thanks to such ties, Phetxarāt lived in dignity in Thailand and married a Thai.

Following the signing of the Franco-Lao convention in July 1949 creating the Associated State of Laos, **Khammao Vilai** disbanded the Lao Issara and most of its members returned to join the new government in Laos. Phetxarāt, however, refused to join the French counter-revolutionary project, demanding fuller independence and the return of his titles. King Sīsāvangvong also refused to countenance his return. Phetxarāt simultaneously rebuffed an invitation from **Ho Chi Minh** to join in building a new **Lao Resistance Government** to replace the Lao Issara and compete with the Associated State of Laos. The Vietnamese finally decided to work with his half-brother, Prince **Suphānuvong.** From 1950, Prince Phetxarāt was on his own and was increasingly sidelined from Lao politics. He ultimately returned to Laos in March 1957 and regained his title of *Tiao Maha Oupahat*. He passed away in October 1959.

**PHÓNG.** *See* HOÀNG VĂN HOAN.

**PHOTOGRAPHY.** If the Indochina War was not yet a "television" war, it was certainly a photographed one, by both military and professional photographers. The French army's *Service Presse Information* employed famous war photographers such as Daniel Camus, André Lebon, **Pierre Schoendoerffer**, **Jean Péraud**, and **Pierre Ferrari** among others. Military photographers such as Schoendoerffer and Ferrari were instructed and expected to show the heroic and valiant side of the **Expeditionary Corps's** fighting troops. They did not disappoint. Non-military photographers were given a freer rein and could travel with local combat units without having to deal with handlers. Some of the most poignant and original photography of the Indochina War came from the likes of **Robert Capa**. Ironically, one of the least photographed or filmed combats of the Indochina War was the battle of **Dien Bien Phu**. Contrary to widespread opinion, Dien Bien Phu is, as the French military writer Eric Déroo puts it, "an episode without an image, or almost". The **Democratic Republic of Vietnam** also produced an exceptional war photographer, Trieu Dai. Like his French counterparts, he worked for the army and the state supporting it. However, Trieu Dai produced some remarkably poignant pictures of men in battle, Vietnamese ones. And the subjects of his photos did not always please the propaganda machine of which he was a part. Those he took during the battle of Dien Bien Phu are a case in point. *See also* CINEMA; CULTURE; EXPERIENCE OF WAR, DIEN BIEN PHU; NOVEL; MYTH OF WAR; RAOUL COUTARD.

**PHOUY PANYA (PHAO PANYA, 1897–?).** Influential non-communist minister in Lao politics during the Indochina War. He studied at the *Collège Sisowath* in Phnom Penh before beginning his colonial career as a secretary – interpreter in the French administration in Laos. Between 1914 and 1919, he took part in military operations against a Hmong revolt in upper Laos and was named provincial head there in 1927. In 1929, he became deputy head of the Office of Lao Affairs in the *Résidence supérieure*. After serving in the local administration in Savannakhet, he worked in 1932 as the secretary general of the Royal Palace in Luang Prabang and was appointed 1[st] Level presiding judge. In 1936, he attained the rank of governor of Samneau province, and became a member of the *Grand Conseil des intérêts économiques et financiers* between 1937 and 1940. Little is known of his activities during World War II other than that he served as an alternate member in Vichy's Indochinese Federation and was provincial governor of Phongsaly until the Japanese overthrew the French in March 1945. He then joined French troops fleeing into southern China and received training from the Allies in Calcutta and subsequentely in France. He left Indochina in the company of Prince **Kindavong.** Phouy Panya returned to Laos with the French occupying forces in July 1946 as an officer in the French army. He served as governor of Luang Prabang province in 1946 and 1947. In January 1948, he was elected vice president of the Lao National Assembly (as a deputy from Luang Prabang or Sayaboury) and served as minister of Finance in the **Bunum** cabinet (March 1949 – February 1950). In May 1949, he helped create the Lao Renovation Party and was re-elected to the National Assembly in October. He was renamed minister of Finance in the **Xananikôn** government of 27 February 1950. In March 1950, he was elected president of the National Assembly of the Associated State of Laos.

**PHŪMĪ NÔSAVAN (1920–1985).** Leading non-communist Laotian politician during the Indochina War. Born in Savannakhet province, he worked in the offices of the French colonial police in Laos during the interwar period. While little is known about his activities during World War II, he joined the Lao for the Lao (*Lao Pen Lao*) nationalist movement in northeast Thailand in 1945 and then the **Lao Issara** government in late 1945. He followed it into exile in Thailand when the French retook all of Laos by force in mid-1946. He also traveled to central Vietnam where he collaborated with representatives of the **Democratic Republic of Vietnam** (DRV) in **Inter-Zone IV** (*Lien Khu IV*). His work with the Vietnamese triggered a serious rupture within the Lao Issara in 1948, one which led the Vietnamese to end their collaboration with him. Angered, Phūmī Nôsavan crossed over to the French side and became one of the DRV's staunchest Lao opponents well into the 1960s. He returned to Laos sometime in 1949 to join the new Lao National Army in 1950 as a lieutenant. In 1955, he was chief of staff of the Royal Lao Army and a virulent anti-communist, attracting the attention and soon the strong support of the Americans as the **Cold War** heated up again in Indochina soon after the signing of the **Geneva Accords.** *See also* CROSSOVERS; DESERTION.

**PHŪMĪ VONGVICHIT (1909–1994).** Influential, behind-the-scenes leader in the **Pathet Lao** communist movement. The son of a civil servant born in Xieng Khouang, he entered the colonial bureaucracy and became local governor of Xieng Khouang in 1939 and Vientiane in 1940. During World War II, he was an active member of the Lao Renovation Movement. In January 1945, he became provincial governor of Sam Neua. Following the Japanese ***coup de force* of 9 March 1945**, he collaborated with Franco-Lao **guerrilla** teams in the *maquis* and replaced the French Resident of Sam Neau until the creation of the **Lao Issara** government in October 1945, at which time he switched his allegiance to the nationalist forces. In December 1945, he returned to govern Sam Neau province with the military backing of the **Democratic Republic of Vietnam**. Following the return of the French in mid-1946, he fled to northern Thailand to run clandestinely the Lao Issara Committee for Northern Laos between 1946 and 1949. He refused to return to Laos upon the dissolution of the Lao Issara in Thailand in 1949. Instead he joined ranks with Prince **Suphānuvong**, travelled to northern Vietnam, and participated in the creation of the **Lao Resistance Government** in mid-1950 and of the new national front, the Pathet Lao, of which he soon became general secretary. Between 1951 and 1953, he served as minister of the Interior in the resistance government and as deputy prime minister. *See also* COLLABORATION; CROSSOVER; DESERTION.

**PHƯƠNG.** *See* TRƯỜNG CHINH; TRƯƠNG TỬ ANH.

**PHUY XANANIKÔN (1903–1983).** Anti-communist, Lao politician, and nationalist during the Indochina War. Brother of **Un Xananikôn**, Phuy studied at the *Collège Pavie* before entering the colonial civil service in 1923 as a secretary in the *Résidence supérieure* in Laos. Between 1924 and 1932, he worked as a clerk in the same office in Vientiane. He helped quell the revolt of the Khas in northern Laos in 1943. Between 1942 and 1945, he was province chief for Houa Khong province in northern Laos. Following the Japanese ***coup de force* of 9 March 1945**, he joined the Franco-Lao underground resistance, retreating with French troops into China before making his way to Calcutta. He returned with the French occupying forces to Laos in 1946. In 1947, he served as minister of Education and Health in the Royal Lao government, became a deputy for Pakse in that same year, and served as the first president of the National Assembly of Laos between 1947 and 1950. In 1950, he briefly served as prime minister of the Associated State of Laos and minister of Defense. He led the Lao delegation to the **Pau conference** in June 1950. He was president of the Independent Party and served as minister of the Interior and Defense in 1953 and then as minister of the Interior and Foreign Affairs in 1954. He led the Lao delegation to the **Geneva Conference** of mid-1954, fiercely opposed to the **Pathet Lao**'s claim to represent any part of Laos. *See also* GENEVA ACCORDS, LAOS.

**PIASTRE AFFAIR.** *See* CURRENCY, FRENCH INDOCHINA.

**PIASTRE INDOCHINOISE.** *See* CURRENCY, FRENCH INDOCHINA.

**PIBUN SONGGRAM (PLAEK KHITTA-SANGKHA, 1897–1964).** Thai nationalist and statesman who supported the Vietnamese, Lao, and Cambodian struggle against the French until the **Cold War** led him to join anti-communist forces with the Americans and their French allies in Indochina. Born into a Sino-Thai family, Pibun Songgram studied at Chulachomklao Royal Military Academy, joined the Thai artillery corps in 1914, and then pursued advanced military training in France at the *École d'artillerie* in Fontainebleau between 1920 and 1927. Upon his return to Thailand, he supported the *coup d'état* of 1932 creating a constitutional monarchy. Between 1938 and 1944, he served as prime minister of Thailand. Alhough he promoted the modernization of the country, he also moved the political system away from its democratic goals towards those of a military dictatorship and allied Thailand with the Japanese during World War II. Thanks to this alliance with the Japanese, he was able to retake territories "lost" to the French in western Laos and Cambodia. Even when he returned to power in 1948, Pibun continued to support Vietnamese, Lao, and Cambodian anti-colonialist groups against the French. He allowed the **Democratic Republic of Vietnam** (DRV) to continue administering its unofficial diplomatic office out of Bangkok. He also tolerated unofficial Thai military and commercial aid to these groups. However, with the victory of the Chinese communists to the north and under pressure from the U.S. to halt communist expansion at the Indochinese line, from 1950 he cracked down on Indochinese anti-colonialists operating from Thailand and increased controls over the Vietnamese living in northeast Thailand. In 1950, his government was the only Asian government to recognize the Associated State of Vietnam led by **Bao Dai**. In 1951, he finally expelled **Nguyen Duc Quy**, the head of the DRV's diplomatic mission. He was prime minister from 1948 to 1957, when Field Marshal Sarit Thannarat forced him from office and allied Thailand even more closely with the United States.

**PIGNON, LÉON ADOLPHE MARIE PASCAL (1908–1976).** Career French colonial servant in Indochina and the mastermind of the **Bao Dai Solution**. Pignon was no stranger to Indochina. His uncle had worked in the customs service in Indochina and his sister taught at the *Lycée Albert Sarraut* in **Hanoi**. Pignon graduated in 1931, first in his class, from the **Colonial Academy** (*École coloniale*). He took his studies seriously, specializing in colonial law and studied Asian languages at the ***École nationale des langues orientales vivantes***. Besides holding a doctorate in law, he also specialized in political economics and studied at the *Institut d'ethnographie*. After completing his military service, in 1932 he began a long colonial career in **Tonkin** in French Indochina. Between 1932 and 1936, he served as cabinet director to the *résident supérieur* for Tonkin (1932), deputy to the *résident* to Ha Dong (1933), Son Tay (1934), and deputy to the cabinet of the *résident supérieur* for Tonkin (1934–1936). In 1936, he was recalled to France where he served in the Political Affairs Section of the Ministry of Colonies. In 1939, he was named lieutenant and sent to Senegal to form a company of *tirailleurs*. During the Battle of France in May–June 1940, he served as a lieutenant in the *53ème régiment d'infanterie coloniale mixte sénégalais*. On 5

June, he commanded his company in intensive fighting against the advancing Germans in the Somme. He was taken prisoner, but repatriated to France in January 1942 because of poor health. He refused to serve as chief secretary to Admiral Platon, then state secretary for the Colonies under Vichy. Pignon asked instead to be transferred to Algiers. In March 1942, he arrived in Algeria and began work in the *Bureau des colonies d'Alger* as deputy director. He crossed over to Free French forces after the Allied Landing in North Africa in November 1942. In Algiers, he headed the 1st Office of the Direction for Political Affairs in the Commission for Colonial Affairs of the *Comité français de Libération nationale*, in short the alternative French government run by **Charles de Gaulle**.

Pignon played a crucial role in the development of the future 4th Republic's colonial policy. For example, he served as secretary of the **Brazzaville conference** organized by **René Pleven** in January–February 1944. In October 1944, he went to work on Indochinese matters for the minister of Colonies in Algiers. While Pignon was aware of the historical shift towards decolonization as World War II drew to an end, he would back away from recognizing the independence of the French colonies. He helped draft the government's **Declaration on Indochina** of March 1945 which promoted a more liberal **Indochinese Federation** but failed to address building Vietnamese independence aspirations.

With the creation of the Provisional Government of the French Republic in Paris, Pignon returned to France to serve as director of the Indochinese Section in the Political Office of the Ministry of Overseas France, in light of his earlier colonial experience in Indochina. He volunteered to serve in the resistance against the Japanese and was sent to Kunming where he joined the Military Mission led by **Jean Sainteny** in April 1945. There he served as deputy to General **Marcel Alessandri** and political advisor to the commissioner for the Republic to **Tonkin** and Southern **Annam**[10], Jean Sainteny. During this time, Pignon cultivated contacts with the various Vietnamese nationalist parties active in southern China, including the **Viet Minh**. Between October 1945 and April 1946, he served as the political advisor to Jean Sainteny, commissioner for the Republic to Tonkin and Northern Annam, and continued meeting discreetly with representatives of the **Democratic Republic of Vietnam** (DRV) and other Vietnamese nationalists. He was deeply involved in the negotiations leading to the **Accord of 6 March 1946**. According to Sainteny, Pignon was "without a doubt the one who contributed the most to making it possible to reach the accord I was able to realize on 6 March 1946 with President **Ho Chi Minh**". Pignon was federal commissioner for Political Affairs between April 1946 and May 1947. In July 1946, he was a member of the French delegation attending the **Fontainebleau Conference**.

However, in mid-1946, Pignon's position on decolonization and nationalism hardened; his willingness to negotiate along liberal lines with the Vietnamese diminished notably. He increasingly supported **Georges Thierry d'Argenlieu**'s aggressive policy towards the DRV and began devising ways to replace Ho Chi Minh's government with a more amenable, pliant non-communist, indeed royalist one. Pignon was infuriated by Colonel **Jean Crépin**'s participation in the elimination of anti-French parties such as the **Vietnamese Nationalist Party** and the Dong Minh Hoi, since it left the French with no other partner than the DRV. He overlooked the fact that these two parties were more anti-French than the Viet Minh. During the summer of 1946, Pignon began developing plans to use the former emperor **Bao Dai** (now in China) to create a counter-revolutionary French-backed Vietnamese state. The **Bao Dai Solution** was born at this time and it was largely masterminded by Léon Pignon and his close collaborators from the pre-World War II Indochinese colonial administration, including **Jean Cousseau**, **Charles Bonfils,** and **Albert Torel**. For Pignon, the French would direct the degree of political reform; but national independence would not be imposed upon them. Pignon served as a political advisor to High Commissioner Thierry d'Argenlieu during the crucial year of 1946.

Pignon's association with the outbreak of war in 1946 led the new high commissioner, **Émile Bollaert**, to transfer him to Cambodia where he worked as the commissioner for the French Republic in Cambodia between May 1947 and September 1948. During this time, Pignon continued to play a behind-the-scenes role in winning over Bao Dai to the creation of a counter-revolutionary, pro-French state. Pignon's influence grew when

10. The French used the term 'southern Annam' at this point because the establishment of the 16th parallel in mid-1945 effectively divided former colonial 'Annam' into two halves.

the more colonially minded ***Mouvement républicain populaire*** (MRP) took control of the Ministry of Overseas France. On 20 October 1948, Pignon was himself named high commissioner for Indochina on the suggestion of the MRP's minister of Overseas France, **Paul Coste-Floret.** Pignon held the position until December 1950, when the **Cao Bang** disaster brought his Indochinese career to an end. But not before he got counter-revolutionary **Associated States of Indochina** off the ground in Vietnam, Laos, and Cambodia. In early 1950, the West accorded diplomatic recognition to these states, marking a victory for Pignon's state-building project and efforts to win over American **Cold War** support for French colonial policy.

In May 1951, he became the French representative on the **United Nations** Trusteeship Council. He later returned to the Direction of Political Affairs in the Ministry of Overseas France as decolonization caught up with him again in French Africa. He ended his career as a member of the French *Conseil d'État*, played a pivotal role in the activities of the *Académie des Sciences d'Outre-mer* in Paris, and was president of the *Association des anciens élèves de l'ENFOM* (1960–1966).

**PIM (*personnels internés militaires*).** *See* PRISONERS OF WAR.

**PISIER, GEORGES LÉON PIERRE (1910–1986).** Born in **Saigon**, Pisier graduated from the Paris ***École nationale des langues orientales vivantes*** with an undergraduate degree in law. Between 1933 and 1944, he served in various administrative posts in colonial Indochina. Between 1941 and 1944, he ran the office for the Direction of Information and headed up *Indochine, hebdomadaire illustré* for the colonial government. He was *résident* to Quang Yen, when the Japanese interned him. Upon liberation, he collaborated with the commissioner for **Tonkin** and Northern **Annam, Jean Sainteny**. Between 1948 and 1950, Pisier worked with the political advisor to the high commissioner for Indochina before leaving to take up a post in New Caledonia. Although **Léon Pignon** considered him to be one of the best specialists of Vietnam, Pisier dedicated his numerous historical studies to New Caledonia, whither he moved to live in 1966. *See also* JEAN COUSSEAU.

**PLAN Z.** Following the signing of the **Geneva Accords** dividing Vietnam at the **17th parallel** into two provisional states, the **Democratic Republic of Vietnam** received secret military aid from China and the Soviet Union. This plan had to be enacted secretly in light of restrictions in the Geneva declaration prohibiting such foreign military assistance. The General Military Party Committee and the Ministry of Defense organized this secret transfer under the code name of Plan Z (*ke hoach Z*). In July and August 1954, the headquarters agencies of the High Command, and principally the General Supply Department and the Military Personnel Department, received the remainder of the assistance allocated by Beijing and Moscow for the rest of 1954 (no one knew, when budgeting aid for the DRV, that the Indochina War would end in July 1954). This remaining military assistance was secretly shipped to the DRV via Thuy Khau in Cao Bang and Dong Dang in Lang Son. By early September 1954, Plan Z was completed. Between July and September, the DRV received via Plan Z 11,546 tons of weapons and equipment and 1,116 motor vehicles of all types. Almost all of this military assistance arrived undetected in the DRV before the **International Commission for Supervision and Control** arrived in northern Vietnam. As one of the officials directly involved in this mission later wrote: "The weapons and equipment that we received via 'Plan Z' provided the foundation that enabled our army to undertake a program of replacing our weapons and equipment during the first years of peace. Our old weapons were issued to local force troops and self-defense militia units". *See also* AID, CHINESE; AID, SOVIET.

**PLATON, ALEXANDROVICH (NGUYỄN VĂN THÀNH, 1922–).** Born and raised in the Ukraine, Platon was one of the **Democratic Republic of Vietnam**'s (DRV) best known **crossovers**. Inducted into the Soviet Red Army in 1941, he saw combat against the Germans, who captured him in May 1942 and transferred him to Western Europe as a forced laborer. At the end of the war, he landed in France or Denmark with no place to go. Uninterested in returning to the Soviet Union, in April 1946 he joined the French **Foreign Legion** and soon found himself in Indochina as the French and the Vietnamese moved towards full-scale war. Opposed to what he saw as an unjust colonial war, he deserted his unit in southern Vietnam on 17 August 1947 and joined the DRV's ranks. He was inducted and served in the Vietnamese army between 1947 and 1955, active mainly on the southern front. He married a Vietnamese woman from Thu Dau Mot, had a daughter, and adopted the Vietnamese name, Nguyen Van Thanh. In 1954, following the division of Vietnam into two provisional states at the **Geneva Conference**, he and his daughter moved to the north and were soon presented as an official symbol of Soviet – Vietnamese friendship. When **Ho Chi Minh** made a major public appearance in **Hanoi** in January 1955, Platon's daughter, Béatrice, was perched gently upon Ho's knee. Later in 1955, father and daughter repatriated to the Soviet Union. Fluent in Vietnamese, Alexandrovich became the first head of the Vietnamese Section of *Moscow Radio*, a position he held until retiring in the 1990s. He translated into Russian Phung Quan's *Breaking out of Poulo Condor* (*Vuot Con Dao*).

**PLEVEN, RENÉ (1901–1993).** French minister of Defense opposed to dealing with the **Democratic Republic of Vietnam** (DRV). A French businessman, he joined **Charles de Gaulle** in London in mid-1940 and moved to Algiers to serve as minister of Overseas France in the *Comité français de Libération nationale*. Pleven was in charge of organizing the **Brazzaville Conference** to define a new French colonial policy for the future 4th Republic. With the creation of the Provisional Government of the French Republic in Paris in 1944, he became a deputy and loyal Gaullist. For the first five years of the Indochina War, he was a particularly staunch supporter of de Gaulle's colonial policy, one that could reform the Empire but would not decolonize it. Pleven was strongly opposed to dealing with **Ho Chi Minh**'s DRV or even with non-communist nationalist demands endangering the reality of the **French Union**. He held a host of governmental posts between 1944 and 1954, including *président du Conseil* between July 1950 and February 1951 and again between August 1951 and January 1952. In 1950, he put his name to a French project to create a European army, the start of what would become the **European Defense Community**. However, the increasing cost of the Indochina War hampered Pleven's European ambitions. He first considered a negotiated settlement of the Indochina War in November 1951 as *président du Conseil*, when he conceded that "the conclusion of an armistice in Korea would create a favorable climate for making contact with China". The armistice in Korea occurred in July 1953, leading the French and the DRV to move towards direct negotiations but not before trying to strengthen their positions in the Indochinese battlefield. Pleven made a fact-finding visit to Indochina between 9 and 28 February 1954, inspecting the camp at **Dien Bien Phu** and meeting with the relevant French and Vietnamese military and political leaders. In his personal report to the **Joseph Laniel** government in early March, Pleven warned that the DRV's armed forces were rapidly increasing in strength and that the balance of force could soon change in their favor, to the point that Pleven doubted the French could impose a negotiated solution on French terms. He underscored the importance of developing and engaging the **army of the Associated State of Vietnam** in the war in order to relieve the French military burden. He concluded that the French had to explore all possible avenues that could lead to a negotiated settlement of the war at Geneva. Ending it was also essential to the implementation of his European plans, above all the creation of the **European Defense Community.**

**POC KHUN (PHRA PHISET PHANIT, 1904–?).** Born in Phnom Penh, he was related to the powerful Thai family of Cambodian origin, the Aphaiwong. Poc Khun spoke Thai and French fluently. In the 1930s, he became involved in nationalist politics and, with the outbreak of World War II, he set up the Independent Khmer Party along the Thai–Cambodia border with the aim of dislodging the French and creating an independent Cambodia. Determined to roll back the French in western Indochina, Thai leaders **Pibun Songgram** and **Khuang Aphaiwong** supported him in areas of Surin and Battambang provinces. Poc Khun continued working among various **Khmer Issarak** clans following the end of World War II.

**POL POT (SALOTH SAR, 1925–1998).** Pol Pot became infamous for the terror he unleashed against his own people in the late 1970s, but he had little if any influence in the Cambodian communist movement during the Indochina War. Besides the six months he spent as a Buddhist novice in the 1930s, Saloth Sar received a French education in colonial Cambodia. Between 1937 and 1942, he pursued his elementary studies at the *École Miche* before continuing them at the *Collège Preah Sihanouk* between 1942 and 1947. Between 1947 and 1949, he attended a technical school in Phnom Penh. He was a mediocre student at best. His life changed, however, when he met **Ieng Sary**, who introduced him to national and more radical politics in Phnom Penh. The Franco-Vietnamese war was underway to the east and the abosolute monarchy was coming under fire in Cambodia. Both joined the **Democrat Party**. In 1949, Saloth Sar obtained a government scholarship to study in France, where he enrolled at the *École d'ingénieurs des technologies de l'information et du management* in Paris. However, studies were not high on his list of priorities and he never received a diploma before returning to Cambodia in January 1953. Instead he became increasingly involved in left-wing politics in Paris, agitating with French and Vietnamese communists active in France at the time. In 1951, he joined a communist cell, affiliated with the **French Communist Party**, called the *Cercle marxiste*. Upon his return to Cambodia in 1953, he briefly served in a Vietnamese–Cambodian military unit. However, Saloth Sar had little influence in a Cambodian communist movement that had developed in alliance with Vietnamese communists. He was probably unknown to the powerful **Party Affairs Committee** (*Ban Can Su*) that ran the Cambodian communist movement under **Son Ngoc Minh** and **Nguyen Thanh Son**. At the end of the Indochina War, Saloth Sar was among those who demobilized and returned to Phnom Penh instead of regrouping to north Vietnam. This allowed him to assert his influence and ultimately take over the communist movement in Cambodia and divorce it from its Indochinese past and framework. *See also* ADMINISTRATIVE OFFICE FOR THE FRONTIER; COMMITTEE FOR EXTERNAL AFFAIRS; COMMITTEE FOR THE EAST, LAO ISSARA.

**PONCHARDIER, PIERRE (1909–1961).** French naval officer who distinguished himself in naval air defense operations (***aéronavale***) during the Indochina War. Born in Saint-Étienne in the Loire, he graduated from the Naval Academy (*École navale*) in 1927 and worked in various positions in the navy. He refused to join Vichy and, with his brother, organized some of the most audacious intelligence networks in France during World War II. Their specialty was providing intelligence to the Allies on German movements along the long French coasts and in Alsace-Lorraine as the war drew to an end. At the end of the war, Ponchardier led the French Naval Air Defense Forces (*aéronautique navale française*) with the task of creating and training paratroopers for the Far East (***Commando** parachutiste d'Extrême-Orient*) to fight the Vietnamese in Indochina in 1945–1946. In 1946, named naval commander, Ponchardier headed up the Commando Paratroopers for Naval Air Defense Forces (*Groupe de commandos parachutistes de l'Aéronavale*) and the ship *Commandant Robert Giraud* between 1947 and 1948. He served as deputy commander for the **Navy** in the Mekong Delta between 1948 and 1950 and then as the naval attaché to the High Command for the French Armed forces in the Far East between 1950 and 1952.

**PONGE, JACK ÉTIENNE (1904–1959).** French colonial administrator who made his career in Indochina. Between 1927 and 1945, he held diverse administrative posts in **Tonkin**, **Annam**, and Cambodia. After World War II, he returned to France where he ran the Colonial Service for Marseilles (1947–1948) before becoming director of the *Agence Indochine* in Paris (1948–1950). He headed the economic service in the ministry in charge of Relations with the Associated States between 1951 and 1952.

**POPULAR FRONT OF SOUTHERN VIETNAM (*Mặt Trận Bình Dân Nam Phần*).** Following the failure of the French-conceived **Provisional Government of the Republic of Cochinchina**, this southern front was designed to attract support for an evolving non-communist Vietnamese government under the control of pro-French leaders such as **Tran Van Huu**. It numbered some 20,000 members in and around **Saigon**-Cholon by the late 1940s.

**POTSDAM CONFERENCE.** Allied conference held in defeated Germany between 17 July and 2 August 1945 to discuss, among other things, the future of Germany and the course of the war against Japan. French leader **Charles de Gaulle** was not, however, a participant in this meeting. This explains his surprise when he learned that Allied leaders had agreed to divide former French Indochina into two zones at the **16th parallel**, with **Chiang Kai-shek**'s China theatre encompassing all of Indochina north of that line and Mountbatten's South East Asia Command in charge of all areas south of it. When Japan announced its decision to surrender in August, the result of the Postdam conference's *ad hoc* compromise decision was that Chiang Kai-shek's republican troops were allowed to occupy and disarm Japanese troops above the 16th parallel, while British troops would do the same to the south. The Postdam conference's decision to demarcate Indochina into these two zones was made on 23 July 1945. The implications of this decision would turn out to be immense. *See also* 23 SEPTEMBER 1945; 19 DECEMBER 1946; ACCORDS OF 6 MARCH 1946; BAO DAI SOLUTION; OCCUPATION, CHINESE.

**POUGET, JEAN (1920?–2007).** He joined the French resistance during World War II and the French army, which sent him to Indochina. In 1954, he served as aide-de-camp to General **Henri Navarre**. As the **Democratic Republic of Vietnam**'s forces threatened to overrun **Dien Bien Phu**, Pouget parachuted into the valley and was taken prisoner when the fortress fell on 7 May 1954. Following his liberation, he became a leading reporter for the French center-right newspaper, *Le Figaro*, covering the American War in Vietnam. He published *Nous étions à Dien Bien Phu* (1964).

**POULLARD, JEAN ROBERT (1917–1998).** French colonial administrator in charge of Indochinese workers in France between 1943 and 1946. He transferred to Laos where he was chief of cabinet for the commissioner to the Republic there. In 1948, he worked for the French high commissioner's office of the economy in charge of the section for internal trade. Between 1949 and 1950, he was chief of cabinet to the commissioner for the Republic to Cambodia, the high commissioner's delegate to Battambang province in 1951, and head of the French Information Service in Phnom Penh. Between 1954 and 1961, he was the high commissioner's delegate to Kampot province, then deputy and head of the *Mission d'aide économique et technique* between 1955 and 1961 in Cambodia.

**POULO CONDOR.** Situated off the coast of southern Vietnam, the prison of Poulo Condor, or Con Dao in Vietnamese, was the most notorious of the French colonial penitentiaries. Created in 1862, Poulo Condor held on average some 1,500 prisoners, although revolts on the mainland could overflow the cells as the French made large-scale arrests. The prison cells often mixed political prisoners with a large majority of common law offenders. Working conditions were often deadly. Disease was rampant and violence common. The mortality rate averaged between 3 and 4 percent, moving as high as 15 percent in 1930. In August 1936, the leftwing Popular Front government in France authorized a massive amnesty, freeing many communist and non-communist political prisoners. However, the fall of the Popular Front government and the outbreak of World War II saw the French colonial authorities renew their crackdown on nationalists and communists. According to **Paul Mus**, as of 9 March 1945 (when the Japanese overthrew the French and freed thousands of political prisoners on the mainland), between 8,000 and 10,000 political prisoners were being held in French Indochinese jails and labor camps, most of them Vietnamese. 5,000 political prisoners had been sent to Poulo Condor following the failed communist uprising in **Cochinchina** in 1940.

Paradoxically, prison experience in Poulo Condor and elsewhere in the Indochinese penal universe contributed to the development of Vietnamese nationalism by bringing together in one crowded place revolutionaries from all over the country. Years behind bars also forged some of the tightest bonds within the **Indochinese Communist Party** (ICP), ones that would make themselves felt within the party, army, and especially in the **Public Security Services**. The lifelong friendship among **Le Duan**, **Pham Hung**, and **Nguyen Van Linh** began on the island of Poulo Condor. They returned together to mainland Vietnam on **23 September 1945**, the day war broke out in the south. These men would go on to become the most important communist leaders in southern Vietnam during the Indochina War and in all of Vietnam during the war with the Americans. In all, boats returned about 1,200–1,800 political prisoners to Vietnam between August and October 1945. (**Bao Dai** had ordered the release of prisoners from Poulo Condor before the Japanese defeat; however, it is not known how many returned to Vietnam.) Prison time also divided communist and non-communist nationalists violently. In many ways, the seeds of the civil war that broke out between the ICP and the **Vietnamese Nationalist Party** (*Viet Nam Quoc Dan Dan*, VNQDD) in 1945–1946 had been planted in Poulo Condor in the 1930s. Nationalists and communists often came to violent blows in the island's cellblocks.

Having returned to southern Vietnam, the French retook Poulo Condor by force on 18 April 1946 and used it again as the major colonial prison during the Indochina War. In May 1946, the French dispatched some 300 prisoners from **Saigon** to Poulo Condor, including combatants of the DRV armed forces as well as workers, students, and intellectuals who had taken part in the resistance. Between 1946 and 1950, not technically at war, the French transferred to Poulo Condor "political prisoners" who had taken part in anti-French activities. As of January 1950, Poulo Condor held 1,392 prisoners. The majority were Vietnamese numbering 1,157, but there were also 95 Cambodians, 9 Lao, 66 Chinese, 3 Thai, as well as 72 Japanese **prisoners of war**. Of the Vietnamese prisoners, 751 came from southern Vietnam, 233 from the north, 161 from the center, and two from the highlands. However, only 2 percent of these Vietnamese prisoners were members of the communist party. From April 1951, as full-scale battles raged on the mainland, the French began to dispatch hundreds of Vietnamese prisoners of war (*tu binh*) to Poulo Condor. While the communist party continued to organize and recruit among political and common law prisoners, the violence that had characterized Poulo Condor since the colonial period resumed, including the use of **torture.** And, as in the 1930s, communist and non-communist nationalists found themselves spending time together behind bars because of their opposition to the French. Heated exchanges were not uncommon. On 20 August 1954, 512 political prisoners were freed from Poulo Condor and transferred to the **Democratic Republic of Vietnam** (DRV). One month later, another 1,050 political prisoners were returned to the DRV via Sam Son. *See also* PRISONERS OF WAR; SON LA.

**POUPAERT, JEAN-JACQUES CHARLES (1920–1981).** Behind-the-scenes colonial administrator active during the Indochina War. Graduated from the **Colonial Academy** (*École coloniale*) in 1939, he made his career in the Indochinese colonial service. In 1943, he joined the Free French forces in North Africa and took part in the liberation of France. Discharged honorably from the Army, he transferred to Indochina where he went to work in the cabinet of the commissioner for the Republic to **Annam** between 1945 and 1946, serving as a delegate of Blao and head of the province of Ninh Thuan between 1946 and 1948. Between 1948 and 1950, he headed the administrative service of the commissioner for the Republic to Annam and served as a provincial advisor to Khanh Hoa. Between 1950 and 1954, he served as the deputy chief then the chief of cabinet of the high commissioner for Indochina. In 1955, he was the chargé d'affaires for administrative and consular questions for the High Commissioner's Office. He thereafter continued his colonial career in Africa until 1961 when he went into the private sector.

**POUSSIN, JACQUES EUGÈNE HENRI (1920–2002).** He was in charge of Indochinese workers in France between 1943 and 1945, when he was transferred to Cambodia. There, he worked in various posts for the commissioner for the Republic. Between 1952 and 1958, he served in the French ministry in charge of relations with the Associated States.

**PRASERT PHINIKORN.** *See* TRẦN MAI.

**PRIDI BANOMYONG (1900–1983).** Prominent Thai statesman and strong supporter of Vietnamese, Lao, and Cambodian anti-colonialists during the early stages of the Indochina War. He studied in France between 1920 and 1927 during which time he obtained his doctorate in law from the Sorbonne. He met with Vietnamese nationalists in France, including Duong Van Giao, **Tran Van Giau,** and possibly **Ho Chi Minh**. He took part in the *coup d'état* ending the absolute monarchy in Thailand in 1932 and held important cabinet positions during the 1930s. During World War II, he led the Free Thai (*Seri Thai*) movement secretly from Bangkok. He worked closely with ethnic Lao politicians in northeastern Thailand, such as **Tiang Sirikhan** and **Thongin Buriphat**. After World War II, Pridi served as prime minister between August 1945 and January 1946 and was a strong supporter of the anti-colonialist causes of the **Democratic Republic of Vietnam** (DRV), **Khmer Issarak**, and **Lao Issara.** He allowed DRV agents to trade clandestinely in Thailand and to administer an unofficial diplomatic office for Southeast Asia in Bangkok. He was forced from power by a *coup d'état* in November 1947 and the return of **Pibun Songgram** in April 1948. He lived in exile in China between 1949 and 1970, when he moved to France where he passed away.

**PRISONERS OF THE JAPANESE.** Following the ***coup de force* of 9 March 1945**, the Japanese incarcerated an estimated 683 French civilians and high-ranking officers (242 in **Hanoi**, 82 in Hue, 150 in **Saigon**, 150 in Haiphong and 59 in Phnom

Penh). The Japanese interned 15,000 members of the French colonial army, 12,000 of them Europeans. Between mid-March and mid-August 1945, 400 French civilians and 1,800 French military personnel died at Japanese hands (though it is not clear exactly how many died in combat, due to execution, or because of illness). The French estimated that some 6,000 "Indochinese" civilians and 700 military personnel perished because of the Japanese. The French estimated Japanese damages to the French community at 2.7 million piastres. No statistics exist for the "Indochinese" or the Japanese financial losses. *See also* FOREIGN LEGION; PRISONERS OF WAR.

**PRISONERS OF WAR, DEMOCRATIC REPUBLIC OF VIETNAM.** According to the December 1954 declaration made by Jacques Chevallier, French state secretary for War,[11] the French returned to the **Democratic Republic of Vietnam** (DRV) 67,000 detainees (*détenus*), including 59,700 internees and 8,000 war prisoners. The French had classified the majority of these enemy Vietnamese prisoners as *personnels internés militaires* or PIM. This status technically refers to enemy prisoners taken by the **Expeditionary Corps** and used for various types of *corvée* labor. The French army used them behind the lines doing manual jobs and even deployed them as workers during the battle of **Dien Bien Phu** during which the PIM suffered heavy casualties. According to a separate source, the French returned 64,000 PIM. *See also* EXECUTIONS.

**PRISONERS OF WAR, FRENCH UNION FORCES.** Between 1945 and 1954, according to French statistics, the **Democratic Republic of Vietnam** (DRV) held around 20,800 **French Union** prisoners. Most of them were taken prisoner during the battles of **Cao Bang** in 1950 and **Dien Bien Phu** in 1954. According to the December 1954 declaration made by Jacques Chevallier, French state secretary for War,[12] prior to 18 August 1954 the DRV returned 5,442 prisoners belonging to the forces of the French Union and another 13,739 were returned between 18 August and 17 October 1954. Of the 13,739, there were 13,029 military personnel coming from French Africa and France and 710 civilians. The total number of "absentees, missing or unreturned" (*absents, disparus ou non rentrés*) from the military forces of the French Union was numbered at 20,661 as of 17 October 1954. The number for the armed forces of the Associated States was about 9,000. The French revealed that 3,266 military men from the army of the Associated State of Vietnam had been liberated as well as 683 Vietnamese civilians. Few French Union forces fell into the hands of the enemy before 1950. The DRV had little if any experience of holding prisoners and it hardly had the medical infrastructure, medicines, or doctors to take care of the wounded and increasingly sick soldiers now living in the insalubrious jungles of Vietnam. Around 50 percent of the non-Vietnamese prisoners taken by the DRV died in captivity, while those who were liberated after being taken prisoner at Dien Bien Phu were often in an appalling state of health. Deadliest of all for these thousands of men was the lack of medical attention, medicines, and the hostile jungle environment into which they were plunged. This was especially the case for the thousands of men taken prisoner at Dien Bien Phu, who were forced on a 600 km death march in the rainy season. Dysentery, dehydration, and **disease** soon set in and continued once the prisoners were concentrated in largely unprotected camps, but ones located so deeply in the jungle that no man could get out alive without a guide. However, the DRV never reached out to the international community for help in taking care of these soldiers, nor did the government allow the **Red Cross** to provide relief for these prisoners or even visit the camps. The DRV had not signed the Geneva Convention.

**PRISONERS OF WAR, LEGAL STATUS.** Neither the French Republic nor the **Democratic Republic of Vietnam** (DRV) ever formally declared war upon the other. For the French, at least at the start of hostilities in southern Vietnam on **23 September 1945**, it was not an internationally recognized war but rather an "insurrection" or a "revolt" against the protecting state, that is, France. According to this legal definition, French military operations constituted an internal police action, a **pacification** operation. Those mainly Vietnamese opposing French troops were technically labeled "insurgents" or "rebels", threatening the internal security of the French colonial state. Until 30 October 1946, the French made no distinction between common law criminals and politically motivated individuals. Nor did the French accord to the DRV's soldiers a military status. Instead, "any individual arrested" by the

11. *Le Monde,* 19–20 December 1954
12. *Le Monde,* 19–20 December 1954

French army or police could be tried in military or civilian courts.

The Franco-Vietnamese ***modus vivendi*** reached in mid-September 1946 changed this by making a legal distinction between common law criminals and political prisoners. Article 9 stipulated that "prisoners currently detained for political motives will be released except for those charged with crimes and common law misdemeanors". This applied to prisoners taken during military operations. The French released most of their "political prisoners" after the modus vivendi came into effect on 30 October 1946. However, the outbreak of full-scale war on **19 December 1946** ensured that the question of the legal status of enemy combatants would not go away as the French began to take an unprecedented amount of prisoners. Indeed, on 27 December 1946, the French Commissioner for Ban Me Thuat requested instructions concerning the status to accord to "forty Annamese prisoners of war" taken by the **Expeditionary Corps**.

With the *modus vivendi* no longer in effect, French authorities had to establish in legal terms how they would define captured enemy combatants. Given that the French refused to acknowledge that the outbreak of "hostilities" on 19 December constituted a "war" in internationally recognized legal terms, or in terms of their political goal to deny the national and international existence of the DRV, French authorities argued that they could not accord "prisoner of war" status to captured individuals claiming to be soldiers of the DRV. In February 1947, French authorities advanced that captured soldiers could not be considered to be "prisoners of war" because the DRV was not an internationally recognized independent state. According to this logic, by the fact that the 6 March Accords of 1946 recognized "Vietnam" as a "free state within the Indochinese Federation and the French Union (*un Etat libre faisant partie de la fédération indochinoise et de l'Union française*), the state of hostilities between the French state in charge of the Union and Federation and the DRV was an "internal legal" matter (*relèvent du droit interne*). As a result, these legal instructions continued, the French were legally entitled to try "Annamese prisoners" captured in **Tonkin, Annam,** and **Cochinchina** (the word "Vietnam" could not be used technically since it implied the existence of a viable nation-state) for "treason" and "a threat to the internal security of the State".

That was the legal brief. In practice and for political reasons, the French had to be more flexible, since many of the individuals their army captured were in military uniform. As a result, it was decided that despite the French legal argument denying the existence of an enemy state and its army, the reality was such that it was agreed to provide uniformed captives with the status of "prisoner of war". This was to be done in accordance with the Geneva Convention, however, it was carefully stipulated internally that "on no occasion" will captured enemy combatants actually receive the status of "prisoner of war" (*cette qualification de "prisonniers de guerre"*). It was thus implicitly, not explicitly, conceded. For captured "irregular troops" (guerillas, *franc tireurs*), the French would investigate first in order to determine whether they were political detainees or common law ones. Those judged to be political prisoners would be "interned purely and simply".

As of 2010, this writer was unable to determine how the DRV or the **Associated States of Indochina** defined their prisoners in legal terms. The DRV was not a signatory to the Geneva Convention.

**PROPAGANDA, DEMOCRATIC REPUBLIC OF VIETNAM.** *See* ART, DEMOCRATIC REPUBLIC OF VIETNAM; CULTURE; EMULATION CAMPAIGN; INDOCTRINATION; NEW HERO; PROSELYTIZING THE ENEMY; PSYCHOLOGICAL WARFARE; RECTIFICATION.

**PROPAGANDA, FRENCH.** *See* INDOCTRINATION; PROSELYTIZING THE ENEMY; PSYCHOLOGICAL WARFARE; REVOLUTIONARY WARFARE.

**PROSELYTIZING THE ENEMY (*Địch Vận*).** Refers to the branch of the **Democratic Republic of Vietnam**'s (DRV) armed forces in charge of mobilizing, propagandizing, and rallying enemy soldiers and officers throughout the Indochina War. *Dich Van* propaganda underscored the "righteous" cause of the DRV's struggle in an attempt to sow doubts and dissension within the enemy's ranks. These propaganda teams relied on pamphlets, papers, tracts, and loudspeakers. To be more effective, they also turned to **deserters** from the **French Union** forces, especially **North African** and African troops, to entice in their native languages colonial troops and Germans from the **Foreign Legion**. European **crossovers** such as **Erwin Börchers**, **Kostas Sarantidis**, **Ernst Frey**, and **Georges Boudarel** conducted propaganda courses in a cacophony of different languages among European prisoners taken by the DRV forces. While there were some notable defections, the proselytizing missions were much less successful than Vietnamese propaganda and many French theoricians of "**revolutionary war**" suggest. The most important targets for the DRV were the Vietnamese troops being recruited by the **Army of the Associated State of Vietnam**. As the Associated State came to life and General **Jean de Lattre de Tassigny** pushed it to mobilize in order to win, the DRV countered with its own general mobilization. This meant that there emerged a real competition for young peasant recruits. As a result, not only did the DRV do its best to control territories and the manpower they held, but the government also stepped up its efforts to win over those soldiers drafted into the enemy Vietnamese army. Vietnamese communists behind this strategy were also betting that their regime's defense of the poor, soon to be backed up by **land reform**, would win over soldiers from the Associated State of Vietnam via *Dich Van*. *See also* INDOCTRINATION; PSYCHOLOGICAL WARFARE; REVOLUTIONARY WARFARE; TORTURE.

**PROSTITUTION.** If French authorities moved to close brothels in France at the end of World War II, the same was not true in the colonies. In 1930, colonial medical authorities had officially recorded 500 prostitutes, but estimated the number of unrecorded prostitutes working in the city of **Hanoi** at 5,000. The same numbers were said to be valid as of 1945. During the Indochina War, the army allowed and organized ***Bordels mobiles de campagne*** to tend to the troops of the **Expeditionary Corps**. In **Saigon**, two famous prostitution houses existed during the war. The *Parc à Buffles*, a large military brothel, provided dancing and "taxi girls" and sexual services to a less monied clientele, whereas the *Arc-en-Ciel* tended to the higher classes or richer clients. **Bernard Fall** reported that 73 known French prostitutes residing in Saigon during the Indochina War tended to rich businessmen, ranking officers, and airline pilots. When General **Jean de Lattre de Tassigny** took over in Indochina, with full military and civilian powers, he tried to get rid of them. One of his ranking intelligence chiefs protested on the grounds that many of these prostitutes were on the intelligence payroll. Apparently de Lattre successfully had them expelled from Indochina or forbidden from practicing their trade.

The **Democratic Republic of Vietnam** (DRV) also used prostitutes as a way of infiltrating female spies into the enemy ranks in order to obtain intelligence on troop movements and operations. During the battle of Hanoi in early 1947, Vietnamese military commanders relied upon Vietnamese dancing girls (*Co Dau*), especially in the *Kham Thien* area in southern Hanoi, to serve as guides, liaison agents, and even combatants in the militia (*Tu Ve*) in two months of urban fighting against French forces. Le Thi Luong and Nguyen Thi Anh distinguished themselves in this battle. During the rest of the Indochina War, such women continued to work for the DRV's secret services from within the occupied cities, serving as liaison agents and valuable sources of information. It was only following the installation of the DRV in Hanoi in late 1954 and 1955 that the Party began to impose a new social morality and order, one that was as hostile to the prostitutes as the Confucian order had been. In 1947, following the battle of Hanoi, several militia prostitutes told their commanders that they preferred to remain in Hanoi, despite the French occupation, rather than face the damning gaze of traditional society (*Cac Chi Chiu Chet O Day Con Hon Ve Lang Chiu Nhuc*).

Prostitution increased notably in urban areas between December 1946 and October 1954 as **French Union** soldiers on leave flocked to the cities. An estimated 15,000 prostitutes were working in Hanoi when the DRV retook possession of the capital in 1954. Moreover, French intelligence and security services were as adept as their opponents in using prostitutes for information gathering missions. *See also* CHILDREN; ORPHANS; WOMEN, DEMOCRATIC REPUBLIC OF VIETNAM.

**PROVISIONAL GOVERNMENT OF THE REPUBLIC OF COCHINCHINA.** Cochinchinese local government formed by the French in 1946 as the first bloc in a new **Indochinese Federation** and as a counter to attempts by the **Democratic Republic of Vietnam** (DRV) to incorporate the former French colony of **Cochinchina** into a unitary Vietnamese state under **Hanoi**'s nationalist leadership. The **Tran Trong Kim** government had obtained the incorporation of Cochinchina into the Empire of Vietnam in August 1945, before the Japanese surrender and **Bao Dai's** abdication.

To the nationalist leaders of the DRV, "*Nam Bo*", the new nationalist word for Cochinchina, was also considered to be an historic and natural part of the Vietnamese nation now led by **Ho Chi**

**Minh**. To the French, determined to create the Indochinese Federation demanded by **Charles de Gaulle**, the colony of Cochinchina was seen as the cornerstone of the new federation. Cochinchina was France's only *de jure* colony in Asia, one that had sent deputies to Paris since its creation in the mid-19th century, as with Algeria. While nationalist leaders of the DRV were determined to unify the three colonial entities of **Tonkin**, **Annam,** and Cochinchina into one unitary *Vietnamese* national identity, colonial federalists were committed to regrouping the five colonial units of Laos, Cambodia, Tonkin, Annam, and Cochinchina into a heavily institutionalized *Indochinese* framework. To complicate matters, on **23 September 1945**, the British facilitated the return of the French to southern Vietnam below the **16th parallel**, thereby triggering the start of the Franco-Vietnamese war in southern Indochina.

**Jean Cédile**, commissioner for the French Republic to Cochinchina and Southern Annam, was charged with restoring the French presence along the lines elaborated during the **Brazzaville Conference** of 1944 and in the March 1945 **Declaration on Indochina**, calling for the creation of local governments for each of the five parts. In October 1945, he developed plans for establishing a consultative assembly; joined hands with French settlers to form a Consultative Council to draft a constitution for a future Cochinchinese government; and together they formed the Cochinchinese Party in November 1945. Cédile did his best to associate moderate pro-French Cochinchinese elites with his project, such as Dr. **Nguyen Van Thinh** and his Democratic Party. On 8 February 1946, a Cochinchinese Consultative Council came to life, with four French and eight Cochinchinese members (all but one of whom had been naturalized French). This council had the task of working with the high commissioner for Indochina **Georges Thierry d'Argenlieu**, to produce a constitution. The latter was particularly determined to create a Cochinchinese "free state".

Meanwhile, in the north, Ho Chi Minh negotiated with the French over the questions of the DRV's independence and the importance of keeping Cochinchina/Nam Bo as part of Vietnam. The **6 March Accords of 1946** had left the resolution of this divisive question to the "populations" who would be consulted in a referendum. When Ho Chi Minh agreed that Vietnam could take part in the Indochinese Federation as a "free state" (*État libre*), he was certain that the referendum would confirm "Cochinchina" as a part of a unitary Vietnamese "free state" represented by the DRV based in Hanoi.

For High Commissioner Thierry d'Argenlieu, it was essential that Cochinchina remain a separate entity. The French government, including the socialist minister of the Colonies **Marius Moutet**, shared this point of view. It was in this context that Thierry d'Argenlieu supported the Cochinchinese Consultative Council's vote on 26 March to counter the reality of the DRV by creating a "Provisional Government of the Republic of Cochinchina" with Dr. Nguyen Van Thinh serving as its president. Worried by the concessions made to the DRV in the 6 March Accords, above all the talk of holding a referendum of uniting Cochinchina with the rest of Vietnam (DRV), Thierry d'Argenlieu stepped up his efforts to create a Cochinchinese government as an essential step in forming the Indochinese Federation ordered by de Gaulle.

Significantly, certain colonial specialists in Paris, most importantly **Henri Laurentie**, warned Moutet that Thierry d'Argenlieu's policy could sabotage Franco-DRV relations at a critical moment. In the event of a referendum, Laurentie had no illusions as to the ability of mainly French-naturalized Vietnamese leaders of Cochinchinese autonomy to match the nationalist attraction of someone like Ho Chi Minh. Laurentie favoured a referendum, but on the condition that in the event of a victory for the unionists, Cochinchina had to be guaranteed a special status in a united Vietnam, even as a "free state" within the Indochinese Federation. Thierry d'Argenlieu did not see things this way, convinced that the loss of Cochinchina to Vietnam would bring down the entire Indochinese colonial house. On 1 June 1946, the day after Ho Chi Minh left to negotiate the status of Cochinchina/Nam Bo during a long summer in France, the high commissioner unilaterally proclaimed the provisional government of the Autonomous Republic of Cochinchina as a separate "free state" within the emerging Indochinese Federation. The president of the provisional government was a French citizen, Dr. **Nguyen Van Thinh,** as was his vice president **Nguyen Van Xuan**. On 5 June, metropolitan authorities accepted this *fait accompli* when Moutet informed Thierry d'Argenlieu of the **Cominindo**'s approval. In effect, the high commissioner in **Saigon** had effectively forced Paris's hand and in so doing had set the French on a collision course with the DRV over Cochinchina. The French government shared the high commissioner's hostility to holding a referendum over the future of Cochinchina and, as a result, the **Fontainebleau Conference** ended in a resounding failure.

And yet in Vietnam, popular sentiment among the overwhelming Vietnamese majority, even in the south, was hostile to the division of "Vietnam". None of this was lost on the president of the fledgling southern government, Dr. Nguyen Van Thinh. When the French proved unwilling to grant him real political power, provoking a ministerial crisis, he resigned and committed suicide on 10 November 1946. This event, together with the leftist victory in the French legislative elections, triggered Thierry d'Argenlieu's decision to adopt a more confrontational policy towards the DRV in the north. After Thinh's suicide, the French approved the nomination of **Le Van Hoach**, another French citizen, to lead the government.

The French experiment in Cochinchinese separatism did not long survive the outbreak of full-scale war on **19 December 1946** and the departure of Thierry d'Argenlieu in March 1947. Léon Pignon's desire to play the Bao Dai card was put on hold when he was transferred to Cambodia. The **Paul Ramadier** government and its new high commissioner for Indochina **Emile Bollaert** left open the possibility of negotiating a way out of full-scale war. It was only after **Paul Mus**'s mission to meet Ho Chi Minh failed in May 1947 and Marius Moutet left the Ministry of Overseas France a few months later that Bollaert turned to what would become known as the **Bao Dai Solution** in late 1947. On 5 June 1948, on a vessel anchored in the Bay of Ha Long in the north, the new French high commissioner for Indochina Bollaert initialed a protocol in the presence of Bao Dai, setting the foundation for a new chapter in Franco-Vietnamese relations. The French would soon accord to **Bao Dai** what they had refused to Ho Chi Minh: the territorial unity of Vietnam. Cochinchinese separatism would necessarily have to come to an end, too. *See also* ALGERIAN WAR.

**PSYCHOLOGICAL WARFARE.** During the Indochina War, *guerre psychologique* came to mean for the French army the development and use of methods capable of undermining the morale of the adversary; strengthening that of the French army and its allies against enemy propaganda; reversing the effects of enemy propaganda; and "detoxifying" and then indoctrinating DRV prisoners taken by **French Union** soldiers.

It is unclear when exactly the term "psychological warfare" came into use in French. It had certainly become commonplace in English during World War II even though Western democracies, and the French Third Republic in particular, had always found it harder than single-party states to use the word propaganda. World War II changed this for the French. Vichy officials developed propaganda as part of Philippe Pétain's National Revoution and the alliance with the Nazis against the Allies, just as Free French forces collaborating with the Allies did so against the Axis. Indeed, Free French initiation to Allied methods of psychological warfare during World War II served the Fourth Republic well, as many of the officers trained in such matters deployed them in France's two major wars of decolonization in the 20th century – the Indochinese and Algerian ones. In 1946, the cabinet of the French High Command in Indochina created a propaganda section while the ***Deuxième Bureau*** did the same in its territorial posts. The *Deuxième Bureau* apparently took the lead in developing psychological warfare sections during the course of the conflict.

However, as in the past, the French had a much harder time developing psychological warfare than their communist opponents and Anglo-American allies. The development of a full-blown psychological warfare section in the French army in Indochina was not officialized at the higher level until January 1953, when the Office of Psychological Warfare (*Bureau de la guerre psychologique*) was created within the General Staff of the French commander-in-chief in Indochina (*Etat-Major interarmées des forces terrestres,* EMIFT). It was soon expanded to the general staffs at the territorial level. Until the end of the Indochina War, American specialists in "psyops" worked with the French through this bureau and French officers studied psychological warfare at Fort Bragg in the United States.

The Allied experience in psychological warfare against the Chinese in the **Korean War** also served as a model to which the French looked when creating their bureau in 1953. In order to sap enemy morale or build up that of its allies, the French army dropped millions of tracts over the **Democratic Republic of Vietnam** zones, targeting both troops and civilians. The Office of Psychological Warfare published 47 papers and bulletins, churning out a total of some 700,000 copies. The budget allotted to psychological warfare amounted to 50 millions francs in 1952. In

1953, it increased to 200 million then 355 million in 1954, part of which was financed by the USA.

As Paul and Marie-Catherine Villatoux have demonstrated convincingly, French psychological warfare developed considerably during the Indochinese and **Algerian Wars**; but the roots of this policy are to be found in World War II and in a wider global context, one in which American, British, and Sino-Soviet models were highly influential on French thinking. *See also* CHARLES LACHEROY; EDWARD LANSDALE; GUERRILLA; PAUL MUS; REVOLUTIONARY WARFARE; ROGER TRINQUIER.

**PUBLIC OPINION, FRENCH.** French public opinion was remarkably uninterested in the Indochina War until the early 1950s. Several reasons account for this. Unlike French Algeria, colonial Indochina possessed only a small Franco-European population (some 40,000 Europeans living in Indochina until March 1945 in marked contrast to the one million residing in Algeria in 1954). Unlike Algeria, where obligatory national military service ensured that a greater number of French youth and families were touched by the war, in Indochina a professional and remarkably non-French contingent conducted the war. Third, in the wake of World War II, French people were much more focused on rebuilding their country and their own lives. The war in Indochina remained far from their daily concerns and certainly further removed than Algeria located just across the Mediterranean. In 1945, Alain Ruscio reports, 25 percent of the French polled on the Indochina War had nothing to say. That number increased to 30 percent in January 1947, just following the outbreak of full-scale war on **19 December 1946**. In 1948, a national poll asked the French to rank the most important problems confronting the country. The Indochina War was to be found at the end of the list. In 1951, another national poll asked respondents what were their greatest concerns at the time. One out of three Frenchmen said "the cost of meat". Moreover, if at the outset of the war a slight majority of the French population (52 percent) felt that Indochina should be maintained by force of arms, in February 1954 only 7 percent of those polled believed that troops should be sent to re-establish French rule and 60 percent were now in favor a reaching a negotiated solution to the problem or to abandon the former colony altogether. While the **French Communist Party** did much to sensitize French opinion to the ***sale guerre*** or "dirty war", it was the battle for **Dien Bien Phu** that finally brought the forgotten war to French public attention in somewhat cataclysmic terms. *See also* ANTICOLONIALISM; *ESPRIT*; HENRI MARTIN; INTELLECTUALS; *TÉMOIGNAGE CHRÉTIEN*.

**PUBLIC SECURITY SERVICES, DEMOCRATIC REPUBLIC OF VIETNAM (*Công An*).** On coming to power, the **Democratic Republic of Vietnam** (DRV) immediately went to work creating a public security force in order to establish order and guarantee the new state's security as quickly as possible against real and imagined enemies, above all the French and anti-DRV Vietnamese groups. In the north, the DRV created the Bureau of Security Forces for Northern Vietnam (*So Liem Phong Bac Bo*), modeled largely on the French *Sûreté*. Recently liberated from colonial detention in Madagascar, **Le Gian** directed this bureau with **Tran Hieu** serving as his deputy director. The Bureau of Security Forces for Northern Vietnam consisted of a **Scouting** Intelligence Unit (*Ban Trinh Sat*), a Political Bureau (*Phong Chinh Tri*), a Bureau of Legal Administration (*Phong Hanh Chinh Tu Phap*), and a Bureau of Identification (*Phong Can Cuoc*). In central Vietnam, the DRV started more modestly with a simple Scouting Intelligence Service (*So Trinh Sat*). In Nam Bo, the National Defense Guard (*Quoc Gia Tu Ve Cuoc*) came to life under the leadership of **Duong Bach Mai**, **Nguyen Van Tran**, and later **Cao Dang Chiem**. When war broke out below the **16th parallel** in mid-September 1945, part of the Guard was pushed out of **Saigon**-Cholon while the rest went underground.

From the outset, the **Indochinese Communist Party** (ICP) sought to control and to direct these new police services. In charge of this was a discreet man who oversaw the party's own internal security affairs – **Tran Dang Ninh**. He had served time in the famous **Son La** colonial prison before 1945. In 1947 he assumed the leadership of the Control and Inspection Board (*Ban Kiem Tra*) of the Executive Committee of the Central Committee of the ICP. He served as the deputy director of the party's General Inspectorate for the Government (*Tong Thanh Tra Chinh Phu*). He also headed up the Central Committee's own Surveillance Board (*Ban Trinh Sat*) to oversee and coordinate the emerging security services. On 21 February 1946, with Tran Dang Ninh's backing, the government promulgated decree

23 which unified all security and police forces under the Ministry of the Interior. This was the Vietnamese Public Security Department (*Viet Nam Cong An Vu*). Officially Le Gian headed the new department for the government; but he was secretly answerable to the ICP Central Committee via Tran Dang Ninh. The central governing body of the public security force was referred to as the *Nha Cong An Viet Nam*. It stood between the Ministry of the Interior and the two lower levels of this new security administration. The first was the Public Security Services in northern, central, and southern Vietnam (*So Cong An Bac Bo, Trung Bo* and *Nam Bo*) and the second was the provincial Public Security Services (*Ty Cong An*). The Public Security Department was in charge of collecting information and documentation both inside and outside the country that was vital for ensuring national security. Internal security was the priority at the outset. Police forces were mainly concerned with keeping the state alive and protecting it against its internal and external enemies. This meant maintaining law and order, and neutralizing anti-communist opponents, such as the **Greater Vietnam Nationalist Party** (*Dai Viet Quoc Dan* or *Dai Viet*), the **Vietnamese Nationalist Party** (*Viet Nam Quoc Dan Dang*, VNQDD), and the Alliance League (*Dong Minh Hoi*).

The crucial conjuncture in the modernization and professionalization of Vietnamese intelligence occurred in 1950. Between 8 and 15 January 1950, as the **Cold War** bore down on all of Indochina, the fifth countrywide meeting of public security took place in Tuyen Quang. This important meeting approved the revamping of the service in light of the new international situation and the preparations for the general counter-offensive. Directives were issued to train more cadres, step up espionage and counter-espionage activities (even against American and British targets), and develop better intelligence on the counter-revolutionary government coming into being under the direction of **Bao Dai**. This meeting concluded that the public security forces were to maintain order and security, protect the Vietnamese state, and contribute to the independence struggle. In 1953, **Tran Quoc Hoan** took over as head of the newly created Ministry of Public Security. *See also* ANTOINE SAVANI; INTELLIGENCE SERVICES, ARMY OF THE DEMOCRATIC REPUBLIC OF VIETNAM; MARCEL BAZIN; MAURICE BELLEUX; *SERVICE DE DOCUMENTATION EXTÉRIEURE ET CONTRE-ESPIONNAGE*; *SÛRETÉ FÉDÉRALE*.

**PULOCH (LE), LOUIS JEAN ALAIN (1904–1976).** French colonel who made his career in the colonial army in Indochina. In 1922, he entered the *École spéciale militaire* at Saint-Cyr and graduated fourth in his class. In 1924, he served as a second lieutenant in the Colonial Infantry, in charge of a section of Tonkinese *tirailleurs*. In mid-1925, he was put in charge of the *3ème Régiment de Tirailleurs tonkinois* and landed in Haiphong at the end of that year. He returned to France in 1929 and was assigned to the General Staff of the Colonial Infantry at the *École spéciale militaire* at Saint-Cyr. He returned to Indochina in 1935 in charge of the General Staff for the commander-in-chief of French troops in Indochina before being transferred to the *11ème Régiment d'infanterie coloniale* in April 1938. He was back in France in August 1939, part of the *21ème Régiment d'infanterie coloniale*, and detached to the General Staff for the Colonies in the French Colonial ministry. During the Battle of France in mid-1940, he served as a battalion commander in the *11ème Régiment d'infanterie coloniale* before being wounded and taken prisoner. He returned to France in July 1941 and was transferred by Vichy to command colonial troops in Senegal. In 1942, following the Allied Landing in North Africa in November, he crossed over to Free French forces and served in the *9ème Division d'infanterie coloniale*, leading colonial troops in reconnaissance operations in North Africa before taking part in the liberation of France, during which time he was named colonel. After World War II, he briefly served as commander of the colonial section of the General Staff of the National Defense between August 1945 and August 1946, when he returned to Indochina yet again to serve as the personal chief of cabinet to the new high commissioner for Indochina, **Georges Thierry d'Argenlieu** and, apparently from 1947, served in 1948 as commander of French Forces in Southern **Annam** and the Highlands. He left Indochina in October 1949.

**PUTH CHHAY (1917–1954).** Cambodian patriot–brigand who was able to exploit the Indochina War to his advantage. Born into a poor family in Kandal province, he had no formal education. He got into trouble at a young age and was sentenced to prison for the first of several times in 1937. While little is known of his activities during World

War II, he appeared before a French colonial court again in early 1947 for running a gambling house. He regained his freedom in March 1948 at which time he joined up with **Khmer Issarak** and **Democratic Republic of Vietnam** (DRV) groups operating in Kandal province. The French charged him with murdering a policeman and three undercover agents; a price of 10,000 piastres was put on his head. His relationship with local representatives of the DRV had become equally strained by May 1949, when Puth Chhay launched attacks against Vietnamese living peacefully in Cambodia. Things got so tense that, in 1950, he offered to cross over to the King of Cambodia's side, if he could continue to "rule" Kandal as his home fiefdom. **Norodom Sihanouk** refused and raised the price on his head. It was only in August 1953 that Puth Chhay surrendered to King Sihanouk and a deal was cut, though the details are unknown. *See also* BINH XUYEN; CRIME; LE VAN VIEN.

**PUY-MONTBRUN (DU), DÉODAT (1920–2009).** French **commando** and intelligence officer who helped develop the use of the **helicopter** during the Indochina War. He left Saint-Cyr before graduating in order to fight against the German invasion of Belgium and France in 1940. He was wounded seriously in combat before the Germans took him prisoner in Belgium. He escaped and returned secretly to Toulouse where he became a *résistant* and began work in the emerging resistance intelligence service created in 1940, the *Bureau central de renseignements et d'action*. After the war, he entered the ***Service Action*** of the newly created French external intelligence service, the ***Service de documentation extérieure et de contre-espionnage*** (SDECE). He joined the famous *11ème choc*, created in 1946, to implement clandestine operations for the SDECE. He volunteered for service in Indochina and made three tours of duty there. He served between 1947 and 1950 in the *Troupes Aéroportées d'Indochine*. Between 1951 and 1952, he was an aide-de-camp to General **Jean de Lattre de Tassigny** and played a role in creating the ***Groupement de commandos mixtes aéroportés***. He took part in numerous commando raids all over Indochina. In October and November 1952, he was part of a mission to British Malaya where he worked within the ranks of the British 22nd **Special Air Service**, in charge of developing and carrying out counterinsurgency operations against communist guerrillas there. On his third tour of duty in Indochina between 1953 and 1954, he served as deputy to Captain Crespin, who created the *Groupement des formations d'hélicoptères de l'Armée de terre en Indochine*. Puy-Montbrun commanded the 1st Helicopter Company in charge of medical evacuations. He also led one of the first airborne commando operations using helicopters to drop units in the field (something which was still very rare and would only truly be developed intensively during the Algerian and Vietnam Wars). He served in the **Algerian War** and wrote two novels on his experiences in Indochina and Algeria: *Les chemins sans croix* (1964) and *L'honneur de la guerre* (2002).

**QUÁCH VĨNH CHƯƠNG.** *See* QUÁCH VŨ.

**QUÁCH VŨ (QUÁCH VĨNH CHƯƠNG, 1922–1966).** Born in the southern province of Bac Lieu, this musician worked for the **Democratic Republic of Vietnam**'s *Voice of Nam Bo* and the Information Service of Nam Bo. During the war, he traveled throughout war **Zones VIII** (*Khu VIII*) and **IX** collecting folklore and songs as part of the cultural and nationalist front in the war against the French.

**QUÂN ỦY.** *See* CENTRAL PARTY MILITARY COMMITTEE.

**QUANG ĐÀM.** A former scout-master who held important position in the **Democratic Republic of Vietnam**'s decrypting and communications services. In late August 1945, **Vo Nguyen Giap** assigned Quang Dam to work with the rudimentary bureau of communications run by **Hoang Dao Thuy**, a fellow scout. From 12 September 1945, Quang Dam headed up the Encryption Service (*Phong Mat Ma*), creating the codes and communication network used by the army and its **General Staff**. Following the signing of the **Accords of 6 March 1946**, Vo Nguyen Giap made him a colonel and assigned him to the Franco-Vietnamese liaison team sent to oversee the replacement of Chinese troops by their French counterparts. During the Indochina War, he worked secretly in the party's communications and radio service in the **Secure Zone** (*An Toan Khu*) in northern Vietnam.

**QUANG TRUNG, BATTLE OF.** *See* DAY, BATTLE OF.

**QUERVILLE, JEAN-MARIE (1903–1967).** French naval officer who served in Indochina during most of the war. Graduated from the French Naval Academy in 1925, he served in the **Navy** submarine section until 1939 when he moved on to Indochina and made lieutenant. He worked as a liaison officer with the British in Singapore at the time of the Franco-German armistice in June 1940. In September 1940, he crossed over to Free French forces in Great Britain, was promoted to lieutenant commander and attached to the General Staff of the ***Deuxième Bureau*** of Free French naval forces in London. He held numerous important posts in the Free French Navy during World War II and participated in the Allied Landing at Normandy in 1944, debarking American ground troops at Omaha Beach. In 1945, he was promoted to the rank of captain and took command of the warship *Suffren* in Indochina in 1946. In 1947, he was put in charge of the naval forces for **Tonkin**. In 1951, named rear admiral, he served as the commander-in-chief of the Naval Division for the Far East. In 1953, he led the Navy in North Vietnam before organizing the evacuation of Vietnamese refugees (mainly Catholics) from northern to southern Vietnam. During the **Algerian War**, he joined the *Organisation armée secrète* and was retired in 1962 with the rank of Admiral.

**QUILICHINI, ROBERT (1912–1979).** Graduated from the *École spéciale militaire* at Saint-Cyr in 1932, he began his military command in the *4ème Régiment de tirailleurs sénégalais*. He transferred to Indochina in June 1933, where he joined the *9ème Régiment d'infanterie coloniale*. He left Indochina with the rank of lieutenant in 1936. He was in Senegal when World War II broke out, crossed into British Nigeria, and began working with **Henri Laurentie** and Free French forces within the General Staff of General **Philippe Leclerc.** In 1944, he became battalion leader and took command of the 1st Office of the 2nd Armored Division's General Staff and participated in the liberation of France. Following the war, in 1945, he received the command of *Troupes françaises de Chine au Yunnan* and had led a contingent of some 3,000 troops into northern Indochina by late December 1945, before an accord was signed between the French and the **Republic of China** allowing French troops to enter Indochina above the **16th parallel**. He left Indochina in late 1946 but returned in 1953 to command the *zone autonome du Nord-Ouest*, the sector of Son Tay in northern Vietnam, and *Groupe Mobile no. 7*. In November 1954, he transferred to the *Inspection des forces terrestres d'Extrême-Orient* and left Indochina for good in June 1955.

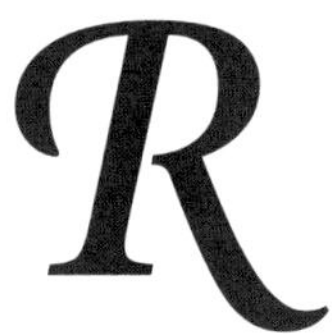

**RADFORD, ARTHUR WILLIAM (1896–1973).** American naval officer who served in World War I before becoming a navy pilot and working himself up to executive officer of the carrier *Yorktown* in 1941. During World War II, he trained thousands of pilots for the navy's rapidly developing air branch. He became rear admiral in 1943, commanding Carrier Division 11. He participated in the attack against the Japanese in the Wake and Gilbert Islands in 1943. After a stint in Washington, he returned to sea duty in November 1944 and participated as commander of Carrier Division 6 in the invasions of Iwo Jima and Okinawa. After the war, in January 1946, he became deputy chief of naval operations for air and took over the Second Task Fleet in the Atlantic in 1947 before becoming commander of the Pacific Fleet in 1948. During the **Korean War**, he remained commander of the Pacific Fleet and supervised naval operations. In 1953, **Dwight D. Eisenhower** named him chairman of the Joint Chiefs of Staff, impressed by his experience in Asia, anti-communist credentials, and firm position towards communist China. In early 1954, as the **Democratic Republic of Vietnam** (DRV) prepared to throw everything it had, including large amounts of artillery, against the French camp at **Dien Bien Phu**, Radford strongly supported the idea of an American air intervention to save the besieged **French Union** forces there. He worked closely with French General **Paul Ely** on what the French called operation **Vautour**. On 22 March 1954, as DRV artillery rained down on the French camp, Ely met with President Eisenhower in the presence of Radford. The latter's plan was to send some 60 B-29 heavy bombers to pound DRV positions at Dien Bien Phu. Radford suggested that the French government send a direct request to the U.S. government along such lines. The French ran with the idea until it became clear that operation Vautour was not going to fly because of Congressional hostility to direct American military intervention.

**RAMADIER, PAUL (1888–1961).** Leader of the ***Section française de l'Internationale ouvrière*** (SFIO) in France at various intervals during the Indochina War. He voted against according "full powers" to Philippe Pétain in 1940 and entered the French resistance. Re-elected to his seat in parliament after World War II, Ramadier served as minister of Justice in **Léon Blum**'s cabinet between December 1946 and January 1947. He succeeded Blum on 21 January 1947, at the head of a fragile coalition government ruled by the SFIO, the **French Communist Party**, and the ***Mouvement républicain populaire***. He remained in power until November 1947. Before his communist ministers resigned in May, Ramadier obtained the vote in the National Assembly to finance the war in Indochina. While he was willing to consider colonial reform, he was opposed to decolonization. He remained a firm believer, like his socialist minister of Overseas France, **Maurius Moutet**, in the **French Union** as a means of maintaining the French Empire and national prestige. *See also* INDOCHINESE FEDERATION; TORTURE.

**RAPHAËL-LEYGUES, JACQUES (1913–1994).** French general commissioner for the **Navy**, he worked in Indochina between 1945 and 1950. Between 1950 and 1958, he served as advisor to the **French Union**. He was favorable to a negotiated solution to the Indochina War, and criticized in November 1950 the "childish Machiavelism" of French policy. In late 1952, he was charged with a mission to open secret contacts with the **Democratic Republic of Vietnam** via **Burma**. To no effect. The French government sent him back to Indochina in 1958 to size up the possibilities for a continued French cultural presence in the former colony. He then served as ambassador to the Ivory Coast for much of the rest of his diplomatic career. In 1976, he published an account of his work in Indochina, *Ponts de lianes*.

**RAVIX, LAURENT (1921–1992).** Joined Free French forces in England in the summer of 1940 and distinguished himself in combat in North Africa and especially in Strasbourg. At the end of the war, he left the army and joined the civil colonial service. He graduated from the **Colonial**

**Academy** (*École coloniale*) and began his colonial career in Indochina. He first served as an administrative liaison representative in the Far East. Between 1946 and 1949, he worked as an advisor to the provincial unit known as the *Sud-des-Lacs*. Between 1949 and 1953, he transferred to southern Vietnam where he administered Chinese Affairs within the cabinet of the Commissioner for the French Republic to Southern Vietnam. He then transferred to the High Commissioner's Office for Indochina to serve as deputy to the diplomatic counselor.

**RAYMOND (DE), JEAN LÉON FRANÇOIS MARIE (1907–1951).** Career colonial civil and military officer in Indochina. The son of a general, de Raymond entered Saint-Cyr in 1925 and graduated two years later. He entered the Regiment of Senegalese *tirailleurs* based in Toulon. In 1929, he began 16 years of service in the colonial infantry in Indochina, serving mainly in the north. In 1933, de Raymond studied Vietnamese at the School for Indochinese Languages in Toulouse. He returned to Indochina in 1934 as the aide-de-camp to General Philippot in **Hanoi**, all the while studying law. Between 1935 and 1938, he served as an administrative delegate in Quang Nguyen, Ta Lung, and Tra Linh along the Sino-Vietnamese border. In 1938–39, he entered the *École supérieure de guerre*. Following the armistice in 1940, he passed the examination to become a colonial civil servant and joined the Ministry of Colonies of Vichy. In 1944, he was still involved in colonial affairs, but he now worked for the Ministry of Overseas France of the Provisional Government of the French Republic. How he shifted from one regime to the other remains unclear. He served the Provisional Government as deputy to the Director of Political Affairs, **Léon Pignon**. In 1945, de Raymond returned to Indochina via Calcutta as the head of the *Mission coloniale française en Extrême-Orient*. He was deputy director of Political Affairs (under Pignon) for the high commissioner to Indochina, **Georges Thierry d'Argenlieu**. De Raymond discreetly met with **Ho Chi Minh**, **Norodom Sihanouk**, and **Bao Dai** among others in a bid to re-establish French sovereignty over Indochina. He declared in January 1946 that the French would not deal with the **Lao Issara** government created in October 1945. Like Pignon and Thierry d'Argenlieu, he opposed the decolonization of Indochina and became increasingly hostile to the **Democratic Republic of Vietnam** (DRV). Between April 1946 and July 1947, he served as commissioner for the Republic to Laos and participated in the French reoccupation of Laos under Colonel **Jean Boucher de Crèvecoeur** in March–April 1946. He subsequently returned to France where he worked on the study commission for the creation of the **French Union** and served as deputy director of Political Affairs in the Ministry of Overseas France. In February 1949, now a colonial governor, he became commissioner for the Republic to Cambodia and served as a member of the French delegation at the signing of the Franco-Cambodian treaty in Paris in 1949. His superiors greatly appreciated his knowledge of and contact with Cambodian elites. His adversaries did not. De Raymond was assassinated by his servant, a Vietnamese agent working for the DRV, on 29 October 1951. On that day, de Raymond was to welcome **Son Ngoc Thanh** back to Cambodia.

**RECTIFICATION (*Chỉnh Huấn*).** Like **land reform**, the application of "rectification" in the **Democratic Republic of Vietnam** (DRV) resulted from the decision of Vietnamese communists in 1950 to align themselves with the communist bloc in general and the Chinese version in particular. Indeed, *cheng feng*, as it is known in Chinese, was something of a Maoist speciality. The Great Helmsman had used it effectively at Yan'an in his indoctrination of the Chinese Communist Party's inner circle, including both political and military cadres.

The main goal of rectification is "reform" (*chinh*) and "instruction" (*huan*) of good elements in the Party. *Chinh huan* was central to shaping likeminded, reliable cadres in the army (*chinh quan*), the Party (*chinh dang*), and mass organizations (*chinh don to chuc*). Rectification was dispensed in sessions in Party schools before being diffused throughout society under the Party leadership via its selected cadres. In these courses, cadres inculcated the major party themes and ideology (land reform, communist theory, new heroes, ideological texts, etc.) starting with ranking and mid-level cadres before working their way down to the local district, even the village levels in territories under DRV control. Cadres then citizens were forced to make rectification "retreats", cut off from the outside, in order to concentrate entirely on readings, exercises, critiques, and auto-critiques.

The main goal of the rectification campaign, as **Georges Boudarel** has described it, was to give rise to an epiphany, a conversion to the Party family and its ideology. For Maoists, rectification allowed the Party to change the ideas, customs, and thinking of its disciples. This type of "education" did not seek to inspire critical or analytical skills, but rather to homogenize thinking and place it under the control of the Party. In order to paralyze attempts at individual thinking, rectification campaigns used group pressure run by a political cadre, backed by police or military force. The cadre teacher could thus force individuals to examine their conscience and confess their shortcomings via self-criticism (*kiem thao*) before being reborn into the wider collective identity.

If **Ho Chi Minh** was uncomfortable with these radical Maoist methods (and new research suggests that this might not have been the case), others in his entourage embraced them as part of the communist recipe. General **Nguyen Son**, who had become a Maoist political cadre in the Chinese Red Army during the Long March and at Yan'an, first applied rectification methods upon his return to Vietnam to work in **inter-zone IV** (*Lien Khu IV*) in the late 1940s. During its second Party congress in early 1951, the newly reborn **Vietnam Worker's Party** openly allied itself with the Chinese methods of rectification, land reform, and new heroes. However, the real intermediaries in the transfer of Maoist rectification practices to Vietnam were the **Chinese Political and Military Advisor Delegations.**

In the spring of 1952, the Vietnamese communist leadership formally approved the launching of rectification campaigns and began organizing sessions for the Party and the army mainly in northern and central areas of the DRV. As the Party consolidated its hold over the DRV, it became increasingly difficult for non-communists working in the state or army to hold out. This was especially the case for independent-minded and colonially trained intellectuals, thousands of whom were working for the DRV on nationalist and anti-colonial grounds. Hundreds began to leave the DRV in the face of this communization of Vietnamese hearts and minds.

Like land reform, the application of Maoist methods could have disastrous effects in the Vietnamese context. The Vietnamese army's Security Department (*Cuc Bao Ve*) has recently acknowledged that in April 1952 the Vietnamese Worker's Party decided to undertake a political "reform" of the army. When it was applied to the Army Officers School operating in Yunnan province in southern China, for example, 4,000 trainees ended up "admitting" under pressure that they were working for the "enemy" or had entertained such connections in the past. This wave of political reform in the army led to a total of 20,000 personnel in the armed forces either admitting or being accused of working for the enemy. While investigations revealed that most of these "admissions" were fabrications designed to placate their accusers, it was clear that the Vietnamese communists, like the Chinese, were intent on politicizing the army, the state, and society. *See also* TORTURE; PSYCHOLOGICAL WARFARE; PROSELYTIZING THE ENEMY; LE THIET HUNG; DESERTION; TRUONG CHINH; INDOCTRINATION; PARALLEL HIERARCHIES.

**RED CROSS.** The Indochina War marked one of the first times the International Committee of the Red Cross (ICRC) became involved in a full-blown war of decolonization. The Red Cross is an international humanitarian organization set up in Europe in the late 19[th] century to assist civilian victims of war as well as to tend to prisoners of war.

In January 1947, following the **Haiphong incident** and the outbreak of full-scale war in Indochina on **19 December 1946**, the Red Cross representative to Indochina, **Charles Aeschlimann**, traveled to Vietnam on behalf of the ICRC to establish contact with civilian and military prisoners of war taken by both belligerents. A specialist in Asia and a man of contacts, Aeschlimann quickly entered into negotiations with **Democratic Republic of Vietnam** (DRV) and French authorities, both of which were reluctant to welcome the Red Cross's presence. While the French argued that this was not a war but an internal security problem, they eventually allowed Aeschlimann to visit Vietnamese prisoners. DRV authorities also allowed Aeschlimann to visit a prisoner camp in Hoa Binh, holding 171 Europeans.

Although Aeschlimann succeeded in gaining the liberation of 29 persons from DRV authorities in early 1947, he had little success thereafter. The DRV was wary of the Red Cross's logistical reliance on the French and possible manipulation by them. With the intensification of the war in 1950, Aeschlimann redoubled his overtures to the DRV to allow the Red Cross to contact the increasing number of **French Union** prisoners. In early 1951, during a visit to **Hanoi**, the ICRC's Paul Ruegger made a radio appeal to **Ho Chi Minh** calling upon the Vietnamese president to allow the Red Cross to provide medical aid to the prisoners. The DRV Red Cross accepted the offer and a meeting occurred outside Hanoi on 26 July 1951 and another in October of that year. However, the DRV rebuffed the Red Cross's requests to establish a physical presence in DRV territory in order to administer exchanges between prisoners and their families, as well as requests to distribute relief. While the DRV broadcast messages from prisoners to their families, the Vietnamese remained wary and un-cooperative. Meanwhile, the French allowed the Red Cross to visit Vietnamese prisoners held by the French in some prisons. It made some 30 visits a year in 1952–53.

Aware of Vietnamese distrust of the organization's reliance on the French, the Red Cross attempted to go through less colonial channels, via the DRV's diplomatic posts in Rangoon, Bangkok, and even Beijing, but to no avail. No Red Cross delegate was able to visit DRV territory. During the battle of **Dien Bien Phu**, the Red Cross failed also to establish a truce between the belligerents. The French accused the Vietnamese of illegally shooting at planes clearly identifiable as belonging to the Red Cross, while the Vietnamese accused the French of flying in arms secretly on those planes. On 27 March 1954, the Red Cross officially responded that according to the Geneva Convention of 1949, "the protection of medical planes is dependent on an agreement between the belligerents". However, General **Vo Nguyen Giap** never approved such an agreement. In terms of international law, the DRV's firing upon the medical planes did not technically violate the Geneva Convention.

In the end, the Red Cross's experience in the Indochina War was a trying one. The organization was unable to tend to prisoners taken during the battle of Dien Bien Phu or to negotiate their return. Morever, the Red Cross's effectiveness was limited by the fact that it could only work with one of the belligerents. The Red Cross did, however, play an important role in organizing relief for hundreds of thousands of Vietnamese deciding to leave North Vietnam for the south following the signing of the **Geneva Accords** of July 1954. The Red Cross's experience in Indochina did awaken it, too, to the unique difficulties of working in wars of decolonization as they moved westwards from Asia to Africa. In 1957, following the signing of the Geneva Accords and the emergence of two Vietnams, the Red Cross recalled its delegate to the DRV. This was something of a mistake since Hanoi refused to accept a new delegate until May 1974. *See also* CATHOLICS, EXODUS FROM NORTH; INTERNATIONAL COMMISSION FOR SUPERVISION AND CONTROL IN VIETNAM; MIGRATION; PRISONERS OF WAR; REFUGEES, FRANCE; REGROUPING TO THE NORTH.

**RED CROSS, DEMOCRATIC REPUBLIC OF VIETNAM.** The first Vietnamese Red Cross (*Hoi Hong Thap Tu*) emerged in 1945, when Vietnamese members of the former French Red Cross branch in **Hanoi** began to transform it into a postcolonial one. In mid-1945, dozens of volunteers, many of them women, spontaneously joined together to tend as best they could to the thousands of starving Vietnamese flooding into Hanoi because of the **famine**. Upon coming to power in September, the **Democratic Republic of Vietnam** (DRV) supported the Red Cross's activities. This was especially the case as relations between the French and the Vietnamese soured and war became increasingly likely from mid-1946. When local Vietnamese Red Cross leaders complained to **Ho Chi Minh** that they wanted to change the name of the association in order to break with its colonial past, Ho Chi Minh advised them against it, pointing out that what mattered most was its work and the fact that the Red Cross was also an internationally recognized humanitarian organization and name. On 23 November 1946, the Association of the Vietnamese Red Cross came to life. Vu Dinh Tung, minister of War Invalids was president and Nguyen Thi Thinh, wife of Dr. **Do Xuan Hop**, became vice president. Vietnamese Red Cross workers risked their lives tending to wounded soldiers during the battle of Hanoi. While no study of the colonial or postcolonial Vietnamese Red Cross exists, it is quite clear that as early as 1945–1947 Vietnamese participation in this organization during the famine of 1944–1945 and during the DRV's short presence in **Saigon** and especially Hanoi in 1945–1947 contributed to a growing sense of modern civic duty. The nature of the Red Cross in the Associated State and Republic of Vietnam remains unknown.

**REDON (DE), RAOUL GUILLAUME HENRI (1908–1997).** Graduated from the ***École nationale des langues orientales vivantes*** and the *Institut d'ethnologie*, in 1933 he joined the colonial civil service in Indochina. Between 1933 and 1946, he served as deputy to the *résidents supérieurs* in Vinh, Thanh Hoa, Hue, and Thua Thien. After World War II, he briefly served as mayor and chief of the province of Vientiane in Laos. Between 1951 and 1952, he returned to central Vietnam to work as the chief of cabinet for the commissioner for the Republic for central Vietnam before returning to France to work in the French ministry in charge of relations with the **Associated States of Indochina** between 1952 and 1954.

**REDON, MAURICE PAUL (1905–2000).** Graduated from Saint-Cyr in 1926 and served in the colonial armies in Indochina and Madagascar during the interwar period. He first worked in Indochina in the Geographical Service between 1929 and 1931. He returned to France in 1932 and taught at the Artillery Academy at Fontainebleau. He was taken prisoner during the Battle of France in 1940, but escaped to southern France in September 1940. Vichy dispatched him to colonial Africa where he worked until he joined the *Forces françaises d'l'intérieur* (FFI) following the Allied liberation of North Africa. In 1944, he was head of the FFI within the 2nd corps of the 1st French Army under the command of **Jean de Lattre de Tassigny**. In May 1945, the French government named Redon a special advisor to the delegation to the Franco-Siamese negotiations in Washington. He served in Indochina between 1948 and 1950, during which time he headed the Western Zone in southern Vietnam and the *Zone opérationnelle du Tonkin*. General de Lattre recalled him to Indochina in 1951. Between 1951 and early 1953, Redon was deputy commander of French Troops to North Vietnam and the *Zone opérationnelle du Tonkin*. He led the *Forces du Laos* and briefly directed the *Mission militaire française* in **Saigon**. Between June 1954 and February 1955, he was the chief of staff to minister of Overseas France Robert Buron.

**REED, CHARLES SHADRACH, 2nd (1898–1973)**. American diplomat and consul in **Saigon** at the start of the Indochina War. Graduated from Harvard University and Law School, Reed was admitted to the Ohio State Bar in 1925. After working with a rubber company in Sumatra between 1925 and 1927, he entered the Foreign Service in 1927. He served in Tokyo, Kunming, Shanghai, Belgrade, Beijing, and was consul at Saigon (on detail at **Hanoi**) between 20 July 1939 and 7 December 1941. He returned to the United States and was re-assigned to Canada and Spain. In September 1945, he returned to Asia as Deputy Political Advisor Commanding General, India–Burma Theater, before being dispatched to Saigon to take up his new assignment as consul at this same date. In early 1946, the United States Department of State authorized Reed to open a consulate in Saigon accredited to the French government, as well as the first United States Information Service Office there. Despite French efforts to limit American influence, the cultural center was a real success with the Vietnamese. Several thousand Vietnamese were said to the use the American library each month and American films and popular culture attracted younger crowds. Reed left his position as consul on 25 November 1947 and returned to the U.S. early the following year. In April 1948, he became chief of the Division of South East Asia Affairs in the Department of State and, in October 1949, Director, Office of Philippine and Southeast Asia Affairs. During this time, he was involved in American policy-making towards Vietnam, Laos, and Cambodia. He ended his long association with Asia when the State Department reassigned him to Italy in February 1950.

**REESE, EVERETTE DIXIE (1923–1955).** American army photographer who covered World War II for the *Houston Post*. He travelled to **Saigon** in 1951 for the forerunner of the United States Information Agency covering political, military, and cultural affairs in Indochina. He photographed the preparations of the French battle of **Dien Bien Phu** as well as the exodus of hundreds of thousands of northern Vietnamese to the south after the signing of the **Geneva Accords**. He died in a plane crash over Cholon in 1955.

**REFUGEES, VIETNAMESE.** *See* CATHOLICS, EXODUS FROM NORTH; MIGRATION; REFUGEES, FRANCE; REGROUPING TO THE NORTH.

**REGNIER, ROBERT.** Served as French Commissioner for Laos between December 1949 and April 1953.

**REGROUPING TO THE NORTH (*Tập Kết Ra Bắc*).** In accordance with the **Geneva Accords** of July 1954, the **Democratic Republic of Vietnam** agreed to regroup its soldiers heretofore located in southern Indochina (including Cambodia) to areas in Vietnam located above the newly established partition line at the **17th parallel**. Between 80 and 90,000 individuals moved to northern Vietnam in the wake of the signing of the Geneva Accords. However, the **Vietnamese Workers' Party** (VWP) authorized some 5 to 10,000 cadres to remain secretly in southern Vietnam and Cambodia in the event that war resumed. In September 1954, **Le Duan** returned to the south to oversee the relocation of soldiers and cadres to the north and to decide who stayed on and how the Party's Territorial Committee for the South would operate in the new circumstances. Sometime in January 1955, as the relocation process wound down, Le Duan boarded the Polish ship *Kilinski* to escort high-ranking communists to North Vietnam. However, with the agreement of the Polish skipper, Le Duan left the boat secretly in the middle of the night and secretly returned to southern Vietnam to continue running the party's clandestine affairs. A handful of Cambodian allies of the DRV/VWP, including **Son Ngoc Minh**, also relocated to **Hanoi** at this time. Most, however, remained in Cambodia, where they demobilized and laid down their arms. *See also* REFUGEES, FRANCE; CATHOLICS IN VIETNAM AND THE WAR; CATHOLICS, EXODUS FROM NORTH; REPATRIATION, JAPANESE TROOPS.

**RELIGION AND WAR.** *See* CAO DAI; HOA HAO; CATHOLICS IN VIETNAM AND THE WAR; CATHOLICS, EXODUS FROM NORTH; CHRISTIANS AND FRENCH OPPOSITION TO THE WAR.

**REMAINS, DEMOCRATIC REPUBLIC OF VIETNAM.** Since the end of the American War in Vietnam in 1975, and especially since the application of the policy of *doi moi* or "renovation" in 1986, Vietnamese authorities and families have accelerated their attempts to locate the remains of civilians and soldiers killed in the Indochina War. American efforts to locate their "**missing in action**" (MIA) in the 1980s and 1990s also made this an issue for the Vietnamese communist side. In 1993, the Vietnamese spoke of 300,000 MIAs for the Vietnam War. The government has never released the number of MIAs stemming from the Indochina War. This has not stopped Vietnamese friends and family from trying to locate their loved ones. And given the importance of this domestic issue, the government is now deeply involved. In December 2003, local residents working in collaboration with the Kontum Province Military Headquarters and the Province Veterans Association located graves of dozens of soldiers killed during the battle of Mang Den in January 1954. Increasingly sophisticated scientific methods, especially forensic methods for DNA testing, are being used to identify the remains found across former French Indochina. The Bio-Industry Institute of the National Industrial and Natural Sciences Center is currently establishing a data bank to identify the remains of unknown soldiers, and is now capable of identifying hundreds of cases each year. Relatives of missing soldiers and civilians provide information about their loved ones and supply blood samples for use in DNA identification. The MIA issue became a particularly important one following the 1991 Party congress, when veterans groups and Party members forced the Party to take concrete action to help family members and veterans recover their loved ones' remains. *See also* REMAINS, FRENCH UNION; CAM LY, MASSACRE; CEMETERIES; PENSION; MYTH OF WAR; EXPERIENCE OF WAR; LOVE AND WAR; LANGUAGE OF WAR; MEMORIAL DAY, INDOCHINA WAR; MARTYR; WAR MEMORIAL, DIEN BIEN PHU; ASSOCIATION OF MOTHERS OF SOLDIERS; *ASSOCIATION NATIONALE DES ANCIENS D'INDOCHINE ET DU SOUVENIR INDOCHINOIS*; *ASSOCIATION NATIONALE DES ANCIENS ET AMIS DE L'INDOCHINE ET DU SOUVENIR INDOCHINOIS*; *ASSOCIATION NATIONALE DES COMBATTANTS DE DIEN BIEN PHU*; NECROPOLIS; MEMORIAL CAO BANG; *ASSOCIATION NATIONALE DES ANCIENS PRISONNIERS INTERNÉS D'INDOCHINE*; COMICS AND WAR.

**REMAINS, ASSOCIATED STATE OF VIETNAM.** *See* REMAINS, FRENCH UNION; NECROPOLIS; ARMY, ASSOCIATED STATE OF VIETNAM.

**REMAINS, FRENCH UNION.** The **Geneva Accords** ending the Indochina War in July 1954 contained a clause obliging the belligerants to search, locate, and exhume the remains of soldiers killed during the war. The French authorities and those of the **Democratic Republic of Vietnam** (DRV) signed "protocol no. 24" on 1 February 1955, allowing for the location and regrouping of remains and the erection of necropolises to hold them throughout all of Vietnam, meaning the DRV above the **17th parallel** and the State of Vietnam (the **Republic of Vietnam** from October 1955) below that line. The remains of DRV personnel were to be relocated to the north while those of the State of Vietnam were to be transferred to the south.

However, because the State of Vietnam led by **Ngo Dinh Diem** and **Bao Dai** was not privy to this protocol (or the Geneva convention) and because the State of Vietnam refused to allow DRV search teams access to its territory, the DRV retaliated in July 1955 by denying the French the right to dispatch search teams to its territory. Negotiations on this delicate subject resumed on 14 December 1959, when an agreement was signed by the French and the DRV authorities allowing for the repatriation of 213 remains and the relinquishing by the French of three cemeteries in Bac Ninh provinces. The French agreed to transfer the remains held in these cemeteries to a new necropolis to be built at French expense. In all, some 30,000 bodies had to be regrouped and moved to a necropolis where they would await eventual repatriation to France. However, the agreement did not require DRV compliance and the war with the Americans took priority over everything else. Between 1954 and 1975, the French only repatriated 1,200 bodies, leaving over 25,000 remains in Vietnam.

After the unification of the country and the establishment of the Socialist Republic of Vietnam in 1976, these cemeteries and others (home to missionaries and colonial figures and families) fell into disrepair, so much so that French authorities decide to repatriate the remains of the **French Union** soldiers killed in the Indochina War as well as Indochinese soldiers allied with the French who had never been claimed by their Vietnamese, Lao, or Cambodian families. On 10 October 1986, then Prime Minister Jacques Chirac personally went to Roissy airport to receive the first coffins. Within a year, some 25,000 remains were transferred to France. Except for those claimed by their families, most of the remains representing the French Union were inhumed at the Indochina War **necropolis** at Fréjus.

Between 1954 and 1956, French authorities transferred hundreds of unclaimed Lao and Cambodians killed during the war to **Saigon** before moving most of them them to France from the late 1980s. That said, individual families repatriated hundreds of remains in the 1960s and 1970s without government assistance. The French Ministry of Veteran Affairs reported that in all 24,632 remains were repatriated at this time, of which 17,830 were those of soldiers killed in the line of duty, 3,407 were soldiers who died for other reasons, and 3,395 were civilians who had died in Indochina. *See also* MEMORIAL DAY, INDOCHINA WAR; MISSING IN ACTION; COMICS AND WAR; BOUDAREL AFFAIR; REMAINS, DEMOCRATIC REPUBLIC OF VIETNAM; CAM LY, MASSACRE; CEMETERIES; MYTH OF WAR; EXPERIENCE OF WAR; LOVE AND WAR; LANGUAGE OF WAR; MARTYR; WAR MEMORIAL, DIEN BIEN PHU; ASSOCIATION OF MOTHERS OF SOLDIERS; *ASSOCIATION NATIONALE DES ANCIENS D'INDOCHINE ET DU SOUVENIR INDOCHINOIS*; *ASSOCIATION NATIONALE DES ANCIENS ET AMIS DE L'INDOCHINE ET DU SOUVENIR INDOCHINOIS*; *ASSOCIATION NATIONALE DES COMBATTANTS DE DIEN BIEN PHU*; *ASSOCIATION NATIONALE DES ANCIENS PRISONNIERS INTERNÉS D'INDOCHINE*; MEMORIAL CAO BANG.

***RENDEZ-VOUS DES QUAIS***. Film made by Paul Carpita in 1953 about the strikes organized by militant French communist dockers in Marseilles against the Indochina War in 1950. While his story revolves around the activities of a young communist couple dedicated to the strike, Carpita links the smashing of the strike on the waterfront to the government's war in Indochina through shots of returning coffins and departing soldiers for Indochina. On 12 August 1955, the French Ministry of Industry and Trade in charge of Information banned the film. The ministry claimed the film's message constituted a "threat to order", but the film also coincided with the government's involvement in yet another colonial war, that of Algeria. The son of a docker, Carpita was a militant in the CGT or *Confédération générale du Travail* and the **French Communist Party** at the time of the making of his film. The film was openly shown in France in 1990, the first time since its banning by the government. Jean-Pierre Daniel had stumbled across it in the *Archives de Bois d'Arcy*. *See also* ALGERIAN WAR; CINEMA; NOVELS; CULTURE; INTELLECTUALS; PUBLIC OPINION; MYTH OF WAR; PIERRE SCHOENDOERFFER.

**REPATRIATION, FRANCE**. Refers to the approximately 35,000 people the French government repatriated to the metropole after 1954. In 1956, two years after the signing of the **Geneva Accords** and faced with Ngo Dinh Diem's new citizenship laws, the French repatriated more than 20,000 ***Français d'Indochine*** – literally, "French from Indochina" – to receiving camps in France called *Centres d'accueil des Français d'Indochine* (CAFI). Most of the Europeans and naturalized citizens had the financial means and family connections to support themselves upon arrival in France. Three of the most important repatriation centers were located in Noyant d'Allier, with 1,700 people, including 740 children; 700 in Bias (Lot-et-Garonne); and 1,200 located in Sainte-Livrade-sur-Lot (Lot-et-Garonne).

Most of these *Français d'Indochine* included the ethnic Vietnamese wives of French soldiers and administrators as well as their ***métis*** children. It appears that they were referred to as *Français d'Indochine* by the fact that they possessed or acquired French citizenship upon arriving in France. The French minister of the Interior provided each family with a small apartment, cooking utensils, and some clothes. These *Français d'Indochine* worked in local shops and industries. A French missionary who had long lived and worked in Indochina even tended to their religious needs since many of them were Catholics. While the children and grandchildren studied in CAFI schools, many went on to higher education and successful careers, returning regularly to visit their parents in these camps. As of 2010, some of these families were still living in the grounds of the *Centre d'accueil* in Sainte-Livrade-sur-Lot.

In contrast to the compensation provided to the "*Harkis*" of the Algerian War, few of these Indochinese families received such benefits from the French state. However, emboldened by the example of the *Harkis*, since the late 1990s many of the children of the *Français d'Indochine* filed for compensation of 30,000€ from the French government. This also led to a greater awareness of the plight of the *Français d'Indochine*, symbolized by the creation of the *Association art et culture d'Indochine* at Sainte-Livrade, the organization of conferences on their history, and the establishment of the *Association des résidents et amis du CAFI*. This mobilization of the CAFI and the memory of the "forgotten" *Français d'Indochine* was also linked to a wider debate in France over its colonial past. Created in May 2002, the *Mission interministérielle aux rapatriés* (MIR) recognized that the *Français d'Indochine* in the CAFI had been forgotten unjustly. The president of the MIR stated that this would change with the preparation of a new law designed to recognize and promote the work and the memory of all the French coming from the former colonies. But the cause of the *Français d'Indochine* seems to have taken second place to that of the many more who fled Algeria in 1962. The first draft of the bill introduced on 11 June 2004 to recognize the memory and accomplishments of the French coming from the colonies failed to mention those from Indochina. A deputy from Allier, home to one of the first of the CAFI, corrected this problem in the second bill.

Since the 1950s, some 1.5 million overseas French have been repatriated to the home country and have received 14.2 billion euros in compensation. It is unclear how much of that sum the *Français d'Indochine* have received. *See also* MYTH OF WAR; CATHOLICS IN VIETNAM AND THE WAR; CATHOLICS, EXODUS FROM NORTH; REGROUPING TO THE NORTH; WAR MEMORIAL, DIEN BIEN PHU; ASSOCIATION OF MOTHERS OF SOLDIERS; *ASSOCIATION NATIONALE DES ANCIENS D'INDOCHINE ET DU SOUVENIR INDOCHINOIS*; *ASSOCIATION NATIONALE DES ANCIENS ET AMIS DE L'INDOCHINE ET DU SOUVENIR INDOCHINOIS*; *ASSOCIATION NATIONALE DES COMBATTANTS DE DIEN BIEN PHU*; MEMORIAL DAY, INDOCHINA WAR.

**REPATRIATION, JAPANESE TROOPS.** As of 15 August 1945, Japanese historian Masaya Shiraishi has estimated there were some 83,000 Japanese soldiers stationed in Indochina. According to Japanese and American sources, in September–October 1945 there were around 48,000 soldiers and 2,000 civilians located in Vietnam north of the **16th parallel**. Approximately 30,500 Japanese located in northern Indochina were repatriated to Japan through the port of Haiphong from 29 April 1946. As for southern Indochina, on 20 May 1946, the French reported that over the previous five weeks 68,084 Japanese had been shipped to Japan. The British handed over to the French at the same time 1,596 Japanese, including 427 who were wanted for war crimes committed during World War II in Asia. Except for deserters and **crossovers**, almost all of the Japanese troops had been repatriated by late 1946, including some 7,000 civilians in April 1946. A Vietnamese history of the colonial prison at **Poulo Condor**

reported that the French deported some 75 Japanese prisoners of war to the island penitentiary. They remained there during most of the Indochina War. What became of them when the **Republic of Vietnam** assumed the prison remains unknown to this author. *See also* DESERTION, JAPANESE.

**RÉPITON-PRENEUF, PAUL (1904–1962).** French oil man who had visited Indochina during the interwar period for Shell. During World War II, he joined Free French forces in the Middle East and obtained the rank of colonel. In 1943, he joined the general staff of General **Philippe Leclerc**'s 2nd Armored Division and took part in the liberation of France and Germany. He was among those who took Hitler's Eagle's Nest on 5 May 1945 after heavy fighting. He accompanied Leclerc to Tokyo for the Allied signing of the Japanese surrender on 2 September 1945. During his service in Indochina between October 1945 and July 1946, he worked as Leclerc's liaison officer with the **Democratic Republic of Vietnam** and chief of the ***Deuxième Bureau***.

**REPUBLIC OF CHINA**. The Republic of China came to life in early 1912 following the implosion of the Qing dynasty. However, in the absence of an effective central power, provincial warlords continued to run China while foreign powers looked on as Republicans led by Sun Yat-sen tried hold China together. Things changed in the early 1920s. Thanks to Soviet assistance, Chinese communists and nationalists (*Guomindang*, GMD) created a united front to defeat the warlords. However, when the defeat of the warlords became imminent in early 1927, **Chiang Kai-shek**, leader of the GMD and the army, turned violently on the Chinese communists and drove them out of the cities and into the countryside in a bloody civil war. In 1928, he took power, established his capital in Nanjing, and ruled the Republic of China with an iron fist. He also dedicated himself to destroying the communists. In 1934, he forced his adversaries on a perilous Long March taking them from southern China to the remote area of Yan'an in the north a year later. However, the Japanese invasion of China in 1937 forced Chiang Kai-shek to renew his collaboration with the communists against the foreign invader. The Americans threw their support behind Chiang Kai-shek, himself forced by the bloody Japanese occupation of Nanjing to set up his wartime capital in Chongqing. Following the Japanese defeat, the United States pressed Chinese nationalists and communists to build a coalition government. Their differences were too great and civil war resumed in 1946.

Meanwhile, in accordance with the decision taken at the **Potsdam conference**, the Republic of China dispatched troops into Indochina above the **16th parallel** to accept the Japanese surrender there. Chiang Kai-shek appointed the Yunnanese general, **Lu Han**, to command the occupation forces, which peaked in late 1945 at about 100,000 troops (attended to by some 10,000 porters, stragglers, and petty merchants). While nationalist China was hardly sympathetic to communism, southern Chinese leaders sent to Indochina knew Vietnam and several of its nationalist leaders, including **Ho Chi Minh**. They were reluctant to overthrow the **Democratic Republic of Vietnam** (DRV), preferring stability that would allow them to concentrate on their own mission and interests. This is also why the Chinese commanders were in no rush to see the French return to the north, especially if it meant setting off a destabilizing Franco-Vietnamese war as had occurred under the British in the south on **23 September 1945**. Chinese troops thus remained in northern Indochina while the central government negotiated the end of French concessions and privileges in China in exchange for an eventual Chinese troop withdrawal from northern Indochina.

On 28 February 1946, the signing of the **Franco-Chinese Accords** allowed for France to assume responsibility for the occupation of Indochina above the 16th parallel before the end of March. With civil war reigniting in northern China, Chiang Kai-shek needed to move his troops from Indochina towards Manchuria. However, when the French tried to force the Chinese hand by debarking troops at Haiphong as early as 6 March, local Chinese forces repulsed them by force, insisting that a Franco-Vietnamese agreement should first be reached. Again, local Chinese authorities had no desire to get bogged down in a colonial war. Under intense Chinese pressure, the French and the Vietnamese signed the **Accords of 6 March 1946** in **Hanoi**. French troops landed safely thereafter in Haiphong and marched into Hanoi on the 18th but could not immediately overthrow the DRV government based in Hanoi. In June, the Chinese pulled the bulk of their troops out of Indochina and on 18 September 1946 the last remaining Chinese contingent left Haiphong.

While Chiang Kai-shek remained sympathetic to the Vietnamese nationalist cause, his attention was more focused on the Chinese communists and this increasingly meant maintaining acceptable relations with the French. This was even more the case following the Chinese communist victory on the mainland in 1949 and the transfer of the Republic of China to Taiwan. Chiang Kai-shek's government now supported the French-backed **Associated States of Indochina** and dispatched diplomats there to tend to the thousands of Chinese nationalist troops held in refugee camps in Indochina following their defeat by the Chinese communists in 1949–50. *See also* REFUGEES, REPUBLIC OF CHINA; VIETNAMESE NATIONALIST PARTY.

**REPUBLIC OF VIETNAM (*Việt Nam Cộng Hòa*).** The Republic of Vietnam was the postcolonial nation-state that emerged from the 4th Republic's failed efforts to hold on colonially to eastern Indochina via the Associated State of Vietnam. In line with the **Geneva Accords** of July 1954, the **Democratic Republic of Vietnam** (DRV) dismantled its administration and withdrew its military personnel from Vietnamese territory located below the 17th parallel, while the State of Vietnam did the same in areas it had formerly administered north of that line. Also in accordance with the Geneva agreements, the French moved their troops and colonial administration to areas below the 17th parallel (or back to France or elsewhere in the French Empire). Although the division of Vietnam at the 17th parallel was provisional, two Vietnamese states continued to exist into the post-accords period, a communist-led one in the north and a non-communist one in the south. A referendum held in the south on 23 October 1955 transformed the State of Vietnam into a Republic with **Ngo Dinh Diem** as president. Diem had served as prime minister under **Bao Dai** since June 1954. He used the election to depose the former Vietnamese emperor and head of state since 1949. Despite French efforts to block Ngo Dinh Diem's ascendancy, they could do little in the end as the Americans stood behind him and his Republic and the French needed to focus on Europe and the **Algerian War.** In 1956, the French officially withdrew the **Expeditionary Corps** from Indochina as Ngo Dinh Diem consolidated his hold over the army and police. Moreover, Ngo Dinh Diem, like Bao Dai, had not signed the Geneva agreements and he had no intention of allowing any referendum to occur except on his terms. Indeed, Diem entertained the hope of reuniting all of Vietnam on non-communist terms. This never occurred, nor did the elections of 1956, as the Vietnamese territories situated below the 17th parallel became de facto "South Vietnam", even though this term had never existed as such in Vietnamese or French colonial history. On 30 April 1975, the point became moot when the DRV vanquished the Republic of Vietnam militarily and unified all of Vietnam under one unitary communist state, officially proclaimed in 1976 as the Socialist Republic of Vietnam. *See also* COCHINCHINA; ANNAM; TONKIN; INDOCHINESE FEDERATION; ASSOCIATED STATES OF INDOCHINA; BAO DAI SOLUTION.

***RÉPUBLIQUE (LA) EST MORTE À DIEN BIEN PHU.*** Documentary film directed by **Philippe Devillers**, **Jean Lacouture**, and Jérôme Kanapa. It was released in 1974, as the American war drew to a close. The authors relied on interviews and newsreel to provide a critical account of the 4th Republic's incapacity to take Vietnamese nationalism and decolonization seriously, although the film's conclusion that the 4th Republic fell because of the battle of **Dien Bien Phu** or the French colonial war in Indochina is an oversimplification. The film was shown for the first time on French television in 1999. *See also* CINEMA; NOVELS; HISTORY; CULTURE; PIERRE SCHOENDOERFFER; MYTH OF WAR.

**REVERS, GEORGES (1891–1974).** Trained as a telecommunications engineer, Revers served in World War I as a captain and remained in the army after the armistice. In 1940, he served as chief of staff to Admiral Darlan and encouraged the army to resist following the German invasion of the southern zone of France in 1942. He joined the resistance that same year. In 1944, **Charles de Gaulle** assigned him the direction of the military region of Paris. In March 1947, he became chief of staff of the French army. In 1949, as **Mao Zedong**'s communist forces were crossing the Yangzi on their way to victory in China, Revers led an important inspection tour of Indochina to determine the best military strategy to adopt in light of the changing international situation. He visited Indochina between 16 May and 17 June 1949. On 29 June he sent a detailed report to the government in which he exposed not only French military problems, but political errors as well. He proposed the application of clear political and strategic policies, including the concentration of civilian and military powers in the hands of one, effective leader. Nonetheless, Revers concluded in his report that it was impossible to resolve the Indochina war by purely military means. It was a political matter at the core. The army should be used to create better conditions for reaching a favorable negotiated settlement. His report was anything but optimistic about the **Bao Dai Solution**: "If **Ho Chi Minh** has been able to hold off French intervention for so long, it is because the **Viet Minh** leader has surrounded himself with a group of men of undeniable worth [...]". His top secret report on the situation in Vietnam triggered the famous "**Generals Affair**", when it ended up in enemy hands. In December 1949, the French government relieved Revers of his duties for this indiscretion and he retired from the army in June 1950. *See also* CAO BANG.

**REVOLUTIONARY WARFARE.** The French term *guerre révolutionnaire* refers to the emergence within the French army in the last years of the Indochina War of a way of understanding and reacting to a "new" type of warfare conceived and implemented by **Mao Zedong** during the Sino-Japanese and Chinese Civil Wars and then taken up against the French army in Indochina by the communist leadership of the **Democratic Republic of Vietnam** (DRV). The term "revolutionary warfare" was directly borrowed from Mao Zedong's 1936 treatise on "revolutionary war" in China, first translated into French in 1950 as *Problèmes stratégiques de la guerre révolutionnaire en Chine*. While no one French theoretician coined the term, it was picked up by a handful of officers seeking to understand the adversary's ability to hold on to the "masses" in Vietnam and the French inability to knock out the guerrillas despite their military superiority.

At the head of this shift in French military thinking were officers working above all in southern Vietnam, where French **pacification** and military operations had failed to defeat the **Viet Minh** and where the ***Deuxième bureau***'s intelligence files on the enemy's methods were most voluminious. Moreover, the DRV never developed main force **divisions** in the south. Nor did southerners succeed in engaging the French in set piece battles as in northern and central Vietnam. It remained a guerrilla war there. Some of the most important French believers in "revolutionary warfare" were **Charles Chanson**, **Guillaume Chassin, Jean Boucher de Crèvecoeur**, **Charles Lacheroy**, **Albert Fossey-François**, and **Jacques Hogard**. (All of them had either worked in intelligence in southern Vietnam during the Indochina conflict or had been guerrillas themselves harassing the Japanese army during World War II.)

So enamored of revolutionary warfare was General Guillaume Chassin that he published the first biography in French of Mao Zedong. In early 1951, he also published an influential essay in the *Revue militaire d'information* entitled *La conquête de la Chine par Mao Tsé Toung*. To understand Mao's surprising victory over the *Guomindang*, Chassin explained, one must understand the "strategy of revolutionary warfare" deployed by the Chinese communists. For Chassin, what made the Chinese Red Army so effective was its control of the "spirit". Morale explained why the Chinese won battles against all odds. Everything, Chassin concluded, depended on education, indoctrination, propaganda, in short on the "conditioning of the individual". De Crèvecoeur would extend this analysis to the Vietnamese communists in his lectures given at the *Centre d'études asiatiques et africaines de la direction des troupes coloniales* in Paris, above all at his seminars entitled *Aperçus sur la stratégie du Viet Minh* (1953) and *Le problème militaire français en Indochine* (1952).

With the French defeat in Indochina, Charles Lacheroy further promoted the idea that, in order to win this new type of "revolutionary" war, the French army had to adopt the practices of its enemies, especially those of indoctrination, vying for control of the population, their "hearts and minds". Lacheroy led the way by "theorizing" the *Deuxième Bureau*'s ideas on **parallel hierarchies**, revealing the control the communists exercised upon the population, down to the village and indeed the individual level. It was "a total war", he and his disciples declared, driven by a group bent on controlling the society. Propaganda allowed the communists to "change the soul" of the person. This gave rise, Lacheroy said, to a "new arm", the most important one of the *guerre révolutionnaire*, the control and transformation of the population through mass mobilization techniques, **emulation** drives, and propaganda sessions.

Advocates of "*la guerre révolutionnaire*" never spoke of the Sino-Vietnamese success in tapping into the power of nationalism. In a series of lectures and publications, Lacheroy was able to make revolutionary warfare *the* lesson to be learned from the Indochina War, as Marie-Catherine and Paul Villatoux have shown. Soon, young French officers saw in the "*École Lacheroy*" the birth of a new type of warfare, *la guerre moderne*, as opposed to the conventional military science taught since World War I in French military academies. The ground was now prepared for the application of "counter-revolutionary warfare" in France's future wars.

In this sense, the effect of France's first war of decolonization on military thinking was to some extent at least "revolutionary". That said, the emergence of *guerre révolutionnaire* in French military thinking was not the result of a uniquely French experience in Indochina. The Americans and the British were deeply involved in fighting this new type of warfare that they had encountered in the **Korean War** and in Malaya. In all three cases, the discovery of revolutionary warfare led the French, the Americans, and the British to "revolutionize" their military tactics to deny the adversary control over populations and to put them under their own control. The importance of this military reorientation is still to be felt to this day. *See also GROUPEMENT DE COMMANDOS MIXTES AÉROPORTÉS*; EDWARD LANSDALE; ALGERIAN WAR; NEW HERO; PIERRE LANGLAIS; RECTIFICATION.

**REY-COQUAIS, FRANÇOIS (1929–).** French colonial administrator and diplomat in Indochina, where he began working for the high commissioner for Indochina in **Saigon** in 1952. Between 1953 and 1954, he was deputy delegate for the high commissioner in Laos to Savannakhet (1953) and Xieng Khouang (1954). Between 1955 and 1958, he served as chief of cabinet to the high commissioner to Cambodia (1955–57) and then as 2[nd] secretary to the newly created French Embassy in Phnom Penh (1958).

**REYNAUD, PAUL (1878–1966).** Deputy in the French National Assembly between 1928 and 1940 and staunch Republican believer in France's colonial destiny during the interwar period. He refused to collaborate with the Germans in 1940, resigning from his post as head of state. His replacement, Philippe Pétain, had him arrested and imprisoned. After World War II, Reynaud was re-elected deputy in the 4[th] Republic's National Assembly. He remained opposed to decolonization and negotiations with the **Democratic Republic of Vietnam** although he was not opposed to colonial reformism. He affirmed in 1947 that France's position as a world power would be diminished if it lost Indochina. He would change his position over time, especially as the **Cold War** affected France's position in both Europe and Asia. In 1953, serving in the **Joseph Laniel** cabinet, he supported a more liberal colonial policy for France, one which would accord more independence to the Vietnamese state associated with **Bao Dai**, but not to **Ho Chi Minh**'s Vietnam.

**RICHONNET, FRANCISQUE (?–1952).** Former paratrooper in the French resistance during World War II. He joined the ***Groupement de commandos mixtes aéroportés*** and served in central Vietnam where he perished during an attempt to infiltrate enemy territory in September 1952.

**RIDGWAY, MATTHEW B. (1895–1993).** Graduated from West Point in 1917, he served in the Philippines and Latin America in the 1920s before graduating from the United States Command and General Staff School at Fort Leavenworth, Kansas, in 1935. He served as deputy chief of staff of the Second U.S. Army and then the Fourth. During World War II, he commanded the then rather revolutionary 82[nd] Airborne Division, organizing the airborne invasion of Sicily in 1943 and Operation Overlord during the Allied landing in Normandy a year later. He returned to the Philippines after the Pacific War and then assumed command of United States forces in the Mediterranean Theater. He received command of the 8[th] Army as it made a tactical retreat following the Chinese entry into the **Korean War** in November 1950. Between 1952 and 1955, he served as chief of staff of the United States Army. In 1954, during preparations for operation **Vautour** to save the French troops besieged at **Dien Bien Phu**, Ridgway counseled President **Dwight D. Eisenhower** against American intervention in Indochina on the grounds that the army would need at least eight divisions to beat the **Democratic Republic of Vietnam** and even then it might provoke the Chinese into entering the war. The army, Ridgway argued, could not provide such unlimited amounts of manpower in light of its other global commitments. In 1952, while serving as the head of the **North Atlantic Treaty Organization**, then based in France, he was confronted with massive demonstrations organized by the **French Communist Party** against him and American involvement in the Korean and Indochina Wars. *See also* HENRI MARTIN; PUBLIC OPINION, FRENCH.

**RISTERUCCI, JEAN (1911–1982).** Ranking French colonial administrator who made his career in Indochina as an economics specialist. Between 1935 and 1939, he headed up financial and personnel questions for the *résident supérieur* in **Annam**. Following World War II, Risterucci remained in Indochina and served as chief of cabinet to Colonel **Henri Lorillot**, commissioner for the Republic to Southern Annam. In 1947, Risterucci returned to France, where he played an important behind-the-scenes role in building the **Bao Dai Solution**. In August 1949, he was general secretary of the French delegation appointed to study the application of the March 1949 agreements on the creation of the Associated State of Vietnam and attended the **Pau Conference** in June 1950 consecrating the creation of the three **Associated States of Indochina**. Between about 1950 and 1953, thanks in part to the support of **Léon Pignon**, he served as the commissioner for the Republic to Cambodia and oversaw "**pacification**" operations there against the **Khmer Issarak** and the forces of the **Democratic Republic of Vietnam**. He was also at the helm in Cambodia when **Norodom Sihanouk** launched his **royal crusade for independence**. In 1954, Risterucci returned to France where he became director of the cabinet for the French ministry in charge of relations with the Associated States of Indochina.

**RIVET, PAUL (1876–1958).** French anthropologist and outspoken critic of French colonial policy in Indochina. In 1925, he created the *Institut d'ethnologie* in Paris together with Émile Durkheim and Lucien Levy-Bruhl. In 1929, Rivet became director of the *Musée d'ethnographie du Trocadéro* and helped found the *Musée de l'homme* in 1937. He mobilized during World War I and saw combat on the Western Front. He was anti-fascist and an active member in the ***Section française de l'Internationale ouvrière*** (SFIO). Vichy removed him of his functions in the fall of 1940. Rivet immediately joined the resistance and took part in the famous *réseau du Musée de l'homme*. Faced with imminent incarceration by the Germans, he fled to South America and joined Free French forces. He became a socialist deputy after World War II. He was one of a handful of French **intellectuals** at the time to break publicly with official French colonial policy in and on Indochina. Named *in extremis* to the French delegation to the **Fontainebleau Conference** in mid-1946, Rivet resigned from his position after the first meeting, disgusted by what he saw as French bad faith. He met with **Ho Chi Minh** during this time and the two became friends. During a speech in Paris marking the second anniversary of the founding of the **Democratic Republic of Vietnam** (DRV), Rivet implored the French government to take up negotiations with the Vietnamese president to end the war. His August 1947 speech critical of the French role in provoking the outbreak of full-scale war in Indochina on **19 December 1946** ended with his expulsion from the SFIO. He wrote numerous articles in ***Témoignage Chrétien,*** *Franc-Tireur,* and *L'Observateur* calling upon the government to negotiate with the DRV. In January 1950, he sent a letter to President **Vincent Auriol** proposing the immediate end of hostilities in Vietnam and the organization of a referendum under **United Nations** auspices. A number of leading French intellectuals signed the proposal. Like **Paul Mus** and **Jean-Marie Domenach** (father of the French China specialist of the same family name), Rivet contributed to a non-communist opposition to the French war in Indochina. However, Rivet was hostile to the Algerian nationalists leading the *Front national de libération* and supported "*Algérie française*". *See also* ALGERIAN WAR.

**ROBIN, YVES HERMELAND FRANÇOIS MARIE (1926–1985).** Between 1951 and 1952, he served as deputy to the head of the Bureau of Chinese Affairs in the office of the high commissioner for Indochina in **Saigon**. Between 1952 and 1953, he was deputy to the director of the Political Cabinet for the commissioner for the Republic to Northern Vietnam. Between 1954 and 1955, Robin served as head of the Press Office for the high commissioner, then as the deputy to the director of the Information Service at the French Embassy in Saigon (1955–1956). *See also* OVERSEAS CHINESE; OVERSEAS VIETNAMESE.

**ROCHOIR, JEAN (TILLARD).** French journalist who wrote prolifically on the Indochina War in the papers *Climats* and *Combat.* During the interwar period, he served as an inspector of Primary Education in **Annam**. In the 27 December 1947 issue of *Combat* he applauded the work of the high commissioner for Indochina, **Émile Bollaert**, and his desire to maintain France's permanent presence in Indochina. Rochoir was an ardent supporter of **Bao Dai** and a devoted anti-communist. He accepted, however, that Vietnam had to be unified territorially into one state, the Associated State of Vietnam, in order to combat the nationalist pull of the **Democratic Republic of Vietnam**. *See also* BAO DAI SOLUTION.

**ROMAIN-DESFOSSÉS, JACQUES (1908–1998).** Born in **Hanoi**, Romain-Desfossés graduated from Saint-Cyr in 1930 and joined the colonial troops in French West Africa. In 1938, he transferred to Indochina and was stationed on the Sino-Vietnamese border where he remained on watch until the Japanese overthrew the French in the ***coup de force* of 9 March 1945**. He moved to southern China with General **Marcel Alessandri**'s retreating troops. Romain-Defossés returned to Indochina following the Japanese defeat in August 1945 and the French reoccupation of Indochina below the **16th parallel**. He joined **Jacques Massu**'s forces in charge of retaking southern Vietnam and then joined the colonial paratroopers. In November 1949, Romain-Desfossés took over from **Edmond Grall** the command of the *5ème Bataillon colonial de* ***commandos*** *parachutistes* (*5ème* BCCP). In July 1950, he and his troops returned to France upon the dissolution of the *5ème* BCCP. Romain-Desfossés returned to Indochina as a lieutenant colonel in early 1954 and took part in airborne operations to evacuate troops in the battle of An Khe under heavy attack from the forces of the **Democratic Republic of Vietnam**. He participated in the **Algerian War** and was an ardent defender of French Algeria.

**ROQUE.** French colonel and doctor who arrived in southern Vietnam in February 1946 to create a military medical unit there. He accompanied **Philippe Leclerc**'s troops to **Hanoi** in March 1946 and was decorated for his work in establishing a medical unit in Haiphong. He was said to be the chief doctor of the de Lannessan Hospital in Hanoi when he returned to France in September 1948. *See also* DISEASE; EXPERIENCE OF WAR.

**ROY, JULES (1907–2000).** Born in Algeria, Jules Roy praised Philippe Pétain for saving France following the debacle of 1940. However, he quickly changed positions and joined the Allied cause upon the liberation of North Africa in 1942. And he was soon an ardent support of **Charles de Gaulle** and his nationalist project. Roy joined the Royal Air Force in Great Britain and took part in bombing missions over the Ruhr Valley in Germany. After World War II, he transferred to the French **Air Force** and became a lieutenant colonel. He asked to serve in Indochina and his wish was granted in April 1952. However, he left the armed forces in Indochina in June 1953, citing his opposition to the army's use of unacceptable methods including **torture**. He subsequently wrote of the army as "the Nazis of Indochina". He began a new career as a novelist and essayist. His work reflects the themes of honor, heroism, and camaraderie, like **Jean Lartéguy** and **Pierre Schoendoerffer**; but Roy was one of the rare French **intellectuals** of the time to take up the themes of decolonization and nationalism. In 1960, back in Algiers, Roy publicly denounced the army's use of torture in Algeria. In 1963, he published a famous account of the battle of **Dien Bien Phu** (*La bataille de Dien Bien Phu*). *See also* ALGERIAN WAR; PAUL MUS; PAUL RIVET.

**ROYAL CRUSADE FOR INDEPENDENCE.** Between February and November 1953, as the Indochina War entered its most intensive phase in Vietnam, King **Norodom Sihanouk** launched a "royal crusade for independence" that took him across the world and throughout Cambodia. At the heart of his sudden decision to push the French for the full independence of Cambodia was Sihanouk's need to recast himself as *the* national leader of Cambodia; it was essential to his ability to remain a power player in postcolonial Cambodia. Like **Bao Dai**, Sihanouk was something of a colonial king, having been selected by Governor General Jean Decoux in 1941. Sihanouk had remained loyal to the French and their return to Indochina after World War II. The problem was that he had national competition. The Cambodian **Democrat Party** began pushing for greater independence from the French as well as political pluralism vis-à-vis the monarchy. The well known nationalist, **Son Ngoc Thanh**, returned to Cambodia in 1950 and soon positioned himself as Cambodia's true modern nationalist leader, contrasting himself to Sihanouk's longstanding relationship with the French and their colonial project. Faced with such challenges, Sihanouk realized he had to break with the past or risk being sidelined for good. His decision to move was also motivated by his frustration at the inept, corrupt revolving door governments in the late 1940s.

It was in this context that Sihanouk decided to go on the move to recast himself as the "father of the nation", even it meant forcing the French colonial hand. The increasing intensity of the Franco-Vietnamese war provided Sihanouk with a favorable conjuncture and the leverage he needed to pressure Paris more effectively in light of the French need to win against the **Democratic Republic of Vietnam** (DRV). In February 1953, as the DRV prepared to disperse the French army across all of Indochina, Sihanouk made his move when he dissolved the Democrat-dominated National Assembly and embarked upon a national and international campaign to force the French to accord Cambodia full independence with himself at the helm. At first, the French refused to take him seriously when he arrived in France and informed **Vincent Auriol** of his call for full independence of Cambodia. The Americans asked Sihanouk not to bother the French with this right now in light of the more urgent need to fight communism at this dire point in the Indochina War. **John Foster Dulles** told Sihanouk that by creating problems with France he was only helping the communists. Miffed by the French and angered by the Americans, Sihanouk turned to the media to advance his case. In an interview he accorded to the *New York Times*, he threatened to lean the other way, towards the Vietnamese communists, if the French did not grant Cambodia independence.

Sihanouk then returned to Cambodia, but left the capital for remote Battambang province. From there, he began to mobilize popular sentiment behind him. He set up base in the temples of Angkor Wat and prepared a national march on Phnom Penh. Although admittedly difficult to gauge accurately, Cambodian support for Sihanouk's crusade was real or at least sufficient enough to convince the French to compromise. The French needed to keep Cambodia on board in the struggle against the DRV. On 17 October 1953, French and Cambodian delegates signed a political convention. Sihanouk resumed contacts with the French and left Battambang to make a triumphal return to Phnom Penh on 8 November 1953. In early 1954, continued negotiations ensured the full independence of Cambodia from the French. "*Messieurs, le roi est fou*", the French commander for Cambodia **Paul de Langlade** said of Sihanouk, "*mais c'est un fou génial*" (Messieurs, the king is a nutter, but a brilliant one).

While the French army remained in control of major military operations, by late 1953 Cambodia had recovered its independence and Sihanouk had successfully recast himself as a nationalist monarch, although his claim to this mantle would continue to be contested into the postwar period. *See also* BAO DAI SOLUTION; PHETXARAT.

**ROYÈRE, JEAN (1909–?).** He served as French consul in Kunming, China, in 1943 and 1944, during which time he established contacts with **Viet Minh** officials. In 1947 and 1948, he served as diplomatic advisor to **Émile Bollaert** and was involved in negotiations with **Bao Dai**.

**SAIGON.** The war for Vietnam began in Saigon on **23 September 1945** and ended there on 31 April 1975, when the **Democratic Republic of Vietnam** (DRV) defeated the **Republic of Vietnam** and unified the country under communist rule.

Under French rule from the mid-19th century, Saigon became the commercial center of Indochina and home to most of the 35,000 Europeans living there on the eve of World War II. The **overseas Chinese** were also most numerous in Saigon and in the neighboring agglomeration of Cholon ("big market"). Throughout the Indochina War, this urban area became known as Saigon-Cholon. French estimates put its total population in 1948 at 1,179,000, including 22,000 Europeans, 840,000 Vietnamese, and 310,000 Chinese among others. In 1954, the total population of Saigon-Cholon was estimated at two million people, most of whom were Vietamese who had arrived from the countryside during the later half of the conflict.

Until 9 March 1945, the European population in French Indochina lived in relative peace thanks to the condominium between France, Germany, and by extension Germany's ally, Japan. On 9 March 1945, worried that leaderless Vichy authorities would rally to Gaullists, the Japanese overthrew the French in Indochina. For some five months, European settlers lived in precarious, humiliating, and often very dangerous circumstances. Things became even more complicated when the Allies defeated the Japanese a few months later. Vietnamese nationalist groups pledging loyalty to the **Viet Minh** took power in Saigon in the week following the **August Revolution** in **Hanoi.** However, the **Indochinese Communist Party** (ICP) at the helm of the Viet Minh in the north was but one nationalist player among several working in a fragile southern coalition with **Cao Dai, Hoa Hoa**, and **Binh Xuyen** leaders. British troops under General **Douglas Gracey** began arriving in mid-September to disarm the Japanese and maintain order. For about a month, the French community living in Saigon found the tables turned on it as the former colonized sought to assert national control over the colonial city. The Japanese mainly looked on as they awaited the arrival of British forces sent to disarm them below the **16th parallel** in Indochina. The Japanese had refused to free the colonial and foreign legion troops they had incarcerated in March. Meanwhile, Viet Minh leaders had a hard time preventing Vietnamese from humiliating and attacking the vulnerable European community. On 2 September 1945, for example, mobs attacked the French in Saigon during festivities organized to celebrate the declaration of Vietnam's independence by **Ho Chi Minh**.

Many French promised to take revenge once they re-established control of the city. That day came on **23 September** when British forces under Gracey backed a French *coup d'état* to oust the Vietnamese, using colonial forces incarcerated by the Japanese. The French coup unleashed months of pent-up fears and frustrations among many in the European community and the newly freed colonial troops. Some took out their anger on any Vietnamese they could find. But such violence only generated more of it. During the night of 24–25, Vietnamese attackers entered the district of **Hérault** in the Tan Dinh and Dakao suburbs of Saigon, and perpetrated one of the most gruesome massacres of the entire Indochina War against French, ***métis,*** and Vietnamese civilians.

The arrival of the **Expeditionnary Corps** ensured French control over Saigon-Cholon. However, the DRV was determined to use the city as one of its main battlefields for a war of terrorism. This urban violence would signal the reality of the DRV's national presence and serve to deter **collaboration** among Vietnamese tempted by French political projects. Between 1946 and 1950, **Nguyen Binh**, supported by Vietnamese communists in charge of Saigon-Cholon, ran an angry urban war in Saigon, targeting the assassination of French officials, Vietnamese allies of the French, and military points of strategic interest. The Viet Minh planted bombs, lobbed grenades, and distributed propaganda via an underground city they knitted together.

While this "grenading" of the Saigon did not stop its myriad of activities, it did directly affect the way people went about their daily lives in downtown Saigon. In 1949, **Lucien Bodard** tells us, as many as a hundred small grenades could go off in one night, usually around dusk, and mainly in the European quarters located along the *rue Catinat* in Saigon and the *rue des Marins* in Cholon. Shopkeepers responded accordingly. Protective fencing and iron mesh went up around establishments. "*Tout Saigon se cloître derrière des barreaux*", Bodard recalled: *C'est alors que le Saigon bien prend l'aspect d'une prison. Il s'enveloppe de grillages – boutiques, bistrots et dancings s'enferment dans des voiles métalliques. Bien à l'abri, les Français en traîn de boire ou de manger écoutent les détonations*. One Chinese restaurant owner serving poor white settlers in the city finally decided to "*enferme son établissement dans un épais rideau de fer*". One dined in peace, Bodard observed, but one did so "in a cage". People were cognizant of their vulnerability. It weighed on their minds even if they got used to it being there.

At the same time, the Viet Minh needed Saigon-Cholon as one of its major sources of imports and trade. True, the DRV did its best to burn down the colonial cities upon withdrawing in 1945–46 and subsequently issued orders to embargo them as a part of its own politico-economic offensive to render enemy life unbearably expensive and to sow a climate of terror. However, the paradox was that the rural-based Viet Minh badly needed access to enemy urban centers to survive and in the end refrained from trying to destroy one of its most important commercial centers. Commanders carefully targeted urban sabotage. Intimidation often worked better than scorched earth tactics. Blind terrorism only served to alienate Vietnamese civilians, who would turn to the French and their Vietnamese allies. Undercover operatives soon received orders to cultivate relations with Western, Asian, and Vietnamese capitalists. The Viet Minh cut deals with Chinese merchants and the owners of the biggest gambling casino in town, *Le grand monde*. Viet Minh underground officials in Hanoi and Saigon were constantly on the look out for ways to buy the paper and ink required to ensure the continued operation of printing presses, the medicine and antibiotics to keep the state's personnel, leadership, and fledgling army healthy, and the hard to find radio parts to guarantee real time communications.

When the French finally shut down the urban terrorism and dismantled much of the underground cities in Hanoi and Saigon by 1951, most of the urban population welcomed peace. Moreover, there is no evidence indicating that the urban populations in Saigon or Hanoi were ripe for or much less predisposed to rising up against Franco-Vietnamese forces. By late 1952, the Viet Minh could only count a few dozen operatives in Saigon. In the end, the best the DRV could hope for on the urban front in Saigon was that it could keep the civilians and non-communists nationalists on the fence, prevent them from supporting the **Bao Dai solution** or joining the Associated State of Vietnam's army, and maintain its commercial activities in the city.

**SAINTENY, JEAN (né ROGER[13], 1907–1978).** French resistance leader and Gaullist sent to Indochina at the end of the Pacific War to help restore French colonial sovereignty. Married to the daughter of **Albert Sarraut**, one of France's most powerful politicians and colonial thinkers, Sainteny began his career working in the *Banque de l'Indochine* in Indochina between 1929 and 1931 then in France between 1932 and 1939. He joined the resistance following the French defeat in 1940 and served as one of the leaders of the *Alliance* network which collaborated with the British Intelligence Service. He escaped incarceration by the Gestapo in June 1944.

In 1945, **Charles de Gaulle** sent him to Kunming to help create Military Mission 5 in charge of gathering intelligence and organizing resistance work against the Japanese inside Indochina. The Japanese capitulation in mid-August 1945 took the French by surprise, however. After failed attempts, Sainteny returned to **Hanoi** in late August 1945 where he later became commissioner for the French Republic in **Tonkin** and Northern **Annam** above the **16th parallel** (replacing **Pierre Messmer** who had been captured by the Vietnamese). Sainteny held that position until December 1947 (except for a long interim from May to November 1946 when he was in France).

Shortly after his arrival in Hanoi in August 1945, he met with representatives of the **Democratic Republic of Vietnam** (DRV), including **Ho Chi Minh** and other Vietnamese elite and nationalist leaders, communist and non-communist alike. He understood that Ho Chi Minh and his entourage were open to negotiations and less anti-French than the **Vietnamese Nationalist Party** or the Dong Minh Hoi. On 6 March 1946, faced with the real possibility of Chinese opposition to the

13. His name change was legally accepted in 1949.

landing of French troops in Haiphong, Sainteny received authorization to sign the **Accords of 6 March 1946** with Ho Chi Minh and **Vu Hong Khanh**. In this light, Stein Tønnesson has argued, Sainteny was perhaps not quite the prescient liberal decolonizer some have thought. In any case, Sainteny escorted Ho Chi Minh to France for the **Fontainebleau Conference** and entertained him during that long summer of 1946.

In November 1946, **Georges Thierry d'Argenlieu** sent Sainteny back to Hanoi in an attempt to put pressure on Ho Chi Minh to replace key members of the Vietnamese government with more amenable ones. Sainteny followed those orders leading down a dangerous path to full-scale confrontation. He was wounded when his car struck a mine at the start of hostilities on **19 December 1946**, but survived and expressed his expectation that the Viet Minh's house of cards would come tumbling down at its first serious defeat. While this proved seriously wrong, he continued to remain involved in Vietnamese affairs. In 1946, he received the title of *gouverneur des colonies*, one which he maintained until his retirement in 1968.

After the signing of the **Geneva Accords** and the division of Vietnam at the **17th parallel** in 1954, Sainteny became general delegate for France in Hanoi to the DRV (not an ambassador). Following a mission to Hanoi, he advocated a *rapprochement* with the DRV, explaining in a 16 September 1954 report that any effort to play the south against Hanoi would "end in failure and perhaps even a new conflict". However, General **Paul Ely** and others convinced **Pierre Mendès France** of the naïveté of Sainteny's proposal and the anger this might provoke in Washington. Mendès France felt obligated to make up to the Americans for the French National Assembly's sinking of the **European Defense Community** earlier that year. In the end, despite an impressive array of contacts spanning the **Cold War** divide in Hanoi, Sainteny had to content himself with rather consular affairs of an economic and cultural order. He held his post in Hanoi until 1958. His contacts and knowledge of the DRV later allowed him to play an intermediary role in secret negotiations between Washington and Hanoi during the **Richard Nixon** presidency. Sainteny wrote two books about his time in Indochina and negotiations with Ho Chi Minh: *Histoire d'une paix manquée: Indochine 1945–1947* (1953) and *Face à Ho Chi Minh* (1970).

**SAINT-MARC (DE), HÉLIE DENOIX (1922–).** Entered Saint-Cyr but interrupted his studies to join the resistance against the Germans. Arrested in 1943, he was deported to the Nazi concentration camp of Buchenwald then Langestein. He was barely alive when the Americans liberated the camp. After the war, Saint-Marc joined the **Foreign Legion** and arrived in Indochina in 1948 to fight the forces of the **Democratic Republic of Vietnam**. In all, he served three tours of duty during the Indochina War. He commanded in the **Algerian War**, took part in the Putsch of Algiers, and was condemned to 10 years in prison for doing so.

**SALA, VITO (1925–?)**. Born in Brooklyn, New York, Sala served as a private in the U.S. army during World War II, taking part in combat operations in Germany in April 1945. He apparently went absent without leave and joined the French **Foreign Legion**. He served in the Indochina War and Foreign Legion records confirm that he participated in and was wounded during the battle of **Dien Bien Phu** in 1954, though it is very unclear how he escaped enemy capture or returned to friendly zones. After 11 years of absence without leave from the U.S. army, in 1956 he contacted American authorities in Paris and returned to the United States. *See also* CROSSOVERS; DESERTION.

**SALAN, RAOUL ("LE MANDARIN", 1899–1984).** One of France's most distinguished yet controversial soldiers, who served in every major French war of the 20th century. Salan joined the army in 1917 and fought in World War I until the end. During the interwar period, he made his career in the colonial army in Indochina, where he served in 1924, 1929, and in the highlands of northern Vietnam between 1934 and 1937. According to one of his close collaborators in Indochina, **Roger Trinquier**, Salan admired Galliéni and was fascinated by Indochinese cultures and peoples. As a young officer, Salan traveled throughout northern Indochina by horse and on foot. He knew **Tonkin** and Upper Laos intimately. In June 1937, he transferred to the Ministry of the Colonies to create, upon the request of Georges Mandel, the *Service de renseignements intercolonies* (S.R.I.). Salan shone in his new job and returned to intelligence after the armistice of 1940, commanding the ***Deuxième Bureau*** for Vichy's Ministry of Overseas France. In January 1942, he left for French (Vichy) West Africa to head the *Deuxième Bureau* in Dakar, where he crossed over to Free French forces in Algiers following the Allied Landing in November 1942. He was named colonel in 1943 and served under General **Jean de Lattre de Tassigny** during the Allied landing in Provence and during the liberation of France and Germany.

Promoted to brigadier general, in October 1945 he left for Indochina and was named commander of French troops in Tonkin and China (those who had escaped the Japanese onslaught in March 1945). In Chongqing, he helped negotiate the 28 February 1946 **Franco-Chinese accord** securing the rapid withdrawal of Chinese Nationalist troops from Indochina above the **16th parallel**. He then landed in **Hanoi**, where he helped Jean Sainteny and Léon Pignon with negotiations leading to the **Accords of 6 March 1946**. His mission was also to take command of military operations in Hanoi in case no agreement could be reached. In such an event, he was authorized to arm French troops interned by the Japanese in the Hanoi citadel since 9 March in order to take control of the city in conjunction with a French landing in Haiphong. On 3 April 1946, in accordance with the March Accords and the peaceful arrival of French troops in Hanoi on 18 March, Salan signed a military convention confirming that a maximum of 15,000 French troops could be stationed in Vietnam above the **16th parallel**. Two days earlier, on 1 April 1946, he bequeathed his post at the head of French troops in northern Indochina to General **Jean Valluy**.

Between 17 April and 11 May 1946, Salan helped prepare the first **Dalat Conference**, as head of the French Military Mission. **Georges Thierry d'Argenlieu** designated him to accompany **Ho Chi Minh** to France in late May 1946 and Salan participated in the French delegation to the failed **Fontainebleau Conference**. He resumed command of French troops in northern Indochina in May 1947 and became general later that year. He played a pivotal role in the preparation and execution of operation **Léa**, which almost captured the **Democratic Republic of Vietnam**'s (DRV) leadership at Bac Kan in October 1947. In 1948, he took over as commander of French Ground Forces in the Far East and then served as interim supreme commander of troops in the Far East. He returned to France in mid-1948.

In late 1950, he returned to Indochina to serve as acting commissioner for the Republic to North Vietnam and took command of the Operational Zone for **Tonkin**. Under de Lattre, he commanded the battles of **Vinh Yen**, **Nghia Lo**, and **Hoa Binh** in 1951. When de Lattre fell ill, he assumed the provisional command of the armed forces in Indochina and was named commissioner for the Republic to South Vietnam from 1 August 1951. Following de Lattre's death in January 1952, Salan became commander-in-chief of Ground, Air, and Naval Forces in the Far East. He held the post until May 1953, when he returned to France. He came back to Indochina in the wake of the French defeat at **Dien Bien Phu**, serving as the military deputy to General **Paul Ely**. He oversaw the evacuation of Nung populations and troops who had fought with the French in northern Vietnam.

He returned to France on 27 October 1954 and went on to fight in France's last major colonial war, the Algerian one. Determined to keep Algeria French and thus avoid another military debacle, Salan turned against the French Republic and General **Charles de Gaulle** by creating the *Organisation armée secrète* and attempting a failed putsch in 1961. In 1962, Salan was arrested, tried by a military court, and imprisoned until he benefited from a general amnesty in 1968. *See also* ALGERIAN WAR.

**SALE GUERRE.** French term meaning "dirty war", first used as a headline in the 17 January 1948 issue of *Le Monde* by its founder Hubert Beuve-Méry to describe the Indochina War. Marcel Cachin of the **French Communist Party** (FCP) picked up on it in an article he wrote in *L'Humanité*, entitled *La guerre du Vietnam, une sale guerre* (21 January 1948). The communists would use this term effectively in their propaganda campaigns against the Indochina War and popularized it in so doing. In May 1949, the FCP used for the first time the slogan: *Plus un homme, plus un sou pour la sale guerre en Indochine. See also* LANGUAGE OF WAR; PUBLIC OPINION.

**SALOTH SAR.** *See* POL POT.

**SAM SARY (1917–1961).** Born in Kompong Cham province in Cambodia, Sam Sary studied at the *Collège Sisowath* before becoming a judge in Kompong Cham. He later transferred to the Court of Appeals in Phnom Penh as deputy commissar for the king of Cambodia to the prosecution service (*parquet general*). His activites during World War II and into the late 1940s remain unclear. In

1950, he was director of economic and financial affairs in the Council of the Presidency. He served as under-secretary of state for the Presidency in the cabinet of Oum Chheang Sun's cabinet of March 1951. He was on good terms with **Norodom Sihanouk** during the Indochina War (though this would change later). Sam Sary is best known for arguing ardently and successfully against the admission of the Cambodian Resistance Government as delegates to the **Geneva conference.** As Sihanouk's personal delegate to the meeting, Sam Sary declared that the "democratic government of Cambodia only exists in the imagination of the ministers from the Asian bloc". He even asked the Soviet Foreign Minister **Viatcheslav Molotov** if, in a hypothetically similar situation, he would accept the presence of the Polish government-in-exile in London. Sam Sary surprised the negotiators at the eleventh hour of the Geneva negotiations, when he refused to sign the armistice unless Cambodia obtained the right to ally the country as it saw fit and even allow foreign bases upon its territory. While Molotov initially thought this was an American ploy, the Soviet diplomat conceded by agreeing that Cambodia could conclude any accord in conformity with the United Nations' charter.

**SAMUEL, RAYMOND.** *See* RAYMOND AUBRAC.

**SANG, MICHEL.** *See* NGUYỄN BA SANG.

**SAO ĐỎ.** *See* NGUYỄN LƯƠNG BẰNG.

**SARANTIDIS, KOSTAS (NGUYỄN VĂN LẬP, 1927–).** Greek national who crossed over to the **Viet Minh** after World War II. Following the German occupation of Greece in 1942, the young Kostas Sarantidis and his siblings fanned out to find work to help their parents make ends meet in the difficult wartime conditions. In 1943, the Germans arrested Kostas for selling cigarettes illegally on the blackmarket. Badly in need of manpower, the Germans forcibly inducted him into the army rather than releasing him. In 1944, the young Greek found himself in German uniform in Austria. At the end of the war in 1945, Sarantidis's presence among the defeated Germans landed him in a prisoner of war camp in Austria. Unwilling to return to wartorn Greece, he signed a five-year contract with the French **Foreign Legion** to get out of the camp. In February 1946, he found himself in the middle of France's colonial war in Vietnam as a member of the 2nd Foreign Legion Regiment guarding Vietnamese prisoners. This was not what he had signed up for. He informed one of his Viet Minh prisoners of his desire to desert and the two of them took off in June 1946 making their way to Ninh Binh to join the armed forces of the **Democratic Republic of Vietnam** (DRV). Sarantidis adopted Vietnamese nationality and learned Vietnamese. During this time, he transferred to **Inter-Zone V** (*Lien Khu V*), where he executed propaganda and **proselytizing the enemy** (*Dich Van*) tasks. In exchange for his support, he was named first lieutenant and served as an "internationalist soldier" (*Chien Si Quoc Te*) in the **People's Army of Vietnam** between 1946 and 1958. He briefly led a platoon in 1951 before serving in 1952 as an overseer in prison camp no. 5 in Quang Ngai province, holding French and African prisoners. Following the **Geneva Accords**, he relocated to northern Vietnam and served in the 354th Regiment. In 1965, he returned to Greece where he continued to support the Vietnamese cause in the war against the Americans.

**SARRAUT, ALBERT PIERRE (1872–1962).** One of the Third Republic's most important colonial politicians and minds. He got his colonial start in Indochina where he served as governor general between 1911 and 1914 and again between 1917 and 1919. During his two mandates, he developed a dual policy designed to win over the support of Vietnamese elites and crush those who continued to oppose French colonial rule. On the first note, he developed the policy of "Franco-Annamese **Collaboration**" and spoke of creating a political charter and federation for Vietnamese working with the French. On the second count, he played a pivotal role in creating the efficient colonial police. Besides ensuring order, it also monitored and arrested scores of nationalists and communists who threatened the colonial order in Indochina. Sarraut left Indochina in 1919 and became minister of Colonies in 1920, a position he held for four years. During this time, he met briefly in Paris a young Vietnamese nationalist named Nguyen Ai Quoc (better known as **Ho Chi Minh**), but thought little of the meeting at the time. Instead, Sarraut joined together with Pierre Pasquier to create what was essentially the first **Bao Dai Solution**. As minister of Colonies, Sarraut sought to craft the young emperor into the living incarnation of his policy of Franco-Annamese collaboration. Sarraut personally presided over the young man's education and upbringing in France, before sending him back to Vietnam in 1932 to help win over the Vietnamese population, tempted by nationalist and communist rebellions. The experiment was a failure long before it was resurrected after World War II. Sarraut was also determined to promote his ideas within the **Colonial Academy** (*École coloniale*), calling upon French cadres to help the "under-developed" colonial peoples. During World War II, the Nazis deported him to Neuengamme, at the age of 72. Upon his liberation in 1945, he returned to France where he was named in 1947 a representative to the Assembly of the **French Union**.

In July–August 1946, during the **Fontainebleau Conference**, Sarraut renewed contact with Ho Chi Minh. In 1950, he presided over the **Pau Conference** between France and her newly created **Associated States of Indochina**. As a member of the French Union Assembly, he opposed decolonization in favor of creating a colonial federation. He was the founder of the *Académie des sciences d'Outre-mer* and inspired a number of French administrators in Indochina such as **Léon Pignon**. His daughter was married to **Jean Sainteny**, who negotiated the **Accords of 6 March 1946** with Ho Chi Minh. On 30 December 1946, in order to underscore the legitimacy of his actions, Admiral **Georges Thierry d'Argenlieu**, high commissioner for Indochina, informed Sarraut by telegraph that he "had the satisfaction of being received in the residence of the governor general that was a long time ago your dwelling". In 1953, Sarraut published an article in *L'Express* in which he called upon Ho Chi Minh to negotiate with, in his view, the fully independent Associated State of Vietnam. His point of view was echoed at the same time by **Pierre Mendès France**, who gave an interview in the same paper in favor of opening direct negotiations with the adversary once a cease-fire was implemented. Sarraut would meet privately with Pierre Mendès France during the **Geneva Conference** of 1954. *See also* ASSOCIATED STATES OF INDOCHINA.

**SARTRE, JEAN-PAUL (1905–1980).** Jean-Paul Sartre supported and published anti-colonialist intellectuals in his review, *Les temps modernes*. **Tran Duc Thao** and **Paul Mus,** for example, published articles on the Indochina War. The **Henri Martin** affair led by the **French Communist Party** radicalized Sartre's interests in defending anti-colonial causes as part of the wider struggle against capitalist domination. He went on to become a particularly outspoken critic of the **Algerian War**. *See also* ANTICOLONIALISM; INTELLECTUALS.

**SASSI, JEAN (1917–2009).** French colonel and special operations officer during the Indochina War. Few details are known of Sassi's activities before World War II. After having taken part in the failed Battle of France in 1940, he joined Free French forces. In 1943 or 1944, he entered the *Jedburghs*, the elite special operations unit created by the Allies to fight the Germans. He parachuted into France and, when the war ended there, transferred to Asia where British Force 136 dropped him into Laos to help create a ***Service Action*** to work against the Japanese. With the end of the Pacific War, he joined the *11ème Bataillon de choc* and left Indochina. He returned sometime in the early 1950s to lead a **commando** section of *11ème Régiment parachutiste de choc* before joining the ***Groupement de commandos mixtes aéroportés***. In this capacity, he ran a Hmong *maquis* operating behind enemy lines between 1953 and 1955, located mainly in Laos. In April 1954, Sassi led Hmong partisans in *Opération Condor* as part of operations to harass Vietnamese forces attacking the French camp at **Dien Bien Phu**. He was also part of a failed operation to help besieged **French Union** forces fighting at Dien Bien Phu. He went on to fight in Algeria as part of the *11ème Bataillon de choc*. *See also* MINORITY ETHNIC GROUPS.

**SÁU BÚA.** *See* LÊ ĐỨC THỌ.

**SÁU PHÁT.** *See* HUỲNH TẤN PHÁT.

**SÁU THANH.** *See* NGUYỄN VĂN THANH.

**SAUVAGNAC, HENRI (1905–?).** Graduated from Saint-Cyr in 1926, he served in the Middle East between 1928 and 1935. In 1937, he joined Captain Frédéric Geille in the development of airborne troops and was the first certified paratrooper officer in the French army. When war broke out in Europe, Sauvagnac was in Algeria where he created the *Compagnie d'infanterie de l'Air no. 1* and joined Free French forces following the Allied landing in 1942. In February 1943, Sauvagnac revamped this company to create the *Bataillon de chasseurs parachutistses*, which became the *1er Régiment de chasseurs parachutistes* (1er RCP) the following year and participated in the liberation of Europe. In 1947, he left his command of the 1er RCP to join the *Demi brigade de marche de parachutistes* in Indochina. At the head of this unit, his troops played important roles in operations **Léa**, Ceinture, and Terminus. In 1948, he left for Algeria but returned to Indochina for a second tour of duty in February 1954 to oversee all airborne missions in Indochina. He left Indochina in January 1955 and became brigadier general. *See also* ALGERIAN WAR.

**SAVĀNGVATTHANĀ.** Crown Prince of Laos who worked closely with the French. He was the oldest son of **Sīsāvangvong** and Thai Kham Ouan. He studied law at the *Institut d'Études Politiques* in Paris in the late 1920s before returning to Laos where in March 1930 he became general secretary of the Luang Prabang Kingdom. In November 1941, he became president of the Privy Council of the same Kingdom and entered into increasing conflict with the Viceroy and Prime Minister for the government of Luang Prabang, Prince **Phetxarāt**. Like his father, Savāngvatthanā opposed Phetxarāt's independent line and favored close collaboration with the French. Both the king and his son opposed Phetxarāt's independence aspirations following the Japanese overthrow of the French in March 1945, symbolized by Phetxarāt's decision to join the **Lao Issara** and sideline the royal family. Savāngvatthanā did, however, agree with Phetxarāt's desire to unify all of French colonial Laos under the royal family of Luang Prabang. But this had to be done under the king's rule and in collaboration with the French, not against them. It occurred officially in 1947.

**SAVANI, ANTOINE MARIE (1909–?).** Influential, behind-the-scenes French military intelligence officer stationed in southern Vietnam during most of the Indochina War. He graduated from Saint-Cyr in 1932 in the same class as **Roger Trinquier**, a close friend and fellow intelligence officer in Vietnam. A Corsican, Savani became a lieutenant in 1934 and made his first tour of duty in Indochina in 1938. His activities during World War II remain unknown. He returned to Indochina sometime in late 1945 or 1946. By 1948, he was running the ***Deuxième Bureau*** for French forces in southern Vietnam. In 1947–1948, he masterminded the defection of non-communist religious, nationalist, and criminal groups to French forces fighting the **Democratic Republic of Vietnam** (DRV) in the south, including the **Hoa Hao**, **Cao Dai**, and **Binh Xuyen**. (Trinquier tried to do much the same in the north in the early 1950s among **minority ethnic groups**.) Savani was married to a southern Vietnamese and apparently spoke the language well. In 1955, he published *Visages et images du Sud Viet Nam* and from 1956 drew upon his experiences in southern Vietnam in lectures he delivered at the *Centre des hautes études d'administration musulmane* as France took up another colonial war in Algeria. *See also* ALGERIAN WAR; MAURICE BELLEUX; MARCEL BAZIN; PIERRE PERRIER; *SERVICE DE DOCUMENTATION EXTÉRIEURE ET CONTRE-ESPIONNAGE*; *SÛRETÉ FÉDÉRALE*; OPIUM; PUBLIC SECURITY SERVICES; INTELLIGENCE SERVICES, DEMOCRATIC REPUBLIC OF VIETNAM.

**SAVARY, ALAIN (1918–1988).** Born in Algiers, Savary served as a naval officer during the interwar period. With the fall of France, he joined Free French forces in 1940. After the war, he became a member of the Consultative Assembly, served as secretary general for Austrian and German affairs 1946–1947, joined the ***Section française de l'Internationale ouvrière*** (SFIO), and was elected to the Assembly of the **French Union** during which time he became interested in colonial affairs. In 1949, as the Chinese communists moved to take all of China, the SFIO – then part of the ruling coalition government – sent Savary to Indochina and authorized him to enter into contact with the **Democratic Republic of Vietnam** (DRV). With a green light from **Léon Pignon,** high commissioner for Indochina, and **Paul Coste-Floret**, minister of Overseas France, Savary used his socialist connections in Indochina to organize a meeting with General **Nguyen Binh**, the commander-in-chief of the DRV's armed forces in the south. Savary sounded out the Vietnamese as to talks to resolve the war diplomatically. The DRV was open to the idea of arranging a meeting between Savary and **Ho Chi Minh**. However, when Savary asked for permission to meet with Ho Chi Minh, the Henri Queuille government refused. In his meetings and speeches to the SFIO leadership, Savary insisted that the French should negotiate a way out of the Indochina War. DRV nationalism, he insisted, was for real and the majority of Vietnamese wanted an end to French colonial rule. He also underscored the lack of popular Vietnamese support for the **Bao Dai solution**. Savary called on his party to make an attempt to contact the resistance, "*c'est la seule chance d'arrêter la guerre*", he insisted. But given that the SFIO was still part of the ruling coalition, the leadership did not want to open discussions with the DRV and thereby make itself vulnerable to attacks from the Right and even from the conservative, colonially minded wing of the socialist party. It was only when the SFIO entered into opposition in 1952 that Savary was able to push his party, with **Louis Caput** and others, towards the idea of negotiating an end to the war. Despite Savary's offer to use his socialist contacts to help open talks with the DRV, **Georges Bidault** only accepted when things turned bad during the battle of **Dien Bien Phu**. In April 1954, Bidault authorized Savary to travel to Moscow to open meetings with the DRV ambassador **Nguyen Luong Bang** before moving on to meet the DRV leadership in northern Vietnam. Determined to winning at Dien Bien Phu, the Vietnamese were not interested. Savary returned to France empty handed. The endgame would be negotiated at Geneva. *See also* GENEVA CONFERENCE.

**SCHEURER, JOSEPH LOUIS ANDRÉ (1911–1948).** Joined the *Corps de liaison administrative pour l'Extrême-Orient* and was initiated into Indochinese affairs in Kunming before being transferred to central Vietnam following the Japanese defeat. There he became the delegate for the *Populations montagnardes du Sud Indochinois* in 1946, French *résident* to Pleiku (1947), and *résident* to Ban Me Thuot in 1947–1948. He died in a fire in 1948.

**SCHLUMBERGER, ÉTIENNE (1915–).** Joined Free French forces in England in July 1940 and distinguished himself as deputy to Admiral **Georges Thierry d'Argenlieu** when the ship they were navigating came under fire off the coast of Vichy Dakar in Senegal. He continued to serve Thierry d'Argenlieu in French Africa before running commando missions against the Nazis along the European coastline. In 1945, he rejoined the Admiral, followed him to Indochina where the latter became high commissioner. Schlumberger remained one of Thierry d'Argenlieu's closest advisors and personal friends during this time. In the early days of the French return, he headed up the high commissioner's intelligence service, the ***Bureau fédéral de documentation***. Schlumberger was a partisan of the high commissioner's aggressive policy towards the **Democratic Republic of Vietnam**.

**SCHNEYDER, RENÉ FRANÇOIS (1894–1973).** Decorated veteran of Verdun and career colonial civil servant in Indochina. Educated in law, he first worked in the Ministry of War but successfully transferred to the Ministry of Colonies. Having passed the entry examination, he began a long colonial career when he arrived in **Tonkin** in 1924. He served as deputy administrator in **Hanoi**, Son La, Cho Bo, and Phu Lang Thuong before serving as the French *résident* to the Cambodian provinces of Stung Treng, Takeo Pursat, Kompong Chnang, and Battambang. Transferred to **Cochinchina**, he worked as the mayor-resident of Ba Ria–Cap Saint Jacques. Between 1937 and 1941, he was chief of Gia Dinh province. During the Vichy period, he served as chief of staff to Admiral Jean Decoux and inspector for Labor in Cochinchina. The Japanese arrested and incarcerated Schneyder following the ***coup de force* of 9 March 1945**. Upon liberation, he remained in Indochina. Between January 1946 and April 1947, he served as inspector of Political and Administrative Affairs and inspector of Labor. He was charged with rebuilding the pre-existing colonial structures in line with **Charles de Gaulle's** new policy towards Indochina. Schneyder returned to France in 1947, but continued working in an advisory capacity for the high commissioner for Indochina, who in 1949 designated him to lead the French delegation in its finalization of the Franco-Laotian Accords signed that year. Schneyder then became director of the Centre for Scientific and Technical Research for the **Associated States of Indochina**, though this did not last long.

**SCHOENDOERFFER, PIERRE (1928–).** French novelist, film director, and veteran of the Indochina War. In 1947, looking for adventure, Schoendoerffer began working as a sailor on a Swedish cargo ship, but yearned for something more exciting. His grandparents, father, and oldest brother had served in both World Wars. In 1952, following the death of the French army's photographer in Indochina, **Georges Kowal**, Schoendoerffer entered the *Service cinématographique des armées* and began work as an official cameraman with the rank of corporal. He was wounded at the start of the battle of **Dien Bien Phu**, evacuated but parachuted back in on 21 March 1954 as part of the 5th Battalion of Vietnamese Paratroopers. He went down with the camp on 7 May and was marched to a prison camp by the **Democratic Republic of Vietnam**'s (DRV) forces.

Freed from captivity four months later, Schoendoerffer began a new career as a novelist and film director. He focused his work mainly on men at war – comradeship, heroism, virility, sacrifice, and most of all honor, all major themes in his novels and films and in his work for the army's information service during the Indochina War. Like **Jean Lartéguy**, Schoendoerffer's men are brave, tragic "centurions" who keep marching on against all odds. Schoendoerffer first gained notoriety for his film, the *317ème section* (1964), which followed the flight of a heroic French-led platoon trying to make its way to safety as Dien Bien Phu and the French army's time in Indochina came to a tragic end (**Norodom Sihanouk** loaned Schoendoerffer troops for the film and authorized him to film in Cambodia). The film won a prize for best scenario at Cannes in 1964. He gained further notoriety for *La section Anderson* (1967), when he followed an American platoon into battle during the Vietnam War. He received an Oscar for this soldier's view of war. In 1976–1977, he produced with **Raoul Coutard** *Le crabe tambour*, which re-joined his "centurions" as older, seemingly rudderless men, as they flash-backed to the Indochinese and Algerian Wars and reflected on the tragic turn of the French Army in these colonial wars.

Schoendoerffer's work does not seek to question the reasons for the French involvement in Indochina or Algeria. To Schoendoerffer, the soldiers of France's colonial wars were unsung heroes, who had been sacrificed by inept politicians. When asked what he felt about the Indochina debacle, he replied: *La honte. La rage d'avoir été abandonné par la France*, a message that comes through clearly in the *317ème section*.

Schoendoerffer was no proponent of Vietnamese or Algerian decolonization. He declared in an interview in 1989 in *Hommes de guerre* that the DRV had not really won the war. He disdained the Algerian *Front de libération nationale* for failing to take on the French army in battle. Anticommunist, Schoendoerffer declared in 1984 that he would never return to Vietnam. He did, however, in order to film *Dien Bien Phu* (1992), another heroic commemoration of the besieged French men fighting on during the battle of Dien Bien Phu. Tragedy serves as his trope for restoring national honor. As he put it to the *Association nationale des anciens d'Indochine* on the meaning of Dien Bien Phu and his film on it 40 years later: "*tout était donc perdu. Alors, dans un ultime sursaut, des centaines et des centaines d'hommes obscurs et ordinaires vinrent, non pour redresser une situation désormais sans espoir, mais pour maintenir jusqu'au bout et le plus haut possible quelque chose qui ressemblait à une certaine idée de la France".*

Schoendoerffer sympathized with and contacted the wayward French generals who had turned against the French Republic during the Algerian War – **Raoul Salan**, André Zeller, **Edmond Jouhaud**, Maurice Challe, and **Pierre Guillaume**. Schoendoerffer sent Salan his novel *La 317ème section,* with a photo of Salan in Indochina in the 1930s. Schoendoerffer's favorite American film on Vietnam is *The Deer Hunter,* "a simply remarkable film" he said. This film traces the lives of a group of American young men drafted into the Vietnam War, who ended up in a Vietnamese communist prison camp and were tortured. Schoendoerffer also produced a film on **prisoners of war** in Vietnam. Despite his animosity towards Vietnamese communists, he accompanied François Mitterrand to Vietnam in 1993, thereby legitimating the French renewal with their former colonial adversary. *See also* ANTICOLONIALISM; CINEMA; EXPERIENCE OF WAR, DIEN BIEN PHU; MYTH OF WAR; NOVELS; PHOTOGRAPHY.

**SCHRÖDER, RUDY (1911–?).** Former German professor at the Sociology Institute of Frankfurt who crossed over to the **Democratic Republic of Vietnam** (DRV) in 1945. As a communist in the politically charged atmosphere of the 1930s, Schröder loathed fascism. He fled to France to escape the Nazis and joined the **Foreign Legion** to carry on the fight against them. However, with the fall of France and the collaboration of Vichy with the Germans, Schröder suddenly found himself in a pro-Vichy Foreign Legion and on his way to colonial Indochina in 1941. Once there, he immediately began organizing anti-fascist cells among a handful of like-minded soldiers in the Foreign Legion. Based in the north, he met secretly with socialists, Gaullists, and Vietnamese opposed to the Japanese. Following the formation of the DRV in September 1945, Schröder joined the **Viet Minh** and actively supported the Vietnamese anti-colonial war and shared the beliefs of the communist leadership. Schröder saw himself as an internationalist and opted for Vietnamese citizenship as a "New Vietnamese" (***Viet Nam Moi***). He took the name of Nguyen Duc Nhan and began work in propaganda matters in **Hanoi** until war broke out in all of Indochina on **19 December 1946**. This young German also had the military confidence of the Viet Minh. In 1947, he commanded a Vietnamese combat unit of 100 men, including 40 foreigners, which engaged the **Expeditionary Corps** in small-scale battles. This Vietnamese–German unit was known as the William Tell combat platoon. From 1950, with the arrival of Chinese advisors and communist ideas, Schröder and other Europeans were moved out of military positions and transferred to help rally and run propaganda and **indoctrination** units in DRV camps holding **French Union** prisoners. Schröder and his Vietnamese family eventually returned to the then East Germany in the early 1960s, a casualty of the ideological differences splitting the communist world and of mistrust on the part of the Vietnamese brothers. *See also* REVOLUTIONARY WARFARE; RECTIFICATION; INDOCTRINATION.

**SCHULZE, WERNER (NGUYỄN ĐỨC VIỆT).** German pilot who served in World War II and in the fledgling **Air Force** of the **Democratic Republic of Vietnam** (DRV). He crossed over to the DRV in early 1946, working as a pilot, technical translator, and weapons manufacturer. In 1949, he worked in the Ordinance Technical Research Office (*Nha Nghien Cuu Ky Thuat Quan Gioi*) of the nascent Vietnamese Air Force. He was charged with obtaining and translating French, American, and German materials on military affairs in general and the development of the air force in particular. As part of the Air Force Research Section, he provided military courses on how to identify different types of planes, develop anti-aircraft weapons, and began training the first pilots for the DRV. At this time, thanks to a gift from **Bao Dai** in the early days of the revolution, the Vietnamese had two (civilian) airplanes stashed away in Chiem Hoa in northern Vietnam. Schulze returned to the then East Germany in 1955, but, like many other Japanese **crossovers**, could not take his Vietnamese family with him. *See also* REPATRIATION, JAPANESE TROOPS; RUDY SCHRÖDER.

**SCOUTING, INDOCHINA WAR.** Thanks to scouting associations backed by the French during the colonial period and mobilized by Vichy and the Japanese during World War II, the **Democratic Republic of Vietnam** (DRV) was able to find enthusiastic recruits to fill its ranks upon its establishment on 2 September 1945. Scouting took off in Vietnam in the 1930s led by Tran Van Khac and **Hoang Dao Thuy**. Many of the former Vietnamese leaders of the colonial scouting movement had no trouble switching over to the DRV's nationalist cause and brought with them hundreds if not thousands of scouts who were running on high levels of patriotism. Hoang Dao Thuy was a notable case. He had been general commissioner of Vietnam's lively scouting movement during World War II and had secretly worked with **Truong Chinh** to bring over the scouts to the revolutionary cause as World War II drew to a close. Hoang Dao Thuy then put his scouting knowledge of communications in the service of the armed forces of the DRV. He worked in the **General Staff** and was the first director of the Ministry of Defense's Bureau of Communications. He created the government and military's first radio codes and encryptions, telegram dispatching system, and began teaching the first courses for a new generation of Vietnamese communications, radio, and intelligence specialists. Scouts were some of the first to sign up in the southern **Vanguard Youth League** led by **Pham Ngoc Thach** and they were present in the first combat units sent to fight in the south. During preparations for the battle of **Hanoi**, scouts in the Hanoi area were divided into two groups: those over 18 joined the army whereas scouts between 12 and 17 took part in helping to evacuate people from the cities and assisted in transporting supplies and setting up defenses. **Hoang Huu Nam**, himself a former scout, visited Dong Da in late 1946 to praise the work of scouts there who were preparing the city for war. Some of these young scouts also joined the Children's Guard. *See also* CHILDREN; RED CROSS; ORPHANS; WOMEN.

***SECTION FRANÇAISE DE L'INTERNATIONALE OUVRIÈRE* (SFIO).** The creation of the SFIO in 1905 marked the unification of French socialist groups and tendencies into one party. While the SFIO was initially critical of colonial excesses, the socialists were reformers, not decolonizers or even anti-colonialists. Local chapters of the SFIO emerged throughout the Empire during the first half of the 20th century. In 1937, French socialist **Louis Caput** created the SFIO's first Indochinese branch in **Hanoi** and strongly advocated the opening of its doors to the Vietnamese. Indeed, he was instrumental in admitting **Hoang Minh Giam** – future minister in the **Democratic Republic of Vietnam** (DRV) – to the SFIO in Hanoi. During the Vichy period and the Japanese occupation during World War II, the SFIO's political activities were pushed underground, where a number of socialists, such as Caput, joined the internal resistance and began to think in anti-colonial terms.

The SFIO emerged from World War II in France in a fairly strong position. However, unable to win a majority vote in the legislative elections of 1945, the party had to join a coalition government with the **French Communist Party** and the ***Mouvement républicain populaire***. This "tripartisme" marked French politics between 1945 and 1947, the period during which the war in Indochina broke out. Caput came down in favor of Vietnamese independence, but ranking socialists were divided over the Vietnam problem and had no clear-cut policy on decolonization. The conservative wing of the party, led by **Marius Moutet**, minister of the Colonies, found it hard to imagine an independent Vietnam. Colonial reform, certainly, but decolonization, no. More liberal thinkers such as Caput and **Paul Rivet** argued in favour of respecting the reality of colonial nationalism and decolonization. The problem was that despite the SFIO's hostility to High Commissioner **Georges Thierry d'Argenlieu**'s aggressive policy towards the DRV in Indochina, French national politics were such that the leadership did not want to endanger its political interests in France by taking too risky a stand on the Indochina problem, preferring instead to turn a blind eye to Thierry d'Argenlieu's actions. While the SFIO, once it was in the opposition, would become critical of the Indochina War and push for a negotiated solution, it was unable to prevent war from breaking out on **19 December 1946**. *See also* ALAIN SAVARY.

**SECURE ZONE (*Ăn Toàn Khu*).** Refers to the secure area first set up by **Indochinese Communist Party** (ICP) leaders outside of **Hanoi** during World War II and then in remote northern Vietnam as the outbreak of full-scale war in Hanoi became increasingly likely by late 1946. The Provisional General Secretary of the ICP **Truong Chinh** played the pivotal role in creating and running the secure zone outside of Hanoi from around 1941. The Standing Committee of the Central Committee operated from there and was in secret contact with **Ho Chi Minh** who operated near the Sino-Vietnamese border. The secure zone was located on both sides of the Red River in the areas of Ha Dong, Dong Anh, Hoai Duc, and Phuc Yen. In late 1942 and early 1943, the Central Committee developed the secure zone further into Bac Giang, Phu Binh, and Thai Nguyen, and began training cadres and militia in preparation to take power in Hanoi at the propitious moment. Following the Japanese overthrow of the French, the secure zone was well positioned to move cadres into positions of power following the Japanese capitulation. The secure zone was revitalized as war with the French became increasingly likely by late 1946. In the fall of 1946, for example, the ICP created the Committee for Communications and Liaison for the Secure Zone (*Ban Giao Thong Lien Lac An Toan Khu*). Led by **Nguyen Luong Bang**, it counted among its members some of the most important intelligence and security leaders of the ICP/**Democratic Republic of Vietnam**, including **Tran Dang Ninh**, **Tran Quoc Hoan,** and **Tran Quoc Huong**. Its first major task was to create a new and secret communication and radio network for the Party in charge of all of Vietnam down to **Inter-Zone V** (*Lien Khu V*) in the event that full-scale war commenced. This party communication center was to work closely with the government and the army. The second task was to scout out and organize a new safe area in northern Vietnam where the party, the state, and the army could continue to exist free from French attacks in the event of war. In early 1947, this committee set up the new secure zone in Dinh Hoa in Thai Nguyen province in the hills of northern Vietnam. It housed the government and the ICP Standing Committee, the General Directorate of the ***Tong Bo Viet Minh***, the **Lien Viet** Association, the Ministry of Defence and the Military High Command. *See also* LEA, OPERATION.

**SEGUINS PAZZIS (DE), HUBERT MARIE JEAN AMBERT (1913–1994).** French military officer involved in **commando** operations in northern Vietnam. In the late 1940s, he joined the 3rd Office of 2nd Colonial Light Brigade of Paratroopers (*2ème demi brigade coloniale de commandos parachutistes)*. After a tour of duty in North Africa, he returned to Indochina in the early 1950s as lieutenant colonel and chief of staff of the *Groupement d'opération de la région Nord Ouest* in January 1954. He also served as chief of staff to General **Christian de Castries** during the battle of **Dien Bien Phu** and was taken prisoner before being liberated and returned to France.

**SEH.** *See SERVICE D'ÉTUDES HISTORIQUES.*

**SEHAN.** *See SERVICE D'ÉTUDES HISTORIQUES.*

**SERGENT, PIERRE ("ARTHUR", 1926–1992).** French **Foreign Legion** veteran of the Indochina War and right-wing politician in France. During World War II, he joined the French resistance as a teenager. Following the war, he trained to become an officer in the French Foreign Legion and graudated from the *École spéciale militaire* at Saint-Cyr in 1949 before transferring to the *1er Régiment Étranger* in Algeria. In 1951, he debarked in Indochina as part of the *1er Bataillon Étranger de Parachutistes* where he served as a captain until 1953. He later returned to Algeria where he opposed decolonization and participated actively in the *Organisation armée secrète*. His actions put him on the wrong side of the French law. He was tried in abstentia in 1962 and again in 1964, and sentenced to death each time. Sergent became a fugitive moving across Europe using the alias of "Arthur" to escape detection. He was amnestied in 1968, returned to France, and became involved in center-right then right-wing politics, serving as a deputy for the *Front National* between 1986 and 1988. He was a prolific writer of military books on the Legion, the French Army, Algeria and his own itinerary. As he put it in the title of one of his books published in 1972, *Je ne regrette rien*. In what has to be one of the most fascinating connections in the memory of the Indochina War, Sergent wrote an absorbing biography of one of his former enemies during the Indochina War, an Austrian deserter, communist, supporter of the **Viet Minh**, turned Catholic and right winger himself at the end of his life, **Ernest Frey**. *Un étrange M. Frey* is how Sergent entitled the biography of his counterpart. *See also* ALGERIAN WAR.

**SERVANT, HENRI ÉDOUARD JEAN-MARIE (1924–).** French colonial administrator during the Indochina War. Between 1948 and 1950, he served in the Press and Information Service in **Hanoi** before taking up a new post in the General Secretariat of the high commissioner's in **Saigon** between 1951 and 1952. He transferred to the diplomatic section of the high commissioner's office between 1952 and 1954. He remained in Saigon after the end of the war, working in the Economic and Technical Assistance Mission between 1954 and 1957.

***SERVICE ACTION* (SA).** French **commando** units working within Britain's Special Operations Executive (SOE) during World War II. The first Franco-British *Service Action* or SA teams appeared in Japanese occupied Laos towards the end of the Pacific War. They answered both to the SOE and to Free French authorities. The SA's main mission was to prepare and direct subversive activities in enemy territory by creating insecurity behind the enemy's lines through sabotage, ambushes, destructive actions, and assassination. It was also designed to solicit favour among local people, generate complicities, and develop contacts.

During the first half of the Indochina War, French military strategists showed little interest in SA operations. This changed in 1950, when the Americans, worried by communist advances in China, Korea, and Indochina, pressured the French to resume such World War II type of actions in Indochina. In April 1950, the French renewed their interest in SA operations when the ***Direction générale de documentation*** and the ***Service de documentation extérieure et de contre-espionnage*** produced a document entitled *Étude sur l'organisation d'un Service Action*. However, nothing apparently came of these efforts until the Americans tried to create their own separate SA in upper Indochina for using upland **minority ethnic groups** to harass the communists on their own turf, even into southern China. The French refused to let them take over SA operations in Indochina, but countered by establishing the ***Groupement de commandos mixtes aéorportés*** (GCMA), which retrieved a number of officers who had first worked in Japanese-occupied Laos during World War II, including **Jean Sassi.**

"*Action*", according to **Edmond Grall** of the GCMA, was designed to "create favourable conditions for the realisation of an act of war" when the moment came. In Indochina, he said, this meant two things mainly: (1) creating a permanent sense of insecurity behind the DRV's lines and (2) developing contacts with local populations hostile to the Vietnamese. *See also* REVOLUTIONARY WARFARE; OFFICE OF STRATEGIC STUDIES.

***SERVICE D'ÉTUDES HISTORIQUES* (SEH, SEHAN, SESAG).** Created in December 1945, the *Service d'études historiques* (SEH), with a branch in **Hanoi** (SEHAN) and another in **Saigon** (SESAG), was designed to provide mainly operational intelligence for French ground forces in charge of retaking Indochina. Indeed, the SEH replaced the *Service de renseignements opérationnels* or the Operational Intelligence Service created by Lieutenant-Colonel **Jean Augustin Trocard,** who had worked in the army's colonial intelligence service in Indochina before World War II. The SEH faded away in 1949–1950 to become a true *Service de renseignement opérationnel* as the war entered a new and more intensive military stage.

***SERVICE DE DOCUMENTATION EXTÉRIEURE ET DE CONTRE-ESPIONNAGE* (SDECE).** The French foreign intelligence service that played a very important role in the war in Indochina. The SDECE was created at the end of 1945 at the national level to undertake counter-intelligence and conduct foreign intelligence outside of France. The SDECE effectively replaced the ***Direction générale des études et des recherches***. The SDECE was unique in that it answered directly to the *Présidence du Conseil* and not just to the General Staff.

Sometime in early 1946, the SDECE began operating in Indochina under the direction of a certain Barada. Following his transfer in December 1947, Colonel **Maurice Belleux** took over and would direct SDECE's intelligence operations in Indochina until 1956. While the Indochinese branch of the SDECE was attached administratively to the high commissioner's office, the French central government was in charge of its personnel, financed an important part of its budget, and oversaw its grand strategy and organization. The SDECE in Indochina consisted of two main services. The "***service technique de recherches***" was vital in that it translated all coded intelligence intercepted by the ***Groupe de contrôle radioélectrique***, and provided crucial intelligence for political, diplomatic, and especially military operations. The SDECE's "*service de renseignements*" gathered intelligence outside of Indochina, mainly from China, Thailand, **Burma**, **Indonesia**, etc.

The SDECE was particularly successful in providing military and civilian leaders with invaluable intelligence on their Indochinese adversaries and was especially effective in intercepting and decrypting communications coming from lower and middle levels of the **Democratic Republic of Vietnam**'s political and military services. It sometimes reached as high as General **Vo Nguyen Giap**'s General Staff. Thanks to SDECE intercepts, the military was able to maintain remarkably accurate orders of battle on the adversary. However, this did not always mean that the French knew their enemy's intentions. The Vietnamese Politiburo never had the intention of "taking" Laos in 1954, the reason for which General **Henri Navarre** justified sending troops into **Dien Bien Phu**. The real Vietnamese strategy was to disperse French troops as far across Indochina as possible, hoping to draw the French into a much-needed battle in the highlands.

The wartime SDECE apparatus was withdrawn from Indochina in 1956, though the listening station remained operational in Dalat until 1960. On 2 April 1982, SDECE became the *Direction Générale de la Sécurité Extérieure*. *See also* OFFICE OF STRATEGIC SERVICES.

***SERVICE DE PROTECTION DU CORPS EXPÉDITIONNAIRE.*** *See SÛRETÉ FÉDÉRALE.*

***SERVICE DE RENSEIGNEMENTS OPÉRATIONNELS.*** French military intelligence service in charge of providing tactical intelligence to territorial commanding officers to execute military operations. *See also SERVICE D'ÉTUDES HISTORIQUES; SERVICE TECHNIQUE DES RECHERCHES.*

***SERVICE TECHNIQUE DES RECHERCHES* (STR).** The main French technical body in charge of direction finding, intercepting, and decrypting enemy communications during the Indochina War. While it had begun functioning in southern Vietnam before the outbreak of full-scale war in the north on **19 December 1946**, it became fully and officially operational in June 1947. It operated two main stations in **Saigon** and, from February 1947, **Hanoi**. The STR's main target was of course the **Democratic Republic of Vietnam**. The STR served as the central organ through which all requests for interceptions, direction finding, and decrypting passed, including its technical collaboration with ***Groupement des contrôles radioélectriques***. The STR's main decrypting center was set up in Dalat in 1948. This was where the core of French code-breaking occurred. In 1954, it moved to Vung Tau (Cap Saint Jacques) and continued operations until 1956 and apparently left Vietnam definitively in 1957.

**SESAG.** *See SERVICE D'ÉTUDES HISTORIQUES.*

**SETTLERS.** *See FRANÇAIS D'INDOCHINE.*

**SHELDON, GEORGE.** American intelligence officer in **Saigon** after World War II. He was favorably impressed by the Vietnamese and the **Democratic Republic of Vietnam** (DRV). Sheldon felt that **Ho Chi Minh** was "recognized and desired by most of the people of **Cochinchina**" and that despite French efforts to restore colonial rule, the Vietnamese resistance would "survive and succeed in the end". On 18 December 1946, the day before full-scale war broke out, Sheldon published an article favorably disposed towards the DRV in the *Far Eastern Survey*. He later returned to Indochina as a *United Press* correspondent. *See also* OFFICE OF STRATEGIC SERVICES.

**SIAO WEN (c. 1890–?).** Intelligence and political officer to **Zhang Fakui** during the **Republic of China**'s occupation of northern Indochina in 1945–1946. During World War II, this native of Guangdong province served as deputy chief for the Foreign Affairs section in Zhang Fakui's Fourth War Area Command and met **Ho Chi Minh**, then held as a political prisoner there. Siao Wen also worked as Zhang Fakui's pointman in relations with non-communist Vietnamese nationalist groups in southern China, most importantly the Dong Minh Hoi or the Alliance League. With the defeat of the Japanese in August 1945, Zhang Fakui transferred Siao Wen to **Hanoi** where he arrived in September and served as deputy commander to **Lu Han**, commander of the 62nd Guangxi Army and head of the Political Office. During his time in Vietnam, Siao Wen protected **overseas Chinese** interests in northern Indochina and worked closely with communist and non-communist Vietnamese nationalists, above all Ho Chi Minh. Rather than overthrowing the **Democratic Republic of Vietnam** (DRV) in favor of anti-communist nationalists, Siao Wen advocated a coalition government and urged non-communist groups like the **Vietnamese Nationalist Party** and the Alliance League to join it. *See also* OCCUPATION, CHINESE; FRANCO-CHINESE ACCORDS.

**SICURANI, JEAN (1915–1977).** French colonial civil servant born in Algeria and graduated from the **Colonial Academy** (*École coloniale*) in the late 1930s. Prisoner of war during World War II, he started his career in Indochina in 1945 when he became deputy to the advisor for the Southern Mekong Region (*la région du Sud-Mékong*). He studied the Khmer language intensively (the lower Mekong has a large **Khmer Krom** population). Between October 1946 and May 1948, Sicurani served as a regional advisor to the territories of Siemreap and Angkor, returned by the Thais in late 1946 and home to **Khmer Issarak** bands. Between December 1948 and May 1950, he headed up the Cambodian Information Service (*Service Information Cambodge*) before being named the high commissioner's delegate to Battambang (May–October 1950) and Kompong Cham (November 1950–June 1951). Between December 1951 and April 1952, he worked as a deputy to the head of the information service in the ministry in charge of relations with the **Associated States of Indochina** before assuming the post of delegate for the high commissioner to Phnom Penh and then advisor for the high commissioner to Cambodia between October 1954 and January 1955. He finished his colonial career in French Africa and Algeria before serving as the ambassador for the Prince of Monaco to Paris in the 1970s.

**SIEU HENG (1922–1975).** Leader of the Khmer People's Revolutionary Party during the Indochina War. He grew up in Battambang province in the 1930s. He was fluent in Vietnamese, thanks no doubt to the fact that his parents had come from colonial Cochinchina. When the Thais annexed Battambang province at the start of World War II, Sieu Heng joined the Thai-backed **Khmer Issarak** movement. In 1946, the Thais returned the province to Cambodia. Sieu Heng continued his anti-colonialist activities but shifted his alliance to the Vietnamese. In 1946, he allegedly joined the **Indochinese Communist Party**. He certainly gained the trust of the Vietnamese communists in charge of Cambodia, most importantly **Nguyen Thanh Son**. In 1951, Sieu Heng joined up with **Son Ngoc Minh** to be the two leading Cambodian radicals of the time and the closest allies of the Vietnamese communists. *See also* KHMER KROM; PARTY AFFAIRS COMMITTEE; CAMBODIAN RESISTANCE GOVERNMENT.

**SIHANOUK.** *See* NORODOM SIHANOUK.

**SIM VAR (1906–1989).** Completed his secondary studies at the *Collège Sisowath* in Phnom Penh and worked in the colonial judicial system as a secretary–interpreter. During World War II, he joined his longtime friend, **Pach Chhoeun**, and served on the editorial board of the nationalist newspaper, *Nagaravatta*. Through family connections, Sim Var also developed a wide array of contacts in royal circles, including the support of the mother of **Norodom Sihanouk**. Following the Japanese ***coup de force* of 9 March 1945**, Sim Var became minister of Foreign Affairs to **Son Ngoc Thanh**. He navigated the return of the French in late 1945 and helped create the **Democrat Party** in 1946. The French arrested him in February 1947 on the grounds that he was planning an insurrection in concert with the **Khmer Issarak** and transferred him to the *Maison centrale* in **Saigon**. He regained his freedom on the king's birthday on 25 November 1947 and resumed his activities within the Democrat Party in Phnom Penh. He travelled to Paris in 1948 as a Cambodian delegate to the **French Union**'s Assembly. In November 1951, back in Cambodia, he became under-secretary of state to the National Police. He was minister of the Economy in the cabinet formed in June 1952 by Norodom Sihanouk and was minister of Foreign Affairs between September and October of the same year. **Penn Nouth** made him minister of the Economy and Public Works in January 1953 and minister of National Defence in a reshuffle in July 1953. Sim Var served finally as minister of Public Works and Telecommunications in the Penn Nouth cabinet of April 1954.

**SIMONDET, JEAN (1919–).** Colonial administrator active in central Vietnam during the Indochina War. He began his colonial career in France attending to questions of Indochinese workers between 1943 and 1945, all the while taking part secretly in the French resistance movement. In 1945, he transferred to **India** as part of the *Corps de liaison administrative pour l'Extrême-Orient* designed to restore colonial administrative rule to Indochina after Japanese defeat. Simondet arrived in Indochina in 1945 and worked in the high commissioner's office until 1946. Between 1946 and 1947, he undertook administrative tasks among the highland peoples of southern Indochina, referred to by the French administratively as *les populations montagnardes du Sud-Indochine*. He moved to Hue where he worked in the Financial Services of the high commissioner's office for central Vietnam between 1947 and 1949. He returned to France in 1949 where he held a post in the Ministry of Overseas France, Indochina Section, until 1950. Between 1955 and 1959, he worked in the French ministry in charge of relations with the **Associated States of Indochina** concerning financial and economic matters and the repatriation of Europeans following the Indochina War. In 1956, he wrote a study of the question entitled *Les rapatriés français d'Indochine et d'Afrique du Nord*. *See also PAYS MONTAGNARDS DU SUD.*

**SIMPSON-JONES, PETER.** British naval officer and member of the British Special Operations Executive during World War II and in Indochina. He was involved in a number of audacious naval and intelligence operations in Africa and Asia during World War II, one of which landed him in a Japanese prisoner of war camp near **Hanoi**. With the war over, the Japanese allowed Simpson-Jones to board an inbound airplane carrying the head of the American **Mercy Team**, **Archimedes Patti**, and **Jean Sainteny**. Lieutenant Commander Simpson-Jones stayed on in Hanoi after his liberation to serve as a British government observer. He was also involved in intelligence gathering. Fluent in French, he developed cordial working relationships with French leaders in northern Vietnam such as **Jean Sainteny** and met on several occasions with **Ho Chi Minh**. For unclear reasons, Simpson-Jones was also the object of several assassination attempts by non-communist Vietnamese groups. It is not clear in what capacity he was truly working in Hanoi at this time. He left sometime in early 1946 and would go on to be a very successful businessman in France. *See also* ARTHUR GOEFFREY TREVOR-WILSON; DOUGLAS GRACEY.

**SINGKAPO SIKHOT CHOUNLAMANY.** *See* SINGKAPŌ SĪKHŌTCHUNNAMĀLĪ.

**SINGKAPŌ SĪKHŌTCHUNNAMĀLĪ (SINGKAPO SIKHOT CHOUNLAMANY, 1913–?).** Senior **Pathet Lao** military leader and close collaborator with the **Democratic Republic of Vietnam**. Born in Thakhek, he trained as a teacher and worked as a youth leader following the Japanese overthrow of the French in March 1945. Prince **Suphānuvong** relied upon him to bring over youth to the nationalist cause following the Japanese defeat. Singkapō joined the **Lao Issara** government and became chief of staff of the Army of Liberation and Defense on 1 November 1945. Following the return of the French in mid-1946, he followed the Lao Issara government into exile in Thailand where he continued to run military affairs for the Thakhek region from bases in Thailand. Following the return of **Pibun Songgram** in late 1947 and early 1948, he left Thailand for central Vietnam to join the Lao Issara **Committee for the East**. In 1950, he joined in the creation of the **Lao Resistance Government** and became vice president of the Pathet Lao national front. He continued collaborating militarily with the Vietnamese in **Inter-Zone IV** (*Lien Khu IV*). He served as president of the Lao–Vietnamese Military Committee based in Do Luong. When the Vietnamese army invaded large parts of Laos from 1953, he moved his residence to Sam Neua with the rest of the Pathet Lao leadership. He worked as a political–military cadre and became in 1953 president of the People's Court for Sam Neau before accompanying the Vietnamese army in its brief occupation of Thakhek later that year. He was named a colonel in the Pathet Lao army. *See also* PARTY AFFAIRS COMMITTEE.

**SĪSĀVANGVONG (1885–1959).** Lao king and dedicated ally of the French throughout the entire Indochina War. He studied in **Saigon** and then at the **Colonial Academy** (*École coloniale*) in Paris between 1900 and 1901. He returned to Laos where he was officially crowned King of Luang Prabang on 4 March 1905. He ruled over Luang Prabang until the Japanese overthrew the French in March 1945. Under Japanese pressure, he agreed to initialize a declaration of independence for Laos and the nullification of the French protectorate. However, he remained faithful to the French and bet his future on their return. To this end, he named Prince **Kindavong** his personal representative to the Provisional Government of the French Republic led by General **Charles de Gaulle.** On 30 August 1945, the king declared null and void the independence forced upon him by the Japanese and reaffirmed the legal validity and continuity of the French protectorate. He was adamantly opposed to the **Lao Issara** and Prince **Phetxarāt**, whom he stripped of his rank and titles. In return, the Lao Issara deposed the king by popular vote of the Provisional People's Assembly (though this decision was reversed in April 1946). The king fully supported the return of the French in 1946 and counted on them to protect Lao interests within the **Indochinese Federation**. In 1946, he approved a constitution for what became a unified Royal Lao government and in 1947 the French allowed Sīsāvangvong to become King of Laos. In July 1949, he signed the Franco-Lao convention by which Laos became an Associated State, the Lao Issara government was dissolved, and its members were allowed to return to Laos, except for Phetxarāt. The French bestowed on the king the *Croix de guerre* in recognition of his services to the French during World War II. *See also* ASSOCIATED STATES OF INDOCHINA.

**SISOWATH MONIPONG (1912–1956).** The uncle of King **Norodom Sihanouk** and one of his strongest political supporters. At the age of 15, Sisowath Monipong travelled to France to study under the supervision of the former *Résident Supérieur* François-Marius Baudoin. Between 1927 and 1930, Sisowath Monipong attended high school in Nice before returning to Cambodia to don the yellow Buddhist robe as a novice. He returned to France to complete his education and entered Saint-Cyr where he specialized in aviation. At the outbreak of World War II, he served as a second lieutenant in the French **Air Force** and was cited for bravery during the Battle of France. Following the armistice, he returned to Cambodia to serve as deputy general secretary of the Royal Palace. In January 1946, he signed the Franco-Khmer ***modus vivendi*** and served as prime minister in the Royal Government of Cambodia. In March 1950, the king named him chief of staff of the Royal Khmer Army, before Monipong became a few months later Cambodian prime minister and minister of the Interior and Information. He was a member of the Cambodian delegation to the **Pau Conference** that same year. In January 1951, he was renamed prime minister and held the portfolios of Health, Labor, and Social Action.

**SISOWATH SIRIK MATAK (1914–1975).** Graduated in 1938 from the *École nationale d'administration du Cambodge.* Little is known of his activities during World War II. He joined the **Democrat Party** in 1946 before moving on to the Renewal Party. In August 1949, he was put in charge of military affairs in the autonomous zone in Siemreap province but lost his post following a fall-out with **Dap Chhuon**. Sirik Matak was a member of the Cambodian delegation to the **Pau Conference** in 1950 and served as director of the Bureau of the Ministry of the Interior. Between June 1952 and January 1953, he was state secretary for National Defense. Between January and July 1953, he served as minister of Defence, Posts, and Telecommunications. He was a member of the Franco-Khmer military committee created by King **Norodom Sihanouk**.

**SISOWATH YOUTEVONG (1913–1947).** Completed his primary and secondary studies in Phnom

Penh and **Saigon** before pursuing his university education at the *Faculté des sciences de Montpellier*, from which he graduated in mathematics in 1941. He married a French woman. He joined the **Democrat Party** in 1946 and briefly served as prime minister and minister of the Interior in December 1946. He was one of the main architects of the constitution approved by King **Norodom Sihanouk** in 1947. He died of illness in 1947.

**SĪTHON KOMMADAM (1908–1977).** Important ethnic minority leader of the **Pathet Lao** and ally of the Vietnamese in charge of operations against the French in southern Laos during the Indochina War. Born in Attopeu province, he came from a family known for its opposition to the French during a famous revolt in the Bolavens. Little is known of his activities before or during World War II, except that he was incarcerated by the French and liberated by the Japanese following their ***coup de force*** **of 9 March 1945**. He joined the **Lao Issara** upon its creation in October 1945 and was active in **guerrilla** operations in southern Laos and north-eastern Thailand, where he worked closely with Vietnamese communists based out of Ubon. Following the dissolution of the Lao Issara in 1949, he refused to return to Laos and worked with the dissident Princes **Phetxarāt** and **Suphānuvong**. In 1950, he participated in the congress that created the **Lao Resistance Government** and national front. He became a minister without portfolio. *See also* PARTY AFFAIRS COMMITTEE; COMMITTEE FOR THE EAST, LAO ISSARA.

**SKRZHINSKY, PLATON ALEXANDROVICH (NGUYEN VAN THANH, 1922–2003).** Born and raised in the Ukraine, Skrzhinsky was one of the **Democratic Republic of Vietnam**'s (DRV) best known **crossovers**. Inducted into the Soviet Red Army in 1941, he saw combat against the Germans, who captured him in May 1942 and transferred him to Western Europe as a forced laborer. At the end of the war, he landed in France or Denmark with no place to go. Uninterested in returning to the Soviet Union, in April 1946 he joined the French **Foreign Legion** and soon found himself in Indochina as the French and the Vietnamese moved towards full-scale war. Opposed to what he saw as an unjust colonial war, he deserted his unit in southern Vietnam on 17 August 1947 and joined the DRV's ranks. He was inducted and served in the Vietnamese army between 1947 and 1955, active mainly on the southern front. He married a Vietnamese woman from Thu Dau Mot, had a daughter, and adopted the Vietnamese name, Nguyen Van Thanh. In 1954, following the division of Vietnam into two states at the **Geneva Conference**, he and his daughter regrouped to the north and were soon presented as an official symbol of Soviet-Vietnamese Friendship. When **Ho Chi Minh** made a major public appearance in **Hanoi** in January 1955, Skrzhinsky's daughter, Béatrice, was perched gently upon Ho's knee. Later in 1955, father and daughter were repatriated to the Soviet Union. Fluent in Vietnamese, Skrzhinsky became the first head of the Vietnamese Section of *Moscow Radio*, a position he held until retiring in the 1990s. He translated into Russian Phung Quan's *Breaking out of Poulo Condor* (*Vuot Con Dao*).

**SMITH, WALTER BEDELL (1895–1961).** Bedell Smith served on the Western Front in France during World War I and rose to the rank of lieutenant general in the United States Army during World War II. He owed his rapid ascent during this time to his effective work for General George Marshall, the army's chief of staff. In 1942, Smith became secretary of the combined chiefs of staff. In March 1944, the Supreme Allied Commander in Europe, **Dwight D. Eisenhower**, named him chief of staff, a position he held until the German surrender in May 1945. After the war, Smith served as ambassador to Moscow between 1946 and 1949. In 1950, President **Harry S. Truman** named him to lead the Central Intelligence Agency. He left this post in 1953, retired from the army, and turned to creating the National Security Agency. In 1953–54, Eisenhower, now president, named him under-Secretary of State. As negotiators at the **Geneva Conference** moved towards an agreement in mid-July, **Pierre Mendès France**, who had staked his position on making a deal on Indochina, pleaded with the Americans to send a high-ranking official to be present during the final act. Mendès France wanted the communist camp to see that the Americans were on board and that the Western camp was of the same mind on Indochina. **John Foster Dulles**, who had left the conference early on, agreed to send General Bedell Smith to head the American delegation at Geneva during the final sessions of the conference. Smith had already served as a ranking diplomat in the American delegation to the Geneva Conference earlier on. He had also worked as a deputy to Dulles on American policy towards Indochina, including operation **Vautour** and at the head of a special committee on Indochina. Smith left for Geneva. In line with Dulles' policy, at the end of the conference, he indicated that the United States took note of the agreement. However, he issued an official communiqué clarifying the American position. In it, he said that the United States abstained from taking note of Article 13 of the final declaration, meaning that the United States would not take part in consultations for implementing the execution of the accords. He added that Washington would only recognize elections organized under United Nations supervision, knowing that communist China was not part of the Security Council.

**SOCIALISTS, FRANCE.** *See SECTION FRANÇAISE DE L'INTERNATIONALE OUVRIÈRE.*

**SOK CHHONG (1918–1995).** Prominent economist and nationalist leader in Cambodia during the Indochina War. Born in Battambang province, he studied medicine at the *Faculté de medicine* in **Hanoi**, but did not graduate. He returned to Cambodia and entered the School of Forestry in 1942. Little is known of his activities during World War II. He served briefly in the police services of **Son Ngoc Thanh**'s government following the Japanese overthrow of the French in the ***coup de force* of 9 March 1945**. After the Pacific War, he helped create the **Democrat Party** in 1946 and became a deputy from Kompong Thom province in the National Assembly. In 1948, he served as counsellor to the Assembly of the **French Union** in Paris as a Democrat nominee, where he resided until 1951. He returned to Cambodia that year and resumed his activities in the Democrat Party. He served as minister for the National Economy in the **Huy Kanthoul** government between October 1951 and June 1952. When **Norodom Sihanouk** moved to consolidate his power against the Democrat party, the king had Sok Chhong arrested and imprisoned in January 1953 on anti-monarchist grounds.

**SOLOVIEFF, STEPHAN.** French-naturalized Russian who lived in Indochina from 1934 and ran the **Hanoi** office for Asia Life Insurance Company. After World War II, he helped the Soviet Union trace missing soldiers, including in Indochina. During this time, he worked with **Jean Sainteny**, commissioner for the French Republic to **Tonkin** and Northern **Annam**, especially during the negotiation of the **Accords of 6 March 1946**. He returned to France "as a friend" of the French in June 1946. *See also* JOSEPH STALIN; AID, SOVIET.

**SOM PHOMMACHAN.** Member of the **Lao Issara** and close ally of the Vietnamese in the resistance against the French. Born in Vientiane province, he joined the Lao Issara after World War II. He was one of the core members of the Lao Issara's **Committee for the East**, which collaborated closely with Vietnamese communists in **Inter-Zone IV** (*Lien Khu IV*). Following the dissolution of the Lao Issara in 1949, he joined the **Lao Resistance Government** in August 1950 and the **Pathet Lao** national front.

**SOMSANIT VONGKOTRATANA (1913–1975).** Non-communist Lao nationalist and politician. He began his career in the colonial bureaucracy in 1942, working as a local governor and a clerk in the *Résidence supérieure* in Vientiane. Little is known of his activities during World War II. Following the overthrow of the French in March 1945 and the defeat of the Japanese shortly thereafter, he joined the **Lao Issara** created in October 1945. He served as minister before following the government into exile in Thailand following the return of the French in mid-1946. With the dissolution of the Lao Issara in 1949, he returned to join the newly created Associated State of Laos. In 1950, he became chief of cabinet of the minister of Justice and in 1952 he was named chief of Nam Tha. In 1954, he took over as general director of the National Police for the Associated State of Laos.

**SON LA PRISON.** Created by the French at the turn of the 20th century, this northern prison located in northern Vietnam held some of the highest ranking Vietnamese communists until the Japanese overthrew the French during the ***coup de force* of 9 March 1945**. Those held included **Nguyen Luong Bang, Tran Quoc Hoan, Le Thanh Nghi, Le Gian**, **Le Duc Tho**, **Xuan Thuy**, **Van Tien Dung**, and **Nguyen Van Tran** among others. *See also* POULO CONDOR; JEAN COUSSEAU.

**SƠN NGỌC MINH (PHẠM VĂN HUA, 1908–1977).** Close ally of Vietnamese communists instrumental in developing communism in Cambodia during the Indochina War. Born to a Vietnamese father and a Cambodian mother, he spoke Vietnamese as fluently as his native Khmer. In the early 1930s, Son Ngoc Minh worked on the Tonle

Sap in Cambodia as a fisherman. In 1936, he began collaborating with **Nguyen Thanh Son** in My Tho province and was increasingly attracted to radical politics. With the help of Nguyen Thanh Son, Son Ngoc Minh created something of a communist cell in Svay Rieng in 1939. During World War II, he moved to Thailand but returned to Cambodia following the ousting of the French to support **Son Ngoc Thanh**'s government. With the return of the French to southern Indochina in late 1945, Son Ngoc Minh took refuge in Rach Gia and renewed his collaboration with Nguyen Thanh Son. According to French intelligence, in 1948 he changed his name to Son Ngoc Minh and began reorganizing the Khmer resistance movement in cooperation with Nguyen Thanh Son. The latter relied heavily upon Son Ngoc Minh to build up a revolutionary movement in Cambodia under the guidance of the **Indochinese Communist Party** and in alliance with the **Democratic Republic of Vietnam**'s Indochinese-wide struggle against the French. Son Ngoc Minh studied in the **Truong Chinh Academy** in Rach Gia sometime in the late 1940s, the equivalent of the Nguyen Ai Quoc Academy in the north. He led the **Cambodian Resistance Government** and the Revolutionary Party created in 1950 in collaboration with the Vietnamese. He attended the **Geneva Conference** as an observer and was repatriated when the subsequent **Geneva Accords** failed to provide the Cambodian Resistance Government with regrouping zones. *See also* SIEU HENG; *MÉTIS*; PARTY AFFAIRS COMMITTEE; KHMER KROM.

**SƠN NGỌC THANH (1908–1977).** Prominent Cambodian nationalist and politician during the entire Indochina War. Born in the Khmer-populated province (Tra Vinh) of colonial **Cochinchina** (known to many Cambodians as *Kampuchea Krom*), he completed his secondary studies in **Saigon** before moving to Phnom Penh where he became active in nationalist politics at the head of the paper *Nagaravatta* and in the *Institut bouddhique* under Suzanne Karpelès. During World War II, Son Ngoc Thanh played a pivotal role in organizing monks in nationalist ways to the consternation of Vichy authorities. Following the French repression of such a demonstration in 1942, Son Ngoc Thanh fled to Thailand where he took refuge in the Japanese Embassy in Bangkok. The latter hurried him off to Japan (where he became a captain in the army) until the ***coup de force* of 9 March 1945** ousting the French from Indochina.

Back in Cambodia, he declared the country independent on 13 March 1945. On 14 August 1945, he became prime minister and minister of Foreign Affairs in the first Cambodian government independent of the French since the 19th century. All of this was shortlived, however. Under orders to retake all of French Indochina, General **Philippe Leclerc** flew to Phnom Penh and delivered Son Ngoc Thanh to a Military Court in Saigon, where the latter received a sentence of 20 years of hard labor for "high treason". The French ended up bundling him off to France, putting him under a rather lax *résidence surveillée* at Poitiers, where he studied at the *Faculté de droit* between 1947 and 1950. His surveillance in France ended on 29 October 1951 upon the request of **Norodom Sihanouk.**

Two months later, Son Ngoc Thanh returned to Cambodia before a large crowd of supporters and resumed his nationalist activities. He renewed his call for the full independence of Cambodia. He was a natural born orator, capable of mesmerizing his Cambodian audiences, much to the concern of the French and the Cambodian Royal family, not least of all Sihanouk. Son Ngoc Thanh also communicated his ideas effectively through the modern press, resurrecting *Nagaravatta* in the form of a new nationalist paper, the *Khmer Krok* (The Awakening of the Khmer). When the paper was closed down in February 1952, Son Ngoc Thanh fled to the *maquis* in Siemreap where he continued to use the radio and the newspaper to exhort the population and Cambodians working in the French and Royal army to join his nationalist project. Before leaving Phnom Penh, Son Ngoc Thanh had also developed good working relations with two important nationalist forces in Cambodian politics – the **Democrat Party** and **Dap Chhuon**. Thanks to his contacts with the Democrats, Son Ngoc Thanh succeeded in organizing student demonstrations in Phnom Penh in May 1952 calling for the full independence of Cambodia.

Determined to maintain control of the political situation, in June 1952 King **Norodom Sihanouk** relieved one of Son Ngoc Thanh's Democrat allies, **Huy Kanthoul**, of his post as prime minister and began preparing his own **royal crusade for independence**. On the defensive, Son Ngoc Thanh entered into limited contact with the forces of the **Democratic Republic of Vietnam** but little came of this. With the end of the Indochina War in 1954, Son Ngoc Thanh returned to legal politics but, as one French intelligence officer confided at the time, the Royal Government of Cambodia had only partially won him over to its side. In 1972, he briefly served as prime minister when **Lon Nol** did away with the monarchy and Sihanouk. *See also* KHMER KROM.

**SON SANN (1911–2000).** Born in the Khmer-populated province of **Cochinchina** (Tra Vinh), he studied at the *École Miche* in Phnom Penh before entering the *Collège de St-Aspais* in Melun, France. From there, he entered the elite Parisian school, the *Lycée Louis-le-Grand*. Upon graduating from the *École des hautes études commerciales* in 1933, he returned to Cambodia, entered the colonial administration in 1935, and served as governor of Battambang province. Son Sann was active in creating and developing the **scouting** movement in Prey Veng province. In 1939, he left his bureaucratic post to work in the *Maison Denis Frères* in Phnom Penh. Nasir Carime-Abdoul states that he worked in the *Au Petit Paris* in Phnom Penh and remained there until 1945. During World War II, Son Sann travelled to Tokyo to participate in an economic conference involved in negotiating rice exports to Japan. He was also active in the patriotic and mobilization movements let loose by the Japanese and the Vichy regime. At the same time, he was among those who served as educators to the new boy king, **Norodom Sihanouk**. Son Sann dispensed lessons in economics.

After World War II, in 1946, he became a member of the **Democrat Party**. In December 1946, he joined the **Sisowath Youtevong** cabinet as minister of Finance and served in the Sisowath Watchayvong cabinet as vice president in July 1947. He held the same post in the **Penn Nouth** cabinet constituted in August 1948 and again in March 1949. In 1949, as separate associated states came into being for Cambodia, Laos, and Vietnam, Son Sann was involved in negotiations over the status of **Khmer Krom** populations living in southern Vietnam. Between May 1950 and March 1951, he served as minister of Foreign Affairs in the **Sisowath Monipong** cabinet and attended the **Pau Conference**. In October 1951, he was elected president of the National Assembly, serving as a Democrat deputy for Phnom Penh. Following **Norodom Sihanouk**'s dismissal of **Huy Kanthoul** in 1952, Son Sann withdrew from the Democrat Party and politics for the rest of the Indochina War.

**SONG HÀO (NGUYỄN VĂN KHƯƠNG, 1917–2004).** Prominent Vietnamese general in the **Democratic Republic of Vietnam**. Born in Nam Ha province in northern Vietnam, he became politically active during the Popular Front period in the late 1930s and joined the **Indochinese Communist Party** (ICP) in 1939. In 1940, he was arrested and imprisoned by the French. He escaped in August 1944 and became a political commissar in the emerging Vietnamese **National Salvation Army**. He attended the conference in Tan Trao in August 1945 and was responsible for taking power in Tuyen Quang and Ha Giang provinces. In late 1945, he became a member of the ICP's Territorial Committee for northern Vietnam (*Xu Uy Bac Bo*) responsible for the provinces of Ha Giang, Tuyen Quang, and Thai Nguyen. During the Indochina War, he was a political commissar in **Inter-Zone X** (*Lien Khu X*), the northwestern zone, and was the secretary for the powerful **Party Affairs Committee** for Vietnamese volunteer troop in upper Laos. With the decision to rename the ICP the **Vietnamese Worker's Party**, in 1950 he led a party delegation to Laos to hold discussions with counterparts there concerning the need to create a separate Lao communist party. Between 1951 and 1954, he was a political commissar in the 308th Division, the secretary of the Division's Party Committee, and a member of the **International Commission for Supervision and Control in Vietnam** for the implementation of the **Geneva Accords**.

**SONN VOEUNSAI (1911–1986).** Born in Phnom Penh, he completed his secondary studies at the *Collège Sisowath* in Phnom Penh and *Lycée Chasseloup Laubat* in **Saigon** before graduating as an engineer from the *École centrale des arts et manufactures* in Paris. He became a French citizen in 1928 and resided in France between 1931 and 1939. As a reserve officer in the French army in Indochina, he was mobilized between 1939 and 1942 in the *Régiment des tirailleurs cambodgiens*. Relieved of active duty that year, he worked in the colonial Public Works Department in Phnom Penh until the end of World War II. Between October 1945 and December 1946, he served as deputy minister of National Defence in the cabinet of Prince Sisowath Monireth. He held the same post in the **Sisowath Youtevong** cabinet (December 1946–July 1947) and the Sisowath Watchayvong government (July 1947–February 1948). Sonn Voeunsai was minister of the National Economy, Public Works, and Communications in the **Chhean Vam** cabinet (February–August 1948) and in the **Penn Nouth** government (August 1948–January 1949). He was involved in negotiations over the status of parts of Khmer-populated areas in former colonial **Cochinchina**, now a part of the emerging Associated State of Vietnam. In 1950–1951, he served **Norodom Sihanouk** and **Sisowath Monipong** as minister of Defence. Under **Huy Kanthoul**, he served as minister of the Interior and National Defence between October 1951 and June 1952. In June 1952, he was re-elected Deputy General Secretary of the Democrat Party. One month later, with the departure of Son Sann, Sonn Voeunsai took charge of the Democrat Party. His influence waned, however, with Sihanouk's consolidation of political power in 1953. *See also* ROYAL CRUSADE FOR INDEPENDENCE

**SOULAT, HENRI (1918–1989).** Joined the French **Air Force** in 1937 and distinguished himself in the resistance during World War II. He took part in the Allied landing at Normandy in 1944. In September 1950, the Air Force transferred him to Indochina to work as a transport pilot. After a short stint in France, he returned to Indochina in September 1952 to lead the 2nd squadron of C-119s based at Cat Bi airbase. He made the first and last supply mission over **Dien Bien Phu** in 1954.

**SOUTH EAST ASIA TREATY ORGANIZATION (SEATO)**. As the Chinese moved to neutralize non-communist Asia against the Americans during the **Geneva Conference**, the Americans, led by **John Foster Dulles**, accelerated their efforts to create an anti-communist collective security organization for Southeast Asia. Hardly a month after the ink had dried on the **Geneva Accords**, the Americans presided over the signing of the Manila Treaty on 8 September 1954, creating the South East Asia Treaty Organization or SEATO as it is more commonly known. Its members included: the United States, France, the United Kingdom, Australia, New Zealand, the Philippines, Pakistan, and Thailand.

Together with the Bagdad Pact, the **North Atlantic Treaty Organization** (NATO), and the treaty signed with Taiwan at about the same time, SEATO was the Southeast Asian link in Washington's global containment of Sino–Soviet communist expansion via the South. As Dulles put it, SEATO was a "no trespassing" sign telling the Soviet Union and China to keep out of Southeast Asia. While Laos, Cambodia, and the **Republic of Vietnam** had been barred by the Geneva agreements from joining such a foreign military pact, a special protocol in the Manila Treaty included these countries within the SEATO zone (even though they were not officially members of the pact). Based in Bangkok, SEATO was in the end more of a deliberative and consultative body. Unlike NATO, SEATO had no troops under its command, no military structure, nor did it bind its members to respond if one member state were attacked. They would consult and respond as dictated by their own national political systems.

If certain Asian states, such as **India**, **Burma,** and **Indonesia**, did not take part in SEATO, it was largely because they had opted for a neutral path, something which membership in SEATO would have denied them. On 29 September 1954, **Jawaharlal Nehru** told his parliament that the Manila Treaty was "dangerous" for "any Asian state". Not everyone saw it this way, however. Membership in SEATO and the continued presence of the **Expeditionary Corps** in lower Vietnam allowed the French to maintain their claim to being a world power on the same level as the British. In April 1956, the French withdrew the Expeditionary Corps from Indochina and concentrated their attention on the **Algerian War.** It was only after the Evian Accords in 1962 that Charles de Gaulle, the man who had led France into the Indochina War, could distance France from the Americans, their war in Vietnam, and SEATO. *See also* NEUTRALIZATION OF INDOCHINA.

**SOUTH VIETNAM.** *See* REPUBLIC OF VIETNAM.

**SPCE.** *See SERVICE DE PROTECTION DU CORPS EXPÉDITIONNAIRE.*

**SPECIAL AIR SERVICE (SAS).** This term, as used by the French, referred to "British paratrooper **commandos"** (*commandos-parachutistes britanniques*) with whom Free French forces trained and fought during World War II, mainly in Europe. Indeed, the English term "SAS" entered the French military vocabulary via French officers trained in SAS operations in Ringway in Great Britain in 1944–1945. After the war, French officers, notably **Pierre Ponchardier** and **Jacques-Pâris de Bollardière**, modeled the creation of their commando paratrooper teams for Indochina on the SAS model of World War II. Ponchardier's unit was referred to as the SASB (B for battalion), while Bollardière created the *Demi-Brigade* SAS. Over time, during the Indochina War, the French SAS was incorporated into the Colonial Paratroopers (*paras coloniaux*). The French SAS disappeared in 1948.

**SPECIAL FORCES, DEMOCRATIC REPUBLIC OF VIETNAM (*Biet Dong*).** Clandestine, **commando** troops employed by the **Democratic Republic of Vietnam** (DRV) behind enemy lines. These undercover troops lived within the heart of French controlled zones, especially in urban centers. Each combatant practiced a legitimate profession as a cover (worker, soldier, policeman, secretary, taxi-girl, etc.). On a signal, these forces would launch surprise commando attacks against pre-ordained targets. Secrecy and their undercover identities transformed the element of surprise into an effective military tactic for striking otherwise unattainable installations or enemies for the DRV's regular forces. This meant that *Biet Dong* troops had to attain a perfect "integration in the masses" (*quan chung hoa*) and obtain a waterproof legal situation (*hop phap hoa*). Such commando teams struck down French and collaborating Vietnamese enemies, launched sabotage operations, and, more rarely, destroyed enemy ships, tanks, or airplanes. One of the most famous *biet dong* operations was the audacious attack on the French military airbase at Gia Lam on 8 March 1954, part of a wider effort to block the aerial supplying of **Dien Bien Phu**. One of the members of this special force team was **Hoang Minh Chinh**, an eminent intellectual who the DRV placed under communist arrest in the 1960s. *See also GROUPEMENT DE COMMANDOS MIXTES AÉROPORTÉS*; *SERVICE ACTION*; SPECIAL AIR SERVICE.

**SPILLMANN, GEORGES JOSEPH ROGER ANDRÉ (1899–1980).** A graduate of Saint-Cyr in 1917, Spillmann first distinguished himself in battle during World War I. During the interwar period, he joined the colonial army in French Africa, where he served in the intelligence services and "indigenous affairs" offices between 1920 and 1945. A trusted advisor to Marshal Louis Hubert Lyautey, Spillmann participated in the "**pacification**" of rebellious parts of Morocco in the late 1920s and early 1930s. Promoted to battalion leader shortly after the outbreak of World War II, he led the 6th Regiment of Tabor Moroccans (*6ème régiment de Tabors marocains*) in May 1940. He joined the chief of cabinet to General Catroux in Algiers in September 1943 and took part in the **Brazzaville Conference** in January 1944. In 1945, Spillmann returned to France where he worked with General **Jean de Lattre de Tassigny** and followed him to Indochina in 1950, when the latter became high commissioner and commander-in-chief of the armed forces in Indochina. General de Lattre put Spillman in charge of the French Military Mission attached to the Associated State of Vietnam. Spillman left Indochina in 1952 for health reasons and returned to France as a brigadier general. He would serve in Algeria as the head of the military division of Constantine.

**STALIN, JOSEPH (1878–1953).** Between 1922 and 1953, Stalin served as General Secretary of the Communist Party of the Union of Soviet Socialist Republics (USSR) and ruled the massive Eurasian state with an iron fist following the death of Lenin in 1924. During the interwar period, Stalin focused mainly on the communist transformation of the USSR. While he supported the Comintern's activities in Asia, he was never a great believer in the socio-economic prospects for socialist revolution in the non-industrialized East. With the rise of the Nazis in Germany and the expansion of the Japanese into Manchuria in the early 1930s, Stalin placed greater emphasis on security in defining his dealings in Asia. Like the United States, he maintained his diplomatic relations with **Chiang Kai-shek**'s **Republic of China** in order to check the Japanese, now in charge of a Manchurian government bordering the Soviet Union. Ties existed between Stalin and **Mao Zedong**, now holed up in the caves of Yan'an; but as the world slid into war and the Nazis invaded the USSR, Stalin's main Asian partner was Chiang Kai-shek, not Mao Zedong. As for Vietnamese communists, Stalin gave little if any real thought to them or their plight in light of his larger wartime concerns. Moreover, in 1943, Stalin disbanded the Comintern to reassure the Allies of his good intentions, but in so doing removed an important network linking Asian communists and information to Moscow.

With the end of World War II and the advent of the **Democratic Republic of Vietnam**, **Ho Chi Minh** fired off letters to **Harry Truman**, Chiang Kai-shek, and Joseph Stalin, pleading with them to support Vietnamese independence. Long out of touch, the Soviets knew little about Vietnam and Stalin certainly did not give much thought to Ho Chi Minh and his problems with the French. Stalin was much more focused on Europe and had little desire to annoy the French at a time when the **French Communist Party** (FCP) was strong. When Ho Chi Minh's request arrived on the desk of S. P. Kozyrev, chief of the European section of the Ministry of Foreign Affairs in Moscow, the latter wrote on it simply: "Not to answer." Like the United States, Stalin had no intention of forcing the French hand on decolonization via the **United Nations**.

Stalin's obsession with Tito from 1948 complicated the DRV's isolation from the USSR. In fact, Stalin was one of Ho Chi Minh's doubters. **Maurice Thorez**, general secretary of the FCP at the time, tried to convince Stalin that Ho was a reliable and authentic communist believer. According to Thorez, Stalin felt that Ho Chí Minh had gone too far in his collaboration with the Americans during World War II and was annoyed by Ho Chi Minh's failure to solicit advice from him before making major decisions. Stalin cited Ho Chi Minh's decision to dissolve the ICP in 1945. According to Ilya Gaiduk, in a memo on the DRV dated 14 January 1950, the Soviet Foreign Ministry pointed out that in Ho Chi Minh's interviews "there is some ambiguity … Speaking about the Vietnam government's attitude towards the U.S., Ho Cho Minh evades the issue of U.S. expansionist policy towards Vietnam. … Until now Ho Chi Minh has abstained from the assessment of the imperialist nature of the North Atlantic Pact and of the U.S. attempt to establish a Pacific bloc as a branch of this pact." Stalin had also suspected Mao Zedong of Titoism. The Soviet leader feared that these "Asian" leaders were, at the core, more nationalist than internationalist and, like Tito, would not necessarily toe the Soviet line in this tense time in the **Cold War**.

In the end, victorious Chinese communists played the decisive role in convincing a reluctant Stalin to take sides by diplomatically recognizing the DRV in January 1950. Had Chinese communists agreed with Stalin and balked at recognizing the DRV, it would have dealt a catastrophic blow to the DRV in its drive for independence. In exchange for his support, however, Stalin insisted in meetings with Ho Chi Minh in 1950 and again in 1952 that the Vietnamese could not have it both ways. They had to adopt communist policies, the most important of which was **land reform**. Vietnamese communists complied.

**STR.** *See SERVICE TECHNIQUE DES RECHERCHES.*

**SƯ RĨ.** *See* NGUYỄN CHÍ THANH.

**SUK VONGSAK (1913–1983)**. Senior member of the **Lao Issara** government. Born in Luang Prabang, he was educated in the *École de droit et d'administration* before joining the colonial administration in Laos. After serving in the Secretariat of the Royal Palace of Luang Prabang, he became personal secretary to the governor of Vientiane, **Xieng Mao.** Following the Japanese overthrow of the French in March 1945, he served as governor of Paksane. He joined the Lao Issara government in October 1945. Following the return of the French to all of Laos in mid-1946, he followed the national government into exile in Thailand, where he was responsible for propaganda and information. Upon the dissolution of the Lao Issara in 1949, representatives of the **Democratic Republic of Vietnam** and Prince **Suphānuvong** persuaded him to travel to northern Vietnam, where he participated in the congress that produced the **Lao Resistance Government** and the new national front, the **Pathet Lao**. Suk Vongsak represented the province of Paksane in the new government and became minister of Education and Propaganda. He went on to become an important leader of the Pathet Lao. *See also* PARTY AFFAIRS COMMITTEE; ADVISOR GROUP 100.

**SUPHĀNUVONG, Prince (CHINH, 1912–1995).** Leading royalist leader of the **Pathet Lao**. Related to the royal branch of Luang Prabang, he was a half-brother to Prince **Phetxarāt** and **Suvanna Phūmā**. He undertook his primary and secondary studies in **Hanoi** between 1921 and 1931, where he graduated from the *Lycée Albert Sarraut*. He then travelled to France to study at the *Lycée Saint Louis*. In 1934, he entered the prestigious *École nationale des ponts et chaussées* from which he graduated in 1937 as a civil engineer. After completing several internships in France, he returned to Indochina and in 1938 joined the *Administration des travaux publics d'Indochine*. He worked as an engineer in Nha Trang, Muong Phin, and Vinh into the early 1940s. In 1943, he published an article in the Vichy cultural magazine, *Indochine* (no. 133, 18 March 1943) in which he praised the national revolution let loose by Vichy during World War II. Fluent in Vietnamese, he married a Vietnamese woman from Nha Trang during his work there, Nguyen Thi Ky Nam (Vieng Kham was her adopted Lao name).

Following the defeat of the Japanese in August 1945, his older half-brother, Prince Phetxarāt, cabled to ask him to return to Laos immediately to take part in the making of a postcolonial Laos. **Viet Minh** representatives contacted him at about the same time and invited him to Hanoi to visit **Ho Chi Minh** to discuss similar things. Suphānuvong travelled to Hanoi by car from Hue in the company of **Le Van Hien**, future minister of Finances in the **Democratic Republic of Vietnam** (DRV) and later ambassador to Laos. After a brief meeting with Ho Chi Minh and others in Hanoi, Suphānuvong returned to Laos and began creating anti-colonialist committees in Thakhek and Savannakhet. He joined the **Lao Issara** government in October 1945, serving as foreign minister.

From the outset, he worked closely with DRV representatives active among the **overseas Vietnamese** in northeast Thailand. Together they organized the defence of Thakhek against the return of French forces in March 1946. The Prince was injured while escaping to Thailand across the Mekong. A young soldier, Le Thieu Huy,[14] threw himself over the prince to protect him from gunfire; the young Vietnamese man died in Suphānuvong's arms. Suphānuvong continued to serve as minister of Foreign Affairs in the Lao Issara government-in-exile and was commander-in-chief of Lao Issara troops from December 1946. He became general secretary of the short-lived South East Asia League upon its creation in September 1947. In 1948 and 1949, he commanded troops positioned along the northern Thai–Lao–Burmese border.

However, working relations between the independent-minded prince and the Lao Issara leadership turned from bad to worse as the French stepped up the pressure to reach a deal putting an end to their dissidence. On 16 May 1949, the Lao Issara relieved Suphānuvong of his functions as minister of Foreign Affairs and of Defence. When the Franco-Lao Treaty of 1949 gave birth to the Associated State of Laos and the dissolution of the Lao Issara, Suphānuvong refused to return to Laos. Instead he intensified his reliance on DRV delegates in Thailand. In late 1949, he travelled to northern Vietnam on the invitation of Ho Chi Minh to build a new Lao revolutionary government in collaboration with the Vietnamese. In August 1950, he helped create the **Lao Resistance Government** and the Pathet Lao nationalist front. When Prince Phetxarāt refused to serve as president, Suphānuvong became the chief of the new resistance government. In 1953, as the DRV's divisions occupied large swaths of eastern Laos, Suphānuvong returned to Laos from Vietnam to run the "resistance government".

Suphānuvong was one of the DRV's closest Lao collaborators during the entire Indochina War, third only to **Kaisôn Phomvihān** and **Nūhak Phūmsavan**. The Vietnamese called him *Chinh* and *Cu*, meaning venerable one. The communist leadership of Laos has recently unveiled a monument in Luang Prabang in honor of the "Red Prince". *See also* ASSOCIATED STATES OF INDOCHINA; METIS; PARTY AFFAIRS COMMITTEE.

***SÛRETÉ FÉDÉRALE.*** The colonial security and police service in charge of French Indochina until the withdrawal of the French following the **Geneva Accords** of July 1954. The *Sûreté* was first created in Indochina during World War I thanks to the efforts of Governor General **Albert Sarraut** and his allies, most notably Louis Marty. The *Sûreté* closely tracked the birth, growth, and activities of Vietnamese communists and nationalists inside and outside of French Indochina. It was on a number of occasions remarkably effective in shutting down anti-colonial activities, especially in 1930–1931 and again in 1940–1941. One ranking French intelligence officer in Indochina considered it to be "all powerful" (*toute puissante*) until early 1945.

The Japanese ***coup de force* of 9 March 1945** changed all that. Not only did the Japanese bring down French Indochina in that month, but with it they put an end to the existing French colonial police services. Following the Japanese defeat a few months later, Vietnamese nationalists in the south and especially above the **16th parallel** took over French *Sûreté* offices, files, archives, and often their techniques. When the French returned to southern Indochina in late 1945, they moved to rebuild their civil police and security services. However, the *Sûreté* would never regain its prewar effectiveness. Too many of its Vietnamese personnel were compromised in 1945; some of its best French officers were purged by Gaullists for their collaboration with Vichy, including Paul

14. Le Thieu Huy, educated in France, was the son of the interwar Vietnamese intellectual, politician, and journalist, Le Thuoc.

Arnoux; and the colonial police apparently never regained the financing it had during the interwar period.

Nevertheless, if the Indochinese colonial state were to function again, the *Sûreté* had to be remade as well. On 14 September 1945, the French created the *Service de Sûreté de la Cochinchine*, relying upon recently liberated French and Vietnamese security personnel. On 17 September 1945, an attempt to recreate the Indochinese Security Service occurred when nine bureaucrats of the colonial police created the *Direction de la Police et de la Sûreté générale,* which returned to its earlier address once the French retook **Saigon** on **23 September 1945**. However, since March 1945, this service had lost some 800 Indochinese personnel. Like the ***Deuxième Bureau***, the territorial reach of the *Sûreté* became more concrete and geographically complete as the French extended their military and political presence into Cambodia and then, in 1946, discreetly into areas above the 16th parallel.

Squadron Leader **Georges Buis** assumed the interim direction of the reconstituted *Sûreté* in 1945. In December 1945, **André Moret**, who had previously directed the political section of the French police in Shanghai, took charge of reorganizing the *Sûreté*'s activities in **Tonkin**, while a certain M. Thierry did the same in Cambodia from late September. **Pierre Perrier** became the new director of the federal police and security forces. He was in direct liaison with other civil and military intelligence services, including the *Deuxième Bureau* and the ***Bureau fédéral de documentation***.

The French colonial security and police services operated out of the main capitals of each of the five parts of Indochina, each of which was in charge of smaller posts throughout their territories. With the creation of the **Provisional Government of the Republic of Cochinchina**, on 8 July 1946 there came also a separate *Sûreté nationale cochinchinoise*. However, in light of its limited resources and under attack from the **Democratic Republic of Vietnam** (DRV), the French *Direction de la Police et de la Sûreté générale* supported it and would continue to do so as the *Sûreté nationale cochinchinoise* eventually morphed into the national intelligence service for the Associated State of Vietnam from 1949.

A national police force in Cambodia came to life in September 1945, in the absence of the French. The French were able to ally their security forces with this nationally inspired one in the ***modus vivendi*** of March 1946. Despite some friction at the outset, collaboration became increasingly effective in light of the wider struggle against the DRV and its Indochinese-wide pretensions. Following the return of the French to all of Laos in mid-1946, an accord was struck in July according to which a national police service would be created in Laos. Until then, the French services filled in.

As for Tonkin/Bac Bo and **Annam**/Trung Bo north of the 16th parallel, the DRV refused to recognize, much less allow the overt extension of, the colonial police and security services in nationally controlled territory. The DRV only tolerated Moret's work in **Hanoi** in order to avoid triggering a premature war. Following the outbreak of full-scale war on **19 December 1946**, however, the French obviously felt no qualms about extending their federal services to all of Annam and Tonkin. Although the idea of creating an **Indochinese Federation** was rapidly fading by late 1947, the name "federal" continued to be used when referring to the *Sûreté*.

This changed with the creation of the Associated State of Vietnam under **Bao Dai** in 1949, when the French began decolonizing their police and security services. The French transferred control of the federal police and security services to their counterparts in northern (15 June 1950), central (18 July 1950), southern Vietnam (10 March 1950), and early 1951 for the highlands. However, it was harder to hand over more sensitive parts of the colonial security apparatus, including a secret section called the "territorial surveillance" (*surveillance du territoire*), military security, the highly sensitive 5th Section in charge of controlling postal and telegraph communications, and the equally secretive "*Police spéciale*". As a result, on 5 April 1950, the French created the *Services de Sécurité du Haut-Commissariat en Indochine*, complete with its territorial subdivisions, in order to ensure some of the main tasks of the former security service and to run the "non-transferable" parts of the former colonial *Sûreté*. Pierre Perrier ran this new service and much of the show.

However, the Associated State of Vietnam increasingly asserted its prerogatives and cooperation was not always ensured between the French and the Vietnamese fighting the **Viet Minh**. In October 1953, as the French were forced to decolonize further, the *Service de Sécurité du Haut-Commissariat* was dissolved and integrated into the *Service de Protection du Corps expéditionnaire*, whose archives can be consulted in part in the *Centre des Archives d'Outre-Mer* in Aix-en-Provence, France. *See also* PUBLIC SECURITY SERVICE; *SERVICE DE DOCUMENTATION EXTÉRIEURE ET DE CONTRE-ESPIONNAGE*; MAURICE BELLEUX; ANTOINE SAVANI; LE GIAN; TRAN HIEU.

**SURLEAU, MARCEL-ANDRÉ (1900–1976).** Career colonial civil servant in Indochina. Born in New Caledonia into a protestant family, he graduated at the top of his class at the **Colonial Academy** (*École coloniale*) in 1921. He was a **Freemason**. In 1925, he obtained his degree in law and in the Vietnamese language and left to begin a long Indochinese career. He served as a colonial administrator in Long Xuyen in southern Vietnam (1925–1926), as deputy to the French *résident* at Pakse in Laos (1926–30), as chief of cabinet of the *résident supérieur* to Laos (1934), and *résident* to Savannakhet (1934–1936). He directed the *Service Radiophonique Indochine* (*Radio* ***Saigon***) between 1939 and 1941 before serving as governor of My Tho province in 1941–1942, when Vichy relieved him of his functions in 1942 because of his Freemason affiliation. To make ends meet, Surleau turned to business interests in Can Tho and then became the director of a business group selling soap and bottled oil and vinegar in southern Indochina during the rest of the war. In 1945, he was recalled to the colonial service. He served as colonial administrator of Cholon, in charge of Political Affairs, and took charge of *Radio Saigon.* In October 1945, a grenade explosion injured him during his work to re-establish the police force in the area. He returned to France and between 1946 and 1955 headed up the Indochinese Section of the Intercolonial Information Service and then entered the ministry in charge of relations with the **Associated States of Indochina**. In 1952–1954, at the personal request of **Nguyen Van Tam**, Surleau worked in the Embassy of the Associated State of Vietnam to Paris in the Press and Information Service. During this time, he was most preoccupied with repatriating the French population leaving Indochina. Between 1955 and 1959, he was vice president of the Interministerial Commission involved in repatriating these populations.

**SUVANNA PHŪMĀ (1901–1984).** Prominent non-communist Lao nationalist who pushed the French to decolonize and tried to steer Laos down a neutral path as the **Cold War** bore down upon Indochina. Born in Luang Prabang of royal blood, he completed his primary and secondary schooling in Luang Prabang and in colonial **Hanoi** at the *Lycée Albert Sarraut* before pursuing advanced studies in France from 1927. He graduated in 1928 from the *École des travaux publics et du bâtiment de Paris* and then in 1930 from the *École supérieure d'électricité de Grenoble*. Suvanna Phūmā returned to Laos in 1931 to work as an engineer. He was the younger brother of Prince **Phetxarāt** and a half-brother of Prince **Suphānuvong**. In August 1933, he married a school-teacher, Aline Claire Allard, born in Phongsaly province to a French father and Lao mother. Until 1940, Suvanna Phūmā worked in the Department of Architecture and Public Works in Vientiane. He was involved in road building projects and the restoration of Lao monuments, including *Wat Phra Keo* in Vientiane. During World War II, he worked in the colonial public works administration in Laos.

Following the overthrow of the French and the defeat of the Japanese in 1945, Suvanna Phūmā joined the **Lao Issara** government in October 1945, serving as minister of Public Works. He fled Laos in April 1946 for Bangkok following the return of the French by force. There he served in the Lao Issara government in exile as vice president of council and was in charge of economic planning. In July 1949, when a Franco-Lao accord was reached to create the Associated State of Laos, Suvanna Phūmā accepted the dissolution of the Lao Issara and returned to Laos, making his way to Vientiane in October or November 1949, when he became minister of Public Works in the **Phuy Xananikôn** government and succeeded him as prime minister in November 1951. Suvanna Phūmā attended the signing of the Franco-Lao Treaty in July 1949 and was a member of the Lao Progressive Party.

In October 1953, faced with the invasion of **Democratic Republic of Vietnam** troops into Laos and their support of the **Pathet Lao** led by his half-brother Suphānuvong, Suvanna Phūmā pressured the French to accord Laos its full independence in a Treaty of Friendship and Association signed on 22 October 1953. This occurred as the battle for **Dien Bien Phu** was shaping up. Laos remained within the **French Union**, however, and signed a defense accord with Paris. Suvanna Phūmā resigned his premiership in October 1954, following the signing of the **Geneva Accords** and the withdrawal of Vietnamese troops. *See also* ASSOCIATED STATES OF INDOCHINA.

**SUVANNARĀT, Prince (1893–1960).** Born into the royal family of Luang Prabang, he completed his secondary studies in Phnom Penh between 1908 and 1911 before pursuing advanced studies in France between 1911 and 1914. He entered the Lao section of the Lao Colonial Administration in 1915 and helped in putting down revolts in northern Laos. During World War II, Suvannarāt served as minister of the Royal Government of Luang Prabang. Following the Japanese overthrow of the French in March 1945 and the defeat of the Japanese shortly thereafter, the newly created **Lao Issara** government removed Suvannarāt from his position. Following the return of the French to Laos in 1946, he served twice as prime minister of Laos between 1947 and 1949. He retired from political life with the dissolution of the Lao Issara and the creation of the Associated State of Laos.

# T

**TẠ NGỌC PHÁCH.** *See* TRẦN ĐỘ.

**TẠ QUANG BỬU (1910–1986).** One of the best-known Vietnamese **intellectuals** and diplomats of the **Democratic Republic of Vietnam** (DRV) between 1945 and 1954. Born in Nghe An province in central Vietnam, he studied mathematics and electrical engineering in France and was one of the rare Indochinese, other than Lao Prince **Phetxarāth Rattanavongsā**, to have studied in Great Britain (briefly at Oxford). On his return to Vietnam, Ta Quang Buu taught school and worked as a lamp manufacturer near Hue. During this time, he also became increasingly involved in nationalist politics and youth mobilization, creating a local branch of the Vietnamese **scouting** organization in central Vietnam.

After the overthrow of the French in Indochina in March 1945, he served as assistant to the minister of Youth, **Phan Anh**, in the **Tran Trong Kim** government in the royal capital of Hue. After the Japanese defeat, he joined the DRV bringing with him a good part of the central Vietnamese scouting movement. He was not a member of the **Indochinese Communist Party**. The DRV made him a professor at the University of **Hanoi** and director of the Polytechnical College of Hanoi, where he often taught history. His Oxford English surprised **Archimedes Patti**, who met him in Hanoi in late 1945. In 1946, Ta Quang Buu was an under-secretary of state in the provisional government before being elected deputy to the National Assembly in early 1946. In 1947, he briefly served as minister of Defense, only to relinquish his post to **Vo Nguyen Giap** to become a vice minister, a position he held until 1960 (except for about a year in 1947–1948, when he replaced Vo Nguyen Giap as minister of Defense).

Ta Quang Buu was also deeply involved in the DRV's diplomacy during the Indochina War. He was part of the Vietnamese delegation to the **Fontainebleau Conference** in mid-1946 and to the **Geneva Conference** in 1954, where he worked in tandem with **Ha Van Lau** and was co-president of the military commission with General **Henri Delteil**. In secret military negotiations with his French counterparts, Ta Quang Buu fleshed out positions over the demarcation line, regrouping zones, and the nature of a cease-fire. He signed the cease-fire agreement at Geneva on behalf of Vo Nguyen Giap, the minister of Defense for the DRV. *See also* TRUNG GIA CONFERENCE.

**TẠ THÁI AN.** *See* HOÀNG MINH THẢO.

**TẠ THU THÂU (1906–1945).** Leading Vietnamese Trotskyist killed in revolutionary violence in mid-1945. Born in Long Xuyen province in southern Vietnam, he studied to become a schoolteacher in **Saigon** in 1925. He also became increasingly involved in patriotic and revolutionary politics, taking part in student demonstrations sparked by the death of Phan Chu Trinh in 1926. In 1927, Ta Thu Thau traveled to France and enrolled in the *Faculté des sciences de Paris* and became increasingly involved in left-wing politics, becoming a Trotskyist in 1929. He was expelled for that reason from France in 1929. On his return to southern Vietnam, he joined a common front with "Stalinist" communists and jointly edited *La Lutte*, an influential leftist paper published between 1933 and 1937. He was elected a Municipal Counselor in Saigon in 1935 and commanded considerable popularity at the time. The French arrested him in 1937 and sentenced him to two years in prison. He was released in February 1939 but arrested and deported to **Poulo Condor** in October 1940. Following the Japanese ***coup de force* of 9 March 1945** ousting the French from Indochina, Ta Thu Thau regained his liberty and traveled to northern Vietnam to contact Trotskyites there. Upon his return to the south in the heady days of August and September 1945, he was caught up in the revolutionary violence sweeping parts of Vietnam, and which got badly out of hand in areas of Quang Ngai province. In September, local communist authorities there executed him. However, they were not necessarily working on orders from the central government, the **Indochinese Communist Party** (ICP), or the **Viet Minh**'s General Directorate (***Tong Bo***) all based in **Hanoi**. It was also at this time and in this province where similar local revolutionary councils almost executed **Le Van Hien**, a loyal communist and future minister in the **Democratic Republic of Vietnam**. After heated exchanges, Le Van Hien finally convinced his captors to contact the ICP by telephone or telegraph. They did and it saved him from certain death. *See also* EXECUTIONS; HÉRAULT, MASSACRE.

**TẠ TIẾN.** *See* TẠ XUÂN THU.

**TẠ XUÂN THU (TẠ TIẾU, 1916–1971).** Born in Thai Binh province in northern Vietnam, Ta Xuan Thu joined the **Indochinese Communist Party** in 1938. In 1940, he was arrested and incarcerated by the French. He escaped from prison in September 1944 and joined the **Viet Minh** and its military forces in northern Vietnam. In March 1945, he commanded a platoon of the **National Salvation Army** (*Cuu Quoc Quan*) and was active in the Tuyen Quang area where the Viet Minh was headquartered. Between 1945 and 1950, he served as a political commissar in **Inter-Zone I** (*Lien Khu I*) in northern Vietnam and then in **Zone** X (*Khu X*) in the northwest. He was in charge of the "Western Advance" front along the Vietnamese–Lao border. He also assumed powerful oversight positions in the army: he was a control member (*Uy Vien Kiem Tra*) of the party's Military Committee (*Quan Uy*) and inspectorate for the army (*Thanh Tra Quan Doi*). Between 1950 and 1953, he helped the **Lao Resistance Government** as the **Democratic Republic of Vietnam**'s special delegate and he directly commanded Vietnamese volunteer troops in upper Laos during that time. In 1954, he joined the 335th Division as commander-in-chief and political commissar.

**TAI.** *See* MINORITY ETHNIC GROUPS; *PAYS MONTAGNARDS DU SUD*; TAI FEDERATION.

**TAI FEDERATION.** In order to facilitate their colonial return after World War II and oppose the **Democratic Republic of Vietnam**'s (DRV) attempt to create a new nation-state in eastern Indochina, the French adopted a divide in order to rule policy. This meant turning **ethnic minority groups** against the **Viet Minh** and playing off real and imagined anti-Vietnamese sentiments. In the upland Tai principalities of northern and northwestern Vietnam, the French cultivated the loyalty of White, Red, and Black Tai lords such as **Deo Van Long**. In July 1948, the French reached an agreement with Tai leaders in the strategically important areas in the highlands of northwestern Vietnam. This agreement allowed for the creation of an autonomous Tai Federation nominally located outside of the jurisdiction of the larger counter-revolutionary Vietnamese state the French were building with **Bao Dai**, the Associated State of Vietnam. Led by White Tai leader, Deo Van Long, this Federation regrouped the provinces of Lai Chau, Phong Tho, and Son La. The French also relied on Tai allies in this region to help them organize opposition to the Viet Minh, most notably via the ***Groupement de commandos mixtes aéroportés***. In so doing, the French supported the development of "ethnonationalism", as Oscar Salemink has argued for the central highlands, promoting the teaching of the Tai language, a separate education system, the militarization of the uplands, their political and cultural distinction from the ethnic Vietnamese and their identification with the French. The DRV naturally opposed the French politico-military project to remove this region and these populations from the Vietnamese nation-state it was set on creating. With the withdrawal of the French from northern Vietnam in 1954, the DRV dissolved this federation and crushed those who resisted their efforts to do so. Although the DRV replaced the elites supported by the French with their own, Vietnamese communists maintained a special legal status for the Tai, the Tay Bac Autonomous Region. *See also PAYS MONTAGNARDS DU SUD.*

**TẠM CHÍ.** *See* HUỲNH TẤN PHÁT.

**TẠM NGẠI.** *See* HUỲNH VĂN NGHỆ.

**TÂN HỒNG.** *See* CHU VĂN TẤN.

**TAURIAC, MICHEL (1927–).** An ardent Gaullist, Michel Tauriac served in the **Expeditionary Corps** in Indochina in the early 1950s before becoming a journalist. He published several novels on Vietnam, including *Jade, La Tunique de soie*, and *La Nuit du Têt*. In 2001, he published an indictment of Vietnamese communism and leftists supporting their cause since 1945, entitled *Le livre Vietnam : Le dossier noir du communisme de 1945 à nos jours. See also* CINEMA; NOVELS; CIVIL WAR; POULO CONDOR; CULTURE; LUCIEN BODARD; MYTH OF WAR.

**TÂY NGUYÊN, BATTLE OF.** *See* ATLANTE, OPERATION.

***TÉMOIGNAGE CHRÉTIEN.*** Together with ***Esprit***, the Christian newspaper *Témoignage Chrétien* (Christian Witness) was one of the rare French papers to criticize the war in Indochina and recognize the reality of Vietnamese nationalism. Having emerged clandestinely during World War II and taken a firm stance against Nazism, the hostility of *Témoignage Chrétien* to the Indochina War and its critique of the colonial project had an important impact on its readers, mainly "progressive" Christians, who looked to it for guidance on major issues of the day. Nowhere was this better seen than in the paper's decision to publish a graphic description and indictment of the French army's use of **torture** in Indochina, written by **Jacques Chegaray** on 29 July 1949 (and rejected by his paper, *L'Aube*). It was followed by the publication of a series of essays by **Paul Mus** in late 1949 and early 1950. In them, this specialist of Asia from the ***École française d'Extrême-Orient*** and head of the **Colonial Academy** (*École coloniale*), condemned the French use of torture and took the French to task for failing to see the humanity of the Vietnamese and the historical reality of nationalism. The French right was outraged by *Témoignage Chrétien*'s criticism. Chegaray's piece triggered a formal investigation into the charges of torture in Indochina, some of which were confirmed. In 1957, as the French army resorted to torture to shut down Algerian nationalists in Algiers, *Témoignage Chrétien* renewed its opposition to colonial wars. However, unlike *Esprit*, **intellectuals** working in *Témoignage Chrétien*, such as Robert Barrat and Robert de Montvalon, still believed in a certain idea of colonial humanism and sometimes favored colonial reform and liberalism over outright decolonization. *See also* CAM LY, MASSACRE; HÉRAULT, MASSACRE; JULES ROY.

**TEP PHAN (1905–1978).** Prominent Cambodian politician who played an important role in defending Cambodian interests during the **Geneva Conference**. He completed his studies at the *Collège Sisowath* in Phnom Penh and the *École d'administration cambodgienne* before entering the Cambodian provincial government in 1925. He also served as secretary–interpreter in the colonial administration from 1923, working in the Resident's office for Kandal province until 1931. Until the end of the closing months of World War II, he worked as a district administrator in Kandal, Battambang, and Kompong Thom provinces. With the Japanese overthrow of the French in March 1945, Tep Phan assumed the direction of the *Commission des Prix et du Service du Ravitaillement de Phnom Penh*. In 1946, he ran the Ministry of National Economy. In 1947, he served as governor for Kompong Thom province. Between August 1948 and January 1949, he was state secretary for the Interior in the **Penn Nouth** cabinet before being named governor of Battambang province in February 1949. Between May and September 1950, he was a royal delegate to Siemreap with the rank of minister. From May 1951, he was minister of Trade and Industry in the Oum Chheang Sun cabinet. In 1952, he worked as chief of the Foreign Trade Service for Cambodia and served as president of the Committee for the Implementation of American Aid to Cambodia. In January 1954, he became head of the General Staff of the Khmer Armed National Forces and served as minister of Defence in the **Norodom Sihanouk** cabinet of 6 April 1954 and minister of Foreign Affairs in the Penn Nouth government of 17 April 1954. Together with **Sam Sary**, he was one of the government's main negotiators during the **Geneva Conference** of 1954, and played a pivotal role in denying the representatives of the Vietnamese-backed **Cambodian Resistance Government** a seat at the negotiating table or the right to regroupment zones. At the 11th hour of the negotiations, he supported Sam Sary's ultimately successful demand that Cambodia be given the right to solicit American aid if the government so desired.

**TER SARKISSOFF, ALEXANDRE (1911–1991).** Graduate from the *École militaire spéciale Saint-Cyr* and member of the French resistance during World War II, Ter Sarkissoff landed in Indochina in 1946 and began work in the personnel section of the French high commissioner for Indochina in **Saigon**. Between 1946 and 1948, he served as a provincial advisor in **Thakhek** in Laos before working for the political advisor of the high commissioner's office in Saigon in 1949. Between 1950 and 1951, he served as a regional advisor in the Lai Chau area, working with local Tai populations against the **Democratic Republic of Vietnam**. He transferred to Battambang province to work as the delegate of the commissioner for the French Republic to Cambodia. Between 1949 and his departure in 1952, he also took care of personnel matters for the high commissioner's office. *See also* TAI FEDERATION; *PAYS MONTAGNARDS DU SUD*; MINORITY ETHNIC GROUPS.

**TERRITORIES, RETROCESSION.** On 17 November 1946, a Franco-Thai agreement was signed in Washington by which the Tokyo convention of 9 May 1940 was annulled. This effectively directed the Thai government to return the right-bank provinces of Pak Lay and Bassac to Laos and the provinces of Battambang and Siem Reap to Cambodia. Under Japanese pressure, the French had ceded these territories to the Thais following a short border war in early 1941.

**THÁI LƯƠNG NAM.** *See* HOÀNG VĂN HOAN.

**THÁI VĂN LUNG (1916–1946).** Southern Vietnamese non-communist and Catholic **intellectual** and lawyer actively opposed to the French war in Vietnam. Born into a Catholic family in Gia Dinh province, Thai Van Lung was the younger brother of Thai Thi Lien, the wife of **Tran Ngoc Danh**. A French citizen, Thai Van Lung completed most of his studies in France where he graduated as a lawyer from the *Faculté de droit* in Paris. He also studied at the *Institut d'études politiques* and the **Colonial Academy** (*École coloniale*). Between 1923 and 1938 he lived in France. During the German occupation, his brother was sent to Buchenwald, where he perished. Back in Indochina, Thai Van Lung was in uniform during the short Franco-Thai border war of early 1941. Demobilized, he returned to **Saigon** to work as a lawyer. At the same time, he became increasingly active in nationalist politics. Though he spoke French better than Vietnamese, he joined the **Vanguard Youth League** (*Thanh Nien Tien Phong*), organized by **Pham Ngoc Thach** in southern Vietnam, and was active in paramilitary affairs. With the advent of the **Democratic Republic of Vietnam**, he became president of the Resistance and Administrative Committee for Thu Duc (outside Saigon) and won a seat in the National Assembly in March 1946. Disappointed by the French drive to retake Vietnam militarily instead of negotiating decolonization, he organized the "Thai Van Lung troops" and helped run military matters in Thu Duc province. His talents in military affairs made him a valuable addition to the southern command, where he obtained the rank of major. During an engagement with French forces sometime in 1946, Thai Van Lung fell into enemy hands. He rejected all French attempts to win him over to their side. French forces severely **tortured** him during his incarceration and many were not convinced by the official report that he had taken his life in prison on 2 July 1946. *See also* CATHOLICS IN VIETNAM AND THE WAR; *TÉMOIGNAGE CHRÉTIEN*; *ESPRIT*; PAUL MUS; JULES ROY.

**THAKHEK, BATTLE OF.** Following the signing of the **Franco-Chinese Accords** of 28 February 1946 directing Chinese troops to withdraw from Indochina above the **16th parallel**, French strategists decided to retake all of northern Laos immediately. Chinese officers on the ground did not object. As a result, a major urban battle shaped up, when Vietnamese and Lao leaders, led by Prince **Suphānuvong,** decided to defend the city of Thakhek against French forces. On 21 March 1946, under the command of **Jean Boucher de Crèvecoeur**, European and Lao troops in the *Forces du Laos*, supported with artillery and airpower, attacked their adversaries in what was a short-lived but intense urban battle. British-supplied Spitfires wreaked havoc on the Vietnamese–Lao troops as they tried to withdraw from the city under heavy fire and across the Mekong to safety in Thailand. The French opened fire from the banks and sent Spitfires to machine-gun from the air hundreds of boats and pirogues trying to transport troops and civilians to safety across the river in Thailand. Suphānuvong himself was injured while trying to escape, saved by a young Vietnamese man who died when he threw himself on top of the Lao prince. In all, the French *Forces du Laos* contingent lost 19 men, including 12 Europeans and thirty wounded. The adversary lost 400 men, mostly Vietnamese. De Crevecoeur later wrote that the French counted 250 dead within the city of Thakhek itself, suggesting that perhaps as many as 100 perished in the Mekong. In their propaganda, the **Democratic Republic of Vietnam** accused the French of a massacre. Vietnamese strategists also learned from Thakhek that the defense of **Hanoi** would need to be thought out very carefully. The battle of Thakhek also made it clear that the city would be an integral part of this violent war of decolonization. *See also* CAM LY, MASSACRE; EXECUTIONS; HANOI; HÉRAULT, MASSACRE; PRISONERS OF WAR; SAIGON.

**THẦN.** *See* TRƯỜNG CHINH.

**THAO SING (1879–?).** Active member in the **Lao Issara** government formed in 1945. Born in southern Laos, he was the son of a high court official of the former Kingdom of Champāsak. He pursued his secondary studies at the *Lycée Chas-*

*seloup Laubat* in **Saigon**. He travelled to Paris as an interpreter in 1900, as part of a delegation to the *Exposition coloniale*. He remained there to study briefly at the **Colonial Academy** (*École coloniale*) before returning to Indochina in 1901. He played an energetic role in suppressing the revolt of the Khas in the Bolovens between 1901 and 1904. Although he officially retired in 1932, Thao Sing remained active in public life. In 1942, for example, he was a member of the Lao Consultative Assembly and an associate judge in the provincial court of Pakse. While little is known of his activities during World War II, he broke with the French and joined the Lao Issara government as minister of Defence in April 1946.

**THẬP VẠN ĐAI SƠN, OPERATIONS (June–October 1949).** In early 1949, Chinese and Vietnamese communists met along the Sino–Vietnamese border to discuss the possibility of a joint military action against the likely retreat of Chinese nationalists towards the south and the need to create an opening to the Gulf of **Tonkin** for the **Democratic Republic of Vietnam** (DRV). Plans for a joint operation solidified when the Chinese Red Army began crossing the Yangzi River into southern China in April 1949. On 23 April, the **Indochinese Communist Party** issued the order to assist the Chinese Communist Party in the creation of a free zone in the areas of Dien Que and Viet Que across the border from **Cao Bang** province in southern China. In June 1949, Vietnamese combat units left Cao Bang and Lang Son provinces and took up positions in Longzhou east of Langson and in the districts of Yongzhou, Feng Cheng, and Qinzhou across from Hai Ninh and Lang Son. Fluent in Chinese, Nam Long, **Le Quang Ba**, and **Chu Huy Man** led this operation into Chinese territory, attacking Chinese nationalist forces in Shuikou, Ninh Ming, and joined Chinese communist troops in operations in Longzhou and Truc Son. Further to the east, between July and October 1949, Vietnamese units commanded by Le Quang Ba attacked the nationalists at Qinzhou, Feng Cheng, Giang Binh, and Dong Hung. The Vietnamese withdrew from China in late October. In 1956, the Chinese built a memorial in honor of the Vietnamese who had fought with the Chinese and for those who died during these operations. It still stands in Dong Hung to this day. *See also* MAO ZEDONG; AID, CHINESE; CHINESE MILITARY AND POLITICAL GROUP.

**THI ĐUA.** *See* EMULATION CAMPAIGN.

**THIBAU, JACQUES (1928–1997).** Graduated from the *École nationale d'administration*, Jacques Thibau served as deputy to the delegate of the commissioner of the Republic to Cambodia in Kampot province (1950–51) and as a private secretary to the high commissioner for Indochina between 1952 and 1953.

**THIÊN HỘ, MEETING.** On 25 October 1945, a month after the outbreak of war in southern Vietnam, **Hoang Quoc Viet**, a member of the Standing Committee of the **Indochinese Communist Party**'s (ICP) Central Committee, presided over this important meeting of the ICP's Territorial Committee for Nam Bo (*Xu Uy Nam Bo*). The gathering was designed to re-establish and consolidate the ICP's leadership in the south. Recently released communists from **Poulo Condor** were also present, including **Le Duan**. During this meeting, Le Duan and his Poulo Condor allies, including **Pham Hung** and **Nguyen Van Linh**, occupied important posts in the revamped ICP Territorial Committee for the south. This meeting also decided to take up **guerrilla** warfare as its main strategy in the war against the French in the south.

**THIERRY D'ARGENLIEU, GEORGES LOUIS MARIE (1889–1964).** The controversial French admiral named by General **Charles de Gaulle** on 16 August 1945 to serve as High Commissioner for Indochina. Thierry d'Argenlieu served in the French **Navy** during World War I. In 1920, he entered the *Carmelite* order as a friar until he joined Free French forces under Charles de Gaulle in 1940. A devout Gaullist and Catholic, Thierry d'Argenlieu became the Free French high commissioner of the French Pacific in 1941, head of French naval forces in 1943, and then the new high commissioner to Indochina after the Japanese ***coup de force* of 9 March 1945**. He arrived in Indochina on 31 October 1945 and, on 6 June 1946, he attained the rank of full admiral.

Thierry d'Argenlieu vigorously applied de Gaulle's instructions to retake and rebuild colonial Indochina piece by piece. He was successful in achieving accords with Lao and Cambodians allowing the French to return to western Indochina. Negotiations with the Vietnamese were much more difficult, especially as he adopted a more aggressive policy towards the **Democratic**

Republic of Vietnam (DRV) following the **Accords of 6 March 1946**. While he accepted the necessity of this accord, Thierry d'Argenlieu objected to the idea that the French would have to begin withdrawing their army within five years and that a referendum would be held to determine whether Cochinchina would be unified with the rest of "Vietnam", that is the DRV. At a deeper level, Thierry d'Argenlieu found it difficult to reconcile his determination to create a federal Indochinese colonial state based on **Cochinchina** with the DRV's national claim to all of eastern Indochina – meaning colonial **Tonkin, Annam,** and Cochinchina.

From April, he began to adopt policies that effectively sought to roll back the sovereignty of the DRV in favor of that of the **Indochinese Federation**. To that end, on 1 June 1946, as **Ho Chi Minh** was visiting France and a DRV delegation was preparing to resume negotiations with the French in Fontainebleau, Thierry d'Argenlieu announced the creation of the **Provisional Government of the Republic of Cochinchina**. For the high commissioner, Cochinchina had to remain a separate "free state" within the federation, not a regional part of "Vietnam". He supported the violent take-over of Lang Son and **Haiphong** in November 1946, pushing the DRV into a corner as he effectively assumed control of French policy towards Indochina. Ho Chi Minh hoped that the imminent creation of a new socialist government led by **Léon Blum** – known to be keen on reaching a negotiated solution to the Franco-Vietnamese dispute – would allow Paris to regain the reins on its Indochinese policy and its high commissioner. Instead Thierry d'Argenlieu successfully blocked Ho Chi Minh's last-minute attempts to contact Blum to head off war. On 19 December 1946, with their backs against the wall, the Vietnamese lashed out at the French forces, setting off full-scale war. The **Paul Ramadier** government recalled Thierry d'Argenlieu and relieved him of his position on 4 March 1947; but it did little to change policy.

Significantly, "containing" Vietnamese communism was not the major concern for Thierry d'Argenlieu in his brinksmanship towards the DRV in 1946; regaining France's colonial control over Indochina as instructed by de Gaulle was. In January 1947, he circulated internal orders forbidding the use of the term "Vietnam". After leaving his position in Indochina, Thierry d'Argenlieu returned to the religious life in Avon. General Charles de Gaulle attended his funeral in 1964.

**THIỀU SƠN (LÊ SỸ QUÝ, 1908–1978).** Vietnamese **intellectual** who supported the independence cause of the **Democratic Republic of Vietnam** (DRV). Born in Hai Duong province in northern Vietnam, he began his career in 1929 in the colonial civil service, working in the Posts and Telegraphs Office. He resigned from the colonial bureaucracy during the Vichy period and supported the DRV after World War II as a member of the Vietnamese section of the ***Section française de l'Internationale ouvrière*** (SFIO). In the late 1940s, Thieu Son was editor of the SFIO's **Saigon**-based journal critical of French colonialism, *Cong Ly* (Justice). In 1949, General **Nguyen Binh** invited him to join the *maquis*. Thieu Son accepted and teamed up with a number of other non-communist intellectuals working for the nationalist cause, including Nguyen Ba Luat, **Pham Thieu**, **Ca Van Thinh**, and **Nguyen Ngoc Nhut**. Thieu Son secretly escorted **Alain Savary**, a French national assembly member, to liberated zones to meet with southern DRV leaders such as **Pham Van Bach**, Nguyen Binh, Huynh Tan Phat, and Tran Nam Hung. **Marcel Bazin**'s security forces later arrested Thieu Son, but released him under pressure from the Indochinese SFIO branch. In the *maquis*, Thieu Son worked in *Radio Nam Bo*. Following the war, he remained in Saigon to work as a journalist and latered entered into conflict with **Ngo Dinh Diem**.

**THIRD FORCE.** *See ATTENTISME.*

**THOMAS, PIERRE-ALBAN.** Having fought in the French resistance against the Germans during World War II, this former school teacher landed in **Saigon** on 14 November 1945 in the 9th Colonial Infantry Regiment (*9ème Régiment d'infanterie coloniale*). But instead of fighting the Japanese, as he had thought he was going to do, he was part of the French effort to oust the **Democratic Republic of Vietnam** from southern Vietnam and restore French colonial rule. He participated in his regiment's military operations until February 1948, when he was transferred to Algeria. He later became critical of the legitimacy of France's colonial wars and the army's use of heavy-handed methods, including **torture**. Much later he would write a memoir discussing these matters, entitled *Combat intérieur*. *See also* ALGERIAN WAR.

**THOMPSON, JAMES HARRISON WILSON (1906–1967?).** American businessman and intelligence officer who closely followed Indochinese affairs. Thompson was born into a wealthy and prominent East Coast family. A graduate of Princeton, he majored in architecture and worked in a New York architectural firm between 1931 and 1940, when he became a director in the Monte Carlo Ballet Company, rebaptized later the New York City Ballet.

In 1940, with war looming, he quit his job and joined the National Guard as a private. He attended Officer Candidate School and served in a coastal artillery unit before joining the **Office of Strategic Services** (OSS). In 1942, fluent in French, he was swnt by the OSS to North Africa as part of efforts to liberate Europe from the Germans. He took part in French and Italian campaigns. In 1945, he headed a special unit that was parachuted into Thailand to establish contact with Free Thai forces and obtain intelligence on the Japanese in Thailand and Indochina. Although he arrived after the Japanese capitulation, Thompson, now promoted to the rank of colonel, remained on active duty in Thailand, serving as acting OSS station chief in Thailand and establishing a temporary American "consulate". It was during this time, that he fell in love with the country and stayed.

Thanks to his position in the OSS, his business interests, and his personality, Thompson developed an extraordinary array of Western and Asian contacts in Thailand. Not only did he know ranking Thai leaders such as **Pridi Banomyong** and **Pibun Songgram**, but he was also in contact with the exiled leaders of the **Lao Issara**, such as Thao Oun Sananikone, the **Khmer Issarak**, and the members of the **Democratic Republic of Vietnam**'s diplomatic delegation in Bangkok. Thompson was a member of the Vietnam–American Friendship Association, based in New York, and sympathized with the nationalist aspirations of the Vietnamese, Lao, and Cambodians. He retired from government around 1948 and dedicated himself full time to developing his business interests and projects in Thailand. He and his associates bought the legendary Oriental Hotel in Bangkok knowing that tourism would develop in Thailand after World War II. Thompson himself became legendary when he disappeared without a trace while on a vacation at a former colonial hill station in Malaysia in 1967. No sign of him has ever been found.

**THONGIN BURIPHAT (?–1949).** Northeast Thai politician of Lao origin who supported the **Lao Issara** and the **Democratic Republic of Vietnam** (DRV) during the Indochina War. He served as a deputy for the province of Ubon between 1933 and 1949. During World War II, he was an active member of the Free Thai (*Seri Thai*) movement and a close collaborator of **Pridi Banomyong**, serving as a member of Pridi's cabinet between August 1945 and January 1946. Thongin Buriphat provided arms and assistance to local DRV forces and shelter to Vietnamese populations forced to flee Laos when the French retook the country by force. He was also a firm supporter of the Lao Issara and the idea of creating a wider trans-Mekong Lao nation state. He died in Thai police detention in March 1949.

**THOREZ, MAURICE (1900–1964).** Maurice Thorez was the most important 20th-century leader of the **French Communist Party** (FCP) and a supporter of the Vietnamese nationalist cause. The son of a miner, Thorez joined the FCP at its beginnings in 1920. Thanks to his political acumen and strict adherence to the internationalist communist line enunciated by **Joseph Stalin**, Thorez rose rapidly within the FCP. Between 1930 and 1964, he served as the party's general secretary. Towards the end of World War II, when the FCP emerged as one of the dominant parties in French politics, Thorez returned to France from exile in the Soviet Union and served as minister and deputy prime minister in several coalition governments between 1945 and 1947. It was also during a brief period when **Léon Blum** led a transitory all-socialist government (and Thorez was not in government) that the French went to war with the **Democratic Republic of Vietnam** (DRV), led by another communist, **Ho Chi Minh**. That Thorez was favorable to the independence aspirations of the Vietnamese communists and supported them, there can be no doubt, as Alain Ruscio has shown. However, Thorez's attitude towards the Vietnamese communists at the outset of the Indochina War was complicated by the FCP's success in French national politics. At the head of a political party that in one of the 1946 elections became the largest in France, Thorez did not want to undermine the FCP's chances of eventually leading the government by presiding over the liquidation of the French Empire, something which he feared his nationalist opponents on the right and center could use effectively against the communists. Thorez made this point of view perfectly clear on several occasions, even to the Gaullist high commissioner for Indochina in

1946, Admiral **Georges Thierry d'Argenlieu**. Just after the outbreak of war in December 1946, Thorez made sure that the communist members in the National Assembly voted in favor of a motion of sympathy for French soldiers. The FCP also did not seek to prevent the transfer of funds from one part of the budget to another in order to finance the war. Later in 1947, however, Thorez's party directed members to abstain from voting the military credits for the war against the DRV. However, those communists who held ministerial portfolios (including Thorez) voted in favor of the credits, and against their conscience, in order not to let the Indochina War break "ministerial solidarity". That said, the failure of the FCP to fully support the war in Indochina contributed greatly to the crisis that forced the communists to leave the coalition government in May 1947. The FCP's policy on Vietnam changed from that point as it overcame its reticence and began condemning the ***sale guerre***. When meeting with a Soviet representative in Switzerland in September 1947, Ho Chi Minh's diplomat at large, **Pham Ngoc Thach**, criticized Thorez's failure to be of greater help to Vietnamese communists now engaged in a full-scale war. *See also* JACQUES DUCLOS; DISSOLUTION OF INDOCHINESE COMMUNIST PARTY.

**THƯỢNG UYỂN.** *See* NGUYỄN TIẾN LÃNG.

**TIANG SIRIKHAN (?–1952).** Thai politician from the northeast and of ethnic Lao origin. After completing his studies in Bangkok, he returned to the northeast and was elected deputy for his home province of Sakhon Nakhon between 1938 and 1952. During World War II, he worked closely with **Pridi Banomyong** in the Free Thai movement. He was a strong supporter of greater autonomy for the Lao located in much of northeastern Thailand (*Isaan*). He also supported the **Democratic Republic of Vietnam**, providing shelter to Vietnamese fleeing the violent French re-occupation of Laos in mid-1946 and furnishing arms to Vietnamese soldiers fighting the French in Indochina. He was general secretary of the Thai-Vietnamese-conceived Southeast Asia League in 1947. He disappeared in mysterious circumstances. *See also* THAKHEK, BATTLE OF.

**TỐ.** *See* PHẠM VĂN ĐỒNG.

**TÔ GĨ.** *See* LÊ GIẢN.

**TÔ HOÀI (NGUYỄN SEN, 1920–).** Born in **Hanoi**, To Hoai is one of modern Vietnam's best-known literary figures. With the advent of the **Democratic Republic of Vietnam** (DRV) in 1945, he put his cultural talents in the service of the Vietnamese nationalist movement. In that same year, he joined the National Salvation Cultural Association (*Hoi Van Hoa Cuu Quoc*) and became a member of the **Indochinese Communist Party** around the same time. He worked to mobilize and organize **intellectuals** in favor of the DRV's struggle against the French and its state-building endeavors. During the Indochina War, he worked as a journalist for the **Viet Minh**'s official mouthpiece, *Cuu Quoc*, and eventually became its editor. To Hoai emerged on the Vietnamese literary scene as a realist writer during World War II, when he published *Foreign Land* (*Que Nguoi*) in 1942, in which he had already begun to mix fiction and autobiography, one of his trademarks to this day. While working in the hills of northern Vietnam following the evacuation of Hanoi in late 1946, he published a novel on the Tai people of northwestern Vietnam, where he worked as a cadre as the DRV wrestled the French for control of this strategically important territory. The novel was entitled *Stories from the Northwest* (*Truyen Tay Bac*). In 2006, To Hoai created something of a controversy when he revealed in a semi-autobiographical novel, *Three Others* (*Ba Nguoi Khac*), that not only had he worked as a cadre during the **land reform** launched during the Indochina War, but that terrible errors had been committed by the party in applying this radical social program. Authorities had blocked the publication of the novel for 14 years because of its politically incorrect point of view. In his memoirs, *Dust and Sand at Somebody's Feet (Cat Bui Chan Ai)* and *Every Afternoon (Chieu Chieu),* To Hoai took up the tricky subject of northern Vietnamese intellectuals who had committed themselves to the national resistance led by the communist party and the moral and intellectual compromises this entailed. *See also* TAI FEDERATION; NOVELS; CINEMA; CULTURE; HISTORY.

**TỐ HỮU (NGUYỄN KIM THÀNH, 1920–2002).** Leading poet and propagandist for the **Vietnamese Worker's Party** during and after the Indochina War. Born in Thua Thien province in central Vietnam, he published a large body of nationalist, anti-colonialist, and communist poetry, which he put in the service of the **Democratic**

**Republic of Vietnam** from its inception. He was a member of the **Indochinese Communist Party** and served prison time in northern Vietnam until his release in 1942. He worked in the communist underground outside **Hanoi** until the **Viet Minh** took power in August–September of 1945. To Huu was a close ally of **Truong Chinh**. His communist contacts and artistic talents made him one of the party's most important propagandists and contacts with foreigners. In 1949, he became director of the government's information services for central Vietnam. In 1951, he became director general of Information for the government, taking over from **Tran Van Giau**. During the Second Party Congress held that same year, he joined the Party's Central Committee. From 1953, he played an important role in various literary and cultural organizations under the Party's leadership. In 1954, he became vice minister of Information. *See also* INDOCTRINATION; CULTURE; PSYCHOLOGICAL WARFARE.

**TÔ KÝ (NAM, 1919–1999).** Influential military leader in southern Vietnam during the Indochina War. Born in southern Vietnam, he became politically active during the Popular Front period and joined the **Indochinese Communist Party** (ICP) in 1937. In early 1939, he served as a member of the party's district committee for Hoc Mon. He was arrested on two occasions but apparently escaped both times. In 1945, he served on the ICP's provincial committee for Gia Dinh in charge of military affairs and helped nationalists take power there in August–September 1945. With the outbreak of war in southern Vietnam in September 1945, he led detachment 12 (*Chi Doi 12*) in war **Zone VII** (*Chien Khu VII*). Between 1947 and 1950, he worked closely with **Nguyen Binh** as deputy commander of Zone VII and military commander of the special zone for **Saigon** and Cholon. To Ky also sat on the Party's committee for this zone as well as its committee for war Zone VII. Between 1950 and 1953, he was the Party and military leader for the province of Gia Dinh. In 1954 and 1955, he headed the committee for the Relocation of Party and Military Cadres of the **Democratic Republic of Vietnam** in Ham Tan and Xuyen Moc to northern Vietnam.

**TÔN ĐỨC THẮNG (1888–1980).** Venerated veteran communist leader who held a symbolic place in the revolutionary pantheon second only to **Ho Chi Minh** during the war. He traveled to France where he worked as a sailor. While he became famous in Vietnamese historiography for taking part in the Black Sea Mutiny in 1919, recent research calls into question this allegation and explains it as a myth designed to legitimate communist Vietnam's place in the internationalist communist world. But all was not a myth. What is sure is that he was arrested by the French in 1929, incarcerated at Kham Lon in **Saigon**, and then deported to **Poulo Condor** prison where he remained until September 1945. There, he forged close ties to ranking leaders of the party, including **Le Duan**. He was a member of the Central Committee of the **Indochinese Communist Party**.

**TÔN THẤT TÙNG (1912–1982).** Famous Vietnamese surgeon who worked for the **Democratic Republic of Vietnam** (DRV) during the Indochina War. Born in Hue in central Vietnam, he was a distant relative of **Bao Dai**. Between 1932 and 1939, Ton That Tung studied medicine and graduated as a doctor of medicine from the *Faculté de médicine* in **Hanoi**. He specialized in heart and liver disorders. In the late 1930s, he broke the colonial barrier when he became one of only a handful of surgeons allowed to practice in Indochina. He gained some early valuable experience in war medicine in the early 1940s, treating those wounded by Allied bombing raids over northern Vietnam. It was also during this time that Ton That Tung was deeply moved by the courage of a young **Viet Minh** cadre whom he could not save from the effects of severe torture at the hands of the Japanese. A few weeks later, with the defeat of the Japanese, Dr. Ton That Tung rallied to the nationalist cause of the DRV. When war engulfed Hanoi in late 1946, he joined the government in the hills of northern Vietnam. He worked there in building the government's medical facilities and training centers. He helped establish, run, and teach in the new Medical School that operated in and out of the Chiem Hoa area throughout the war. In 1947, he served as acting minister of Health. In July 1949, he began working as the surgical advisor to the Ministry of Defense and served in numerous battles to aid the wounded and sick, in particular during the battle of **Dien Bien Phu**. He also tended to captured enemy troops. He was a strong supporter of the communist cause, deeply involved in **emulation** and **new hero** campaigns designed to create a "new man" and society in the early 1950s. From 1952, he worked as the government's representative to the International

Committee of the **Red Cross** and was involved in negotiations on prisoner exchanges. Ton That Tung and **Dang Van Ngu** were instrumental in developing an effective penicillin vaccination for use during the resistance. In 1958, he performed the first Vietnamese open heart surgery in Vietnam. *See also* DISEASE; DO XUAN HOP; EXPERIENCE OF WAR; EXPERIENCE OF WAR, DIEN BIEN PHU; PAUL GRAUWIN.

**TỔNG BỘ VIỆT MINH.** The General Directorate of the **Viet Minh** nationalist front created by **Ho Chi Minh** and the **Indochinese Communist Party** (ICP) in 1941. Contrary to what French authorities thought at the time, the *Tong Bo* was not an all-powerful communist decision-making entity. Despite the ICP's desire in November 1945 to transform the *Tong Bo* into some sort of permanent headquarters to oversee and transmit instructions down to local Viet Minh chapters and cadres, this never occurred. It is not even sure a chairman for the *Tong Bo* was ever named, according to David Marr. With the movement of the government to the hills of northern Vietnam following the outbreak of full scale war in late 1946, the *Tong Bo* faded away.

**TONKIN.** Colonial term referring roughly to present day northern Vietnam. Under the Tay Son and during the first half of the Nguyen dynasty, this northern part of today's Vietnam was referred to as *Bac Thanh*. In 1834, following a major administrative reform, the Nguyen renamed it *Bac Ki* (or *Bac Ky* in modern Vietnamese), running as far south as today's Thanh Hoa, Nghe An, and Ha Tinh provinces. When the French colonized all of Vietnam during the second half of the 19th century, they maintained the Vietnamese term *Bac Ki*, referring to it in French as "Tonkin" (meaning capital of the East). The French, however, transferred Thanh Hoa, Nghe An, and Ha Tinh to **Annam** (*Trung Ky*). Following the Japanese ***coup de force* of 9 March 1945** ousting the French from Indochina, the **Tran Trong Kim** government adopted the term "northern section" or *Bac Phan* to refer to former colonial Tonkin. The **Democratic Republic of Vietnam** followed suit but dropped *Phan* in favour of *Bo* to form *Bac Bo*. During the Indochina War, the French would revive the colonial term, "Tonkin", as part of a wider battle over the future of **Vietnam.** Leaders of the **Republic of Vietnam** would use the word *Bac Phan* in order avoid borrowing either the colonial or communist terms. These geographical terms had contested political meanings throughout the Indochina War. *See also* COCHINCHINA.

**TOREL, ALBERT (1895–1987).** French career colonial servant in Indochina and specialist on legal questions. He was secretary to the *résident supérieur* of **Annam** between 1921 and 1924 before serving in 1925–1926 as deputy chief of Qui Nhon province. He then served as secretary to the *résident supérieur* for Cambodia and *directeur des Bureaux* there between 1927 and 1930. After a brief stint in Annam, he served in Laos between 1932 and 1936, working as head of the province and mayor of Vientiane between 1933 and 1936. He returned to Annam yet again to serve as an advisor to the Annamese protectorate government until 1939, when he became cabinet director for Governor General Georges Catroux. Torel supported Catroux's decision to enter into dissidence against Vichy following the fall of the Third Republic. While Vichy leaders in Indochina criticized him for supporting Catroux, Torel remained in Indochina and served loyally during World War II as labor inspector (1940–1941) and as *résident* in Quang Ngai province (1941–1943). Even Catroux's successor, Admiral Jean Decoux, was willing to forget the past: Torel "*mérite cependant d'être utilisé à plein*", Decoux wrote in 1944. In that same year, Torel became Inspector of Administrative Affairs and of Labor in Vientiane, Laos. He was a member of the Indochina Council created by Decoux in December 1944.

His support of Catroux's "treason" in 1940 served Torel well when Gaullists went about retaking and purging the Indochinese colony the French had lost to the Japanese in March 1945. In 1946, Torel became federal commissioner for legal questions (*Commissaire fédéral aux questions juridiques*), a position he held until 1947. He was no liberal, however, when it came to the question of decolonization. As he told **Paul Mus** in the wake of World War II, "*les Annamites n'attendent que notre retour*". He took part in the first **Dalat Conference** of April 1946. During this meeting, he engaged in a heated legal debate with **Vo Nguyen Giap** over the national reality of Vietnam, something which did not exist according to Torel. He also took part in the failed negotiations over the unification of "Vietnam" at **Fontainebleau** during the long French summer of 1946. **Philippe Devillers** says that he was the *éminence grise* to **Georges Thierry d'Argenlieu**.

In 1948, Torel provisionally served as commissioner of the Republic to the Provisional Government of South Vietnam. He was close to **Léon Pignon**: they used the informal *tutoiement* to address each other, and they often worked together on major political questions. Torel was strongly opposed to Vietnamese nationalism and decolonization, to say nothing of communism. On 20 October 1948, he was raised to the rank of governor of the colonies. Between 1948 and 1949, he served as the personnel director for High Commissioner Léon Pignon before being named in 1949 director general of the administration for the high commissioner in Indochina, a post which he occupied until 1950. Torel was involved in the development and application of the **Bao Dai Solution** in collaboration with Pignon. In 1949, Torel assumed the leadership of the French delegation in charge of applying the March 1949 Accords with **Bao Dai**. In so doing, he implicitly accepted the national unity of Vietnam, something that he had strongly denied the **Democratic Republic of Vietnam** in Dalat and Fontainebleau in 1946. *See also* JEAN COUSSEAU.

**TORTURE, DEMOCRATIC REPUBLIC OF VIETNAM.** The Vietnamese intelligence and public security forces used torture during the Indochina War. In the north, the **Democratic Republic of Vietnam**'s (DRV) use of torture got out of hand during the **H122 affair** in 1948, when the party suspected the French of having planted a mole in the army's **General Staff**. In southern Vietnam, torture became a real problem in 1949 when it was learned or feared that French-backed "reactionary" nationalist party spies had penetrated the **Public Security Services**. Again, officials turned to torture and heavy-handed interrogations to ferret out these suspected moles.

From the evidence currently available, it appears unlikely that the Vietnamese intelligence services used physical torture systematically, fearful of its negative impact on their popular base. However, there is no denying that it existed; communist sources confirm it. The problem, at least at the beginning, is that it often spun out of control when paranoia and hysteria quickly got the best of the security officials. Indeed, the excessive use of torture seems to have done serious damage on several occasions, resulting in the deaths of dozens if not hundreds of innocent people in the north and south. The situation got so bad that in 1951 the Public Security Service issued a regulation banning the use of physical violence in interrogations for fear of its possible manipulation by the enemy, alienation of local Vietnamese support, and danger to the legitimacy of the party's cause. The DRV's physical torture was mainly directed against Vietnamese, not French prisoners. Recently the Vietnamese Communist Party has acknowledged that torture was used against Vietnamese based on class. This occurred during the land **reform begun** in upper Vietnam from 1953. *See also* CIVIL WAR; EXECUTION; HÉRAULT, INDOCTRINATION; LANGUAGE OF WAR; MASSACRE; PROSELYTIZING THE ENEMY; RECTIFICATION; VIETNAMESE NATIONALIST PARTY.

**TORTURE, FRENCH.** The French Army practiced torture during the Indochina War. How widely? No one knows for sure. The army, however, was not the first to do so in Indochina. During the colonial period, the *Sûreté* did so with considerable impunity. In 1933, ***Esprit*** published the notes of Andrée Viollis's detailed investigation into the official use of torture against the Vietnamese who had revolted against the French in 1930–1931. **Marcel Bazin** was known for the harsh methods he used on Vietnamese political prisoners. After his liberation from a Japanese prison camp (where he himself was tortured), Bazin resumed his harsh methods against the **Democratic Republic of Vietnam**'s men and women who fell into his hands. He was the head of the ***Sûreté Fédérale*** in southern Vietnam.

There was continuity in the use of this practice flowing out of the colonial period and World War II. The French army practiced torture during the colonial reconquest of southern Vietnam, especially in mid-1946 when General **Jean Valluy** had to issue orders to stop it. The French public became aware of the use of torture when, in July 1949, the influential Catholic newspaper, ***Témoignage Chrétien***, published **Jacques Chegaray**'s account of its use within the army. Outraged by what Chegaray described, the French specialist of Indochina and then head of the **Colonial Academy**, **Paul Mus** wrote a series of famous essays in which he publicly condemned the use of torture (*Non pas ça!* is how he titled it). The Right and military circles in Indochina, notably General **Roger Blaizot**, condemned the articles. However, **Paul Ramadier,** then minister of Defence, issued secret instructions to authorities in Indochina proscribing the use of torture. High Commissioner

**Léon Pignon** was appalled, writing in September 1949 that torture was contrary to everything that the French were trying to do in Indochina in the name of *une valeur essentiellement humaine et de civilisation*. It had to be stopped at all levels. In fact, Chegaray's article coincided with internal investigations into the use of torture and summary executions in the *Service de sécurité d'Air* in **Hanoi** on at least two separate occasions in mid-1949. Ramadier and Pignon were referring to this as much as to Chegaray's article.

How widespread was the use of torture during the Indochina War? **Jules Roy** left the army disgusted by the army's use of it. Vietnamese-language memoirs and histories of the conflict leave no doubt as to its existence. However, in the absence of any methodologically reliable study of the question, it is impossible to gauge how widespread the use of torture was in the army and security services across all of Indochina. Was the Algerian experience engraved in the Indochinese one? In an internal *Étude sur les renseignement tirés de la campagne d'Indochine en matière de "renseignements"*, the ***Deuxième Bureau*** for North Vietnam concluded in 1955 that when it came to interrogating **Viet Minh** prisoners during the Indochina War, the use of torture had in no way improved the quality of the intelligence provided (*les mauvais traitements n'améliorent nullement le rendement des interrogatoires*). The opposite was often true, as the DRV's services had also learned the hard way. *See also* ALGERIAN WAR; CAM LY, MASSACRE; MY THUY, MASSACRE; MOTHERS OF GIO LINH; PHAM DUY; TORTURE, DEMOCRATIC REPUBLIC OF VIETNAM.

**TOSHIO KOMAYA (NGUYEN QUANG THUC).** Japanese soldier who crossed over to the **Democratic Republic of Vietnam** (DRV) in northern Vietnam at the end of World War II. There, he worked as a military advisor to the Chinese-trained Vietnamese officer, Nam Long. He accompanied **Le Quang Ba** into southern China in mid-1949 to help the **Chinese Communist Party** defeat Chinese nationalist forces on the run. As the Chinese communist victory approached, the Vietnamese moved Toshio to the operations section of the DRV **General Staff** in the newly formed **Inter-Zone Viet Bac** (*Lien Khu Viet Bac*). He played a particularly important role in helping to organize and plan a new level of modern military operations against the French, thanks to the aid now being provided by the Chinese. Toshio Komaya participated in organizing the frontier battles designed to open the border to China via **Cao Bang** in mid-1950. His most important contributions were in the training of cadres and officers, the development of Viet Bac's Military Intelligence, and his operational work in the planning and mapping of major northern battles. *See also* DESERTION, JAPANESE; THẬP VẠN ĐAI SƠN, OPERATIONS.

**TRAITOR.** *See* VIET GIAN.

**TRAMIER, ALBERT (1917–).** Between 1945 and 1949, he worked in the Economic Affairs section of the high commissioner's office for Indochina.

**TRẦN BẠCH ĐẰNG (TƯ ÁNH, TRẦN QUANG, TRƯƠNG GIA TRIỀU, NGUYỄN TRƯỜNG THIÊN LÝ, 1926–2007).** A powerful behind-the-scenes southern communist during the wars for Vietnam between 1945 and 1975. Born in the province of Kien Giang, he became politically active as a journalist during World War II and secretly joined the **Indochinese Communist Party** at this time. He worked in clandestine operations for the **Democratic Republic of Vietnam** in the **Saigon**-Cholon area and was a member of the secretariat of the party's Territorial Committee for Nam Bo (*Xu Uy Nam Bo*) under **Le Duan**. His activities landed him in jail in 1948 when Indochina's master security chief, **Marcel Bazin** captured him. Upon his release, Tran Bach Dang became the deputy director of the Information Service for Saigon run by the Resistance and Administrative Committee for Nam Bo. In 1954, he was secretary of the permanent bureau of the **Lien Viet** national front. He would go on to play a pivotal role in the war against the Americans in southern Vietnam in general and in Saigon-Cholon in particular.

**TRẦN BỘI CƠ (1932–1950).** The name of the young Chinese girl killed during Vietnamese anticolonialist demonstrations in **Saigon** in 1950. One of Saigon's leading high schools is now named after her. She was from the Fujian community. Her death allowed the partisans of the **Democratic Republic of Vietnam**'s nationalist cause to mobilize **intellectuals** and students in Saigon and elsewhere against the war and its internationalization, marked by the arrival at the port of Saigon of an American ship delivering arms to the French army. *See also* OVERSEAS CHINESE.

**TRẦN BỬU KIẾM (1921–).** One of the founders of the **Vietnamese Democratic Party** (*Dang Dan Chu Viet Nam*). Born in Can Tho province in southern Vietnam, Tran Buu Kiem graduated as a lawyer from the *Faculté de droit* in **Hanoi**. During World War II, he helped create the Democratic Party and was active in the General Association of Indochinese Students. He was arrested by the French but escaped in early 1945. He returned to **Saigon** following the Japanese overthrow of the French in March, resuming his activities in the Democratic Party and participating in the **Vanguard Youth League** (*Thanh Nien Tien Phong*) led by **Pham Ngoc Thach**. Tran Buu Kiem was a firm supporter of the independence cause of the **Democratic Republic of Vietnam** (DRV). Between 1946 and 1949, he was the general secretary for the Resistance and Administrative Committee for the south. From 1950, he served as the deputy director of Economic Services of Nam Bo. He was simultaneously active among student and **intellectual** groups agitating in favor of the DRV's cause.

**TRẦN ĐẠI BIÊN.** *See* TRẦN QUANG VỊNH.

**TRẦN ĐẠI NGHĨA (PHẠM QUANG LỄ, 1913–1997).** Vietnamese engineer and specialist in armaments production for the **Democratic Republic of Vietnam** (DRV) during the Indochina War. He was born in Vinh Long province in southern Vietnam. Between 1926 and 1930, he studied at the provincial elementary school of My Tho, where one of his classmates was the future head of the DRV's southern security forces, **Pham Hung**. Between 1930 and 1935, Tran Dai Nghia was in **Saigon** completing his secondary studies at the *Lycée Pétrus Ky*. Thanks to a locally provided scholarship, he traveled to France in September 1935 to study engineering and mathematics, and apparently successfully completed his studies in 1939, graduating from the *École centrale des arts et manufactures*. Despite repeated requests to study weapons engineering, the French turned him down. This was off limits to colonial "subjects". On the eve of World War II, however, he found himself working in a French aviation factory. Following the French defeat in June 1940, the occupying Germans sent him to work in a central German aviation plant in Halle in 1942. He also studied and worked in a weapons research institute there and was thus initiated into basic German research in avionics. He returned to work in France towards the end of the war (leaving just before the Allied bombing of Halle).

During his visit to France in mid-1946, **Ho Chi Minh** persuaded Tran Dai Nghia to return to Vietnam to join the nationalist cause. As war looked increasingly likely, the Vietnamese badly needed weapons specialists and engineers. In October 1946, Tran Dai Nghia returned to northern Vietnam in Ho Chi Minh's entourage and joined the armaments section in the DRV Ministry of National Defense. He put his French and German engineering and wartime training in Europe to work making home-made bazookas, mortars, grenades, and recoilless guns for the DRV's nascent army. On 5 December 1946, he headed up the newly established Bureau of Armaments Production (*Cuc Quan Gioi*). He oversaw the creation of a network of weapons-making workshops across the country, though mainly located in central and northern resistance zones. In mid-1948, these workshops began producing hand-grenades and the first 60mm and 81mm mortars. In late 1949, his recoilless guns appeared in northern skirmishes. However rudimentary they certainly were, these weapons often worked. Even French military authorities recognized their effectiveness and the quality of Tran Dai Nghia.

He joined the **Indochinese Communist Party** in 1949, having already been named major general in 1948. In 1949, Tran Dai Nghia assumed the leadership of the Office of Artillery (*Cuc Phao Binh*), became deputy director of the General Technical Bureau (*Tong Cuc Ky Thuat*), and served as deputy director of the General Directorate of the Rearguard of the **People's Army of Vietnam** (*Tong Cuc Hau Can Quan Doi Nhan Dan Viet Nam*). In September 1950, as the battles intensified with the arrival of the **Cold War** and increased military aid for the belligerents, he became vice minister for Heavy [Armaments] Industry, a post he held until 1963. He was also a founding member of the Vietnam–USSR Friendship Association.

**TRẦN DẦN (TRẦN VĂN DẦN, 1926–1997).** Vietnamese poet and writer who supported the nationalist cause of the **Democratic Republic of Vietnam** and published perhaps the most important war novel of the Indochina War in any language. Born into a wealthy family in Nam Dinh province, Tran Dan studied French literature in high school, where he discovered the work of Baudelaire, Verlaine, and the symbolists.

According to **Georges Boudarel**, Tran Dan began writing in earnest during World War II, but was less interested in politics than in art for its own sake. Little else is known of his activities during the war or during the events that brought the **Democratic Republic of Vietnam** (DRV) into being in September 1946. In Nam Dinh in late 1946, he joined with a group of symbolist poets to publish the first issue of their literary review, *Dia nguc/Hell*. As the founding manifesto read: "We are a band of wanderers, without a light or a place, reincarnated accidentally at the very time when the stars are fading".

His life indeed his perspective on art changed, however, with the outbreak of full-scale war on **19 December 1946**. Unlike some of his friends, Tran Dan not only chose to support the DRV against the return of French colonialism, he also agreed to put his art in the service of the party's nationalist cause. The **Viet Minh** put him to work tending to matters of information and propaganda. In early 1948, he joined the army in **Son La** province and became a member of the **Indochinese Communist Party** (ICP) in August of that year. He worked on propaganda within the army in Son La and took part in the creation of the literary and artistic Black River Group and contributed regularly to its review. He soon stood out for the originality of his writings on the war and also his drawings of soldiers (some of which drew criticism from political cadres unable to understand his cubist style). After undergoing cadre **rectification** in 1951, he was promoted to the committee in charge of artistic questions for the army. When this did not work out, he transferred to the people's army magazine and covered a number of the major battles in the north. In late 1953, he volunteered to go to **Dien Bien Phu**. Tran Dan travelled to the front with the composer Do Nhuan and the painter To Ngoc Van.

Based on his first-hand experience of seeing men engaged in this epic battle, in April 1955 he published his famous novel about the war as seen from the Vietnamese soldier's point of view *Nguoi Nguoi Lop Lop* or *Man after man, wave after wave*. However, before publishing his novel, he made a two-month trip to China to work on a documentary film of the same battle. During this time, he rejected the efforts of the political commissar accompanying him to impose a crude propagandistic stamp on the film. He also journeyed in China at a time when the Chinese Communist Party allowed intellectuals to criticize the party. According to **Georges Boudarel**, Tran Dan was influenced by the ideas of Hu Feng and, like him, rejected Maoism and the party's right to define art so directly. His war novel reflected this new way of thinking. In it, soldiers certainly fight heroically, and the party is there; but we see some of the human side of the soldiers, their doubts, fears, and fatigue. The party criticized his realistic accounts of the war, preferring heroic and ideological representations. Tran Dan left the party in April 1955, was arrested for his participation in *Nhan Van Giai Pham* movement, accused of being "anti-party" (*chong Dang*), and forced to undergo re-education. His work would not be rehabilitated, like that of Hung Feng, until the 1980s. *See also* CINEMA; CULTURE; EMULATION; EXPERIENCE OF WAR; HISTORY; MYTH OF WAR; NEW HERO; NOVELS.

**TRẦN ĐĂNG NINH (1910–1955).** Powerful, behind-the-scenes leader in the **Indochinese Communist Party** (ICP) in charge of high-level and sensitive intelligence, security, and internal investigative matters. Born in Ha Tay province near **Hanoi**, Tran Dang Ninh was a printer by profession who became politically active in the early 1930s. He joined the ICP in 1936. In 1939, he was a member of the party's underground Committee for Hanoi. During World War II, he joined the ICP's Territorial Committee for **Tonkin** (*Xu Uy Bac Ky*) and worked closely with the likes of **Truong Chinh**, then acting general secretary of the party. In May 1941, Tran Dang Ninh became the secretary of the same Territorial Committee and entered the ICP's Central Committee. He participated in the 8th Plenum in May 1941 which gave birth to the **Viet Minh**. The French arrested him shortly thereafter and incarcerated him in **Son La** and Hoa Lo prisons following an escape in 1943. He regained his freedom following the Japanese ***coup de force* of 9 March 1945** and resumed his activities in northern Vietnam. During a party plenum adopted during the Tan Trao Conference in August 1945, he joined the General Directorate or the ***Tong Bo* Viet Minh.** As a senior leader in the ICP, he was in charge of the Party's own internal security affairs and its control over the government of the **Democratic Republic of Vietnam**. In 1947, he assumed the leadership of the Control and Inspection Board (*Ban Kiem Tra*) of the Executive Committee of the ICP's Central Committee, a powerful position. He served as the deputy director of the Party's General Inspectorate for the Government (*Pho Truong Ban Thanh Tra Chinh Phu*). And he headed up the ICP's Central Committee's own Surveillance Board (*Ban Trinh Sat*), designed to oversee and coordinate all security services.

While Tran Dang Ninh was a committed communist, he was also a cool-headed, rational, and organized leader and thinker. This helps explain why **Ho Chi Minh** brought him in to handle the sensitive **H122 Affair**, which had generated a climate of paranoia within the army and even the Party as security services tried to ferret out an alleged French mole, H122. After close investigation, Tran Dang Ninh concluded that there was no spy. H122 was, he concluded, a French deception operation. Party and military unity was re-established in large part due to Tran Dang Ninh, and this at a crucial point in the Indochina War. He accompanied Ho Chi Minh on the latter's voyage to China in late 1949 and early 1950. He also met with the nationalist archbishop **Le Huu Tu** in an effort to keep Catholics from leaning to the French side. Soon thereafter, he joined the Party's General Military Commission (*Quan Uy*) (together with **Vo Nguyen Giap** and **Nguyen Chi Thanh**) and attended to questions of logistics and supply. In 1951, he became a member of the Central Committee of the **Vietnam Worker's Party.**

**TRẦN ĐÌNH VỸ.** Sergeant and second-in-command to **Roger Vandenberghe**'s ***Commando*** *Nord Vietnam no. 2* during the Indochina War. Tran Dinh Vy accompanied Vandenberghe on some of the most audacious commando operations of the Indochina War and was apparently the only survivor of the **Viet Minh** attack that assassinated Vandenberghe. After the war, Tran Dinh Vy served in the army of the **Republic of Vietnam** before evacuating his family to the United States in 1975 while he went to France and attained the rank of colonel in the French **Foreign Legion**. He retired in 1988 and was present in 1989 when Vandenberghe's remains were deposited in a monument erected in the latter's honor at the National Non-Commissioned Officers' Academy in Pau, France.

**TRẦN ĐỘ (TẠ NGỌC PHÁCH, 1924–2002).** Born in northern Vietnam, he joined the **Indochinese Communist Party** in 1940. The French incarcerated him at **Son La** the following year. In 1944, he escaped from prison and resumed his work for the party in the Red River Delta, where he collaborated closely with **Truong Chinh** (serving briefly as the latter's body guard). Tran Do helped the Party take power in the Vinh Phuc area and became a member of the Revolutionary Military Committee for **Hanoi**. He joined the army in 1945 and helped edit the *Liberation Army Paper* in 1946. Between January 1947 and 1950, he served as deputy political commissar for **Zone** II (*Khu II*), which covered Hanoi, before being named head of the Bureau of Propaganda in the army's political section as well as editor of the army paper *Ve Quoc Doan*. In March 1950, he served as the political commissar to the 209th Regiment. In April 1951, he became deputy, then chief, political commissar in the 312th Division. Between October 1955 and 1964, he was political commissar as well as secretary of the party's Military Committee for the Right Bank [of the Red River] War zone.

**TRẦN ĐỨC THẢO (1917–1993).** Vietnamese philosopher and supporter of the nationalist cause of the **Democratic Republic of Vietnam** (DRV) during the Indochina War. Born in **Hanoi**, Tran Duc Thao grew up in a civil service family in colonial Indochina. He arrived in Paris in 1936, after having completed an academic year at the *Faculté de droit* in Hanoi. He completed his secondary studies at the select Paris schools *Lycée Louis le Grand* and *Henri IV*. In 1939, he was admitted to the elite French *École normale supérieure* on the rue d'Ulm in Paris, entering third in his class. In 1943, he successfully passed the exam to obtain his specialization in philosophy (*agrégation de philosophie*). He was the top-ranked candidate and submitted a thesis on Edmund Husserl's phenomenology. While Vichy France heralded this as a sign of the French *génie colonisateur*, Tran Duc Thao also became an ardent supporter of Vietnamese nationalism and French decolonization. In 1944, he was elected to the General Delegation of the Indochinese living in France.

Although he remained in France after World War II, he publicly supported the DRV's quest for independence and (moderate) social revolution. When he warned in an interview that the Vietnamese would and should resist the return of the French to Vietnam, he was arrested and spent three months behind bars in the Parisian jail *La Santé* in late 1945. It was during this time that he wrote a celebrated article criticizing French colonialism, published in *Les Temps Modernes* edited by **Jean-Paul Sartre** (*Les relations franco-vietnamiennes*, February 1946). It was also during this time that he emerged as a world-class philosopher. He collaborated with Sartre as a debater and contributor to *Les Temps Modernes*. Their collaboration broke down, however, when differences in 1949 and 1950 over Marxism and existentialism divided them. Tran Duc Thao published important philosophical works, above all his famous *Phénoménologie et matérialisme dialectique* (1951).

In 1951, he returned to Vietnam by way of Prague, Moscow, and Beijing to take part in the resistance. He arrived in early 1952. He was commissioned to write a number of reports for the government on the education program in the north and the status of two industrial workshops. During the spring of 1953, he translated several works of **Truong Chinh** into French, all the while undergoing political **indoctrination** sessions himself. In 1953 and 1954, he was involved in **land reform** efforts in Phu Tho province. Following the end of the war in mid-1954, he was named professor at the University of Hanoi. Between 1954 and 1955 he held the Chair in Ancient History, the Chair in the History of Philosophy between 1955 and 1958, and was dean of the Faculty of History between 1956 and 1958. However, his disillusionment with the non-democratic nature of Vietnamese communism became increasingly evident after the Indochina War ended. His critical voice during the *Nhan Van Giai Pham* movement in 1956 cost him his right to teach at the University of Hanoi and isolated him professionally and personally. *See also* CULTURE; COLLABORATION; HISTORY; INTELLECTUALS; RECTIFICATION.

**TRẦN DUY HƯNG (1912–1988, PHẠM THƯ).** Born near **Hanoi**, Tran Duy Hung was a member of the **Indochinese Communist Party** and served on the party section for the city of Hanoi in 1945–1946. He was thus involved in efforts to head off war with the French in the explosive month of December 1946, all the while preparing the city for war. He was a deputy to the National Assembly of the **Democratic Republic of Vietnam.**

**TRẦN HIỆU (HOÀNG MỸ, VŨ VĂN ĐÍCH, 1914–1997).** Born in Ha Dong province near **Hanoi**, he was one of the most secret and important architects of the **Democratic Republic of Vietnam**'s (DRV) early military intelligence apparatus. He studied at the *École pratique industrielle* in Hanoi. As a youngster in Hanoi, he witnessed the nationalist outpouring surrounding the death of Phan Chu Trinh in 1925. He drifted leftwards in the late 1920s, joining a communist-oriented youth group in 1929. Though trained as a mechanic, he became actively involved in journalism and radical politics during the Popular Front period. In 1938, **Truong Chinh** and Dao Duy Ky introduced him into the **Indochinese Communist Party** (ICP). In September 1939, with the end of this liberal period, the French police arrested him and shipped him off to Son La prison. In June 1941, the French deported him to a jail in Madagascar with seven other communists, including **Le Gian**, **Hoang Huu Nam**, and **Hoang Dinh Giong**.

Following the overthrow of the Vichy regime there in 1942, these political prisoners, including Tran Hieu, regained their freedom but were blocked from returning to Vietnam because of the Japanese occupation of Indochina. In 1943, however, Gaullist authorities allowed the British Intelligence Service MI6 to recruit these Vietnamese men. Tran Hieu, Hoang Huu Nam, and Hoang Dinh Giong agreed that this was the only way for them to return to Vietnam and justified their actions in light of the wider communist approved anti-fascist struggle. In 1944, the British trained Tran Hieu in New Delhi in intelligence, radio, and cipher operations before parachuting him in March 1945 to a village near Hanoi. From there, he provided intelligence on the Japanese to the Allies and went to work to help the ICP take power. With the help of **Tran Quoc Hoan**, the deputy Party secretary of the Tonkin regional committee, Tran Hieu was provided with access to a radio in order to communicate with the Allies in Calcutta, administer radio communications for the Tonkin committee with the ICP central committee to the north, and teach a class on military reconnaissance operations for the Tonkin committee. This he did.

With the birth of the DRV in September 1945, he put his clandestine communist experience, prison contacts, and recently acquired modern intelligence knowledge to work for the nationalist cause. When the government created the Bureau of Security Forces for Northern Vietnam (*So Liem Phong Bac Bo*) in late 1945, he seconded Le Gian as deputy director. He remained deputy director when this bureau was replaced in February 1946 by the Public Security Department (*Cong An Vu*). In this capacity, he played a pivotal role in combating non-communist nationalist efforts to contest communist power in 1946. Tran Hieu headed up the Ministry of Defense and High Command's intelligence bureau (*Cuc Tinh Bao*) between 1947 and 1948. In early 1948, the DRV officially named him Director of the Intelligence Department of the Vietnamese National Army's High Command. This department was disbanded in April 1950. Tran Hieu became the Deputy Director of Vietnam Public Security Directorate and served concurrently as Chief of the Public Security Directorate's Intelligence Buerau. In July 1951, a strategic intelligence agency for the party and the government emerged, called the Liaison Department, directly subordinate to the Prime Minister's office. Tran Hieu was director of this powerful department. In June 1967, the Liaison Department merged with the General Staff's Military Intelligence Department to create the Intelligence Department, the Party, and army's overall strategic intelligence agency. Tran Hieu, the man who got his intelligence start with the help of the allies, was in charge. *See also DEUXIÈME BUREAU;* H122; MAURICE BELLEUX; PUBLIC SECURITY SERVICES; *SERVICE DE DOCUMENTATION EXTÉRIEURE ET DE CONTRE-ESPIONNAGE.*

**TRẦN HƯNG ĐẠO, BATTLE.** *See* VINH YEN, BATTLE.

**TRẦN HỮU MAI.** *See* HỮU MAI.

**TRẦN HUY LIỆU (1901–1969).** Born in Nam Dinh province in northern Vietnam, Tran Huy Lieu became a prolific journalist and nationalist in southern Vietnam during the 1920s, writing for the Vietnamese newspaper *Dong Phap*. He also joined the **Vietnamese Nationalist Party** (*Viet Nam Quoc Dan Dang*, VNQDD) around 1927. In 1928, the French arrested him and deported him to **Poulo Condor** where he crossed over to the **Indochinese Communist Party** (ICP). Before his arrest, he had helped recruit into the nationalist party the future general of the southern army of the **Democratic Republic of Vietnam** (DRV), **Nguyen Binh**. The two were particularly close during their time behind bars at Poulo Condor. Tran Huy Lieu emerged from prison in 1935 and resided thereafter in northern central Vietnam where he worked as a journalist during the Popular Front period. He was the editor in 1938 of the communist paper *Tin Tuc* in **Hanoi** and worked closely with **Truong Chinh**. In 1939, the French arrested and sent Tran Huy Lieu to prison in **Son La** and then Nghia Lo, where he remained until his release in March 1945 following the Japanese overthrow of the French. He contributed to the **Viet Minh**'s newspaper, *Cuu Quoc*, and attended the Conference of the ICP at Tan Trao, when he was elected vice president of the National Liberation Committee. He served as minister of Communications and Propaganda in the first DRV Provisional Government. He accompanied **Nguyen Luong Bang** and Cu Huy Can to Hue to receive the abdication of the Emperor **Bao Dai** on 29–30 August 1945. He was secretary of the Viet Minh's General Directorate or the ***Tong Bo* Viet Minh** in 1945. He joined the DRV's National Assembly in 1946 as a deputy for Nam Dinh province. However, his public interference in major foreign policy issues handled by **Ho Chi Minh**, especially his criticism of negotiations with the French in 1945 and 1946, probably ended his career as minister. Like **Tran Van Giau**, Tran Huy Lieu would turn to writing the party's national and official history. In 1953, Tran Huy Lieu ran the DRV's new Social Sciences Committee, the *Ban Nghien Cuu Van Su Dia*. He eventually became head of the *Vien Su Hoc* (Historical Studies Institute) in 1959 and editor of *Nghien Cuu Lich Su* (Historical Research). *See also* HISTORY.

**TRẦN KHÁNH GIƯ.** *See* KHÁI HƯNG.

**TRẦN KHUY.** *See* TRẦN NAM TRUNG.

**TRẦN KIM TUYẾN (1925–1995).** Born in Thanh Hoa province to a Catholic family, Tran Kim Tuyen received a religious education and briefly studied to become a priest in a northern seminary before shifting to education. He returned to Thanh Hoa and taught at a Catholic school there until 1949, when he renewed his studies at the *Facultés de medecine et de droit* at the Indochinese University in 1949. He obtained his degree in law but was drafted into the **army of the Associated State of Vietnam** before finishing his medical studies. He became a physician's assistant in the military medical school in **Hanoi**. There he became close friends with **Ngo Dinh Nhu** and eventually his brother, **Ngo Dinh Diem**. Upon taking charge of the State of Vietnam in mid-1954 and becoming president of the **Republic of Vietnam** a year later, Ngo Dinh Diem selected Tran Kim Tuyen to serve as one of his most trusted advisors, in charge of the Social and Political Research Bureau (*So Nghien Cuu Chinh Tri Xa Hoi*). In short, Tran Kim Tuyen became the chief of intelligence and security in the office of the President. *See also* CATHOLICS

IN VIETNAM AND THE WAR; LE GIAN; PUBLIC SECURITY SERVICE; TRAN HIEU; TRAN QUOC HOAN; TRAN QUOC HUONG.

**TRẦN LƯƠNG.** *See* TRẦN NAM TRUNG.

**TRẦN MAI (TRẦN VĂN MAI, LÊ VĂN LẠC, NAI PRASERT PHINIKORN, 1915–?).** Prominent diplomat in Asia for the **Democratic Republic of Vietnam** (DRV) during the Indochina War. Born in Thai Binh province in northern Vietnam, he studied at the *Lycée Albert Sarraut* in **Hanoi** in the mid-1920s before returning home to work in the family business. He reappeared on the political scene following the Japanese overthrow of the French in the ***coup de force*** **of 9 March 1945** and their defeat shortly thereafter. He joined the nationalist cause of the DRV, became a member of the government's National Assembly in 1946, and worked in the newly founded **Public Security Services** (*Cong An*) section in Nghe An province. For unclear reasons, he moved to Bangkok in 1948 and began a diplomatic career in the DRV's delegation, where he took over the direction of the *Viet Nam News Service* from **La Vinh Loi** (Le Hy). In this position, Tran Mai agitated against French colonialism and their moves to create a counter-revolutionary government in the person of **Bao Dai**. In May 1950, he moved to Jakarta to plead the DRV's cause to a sympathetic Indonesian public and government. In the end, however, the Indonesian government preferred not to recognize either of the two Vietnams. *See also* INDONESIA; INDIA; NEUTRALIZATION OF INDOCHINA.

**TRẦN MAI NAM.** *See* HỮU MAI.

**TRẦN NAM HÙNG (1915–1993).** Born in Tien Giang province in southern Vietnam, Tran Nam Hung was admitted to the *Faculté de médecine* in the late 1930s and graduated as a doctor in 1943. He immediately went to work in a French military hospital in Phnom Penh with the rank of surgeon captain. He supported the nationalist cause of the **Democratic Republic of Vietnam** (DRV) in September 1945 and served it as the director of the medical service for his home province of Tien Giang. The French arrested him in October 1945 while he was at work in a My Tho hospital. He was released and put to work by the French in a military hospital near Cho Ray where he honed his medical skills in treating war-related injuries. He also kept in close contact with other patriotic **intellectuals** in **Saigon**, such as **Luu Van Lang** and Bui Thi Cam. Following a secret trip to the *maquis*, he returned to Saigon determined to help the DRV clandestinely. He helped smuggle vital medicines to his friends and resistance doctors, **Ho Van Hue** and Nguyen Van Hoa. He signed the 1950 petition of intellectuals calling on the French to negotiate directly with **Ho Chi Minh**.

**TRẦN NAM TRUNG (TRẦN KHUY, TRẦN LƯƠNG, 1913–2009).** Born into a peasant family in Quang Ngai province in central Vietnam, Tran Nam Trung was an active union leader and worker by the late 1920s. He joined the **Indochinese Communist Party** in 1931. Until 1943, he was in and out of colonial prisons for a variety of different reasons. In 1944 and 1945, he was active in the creation of the Committee for the Mobilization of the National Salvation Front of Quang Ngai province and took part in the Ba To uprising. With the advent of the **Democratic Republic of Vietnam** in September 1945, he became the Party's provincial secretary for Quang Ngai and Binh Dinh. Between September 1945 and 1946, he served as a member of the Party's Territorial Committee for Trung Bo (*Xu Uy Trung Bo*), in charge of military matters. In September 1946, he became a political commissar and joined the Party's Standing Committee for **Inter-Zone V** (*Lien Khu V*). Between 1951 and 1954, he served under **Nguyen Chi Thanh** in the General Political Bureau as his deputy. He oversaw the mobilization of local populations in support of the battle of **Dien Bien Phu**.

**TRẦN NGỌC DANH (LÊ DUY NGHĨA, BLOKOV).** Ranking Vietnamese communist leader expelled from the **Indochina Communist Party** (ICP) in 1951 for unilaterally closing the Vietnamese diplomatic delegation in Paris in 1949 and criticizing **Ho Chi Minh** and the Party in reports to the Soviets. Born in central Vietnam, Tran Ngoc Danh was the younger brother of Tran Phu, the first general secretary of the ICP, who had criticized Ho Chi Minh's "narrow nationalism" in the early 1930s. Tran Ngoc Danh completed his primary and secondary studies in colonial Indochina before studying in the Soviet Union in the late 1920s. He returned to Indochina in the early 1930s and joined the ICP in 1931 before the French arrested him about a year later. He was not released from prison until the Japanese overthrew the French in 1945. He immediately joined the **Democratic Republic of Vietnam** (DRV) in September, serving as a deputy in the National Assembly, and was named an alternate member in the ICP's Central Committee. In 1946, during his trip to France, Ho Chi Minh named **Hoang Minh Giam** and Tran Ngoc Danh to create and lead the DRV's Permanent Delegation to France. Tran Ngoc Danh assumed direction of the delegation in late 1946 and held this position until he dissolved the mission in 1949. During his time in France, he worked to win over the support of the Vietnamese living in France, the French people, and world opinion to the Vietnamese independence cause. He also maintained good relations with **Jacques Duclos** and other ranking members of the **French Communist Party**. Duclos helped him escape the French police and make his way to Prague in 1949 where Tran Ngoc Danh created another diplomatic delegation. It was also during this tense time in the **Cold War** that Tran Ngoc Danh sent a series of letters to the French, Chinese, and Soviet communist parties criticizing the "nationalist" and "bourgeois" tendencies of the ICP in general and of Ho Chi Minh in particular. The ICP expelled him in 1951 for having endangered the country's foreign relations, for having dissolved the delegation in France without authorization, and for criticizing a senior member of the party. *See also* H122 AFFAIR; HOANG VAN HOAN; JOSEPH STALIN; LA VINH LOI; NGUYEN DUC QUY.

**TRẦN NGỌC NGHIÊM.** *See* HOÀNG MINH CHÍNH.

**TRẦN QUANG.** *See* TRẦN BẠCH ĐẰNG.

**TRẦN QUANG VINH (TRẦN ĐẠI BIÊN, TRƯƠNG VỊNH THANH, 1897–1975).** One of the prime movers of the **Cao Dai** religious movement, born in Long Xuyen province in southern Vietnam. He began working in the colonial offices of Phnom Penh as a secretary in Cambodian Arts. He joined the Cao Dai movement in 1930 and served as head of the movement's mission in Cambodia until 1941. In September 1941, the French took him into custody but he walked free thanks to Japanese protection. At this time, he also joined the Vietnamese Restoration Society (*Viet Nam Phuc Quoc Hoi*) and, with the overthrow of the French in March 1945, helped create the first Cao Dai combat force with Japanese backing. Following the Japanese defeat, **Viet Minh** forces arrested him briefly. On 9 May 1946, French security forces then arrested him and succeeded in winning over his support in the war against the **Democratic Republic of Vietnam** in the south. Tran Quang Vinh brought over his troops to the French side and recognized the legitimacy of the **Provisional Government of the Republic of Cochinchina** created by the French on 1 June 1946. The French named him commander-in-chief of the Cao Dai Armed Forces and helped him arm, train, and reorganize his troops. On 23 May 1948, he became under-secretary in the National Defense of the provisional government of South Vietnam. Between May 1950 and March 1951, Tran Quang Vinh served as minister of the Armed Forces in **Tran Van Huu**'s first government. In August 1951, he returned to the "Holy See" of the Cao Dai in Tay Ninh province. A rival, **Trinh Minh The**, held him prisoner until May 1954.

**TRẦN QUỐC HOÀN (NGUYỄN TRỌNG CẢNH, NAM ĐÀN, 1916–1986).** Became one of the **Democratic Republic of Vietnam**'s most powerful public security officers during the Indochina War. Born in Nghe An province, Tran Quoc Hoan became involved in radical politics in the early 1930s while working as a miner in the silver mines of Laos. In March 1934, he joined the **Indochinese Communist Party** (ICP) in Laos. The French arrested him later that year and placed him under surveillance in Ha Tinh until the Popular Front period allowed him to relocate to **Hanoi** where he worked in communist papers such as *Ban Dan, Thoi The,* and the *Ha Thanh Thoi Bao*. During World War II, he worked clandestinely in the Hanoi area in close collaboration with **Truong Chinh** and served as the secretary of the Party's Urban Committee for Hanoi. In June 1941, with the French police closing in on him, Tran Quoc Hoan organized the withdrawal of the party to "**Secure Zones**" (*An Toan Khu*) outside the city. While working as liaison between the Party and cells inside Hanoi, he fell into French hands in 1941 and ended up in **Son La prison**. There he rubbed shoulders with the likes of **Tran Dang Ninh** and **Le Duc Tho.**

Tran Quoc Hoan walked out of Son La following the Japanese overthrow of the French on 9 March 1945. He secretly returned to Hanoi where he became secretary of the ICP's Territorial Committee for **Tonkin** (*Xu Uy Bac Ky*) and served as the Central Committee's Special Committee envoy to Hanoi (*Thanh Uy*). He helped in preparations for the battle of Hanoi and was the handler for the agent that cut the electricity on the evening of **19 December 1946**. He stayed in the capital city during much of the sixty-day battle of Hanoi, serving as the ICP's special delegate. He remained undercover in Hanoi as the Central Committee's special delegate to the occupied city, running a network of operatives and secretly mobilizing **intellectuals** and the youth against the French.

Between 1949 and 1951, he was political commissar for the provinces of Hanoi and Ha Dong. In 1949, he also became the director of the ICP's "special zone" for Hanoi, a position he held until 1977. In 1951, during the Second Party Congress, he joined the Executive Committee of the **Vietnamese Worker's Party**'s Central Committee. He was deeply involved in setting up and running the public security system in Hanoi. In 1952, the ICP appointed him to run the national security services. In 1953, he became the director of the newly created Ministry of Public Security, a position he would hold for years to come. In 1954–1955, he served on the Central Committee's board in charge of the **land reform.** He presided over the Party and government's return to Hanoi in late 1954. Rising to the top of the security forces during the Indochina War, he became one of the most powerful Vietnamese communists until his death in 1986. *See also* JEAN COUSSEAU; LE GIAN; POULO CONDOR; REEDUCATION; TRAN HIEU.

**TRẦN QUỐC HƯƠNG (MƯỜI HƯƠNG, TRẦN NGỌC BAN, 1924–).** One of communist Vietnam's best spy masters during both Indochina Wars. Born in Ha Nam province in northern Vietnam, he became active in revolutionary politics during the Popular Front period, when he worked in the Vietnamese Youth Union. In 1943, after serving time in prison, he joined the **Indochinese Communist Party** (ICP). During World War II, he remained in the north collaborating closely with **Truong Chinh** and **Le Duc Tho** in the outskirts of **Hanoi**. He distinguished himself in the Department for the **Secure Zone** (*An Toan Khu*), run by the Party's Standing Central Committee. From there, Tran Quoc Huong was in charge of running secret missions, operations, and preparations for taking power in Hanoi. Truong Chinh authorized him to enter into contact with European leftist **crossovers** in the French **Foreign Legion** based in the Hanoi area, in particular **Erwin Börchers** *(Chien Si)*. In 1945–1946, Tran Quoc Huong served as Truong Chinh's private secretary. From 1949, Tran Quoc Huong entered the **Democratic Republic of Vietnam**'s Military Intelligence Service (*Cuc Tinh Bao*) and became deputy director of the Central Intelligence Department. After the **Geneva Accords** divided Vietnam in 1954, the Party dispatched Tran Quoc Huong to southern Vietnam to create a secret secure zone outside of **Saigon**-Cholon and to create and run top secret intelligence operations for the Territorial Committee of Nam Bo, as he had done for the ICP from outside Hanoi in 1944–1945. From December 1954, he helped operate a newly created southern espionage network designed to follow developments in the south, the southern Party Commission's Research Branch Responsible for Following the Enemy Situation (*Ban Nghien Cuu Dich Tinh Xu Uy*). He was the ranking case-officer for **Pham Ngoc Thao**, **Pham Xuan An**, **Vu Ngoc Nha,** and Le Huu Thuy, all of whom penetrated the **Republic of Vietnam** led by **Ngo Dinh Diem**. The Republic of Vietnam's security forces arrested and incarcerated Tran Quoc Huong in the late 1950s. However, he regained his freedom in 1964, shortly after Ngo Dinh Diem's assassination. In 1968, Tran Quoc Huong returned to southern Vietnam where he worked as a ranking security officer in the party's Saigon regional committee. Tran Quoc Huong later became secretary of the Central Committee of the Vietnamese Communist Party.

**TRẦN QUỐC TUẤN MILITARY ACADEMY (*Trường Võ Bị Trần Quốc Tuấn*).** The first and most important military academy of the **Democratic Republic of Vietnam**. Created on 17 April 1946, it began teaching its first class of over 250 officer cadets in May 1946. The first director of the academy was **Hoang Dao Thuy**, with **Tran Tu Binh** serving as political commissar. *See also* ACADEMY, ASSOCIATED STATE OF VIETNAM; SCOUTING, INDOCHINA WAR.

**TRẦN QUÝ HAI (BÙI CHẤN, 1913–1985).** Born in Quang Ngai province in central Vietnam, he joined the **Indochinese Communist Party** in 1930. He was arrested by the French and incarcerated in the prison of Ba To in the central highlands. Following the Japanese overthrow of the French in March 1945, Tran Quy Hai regained his freedom and joined other prisoners to form an ultra-leftist group in Quang Ngai and helped communists take power in Quang Ngai province. He became the Party provincial secretary for Quang Ngai and a member of the Standing Committee of the People's Committee for Quang Ngai. In 1946, he became an alternate member of the Territorial Committee for Trung Bo (*Xu Uy Trung Bo*) in charge of the provinces of Binh Dinh, Phu Yen, and Khanh Hoa. Between 1947 and 1952, he was a political commissar in the 101st Regiment and then political commissar in the Binh Tri Thien Front. Between 1953 and 1954, he was divisional leader as well as the first political commissar to the 325th division. He also served as political commissar to the Central Lao front and commander of the battle of lower **Laos** in 1953–1954. He adopted a Maoist line in the 1950s.

**TRẦN THIỆN KHIÊM (1925–).** Following the overthrow of the French in March 1945, the Japanese named him acting governor of Tan Binh province in southern Vietnam. He graduated from the sole class of the *École militaire d'Extrême-Orient* in Dalat and served as under-secretary in the **Nguyen Van Xuan** southern Vietnamese government. From May 1948, he worked as his general secretary. By the end of the Indochina War, Tran Thien Khiem was a lieutenant colonel and deputy chief of staff in the Associated State of Vietnam's Joint Chiefs of Staff. He was later involved in a number of coups in **Saigon** in the mid-1960s and served as prime minister to Nguyen Van Thieu between 1969 and 1975.

**TRẦN THIỆN VANG.** Catholic politician in the French-backed governments during the Indochina War. He was related to Empress **Nam Phuong** and served as counselor for **Cochinchina** and My Tho province during the Vichy period. Anti-communist, he cooperated closely with the French following World War II. He was a member of the Cochinchina Democrat Party representing mainly Catholic constituents. In October 1947, he served as minister for Agriculture in **Nguyen Van Xuan**'s cabinet and traveled to Hong Kong to help convince **Bao Dai** to return to lead a non-communist, pro-French Vietnamese government. *See also* ASSOCIATED STATES OF INDOCHINA; BAO DAI SOLUTION.

**TRẦN THỌ.** *See* HOÀNG TÙNG.

**TRẦN THÚC KÍNH.** *See* TRẦN VĂN QUANG.

**TRẦN TRỌNG KIM (1883–1953).** Vietnamese educator, **intellectual**, and non-communist nationalist leader. Born in Ha Tinh province in central Vietnam, he was first trained in the *Collège des interprètes* in **Hanoi** before studying to become an educator at the *École normale d'instituteurs* in France. Upon his return to Vietnam, he taught as a professor in the *Collège du Protectorat* and the *École normale d'instituteurs*, both in Hanoi, and was inspector for Franco-Annamese Primary Schools. He wrote widely on Vietnamese culture and history, incorporating both subjects into the educational curriculum. He founded and ran the educational journal *Hoc Bao* and served as vice president of the *Association pour la formation intellectuelle et morale des Annamites* (AFIMA). Vichy authorities placed him under surveillance during World War II. The governor general, Jean Decoux, even had him removed from his position on the *Conseil du gouvernement*. Tran Trong Kim escaped to Singapore in 1944 thanks to the protection of the Japanese and became prime minister in the first Vietnamese government formed after the Japanese ***coup de force* of 9 March 1945** ousted the French. With the birth of the **Democratic Republic of Vietnam**, he holed himself up in Hanoi, refusing offers to join the new government. He left for Nanjing on 9 July 1946 as part of an attempt to create a non-communist, nationalist alternative to French neo-colonialism and Vietnamese communism. He entered into contact with **Bao Dai** along these lines and returned to Vietnam to put the idea to the French. When High Commissioner **Georges Thierry d'Argenlieu** sent him packing, Tran Trong Kim moved to Cambodia and swore never to take up politics again. Nevertheless, in October 1953, he agreed to take part in the organization of the first National Assembly for the Associated State of Vietnam, of which he was elected unanimously president that year. He died, however, shortly thereafter on 2 December 1953.

**TRẦN TỬ BÌNH (PHẠM VĂN PHU, 1907–1967).** Born into a Catholic family in northern Vietnam, he was expelled from his seminary for taking part in nation-wide student strikes following the death of Phan Chu Trinh in 1926. In 1927, he moved to southern Vietnam to work as a laborer on a rubber plantation and joined the Vietnamese Youth League in 1929 and the **Indochinese Communist Party** (ICP) about a year later. Following his participation in a demonstration of plantation workers against their harsh working and living conditions, he ended up serving time in **Poulo Condor** prison cell. In 1936, thanks to the

Popular Front, he left the island, but remained under *résidence surveillée* in the north. In 1941, he joined the ICP's Territorial Committee for **Tonkin** (*Xu Uy Bac Ky*). In late 1943, the French arrested him again and incarcerated him in three different prisons. Following the Japanese overthrow of the French, Tran Tu Binh regained his freedom and resumed his political activities in the north. As a member of the Standing Committee of the Territorial Committee for Tonkin, he took part in the insurrection of August 1945 and used the colonial telegraph network to inform other areas and issue orders to turn power over to the **Viet Minh**. During the Indochina War, he served in the army and became a major general in January 1948. He also served as the deputy general director of the Army Investigative Board (*Pho Tong Thanh Tra Quan Doi*) and was involved in the investigation of the **H122** incident. Tran Tu Binh later served as the **Democratic Republic of Vietnam**'s ambassador to China during the height of the Vietnam War.

**TRẦN VĂN.** *See* TRẦN VĂN GIÀU.

**TRẦN VĂN ÂN (1903–2002).** Born in Long Xuyen province in southern Vietnam, Tran Van An completed his secondary studies at the *Lycée Chasseloup Laubat* in **Saigon**. Between 1923 and 1928, he studied in Aix-en-Provence, where he became involved in nationalist politics. He published articles in favor of Vietnamese independence in a paper he set up at that time, *l'Annam scolaire*. Upon his return to Saigon, he joined the editorial board of the *Duoc Nha Nam* until it went under in 1934. In 1935, he turned to more radical politics when he joined the communist paper, *La Lutte*, run by one of his friends, **Ta Thu Thau**. Tran Van An also made ends meet as the manager of a distillery until 1940. In February 1941, the French arrested him briefly as a threat to "national security". Although he was released a few months later, colonial authorities placed him in a special worker's unit (*Formation spéciale de travailleurs*) in southern Vietnam. During World War II, in 1942, he joined the Japanese police force in Indochina and actively agitated for the independence of Vietnam as one of the leaders of the Cochinchinese branch of the Vietnamese Restoration Association (*Viet Nam Phuc Quoc Dong Minh Hoi*). The Japanese transferred him to Singapore around September 1944. He broadcast there in Vietnamese for the Japanese. He returned to Indochina following the Japanese ***coup de force* of 9 March 1945** and led the Vietnamese Nationalist Independence Party (*Viet Nam Quoc Gia Doc Lap Dang*). He also collaborated closely with the head of **Cao Dai** armed forces, **Tran Quang Vinh**, in a failed attempt to bring Prince Cuong De back to Vietnam to serve as emperor of a constitutional monarchy. With the advent of the **Democratic Republic of Vietnam**, Tran Van An withdrew briefly from politics. In September 1946, however, he joined efforts with **Nguyen Van Sam** to create a non-communist Front of National Unity and then the Vietnamese National-Socialist Party (*Dang Viet Nam Dan Chu Xa Hoi*, or *Dang Dan Xa* for short) in alliance with the head of the **Hoa Hao**, **Huynh Phu So**. His anti-communism was virulent. In October 1947, he became minister of Information in the government of **Nguyen Van Xuan**. However, he thereafter faded from the political scene for unclear reasons.

**TRẦN VĂN ĐÔN (1917–).** Born in Bordeaux, France, Tran Van Don was a French national and a Vietnamese non-communist nationalist. He graduated from the *Hautes études commerciales* (HEC) in Paris in 1939 and served in the French army. He was captured during the Battle of France in 1940 and returned to Vietnam in 1942 in the colonial army now in the service of Vichy. He served with General **Philippe Leclerc** during the French reoccupation of Indochina in 1945 and 1946. With the creation of the Associated State of Vietnam in 1949, he left the French army to serve in the emerging Vietnamese one. He studied General Staff work at the *École de guerre* in France in 1950–1951. In Vietnam, he headed the army's Military Security between 1951 and 1953, when he became colonel. Between 1953 and 1957, he served on the Joint Chiefs of the General Staff of the **Republic of Vietnam** following the signing of the **Geneva Accords**.

**TRẦN VĂN GIÀU (HỒ NAM, HOÀNG, TRẦN VĂN, 1911–2010).** Leading Western-trained Vietnamese communist who helped Vietnamese nationalists take over in **Saigon** in August 1945. Born in Tan An province in southern Vietnam, Tran Van Giau pursued his secondary studies in Toulouse, France, where he became involved in radical politics. He joined the **French Communist Party** in May 1929 and in 1931 he traveled to the Soviet Union, where he studied at the University of Toilers in the Far East. After pursuing advanced ideological training there, he joined the

Comintern which dispatched him to **Cochinchina** in 1935 to build up the Territorial Committee for Cochinchina on behalf of the **Indochinese Communist Party** (ICP). Shortly after his return, the colonial police arrested him for illegal political activities. Tran Van Giau regained his liberty after four months. In 1935, the French sentenced him to five years of prison for his involvement in the "Deschamps affair". Upon his release in 1940, he was interned in a "Special Workers Unit" (*Formation spéciale de travailleurs*) in southern Vietnam, from which he escaped shortly thereafter.

Following the Allied liberation of France and General **Charles de Gaulle**'s rapprochement with the Soviet Union, Tran Van Giau entered into contact with French Gaullists in Indochina concerning the need to collaborate against the common enemy, the Japanese. In December 1944, he contacted secretly the ***Section française de l'Internationale ouvrière*** leader in Indochina **Louis Caput** along similar lines, just as **Truong Chinh** was doing in the north. From this time, Tran Van Giau produced brochures and published clandestine papers explaining why the Indochinese should collaborate with the New France led by De Gaulle against the Japanese in exchange for French colonial reform and eventual decolonization. During this time, he was not in direct contact with the ICP leadership located in northern Vietnam, nor was he a member of the **Viet Minh**, which was also located far to the north. Tran Van Giau worked closely with **Pham Ngoc Thach** in mobilizing the youth in the Saigon area and would use Thach and his **Vanguard Youth League** (*Thanh Nien Tien Phong*) to promote the communist position in the south following the Japanese defeat in August 1945. Relations, however, between communists such as Tran Van Giau and non-communist political, national, and religious groups, such as the **Cao Dai**, **Hoa Hao**, and **Binh Xuyen**, were difficult from the start.

In August and September 1945, Tran Van Giau served as chairman of the Provisional Administrative Committee for Nam Bo and supported the **Democratic Republic of Vietnam** (DRV) declared in **Hanoi** by **Ho Chi Minh** on 2 September 1945. Recalled to Hanoi in November 1945, Tran Van Giau headed a special Bureau for Nam Bo (*Phong Nam Bo*). While he advised the government on southern affairs, he ceded his communist leadership position in the south to **Le Duan**, who headed up the revamped Territorial Committee for Nam Bo (*Xu Uy Nam Bo*) from October, and **Nguyen Binh**, who ran military affairs for all of the south from December. In 1946, the government sent Tran Van Giau to Thailand to procure arms for the southern resistance and to win over Thai support (Tran Van Giau had known Prime Minister **Pridi Banomyong** since their days in France). Tran Van Giau represented the DRV at the Asian Relations Conference held in New Delhi in 1947. For unclear reasons, he was recalled to Vietnam in 1948 and arrived in **Inter-Zone IV** (*Lien Khu IV*) sometime in 1949. He briefly served as the director of Communications and Propaganda in this zone before dedicating himself to educational and intellectual matters. Until the end of the Indochina War in 1954, he worked in central Vietnam as the vice director of the Provisional University of Inter-Zone IV. It remains unclear why he was removed from important political and diplomatic positions in the government, Party, and in Southeast Asia. *See also* HOANG VAN HOAN; LE HY; TRAN NGOC DANH.

**TRẦN VĂN HỮU (1896–1984).** Prominent and active non-communist politician during the Indochina War. Born in Vinh Long province in southern Vietnam, he completed his secondary studies at the *Lycée Chasseloup Laubat* in **Saigon** and then studied agricultural engineering at the *École coloniale d'agriculture* in French Tunisia and in Nogent-sur-Marne in France, from which he graduated as an engineer in tropical agronomics. He married a Vietnamese French national and was naturalized as a French citizen himself on 6 February 1925. In Indochina, he worked in the colonial agricultural service in southern Vietnam between 1915 and 1929. In that year, he went to work as an inspector in the *Crédit hypothécaire de l'Indochine* (also known as *Crédit foncier d'Indochine*) in Saigon and became in 1931 a member of the *Grand conseil des intérêts économiques et financiers de l'Indochine*. He was also an important landowner in **Cochinchina**. In 1935, he ran for election to the Colonial Council in Cochinchina and was a corresponding member of the *Académie des sciences coloniales*. In 1939, he joined the Indochinese Democrat Party (*Dang Dan Chu*). His activities during World War II are unknown. The French reported that he collaborated neither with the Japanese nor with the **Viet Minh**.

Following the Japanese defeat in August 1945, he was hostile to the advent of the **Democratic Republic of Vietnam** (DRV) and supported the southern autonomy being pushed by High Commissioner **Georges Thierry d'Argenlieu** against **Ho Chi Minh**. On 6 December 1946, the French named Tran Van Huu minister of Finances in the **Provisional Government of the Republic of Cochinchina**. He held this post until October 1947. On 8 October 1947, he became the first vice president of the provisional government of Cochinchina and minister of Finances and of the National Economy and remained in those positions until 1948. In April of that year, he became state minister and vice president of the Council of the Provisional Government of Vietnam as well as governor of Southern Vietnam. He played an active part in the Bay of Ha Long negotiations aimed at creating an independent, non-communist Vietnam under **Bao Dai** but allied closely with France.

In May 1950, with the advent of the Associated State of Vietnam, he became president of the Vietnamese Council of Government, minister of Foreign Affairs and minister of National Defense. With the support of Robert Schuman, Tran Van Huu obtained his government's participation in the San Francisco Conference officially ending a state of war between the Associated State of Vietnam and Japan. Bao Dai confided special powers to Tran Van Huu to destroy "terrorist" networks operating in southern Vietnam. Tran Van Huu traveled to France with Bao Dai on 20 June 1950 to attend the **Pau Conference**, during which time he openly criticized the French delegation in an interview, saying that that the **French Union** must not be used as a "cover" to return to a "disguised protectorate for Vietnam". He also solicited American help in promoting full Vietnamese independence. He remained president of the government following a ministerial shakeup in February 1951 and headed the Ministry of Foreign Affairs and that of the Interior. He also presided over the defeat of **Nguyen Binh's** urban war of terror in Saigon in 1949–1950. In another shakeup in March 1952, he remained at the head of the government and took charge of the Ministry of Finances and that of National Defense. He withdrew from the political scene when **Nguyen Van Tam** replaced him as president of the government council in June 1952. With the rise of **Ngo Dinh Diem** in 1955 he went into exile in France where he came to favor the DRV's cause and the neutralization of Vietnam. He died at Val-de-Grâce in France in 1984. *See also* BAO DAI SOLUTION.

**TRẦN VĂN KHA (1894–?).** Leading non-communist politician during the Indochina War. Born in **Saigon**, he completed his primary education at the Catholic school *Taberd* in Saigon. In 1909, he left for France where he pursued his secondary studies at the *Lycée Lakanal* near Paris. Upon graduation, he worked in the French Ministry of War between 1911 and 1921 in the Section for Colonial Workers. During this time, he became active in patriotic politics and met with leading nationalists such as Phan Chu Trinh, Phan Van Truong, and even the future **Ho Chi Minh**. Upon his return to **Cochinchina** in 1921, he married a Vietnamese woman of French nationality. He was president of the Federation of Boy Scouts, a member of the Colonial Council between 1926 and 1939, and joined the *Grand conseil des intérêts économiques et financiers de l'Indochine*. Little is known about his activities during World War II, other than the fact that he was very active in **scouting** and sports. During negotiations leading up to the **Accords of 6 March 1946**, he sent a telegram to the minister of Overseas France asking the French to take the Vietnamese desire for independence seriously. However, he was no supporter of the **Democratic Republic of Vietnam**. In 1946, Tran Van Kha became a titular member of the Cochinchinese Council for the province of Gia Dinh and actively supported the non-communist Associated State of Vietnam. **Bao Dai** named him the Vietnamese representative to the Assembly of the **French Union** in early January 1950 and in January 1951 he was elected vice president of the Assembly of the **French Union**. On 18 February 1951, Tran Van Kha became minister of National Economy in the second **Tran Van Huu** government. In 1952, he became the Associated State of Vietnam's minister to the United States, the first Vietnamese to hold the title. In July 1952, Tran Van Kha presented his credentials to President **Harry Truman** at the White House in Washington, D.C.

**TRẦN VĂN KỲ.** *See* HOÀNG SÂM.

**TRẦN VĂN LUẬN (1910–?).** Vietnamese diplomat stationed in Southeast Asia during the Indochina War. Born in **Saigon**, Tran Van Luan completed his secondary education in Aix-en-Provence before studying to become a pharmacist in Montpellier. He also studied painting under the direction of André Lhote. In 1938, after 13 years in France, he returned to Saigon to work as a pharmacist. During World War II, Tran Van Luan participated in youth movements organized by Vichy and then in **Pham Ngoc Thach**'s **Vanguard Youth League**

(*Thanh Nien Tien Phong*). He also joined the **Indochinese Communist Party** sometime during World War II. With the advent of the **Democratic Republic of Vietnam** (DRV) in September 1945, he served briefly in 1945 in the Resistance and Administrative Committee for Rach Gia province and became a deputy in the DRV's constituent assembly for Rach Gia Province. Following the signing of the **Accords of 6 March 1946,** the DRV dispatched him to Thailand to work in the newly created delegation there. He attended the Asian Inter-Relations Conference in New Delhi in 1947 before moving on to Rangoon to set up the DRV's diplomatic delegation in February 1948. He was active in garnering support in South and Southeast Asia for the DRV's nationalist cause and war against the French. He maintained excellent relations with leading Burmese politicians and military leaders. He also met major regional and international leaders, including American Ambassador-at-large **Philip Jessup** during his visit to the region in January 1950. Tran Van Luan remained in his post in **Burma** throughout the Indochina War.

**TRẦN VĂN MAI.** *See* TRẦN MAI.

**TRẦN VĂN QUANG (TRẦN THÚC KÍNH, 1917–).** Born in Nghe An province in central Vietnam, Tran Van Quang became active in nationalist politics during the Popular Front period. He joined the **Indochinese Communist Party** in 1936 and served as a member of the party's Committee for **Saigon**-Cholon, organizing workers in the city. In 1939, the French arrested him, but he escaped in October 1940 to make his way to Nghe An province, where he served on the party's Provincial Committee. He was arrested again in April 1941 and incarcerated in Buon Me Thuot. Following the Japanese overthrow of the French in the ***coup de force* of 9 March 1945**, Tran Van Quang returned again to Nghe An to help the Party take power there. He rejoined the Party Provincial Committee in Nghe An before transferring to military affairs and the start of a long military career in **Inter-Zone IV** (*Lien Khu IV*). Between November 1946 and 1947, he was a political commissar there. Between 1948 and 1949, he was commander as well as political commissar for the Zonal Section of Binh Tri Thien (*Phan Khu Binh Tri Thien*). He was the first political commissar for the 304$^{th}$ Division between May 1950 and 1951. Between June 1951 and 1953, he was deputy then chief of the Bureau for **Proselytizing the Enemy** (*dich van*). Between August 1953 and 1958, he headed the Strategic Office of the **General Staff**. *See also* INDOCTRINATION; PEOPLE'S ARMY OF VIETNAM; PSYCHOLOGICAL WARFARE; RECTIFICATION.

**TRẦN VĂN SOÁI (NĂM LỬA, TRẦN VĂN XÁI, LÊ VĂN SÁNG, 1894–?).** Prominent **Hoa Hao** leader opposed to the forces of the **Democratic Republic of Vietnam** (DRV) during the Indochina War. Born in Long Xuyen province in southern Vietnam, Tran Van Soai worked as a mechanic and bus driver for a number of southern companies during the interwar period. Illiterate and poor, he grew up on the rougher sides of southern Vietnamese society. But he was also streetwise and savvy, something that would take him far in a time of war. In the late 1930s, he began his own bus service and ran two main lines in Vinh Long and Can Tho provinces.

In 1940, after being wounded in a brawl, he converted to the Hoa Hao faith and served as the personal bodyguard to **Huynh Phu So** during the latter's movements throughout the Mekong Delta. During World War II, Tran Van Soai joined the Japanese police force, whose protection allowed him to act largely with impunity in Can Tho province. Together with Huynh Phu So, he was deeply involved in the politicization and militarization of the Hoa Hao faith. Following the defeat of the Japanese, he rejoined Huynh Phu So as his first lieutenant and became the head of the movement's military forces.

Like his mentor, Tran Van Soai was hostile to the **Viet Minh**'s efforts to monopolize control over political and armed forces in the south. When DRV agents assassinated Huynh Phu So in mid-1947, Tran Van Soai crossed over to the French side on 15 May in an agreement reached with French Colonel Cluzet, commander of the Western Zone in **Cochinchina**. On 18 May 1947, Tran Van Soai signed a convention with the French establishing the terms of cooperation between the French and Hoa Hao forces. He assumed the title of general and set up his headquarters in his old stomping grounds in Can Tho.

In May 1950, Tran Van Soai attended an important military conference in Dalat aimed at unifying various non-communist military forces into one national army under the Associated State of Vietnam. But the national integration of the armed forces remained difficult. As of July 1951, Tran

Van Soai's forces numbered 4,441 men. By October, they totalled 7,463. In January 1953, **Bao Dai** promoted him to major general to induce him to integrate his troops into the national army. In March 1953, still desirous to maintain his forces under his control, Tran Van Soai informed **Nguyen Van Tam** that such national integration was unacceptable. His then almost 10,000-strong Hoa Hao troops remained linked by convention to the French Army until the end of the Indochina War in mid-1954 and were never integrated into the **Army of the Associated State of Vietnam** or that of the DRV. *See also* ANTOINE SAVANI; BINH XUYEN; CAO DAI; COLLABORATION; CRIMINALITY; LE VAN VIEN; MARCEL BAZIN; PHAM CONG TAC; ASSOCIATED STATES OF INDOCHINA.

**TRAN VAN THINH (1926–)**. One of the very first agents of the **Democratic Republic of Vietnam** (DRV) to infiltrate the French ranks as a deep-cover penetration. A graduate of the Faculty of Fine Arts at the University of **Hanoi**, he joined the Viet Minh in 1945 and put his artistic abilities in the service of the new nation-state. In late 1947, because of his knowledge of French and some English, Tran Van Thinh attracted the attention of the head of military intelligence, **Tran Hieu**, who recruited him. A few years later, the latter assigned Tran Van Thinh the task of infiltrating the ranks of the emerging Associated State of Vietnam. Tran Van Thinh successfully passed qualifying entry exams for working for the Ministry of Defense in the Associated State in late 1949. In early 1950, he transferred to **Saigon** where he worked in the J-1 (Personnel) section of the new Vietnamese National Army headquarters. In 1953, the Associated State's National Defence sent him to officer training school at the Military Academy in Dalat. He ended up working as a liaison officer between the Vietnamese Army's J-1 Office and the Training Relations and Instruction Mission (TRIM), the joint Franco–American training mission formed after the **Geneva accords**. During this time, he passed on secret information to his handlers in the north on the **Army of the Associated State of Vietnam**, its tactics and strategy, as well as its relationship with the French and the Americans. His wife was particularly instrumental in passing secret information from Saigon to Hanoi and on to the DRV thanks to her cover as a trader.

**TRẦN VĂN TRÀ (NGUYỄN CHẤN, LÊ VĂN THẮNG, 1919–1996).** Increasingly powerful and influential Vietnamese communist general in southern Vietnam during the Indochina War. Born into a peasant family in Quang Ngai province in central Vietnam, Tran Van Tra studied in the *École industrielle* in Hue and became active in nationalist politics during the Popular Front period. In August 1938, he joined the **Indochinese Communist Party** (ICP) in Hue. Between 1936 and 1939, he was apparently a member of the *Mouvement de la jeunesse républicaine de la Capitale*. In December 1939, the French arrested him in **Saigon**. They sentenced him to six months of prison, incarcerated him in Hue, and then placed him under house arrest until his escape in 1941. Tran Van Tra worked clandestinely for the party in Saigon under the name of Le Van Thang. He was arrested again in June 1944 and did not regain his release from the Saigon's Kham Lon prison until mid-1945, when the Japanese overthrew the French. At this time, Tran Van Tra immediately returned to his political activities. In March 1946, he formed, trained, and led Detachment 14 (*Chi Doi 14*) in the war against the French in southern Vietnam.

In that same year, when three military zones were created for the south, he assumed command of war **Zone VIII** (*Chien Khu VIII*), which he ran until late 1949. He also joined the Party's Territorial Committee of Nam Bo (*Xu Uy Nam Bo*) and worked closely with **Le Duan** throughout the entire conflict. In 1948, the ICP's Territorial Committee for Nam Bo designated him to lead a special delegation to northern Vietnam to report to **Ho Chi Minh** and the Central Committee on the situation in the south. He duly executed the mission. Back in the south in late 1949 or early 1950, a decree of 22 May 1950 appointed him the government's military delegate for war **Zone VII** (*Khu Chien VII*) and another of 4 August 1950 made him deputy commander of the Armed forces in the south. He maintained the military command of Zone VII and was its top political commissar as well. The ICP leadership had clearly decided to impose one of their own in order to take greater control over this strategically important zone ruled by General **Nguyen Binh** since 1946. Tran Van Tra served as deputy commander-in-chief of Zone VII until the death of Nguyen Binh in September 1951. Since November 1949 he had also been political commissar to the special region of Saigon-Cholon. Between 1952 and 1954, he served as military commander of the **Inter-Zone for Eastern Nam Bo** (*Phan Lien Khu Mien Dong*

*Nam Bo*). He became a member of the **Central Office for the Southern Region** (*Trung Uong Cuc Mien Nam*, better known by its American acronym, COSVN) when it replaced the Party's Territorial Committee for Nam Bo in 1951. From this point, he worked closely with its director and deputy director, **Le Duan** and **Le Duc Tho**, respectively. Tran Van Tra's rise was linked to the support of these two men and the Party's move to increase its hold over southern forces which had until then escaped the ICP's direct control. Tran Van Tra was regrouped to northern Vietnam in 1954, but would return to play a leading role in military operations during the war against the Americans.

**TRẦN VĂN TRUNG (1926–).** Born in Hue in 1926, Tran Van Trung completed his secondary studies at the Catholic Redemptorist school between 1935 and 1946. He joined the **French Union** forces in August 1947. In December 1948, he entered the First Class of the French-backed Vietnamese National Military Academy in Hue. He graduated in June 1949 and was commissioned as a second lieutenant in the emerging Vietnamese National Army (August 1949). He took advanced officer training courses at Saint Cyr during the second half of 1949. Upon his return to Vietnam, he joined the 2nd Reenforced Company in 1950. In 1952, he studied at the Command and Strategy Course at the Command and Staff College in **Hanoi**. In 1953, he joined the *Groupe Mobile 21* before moving on to the 1st Vietnamese Regiment in July 1954. *See also* ACADEMY, ASSOCIATED STATE OF VIETNAM; ARMY, ASSOCIATED STATE OF VIETNAM.

**TRẦN VĂN TUYÊN.** *See* TRẦN VĨNH PHÚC.

**TRẦN VĂN TỴ (1888–?).** Non-communist nationalist in favor of the increased autonomy of **Cochinchina** during the early stages of the Indochina War. Born in Bac Lieu province, Tran Van Ty studied law successfully to become a leading magistrate in **Saigon** between 1932 and 1946. He volunteered in January 1916 and served in France during World War I. He demobilized in January 1920. A French citizen, he was one of the few Vietnamese to enter the ranks of the French **Colonial Academy** (*École coloniale*) during this time. He was an outspoken and fervent supporter of Cochinchinese autonomy after the defeat of the Japanese in August 1945 and the difficult return of the French to southern Vietnam. He served as minister of Justice in the **Provisional Government of the Republic of Cochinchina** spearheaded by **Georges Thierry d'Argenlieu** and led by Dr. **Nguyen Van Thinh**. Following the suicide of the latter in late 1946, Tran Van Ty became vice president of the Council of Ministers (1946–1948) and minister of Interior under the premiership of **Le Van Hoach**. As late as May 1949, Tran Van Ty was still president of the Saigon Court of Appeals (he was the first to hold the position). He was virulently opposed to **Ho Chi Minh** and communism. He also felt, at least in the wake of World War II, that it was impossible to disassociate Cochinchina from French interests there.

**TRẦN VĂN XÁI.** *See* TRẦN VĂN SOÁI.

**TRẦN VĨNH PHÚC (TRẦN VĂN TUYÊN, 1913–1976).** Active member of the **Greater Vietnam Nationalist Party** (*Dai Viet Quoc Dan*) opposed to the restoration of French rule to Vietnam during the Indochina War. Born in Tuyen Quang province in northern Vietnam, he joined the Greater Vietnam Nationalist Party in 1941. Following the overthrow of the French and the subsequent defeat of the Japanese in mid-1945, he created, in **Hanoi**, the Party of Nationalist Youth of Vietnam (*Viet Nam Quoc Gia Thanh Nien Dang*). During the shaky alliance among non-communist Vietnamese nationalist groups in 1945 and 1946, Tran Vinh Phuc served as personal secretary to **Nguyen Tuong Tam**, then minister of Foreign Affairs in the **Democratic Republic of Vietnam** (DRV) in spite of the latter's membership in the **Vietnamese Nationalist Party** (*Viet Nam Quoc Dan Dang*, VNQDD).

In June 1946, as civil war broke out between the Vietnamese in the north and the French and the DRV moved against the non-communist Vietnamese nationalists, Tran Vinh Phuc took refuge in China (the DRV had sentenced him to death). There, he joined the Directing Committee of the National Union Front, created by **Nguyen Hai Than** and Nguyen Tuong Tam to take on the **Viet Minh** in the fight for the nationalist mantle. In July 1948, hopeful that the French were serious about building a truly nationalist, non-communist government, Tran Vinh Phuc returned to **Saigon** from Hong Kong to work in the provisional government of South Vietnam. He served as undersecretary of state in the Ministry of Information between July 1949 and January 1950. In January 1950, the government named him a delegate to the Assembly of the **French Union**. In May 1950, with the advent of the Associated State of Vietnam, he served as under-secretary of state to the Presidency in the cabinet of **Tran Van Huu** (and became state secretary to the Presidency in the second Tran Van Huu cabinet as well). He was a member of this government's delegation to the **Pau Conference** in 1950.

**TRAPNELL, THOMAS J. H. (1902–2002).** Graduated from the United States Military Academy in 1927 and served in the U.S. Army during World War II in the Asian theatre. Taken prisoner in the Philippines, Thomas Trapnell survived a Japanese death camp to return to duty after World War II. He led the 187th Airborne Regimental Combat Team in Korea from 1951 to 1952. He then served as chief of the **Military Assistance and Advisory Group** for Indochina, created in September 1950, to advise and assist French-led forces in the war against the **Democratic Republic of Vietnam**. In November 1953, he accompanied General **Henri Navarre** to inspect French preparations for the camp at **Dien Bien Phu**, and returned again on 14 January. Trapnell was one of the few military strategists at the time to understand the nature of the risks Navarre was taking at Dien Bien Phu. For one, he worried that Navarre had dispersed his troops too far throughout Indochina to make a successful stand at Dien Bien Phu. Second, he doubted that French air power could keep the remote camp supplied sufficiently to hold off an enemy with a superior battle corps. In January 1954, with this in mind, Trapnell gave the **French Union** forces defending Dien Bien Phu a fifty-fifty chance of surviving the attack. He had his experience in Korea in mind. Lastly, Trapnell felt that the French could not deliver a decisive military blow to the adversary in Indochina given their increasing troop commitments to European defense. *See also* EUROPEAN DEFENSE COMMUNITY; NORTH ATLANTIC TREATY ORGANIZATION; AID, AMERICAN; KOREAN WAR; WAVE TACTICS.

**TREVOR-WILSON, ARTHUR GEOFFREY.** Fluent in French and the son of a prominent Barclay's Bank manager, Trevor-Wilson worked for seventeen years during the interwar period in finance in France and North Africa. Upon the outbreak of World War II, he joined the British army, became a lieutenant, and served as a liaison officer with the French for the British 2nd Division until his evacuation from Dunkirk. Because of his fluent French, Trevor-Wilson joined Special Operations Executive and moved into the Secret Intelligence Service (SIS or MI6). He specialized in North African affairs and trained under Kim Philby, his boss at the time. In mid-1942, Trevor-Wilson went undercover to Tangiers as a Swiss businessman to determine how the British would be received locally as the Allies prepared to land in North Africa. He returned to Britain after the landing and joined Section V at St. Albans to train as a Special Counter-Intelligence Unit officer. He landed with the American armada in Algiers on 8 November 1942, in charge of the four British special counter-intelligence units sent into the French colony. For almost a year, he performed liaison work with the French ***Deuxième Bureau*** before being sent to France for the liberation of Paris as part of the American Task force of forty people who stayed put at the *Gare Montparnasse* (including Malcolm Muggeridge) until General **Philippe Leclerc's** 2nd Armored Division (*2ème Division blindée*) entered Paris. Leclerc personally bestowed upon Trevor-Wilson the French *Croix de guerre* for his services rendered. Trevor-Wilson then returned to Britain to work in Section V of the SIS now located in Ryder Street in London.

In mid-1945, with the rank of lieutenant colonel, the SIS dispatched Trevor-Wilson to work for General **Douglas Gracey** in charge of the British occupation of Indochina below the **16th parallel.** Trevor-Wilson served as a staff officer on Gracey's headquarter's staff. Gracey sent him on a private mission to determine whether Leclerc's forces could reoccupy Phnom Penh. Trevor-Wilson responded positively and Leclerc's forces arrested **Son Ngoc Thanh.** In late 1945, Gracey sent Trevor-Wilson to **Hanoi** to serve as the director of the British Military Mission attached to the headquarters of the Chinese occupying forces in northern Indochina led by General **Lu Han.** During his time in Hanoi, Trevor-Wilson helped liberate French officers, met often with **Ho Chi Minh** and, thanks to the support of the latter, had Chandra Bose's deputy, Major-General A. C. Chatterjee, arrested and deported to British custody. Trevor-Wilson drove General **Raoul Salan** to Haiphong as Chinese and French forces prepared to clash in early March. General Leclerc thanked Trevor-Wilson and **Peter Simpson-Jones** of the British Military Mission for the behind-the-scenes role they played in the realization of the **Franco-Chinese accord** and in heading off a major clash with local Chinese forces in Haiphong in early March.

In mid-1946, having joined the Foreign Service, Trevor-Wilson returned to France in the company of Ho Chi Minh to cover the **Fontainebleau Conference**. In July 1946, he flew back to Hanoi to open and lead the new British Consulate in Hanoi. During the battle of Hanoi in late 1946 and early 1947, he tended to the **Indian** population caught in the cross-fire and helped negotiate a truce to evacuate civilians. Trevor-Wilson remained in Indochina until 1951, establishing an impressive network of contacts with the French, Americans, and various sides of the Vietnamese nationalist movement. He was a personal friend of **Graham Greene**. Trevor-Wilson was also on good terms with French political, military, and intelligence figures in Indochina, most importantly General Raoul Salan and Colonel **Maurice Belleux** at the head of the ***Service de Documentation extérieure et de contre-espionnage***. In 1949, Trevor-Wilson was one of two witnesses to the marriage of **Paul Aussaresse**, a French military intelligence officer at the time. However, Trevor-Wilson's relationship with General **Jean de Lattre de Tassigny** and the ***Sureté fédérale*** in Indochina was much less cordial. So much so that de Lattre personally asked for Trevor-Wilson's transfer out of Indochina. In 1952, Arthur Trevor-Wilson returned to England. He later served as First Secretary in the British Embassy in Laos between 1960 and 1968, when he retired. *See also* NOVELS.

**TRIỆU CÔNG MINH (TRIỆU TRỪNG THẾ, TRIỆU TỬ LONG, BAO KÉO, TƯ GIO, TRỤM NỘC, CHỊ BA SỪNG RĂNG, CHỊ TƯ XÓM GÀ, TRƯƠNG CA PHONG, 1909–1975).** Vietnamese journalist during the Indochina War. Born in Bac Lieu province in southern Vietnam, Trieu Cong Minh graduated from the pedagogical school in **Saigon**. After teaching for a few years, he switched careers to work as a journalist during the interwar period. Together with his wife, Ai Lan, he freelanced in numerous southern papers including *Luc Tinh Tan Van, Dong Phap Thoi Bao,* and *Phu Nu Tan Van*. Little is known of the couple's activities during World War II. Following the Japanese defeat and the advent of the **Democratic Republic of Vietnam** (DRV), they joined the resistance in the south. In late 1945, following the French reoccupation of Saigon, they worked in southwestern Vietnam before returning to Saigon to agitate as journalists in favor of Vietnamese independence. Both took part in the United Newspaper Movement in Saigon (*Phong Trao Bao Chi Thong Nhat*), and were fervent defenders of the freedom of the press and of the nationalist cause led by **Ho Chi Minh**. Sometime around 1950, Trieu Cong Minh moved to **War Zone D** (*Chien Khu D*) and joined the editorial staff of the DRV's clandestine Radio Saigon-Cholon (*Dai Phat Thanh Saigon Cholon*). He worked there until 1953 when he joined the staff of the paper *Cuu Quoc Nam Bo*. He left this post with the end of the war and the partition of Vietnam by the **Geneva Accords** in July 1954.

**TRIỆU TRỪNG THẾ.** *See* TRIỆU CÔNG MINH.

**TRIỆU TỬ LONG.** *See* TRIỆU CÔNG MINH.

**TRỊNH ĐÌNH HUẤN**. *See* LÊ LIÊM.

**TRỊNH ĐÌNH THẢO (c. 1902–1986).** Born in Ha Dong province in northern Vietnam, Trinh Dinh Thao studied law in Marseilles and defended his doctorate in 1929. He became active in Vietnamese nationalist politics in the 1920s and was said to be a **Freemason**. He returned to Vietnam in 1929 where he worked as a lawyer in the Superior Court in **Saigon**. During the Popular Front period, he participated in the Indochinese Congress and political front. He also worked as a legal advisor to the head of the **Cao Dai** religious movement, **Pham Cong Tac**. Following the Japanese overthrow of the French in March 1945, he served as minister of Justice in the **Tran Trong Kim** government until the Allied defeat of the Japanese in August. During this time, he approved the release of scores of Vietnamese political prisoners in central Vietnam. He supported the nationalist cause of the **Democratic Republic of Vietnam**, but remained on the sidelines and in the colonial city. He called on the French to negotiate with **Ho Chi Minh** or to accord real independence to **Bao Dai**. In 1949, he joined with the French socialist party leader, **Alain Savary**, to make a secret trip to southern resistance zones. *See also ATTENTISME*; INTELLECTUALS.

**TRỊNH MINH THẾ (THOÁI VĂN TRƯƠNG, 1920–1955).** Born in Tay Ninh province in southern Vietnam, Trinh Minh The was a military leader in the **Cao Dai** politico-religious movement during the Indochina War. During World War II, he was a member of the Japanese-backed anti-colonialist movement, the Association for the Restoration of Vietnam (*Viet Nam Phuc Quoc Hoi*). He worked as a non-commissioned officer in the Japanese police force during this time. He was a staunch supporter of Vietnamese independence, but was distrustful of and hostile to the aims of Vietnamese communists. He collaborated briefly with the forces of the **Democratic Republic of Vietnam**; however, when relations broke down violently, he crossed over to the French side in November 1946 and became a major in the French army (though he would entertain secret contacts with the **Viet Minh** into 1948). Although the French named him colonel in 1949, Trinh Minh The defected on 6–7 June 1951 with 2,000 men and assumed the rank of "brigadier general". He called for the creation of the Union of Nationalist Forces of Vietnam, a third force of sorts, opposed both to French colonialism and to Vietnamese communism. After the Indochina War, he came into contact with **Edward Lansdale**, who helped finance his troops in support of **Ngo Dinh Diem**. Tran Minh The was shot dead in 1955 by a sniper, while helping Ngo Dinh Diem neutralize the **Binh Xuyen** as a politico-military force. The exact circumstances of his death and those responsible for it remain unclear. Although never stated as such, Trinh Minh The and his "third force" figure prominently in **Graham Greene**'s classic, *The Quiet American. See also* ANTOINE SAVANI; *ATTENTISME*; CIVIL WAR; HOA HAO; LE VAN VIEN; MARCEL BAZIN; NGUYEN BINH; NOVELS.

**TRỊNH NGỌC ANH.** *See* NGÔ THẤT SƠN.

**TRINQUIER, ROGER (1908–1986).** Born into a rural family in southern France, Trinquier became one of France's leading specialists in **revolutionary warfare** during the Indochina War. In 1932, upon graduating from Saint-Cyr, he began his military career in the colonial infantry in Indochina as a second lieutenant assigned to a border post in northern **Tonkin**. During this time, he came to know and work with the then Captain **Raoul Salan**, his future commander during the latter part of the Indochina War. Between 1937 and 1938, Trinquier returned to France and was assigned to the Maginot Line facing Nazi Germany. In 1938, he assumed command of a company assigned to guard the French Embassy in China before transfering to Shanghai where he became the deputy to the commanding colonel of French Troops in Shanghai (under Vichy). He remained in Shanghai until the defeat of the Japanese in mid-1945.

On his way back to France, he stopped over in **Saigon**, where his long-time friend Raoul Salan, now a general, persuaded him to stay and help with the French reoccupation of Indochina. During this time, Trinquier joined the ***Commandos** parachutistes d'Extrême-Orient* led by **Pierre Ponchardier** and commanded the "sub Commando B4" in southern Vietnam. It was an initiation for Trinquier to commando and action operations and a turning point in his thinking and military career. He traveled to France in the summer of 1946 to recruit and train volunteers for the creation of a battalion of colonial paratroopers – the *2ème Bataillon Colonial de Commandos parachutistes*. Upon returning to Indochina in November 1947, he became the second-in-command of this battalion as it went immediately into action against the forces of the **Democratic Republic of Vietnam** (DRV) in areas near Saigon as well as in Cambodia and Central Vietnam.

During this time, Trinquier became increasingly interested in "revolutionary warfare". He read **Mao Zedong**'s political and military writings and took a keen interest in the communist reliance on **guerrilla** warfare and control of the masses for extending their military and political reach. In 1948, he suggested to General **Boyer de la Tour** that the French army turn these "revolutionary" techniques against the **Viet Minh**. With a green light, Trinquier began launching guerrilla operations by night and using ambushes instead of large-scale troop movements in order to break the adversary's control over the populations.

In December 1949, after a brief stint back in France, Trinquier returned to Indochina to join the ***Groupement des commandos mixtes aéroportés*** and lead the ***Service Action***'s operational antenna in northern Vietnam. In January 1952, he assumed command of the Regional Representation [Office] for North Vietnam (*Commandement de la représentation régionale du Nord Vietnam*). In this capacity, he went beyond simple guerrilla activities to creating autonomous *maquis* zones to harass the DRV from rear areas. From May 1953, he headed the *Service Action* for all of Indochina. He personally led combat missions far behind the enemy's lines in northern Vietnam and relied on Tai populations to create hostile guerrilla zones and partisans to take the war to the DRV. At one point, he was allegedly in charge of some 30,000 partisans. He returned to France in January 1955 as a lieutenant colonel. Trinquier would go even further in developing his counter-insurgency ideas and actions during the **Algerian War.** *See also* ANTOINE SAVANI; *PAYS MONTAGNARDS DU SUD*; TAI FEDERATION.

**TROCARD, JEAN AUGUSTIN (?–1947).** Began his career in colonial intelligence before World War II. He first worked in this capacity in French Indochina in 1929 before serving in the *Service de renseignement intercolonial* where he befriended **Raoul Salan**. In 1940, Trocard was injured, taken prisoner, and incarcerated by the Germans in Lübeck until 1945 when he rejoined the 9th Colonial Infantry Division (*9ème Division d'infanterie coloniale*) at the head of its ***Deuxième Bureau***. In 1946, he arrived in Indochina and served under the command of General **Jean Valluy**. Trocard ran the *Deuxième Bureau* for the *Commandement supérieur des troupes françaises en Extrême-Orient*. His intelligence services, the ***Service des études historiques***, warned the French High Command of Vietnamese preparations to attack on the evening of **19 December 1946**. He perished in a **Viet Minh** ambush in 1947.

**TROOPS, DEMOCRATIC REPUBLIC OF VIETNAM.** *See* PEOPLE'S ARMY OF VIETNAM.

**TROOPS, FRANCE.** *See* EXPEDITIONARY CORPS.

**TRỤM NỘC.** *See* TRIỆU CÔNG MINH.

**TRUMAN, HARRY S. (1884–1972).** After serving in France during World War I, Truman returned to his native Kansas City, became a judge in Jackson County, and rose rapidly in the local Democratic Party. In 1934, with the backing of the powerful Pendergast political machine, he became a United States senator and maintained that position until 1944, when he ran as President Franklin Roosevelt's vice presidential candidate. Truman became president of the United States upon Roosevelt's death in April 1945 and presided over the final acts of World War II, first in Europe then in Asia. While Truman was no advocate of French colonialism, he allowed his administration to reverse his predecessor's desire to bar the French from restoring their rule to Indochina by placing the former colony under an international Trusteeship. The U.S. government also allowed France to use Lend–Lease supplies, initially earmarked for operations against Germany and Japan, to outfit French troops used to retake southern Indochina. American ships even transported over ten thousand French troops to **Saigon**. In 1946, Truman increasingly rejected Roosevelt's belief that that the "grand alliance" between the United States and the Soviet Union established in 1941 could serve as the foundation for a new post–1945 international order. By March 1947, he had adopted a much more hostile policy towards Moscow and decided to "contain" Soviet expansionism. This also meant that Truman was much more concerned with supporting French reconstruction rather than pushing them hard on postwar decolonization. Like **Joseph Stalin**, Truman attached more importance to France and its place in Europe than to supporting Vietnamese nationalists in Asia. And like Stalin, Truman refused to respond to **Ho Chi Minh**'s letters appealing to American anti-colonialism and the need to thwart the restoration of European colonialism. Truman went ahead with the containment policy and the Marshall Plan (some of which was used by the French to finance the war in Indochina War) and he recognized the French right to return to Indochina. Although Truman was unwilling to spend the necessary resources to bolster **Chiang Kai-shek** against the Chinese communists, the rapid shift of the **Cold War** to Asia in 1950 and the rise of McCarthyism in the United States led him to support more vigorously the French presence in Indochina in order to hold the line against any further spread of communism into the region. The British and the French actively urged Truman to defend Southeast Asia against the communist threat, while Republicans accused him of being too soft after having "lost China". In January 1950, despite efforts to pressure the French to decolonize fully in Indochina, the Truman administration diplomatically recognized the three French-backed **Associated States of Indochina**, none of which was completely independent at the start. In May 1950, Truman also initiated military and economic aid to the French to hold the line against communism in Indochina. The North Korean attack upon the south in June 1950 further reinforced Truman's commitment to the French in order to stop communism from spreading into Southeast Asia. In his declaration on the **Korean War** delivered on 27 June 1950, Truman explicitly linked the American commitment in Korea to his decision to speed up military aid to the French and the Associated States of Indochina.

**TRUNG BỘ.** *See* ANNAM.

**TRUNG GIA CONFERENCE.** During the **Geneva Conference** in mid-1954, from 4 July 1954 a joint military commission consisting of French and Vietnamese officers began meeting in the town of Trung Gia located 40 km north of **Hanoi**. Discussions focused on the application of the possible accords and above all on the exchange of prisoners. Colonel Marcel Lennuyeux led the French delegation while General **Van Tien Dung** represented the **People's Army of Vietnam**. The three **Associated States of Indochina** also sent delegates to the conference, but they were relegated to second rank by both the French and **Democratic Republic of Vietnam**.

**TRUNG KỲ.** *See* ANNAM.

**TRUNG NAM.** *See* NGUYỄN VĂN KINH.

**TRUONG CANG (1913–?).** Other than the fact that he was born in today's southern Vietnam, we know little about Truong Cang before 1945. In 1946, he served as governor of Svayrieng. In 1947, he resigned from this post in order to lead the *Parti de la minorité khmère du Sud-Vietnam* until 1948. He left to study in France in 1950, where he obtained his *licence* or bachelor's degree in law at Aix-en-Provence. He obtained his doctorate in law in 1957 in Paris. **Penn Nouth** entrusted him during his time in France to mobilize Khmer students in favor of **Norodom Sihanouk**. *See also* KHMER KROM.

**TRƯƠNG CAO PHONG.** *See* TRIỆU CÔNG MINH.

**TRƯỜNG CHINH (ĐẶNG XUÂN KHU, THÂN, QUYẾT, PHƯƠNG, QUA NINH, SÓNG HỒNG, 1907–1988).** The acting general secretary of the **Indochinese Communist Party** (ICP) until 1951, when the **Vietnamese Worker's Party** officially made him head of the Party. Born in Nam Dinh province in upper central Vietnam, Truong Chinh took up radical politics in the late 1920s. In 1927, he joined the Vietnamese Revolutionary Youth Party and became a member of the ICP upon its official creation in 1930. He worked in the Propaganda Campaign Committee for the Party's Central Committee. He was arrested in late 1930, sentenced to 12 years of prison, and shipped off to the **Son La** colonial prison in late 1931. In late 1936, thanks to the liberal policies of the Popular Front government, he regained his freedom and resumed his communist activities in the **Hanoi** area. He wrote assiduously in *Notre Voix* and *Le Travail*. He joined the Party's Territorial Committee for **Tonkin** *(Xu Uy Bac Ky*) and represented the northern committee in the Indochinese Democratic Front. In 1938, he co-authored a famed treatise on the "Peasant Question" (*Van de dan cay*) with **Vo Nguyen Giap**.

In 1940, with World War II now underway, Truong Chinh went underground in charge of the Tonkin committee. As one of the rare ranking communists still free, he assumed de facto leadership of the Party during a meeting held in November 1940 (later called the "Central Committee's 7th plenum"). Over the next year, in his function as head of the regional Party committee for Tonkin, Truong Chinh developed underground Party networks in the Red River Delta and Hanoi and linked up with the **Viet Minh** movement (over which **Ho Chi Minh** presided) in May 1941 on the Sino-Vietnamese border.

During the Central Committee's 8th plenum, Truong Chinh was elected to the Executive Committee. However, it is unclear whether this plenum elected him officially the general secretary of the ICP. It would be more accurate to describe him as the acting head of the Party until a proper congress could officially elect a new general secretary (this occurred officially in 1951). In any case, during World War II, Truong Chinh served as editor of the Party paper *Co Giai Phong*; consolidated his position within the Tonkin Territorial Committee; and headed the ICP's board for political propaganda and ideological education. He also worked on the cultural front as general secretary of the Association for the Promotion of Quoc Ngu (*Hoi Truyen Ba Quoc Ngu*) and as the author of the seminal 1943 outline for the development of a new Vietnamese **culture** (*De Cuong Van Hoa*), both nationalist and internationalist.

In 1943, the French condemned Truong Chinh to death *in absentia* for his various activities. Working from "**Secure Zones**" (*An Toan Khu*) outside of Hanoi, he presided over preparations for taking power once the favorable moment arrived. This meant closely monitoring French and Japanese military and political developments in Hanoi. It also meant secretly penetrating and mobilizing **intellectuals**, workers, and colonial and European soldiers. Truong Chinh oversaw the construction of a secret network of party cells and activists ready to act when the time came. To this end, he collaborated closely with Hoang Van Thu, **Hoang Quoc Viet**, **Le Duc Tho**, **Tran Dang Ninh**, and **Tran Quoc Hoan** among others. The Party's center of gravity effectively shifted during World War II from the south to the north and into the Red River Delta outside Hanoi. Disguised, Truong Chinh met secretly in Hanoi with the French socialist leader, **Louis Caput** in late 1944, as well as with the European leftists in the **Foreign Legion**, **Erwin Börchers** and **Ernst Frey**, and Gaullists such as Seyberlich and Auriol (General Mordant's representative to this secret meeting).

Three days after the Japanese ***coup de force* of 9 March 1945**, Truong Chinh issued a new directive calling on all the people of Indochina to oppose the Japanese, but not the French on the condition that the latter did not oppose Vietnamese independence aspirations. Truong Chinh returned officially to Hanoi on 19 August 1945 to consolidate the **Viet Minh**'s takeover of the city and to make preparations for the creation of the **Democratic Republic of Vietnam**. He collaborated closely with **Ho Chi Minh** upon the latter's return to Hanoi shortly thereafter. Until the **dissolution of the Indochinese Communist Party** in November 1945, Truong Chinh continued to run the Party's paper, *Co Giai Phong*, and its successor *Su That*. Following the outbreak of war on **19 December 1946**, he retreated with the government and the Party to bases in the Viet Bac region and continued to serve as the acting head of the Party. He was a fervent Maoist and vigorously applied Chinese **land reform** in Vietnam from 1953. He headed the ICP's Special Committee for Land Reform, together with Hoang Quoc Viet, **Le Van Luong,** and Ho Viet Thang. In 1956, Truong Chinh lost his position as General Secretary of the Party because of errors committed during the land reform.

**TRƯỜNG CHINH ACADEMY (*Trường Trường Chinh*).** Political training academy for high level cadres in southern and lower central Vietnam and Cambodia. Created in 1950, the Truong Chinh Academy operated in southwestern Vietnam under the direction of the **Indochinese Communist Party**'s Territorial Committee for Nam Bo (*Xu Uy Nam Bo*). Its main task at the time was to train cadres who would run the main administrative levers of the Party and government administration. This was all the more important given that the Party was determined from 1950–1951 to consolidate its hold on the southern resistance administration and army and to expand the Party's presence. The Academy functioned until the implementation of the cease-fire in 1954 in line with the **Geneva Accords.** Several hundred middle and high-level communist cadres are said to have been trained in this political academy, including the Cambodian revolutionary **Son Ngoc Minh**. *See also* ACADEMY, ASSOCIATED STATE OF VIETNAM; COLONIAL ACADEMY.

**TRƯƠNG GIA TRIỀU.** *See* TRẦN BẠCH ĐẰNG.

**TRƯƠNG LAI.** *See* PHẠM ĐÀN.

**TRƯỜNG SƠN.** *See* NGUYỄN CHÍ THANH.

**TRƯƠNG TỬ ANH (TRƯƠNG KHÁN, PHƯƠNG, 1914–1946).** Born in Phu Yen province, Truong Tu Anh became active in nationalist politics in the late 1920s and 1930s. He studied at the *Faculté de droit* at the Indochinese University in **Hanoi**. In 1938, he created the non-communist and fiercely anti-colonialist **Greater Vietnam Nationalist Party** (*Dai Viet Quoc Dan Dang*). In 1942, the French incarcerated him in Hoa Binh. The French were not the only problem, however. Truong Tu Anh was also strongly opposed to the **Democratic Republic of Vietnam**, which he considered to be dominated by the **Indochinese Communist Party**. Vietnamese communists suspected him of being behind an attempt to provoke the French into attacking the **Viet Minh** on 14 July 1946, during French national day celebrations. Truong Tu Anh disappeared during the outbreak of full-scale war in Vietnam on **19 December 1946** in unclear circumstances. *See also* CIVIL WAR; POULO CONDOR.

**TRƯỜNG VĂN GIÀU (1913–1984).** Born in Vinh Loi province in southern Vietnam, Truong Van Giau worked in the offices of the Shell Oil Company in **Saigon** in 1930–1931 before joining the colonial army in 1933 to make ends meet. He remained there until the end of World War II and the advent of the **Democratic Republic of Vietnam** (DRV) in 1945. During the 1930s, Truong Van Giau drifted leftwards towards anti-colonialist politics and collaborated with southern communists during World War II, in particular **Tran Van Giau**.

In exchange for his **collaboration**, Truong Van Giau became head of the pro-DRV Republican Guard in August–September 1945. Following the return of the French to Saigon on **23 September 1945**, he helped create the southwestern military **Zone IX** (*Khu IX*). In December 1947, he became the head of this zone and held the position until September 1950, when he became the head of the **Tran Quoc Tuan Military Academy** in Nam Bo as well as the director of the Selective Service and Recruiting Offices (*So Tuyen Quan va Truong Tan Binh*). Because of poor health, he was named the special delegate to the high commander for the south in 1951 apparently following General **Nguyen Binh**'s death. The Party also included him in the making of the powerful **Central Office for the Southern Region** (*Trung Uong Cuc Mien Nam*, better known by its American acronym, COSVN) in that same year. In 1954, following the division of Vietnam into two provisional halves during the **Geneva Conference**, he relocated to the north and worked in the Ministry of Communications and Postal Service. Little is known of what became of him thereafter.

**TRƯỜNG VĂN HUỆ (1903–?).** Born into a Catholic family in Thua Thien province in central Vietnam, Truong Van Hue studied at the Catholic school *École Pellerin* in Hue to become a certified primary school teacher in 1921. He taught school until 1925, but switched professions to work in the colonial Public Works bureau. In 1938, he joined the Railway Service in Dalat and circulated throughout French Indochina until the overthrow of the French in March 1945. With the emergence of the **Democratic Republic of Vietnam** (DRV) in September 1945, he resigned his position in the Public Works department to dedicate himself to Catholic organizational work. He led the Vietnamese Catholic League (*Lien Doan Cong Giao*) and its nationalist journal, *To Quoc*. He maintained a fragile relationship with the DRV, which controlled Hue until early 1947. If there was no questioning his nationalism and anti-colonialism, the Vietnamese communist leadership was wary of his possible anti-communism. Following the French occupation of Hue, he tried to steer a middle course between the Vietnamese communists and the French colonialists, but not without difficulties. He became a partisan of **Ngo Dinh Diem** and on 4 January 1950 he almost succumbed to an assassination attack organized by DRV forces convinced that he was leaning too far the other way. With the arrival of the **Cold War**, he gravitated towards the Associated State of Vietnam led by the ex-emperor **Bao Dai.** *See also* CATHOLICS IN VIETNAM AND THE WAR; CATHOLICS, EXODUS FROM NORTH; CHRISTIANS AND OPPOSITION TO THE INDOCHINA WAR; LE HUU TU; VATICAN.

**TRƯỜNG VĨNH THANH.** *See* TRẦN QUANG VỊNH.

**TƯ ANH.** *See* TRẦN BẠCH ĐẰNG.

**TƯ GIO.** *See* TRIỆU CÔNG MINH.

**TƯ VŨ.** *See* VŨ HỒNG KHANH.

**TŪBĪ LĪFUNG (1919–1978).** Ethnic Hmong born in Nong Het in Laos, he completed his secondary studies in Vinh in central Vietnam and in Vientiane, where he began working as a colonial civil servant. In 1939 or 1940, he was elected chief of Nong Het district in Xieng Khouang province. In 1940, as the only Hmong on the Opium Purchasing Board, he was involved in the decision to institute a new tax payable in opium for mainly Hmong farmers unable to pay in cash. During World War II, the French worked with Tūbī to increase opium production. Following the Japanese ***coup de force* of 9 March 1945**, overthrowing French rule in Indochina, Tūbī Līfung joined French **guerrillas** in Laos against the Japanese. Tūbī continued to work with the French following the return of the latter to all of Laos in mid-1946, becoming deputy governor of Xieng Khouang and chief of the Hmong population living there. He joined the French and the Royal Government of Laos led by **Sīsāvangvong** against the forces of the **Democratic Republic of Vietnam** during the Indochina War, especially during the latter's invasion of Laos in 1953 and 1954. *See also* MINORITY ETHNIC GROUPS; *PAYS MONTAGNARDS DU SUD*; TAI FEDERATION.

**TUTENGÈS, ÉMILE (1902–1989).** Senior French officer who developed cordial relations with **Ho Chi Minh** during the troubled period preceding the outbreak of war on **19 December 1946**. Graduated from the ***École nationale des langues orientales vivantes*** in Paris, Tutengès joined and made his career in the colonial army, including two assignments in French Indochina before the outbreak of World War II. In 1940, he joined the French resistance and became chief of staff to General **Philippe Leclerc** in French Africa, but asked to be relieved of his post following differences with Leclerc. Tutengès became a battalion leader in the infantry. In September 1941, General **Charles de Gaulle** selected him to lead the Free French Military Mission to Singapore (*Mission Militaire Française Libre à Singapour*) before being transferred to Chongqing where he continued in the same functions as lieutenant colonel between 1942 and 1943. He played a pivotal role in reorganizing Free French intelligence operations in China (*Service de renseignements-Extrême-Orient*), working secretly with **François de Langlade**. In July 1943, **Zinovi Pechkoff** replaced Tutengès at the head of the French Military Mission in Chongqing. In 1944, Tutengès became chief of the ***Deuxième Bureau*** for French Forces in the Far East under General **Roger Blaizot.** A discreet and diplomatic officer, Tutengès traveled to the United States in September 1944 to plead in favor of an American landing in Indochina to head off an imminent, in his view, Japanese *coup d'État*.

Following the end of the Pacific War, Tutengès served as deputy chief of Staff to the new high commissioner to Indochina, Admiral **Georges Thierry d'Argenlieu**. The latter entrusted him with the investigation of the conditions in which the **Accords of 6 March 1946** had been reached and to which Thierry d'Argenlieu was increasingly hostile. Tutengès accompanied Ho Chi Minh and **Pham Van Dong** during the **Fontainebleau Conference** in mid-1946. He also accompanied Ho Chi Minh on his long return to Vietnam following the signing of the September 1946 ***modus vivendi***. Tutengès was present in **Hanoi** when full-scale war broke out on 19 December 1946 and took charge of the Chinese quarter of Hanoi for General **Louis Morlière.** In spite of the rupture between the French and the Vietnamese at this time, Tutengès was said to command the trust of Ho Chi Minh and members of the latter's entourage. He left the army in January 1948 and served with the rank of colonel in the reserves. He offered his services in June 1954 as a go-between with Ho Chi Minh. His offer was rejected.

**U NU (1907–1995).** Graduated from the University of Rangoon with a bachelor's degree in 1929, U Nu studied law in the early 1930s and became increasingly involved in nationalist politics. In 1934, he became president of the Burmese student union for Rangoon. He gained national prominence when he and another young nationalist leader Aung San were expelled from university for their involvement in student strikes. In 1937, U Nu joined the We Burmans Association and pushed the British on national independence. With the outbreak of World War II, the British arrested him in 1940 on charges of sedition but the Japanese released him upon taking the colony. In 1943, U Nu briefly served as Foreign Affairs and Information minister in the Japanese-backed Baw Maw government but grew rapidly disillusioned with the Japanese.

Upon the assassination of Aung San in 1947, U Nu agreed to lead the main nationalist party, the Anti-Fascist People's Freedom League and accepted the British offer to serve as premier designate of independent Burma. U Nu became the first prime minister of independent **Burma**, a position he held for ten years. Like India's **Jawaharlal Nehru**, U Nu hoped to navigate a neutral tack in the **Cold War**. A devoted Buddhist, he also wanted to make sure that Laos and Cambodia remained free of communist control and thus sought to roll back any communist pretensions entertained by the **Democratic Republic of Vietnam** in western Indochina. U Nu met with **Zhou Enlai** during the **Geneva Conference**, making these views known to the Chinese statesman. In short, Laos and Cambodia would have to be neutralized and the Chinese had to refrain from supporting internal communist movements in non-communist Asia, if Beijing wanted to keep the Burmese from leaning to the other side. Zhou Enlai understood. Following the Geneva Conference, relations were formally established between the two countries. *See also* GENEVA ACCORDS; INDIA; INDONESIA; NEUTRALIZATION OF INDOCHINA.

**UN XANANIKÔN (1907–1978).** Non-communist Lao nationalist leader and brother to **Ngon** and **Phuy Xananikôn**. He worked as a veterinarian in Indochina in the 1930s. He moved to Thailand upon the outbreak of the Franco-Thai war in 1940–1941, engaged in anti-French propaganda as a speaker for *Radio Bangkok*, and became an officer in the Thai cavalry. He also joined an anti-colonial Lao clandestine political group working along the Thai side of the Mekong – the Movement of Lao for the Lao, better known as *Lao Pen Lao*. Active in southern Laos when the Japanese capitulated, Un Xananikôn joined the **Lao Issara** government and opposed the return of French colonial rule. In April 1946, he became minister of Agriculture and Economy in the government before fleeing into Thailand upon the French occupation of Laos in mid-1946. He broke, however, with Prince **Phetxarāt** and other Lao Issara leaders in Thailand. He returned to Laos in 1949 and joined the Democratic Party. *See also* THAKHEK, BATTLE OF.

**ỨNG HOÈ.** *See* NGUYỄN VĂN TỐ.

**UNG VĂN KHIÊM (BA KHIÊM, 1910–1991).** Born in Long Xuyen province in southern Vietnam, Ung Van Khiem completed his secondary studies at the *Lycée Can Tho*. He became involved in radical politics in the 1920s when widespread student strikes rocked Vietnam. In 1927, he joined the Vietnamese Revolutionary Youth League and traveled secretly to Guangzhou (Canton) to study. In August 1929, back in Vietnam, he helped create the Annamese Communist Party. In late 1930, he joined the **Indochinese Communist Party** (ICP) and served as the secretary of the Territorial Committee for **Annam** (*Xu Uy An Nam*) following the capture of Ngo Gia Tu. In 1931, the French police arrested him and shipped him off to **Poulo Condor** where he stayed until the Popular Front freed him in 1936. He returned to radical politics in **Saigon**, taking part in the Indochinese Congress. In 1939, during a renewed French crack down, he ended up back in prison serving time for two years. Upon his release, Ung Van Khiem joined the Territorial Committee for **Cochinchina** (*Xu Uy Nam Ky*) and was selected to participate in the Tan Trao Conference in northern Vietnam with **Ha Huy Giap**. They did not make it in time. With the birth of the **Democratic Republic of Vietnam**, he became a deputy in the National Assembly in March 1946. Little is known about his activities in the late 1940s, though he seems to have remained on the new Standing Committee of the ICP's Territorial Committee for Nam Bo. During the Second Party Congress held in early 1951, he was elected to the Executive Committee of the **Vietnamese Worker's Party**'s Central Committee. He also joined the Party's new **Central Office for the Southern Region** (*Trung Uong Cuc Mien Nam*, better known by its American acronym as COSVN). During the rest of the Indochina War, he worked as the president of the Resistance and Administrative Committee for Bac Lieu province. He relocated to northern Vietnam after the **Geneva Accords** of 1954 and became in 1955 vice minister in the Ministry of Foreign Affairs and director of the powerful Central Committee's Foreign Affairs Bureau (*Ban Doi Ngoai Trung Uong Dang*).

***UNION FRANÇAISE.*** *See* FRENCH UNION.

**UNITED NATIONS.** In contrast to its intervention in the Dutch–Indonesian conflict, the United Nations never seriously took up the question of the Indochina War between 1945 and 1954. There are several reasons for this. For one, the French held a permanent seat with veto rights on the Security Council and could thus effectively thwart any attempt to bring up the decolonization of Indochina in that body. Second, neither the Americans nor the Soviets, both permanent members, wanted to trouble the French over Vietnam in the wake of World War II. What counted most was France's position in Europe. When the United States received a request from the **Democratic Republic of Vietnam** (DRV) at the outset of the Indochina conflict to bring the Franco-Vietnamese conflict before the UN, the Americans reached an understanding with the UN's secretariat ("Trygve Lie's people") preventing the circulation of the appeal to members of the Security Council. During the first half of the Indochina War, the Soviet Union refused to act on DRV pleas to bring the Vietnamese cause before the UN. Third, during the second half of the Indochina conflict, the globalization of the **Cold War** rivalry between the Soviets and the Americans ensured that any attempt to support the cause of the communist-led DRV would meet with a veto from the Americans as well as the British, French, and most probably the **Republic of China**. The Soviet Union's veto torpedoed the Associated State of Vietnam's attempt to join the UN in 1952 (as was the DRV's application rejected by the American-led bloc). Fourth, given that the historical phenomenon of decolonization was only just getting underway in the "South" in 1945, the number of sovereign "Southern" nation-states present in the General Assembly of the UN and in favor of the DRV's nationalist cause remained small during the period of the Indochina War.

However, some in French ruling circles understood that things were changing. French President **Vincent Auriol** warned one of his generals in 1949 that the days were numbered in the UN for hardline defenders of the colonial order. Decolonization was on the move in Asia, he pointed out: "And then there's the United Nations, do you see what's happening in Indonesia". However, it was only truly during the **Algerian War** that the increasing number of Southern states in the General Assembly allowed for a discussion of Algeria in the General Assembly in spite of French opposition. Nor did the Americans come under the same type of non-Western pressure on Indochina as they would during Algerian conflict in the UN.

Nonetheless, unlike the FLN in Algeria or the Indonesian Republicans fighting the Dutch, the communist core of the DRV also posed problems for non-communist Southern states. Despite direct requests from the DRV, especially from **Pham Ngoc Thach** in 1948, the Indian government led by **Jawaharlal Nehru** refused to bring up the Vietnamese issue in the General Assembly, in striking contrast to Nehru's support of Indonesian Republicans at the UN at the same time. Indian, Burmese, and Indonesian leaders were also distrustful of Vietnamese communist designs on Laos and Cambodia. *See also* BURMA; INDONESIA; NEUTRALIZATION OF INDOCHINA.

***UNITÉS MOBILES POUR LA DÉFENSE DES CHRÉTIENS* (UMDC).** With the support of General **Pierre Boyer de la Tour**, in August 1947 **Jean Leroy** created this mobile militia among Vietnamese Catholics and other religious groups located in Ben Tre province. This followed upon a violent break between the southern forces of the **Democratic Republic of Vietnam** (DRV) and the **Cao Dai** and **Hoa Hao** earlier in the year. Financed by the French army, this unconventional militia soon numbered 3,000 individuals. Its main task was to protect local religious communities hostile to the forces of the DRV. However, Jean Leroy used his militia and the support of the French to build up something of a personal fiefdom. This lasted until 1952, when he had to give up his militia in favor of the creation of the national **army of the Associated State of Vietnam**. Leroy and his militia fascinated the British novelist **Graham Greene** who befriended the Eurasian colonel and later prefaced Leroy's memoirs, *Fils de la rizière*. *See also* CATHOLICS, EXODUS FROM NORTH; CATHOLICS IN VIETNAM AND THE WAR; CHRISTIANS AND OPPOSITION TO THE INDOCHINA WAR; CINEMA; EXECUTION; LE HUU TU; *MÉTIS*; NOVELS; TORTURE; VATICAN.

**UNKNOWN SOLDIER.** *See* MEMORIAL DAY, INDOCHINA WAR.

**URBAN WARFARE.** *See* SAIGON; HANOI.

**UTHONG SUVANNAVONG (1907–?).** Non-communist, pro-French Lao politician during the Indochina War. Graduated from the *Lycée Chasseloup Laubat* in **Saigon** in 1927, he joined the French colonial civil service in Laos. In 1942, he served as minister of Finances in the Royal Government of Luang Prabang. He opposed the **Lao Issara** government created in October 1945 and supported the return of the French in 1946. In 1947, he became minister of Finances in the first Royal Lao government and served as minister of the Interior and Defence between 1947 and 1949. In April 1949, he joined the King's Council. In 1950, he was named minister of External Affairs, Education, and Information. In 1953, he served as minister of Education and Information before becoming minister of Education and Health in 1954.

**VALLADON, JACQUES VINCENT (1920–1992).** French colonial administrator who was in charge of Indochina worker questions in France between 1943 and 1945. He landed in Indochina in 1946 and worked in the Economic Affairs section of the French High Commissioner's Office for Indochina until 1947 when he transferred to Cambodia to work as deputy advisor to the Cambodian minister of the Economy until 1948. Between 1948 and 1949, he worked in the Economic section of the Ministry of Overseas France in Paris. After a short stint in Cambodia as deputy advisor in Kompong Cham in 1949–1950, he returned to France to work in the Political Affairs section of the French ministry in charge of Relations with the **Associated States of Indochina** (1950–1955).

**VALLUY, JEAN ETIENNE (1899–1970).** French general on watch with **Georges Thierry d'Argenlieu** when full-scale war in Indochina commenced on **19 December 1946**. Valluy saw combat and was wounded during World War I. He entered the *École spéciale militaire* at Saint-Cyr in 1917. During the interwar period, he served in the French colonial army in Syria, Morocco, and China. The Germans took him prisoner during the Battle of France, but freed him a year later. Valluy commanded troops in Vichy French Africa until he joined Free French forces in Algiers in 1943 and served as the chief of staff to **Jean de Lattre de Tassigny** during the liberation of France. In February 1945, he assumed command of the 9th Colonial Infantry Division (*9ème Division d'infanterie coloniale*) and took it to Indochina in March to reoccupy and "pacify" lower Vietnam below the **16th parallel**. In early March 1946, boats transported Valluy's troops to upper Vietnam to replace the Chinese occupation force there. Valluy's men were able to march peacefully into **Hanoi** afer an acute crisis had been resolved by the **Accords of 6 March 1946.** On 1 April 1946, Valluy became commander of French Forces in Northern Indochina and Laos. With the departure of General **Philippe Leclerc** in July 1946, Valluy became acting commander of all French Forces in Indochina. This became official on 1 October 1946. As a commander, Valluy supported High Commissioner **Georges Thierry d'Argenlieu** in his hostility to negotiating with the **Democratic Republic of Vietnam** (DRV) and in trying to roll back the Vietnamese government's sovereignty in line with **de Gaulle's** instructions to retake and rebuild French Indochina within the form of the **Indochinese Federation**. In November and December 1946, Valluy served on an interim basis as High Commissioner in Indochina during Thierry d'Argenlieu's absence in France. Valluy supported and encouraged Colonel **Pierre Debès**'s heavy-handed take-over of **Haiphong** in November of that year, presenting it as an entirely premeditated act taken by the DRV. In May 1948, Valluy returned to France and was promoted. In December 1950, he was named military advisor to the Ministry of the **Associated States of Indochina.** *See also* PACIFICATION; 19 DECEMEBER 1946.

**VALMARY, ALFRED VICTOR GABRIEL JOSEPH (1901–1970).** Born in French Pondicherry, Valmary made his career in colonial Indochina. He landed in Cambodia in 1925, where he began work as deputy to the *résident* of Kandal province. Between 1926 and 1937, he held a variety of important administrative posts in Laos, such as cabinet secretary to the French *résident supérieur* to Laos (1926, 1928–29, 1931–32) and provincial head of Luang Prabang (1935–37). After serving as *résident* to Son La province in Tonkin in 1937, he joined the economics section of the governor general's office in **Hanoi** in 1938. In December 1939, he was mobilized as a lieutenant in the reserves. In 1941, he left the army to return to civilian life in Indochina. In March 1941, Jean Decoux named him commissioner to Luang Prabang until he was transferred to Vietnam to serve as *résident* to Quang Tri province. In 1944, Valmary returned to Laos as *résident* to Pakse where he remained until the Japanese ***coup de force*** **of 9 March 1945**. He resumed his colonial career in Laos following the French reoccupation of all of Laos in mid-1946, serving as regional advisor to Luang Prabang (1946–47) and as interim commissioner for Laos between March 1948 and December 1949. After World War II, Valmary played an important role in the revision of the Lao constitution, the Franco-Lao accords of 19 July 1949, the return of the **Lao Issara** from Thailand, the dissolution of its government-in-exile, and the preparation of the Franco-Lao treaty of 1950.

**VĂN.** *See* VÕ NGUYÊN GIÁP.

**VĂN CAO (NGUYỄN VĂN CAO, 1923–1995).** Author of the national anthem of the **Democratic Republic of Vietnam** (DRV), *Bai Tien Quan Ca*. In late 1944, Van Cao worked as a musician in **Hanoi** and entered into secret contact with the editors of the communist-run clandestine nationalist paper, *Doc Lap*, located in the suburbs of the northern capital. During this time, Van Cao began composing a patriotic song, which would be played for the first time on the morning of 17 August 1945 in front of the opera house in Hanoi as the **Viet Minh** moved to take power. It was adopted as the national anthem of the DRV upon the nation-state's creation on 2 September 1945. During the Indochina War, Van Cao wrote scores of other patriotic songs, including *In Praise of President* ***Ho Chi Minh*** (*Ca Nguoi Ho Chu Tich*) and the *Vietnamese Fighter* (*Chien Si Viet Nam*).

**VẠN PHÚC, MEETING.** Meeting of the Standing Committee of the **Indochina Communist Party**'s (ICP) Central Committee held outside **Hanoi** in the village of Van Phuc in Ha Dong province during the night of 18–19 December 1946. **Ho Chi Minh** personally presided over this meeting to discuss the tense situation verging on war. With the incidents in **Lang Son** and **Haiphong** in mind, those assisting this meeting concluded that the French were now looking for a way to take over Hanoi and to oust the **Democratic Republic of Vietnam** (DRV) from power. Participants at the Van Phuc meeting concluded that the French were determined to expand the war and that the DRV and the ICP could make no more concessions. *See also* 19 DECEMBER 1946; 23 SEPTEMBER 1945; ACCORDS OF 6 MARCH 1946.

**VĂN TIẾN DŨNG (LÊ HOÀI, 1917–2002).** Born outside **Hanoi**, Van Tien Dung came from a peasant background and possessed only a sixth-grade education. He worked as a weaver until he became involved in radical politics during the Popular Front period and joined the **Indochinese Communist Party** in 1937. In 1939, the French police arrested him in Hanoi and sentenced him to two years of hard labor at **Son La**. He escaped during his transfer and began rebuilding Party cells in the Ha Dong area, using the cover of a Buddhist monk. He was arrested in 1944 and sentenced to death, but escaped again from detention to build up armed units in the Ninh Binh area in northern Vietnam.

With the advent of the **Democratic Republic of Vietnam** (DRV), he rapidly became one of the party's most dynamic military leaders. He led the famous 320th division into battle against the French in the Red River Delta from 1950. In 1952, he led daring attacks on the Catholic stronghold of Phat Diem, as the French tried to take control of this largely autonomous yet strategically important region. This raid on Franco-Vietnamese forces marked the beginning of Van Tien Dung's use of "the opening of the Lotus" tactic. His men liked to call it the "parachute". During this type of raid (and others thereafter) his men slid between French posts secretly in order to pierce deeply, attack ferociously and hold the inside for 24 hours, then push back out against the protecting enemy forces on the periphery, but hitting them from the inside on their way out. He would use much the same tactic during the attack on **Saigon** in 1975.

He was elected to the **Vietnamese Worker's Party**'s Central Committee in 1951 and, for unclear reasons, took over from **Hoang Van Thai** in 1953, on orders from the Politburo, as chief of the army's **General Staff**. He held this position during the battle of **Dien Bien Phu**. In 1954, during negotiations to end the war, the General Staff named Van Tien Dung head of the **People's Army of Vietnam**'s delegation to the military discussions in **Trung Gia** concerning the application of the cease-fire negotiated in Geneva. In 1955–1956, he served as the DRV's representative to the **International Commission for Supervision and Control in Vietnam**, created during the **Geneva Conference**.

**VANDENBERGHE, ROGER (1927–1952).** One of the most highly decorated **commandos** in the French army during the Indochina War. A huge man, Vandenberghe found his place in the world running highly unconventional commando raids into enemy territory during World War II and the Indochina War. Born dirt poor, Vandenberghe and his brother had been raised by a series of different families in a secluded part of the Pyrenees in southwestern France. The boys had little education: Roger Vandenberghe could barely read or write, according to one of his close military colleagues in Indochina. The deportation of his Jewish mother to the Nazi gas chambers under Vichy left no doubt as to which side the **orphans** would fight for in World War II. The Vandenberghe brothers joined the French resistance, the *Forces françaises de l'intérieur*, and never looked back. Both shone serving in General **Jean de Lattre de Tassigny**'s First French Army in 1944, operating in special commando units conducting perilous missions into enemy territory. In February 1945, Roger obtained the *Croix de guerre* at the age of 18.

The Vandenberghe brothers arrived in Indochina in 1947 in the 49th Infantry Regiment, soon integrated into the 3rd Battalion, 6th Colonial Infantry Regiment. Both chose to continue their daring commando operations in Indochina. In June 1948, Roger's brother was killed doing just that. With little if any family left, Roger now invested himself entirely in the war and in particular high risk commando forays. In Indochina, he formed his own commando unit called the Black Tigers (*tigres noirs*), recruited almost entirely from "reconverted" **Viet Minh** prisoners. His unit struck deep into enemy territory for days using unconventional methods, certainly brutal, bordering on the illegal, and ones which were often disapproved or disavowed by the upper echelons. He rode his men hard and was pitiless with the enemy, including civilians. Desertion in his unit was high. Tension was such that in February 1949 he took a bullet in the back from "friendly" forces. He survived. And after convalescing in France, he returned to Indochina in the 6th Infantry to resume his commando operations in November 1949. Vandenberghe had by now become a legendary figure and for some in the French army an embarrassing one. However, when he personally brought back, at extraordinary personal risk, the body of General de Lattre's son, Bernard, he won sympathy and support in very high places, even though the operation had cost the lives of 15 of his men. De Lattre personally lauded Vandenberghe and, implicitly, his methods. Thanks to this support, Vandenberghe was able to put together and lead another unit, Commando 24, two thirds of which consisted of former Viet Minh partisans who had been indoctrinated. While Vandeberghe's military results were indeed appreciated, his men later revealed that they had had a hard time controlling his violent actions while on operations, "something which was harmful to the populations in certain circumstances". The adversary agreed and the **Democratic Republic of Vietnam**'s (DRV) **special forces** organized and executed an elaborate operation infiltrating their commandos into Vandenberghe's unit in order to eliminate him physically. On 6 January 1952, the DRV's agents gunned down Vandenberghe at the age of 24. The only member of Vandenberghe's unit to survive that violent day was **Tran Dinh Vy**. In 1989, Roger Vandenberghe's remains were returned from Indochina for reinterment under a monument erected in his honor at the National Non-Commissioned Officers Academy in Pau, France. *See also* DESERTION; EXECUTIONS; *GROUPEMENT DE COMMANDOS MIXTES AÉROPORTÉS*; INDOCTRINATION; EXPERIENCE OF WAR; *SERVICE ACTION*; SPECIAL FORCES, DEMOCRATIC REPUBLIC OF VIETNAM; TORTURE.

**VANGUARD YOUTH LEAGUE (*Thanh Niên Tiền Phong*).** The origins of the southern-based Vanguard Youth League can be traced in part to the mobilization campaigns initiated by French Governor General Jean Decoux during the Vichy period in Indochina (1940–March 1945) and his Japanese competitors. Faced with the Japanese occupation of Indochina, Decoux eased controls on patriotic expression and mobilized the Indochinese youth in a bid to hold on in Indochina against Japanese and Thai competitors vying for the French colony and its inhabitants. Ironically, this patriotic mobilization of the Vietnamese youth worked against the French following the Japanese ***coup de force* of 9 March 1945** ousting them from power. In mid-1945, the Japanese looked the other way and certain Japanese supported Vietnamese activists as they began to channel the Vichy-mobilized youth groups in national ways. Tens of thousands of southern youth joined what became known as the Vanguard Youth League. One of its main leaders was Dr. **Pham Ngoc Thach**.

Thanks to his cordial relations with the Japanese leadership in **Saigon**, the latter was able to organize and continue mobilizing youth groups following the March coup – and in much more political and nationalist ways than ever before. The Emperor **Bao Dai** received a Vanguard Youth delegation and named Pham Ngoc Thach as the royal government's delegate for the youth in the south. The latter was also working clandestinely with southern communists, notably **Tran Van**

**Giau**. Both understood that the youth would be a powerful instrument for taking power in Saigon once the Japanese were defeated. Indeed, following the Japanese capitulation in August and the outbreak of war in southern Vietnam on **23 September 1945**, Pham Ngoc Thach put much of the Vanguard Youth League in the service of the new Vietnamese nation, the **Democratic Republic of Vietnam**, and its emerging military and state-building forces in the south. *See also* CHILDREN; ORPHANS; SCOUTING, INDOCHINA WAR.

**VANUXEM, PAUL FIDÈLE FÉLICIEN (1904–1979).** Vanuxem entered the military in 1923 and little during the interwar period indicated that he would go far. World War II changed all that, however, when he ended up in Algeria in late 1940 serving in Vichy's colonial army and then found himself a battalion commander in the Free French army following the Allied liberation of North Africa in late 1942. In 1944–1945, Vanuxem distinguished himself in high-risk intelligence and combat operations running deep in enemy territory in Italy, France, and Germany. He had every intention of doing the same in France's colonial wars. In May 1947, he took command of the *Bataillon de marche du 6ème régiment de tirailleurs marocains en Indochine* before commanding the sector of Son Tay in northern Vietnam from December 1948. He was deeply involved in "**pacification**" operations in northern Vietnam during this time. He became lieutenant colonel in early 1949. He left for France in May only to return for a second tour of duty to Indochina as commander of the military sector of Bien Hoa in June 1950 and commander of *Groupe Mobile no. 3* in January 1951. In June 1952, he was an instructor in tactics for training Vietnamese battalion leaders. He returned to Indochina a third time in July 1953 to serve as operational deputy to the commanding colonel of the *1ère Division de marche du Tonkin*, then as commander of the military sector of Ha Dong in August, and finally as commander of the Southern Zone of the northern delta in June 1954. He left **Saigon** in June 1955 and soon transferred to Algeria where he commanded troops until 1958. The long list of citations noted in his personnel file make it clear that Vanuxem was one of France's best centurions, as **Jean Lartéguy** put it at the time. *See also GROUPEMENT DE COMMANDOS MIXTES AÉROPORTÉS*; MYTH OF WAR; *SERVICE ACTION*.

**VARET, PIERRE (1902–1991).** Career colonial administrator in **Tonkin** during the interwar period and author of a thesis entitled *Le concours apporté à la France par ses colonies et protectorats au cours de la guerre de 1914*. Although a **Freemason**, he emerged unscathed from the Vichy period in Indochina and served as imperial delegate to Tonkin for **Bao Dai** following the ***coup de force* of 9 March 1945** before being interned by the Japanese. Upon his liberation, he advised **Jean Sainteny** then General **Jean Valluy** on political affairs in northern Vietnam before returning to France where he worked in the **Cominindo**, the Assembly of the **French Union**, and as secretariat to the French Union's Upper Council. He was active in the *Fédération des oeuvres de l'enfance en Indochine* and wrote a book on Vietnam entitled *Au pays d'**Annam**: les dieux qui meurent*.

**VATICAN.** Long before the French Republic, the Vatican grasped the historical reality of Vietnamese nationalism and the global dimensions and implications of decolonization. With the Church in decline in much of Europe by the early 20th century, the Vatican realized that much of its future support would come from non-Western parts of the world, vast parts of which had been colonized by European colonial states. Of particular importance was the need to "indigenize" still mainly European-dominated clergies and hierarchies and to disassociate the Vatican and its local hierarchies from European colonialism in the "South", where nationalism was now making itself increasingly felt in the wake of World War I. Pope Benedict XV had already referred to the intermingling of the Church's interests and those of the colonial powers as a "most dangerous plague". In 1919, Benedict began to attack this problem with his apostolic letter *Maximum Illud*, which was followed up by Pius XI's 1926 Encyclical *Rerum Ecclesiae*.

To the shock of French colonial authorities in Vietnam, Rome had publicly and officially rejected a tacit contract between Western colonial states and local missionaries. By the early 1930s, French colonial administrators were hostile to the Vatican's "*politique indigène*", seeing it as an anti-colonialist threat to French rule and one which could call into question the legitimacy of colonial rule among the Vietnamese. While Vietnamese Catholic nationalists heralded Rome's recognition of their nationalist aspirations, French colonial authorities tried to block the Vatican's naming of Vietnamese bishops, who could escape colonial control. The French were even more suprised, in the wake of World War II, when they learned that Rome had sent its best wishes to the new nation state **Ho Chi Minh** declared a reality on 2 September 1945, the **Democratic Republic of Vietnam** (DRV). Rome understood again that this second World War had made decolonization an even more pressing matter and that the Church could not afford to be caught on the wrong side of this historical phenomenon.

Throughout the Indochina War, Vatican officials frustrated French officials by their reluctance to support French demands to bring the Vietnamese **Catholics** and clergy into colonial line. The problem was that the nationalist movement was led by a communist party, antipathetic to Pius XII. In June 1948, as the Cold War heated up, the Vatican went on record saying that the Vietnamese communists were "little by little" showing their real colors: they were not patriots but rather leaders of an anti-religious party who would sooner or later implement "a systematic persecution" of Vietnamese Catholics. On 1 July 1949, as Chinese communists were moving into southern China, Pope Pius XII issued a papal decree prohibiting all collaboration with communists in all parts of the Catholic world, in the north and the south. The French lost no time in Vietnam, dropping thousands of copies of the decree over Catholic populations, especially in the autonomous Catholic zones of Bui Chu and Phat Diem.

Even though Rome proscribed collaboration with the communists, this did not necessarily mean that the Vatican condoned the French. Indeed, during the war, the Vatican remained committed to nationalizing the Vietnamese church, naming six apostolic vicars, including in **Hanoi** and Haiphong. Although the Vatican followed the lead of Vietnamese Catholic leaders, such as **Le Huu Tu**, in recognizing **Bao Dai**'s Associated State of Vietnam on anti-communist grounds, the Vatican kept its distance from the Vietnamese emperor and his Catholic wife, in light of the French reluctance to grant Bao Dai's Vietnam full independence. In December 1954, Pope Pius XII recognized the right of colonized peoples across the world to political freedom. For the Vatican, the future of the Church was in the postcolonial world coming into being whether the colonial powers wanted it or not. The American Catholic Church agreed. In May 1948, Cardinal Spellman arrived in **Saigon** at the head of a large delegation. During this visit, Cardinal Fulton Sheen declared that colonialism was finished and that the Roman Catholic Church now counted on the Far East to serve as a "solid pillar" for developing the Christian faith. *See also* CATHOLICS IN VIETNAM AND THE WAR; CHRISTIANS AND FRENCH OPPOSITION TO THE WAR; *ESPRIT*; LE HUU TU; *TÉMOIGNAGE CHRÉTIEN*.

**VAUTOUR, OPERATION.** On 8 January 1954, the chief of staff of the American Armed Forces, Admiral **Arthur Radford**, spoke to President **Dwight D. Eisenhower** of the possibility of using American planes to bomb the **Democratic Republic of Vietnam**'s artillery positions located in the jungle cliffs overlooking the valley of **Dien Bien Phu**. A little over two months later, with Vietnamese artillery raining down on the besieged French camp, Radford met with French General **Paul Ely** on 24 and 26 March, promising to take up the subject again with the American president. In the meantime, the United States Air Force began secret preparations in the event that Eisenhower approved such a plan. The French referred to this as operation *Vautour*, seeing it increasingly as the only way to save the French camp as the Vietnamese slowly but surely tightened the noose around it. On 4 April, the French government officially requested American air intervention over Dien Bien Phu. Operation *Vautour* would use 98 B-29s based in Okinawa and the Philippines to drop some 1,400 tons of bombs on Vietnamese positions. However, when **John Foster Dulles** consulted congressional leaders about the proposed operation, they imposed conditions making its adoption difficult in such a short period of time. Most importantly, they insisted that such intervention could not be done unilaterally – an Allied coalition consisting of Southeast Asian, Commonwealth, and Western states, especially the United Kingdom, had to be created in order to implement the operation. On 8 April, Washington informed Paris that it could not intervene unless such an enlarged coalition could be formed. It was tantamount to a refusal to intervene. Moreover, some 60 percent of American public opinion was hostile to intervening in the French war in Indochina. While Operation *Vautour* was shelved, the Americans under Eisenhower came surprisingly close to going to war in Vietnam in 1954.

**VENEREAL DISEASE.** Venereal disease was a serious problem during the Indochina War for the **Expeditionary Corps**. As French historian Michel

Bodin has shown, of the 288,036 cases treated, 207,893 were first time infections – 117,943 cases of gonorrhea, 26,486 cases of syphilis, and 58,185 cases of crabs, among other infections. 107,343 Europeans, Africans, North Africans, and **Foreign Legion** troops were hospitalized for venereal diseases. Efforts to control sexually transmitted diseases via the ***Bordel mobile de campagne*** met with some success, thanks to bi-weekly medical check-ups for the women working there.

***VÊPRES HANOÏENNES.*** This term, literally "**Hanoi** vespers", was used by French settlers and the press in Indochina to refer to the Vietnamese killings of Europeans in Hanoi on **19 December 1946.** It was an obvious if fallacious allusion to the Sicilia vespers: the massacre of French occupying troops in Sicily beginning at vespers on 30 March 1282. In January 1950, **Paul Mus** wrote an essay in favor of getting rid of the term "*vêpres hanoïennes*", arguing that it falsified the reality of what really happened, dehumanized the Vietnamese, and in so doing widened the gap between the French and the Vietnamese. *See also* HÉRAULT, MASSACRE; MYTH OF WAR; LANGUAGE OF WAR.

**VETERAN HOSPITALS, DEMOCRATIC REPUBLIC OF VIETNAM.** During the Indochina War, the **Democratic Republic of Vietnam** (DRV) created a few modest camps to receive wounded and disabled soldiers (*trai thuong binh* or *trai an duong*) in the provinces of Thanh Hoa and Nghe An. Following the conflict, the government increased the number of camps across its territories, mainly in northern and central Vietnam where the war had left the most disabled in its path. In 1955, the government counted 4,500 invalids and wounded in its existing veterans facilities. With the regroupment of cadres and soldiers from the south to the north, this number rose to some 15,000 persons by the late 1950s. A typical camp housed between 130 and 200 disabled veterans, divided into two groups, the disabled (*thuong binh*), and the sick (*benh binh*). The staff consisted of doctors and nurses on the one hand and party cadres on the other. Besides caring for the invalids, the DRV also used the camps as platforms for the ideological **indoctrination** of the veterans. *See also* CINEMA; CULTURE; EMULATION; EXPERIENCE OF WAR; MYTH OF WAR; NEW HEROES; NOVELS; DISEASE; TRAN DAN.

**VÉZINET, ADOLPHE ANDRÉ (1906–1996).** Began his military career in the colonies during the interwar period, serving in West Africa and in Indochina (1931–1932). He joined Free French forces in 1940 and led colonial troops for General **Philippe Leclerc** until 1943, when he was put in charge of the *1er Bataillon du régiment de marche du Tchad* and helped Leclerc assemble the 2nd Armored Division, which he joined and in which he served during the French and German campaigns. In early 1945, Vézinet was named colonel and obtained the position of chief of staff of the French **Expeditionary Corps** for the Far East. He remained in France, however, in 1945 to serve briefly as director of colonial troops before resuming his post in mid-1946 as chief of staff to Lerclerc until the latter's death in November 1947 (though he accompanied his boss on a mission to Indochina in December 1946–January 1947). In October 1949, Vézinet returned to Indochina to command the military sector of Southern **Annam** and the *Plateaux* and was named brigadier general in December. He returned to France in the early 1950, serving as deputy general secretary to the National Defense during the endgame of the Indochina War.

**VIALA, MAXIME CHARLES JACQUES (1905–1972).** French colonial administrator active behind the scenes during the Indochina War. He began his Indochinese career in 1932–1933, when he was sent to the upland areas of **Annam**. Between 1933 and 1946, he held a variety of administrative posts in **Cochinchina** (Soc Trang, My Tho, Ca Mau, Ha Tien, and Rach Gia). Little is known, however, about his activities under Vichy or following the Japanese ***coup de force* of 9 March 1945**. His experience was in great need, however, when the French went about restoring their Indochinese colony after World War II. Between 1947 and 1949, Viala was director of political affairs for the commissioner of the French Republic for Cochinchina (the provisional government of South Vietnam) and provincial head of Cap Saint Jacques in 1949–1950.

**VIAN, BORIS. (1920–1959).** French composer and singer opposed to the war in Indochina. In February 1954, as French soldiers prepared for a violent showdown with their Vietnamese opponents during the battle of **Dien Bien Phu**, Vian completed the manuscript of his anti-war song, *The Deserter (Le déserteur)*. In the famous opening line *Mon-*

*sieur le Président*, Vian announces his decision to desert rather than to fight yet another war. He ends on an equally provocative note by telling the French president to go ahead and authorize the police to shoot him. *Le déserteur* was officially released on 7 May 1954, the very day Dien Bien Phu fell to the **Democratic Republic of Vietnam**. Vian insisted that it was not anti-militarist but rather "pro-civil". The ballad nevertheless caused a scandal in official and nationalist-minded circles in France and was banned from French radio while the sale of the record was outlawed. Only with the end of the **Algerian War** in 1962 did Vian's records return to music shelves in France, including *Le déserteur*. Although Vian had died in 1959, this song in particular would go on to become a global anti-war hit, being translated into dozens of languages. As the Vietnam War hotted up in the 1960s, the American folk singers Peter, Paul and Mary, produced a popular version of this song (in English and French). Joan Baez also included it in her anti-war repertoire. Vian's portrayal of the socio-cultural devastation of war on people, wives, and families stood in stark contrast to the heroization of war, the army, and the Indochina War in the works of **Pierre Schoendoerffer**, **Jean Lartéguy**, and the communist **Democratic Republic of Vietnam**. *See also* CINEMA; CULTURE; EXPERIENCE OF WAR; EXPERIENCE OF WAR, DIEN BIEN PHU; LOVE AND WAR; MYTH OF WAR; NOVEL; PUBLIC OPINION.

**VIDAL, PIERRE (1926–1950).** Between 1948 and 1949, he worked as a colonial administrator in **Saigon** dealing with personnel questions. Between 1949 and 1950, he was named administrative delegate for Blao in the uplands of central Vietnam and district chief of Cheo Reo. He died in an ambush in the area of Buon Mung in August 1950.

**VIỆT BẮC.** *See* INTER-ZONE VIET BAC.

**VIỆT CỘNG.** The Americans did not create the term *Viet Cong* during the Vietnam War; the Vietnamese did. One of the earliest appearances of this term probably appeared during the interwar period in southern China, where Vietnamese communist and anti-communist nationalists had escaped from French repression inside Indochina. To distinguish themselves from each other, these Vietnamese referred to each other as the "*Viet Cong*" (Vietnamese communists) and the "***Viet Quoc***" (Vietnamese nationalists), following a similar distinction used in Chinese by Chinese communists and nationalists engaged in full-blown civil war from 1927 in southern China. The two terms were also used by Vietnamese nationalists in heated exchanges while serving time in the French colonial prison of **Poulo Condor**. The term *Viet Cong* entered the Vietnamese lexicon in 1945–1946 when Vietnamese communist nationalists led by **Ho Chi Minh** engaged in a **civil war** against anti-communist nationalists (*Viet Quoc*) led by the likes of **Vu Hong Khanh**, **Nguyen Hai Than**, and **Truong Tu Anh**. These nationalists carried this term with them as they resettled in the south after 1954.

How and when exactly the Vietnamese term *Viet Cong* crossed over into English remains unknown (it never entered French before 1954). We do know that it happened before American combat advisors and ground troops arrived in southern Vietnam. On 10 March 1956, for example, a Vietnamese advocate of the **Republic of Vietnam** wrote to the *Washington Post* to protest Professor Hans Morgenthau's characterization of Ngo Dinh Diem as "ruthless". In this letter to the editor, the author used the term "*Viet Cong*" in English: "It would be a mistake to consider that the war with the *Viet Cong* has ended". In his address (in Vietnamese) celebrating the fifth anniversary of the founding of the Republic, **Ngo Dinh Diem** urged his listeners to "participate actively in the struggle to exterminate the *Viet Cong* traitors …". According to Nicholas Cull, around 1956 Vietnam specialists within the United States Information Service (USIS) in **Saigon** latched on to the term *Viet Cong* in a bid to weaken the nationalist appeal that the term **Viet Minh** continued to evoke in many a Vietnamese mind. USIS Saigon was directly involved in popularizing this term in Ngo Dinh Diem's speeches and in official American statements. By 1958, the term *Viet Cong* had taken hold among American officials in Vietnam and Washington. That said, while the Americans were clearly involved in popularizing the term, they did not create it. *See also* LANGUAGE OF WAR.

**VIỆT GIAN.** Vietnamese term increasingly used by the propaganda organs of the **Democratic Republic of Vietnam** (DRV) and the **Indochinese Communisty Party** to stigmatize their adversaries as "traitors". This term entered the Vietnamese lexicon with force from the early days of the Indochina War when the colonial war was doubled by a civil war among the Vietnamese. Of the hundreds of Vietnamese political enemies captured and executed by the DRV's security forces, most were classified as *Viet Gian* before being killed. Until recently, official Vietnamese communist accounts of the Indochina War refer to the members of the **Vietnamese Nationalist Party** (*Viet Nam Quoc Dan Dang*, VNQDD) or the Associated State of Vietnam as "traitors" and "puppets" (*nguy* or *bu nhin*). Like the use of the term ***Viet Cong*** by anti-communists, *Viet Gian* served to dehumanize and stigmatize the other, excluded the said group or person from the community, and allowed the governing authorities, especially the police forces, to act against this enemy, including the use of torture, imprisonment, and physical elimination. As a new political power, the DRV defined, codified, and used this term and others to categorize undesirable social components in areas under its control. The children of *Viet Gian*, for example, were barred entry to certain educational establishments and occupations. This even applied to the DRV's definition of those constituting the realm of the dead, referring to the family of a puppet soldier as *gia dinh nguy binh*. *See also* COLLABORATION; LANGUAGE OF WAR; *VIET QUOC*.

**VIỆT MINH.** The broad-based nationalist front created by the **Indochinese Communist Party** (ICP) in 1941 that dominated the struggle against the return of French colonial domination from September 1945. In 1938, as World War II got underway in Asia, **Ho Chi Minh** left Moscow for Yan'an before making his way back to southern China. During this time, he closely studied the united front strategy the **Chinese Communist Party** (CCP) was using against the invading Japanese. In Chongqing, he renewed his contacts with **Zhou Enlai**, the CCP's liaison to the **Republic of China** now operating in southern China. Ho Chi Minh also renewed contacts with ICP cadres such as **Vo Nguyen Giap**, **Pham Van Dong**, and **Hoang Van Hoan**. He then turned to building a clandestine base within Vietnam, selecting the limestone caves of Pac Bo in Cao Bang province, next to Guangxi province in China.

With the **collaboration** of the acting secretary general of the ICP, **Truong Chinh**, Ho Chi Minh shifted the party's line to creating broad-based support with a view to taking power as World War II spread across the globe. Ho did this during the Eighth Plenum of the ICP Central Committee that met at Pac Bo on 10–19 May 1941. He presided over the approval of a resolution that ignored the Comintern's line at the time as well as **Joseph Stalin**'s non-aggression pact with Hitler. With the war now underway in Europe and the French knocked out by the Germans, the resolution called for resistance to the Japanese, opposition to the collaborating Vichy authorities in Indochina, and cooperation with the Chinese.

This meeting also created a broad-based nationalist front, the *Viet Nam Doc Lap Dong Minh* (Vietnam Independence League), more commonly known as the Viet Minh. Through the Viet Minh, the ICP abandoned its earlier emphasis on class struggle in favour of creating a broad nationalist front to attract support for the "national liberation revolution" (*Cach Mang Giai Phong Dan Toc*) from all parts of society. A directing committee, the ***Tong Bo Viet Minh***, ran the front from on high, establishing "national salvation" associations in order to organize and mobilize peasants, women, traders, etc. into the movement.

Following the overthrow of the French by the Japanese and then the Japanese by the Allies, the Viet Minh was able to ride a wave of popular discontent to power. With the advent of the **Democratic Republic of Vietnam** (DRV) in August–September 1945, the Viet Minh continued to exist as a political party. However, non-communist parties such as the **Vietnamese Nationalist Party** (*Viet Nam Quoc Dan Dang*, or VNQDD) successfully cast it as a communist front organization, equating it with the ICP. In May 1946, as armed clashes broke out between the forces of the DRV and the ICP on the one hand and the anti-communist nationalist parties on the other, the DRV created a new national front called the Association of United Vietnamese People (*Hoi Lien Hiep Quoc Dan Viet Nam*) or ***Lien Viet*** for short. Ho Chi Minh was honorary president of this "super" national front, which regrouped all patriotic individuals who had not yet joined the Viet Minh front. The Viet Minh continued to exist until it was formally replaced by the Lien Viet organization during the Second Party Congress in early 1951. The term, however, did not disappear and was used by both the French and the Vietnamese throughout the rest of the war, even though it technically no longer existed during the second half of the Indochina War.

**VIỆT NAM MỚI.** Legal term created in late 1945 in order to incorporate European and Japanese

**crossovers** and **deserters** into the **Democratic Republic of Vietnam** as citizens. Hundreds of Japanese, German, Austrian, French and even Moroccans became "New Vietnamese" during the Indochina War. In some cases, they were apparently required to renounce their former citizenship. *See also* FOREIGN LEGION.

**VIỆT QUỐC.** This Vietnamese term referred to the two non-communist nationalist parties, the *Viet Nam Cach Menh Dong Minh Hoi* and the *Viet Nam Quoc Dan Dang* or the **Vietnamese Nationalist Party**. One of the earliest appearances of the term appeared during the interwar period in southern China, where Vietnamese communist and anti-communist nationalists had escaped from French repression inside Indochina. To distinguish themselves from each other, these Vietnamese commonly referred to each other as the "***Viet Cong***" (Vietnamese communists) and the "*Viet Quoc*" (Vietnamese nationalists), following a similar distinction used in Chinese by Chinese communists and nationalists engaged in full-blown civil war from 1927 in southern China. The two terms were also used by Vietnamese nationalists in heated exchanges while serving time in the French colonial prison of **Poulo Condor**. The term *Viet Quoc* entered the Vietnamese lexicon in full force in 1945–1946 when Vietnamese anti-communist nationalists (*Viet Quoc*) led by the likes of **Vu Hong Khanh**, **Nguyen Hai Than, Nguyen Tuong Tam,** and **Truong Tu Anh** engaged in a **civil war** against communist nationalists (*Viet Cong*) led by **Ho Chi Minh**. Communists used *Viet Quoc* in a derogatory fashion in their speeches and papers, often confusing it intentionally with ***Viet Gian*** for "traitor". *See also* LANGUAGE OF WAR.

**VIETNAM–AMERICAN FRIENDSHIP ASSOCIATION.** Formally inaugurated on 17 October 1945, the Vietnam–American Friendship Association was designed to promote better mutual understanding and cooperation in cultural areas. The Association's program included the organization of language courses, a lecture series, the creation of a monthly magazine, *Viet My Tap Chi* (Vietnamese–American Journal), and the construction of a library. Three issues of the Vietnamese–American Journal appeared between October 1945 and February 1946. General **Philip Gallagher** of the **Office of Strategic Services** personally attended the inaugural meeting and encouraged his staff to do so. Both sides saw the association as an important contribution to their "cultural diplomacy". The association also hosted American business representatives interested in the Vietnamese market. The French were hostile to this association and its implicit intrusion into a colonial domain monopolized by them since the mid-19th century. *See also* CULTURE.

**VIETNAMESE DEMOCRATIC PARTY (*Đảng Dân Chủ Việt Nam*).** Created clandestinely on 30 June 1944 in Vichy–Japanese Indochina, the Democratic Party united leading non-communist Vietnamese **intellectuals**, mainly from northern Vietnam. The democrats joined the **Viet Minh** nationalist front in early 1945 and sent delegates to attend the Tan Trao Conference. This party consisted of patriotic students, intellectuals, and civil servants. The provisional government of the **Democratic Republic of Vietnam** counted three Democratic members among its ministers. The party held its first National Congress in **Hanoi** in September 1946. At the time, the Democratic party enjoyed real independence from communist control and was theoretically positioned on the same level as the **Indochinese Communist Party** (ICP) within the Viet Minh front. While the communists infiltrated the Democratic Party, it cannot be said that they controlled the party between 1944 and 1947. The general secretary of the party was **Hoang Minh Chinh**, a communist and considered to be the ICP's insert. Two of the Democratic Party's best known members included the intellectuals **Huy Can** and **Dang Thai Mai.**

**VIETNAMESE NATIONALIST PARTY (*Việt Nam Quốc Dân Đảng,* VNQDĐ).** Created in 1927, the Vietnamese Nationalist Party (*Viet Nam Quoc Dan Dang*) posed the first organized nationalist challenge to colonial rule over Vietnam. At the outset, this party counted among its members a wide range of individuals – disgruntled youth, teachers, journalists as well as soldiers in the colonial army, merchants, and members of the bourgeoisie. Inspired and to a considerable extent modeled on the Chinese nationalist model, the VNQDD sought to create a mass-based party along Leninist lines.

While the Vietnamese Nationalist Party started off as a reform-minded party, a combination of French repression and frustration with failed colonial reformism saw the party adopt a more radical line. In 1930, led by a young school teacher, Nguyen Thai Hoc, nationalists organized and launched a "general uprising" against the French in northern Vietnam designed to throw out the colonialists, unify the country and create a Republic. Initially caught off guard by the revolt, the French responded quickly and crushed the uprising, located mainly in northern Vietnamese colonial garrisons such as Yen Bay. Those who escaped made their way to southern China. Meanwhile, the French sent scores of the arrested to colonial prisons, especially **Poulo Condor**, while they executed the core leadership. Before going to the guillotoine, Nguyen Thai Hoc went down in history when he screamed out *Long Live Vietnam* (*Viet Nam Van tue*)! His fiancée signed a double suicide note, one dedicated to her lover, the other addressed to the nation. Nationalism was real.

This French repression coincided with a second one directed against the **Indochinese Communist Party**, sending hundreds of communists to prison or fleeing into southern China on the heels of the nationalists. Indeed, French repression had the unintended effect of forcing communists and nationalists into fierce competition for the nationalist high ground in the microcosms of the colonial prisons and southern Chinese cites, where fierce debates and even low-intensity violence broke out between the two sides. This violence manifested itself in a **civil war** in the wake of World War II as the VNQDD and the ICP moved to create the nation state they had failed to achieve in the early 1930s. The arrival of the Republican Chinese occupying forces delayed the start of what would have surely become a full-blown civil war by October 1945. The communists at the head of the **Democratic Republic of Vietnam** (DRV) realized that they could not authorize the security forces to attack the nationalist leaders, including the head of the VNQDD, **Vu Hong Khanh**, arriving with or backed by the Chinese from exile in southern China. To do so would be to risk a hostile Chinese take-over. Determined to deny them any pretext for overthrowing the fledgling government, the **Viet Minh** and the communists allowed the opposition to organize propaganda drives, operate newspapers, publish political cartoons satirizing the communists and even Ho Chi Minh, the "father" of the new nation.

Thanks to the Chinese security umbrella, the VNQDD joined forces with the **Greater Vietnam National Party** of **Truong Tu Anh** and the Alliance Party of **Nguyen Hai Than**. These parties organized membership drives, mobilized youth groups, and recruited for their militias. These opposition leaders decried what they considered to be the communist monopoly over the new state. They called for the creation of a truly nationalist coalition, with non-communists holding key ministries. Their wish was granted on several occasions thanks to Chinese pressure. Meanwhile, the opposition organized anti-Viet Minh demonstrations called on the population to boycott elections and urged workers and civil servants to go on strike. It was all part of their bid to roll back communist efforts to define the limits of political participation, citizenship, and power. Things got so bad that in mid-November 1945 the ICP leadership decided to "**dissolve**" its party as a reflection of communist "selflessness" and "authentic" patriotism.

Until the Chinese pulled out, the VNQDD fought its battles for Vietnamese hearts and minds via newspapers, printing presses, and publishing houses. The VNQDD paper *Viet Nam* was particularly effective in late 1945 and early 1946 in portraying the Viet Minh and the DRV leaders as internationalist communists bent on betraying the country. Scathing debates became commonplace in government and opposition papers. Powerfully charged words that had been proffered back and forth privately between the two sides now came into the open in **Hanoi** and in bold print: *Viet gian*, *phan quoc*, *phan dong*, *Viet quoc*, and perhaps even *Viet cong*. Communist hate for the opposition was palpable. The chief of the DRV's security services recalled one memorable encounter: "What paper do you have there?" "*Viet Nam*" a young nationalist replied. Mockingly, the chief of police shot back: "There's nothing Vietnamese in it; their paper is nothing but a traitorous one!" (*Viet Nam gi bao cua chung may la bao Viet Gian!*)

This violent "war of the pens" set the mental stage for the civil violence of mid-1946. The shift began when the Chinese finished pulling the bulk of their troops out of upper Vietnam by 17 June 1946. Within a few weeks, the communists unleashed the security services against the VNQDD and the Greater Vietnam party while Vo Nguyen Giap used his emerging army against nationalist troops located in the northern countryside, with the support of local French troops. By September 1946, Vu Hong Khanh and most of his remaining forces had returned to southern China. Meanwhile, with the Chinese gone, the DRV Ministry of Interior authorized the police to confiscate opposition papers. In a final move to define in the clearest of terms the limits of opposition, the government replaced the original Vietnamese Nationalist Party with a "new" VNQDD, whose leaders and organizations were now tied to the DRV.

The security service's raids against the VNQDD presence in Hanoi, doubled by the army's attacks against the nationalist forces in the countryside, marked the outbreak of the first civil war in Vietnam since the 18th century. It was also the first in a long line of civil conflicts that would dominate modern Vietnamese history for the rest of the 20th century. Vu Hong Khanh would return to northern Vietnam with a few of his men in early 1950 as Chinese communist troops consolidated their hold over southern China and put an end to the **Republic of China**, the VNQDD's most important backer. *See also* AID, CHINESE; BINH XUYEN; CAO DAI; COLLABORATION; HOA HAO; HUYNH PHU SO; LE VAN VIEN; LANGUAGE OF WAR; PHAM CONG TAC.

**VIETNAMESE SOCIALIST PARTY.** The Vietnamese Socialist Party (*Dang Xa Hoi Viet Nam*) got its start as a chapter of the ***Section française de l'Internationale ouvrière***'s (SFIO) Indochinese branch formed by **Louis Caput** in 1937 and open to Vietnamese members. **Hoang Minh Giam** joined it at this time. With the advent of the **Democratic Republic of Vietnam** (DRV) in September 1945, Vietnamese socialists moved to decolonize their relationship with the SFIO by forming a separate, entirely national socialist party for Vietnam. The fact that many of the postwar leaders of the SFIO's Indochina branch did not share Louis Caput's support of the DRV's nationalist aspirations only reinforced the desire of Vietnamese socialists to go their own way. The **Indochinese Communist Party** supported the creation of a separate socialist party, which could not be manipulated by the French and would attract more Vietnamese supporters. On 27 July 1946, as the **Fontainebleau Conference** stalled in France, the Vietnamese Socialist Party came to life. Its founding document disassociated it from the SFIO's chapters in **Hanoi** and **Saigon**.

**VIETNAMESE WORKERS' PARTY (VWP).** The Vietnamese Workers' Party (*Dang Lao Dong Viet Nam*) was the direct heir of the **Indochinese Communist Party** (ICP) created in 1930. In 1945, in order to hold on to power and promote its purely nationalist face to the Vietnamese and Allied powers troubled by communism, **Ho Chi Minh** presided over the **dissolution of the Indochinese Communist Party**. However, the Party never ceased to exist. In 1949, as it became clear to that the Chinese Red Army was going to take all of China, Vietnamese communists began preparations to bring their Party back into the limelight and to stress its internationalist credentials with a view to renewing contact with communist bloc. In early 1950, **Mao Zedong's People's Republic of China**, followed by **Joseph Stalin's** Soviet Union, formally recognized the **Democratic Republic of Vietnam**.

Aware that ranking Chinese and Soviet leaders, above all Stalin, had criticized the Vietnamese decision to dissolve the party in 1945, Vietnamese communists announced the creation of a Workers' Party during the Party's second national congress held in early 1951. The VWP affirmed its communist identity and membership in the wider internationalist family led by Stalin. While the leadership opted in favor of a separate Vietnamese Party instead of an Indochinese one in light of the "advanced" state of the Vietnamese revolution over the Lao and Cambodian ones, Vietnamese communists secretly maintained their revolutionary commitment to the Indochinese model first required by the Comintern in 1930. Vietnamese communists established **Cadres Committees** for building communist parties, resistance governments and cadres' committees in Laos and Cambodia.

The VWP also implemented communist policies and methods in the territories it controlled in Vietnam, notably **rectification** campaigns, **emulation** drives, **new hero** adulation, and **land reform**. During the 1950s, the VWP actively purged the Party, state, and army of its non-communist members and actively moved to recruit workers and peasants into its ranks. In 1951, during the ICP's official second congress, **Truong Chinh** was formally and officially elected general secretary of the Party, a post he held until errors committed during the land reform cost him his post in 1956. *See also* COMMITTEE FOR THE EAST, LAO ISSARA; EXTERNAL AFFAIRS COMMITTEE; LAO RESISTANCE GOVERNMENT; CAMBODIAN RESISTANCE GOVERNMENT; ADVISORY GROUP 100.

**VILLEDIEU, HENRI LUCIEN PAUL (1914–1969).** French colonial administrator who served as deputy director of the *Agence de l'Indochine* in France between 1946 and 1947. He then transferred to Laos where he worked as a provincial advisor in Savannakhet between 1947 and 1950. Between 1951 and 1953, he was the head of the province of Kontum, then Djiring.

**VINCENS, JACQUES MARCEL JOSEPH (1919**–1996). French colonial administrator who worked in Laos during World War II and was interned by the Japanese following the ***coup de force* of 9 March 1945**. Between 1946 and 1950, he served as chief of cabinet of the commissioner of the French Republic to Laos.

**VINCENT, JEAN ANDRÉ LÉON MARIE (1907–1984).** Vincent graduated from the **Colonial Academy** (*École coloniale*) in 1928 and became a colonial administrator in Indochina. He was first assigned to Cambodia where he began working in 1932 as deputy to the *résident* of Takeo then as interim *résident* there (1932–1938). Between 1939 and 1940, he worked as deputy to the *résident* at Kompong Cham. Under Vichy, he served as head of the local Office of Sport and Youth (*Service local du sport jeunesse*) in Cambodia (1941–1945) and was one of the prime French movers of the Cambodian **scouting** movement. He instilled in his Cambodian pupils "a sense of discipline" and "love of Cambodia and gratitude to France" (*amour du Cambodge et reconnaissance envers la France*). He was a strong supporter of Marshal Philippe Pétain and Vichy's *Révolution nationale*. Between 1 January 1942 and July 1942, Vincent was a member of the right-wing Local Union of the *Légion* (*Union locale de la Légion*). Following World War II, he was cleared of wrong-doing under Vichy and stayed on to serve as provincial advisor to the "Eastern Mekong" between 1945–1946 before returning to Cambodia to work as office director for the *Résidence supérieure*. In 1951, he was named delegate for the high commissioner of Indochina to the King of Laos and ended his career in Indochina as cabinet director for the high commissioner to Laos between 1952 and 1953.

**VINCENT, JOHN CARTER (1900–1972).** Born in Seneca, Kansas, John Carter Vincent served in World War I before joining the Foreign Service. As a career diplomat, he served in a variety of posts, especially in Asia. He was vice consul in Changsha, China, between 1926 and 1927 and consul in Mukden in 1932, when the conflict between China and Japanese erupted in Manchuria. Upon his return to the State Department shortly thereafter, he became a strong advocate of helping the **Republic of China** against Japanese aggression. During World War II, he returned to China in 1941 to serve as first secretary in the American Embassy in Chongqing. During this time, he began to write increasingly trenchant and critical reports on the corruption and ineptitude of the Chinese nationalist leaders, not least of all **Chiang Kai-shek**. In 1944, Vincent returned to Washington to direct the Division of Chinese Affairs in the State Department. He counseled against intervention in the Chinese civil war on behalf of the Chinese Republicans, though it is not clear whether Vincent had any real influence on President **Harry Truman**'s policymaking on China.

At the outbreak of the Indochina War, Vincent worked with other "liberals" in the State Department, especially **Abbot Low Moffat** in charge of the Southeast Asian desk. Like Moffat, Vincent warned against the dangers of a French war to restore colonial rule and urged the government to push the French, like the Dutch, to negotiate a peaceful end to the Indochina War. In late 1945, Vincent suggested that the United States initiate such negotiations between the French and the **Democratic Republic of Vietnam**, although he quickly watered down his proposal. Nevertheless, he was prescient when he wrote on 23 December 1946, as the French and Vietnamese went to war, that the "French have tried to accomplish in Indochina what a strong and united Britain has found it unwise to attempt in **Burma**. Given the present elements in the situation, **guerrilla** warfare may continue indefinitely". The **Cold War** would turn Vincent's life into something of a nightmare. Suspected of leftist indeed communist views during the McCarthy years, he was forced to leave the Bureau of Far Eastern Affairs.

**VINCENT, PAUL ROBERT (1921–)**. French colonial administrator in charge of relations with the ***Sûreté fédérale*** within the commissioner's Office for Political Affairs between 1945 and 1946. In 1946, he also served as secretary to General **Raoul Salan** during the **Dalat Conference**. He then worked as deputy to the head of the financial service in the commissioner's office in Cambodia for the French Republic and deputy advisor to the areas of Kandal and Kompong Speu.

**VĨNH THỤY.** *See* BẢO ĐẠI.

**VĨNH YÊN, BATTLE.** Having inflicted a severe defeat upon the forces of the **French Union** in the uplands of **Cao Bang**, General **Vo Nguyen Giap** was convinced that he could repeat his feat in the Red River Delta. It was said that the commanding general had even promised his troops that they would be in **Hanoi** before the lunar New Year in February 1951. With the battle of Trung Hung Dao, as the Vietnamese christened this operation, the General Counter Offensive was underway and the days of the pure **guerrilla** were fading. However, not unlike **Nguyen Binh** in the south, Vo Nguyen Giap badly underestimated the enemy's strength in the deltas. Thanks to their intelligence services, the French were well aware of the adversary's intentions to attack at Vinh Yen. And the new French high commander, General **Jean de Lattre de Tassigny**, was also spoiling for a fight, especially in the Red River Delta. Between 12 and 17 January 1951, Vo Nguyen Giap began the attack at Luc Nam and on the road to Vinh Yen, committing regiments of the 308th division to the battle. This was the first time the Vietnamese had engaged in battle in the open field, applying **wave tactics** they had learned from the Chinese. Against such attacks, de Lattre let loose his artillery and air power, ordering the use of **napalm** against attacking troops. The French scored a resounding victory over the Vietnamese at Vinh Yen. Somewhere between 1,200 and 1,600 Vietnamese were killed during the battle. The French victory increased the confidence of the **Expeditionary Corps** after the loss at **Cao Bang**. De Lattre, it was thought, would indeed turn things around. For the Vietnamese, it was clear that victory would not be immediate, that the General Counter Offensive could not be applied so easily, nor the abandonment of the guerrilla war. General Vo Nguyen Giap also realized that wave tactics in the deltas, against superior French airpower and artillery, could be a recipe for disaster. *See also* DIEN BIEN PHU, BATTLE OF; NA SAN, BATTLE OF; WAVE TACTICS.

**VIRIYA, PRINCE.** Powerful behind-the-scenes supporter of his cousin **Norodom Sihanouk** during the Indochina War. Viriya attended the *Lycée Chasseloup Laubat* in **Saigon**. In 1948, he was the chief of cabinet for the Ministry of National Defence. In 1952, as Sihanouk prepared to consolidate his political power, Viriya was entrusted by the king to create a secret palace police service to follow the activities of various Cambodian political parties. In 1952, Viriya participated in army operations against **Son Ngoc Thanh** and his forces in Siemreap province. In January 1953, Viriya became chief of the Municipal Police for Phnom Penh and in June chief of the Private Staff of the king himself. He accompanied Norodom Sihanouk to Thailand in June 1953 and entered into contact with Thai Police Chief Phao Sryanond. Prince Viriya soon himself became Sihanouk's state secretary in the Ministry of the Interior in charge of all Police Services. He maintained these posts in the April 1954 government reshuffles of **Chan Nak** and Sihanouk.

**VÕ AN NINH (1907–2009).** One of Vietnam's best-known photographers of the 20th century. He covered both everyday and historic events of the colonial and postcolonial period, including the famine and August Revolution of 1945 as well as the two wars for Vietnam. His love of photography began at the age of 16. Legend has it that he spent all his savings on a Zeiss Ikon Y 45.143 to get started. His first photos were of a picnic of students of the *Lycée du Protectorat (École Buoi)* in **Hanoi** and rural scenes of the surrounding city. During a competition held by the Department of Fine Arts in Hanoi, he won first prize for a picture of rafts on the water off Sam Son. In 1938, he won the top prize in a photo exhibition in Paris for his photo *Rowing the Boat Offshore*. Under the influence of the Popular Front period in the late 1930s, he shifted the subjects of his photos to more social matters. While working for the Forestry and Agriculture Department, his travels throughout the countryside provided him with more material on everyday life and society beyond the cities. This shift came through powerfully in 1944–1945 when he published moving pictures of the deadly famine in **Tonkin**. Many of these pictures appeared on the front page of the widely read *Trung Bac Chu Nhat* (*The Sunday Northern Central*). They are among the few available on this historic event. He continued to record the major events of the new Vietnamese nation-state as a photographer for *Vi Nuoc*. He scored a scoop with his pictures of President **Ho Chi Minh** on the French battleship *Dumot Durville* returning from Cam Ranh Bay in October 1946. He also covered the large student demonstrations in **Saigon** in 1950 against increased American involvement in the Indochina War, marked by the visit of the U.S. Navy destroyers *Stickell* and *Richard B. Anderson*. Vo An Ninh is generally considered to be the father of modern Vietnamese photography. *See also* ART; CINEMA; CULTURE; NOVELS; PHOTOGRAPHY.

**VÕ NGUYÊN GIÁP (VĂN, 1911–).** Vietnam's best known general of the 20th century and the victor of the battle of **Dien Bien Phu** over the French **Expeditionary Corps** in 1954. Born in the province of Quang Binh, he first studied at the *Lycée Quoc Hoc* in Hue, where he became involved in nationalist politics. In 1929, he joined the New Vietnamese Revolutionary Party (*Tan Viet Nam Cach Mang Dang*). The French arrested him in 1930 for trying to garner money for the victims of the communist-backed uprising in central Vietnam in 1930. Although sentenced to two years of prison, he was released shortly thereafter and moved to **Hanoi** to finish his secondary studies at the *Lycée Albert Sarraut*. According to one of his former teachers, **Marcel Ner**, Vo Nguyen Giap was extremely hard-working, studious, and sensitive. He pursued higher studies in law at the *Faculté de droit* at the Indochinese University, from which he graduated in 1937. He was also awarded a certificate in political economics. During this time, **Dang Thai Mai** took him under his wing, and provided him with a job teaching history in a private high school in Hanoi, *Thang Long*. During the Popular Front period, Vo Nguyen Giap became involved in nationalist politics, writing for left-wing newspapers in Hanoi such as *Notre voix*, and participated in the Indochinese Congress. He co-wrote with **Truong Chinh** a treatise on the "Peasant Question". He married Nguyen Thi Quang Thai, the younger sister of a prominent member of the **Indochinese Communist Party** (ICP), Nguyen Thi Minh Khai.

Vo Nguyen Giap left the *Thang Long* high school in May 1940, when he was warned that an arrest warrant had been issued against him. Thanks to the assistance of Hoang Van Thu, another ranking ICP leader, Giap escaped to southern China and made his way with **Pham Van Dong** to Kunming where they met **Ho Chi Minh**. The latter recognized the potential of Vo Nguyen Giap and brought him formally into the ICP. With the fall of France and the Japanese move into Indochina in 1940, the ICP sent Vo Nguyen Giap to build up bases along the Sino-Vietnamese border. In May 1941, during the Party's 8th Plenum, he ran the Military Committee for the **Viet Minh**'s General Directorate (*Uy Ban Quan Su Tong Bo Viet Minh*), in charge of creating and training the movement's armed forces. On 12 December 1944, Vo Nguyen Giap presided over the creation of the Armed Propaganda Brigade for the Liberation of Vietnam (*Doi Viet Nam Tuyen Truyen Giai Phong Quan*), the origin of the **People's Army of Vietnam** of today. He attended the Conference in Tan Trao in mid-August 1945, which created the National Committee for the Liberation of Vietnam (*Uy Ban Dan Toc Giai Phong Viet Nam*). He ran its Military Committee and signed the order to begin the general uprising.

From September 1945 to March 1946, with the advent of the **Democratic Republic of Vietnam** (DRV), Vo Nguyen Giap served as minister of the Interior. He served as the deputy leader of the Vietnamese delegation to the **Dalat Conference** of April 1946, led officially by the minister of Foreign Affairs, **Nguyen Tuong Tam**. During Ho Chi Minh's long absence in France in mid-1946, Vo Nguyen Giap proceeded to eliminate the anti-communist and anti-colonial opposition parties, with the support of the French.

In November 1946, he became minister of Defense. In that same year, he headed the ICP's newly created Military Committee (*Quan Uy*) overseeing the entire armed forces. He held both posts until 1977. In 1946 or 1947, he married again, this time to Dang Bich Ha, the daughter of Dang Thai Mai. In 1948, Vo Nguyen Giap became a four-star general and the supreme commander of all the DRV's armed forces. During the Second Party Congress held in early 1951, he was re-elected to the Central Committee of the new **Vietnamese Workers' Party** and its Politburo. In 1954, he oversaw the historic battle of Dien Bien Phu, making him modern Vietnam's greatest general. *See also* COURT MARTIAL; DISEASE; EXPERIENCE OF WAR, DIEN BIEN PHU; MYTH OF WAR.

**VŨ ĐÌNH HÙYNH (1904–1991).** Personal secretary to **Ho Chi Minh** during the Indochina War. Vu Dinh Huynh joined the **Indochinese Communist Party** upon its creation in 1930 and worked as a clandestine liaison agent for the party in northern Vietnam and **Hanoi**. In 1939, his activities attracted the attention of the French *Sûreté*. He was arrested and sent off to **Son La prison** in northern Vietnam, where he rubbed shoulders with ranking leaders in the party and future national government. Upon his liberation in 1941, Vu Dinh Huynh resumed his clandestine activites for the party moving in and around Hanoi, sheltering and connecting Vietnamese revolutionaries in the months and days leading up to the creation of the **Democratic Republic of Vietnam**. During the Tan Trao Conference, which he helped organize, he met Ho Chi Minh and became his personal secretary. He accompanied Ho Chi Minh to Paris for the **Fontainebleau Conference** and remained at his side in northern Vietnam during the rest of the Indochina War. This did not prevent Vu Dinh Huynh from landing in prison in 1967 as part of the "anti-revisionist campaign" stemming from intense differences of strategy leading up to the Tet Offensive of 1968. His son, Vu Thu Hien, published in the 1990s a detailed account of his father's life and tragic fall, entitled *Darkness in the Middle of the Day* or *Dem giua ban ngay. See also* HOANG MINH CHINH; NGUYEN HUU DANG.

**VŨ ĐÌNH LONG.** *See* VŨ NGỌC NHẠ PIERRE.

**VŨ ĐỨC.** *See* HOÀNG ĐÌNH GIỌNG.

**VŨ HẢI THU**. *See* NGUYỄN HẢI THẦN.

**VŨ HỒNG KHANH (VŨ VĂN GIẢNG, GIAO GIẢNG, TƯ VŨ, WU HUNG SINH, 1907–1993).** One of the best-known leaders of the **Vietnamese Nationalist Party** (*Viet Nam Quoc Dan Dang,* VNQDD). Born in Vinh Yen province in northern Vietnam, Vu Hong Khanh entered the *École normale de* ***Hanoi*** in 1921 and graduated in 1925 as a school teacher. He taught school in Kien An province between 1926 and 1929. It was also during this period that he became involved in nationalist politics. In 1929, he joined the VNQDD created by Nguyen Thai Hoc in 1927. With the French crushing of the VNQDD revolt at Yen Bay in 1930, Vu Hong Khang fled to southern China in June 1930 where he became one of the most important leaders of the Party outside French Indochina. He quickly learned Chinese and graduated from a Chinese nationalist military academy in Nanjing as a second lieutenant in the Chinese Republican army. During the Sino-Japanese war, he rose rapidly in the Chinese nationalist hierarchy. He obtained the rank of brigadier general in 1941 and **Chiang Kai-shek** made him the director of the Military Academy of Yunnan. However, he resigned from this post almost immediately to dedicate himself entirely to the VNQDD's return to Vietnam.

Vu Hong Khanh bet on the Chinese nationalists, their anti-communism, and their occupation of northern Vietnam to help him take power against Vietnamese communists. He returned to Hanoi on 6 November 1945 with Chinese occupying forces. However, because the Chinese nationalist leadership decided to keep the **Democratic Republic of Vietnam** (DRV) intact rather than risk setting off a destabilizing Franco-Vietnamese war, Vu Hong Khanh was forced to join a coalition government as part of the DRV. In early 1946, he served as vice president of the High Council of National Defense, led by **Vo Nguyen Giap**. He even signed the **Accords of 6 March 1946** which allowed the French to replace Chinese troops above the **16th parallel**. Vu Hong Khanh was a member of the Vietnamese delegation to the **Dalat Conference**, but kept a low profile.

However, his party's double hostility to French colonialism and Vietnamese communism led certain French officers in Indochina and Vo Nguyen Giap to join forces to eliminate this hostile opposition force. By the time **Ho Chi Minh** returned from France in October 1946, the French and the DRV were *face à face* as one French witness to the events later put it. From bases in the nationalist stronghold of Vinh Yen, Vu Hong Khanh took refuge for a second time in southern China in June 1946. To make matters worse, his relations with other members in the VNQDD were troubled. In 1948, he was relieved of his duties as general secretary of the VNQDD and then expelled from the Party altogether. In December 1949, he joined Chinese nationalist troops seeking refuge in Indochina from the advancing Chinese People's Liberation Army.

When Vu Hong Khanh refused to surrender to the French army in early 1950, he found himself once again under fire from both the DRV and the French (**Air Force**). He and his men finally surrendered on 6 January 1950 in Bac Giang. However, in French eyes, Vu Hong Khanh's anti-communism trumped his longstanding hostility to French colonialism. In April 1950, he began to participate in Franco-Vietnamese attempts to create a national **army for the Associated State of Vietnam**. Politically, however, Vu Hong Khanh and his resurrected VNQDD were a spent force in Vietnamese national politics. He would contact a wide range of Vietnamese non-communist groups and individuals, including the **Binh Xuyen**, **Cao Dai**, and **Bao Dai**; but he never succeeded in developing a political or a military base and his aversion to the French limited his cooperation with them and their Vietnamese allies. By the end of the Indochina War, Vu Hong Khanh and the VNQDD had been overtaken by events. *See also* CIVIL WAR; HOANG VAN HOAN; NGUYEN SON; POULO CONDOR; VUONG THUA VU.**VŨ HỒNG THỦY.** *See* NGUYỄN SƠN.

**VŨ HỮU BÌNH.** Former non-commissioned officer in the colonial *Garde indigène*, based in Vientiane in the 1930s. He was at ease in Lao and Thai. He crossed into Thailand around 1940 and became an officer in the Royal Thai Army. He met Phin Chunhawan and **Pibun Songgram** at this time. He also secretly joined the **Indochinese Communist Party** (ICP) along the Mekong. With the end of the war, he helped the ICP develop its bases among the **overseas Vietnamese** living in northeastern Thailand and in Laos. He played a pivotal go-between role for the **Democratic Republic of Vietnam**'s agents seeking to contact Thai political, military, and commercial leaders. He transferred to work in the Cambodian Front with **Nguyen Thanh Son** in 1950. He would later serve in the diplomatic corps, with assignments in Southeast Asia.

**VŨ LANG (ĐỖ ĐỨC LIÊM, 1921–1988).** Born in the **Hanoi** region, Vu Lang was a carpenter who became involved in nationalist politics during the Popular Front period in Indochina. With the advent of the **Democratic Republic of Vietnam** in 1945, he joined the **Nam Tien** advance units to fight the French in southern Vietnam. He got as far as southern central Vietnam, where he took command of a platoon before becoming deputy chief of military instruction for **Zone** VI (*Khu VI*). In June 1946, he returned to the north where he served as a bodyguard to the government palace and helped evacuate the government from the city with the start of full-scale war on **19 December 1946**. In February 1947, he joined the **Indochinese Communist Party** and returned to his position in the army. Between 1947 and 1954, he rapidly rose in the army taking part in all the major battles in the north. By the time of the battle of **Dien Bien Phu** in 1954, he had risen from a platoon commander to the head of the **General Staff** for the 316th division.

**VŨ NGỌC NHÃ.** *See* VŨ NGỌC NHẠ PIERRE.

**VŨ NGỌC NHẠ PIERRE (VŨ NGỌC NHÃ, HOÀNG ĐỨC NHÃ, VŨ ĐÌNH LONG, HAI LONG, 1928–2002).** Intelligence officer for the **Democratic Republic of Vietnam** (DRV) during the Indochina and Vietnam Wars. A Catholic, Vu Ngoc Nha was born in Thai Nguyen province in northern Vietnam but moved at a young age to the Catholic fiefdom of Phat Diem in lower **Tonkin**. He completed his secondary education in **Hanoi**, where he got caught up in the nationalist fervor of 1945. He joined the **Viet Minh** that year and fought in the battle of Hanoi following the outbreak of full-scale war on **19 December 1946**. He then transferred to his native Thai Nguyen province where he was put in charge of mobilizing Catholics for the DRV. He did this until 1951, when he was sent to Hanoi to work underground. In 1953, thanks to an introduction from Do Muoi, **Tran Quoc Huong** brought Vu Ngoc Nha into the DRV's military intelligence and espionage operations, assigning him the task of training cadres to work among Catholics. When the **Geneva Accords** ended the war and created two de facto states, **Hoang Minh Dao**, head of military intelligence, instructed Vu Ngoc Nha to join the tens of thousands of Vietnamese Catholics fleeing the north in order to go undercover in the south as a DRV operative. He was given a new name, Vu Dinh Long, and a new identity making him a virulent anti-communist Catholic from Phat Diem. His cover was so good that he even had the support of **Le Huu Tu**. In December 1955, Vu Ngoc Nha left Haiphong as a refugee and went on to become one of the DRV's legendary spies during the Vietnam War. *See also* PHAM NGOC THAO; PHAM XUAN AN; TRAN QUOC HOAN.

**VŨ NGUYÊN BÁC.** *See* NGUYỄN SƠN.

**VŨ QUÝ MÃO (1904–?).** Non-communist Vietnamese member of the **Greater Vietnam Nationalist Party** (*Dai Viet Quoc Dan*), born in Gia Dinh province. He worked in the Indochinese colonial administration before serving in the mandarin government in northern Vietnam in the late 1930s. Little is known of his activities during World War II. Following the defeat of the Japanese and the advent of the **Democratic Republic of Vietnam** (DRV), he briefly served as director of Administrative Affairs in the Ministry of the Interior in the DRV. He left the government to join forces with other Greater Vietnam Nationalist Party members rallied around the person of **Nguyen Huu Tri**, governor of North Vietnam in the Associated State of Vietnam. Vu Quy Mao served as chief of cabinet to Nguyen Huu Tri. He refused a French offer to join a Vietnamese delegation to the Assembly of the **French Union**.

**VŨ TÙNG (1917–1968, NGUYỄN VĂN THỌ).** Born in Bac Ninh province in northern Vietnam, in 1938 Vu Tung entered the private high school of *Thang Long* in **Hanoi**. It was also during this time of the Popular Front that he became involved in nationalist politics. He took a job working in an electrical plant in Thanh Hoa province and agitated among workers there. When such activities landed him in trouble, he left for **Saigon** where he lived and worked during World War II and helped nationalist groups eventually allied with the **Viet Minh** to take power in Saigon in August 1945. In late 1945, in opposition to the French reoccupation of southern Vietnam, Vu Tung joined detachment no.11 (*Chi Doi*). In late 1946 or early 1947, he returned to Saigon as a member of the local branch of the ***Section française de l'Internationale ouvrière***, in charge of the Vietnamese section of the party's local paper, *La Justice*. He used his position in the paper to translate and publish articles opposed to the French-created **Provisional Government of the Republic of Cochinchina**. In 1948, Vu Tung escorted French Professor **Jean Chesneaux** to the *maquis* to meet with members of the **Democratic Republic of Vietnam** (DRV). The French arrested and incarcerated both men. The colonial police expelled Chesneaux from Indochina while Vu Tung was eventually released and immediately made his way back to the *maquis*. There he underwent intensive training in the first class of the cadres school in the south, the **Truong Chinh Academy** (*Truong Truong Chinh*). He then joined the special zone of Cholon-Gia Dinh as a member of the Propaganda and Political Indoctrination Committee (*Ban Tuyen Huan*). Following the end of the war and the partition of Vietnam into two halves, he remained in Saigon, sympathetic to the cause of the DRV.

**VŨ VĂN ĐÍCH.** *See* TRẦN HIỆU.

**VŨ VĂN GIẢN.** *See* VŨ HỒNG KHANH.

**VƯƠNG QUANG NHƯỜNG (1902–?).** Born in Go Cong province in southern Vietnam, Vuong Quang Nhuong completed his studies in the *Lycée Chasseloup Laubat* in **Saigon** and the *Lycée de **Hanoi***. He then studied law in the *Faculté de droit* in Bordeaux, France. He served as the president of the *Association mutuelle des Indochinois de Bordeaux et du Sud-Ouest*. He resigned in 1926 following criticism of his reception speech for the minister of the Colonies, which was judged to be too moderate. In 1927, he obtained his undergraduate degree in law and, in 1929, his doctorate in law. Between 1929 and 1931, he worked as an intern in a Parisian law firm. He returned to **Cochinchina** in August 1931, joined the bar in Saigon a year later, and worked in a law firm there. In May 1935, he became a naturalized French citizen. He was a close colleague of the constitutionalist, Bui Quang Chieu, and married his daughter, Dr. Henriette Bui. Between 1927 and 1940, Vuong Quang Nhuong was a member of the Council of the Order of Lawyers in the Appeals Court of Saigon (*Conseil de l'ordre des avocats à la cour d'appel de Saigon*).

After the Japanese ***coup de force* of 9 March 1945**, he became a public prosecutor in Saigon and worked with the Japanese consul and governor of Cochinchina. He successfully navigated the defeat of the Japanese in August 1945, the brief period of nationalist rule in the south until **23 September,** and the return of the French to Saigon thereafter. Having divorced in 1937, he married the daughter of the former emperor Thanh Thai, Mme. Cong Nu Luong Nhan. He was favorable to ending the war and achieving Vietnamese national independence. In April 1947, to the surprise of the French, he joined a number of other prominent Vietnamese to sign the *Manifeste des intellectuels vietnamiens de la région de Saigon Cholon*, calling upon the French to negotiate directly with the government of the **Democratic Republic of Vietnam** (DRV). The French even suspected him of having provided brief asylum in Saigon to the head of the southern army, **Nguyen Binh**. In 1949, Vuong Quang Nhuong signed another petition calling upon the French to negotiate with **Ho Chi Minh**. This clearly did not prevent **Nguyen Phan Long** from naming him minister of National Education in January 1950 or from putting him in charge of convincing nationalists living in the "rebel zones" of the DRV to **crossover** to the Associated State of Vietnam. Vuong Quang Nhuong stayed on as minister of National Education in the **Tran Van Huu** government constituted in May 1950. He was seriously wounded, however, in a "terrorist" attack in June 1950. It was in fact organized by the DRV's security forces operating in Saigon.

Vuong Quang Nhung became deputy minister to the president of the council in the second Tran Van Huu government of February 1951.

**VƯƠNG THỪA VŨ (NGUYỄN VĂN ĐỒI, 1910–1980).** Born in **Hanoi** to a science teacher, he became involved in nationalist politics during the 1920s. He joined the **Vietnamese Nationalist Party** (*Viet Nam Quoc Dan Dang*, VNQDD) in the late 1920s and fled to China following the French crackdown on this party in early 1930. Vuong Thua Vu learned Chinese fast before entering a Chinese nationalist military academy in Yunnan, from which he graduated as an officer sometime in the late 1930s. He returned to Vietnam in the early 1940s and was arrested by the French in late 1941. It was during his time in prison in Thai Nguyen that he defected to the **Indochinese Communist Party** in 1943. Following his liberation in March 1945, he put his military talents in the service of what became the **Democratic Republic of Vietnam**. He joined the army in August 1945. In 1946, he was in charge of training and commanding the troops protecting Hanoi. He did this as the head of **Zone** XI (Hanoi). He answered directly to **Vo Nguyen Giap** during the stormy days leading up to the outbreak of full-scale war on **19 December 1946** and commanded the battle for Hanoi from 19 December 1946 to 17 February 1947. Between 1947 and 1948, he was deputy commander of **Inter-Zone IV** (*Lien Khu IV*) in upper central Vietnam before taking over as head of the Binh Tri Thien zone. Between 1949 and 1954, he led the 308th Division and served simultaneously as its political commissar between 1949 and 1951. He was named major general in 1950. He led the 308th into the battle of **Dien Bien Phu**.

**WAN WAITHAYAKON (1891–1976).** The Thai Prince Waithayakon received his education at Oxford University in Britain and *Sciences Po* in France before entering the Thai Ministry of Foreign Affairs in 1917. In 1924, he became undersecretary for Foreign Affairs and led negotiations ending special Western privileges in Thailand. In the late 1920s, he served as Thai minister to the United Kingdom, the Netherlands, and Belgium and led the Thai delegation to the League of Nations. He returned to Thailand in 1930 and taught at Chulalongkorn University, but remained deeply involved in Thai diplomacy, including the negotiations that saw the Thais join with the Japanese during World War II. At the end of the Pacific War, he successfully negotiated Thailand's international rehabilitation, marked by its admission to the **United Nations** (UN), and its improved relations with the United States in particular. In 1947, he became Thai ambassador to the United States and served also as ambassador to the UN. He held these positions until 1952, when he became Thai minister of Foreign Affairs. During this time, he represented Thai interests during the **Geneva Conference** of 1954 on Indochina. He supported the separation of the Vietnamese question from that of Laos and Cambodia, rejecting the **Democratic Republic of Vietnam**'s (DRV) attempt to get the **Lao** and **Cambodian resistance governments** admitted as conference participants. With the support of the Americans, he also pushed the idea of allowing the UN to serve as future observers of the accords and the elections rather than the **International Commission for Supervision and Control**. On 29 May the Thais officially submitted their proposal to the UN and it was put on the Security Council's agenda on 3 June. Beijing was strongly opposed to the Wan's proposal, insisting that it was designed to sabotage the Geneva Conference and open the way for the United States to intervene. The Soviets immediately vetoed the Thai proposal.

**WANG BINGNAN (1908–1988).** Chinese diplomat and member of the delegation led by **Zhou Enlai** to the **Geneva Conference**. After a short stint in Japan in 1929, Wang Bingnan studied in Germany in the early 1930s, where he collaborated with the German Communist Party and worked among Chinese student groups in Germany. It was also during this time that he married in 1935 the German, Anna von Kleist. He returned to China in 1936 with his wife and until 1949 served as an alternate member of the Southern Bureau of the **Chinese Communist Party** (CCP) and second deputy secretary and spokesman of the Committee of Foreign Affairs to the CCP's delegation operating in Nanjing. He also served as the CCP's deputy director general of the Group of Foreign Affairs. With the advent of the **People's Republic of China** in 1949, he worked closely with Zhou Enlai to create the Ministry of Foreign Affairs. Between 1949 and 1955, he served as general director of the General Office of the Ministry of Foreign Affairs.

During the Geneva Conference of 1954, he was general secretary of the Chinese delegation and played an important behind-the-scenes role with Zhou Enlai in reaching an agreement with the French on ending the Indochina War. His contacts with the former French military attaché to Nanjing, Colonel **Jacques Guillermez**, served him well when Guillermez appeared in Geneva as a member of the French delegation. The two men met often and through their contacts arranged essential meetings between the French and the Chinese delegations and others during the Geneva Conference. Wang and Guillermez were, according to François Joyaux, instrumental in setting in motion Franco-Chinese collaboration at the outset of the Geneva Conference. Wang Bingnan's marriage to Anna von Kleist also opened doors since she was related to the German Countess Asta von Kleist, who was the wife of French Ambassador **Jean Louis Paul-Boncour**. The latter had been *chargé d'affaires* in Chongqing between 1941 and 1943 and was now general secretary of the French delegation to the Geneva Conference. Paul-Boncour and Wang Bingnan also met secretly behind the scenes to push negotiations forward. Indeed, Wang Bingnan informed the French as early as 18 May 1954 that the Chinese were not in Geneva "to support the **Viet Minh**" but rather to "re-establish peace".

He even said that the "Chinese did not encourage necessarily Viet Minh military action towards the delta".

**WAR INVALIDS.** In May 1947, following the outbreak of full-scale war in **Hanoi** on **19 December 1946**, the **Democratic Republic of Vietnam** created a Bureau for War Invalids (*Phong Thuong Binh*) located in northern Vietnam (Dai Tu). The Ministry of Defense administered it and **Van Tien Dung** put Le Thanh An in charge of it. At the outset, this office tended to some 100 wounded soldiers evacuated to Dai Tu following the battle of Hanoi between December 1946 and February 1947. As the war progressed and intensified, this office established branches across the country and was soon overwhelmed with sick, wounded, and disabled soldiers. To honor the sacrifices of the wounded, in July 1947 the government created a national day to commemorate the war wounded. *Ngay Thuong Binh* is held on 27 July of each year and was later expanded to include the war dead – *Ngay Thuong Binh, Liet Si*, the equivalent of veteran's day. This day was selected because of the lucky number 7. On 27 July 1947, to mark the beginning of this national day of commemoration, **Ho Chi Minh** thanked the soldiers for their sacrifices for the nation.

**WAR MEMORIAL, ĐIỆN BIÊN PHỦ, FRANCE.** The French war memorial at Dien Bien Phu was created in 1994 upon the initiative of a former member of the French **Foreign Legion**, veteran of the Indochina War, and putschist during the **Algerian War**, Rolf Rodel. The French minister of Defence and Jacques Chirac supported this initiative and financed its transformation into a war memorial in collaboration with the ***Association Nationale des Anciens Prisonniers et Internés d'Indochine*** (ANAPI). In 1997, during Chirac's participation in the *Francophonie* Summit held in **Hanoi**, he visited the **Dien Bien Phu** war memorial in the company of Rodel. In 1999, the memorial was officially consecrated by the visit of the ANAPI. The Dien Bien Phu site is today an officially recognized French war monument. *See also* ASSOCIATION OF MOTHERS OF SOLDIERS; EXPERIENCE OF WAR; MYTH OF WAR; *ASSOCIATION NATIONALE DES ANCIENS D'INDOCHINE ET DU SOUVENIR INDOCHINOIS*; *ASSOCIATION NATIONALE DES ANCIENS ET AMIS DE L'INDOCHINE ET DU SOUVENIR INDOCHINOIS*; *ASSOCIATION NATIONALE DES COMBATTANTS DE DIEN BIEN PHU*; *ASSOCIATION NATIONALE DES ANCIENS PRISONNIERS ET INTERNÉS D'INDOCHINE*.

**WAR ZONE D (*Chiến Khu D*).** Famous secret warzone used by **Democratic Republic of Vietnam**'s southern forces during the Indochina War. It first came into being in early 1946 as southern forces took up **guerrilla** war against the French **Expeditionary Corps**. It was located in the dense jungles surrounding the villages of Tan Hoa, My Loc, Tan Tich, Thuong Lang, and Lac An. From 1948, it was home to the southern administration and the **Indochinese Communist Party**'s directing organizations and protected armed forces coming from the surrounding provinces of Bien Hoa, Thu Dau Mot as well as **Zone VII** and **Inter-Zone for Eastern Nam Bo**. War Zone D became famous for the Vietnamese fighting the Americans during the Vietnam War.

**WAVE TACTICS.** Besides supplying large amounts of military aid and training from 1950, Chinese advisors also introduced wave tactics to the **General Staff** of the **Democratic Republic of Vietnam** in a bid to overwhelm the French positions, as the Chinese army had done against the **Republic of China** during the Chinese civil war and was trying to do against the Americans in the **Korean War**. However, such human wave tactics were extremely risky when applied in Vietnam. For one, the French **Expeditionary Corps** was a professional army superior to **Chiang Kai-shek**'s armed forces, and both Generals **Vo Nguyen Giap** and **Chen Geng** conceded that the French were no pushover. Though France's **Air Force** in Indochina had serious problems, it was more modern and effective than the Chinese republican one had been. Not only did the French have more advanced artillery, they were also good at using it in complex and coordinated ways and at night. Moreover, compared to China and its armies, the Vietnamese population was so much smaller that it could not support such costly wave tactics without risking the depletion of a relatively small army (around 250,000 in the early 1950s, including 115,000 regular troops). In short, the Vietnamese were applying a Chinese military model against a superior enemy equipped with modern firepower, in different Vietnamese circumstances, in a much smaller country, and at an increasingly important international conjuncture that obliged them to score a big victory against the French at **Dien Bien Phu**. Wave tactics showed their limits in the Vietnamese battles in the Red River Delta in 1951 and even in the uplands. The bloody Vietnamese failure to take **Vinh Yen** was a painful case in point; **Na San** was an equally costly defeat in 1953. And the tactics used in the battle of Dien Bien Phu had much more in common with the trench warfare used at Verdun than the wave tactics the Chinese deployed in Korea. *See also* AID, CHINESE COMMUNIST.

**WEI GUOQING (1913–1989).** Wei Guoqing was a Chinese general in the Chinese People's Liberation Army. He was born in a family of the Zhuang ethnic background in Guangxi province, bordering Vietnam. He took over in late 1950 as the head of the **Chinese Military Advisor Delegation** to Vietnam, replacing **Chen Geng** who had been transferred to Korea. Wei's poor health caused him to return to China frequently, and during his absences either **Luo Guibo** or Wei's deputy, General **Mei Jiasheng**, assumed direct command of the Military Advisory Delegation. After returning from Vietnam, Wei served as the governor of Guangxi province (1955–1975) and the director of the General Political Affairs Department of the People's Liberation Army (1977–1982).

**WIDOWS OF WAR.** *See* ASSOCIATION OF MOTHERS OF SOLDIERS.

**WINTREBERT, MICHEL (1912–1978).** Born and raised in Indochina, Wintrebert served as a colonial administrator mainly in Vietnam. In 1951, he worked briefly as the chief of the civilian cabinet of General **Jean de Lattre de Tassigny**. In 1954, he became acting high commissioner to the State of Vietnam. When the **Geneva Accords** put an end to the war and gave rise to two competing Vietnamese states above and below the **17th parallel**, he became second counsellor to the **Republic of Vietnam** between 1955 and 1959. He was very supportive of **Ngo Dinh Diem** as the new national leader for postcolonial Vietnam and was sympathetic to American efforts to support him. Wintrebert and Ngo Dinh Diem may have studied together during their youth. His enthusiasm for Ngo Dinh Diem led some of his French detractors to refer to Wintrebert as "Ngo Dinh Michel".

**WOMEN, DEMOCRATIC REPUBLIC OF VIETNAM.** Vietnamese communists were not the first to take up the "question of women" (*van de phu nu*) or their emancipation. The place of women in Vietnamese society had been an important subject of debate during the interwar period as a new generation of Vietnamese began to question the oppressive nature of "traditional" society, of its "out-moded customs", and of Confucianism in particular. This was more pronounced in the colonial cities of **Hanoi** and **Saigon**, where Vietnamese intellectuals, journalists, and editors contributed regularly to and ran papers and magazines dedicated to women's issues, most notably *Phu Nu Tan Van* (Modern Women).

The leaders of the **Indochinese Communist Party** (ICP), created in 1930, also attached considerable importance to the liberation of women from traditional Confucian and bourgeois oppression. Vietnamese nationalists also understood that speaking to women about their rights was essential to winning their support as one of the most important untapped political forces in Vietnamese society to date. The French were shocked to learn that following the execution of Nguyen Thai Hoc, the leader of the failed **Vietnamese Nationalist Party** revolt, his wife wrote a double suicide note addressed to her husband and to the nation before she killed herself. Another woman, Nguyen Thi Minh Khai, rose to the highest ranks of the ICP before she was arrested and executed by the French on the eve of World War II.

Communist nationalists certainly had women in mind when they created the **Viet Minh** in 1941, explicitly mentioning the need to win over their support as part of building a broad-based nationalist front to fight for independence. Theoretically, both the ICP and the Viet Minh's political platforms ensured equal rights for women and assigned them a major revolutionary force. Upon coming to power, the **Democratic Republic of Vietnam** (DRV) instituted legal reforms designed to liberate the postcolonial Vietnamese woman. Decrees no. 14 and 51 of 1945 provided women with the right to vote. Elections in January 1946 sent ten women to the National Assembly. The 1946 constitution, the first, proclaimed the equality of the sexes. Article 37 of the 1947 labor law stipulated that equal work meant equal pay. In 1950, as Vietnamese communists renewed their ties with the Sino-Soviet bloc, the DRV issued decrees affirming the equality of boys and girls within the Vietnamese family, in a move designed to roll back Confucianism and its male-centered hold on power. Young women also received the right to choose their marriage partner. In November 1950, the government provided women with the right to divorce.

War itself contributed to changing the status of Vietnamese women, especially for those living within the DRV's territories. Given that women constituted half of the population and that the war state was faced with a chronic shortage of manpower, women were called upon to participate in a wide variety of political, social, economic, administrative, and even military occupations. During the battle of Hanoi in January and February 1947, the Capital Regiment of 1,200 individuals counted 200 women and 170 **children**. The evacuation of the cities in 1945–1947 towards the countryside was such that traditional family hierarchies broke down and the influence of urban ideas on "women's questions" expanded into the countryside.

Meanwhile, the DRV's needs for labor only increased as the fighting carried on. Women worked in village, provincial, and zonal bureaucracies. Many were involved in services in charge of women's, family, and cultural questions and used their positions to promote greater equality between the sexes. The DRV also set in motion an educational and literacy programme that schooled young girls as well as boys. In **Viet Minh** zones, Confucian-minded notables lost their central role at the village level. Meetings no longer excluded women, given their role in mobilizing local girls and women for national salvation fronts and productive power. **Nguyen Thi Ngoc Toan** not only served as a clandestine militant for the Viet Minh in Hue with the advent of the DRV in 1945, but she also studied at the DRV medical school and tended to grievously wounded men during the battle of **Dien Bien Phu**. She also openly challenged the powerful male cadres who had organized a **court marshal** of innocent men, going so far as to call into question the legitimacy of the trial.

Hundreds perhaps even thousands of women carried out dangerous undercover espionage, sabotage, and assassination missions behind enemy lines and in the occupied cities of Saigon and Hanoi. In Hung Yen, 6,700 women enrolled in the militia forces and took part in 680 guerrilla operations. Many paid with their lives and were tortured severely. Nguyen Thi Chien, Mac Thi Buoi, and Bui Thi Cuc died in the line of duty and were recast as **new heros** to emulate.

However, in practice things were not quite as egalitarian as communist nationalist historiography and these statistics would have us believe. Of the "ten essential tasks of the revolution" laid out by the ICP in 1930, women's rights were only contained in the penultimate point. Like the French, the DRV refused women the right to enlist in the national army. For the DRV, women were expected to "replace men in all tasks in the rear" and tend to the family and to children. Remarkably few women truly moved into the upper levels of leadership either in the DRV or the ICP during the Indochina conflict. In the DRV's 1946 National Assembly, women held only ten seats out of a total of 403. As of mid-1948, Le Duc Tho reported that "women comrades" made up less than 8% of total party membership.

The application of more communist-minded reforms and policies from 1953, including **land reform** and a marriage law, severed the hold of male-dominated land holdership and liberated peasant women from the male-centered Confucian order. However, as recent research on Chinese communism suggests, the Party's liberation of women was not always altruistic. By breaking traditional Confucian bonds of domination in the countryside, the Party also sought to insinuate political cadres (mostly men) into villages in order to better control and mobilize women for the Party's sake and ends. *See also* EMULATION; LOVE AND WAR; MINORITY ETHNIC GROUPS; ORPHANS.

**WOMEN, FRENCH ARMED FORCES.** While the number of women serving in the French armed forces (Army, **Navy**, and **Air Force**) during the Indochina War remained small, their size more than doubled between 1946 and 1954, increasing from 1,010 to 2,485 respectively. This suggests a small but important degree of feminization of the French armed forces during the Indochina War. The creation of the ***Personnel Féminin de l'Armée de Terre*** in 1951 contributed to this process. *See also* BELLONE; *BORDELS MILITAIRES DE CAMPAGNE*; PROSTITUTION; WOMEN, DEMOCRATIC REPUBLIC OF VIETNAM.

**WOMEN, FRENCH.** *See PERSONNEL FÉMININ DE L'ARMÉE DE TERRE* (PFAT).

**WORKERS, VIETNAMESE IN FRANCE.** *See* OVERSEAS VIETNAMESE IN FRANCE.

**WU HUNG SINH.** *See* VŨ HỒNG KHANH.

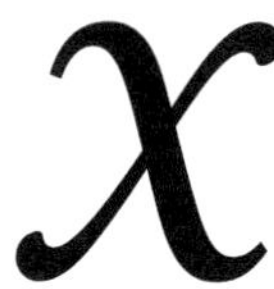

**XERIDAT, LUCIEN (1912–1986).** French colonial administrator during the Indochina War. He began his colonial career in Laos where he worked in a variety of administrative posts in Luang Prabang and Vientiane between 1936 and 1939. Under Vichy, he served as *résident* to Savannakhet (1941–1942) and chief of cabinet to the *résident supérieur* of Laos (1942–1944). He was interned by the Japanese following the ***coup de force* of 9 March 1945**. After the war, Xeridat was assigned to the section in charge of war damages in **Saigon**, where he worked between 1948 and 1955.

**XIANG MAO.** *See* KHAMMAO VILAI.

**XUÂN DIỆU (NGÔ XUÂN DIỆU, 1916–1985).** Vietnamese poet born in Binh Dinh province in central Vietnam. Son of a schoolteacher, he obtained his degree in agricultural engineering in 1943 but found his real calling in the arts when he joined **Nguyen Tuong Tam**'s *Tu Luc Van Doan* (Self Strengthening Movement) in **Hanoi** in the 1930s. Xuan Dieu shone as one of the leaders of the New Poetry movement. He wrote some particularly original and powerful Vietnamese poetry, including the celebrated love poem, *Em Di* (*Go now*). Together with his male partner, the poet **Huy Can**, he put his poetry in the service of the nationalist cause of the **Democratic Republic of Vietnam** (DRV) from 1945. He was involved in cultural associations working for the independence cause and the national resistance in Hanoi in 1945–1946, and elsewhere during the Indochina War. Although the communist authorities disapproved of his homosexuality, Xuan Dieu remained a pre-eminent cultural luminary in the DRV until his death in 1985. His works are studied by high school students in Vietnam to this day and his poetry from the pre–1945 period maintains all its forcefulness. *See also* LOVE AND WAR; LANGUAGE OF WAR.

**XUÂN THỦY (NGUYỄN TRỌNG NHÂM, 1912–1985).** Born in the province of Ha Dong near **Hanoi**, Xuan Thuy joined the Vietnamese Revolutionary Youth League in 1926 and the **Indochinese Communist Party** sometime in the 1930s. In 1939, he was arrested by the French and incarcerated in **Son La prison** in northern Vietnam, where he probably first met **Le Duc Tho**. In late 1943 or early 1944, he was placed under house arrest in Ha Dong. Following the Japanese overthrow of the French in March 1945, he became editor-in-chief of the **Viet Minh**'s newspaper, *Cuu Quoc* (National Salvation). He also joined the General Directorate or the ***Tong Bo* Viet Minh**. In 1946, he was elected a deputy to the National Assembly. He started his diplomatic career in 1953, when he became general secretary of the Committee for Peace in Vietnam and represented the **Democratic Republic of Vietnam** at the World Council of Peace. He would become a close ally of Le Duc Tho and participated in high-level negotiations with the Americans during the Vietnam War and the talks leading up to the Paris Peace Accords of 1973.

**YÈM SAMBAUR (1913–1989).** Devoted supporter of King **Norodom Sihanouk**. Born in Battambang province, he studied at the *Collège Sisowath* in Phnom Penh and the *Lycée Albert Sarraut* in **Hanoi**. Graduated in 1935, he entered the colonial administration as a judge, as deputy commissioner to the king in the Appellate Court (*Sala Outor*), president of the Cambodian Court of Kompong Chhnang and then Kompong Thom. In 1946, he joined the **Democrat Party** and was elected deputy for Kompong Chhang in 1947. He worked as chief of the National Cambodian Police force in 1947–1948. Between February and August 1948, he was state secretary of the Interior in the **Chheam Vam** cabinet. In November of that year, he resigned from the Democrat Party to ally himself with royal forces. From February 1949, he served the king as president of council (*présidence du conseil*) and minister of the Interior and of Information. He oversaw the signing of the Franco-Cambodian Treaty creating the Associated State of Cambodia. In 1949, he entered into open conflict with the democrats in the National Assembly. To solve the gridlock, Norodom Sihanouk dissolved the National Assembly on 17 September and charged Yèm Sambaur to create a new government. Shortly thereafter, Yèm named his new cabinet. He held the presidency of council and the ministries of the Interior and National Defence. He won over **Dap Chhuon** and created the Renovation Party in 1950. He resigned in May 1950 but had little success in getting his party off the ground. His problems with the democrats continued, and Sihanouk's support did not help. In 1952, the Democrat government linked him to the assassination of **Ieu Koeus** two years earlier and incarcerated him, sparking a crisis leading to Sihanouk's dismissal of the **Huy Kanthoul** government. Upon regaining his freedom, Yèm Sambaur became a prominent leader in Sihanouk's Sangkhum party. Sihanouk named him Inspector of Finances in November 1952 and he became minister of the National Economy in **Chan Nak**'s cabinet of November 1953. He served as minister of Finances in Norodom Sihanouk's 6 April 1954 cabinet and in the 17 April cabinet of **Penn Nouth**.

**YOUTH ASSAULT TEAMS (*Thanh Niên Xung Phong*).** These teams came into operation from May 1950 as the Indochina War entered its most intensive phase in eastern Indochina. The government of the **Democratic Republic of Vietnam** used these teams to mobilize, recruit, and support the supplying of large-scale battles now being launched against the French **Expeditionary Corps** and its Vietnamese allies in much of central and northern Indochina. Youth helped open and repair supply routes, ensure communications during battles, and hauled food and military supplies to the front lines. They were first used in real ways during the battle of **Cao Bang** and would be mobilized in even greater ways during the rest of the Indochina War and into the Vietnam War. Statistics on casualties suffered by this unit are unknown. *See also* MYTH OF WAR; EXPERIENCE OF WAR; WOMEN, DEMOCRATIC REPUBLIC OF VIETNAM.

**ZHANG FAKUI (CHANG FA-KWEI, 1896–1980).** First met **Ho Chi Minh** in southern China in the mid-1920s when the first united front saw Chinese communists and nationalists work together against the warlords then dominating most of China. Between 1939 and 1944, General Zhang Fakui commanded troops in the Fourth War Area for the **Republic of China** led by **Chiang Kai-shek**. This zone covered most of Guangdong and Guanxi provinces in southern China. Between 1944 and 1945, he served as commander-in-chief of the 2nd Front Army. *See also* FRANCO-CHINESE ACCORD; CIVIL WAR; 16th PARALLEL.

**ZHANG WENTIAN (1900–1976).** Chinese diplomat who was part of the Chinese delegation to the **Geneva Conference** of 1954. Born in Shanghai, Zhang Wentian joined the **Chinese Communist Party** (CCP) in 1925 and studied at the Sun Yat-Sen University in Moscow. Upon his return to China in 1930, he became minister of the Propaganda Department and eventually a standing member of the CCP's politburo. Despite his support by the Comintern, he survived the **Republic of China**'s attack on the Jiangxi Republic, made the Long March to Yan'an, and carefully survived **Mao Zedong**'s rise to power during this time. Indeed, he served as something of a compromise general secretary of the CCP as Mao Zedong consolidated his power and assumed leadership of the party in 1945. Zhang Wentian's links to the Soviet Union made him a natural choice for ambassador to Moscow, a post he held between 1951 and 1955. He was also vice minister in the Ministry of Foreign Affairs. In 1954, as vice minister and ambassador to the Soviet Union, he served as one of the ranking members in the Chinese delegation led by **Zhou Enlai** to negotiate on Korea and Indochina at the Geneva Conference. He was persecuted during the Cultural Revolution and died in 1976, denied proper health care by Mao. *See also* GENEVA ACCORDS.

**ZHOU ENLAI (1898–1976).** Son of a wealthy Chinese mandarin, Zhou Enlai rose to become one of communist China's greatest diplomats. He studied in Japan and then in France, where he met the future leader of modern Vietnam, **Ho Chi Minh**, for the first time. Zhou Enlai returned to southern China where he joined the **Chinese Communist Party** in 1922 and ran the Whampoa Political Military Academy outside Guangzhou (Canton). There, he renewed his friendship with Ho Chi Minh and supported the latter's efforts to build up a revolutionary movement outside of French Indochina. Following the outbreak of the Chinese civil war, Zhou made the long march to Yan'an and became one of **Mao Zedong**'s closest aides. With the creation of the **People's Republic of China** in 1949, Zhou served long terms as prime minister (1949–1974) and minister of Foreign Affairs (1949–1958).

As director of China's foreign relations, Zhou Enlai supported the Chinese decision to recognize Ho Chi Minh's **Democratic Republic of Vietnam** in January 1950. In 1953, with the death of **Joseph Stalin** and the signing of a cease-fire in Korea, Zhou Enlai joined the Soviets and the French to try to find a peaceful solution to the other hot war in Asia, the Indochinese one. Zhou Enlai played a particularly important role in the **Geneva Conference** of 1954, determined to find a political solution to the war in order to keep the Americans from replacing the French. One of his most important strategies was his move to neutralize former French Indochina as well as the rest of non-communist Asia against the Americans, even if it meant accepting the division of Vietnam in order to realize that goal. While Zhou Enlai did pressure the Vietnamese to rally to this strategy, new documents show that the Vietnamese, in particular Zhou Enlai's longtime ally Ho Chi Minh, shared his fears of American military intervention. By refusing to export "communism" to Asia, as Zhou had promised to **Jawaharlal Nehru** during the Geneva Conference, Zhou was successful in getting communist China accepted as a major player in the Bandung Conference of 1955. *See also* NEUTRALIZATION OF INDOCHINA.

**ZONE (*Khu* or *Khu Chiến*).** In early 1946, the **Democratic Republic of Vietnam** divided the country into 14 administrative zones, each of which was linked by radio or telegraph to the central government located in **Hanoi** until December. The zonal heads would, in turn, rule over a **Resistance and Administrative Committee** reaching down, in theory, to the provincial, district, and village levels of each zone.

**ZONE VII (*Khu VII*).** Created on 10 December 1945, this **Zone** covered roughly the upper swath of **Cochinchina**/Nam Bo for the **Democratic Republic of Vietnam** during the first half of the Indochina War. It included, at the outset, the following provinces: Thu Dau Mot, Bien Hoa, Ba Ria, Cho Lon, Tay Ninh, Gia Dinh, and the city of **Saigon**. To the northeast, Zone VII bordered southern central Vietnam, to the northwest was Cambodia, to the southwest lay **Zone VIII**, and the sea was to the south. In January 1948, the provinces of Tay Ninh, Gia Dinh, Cho Lon, and the city of Saigon were detached from Zone VII in order to create the special zone of Saigon (*Dac Khu Saigon*) under the direction of **To Ki**, deputized by the Political Commissar **Phan Trong Tue**. In May 1950, these territories were returned to Zone VII except for Saigon and its outlying areas, which continued to constitute the special zone of Saigon run by Nguyen Van Thi and **Nguyen Van Linh**. Zone VII was led militarily by General **Nguyen Binh**. In 1946, this zone had 18 military detachments (*Chi Doi*), including those of the **Binh Xuyen**. In 1949, the zone marshalled four main-force regiments. In May 1951, the government dissolved Zone VII and incorporated it into **Inter-Zone for Eastern Nam Bo** (*Phan Lien Khu Mien Dong*).

**ZONE VIII (*Khu VIII*).** Created on 10 December 1945, this **Zone** covered roughly the middle stretch of **Cochinchina**/Nam Bo for the **Democratic Republic of Vietnam** during the first half of the Indochina War. It included, at the outset, the following provinces: Ben Tre, Go Cong, Tan An, My Tho, Sa Dec, Vinh Long, and Tra Vinh. To the east, this zone bordered **Zone VII**, to the north and northwest lay Cambodia, to the southwest was **Zone IX**, and to the south and southeast was the South China Sea. In 1946, Zone VIII was home to five military detachments (*Chi Doi*). In 1949, this zone counted one main-force mobile battalion and two "combined regiments" (*Lien Trung Doan*). **Tran Van Tra** was the first head of Zone VIII, deputized by the Political Commissar **Nguyen Van Vinh**. In March 1951, the government dissolved Zone VIII and incorporated it into the **Inter-Zone for Western Nam Bo** (*Phan Lien Khu Mien Tay*).

**ZONE IX (*Khu IX*).** Created on 10 December 1945, this **Zone** covered roughly the southernmost swath of **Cochinchina**/Nam Bo for the **Democratic Republic of Vietnam** during the first half of the Indochina War. It included, at the outset, the following provinces: Can Tho, Soc Trang, Long Xuyen, Chau Doc, Ha Tien, Bac Lieu, and Rach Gia. To the northeast, this zone bordered **Zone VII**, to the northwest was Cambodia, to the south, southeast and west was the ocean. **Hoang Dinh Giong** (Vu Duc) headed up Zone IX at the outset, deputized by **Phan Trong Tue**, his political commissar. In 1946, this zone had five military detachments (*Chi Doi*). In 1949, the zone marshalled one main-force mobile battalion and two "combined regiments" (*Lien Trung Doan*). In May 1951, **Zones VIII** and IX were dissolved into the **Inter-Zone for Western Nam Bo** (*Phan Lien Khu Mien Tay*).

# Selected Bibliography

This is a selected bibliography of the Indochina War. To have provided a comprehensive bibliography, including the Vietnamese sides, would have meant increasing the size of this bibliography and thus of this dictionary by at least half. I have refrained from doing so for several reasons. First, I preferred to favor the development of a wide range of entries in this dictionary rather than building up a comprehensive bibliography. Second, French scholar Alain Rusico has already provided an in-depth, voluminous bibliography of the Indochina War, focused mainly on French and French-language sources.[1] Third, Edwin Moise's excellent on-line bibliography of the Vietnam Wars complements Ruscio's work nicely, especially for English-language sources.[2] I highly recommend both of these sources to those interested in learning more about the Indochina War. Fourth, a selected bibliography can serve a highly valuable purpose, and one different from that of a comprehensive bibliography, if the selection is made with care. And lastly, David Marr and myself are currently creating an on-line bibliography of Vietnamese-language sources on the Indochina War. The bibliography below aims to provide the reader with the principal secondary and monograph sources on the war.

## Reference Materials, Official Documents, and General Histories

### *Bibliographies*


Brown, F. C. *Annotated Bibliography of Vietnam fiction. 500 Titles Dealing with the Conflict in Vietnam, Cambodia and Laos.* San Francisco, California: Rice Paddy Press, 1986.

Burns, Richard Dean, and Milton Leitenberg. *The Wars in Vietnam, Cambodia and Laos, 1945–1982. A Biographic Guide.* Santa Barbara, California: War / Peace Series, no. 18, A.B.C. Inf. Service, 1984.

Cotter, Michael G. *Vietnam: A Guide to References Sources*. Boston, Massachusetts: G.K. Hall, 1977.

Hickey, John D., and Robert Crispono. *Vietnam Bibliography.* Lexington, Massachusetts: D.C. Heath, 1982.

Jumper, Roy. *Bibliography on the Political and Administrative History of Vietnam 1802–1962.* Saigon, Vietnam: Michigan State Univ., VN Advisory Group, 1962.

Keyes, Charles F. *Southeast Asia Research Tools. Cambodia.* Honolulu, Hawaii: Univ. of Hawaii Press, Southeast Asia Paper, no. 16, 1979.

Keyes, Jane G. (ed.). "A Bibliography of North Vietnamese Publications in the Cornell University Library." *Data Paper*, no. 47. Ithaca, New York: Cornell Univ. Press, Southeast Asia Program, 1962.


1. Alain Ruscio, *La Guerre « Française » d'Indochine (1945–1954). Les Sources de la Connaissance: Bibliographie, Filmographie, Documents Divers.* Paris: Les Indes Savantes, 2002.

2. Edwin Moise, 'Bibliography of the Vietnam War' at http://www.clemson.edu/caah/history/facultypages/EdMoise/bibliography.html.

Lafont, Pierre-Bernard. *Bibliographie du Laos. Tome 1 (1666–1961)*. Paris: École française d'Extrême Orient, Diffusion A. Maisonneuve, 1964.

Marr, David G. *Vietnam Biographical Database.* Canberra, Australia: Research School of Pacific and Asian Studies, 1994.

Marr, David G., and Kristine Alilunas-Rodgers. *Vietnam.* Oxford, England: Clio Press Ltd, Word Bibliographies Series, vol. 147, 1992.

République du Vietnam. *The Republic of Vietnam: A Biography.* Washington, DC: U.S. Department of State, External Research Staff, 1963.

Ruscio, Alain. *La Première Guerre d'Indochine (1945–1954). Bibliographie.* Paris: Ed. L'Harmattan, 1987.

——— (ed.). *La guerre 'française' d'Indochine (1945–1954). Les sources de la connaissance. Bibliographie, filmographie, documents divers.* Paris: Les Indes Savantes, 2002.

Sage, William, and Judith Henchy. *Laos. A Bibliography.* Singapore: Inst. of Southeast Asian St., 1986.

Singleton, Carl. *Vietnam Studies. An Annotated Bibliography.* Lanham, Maryland: The Scarecrow Press, Inc.; Pasadena, California: Salem Press; 1997.

## *Historical Dictionaries, Encyclopedias, Historical Almanacs and Atlases*

Académie des Sciences d'Outre-mer, *Derniers chefs d'un Empire.* Paris: Académie des Sciences d'Outre-mer, 1972.

*Annuaire de l'association des anciens élèves de l'E.N.F.O.M.* Paris: no editor indicated, editions of 1983 and 2003).

*Annuaire diplomatique,* France: Ministère des affaires étrangères.

Bộ Quốc Phòng. *Từ Điển Kỹ Thuật Quân Sự.* Hanoi: Nhà Xuất Bản Tổng Cục Chính Trị, 1990.

———. Vien Lich Su Quan Su Viet Nam, *55 nam Quan Doi Nhan Dan Viet Nam (Bien Nien Su Kien).* Hanoi: Nhà Xuất Bản Quân Đội Nhân Dân, 1999.

———. Vien Lich Su Quan Su Viet Nam, *Viet Nam The Ky XX : Nhung Su Kien Quan Su* . Hanoi: Nhà Xuất Bản Quân Đội Nhân Dân, 2001.

Bodin, Michel. *Dictionnaire de la guerre d'Indochine.* Paris: Commission Française d'Histoire Militaire, Institut de Stratégie Comparée, Economica, 2004.

Clauzel, Jean (ed.). *La France d'Outre-mer (1930–1960): Témoignages d'administrateurs et de magistrats*, Paris: Karthala, 2003.

Corfeld, Justin, and Laura Summers. *Historical Dictionary of Cambodia.* Lanham, Maryland: The Scarecrow Press, 2003.

Coston, Henry *et al. Dictionnaire de la politique française.* Paris: La Librarie Française, 2 vol., 1967 and 1972.

*Current Biography*. Bronx, New York: H. W. Wilson Co., 1940–1985.

Dalloz, Jacques. *Dictionnaire de la guerre d'Indochine, 1945–1954.* Paris: Armand Colin, 2006.

Đào Xuân Chức. *Nguồn Tư Liệu Ảnh về Cuộc Kháng Chiến Chống Thực Dân Pháp (1945–1954).* Hanoi: Nhà Xuất Bản Chính Trị Quốc Gia, 2002.

*Dictionnaire biographique français contemporain.* Paris: Pharos, Centre International de documentation, 1950.

*Dictionnaire des parlementaires français, 1940–1958.* Paris: Assemblée nationale, La Documentation française, 3 vol., 1988, 1992 and 1994.

Đinh Xuân Lâm, Chương Thâu. *Danh Nhân Lịch Sử Việt Nam, Tập Hai.* Hanoi: Nhà Xuất Bản Giáo Dục, 1988.

Duiker, William J., and Bruce Lockhart. *Historical Dictionary of Vietnam.* Lanham, Maryland: The Scarecrow Press, 2006 (3rd edition).

Hội Đồng Quốc Gia Chỉ Đạo Biên Soạn Tử Điển Bách Khoa Việt Nam. *Từ Điển Bách Khoa Việt Nam,* volumes 1–3. Hanoi: Nhà Xuất Bản Từ Điển Bách Khoa, 2003.

*Hommes et Destins. Dictionnaire biographique d'Outre-mer.* Tomes I à IX. Paris: Académie des Sciences d'Outre-mer, 1975–1989.

Julliard, Jacques, Michel Winock *et al. Dictionnaire des intellectuels français. Les personnes. Les lieux. Les moments.* Paris: Seuil, 1996.

Lê Trung Hoa (ed.). *Từ Điển Địa Danh Thành Phố Sài Gòn-Hồ Chí Minh.* Hồ Chí Minh City: Nhà Xuất Bản Trẻ, 2003.

Liauzu, Claude. *Dictionnaire de la colonisation française.* Paris: Larousse, 2007.

Moussay, Gérard, and Brigitte Appavou. *Répertoire des membres de la société des missions étrangères, 1659–2004.* Paris: Archives des Missions étrangères, 2004.

Nguyễn Huyền Anh. *Việt Nam Danh Nhân Từ Điển.* Saigon: Nhà Sách Khai Trí (3rd edition), introduction dated 1970.

Nguyễn Quốc Dũng *et al. 55 Năm Quân Đội Nhân Dân Việt Nam (Biên Niên Sự Kiện).* Hanoi: Nhà Xuất Bản Quân Đội Nhân Dân, 1999.

Nguyễn Quốc Thắng, Nguyễn Bá Thế. *Từ Điển Nhân Vật Lịch Sử Việt Nam.* Hanoi: Nhà Xuất Bản Khoa Học Xã Hội, 1992.

Nha Xuat Ban Chinh Tri Quoc Gia, *Bach Khoa Tri Thuc Quoc Phong Toan Dan,* Ha Noi: Nha Xuat Ban Chinh Tri Quoc Gia, 2003.

Pham, David Lan. *Vietnam History Dictionary.* volume I, Bloomington, Indiana: 1st Book Library, 2001.

———. *Vietnam History Dictionary.* volume II, Bloomington, Indiana: 1st Book Library, 2002.

Phạm Đình Nhân. *Những Sự Kiện Lịch Sử Việt Nam.* Hanoi: Nhà Xuất Bản Văn Hóa Thông Tin, 2002.

Phạm Văn Trà, Nguyễn Huy Hiệu *et al. Bộ Quốc Phòng, 1945–2000, Biên Niên, Sự Kiện.* Hanoi, Việt Nam: Nhà Xuất Bản Quân Đội Nhân Dân, 2003.

Phan Ngọc Liên (ed.). *Từ Điển Tri Thức Lịch Sử Phổ Thông Thế Kỷ XX.* Hanoi: Nhà Xuất Bản Đại Học Quốc Gia Hà Nội, 2002.

Phùng Quang Thanh *et al. Từ Điển Bách Khoa Quân Sự Việt Nam.* Hanoi: Nhà Xuất Bản Quân Đội Nhân Dân, 2004.

Rioux, Jean-Pierre (ed.). *Dictionnaire de la France coloniale.* Paris: Flammarion, 2007.

Sirinelli, Jean François *et al. Dictionnaire historique de la vie politique française au XXe siècle.* Paris: P.U.F., 1995.

*Souverains et notabilités d'Indochine.* Hanoi: Gouvernement général, Imprimerie d'Extrême-Orient, 1943.

Stuart-Fox, Martin, and Mary Kooyman. *Historical Dictionary of Laos.* Lanham, Maryland: The Scarecrow Press, 2001 (2nd edition).

Tertrais, Hugues. *Atlas des guerres d'Indochine, 1940–1990: De l'Indochine française à l'ouverture internationale.* Paris: Autrement, 2004.

Thompson, Virginia, and Richard Adloff. *Who's Who in SE Asia (August 1945–December 1950): Indochina.* microfilm copy Wason DS540 A2 T47, Cornell Univ. Library.

*Thompson-Adloff collection on Southeast Asia, #4398.* Division of Rare and Manuscript Collections, Cornell Univ. Library.

Trần Quỳnh Cư, Nguyễn Hữu Đạo *et al. Việt Nam, Những Sự Kiện Lịch Sử (1945–1975).* Hanoi: Nhà Xuất Bản Giáo Dục, 2002.

Trinh Van Thao. *Les compagnons de Hô Chi Minh: Histoire d'un engagement intellectuel au Viêt-Nam.* Paris: Éditions Karthala, 2004.

Trịnh Vương Hồng, Lê Đình Sỹ *et al. Việt Nam, Thế Kỷ XX, Những Sự Kiện Quân Sự.* Hanoi: Nhà Xuất Bản Quân Đội Nhân Dân, 2001.

Tucker, Spencer C. (ed.). *Encyclopedia of the Vietnam War. A Political, Social and Military History.* 3 vols., Santa Barbara, California: ABC Clio, 1978.

Vaïsse, Maurice (ed.). *Dictionnaire des relations internationales au 20e siècle.* Paris: Armand Colin, 2000.

Viện Khoa Học Xã Hội Việt Nam, Viện Sử Học. *Việt Nam, Những Sự Kiện, 1945–1986.* Hanoi: Nhà Xuất Bản Khoa Học Xã Hội, 1990.

Wayne, Northcutt (ed.). *Historical Dictionary of the French IVth and Vth Republics, 1946–1991.* Westport, Connecticut: Greenwood Press, 1992.

## *Official Document Collections*

Bodinier, Gilbert. *La Guerre d'Indochine, 1945–1954. Textes et documents, Vol. 1, Le retour de la France en Indochine, 1945–1946.* Vincennes: Service historique de l'armée de Terre, 1987.

———. *La Guerre d'Indochine, 1945–1954. Textes et documents français et Viet Minh, Vol. 2, Règlement politique ou solution militaire? 1947.* Vincennes: Service Historique de l'armée de Terre, 1989.

Đảng Cộng Sản Việt Nam. *Văn Kiện Đảng, Toàn Tập, Tập 7, 1940–1945.* Hanoi: Nhà Xuất Bản Chính Trị Quốc Gia, 2000.

———. *Văn Kiện Đảng, Toàn Tập, Tập 8, 1945–1947.* Hanoi: Nhà Xuất Bản Chính Trị Quốc Gia, 2000.

———. *Văn Kiện Đảng, Toàn Tập, Tập 9, 1948.* Hanoi: Nhà Xuất Bản Chính Trị Quốc Gia, 2001.

———. *Văn Kiện Đảng, Toàn Tập, Tập 10, 1949.* Hanoi: Nhà Xuất Bản Chính Trị Quốc Gia, 2001.

———. *Văn Kiện Đảng, Toàn Tập, Tập 11, 1950.* Hanoi: Nhà Xuất Bản Chính Trị Quốc Gia, 2001.

———. *Văn Kiện Đảng, Toàn Tập, Tập 12, 1951.* Hanoi: Nhà Xuất Bản Chính Trị Quốc Gia, 2001.

———. *Văn Kiện Đảng, Toàn Tập, Tập 13, 1952.* Hanoi: Nhà Xuất Bản Chính Trị Quốc Gia, 2001.

———. *Văn Kiện Đảng, Toàn Tập, Tập 14, 1953.* Hanoi: Nhà Xuất Bản Chính Trị Quốc Gia, 2001.

———. *Văn Kiện Đảng, Toàn Tập, Tập 15, 1954.* Hanoi: Nhà Xuất Bản Chính Trị Quốc Gia, 2001.

Hồ Chí Minh. *Oeuvres choisies* (1922–1967). Paris: F. Maspero, Coll. Tricontinentale, 1967.

———. *Toàn Tập.* 7 vols. Hanoi: Nhà Xuất Bản Mac Lê-Nin, Sự Thật.

Truong Chinh. *Écrits*. Hanoi: Éditions Langues Étrangères, 1977.

Ủy Ban Trung Ương Mặt Trận Tổ Quốc Việt Nam. *Văn Kiện Đảng Về Mặt Trận Dân Tộc Thống Nhất Việt Nam, Tập II (1945–1977).* Hanoi: Nhà Xuất Bản Chính Trị Quốc Gia, 2001.

*Văn Kiện Quân Sự Của Đảng, Tập I (Từ 1930 Đến Tháng 8-1945).* Hanoi: Nhà Xuất Bản Quân Đội Nhân Dân, 1969.

*Văn Kiện Quân Sự Của Đảng, Tập II (Từ Ngày 2-9-1945 Đến Ngày 10-10-1950).* Hanoi: Nhà Xuất Bản Quân Đội Nhân Dân, 1976.

*Văn Kiện Quân Sự Của Đảng, Tập III (Từ Tháng 2-1951 Đến Tháng 9-1954).* Hanoi: Nhà Xuất Bản Quân Đội Nhân Dân, 1977.

## Statistical Compilations

Clodfelter, Micheal. *Warfare and Armed Conflicts: A Statistical Reference to Casualty and Other Figures, 1618–1991. volume II: 1900–1991,* Jefferson, North Carolina: McFarland & Company, 1992.

———. *Vietnam in Military Statistics. A History of the Indochina Wars, 1772–1991.* Jefferson, North Carolina: McFarland and Company, 1995.

Viện Lịch Sử Quân Sự Việt Nam, Bộ Quốc Phòng. *Thống Kê Các Chiến Dịch Trong Kháng Chiến Chống Pháp, Kháng Chiếm Chống Mỹ, 1945–1975, Tập 1,2.* Hanoi: Nhà Xuất Bản Quân Đội Nhân Dân, 1993.

## Archival Finding Guides

Devos, Jean-Claude, Jean Nicot, and Philippe Schilinger. *Inventaire des Archives de l'Indochine. Sous-série 10H (1867–1956).* 2 vols. Château de Vincennes, France: Service Historique de l'armée de Terre, 1990.

## General Histories of the Indochina War

Allen, Joe. *Vietnam: The (Last) War the U.S. Lost*. Chicago, Illinois: Haymarket Books, 2008.

Anderson, David L. *The Columbia History of the Vietnam War*. New York: Columbia Univ. Press, 2010.

Arevian, Christian L. *A Conservative View of the Vietnam Era*. Booksurge, 2006.

Ban Chỉ Đạo Tổng Kết Chiến Tranh Trực Thuộc Bộ Chính Trị. *Chiến Tranh Cách Mạng Việt Nam, 1945–1975, Thắng Lợi và Bài Học*. Hanoi: Nhà Xuất Bản Chính Trị Quốc Gia, 2000.

Bodard, Lucien. *La guerre d'Indochine: L'enlisement, l'humiliation, l'aventure*. Paris: Grasset, 1997.

Bradley, Mark Philip. *Vietnam at War*. New York: Oxford Univ. Press, 2009.

Brocheux, Pierre, and Daniel Hémery. *Indochine: La colonisation ambiguë, 1858–1954*. Paris: Éditions la Découverte, 2001, 2nd updated printing.

———. *Indochina: An Ambiguous Colonization, 1858–1954*. Berkeley, California: Univ. of California Press, 2009, 2nd updated printing.

Cesari, Laurent. *L'Indochine en guerre 1945–1993*. Paris: Belin-Sup Histoire, 1995.

Chaffard, Georges. *Les deux guerres du Vietnam, de Valluy à Westmorland*. Paris: La Table Ronde, 1969.

Dalloz, Jacques. *La guerre d'Indochine, 1945–1954*. Paris: Seuil, 1987.

Devillers, Philippe. *Histoire du Vietnam de 1940 à 1952*. Paris: Seuil, 1952.

Devillers, Philippe, and Jean Lacouture. *Vietnam, de la Guerre française à la Guerre américaine*. Paris: Seuil, Coll. Frontière ouverte, 1969.

Đoàn Khuê, Văn Tiến Dũng *et al*. *Tổng Kết Cuộc Kháng Chiến Chống Thực Dân Pháp, Thắng Lợi và Bài Học*. Hanoi: Nhà Xuất Bản Chính Trị Quốc Gia, 1996.

Duiker, William J. *Sacred War. Nationalism and Revolution in a Divided Vietnam*. New York: McGraw Hill, 1995.

Dunn, Peter M. *The First Vietnam War*. London: C. Hurst & Co., 1985.

Elliott, David W. P. *The Vietnamese War: Revolution and Social Change in the Mekong Delta, 1930–1975*. New York: East Gate Books, 2007 [2003].

Fall, Bernard B. *Political development of Viet-Nam, VJ-Day to the Geneva Cease-Fire*. PhD thesis, Graduate School of Syracuse University, October 1954.

———. *Le Viet-Minh, La République démocratique du Viet-Nam, 1945–1960*. Paris: Armand Colin, 1960.

———. *Street without Joy: Indochina at War, 1946–1954*. Harrisburg, Pennsylvania: Stackpole, 1961.

———. *Indochine 1946–1962, Chronique d'une guerre révolutionnaire*. Paris: Laffont, 1962.

Fleury, G. *La guerre en Indochine 1945–1954*. Paris: Plon, 1994.

de Folin, Jacques. *Indochine 1940–1955: La fin d'un rêve*. Paris: Perrin, 1993.

Franchini, Philippe. *Les guerres d'Indochine. La première histoire exhaustive des guerres française et américaine*. 2 vols. Paris: Pygmalion G. Watelet, 1988.

Goscha, Christopher E. *Vietnam: Un Etat né de la guerre*. Paris: Armand Colin, 2011.

Goscha, Christopher E., and Benoît de Tréglodé (eds). *Naissance d'un État-Parti: Le Viêt Nam depuis 1945*. Paris: Les Indes Savantes, 2004.

Gras, Yves. *Histoire de la guerre d'Indochine*. Paris: Denoel, 1992.

Hammer, Ellen J. *The Struggle for Indochina.* Stanford, California: Stanford Univ. Press, 1954.

Hess, Gary R. *Vietnam: Explaining America's Lost War*. Malden, Massachusetts: Blackwell Publishing, 2009.

Hoàng Văn Thái, Trần Văn Quang *et al. Lịch Sử Cuộc Kháng Chiến Chống Thực Dân Pháp, 1945–1954, Tập I.* Hanoi: Nhà Xuất Bản Quân Đội Nhân Dân, 1994.

———. *Lịch Sử Cuộc Kháng Chiến Chống Thực Dân Pháp, 1945–1954, Tập II.* Hanoi: Nhà Xuất Bản Quân Đội Nhân Dân, 1995.

Hunt, David. *Vietnam's Southern Revolution: From Peasant Insurrection to Total War*. Amherst, Massachusetts: Univ. of Massachusetts Press, 2008.

Lancaster, Donald. *The Emancipation of French Indochina.* London: Oxford Univ. Press, 1961.

Langer, Paul F., and Joseph Jeremiah Zasloff. *North Vietnam and the Pathet Lao. Partners in the Struggle for Laos*. Cambridge, Massachusetts: Harvard Univ. Press, 1970.

Lockhart, Greg. *Nation in Arms: The Origins of the People's Army of Vietnam*. Wellington, New Zealand: Allen & Unwin, 1989.

Lưu Văn Lợi, Nguyễn Hồng Thạch. *Pháp Tái Chiếm Đông Dương và Chiến Tranh Lạnh.* Hanoi: Nhà Xuất Bản Công An Nhân Dân, 2002.

MacAlister, John T. Jr. *Vietnam. The Origins of Revolution.* New York: Princeton Univ., The Center of International Studies, A.A. Knopf, Ed., 1969.

Meuleau, Marc. *Des pionniers en Extrême-Orient: Histoire de la Banque de l'Indochine (1875–1975)*. Paris: Fayard, 1990.

Mus, Paul. *Vietnam, sociologie d'une guerre.* Paris: Seuil, Coll. Esprit/Frontière ouverte, 1952.

Pike, Douglas. *Popular Army of Vietnam*. Novato, California: Presidio Press, 1986.

Prados, John. *Vietnam: The History of an Unwinnable War, 1945–1975*. Lawrence, Kansas: Univ. of Kansas Press, 2009.

Ruscio, Alain. *La guerre française d'Indochine*. Bruxelles: Éditions complexes, 1992.

Smith, Ralph B. *Communist Indochina*. London: Routledge, 2008.

Tanham, George K. *Communist Revolutionary Warfare: The Viet Minh in Indochina.* New York: Praeger, 1961.

Tertrais, Hugues. *La piastre et le fusil: Le coût de la guerre d'Indochine, 1945–1954.* Paris: Comité pour l'histoire économique et financière de la France, 2002.

Teulières, André. *L'Indochine, guerres et paix.* Paris: Lavauzelle, 1985.

Toinet, Raymond. *Une guerre de 35 ans. Indochine – Vietnam 1940–1975.* Paris: Lavauzelle, 1998.

Tønnesson, Stein. *Vietnam 1946: How the War Began*. Berkeley & Los Angeles, California: Univ. of California Press, 2010.

Tran Van Don. *Les guerres du Vietnam. Un quart de siècle au Vietnam du Sud.* Paris: Vertiges Publications, 1985.

de Tréglodé, Benoît. *Héros et Révolution au Viêt Nam*. Paris: Ed. L'Harmattan, 2001.

Valette, Jacques. *La guerre d'Indochine, 1945–1954.* Paris: Armand Colin, 1994.

## The French Fourth Republic and the Democratic Republic of Vietnam at War

### *Biographies and Memoirs*

Arrighi, Jean. *Indochine, les combats oubliés.* Paris: Ed. L'Harmattan, 1992.

Auriol, Vincent. *Journal du Septennat.* Vols. I à VII. Paris: Armand Colin, 1991.

Aussaresses, Paul. *Pour la France. Services Spéciaux, 1942–1955.* Paris: Ed. du Rocher, 2001.

Ban Nghiên Cứu Lịch Sử Đảng Trung Ương. *Chủ Tịch Hồ Chí Minh, Tiểu Sử và Sự Nghiệp.* Hanoi: Nhà Xuất Bản Chính Trị Quốc Gia, 2005.

Bergot, Erwan. *Deuxième classe à Dien Bien Phu.* Paris: La Table Ronde, 1964.

Bigeard, Marcel. *Pour une parcelle de gloire.* Paris: Plon, 1975.

———. *Lettres d'Indochine.* Paris: Éditions 1, 1998.

Blagov, Sergei. *Honest Mistakes: The Life and Death of Trình Minh Thế (1922–1955): South Vietnam's Alternative Leader.* Huntington, New York: Nova Science Publishers, Inc., 2001.

Bộ Quốc Phòng, Viện Lịch Sử Quân Sử Quân Sự Việt Nam. *Đại Tướng Nguyễn Chí Thanh, Nhà Chính Trị Quân Sự Lỗi Lạc.* Hanoi: Nhà Xuất Bản Quân Đội Nhân Dân, 1997.

Bộ Tư Lệnh Quân Đội Quân Khu 5. *Nguyễn Chánh, Con Người và Sự Nghiệp.* Hanoi: Nhà Xuất Bản Quân Đội Nhân Dân, 1997.

Boudarel, Georges. *Giap.* Paris: Ed. Atlas, 1977.

———. *Autobiographie.* Paris: Jacques Bertoin, 1991.

Boulet, Luc. *Chroniques indochinoises, 1945–1955.* Steenvoorde, France: Ed. Houtland, 1997.

Bourely, Pierre. *Des canons dans la rizière: combat pour un paradoxe.* Draguignan, France: Association des Amis du Musée du Canon et des Artilleurs, 1996.

Bourry, Jacques. *Itinéraire d'un soldat.* Marseille, France: Chez l'Auteur, P. Tacussel, 1989.

Brett, Gérard. *Les supplétifs en Indochine, 1951–1953.* Paris: Ed. L'Harmattan, Coll. Mémoires asiatiques, 1996.

Brocheux, Pierre. *Ho Chi Minh. Du révolutionnaire à l'icône.* Paris: Payot et Rivages (Biographies Payot), 2003.

Brohard, René. *L'année du Tigre.* Le Gaure Montlar/Gervannes, Nil Ed., 1994.

Bruge, Roger. *Un sergent para.* Paris: Ed. France-Empire, 1959.

Bùi Anh Tuấn *et al. Đồng Chí Trần Quốc Hoàn với Công An Nhân Dân Việt Nam.* Hanoi: Nhà Xuất Bản Công An Nhân Dân, 2004.

Bui Xuan Quang *et al. Ho Chi Minh, l'homme et son héritage.* Paris: Duong Moi – La voie nouvelle, 1990.

Cesca, Pierre. *Journal de marche, Indochine.* Saint-Jean des Mauvrets, France: Chez l'auteur, 1993.

Chang Fa K'uei. *Memoirs of the Resistance War.* Hong Kong: United Revue, 1962.

Chateau-Jobert. *Feux et Lumières sur ma trace. Faits de guerre et de paix.* Paris: Presses de la Cité, 1978.

Chaudron, Roger. *Les allées du Phnom.* Paris: Ed. des Ecrivains, 1998.

Chaumont-Guitry, Guy de. *Lettres d'Indochine. Du Rhin-et-Danube à la Plaine des Joncs.* Paris: Ed. Alsatia, 1951.

Cholet, Raoul. *Planteurs en Indochine française.* Paris: La Pensée Universelle, 1981.

Coudert, Jack. *La dernière luciole. Les Dakotas parachutés à Dien Bien Phu.* Reims, France: Chez l'auteur, 2000.

Đặng Văn Thái. *Hoạt Động Đối Ngoại Của Chủ Tịch Hồ Chí Minh Trong Kháng Chiến Chống Thực Dân Pháp.* Hanoi: Nhà Xuất Bản Chính Trị Quốc Gia, 2004.

Đào Duy Anh. *Hồi Ký Đào Duy Anh (Nhớ Nghĩ Chiều Hôm).* Hồ Chí Minh City: Nhà Xuất Bản Trẻ, 2000.

Duiker, William J. *Ho Chi Minh: A Life.* New York: Hyperion Books, 2001.

Ely, Paul. *Mémoires*, Vol. 1, *L'Indochine dans la tourmente.* Paris: Plon, 1964.

Estival, Bernard. *L'enseigne dans le delta.* Versailles, France: Ed. Editions Les Sept Vents, 1989.

Faure, Edgar. *Mémoires.* Vol. 1. Paris: Plon, 1982.

Froment-Meurice, Henri. *Vu du Quai. Mémoires, 1945–1983.* Paris: Fayard, 1998.

Gaget, Robert. *Commando parachutiste.* Paris: Éditions Jacques Grancher, Coll. Témoignages pour l'Histoire, 1992.

Genty, Robert. *Ultimes secours pour Dien Bien Phu, 1953–1954.* Paris: Ed. L'Harmattan, Coll. Mémoires asiatiques, 1994.

Guillaume, Roger. *La guerre était notre lot.* Nice, France: Chez l'auteur, 1980.

Guillot, Maurice. *La grande occasion.* Paris: Nouvelles Éditions Debresse, 1959.

Guiraud, Georges-Henri. *Aux frontières de l'enfer.* Paris: La Nef de Paris, 1956.

Hémery, Daniel. *Ho Chi Minh. De l'Indochine au Viet Nam.* Paris: Gallimard, 1990.

Hoàng Quốc Việt. *Chặng Đường Nóng Bỏng : Hồi Ký.* Hanoi: Nhà Xuất Bản Lao Động, 1985.

Hoang Van Chi. *From Colonialism to Communism: A Case History of North Vietnam.* New York: Frederick A. Praeger, 1968 (3rd ed.).

Hoàng Văn Thái, Trần Độ. *Trận Đánh Ba Mươi Năm, Ký Sự Lịch Sử, Tập I.* Hanoi: Nhà Xuất Bản Quân Đội Nhân Dân, 1983.

———. *Trận Đánh Ba Mươi Năm, Ký Sự Lịch Sử, Tập II.* Hanoi: Nhà Xuất Bản Quân Đội Nhân Dân, 1985.

Hữu Mai. *Trận Đánh Cuối Cùng.* Hanoi: Nhà Xuất Bản Tác Phẩm Mới, 1977.

Juin, Alphonse. *Mémoires*, Tome II. Paris: Librairie Arthène Fayard, 1960.

Keraly, Hugues. *Hervé de Blignières, Un combattant dans les tourmentes du siècle.* Paris: Albin Michel, 1990.

Lê Giản. *Những Ngày Sóng Gió, Hồi Ký.* Hanoi: Nhà Xuất Bản Thanh Niên, 2003.

Lê Khánh Chi. *Phạm Ngọc Thạch, Le Combattant, L'Homme de Science.* Unknown Publisher, No date.

Lê Văn Hiến. *Nhật Ký Của Một Bộ Trưởng, Tập I-II.* Đà Nẵng, Việt Nam: Nhà Xuất Bản Đà Nẵng, 1995. 2 vols.

Leroy, Jean. *Un homme dans la rizière.* Paris: Éditions de Paris, 1955.

Leroy, Jean. *Fils de la rizière.* Paris: Robert Laffont, 1977.

Loustau, Henri-Jean. *Les derniers combats d'Indochine, 1952–1954.* Paris: Albin Michel, Coll. Les Combattants, 1984.

———. *Les deux bataillons. Cochinchine-Tonkin, 1945–1952.* Paris: Albin Michel, Coll. Les Combattants, 1987.

Mai Chí Thọ. *Hồi Ức Mai Chí Thọ, Tập I-II. Những Mẩu Chuyện Đời Tôi.* T.P. Hồ Chí Minh, Việt Nam: Nhà Xuất Bản Trẻ, 2001. 2 vols.

Marty, André. *L'affaire Marty.* Paris: Ed. des Deux-Rives, 1955.

Minh Quang. *Nguyễn Sơn, Vị Tướng Huyền Thoại.* T.P. Hồ Chí Minh, Việt Nam: Nhà Xuất Bản Trẻ, 2001.

Montaron, Georges. *Quoi qu'il en coûte.* Paris: Libr. Stock, 1975.

Navarre, Henri. *Agonie de l'Indochine* (1953–1954). Paris: Plon, 1956.

Nghiêm Kế Tổ. *Việt Nam Máu Lửa.* Los Alamitos, California: Xuân Thu, 1989.

Ngô Vi Thiện, Nguyễn Hữu Lê *et al. Trần Đăng Ninh, Con Người Và Lịch Sử.* Hanoi: Nhà Xuất Bản Chính Trị Quốc Gia, 1996.

Ngô Vương Anh, Nguyễn Thu Hương, Phạm Chinh *et al. Chúng Tôi Đánh Giặc Như Thế: Truyện Kể Trên Thao Trường.* Hanoi: Nhà Xuất Bản Quân Đội Nhân Dân, 2000.

Nguyễn Đôn. *Bình Minh Ba Tơ.* Hanoi: Nhà Xuất Bản Quân Đội Nhân Dân, 2001.

Nguyên Hùng. *Nguyễn Bình, Huyền Thoại Và Sự Thật.* T.P. Hồ Chí Minh: Nhà Xuất Bản Văn Học, 1995.

———. *Nam Bộ, Những Nhân Vật Một Thời Vang Bóng.* Hanoi: Nhà Xuất Bản Công An Nhân Dân, 2002.

Nguyễn Phúc Luân. *Ngoại Giao Hồ Chí Minh, Lấy Chí Nhân Thay Cường Bạo.* Hanoi: Nhà Xuất Bản Công An Nhân Dân, 2004.

Nguyễn Phương Nam. *Những Viên Tướng Ngã Ngựa.* Hanoi: Nhá Xuất Bản Lao Động, 2004.

Nguyễn Thanh, Lưu Vinh *et al. Những Kỷ Niệm Sâu Sắc Về Bộ Trưởng Trần Quốc Hoàn.* Hanoi: Nhà Xuất Bản Công An Nhân Dân, 2004.

Nguyễn Thế Trường. *Trung Tướng Nguyễn Bình.* Hanoi: Nhà Xuất Bản Quân Đội Nhân Dân, 2002.

Nguyễn Thị Ngọc Hải. *Trần Quốc Hương, Người Thầy Của Những Nhà Tình Báo Huyền Thoại.* Hanoi: Nhà Xuất Bản Công An Nhân Dân, 2004.

Nguyễn Tư Đương. *Đường Mòn Trên Biển, Ký Sự*. Hanoi: Nhà Xuất Bản Quân Đội Nhân Dân, 1986.

Nguyễn Văn Trấn. *Hồi Ký Chúng Tôi Làm Báo*. T.P. Hồ Chí Minh: Nhà Xuất Bản Văn Nghệ, 2001.

Nguyễn Viết Hưng (ed.). *Chân Dung Năm Cố Bộ Trưởng Ngoại Giao*. Hanoi: Nhà Xuất Bản Chính Trị Quốc Gia, 2005.

Nguyễn Xuân Chu. *Hồi Ký* (Mémoires). Houston, Texas: Văn Hoa, 1996.

Nhiều Tác Giả. *Khúc Bi Tráng Trên Sông Vàm Cỏ, Chuyện Chưa Biết Về Người Anh Hùng*. Hanoi: Nhà Xuất Bản Công An Nhân Dân, 2008.

*Những Người Cùng Thời*. T. P. Hồ Chí Minh: Nhà Xuất Bản Trẻ, 2002.

Phạm Chí Nhân. *Nhà Chiến Lược Quân Sự Hồ Chí Minh*. Hanoi: Nhà Xuất Bản Chính Trị Quốc Gia, 2004.

Phạm Khắc Hòe. *Từ Triều Đình Huế Dến Chiến Khu Việt Bắc, Hồi Ký*. Hanoi: Nhà Xuất Bản Hà Nội, 1983.

Phạm Mai Hùng. *Chủ Tịch Hồ Chí Minh Ở Pháp Năm 1946*. Hanoi: Nhà Xuất Bản Thống Kê, 2001.

Phạm Ngọc Thạch. *Những Ngày Tháng Tám*. Hanoi: Nhà Xuất Bản Văn Học, 1961.

Phạm Xuân Xứng, Vũ Thiệt Chủy *et al*. *Hồi Ký Về Đồng Chí Trường Chinh*. Hanoi: Nhà Xuất Bản Chính Trị Quốc Gia, 1997.

Phan Hoàng. *Phỏng Vấn Tướng Lĩnh Việt Nam, Tuyển Tập*. T.P. Hồ Chí Minh: Nhà Xuất Bản Trẻ, 2000.

Phan Văn Hoàng. *Cao Triều Pháp, Nghĩa Khí Nam Bộ*. T.P. Hồ Chí Minh: Nhà Xuất Bản Trẻ, 2001.

Pignon, Léon. *Léon Pignon, 1908–1976: Un homme de coeur au service de l'Outre-mer français*. Paris: Académie des Sciences d'Outre-mer, 1988.

Raphael-Leygues, Jacques. *Ponts de lianes. Missions en Indochine, 1945–1954*. Paris: Hachette, 1976.

Rolland, André. *L'action dans l'ombre: avant Dien Bien Phu*. Paris: Ed. du Dauphin, 1971.

Sabatier, Gabriel. *Le destin de l'Indochine. Souvenirs et documents (1941–1951)*. Paris: Plon, 1952.

Sainteny, Jean. *Histoire d'une paix manquée. Indochine, 1945–1947*. Paris: Fayard, Coll. Les grandes Etudes contemporaines, 1967.

Salan, Dominique. *Raoul Salan: Le destin d'un homme simple*. Biarritz: Atlantica, 2003.

Salan, Raoul. *Mémoires. Fin d'un Empire, Volume I: Le sens d'un engagement, juin 1899–septembre 1946*. Paris: Presses de la Cité, 1970.

———. *Mémoires. Fin d'un Empire, Volume II: Le Viet Minh, mon adversaire, octobre 1946–octobre 1954*. Paris: Presses de la cité, 1971.

Norodom Sihanouk. *Norodom Sihanouk: L'Indochine vue de Pékin*. Paris: Seuil, 1972 (interviews with Jean Lacouture).

Simon, Guy. *Chroniques de Cochinchine (1951–1956)*. Paris: Lavauzelle, 1996.

Song Hào. *Hồi Ký và Tác Phẩm*. Hanoi: Nhà Xuất Bản Quân Đội Nhân Dân, 2005.

Thăng Long. *Thời Gian và Thử Thách*. T.P. Hồ Chí Minh: Nhà Xuất Bản Trẻ, 2002.

Thevenet, Amédée *et al*. *La Guerre d'Indochine racontée par ceux qui l'ont vécue. Un devoir de mémoire assumé ensemble*. Paris: Ed. France-Empire, 2001.

Thierry d'Argenlieu, Georges. *Chroniques d'Indochine*. Paris: Albin Michel, 1985.

Tongas, Gérard. *J'ai vécu dans l'enfer communiste au nord Vietnam*. Paris: Nouvelles Ed. Debresse, 1960.

Trần Công Tấn. *Hà Văn Lâu, Người Đi Từ Bến Làng Sình*. Hanoi: Nhà Xuất Bản Phụ Nữ, 2004.

Trần Đình Nghiêm (ed). *Lê Duẩn, Một Nhà Lãnh Đạo Lỗi Lạc, Một Tư Duy Sáng Tạo Lớn Của Các Mạng Việt Nam (Hồi Ký)*. Hanoi: Nhà Xuất Bản Chính Trị Quốc Gia, 2002.

——— (ed). *Trường Chinh, Một Nhân Cách Lớn, Một Nhà Lãnh Đạo Kiệt Xuất Của Cách Mạng Việt Nam (Hồi Ký)*. Hanoi: Nhà Xuất Bản Chính Trị Quốc Gia, 2002.

Trần Kiếm Qua, Nguyễn Đồng Thoại (translator). *Hoàng Hà Nhớ Hồng Hà Thương, Lưỡng Quốc Tướng Quân Nguyễn Sơn*. Hanoi: Nhà Xuất Bản Văn Học, 2001.

Trần Trọng Kim. *Một Cơn Gió Bụi*. Saigon: Nhà Xuất Bản Vĩnh Sơn, 1969.

Trần Trọng Trung. *Hoàng Văn Thái, Những Năm Tháng Quyết Định*. Hanoi: Nhà Xuất Bản Quân Đội Nhân Dân, 2001.

Trần Văn Trà. *Gọi Người Đang Sống*. T.P. Hồ Chí Minh: Nhà Xuất Bản Trẻ, 1996.

Trịnh Thúc Huỳnh (ed.). *Phạm Hùng, Nhà Lãnh Đạo Trung Kiên, Mẫu Mực*. Hanoi: Nhà Xuất Bản Chính Trị Quốc Gia, 2003.

Trịnh Thúc Huỳnh, Lê Văn Đệ *et al*. *Đồng Chí Trần Quốc Hoàn, Chiến Sĩ Cách Mạng Trung Kiên Của Đảng, Nhà Lãnh Đạo Xuất Sắc Của Công Anh Việt Nam*. Hanoi: Nhà Xuất Bản Công An Nhân Dân, 2006.

Trịnh Vương Hồng (ed.). *Đại Tướng Đoàn Khuê*. Hanoi: Nhà Xuất Bản Quân Đội Nhân Dân, 2002.

Trinquier, Roger. *Les maquis d'Indochine, 1952–1954*. Paris: Albatros, 1976.

———. *Le temps perdu*. Paris: Albin Michel, 1978.

———. *Le 1er Bataillon de Bérêts rouges. Indochine, 1947–1949*. Paris: Plon, 1984.

Vanuxem, Paul. *Mémoires d'un soldat*. Vol. 1, *1951. Le Général vainqueur. Le destin exemplaire de De Lattre en Indochine*. Paris: Soc. Prod. Littéraires, 1977.

Viện Khoa Học Xã Hội Việt Nam, Viện Sử Học. *Hồi Ký Trần Huy Liệu*. Hanoi: Nhà Xuất Bản Khoa Học Xã Hội, 1991.

Võ Chí Công. *Trên Những Chặng Đường Cách Mạng (Hồi Ký)*. Hanoi: Nhà Xuất Bản Chính Trị Quốc Gia, 2001.

Võ Nguyên Giáp. *Những Năm Tháng Không Thể Nào Quên*. Hanoi: Nhà Xuất Bản Quân Đội Nhân Dân, 1970.

———. *Những Chặng Đường Lịch Sử. Hồi Ký*. Hanoi: Nhà Xuất Bản Văn Học, 1977.

———. *Chiến Đấu Trong Vòng Vây*. Hanoi: Nhà Xuất Bản Quân Đội Nhân Dân, 2001.

Vũ Tâm, Lê Bầu. *60 Ngày Đêm, Giữ Chợ Đồng Xuân, Hồi Ký*. Hanoi: Nhà Xuất Bản Hà Nội, 1987.

Vương Thừa Vũ. *Trưởng Thành Trong Chiến Đấu, Hồi Ký*. Hanoi: Nhà Xuất Bản Quân Đội Nhân Dân, 1979.

## Franco-Vietnamese Negotiations

Azeau, Henri. *Hô Chi Minh, dernière chance*. Paris: Flammarion, 1968.

Guillemot, François. *Dai Viêt, indépendance et révolution au Viêt-Nam. L'échec de la troisième voie (1938–1955),* Paris: Les Indes Savantes, 2011.

Hoàng Xuân Hãn, Vũ Văn Hiền *et al. Hội Nghị Việt Pháp, Đà Lạt 1946*. Hanoi: Nhà Xuất Bản Văn Hóa, 1949.

Hoàng Xuân Hãn. *Một Vài Kỳ Vọng Về Hội Nghị Đà Lạt*. Paris: Association vietnamienne d'Action culturelle, 1987.

Học Viện Quan Hệ Quốc Tế. *Đấu Tranh Ngoại Giao Trong Cách Mạng Dân Tộc Dân Chủ Nhân Dân (1945–1954)*. Hanoi: Đại Học Quốc Gia Hà Nội, 2002.

Lin Hua. *Chiang Kai-Shek, De Gaulle contre Hô Chi Minh: Viêt-Nam, 1945–1946*. Paris: Ed. L'Harmattan, 1994.

Nguyễn Đình Bin (ed.). *Ngoại Giao Việt Nam, 1945–2000*. Hanoi: Nhà Xuất Bản Chính Trị Quốc Gia, 2002.

Shipway, Martin. *The Road to War: France and Vietnam, 1944–1947*. Providence, Rhode Island: Berghahn Books, 1996.

Tønnesson, Stein. *1946: Déclenchement de la guerre d'Indochine: Les vêpres tonkinoises du 19 décembre*. Paris: Ed. L'Harmattan, 1987.

Trình Quốc Quang. *Hội Nghị Việt Pháp Fông-Te-Nơ-Bơ-Lô, Tháng Bẩy 1946, Tập I*. Hanoi: Nhà Xuất Bản Văn Hóa, 1950.

———. *Hội Nghị Việt Pháp Fông-Te-Nơ-Bơ-Lô, Tháng Bẩy 1946, Tập II*. Hanoi: Nhà Xuất Bản Văn Hóa, 1950.

Turpin, Frédéric. *De Gaulle, les gaullistes et l'Indochine (1940–1956)*. Paris: Les Indes Savantes, 2005.

## The Franco-Vietnamese Military Context of the War

d'Alzon, Claude. *La présence militaire française en Indochine, 1940–1945*. Château de Vincennes: Publications du Service Historique de l'Armée de Terre, 1985.

Bail, René. *Les Pingouins d'Indochine. L'Aéronavale de 1945 à 1954*. Paris: Ed. Maritimes et d'Outre-mer, 1976.

Ban Chấp Hành Đảng Bộ Tỉnh Ba Rịa – Vũng Tàu. *Lịch Sử Bà Rịa – Vũng Tàu Kháng Chiến (1945–1975)*. Hanoi: Nhà Xuất Bản Quân Đội Nhân Dân, 1995.

Ban Chỉ Đạo và Ban Biên Tập Truyền Thống Tây Nam Bộ. *Tây Nam Bộ, 30 Năm Kháng Chiến (1945–1975)*. Hồ Chí Minh City: Nhà In SCITECH, 2000.

Ban Liên Lạc Bắc Trung Nam. *50 Năm Trường Lục Quân Trung Học, Quảng Ngãi 1.6.1946–1.6.1996*. T.P. Hồ Chí Minh, Việt Nam: Sở Văn Hóa Thông Tin T.P Hồ Chí Minh, 1994.

Báo Quân Đội Nhân Dân. *Chiến Đấu Bảo Vệ Chính Quyền Cách Mạng*. Hanoi: Nhà Xuất Bản Quân Đội Nhân Dân, 2005.

Barjot, Pierre. *Histoire de la guerre aéronavale*. Paris: Flammarion, 1961.

Bergot, Erwan. *Les paras*. Paris: Balland, Coll. Corps d'élite, 1971.

Bộ Chỉ Huy Hà Tây. *Hà Tây, Lịch Sử Kháng Chiến Chống Thực Dân Pháp (1945–1954)*. Hanoi: Nhà Xuất Bản Quân Đội Nhân Dân, 1998.

Bộ Chỉ Huy Quân Sự Tỉnh Hà Bắc. *Lịch Sử Quân Sự Hà Bắc (1945–1954), Tập I*. Hà Bắc: Xí Nghiệp In Hà Bắc, 1990.

Bộ Chỉ Huy Quân Sự Tỉnh Lào Cai. *Lịch Sử Kháng Chiến Chống Thực Dân Pháp Của Quân Và Dân Lào Cai, 1945–1954*. Hanoi: Nhà Xuất Bản Quân Đội Nhân Dân, 1998.

Bộ Chỉ Huy Quân Sự Tỉnh Thái Bình. *Thái Bình, Kháng Chiến Chống Pháp Xâm Lược, 1945–1954*. Thái Bình: Xí Nghiệp In Thái Bình, 1989.

Bộ Chỉ Huy Quân Sự Tỉnh Tiền Giang. *Những Trận Đánh Của Lực Lượng Vũ Trang Tiền Giang (1945–1975), Tập II*. Tiền Giang: Xí Nghiệp In Tiền Giang, 1994.

Bộ Quốc Phòng, Viện Lịch Sử Quân Sự Việt Nam. *Lịch Sử Cuộc Kháng Chiến Chống Thực Dân Pháp, 1945–1954, Tập II*. Hanoi: Nhà Xuất Bản Quân Đội Nhân Dân, 1986.

———. *Lịch Sử Cuộc Kháng Chiến Chống Thực Dân Pháp, 1945–1954, Tập III*. Hanoi: Nhà Xuất Bản Quân Đội Nhân Dân, 1989.

———. *Lịch Sử Cuộc Kháng Chiến Chống Thực Dân Pháp, 1945–1954, Tập IV*. Hanoi: Nhà Xuất Bản Quân Đội Nhân Dân, 1990.

Bộ Quốc Phòng, Viện Lịch Sử Quân Sự Việt Nam. *Lịch Sử Cuộc Kháng Chiến Chống Thực Dân Pháp, 1945–1954, Tập V*. Hanoi: Nhà Xuất Bản Quân Đội Nhân Dân, 1992.

———. *Lịch Sử Cuộc Kháng Chiến Chống Thực Dân Pháp, 1945–1954, Tập VI*. Hanoi: Nhà Xuất Bản Quân Đội Nhân Dân, 1993.

Bộ Quốc Phòng, Viện Lịch Sử Quân Sự Việt Nam. *Công Tác Bảo Đảm Vũ Khí Kỹ Thuật Quân Sự Trong Kháng Chiến Chống Pháp (1945–1954)*. Hanoi: Nhà Xuất Bản Quân Đội Nhân Dân, 1998.

———. *Lịch Sử Chiến Thuật Tập Kích Của Quân Đội Nhân Dân Việt Nam Trong 30 Năm Kháng Chiến (1945–1975)*. Hanoi: Nhà Xuất Bản Quân Đội Nhân Dân, 2001.

———. *Lịch Sử Kỹ Thuật Quân Sự Việt Nam Trong Kháng Chiên Chống Thực Dân Pháp (1945–1954)*. Hanoi: Nhà Xuất Bản Quân Đội Nhân Dân, 2002.

Bộ Tổng Tham Mưu, Ban Tổng Kết – Biên Soạn Lịch Sử. *Lịch Sử Bộ Tổng Tham Mưu Trong Kháng Chiến Chống Pháp (1945–1954)*. Hanoi: Nhà In Bộ Tổng Tham Mưu, 1991.

Bộ Tổng Tư Lệnh. *Những Tài Liệu Chỉ Đạo Các Chiến Dịch của Trung Ương Đảng, Tổng Quân Ủy và Bộ Tổng Tư Lệnh, (Từ Việt-Bắc đến Điện Biên Phủ) Tập I*. Hanoi: Bộ Tổng Tham Mưu Xuất Bản, 1961.

———. *Những Tài Liệu Chỉ Đạo Các Chiến Dịch của Trung Ương Đảng, Tổng Quân Ủy và Bộ Tổng Tư Lệnh, (Từ Việt-Bắc đến Điện Biên Phủ) Tập VI*. Hanoi: Bộ Tổng Tham Mưu Xuất Bản, 1963.

Bộ Tư Lệnh Binh Chủng Đặc Công. *Lược Sử Đặc Công Quân Đội Nhân Dân Việt Nam*. Hanoi: Nhà Xuất Bản Quân Đội Nhân Dân, 1982.

Bộ Tư Lệnh Quân Khu 1. *Tổng Kết Chỉ Đạo Thực Hiện Nhiệm Vụ Chiến Lược Quân Sự Của Liên Khu Việt Bắc Trong Kháng Chiến Chống Thực Dân Pháp (1945–1954), Tập I*. Hanoi: Nhà Xuất Bản Quân Đội Nhân Dân, 1990.

———. *Tổng Kết Chỉ Đạo Thực Hiện Nhiệm Vụ Chiến Lược Quân Sự Của Liện Khu Việt Bắc Trong Kháng Chiến Chống Thực Dân Pháp (1945–1954), Tập II*. Hanoi: Nhà Xuất Bản Quân Đội Nhân Dân, 1991.

———. *Tổng Kết Chỉ Đạo Thực Hiện Nhiệm Vụ Chiến Lược Quân Sự Của Liện Khu Việt Bắc Trong Kháng Chiến Chống Thực Dân Pháp (1945–1954), Tập III*. Hanoi: Nhà Xuất Bản Quân Đội Nhân Dân, 1991.

Bộ Tư Lệnh, Quân Đoàn 2. *Quân Đoàn 2, Những Trận Đánh Trong Chiến Tranh Giải Phóng (1945–1975)*. Hanoi: Nhà Xuất Bản Quân Đội Nhân Dân, 1994.

Bodin, Michel. *Les combattants français face à la guerre d'Indochine, 1945–1954*. Paris: Ed. L'Harmattan, 1998.

Brossard, Maurice de. *Dinassaut*. Paris: Ed. France-Empire, 1952.

Bùi Minh Hải, Vũ Văn Sum. *Quảng Ngãi, Lịch Sử Chiến Tranh Nhân Dân 30 Năm (1945–1975)*, Nghĩa Bình, Việt Nam: Nhà Xuất Bản Tổng Hợp Nghĩa Bình, 1988.

Cao Văn Lương, Nguyễn Văn Nhật *et al*. *Lịch Sử Kháng Chiến Chống Thực Dân Pháp của Quân và Dân Khu Tây Bắc (1945–1954)*. Hanoi: Nhà Xuất Bản Khoa Học Xã Hội, 2003.

Carhart, Tom (ed.). *Battles and Campaigns: Vietnam, 1954–1984*. Greenwich, Connecticut: Bison Books, 1987.

Cauchetier, Raymond. *Ciel de guerre en Indochine*. Lausanne, Switzerland: Édité par le commandement de l'air en Extrême-Orient, 1953.

Chassin, Lionel-Max. *Aviation Indochine. De Koh Chang à Dien Bien Phu*. Paris: Amiot – Dumont, 1954.

*Chiến Thắng Điện Biên Phủ. Ký Sự*. (La bataille victorieuse de Dien Bien Phu. Chronique historique). 2 vol. Hanoi: Nhà Xuất Bản Quân Đội Nhân Dân, 1964.

*Chiến Tranh Cách Mạng Việt Nam, 1945–1975. Thắng Lợi Và Bài Học*. Hanoi: Nhà Xuất Bản Chính Trị Quốc Gia, 2000.

*Chuyen Nhung Nguoi Lam Nen Lich Su, Hoi Uc Dien Bien Phu, 1954*–2009. Hanoi: Nhà Xuất Bản Chính Trị Quốc Gia/Tomorrow Media Company, Ltd., 2009.

Croizat, Victor J. *The Brown Water Navy: The River and Coastal War in Indochina, 1948–1972*. Poole, U.K.: Blandford Press, 1984.

Crosnier, Alain, and Jean-Michel Guhl. *L'armée de l'Air en Indochine, 1945–1954 / French Air Force in Indochina, 1945–1954*. Paris: Sup. Air, 1981.

Cục Công Tác Chính Trị - Bộ Nội Vụ, Vụ Tuyên Truyền – Ban Tư Tưởng Văn Hóa Trung Ưng. *50 Năm Công An Nhân Dân Việt Nam Xây Dựng Chiến Đấu và Trưởng Thành*. Hanoi: Nhà Xuất Bản Công An Nhân Dân, 1995.

Đảng Ủy, Bộ Tư Lệnh Quân Khu 9. *Quân Khu 8, Ba Mươi Năm Kháng Chiến, (1945–1975). Hanoi:* Nhà Xuất Bản Quân Đội Nhân Dân, 1998.

Đảng Ủy, Bộ Tư Lệnh, Hồi Đồng Khoa Học Quân Sự Quân Khu 7. *Miền Đông Nam Bộ Kháng Chiến 1945–1975*. Hanoi: Nhà Xuất Bản Quân Đội Nhân Dân, 1993.

Đảng Ủy, Bộ Tư Lệnh, Hội Đồng Khoa Học Quân Sự Quân Khu 9. *Quân Khu 9, 20 Năm Kháng Chiến (1945–1975)*. Hanoi: Nhà Xuất Bản Quân Đội Nhân Dân, 1996.

Đặng Vũ Hiệp. *Tổ Chức Sự Lãnh Đạo Của Đảng Trong Quân Đội Nhân Dân Việt Nam (Biên Niên) Tập I (1930–1954)*. Hanoi: Nhà Xuất Bản Quân Đội Nhân Dân, 2002.

*Dien Bien Phu vu d'en face, paroles de bo doi*. Paris: Nouveau Monde Editions, 2010.

Đinh Thu Xuân, Nguyễn Danh Khôi *et al*. *Lược Sử Chiến Sĩ Quyết Tử, Sài Gòn – Chợ Lớn – Gia Định, 1945–1954*. T.P. Hồ Chí Minh: Câu Lạc Bộ Truyền Thống Vũ Trang T.P. Hồ Chí Minh, 1992.

Đinh Văn Huệ, Hồ Sơn Đài *et al*. *50 Năm Lực Lượng Vũ Trang Quân Khu 7 (1945–1995)*. Hanoi: Nhà Xuất Bản Quân Đội Nhân Dân, 1995.

Đinh Văn Huệ, Hoàng Kim Sang *et al*. *Lịch Sử Đặc Công Miền Đông Nam Bộ (1945–1975)*. Hanoi: Nhà Xuất Bản Quân Đội Nhân Dân, 1997.

Đoàn Mạnh Lập, Nguyễn Tiến Hùng. *Quân Khu 2, 50 Năm Xây Dựng Chiến Đấu Trưởng Thành (1946–1996)*. Hanoi: Nhà Xuất Bản Quân Đội Nhân Dân, 1996.

Doyon, Jacques. *Les soldats blancs de Ho Chi Minh*. Paris: Fayard, 1973.

Dufour, Pierre. *Deuxième R.E.P., Action immédiate*. Paris: Lavauzelle, 1995.

Estival, Bernard. *La Marine française dans la Guerre d'Indochine*. Nantes, France: Marines-Éditions, 1998.

Favin-Leveque, Bernard. *Souvenirs de mer et d'ailleurs*. Paris: Ed. des Sept Vents, 1990.

Fleury, Georges. *Le 1[er] Régiment de Chasseurs parachutistes*. Paris: Lavauzelle, 1984.

Gaget, Robert. *Commando parachutiste*. Paris: Ed. Jacques Grancher, Coll. Témoignages pour l'Histoire, 1992.

———. *La Saga des Paras*. Paris: Ed. Jacques Grancher, 1998.

Hồ Sơn Đài. *Chiến Khu ở Miền Đông Nam Bộ (1945–1954)*. T.P. Hố Chí Minh: Nhà Xuất Bản T.P. Hố Chí Minh, 1996.

Hoàng Đỉnh, Nguyễn Văn Tạo *et al*. *Tổng Kết Tác Chiến Pháo Binh*. Hanoi: Trường Sĩ Quan Pháo Binh, 1985.

Hoàng Minh Thảo, Nguyễn Khác Phòng *et al*. *Hải Phòng, Những Ngày Đầu Kháng Chiến Chống Thực Dân Pháp, 11/1946–4/1947*. Hải Phòng: Nhà Xuất Bản Hải Phòng, 1996.

———. *Những Ngày Đầu Kháng Chiến Chống Pháp ở Hải Phòng*. Hải Phòng: Nhà Xuất Bản Hải Phòng, 1986.

Hoàng Phương (ed.). *Tổng Kết 60 Ngày Đêm Chiến Đấu Mở Đầu Toàn Quốc Kháng Chiến Chống Thực Dân Pháp Của Quân Và Dân Thủ Đô Hà Nội (19-12-1946–18-12-1947)*. Hanoi: Nhà Xuất Bản Quân Đội Nhân Dân, 1997.

Hoàng Văn Thái, Nguyễn Xuân Hoàng. *Chiến Dịch Tiến Công Hoà Bình (12-1951–2-1952)*. Hanoi: Nhà Xuất Bản Quân Đội Nhân Dân, 1991.

Hoàng Văn Thái, Trần Văn Quang. *Trận Đánh 30 Năm, Ký Sự Lịch Sử, Tập III.* Hanoi: Nhà Xuất Bản Quân Đội Nhân Dân, 1988.

———. *Trận Đánh 30 Năm, Ký Sự Lịch Sử, Tập IV.* Hanoi: Nhà Xuất Bản Quân Đội Nhân Dân, 1990.

———. *Lịch Sử Bộ Tổng Tham Mưu Trong Kháng Chiến Chống Pháp (1945–1954).* Hanoi: Nhà Xuất Bản Quân Đội Nhân Dân, 1991.

Hoàng Văn Thái. *Cuộc Tiến Công Chiến Lược Đông Xuân, 1953–1954.* Hanoi: Nhà Xuất Bản Quân Đội Nhân Dân, 1984.

Hovette, Pierre. *Paras au Vietnam.* Paris: Ed. Franc-Empire, 1969.

Killian, Robert. *Les fusiliers marins en Indochine. La Brigade marine du Corps expéditionnaire d'Extrême-Orient, septembre 1945–mars 1947.* Paris: Ed. Berger-Levrault, 1948.

Koburger, Charles W. Jr. *Naval Expeditions: The French Return to Indochina, 1945–1946.* Westport, Connecticut: Praeger, 1997.

Ladouet, Christian. *Para en Indo.* Paris: Ed. de la Pensée Moderne, 1972.

Lê Đình Cẩm, Hồ Thành Trung *et al. Lịch Sử Trường Sĩ Quan Lục Quân I.* Hanoi: Nhà Xuất Bản Quân Đội Nhân Dân, 1995.

Lê Minh Tân, Nguyễn Huy Long. *Tổng Cục Chính Trị Quá Trình Hình Thành Tổ Chức Và Chỉ Đạo Công Tác Đảng, Công Tác Chính Trị Trong Quân Đội, Tập I (1944–1954).* Hanoi: Nhà Xuất Bản Quân Đội Nhân Dân, 1997.

Le Mire, Henri. *Les Paras français. La Guerre d'Indochine.* Paris: Ed. Princesse, 1977.

Le Sage, Roger. *Tout vient du ciel.* Paris: Ed. de la Pensée moderne, 1958.

Lê Văn Hân, Nguyễn Nhật Kỷ *et al. Lịch Sử Tổng Cục Chính Trị Quân Đội Nhân Dân Việt Nam, Tập I (1944–1975).* Hanoi: Nhà Xuất Bản Quân Đội Nhân Dân, 2004.

Lưu Phương Thanh, Trần Hải Phụng (eds). *Lịch Sử Sài Gòn, Chợ Lớn, Gia Định Kháng Chiến (1945–1975).* T.P. Hồ Chí Minh: Nhà Xuất Bản T.P. Hồ Chí Minh, 1994.

Maestrai, Olivier. *Indochine, autopsie d'un échec. Légion, Paras.* Toulouse: Chez l'auteur, 1993.

Maucleres, Jean. *Marins dans les arroyos.* Paris: J. Peyronnet and Cie, Coll. Guerre navale, 1951.

Michel, Jacques. *La Marine française en Indochine*, 4 vols. Paris: Publ. de l'Etat-major de la Marine, Service historique, 1971–1974.

*Miền Đông Năm Bộ Kháng Chiến, 1945–1975* (L'Est du Nam Bo en guerre de Résistance, 1945–1975). Hanoi: Nhà Xuất Bản Quân Đội Nhân Dân, 1993.

Mordal, Jacques. *Marine Indochine.* Paris: Amiot-Dumont, Coll. Bibliothèque de la Mer, 1953.

Ngô Đăng Tri. *Vùng Tự Do Thanh-Nghệ-Tĩnh Trong Kháng Chiến Chống Pháp (1946–1954).* Hanoi: Nhà Xuất Bản Chính Trị Quốc Gia, 2001.

Nguyễn Cao, Đinh Thu Xuân (eds). *Lịch Sử Quân Giới Nam Bộ (1945–1954).* Hanoi: Nhà Xuất Bản Quân Đội Nhân Dân, 1991.

Nguyễn Chánh Cân, Phạm Vân Thiệu. *Lịch Sử Ngành Cơ Yếu Quân Đội Nhân Dân Việt Nam (1945–1975).* Hanoi: Nhà Xuất Bản Quân Đội Nhân Dân, 1990.

Nguyễn Đăng Vinh, Nguyễn Thị Phương Túy. *60 Năm Quân Đội Nhân Dân Việt Nam Anh Hùng (Hỏi Và Đáp).* Hanoi: Nhà Xuất Bản Chính Trị Quốc Gia, 2004.

Nguyễn Kiến Giang. *Việt Nam, Năm Đầu Tiên Sau Cách Mạng Tháng 8 (Tháng Tám 1945–Tháng Chạp 1946).* Hanoi: Nhà Xuất Bản Sự Thật, 1961.

———. *Thử Nhìnħ Lại Giai Đoạn Đầu Toàn Cuốc Kháng Chiến (Từ Ngày Toàn Quốc Kháng Chiến 19-12-1946 Đến Chiến Thắng Việt Bắc Cuối 1947).* Hanoi: Nhà Xuất Bản Sự Thật, 1962.

Nguyễn Ngọc Thành (ed.). *Lịch Sử Công Binh Việt Nam, 1945–1975.* Hanoi: Nhà Xuất Bản Quân Đội Nhân Dân, 1991.

Nguyễn Phụng Minh (ed.). *Nam Trung Bộ Kháng Chiến 1945–1975.* T.P. Hồ Chí Minh: Viện Lịch Sử Đảng, Hội Đồng Biên Soạn Lịch Sử Nam Trung Bộ Kháng Chiến, 1992.

Nguyễn Phụng Minh *et al. Phú Yên, Kháng Chiến Chống Thực Dân Pháp, 1945–1954.* Phú Yên: Xí Nghiệp In Tổng Hợp Phú Yên, 1994.

Nguyễn Quốc Minh, Vũ Doãn Thành. *Lịch Sử Bộ Đội Đặc Công, Tập Một.* Hanoi: Nhà Xuất Bản Quân Đội Nhân Dân, 1987.

Nguyễn Văn Khoan. *Việt Minh Hoàng Diệu, Tổng Khởi Nghĩa Tháng 8-1945 tại Hà Nội.* T.P. Hồ Chí Minh: Nhà Xuất Bản T.P. Hồ Chí Minh, 2001.

Nguyễn Văn Trân, Văn Tiến Dũng *et al. Lịch Sử Kháng Chiến Chống Thực Dân Pháp của Quân và Dân Liên Khu III (1945–1955).* Hanoi: Nhà Xuất Bản Chính Trị Quốc Gia, 2005.

Phạm Quang Định (ed.). *Phong Trào Nam Tiến (1945–1946), Kỷ Yếu Hội Thảo Khoa Học.* Hanoi: Nhà Xuất Bản Quân Đội Nhân Dân, 1997.

Phạm Xưởng (ed.). 50 Năm *Lịch Sử Cục Quân Huấn (1946–1996).* Hanoi: Nhà Xuất Bản Quân Đội Nhân Dân, 1996.

Phan Long, Doãn Ngọc Liệu. *Quảng Nam – Đà Nẵng, 30 Năm Chiến Đấu và Chiến Thắng (1945–1954), Tập I.* Hanoi: Nhà Xuất Bản Quân Đội Nhân Dân, 1985.

Phạn Văn Chiêu. *Cuộc Kháng Chiến Chống Pháp Của Đồng Bào Gia Định, 1945–1954.* T.P. Hồ Chí Minh: Nhà Xuất Bản T.P. Hồ Chí Minh, 2003.

Phân Viện Lịch Sử Quân Sự. *Chiến Dịch Tiến Công Biên Giới – 1950 (Chiến Dịch Lê Hồng Phong II).* Hanoi: Học Viện Quân Sự Cao Cấp, 1979.

———. *Chiến Dịch Tiến Công Biên Giới – 1950.* Hanoi: Học Viện Quân Sự Cao Cấp, 1979.

Phúc Khánh, Dinh Lục (eds). *Cuộc Kháng Chiến Chống Thực Dân Pháp Xâm Lược (9-1945–7-1954).* Hanoi: Nhà Xuất Bản Sự Thật, 1986.

Pissardy, Jean-Pierre. *Paras d'Indochine, 1944–1954*, 2 vols. Paris: Soc. de Prod. Littéraires, 1982.

Quân Khu 7. *Những Trận Đánh của Lực Lượng Vũ Trang Quân Khu 7, Tập I, 1945–1954.* Hanoi: Nhà Xuất Bản Quân Đội Nhân Dân, 2001.

de Sacy, Sylvestre. *Regards sur l'aviation militaire française en Indochine, 1940–1954.* Vincennes: Service historique de l'armée de l'air, 1999.

Thăng Long (ed.). *Nhớ Nam Bộ Và Cực Nam Trung Bộ Buổi Đầu Kháng Chiến Chống Pháp*. T.P. Hồ Chí Minh: Nhà Xuất Bản Trẻ, 1999.

Thanh Vân, Trần Hoài Long *et al. Thủ Đô Hà Nội, Lịch Sử Kháng Chiến Chống Thực Dân Pháp (1945–1954)*. Hanoi: Nhà Xuất Bản Hà Nội, 1986.

Thế Kỷ. *Lịch Sử Bộ Tham Mưu Phòng Không (Trong Kháng Chiến Chống Pháp và Chống Mỹ)*. Hanoi: Nhà Xuất Bản Quân Đội Nhân Dân, 1999.

Tổng Cục Hậu Cần. *Công Tác Hậu Cần Chiến Dịch Biên Giới, Mùa Thu Năm 1950*. Hanoi: Xưởng In Hậu Cần, 1979.

Trần Bạch Đằng, Trần Văn Trà (eds). *Mùa Thu Rồi Ngày Hăm Ba, Tập I, Trước Lúc Bình Minh*. Hanoi: Nhà Xuất Bản Chính Trị Quốc Gia, 1995.

———. *Mùa Thu Rồi Ngày Hăm Ba, Tập II, Độc Lập Hay là Chết*. Hanoi: Nhà Xuất Bản Chính Trị Quốc Gia, 1996.

———. *Mùa Thu Rồi Ngày Hăm Ba, Tập III, Hào Khí Đồng Nai – Bến Nghé – Cửu Long, Quân Sự Đô Thị*. Hanoi: Nhà Xuất Bản Chính Trị Quốc Gia, 1996.

———. *Mùa Thu Rồi Ngày Hăm Ba, Tập IV, Hào Khí Đồng Nai – Bến Nghé – Cửu Long, Xây ựng Căn Cứ Địa*. Hanoi: Nhà Xuất Bản Chính Trị Quốc Gia, 1996.

Trần Hải Phụng (ed.). *Tự Vệ Thành Sài Gòn – Chợ Lớn, Những Năm Đầu Kháng Chiến Chống Thực Dân Pháp*. Hanoi: Nhà Xuất Bản Quân Đội Nhân Dân, 1995.

Trần Phấn Chấn (ed.). *Lịch Sử Lực Lượng Võ Trang Thành Phố Hồ Chí Minh (1945–1995)*. Hanoi: Nhà Xuất Bản Quân Đội Nhân Dân, 1998.

Trần Phấn Chấn, Hồ Sơn Đài. *Miền Đông Nam Bộ Kháng Chiến, 1945–1975, Tập Một*. Hanoi: Nhà Xuất Bản Quân Đội Nhân Dân, 1990.

Trần Qúy Cát. *Khu 5, 30 Năm Chiến Tranh Giải Phóng, Tập I, Kháng Chiến Chống Thực Dân Pháp*. Quân Khu 5, Vietnam: Nhà Xuất Bản Khu 5, 1986.

Trần Thế Long. *Trung Đoàn Thành Đồng Biên Giới, Ký Sự*. Thanh Hóa: Cục Chính Trị Quân Đoàn Xuất Bản, 1982.

Trình Mưu (ed.). *Lịch Sử Kháng Chiến Chống Thực Dân Pháp Của Quân Và Dân Liện Khu IV (1945–1954)*. Hanoi: Nhà Xuất Bản Chính Trí, Quốc Gia, 2003.

Vaïsse, Maurice (ed.). *L'Armée française dans la guerre d'Indochine (1946–1954): adaptation ou inadaptation?* Bruxelles: Éditions Complexe, 2000.

Van Onsen, Raoul. *Derniers combats pour l'Indochine*. Paris: Scaillet, 1991.

Võ Nguyên Giáp. *Chiến Tranh Nhân Dân và Quân Đội Nhân Dân*. Hanoi: Nhà Xuất Bản Sự Thật, 1959.

Vulliez, Albert. *Aéronavale (1945–1954)*. Paris: Amiot-Dumont, 1955.

Xuân Thiêm, Hàn Thụy Vũ *et al. Đại Đoàn Đồng Bằng*. Hanoi: Nhà Xuất Bản Quân Đội Nhân Dân, 1976.

## *The French Communist Party and the Indochina War*

Caute, David. *Le communisme et les intellectuels français, 1914–1966*. Paris: Gallimard, 1967.

Doyon, Jacques. *Les soldats blancs de Hô Chi Minh: Les transfuges antifascistes et les communistes français dans le camp du Viêt-Minh*. Paris: Fayard, 1973.

Joucelain, Francis. *Le P.C.F. et la première Guerre d'Indochine.* Paris: Maspéro, Cahiers rouges, 1973.

Lafon, Monique. *La lutte du P.C.F. contre le colonialisme.* Paris: Editions Sociales, 1962.

Pigenet, Michel. *Au cœur de l'activisme communisme des années de guerre froide: la manifestation Ridgway.* Paris: Ed. L'Harmattan, 1992.

Rice-Maximin, Edward. *Accomodation and Resistance. The French Left, Indochina and the Cold War, 1944–1954.* Westport, Connecticut: Greenwood Press, Contribution to the Study of World History, no. 2, 1986.

Ruscio, Alain. *La C.G.T. et la guerre d'Indochine, 1945–1954.* Paris: Institut C.G.T. d'histoire sociale, 1984.

———. *Les communistes français et la Guerre d'Indochine (1944–1954).* Paris: Ed. L'Harmattan, 1985.

Wall, Irving M. *French Communism in the Era of Stalin: The Quest for Unity and Integration, 1945–1962.* Westport, Connecticut: Greenwood Press, 1983.

## *French Opposition to the Indochina War*

Biondi, Jean-Pierre, and Gilles Morin. *Les Anticolonialistes (1881–1962).* Paris: Robert Laffont, 1992.

Marty, André. *L'Affaire Marty.* Paris: Edition des Deux Rives, 1955.

Parmelin, Hélène. *Matricule 2078. L'Affaire Henri Martin.* Paris: Ed. Français Réunis, 1953.

Rousseau, Sabine. *La colombe et le napalm: Des chrétiens français contre les guerres d'Indochine et du Vietnam, 1945–1975.* Paris: CNRS Éditions, 2002.

Sartre, Jean-Paul *et al. L'Affaire Henri Martin.* Paris: Gallimard, 1953.

Theolleyre, Jean-Marc. *Ces procès qui ébranlèrent la France.* Paris: Grasset, 1966.

## *Military Medicine*

Accoce, Pierre. *Médecins à Dien Bien Phu.* Paris: Presses de la Cité, Coll. Documents, 1992.

Berger, Jean-François. *L'action du Comité international de la Croix Rouge en Indochine, 1946–1954.* Monteux, France: Corbaz, 1982.

Carre-Tornezy, Hélène. *Infirmière en Indochine 1950–1952. D'amour et de détresse.* Paris: Lavauzelle, 1999.

Cleret, François. *Le cheval du Roi.* Toulon, France: Les Presses du Midi, 2000.

Croix Rouge Française. *La Croix Rouge française en Indochine.* Paris: Croix Rouge française, 1952.

Dambielle, Bernard. *Mes derniers jours en Cochinchine, 1952–1956.* Auch, France: Chez l'auteur, 1995.

Delivre, Jacques. *Le carabin rouge. Témoignage d'un médecin de combat en Indochine et en Algérie devenu médecin du travail chez les sidérurgistes de Longwy.* Les Sables d'Olonne, France: Ed. Le Cercle d'Or / J. Huguet, 1985.

Distinguir, Henry. *Une autre Indochine: Mémoires retrouvés.* Paris: La Pensée Universelle, 1992.

Đỗ Nguyên Phương, Phạm Mạnh Hùng (eds). *Bộ Y Tế Việt Nam, 1945–2000.* Hanoi: Nhà Xuất Bản Chính Trị Quốc Gia, 2001.

Faucon, René. *Mon Indochine.* Paris: Ed. des Ecrivains, 1999.

Giudicelli, Pierre. *Médecin de Bataillon en Indochine, 1947–1951.* Paris: Ed. L'Albatros, 1992.

Grauwin, Paul. *J'étais médecin à Dien Bien Phu.* Paris: Ed. France-Empire, 1954.

———. *Seulement médecin.* Paris: Ed. France-Empire, 1956.

Lemaire, Marc. *Le service de santé militaire dans la Guerre d'Indochine. Le soutien santé des parachitistes (1944–1954).* Paris: Ed. L'Harmattan, Coll. Recherches Asiatiques, 1997.

Mai Văn Duẩn. *Hỏi và Đáp về Chế Độ Chính Sách Đối Với Thương Binh Bệnh Binh Gia Đình Liệt Sĩ Người Có Công và Văn Bản Có Liên Quan.* Hanoi: Nhà Xuất Bản Thống Kê, 2003.

May, Jacques. *Médecin français en Extrême-Orient.* Paris: Ed. de la Paix, 1951.

Merle, Fernand. *Un chirurgien au temps des colonies.* Paris: La pensée Universelle, 1978.

———. *Toubibs et Bons Pères en Indochine.* Paris: Lavauzelle, 1996.

Phạm Văn Hựu (ed.). *30 Năm Phục Vụ Và Xây Dựng Của Ngành Quân Y, Quân Đội Nhân Dân Việt Nam, 1945–1975, Dự Thảo Tóm Tát Lịch Sử.* Hanoi: Nhà Xuất Bản Quân Đội Nhân Dân, 1976.

## *Intelligence, Special Services, and Policing in the Indochina War*

Bergot, Erwan. *Commandos de choc en Indochine. Services secrets en Indochine, 1945–1954.* Paris: Grasset/Fasquelle, 1975.

Currey, Cecil B. *Edward Lansdale: the Unquiet American.* Boston, Massachusetts: Houghton Mifflin, 1988.

Deuve, Jean. *Le Service de Renseignements des Forces françaises du Laos, 1946–1948.* Paris: Ed. L'Harmattan, Coll. Culture du Renseignement, 2000.

Lansdale, Edward Geary. *In the Midst of Wars. An American Mission to Southeast Asia.* New York: Harper and Row, 1972.

Lê Văn Kính, Nguyễn Hoàng Long *et al. Cảnh Vệ Công An Nhân Dân Việt Nam, Lịch Sử Biên Niên (1941–1954).* Hanoi: Nhà Xuất Bản Công An Nhân Dân, 1995.

Mai Chí Thọ, Cao Đăng Chiếm *et al. Công An Nam Bộ Trong Kháng Chiến Chống Thực Dân Pháp Xâm Lược.* Hanoi: Nhà Xuất Bản Công An Nhân Dân, 1993.

Muelle, Raymond, and Eric Deroo. *Services spéciaux. Armes, techniques, missions. G.C.M.A., Indochine, 1950–1954.* Paris: Ed. Crépin-Leblond, 1992.

Nguyễn Đình Thành, Nguyễn Văn Tình *et al. Công An Thủ Đô, Những Chặng Đường Lịch Sử (1945–1954).* Hanoi: Nhà Xuất Bản Công An Nhân Dân, 1990.

Phạm Ngọc Giai, Trần Quang Minh *et al. Hậu Cần Công An Nhân Dân Việt Nam, Lịch Sử Biện Niên (1945–1954).* Hanoi: Nhà Xuất Bản Công An Nhân Dân, 1998.

Phạm Tâm Long, Vũ Văn Bân, *et al. Lịch Sử Công An Nhân Dân Việt Nam (1945–1954), Sơ Thảo.* Hanoi: Nhà Xuất Bản Công An Nhân Dân, 1996.

Phạm Văn Minh, Vũ Văn Bân *et al. Công An Nhân Dân Việt Nam, Nửa Thế Kỷ Chiến Đấu Và Trưởng Thành (1945–1995).* Hanoi: Nhà Xuất Bản Công An Nhân Dân, 1995.

Phạm Xuân Trường. *Sổ Tay Tư Liệu Đặc Công.* Hanoi: Nhà Xuất Bản Quân Đội Nhân Dân, 1992.

Porch, Douglas. *The French Secret Service: From the Dreyfus Affair to the Gulf War.* New York: Farrar, Straus and Giroux, 1995.

Rolland, André. *L'action dans l'ombre : avant Dien Bien Phu.* Paris: Ed. du Dauphin, 1971.

Trần Liêu (ed.). *Lịch Sử Cảnh Sát Nhân Dân Việt Nam, Tập I (1945–1954).* Hanoi: Nhà Xuất Bản Công An Nhân Dân, 1995.

Trần Quốc Hoàn. *Một Số Vấn Đề Xây Dựng Lực Lượng Công An Nhân Dân.* Hanoi: Nhà Xuất Bản Công An Nhân Dân, 2004.

Villatoux, Paul, and Marie-Catherine Villatoux. *La République et son armée face au "péril subversif": Guerre et actions psychologiques (1945–1960).* Paris: Les Indes Savantes, 2005.

Vũ Văn Bân, Đặng Mạnh Hoàn. *Công An Nhân Dân Việt Nam, Lịch Sử Biên Niên (1945–1954).* Hanoi: Nhà Xuất Bản Công An Nhân Dân, 1994.

### *The Battle of Dien Bien Phu*

Bail, René. *Dernier baroud à Dien Bien Phu.* Paris: Ed. Jacques Grancher, 1990.

Bornert, Lucien. *Dien Bien Phu, citadelle de la gloire.* Paris: Nouv. Presses Mondiales, Coll. Documents du Monde, 1954.

Bruge, Roger. *Les hommes de Dien Bien Phu.* Paris: Perrin, 1999.

Cao Tiến Lê. *Nếm Trải Điện Biên Phủ.* Hanoi: Nhà Xuất Bản Quân Đội Nhân Dân, 1994.

Dalloz, Jacques. *Dien Bien Phu.* Paris: La Documentation française, 1991.

Đảng Ủy Quân Sự Trung Ương Bộ Quốc Phòng. *Một Số Văn Kiện Chỉ Đạo Chiến Lược Cuộc Đông Xuân 1953–1954 và Chiến Dịch Điện Biên Phủ.* Hanoi: Nhà Xuất Bản Quân Đội Nhân Dân, 2004.

Đỗ Gia Nam, Nguyễn Đăng Vinh. *Điện Biện Phủ, Sự Kiện, Tư Liệu.* Hanoi: Nhà Xuất Bản Quân Đội Nhân Dân, 2004.

Fall, Bernard B. *Hell in a Very Small Place: The Siege of Dien-Bien-Phu.* New York: Lippincott, 1967.

Genty, Robert. *Ultimes secours pour Dien Bien Phu, 1953–1954.* Paris: Ed. L'Harmattan, Coll. Mémoires asiatiques, 1994.

Georges, Marcel. *Go sur Dien Bien Phu!.* Paris: Ed. France-Empire, 1971.

Hoàng Liên. *Quân Dân Đồng Bằng Bắc Bộ, Góp Phần Làm Nên Chiến Thắng Lịch Sử Điện Biên Phủ.* Hanoi: Nhà Xuất Bản Chính Trị Quốc Gia, 2004.

Hoàng Minh Thảo (ed.). *Điện Biên Phủ, Trận Thắng Thế Kỷ.* Hanoi: Nhà Xuất Bản Chính Trị Quốc Gia, 2004.

Hữu Mai. *Con Ngựa Sang Sông*. Hanoi: Nhà Xuất Bản Kim Đồng, 1974.

———. *Điện Biên Phủ, Thời Gian và Không Gian*. Hanoi: Nhà Xuất Bản Thanh Niên, 1979.

Journoud, Pierre, and Hugues Tertrais. *1954–2004: La bataille de Dien Bien Phu, entre histoire et mémoire*. Paris: Publications de la Société française d'histoire d'Outre-mer, 2004.

Langlais, Pierre. *Dien Bien Phu*. Paris: France-Empire, 1963.

Lê Mạnh Thái. *Điện Biên Phủ, Một Góc Nhìn, Hồi Ký*. Hanoi: Nhà Xuất Bản Thanh Niên, 2004.

Lê Mậu Hãn (ed.). *Điện Biên Phủ, Văn Kiện Đảng, Nhà Nước*. Hanoi: Nhà Xuất Bản Chính Trị Quốc Gia, 2004.

Lê Trọng Tấn. *Từ Đồng Quan Đến Điện Biên*. Hanoi: Nhà Xuất Bản Quân Đội Nhân Dân, 2002.

Morgan, Ted. *Valley of Death: The Tragedy at Dien Bien Phu That Led America into the Vietnam War*. New York: Random House, 2010.

Phạm Kiên *et al. Vài Hồi Ức về Điệ Biên Phủ*. Hanoi: Nhà Xuất Bản Quân Đội Nhân Dân,, 1973.

Phạm Quang Định, Phạm Bá Toàn *et al. Đại Tướng Lê Trọng Tấn với Chiến Dịch Điện Biên Phủ*. Hanoi: Nhà Xuất Bản Quân Đội Nhân Dân, 2004.

Phan Ngọc Liên. *Chiến Thắng Lịch Sử Điện Biên Phủ, Toàn Thư*. Hanoi: Nhà Xuất Bản Từ Điển Bách Khoa, 2004.

Rocolle, Pierre. *Pourquoi Dien Bien Phu?* Paris: Flammarion, Coll. L'Histoire, 1968.

Roy, Jules. *La bataille de Dien Bien Phu*. Paris: Julliard, 1963.

Ruscio, Alain. *Dien Bien Phu: La fin d'une illusion*. Paris: Ed. L'Harmattan, 1986.

———. *Dien Bien Phu: Mythes et réalités, 1954–2004*. Paris: Les Indes Savantes, 2005.

Tagliazucchi, Pino. *Dien Bien Phu tremila giorni*. Turin, Italy: Musolini Ed., 1969.

Trần Trọng Trung. *Hoàng Văn Thái, Điện Biên Phủ, Chiến Dịch Lịch Sử, Hồi Ức*. Hanoi: Nhà Xuất Bản Quân Đội Nhân Dân, 2001.

Ủy Ban Khoa Học Xã Hội Việt Nam, Viện Sủ Học. *Mấy Vấn Đề Về Chiến Thắng Lịch Sử Điện Biên Phủ*. Hanoi: Nhà Xuất Bản Khoa Học Xã Hội, 1985.

Võ Nguyên Giáp. *Điên-Biên-Phủ*. Hanoi: Nhà Xuất Bản Sự Thật, 1959.

———. *Báo Cáo Về Kế Hoạch Tác Chiến Và Tổng Kết Kinh Nghiệm Trong Các Chiến Dịch Lớn, Tập III, Chiến Dịch Điện Biên Phủ*. Hanoi: Bộ Tổng Tham Mưu, 1959.

———. *Vài Hồi Ức về Diện Biên Phủ*. (Quelques anecdotes sur Dien Bien Phu). Hanoi: Nhà Xuất Bản Quân Đội Nhân Dân, 1977.

———. *Điện Biên Phủ*, 6th edition. Hanoi: Nhà Xuất Bản Thế Giới, 1999.

———. *Đường Tới Điện Biên Phủ*. Hanoi: Nhà Xuất Bản Quân Đội Nhân Dân, 1999.

———. *Điện Biên Phủ, Điểm Hẹn Lịch Sử*. Hanoi: Nhà Xuất Bản Quân Đội Nhân Dân, 2001.

———. *Đại Tướng Võ Nguyên Giáp Với Chiến Dịch Điện Biên Phủ.* Hanoi: Nhà Xuất Bản Quân Đội Nhân Dân, 2004.

Windrow, Martin. *The Last Valley: Dien Bien Phu and the French Defeat in Vietnam: The Battle that doomed the French Empire and led America into Vietnam.* Cambridge, Massachusetts: Da Capo Press, 2004.

## The Geneva Accords

Cable, James. *The Geneva Conference of 1954 on Indochina.* New York: St Martin's Press, 1986.

Devillers, Philippe, and Jean Lacouture. *End of a War: Indochina, 1954.* London: Pall Mall Press, 1969.

« Documents relatifs à la Conférence de Genève sur l'Indochine (21 juillet 1954). » *Notes et Etudes doc.,* no. 1909. Paris: La Documentation française, 30 juillet 1954.

Joyaux, François. *La Chine et le règlement du premier conflit d'Indochine, Genève, 1954.* Paris: Publ. de la Sorbonne, 1979.

Randle, Robert F. *Geneva 1954. The Settlement of the Indochinese War.* Princeton, New Jersey: Princeton Univ. Press, 1969.

## Prison Camps and Prisoners of War

Bayle, Claude. *Prisonnier au Camp 113. Le camp de Boudarel.* Paris: Perrin, 1991.

———. *Cinq mois captifs au sein de la force opérationnelle Viet Minh: fin novembre 1952 à fin mars 1953.* Paris: Ed. des Ecrivains, 1999.

Bergot, Erwan. *Convoi 42* (La marche à la mort des prisonniers de Dien Bien Phu). Paris: Presses de la Cité, 1986.

Bonnafous, Robert. *Les prisonniers français dans les camps Viêt Minh (1945–1954).* Paris: Éditions des Écrivains, 2000.

Goeldhieux, Claude. *Quinze mois prisonnier chez les Viets. Choses vues.* Paris: Julliard, 1953.

Ky Thu. *Khep lai qua khu dau thuong hoi ky ve trai tu binh si quan Phap so Mot.* Hanoi: no publisher indicated, 1994.

Lê Mạnh Thái. *Hỏi Cung Tù Binh Điện Biên : Hồi Ký.* T.P. Hồ Chí Minh: Nhà Xuất Bản Văn Nghệ, 1987.

Moreau, René. *Huit ans otage chez les Viets, 1946–1954.* Paris: Ed. Pygmalion/Gérard Watelet, 1982.

Richard, Pierre. *Cinq ans prisonnier chez les Viets.* Paris: Nouvelle Ed. Latines, 1975.

Stein, Louis. *Les soldats oubliés. De Cao Bang aux camps de rééducation du Viet Minh.* Paris: Albin Michel, Coll. Les Combattants, 1993.

Theresin, Maurice. *Mémoires de captivité.* Paris: La Pense universelle, 1992.

Thevenet, Amédée. *Goulags indochinois. Carnets de guerre et de captivité, 1949–1952.* Paris: Ed. France-Empire, 1997.

Vidal, Robert. *Les îles de la nuit. Un Goulag jaune, 21 mois prisonnier chez les Viets.* Paris: Olivier-Orban, 1976.

## The Associated States[3] and the Indochina War

Adams, Nina S., and Alfred McCoy (eds). *Laos: War and Revolution.* New York: Harper and Row, 1970.

Blanchet, Marie Thérèse. *La naissance de l'Etat associé du Vietnam.* Paris: Génin, 1954.

Boucher de Crèvecoeur, Jean. *La Libération du Laos, 1945–1946.* Château de Vincennes: Serv. Hist. de l'armée de Terre, 1985.

Chandler, David P. *A History of Cambodia.* Boulder, Colorado: Westview Press, 1983.

Chandler, David P., and Ben Kiernan (eds). *Revolution and Its Aftermath in Kampuchea: Eight Essays.* New Haven, Connecticut: Yale Univ. Press,1983.

Cixoux, Hélène. *L'histoire terrible mais inachevée de Norodom Sihanouk, roi du Cambodge.* Paris: Théâtre du Soleil, 1985.

Colombani, Antoine. *Vietnam, 1948–1950. La solution oubliée.* Paris: Ed. L'Harmattan, 1997.

Deuve, Jean. *Histoire de la Police nationale du Laos.* Paris: Ed. L'Harmattan, 1998.

———. *Le Laos, 1945–1949: Contribution à l'histoire du mouvement Lao Issala.* Montpellier, France: Les Presses de l'imprimerie de Recherche - Université Paul Valéry, 2000.

———. *Le royaume du Laos, 1949–1965: Histoire événementielle de l'indépendance à la guerre américaine.* Paris: Ed. L'Harmattan, 2003.

Dommen, Arthur J. *The Indochinese Experience of the French and the Americans: Nationalism and Communism in Cambodia, Laos, and Vietnam.* Bloomington, Indiana: Indiana Univ. Press, 2001.

Evans, Grant. *A Short History of Laos: The Land in between.* Crows Nest, Australia: Allen & Unwin, 2002.

Guillemot, François. *Dai Viêt, indépendance et révolution au Viêt-Nam. L'échec de la troisième voie (1938–1955),* Paris: Les Indes Savantes, 2011.

Gunn, Geoffrey C. *Political Struggles in Laos, 1930–1954: Vietnamese Communist Power and the Lao Struggle for National Independence.* Bangkok, Thailand: Editions Duang Kamol, 1988.

Grandclément, Daniel. *Bao Dai ou les derniers jours de l'Empire d'Annam.* Paris: Jean-Claude Lattès, 1997.

Hamilton-Merritt, Jane. *Tragic Mountains: The Hmongs, the Americans and the Secret Wars for Laos, 1942–1992.* Bloomington, Indiana: Indiana Univ. Press, 1993.

Heder, Steve. *Imitation and Independence*, 1930–1975. Vol. I, dans *Cambodian Communism and the Vietnamese Model*, Bangkok: White Lotus Press, 2004.

Kiernan, Ben. *How Pol Pot came to Power: A History of Communism in Kampuchea, 1930–1975.* London: Verso, 1987.

———. *The Pol Pot Regime: Race, Power and Genocide in Cambodia under the Khmer Rouge, 1975–79.* London: Yale Univ. Press, 2002 (2nd ed.).

3. I include the states associated with both the French and the Democratic Republic of Vietnam.

Langer, Paul F. and Joseph J. Zasloff. *North Vietnam and the Pathet Lao: Partners in the Struggle*. Cambridge, Massachusetts: Harvard Univ. Press, 1970.

Lockhart, Bruce McFarland. *The End of Vietnamese Monarchy*. Yale, Connecticut: Lac Viet Series, 1993.

Osborne, Milton B. *Politics and Power in Cambodia: The Sihanouk Years*. Camberwell, Australia: Longmans, 1973.

———. *Sihanouk: Prince of Light, Prince of Darkness*. Honolulu, Hawaii: Univ. of Hawaii Press, 1994.

Sihanouk, Norodom. *Souvenirs doux et amers*. Paris: Hachette, Stock, 1981.

Simms, Peter, ans Sandra Simms. *The Kindom of Laos*. Richmond, Virginia: Curzon Press, 1999.

Sisouk, Na Champassak. *Tempête sur le Laos*. Paris: La Table Ronde, 1961.

Souvannaphouma, Prince Mangkra. *L'agonie du Laos*. Paris: Plon, 1976.

Stuart-Fox, Martin. *Laos: Politics, Economics and Society*. Boulder, Colorado: Lynne Tienner Publ., 1986

———. *A History of Laos*. Cambridge, Massachusetts: Cambridge Univ. Press, 1997.

Tong, André. *Sihanouk, la fin des illusions*. Paris: La Table Ronde, Coll. L'Ordre du Jour, 1972.

Toye, Hugh. *Laos, Buffer State of Battleground*. Oxford, U.K.: Oxford Univ. Press, 1968.

## The International Context of the Indochina War

Bartholomew-Feis, Dixee R. *The OSS and Ho Chi Minh: Unexpected Allies in the War against Japan*. Lawrence, Kansas: Univ. Press of Kansas, 2006.

Beloff, Max. *Soviet Policy in the Far East, 1944–1951*. London: Oxford Univ. Press, 1953.

Berger, Jean-François. *L'action du Comité international de la Croix-Rouge en Indochine 1946–1954*. Montreux, France: Editions Corbaz, 1982.

Billings-Yun, Melanie. *Decision against War: Eisenhower and Dien Bien Phu, 1954*. New York: Colombia Univ. Press, 1988.

Bodin, Michel. *Les Africains dans la guerre d'Indochine, 1947–1954*. Paris: Ed. L'Harmattan, 2000.

Bradley, Mark Philip. *Imagining Vietnam and America: The Making of Postcolonial Vietnam, 1919–1950*. Chapel Hill, North Carolina: Univ. of North Carolina Press, 2000.

Brown, Mac Alister, and Joseph Jeremiah Zasloff. *Prelude to Disaster: The American Role in Vietnam, 1940–1963*. Port Washington, New York: Kennikat Press, National Univ. Publications, 1975.

Cable, James. *The Geneva Conference of 1954 on Indochina*. New York: St Martin's Press, 1986.

Chang Fa K'uei. *Memoirs of the Resistance War*. Hong Kong: United Revue, 1962.

Chen Jian. *Mao's China and the Cold War*. Chapel Hill, North Carolina: Univ. of North Carolina Press, 2001.

Chen King C. *Vietnam and China, 1938–1954*. Princeton, New Jersey: Princeton Univ. Press, 1969.

Colbert, Evelyn S. *Southeast Asia in International Politics, 1941–1956*. Ithaca, New York: Cornell Univ. Press, 1977.

Croix Rouge Française. *La Croix Rouge française en Indochine*. Paris: Croix Rouge française, 1952.

Delanoë, Nelcya. *Poussières d'Empires*. Paris: P.U.F, 2002.

Dunn, Peter M. *The First Vietnam War*. New York: St Martin's Press; London: C. Hurst; 1985.

Freymond, Jacques. *Guerres, révolutions, Croix Rouge. Réflexions sur le rôle du Comité international de la Croix Rouge*. Geneva: Institut Universitaires des Hautes Etudes Internationales, 1976.

Gaiduk, Ilya V. *The Soviet Union and the Vietnam War.* Chicago, Illinois: Ivan Dee, 1996.

Gardner, Lloyd C. *Approaching Vietnam: From World War II through Dienbienphu (1941–1954)*. New York: W.W. Norton & Company, 1988.

Goscha, Christopher E., and Christian F. Ostermann (eds), *Connecting Histories: Decolonization and the Cold War in Southeast Asia, 1945–1962.* (Stanford: Stanford University Press, 2009).

Goscha, Christopher E., and Karine Laplante (eds), *The Failure of Peace in Indochina,* (Paris: Les Indes Savantes, 2010).

Gurtov, Melvin. *The First Vietnam Crisis. Chinese Communist Strategy and United States Involvment, 1953–1954*. New York: Columbia Univ. Press, 1967.

Hoàng Thanh. *Hồ Chí Minh Với Trung Quốc*. Hanoi: Nhà Xuất Bản Sao Mai, 1990.

Hoàng Văn Hoan. Một Giọt Nước ở trong Biển Cả. Beijing: Nhà Xuất BảnTin Việt Nam, 1982.

Jacobs, Seth. *America's Miracle Man in Vietnam: Ngo Dinh Diem, Religion, Race, and U.S. Intervention in Southeast Asia, 1950–1957*. Durham, North Carolina: Duke Univ. Press, 2004.

———. *Cold War Mandarin: Ngo Dinh Diem and the Origins of America's War in Vietnam, 1950–1963*. Lanham, Maryland: Rowman & Littlefield, 2006.

Joyaux, François. *La Chine et le règlement du premier conflit d'Indochine, Genève, 1954*. Paris: Publ. De la Sorbonne, 1979.

Lawrence, Mark Atwood. *Assuming the Burden: Europe and the American Commitment to War in Vietnam*. Los Angeles, California: Univ. of California Press, 2005.

Lawrence, Mark Atwood, and Fredrik Logevall (eds). *The First Vietnam War: Colonial Conflict and the Cold War Crisis*. Cambridge, Massachusetts: Harvard Univ. Press, 2007.

Lin Hua. *Chiang Kai-Shek, De Gaulle contre Ho Chi Minh, Vietnam 1945–1946.* Paris: Ed. L'Harmattan, 1994.

Neville, Peter. *Britain in Vietnam: Prelude to Disaster, 1945–6*. London: Routledge, 2007.

Nguyễn Trọng Hậu. *Hoạt Động Đối Ngoại Cuả Nước Việt Nam Dân Chủ Cộng Hòa, Thời Kỳ 1945–1950*. Hanoi: Nhà Xuất Bản Chính Trị Quốc Gia, 2004.

Patti, Archimedes L. A. *Why Viet Nam? Prelude To America's Albatross*. Los Angeles, California: Univ. of California Press, 1982.

Pike, Douglas. *Vietnam and the Soviet Union. Anatomy of an Alliance*. London: Westview Press, 1987.

Qiang Zhai. *China and the Vietnam Wars, 1950–1975*. Chapel Hill and London: Univ. of North Carolina Press, Coll. The New Cold War History, 2000.

Rosie, George. *The British in Vietnam. How the Twenty-five years War began*. London: Panther Books Ltd, 1970.

Rotter, Andrew Jon. *The Triangular Route to Vietnam: the United States, Great Britain and Southeast Asia*. Ithaca, New York: Cornell Univ. Press, 1987.

Smith, T. O. *Britain and the Origins of the Vietnam War: UK Policy in Indo-China, 1943–50*. Basingstoke and New York: Palgrave Macmillan, 2007.

Spector, Ronald H. *United States Army in Vietnam. Advice and Support: The Early Years, 1941–1960*. Washington, DC: U.S. Army Center of Military History, 1983.

Statler, Kathryn C. *Replacing France: The Origins of American Intervention in Vietnam*. Lexington, Kentucky: Univ. Press of Kentucky, 2007.

Ton, That Thien. *India and Southeast Asia, 1947–1960. A Study of India's Policy towards the Southeast Asian Countries in the period 1947–1960*. Geneva: Libr. Droz, Coll. Etudes d'Hist. économique, politique et sociale, 1963.

Tønnesson, Stein, and Hans Antlov (eds). *Imperial Policy and Southeast Asian nationalism, 1930–1957*. Copenhagen and London: NIAS/Curzon Press, Studies in Asian Topics, no. 19, 1995.

Vũ Xuân Hồng. *Hoạt Động Đối Ngoại Nhân Dân Việt Nam*. Hanoi: Nhà Xuất Bản Chính Trị Quốc Gia, 2003.

Worthing, Peter. *Occupation and Revolution: China and the Vietnamese August Revolution of 1945*. Berkeley, California: Institute of East Asian Studies, 2001.

Zagoria, Donald (ed.). *Soviet Policy in East Asia*. New Haven, Connecticut: Yale Univ. Press, 1982.

## War and State Formation in the Democratic Republic of Vietnam

Ban Tài Chính Quản Trị Trung Ương. *Biên Niên Sử Hoạt Động Tài Chính Cuả Đảng Cộng Sản Việt Nam*. Hanoi: Nhà Xuất Bản Chính Trị Quốc Giá, 2000.

Đặng Phong. *Lịch Sử Kinh Tế Việt Nam, 1945–2000, Tập I: 1945–1954*. Hanoi: Nhà Xuất Bản Khoa Học Xã Hội, 2002.

Đặng Văn Thân, Vũ Tuyến *et al*. *Lịch Sử Ngành Bưu Điện Việt Nam, Tập I*. Hanoi: Nhà Xuất Bản Bưu Điện, 1990.

Đỗ Khắc Quảng, Lê Chân *et al*. *Lịch Sử Bộ Đội Thông Tin Liên Lạc, Ghi Tóm Tắt Theo Năm Tháng*. Hanoi: Bộ Tư Lệnh Thông Tin Liên Lạc, 1982.

Doan Trong Nguyen and Thanh Vinh Pham. *L'édification d'une économie nationale indépendante au Vietnam, 1945–1965*. Hanoi, Vietnam: Ed. Langues Etrangères, 1964.

Goscha, Christopher E. *Vietnam: Un Etat né de la guerre*. Paris: Armand Colin, 2011.

Guillemot, François. *Dai Viêt, indépendance et révolution au Viêt-Nam. L'échec de la troisième voie (1938–1955),* Paris: Les Indes Savantes, 2011.

de Hartingh, Bertrand. *Entre le peuple et la nation: La République démocratique du Viet Nam de 1953 à 1957.* Paris: Ecole française d'Extrême-Orient, 2003.

Hồng Chương. *Báo Chí Việt Nam*. Hanoi: Nhà Xuất Bản Sự Thật, 1985.

Lê Ngọc Trác, Huỳnh Văn Mai *et al. Lịch Sử Truyền Thống 30 Năm Giao Bưu Vận Nam Bộ (1945–1975). Hanoi*: Nhà Xuất Bản Bưu Điện, 2003.

Lê Ngọc Trác, Huỳnh Văn Mai *et al. Lịch Sử Truyền Thống 30 Năm Thông Tin Vô Tuyến Điện Nam Bộ (1945–1975).* Hanoi: Nhà Xuất Bản Bưu Điện, 2003.

Mai Văn Bộ *et al. Kỷ Niệm 50 Năm Đài Phát Thanh Tiếng Nói Năm Bộ Kháng Chiến (1947–1997)*. T.P. Hồ Chí Minh, Việt Nam: Nhà Xuất Bản Trẻ, 1997.

Moise, Edwin B. *Land Reform in China and North Vietnam. Consolidating the Revolution at the Village Level.* Chapel Hill, North Carolina: Univ. of North Carolina Press, 1983.

Nguyễn Bích Huệ. *Đồng Bạc Việt Nam và Các Vấn Đề Liên Hệ*. Saigon: Phạm Quang Khải, 1968.

Nguyễn Chiến, Nguyễn Diệp *et al. Lịch Sử Bô Đội Thông Tin Liện Lạc, 1945–1995.* Hanoi: Nhà Xuất Bản Quân Đội Nhân Dân, 1996.

Nguyễn Lương Hoàng (ed.). *Ngành In Việt Nam, Phong Trào Công Nhân, 1930–1945.* Hanoi: Liên Hiệp Các Xí Nghiệp In Việt Nam, 1987.

——— (ed.). *Lịch Sử Ngành In Việt Nam, Tập 2, Sơ Thảo.* Hanoi: Cục Xuất Bản Bộ Văn Hóa Thông Tin, 1992.

Nguyễn Ngọc Minh (ed.). *Kinh Tế Việt Nam, từ Cách Mạng Tháng Tám Đến Kháng Chiến Thắng Lợi, 1945–1954*. Hanoi: Nhà Xuất Bản Khoa Học, 1966.

Nguyễn Ngọc Oánh, Phạm Ngọc Phòng (eds). *Ngân Hàng Việt Nam Quá Trình Xây Dựng và Phát Triển.* Hanoi: Nhà Xuất Bản Chính Trị Quốc Gia, 1996.

Nguyễn Văn Canh. *Nông Dân Bắc Việt Những Năm 1945–1970*. San José, California: A.C.S.A.V., Center for Vietnamese Studies, 1987.

Nguyễn Văn Khánh (ed.). *Trí Thức Với Đảng, Đảng Với Trí Thức Trong Sự Nghiệp Giải Phóng Và Xây Dựng Đất Nước.* Hanoi: Nhà Xuất Bản Thông Tấn, 2004.

Phạm Gia Đức (ed.). *Lịch Sử Nhà Xuất Bản Quân Đội Nhân Dân, 1950–2000.* Hanoi: Nhà Xuất Bản Quân Đội Nhân Dân, 2000.

Tổng Cục Chính Trị, Cục Dân Vận và Tuyên Truyền Đặc Biệt. *Công Tác Dân Vận Và Tuyên Truyền Đặc Biệt Trong Quân Đội Nhân Dân Việt Nam (1947–2002), Biên Niên.* Hanoi: Nhà Xuất Bản Quân Đội Nhân Dân, 2003.

*Trí Thức Kháng Chiến*. Thanh Hóa: Trường Dự Bị Đại Học Thanh Hóa, 1952.

Viện Kinh Tế Thuộc Ủy Ban Khoa Học Nhà Nước. *Kinh Tế Việt Nam, 1945–1960.* Hanoi: Nhà Xuất Bản Sự Thật, 1960.

Vo Nhan Tri. *Croissance économique de la République Démocratique du Vietnam (1945–1965).* Hanoi: Ed. Langues Etrangères, 1967.

Vũ Ngọc Khuê. *Pháp Luật về Tài Chính (1945–1954)*. Hanoi: Nhà Xuất Bản Pháp Lý, 1985.

Vũ Văn Hiền. *Tiền Vàng và Tiền Giấy (Đồng Tiền Trong Nước Việt Nam và Ở Nước Ngoài Trước và Sau Chiến Tranh).* Saigon: Nhà Sách Vĩnh Bảo, 1949.

## Culture, Society, and Religion in a Time of War

Capa, Robert. *Images of War. With texts of his own writings.* London: Paul Hamlyn; New York: Chanticleer Press; Milan: Impr. A. Pizzi; 1964.

Copin, Henri. *L'Indochine dans la literature française des années 20 à 1954. Exotisme et altérité.* Paris: Ed. L'Harmattan, Coll. Critiques littéraires, 1996.

Dallet, Sylvie *et al. Guerres Révolutionnaires. Histoire et Cinéma.* Paris: Publ. De la Sorbonne/Ed. L'Harmattan, 1984.

Darcourt, Pierre. *Bay Vien, le maître de Cholon.* Paris: Hachette, 1977.

Dissanayake, Wimal (ed.). *Colonialism and nationalism in Asian Cinema.* Bloomington, Indiana: Indiana Univ. Press, 1994.

Đoàn Đức Thu, Xuân Huy. *Giám Mục Lê Hữu Tư và Phát Diệm, 1945–1954, Những Năm Tranh Đấu Hào Hùng.* Saigon: Ed. Histoire moderne, 1973.

Dooley, T. A. *Deliver us from Evil. The Story of Vietnam's Flight to Freedom.* New York: Farrar, Straus and Cudahy, 1956.

Faas, Horst, and Tim Page. *Requiem by the photographers who died in Vietnam and Indochina.* London: Jonathan Cape, 1997.

Ferré, Léo. *Poète...vos papiers!* Paris: La Table ronde, 1956.

Flament, Marc. *Les beaux-arts de la guerre.* Paris: Ed. de la Pensée moderne, 1974.

Greene, Graham. *The Quiet American.* New York: Bantam, 1955.

Handache, Gilbert. *L'œil de Cao Dai.* Paris: Julliard, 1958.

Hồ Sơn Đài, Đỗ Tầm Chương *et al. Bộ Đội Bình Xuyên.* Hanoi: Nhà Xuất Bản Lao Động, 2005.

Lanning, Michael Lee. *Vietnam at the Movies.* New York: Fawcett Columbine, 1994.

Lê Tiến Giang. *Công Giáo Kháng Chiến Nam Bộ 1945–1954, Hồi Ký.* Paris: Hồi Ký, 1972.

Malle, Louis. *Un souffle au cœur.* Paris: Gallimard, 1971.

Nguyễn Đình Thi. *Mấy Vấn Đề Nghệ Thuật.* Hanoi: Hội Văn Nghệ Việt Nam, 1950.

Nguyễn Hùng. *Người Bình Xuyên.* T.P. Hồ Chí Minh: Nhà Xuất Bản Công An Nhân Dân, 1988.

Panivong, Norindr. *Phantasmatic Indochina. French Colonial Ideology in Architecture, Film and Literature.* Durham, North Carolina: Duke Univ. Press, 1996.

Phạm Mục. *Phim Truyện và Phim Hoạt Hình Việt Nam.* Hanoi: Cục Điện Ảnh, 1983.

Phan Kế Hoành, Vũ Quang Vinh. *Bước Đầu Tìm Hiểu Lịch Sử Kịch Nói Việt Nam, 1945–1975.* Hanoi: Nhà Xuất Bản Văn Hóa, 1982.

Rousseau, Sabine. *La colombe et le napalm : des chrétiens français contre les guerres d'Indochine et du Vietnam, 1945–1975.* Paris: CNRS Editions, 2002.

Saint Julien, Albert de. *Loin. Poèmes glanés aux durs chemins d'Indochine.* Paris: Nouv. Presses Mondiales, 1954.

Schoendoerffer, Pierre *et al. Dien Bien Phu, 1954–1992. De la bataille au film*. Paris: Ed. Lincoln-Fixot, 1992.

Schoendoerffer, Pierre. *Le crabe-tambour*. Paris: Ed. Grasset, 1976.

———. *Là-haut*. Paris: Ed. Grasset and Fasquelle, 1981.

Vũ Ngọc Phan. *Nhà Văn Hiện Đại, Phê Bình Văn Học, Quyển Tư (Tập Hai)*. Hanoi: Nhà Xuất Bản Vĩnh Thịnh, 1951.

Wargnier, Régis, and Jean-Marie Leroy. *Indochine*. Paris: Ed. Ramsay, Coll. Cinéma, 1992.

Werner, Jayne S. *Peasant Politics and Religious Sectarianism – Peasant and Priest in the Cao Dai in Vietnam*. New Haven, Connecticut: Yale Univ. Press, 1981.

## Minorities and the War

Bộ Tư Lệnh Quân Khu 7, Tỉnh Ủy Lâm Đồng. Vai Trò Đồng Bào Các Dân Tộc Thiểu Số ở Đông Nam Bộ và Cực Nam Trung Bộ Trong Chiến Tranh Giải Phóng (1945–1975), Kỷ Yếu Hội Thảo Khoa Học. Hanoi: Nhà Xuất Bản Chính Trị Quốc Gia, 2004.

Chu Văn Tân. *Kỷ Niệm Cứu Quốc Quân, Hồi Ký*. Hanoi: Nhà Xuất Bản Quân Đội Nhân Dân, 1971.

Condominas, Georges. *L'exotique est quotidien. Sar Luk, Vietnam central*. Paris: Plon, Coll. Terre humaine, 1965.

Coutaz, Bernard. *Les dents agacées*. Paris: Ed. Témoignages Chrétien, 1952.

Dasse, Martial. *Montagnards, révoltes et guerres révolutionnaires en Asie continentale*. Bangkok, Thailand: DK Book House, 1976.

Đinh Xuân Lâm et al. Những Trang Sử Vẻ Vang Của Các Dân Tộc Ít Người: Miền Nam. Hanoi: Nhà Xuất Bản Giáo Dục, 1968.

Eisen, Arlene. *Women and Revolution in Vietnam*. London: Zed, 1984.

Eisen-Bergman, Arlene. *Women of Vietnam*. San Francisco, California: People's Press, 1974.

Franchini, Philippe. *Continental-Saigon*. Paris: Olivier Orban, 1976.

———. *Métis*. Paris: Ed. Jacques Bertoin, 1993.

Gaubry, Juliette. *Tricornes et Bérets*. Paris: Ed. Pierre Horay, 1954.

Gicquel, Pierre. *Sur la piste Méos*. Paris: Ed. du Gerfaut, 1972.

Gough, Kathleen. *Vietnamese Women Today and Women in Revolution*. New York: W.I.R.E. Service, 1979.

Hamilton-Merritt, Jane. *Tragic Mountains: The Hmongs, the Americans and the Secret Wars for Laos, 1942–1992*. Bloomington, Indiana: Indiana Univ. Press, 1993.

Hickey, Gerald C. *Sons of the Mountain. Ethnohistory of the Vietnamese Central Highlands to 1954*. Yale, Connecticut: Yale Univ. Press, 1982.

Hội Hữu Nghị Việt Pháp T.P. Hồ Chí Minh. *Tâm Hồn và Trí Tuệ Phụ Nữ Việt Nam*. T.P. Hồ Chí Minh: Nhà Xuất Bản Trẻ, 1999.

L'Herbier-Montagnon, Germaine. *Jusqu'au sacrifice*. Paris: Ed. E.C.L.A.I.R., 1960.

La Renaudie, Valérie. *Sur les routes du ciel. Les convoyeuses de l'Air*. Paris: Nouv. Ed. Latines, 1996.

Lefèvre, Kim. *Métisse blanche*. Paris: Ed. Barrault, 1989.

Maloire, Albert. *Femmes dans la guerre*. Paris: Ed. Louvois, Coll. Actualités mondiales, 1957.

Marchand, Jean. *Dans la jungle Moï*. Paris: J. Peyronnet and Cie, 1951.

Muelle, Raymond. Combats en pays Thai, de Lai Chau à Dien Bien Phu (1953–1954). Paris: Presses de la Cité, 1999.

Nguyễn Thị Được. Phòng Trào Cách Mạng Phụ Nứ Minh Hải trong Kháng Chiến Chống Pháp: Ký Sự. Minh Hải, Việt nam: Nhà Xuất Bản Mũi Cà Mau, 1994.

Nguyễn Thị Thập. *Lịch Sử Phong Trào Phụ Nữ Việt Nam*. Hanoi: Nhà Xuất Bản Phụ Nữ, 1980.

Nguyen, Thi Thu Lam. *Fallen Leaves : the Memoirs of a Vietnamese Woman from 1945 to 1975*. New Haven, Connecticut: The Council of Southeast Asian St., 1989.

Nguyen, Thi Tuyet Mai. *The Rubber Tree: Memoir of a Vietnamese Woman Who Was an Anti-French Guerilla, a Publisher and a Peace Activist*. Jefferson, North Carolina: Mac Farland, 1994.

Nông Minh Châu. *Muối Lên Rừng* (*Le sel a atteint la jungle*). Hanoi: Nhà Xuất Văn Học, 1964.

Quincy, Keith. *Hmong. History of a People*. Cheney, Washington: Eastern Washington Univ. Press, 1995.

Sassi, Jean, and Jean-Louis Tremblais. *Opérations spéciales: 20 ans de guerres secrètes (Résistance, Indochine, Algérie)*. Nimrod, 2009.

Sauzeau, Jean. *Lieutenant en pays Thai. Indochine (1949–1951)*. Paris: Ed. Mémoires d'Hommes, 2000.

Tetreault, Mary Ann. *Women and Revolution in Vietnam*. East Lansing, Michigan: Michigan State Univ. Press, 1991.

Thompson, Virginia M., and Richard Adloff. *Minority Problems in Southeast Asia*. Stanford, California: Stanford Univ. Press, 1955.

Trần Khánh. *Người Hoa Trong Xã Hội Việt Nam (Thời Pháp Thuộc và Dưới Chế Độ Sài Gòn)*. Hanoi: Nhà Xuất Bản Khoa Học Xã Hội, 2002.

## Comics and Cartoons

Giroux Frank, and Christian Lax. *Les oubliés d'Annam*. Dupuis, Collection Aire Libre, 2000 [1990].

Rullier, Laurent, and Stanislas Barthélémy. *La vie de Victor Levallois: Trafic en Indochine*. Genève: Les Humanoïdes Associés, 2002 [1990].

———. *La vie de Victor Levallois: La route de Cao Bang*. Genève: Les Humanoïdes Associés, 2003 [1992].

# Name Index

(Main entries for person indicated by bold text.)


Abalan, Michel Henri Charles **27**
Abbott, George Manlove **27**
Achard, Jacques Augustin **28**
Aeschlimann, Charles **30**, 288, 400
Albinet, Louis Casimir Henri **34**
Alessandri, Marcel Jean Marie **35**, 73, 87, 383, 411
Allard, Jacques Marie Paul **38**, 189
Amiel, Henri **38**
André. *See* Jean Maranne
André, Max **38**, 61, 173
André, Valérie **38**, 367
Andrieu, Georges **39**
Anh Ba. *See* Lê Duẩn
Anh Ba. *See* Nguyễn Bình
Anh Cả. *See* Nguyễn Lương Bằng
Anh Sáu. *See* Lê Đức Thọ
Anh Sáu. *See* Nguyễn Chí Thanh
Anh Út. *See* Nguyễn Văn Linh
Anh Út. *See* Nguyễn Hữu Thọ
Anthonioz, Pierre **40**
Appert, Raymond Paul Etienne Marie **42**
Argenlieu (d'). *See* Thierry d'Argenlieu, Georges
Arnaud, Andre Jean Laurent **43**
Arnaud, Georges Victor Maurice **43**
Aron, Raymond Claude Ferdinand **43**, 153, 229
Arsenen Lapin. *See* Katāy Dōn Sasōrit
Au Chhuen **47**
Auboyneau, Philippe **47**, 56, 353
Aubrac, Lucie **47–48**
Aubrac, Raymond **48**
Aurillac, Jean Honoré Charles **48–49**
Auriol, Vincent **49**, 53, 54, 67, 87, 285, 410, 412, 472, 476
Aussaresse, Paul Louis **49**, 96, 468
Axelrad, Édouard **49**, 346
Ayrolles, Léopold-Henry **50**

Ba Cụt. *See* Lê Quang Vinh
Ba Dương. *See* Dương Văn Dương
Ba Khiêm. *See* Ung Văn Khiêm
Baillet, Marcel **51**
Bailly, Camille Victor **51**
Balmont. *See* Raymond Aubrac
Bảo Đại 9, 14, 19, 27, 33, 36, 40, 44, 47, 49, **52–55**, 57–492 *passim*
Bao Keo. *See* Triệu Công Minh
Barbeau, Henri **55**
Bartlett, F. **55**
Bastid, Hélène **55**
Bastid, Paul **55**
Battet, Robert **56**, 198
Baudet, Philippe **56**
Bảy Chiếm. *See* Cao Đăng Chiếm
Bảy Viễn. *See* Lê Văn Viễn
Bayen, Maurice **56**
Bazé, William **56–57**, 67, 174, 175, 292
Bazin, Marcel Marshal **57**, 63, 282, 445, 450, 451
Beaufre, André **57–58**
Beauvais, André Antoine Marcel **58**
Belleux, Maurice **58**, 65, 191, 351, 425, 468
Bergot, Erwan **59**, 303
Bernard, Lucie. *See* Lucie Aubrac
Bert, Marcel **59**
Bertin, Maurice **59–60**
Beucler, Jean Jacques **60**, 69
Bevin, Ernest **60**
Beziat, Maître Joseph **60**
Bidault, Georges Augustin **61**, 96, 114, 182, 255, 273, 300, 420

Bier, René **61**

Bigeard, Marcel **61–62**, 67, 70, 80, 254

Binoche, François Alphonse **63**

Biros, Casimir **63**

Blaizot, Roger **63–64**, 165, 218, 450, 474

Blanc, Clément **64**

Blignières (de), Hervé Le Barbier **64**

Bloch-Lainé, François **64**, 123

Blum, Léon 25, 49, 61, **64–65**, 114, 134, 205, 300, 398, 445, 446

Bodard, Lucien 58, **65**, 107, 273, 320, 414

Bodet, Pierre **65**

Bollaert, Émile 54, 64, **65–66**, 118, 126, 148, 242, 270, 271, 279, 291, 293, 301, 367, 383, 393, 410, 412

Bollardière (de), Jacques-Pâris **66**, 433, 434

Bollot, Michel **66**

Bondis, Paul-Louis **66**, 338

Bonfils, Charles-Henri 54, **66–67**, 112, 383

Bong Suvannavong **67**

Bông Văn Dĩa **67**, 94

Bonnafous, Robert **67**, 70

Bonvissini, Henri 67

Börchers, Erwin **67–68**, 87, 120, 178, 390, 459, 472

Bordier, Louis **69**

Boucher de Crèvecoeur, Jean Marie Charles **69**, 74, 236, 273, 399, 408, 443

Boudarel, Georges 6, 59, 60, **69–71**, 98, 113, 196, 228, 303, 372, 390, 399, 453

Boudier, Michel **71**

Boulle, Pierre **71–72**

Bourgoin, Jean **72**

Bourgund, Gabriel **72**

Bourlier, François **72**

Boussarie, Armand **72**, 192

Boussarie, Marcel Marie **73**, 139

Boutbien, Léon **73**

Boyer de La Tour Du Moulin, Pierre Georges Jacques Marie **73**, 95, 132, 188, 203, 270, 291, 469, 476

Boyer, Pierre Jean Gabriel **73**

Brébisson (de), Michel Marie René 69, **74**, 197, 236

Brink, Francis Gerard **75**, 293, 294

Brohon, Raymond **75**

Brotherton, Alexander **75**, 249

Bruce, David Kirkpatrick Este **75**, 80

Brunet, Félix **75–76**

Buis, Georges Paul Gabriel **76**, 437

Bunchhan Mol **76**

Bunum Champāsak **76**

Burchett, Wilfred **77**

Buttinger, Joseph A. **79**

Bửu Hội. *See* Nguyễn-Phước Bửu Hội

Bửu Lộc. *See* Nguyễn-Phước Bửu Lộc

Cadière, Léopold **80**

Caffery, Thomas Jefferson 75, **80**

Caillaud, Robert **80**

Canac, André **81–82**

Cao Đăng Chiếm **84**, 336, 394

Cao Phá **84–85**

Cao Thắng. *See* Đặng Văn Sung

Cao Triệu Phát **85**, 327

Cao Văn Khánh 85, 277, 331

Cao Văn Thỉnh **85–86**, 333

Cao Văn Viên **86**, 128, 325

Capa, Robert **86**, 380

Caply, Michel. *See* Jean Deuve

Caput, Louis 68, 82, **86–87**, 176, 178, 212, 420, 422, 423, 462, 472, 488

Carle, Pierre Louis Joseph **87**

Carpentier, Marcel Maurice 35, 64, **87–88**, 194

Cassaigne, Marie Pierre Jean, Mgr **88**

Castries (de), Christian Marie Ferdinand De La Croix **88**, 423

Catala, Jean-Marie **89**

Catherine. *See* Lucie Aubrac

Cédile, Jean Marie Arsène 24, 51, 57, **91–92**, 112, 129, 140, 189, 202, 224, 243, 372, 392

Chabalier, Jean-Baptiste **93**
Chaleun Phouangchan **93**
Chalier, Pierre **93**
Chan Mun Boy 32, **94**
Chan Nak 94, 242, 490, 501
Chang Fa-Kwei. *See* Zhang Fakui
Chanson, Charles Marie Ferreol **94–95**, 408
Chanto Tres **95**
Chapuis **95**
Charret, Henri Roger Charles **95**
Chassin, Guillaume Jean Max **95**, 408
Château-Jobert, Pierre **96**
Châu Quang Lộ **96**, 101, 294
Châu Sen Cocsal **96**
Chauvel, Jean **96–97**
Chea Chinkoc **97**
Chegaray, Jacques **97**, 102, 442, 450, 451
Chen Geng 82, **97**, 497, 498
Chesneaux, Jean 71, **97–98**, 102, 140, 494
Chevance-Bertin, Maurice **98**
Cheysson, Claude **98**
Chhean Vam **98**, 220, 433
Chhum. *See* Chau Sen Cocsal
Chhuon Mchhulpich. *See* Dap Chhuon
Chị Ba Sưng Răng. *See* Triệu Công Minh
Chí Thuận. *See* Nguyễn Chánh
Chị Tư Xóm Gà. *See* Triệu Công Minh
Chiang Kaishek **98–99**, 502
Chín. *See* Lê Duẩn
Chính Hữu **102**
Chu Bá Phượng **102–103**
Chu Huy Mân 29, **103**, 325, 444
Chu Văn Điều. *See* Chu Huy Mân
Chu Văn Tấn **103**, 232, 233, 295, 306
Chuan Kem Piket. *See* Dap Chhuon
Chuiton (le), Raymond **103**
Chuon Kemphetchr. *See* Dap Chhuon
Churchill, Winston 99, **103–104**, 162, 183, 299
Clarac, Achille Marie **107**
Clark, Mark Wayne **107**
Clémentin, Jean Manan **107**, 118
Clos, Max **107**
Cogny, René Jules Lucien **108**, 136, 343
Collet, François **112**
Collins, Joseph Lawton **112**, 163
Colonna, Côme Damien **113**
Compain, Jacques Marie Julien **115**
Conein, Lucien E. **115**
Cornevin, Robert **116**
Coste-Floret, Paul **116**, 384, 419
Cousseau, Jean Germain Noël Bernard 3, 53, 54, 65, **117–118**, 215, 261, 262, 319, 383
Coutard, Raoul 26, **118–119**, 421
Crépin, Jean Albert Émile **119–120**, 271, 383
Cung Đình Quỳ **122**

D'Argenlieu. *See* Thierry d'Argenlieu
Dalloz, Jacques 5, 40, **125**, 176, 236, 371
Đàm Ngọc Lưu. *See* Đàm Quang Trung
Đàm Quang Trung **125**
Đàm Văn Mông. *See* Lê Quảng Ba
Đặng Chân Liệu **125**, 127
Đặng Hoán Bổn **125–126**
Đặng Hữu Chí **126**
Đặng Kim Giang **126**
Đặng Minh Trứ **126**, 333
Đặng Ngọc Chân **127**
Đặng Phúc Thông **127**
Đặng Thai Mai 85, **127**, 196, 204, 333, 486, 491
Đặng Tính **128**
Đặng Văn Ngữ **128**, 331, 449
Đặng Văn Quang **128**
Đặng Văn Sung **128–129**, 377
Đặng Văn Tĩ. *See* Đặng Tính
Đặng Văn Việt **129**
Đặng Vũ Lặc **129**, 266
Đặng Xuân Khu. *See* Trường Chinh
Dannaud, Jean-Pierre **129–130**

Đào Duy Anh **130**, 204
Đào Phúc Lộc. *See* Hoàng Minh Đào
Đào Xuân Mai **130**
Dap Chhuon 93, **130–131**, 243, 344, 428, 431, 501
Darcourt, Pierre **131**
Daridan, Jean Henri **131**
Davée, Robert **131**
De Gaulle, Charles 7–12 *passim*, 24–114 *passim*, **132**, 134–478 *passim*
De Lattre de Tassigny, Bernard 132–133
De Lattre de Tassigny, Jean Joseph Marie Gabriel 14, 31, 38, 42, 49, 58, 65, 73, 83, 87, 90, 108, 129, 131, 132, **133**, 149–498 *passim*
Debès, Pierre Louis **133–134**, 198, 199, 251, 252, 298, 478
Defferre, Gaston Paul Charles **134**
Dejean, Maurice **134**, 343
Delpey, Roger 105, **134**, 254, 303
Delteil, Henri Noël Barthélemy **135**, 163, 185, 186, 440
Delvert, Jean **135**
Dening, Maberly Esler **136**
Đèo Văn Long 69, **136**, 294, 441
Dequeker, Jacques **136–137**
Descoeuvres, Dr. **137**
Deuve, Jean **138–139**
Deux cents bougies. *See* Lê Duẩn
Devaux, Max Alexandre Henri **139**
Devillers, Philippe 5, 25, 79, 97, 98, **139–140**, 169, 199, 250, 301, 360, 407, 449
Devinat, Paul **140**
Dewey, Albert Peter **140–141**, 351
Diệp Ba **147**
Diệp Tư **147–148**
Diethelm, André **148**
Digo, Yves **148**
Dillon, C. Douglas **148**
Đinh Ngọc Liên **148**
Đinh Thị Cẩn **148**
Đinh Xuân Quảng **148–149**
Đinh Xuân Tín. *See* Lê Trọng Nghĩa
Dio, Louis Joseph Marie **149**
Đỗ Đức Liêm. *See* Vũ Lang
Đỗ Mười **151**, 232, 493
Đỗ Văn Năng **151**
Đỗ Xuân Hợp **151–152**, 401
Đoàn Khuê **152**
Đoàn Quân Tấn **152**
Domenach, Jean-Marie 41, 140, **152–153**, 164, 229, 410
Đồng Sĩ Hua **153**
Đồng Sĩ Nguyên **153**
Donovan, William Joseph 75, **154**, 350
Dooley, Thomas **154**
Drapier, Antonin-Fernand, Mgr. **155**
Dronne, Raymond **155**
Duclos, Jacques **155**, 458
Dufour, Robert **155**
Dugardier, Robert 155
Dulac, Léon Hippolyte Guillaume André **155–156**
Dulles, John Foster **156**, 162, 165, 182, 184, 185, 412, 429, 430, 433, 482
Dương Bá Lộc. *See* Jean Moreau
Dương Bạch Mai **156–157**, 394
Dương Đức Hiền **157**
Dương Quốc Chính **157**
Dương Tấn Tài **157**
Dương Văn Dương 120, **158**
Dương Văn Minh **158**
Dupin, Roger Émile Lucien **158**
Dupont d'Isigny, Paule **158**, 367
Durand, Maurice **158–159**

Ea Sichau **160**
Écarlat, Pierre Eugène **160**
Eden, Anthony 104, **161–162**, 183, 184, 290, 297
Eiji Wajima **162**
Eisenhower, Dwight D. 42, 87, 105, 107, 112, 147, 148, 153, 154, 156, **162**, 183, 245, 343, 346, 350, 398, 409, 429, 482

Ely, Paul Henri Romuald 75, 112, **162–163**, 170, 171, 218, 306, 350, 398, 415, 416, 482

Emiry, Olivier Jean **163**

Erskine, Graves B. *See* Melby–Erskine Mission (general index)

Faget, Jean **168**

Faidāng Lôbliayao **168**

Fall, Bernard 37, 46, 77, 79, 117, **168–169**, 179, 189, 199, 250, 391

Fargue, Jean-Paul **169**

Farinaud, Marie-Étienne **169**

Faugere, Fernand Dominique **169**, 292

Faure, Edgard **170**

Fay, Pierre Joseph Armand Léon **170**

Fenn, Charles **170**

Ferrandi, Jean **170–171**

Ferrari, Pierre **171**, 380

Figuères, Léopold 98, **171**, 177, 284

Fleurquin, Pierre Albérie Gabriel **172**

Foccart, Jacques 172

Fonde, Julien Roger Jean Pierre **172–173**, 298

Fong Sitthitham **173**

Fossey-François, Albert **174**, 408

Francès, Robert **175**

Frédéric-Dupont, Édouard 74, **175**

Frey, Ernst 120, **178–179**, 390, 424, 472

Friang, Brigitte **179**, 359

Gabarre, Marcel Antoine Henri **180**

Gabrillagues, Fernand Frédéric **180**

Galard (de), Geneviève-Terraube 68, **180**

Gallagher, Philip E. **180**, 486

Gambiez, Fernand Charles Louis 38, **180–181**, 359

Gannay, Paul 51, **181**

Gardet, Roger **181**

Gaudart, Joseph Frank **181**

Gaultier de la Ferrière, Jacques Marie Georges **181**

Gentil, Pierre Aristide Marie Gaston **186**

Geyre, Georges **186**

Giao Giăng. *See* Vũ Hồng Khanh

Gilles, Jean Marcellin Joseph Calixte 88, 136, 143, **186–187**, 253

Gimbert, Robert 187

Godard, Yves 119, **187**

Gonçalvès-Caminha, Pedro Mario **187**

Gonzalez de Linarès, François Jean Antonin Marie Amédée 132, **187–188**

Gorce, Pierre Marie Martial **188**

Gourou, Pierre **188**

Gracey, Douglas David (Sir) 23, 24, 25, 92, 140, **188–189**, 202, 225, 235, 288, 413, 467

Gracieux, Jean **189**

Grall, Edmond 101, 104, **189**, 192, 411, 424

Gras, Yves 101, **189**, 209

Grauwin, Paul, M.D. **189**

Greene, Graham **190**, 272, 346, 468, 469, 477

Griffin, Robert Allen **190–191**, 293

Guillaume, Pierre 70, 199, **194**, 421

Guillermaz, Jacques **194–195**

Guiriec, Hyacinthe Antoine Jules **195**

Gullion, Edmund Ashbury **195**, 239–240

Hạ Bá Cang. *See* Hoàng Quốc Việt

Hà Huy Giáp 93, 156, **196–197**, 476

Hà Kế Tấn **197**

Hà Văn Lâu 74, 120, **197**, 440

Haas, Émile Auguste **197**

Hai Hùng. *See* Phạm Hùng

Hai Long. *See* Vũ Ngọc Nhạ Pierre

Hak Mong Sheng **198–199**

Hammer, Ellen 6, 79, 98, **199**, 250, 342

Hán Thư. *See* Nguyễn Tiến Lãng

Hartemann, André **200**

Heath, Donald R. 118, **200**, 240

Hébert, René **201**

Hentic, Pierre **201**
Herckel, Raoul **202–203**, 211
Hermitte (L'), René 203
Hiroo Saito 138, **203**, 233
Hồ Chí Minh 4–203 *passim*, **204–206**, 207–502 *passim*
Hồ Chí Toán. *See* Stefan Kubiak
Hồ Đắc Di 152, **206–207**, 230
Hồ Đắc Diễm 206, **207**
Hồ Nam. *See* Trần Văn Giàu
Hồ Thanh Biển **207**
Hồ Thị Bi **207**
Hồ Thị Hoa. *See* Hồ Thị Bi
Hồ Thị Sáu. *See* Hồ Thị Bi
Hồ Tùng Mậu 207–208
Hồ Văn Huê **208**, 457
Hoàng. *See* Trần Văn Giàu
Hoàng Anh Kiệt. *See* Hoàng Nam Hùng
Hoàng Chung **209**
Hoàng Đạo Thúy 164, **209–210**, 397, 422, 459
Hoàng Đình Giọng 38, **210**, 211, 262, 295, 455, 503
Hoàng Đình Tùng **210**
Hoàng Đức Nhã. *See* Vũ Ngọc Nhã Pierre
Hoàng Hai Đình. *See* Hoàng Nam Hùng
Hoàng Hữu Nam 203, **211**, 262, 296, 422, 455
Hoàng Lung **211**
Hoàng Minh Chính **211**, 434, 486
Hoàng Minh Đạo **211–212**, 230, 373, 493
Hoàng Minh Giám 86, 87, 127, 176, **212**, 296, 422, 458, 488
Hoàng Minh Phụng. *See* Hoàng Minh Đạo
Hoàng Minh Thảo **212**
Hoàng Mỹ. *See* Trần Hiệu
Hoàng Nam Hồng. *See* Hoàng Nam Hùng
Hoàng Nam Hùng **213**
Hoàng Quân Bình. *See* Nguyễn Đình Luyện
Hoàng Quốc Việt 91, **213–214**, 274, 444, 472
Hoàng Sâm **214**, 232
Hoàng Thị Nghị **214**
Hoàng Tích Trí **214**
Hoàng Tùng **214–215**
Hoàng Văn Chí 121, **215**, 230
Hoàng Văn Hoan 114, 184, **215–216**, 243, 275, 282, 328, 357, 359, 360, 372, 485
Hoàng Văn Thái 33, 181, 197, 212, **216**, 236, 288, 479
Hoàng Văn Xiêm. *See* Hoàng Văn Thái
Hoàng Xuân Bình **216**, 277
Hoàng Xuân Hãn 121, 130, 196, **216–217**, 230, 316, 370
Hoàng Xuân Nhị **217**
Hogard, Jacques Claude Émile Michel 37, **217–218**, 317, 408
Hồng Lĩnh. *See* Nguyễn Khánh Toàn
Hoppenot, Henri **218**
Huang Hua 195, **218**
Huard, Paul Marie Léon **218**
Huard, Pierre 151, 152, **218–219**, 274
Hunt, Pierre **219**
Hunter, William H. **219**, 351
Hữu Mai **219**
Huy Cận **219–220**, 486, 500
Huy Kanthoul 160, **220**, 276, 345, 358, 430, 431, 432, 433, 501
Huy Mong **220**
Huỳnh Cường **220**
Huỳnh Đắc Hương **220**
Huỳnh Phan Hộ **220–221**, 268, 333
Huỳnh Phú Sổ 165, 209, **221**, 317, 461, 464
Huỳnh Tấn Phát **221**, 445
Huỳnh Thúc Kháng 130, **222**, 275
Huỳnh Văn Nghệ 57, **222**
Huỳnh Văn Trì **222**

Iehlé, Pierre **223**
Ieng Sary 81, **223**, 386
Ieu Koeus 94, 98, 135, **223–224**, 276, 501

Imfeld, Hans **224**

Isaacs, Harold **233**

Ishii Takuo 120, **233**

Ith Seam **233–234**

Jacq, Bishop, O. **235**

Jacquet, Marc 74, **235**

Jahan, Pierre **235**

Jaquin, Henri **235**

Jessup, Philip **236**, 464

Jiang Jieshi. *See* Chiang Kai-Shek

Jouhaud, Edmond 69, 74, **236**, 421

Jubelin, André **236**

Juglas, J. J. 237

Juin, Alphonse Pierre 87, **237**, 249, 306, 358

Jumeau, Henri 81, **237**

Kaisôn Phomvihãn 114, **238**, 241, 292, 325, 352, 365, 436

Kamath, Mello **238**

Karmen, Roman Lazarevitch 104, **238–239**

Katāy Dōn Sasōrit **239**

Keller, Rene Paul Léon Jules **239**

Kennedy, John F. **239–240**

Kha Vạn Cân **240**, 372

Khái Hưng **240**

Khamfeuane Tounarom **240–241**

Khammao Vilai **241**, 380

Khamtai Sīphandôn **241**

Khim Tith 47, 94, **241–242**

Khuang Aphaiwong 242, **244**, 385

Khương Mê 104, **244**

Kindavong, Prince **245**, 381, 428

Kinim Phosēnā **245**

Knowland, William Fife **245**

Koenig, Marie Pierre **245**

Komaki Oomiya **245–246**

Kosal **246**

Koshiro Iwai **246–247**

Kowal, Georges **247**, 420

Krull, Germaine **247**

Ku Aphai **247**

Ku Vôravong **247–248**

Kubiak, Stefan **248**

La Chambre, Guy 107, **249**

Lã Vĩnh Lợi **249**, 457

Labrouquère, André **249**

Lacharrière (de), Ladreit **249**

Lacheroy, Charles 37, 155, **249–250**, 253, 290, 359, 360, 408

Lacouture, Jean 79, 97, 98, 139, 140, 199, 221, **250**, 360, 407

Lalande, André 71, 117, **250**

Lâm Thành Nguyên **250–251**

Lami, Pierre 211, **251**, 368

Langlade (de), François Giron 112, **252–253**, 274, 276, 301, 474

Langlade (de), Paul Annet Joseph Alexandre Girot **253**, 412

Langlais, Pierre Charles Albert Marie 45, 62, **253–254**

Laniel, Joseph 44, 104, 170, 182, 183, 235, **255**, 306, 307, 385, 409

Lansdale, Edward Geary 115, **255–256**, 376, 469

Lapierre, Henri Gustave Léon **258**

Lartéguy, Jean 37, 65, 129, **258**, 303, 346, 411, 421, 481, 484

Laurentie, Henri 8, 74, 134, 178, **258–259**, 392, 397

Lê Chinh. *See* Jean Marrane.

Lê Cộng Trinh **259**

Lê Đình Chi **259**

Lê Duẩn 67, 78, 84, 93, 114, 128, 156, 206, 213, 214, 243, **260–261**, 262, 269, 277, 281, 335, 336, 368, 370, 373, 378, 387, 403, 444, 451, 462, 465, 466

Lê Đức Anh **261**

Lê Đức Thọ **261–262**

Lê Duy Nghĩa. *See* Trần Ngọc Danh

Lê Giản 83, 118, 130, 211, 261, **262**, 368, 394, 395, 430, 455

Lê Hiến Mai. *See* Dương Quốc Chính

Lê Hồng. *See* Hoàng Minh Chính

Lê Hữu Từ 90, 91, 132, 230, **262–263**, 340, 371, 454, 482, 493
Lê Hy. *See* Lã Vĩnh Lợi
Lê Liêm **263**, 274
Le Puloch, Louis **263–264**
Lê Quảng Ba 233, **264**, 444, 451
Lê Quang Đạo **264**
Lê Quang Hòa 232, **264**
Lê Quang Huy **264–265**
Lê Quang Vinh 209, **265**
Lê Quốc Lộc **265**
Lê Quốc Sản **265**
Lê Sỹ Quỳ. *See* Thiếu Sơn
Lê Tấn Nam **265–266**
Lê Thắng **266**
Lê Thanh Kim. *See* Lê Quang Hoà
Lê Thanh Nghị **266**, 430
Lê Thị Xuyền **267**
Lê Thiết Hùng **267**
Lê Trọng Nghĩa 231, **267–268**
Lê Trọng Tấn 84, **268**
Lê Trọng Tố. *See* Lê Trọng Tấn
Lê Văn Chi **268**
Lê Văn Hiến 39, 210, **268**, 436, 441
Lê Văn Hoạch 111, **268–269**, 337, 341, 393, 466
Lê Văn Lạc. *See* Trần Mai
Lê Văn Lương **269**, 370, 472
Lê Văn Nghiệm. *See* Lê Thiết Hùng
Lê Văn Sửu. *See* Lê Thiết Hùng
Lê Văn Thắng. *See* Trần Văn Kha
Lê Văn Viễn 63, 120, 131, **269–270**, 282, 317, 353
Lê Vang Sang. *See* Trần Văn Soái
Lê Vang Thắng. *See* Lê Thắng
Lebris 63, **271**
Leclerc, Philippe Marie de Hautecloque 10, 11, 27, 28, 39, 47, 62, 73, 76, 91, 119, 129, 132, 139, 149, 155, 165, 172 ,173 ,187, 242, 250, 253, 258, 259, **271–272**, 284, 285, 286, 295, 299, 301, 317, 345, 397, 406, 411, 431, 461, 467, 474, 478, 483
Lecuir, Henri **272**
Léger, Paul-Alain **272**
Lejay-Cler. *See* Guillaume Chassin
Leroy, Jean **272–273**, 476, 477
Lesseps (de), Louis **273**
Letourneau, Jean 38, 53, 74, 101, 107, **273**, 351
Leuam Insīxiangmai **273**
Leuba, Jeanne **274**
Levain, Marcel **274**
Lévy, Paul 97, 160, **274**
Li Bishan. *See* Lý Ban
Li Peiwen. *See* Lý Ban
Li Ying. *See* Lý Ban
Lon Nol 96, **275–276**, 343, 432
Longeaux, Louis **276**
Lorillot, Henri Augustin **276**, 410
Loubet, Lucien Vincent **277**
Lozeray, Rodolphe Henri 177, **277–278**
Lu Han 25, 99, 180, **278**, 406, 426, 467
Luang Kovit Aphaiwong. *See* Khuang Aphaiwong
Luo Guibo 101, 102, **278**, 498
Lưu Đoàn Huỳnh **278–279**
Lưu Đức Phó. *See* Nguyễn Duy Trinh
Lưu Văn Lang 126, **279**, 457
Lưu Văn Lợi 203, **279**, 284, 326
Lý Anh Tư. *See* Nguyễn Sơn
Lý Bá Phẩm **280**
Lý Ban 121, 136, **280**, 318, 369
Ly Seo Nung 209, **280**

Mā Khaikhamphithūn **281**
MacDonald, Malcolm **281**
Mai Chí Thọ 84, **281**, 370
Mai Hữu Xuân **282**
Mai Lâm **282**
Mai Thế Châu **282**
Mai Văn Hiến **282**
Maisonneuve, Regis Bouvet **282–283**
Malleret, Louis **283**, 374
Mansfield, Michael Joseph 245, **283**

Mao Zedong 14, 15, 32, 95, 101, 102, 193, 200, 206, 218, 226, 250, 251, **283–284**, 328, 329, 366, 407, 408, 434, 435, 469, 488, 502

Marchal, Léon **284**

Marion, Roger François Marie Maurice **284**

Marneffe, Hubert **284**

Marrane, Jean 177, 259, 279, **284**, 326

Marson, Paul **284–285**

Martin, Henri 42, 153, 177, 229, **285**, 418

Martinet, André **285**

Martini, François Joseph **285–286**

Martinoff, Raymond **286**

Massu, Jacques Émile Charles Marie 65, 165, 187, **286–287**, 358, 363, 411

Mast, Charles 30, **287**

Mathivet de la Ville de Mirmont, Pierre Antoine **287**

Mayer, René 142, 172, **287**, 306, 350

McGovern, James B., Jr. 106, **287–288**

Mehta, A. N. **288**

Mei Jiasheng **288**, 498

Meiklereid, Ernest William **288**

Melby, John F. *See* Melby–Erskine Mission

Mendès France, Pierre Isaac Isidore 18, 19, 56, 61, 62, 82, 83, 96, 98, 116, 163, 165, 166, 170, 171, 183, 184, 206, 230, 245, 249, 255, 273, **290**, 415, 418, 429

Menon, Krishna Vengalil Krishnan 182, **290–291**

Méric, Édouard **291**

Messmer, Pierre Auguste Joseph 112, **291**, 414

Michaudel, Maurice Marie Auguste **293**

Michel, Étienne Didier 67, **293**

Minh Viên. *See* Huỳnh Thúc Kháng

Missoffe, François **295**

Mistral, Jean Édouard **295**

Moffat, Abbot Low **296–297**, 489

Molotov, Viatcheslav Skriabine 162, 183, 184, 290, **297**, 417

Moneglia, Vincent **297**

Monthéard, Henri Denis Alfred 78, **297**

Moreau, Jean 292, **297–298**

Moreau, Louis Guy Marle **298**

Morel, André **298**

Moret, André **298**, 368, 437

Morlière, Louis Constant 120, 134, 198, 251, 252, **298–299**, 474

Motais de Narbonne, Léon **299**

Mountbatten, Louis, Lord 91, 99, 136, 235, 285, **299**, 386

Moutet, Marius 12, 61, 65, 73, 87, 173, 249, 291, 296, **300**, 392, 393, 398, 423

Mune **300–301**

Mười Cúc. *See* Nguyễn Văn Linh

Mười Hương. *See* Trần Quốc Hương

Mus, Paul 5, 9, 41, 65, 87, 97, 98, 102, 113, 116, 127, 140, 153, 160, 164, 169, 178, 188, 198, 199, 229, 250, 259, **301–302**, 310, 339, 387, 393, 410, 418, 442, 449, 450, 483

Naison Sichan. *See* Ngô Thất Sơn

Nam *See* Tô Ký

Năm Bi. *See* Hồ Thị Bi

Nam Cao **304**

Năm Đạo. *See* Hoàng Minh Đạo

Năm Đời. *See* Hoàng Minh Đạo

Nam Hùng. *See* Nguyễn Chí Thanh

Năm Lửa. *See* Trần Văn Soái

Nam Phương 52, 81, **305**, 332, 460

Năm Thu. *See* Hoàng Mình Đạo

Nam Xuân. *See* Mai Chí Thọ

Navarre, Henri Eugène 34, 46, 86, 105, 134, 141–144, 147, 162, 163, 170, 172, 182, 192, 255, 257, 258, 287, 304, **306–307**, 343, 346, 350, 353, 379, 387, 425, 467

Nehru, Jawaharlal 109, 182, 183, 184, 224, 225, 228, 238, 275, 282, 288, 290, **309–310**, 337, 359, 433, 475, 476, 502

Ner, Marcel **310**, 491
Nghiêm Kế Tổ **312**
Nghiêm Văn Trị **312–313**
Nghiêm Xuân Yểm **313**
Ngô Đình Diệm, Jean-Baptiste 4, 18, 19, 26–295 *passim*, **313–314**, 315–498 *passim*
Ngô Đình Nhu, Jacob 47, 140, **314**, 315, 456
Ngô Đình Thục, Pierre Martin 155, **314–315**, 373
Ngô Gia Khẩm **315**
Ngô Mạnh Gương. *See* Ngô Thất Sơn
Ngô Thất Sơn **315–316**
Nguyễn Ái Quốc. *See* Hồ Chí Minh
Nguyễn Bá Sang **316**
Nguyễn Bắc 232, 254, **316**
Nguyễn Bình 10, 29, 36, 38, 57, 63, 64, 65, 66, 73, 83, 95, 111, 132, 157, 158, 165, 194, 202, 206, 211, 212, 218, 222, 232, 260, 261, 266, 270, **316–317**, 322, 340, 370, 373, 413, 419, 445, 448, 456, 462, 463, 473, 490, 494, 503
Nguyễn Cẩm Giang. *See* Nguyễn Hải Thần
Nguyễn Cao Kỳ **317**
Nguyễn Chấn. *See* Trần Văn Trà
Nguyễn Chánh (central commander) 85, 232, **318**, 371
Nguyễn Chánh (southern commander) 138, **318**
Nguyễn Chí Thanh 85, 181, **318–319**, 454, 457
Nguyễn Cơ Thạch 215, **319**
Nguyễn Công Hoan 118, 269, **319**
Nguyễn Công Miều. *See* Lê Văn Lương
Nguyễn Đệ **319–320**
Nguyễn Đình Luyện **320**
Nguyễn Đình Ưu **320**
Nguyễn Đôn **320**
Nguyễn Đức Nguyễn. *See* Lê Quang Đạo
Nguyễn Đức Quỳ 279, **320–321**, 382
Nguyễn Đức Thụy **321**
Nguyễn Đức Việt. *See* Werner Schulze
Nguyễn Duy Thanh **321**
Nguyễn Duy Trinh 130, 215, **321**
Nguyễn Giác Ngộ **322**
Nguyễn Hải Thần **322**, 466, 484, 486, 487
Nguyễn Hoài Thanh. *See* Nguyễn Văn Thanh
Nguyễn Hữu Đang **323**
Nguyễn Hữu Thị Lan, Marie-Thérèse. *See* Nam Phương
Nguyễn Hữu Thọ 216, **323**, 330, 341
Nguyễn Hữu Trí **323–324**, 493, 494
Nguyễn Hữu Vũ. *See* Đồng Sĩ Nguyên
Nguyễn Huy Lai **324**
Nguyễn Ken. *See* Nguyễn Thế Lam
Nguyễn Khắc Vệ **324**
Nguyễn Khắc Viện **324–325**
Nguyễn Khắc Xứng. *See* Lê Thanh Nghị
Nguyễn Khải **325**
Nguyễn Khang 29, **325**, 360
Nguyễn Khanh 128, **325**
Nguyễn Khánh Toàn 121, 204, **325–326**, 329
Nguyễn Kinh Chi **326**
Nguyễn Lương Bằng 279, **326**, 420, 423, 430, 456
Nguyễn Mạnh Hà 121, 217, 230, 284, 292, **326–327**
Nguyễn Mạnh Khải. *See* Nguyễn Khải
Nguyễn Nam Hùng. *See* Hoàng Nam Hùng
Nguyễn Ngọc Nhứt **327**, 445
Nguyễn Ngọc Vỹ **327**
Nguyễn Phan Long 149, 265, 266, **327–328**, 377, 379, 494
Nguyễn Phúc Vĩnh Thụy. *See* Bảo Đại
Nguyễn Phương Thảo. *See* Nguyễn Bình
Nguyễn Quốc Trị. *See* Kaison Phomvihan.
Nguyễn Quyết **328**
Nguyễn Sơn 120, 127 178, 215, 232, 233, 279, 292, 326, **328–329**, 332, 369, 400

Nguyễn Tấn Cường 272, **329**
Nguyễn Thanh Giưng, Henri **329**
Nguyễn Thành Lập **329**
Nguyễn Thanh Sơn 114, 242, **329–330**, 360, 369, 386, 426, 431, 493
Nguyễn Thế Lâm 232, **330**
Nguyễn Thế Lương. *See* Cao Phá
Nguyễn Thị Ba **330**
Nguyễn Thị Bình **330**
Nguyễn Thị Định **330–331**
Nguyễn Thị Ngọc Toàn 85, 117, 128, 146, 277, **331**, 499
Nguyễn Thị Ngọc Tốt. *See* Nguyễn Thị Thập
Nguyễn Thị Thập **331**
Nguyễn Tiến Lãng **331–332**
Nguyễn Tôn Hoàn 314, **332**
Nguyễn Trọng Cảnh. *See* Trần Quốc Hoàn
Nguyễn Trọng Vinh **332**
Nguyễn Trung Vịnh **332**
Nguyễn Tú Minh. *See* Nguyễn Văn Thanh
Nguyễn Tường Tam 126, 190, 240, **333**, 375, 466, 486, 491, 500
Nguyễn Văn Ban. *See* Nguyễn Xuân Hoàng
Nguyễn Văn Chí (educator) **333**
Nguyễn Văn Chí (spokesman) **333–334**
Nguyễn Văn Cúc. *See* Nguyễn Văn Linh
Nguyễn Văn Đôi. *See* Vương Thừa Vũ
Nguyễn Văn Đồng. *See* Đồng Sĩ Nguyên
Nguyễn Văn Hình 43, 107, 313, **334–335**, 336, 340, 377
Nguyễn Văn Hương 126, 230, **335**
Nguyễn Văn Huyên **335**
Nguyễn Văn Khương. *See* Song Hào
Nguyễn Văn Kỉnh **335**
Nguyễn Văn Lập. *See* Kostas Sarantıdis
Nguyễn Văn Linh 84, 260, 261, 281, **336**, 370, 378, 387, 444, 503
Nguyễn Văn Long **336**
Nguyễn Văn Luyện. *See* Nguyễn Đình Luyện
Nguyễn Văn Sâm **336**, 461
Nguyễn Văn Tâm 98, 122, 162, 213, 266, 269, 313, 324, 329, 324, **336–337**, 342, 377, 379, 438, 463, 465
Nguyễn Văn Tạo **337–338**
Nguyễn Văn Tây. *See* Nguyễn Thanh Sơn
Nguyễn Văn Thắng. *See* Nguyễn Hải Thần
Nguyễn Văn Thanh **338**, 385, 429
Nguyễn Văn Thích, Jean-Marie **338**
Nguyễn Văn Thiệu 27, 86, 128, 325, 334, **338**, 460
Nguyễn Văn Thịnh 111, 198, 269, 329, 337, **339**, 392, 393, 466
Nguyễn Văn Thọ. *See* Vũ Tùng
Nguyễn Văn Tố 160, 268, 271, 333, **339–340**
Nguyễn Văn Vịnh 232, 266, **340**, 503
Nguyễn Văn Vỹ 334, **340**
Nguyễn Văn Vỹ, Michel **340–341**
Nguyễn Văn Xuân 30, 54, 126, 266, 312, 313, 319, 324, **341**, 379, 392, 460, 461
Nguyễn Xiển 196, 267, **341**
Nguyễn Xuân Hoàng **341–342**
Nguyễn Xuân Mai. *See* Mai Chí Thọ
Nguyễn-Phước Bửu Hội **342**
Nguyễn-Phước Bửu Lộc **342**
Nhiek Tioulong 96, 186, 276, 316, **342–343**
Nixon, Richard Milhous **343**, 415
Nong Kimny **343**
Nordlinger, Stephen **343–344**
Norodom Chantaraingsey 95, **344**
Norodom Montana 97, **344**
Norodom Sihanouk 9, 26, 42, 44, 47, 76, 81, 94, 96, 98, 130, 135, 160, 220, 242, 244, 255, 256, 276, 287, 295, 315, 343, **344–345**, 364, 396, 399, 410, 411, 417, 421, 427–433, 442, 471, 490, 501

Nūhak Phūmsavan 29, 114, **347–438**, 436
Nyiaveu Lôbliayao **348**
Nyo, Georges Yves **348**
Nyūy Aphai **348**

O'Connell, Madeleine **349**
O'Daniel, John W. 170, **350**
Offroy, Raymond **351**
Ogburn, Charlton 233, **351–352**
Ōkham Anurak 114, **352**
Ortoli, Paul 56, **353**
O'Sullivan, James O. 198, **354**
Ourot Souvannavong **354**

Pach Chhoeun 96, **358**, 426
Pagniez, Yvonne **359**
Panikkar, Kavalam Madhava **359**
Parisot, Jean-Paul **360**
Patti, Archimedes L. A. 23, 115, 291, 295, 351, **361**, 427, 440
Paul-Boncour, Jean Louis **362**, 496
Pechkoff, Zinovi **363**, 474
Penavaire, Romain Victor Joseph **364**
Penn Nouth 47, 98, 242, 343, 344, **364–365**, 427, 432, 433, 442, 471, 501
Peraud, Jean **366–367**, 380
Pereyra (de), Miguel-Joaquin **367**
Perrier, Pierre 95, **367**, 437
Petit, Charles Eugène Fernand 292, **367–368**
Phạm Công Tắc 83, 120, 262, 269, **368**, 468
Phạm Đàn **368**
Phạm Đang Cao **368–369**
Phạm Duy 121, 230, 299, **369**, 376
Phạm Hùng 84, 93, 222, 232, 249, 260, 261, 269, 281, 336, **369–370**, 379, 387, 444, 452
Phạm Huy Thông **370**
Phạm Khắc Hòe 251, **370–371**
Phạm Kiệt **371**
Phạm Ngọc Chi, Pierre-Marie 91, **371**
Phạm Ngọc Mậu **371**
Phạm Ngọc Quyết. *See* Phạm Ngọc Mậu
Phạm Ngọc Thạch 71, 130, 140, 141, 155, 176, 177, 224, 230, 249, 292, 320, 329, **371–372**, 373, 374, 376, 422, 443, 447, 452, 462, 476, 480, 481
Phạm Ngọc Thảo, Albert **372–373**
Phạm Ngọc Thuần, Gaston **373–374**
Phạm Quang Khánh. *See* Phạm Kiệt
Phạm Quang Lễ. *See* Trần Đại Nghĩa
Phạm Thiều 85204, 230, 373, **374**, 445
Phạm Thư. *See* Trần Duy Hưng
Phạm Văn Bạch 140, 233, 324, 333, 373, **374**, 445
Phạm Văn Bình **374–375**
Phạm Văn Cương. *See* Nguyễn Cơ Thạch
Phạm Văn Đồng 125, 127, 128, 173, 183, 184, 196, 197, 213, 220, 222, 260, 281, 296, 328, 334, **375**, 376, 474, 485, 491
Phạm Văn Hua. *See* Song Ngọc Minh
Phạm Văn Khoa **375–376**
Phạm Văn Khương. *See* Lê Văn Lương
Phạm Văn Phu. *See* Trần Tử Bình
Phạm Văn Thiện. *See* Phạm Hùng
Phạm Xuân Ẩn 84, 256, 372, **376**, 459
Phan Anh 217, **376**, 440
Phan Bội. *See* Hoàng Hữu Nam
Phan Đình Khải. *See* Lê Đức Thọ
Phan Huy Dân **377**
Phan Huy Quát 190, **377**
Phan Kế Toại **377–378**
Phan Khắc Hy **378**
Phan Khắc Sửu **378**
Phan Trọng Hộ. *See* Huỳnh Phan Hộ
Phan Trọng Tuệ 232, **378–379**, 503
Phan Văn Giáo 120, 197, **379**
Phao Panya. *See* Phouy Panya
Phetxarāt Rattanavongsā **379**
Phóng. *See* Hoàng Văn Hoan
Phouy Panya **380–381**

Phūmī Nôsavan **381**
Phūmī Vongvichit 241, **381**
Phương. See Trường Chinh; Trương Tử Anh
Phuy Xananikôn 241, **381–382**, 438, 475
Pibun Songgram 173, 244, 321, 336, 357, **382**, 385, 388, 427, 446, 493
Pignon, Léon Adolphe Marie Pascal 3, 8, 13, 14, 53, 54, 55, 63, 65, 66, 67, 74, 87, 92, 97, 106, 112, 115, 118, 120, 127, 134, 151, 157, 161, 169, 191, 198, 227, 236, 242, 256, 258, 277, 281, 292, 296, 351, **382–384**, 393, 399, 410, 416, 418, 419, 450, 451
Pisier, Georges Léon Pierre **384**
Platon, Alexandrovich 383, **384–385**
Pleven, René 17, 30, 91, 163, 164, 170, 171, 235, 255, 258, 383, **385**
Poc Khun 242, 243, **385**
Pol Pot 81, 223, 342, **385–386**
Ponchardier, Pierre **386**, 433, 434, 469
Ponge, Jack Étienne **386**
Pouget, Jean **387**
Poullard, Jean Robert **387**
Poupaert, Jean-Jacques Charles **388**
Poussin, Jacques Eugène Henri **388**
Prasert Phinikorn. *See* Trần Mai
Pridi Banomyong 321, 336, **388**, 446, 447, 462
Puloch (Le), Louis Jean Alain **395**
Puth Chhay 242, **395–396**
Puy-Montbrun (Du), Déodat 70, **396**

Quắch Vĩnh Chương. *See* Quắch Vũ
Quắch Vũ **397**
Quang Đàm **397**
Querville, Jean-Marie **397**
Quilichini, Robert **397**

Radford, Arthur William 163, **398**, 482
Ramadier, Paul 53, 65, 177, 393, **398**, 445, 450, 451
Raphaël-Leygues, Jacques **398**
Ravix, Laurent **398–399**
Raymond (de), Jean Léon François Marie **399**
Redon (de), Raoul Guillaume Henri **401–402**
Redon, Maurice Paul 194, **402**
Reed, Charles Shadrach, 2nd 354, **402**
Reese, Everette Dixie **402**
Regnier, Robert **402**
Répiton-Preneuf, Paul **406**
Revers, Georges 30–31, 55, 64, 82, 87, 287, **407–408**
Rey-Coquais, François **409**
Reynaud, Paul 157, 255, **409**
Richonnet, Francisque **409**
Ridgway, Matthew B. **409**
Risterucci, Jean **410**
Rivet, Paul 53, **410**, 423
Robin, Yves Hermeland François Marie **410**
Rochoir, Jean **410–411**
Romain-Desfossés, Jacques **411**
Roque **411**
Roy, Jules **411**, 451
Royère, Jean **412**

Sainteny, Jean 24, 28, 55, 87, 115, 163, 173, 198, 205, 273, 274, 291, 295, 296, 298, 361, 383, 384, **414–415**, 416, 418, 427, 430, 481
Saint-Marc (de), Hélie Denoix **415**
Sala, Vito **415**
Salan, Raoul 37, 45, 107, 108, 134, 162, 170, 171, 187, 188, 190, 208, 235, 257, 271, 272, 304, 306, 312, **415–416**, 421, 467, 468, 469, 470, 489
Saloth Sar. *See* Pol Pot
Sam Sary 242, **416–417**, 442
Samuel, Raymond. *See* Raymond Aubrac
Sang, Michel. *See* Nguyễn Bá Sang
Sao Đỏ. *See* Nguyễn Lương Bằng
Sarantidis, Kostas 390, **417**

Sarraut, Albert Pierre 3, 52–56 *passim*, 110, 111, 125, 131, 149, 158, 188, 215, 216, 247, 301, 310, 319, 322, 323, 331, 340, 342, 361, 371, 374, 382, 414, **417–418**, 435, 436, 438, 457, 491, 501

Sartre, Jean-Paul 43, 153, 229, 285, 310, **418**, 454, 455

Sassi, Jean **418**, 424

Sáu Búa. *See* Lê Đức Thọ

Sáu Phát. *See* Huỳnh Tấn Phát

Sáu Thanh. *See* Nguyễn Văn Thanh

Sauvagnac, Henri 270, **418–419**

Savāngvatthanā **419**

Savani, Antoine Marie 63, 203, 221, **419**

Savary, Alain **419–420**, 445, 468

Scheurer, Joseph Louis André **420**

Schlumberger, Étienne 78, **420**

Schneyder, René François **420**

Schoendoerffer, Pierre 26, 37, 41, 105, 119, 129, 146, 303, 346, 347, 367, 380, 411, **420–421**, 484

Schröder, Rudy 120, **421–422**

Schulze, Werner 33, 321, **422**

Seguins Pazzis (de), Hubert Marie Jean Ambert **423**

Sergent, Pierre 179, **424**

Servant, Henri Édouard Jean-Marie **424**

Sheldon, George **426**

Siao Wen 349, **426**

Sicurani, Jean **426**

Sieu Heng **426**

Sihanouk. *See* Norodom Sihanouk

Sim Var 98, 135, **426–427**

Simondet, Jean **427**

Simpson-Jones, Peter **427**, 467

Singkapo Sikhot Chounlamany. *See* Singkapō Sīkhōtchunnamālī

Singkapō Sīkhōtchunnamālī **427–428**

Sīsāvangvong, King 9, 76, 245, 380, 419, **428**, 473

Sisowath Monipong 47, 98, 220, **428**, 432, 433

Sisowath Sirik Matak **428**

Sisowath Youtevong 47, 98, 198, 220, 364, **428–429**, 432

Sīthon Kommadam 241, 348, **429**

Skrzhinsky, Platon Alexandrovich **429**

Smith, Walter Bedell 165, 185, 290, **429–430**

Sok Chhong **430**

Solovieff, Stephan **430**

Som Phommachan 114, **430**

Somsanit Vongkotratana **430**

Sơn Ngọc Minh 81, 94, 138, 243, 292, 386, 403, 426, **430–431**, 472

Sơn Ngọc Thành 9, 76, 94, 95, 96, 131, 160, 218, 223, 242, 243, 276, 295, 342, 343, 344, 358, 399, 411, 427, 430, **431–432**, 467, 490

Son Sann **432**, 433

Song Hào 238, 365, **432**

Sonn Voeunsai **432–433**

Soulat, Henri **433**

Spillmann, Georges Joseph Roger André 358, **434**

Stalin, Josef 14, 15, 18, 32, 41, 52, 99, 104, 109, 143, 155, 156, 182, 206, 251, 283, 297, 366, **434–435**, 446, 470, 485, 488, 502

Sư Rĩ. *See* Nguyễn Chí Thanh

Suk Vongsak **435**

Suphānuvong, Prince 91, 216, 238, 257, 292, 300, 336, 341, 347, 380, 381, 427, 429, **435–436**, 438, 443

Surleau, Marcel-André **438**

Suvanna Phūmā 241, 248, 343, 348, 435, **438–439**

Suvannarāt, Prince 273, **439**

Tạ Ngọc Phách. *See* Trần Độ

Tạ Quang Bửu 33, 74, 84, 135, 183, 185, 186, 197, 209, **440**

Tạ Thái An. *See* Hoàng Minh Thảo

Tạ Thu Thâu **440**, 461

Tạ Tiến. *See* Tạ Xuân Thu

Tạ Xuân Thu **441**

Tạm Chí. *See* Huỳnh Tấn Phát

Tạm Ngại. *See* Huỳnh Văn Nghệ

Tân Hồng. *See* Chu Văn Tấn

Tauriac, Michel **441**
Tep Phan 220, **442**
Ter Sarkissoff, Alexandre **442**
Thái Lương Nam. *See* Hoàng Văn Hoan
Thái Văn Lung 268, 333, 372, 373, **443**
Thần. *See* Trường Chinh
Thao Sing **443–444**
Thibau, Jacques **444**
Thierry d'Argenlieu, Georges Louis Marie 9, 12, 24, 28, 40, 42, 53, 54, 61, 64, 65, 66, 67, 77, 78, 92, 103, 107, 111, 114, 118, 124, 125, 127, 131, 132, 134, 137, 172, 173, 187, 192, 197, 199, 202, 205, 223, 224, 227, 237, 249, 252, 253, 259, 263, 264, 269, 270, 271, 276, 291, 298, 300, 305, 339, 362, 363, 372, 383, 392, 393, 395, 399, 415, 416, 418, 420, 423, **444–445**, 447, 449, 460, 463, 466, 474, 478
Thiếu Sơn **445**
Thomas, Pierre-Alban **445**
Thompson, James Harrison Wilson 247, **445–446**
Thongin Buriphat 388, **446**
Thorez, Maurice 155, 435, **446–447**
Thượng Uyển. *See* Nguyễn Tiến Lãng
Tiang Sirikhan 388, **447**
Tố *See* Phạm Văn Đồng
Tô Gĩ. *See* Lê Giản
Tô Hoài **447**
Tố Hữu **447–448**
Tô Ký **448**
Tôn Đức Thắng 249, 275, **448**
Tôn Thất Tùng 152, 230, **448–449**
Torel, Albert 3, 54, 136, 383, **449–450**
Toshio Komaya (Nguyen Quang Thuc) **451**
Tramier, Albert **451**
Trần Bạch Đằng **451**
Trần Bội Cơ **451**
Trần Bửu Kiếm **452**
Trần Đại Biên. *See* Trần Quang Vịnh
Trần Đại Nghĩa 230, **452**
Trần Dần 302, 347, **452–453**
Trần Đăng Ninh 118, 126, 196, 263, 394, 395, 423, **453–454**, 458, 472
Trần Đình Vỹ **454**, 480
Trần Độ **454**
Trần Đức Thảo 121, 204, 230, 370, 418, **454–455**
Trần Duy Hưng **455**
Trần Hiệu 83, 231, 262, 368, 394, **455–456**, 465
Trần Hữu Mai. *See* Hữu Mai
Trần Huy Liệu 13, 106, 121, 204, 219, 306, 316, 323, **456**
Trần Khánh Giư. *See* Khái Hưng
Trần Khuy. *See* Trần Nam Trung
Trần Kim Tuyến **456**
Trần Lương. *See* Trần Nam Trung
Trần Mai **457**
Trần Mai Nam. *See* Hữu Mai
Trần Nam Hùng 445, **457**
Trần Nam Trung **457**
Trần Ngọc Danh 54, 125, 156, 157, 226, 249, 334, 443, **457–458**
Trần Ngọc Nghiêm. *See* Hoàng Minh Chính
Trần Quang. *See* Trần Bạch Đằng
Trần Quang Vinh 338, **458**, 461
Trần Quốc Hoàn 261, 262, 316, 319, 395, 423, 430, 455, **458–459**, 472
Trần Quốc Hương 84, 373, 376, 423, **459**, 493
Trần Qúy Hai 120, **459–460**
Trần Thiện Khiêm **460**
Trần Thiện Vang **460**
Trần Thọ. *See* Hoàng Tùng
Trần Thúc Kính. *See* Trần Văn Quang
Trần Trọng Kim 9, 12, 40, 108, 149, 190, 217, 222, 305, 320, 375, 376, 378, 391, 440, 449, **460**, 468
Trần Tử Bình 267, 459, **460–461**
Trần Văn. *See* Trần Văn Giàu
Trần Văn Ẩn **461**
Trần Văn Đôn 282, 340, **461**
Trần Văn Giàu 57, 92, 204, 214, 260, 374, 388, 448, 456, **461–462**, 472

Trần Văn Hữu 122, 149, 157, 265, 269, 272, 321, 324, 329, 332, 334, 337, 361, 375, 377, 386, 458, **462–463**, 467, 494, 495

Trần Văn Kha 89, 422, **463**

Trần Văn Kỳ. *See* Hoàng Sâm

Trần Văn Luận 78, 79, **463–464**

Trần Văn Mai. *See* Trần Mai

Trần Văn Quang 232, **464**

Trần Văn Soái 209, 251, **464–465**

Trần Văn Thình **465**

Trần Văn Trà 232, 340, 373, **465–466**, 503

Trần Văn Trung (spy). *See* Phạm Xuân Ẩn

Trần Văn Trung (French Union officer) **466**

Trần Văn Tuyên. *See* Trần Vĩnh Phúc

Trần Văn Tỵ **466**

Trần Văn Xái. *See* Trần Văn Soái

Trần Vĩnh Phúc **466–467**

Trapnell, Thomas J. H. 75, **467**

Trevor-Wilson, Arthur Geoffrey 58, **467–468**

Triệu Công Minh **468**

Triệu Trừng Thế. *See* Triệu Công Minh

Triệu Tử Long. *See* Triệu Công Minh

Trịnh Đình Huân. *See* Lê Liêm

Trịnh Đình Thảo **468**

Trịnh Minh Thế 95, 255, 458, **468–469**

Trịnh Ngọc Anh. *See* Ngô Thất Sơn

Trinquier, Roger 37, 101, 192, 352, 353, 415, 419, **469–470**

Trocard, Jean Augustin 425, **470**

Trụm Nộc. *See* Triệu Công Minh

Truman, Harry S. 10, 25, 31, 52, 75, 107, 108, 109, 112, 162, 245, 246, 293, 347, 361, 362, 429, 434, 463, **470–471**, 489

Trung Nam. *See* Nguyễn Văn Kinh

Truong Cang **471**

Trương Cao Phong. *See* Triệu Công Minh

Trường Chinh 13, 38, 48, 52, 57, 68, 86, 109, 121, 171, 178, 194, 203, 209, 213, 214, 215, 226, 249, 252, 259, 262, 269, 274, 275, 306, 311, 323, 340, 374, 376, 422, 423, 431, 448, 453–459 *passim*, 462, **471–472**, 485, 488, 491, 494

Trương Gia Triều. *See* Trần Bạch Đằng

Trương Lai. *See* Phạm Đàn

Trường Sơn. *See* Nguyễn Chí Thanh

Trương Tử Anh 190, **472**, 484, 486, 487

Trường Văn Giàu **472–473**

Trường Văn Huệ **473**

Trường Vĩnh Thanh. *See* Trần Quang Vịnh

Tư Anh. *See* Trần Bạch Đằng

Tư Gio. *See* Triệu Công Minh

Tư Vũ. *See* Vũ Hồng Khanh

Tūbī Līfung 352, **473**

Tutengès, Émile **473–474**

U Nu **475**

Un Xananikôn 241, 381, 438, **475**

Ứng Hòe. *See* Nguyễn Văn Tố

Ung Văn Khiêm 57, 93, 221, 369, **475–476**

Uthong Suvannavong **477**

Valladon, Jacques Vincent **478**

Valluy, Jean Étienne 63, 108, 119, 134, 165, 170, 198, 199, 237, 251, 252, 271, 298, 416, 450 ,470, **478**, 481

Valmary, Alfred Victor Gabriel Joseph **478–479**

Văn *See* Võ Nguyên Giáp

Văn Cao 305, 369, **479**

Văn Tiến Dũng 181, 216, 236, **479**, 497

Vandenberghe, Roger 95, 114, 454, **479–480**

Vanuxem, Paul Fidèle Félicien **481**

Varet, Pierre **481**

Vézinet, Adolphe André **483**

Viala, Maxime Charles Jacques **483**

Vian, Boris 295, **483–484**

Vidal, Pierre 153, **484**

Villedieu, Henri Lucien Paul **488–489**

Vincens, Jacques Marcel Joseph **489**

Vincent, Jean André Léon Marie **489**

Vincent, John Carter **489**

Vincent, Paul Robert **489**

Vĩnh Thụy. *See* Bảo Đại

Viriya, Prince **490**

Võ An Ninh **490–491**

Võ Nguyên Giáp 7–490 *passim*, **491**, 492, 495, 497

Vũ Đình Huỳnh **491–492**

Vũ Đình Long. *See* Vũ Ngọc Nhạ Pierre

Vũ Đức. *See* Hoàng Đình Giọng

Vũ Hải Thu. *See* Nguyễn Hải Thần

Vũ Hồng Khanh 28, 205, 322, 415, 484, 486, 487, 488, **492–493**

Vũ Hồng Thủy. *See* Nguyễn Sơn

Vũ Hữu Bình 330, **493**

Vũ Lang **493**

Vũ Ngọc Nhã. *See* Vũ Ngọc Nhạ Pierre

Vũ Ngọc Nhạ Pierre 459, **493**

Vũ Nguyên Bác. *See* Nguyễn Sơn

Vũ Qúy Mão **493–494**

Vũ Tùng **494**

Vũ Văn Đích. *See* Trần Hiệu

Vũ Văn Giản. *See* Vũ Hồng Khanh

Vương Quang Nhường **494–495**

Vương Thừa Vũ 100, 178, 199, 278, 353, **495**

Wan Waithayakon **496**

Wang Bingnan 195, **496–497**

Wei Guoqing 97, 101, 145, 278, 288, **498**

Wintrebert, Michel **498**

Wu Hung Sinh. *See* Vũ Hồng Khanh

Xeridat, Lucien **500**

Xiang Mao. *See* Khammao Vilai

Xuân Diệu 203, 219, 220, 306, **500**

Xuân Thủy 306, 430, **500**

Yèm Sambaur 47, 220, 246, **501**

Zhang Fakui 426, **502**

Zhang Wentian 502

Zhou Enlai 15, 79, 143, 156, 171, 182, 183, 184, 204, 206, 216, 218, 225, 275, 283, 290, 309, 310, 311, 328, 366, 475, 485, 496, **502**

# *Place Index*

(Main entries only.)

16th Parallel 25
17th Parallel 26

Annam 39
Associated States of Indochina 44

Bắc Bộ. *See* Tonkin
Bắc Kỳ. *See* Tonkin
Burma 78

Cambodia, Associated State of. *See* Associated States of Indochina.
China. *See* People's Republic of China; Republic of China
Cochinchina 107

Democratic Republic of Vietnam (DRV) 135
Điện Biên Phủ. *See* event and general indexes

*Fédération Indochinoise*. *See* Indochinese Federation

Hanoi 199
Hồ Chí Minh Trail 206

India 224
Indochinese Trail. *See* Ho Chi Minh Trail
Indonesia 228
Inter-Zone (*Liên Khu*) 231
- for Eastern Nam Bộ (*Phần Liên Khu Miền Đông*) 231
- I (*Liên Khu I*) 232
- III (*Liên Khu III*) 232
- IV (*Liên Khu IV*) 232
- V (*Liên Khu V*) 232
- Việt Bắc (*Liên Khu Việt Bắc*) 233
- for Western Nam Bộ (*Phần Liên Khu Miền Tây*) 232

Laos
- Associated State of. *See* Associated States of Indochina.
- battles of. *See* events index

Liên Khu. *See* Inter-Zone

Nam Bộ. *See* Cochinchina
Nam Kỳ. *See* Cochinchina

*Pays Montagnards du Sud* (PMS) 362
People's Republic of China 366
PMS. *See Pays Montagnards du Sud*

Republic of China 406
Republic of Vietnam. *See* Vietnam

Saigon 413
Secure Zone (*An Toàn Khu*) 423
South Vietnam. *See* Vietnam, Republic of

Tonkin 449
Trung Bộ. *See* Annam
Trung Kỳ. *See* Annam

Việt Bắc. *See* Inter-Zone Việt Bắc.
Vietnam
- Associated State of. *See* Associated States of Indochina.
- Republic of (*Việt Nam Cộng Hòa*) 407

War Zone D (*Chiến Khu D*) 497

Zone
- *Khu* or *Khu Chiến* 502
- VII (*Khu VII*) 503
- VIII (*Khu VIII*) 503
- IX (*Khu IX*) 503

# *Events Index*

(Main entries only.)


2 September 1945 23
23 September 1945 23
19 December 1946 24

*Affaire Boudarel*. *See* Boudarel Affair
*Affaire des Généraux* 30
Algerian War 36
All Country Military Meeting (*Hội Nghị Quân Sự Toàn Quốc*) 37
An Phú Xã Meeting 38
Atlante, Operation 46
August Revolution (*Cách Mạng Tháng Tám 1945*) 48

Bắc Kạn, Operation. *See* Lea, Operation
Bắc Ninh Incident 51
Berlin Conference. *See* Geneva Accords
Boudarel Affair 69
Brazzaville Conference (30 January–8 February 1944) 74

Call to National Resistance (*Lời Kêu Gọi Toàn Quốc Kháng Chiến*) 81
Cam Ly, Massacre 81
Cao Bằng, Battle of 82
Cây Mai Meeting 91
*Coup de Force* of 9 March 1945 116

Dalat Conference
  first meeting, April–May 1946 124
  second meeting, August 1946 124
Day, Battle of (*Chiến Dịch Quang Trung*, 28 May–20 June 1951) 131
Declaration on Indochina 134
Điện Biên Phủ, Battle of 141
  cancellation of first attack 144
  experience of battle 145
  prcparation and contcxt 142
  significance of 146
  *see also* Điện Biên Phủ, Film (general index)

Dissolution of the Indochinese Communist Party 150
Đông Triều, Battle of (*Hoàng Hoa Thám*, 23 March–7 April 1951) 154

Fontainebleau Conference 173

Generals Affair. *See Affaire des Généraux*
Geneva Conference. *See* Geneva Accords (general index)

H122 Affair 196
Haiphong Incident 197
Hérault, Massacre 201
Hòa Bình, Battle of (10 December 1951–25 February 1952) 208
Hoàng Hoa Thám. *See* Dong Trieu, Battle of

Lang Son Incident 252
Laos, First Battle of (13 April–18 May 1953) 257
Laos, Second Battle of (15 December 1953–May 1954) 257
Léa, Operation 270
Liuzhou Conference 275
Lý Thượng Kiệt, Battle of. *See* Nghĩa Lộ, Battle of

Massacres. *See* Cam Ly, Massacre; Experience of War; Hérault, Massacre; Khmer Krom; Mỹ Thủy, Massacre; Myth of War; Sơn Hà, Massacre
Mỹ Thủy, Massacre 302

Na San, Battle of 304
Nghĩa Lộ, Battle of 312

Pau Conference 361
Piastre Affair. *See* Currency, French Indochina (general index)
Potsdam Conference 386

Quang Trung, Battle of. *See* Day, Battle of

Tây Nguyên, Battle of. *See* Atlante, Operation

Thakhek, Battle of 443

Thap Van Dai Son, Operations (June–October 1949) 444

Thien Ho, Meeting 444

Trần Hưng Đạo, Battle. *See* Vĩnh Yên, Battle

Trung Gia Conference 471

Vạn Phúc, Meeting 479

Vĩnh Yên, Battle 490

# General Index

(Main entries only.)

*2ème Bureau. See Deuxième Bureau* 26
*317ème Section* 26

A 27
Academy, Associated State of Vietnam 27
Accords
- of 6 March 1946 27
- of 8 March 1948. *See* Bao Dai Solution
- of Ha Long Bay. *See* Bao Dai Solution
- *see also* Ely–Collins Agreement; Franco-Chinese Accord; Geneva Accords; *Modus Vivendi*

Administrative Office for the Frontier (*Phòng Biến Chính*) 28
Advance Southern Units (*Nam Tiến*) 29
Advisory Group 100 (Đòan 100) 29
*Aéronavale* 29
African Troops 31
Aid
- American 31
- Chinese Communist 32
- Malaysia 32
- Soviet 32

Air America. *See* Civil Air Transport
Air Force
- Democratic Republic of Vietnam (DRV) 33
- France 34

Alcoholism 35
American Aid. *See* Aid, American
ANAI. *See Association Nationale des Anciens d'Indochine et du Souvenir Indochinois*
ANAPI. *See Association Nationale des Anciens Prisonniers et Internés d'Indochine*
Animals and War 39
Anti-colonialism 40
Anti-communism. *See* Civil War
ANZUS 42
Army
- Associated State of Cambodia 42
- Associated State of Laos 42
- Associated State of Vietnam (*Vệ Binh Quốc Gia*) 42

Art, Democratic Republic of Vietnam 43
*Association Nationale des Anciens et Amis de l'Indochine et du Souvenir Indochinois* (ANAI) 44
*Association Nationale des Anciens Prisonniers et Internés d'Indochine* (ANAPI) 45
*Association Nationale des Combattants de Dien Bien Phu* 45
Association of Mothers of Soldiers (*Hội Mẹ Chiến Sĩ*) 45
*Attentisme* 46

Bà Mẹ Gio Linh. *See* Mothers of Gio Linh
Bank of Indochina 51
Bao Dai Solution 53–55
*Bataillon d'Infanterie Légère d'Outre-Mer* (BILOM) 55
BCRI. *See Bureau Central de Renseignements de l'Indochine*
BD. *See* Comics and War; Culture; Novels
*Bellone* 58
BFDOC. *See Bureau Fédéral de Documentation*
Bicycles 60
*Biet Dong*. *See* Special Forces, Democratic Republic of Vietnam
BILOM. *See Bataillon d'Infanterie Légère d'Outre-Mer*
Bình Xuyên 62
*Bordels Mobiles de Campagne* 68

*Bù Nhìn*. *See* Việt Gian
*Bureau Central de Renseignements de l'Indochine* (BCRI) / Central Intelligence Office for Indochina 77
*Bureau des Archives Techniques* (BAT) / Office of Technical Archives 77
*Bureau Fédéral de Documentation* (BFDOC) / Federal Bureau of Intelligence 77
Bureau for Overseas Chinese Affairs for Nam Bo (*Phòng Huệ Kiều Vụ Nam Bộ*) 78
*Bureau Technique de Liaison et de Coordination d'Êxtrème-Orient* (BTLCEO) 78

C 80
Cambodian Resistance Government 81
Cao Đài 83
*Caravelle* 87
Casualties, Indochina War 88
Catholics
  exodus from North 91
  in Vietnam and the War 90
  *see also* Christians and French Opposition to the Indochina War; Le Huu Tu (name index); Vatican
CCP. *See* People's Republic of China (place index)
Cemeteries
  Democratic Republic of Vietnam 92
  French Union Forces. *See* Myth of War; Necropolis; Remains, French Union; War Memorial, Dien Bien Phu
Central Intelligence Agency. *See* Office of Strategic Services
Central Office for the Southern Region (*Trung Ương Cục Miền Nam*) 92
Central Party Military Committee (*Quân Ủy Trung Ương*) 93
Children 99
Chinese
  Communist Party. *See* People's Republic of China (place index)
  Military Advisory Delegation 101
  Military Intervention, French Allegation of 101
  Political Advisory Delegation 101
Christians and French Opposition to the War 102
CIA. *See* Office of Strategic Services
Cinema
  Democratic Republic of Vietnam 104
  France 104
City at War. *See* Hanoi; Saigon (both place index)
Civil Air Transport (CAT) 105
Civil War 106
Cochinchinese Civil Guard 108
Cold War 108
Collaboration 109
Colonial Academy 112
*Colons. See Français d'Indochine*
Combat. *See* Casualties; Experience of War; Myth of War.
Comics and War 113
Cominindo 113
*Comité Interministériel de l'Indochine*. *See* Cominindo
Commando 114
Committee for External Affairs (*Ban Ngoai Vu*) 114
Committee for the East, Lao Issara 114
Công An. *See* Public Security Services, Democratic Republic of Vietnam.
Congregations. *See Groupements Administratifs Chinois Régionaux* (G.A.C.R.) / Administrative Chinese Regional Groupings.
*Corps Expéditionnaire*. *See* Expeditionary Corps
COSVN. *See* Central Office for the Southern Region
Court Martial, Democratic Republic of Vietnam 117
Court Martial, French Union 117
*Crabe Tambour, Le* 119
Crime 120
Crossovers 120

Culture, Democratic Republic of Vietnam 121
Currency
 Associated States of Indochina 122
 Democratic Republic of Vietnam 122
 French Indochina 122

D 124
Đại Việt. *See* Greater Vietnam Nationalist Party
Đảng Xã Hội Việt Nam. *See* Vietnamese Socialist Party
De La Tour Plan 132
Democrat Party, Cambodia 135
Department of Overseas Chinese Affairs (*Hoa Kiều Vụ*) 136
Desertion
 Democratic Republic of Vietnam 137
 French Union Forces 137
 Japanese 138
Detachment Tran Phu (*Chi Đội Trần Phú*) 138
*Deuxième Bureau* (*2ème Bureau*) 139
Diaspora, Vietnamese. *See* Overseas Vietnamese
*Địch Vận*. *See* Proselytizing the Enemy
Điện Biên Phủ
 film 146. *See also* Điện Biên Phủ, battle of (events index)
 war memorial. *See* War Memorial
DINASSAUT. *See Division Navale d'Assaut*
*Direction Générale de la Documentation* (DGD) 149
Dirty War. *See Sale Guerre*
Disease, Democratic Republic of Vietnam 149
*Division Navale d'Assaut* (DINASSAUT) 150
Divisions, Associated State of Vietnam. *See* Army of the Associated State of Vietnam; French Union
Divisions, Democratic Republic of Vietnam 151
Doan 100. *See* Advisory Group 100
Domino Theory 153
Đông Triều, Battle of (*Hoàng Hoa Thám*, 23 March – 7 April 1951) 154
Đồng. *See* Currency, Democratic Republic of Vietnam
Draft, Associated State of Vietnam. *See* Army, Associated State of Vietnam.
Draft, Democratic Republic of Vietnam 154

*École Coloniale*. *See* Colonial Academy
*École d'Enfants de Troupe Indochinoise*. *See* Children
*École Française d'Êxtrême-Orient* (EFEO) 160
*École Nationale des Langues Orientales Vivantes* (ENLOV) 161
Economy of War, France 161
Ely–Collins Agreement 163
Emulation Campaign 163
*Esprit* 164
Eurasians. *See Métis*
European Defense Community (EDC) 164
Executions 165
Expeditionary Corps 165
Experience of War 166. *See also* Massacres (events index)

Famine 169
*Fédération Indochinoise*. *See* Indochinese Federation
Financial Cost of Indochina War, France 171
Flag, Democratic Republic of Vietnam 172
Fontainebleau Conference 173
Foreign Legion 173
*Français d'Indochine* 174
Franco-Chinese Accord (28 February 1946) 175
Freemasons 176
Fréjus. *See* Necropolis
French Communist Party 177
French Union 177

G.A.C.R. *See Groupements Administratifs Chinois Régionaux* (G.A.C.R.) / Administrative Chinese Regional Groupings

General Political Bureau (*Tong Cuc Chinh Tri*) 181

General Staff, Democratic Republic of Vietnam 181

Generals Affair. *See Affaire des Généraux*

Geneva Accords 182
  Cambodia 185
  Laos 186

GMD. *See* Republic of China (place index)

Gold Week 187

Greater Vietnam Nationalist Party (*Đại Việt Quốc Dân Or Đại Việt*) 190

Griffin Mission. *See* Robert Allen Griffin (name index)

Group 100. *See* Advisory Group 100

*Groupement de Commandos Mixtes Aéroportés* (GCMA) 191

*Groupement des Contrôles Radio-Électroniques* (GCR) 192

*Groupements Administratifs Chinois Régionaux* (G.A.C.R.) / Administrative Chinese Regional Groupings 193

*Groupements Aériens Tactiques* (GATAC) 193

*Guerre Révolutionnaire*. *See* Revolutionary Warfare.

Guerrilla 193

Guomindang. *See* Republic of China (place index)

Helicopters 201

Hero. *See* New Hero

*Hiérarchies Parallèles*. *See* Parallel Hierarchies

History, Democratic Republic of Vietnam 203

Hmong. *See* Minority Ethnic Groups

Hồ Chí Minh Trail 206

Hoa Hảo 209

Hoàng Hoa Thám. *See* Dong Trieu, Battle of

ICC. *See* International Commission for Supervision and Control in Vietnam

INALCO. *See École Nationale des Langues Orientales Vivantes*

Indians, Indochina War 225

Indochinese Communist Party (ICP) 225. *See also* Dissolution of the Indochinese Communist Party (events index)

Indochinese Federation 227

Indochinese Trail. *See* Hồ Chí Minh Trail

Indoctrination 228

Industrialization. *See* Economy of War, France.

Instructions for "People's Total Resistance" (*Chỉ Thị "Toàn Dân Kháng Chiến"*) 229

Intellectuals, French 229

Intellectuals, Democratic Republic of Vietnam 230

Intelligence Services, Army of the Democratic Republic of Vietnam. 230

International Commission for Supervision and Control in Vietnam (ICSC or ICC) 231

Japanese Troops, Indochina War 235

Jarai. *See* Minority Ethnic Groups; *Pays Montagnards du Sud* (PMS)

*Jaunissement* 236

Joint Chiefs of Staff, Democratic Republic of Vietnam (*Bộ Tổng Tham Mưu*) 236

K. *See* D.

Khmer Issarak 242

Khmer Krom 243

KMT. *See* Republic of China

Korean War 246

Kuomintang. *See* Republic of China

Land Reform 251

Language and War 254

Lao Issara 256

Lao Resistance Government 257

*Légion Étrangère*. *See* Foreign Legion

*Les Viet* 273
Liberation Flag (*Cờ Giải Phóng*) 274
Liên Việt (*Hội Liên Hiệp Quốc Dân Việt Nam*) 275
Love and War 277

Martyr 286
Massacres. *See* Experience of War; (and in events index) Cam Ly; Hérault; Mỹ Thủy; Sơn Hà
Medical Evacuations, French 288
Medical Treatment, French Union 288
Melby–Erskine Mission 288
Memorial
  Cao Bang 289
  France *See* Necropolis, Fréjus
  War. *See* War Memorial
Memorial Day, Indochina War 289
*Mémorial des Guerres en Indochine de Fréjus*. *See* Necropolis, Fréjus
Meo. *See* Minority Ethnic Groups
Mercy Team, Hanoi 291
*Métis* 291
Migration. *See* Desertion; Hanoi; Saigon (both places index)
Military Assistance Advisory Group (MAAG), Indochina 293
Military Regions, Associated State of Vietnam 294
Minority Ethnic Groups 294
Missing in Action 295
Mixed Marriage. *See* Love and War; *Métis*
Mobile Field Brothel. *See* Bordels Mobiles de Campagne
*Modus Vivendi*
  Franco-Cambodian 295
  Franco-Vietnamese 296
*Mort en Fraude* 299
Mothers of Gio Linh 299
*Mouvement Républicain Populaire* (MRP) 300
Mutiny. *See* Court Martial
Myth of War
  Democratic Republic of Vietnam 302
  France 303
Nam Tiến. *See* Advance Southern Units
Napalm 305
National Anthem
  Democratic Republic of Vietnam 305
  Republic of Vietnam 305
National Defence Review (*Quốc Phòng Toàn Dân*) 305
National Military Academy, Associated State of Vietnam. *See* Academy, Associated State of Vietnam
National Salvation Army (*Cứu Quốc Quân*) 306
National Salvation Newspaper (*Báo Cứu Quốc*) 306
Navarre Plan 306
Navy
  Associated State of Vietnam 307
  Democratic Republic of Vietnam 308
  French 308
Necropolis, Fréjus 308
Neutralization of Indochina 310
New Hero 311
New Man *See* New Hero; Rectification 312
New Vietnamese. *See* New Hero; Rectification; Việt Nam Mới
Nghĩa Lộ, Battle of 312
North Africans 345
North Atlantic Treaty Organization (NATO) 345
Novels, French 346
Novels, Vietnamese 346
NSC-5405 347
NSC-64 347
Nùng. *See* Minority Ethnic Groups

Occupation, Chinese 349
O'Daniel Missions. *See* John O'Daniel
Office For Nam Bo (*Phòng Nam Bộ*) 350
Office of Strategic Services (OSS) 350
Opium 352
Opposition to the War. *See* Anti-colonialism; Boudarel Affair;

Christians and Opposition to the Indochina War; Civil War; *Esprit*; French Communist Party; Henri Martin; Jean Chesneaux; Paul Mus; *Témoignage Chrétien*

Orphans 353

OSS. *See* Office of Strategic Services

Overseas Chinese 354

Overseas Vietnamese
- in France 355
- in Japan 356
- in Thailand 356

Pacification 358

Parallel Hierarchies 359

Paratroopers. *See* Special Air Service (SAS)

*Paris–Saigon* 360

Party Affairs Committee (*Ban Cán Sự*) 360

Pathet Lao 361

Peace in Order to Advance Instructions (*Hòa Để Tiến*) 363

Pension, Democratic Republic of Vietnam 365

People's Army
- of Cambodia 365
- of Laos 365
- Newspaper (*Báo Quân Đội Nhân Dân Việt Nam*) 365
- Publishing House (*Nhà Xuất Bản Quân Đội Nhân Dân*) 366
- of Vietnam (*Quân Đội Nhân Dân Việt Nam*) 365

People's Paper (*Nhân Dân*) 366

People's Revolutionary Party of Cambodia. *See* Indochinese Communist Party; Khmer Issarak

Personnel Féminin de l'Armée de Terre (PFAT) 367

Personnels Internés Militaires (PIM). *See* Prisoners of War, Democratic Republic of Vietnam

Photography 380

*Piastre Indochinoise*. *See* Currency, French Indochina

PIM (Personnels Internés Militaires). *See* Prisoners of War

Plan Z 384

Popular Front of Southern Vietnam (*Mặt Trận Bình Dân Nam Phần*) 386

Poulo Condor 387

Prisoners of the Japanese 388

Prisoners of War, Democratic Republic of Vietnam 389

Prisoners of War, French Union Forces 389

Prisoners of War, Legal Status 389

Propaganda, Democratic Republic of Vietnam. *See* Art, Democratic Republic of Vietnam; Culture; Emulation Campaign; Indoctrination; New Hero; Proselytizing the Enemy; Psychological Warfare; Rectification

Propaganda, French. *See* Psychological Warfare; Indoctrination; Revolutionary Warfare

Proselytizing the Enemy (*Địch Vận*) 390

Prostitution 391

Provisional Government of the Republic of Cochinchina 391

Psychological Warfare 393

Public Opinion, French 394

Public Security Services, Democratic Republic of Vietnam (*Công An*) 394

Quân Ủy. *See* Central Party Military Committee

Quang Trung, Battle of. *See* Day, Battle of

Rectification (*Chỉnh Huấn*) 399

Red Cross 400

Red Cross, Democratic Republic of Vietnam 401

Refugees, Vietnamese. *See* Catholics, Exodus from North; Migration; Regrouping to the North

Regrouping to the North (*Tập Kết Ra Bắc*) 402

Religion and War. *See* Cao Dai; Catholics; Christians and French Opposition to the War; Hoa Hao

Remains
- Associated State of Vietnam. *See* Remains, French Union; Necropolis; Army, Associated State of Vietnam
- Democratic Republic of Vietnam 403
- French Union 403

*Rendez-Vous des Quais* 404

Repatriation, France 404

Repatriation, Japanese Troops 405

*République (La) est Morte à Dien Bien Phu* 407

Revolutionary Warfare 408

Royal Crusade for Independence 411

*Sale Guerre* 416

Scouting, Indochina War 422

*Section Française de l'Internationale Ouvrière* (SFIO) 422

Secure Zone (*An Toàn Khu*) 423

SEH. *See Service d'Études Historiques*

SEHAN. *See Service d'Études Historiques*

*Service Action* (SA) 424

*Service d'Études Historiques* (SEH, SEHAN, SESAG) 424

*Service de Documentation Extérieure et de Contre-Espionnage* (SDECE) 425

*Service de Protection du Corps Expéditionnaire. See Sûreté Fédérale*

*Service de Renseignements Opérationnels* 425

*Service Technique des Recherches* (STR) 425

SESAG. *See Service d'Études Historiques*

Settlers. *See Français d'Indochine*

Socialists, France. *See Section Française de l'Internationale Ouvrière*

Sơn La Prison 430

South East Asia Treaty Organization (SEATO) 433

SPCE. *See Service de Protection du Corps Expéditionnaire*

Special Air Service (SAS) 433

Special Forces, Democratic Republic of Vietnam (*Biệt Động*) 434

STR. *See Service Technique des Recherches*

*Sûreté Fédérale* 436

Tai. *See* Minority Ethnic Groups; *Pays Montagnards du Sud*; Tai Federation

Tai Federation 441

*Témoignage Chrétien* 442

Territories, Retrocession 443

Thi Đua. *See* Emulation Campaign

Third Force. *See Attentisme*

Tong Bo Viet Minh 449

Torture
- Democratic Republic of Vietnam 450
- French 450

Traitor. *See* Viet Gian

Trần Quốc Tuấn Military Academy (*Trường Võ Bị Trần Quốc Tuấn*) 459

Troops
- Democratic Republic of Vietnam. *See* People's Army of Vietnam
- France. *See* Expeditionary Corps

Trương Chinh Academy (*Trường Trường Chinh*) 472

*Union Française*. *See* French Union

United Nations 476

*Unités Mobiles pour la Défense des Chrétiens* (UMDE) 476

Unknown Soldier. *See* Memorial Day, Indochina War

Urban Warfare. *See* Hanoï ; Saigon

Vanguard Youth League (*Thanh Niên Tiền Phong*) 480

Vatican 481. *See also* Catholics

Vautour, Operation 482

Venereal Disease 482

*Vêpres Hanoïennes* 483

Veteran Hospitals, Democratic Republic of Vietnam 483

Việt Cộng 484

Việt Gian 484

Việt Minh 485

Việt Nam Mới 485

Việt Quốc 486

Vietnam-American Friendship Association 486

Vietnamese Democratic Party. (*Đảng Dân Chủ Việt Nam*) 486

Vietnamese Nationalist Party (*Việt Nam Quốc Dân Đảng*, VNQDD) 486

Vietnamese Socialist Party 487

Vietnamese Workers' Party (VWP) 488

War Invalids 497

War Memorial, Dien Bien Phu, France 497

Wave Tactics 497

Widows of War

Women
- Democratic Republic of Vietnam 498
- French. *See Personnel Féminin de l'Armée de Terre*
- French Armed Forces 499

Workers, Vietnamese in France. *See* Overseas Vietnamese in France

Youth Assault Teams (*Thanh Niên Xung Phong*) 501